UNDERSTANDING PSYCHOLOGY

McGraw-Hill, Inc.
New York   St. Louis
San Francisco
Auckland
Bogotá   Caracas
Lisbon   London   Madrid
Mexico   Milan   Montreal
New Delhi   Paris
San Juan
Singapore   Sydney
Tokyo
Toronto

THIRD EDITION

UNDERSTANDING PSYCHOLOGY

Robert S. Feldman
University of Massachusetts at Amherst

UNDERSTANDING PSYCHOLOGY

2 3 4 5 6 7 8 9 0 VNH VNH 9 0 9 8 7 6 5 4 3

ISBN 0-07-020659-7

This book was set in New Baskerville by Waldman Graphics, Inc.
The editors were Christopher Rogers, Rhona Robbin, and David Dunham;
the designer was Jo Jones;
the production supervisor was Friederich W. Schulte.
The photo editor was Elsa Peterson.
New drawings were done by Fine Line Illustrations, Inc.
Cover photograph © Michael de Camp, The Image Bank.
Von Hoffmann Press, Inc., was printer and binder.

Library of Congress Cataloging-in-Publication Data

Feldman, Robert S. (Robert Stephen), (date).
  Understanding psychology / Robert S. Feldman. — 3rd ed.
    p.   cm.
  Includes bibliographical references and indexes.
  ISBN 0-07-020659-7
  1. Psychology.   I. Title.
BF121.F35   1993
150—dc20   92-13181

ABOUT THE AUTHOR

Robert S. Feldman is Professor of Psychology at the University of Massachusetts at Amherst, where he is director of the Personality and Social Psychology program. A graduate of Wesleyan University and the University of Wisconsin-Madison, he is a former Fulbright Senior Research Scholar and Lecturer. He is a Fellow of the American Psychological Association and the American Psychological Society and author of more than 90 scientific articles, book chapters, and papers. He has also written or edited ten books, including *Social Psychology* (McGraw-Hill) and *Fundamentals of Nonverbal Behavior* (Cambridge University Press). His research interests include nonverbal behavior and the social psychology of education. His spare time is most often devoted to serious cooking and earnest, but unpolished, piano playing. He lives with his wife, also a psychologist, and three children overlooking the Holyoke mountain range in Amherst, Massachusetts.

To
Jonathan,
Joshua,
Sarah,
and
Kathy

CONTENTS IN BRIEF

CONTENTS

LIST OF BOXES

REVIEWERS

The following individuals reviewed all or part of the manuscripts of this or one of the previous editions of *Understanding Psychology*:

Phillip Ackerman, University of Minnesota

Louis E. Banderet, Northeastern University

Gordon Barr, Hunter College

Robert C. Beck, Wake Forest University

Brenda Bennett, Vincennes University

David Berg, Community College of Philadelphia

Allen E. Bergin, Brigham Young University

Jeanine Bloyd, Spoon River College

Terry D. Blumenthal, Wake Forest University

Craig Bowman, California State University–Fullerton

Allen R. Branum, South Dakota State University

David M. Brodzinsky, Rutgers University

Peter Burzynski, Vincennes University

Jay Caldwell, California State University

Bernardo Carducci, Indiana University Southeast

Steve Coccia, Orange County Community College

Lorry Cology, Owens Technical College

Helen Joan Crawford, Virginia Polytechnic Institute and State University

James Dailey, Vincennes University

Patrick T. DeBoli, Nassau Community College

Joyce Dennis, Southern Union State University

Barbara Dickson-Parnell, Independent Practice

William Dwyer, Memphis State University

Marsha Epstein, Middlesex Community College

Walter Essman, Queens College

Richard Ettinger, Eastern Oregon State College

William Ford, Bucks County Community College

Judith Gentry, Columbus State Community College

Marvin W. Goldstein, Rider College

David A. Griesé, SUNY at Farmingdale

Gloria Griffith, Tennessee Tech University

David Harnison, Virginia Polytechnic Institute

Earl Harper, Bunker Hill Community College

Lynn Hasher, Temple University

Donna Hummel, Trinity College

Janet Shibley Hyde, University of Wisconsin–Madison

Carroll Izard, University of Delaware

Tom Jackson, Fort Hays State University

Kenneth D. Kallio, SUNY at Geneseo

Don Kaesser, Des Moines Area Community College

Lynn Kiorpes, New York University

Michael Knight, Central State University

Angela La Sala, Suffolk Community College

Kenneth B. LeSure, Cuyahoga Community College

David F. Lohman, University of Iowa

Kevin McCaul, North Dakota State University

Harold Mansfield, North Dakota State University

Frederick Meeker, California State Polytechnic University

Linda Musun-Miller, University of Arkansas

Gary Naseth, Oregon Institute of Technology

Steve Noble, North Georgia College

Fay-Tyler Norton, Cuyahoga Community College

Frances O'Keefe, Tidewater Community College

Joseph J. Palladino, University of Southern Indiana

Holly Pennock, Hudson Valley Community College

James Perry, East Tennessee State University

Edward Pflaumer, Loma Linda University

James Polyson, University of Richmond

Laura Puckett, North Hennepin Community College

Richard Rasor, American River College

Michael Rodman, Middlesex Community College

Richard M. Ryckman, University of Maine–Orono

Valerie J. Sasserath, Chatham Township Schools

Joyce Schaeuble, Sacramento City College

Alan Searleman, St. Lawrence University

Peggy Skinner, South Plains College

Harold I. Siegel, Rutgers University

Luella Snyder, Parkland College

Norman R. Simonson, University of Massachusetts–Amherst

Robert D. Sorkin, University of Florida–Gainesville

Robert Stern, Pennsylvania State University

Alfred W. Stone, Edinboro University of Pennsylvania

Michael J. Strube, Washington University

John Suller, Rider College

Granville L. Sydnor, San Jacinto College

Robert Thompson, Hunter College

David Tuber, Ohio State University

Carol Vitiello, Kirkwood Community College

Benjamin Wallace, Cleveland State University

Charles Weichert, San Antonio College

Richard Williams, Imperial Valley College

Fred Wright, John Jay College of Criminal Justice

Stephen Zaccaro, George Mason University

Philip Sanford Zeskind, Virginia Polytechnic Institute and State University

In addition to the preceding professionals, I met with a panel of undergraduate students who had used the second edition of *Understanding Psychology* during their introductory psychology course. Over the course of a subsequent semester, we reviewed the second edition, literally line-by-line. Their insights and suggestions were invaluable in preparing this revision, and I am very appreciative of their efforts: Shannon O'Hearn, Risa Chudnofsky, Laura Verrette.

Robert S. Feldman

PREFACE

As I look out the window, the form of Mount Norwottock, an ancient volcanic mountain, rises above the landscape. I can see a farmer in the valley below Norwottock methodically plowing his fields, as, closer to home, a mother walks her child to school. A crew of carpenters is building a new house on land nearby, working together and following complicated architectural plans.

At the same time as I look out on this peaceful scene, the morning newspaper lying across my desk reports another terrorist attack, a Mideast treaty broken, and a murder in a small town nearby. It tells of a march of members of a Nazi-like organization who want to expel minorities from the United States, and of the upcoming release from a mental hospital of a killer judged innocent by reason of insanity.

Although nearly a decade has passed since I wrote these words at the beginning of the first edition of *Understanding Psychology*, the fundamental elements of the scene I describe are little changed today. The view from my study window continues to be dominated by the outline of Mount Norwottock and the tranquil fields that dot its base, while my daily newspaper is still filled with incidents of irrationality, selfishness, and violent competition among the world's people. For better or worse, the essential characteristics of human behavior have changed little over the last ten years.

What has changed, though, is the field of psychology. The discipline has made important advances that have brought us closer to understanding people's behavior and thought processes. This book, now in its third edition, is a testament to the field's progress, as well as to the basic principles on which the discipline of psychology is built.

THE THIRD EDITION OF UNDERSTANDING PSYCHOLOGY

Like its predecessors, the third edition of *Understanding Psychology* has three major goals. First, it is intended to provide effective and broad coverage of the field of psychology, introducing readers to the theories, research, and applications that constitute the science. Second, it is meant to provide an impetus for students to begin to think as psychologists, even after the recall of specific content has waned, and to foster an appreciation for the scientific basis of psychology. Finally, this book is designed to be engaging and interesting, arousing students' intellectual curiosity and building an appreciation of how psychology can increase their understanding of the world around them.

These goals, of course, are interdependent. In fact, I would argue that if the text is successful in accurately communicating the nature of psychology, an understanding of and interest in the field will follow naturally. To that end, the writing style of this book has received considerable attention. The style is intended to provide as close a facsimile to two people sitting down and discussing psychology as can be conveyed by the written word.

Furthermore, this text has special features that are designed to challenge students (Cutting Edge boxes with the latest findings), demonstrate the everyday relevance of psychology (Psychology at Work boxes), and improve the quality of readers' own lives (Informed Consumer of Psychology sections). It is also a book that has been carefully designed to promote learning. Material is presented in rational, manageable chunks, each of which is followed by a succinct summary (called a "Recap") and a set of questions on the material (a "Review"). A reader who answers these questions—and then checks the answers, which are provided on a following page—will be able to assess the degree of initial mastery of the material, as well as having a head start on long-term recall and understanding of the information.

In sum, *Understanding Psychology* is, as I emphasize in the first chapter, designed to be user-friendly. It is a book that is meant not to merely expose readers to the content—and promise—of psychology, but to do so in a way that will bring alive the excitement of the field, and to keep that excitement alive long after readers have completed their introduction to the discipline.

WHAT'S NEW IN THE THIRD EDITION?

Much thought has gone into the changes incorporated into this edition of *Understanding Psychology*. Because the basic structure and features of the first two editions met with such a positive response from both students and professors, the fundamental attributes of the book remain intact. At the same time, additions that reflect important advances in the field of psychology have been incorporated.

To begin with, there are two new chapters—one that focuses on research methods (Chapter 2) and another that is devoted to consumer and industrial-organizational psychology (Chapter 21). The research methods chapter spotlights the role of research in shaping the field of psychology, and the consumer and industrial-organizational reflects the growing importance of these topics within the discipline.

Several new themes also emerge in this edition. Explicitly acknowledging the multicultural nature of U.S. society, greater emphasis has been placed on the influence of race and culture on human behavior, both from a subcultural and cross-cultural perspective. Rather than relegating this information to a chapter of its own, multicultural material is included throughout the book. To cite just a few examples, the chapter on sensation outlines cultural differences in the experience of pain; child-rearing practices of Japanese mothers are discussed in one of the chapters on development; and racial and ethnic differences in consumer behavior are discussed in Chapter 21.

The increasingly influential cognitive and cognitive neuroscientific perspectives have also provided a focal point for revision. Significant new material on cognition has been added throughout this edition. For example, the chapter on biopsychology discusses computational neuroscience and neural networks; the states of consciousness chapter discusses how cognitive expectations relate to the effect of alcohol; and gender differences in cognitive abilities are examined in the chapter on gender and sex. In addition, the chapter on cognition has been expanded and updated.

Overall, a wealth of contemporary research is cited in this edition. More than 750 new citations have been added, most of them published since 1990. Furthermore, an extensive array of new topics has been incorporated, along with information updating existing material. A sample of the new and revised topics featured in this edition provides a good indication of the currency of the revision: minority representation in the field of psychology, meta-analytic research techniques, circadian rhythms, development of taste preferences, sex differences in smell, speech perception, new theories of dreaming, priming, bilingual training, implicit memory, everyday memory, emotional intelligence, cultural difference in emotion, sexual harassment, date rape, the world AIDS epidemic, genetic determinants of personality traits, homelessness, cultural factors in treatment, violence and pornography, and consumer psychology.

One of the distinctive characteristics of *Understanding Psychology* has always been its inclusion of substantial information designed to have a lasting impact on students' lives. This edition continues this tradition, including new material on such topics as breast and testicular self-examination (sensation chapter), the prevention of date rape and the use of safer sex practices (gender and sexuality chapter), and consideration of the social-influence tactics of advertisers (consumer and industrial-organizational psychology chapter).

AN OVERVIEW OF UNDERSTANDING PSYCHOLOGY

Understanding Psychology includes extensive coverage of the traditional topical areas of psychology, including the biological foundations of behavior, sensation and perception, learning, memory, cognition, human development, personality, abnormal behavior, and social psychological foundations of behavior. Notably, however, it also includes several distinctive chapters that focus primarily on applications of psychological theory and research in nonlaboratory, field settings. For example, there are separate chapters on health psychology and psychology in the workplace and the marketplace—burgeoning areas that represent the most important applied topics currently undergoing investigation.

The flexibility of this text's organizational structure is considerable. Each chapter is divided into three or four manageable, self-contained units, allowing instructors to choose and omit sections in accordance with their syllabus. Furthermore, because chapters are self-contained, it is possible to use this book in either biologically oriented or socially oriented introductory psychology courses by choosing only those chapters that are relevant. In addition, because the applications material is well-integrated throughout, even in the chapters that cover the most traditional, theoretical topics, those courses that omit the more applied topical chapters will still be successful in conveying the relevance of psychology to readers.

Overall, then, the book reflects a combination of traditional core topics and contemporary applied subjects, providing a broad, eclectic—and current—view of the field of psychology. It should be apparent that the volume is *not* an applied psychology text; nor is it a theories-oriented volume. Instead, it draws from theoretical and applied approaches, and integrates the two along with objective presentations of research that illustrate the way in which the science of psychology has evolved and grown. Indeed, the book exemplifies the view that a theory-application dichotomy is a false one. Applications are not presented as devoid of theory, but rather are placed in a theoretical context, grounded in research findings. Likewise, when theoretical material is presented, practical implications are drawn from it.

Some examples can illustrate this approach. If you turn to Chapter 4, you will find that it includes the traditional material on sight and the eye. But the text moves beyond a mere recitation of the various parts of the eye and theories of vision. It also explores current work involving laser surgery in which a slice of the eye's cornea is removed, permitting improved vision that makes eyeglasses and contact lenses obsolete. Similarly, Chapter 13 includes a presentation of the theories behind the nature-nurture issue and a discussion of developmental research strategies. These are tied to a presentation of exciting new findings on genetic influences on temperament and shyness and to contemporary issues such as the effects of day-care on children's development. Finally, the chapter on abnormal behavior not only explores the development of models of abnormality but considers how they apply to homelessness, one of the major social problems of the 1990s. In each of these instances, the text demonstrates how applications grow out of the theoretical and research base of the field.

LEARNING AIDS AND FEATURES OF UNDERSTANDING PSYCHOLOGY

Understanding Psychology has been designed with its ultimate consumer—the student—in mind. As you can see from the following list of elements that are common to every chapter, the book incorporates educational features, based on learning and cognitive instructional design theory and research, that are meant to make the book an effective learning device and, at the same time, enticing and engaging:

■ *Chapter Outline.* Each chapter opens with an outline of the chapter structure. Not only does the outline provide a means of understanding the interrelationships of the material within the chapter, but it serves as a chapter organizer, helping to bridge the gap between what a reader already knows and the subsequent chapter content.

■ *Prologue.* Each chapter starts with an account of a real-life situation that involves major aspects of the topics of the chapter. These scenarios demonstrate the relevance of basic principles and concepts of psychology to actual issues and problems. For example, the chapter on sensation discusses rock star Pete Townshend's hearing loss; the chapter on health and stress describes the psychological impact of participation in the war in the Persian Gulf; and the chapter on attitudes and social cognition discusses the case of Rodney King, who was stopped by Los Angeles police and beaten in a racial incident.

■ *Looking Ahead.* A chapter overview follows the prologue. It articulates the key themes and issues and lists a set of questions that are answered in the chapter.

■ *Psychology at Work.* The Psychology at Work boxes illustrate an application of psychological theory and research findings to a real-world problem. For example, Chapter 2 discusses how psychologists' theoretical findings on the brain are used by advertisers to analyze commercials; the chapter on states of consciousness considers how a psychologist analyzed the speech of the captain of the Exxon Valdez, a ship involved in a major Alaskan oil spill, to determine if he was intoxicated; and Chapter 19 discusses the way in which prejudice reduction techniques have been employed on college campuses.

■ *The Cutting Edge.* These boxed inserts describe a contemporary research program that is in the forefront of the discipline—suggesting where the field of psychology is heading. This feature helps provide a sense of the growing and developing status of the science of psychology. For instance, the biopsychology chapter explores current work on gender differences in the brains of males and females; the memory chapter discusses the evidence for implicit memory while anesthetized; the chapter on adolescence and adulthood presents findings relating the use of drugs to social adjustment; and the chapter on attitudes and social cognition discusses new evidence regarding the prevalence of stereotypes.

■ *The Informed Consumer of Psychology.* Every chapter includes information designed to make readers more informed consumers of psychological information and knowledge by giving them the ability to evaluate critically what the field of psychology offers. For example, these sections discuss treatment for dyslexia (perception chapter), dealing with drug- and alcohol-related problems (states-of-consciousness chapter), using behavior modification techniques for time management (learning chapter), personality and vocational testing (personality chapter), choosing a physician (health and stress chapter), and evaluating psychological therapy (treatment chapter).

■ *Recap and Review.* Research clearly indicates the importance of careful organization of textual material, learning material in relatively small chunks, and actively reviewing material. Consequently, each chapter is divided into three or four sections, each of which concludes with a Recap and Review. A Recap summarizes the key points of the previous section, and a Review presents a variety of types of questions for students to answer—including multiple choice, fill-in, short answer, and critical thinking questions—in order to test both recall and higher-level understanding of the material.

■ *Running Glossary.* Key terms are highlighted in boldface type when they are introduced, and they are defined in the margin of the text, with pronunciation guides for difficult words. There is also an end-of-book Glossary.

■ *Looking Back.* To facilitate the review of the material covered in each chapter and to aid in the synthesis of the information covered, a numbered summary is included at the end of every chapter. The summary emphasizes the key points of the chapter and is organized according to the questions asked in the "Looking Ahead" section at the beginning of the chapter.

■ *Key Terms and Concepts.* A list of key terms and concepts, including the page numbers where they were first introduced, is also provided at the end of each chapter.

■ *A full-color graphic design.* To support the instructional design features of the text, a team of graphic designers has developed a design structure to enhance the pedagogy of the text. The beautiful design and photos make the text inviting and a book from which it is easy to learn.

ANCILLARY MATERIALS

The third edition of *Understanding Psychology* is accompanied by an extensive, integrated set of supplemental materials designed to support the classroom teaching of both new and veteran instructors. The centerpieces of the supplements are the student Study Guide, Instructor's Manual, and Test Bank, all written by Professor Mark Garrison of Kentucky State University. A master teacher and experienced author, Professor Garrison's materials provide a consistent pedagogical framework for students and professors using *Understanding Psychology*.

The Study Guide has been completely revised and reorganized to provide a streamlined, integrated review of the material in each textbook chapter. Each *Study Guide* chapter contains a chapter outline with highlighted key terms, a detailed chapter summary, learning objectives keyed to page numbers in the text, and a set of self-study questions of various types and levels of difficulty. New to this edition are essay questions with detailed sample answers and an introductory essay which provides the student with suggestions for how best to utilize the *Study Guide* and covers the SQ3R study and review method.

The *Instructor's Manual* contains a wide variety of lecture ideas and resources for both first-time and experienced instructors. Designed to complement the *Study Guide* and *Test File*, each chapter in the *Instructor's Manual* includes a detailed chapter outline, a chapter summary, learning objectives, and a set of Lecture Resources including discussion topics, ideas for classroom demonstrations, a list of relevant films and videos, and suggestions for activities and projects that can be used both in and out of the classroom. New features in this edition include learning objectives, as well as chapter summaries that are indexed to the text and keyed to student learning objectives and the relevant test bank questions.

The *Test File* contains a mix of factual and conceptual multiple-choice questions indexed to the text and keyed to learning objectives for a total of over 3000 items. In addition, there are approximately twenty-five true-false questions per chapter. *Computerized Test Banks* are available in IBM (on both 5.25″ and 3.5″ disks).

In addition to the student Study Guide, Instructor's Manual, and Test Bank, McGraw-Hill provides a wide variety of audiovisual and computerized teaching aids. For example, Philip G. Zimbardo of Stanford University and Allen Funt have developed an innovative set of laser discs and videotapes using clips from *Candid Camera*, available exclusively through McGraw-Hill. Furthermore, the Instructor's Manual includes a list of the films available for use with each chapter, along with information about how these films can be acquired. Finally, a Transparency and Slide Set is available to instructors using the text.

Several software packages also accompany this text. These include *Psych-World*, 2d ed. (for IBM 3½ and 5¼); *Computer Activities for Psychology*, 4th ed. (CAPS IV, for IBM); and *Statistical Computation Program for Students* (for IBM).

Finally, professors using the third edition of *Understanding Psychology* will receive a monthly *Update*, written by this book's author. The *Update* will include reports of new psychological findings and will discuss the psychological implications of current events in the news. The *Update* can be distributed to students or incorporated into lectures. In order to ensure timeliness, the newsletter will be sent to instructors via FAX.

ACKNOWLEDGMENTS

As the long list of reviewers on pages xxvii–xxviii attests, this book involves the efforts of many people. They lent their expertise to evaluate all or part of the manuscript, providing an unusual degree of quality control. Their careful work and thoughtful suggestions have improved the manuscript many times over from its first-draft incarnations. I am grateful to them all for their comments.

My thinking has been shaped by many teachers along the way. I was introduced to psychology at Wesleyan University, where several committed and inspiring teachers—and in particular Karl Scheibe—made the excitement and relevance of the field clear to me. By the time I left Wesleyan I could envision no other career but that of psychologist. Although the nature of the University of Wisconsin, where I did my graduate work, could not have been more different from the much smaller Wesleyan, the excitement and inspiration were similar. Once again, a cadre of excellent teachers—led, especially, by the late Vernon Allen—molded my thinking and taught me to appreciate the beauty and science of the discipline of psychology.

My colleagues and students at the University of Massachusetts at Amherst provide ongoing intellectual stimulation, and I thank them for making the University a very fine place to work. Several people also provided extraordinary research and editorial help; they include John Graiff, Nancy Goff, Sean Donovan, Lee Rosen, Carolyn Dash, Richard Fleming, Wendy Copes, Frances Ramos, Lisa Beck, and the late Kate Cleary. I also thank James M. Royer, who provided a draft of the material in the statistics appendix.

Every reader of this book owes a debt of gratitude to Rhona Robbin, senior developmental editor for this edition of *Understanding Psychology*. Her relentless pursuit of excellence shaped the underlying quality of this book. Chris Rogers, executive editor, is a throwback to the old-fashioned days of publishing. Chris's creativity and concern about quality are increasingly rare commodities in a world of publishing conglomerates. I'm thankful to both Rhona and Chris, and I'm pleased to count them as friends.

Other people at McGraw-Hill were central to the design and production process; these include David Dunham, editing supervisor, Jo Jones, designer, Fred Schulte, production supervisor, and Elsa Peterson, photo editor. I am proud to be a part of this first-class team.

Finally, I am, as always, indebted to my family. My parents, Leah Brochstein and the late Saul D. Feldman, provided a lifetime foundation of love and support. My extended family also play a central role in my life. They include, more or less in order of age, my nieces and nephews, my brother, various brothers- and sisters-in-law, Ethel Radler, and Harry Brochstein. I'm thankful for all that they add to my life. Finally, my late mother-in-law, Mary Evens Vorwerk, had an important influence on this book, and I remain ever grateful to her.

Ultimately, my children, Jonathan, Joshua, and Sarah, and my wife, Katherine, remain the focal point of my life. I thank them, with great love.

Robert S. Feldman

INTRODUCTION TO PSYCHOLOGY

The consequences of the devastating California fires can be considered from a variety of psychological perspectives.

FIRE!

No one knows for sure how the fire began. Some reports said the flames started in a small brushfire close to an illegally built shack. But to those Californians living in the Oakland and Berkeley hills who lost their homes, the cause of the fire was secondary. What counted was the horror of finding that a lifetime of possessions vaporized in a few short minutes.

The fire, the worst in recent U.S. history, flared up in an area that just two years earlier had suffered a devastating earthquake. The fire caused dozens of deaths. Over 3000 homes and apartments were destroyed, and more than $1.5 billion dollars in property damage was left in its aftermath.

No resident of the area emerged unscathed from the fire. Although the majority of the inhabitants were not physically harmed, most experienced continuing degrees of anxiety. Every resident knew that, in an area that suffers periodic droughts, new fires are possible at any time (Rogers, 1991).

LOOKING AHEAD

Although the fires that ravaged the California landscape brought incredible physical destruction, much of the lingering outcomes would be psychological. Consider, for example, some of the ways that different types of psychologists might view the catastrophic fires:

■ Psychologists who specialize in the biology underlying behavior would examine changes in the body's internal activity as a consequence of suddenly fleeing from the threatening fire.

■ Those psychologists who specialize in the study of learning and memory could investigate the kinds of details concerning the fire that people were most apt to recall.

■ Psychologists who study people's thinking processes might consider why people choose to live in an area that was prone to devastating fires.

■ Developmental psychologists, who study children, would investigate how the loss of shelter and a lifetime of possessions would affect later emotional growth and development.

■ Health psychologists, who study the relationship between physical and psychological factors, would examine the ways in which experiencing apprehension and terror due to the fires might produce later illness.

■ Clinical and counseling psychologists, who provide therapy, could investigate ways to reduce people's continuing anxiety following the fires.

■ Social psychologists, who study questions related to interpersonal interaction, would try to understand the reasons behind the helpfulness and heroism of some individuals, who aided and sheltered those who had lost their homes, and contrast it with the uncaring, indifferent behavior of looters.

THE STUDY OF BEHAVIOR AND MENTAL PROCESSES: THE COMMON LINK AMONG PSYCHOLOGISTS

Psychology: The scientific study of behavior and mental processes

Although the approaches that different psychologists would take in contemplating the fire are diverse, there is a common link: Each represents a specialty area within the general area of study called psychology. **Psychology** is the scientific study of behavior and mental processes.

This definition, although clear-cut, is also deceptively simple. In order to encompass the breadth of the field, "behavior and mental processes" must be understood to mean many things: It includes not just what people do but also their thoughts, feelings, perceptions, reasoning processes, and memories, and even the biological activities that keep their bodies functioning.

When psychologists speak of "studying" behavior and mental processes, their interests are equally broad. To psychologists, it is not enough simply to describe behavior. As with any science—and psychologists clearly consider their discipline a science—psychology attempts to explain, predict, modify, and ultimately improve the lives of people and the world in which they live.

By using scientific procedures, psychologists are able to find answers to questions about the nature of human behavior that are far more valid than those resulting from mere intuition and guesses. And what a variety and range of questions psychologists pose. Consider these examples: How do we see colors? What is intelligence? Can abnormal behavior be cured? Is a hypnotic trance the same as sleep? Can aging be delayed? How does stress affect us? What is the best way to study? What is normal sexual behavior?

These questions—whose answers you will know by the time you finish reading this book—provide just a hint of the various topics that will be presented as we explore the field of psychology. Our discussions will take us across the spectrum of what is known about behavior and mental processes. At times, we will leave the realm of humans to explore animal behavior, because many psychologists study nonhumans in order to determine general laws of behavior that pertain to *all* organisms. Animal behavior thus provides important clues to answering questions about human behavior. But we will always return to the usefulness of psychology in helping to solve the everyday problems that confront all human beings.

In this introductory chapter, we discuss a number of topics that are central to an understanding of psychology. We begin by describing the different types of psychologists and the various roles they play. Next, we examine the major approaches and models that are used to guide the work psychologists do. Finally, we identify the major issues that underlie psychologists' views of the world and human behavior.

In covering this preliminary material, you'll also be introduced to the text itself. This book is intended to provide as close a facsimile to two people sitting down and discussing psychology as one can convey with the written word; when I write "we," I am talking about the two of us—reader and writer. To borrow a phrase from folks who spend much of their time with computers, the book is meant to be user-friendly.

You will find material to demonstrate the ways in which psychologists apply what they have learned to everyday life (Psychology at Work boxes) and discussion of what the future of psychology holds (Cutting Edge boxes). You will also come across sections in each chapter that are intended to make you a more knowledgeable consumer of psychological information by enhancing your ability to critically evaluate the contributions psychologists offer society. Called "The Informed Consumer of Psychology," these sections include concrete recommendations for incorporating psychology into your life.

The book itself has been designed to make it easier for you to learn the material we discuss. Based on the principles developed by psychologists who specialize in learning and memory, it presents information in relatively small chunks, with each chapter including three or four major sections. Each of these segments is followed by a Recap and Review that lists the key points that have been covered and asks you a series of questions. Some questions provide a quick test of recall and are answered on the page following the review. Other questions, designated "Ask Yourself," are broad queries designed to elicit critical analysis of the information. This kind of immediate drill will help you in learning, and later recalling, the material. To further reinforce your understanding of the material, each chapter ends with a summary and list of key terms.

After reading this chapter, then, you will be able to answer the following questions:

What is psychology and why is it a science?
What are the different branches of the field of psychology?
Where are psychologists employed?
What are the historical roots of the field?
What are psychology's key issues and controversies?

PSYCHOLOGISTS AT WORK

Wanted: Assistant professor at a small liberal arts college. Teach undergraduate courses in introductory psychology and courses in specialty areas of cognitive psychology, perception, and learning. Strong commitment to quality teaching and student advising necessary. The candidate must also provide evidence of scholarship and research productivity or potential.

Wanted: Industrial/organizational consulting psychologist. International firm is seeking psychologists for full-time career positions as consultants to management. Candidates must have the ability to establish effective rapport with senior business executives and to assist them with innovative, practical, and psychologically sound solutions to problems concerning people and organizations.

Wanted: Clinical psychologist. Ph.D., internship experience, and license required. Comprehensive clinic seeks psychologist to work with children and adults providing individual and group therapy, psychological evaluations, crisis intervention, and development of behavior treatment plans on multidisciplinary team. Broad experience with substance abuse problems is desirable.

Many people mistakenly believe that almost all psychologists analyze and treat abnormal behavior. However, as the job descriptions reprinted above indicate, the range and scope of the field of psychology are much broader than this common misconception would suggest.

We will examine the major specialty areas of psychology by describing them in the general order in which they are discussed in subsequent chapters of this book. The proportion of psychologists who identify themselves as belonging to each of these specialty areas is shown in Figure 1-1.

Biopsychologists: The Biological Foundations of Psychology

Biopsychology: The branch of psychology that specializes in the biological basis of behavior

In the most fundamental sense, people are biological organisms, and some psychologists emphasize how the physiological functions and structures of our body work together to influence our behavior. **Biopsychology** is the branch of psychology that specializes in the biological bases of behavior. Biopsychologists study a broad range of topics, with a focus on the operation of the brain and nervous system. For example, they may investigate the ways in which specific sites in the

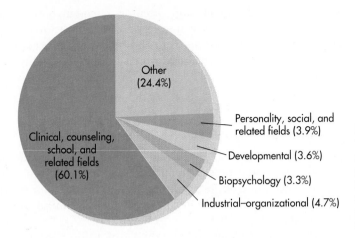

FIGURE 1-1

The percentage of psychologists falling into the major specialty areas of the field. (Source: ODEER, 1991; data combine masters and doctoral psychologists, whose specialty areas vary according to training.)

brain are related to a disorder such as Parkinson's disease (see Chapter 3), or they may attempt to determine how bodily sensations are related to emotion (see Chapter 11).

Experimental Psychologists: Sensing, Perceiving, Learning, and Thinking

If you have ever wondered how acute your vision is, how you experience pain, or how you can most effectively study, you have raised a question that is most appropriately answered by an experimental psychologist. **Experimental psychology** is the branch of psychology that studies the processes of sensing, perceiving, learning, and thinking about the world.

    The work of experimental psychologists overlaps that done by biopsychologists, as well as that done by other types of psychologists. Actually, the term "experimental psychologist" is somewhat misleading, since psychologists in every specialty area use experimental techniques, and experimental psychologists do not limit themselves solely to experimental methods.

    Several subspecialties have grown out of experimental psychology to become central branches of the field in their own right. One example of such a specialty area is **cognitive psychology**, which focuses on the study of higher mental processes, including thinking, language, memory, problem solving, knowing, reasoning, judging, and decision making. Cutting a wide swath across human behavior, cognitive psychologists have, for instance, identified more efficient ways of remembering and better strategies for solving problems involving logic (as discussed in Chapters 8 and 9).

Developmental and Personality Psychologists: Understanding Change and Individual Differences

A baby producing her first smile . . . taking her first step . . . saying her first word. These events, which can be characterized as universal milestones in development, are also singularly special and unique for each person. Developmental psychologists, whose work is discussed in Chapters 13 and 14, trace the changes in behavior and in people's underlying capabilities throughout their lives.

    Developmental psychology, then, is the branch of psychology that studies how people grow and change throughout the course of their lives. Another

Experimental psychology: The branch of psychology that studies the processes of sensing, perceiving, learning, and thinking about the world

Cognitive psychology: The branch of psychology that focuses on the study of higher mental processes, including thinking, language, memory, problem solving, knowing, reasoning, judging, and decision making

Developmental psychology: The branch of psychology that studies how people grow and change throughout the course of their lives

Personality psychology: The branch of psychology that studies consistency and change in a person's behavior over time, as well as the individual traits that differentiate the behavior of one person from another

Health psychology: The branch of psychology that explores the relationship of psychological factors and physical ailments or disease

Clinical psychology: The branch of psychology that deals with the study, diagnosis, and treatment of abnormal behavior

Counseling psychology: The branch of psychology that focuses on educational, social, and career adjustment problems

Educational psychology: The branch of psychology that considers how the educational process affects students

School psychology: The branch of psychology devoted to assessing children in elementary and secondary schools who have academic or emotional problems and to developing solutions to such problems

branch, **personality psychology**, attempts to explain both consistency and change in a person's behavior over time, as well as the individual traits that differentiate the behavior of one person from another when each confronts the same situation. The major issues relating to the study of personality will be considered in Chapter 15.

Health, Clinical, and Counseling Psychologists: Physical and Mental Health

If you have difficulty getting along with others, continuing unhappiness in your life, or a fear that prevents you from carrying out your normal activities, you might consult one of the psychologists who devote their energies to the study of physical or mental health: health psychologists, clinical psychologists, and counseling psychologists.

Health psychology explores the relationship between psychological factors and physical ailments or disease. For instance, health psychologists are interested in how long-term stress (a psychological factor) can affect physical health. They are also concerned with identifying ways of promoting behavior related to good health (such as increased exercise) or discouraging unhealthy behavior such as smoking, as we will discuss in Chapter 16.

For clinical psychologists, the focus of activity is on the treatment and prevention of psychological disturbance. **Clinical psychology** is the branch of psychology that deals with the study, diagnosis, and treatment of abnormal behavior. Clinical psychologists are trained to diagnose and treat problems ranging from the everyday crises of life such as grief due to the death of a loved one to more extreme conditions, such as loss of touch with reality. Some clinical psychologists also conduct research, investigating issues that range from identifying the early signs of psychological disturbance to studying the relationship between how family members communicate with one another and psychological disorder.

As we will see when we discuss abnormal behavior and its treatment in Chapters 17 and 18, the kinds of activities carried out by clinical psychologists are varied indeed. It is clinical psychologists who administer and score psychological tests and who provide psychological services in community mental health centers. Even sexual problems, as we will see when we consider human sexuality in Chapter 12, are often treated by clinical psychologists.

Like clinical psychologists, counseling psychologists deal with people's psychological problems, but they are problems of a particular sort. **Counseling psychology** is the branch of psychology that focuses primarily on educational, social, and career adjustment problems. Almost every college has a counseling center staffed with counseling psychologists, where students can get advice on the kinds of jobs they might be best suited for, on methods of studying effectively, and on strategies for resolving everyday difficulties, from problems with roommates to concerns about a specific professor's grading practices. Many large business organizations also employ counseling psychologists in order to help employees with work-related problems.

Two close relatives of counseling psychology are educational psychology and school psychology. **Educational psychology** considers how the educational process affects students; it is, for instance, concerned with ways of understanding intelligence, developing better teaching techniques, and understanding teacher–student interaction. **School psychology**, in contrast, is the specialty area devoted to assessing children in elementary and secondary schools who have academic or emotional problems and to developing solutions to such problems.

College counseling centers help students cope with studying difficulties, personal problems, and career decisions.

Social, Industrial-Organizational, Consumer, and Cross-Cultural Psychologists: Understanding the Social World

None of us lives in isolation; rather, we are all part of a complex network of interrelationships. These networks with other people and with society as a whole are the focus of study for many different kinds of psychologists.

Social psychology, as we will see in Chapters 19 and 20, is the study of how people's thoughts, feelings, and actions are affected by others. Social psychologists focus on such diverse topics as understanding human aggression, learning why people form relationships with one another, and determining how we are influenced by other people.

Industrial-organizational psychology is concerned with the psychology of the workplace. Specifically, it considers issues such as productivity, job satisfaction, and decision making. A related branch is **consumer psychology**, which considers people's buying habits and the effects of advertising on buyer behavior. As we will discuss in Chapter 21, an industrial-organizational psychologist might ask a question such as "How do you influence workers to improve the quality of products they produce?" while a consumer psychologist might ask the corresponding question of "How does product quality enter into decisions to purchase a product?"

Finally, **cross-cultural psychology** investigates the similarities and differences in psychological functioning in various cultures and ethnic groups. As we discuss throughout this book, psychologists specializing in cross-cultural issues investigate such questions as the following: How do the ways in which people in different cultures attribute their academic successes or failures lead to differences in scholastic performance (a factor that may account for differences in academic achievement between Americans and Japanese students)? How do child-rearing practices, which are substantially different among various cultures, affect subsequent adult values and attitudes? And why do cultures vary in their standards of physical attractiveness?

Social psychology: The branch of psychology that studies how people's thoughts, feelings, and actions are affected by others

Industrial-organizational psychology: The branch of psychology that studies the psychology of the workplace, considering productivity, job satisfaction, and decision making

Consumer psychology: The branch of psychology that considers our buying habits and the effects of advertising on buyer behavior

Cross-cultural psychology: The branch of psychology that investigates the similarities and differences in psychological functioning in various cultures and ethnic groups

A cross-cultural psychologist observing these young Moslem women as they read the Koran might note the influence of religion in their culture.

Environmental psychology: The branch of psychology that considers the relationship between people and their physical environment

Forensic psychology: The branch of psychology that focuses on legal issues, such as deciding what criteria indicate that a person is legally insane and whether larger or smaller juries make fairer decisions

Program evaluation: The assessment of large-scale programs to determine whether they are effective in meeting their goals

Emerging Areas

As the field of psychology matures, the number of specialty areas continues to increase (Schneider, 1990). For example, **environmental psychology** considers the relationship between people and their physical environment. Environmental psychologists have made significant progress in understanding how our physical environment affects, for example, the way we behave toward others, our emotions, and how much stress we experience in a particular setting.

   Forensic psychology focuses on legal issues, such as deciding what criteria indicate that a person is legally insane and whether larger or smaller juries make fairer decisions. Psychologists interested in **program evaluation** also constitute a growing body; they focus on assessing large-scale programs, usually run by the government, to determine whether they are effective in meeting their goals. For example, psychologists specializing in evaluation have examined the effectiveness of such governmental social services as the Head Start day-care program and Medicaid.

   To conclude our discussion of specialty areas, consider the work being done by psychologists interested in one of the frontiers of the 1990s: space psychology (described in the accompanying Cutting Edge box).

The Demographics of Psychology

Not only are the subfields of psychology diversified; the kinds of people who make up the field are also varied. Some basic demographic statistics begin to tell the story. For example, about two-thirds of American psychologists are men and about one-third women. These figures are not static, however: Among psychologists who recently received their degrees, the proportion of men to women is about equal, and in fact the number of women currently enrolled in psychology graduate schools is higher than that of men (ODEER, 1991).

   Psychologists are also found in all parts of the world. Although the majority are based in North America, about one-third are found in other areas of the globe (see Figure 1-2).

   Within the United States, one area in which there is relatively little diversity is that of race and ethnic origin. According to figures compiled by the American Psychological Association, of those psychologists who identify themselves by race

The writers of "Star Trek: The Next Generation" were on the right track when they included a psychologist among the crew of the starship *Enterprise*. As space flight becomes more common (by the turn of the century some 1000 people will have rocketed into space) and space flights grow longer, the psychological concerns of those on board will become increasingly important.

Several aspects of the exploration of outer space raise psychological issues, ranging from biological to social factors. Among the most critical factors are the following (Adler, 1990; Afari, 1989):

- Space flights are becoming longer—a possible Mars mission, for instance, is expected to last three years. In addition, flight crews are becoming increasingly diverse in terms of age, sex, and ethnic background. As the flight length and diversity of crew members increase, the possibility of conflict in cramped, public quarters also grows. The result is a need for rigorous psychological screening of astronauts to weed out people who are most vulnerable to discord.
- Space sickness, a close cousin of motion sickness, is a frequent affliction encountered by space travelers. The symptoms include

PSYCHOLOGY IN SPACE

a grim combination of nausea, vomiting, drowsiness, and headaches, and they affect about half of all space travelers. Although the symptoms usually fade after a few days, space sickness at best represents an unpleasant introduction to space and at worst interferes with mission duties. However, psychologists have developed a way of training potential astronauts to control their biological response. By using biofeedback techniques that we discuss in Chapter 3, in which people learn to control their physical responses, almost two-thirds of potential space travelers have been able to elude the symptoms of space sickness (Afari, 1989).

- Research in environmental psychology has shown that one of the ways in which crews deal with stress is by looking outside and observing the earth below. Crew members are now given the opportunity simply to look outside of the spacecraft. In addition, environmental psychologist Yvonne Clearwater is leading a team to increase the livability of future space stations (Clearwater, 1985). Her research to date has found that configurations that em-

phasize openness and depth—and allow people to look out a window—are crucial. She has also determined that the color scheme of the ship interior is important, not that one particular color is better than another, but that it is necessary to provide a variety of colors.

- Isolated groups may be subject to poor decision making, a phenomenon called "groupthink" that we discuss in Chapter 21 (Janis & Mann, 1976). Consequently, the decisions made by astronauts in flight must be monitored carefully to ensure their soundness.
- Finally, sex: The existence of mixed-sex crews raises the likelihood that sexual issues will need to be addressed. On long flights, sexual tensions and even liaisons may occur, and, as we consider in our discussion of sex and gender in Chapter 12, psychologists can provide assistance in dealing with these possibilities (Broad, 1992).

Issues such as these suggest that psychologists will come to play an increasingly important role in the space exploration program. Indeed, it is not farfetched to assume that psychology texts of the future will include "space psychology" among the branches of the field.

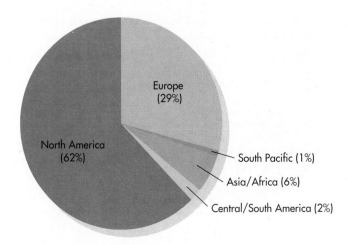

FIGURE 1-2

Origin of published research. (Source: Psychinfo, 1991.)

▶ **9**

and ethnic origin in surveys—and one-third don't respond to the question—almost 95 percent are white. Two percent are African-American and 2 percent Hispanic, while 1 percent are Asian. Although the number of nonwhite psychologists currently in graduate school is higher, approaching 11 percent, the numbers are still not representative of the proportion of minorities in society at large.

The underrepresentation of racial and ethnic minorities among psychologists is significant for several reasons. First, the field of psychology may be harmed by a lack of the diverse perspectives and talents provided by minority group members. Furthermore, minority group psychologists serve as role models for members of minority communities, and their lack of representation within the profession may deter additional minority group members from seeking to enter the field. Finally, members of minority groups frequently prefer to receive psychological therapy and counseling from treatment providers of the same race or ethnic group as their own. The relative rarity of minority psychologists therefore may hinder their ability to obtain treatment successfully. Consequently, vigorous efforts are being made to increase the numbers of psychologists from underrepresented groups (Stricker et al., 1990; Sue & Sue, 1990).

Psychology's Workplace

Given the diversity of roles that psychologists play, it is not surprising that they are employed in a variety of settings. As you can see in Figure 1-3, many psychologists are employed by institutions of higher learning (universities, two- and four-year colleges, and medical schools) or work as independent practitioners treating clients. The next most frequent employment settings are hospitals, clinics, community mental-health centers, and counseling centers. Other settings include human-services organizations, research and consulting firms, and business and industry (ODEER, 1991).

Why are so many psychologists found in academic settings? The answer is that the three major roles played by psychologists in society—teacher, scientist, and clinical practitioner—are easily carried out in such an environment. Very often professors of psychology are also actively involved in research or in serving clients. Whatever their particular job site, however, psychologists share a commitment to better both individual lives and society in general (DeLeon, 1988; Peterson, 1991).

FIGURE 1-3

Where psychologists work: The major settings in which psychologists are employed. (Source: ODEER, 1991; data comprise masters and doctoral psychologists, whose employment settings vary according to training.)

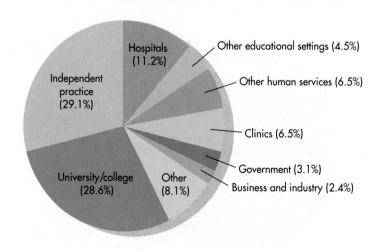

RECAP

◀ Psychology is the scientific study of behavior and mental processes.

◀ Among the major kinds of psychologists are biopsychologists; experimental psychologists; cognitive psychologists; developmental and personality psychologists; health, clinical, and counseling psychologists; education and school psychologists; and cross-cultural psychologists.

◀ Many psychologists are employed by institutions of higher learning, and most of the balance are employed by hospitals, clinics, and community health centers or are engaged in independent practice.

REVIEW

1. The foundation of psychology today lies in
   a. intuition.
   b. observation and experimentation.
   c. trial and error.
   d. metaphysics.
2. It is pointless to consider animal behavior when you are interested in learning about human behavior. True or false? _____F_____
3. A large proportion of psychologists are employed in academic institutions because that type of environment makes it easier for them to carry out the roles of _____teacher_____, _____scientist_____, and _____clinical_____ _____practitioner_____.
4. Match each branch of psychology with the issues or questions posed in the next column.
   _4_ a. Biopsychology
   _9_ b. Experimental psychology
   _11_ c. Cognitive psychology
   _2_ d. Developmental psychology
   _5_ e. Personality psychology
   _8_ f. Health psychology
   _10_ g. Clinical psychology
   _1_ h. Counseling psychology
   _12_ i. Educational psychology
   _7_ j. School psychology
   _3_ k. Social psychology
   _13_ l. Industrial psychology
   _6_ m. Consumer psychology

1. Joan, a college freshman, is panicking. She needs to learn better organizational skills and study habits to cope with the demands of college.
2. At what age do children generally begin to acquire an emotional attachment to their fathers?
3. It is thought that pornographic films that depict violence against women may prompt aggressive behavior in some men.
4. What chemicals are released in the human body as a result of a stressful event? What are their effects on behavior?
5. John is fairly unusual in his manner of responding to crisis situations, with an even temperament and a positive outlook.
6. The general public is more apt to buy products that are promoted by attractive and successful actors.
7. Eight-year-old Jack's teachers are concerned that he has recently begun to withdraw socially and to show little interest in school work.
8. Janet's job is demanding and stressful. She wonders if this lifestyle is leaving her more prone to certain illnesses such as cancer and heart disease.
9. A psychologist is intrigued by the fact that some people are much more sensitive to painful stimuli than others.
10. A strong fear of crowds leads a young woman to seek treatment for her problem.
11. What mental strategies are involved in solving complex word problems?
12. What teaching approaches most effectively motivate elementary school students to successfully accomplish academic tasks?
13. Jessica is asked to develop a management strategy that will encourage safer work practices in an assembly plant.

Ask Yourself

Imagine you had a seven-year-old child who was having problems learning to read. Imagine further that you could consult as many psychologists as you wanted. How might each type of psychologist approach the problem?

Are intuition and common sense sufficient for understanding why people act the way they do? Why is a scientific approach appropriate for studying human behavior?

(Answers to review questions are on page 12.)

A SCIENCE EVOLVES: THE PAST AND THE FUTURE

Some half-million years ago, primitive peoples assumed that psychological problems were caused by the presence of evil spirits. To allow these spirits to escape, an operation called trephining was performed. Trephining consisted of chipping away at the

According to Descartes, nerves were hollow tubes through which impulses would flow.

skull with crude stone instruments until a hole was cut through the bone. Because archaeologists have found skulls with signs of healing around the opening, we can assume that patients sometimes survived the cure.

The famous Greek physician Hippocrates thought that personality was made up of four temperaments: sanguine (cheerful and active), melancholic (sad), choleric (angry and aggressive), and phlegmatic (calm and passive). These temperaments were influenced by the presence of "humors," or fluids, in the body. For instance, a sanguine person was thought to have more blood than other people.

Franz Josef Gall, an eighteenth-century scientist, argued that a trained observer could discern intelligence, moral character, and other basic personality traits from the shape and number of bumps on a person's skull. His theory gave rise to the "science" of phrenology, employed by hundreds of practitioners in the nineteenth century.

According to the philosopher Descartes, nerves were hollow tubes through which "animal spirits" conducted impulses in the same way that water is transmitted through a pipe. When a person put a finger too close to the fire, the heat was transmitted via the spirits through the tube and directly into the brain.

Although these "scientific" explanations sound farfetched to us, at one time they represented the most advanced thinking regarding what might be called the psychology of the era. Even without knowing much about modern-day psychology, you can surmise that our understanding of behavior has advanced tre-

---

ANSWERS (REVIEW I):

1. b **2.** False; by studying animal behavior, we can learn general behavioral laws that may apply to humans as well. **3.** Teacher; scientist; clinical practitioner **4.** a-4; b-9; c-11; d-2; e-5; f-8; g-10; h-1; i-12; j-7; k-3; l-13; m-6

mendously since these earlier views were formulated. Yet most of the advances have been recent, for, as sciences go, psychology is one of the newcomers on the block.

Although its roots can be traced back to the ancient Greeks and Romans, and although philosophers have argued for several hundred years about some of the same sorts of questions that psychologists grapple with today, the formal beginning of psychology is generally set at 1879. In that year, the first laboratory devoted to the experimental study of psychological phenomena was established in Germany by Wilhelm Wundt; at about the same time, the American William James set up his laboratory in Cambridge, Massachusetts.

Throughout some eleven decades of formal existence, psychology has led an active life, developing gradually into a true science (Hilgard, Leary, & McGuire, 1991). As part of this evolution, it has produced a number of conceptual **models**, systems of interrelated ideas and concepts used to explain phenomena, that have guided the work being carried out. Some of these models have been discarded—just as the views of Hippocrates and Descartes have—but others have been developed and elaborated on and provide a set of maps for psychologists to follow.

Models: Systems of interrelated ideas and concepts used to explain phenomena

Each of the models provides a distinct perspective, emphasizing different factors. Just as we may employ not one but many maps to find our way around a particular geographical area—one map to show the roads, one the major landmarks, and one the topography of the hills and valleys—psychologists also find that more than one approach may be useful in understanding behavior. Given the range and complexity of behavior, no single model will invariably provide an optimal explanation—but together, the models provide us with a means for explaining the extraordinary breadth of behavior.

The Roots of Psychology

When Wilhelm Wundt set up the first psychology laboratory in 1879, he was interested in studying the building blocks of the mind. Formally defining psychology as the study of conscious experience, he developed a model that came to be known as structuralism. **Structuralism** focused on the fundamental elements that form the foundation of thinking, consciousness, emotions, and other kinds of mental states and activities.

Structuralism: An early approach to psychology which focused on the fundamental elements that form the foundation of thinking, consciousness, emotions, and other kinds of mental states and activities

To come to an understanding of how basic sensations combined to produce our awareness of the world, Wundt and other structuralists used a procedure called **introspection** to study the structure of the mind. In introspection, people were presented with a stimulus—such as a bright green object or a sentence printed on a card—and asked to describe, in their own words and in as much detail as they could manage, what they were experiencing as they were exposed to it. Wundt argued that psychologists could come to understand the structure of the mind through the reports that people offered of their reactions.

Introspection: A procedure used to study the structure of the mind, in which subjects are asked to describe in detail what they are experiencing when they are exposed to a stimulus

Wundt's structuralism did not stand the test of time, however, for psychologists became increasingly dissatisfied with the assumption that introspection could unlock the fundamental elements of the mind. For one thing, people had difficulty describing some kinds of inner experiences, such as emotional responses. (For example, the next time you experience anger, try to analyze and explain the primary elements of what you are feeling.) Moreover, breaking down objects into their most basic mental units sometimes seemed to be a most peculiar undertaking. A book, for instance, could not be described by a structuralist

Wilhelm Wundt, in the center of this photo, established the first laboratory to study psychological phenomena in 1879.

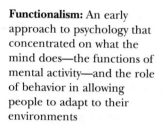

Functionalism: An early approach to psychology that concentrated on what the mind does—the functions of mental activity—and the role of behavior in allowing people to adapt to their environments

Gestalt (geh SHTALLT) **psychology:** An approach to psychology that focuses on the organization of perception and thinking in a "whole" sense, rather than on the individual elements of perception

as merely a book, but instead had to be broken down into its various components, such as the material on the cover, the colors, the shapes of the letters, and so on. Finally, introspection was not a truly scientific technique; there was little way that an outside observer could verify the accuracy of the introspections that people did make. Such drawbacks led to the evolution of new models, which largely supplanted structuralism.

Interestingly, however, important remnants of structuralism still exist. As we shall see in Chapter 9, the past twenty years have seen a resurgence of interest in people's descriptions of their inner experience. Cognitive psychologists, whose interests center on higher mental processes such as thinking, memory, and problem solving, have developed innovative techniques for understanding people's conscious experience that overcome many of the difficulties inherent in introspection.

The model that largely replaced structuralism in the evolution of psychology was known as functionalism. Rather than focusing on the mind's components, **functionalism** concentrated on what the mind *does*—the functions of mental activity. Functionalists, whose model rose to prominence in the early 1900s, asked what roles behavior plays in allowing people to adapt to their environments better. Led by the American psychologist William James, the functionalists, rather than raising the more abstract questions about the processes of mental behavior, examined the ways in which behavior allows people to satisfy their needs (Johnson & Henley, 1990). The famous American educator John Dewey took a functionalist approach and from it developed the field of school psychology, theorizing about how students' needs could best be met through the educational system.

Another reaction to structuralism was the development of gestalt psychology in the early 1900s. **Gestalt psychology** is a model of psychology focusing on the study of how perception is organized. Instead of considering the individual parts that make up thinking, gestalt psychologists took the opposite tack, concentrating on how people consider individual elements as units or wholes. Their credo was "The whole is greater than the sum of its parts," meaning that, when considered together, the basic elements that comprise our perception of objects produce something greater and more meaningful than those individual elements alone. As we shall see when we examine perception in Chapter 5, the contributions of gestalt psychologists to the understanding of perception are substantial.

Despite societal constraints that limited women's participation in many professions—and psychology was no exception—several women made major contributions to psychology in the early years of the field (Russo & Denmark, 1987). For example, in the early part of the century Leta Stetter Hollingworth coined the term "gifted" in reference to unusually bright children, and she wrote a book on adolescence that became a classic (Hollingworth, 1928). She also was one of the first psychologists to focus particularly on women's issues. For instance, she collected data to refute the view, popular in the early 1900s, that women's abilities regularly declined during parts of the menstrual cycle (Benjamin & Shields, 1990; Hollingworth, 1943/1990).

Another influential figure was June Etta Downey, who spearheaded the study of personality traits in the 1920s. She also developed a widely disseminated personality test and became the first woman to lead a psychology department at a state university (Stevens & Gardner, 1982).

Despite the contributions of such women, psychology was largely a male-dominated field in its early years. Still, although their absolute numbers were low, the proportion of prominent women in psychology was greater than in other scientific fields (Simonton, 1992). Furthermore, the situation has undergone a dramatic turnaround over the past decade, and, as we mentioned earlier, the number of women in the discipline has been increasing rapidly in recent years. Consequently, when future historians of science write about psychology in the 1990s, they are likely to be recording a history of men *and* women (Cohen & Guntek, 1991).

Today's Models

The early roots of psychology are complex and varied, and consequently it is not surprising that the field is so diverse today. However, it is possible to encompass the breadth of psychology using just a few basic models. Each of these broad models, which continue to evolve, emphasizes different aspects of behavior and mental processes and steers the thinking of psychologists in somewhat different directions.

The five major models that make up the field are the biological, psychodynamic, cognitive, behavioral, and humanistic models. We discuss each in turn.

Biological Models: Blood, Sweat, and Fears.   When we get down to the basics, behavior is carried out by living creatures made of skin and guts. According to the **biological model**, the behavior of both people and animals should be considered from the perspective of their biological functioning: how the individual nerve cells are joined together, how the inheritance of certain characteristics from parents and other ancestors influences behavior, how the functioning of the body affects hopes and fears, what behaviors are due to instincts, and so forth. Even more complex kinds of behaviors—emotional responses such as anxiety, for example—are viewed as having critical biological components by psychologists using the biological model.

Biological model: The psychological model that views behavior from the perspective of biological functioning

Because every behavior can at some level be broken down into its biological components, the biological model has broad appeal. Psychologists who subscribe to this model have made major contributions to the understanding and betterment of human life, ranging from developing cures for certain types of deafness to identifying drugs to treat people with severe mental disorders.

Sigmund Freud, a Viennese physician, developed the psychodynamic model in which people's behavior was considered to be determined by unconscious processes.

Psychodynamic model: The psychological model based on the belief that behavior is motivated by inner forces over which the individual has little control

Cognitive model: The psychological model that focuses on how people know, understand, and think about the world

Behavioral model: The psychological model that focuses on observable behavior

Rejecting psychology's initial emphasis on the inner workings of the mind, John B. Watson emphasized observable behavior.

Psychodynamic Models: Understanding the Inner Person.   To many people who have never taken a psychology course, psychology begins and ends with the **psychodynamic model**. Proponents of the psychodynamic perspective believe that behavior is motivated by inner forces over which the individual has little control. Dreams and slips of the tongue are viewed as indications of what a person is truly feeling within a seething cauldron of subconscious psychic activity.

The psychodynamic view is intimately linked with one individual: Sigmund Freud. Freud was a Viennese physician in the early 1900s whose ideas about unconscious determinants of behavior had a revolutionary effect on twentieth-century thinking, not just in psychology but in related fields as well. Although many of the basic principles of psychodynamic thinking have been roundly criticized, the model that has grown out of Freud's work has provided a means not only for treating mental disorders but also for understanding everyday phenomena such as prejudice and aggression.

Cognitive Models: Comprehending the Roots of Understanding.   The route to understanding behavior leads some psychologists straight into the mind. Evolving in part from structuralism, which, as we noted earlier, was concerned with identifying the various parts of the mind, the **cognitive model** focuses on how people know, understand, and think about the world. The emphasis, though, has shifted away from learning about the structure of the mind itself to learning how people understand and represent the outside world within themselves and how this understanding influences their behavior (Rouse & Morris, 1986).

Psychologists relying on this model ask questions ranging from whether a person can watch television and study a book at the same time (the answer is "probably not") to how people figure out for themselves the causes of others' behavior. The common elements that link cognitive approaches are the emphasis on how people understand and think about the world and a concern about describing the patterns and regularities of the operation of our minds.

Behavioral Models: Observing the Outer Person.   While the biological, psychodynamic, and cognitive approaches look inside the organism to determine the causes of its behavior, the behavioral model takes a very different approach. The **behavioral model** grew out of a rejection of psychology's early emphasis on the inner workings of the mind, suggesting instead that observable behavior should be the focus of the field.

John B. Watson was the first major American psychologist to advocate a behavioral approach. Working in the 1920s, Watson was firm in his view that a full understanding of behavior could be obtained by studying and modifying the environment in which people operated. In fact, he believed rather optimistically that by properly controlling a person's environment, any desired sort of behavior could be obtained, as his own words make clear: "Give me a dozen healthy infants, well-formed, and my own specified world to bring them up in and I'll guarantee to take any one at random and train him to become any type of specialist I might select—doctor, lawyer, artist, merchant-chief, and yes, even beggar-man and thief, regardless of his talents, penchants, tendencies, abilities, vocations and race of his ancestors" (Watson, 1924). In more recent time, the behavioral model was championed by B. F. Skinner, who until his death in 1990 was the best-known contemporary psychologist. Much of our understanding of how people learn new behaviors is based on the behavioral model.

As we will see, the behavioral model crops up along every byway of psychology. Along with the influence it has had in the area of learning processes, this model has also made contributions in such diverse areas as the treatment of

The story began with a case of fatigue and a stubborn rash in the folds of her groin. The physician examined her carefully. The fatigue was easily explained away. She was working too hard. As for the rash, nylon stockings and relentless humidity made it a common summertime affliction. Still, the rash struck him as meaner than most. He ordered a blood workup for the patient.

"So," he said, . . . tell me about your sex life." She had lost her virginity at twenty, the oldest among her friends, and married the first man she slept with, but divorced him two years later. Depression dulled her . . . sensibilities and she "got wild" for about two years. Though she had been celibate for the nine months before the examination, there had been fifteen partners before that. For the most part, they were friends who became lovers or lovers who became friends. And no condoms; they didn't seem necessary. There is, to this day, no reason to think that any of her partners were bisexual or users of intravenous drugs or frequenters of prostitutes.

The doctor asked her if she would like him to order an AIDS test. He had no particular reason to suggest it, but was mindful of the times. (Kroeger, 1989, p. 158.)

The test would be repeated twice over the next few weeks, and each time it would produce the same result: The woman had AIDS.

The story is not a rare one. One out of every 500 college students now carries the virus, and it is predicted that by the year 2000 there will be more than 1 million reported cases just in the United States (Cowley, 1990b; Alumnus, 1989).

Yet the AIDS epidemic has not gone unchallenged. Evidence suggests that the rate of increase in new cases has started to decline as sci-

PSYCHOLOGY AND THE PREVENTION OF AIDS

Psychologists have made a concerted effort to halt the spread of AIDS and to deal with the aftermath of the disease through counseling, as with AIDS sufferer Tom White.

entists in a variety of fields have begun to address the disease.

The field of psychology has come to play a key role in the war against AIDS. Psychologists have worked to quell the spread of the disease and to deal with its aftermaths. Their work can be seen along several fronts:

- Counseling and treating people with the AIDS virus. People who learn they carry the AIDS virus face major psychological difficulties in addition to their medical ones. They must decide who to tell of the test results, may face eviction from their homes and loss of insurance coverage, and—most fundamentally—must adjust to the uncertainty of the disease and the very real possibility of their own death in the not-too-distant future. Coping with such a terrifying set of circumstances typically requires major psychological adjustment, and psychologists are devising innovative treatment techniques.

- Understanding the biological basis of AIDS. Some psychologists, using the biological model, are working toward understanding the physiological aspects of the disease better. For example, patients in the advanced stages of AIDS sometimes show signs of

brain damage, leading to loss of intellectual abilities. Deciphering how the disease progresses as it increasingly involves the brain may help to better treatment programs and slow the course of the virus.

- Preventing the spread of AIDS. Although the term "safer sex" is becoming a familiar one, this has not always been the case. Psychologists, especially those employing the cognitive and behavioral models, have been in the forefront of developing ways to lead people to modify their sexual practices to reduce the danger of contracting and spreading the AIDS virus (Coates, 1990). In addition, psychologists using approaches derived from the biological model are investigating the actual means of viral transmission. (We will speak more of specific safer-sex practices in Chapter 12.)

- Supporting rational decision making in testing for AIDS. Should people who feel themselves at risk be tested for AIDS, or are they better off with the uncertainty of the disease? Should testing be mandatory for some people, such as health-care workers? Questions such as these are being addressed with the assistance of psychologists concerned with social processes, decision making, and ethics, primarily using cognitive models as a guide.

As you can see, psychologists are playing important and quite varied roles in combating the AIDS epidemic. And this is not the only societal problem in which their expertise is being called upon to help alleviate human suffering. As we will see throughout this book in other Psychology at Work boxes, the basic principles of the science of psychology are being used to address a wide range of social problems.

mental disorders, the curbing of aggression, the resolution of sexual problems, and even the halting of drug addiction.

Humanistic Models: The Unique Qualities of Homo Sapiens.   Although it emerged several decades ago, the **humanistic model** is still considered the newest of the major approaches. Rejecting the views that behavior is determined largely by automatic, biological forces, unconscious processes, or solely by the environment, it suggests instead that people are in control of their lives. Humanistic psychologists maintain that people are naturally inclined to develop toward higher levels of maturity and fulfillment and that, if given the opportunity, they will strive to reach their full potential. The emphasis, then, is on **free will**, the human ability to make decisions about one's life.

More than any other approach, the humanistic model stresses the role of psychology in enriching people's lives and helping them to achieve self-fulfillment. While not as all-encompassing as some of the other general models, the humanistic perspective has had an important influence on psychologists, reminding them of their commitment to the individual person and society.

It is important not to let the abstract qualities of the humanistic model, as well as the other models we have discussed, lull you into thinking that they are purely theoretical: They underlie ongoing work in psychology that has very practical implications, implications that will concern us throughout this book. As a start, consider the Psychology at Work box on p. 17.

Humanistic model: The psychological model that suggests that people are in control of their lives

Free will: The human ability to make decisions about one's life

---

RECAP AND REVIEW II

RECAP

◄ Traces of the early models of structuralism, functionalism, and gestalt psychology can be seen in the major models used by psychologists today.

◄ The dominant psychological models encompass biological, psychodynamic, cognitive, behavioral, and humanistic approaches.

REVIEW

1. Wundt described psychology as the study of conscious experience, a model he termed _structuralism_ .
2. Early psychologists studied the mind by asking people to describe what they were experiencing when exposed to various stimuli. This procedure was known as _introspection_ .
3. The model of psychology which largely replaced structuralism was _functionalism_ , a model concerned with the purposes of mental activity.
4. The statement, "In order to study human behavior, we must consider the whole of perception rather than its component parts" is one that might be made by a person subscribing to which model of psychology? _Gestalt_
5. Jeanne's therapist asks her to recount a violent dream she recently experienced in order to gain insight into the un-

conscious forces affecting her behavior. Jeanne's therapist is working from a _psychodynamic_ model.
6. "It is behavior that can be observed which should be studied, not the suspected inner workings of the mind." This statement was most likely made by someone following the perspective of a
   a. cognitive model.
   b. biological model.
   c. humanistic model.
   d. behavioral model.
7. Recent studies of schizophrenia have identified peculiar arrangements of nerve cells, possibly inherited, as a suspected cause of that mental illness. Research such as this is typical of a _biological_ model.
8. "My therapist is wonderful! She always points out my positive traits. She dwells on my uniqueness and strength as an individual. I feel much more confident about myself— as if I'm really growing and reaching my potential." The therapist referred to above probably practices from a _humanistic_ model.

Ask Yourself

How are today's major models of psychology related to the earlier models of structuralism, functionalism, and gestalt psychology?

(Answers to review questions are on page 20.)

As you consider the many diverse topical areas and models that make up the field of psychology, you may find yourself thinking that you've embarked on a journey into a fragmented discipline that lacks any cohesion. You may be anticipating a field of study consisting of a series of unrelated, separate subject areas, no closer to one another than physics is to chemistry. In fact, such a conclusion is not illogical, given that psychology covers so many diverse areas, ranging from such topics as narrowly focused as the minute biochemical influences on behavior to social behavior in its broadest sense.

Yet despite the seeming disparity between the various topics and models, the differences in some ways are more apparent than real. The field is actually more unified than a first glimpse may imply, because the five models actually help to integrate the various branches of the discipline. Thus a psychologist from any given branch might choose to employ any one, or more, of the major models.

For example, a developmental psychologist might subscribe to a psychodynamic model *or* a behavioral model *or* any of the other models. Similarly, a clinical psychologist might use a behavioral model *or* a cognitive model *or* one of the other models. The models may be used in different ways by various psychologists, but the assumptions of a given model are similar regardless of the subfield to which it is applied.

Of course, not every branch of psychology is equally likely to employ a particular model. Historically, some kinds of psychologists have been more apt to use certain models, and some models have proven more useful than others when attempting to deal with a particular topical area.

For example, biopsychologists interested in the brain are most likely to employ a biological model, given its emphasis on the biological foundations of behavior. At the same time, most biopsychologists reject the psychodynamic model's reliance on unconscious determinants of behavior. Similarly, social psychologists who are interested in explaining the roots of prejudice are more apt to find cognitive models of use than biological models.

Table 1-1 indicates which major models of psychology are most likely to be used by the different types of psychologists. Keep in mind, though, that at least in theory, each of the models is available to any psychologist who chooses to employ it.

Psychology's Key Issues and Questions

Another link exists among the various branches and models of psychology: a shared agreement on what the key issues and questions of the field are. At the same time, universal accord on how best to resolve and answer them is lacking; indeed, each represents a major set of controversies within the discipline. However, what makes psychology a unified science is the collective acknowledgment that these issues and questions must be addressed in order for the field to move forward. Among the most important are the following:

■ *Nature (heredity) versus nurture (environment).* How much of our behavior is due to heredity ("nature") and how much is due to environment ("nurture")? This question infuses many of the models and branches of psychology, and in fact has deep philosophical and historical roots.

The particular model to which a psychologist subscribes determines in part how this issue is addressed. For example, developmental psychologists whose focus is on how people grow and change throughout the course of

TABLE 1-1

MAJOR MODELS OF PSYCHOLOGY AS USED BY DIFFERENT KINDS OF PSYCHOLOGISTS

Type of Psychologist	Model[a]				
	Biological	**Psychodynamic**	**Cognitive**	**Behavioral**	**Humanistic**
Biopsychologist	✓			✓	
Experimental	✓		✓	✓	
Cognitive			✓		
Developmental	✓	✓	✓	✓	✓
Personality	✓	✓	✓	✓	✓
Health	✓		✓	✓	
Clinical	✓	✓	✓	✓	✓
Counseling		✓	✓	✓	✓
Educational			✓	✓	✓
School			✓	✓	✓
Social		✓	✓	✓	
Industrial-organizational			✓	✓	
Consumer			✓	✓	
Cross-cultural		✓	✓	✓	✓

[a] Models that are used most frequently by a particular type of psychologist are checked.

their lives would concentrate most on the hereditary side of the issue if they were oriented toward employing a biological model. On the other hand, developmental psychologists who are proponents of the behavioral model would be more apt to focus on the environmental determinants of behavior.

■ *Conscious versus unconscious determinants of behavior.* How much of our behavior is produced by forces of which we are fully aware, and how much is due to unconscious activity—mental processes not available to the conscious mind—about which we are oblivious?

The degree to which behavior is influenced by unconscious forces represents one of the great controversies in the field of psychology. For example, clinical psychologists subscribing to the psychodynamic model argue that much of abnormal behavior is produced by unconscious factors, while others employing cognitive models suggest that abnormal behavior is largely the result of faulty thinking processes. The specific approach taken has a clear impact on how abnormal behavior is treated.

■ *Observable behavior versus internal mental processes.* Should psychology concentrate solely on behavior that can be seen by outside observers, or should unseen thinking processes represent the focus of the field?

Some psychologists, particularly those relying on behavioral models, contend that the only legitimate source of information for psychologists is behavior that can be observed. Other psychologists, building on a cognitive model, argue that what goes on inside a person's head is most critical and

ANSWERS (REVIEW II):
1. structuralism   **2.** introspection   **3.** functionalism   **4.** Gestalt   **5.** psychodynamic   **6.** d
7. biological   **8.** humanistic

that we cannot understand behavior without concerning ourselves with mental processes.

■ *Freedom of choice versus determinism.* How much of behavior is a matter of choices made freely by an individual, and how much is subject to **determinism**, the notion that behavior is largely produced by factors beyond people's willful control?

Determinism: The notion that behavior is largely produced by factors beyond people's willful control

An issue long argued by philosophers, the freedom–determinism argument is central to the field of psychology as well (Kimble, 1989). For example, some psychologists specializing in abnormal behavior argue that behavior is governed by the intentional choices people make, and hence those who display so-called "abnormal behavior" should be considered responsible for their actions. Other psychologists take an opposing position, contending that such individuals are the victims of forces beyond their control. The stance taken on this issue has important implications for the nature of treatment, particularly when deciding whether treatment should be forced on those who say they do not want it.

■ *Individual differences versus universal principles.* How much of behavior is a consequence of the unique and special qualities that each of us possesses, and how much is due to the fact that we are all human beings, sharing a similar biological makeup and to some degree similar experiences?

This question bears on the issue of to what extent people behave similarly to one another. Psychologists relying on biological models tend to look for the universals in behavior, such as how our nervous system operates or in the way certain hormones automatically prime us for sexual activity. Such psychologists concentrate on the similarities in our behavioral destinies, despite vast differences in upbringing. In contrast, psychologists employing humanistic models focus more on the uniqueness of every individual. They consider how every person's behavior is a reflection of distinct and special qualities.

As you contemplate these five key psychological issues, summarized in Table 1-2, keep in mind that they should not be looked upon in "either-or" terms. For example, as suggested earlier, a psychologist would not argue that behavior is due solely to nature *or* solely to nurture; instead, the question would be one of degree. Each of these issues, then, should be considered as opposite ends of a continuum, with the positions of individual psychologists falling somewhere between the two extremes of the issue.

Psychology's Future

We've visited the foundations from which the field of psychology has evolved. But what does the future hold in store for the discipline? Although the course of scientific development is notoriously difficult to predict, several trends do seem likely to emerge in the not-so-distant future:

■ Psychology will become increasingly specialized. In a field in which practitioners must be experts on such diverse topics as the intricacies of the transmission of electrochemical impulses across nerve endings and the communication patterns of employees in large organizations, no one individual can be expected to master the field. Thus, it is likely that specialization will increase as psychologists delve into new areas.

TABLE 1-2

POSITIONS TAKEN BY PSYCHOLOGISTS USING THE MAJOR MODELS OF PSYCHOLOGY

	Model				
	Biological	*Psychodynamic*	*Cognitive*	*Behavioral*	*Humanistic*
Conceptual Focus: **Issue**	Biological functions as bases of behavior	Unconscious determinants of behavior	Nature of thought processes and under-standing	Observable behavior	Human desire to reach potential
Nature (heredity) vs. nurture (environment)	Nature (heredity)	Nature (heredity)	Both	Nurture (environment)	Nurture (environment)
Conscious vs. unconscious determinants of behavior	Unconscious	Unconscious	Both	Conscious	Conscious
Observable behavior vs. internal mental processes	Internal emphasis	Internal emphasis	Internal emphasis	Observable emphasis	Internal emphasis
Freedom vs. determinism	Determinism	Determinism	Freedom	Determinism	Freedom
Individual differences vs. universal principles	Universal emphasis	Universal emphasis	Individual emphasis	Both	Individual emphasis

■ New models will evolve. As a growing, maturing science, psychology will produce new models to supplant current approaches. Moreover, older models may be merged to form new ones. We can be certain, then, that as psychologists accumulate more knowledge they will become increasingly sophisticated in their understanding of behavior and mental processes.

■ Psychological treatment will become more accessible as the number of psychologists increases. In addition, psychologists will increasingly act as consultants to volunteer and self-help groups that are becoming more common, permitting members of such groups to help themselves more effectively (Jacobs & Goodman, 1989).

■ Psychology's influence on issues in the public interest will grow. Each of the major problems of our time—such as racial and ethnic prejudice, poverty, environmental and technological disasters—have important psychological aspects. While psychology alone will not solve these problems, its major accomplishments in the past (many of which are documented in future chapters) foretell that psychologists will make important practical contributions toward their resolution.

THE INFORMED CONSUMER OF PSYCHOLOGY:
Distinguishing Professional Psychology from Pseudo-Psychology

■ An advertisement on the back pages of a national magazine proclaims a cure for a major psychological problem: "The 8-week Phobia Treatment: A Complete Home-Treatment Guide to Phobia and Stress Relief." For only $29.95 (plus $3.05 for postage), a reader is furnished with an "amazing" book covering topics such as "why pills and medication won't help," "your own tests," and "much, much more."

■ A self-proclaimed expert on an Oprah Winfrey show provides advice to a woman whose husband left her after thirty-three years of marriage: "I sense some anger," he says. "Let the anger out, let the anger out." Just how the anger is to be let out is left to the viewer's imagination.

■ "Penetrate the Minds of Others—with Mind Prober!" declares the sales pitch that arrives in the mail with the day's bills and catalogs. "Now you can use the power of your personal computer to unlock those hidden truths about anyone in your life. With Mind Prober software, you'll gain useful, accurate insight into anyone you choose as a subject. There is no limit to the number of people you may analyze. If you'd like to reveal hidden truths about people you know (or think you know), order Mind Prober today!"

From advertisements to television and radio talk shows, we are subjected to a barrage of information in the media about psychology. We are told how to become better adjusted, smarter, happier, and more insightful about others by learning the secrets that psychologists have revealed.

Yet the promises are usually empty ones. If self-improvement were this easy, we would live in a country of happy-go-lucky, fully satisfied, and fulfilled individuals. Obviously the world is not quite so simple, and the quality of advice supposedly based on psychological truths, provided by self-styled experts—and even, on occasion, by some less than reputable psychologists—varies widely. For this reason, there are several points to keep in mind when you evaluate information of a psychological nature, whether the source is an advertisement, a television show, a magazine article, or even a book as seemingly reliable as a college text.

■ For starters, know who the information and advice is coming from. Are the purveyors of the information trained psychologists? What kind of degree do they have? Are they licensed? Are they affiliated with a particular institution? Before seriously relying on experts' advice, check out their credentials.

From ads to popular books to radio and television talk shows, we receive a barrage of information about psychology, not all of which is based on sound research.

■ There's no free ride. If it were possible to solve major psychological ills through the purchase of a $29.95 book, why do many people who suffer from such problems typically expend a considerable amount of time and money before they can be helped? If you could erase the pain of divorce by "letting your anger out," why aren't more recently divorced people venting their anger from the rooftops? If you could, in fact, buy a computer program that would really "unlock the hidden truths" about others, wouldn't it be in widespread use? The point is that difficult problems require complex solutions, and you should be wary of simple, glib responses to the question of how to resolve major difficulties.

■ Few universal cures for all of humankind's ills exist. No method or technique works with everyone. The range of difficulties bound up with the human condition is so broad that any procedure that purports to resolve all problems is sure to be a disappointment for many who attempt to employ it.

■ Finally, remember that no source of information or advice is definitive. The notion of infallibility is best left to religious realms, and you should approach psychological information and advice from a critical and thoughtful perspective.

Despite these cautions, the field of psychology has produced a wealth of important information that can be drawn upon for suggestions about every phase of people's lives. As discussed earlier, one of the major goals of this book is to make you an informed consumer of psychological knowledge by enhancing your ability to evaluate what psychologists have to offer. Ultimately, this book should provide you with the tools you need to critically analyze the theories, research, and applications that psychologists have developed. In doing so, you will be able to appreciate the contributions that the field of psychology has made in improving the quality of human life.

▶ RECAP AND REVIEW III

RECAP

◀ Underlying the work of all psychologists are the issues of heredity (nature) versus environment (nurture), conscious versus unconscious determinants of behavior, observable behavior versus internal mental processes, freedom versus determinism, and individual differences versus universal principles.

◀ Future trends suggest that the field of psychology will become more specialized, psychological treatment will become more accessible, and psychology's influence over the public interest will grow.

REVIEW

1. Each branch of psychology has a model unique to it. True or false? _____

2. "It can be shown that all behavior can be traced to purely environmental causes." Would you agree or disagree, and why?

3. Identify the model that suggests that abnormal behavior may be the result of largely unconscious forces.

4. "Psychologists should only worry about behavior that is directly observable." This statement would most likely be made by a person using which model of psychological research?

5. Psychology is currently moving toward increased specialization and differentiation. True or false? _____

Ask Yourself

"Computer programs which read minds and at-home cures for mental illness show the great progress psychology has made as of late." Criticize this statement in light of what you know about professional and pseudo-psychology.

(Answers to review questions are on page 26.)

■ *What is psychology and why is it a science?*

1. Although the definition of psychology—the scientific study of behavior and mental processes—is clear-cut, it is also deceivingly simple, since "behavior" encompasses not just what people do, but also their thoughts, feelings, perceptions, reasoning, memory, and biological activities.

■ *What are the different branches of the field of psychology?*

2. Psychology has a number of major areas in which psychologists specialize. Biopsychologists focus on the biological basis of behavior, while experimental psychologists study the processes of sensing, perceiving, learning, and thinking about the world. Cognitive psychology, an outgrowth of experimental psychology, considers the study of higher mental processes, including thinking, language, memory, problem solving, knowing, reasoning, judging, and decision making.

3. The branches of psychology that study change and individual differences are developmental and personality psychology. Developmental psychologists study how people grow and change throughout their life span. Personality psychologists consider the consistency and change in an individual's behavior as he or she moves through different situations, as well as the individual differences that distinguish one person's behavior from another's when each is placed in the same situation.

4. Health, clinical, and counseling psychologists are primarily concerned with promoting physical and mental health. Health psychologists study psychological factors that affect physical disease, while clinical psychologists consider the study, diagnosis, and treatment of abnormal behavior. Counseling psychologists focus on educational, social, and career adjustment problems.

5. Educational psychologists investigate how the educational process affects students, while school psychologists specialize in assessing and treating children in elementary and secondary schools who have academic or emotional problems.

6. Social psychology is the study of how people's thoughts, feelings, and actions are affected by others. Industrial-organizational psychologists focus on how psychology can be applied to the workplace, while consumer psychologists consider people's buying habits. Cross-cultural psychology examines the similarities and differences between various cultures in psychological functioning.

■ *Where are psychologists employed?*

7. Psychologists are employed in a variety of settings. Although the primary employment sites are universities and colleges, many psychologists are found in hospitals, clinics, community mental health centers, and counseling centers. Many also have independent practices.

■ *What are the historical roots of the field of psychology?*

8. The foundations of psychology were established by Wilhelm Wundt in Germany in 1879. Early conceptual models that guided the work of psychologists were structuralism, functionalism, and gestalt theory. Structuralism focused on identifying the fundamental elements of the mind, largely by using introspection. Functionalism concentrated on the functions played by mental activities. Gestalt psychology focused on the study of how perception is organized into meaningful units. Modern-day psychologists rely primarily on five models: the biological, psychodynamic, cognitive, behavioral, and humanistic models.

■ *What are the major models psychologists use?*

9. The biological model focuses on the biological functioning of people and animals, reducing behavior to its most basic components. The psychodynamic model takes a very different approach; it suggests that there are powerful, unconscious inner forces of which people have little or no awareness and which are primary determinants of behavior.

10. Cognitive approaches to behavior consider how people know, understand, and think about the world. Growing out of early work on introspection and later work by the gestaltists and functionalists, cognitive models study how people understand and represent the world within themselves.

11. Behavioral models de-emphasize internal processes and concentrate instead on observable behavior. They suggest that an understanding and control of a person's environment are sufficient to fully explain and modify behavior.

12. Humanistic models are the newest of the major models of psychology. They emphasize that humans are uniquely inclined toward psychological growth and higher levels of functioning and that human beings will strive to reach their full potential.

13. Several major trends seem to be emerging in terms of the future of psychology. Psychology will become increasingly specialized, psychological treatment will become more accessible, and the influence of psychology over the public interest will grow.

■ *What are psychology's key issues and controversies?*

14. Among the key issues that psychologists grapple with are the questions of nature versus nurture, conscious versus unconscious determinants of behavior, observable behavior versus internal mental processes, freedom versus determinism, and individual differences versus universal principles. Each of these questions is considered in terms of the opposite ends of a continuum, with psychologists falling somewhere between the two extremes of a given issue.

KEY TERMS AND CONCEPTS

psychology (p. 2)
biopsychology (p. 4)
experimental psychology (p. 5)
cognitive psychology (p. 5)
developmental psychology (p. 5)
personality psychology (p. 6)
health psychology (p. 6)
clinical psychology (p. 6)
counseling psychology (p. 6)
educational psychology (p. 6)
school psychology (p. 6)

social psychology (p. 7)
industrial-organizational
   psychology (p. 7)
consumer psychology (p. 7)
cross-cultural psychology (p. 7)
environmental psychology (p. 8)
forensic psychology (p. 8)
program evaluation (p. 8)
models (p. 13)
structuralism (p. 13)

introspection (p. 13)
functionalism (p. 14)
gestalt psychology (p. 14)
biological model (p. 15)
psychodynamic model (p. 16)
cognitive model (p. 16)
behavioral model (p. 16)
humanistic model (p. 18)
free will (p. 18)
determinism (p. 21)

ANSWERS (REVIEW III):

1. False; nearly every branch of psychology can and does make use of all five major models of psychology. **2.** Disagree; much research has shown that it is the interaction between genetic and environmental influences (nature and nurture) which produce the unique behavior of each person. **3.** Psychodynamic **4.** Behaviorist **5.** True

PSYCHOLOGICAL RESEARCH

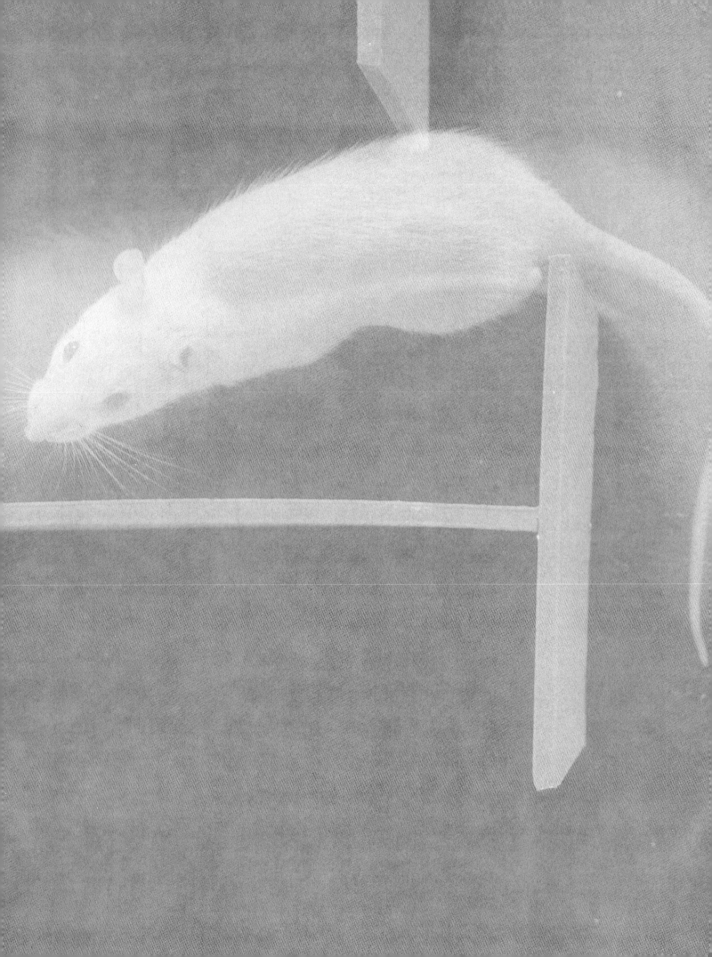

2

PSYCHOLOGICAL RESEARCH

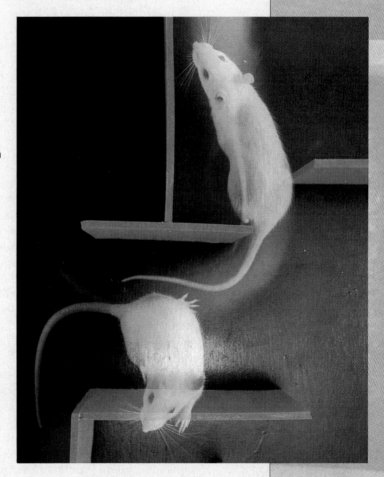

ERICA MORRIS

The Accused, starring Jodie Foster, was a fictionalized account of a rape similar to an actual incident in New Bedford, Massachusetts.

It was a warm spring evening in a small New England city when Erica Morris[1] was savagely raped. But it was not just the rape that made the headlines in the next day's newspapers. What aroused the most public horror was the fact that the rape had occurred in front of scores of bystanders—not one of whom bothered to help Morris, despite her pleas for assistance.

As the victim later recounted the event, the nightmare began when she tried to leave the bar. One man stopped her, blocking the door and ripping off all her clothing but a sweater. She struggled to get away, screaming for help from anyone in the crowded bar, but the only consequence of her pleas was that several other men joined in the attack. They carried her to a pool table and raped her repeatedly.

According to police accounts, she "cried for help, she asked for help, she begged for help—yet no one helped her." The closest anyone came to assisting her was a customer who tried to call the police. Even this effort proved inadequate, however; the customer dialed a wrong number and then gave up. The bartender claimed no one responded because Morris's attackers kept potential helpers at bay with a butter knife.

Eventually, Morris broke away from the rapists and ran out of the bar, half naked and dazed. This time, though, she had better luck: A passing driver picked her up and brought her to a telephone, where she was able to call for help.

LOOKING AHEAD

Were this an isolated incident, we might be able to attribute the behavior of the bystanders to something peculiar about the situation. However, events such as this one—which became the subject matter of the film *The Accused*, starring Jodi Foster—unfortunately are not uncommon.

For example, in one famous case, a woman named Kitty Genovese was attacked near an apartment building in New York in the mid-1960s. At one point during the assault, which lasted thirty minutes, she managed to free herself and screamed, "Oh, my God, he stabbed me. Please help me!" In the stillness of the night, no fewer than thirty-eight neighbors heard her screams. Windows opened and lights went on. One couple pulled chairs up to the window and turned off the lights so they could see better. Someone called out, "Let that girl alone." But shouts were not enough to scare off the killer. He chased her, stabbing her eight more times and sexually molesting her before leaving her to die. And how many of those thirty-eight witnesses came to her aid? As with Erica Morris, not one person helped.

The cases of Erica Morris and Kitty Genovese both remain dismaying—and puzzling—examples of "bad Samaritanism." The general public, as well as psychologists, found it difficult to explain how so many people could stand by without coming to the aid of innocent victims.

One easy explanation, supplied by many editorial writers, was that the incidents could be attributed to the basic shortcomings of "human nature." But such a supposition is woefully inadequate. For one thing, there are numerous

---

[1] In the interest of preserving the victim's privacy, this is not her real name.

examples of people who have placed their own lives at risk to help others in dangerous situations. We all have heard stories, for example, of people who risked their own well-being in order to help total strangers.

Clearly, then, "human nature" consists of an array of both negative and positive responses, and consequently it does not provide a very satisfying explanation for the unhelpful behavior of the bystanders. The mystery remained, then, of how to explain the lack of bystander intervention in both incidents.

Psychologists in particular puzzled over the problem for many years, and they finally reached an unexpected conclusion: Both Erica Morris and Kitty Genovese might well have been better off had there been just a few people who heard their cries for help rather than the many who did. In fact, had there been just one bystander present in each instance, the chances of that person intervening might have been fairly high. It turns out that the *fewer* witnesses present in a situation such as the two in question, the better the victim's chances of getting help.

But how did psychologists come to such a curious conclusion? After all, logic and common sense would clearly suggest that more bystanders would mean a greater likelihood that someone would help a person in need. This seeming contradiction—and the way psychologists resolved it—illustrates a task central to the field of psychology: the challenge of asking and answering questions of interest.

In this chapter, we examine the ways in which psychologists reach conclusions about the world. We begin by examining the scientific method used to pose and answer questions of psychological interest. We discuss how psychologists develop suppositions and theories that can be tested through research. We then consider the specific means of doing research, using, as one example, psychologists' investigations into bystander-helping behavior. We discuss the major techniques by which research is carried out, considering each method's benefits and limitations. Finally, we examine the ethics of research and the ways in which we can become knowledgeable and critical consumers of research findings.

After reading and studying this chapter, then, you will know the answers to these questions:

■ What is the scientific method, and how do psychologists use theory and research to answer questions of interest?

■ What are the different research methods employed by psychologists?

■ How do psychologists establish cause-and-effect relationships in research studies?

■ What are the major issues that underlie the process of conducting research?

POSING QUESTIONS: THE SCIENTIFIC METHOD

Consider the following ten statements. Which of them do you think are correct?

1. Geniuses usually have poor social adjustment.
2. Spare the rod and spoil the child.
3. A person with schizophrenia has at least two distinct personalities.
4. If you are having trouble sleeping, the best way to get to sleep is to take a sleeping pill.
5. Frequent masturbation can lead to mental illness.

6. Once people reach old age, their leisure activities change radically.
7. Satisfied workers are more productive than dissatisfied workers.
8. Most people would refuse to give painful electric shocks to others.
9. People's looks have little to do with how much they are liked.
10. Children's IQ scores are related only minimally to their school performance.

If you agreed with any of them, you answered incorrectly: Despite the apparent reasonableness of these statements, not one of them is accurate. Each has been proven false by psychological research employing methodical, well-controlled scientific techniques. Don't be too concerned if you guessed wrong, though; both the general public and students enrolled in introductory psychology classes typically make similar errors (Gage, 1991; Lamal, 1979; Kohn, 1990; Locke & Latham, 1991).

Determining which of our suppositions about behavior are accurate represents one of the major undertakings for the field of psychology. But in order to understand how this task can be accomplished, we first need to consider how psychologists come to develop such suppositions in the first place.

The challenge of appropriately framing those questions of interest to psychologists and properly answering them has been met through reliance on the scientific method. The **scientific method** is an approach that practitioners of psychology, as well as those engaged in other scientific disciplines, use to come to an understanding about the world. As illustrated in Figure 2-1, it consists of three main steps: (1) identifying questions of interest; (2) formulating an explanation; and (3) carrying out research designed to lend support or refute the explanation.

Scientific method: The process of appropriately framing and properly answering questions, used by practitioners of psychology and those engaged in other scientific disciplines, to come to an understanding about the world

Developing Theories: Specifying Broad Explanations

In using the scientific method, psychologists start with the kind of observations about behavior with which we are all familiar. If you have ever asked yourself why a particular teacher is so easily annoyed, why a friend is always late for appointments, or how your dog understands your commands, you have been formulating questions about behavior. Psychologists, too, ask questions about the nature and causes of behavior, although their questions are typically more abstract.

Once a question has been formulated, the next step in the scientific method involves developing theories to explain the phenomenon that has been observed. **Theories** are broad explanations and predictions of phenomena of interest. Growing out of the diverse models of psychology that we discussed in Chapter 1, theories vary both in their breadth and in the particular level of detail they employ. For example, one theory might seek to explain and predict as broad a phenomenon as emotional experience in general. A narrower theory might purport to predict how people display the emotion of fear nonverbally after receiving

Theories: Broad explanations and predictions concerning phenomena of interest

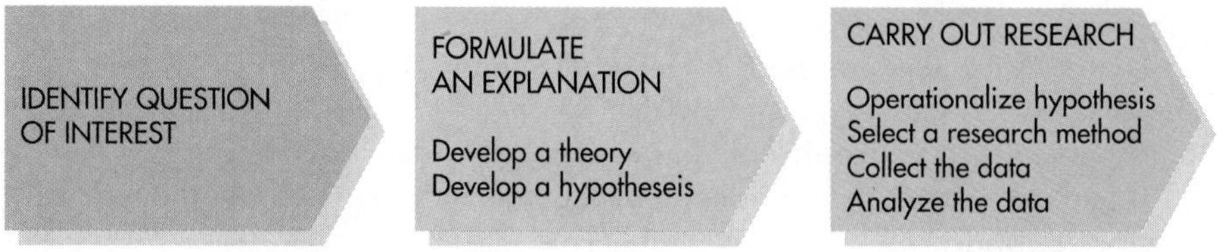

FIGURE 2-1
Steps in the scientific method.

IDENTIFY QUESTION OF INTEREST

FORMULATE AN EXPLANATION

Develop a theory
Develop a hypotheseis

CARRY OUT RESEARCH

Operationalize hypothesis
Select a research method
Collect the data
Analyze the data

Diffusion of responsibility is the tendency for individuals in a crowd to refrain from helping in an emergency since they assume that others will do so. A lone bystander might therefore be more likely to take action to aid the victim.

a threat. An even more specific theory might attempt to explain how the muscles of the face work in tandem to produce expressions of fear when people are afraid.

All of us have developed our own informal theories of human behavior, such as "People are basically good" or "People's behavior is usually motivated by self-interest" (Sternberg, 1985b). However, psychologists' theories are more formal and focused. They are established on the basis of a careful reading of the psychological literature to identify relevant theory and research done previously, as well as psychologists' general knowledge of the field.

For example, psychologists Bibb Latané and John Darley responded to the situations exemplified by the Erica Morris and Kitty Genovese cases by developing a theory based on a phenomenon they called *diffusion of responsibility* (Latané & Darley, 1970). According to their theory, the greater the number of bystanders or witnesses to an event that requires helping behavior, the more the responsibility for helping is perceived to be shared by all the bystanders. Because of this sense of shared responsibility, then, the more people present in an emergency situation, the less personally responsible each person feels—and the less likely it is that any single person will come forward to help.

Hypotheses: Crafting Testable Predictions

Although such a theory makes sense, it represented only the beginning phase of Latané and Darley's investigative process. Their next step was to devise a way of testing whether their reasoning was correct. To do this, they needed to derive a hypothesis. **Hypotheses** are predictions stated in a way that allows them to be tested. Just as we have our own broad theories about the world, so do we develop hypotheses about events and behavior (ranging from trivialities, such as why our English professor is such an eccentric, to what the best way is for people to study).

Hypothesis (hy POTH eh sis): A prediction stated in a way that allows it to be tested

Although we rarely test them systematically, we do try to determine whether they are right or not. Perhaps we might try cramming for one exam but studying over a longer period of time for another. By assessing the results, we have created a way to compare the two strategies.

Latané and Darley's hypothesis was a straightforward derivation from their more general theory of diffusion of responsibility: The more people who witness an emergency situation, the less likely it is that help will be given to a victim. They could, of course, have chosen another hypothesis (for instance, that people with greater skills related to emergency situations will not be affected by the presence of others), but their initial derivative seemed to offer the most direct test of the theory.

There are several reasons psychologists rely on formal theories and hypotheses. For one thing, theories and hypotheses allow them to make sense of unorganized, separate observations and bits of information by permitting them to be placed within a structured and coherent framework. In addition, they offer psychologists the opportunity to move beyond facts that are already known about the world and to make deductions about phenomena that have not yet been explained. In this way, theories and hypotheses provide a reasoned guide to the direction that future investigation ought to take.

In sum, then, theories and hypotheses help psychologists pose the appropriate questions. But how are such questions answered? As we shall see, the answers come from research.

RECAP AND REVIEW I

RECAP

◀ The scientific method used by psychologists proceeds in three steps: identifying questions of interest, formulating an explanation, and carrying out research that is designed to lend support to or refute the explanation.

◀ Theories are broad explanations and predictions of phenomena of interest.

◀ Hypotheses grow out of theories, stating assumptions derived from a theory in a way that allows the assumptions to be tested through research.

REVIEW

1. An explanation about a phenomenon of interest is known as a _the ory_ .
2. To test this explanation, it must be stated in terms of a testable question known as a _hypotheses_ .

Ask Yourself

Starting with the theory that responsibility for helping is shared by bystanders due to diffusion of responsibility, Latané and Darley derived the hypothesis that the more people who witness an emergency situation, the less likely it is that help will be given to a victim. How many other hypotheses can you think of based on this same theory of diffusion of responsibility?

(Answers to review questions are on page 36.)

FINDING ANSWERS: PSYCHOLOGICAL RESEARCH

Research: Systematic inquiry aimed at discovering new knowledge

Operationalization: The process of translating a hypothesis into specific testable procedures that can be measured and observed

Research, systematic inquiry aimed at the discovery of new knowledge, represents a central ingredient of the scientific method in psychology. It provides the key to understanding the degree to which theories and hypotheses are correct.

Just as we can derive several theories and hypotheses to explain particular phenomena, so we can use a considerable number of alternate means to carry out research. First of all, though, the hypothesis must be restated in a way that will allow it be tested, a procedure known as operationalization. **Operationalization** is the process of translating a hypothesis into specific, testable procedures that can be measured and observed.

There is no single way to go about operationalizing a hypothesis; it depends on logic, the equipment and facilities available, the psychological model being employed, and ultimately the ingenuity of the researcher. For example, one researcher might develop a hypothesis in which she operationalizes "fear" as an increase in heart rate. In contrast, another psychologist might operationalize "fear" as a written response to the question, "How much fear are you experiencing at this moment?"

We will consider several of the major weapons in the psychologist's research arsenal. As we discuss these research methods, keep in mind that their relevance extends beyond testing and evaluating theories and hypotheses in psychology (Aronson et al., 1990). Even if they do not have a degree in psychology, for instance, people often carry out rudimentary forms of research on their own. For example, a boss may need to evaluate her employee's performance. A physician might systematically test the effects of different dosages of a drug on a patient. A salesperson may compare different persuasive strategies. Each of these situations calls for the use of the research practices we are about to discuss.

Furthermore, a knowledge of the research methods used by psychologists permits us to evaluate the research that others conduct better. We are constantly bombarded in the media with information about research studies and findings; knowledge of research methods allows us to sort out what is credible from what should be ignored. Finally, there is evidence that studying some kinds of research methods in depth allows people to learn to reason more critically and effectively (Lehman, Lempert, & Nisbett, 1988). Understanding the methods by which psychologists conduct research may enhance our ability to analyze and evaluate the situations we encounter in our everyday lives.

Archival Research

Suppose, like psychologists Latané and Darley, you were interested in finding out more about emergency situations in which bystanders did not provide help. One of the first places to which you might turn would be historical accounts. By using newspaper records, for example, you might find support for the notion that a decrease in helping behavior has accompanied an increase in the number of bystanders.

Using newspaper articles is an example of archival research. In **archival research**, existing records, such as census data, birth certificates, or newspaper clippings, are examined to confirm a hypothesis. Archival research is a relatively inexpensive means of testing a hypothesis, since someone else has already collected the basic data. Of course, the use of already existing data has several drawbacks. For one thing, the data may not be in a form that allows the researcher to test a hypothesis fully. The information may be incomplete, or it may have been collected haphazardly.

Archival research: The examination of existing records for the purpose of confirming a hypothesis

In most cases, though, archival research is stymied by the simple fact that records with the necessary information simply may not exist. In these instances, researchers often turn to another research method: naturalistic observation.

Naturalistic Observation

In **naturalistic observation**, the investigator simply observes some naturally occurring behavior and does not intervene in the situation. For example, a researcher investigating helping behavior might turn to a high-crime area of a city and observe the kind of help that is given to victims of crime. The important point to remember about naturalistic observation is that the researcher is passive and simply meticulously records what occurs.

Naturalistic observation: Observation without intervention, in which the investigator records information about a naturally occurring situation and does not intervene in the situation

Naturalistic observation might involve watching a busy city street during certain hours of the day and recording incidents of delinquent or criminal behavior.

Although the advantage of naturalistic observation is obvious—we obtain a sample of what people do in their "natural habitat"—there is also an important drawback: the inability to control any of the factors of interest. For example, we might find so few naturally occurring instances of helping behavior that we would be unable to draw any conclusions. Because naturalistic observation prevents researchers from making changes in a situation, they must wait until appropriate conditions occur. Similarly, if people know that they are being watched, they may alter their reactions, resulting in behavior that is not truly representative of the group in question.

Survey Research

Survey research: Sampling a group of people by assessing their behavior, thoughts, or attitudes, then generalizing the findings to a larger population

There is no more straightforward way of finding out what people think, feel, and do than by asking them directly. For this reason, surveys represent an important research method. In **survey research**, people chosen to represent some larger population are asked a series of questions about their behavior, thoughts, or attitudes. Survey methods have become so sophisticated that even using a very small sample is sufficient to infer with great accuracy how a larger group would respond. For instance, sampling just a few thousand voters is sufficient to predict within one or two percentage points who will win a presidential election—if the sample is chosen with care.

Researchers investigating helping behavior might conduct a survey asking people to indicate their reasons for not wanting to come forward to help another individual. Similarly, researchers interested in learning about sexual practices have carried out surveys to learn which ones are common and which are not, and to chart changing notions in sexual morality over the past several decades (as we discuss in Chapter 12).

ANSWERS (REVIEW I):

1. Theory **2.** Hypothesis

While asking people directly about their behavior seems in some ways like the most straightforward approach to understanding what people do, survey research has several potential drawbacks. For one thing, people may give inaccurate information because of memory lapses or because they don't want to let the researcher know what they really believe about a particular issue. Moreover, people sometimes offer responses they think the researcher wants to hear—or, in just the opposite instance, responses they assume the researcher *doesn't* want to uncover (Hyman, 1991; Miller, 1991).

In addition, as people have found themselves deluged by researchers asking for their cooperation, they have become increasingly reluctant to participate in surveys. In some parts of the United States, for instance, less than half of those contacted consented when asked to cooperate in a survey (Rothenberg, 1990). The difficulty with such low rates of participation is that there may be some difference in attitudes and opinions between those who agree to be surveyed and those who do not. If so, any survey results apply only to those people willing to be queried and not to those who refused. Such results, then, are not representative of the population as a whole.

The Case Study

When Erica Morris's rapists were arrested, many people found themselves wondering what it was about their personalities or backgrounds that might have led to their conduct. In order to answer this question, psychologists might conduct a case study. In contrast to a survey, in which many people are studied, a **case study** is an in-depth, intensive investigation of an individual or small group of people. Case studies often include psychological testing, in which a carefully designed set of questions is used to gain some insight into the personality of the individual being studied.

When case studies are used as a research technique, the goal is often not only to learn about the few individuals being examined, but also to use the insights gained to understand people in general better. However, such extrapolation must be done cautiously. For instance, the degree to which the rapists in the Erica Morris case are representative of the general population is certainly open to question.

Case study: An in-depth interview of an individual in order to understand that individual better and to make inferences about people in general

Correlational Research

In using the research methods that we have described, researchers often wish to determine the relationship between two behaviors or between responses to two questions on a questionnaire. For example, we might want to find out if people who report that they attend religious services regularly also report that they are more helpful to strangers in emergency situations. If we did find such a relationship, we could say that there was an association—or correlation—between attendance at religious services and being helpful in emergencies.

In **correlational research**, the relationship between two sets of factors is examined to determine whether they are associated, or "correlated." The strength of a relationship is represented by a mathematical score ranging from $+1.0$ to -1.0. A positive score indicates that as the value of one factor increases, we can predict that the value of the other factor will also increase.

For example, if we predicted that the *more* studying students do for a test, the *higher* their subsequent grades on the test, and that the *less* studying they do,

Correlational research: Research to determine whether there is a relationship between two sets of factors, such as certain behaviors and responses

the *lower* their test scores, we would expect to find a positive correlation. (Higher values of the factor of amount of time studying would be associated with higher values on the factor of test scores, and lower values of time spent studying would be associated with lower values of test scores.) The correlation, then, would be indicated by a score that was a positive number, and the closer the association between studying and grades, the closer the score would be to +1.0.

On the other hand, a correlation with a negative value tells us that as the value of one factor increases, the other decreases. For instance, we might predict that as the number of hours spent studying *increased*, the number of hours spent in recreational activities would *decline*. Here, we are expecting a negative correlation, ranging between 0 and −1: more studying is associated with less recreation, and less studying is associated with more recreation. The stronger the association between study and play, the closer to −1.0 the score would be.

Of course, it's quite possible that no relationship exists between two factors. For instance, we would probably not expect to find a relationship between number of hours studied and height. Lack of a relationship would be indicated by a correlation of close to 0; knowing how much someone studies does not tell us anything about how tall he or she is. (You can read more about the concept of correlation, and how statistics in general are used by psychologists, in the appendix at the end of this book.)

When we find that two variables are strongly correlated with one another, it is tempting to presume that one factor causes the other. For example, if we find that more study time is associated with higher grades, we might guess that more studying *causes* higher grades. Although not a bad hunch, it remains just a guess—because finding that two factors are correlated does not mean that there is a causal relationship. The strong correlation suggests that knowing how much a person studies can help us predict how he or she will do on a test, but it does not mean that the studying caused the test performance. It might be, for instance, that people who are more intelligent tend to study more than those who are less intelligent, and it is intelligence that causes test performance, not the

Children who habitually watch television programs depicting violence demonstrate a higher degree of aggression than children who do not watch such programs.

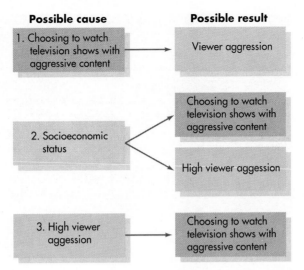

FIGURE 2-2

If we find that frequent viewing of television programs having aggressive content is associated with high levels of aggressive behavior, we might cite several plausible causes, as suggested in this figure. Correlational findings, then, do not permit us to determine causality.

number of hours spent studying. Just because two factors occur together does not mean that one causes the other.

Another example illustrates the critical point that correlations tell us nothing about cause and effect but only provide a measure of the strength of a relationship between two factors. For instance, we might find that children who watch a lot of television programs containing high levels of aggression are apt to demonstrate a relatively high degree of aggressive behavior, while those who watch few television shows that portray aggression are apt to exhibit a relatively low degree of such behavior (see Figure 2-2). We cannot say that the aggression is *caused* by the TV viewing, since it is just as likely to be caused by some other factor. For example, we may learn that children of low socioeconomic status watch more programs having aggressive content *and* are more aggressive. Factors relating to a family's socioeconomic status, then, may be the true cause of the children's higher incidence of aggression. In fact, there may be several factors that underlie both the aggressive behavior and the television viewing. It is even possible that people who show high aggressiveness choose to watch shows with high aggressive content *because* they are aggressive. Clearly, then, any number of causal sequences are possible—none of which can be ruled out by correlational research.

The inability of correlational research to answer questions of a cause-and-effect nature represents a crucial drawback to its use. There is, however, an alternative technique that does establish causality: the experiment.

Experimental Research

The *only* way that psychologists can establish cause-and-effect relationships through research is by carrying out an experiment. In a formal **experiment**, the relationship between two (or more) factors is investigated by deliberately producing a change in one factor and observing the effect that change has on other factors. The change deliberately produced is called the **experimental manipulation**. Experimental manipulations are used to detect relationships between **variables**, behaviors, events, or other characteristics that can change, or vary, in some way.

There are several steps in carrying out an experiment, but the process typi-

Experiment: A study carried out to investigate the relationship between two or more factors by deliberately producing a change in one factor and observing the effect that change has upon other factors

Experimental manipulation: The change deliberately produced in an experiment to affect responses or behaviors in other factors to determine causal relationships between variables

Variable: A behavior or event that can be changed

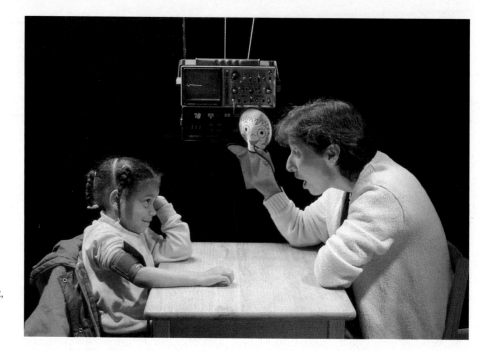

In this psychological experiment, preschoolers' reactions to the activity of the puppet are monitored.

cally begins with the development of one or more hypotheses for the experiment to test (Broota, 1990). Recall, for example, the hypothesis derived by Latané and Darley to test their theory of helping behavior: The more people who witness an emergency situation, the less likely it is that any of them will help a victim. We can trace the way they developed an experiment to test this hypothesis.

The first step was to operationalize the hypothesis by conceptualizing it in such a way that it could be tested. Doing so required that Latané and Darley take into account the fundamental principle of experimental research that we mentioned earlier. There must be a manipulation of at least one variable in order to observe what effects the manipulation has on another variable. But this manipulation cannot be viewed in isolation; if a cause-and-effect relationship is to be established, the effects of the manipulation must be compared with the effects of no manipulation or a different manipulation.

Treatment: The manipulation implemented by the experimenter to influence results in a segment of the experimental population

Treatment group: The experimental group receiving the treatment, or manipulation

Control group: The experimental group receiving no treatment

Experimental research requires, then, that the responses of at least two groups be compared with each other. One group will receive some special **treatment**—the manipulation implemented by the experimenter—while another group receives either no treatment or a different treatment. Any group receiving a treatment is called a **treatment group**, while a group that does not is called the **control group**. (In some experiments, however, there are multiple treatment and control groups, each of which is compared with another.)

By employing both treatment and control groups in an experiment, researchers are able to rule out the possibility that anything other than the experimental manipulation produced the results seen in the experiment. If we didn't have a control group, we couldn't be sure that some other factor, such as the temperature at the time we were running the experiment or the mere passage of time, wasn't causing the changes observed. Through the use of control groups, then, researchers can isolate specific causes for their findings—and cause-and-effect inferences can be drawn.

To Latané and Darley, a means of operationalizing their hypothesis, based on the requirement of having more than one treatment group, was readily available. They decided they would create a bogus emergency situation which would require the aid of a bystander. As their experimental manipulation, they decided to vary the number of bystanders present. They could have just had an experimental group with, for instance, two people present, and a control group for comparison purposes with just one person present. Instead, they settled on a more complex procedure in which there were three groups that could be compared with one another, consisting of two, three, and six people.

Latané and Darley now had identified what is called the experimenter's **independent variable**, the variable that is manipulated. In this case, it was the number of people present. The next step was to decide how they were going to determine what effect varying the number of bystanders had on participants' behavior. Crucial to every experiment is the **dependent variable**, which is the variable that is measured and is expected to change as a result of changes caused by the experimenter's manipulation. Experiments have, then, both an independent and a dependent variable. (To remember the difference, you might recall that a hypothesis predicts how a dependent variable *depends* on the manipulation of the independent variable.)

How, then, should the dependent measure be operationalized for Latané and Darley's experiment? One way might have been to use a simple "yes" or "no" measure of whether a **subject**—as a participant in research is known—helped or didn't help. But the two investigators decided they also wanted a measure that provided a more precise analysis of helping behavior, so they assessed the amount of time it took for a subject to provide help.

Latané and Darley now had all the components of an experiment. The independent variable, manipulated by them, was the number of bystanders present in an emergency situation. The dependent variable was whether the bystanders in each of the groups provided help and the amount of time it took for them to do so. *All* true experiments in psychology fit this straightforward model.

The Final Step: Random Assignment of Subjects to Treatments. To make the experiment a valid test of the hypothesis, the researchers needed to add a final step to the design: properly assigning subjects to a specific treatment group.

The significance of this step becomes clear when we examine various alternative procedures. For example, the experimenters might have considered the possibility of assigning just males to the group with two bystanders, just females to the group with three bystanders, and both males and females to the group with six bystanders. Had they done so, however, it would have become clear that any differences they found in helping behavior could not be attributed with any certainty solely to the group size, since they might just as well be due to the makeup of the group. A more reasonable procedure would be to ensure that each group had the same composition in terms of gender; then they would be able to make comparisons across groups with considerably more accuracy.

Subjects in each of the treatment groups ought to be comparable, and it is easy enough to create similar groups in terms of gender. The problem becomes a bit trickier, though, when we consider other subject characteristics. How can we ensure that subjects in each treatment group will be equally intelligent, extroverted, cooperative, and so forth, when the list of characteristics—any one of which may be important—is potentially endless?

The solution to the problem is a simple but elegant procedure called random assignment to condition. In **random assignment to condition**, a group of subjects are assigned to a different experimental group, or "condition," on the basis of

Independent variable: The variable that is manipulated in an experiment

Dependent variable: The variable that is measured and is expected to change as a result of experimenter manipulation

Subject: A participant in research

Random assignment to condition: The assignment of subjects to given groups on a chance basis alone

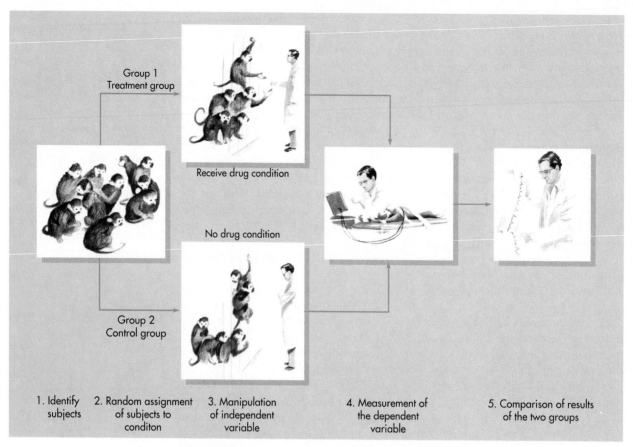

Group 1
Treatment group

Receive drug condition

No drug condition

Group 2
Control group

1. Identify
   subjects

2. Random assignment
   of subjects to
   conditon

3. Manipulation
   of independent
   variable

4. Measurement of
   the dependent
   variable

5. Comparison of results
   of the two groups

FIGURE 2-3

In this depiction of a study investigating the effects of the drug propranolol on stress, we can see the basic elements of all true experiments. The subjects of the experiment were monkeys, who were randomly assigned to one of two groups. Monkeys assigned to the treatment group were given a drug, propranolol, hypothesized to prevent heart disease, while those in the control group were not given the drug. Administration of the drug, then, was the independent variable.

All the monkeys were given a high-fat diet that was the human equivalent of two eggs and bacon every morning, and they were occasionally reassigned to different cages to provide a source of stress. To determine the effects of the drug, the monkeys' heart rates and other measures of heart disease were assessed after twenty-six months. These measures constituted the dependent variable. (The results? As hypothesized, monkeys who received the drug showed lower heart rates and fewer other symptoms of heart disease than those who did not.) (Based on a study by Kaplan & Manuck, 1989.)

chance and chance alone. The experimenter might, for instance, put the names of all potential subjects into a hat and draw names to make assignments to specific groups. The advantage of this technique is that subject characteristics have an equal chance of being distributed across the various groups. By using random assignment, the experimenter can be confident that each of the groups will have approximately the same proportion of intelligent people, cooperative people, extroverted people, males and females, and so on.

Figure 2-3 provides another example of an experiment. Like all experiments, it includes the following set of key elements, which are important to keep in mind as you consider whether a research study represents a true experiment:

■ An independent variable, the factor that is manipulated by the experimenter

■ A dependent variable, the variable that is measured by the experimenter and expected to change

■ A procedure that randomly assigns subjects to different experimental groups or "conditions" of the independent variable

■ A hypothesis that ties the independent and dependent variable together.

Only if each of these elements is present can a research study be considered a true experiment in which cause-and-effect relationships can be determined.

Choosing the Appropriate Subjects.   Latané and Darley, both college professors, turned to the people who were most readily accessible to them when they were looking for participants in their experiment: college students. In fact, this group is used so frequently in experiments that psychology has sometimes been called the "science of the behavior of the college sophomore" (Rubenstein, 1982).

The use of college students as subjects has both advantages and drawbacks. The big benefit is their availability: Since most research occurs in university settings, college students are readily available. Typically, they participate for either extra course credit or a relatively small monetary payment, making the cost to the researcher minimal.

The problem with relying on college students for subjects is that they may not adequately represent the general population. College students tend to be disproportionately white and middle class, younger and better educated than a significant percentage of the rest of the population of the United States. Moreover, their attitudes are likely to be less well formed, and they are apt to be more susceptible to social pressures from authority figures and peers than older adults (Sears, 1986). Given these characteristics, the degree to which we may generalize beyond college students is open to question, and many researchers strive to use subjects who are more representative of the general population.

Were Latané and Darley Right?   By now, you must be wondering whether Latané and Darley were right when they hypothesized that increasing the number of bystanders present in an emergency situation would lower the degree of helping behavior.

According to the results of the experiment they carried out, their hypothesis was right on target. In their test of the hypothesis, they used a laboratory setting in which subjects were told that the purpose of the experiment was to hold a discussion about personal problems associated with college. The discussion was to be held over an intercom supposedly in order to avoid the potential embarrassment of face-to-face contact. Chatting about personal problems was not, of course, the true purpose of the experiment, but subjects were told that it was in order to keep their expectations about the experiment from biasing their behavior. (Consider how they would have been affected had they been told that their helping behavior in emergencies was being tested. The experimenters could never have gotten an accurate assessment of what the subjects would actually do in an emergency; by definition, emergencies are rarely announced in advance.)

The sizes of the discussion groups were two, three, and six people, which constituted the manipulation of the independent variable of group size. Subjects

Confederate: A participant in an experiment who has been instructed to behave in ways that will affect the responses of other subjects

were randomly assigned to one of these groups upon their arrival at the laboratory.

As the subjects in each group were holding their discussion, they suddenly heard one of the other participants (in reality a trained **confederate**, or employee, of the experimenters) lapse into what sounded like an epileptic seizure:

> I-er-um-I think I-I need-er-if-if-could-er-er-somebody er-er-er-er-er-er-er give me a little-er give me a little help here because-er-I-er-I'm-er-er-h-h- having a-a-a real problem-er-right now and I-er-if somebody could help me out it would-it-would-er-er s-s-sure be-sure be good . . . because-er-there-er-er-a cause I-er-I-uh-I've got a-a one of the-er-sei—er-er-things coming on and-and-and I could really-er-use some help so if somebody would-er-give me a little h-help-uh-er-er-er-er c-could somebody-er-er-help-er-us-us-us [choking sounds]. . . . I'm gonna die-er-er-I'm . . . gonna die-er-help-er-er-seizure-er- [choking sounds, then silence] (Latané & Darley, 1970, p. 379).

The subject's behavior was now what counted. The dependent variable was the time that elapsed from the start of the "seizure" to the time a subject began trying to help the "victim." If six minutes went by without a subject's offering help, the experiment was ended.

As predicted by the hypothesis, the size of the group had a significant effect on whether a subject provided help (Latané & Darley, 1970). In the two-person group (in which subjects thought they were alone with the victim), the average elapsed time was fifty-two seconds; in the three-person group (the subject, the victim, and one other person), the average elapsed time was ninety-three seconds; and in the six-person group (the subject, the victim, and four others), the average time was 166 seconds. Considering a simple "yes" or "no" measure of whether help was given corroborates the elapsed-time pattern. Eighty-five percent of the subjects in the two-person-group condition helped; 62 percent helped in the three-person-group condition; and only 31 percent helped in the six-person group (see Figure 2-4).

Because these results are so straightforward, it seems clear that the original hypothesis was confirmed. However, Latané and Darley could not be sure that the results were truly meaningful until they examined their data using formal statistical procedures. As discussed in this book's appendix, statistical procedures—which entail several kinds of mathematical calculations—allow a researcher to determine precisely the likelihood that results are meaningful and not merely the outcome of chance.

The Latané and Darley study contains all the elements of an experiment: an independent variable, a dependent variable, random assignment to conditions, and multiple treatment groups. Because it does, we can say with some confidence that group size *caused* changes in the degree of helping behavior.

Of course, one experiment alone does not resolve forever the question of bystander intervention in emergencies. Psychologists require **replication**, or repetition, of findings, using other procedures in other settings, with other groups of subjects, before full confidence can be placed in the validity of any single experiment. [In this case, the experiment has stood the test of time: In a review of some fifty studies that were carried out in the ten years following their original experiment, the finding that an increase in bystanders leads to decreased helping has been replicated in numerous other studies (Latané & Nida, 1981).]

In addition to replicating experimental results, psychologists also need to test the limitations of their theories and hypotheses in order to determine under which specific circumstances they do and do not apply. It seems unlikely, for

Replication: The repetition of an experiment in order to verify the results of the original experiment

FIGURE 2-4

The results of the Latané and Darley experiment showed that as the size of the group witnessing an emergency increased, helping behavior decreased. (Based on Latané & Darley, 1968.)

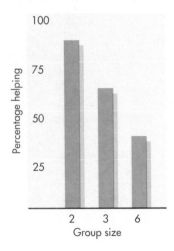

instance, that increasing numbers of bystanders *always* results in less helping; therefore it is critical to understand the conditions in which exceptions to this general rule occur. For example, we might speculate that under conditions of shared outcomes, in which onlookers experience a sense that a victim's difficulties may later affect them in some way, help would be more readily forthcoming (Aronson, 1988). To test this hypothesis (for which, in fact, there is some support) requires additional experimentation. Like any science, then, psychology increases our understanding in small, incremental steps, with each step building upon previous work.

RECAP AND REVIEW II

RECAP

◄ Among the key research methods are archival research, naturalistic observation, survey research, and the case study.

◄ In correlational research, the relationship between two variables is examined to determine whether they are associated, although cause-and-effect relationships cannot be established.

◄ In a formal experiment—which is the only means of determining cause-and-effect associations—the relationship between factors is investigated by deliberately producing a change in one factor and observing the effects of the change in the other.

REVIEW

1. An experimenter is interested in studying the relationship between hunger and aggression. He defines aggression as the number of times a subject will hit a punching bag. What is the process of defining this variable called?

2. Match the following forms of research to their definition:

   _b_ 1. Archival research
   _c_ 2. Naturalistic observation
   _a_ 3. Survey research
   _d_ 4. Case study

   a. Directly asking a sample of people questions about their behavior.
   b. Examining existing records to confirm a hypothesis.
   c. Looking at behavior in its true setting without intervening in the results.
   d. In-depth investigation of a person or small group.

3. Match each of the following research methods with a problem basic to it:

   _c_ 1. Archival research
   _b_ 2. Naturalistic observation
   _d_ 3. Survey research
   _a_ 4. Case study

   a. May not be able to generalize to the population at large.
   b. People's behavior may change if they know they are being watched.
   c. The data may not exist or may be unusable.
   d. People may lie in order to present a good image.

4. A correlation of +2.0 shows that two variables are highly related. True or false? _____f_____

5. Your professor tells you that "Anxiety about speaking in public and performance are negatively correlated. Therefore, high anxiety must cause low performance." Is this statement true or false, and why?

6. A psychologist wants to study the effect of attractiveness on willingness to help a person with a math problem. Attractiveness would be the __dependent__ variable, while amount of helping would be the __independent__ variable.

7. The group in an experiment which receives no treatment is called the __controlled__ group.

8. Experiments, archival research, and case studies can all establish cause-and-effect relationships between variables. True or false? _____f_____

Ask Yourself

In running an experiment, you decide to take the first twenty available subjects and assign them to the experimental group and assign the next twenty to the control group. Why might this not be a good idea?

(Answers to review questions are on page 46.)

RESEARCH ISSUES

It is probably apparent by now that there are few simple formulas that psychologists can follow as they carry out research. Choices must be made about the type of study to conduct, the measures to be taken, and the means of analyzing the results. Even after these essential questions have been answered, several critical issues still need to be considered. We turn first to one of the issues that is most fundamental: ethics.

The Ethics of Research

If you were to put yourself in the place of one of the subjects in the Latané and Darley experiment, how would you feel when you learned that the person you thought was having a seizure was in reality a paid accomplice of the experimenter?

Although at first you might experience relief that there was no real emergency, you might also feel some resentment that you were deceived by the experimenter. And you might also experience concern that you were placed in an unusual situation in which, depending on how you behaved, you may have suffered a blow to your self-esteem.

Most psychologists argue that the use of deception is sometimes necessary in order to avoid having subjects influenced by what they think is the study's true purpose. (If you knew the Latané and Darley study was actually concerned with your helping behavior, wouldn't you automatically be tempted to intervene in the emergency?) In order to avoid such outcomes, researchers must occasionally use deception.

Nonetheless, because research has the potential to violate the rights of participants, psychologists are expected to adhere to a strict set of ethical guidelines aimed at protecting subjects (American Psychological Association, 1990). These guidelines advocate the protection of subjects from physical and mental harm, the right of subjects to privacy regarding their behavior, the assurance that participation in research is completely voluntary, and the necessity of informing subjects about the nature of procedures prior to participation in the experiment. Although the guidelines do allow the use of deception, the experiment must be reviewed by an independent panel prior to its use—as must all research that uses human beings as subjects (Ceci, Peters, & Plotkin, 1985; Keith-Spiegel & Koocher, 1985; Aronson et al., 1990).

Informed consent: A document signed by subjects prior to an experiment in which the study and conditions and risks of participation are explained

One of the key ethical principles followed by psychologists is that of **informed consent**. Prior to participating in an experiment, subjects must sign a document affirming that they have been told the basic outlines of the study and are aware of what their participation will involve, what risks the experiment may hold, and the fact that their participation is purely voluntary and may be terminated at any time. The only time informed consent can be dispensed with is in experiments in which the risks are minimal, as in a purely observational study on a street corner or other public location.

Should Animals Be Used in Research?

It is not just psychologists working with humans who operate under strict ethical constraints; researchers who use animals as subjects have their own set of exacting guidelines to ensure that animals do not suffer (APA, 1986; APA, 1990).

ANSWERS (REVIEW II)

1. Operationalization **2.** 1-b; 2-c; 3-a; 4-d **3.** 1-c; 2-b; 3-d; 4-a **4.** False; the highest possible correlation is +1.0. A correlation of 2 means that you need a new calculator. **5.** False; correlation does not imply causation. Just because two variables are related does not mean that one causes the other. It could be the case that poor performance causes people to become more anxious, or that a third factor causes both of these effects. **6.** Independent; dependent **7.** control **8.** False; only true experiments can do this.

Specifically, they must make every effort to minimize discomfort, illness, and pain, and procedures subjecting animals to distress are used only when an alternative procedure is unavailable and when the goal of research is justified by its prospective value. Moreover, there are federal regulations specifying how animals are to be housed, fed, and maintained. Not only must researchers strive to avoid physical discomfort, they are also required to promote the *psychological* well-being of some kinds of animals such as primates that are used in research (Novak & Suomi, 1988; Adler, 1991; Novak & Petto, 1991).

Why should animals be used for research in the first place? How can we dare to infer human behavior from the results of research employing rats, gerbils, and pigeons? The answer is that the 7 or 8 percent of psychological research that does employ animals has a different focus and is designed to answer different questions from research that uses humans. For example, the shorter life span of animals (rats live an average of two years) allows us to learn about the effects of aging in a much more rapid time frame than if we studied aging directly on humans. Moreover, the very complexity of human beings may obscure information about fundamental phenomena that can be identified more plainly in animals. Finally, some studies require large numbers of subjects who share similar backgrounds or who have been exposed to particular environments—conditions that could not practically be met with human beings (Gill, Smith, Wissler, & Kunz, 1989).

Research using animals as subjects has provided psychologists with information that has profound benefits for humans (Viney, King, & Berndt, 1990). For instance, animal research has furnished us with the keys to learning how to detect eye disorders in children early enough to prevent permanent damage, how to communicate more effectively with severely retarded children, and how to reduce chronic pain in people, to name just a few results (American Psychological Association, 1988).

Despite the demonstrated value of research that uses animals as subjects, their use in psychological research remains controversial (Devenport & Devenport, 1990; Ulrich, 1991; Plous, 1991), with some people calling for a complete ban on the practice. However, most psychologists believe that existing ethical guidelines are sufficiently stringent to provide protection for animals while still allowing valuable animal research to continue.

Although animals have been employed in experimental research for many years, their use by the scientific community recently has become exceptionally controversial.

Threats to Experiments: Experimenter and Subject Expectations

Even the best-laid experimental plans are susceptible to **experimental bias**—factors that distort an experimenter's understanding of how the independent variable affected the dependent variable. One of the most common forms of experimental bias that experimenters need to elude is **experimenter expectations**, whereby an experimenter unintentionally transmits cues to subjects about the way they are expected to behave in a given experimental condition. The danger is that these expectations will bring about an ''appropriate'' behavior—one that might not have otherwise occurred. For example, if Latané and Darley had behaved toward subjects in the two-bystander condition as if they expected them to help, but let on that they had low expectations for helping in the six-person bystander condition, such variations in experimenter behavior—no matter how unintentional—might have affected the results.

A related problem is **subject expectations** about what is appropriate behavior. If you have ever been a subject in an experiment, you know that you quickly develop ideas about what is expected of you, and it is typical for people to develop

Experimental bias: Factors that could lead an experimenter to an erroneous conclusion about the effect of the independent variable on the dependent variable

Experimenter expectations: An experimenter's unintentional message to a subject about results expected from the experiment

Subject expectations: A subject's interpretation of what behaviors or responses are expected in an experiment

their own hypotheses about what the experimenter hopes to learn from the study. If these expectations influence a subject's behavior, it becomes a cause for concern, since then it is no longer the experimental manipulation producing an effect, but rather the subject's expectations.

To guard against the problem of subject expectations biasing the results of an experiment, the experimenter may try to disguise the true purpose of the experiment. Subjects who do not know that helping behavior is being studied, for example, are more apt to act in a "natural" way than if they are told their helping behavior is under scrutiny. Latané and Darley decided to misinform their subjects, then, telling them that the purpose of the experiment was to hold a discussion among college students about their personal problems. In doing so, they expected that their subjects would not suspect the true purpose of the experiment.

In some experiments, it is impossible to hide the actual purpose of the research. In cases such as these, other techniques are available. For example, suppose you were interested in testing the ability of a new drug to alleviate the symptoms of severe depression. If you simply gave the drug to half your subjects and not to the other half, subjects given the drug might report feeling less depressed merely because they knew they were getting a drug. Similarly, the subjects who got nothing might report feeling no better because they knew that they were in a no-treatment control group.

To solve this problem, psychologists typically use a procedure in which subjects in the control group do receive treatment, sometimes in the form of a pill called a placebo. A **placebo** is a pill without any significant chemical properties or active ingredient. Because members of both groups are kept in the dark as to whether they are getting a real or a bogus pill, any differences that are found can be attributed to the quality of the drug and not to the possible psychological effects of being administered a pill.

But there is still one more thing that a careful researcher must do in an experiment such as this. In order to overcome the possibility that experimenter expectations will affect the subject, the person who administers the drug shouldn't know whether it is actually the true drug or the placebo. By keeping both the subject and the experimenter who interacts with the subject "blind" as to the nature of the drug that is being administered, researchers can more accurately assess the effects of the drug. This method is known as the **double-blind procedure**.

Placebo (pla SEE bo): A biologically ineffective pill used in an experiment to keep subjects, and sometimes experimenters, from knowing whether or not the subjects have received a behavior-altering drug

Double-blind procedure: The technique by which both the experimenter and the subject are kept from knowing which subjects received a drug, making any observed behavior variations more reliable

The Significance of Research

If you turn back for a moment to the bar graph of Latané and Darley's results shown in Figure 2-3, you'll note how convincing the results appear. Surely, it seems, there can be little doubt that as the size of the group increased, the amount of helping behavior decreased significantly.

Suppose, though, that the differences between each of the three group sizes were less pronounced. If this were the case, we might be less confident that the differences were meaningful. In fact, as the magnitude of the difference among the three groups decreased, we would become increasingly uncertain that the differences were, in fact, supportive of the hypothesis.

But how would we know at what point the differences would be so small as not to be meaningful? The answer to the question is that we wouldn't be able to tell—not from looking at the graph, that is. Casual inspection of data is simply too inexact an enterprise to tell us whether the differences we find between conditions are consequential.

Does therapy for psychological problems really help? Do groups make better decisions than individuals? Is it better to study in the same room in which a test will be administered than to study elsewhere? Do males score higher on tests of mathematics skills than females?

Even the most ingenious researcher would be hard-pressed to design a single experiment that would be able to answer questions as broad as these. Consequently, most psychologists traditionally would turn to the psychological literature, thoroughly review studies that spoke to the issue, and ultimately attempt to make sense of the findings.

But imagine that they found that not all the studies agreed with one another. Suppose, for instance, they were trying to answer the question of whether gender differences existed in mathematics performance, and half the studies found that males outperformed women, while the other half found just the opposite. Then what could they conclude?

Rather than giving up in frustration, they might well turn to a new research technique called meta-analysis. **Meta-analysis** is a procedure in which the outcomes of different studies are quantified so that they may be compared and summarized.

The basic procedure used to carry out a meta-analysis is straightforward. All research studies relevant to the issue in question are identified,

INTEGRATING RESEARCH USING META-ANALYSIS

and each is inspected to ensure that the study meets certain minimal criteria. For example, a researcher might decide to include only those studies that used more than some minimum number of subjects, or include only those studies that had members of several racial groups as subjects (Beaman, 1991).

Once the body of studies has been identified, the statistics reported in each of the individual studies are combined according to one of several complex formulas and an overall finding is derived. This is a particularly critical step, because it takes into account not just the direction of the findings of each study, but also their strength.

For example, to return to the question of gender differences in mathematics, it may be that studies showing that men perform better than women report relatively large performance differences, while those showing that women perform better than men show only small performance differences. In such a case, the statistical techniques employed in the meta-analysis can summarize and combine the individual findings into a general statistic, which can then be interpreted by the researcher.

Meta-analysis represents a sig-

nificant improvement over traditional reviews of the psychological literature. In conventional reviews, researchers gather a group of studies together, evaluate them, and then come up with a conceptual summary. Often, the criteria used to develop the summary are vague and the way in which the studies are combined is often unspecified.

Meta-analysis is not without its critics, however. Some researchers argue that combining different studies, some of which are quite rigorous and some of which are only marginally sound, results in a whole that is less than the sum of its parts. Furthermore, some detractors suggest that the use of meta-analysis removes the role of insight and intuition from the research evaluation process, casting the literature reviewer into the role of a mere bookkeeper (Wachter, 1988).

Despite these criticisms, however, most researchers feel the benefits of meta-analysis outweigh its drawbacks, and its use is continuing to grow. In fact, in many areas of psychology, meta-analysis has become the only acceptable means of reviewing and combining research studies. As we will see in several places in this book, it is used widely in psychology. (As to the question of whether men outperform women in mathematics—we'll discuss the results of a meta-analysis on the issue in Chapter 12.)

However, psychologists, following the lead of statisticians, have devised ways of knowing when results are meaningful, representing a **significant outcome**. Through various kinds of statistical analyses—which we discuss further in the Appendix—researchers are able to determine whether a numeric difference is a meaningful one or whether it is trivial. Only when differences between groups are of a large enough magnitude that statistical tests deem them "significant" is it possible for researchers to feel confident that they have confirmed their hypotheses.

We need to keep in mind, though, that even when differences are sufficiently large to be labeled significant, there is still the possibility that the results of an experiment are simply due to chance. All that finding statistical significance tells us is this: The differences a researcher has found are overwhelmingly likely to be true differences.

Meta-analysis: A procedure in which the outcomes of different studies are quantified so that they may be compared and summarized

Significant outcome: Statistically meaningful results from an experiment that confirm a hypothesis

Moreover, statistical significance does not necessarily imply that the results of an experiment have real-world importance. An experiment may demonstrate that two groups differ significantly from one another, but the meaning of the differences in terms of what occurs outside the laboratory may be limited. For example, a large body of studies found in the 1960s and 1970s that women are more susceptible to social influence than men—a conclusion that would later come to be quite controversial, as we discuss in Chapter 12 (Eagly, 1978). Careful scrutiny of the studies ultimately showed that although the differences between men and women in many of the studies met the criteria necessary to be labeled "significant," such differences were so small as to be insignificant when it came to predicting the behavior of women and men in their day-to-day activities. Just because a finding in a study is statistically significant, then, doesn't make it a meaningful or important finding.

In recent years, psychologists have tried to develop techniques that avoid reliance on a single experiment in drawing their conclusions. For example, they have developed ways of combining the results of several separate studies into one overall conclusion. The result, as we see in the accompanying Cutting Edge box, is a procedure that allows psychologists to have considerably more confidence in a particular finding than when it is confirmed by only one experiment.

THE INFORMED CONSUMER OF PSYCHOLOGY:
Critical Thinking about Research

If you were about to purchase an automobile, it is unlikely that you would stop at the nearest car dealership and drive off with the first car a salesman recommended. Instead, you would probably mull over the purchase, read about automobiles, consider the alternatives, talk to others about their experiences, and ultimately put in a fair amount of thought before you made such a major purchase.

In contrast, many of us are considerably less conscientious when it comes to the expenditure of intellectual assets than when we disperse our financial resources. People jump to conclusions on the basis of incomplete and inaccurate information, and it is relatively rare that they take the time to evaluate critically the research and data to which they are exposed.

Because the field of psychology is based on an accumulated body of research, it is crucial to scrutinize the methods, results, and claims of researchers thoroughly. Yet it is not just psychologists who need to know how to evaluate research critically; all of us are constantly exposed to the claims of others. Knowing how to approach research and data can be helpful in areas far beyond the realm of psychology.

Several basic questions can help us sort through what is valid and what is not. Among the most important to ask are the following:

■ What are the foundations of the research? Research studies should evolve from a clearly specified theory. Furthermore, the specific hypothesis that is being tested must be taken into account. Unless we know what hypothesis is being examined, it is not possible to judge how successful a study has been. We need to be able to see how the hypothesis has been derived from an underlying theory, and in turn we need to consider how well the design of the study tests that hypothesis.

■ How well was the study conducted? Consider who the subjects were, how many of them there were, what methods were employed, and what problems in collecting the data the researcher encountered. For instance, there are important differences between a case study reporting the anecdotes of a handful of respondents and a survey collecting data from several thousand people.

■ What are the assumptions behind the presentation of the results of the study? It is necessary to assess how well the statements being made reflect the actual data, as well as the logic of what is being claimed. For instance, when the manufacturer of Brand X aspirin boasts that "no other aspirin is more effective in fighting pain than Brand X," this does not mean that Brand X is any better than other kinds of aspirin. It just means that no other brand of aspirin works better—or, stated another way, that Brand X is no better than any other kind of aspirin. Expressed in the latter fashion, the finding doesn't seem worth bragging about.

These basic principles can help you assess the validity of research that you come across—both within and outside the field of psychology. In fact, the more you know about the evaluation of research generally, the better able you will be to assess what the field of psychology has to offer.

> **RECAP AND REVIEW III**

RECAP

◄ Among the major ethical issues faced by psychologists are deception in experiments and the use of animals as subjects.

◄ Threats to experiments include experimenter expectations and subject expectations.

◄ Psychologists use mathematical formulas to determine whether research is significant in a formal statistical sense.

REVIEW

1. Ethical research begins with the concept of informed consent. Before signing up to participate in an experiment, subjects should be informed of
   a. The procedure of the study, stated generally
   b. The risks that may be involved
   c. Their right to withdraw at any time
   d. All of the above
2. Each psychologist must determine his or her own guidelines for ethics in research. True or false? _____

3. List three benefits of using animals in psychological research.
4. Deception is one means experimenters can use to try and eliminate subjects' expectations. True or false? _True_
5. _Experimenter bias_ occurs when the experimenter unintentionally gives subjects clues about how to behave in an experiment.
6. A procedure whereby the experimenter does not know whether subjects are receiving an actual treatment or not is known as the _double_ - _blind_ procedure.
7. In the procedure described in No. 6, a pill without significant chemical properties sometimes is used in the control group. What is this pill commonly called? _Placebo_
8. A study is reported which shows that men differ from women in their preference of ice cream flavors. This study was based on a sample of two men and three women. What might be wrong with this study?

Ask Yourself
A psychologist tells you that because the results of his study are statistically significant, he can be sure that they are absolutely correct. Is he right or not, and why?

(Answers to review questions are on page 52.)

■ *What is the scientific method, and how do psychologists use theory and research to answer questions of interest?*

1. The scientific method is an approach psychologists use to understand the world. It contains three steps: identifying questions of interest, formulating an explanation, and carrying out research that is designed to lend support to the explanation.

2. Research in psychology is guided by theories (broad explanations and predictions of phenomena of interest) and hypotheses (derivations of theories that are predictions stated in a way that allows them to be tested).

■ *What are the different research methods employed by psychologists?*

3. Archival research uses existing records such as old newspapers or other documents to confirm a hypothesis. In naturalistic observation, the investigator acts mainly as an observer, making no change in a naturally occurring situation. In survey research, people are asked a series of questions about their behavior, thoughts, or attitudes. The case study represents an in-depth interview and examination of one person. These methods rely on correlational techniques which describe associations between various factors but cannot determine cause-and-effect relationships.

■ *How do psychologists establish cause-and-effect relationships in research studies?*

4. In a formal experiment, the relationship between factors is investigated by deliberately producing a change—called an experimental manipulation—in one of them and observing the change in the other. The factors that are changed are called variables—behaviors, events, or persons that can change, or vary, in some way. In order to test a hypothesis, it must be operationalized: The abstract concepts of the hypothesis are translated into the actual procedures used in the study.

5. In an experiment, at least two groups must be compared with each other in order to assess cause-and-effect relationships. The group receiving the treatment (the special procedure devised by the experimenter) is the treatment group, while the second group (which receives no treat-

ment) is the control group. There also may be multiple treatment groups, each of which is subjected to a different procedure and can then be compared with the others. The variable that is manipulated is the independent variable; the variable that is measured and expected to change as a result of manipulation of the independent variable is called the dependent variable.

6. In a formal experiment, subjects must be assigned to treatment conditions randomly so that subject characteristics are evenly distributed across the different conditions.

7. Although the use of college students as subjects has the advantage of easy availability, there are drawbacks to their use. For instance, students do not necessarily represent the characteristics of the general population. The use of animals as subjects also has costs in terms of generalizability, although the benefits of using animals in research have been profound.

■ *What are the major issues that underlie the process of conducting research?*

8. One of the key ethical principles followed by psychologists is that of informed consent. Subjects must be told, prior to participation, what the basic outline of an experiment is and what the risks and potential benefits of their participation are. Researchers working with animals must also follow a rigid set of ethical guidelines for the protection of the animals.

9. Experiments are subject to a number of threats, or biases. Experimenter bias occurs when an experimenter unintentionally transmits cues to subjects about his or her expectations regarding their behavior in a given experimental condition. Subject expectations can also bias an experiment. To help eliminate bias, researchers use placebos and double-blind procedures.

10. Psychologists use statistical procedures to determine if the results of an experiment represent a significant outcome. However, obtaining formal statistical significance does not ensure that results have real-world importance.

11. Meta-analysis is a procedure for statistically combining the results of different studies. Meta-analysis has begun to replace more traditional, less formal methods of reviewing groups of studies done by psychologists.

ANSWERS (REVIEW III):

1. d **2.** False; there is a universal set of strict guidelines, developed by the American Psychological Association, to which all psychologists must adhere. **3.** (1) We can study simple phenomena in animals more easily than we can in people. (2) Large numbers of similar subjects can easily be obtained. (3) We can look at generational effects much more easily in animals with a shorter life span than we could with people. **4.** True **5.** Experimenter bias **6.** double-blind **7.** Placebo **8.** There are far too few subjects. Without a larger sample, no valid conclusions can be drawn about ice cream preferences.

KEY TERMS AND CONCEPTS

scientific method (p. 32)
theories (p. 32)
hypothesis (p. 33)
research (p. 34)
operationalization (p. 34)
archival research (p. 35)
naturalistic observation (p. 35)
survey research (p. 36)
case study (p. 37)
correlational research (p. 37)
experiment (p. 39)

experimental manipulation (p. 39)
variable (p. 39)
treatment (p. 40)
treatment group (p. 40)
control group (p. 40)
independent variable (p. 41)
dependent variable (p. 41)
subject (p. 41)
random assignment to condition (p. 41)

confederate (p. 44)
replication (p. 44)
informed consent (p. 46)
experimental bias (p. 47)
experimenter expectations (p. 47)
subject expectations (p. 47)
placebo (p. 48)
double-blind procedure (p. 48)
meta-analysis (p. 49)
significant outcome (p. 49)

Monopolar Z Score Maps: Age - 74.5

Delta   Theta

Absolute
Power

Relative
Power

Power
Asymmetry

Coherence

THE BIOLOGY UNDERLYING BEHAVIOR

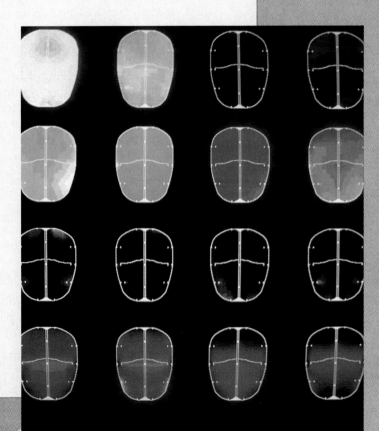

ANDREA FYIE

Andrea Fyie.

Relax. Sit still for a few moments—perfectly still. Imagine that you are lounging comfortably on an easy chair, and resting dreamily.

But now suppose that, without warning, your body is racked with sudden tremors. You stiffen, your limbs twitch, your tongue hangs outside your mouth. Your body takes on a mind of its own. You flail about, falling to the floor.

You can't speak or call for help, but it doesn't matter, since you've lost consciousness. When you do once again become aware of your surroundings, you find yourself on the ground, bruised, with your tongue bitten and bleeding.

For some people, the events described above are a routine part of their lives. Take, for example, Andrea Fyie. When she was first brought to the medical center at the University of Los Angeles, she was just under a year of age. But it had not been an easy first year of life for her: Every day, she was racked with between thirty and forty seizures.

At a loss to understand the reason for her tremors, Andrea's physicians turned to increasingly sophisticated diagnostic measures. Finally they selected a new procedure: positron emission tomography, or PET. This advanced brain scanning technique provides an image of the innermost workings of the brain.

A PET scan begins with the insertion of radioactive chemical elements into the bloodstream. These are then carried by the blood to the interior of the brain. Employing computer-generated images, a PET scanner uses the radioactive elements to produce a snapshot of how the farthest reaches of the brain are functioning at a given moment.

In Andrea's case, the PET scan supplied her physicians with the clue they needed to determine the cause of her seizures. The scan revealed that the use of glucose, a chemical crucial to normal functioning, was impaired in a minute portion of her brain. Her physicians theorized that removing this part of the brain would halt her seizures.

The operation was a tricky one. As with all brain surgery, a false move by so much as the width of a hair could have caused permanent, irreversible damage. But Andrea was lucky: Her surgeons were able to remove just the tiny piece of the brain that was abnormal without producing new problems. Andrea's seizures disappeared immediately, and today, four years after the operation, Andrea is a completely normal five-year-old (Freudenheim, 1990).

LOOKING AHEAD

Andrea Fyie's success story is mirrored in the stories of many others, as surgery that extracts minute portions of the brain becomes almost routine. Even more extraordinary are operations in which malfunctioning parts of the brain are replaced by tissue from other parts of the body. For example, some people who suffer from Parkinson's disease, an illness that also causes seizures, have successfully had tissue from their adrenal gland, located near their kidneys, implanted into their brains. The implanted tissue then begins to produce chemicals that are capable of putting an end to the seizures (Rohter, 1987; Weiss, 1990; Blakeslee, 1991).

The results of operations like these are little short of miraculous. But the greater miracle is the object of the surgical procedure: the brain itself. As we shall see in this chapter, the brain, an organ roughly half the size of a loaf of bread, controls our behavior through every waking and sleeping moment. The brain and its pathways extending throughout the body compose the human **nervous system**. Our movements, thoughts, hopes, aspirations, dreams—the very awareness that we are human—are all intimately related to this system.

Because of the importance of the nervous system in controlling behavior, and because human beings at their most basic level are biological entities, psychologists and researchers from other fields as diverse as computer science, zoology, and medicine—experts collectively called **neuroscientists**—have paid special attention to the biological underpinnings of behavior (Cacioppo & Tassinary, 1990; Body, 1989; Lister & Weingartner, 1991).

Psychologists who specialize in considering the ways in which biological structures and functions of the body affect behavior are known as **biopsychologists**. These specialists seek to answer questions such as these: What are the bases for voluntary and involuntary functioning of the body? How are messages communicated from one part of the body to another? What is the physical structure of the brain, and how does this structure affect behavior? Can the causes of psychological disorders be traced to biological factors, and how can such disorders be treated?

This chapter addresses such questions, focusing on those biological structures of the body of interest to biopsychologists. Initially, we discuss nerve cells, called neurons, which allow messages to travel from one part of the body to another. We learn that through their growing knowledge of neurons and the nervous system, psychologists are increasing their understanding of human behavior and are uncovering important clues in their efforts to cure certain kinds of diseases. The structure and main divisions of the nervous system are then presented, with explanations of how they work to control voluntary and involuntary behaviors. In the process we also examine how the various parts of the nervous system operate together in emergency situations to produce life-saving responses to danger.

Next, we consider the brain itself, examining its major structures and the ways in which these affect behavior. We see how the brain controls movement, the five senses, and our thought processes. We also consider the fascinating notion that the two halves of the brain may have different specialties and strengths. Finally, we examine the chemical messenger system of the body, the endocrine system.

As we discuss these biological processes, it is important to keep in mind the rationale for doing so: Our understanding of human behavior cannot be complete without knowledge of the fundamentals of the brain and the rest of the nervous system. As we shall see, our behavior—our moods, motivations, goals, and desires—has a good deal to do with our biological makeup.

In sum, after reading this chapter, you will be able to answer these questions:

Why do psychologists study the brain and nervous system?

What are the basic elements of the nervous system?

How does the nervous system communicate electrical and chemical messages from one part to another?

In what way are the structures of the nervous system tied together?

What are the major parts of the brain, and what are the behaviors for which each part is responsible?

Nervous system: The brain and its pathways, extending throughout the body

Neuroscientists: Psychologists and researchers from diverse fields who study the nervous system

Biopsychologists: Psychologists who study the ways biological structures and body functions affect behavior

How do the two halves of the brain operate interdependently?

How can an understanding of the nervous system help us to find ways to alleviate disease and pain?

NEURONS: THE ELEMENTS OF BEHAVIOR

If you have ever watched the precision with which a well-trained athlete or dancer executes a performance, you may have marveled at the complexity—and wondrous abilities—of the human body. But even the most everyday tasks, such as picking up a pencil, writing, and speaking, require a sophisticated sequence of activities that is impressive. For instance, the difference between saying the words "dime" and "time" rests primarily on whether the vocal cords are relaxed or tense during a period lasting no more than one-hundredth of a second. Yet it is a distinction that almost everyone can make with ease.

The nervous system provides the pathways that permit us to carry out such precise activities. To understand how it is able to exert such exacting control over our bodies, we must begin by examining neurons, the most basic parts of the nervous system, and considering the way in which nerve impulses are transmitted throughout the human body.

The Structure of the Neuron

The ability to play the piano, drive a car, or hit a tennis ball depends, at one level, merely on muscle coordination. But if we consider *how* the muscles involved in such activities are activated, we see that there are more fundamental processes involved. It is necessary for the body to provide messages to the muscles and to coordinate those messages to enable the muscles to produce the complex movements that characterize successful physical activity.

Neurons: Specialized cells that are the basic elements of the nervous system that carry messages

Such messages are passed through specialized cells called **neurons**, the basic elements of the nervous system. Their quantity is staggering; it is estimated that there are between 100 billion and 200 billion neurons in the brain alone. Although there are several types of neurons, each has a similar basic structure, as illustrated in Figure 3-1 (Levitan & Kaczmarek, 1991). Like all cells in the body, neurons have a cell body, containing a nucleus. The nucleus incorporates the inherited material that establishes how the cell will function.

Dendrites: Clusters of fibers at one end of a neuron that receive messages from other neurons

Unique among the body's cells, however, neurons have a distinctive feature: the ability to communicate with other cells. As you can see in Figure 3-1, neurons have a cluster of fibers called **dendrites** at one end; these fibers, which look like the twisted branches of a tree, receive messages from other neurons. At the opposite end, neurons have a long, slim, tube-like extension called an **axon**, which carries messages destined for other cells through the neuron. The axon is considerably longer than the rest of the neuron; most axons are 1 to 2 inches long, though some may reach 3 feet in length. In contrast, the remainder of the neuron is only a fraction of the size of the axon. (The scale drawing of the neuron in Figure 3-2 illustrates the relative proportions of the various parts.) Finally, at the end of the axon are small branches ending in bulges called **terminal buttons** through which messages are relayed to other cells.

Axon: A long extension from the end of a neuron that carries messages to other cells through the neuron

Terminal buttons: Small bulges at the end of axon branches that relay messages to other cells.

The messages that travel through the neuron are purely electrical in nature. They generally move across neurons as if they were traveling on a one-way street, following a route that begins with the dendrites, continues into the cell body, and leads ultimately down the tube-like extension, the axon. *D*endrites, then, *d*etect messages from other neurons; *a*xons carry signals *a*way from the cell body.

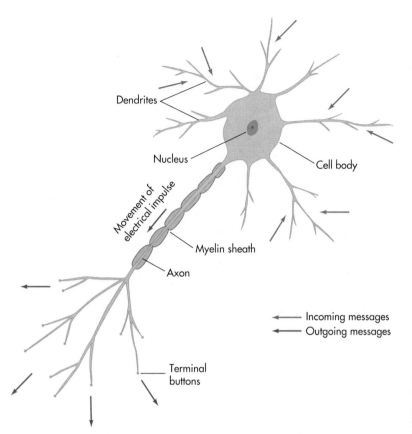

Dendrites

Nucleus

Cell body

Movement of
electrical impulse

Myelin sheath

Axon

⟵ Incoming messages
⟵ Outgoing messages

Terminal
buttons

FIGURE 3-1

The primary components of the
specialized cell called the neuron,
the basic element of the nervous
system.

These two photographs, made with an electron microscope, show a group of
interconnected neurons in the cerebral cortex, a part of the brain (L), and a close-up
of a single neuron (R).

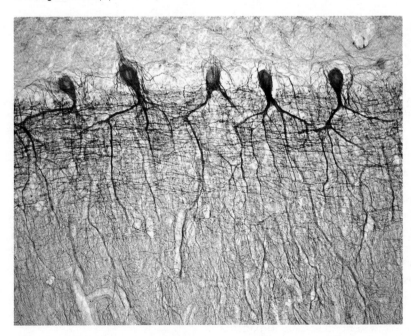

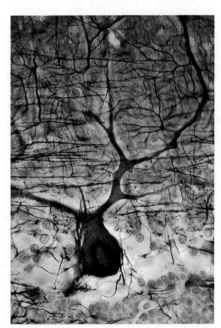

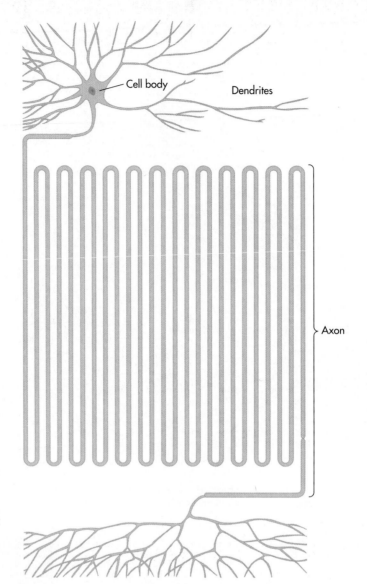

Cell body

Dendrites

Axon

FIGURE 3-2

This representation of a neuron, enlarged 250 times, shows the proportions of its various parts drawn to scale. As you can see, the axon, which is folded so that it can fit within the diagram, is considerably longer than the other parts of the neuron. (Stevens, 1979, p. 56.)

Myelin sheath: An axon's protective coating, made of fat and protein

In order to prevent messages from short-circuiting one another, it is necessary for the axons to be insulated in some fashion (analogous to the way in which electrical wires must be insulated). In most axons, this is done with a protective coating known as the **myelin sheath**, made up of a series of specialized cells of fat and protein that wrap themselves around the axon.

The myelin sheath also serves to increase the velocity with which the electrical impulses travel through the neurons. Those neurons that carry the most important and urgently required information have the greatest concentrations of myelin. If your hand touches a painfully hot stove, for example, the information regarding the pain is passed through neurons in the hand and arm that contain a relatively large quantity of myelin, speeding the message of pain to the brain. In certain diseases, such as multiple sclerosis, the myelin sheath surrounding the axon deteriorates, exposing parts of the axon that are normally covered. The result is a kind of short circuit that causes a disturbance in messages between the brain and muscles and results in symptoms such as the inability to walk, vision difficulties, and general muscle impairment.

Although the electrical impulse always moves across the neuron in a dendrite-to-cell body-to-axon sequence, certain substances travel through the neuron in the opposite direction. For instance, axons allow chemical substances needed for nourishment of the cell nucleus to move toward the cell body in a reverse flow. Certain diseases, such as amyotrophic lateral sclerosis (ALS)—also known as Lou Gehrig's disease for its most famous victim—may be caused by the inability of the neuron to transport vital materials in this reverse direction. When this occurs, the neuron eventually dies from starvation. Similarly, rabies is caused by the transmission of the rabies poison by reverse flow along the axon from the terminal buttons.

The movement of material along the dendrite may also be multidirectional: Rather than consistently transmitting information from other neurons to the cell body, a dendrite may occasionally "leak" information intended for its cell body, thereby inadvertently sending messages to other neurons. In fact, some scientists now suspect that such leaks may cause epilepsy, the disorder in which a person suffers from periodic seizures and convulsions. When electrical discharges are leaked from dendrites, communicating unintended messages in an uncontrolled manner, furious electric storms are produced in the brain.

Firing the Neuron

Like a gun, a neuron either fires or doesn't fire; there is no in-between stage. Pulling harder on the trigger is not going to make the bullet travel faster or more surely. Similarly, neurons follow an **all-or-none law**: They are either on or off; once triggered beyond a certain point, they will fire. When they are off—that is, in a **resting state**—there is a negative electrical charge of about − 70 millivolts within the neuron (a millivolt is one-thousandth of a volt). This charge is caused by the presence of more negatively charged ions (a type of molecule) within the neuron than outside it. You might think of the neuron as one of the poles of a miniature car battery, with the inside of the neuron representing the negative pole and the outside of the neuron the positive pole.

However, when a message arrives for a neuron, the cell walls in the neuron allow positively charged ions to rush in suddenly. The arrival of these positive ions causes the charge within that part of the cell to change momentarily from negative to positive. When the charge reaches a critical level, the "trigger" is pulled, and an electrical nerve impulse, known as an **action potential**, then travels down the neuron (see Figure 3-3).

All-or-none law: The principle governing the state of neurons, which are either on (firing) or off (resting)

Resting state: The nonfiring state of a neuron when the charge equals about − 70 millivolts

Action potential: An electric nerve impulse that travels through a neuron when it is set off by a "trigger," changing the cell's charge from negative to positive

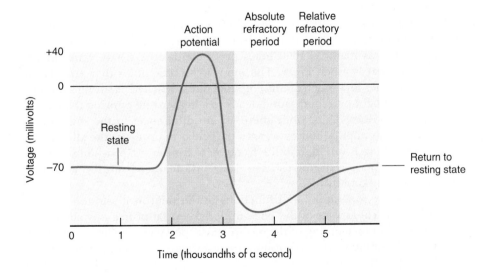

FIGURE 3-3

Changes in the electrical charge of a neuron during the passage of an action potential. In its normal resting state, a neuron has a negative charge of about − 70 millivolts. When an action potential is triggered, however, the cell charge becomes positive, increasing to about + 40 millivolts. Following the passage of the action potential, the charge becomes even more negative than it is in its typical state. It is not until the charge returns to its resting potential that the neuron will be fully ready to be triggered once again.

FIGURE 3-4

Movement of an action potential across a neuron can be seen in this series of three drawings. Just prior to time 1, positively charged ions enter the cell walls, changing the charge within that part of the cell from negative to positive. The action potential is thus triggered, traveling down the neuron, as illustrated in the changes occurring from time 1 to time 3 (from top to bottom in this drawing). Following the passage of the action potential, positive ions are pumped out of the neuron, restoring its charge to negative. The change in voltage illustrated at the top of the neuron can be seen in greater detail in Figure 3-3.

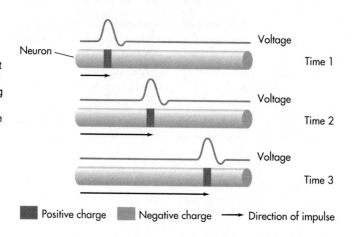

Absolute refractory period:
The recovery period following the triggering of a neuron in which the neuron cannot fire again, no matter how much stimulation it receives

Relative refractory period:
The period during which a neuron, not having returned to its resting state yet, requires more than the normal stimulus to be set off

The action potential moves from one end of the neuron to the other like a flame moves across a fuse toward an explosive. As the impulse moves toward the end of the neuron, the movement of ions causes a sequential change in charge from negative to positive along the cell (see Figure 3-4). After the passage of the impulse, positive ions are pumped out of the neuron, and the neuron charge returns to negative.

Just after an action potential has passed, the neuron cannot be fired again immediately; it is in its **absolute refractory period**. During the absolute refractory period, the neuron is incapable of being triggered, no matter how much stimulation it receives. It is as if the gun has to be painstakingly reloaded after each shot.

Following the absolute refractory period, there is also a **relative refractory period**, in which it is more difficult than usual, although possible, to fire the neuron. While an impulse can pass through the neuron during this period, it takes a stronger stimulus to set it off than if the neuron had been given sufficient time to reach its normal resting potential. Eventually, though, the neuron returns to its resting state and is ready to be fired once again.

These complex events may occur at dizzying speeds, although there is great variation among different neurons. The particular speed at which an action potential passes through an axon is determined by the axon's size and the thickness of the myelin sheath. Neurons with small diameters carry impulses at about 2 miles per hour; longer and thicker ones can average speeds of more than 225 miles per hour.

In addition to varying according to how quickly an impulse moves across them, neurons differ in their potential rate of firing. Some neurons have the potential to fire as many as 1000 times per second; others have a maximum potential rate that is much lower. The intensity of a stimulus that provokes a neuron determines how much of this potential rate is reached: A strong stimulus, such as a bright light or a loud sound, leads to a higher rate of firing than a less intense stimulus does. Thus, while there are no differences in the strength or speed at which an impulse moves across a particular neuron—as the all-or-none law suggests—there is variation in the frequency of impulses, providing a mechanism by which we can distinguish the tickle of a feather from the weight of someone standing on our toe.

The structure, operation, and functions of the neuron illustrate how fundamental biological aspects of the body underlie several primary psychological processes. Our understanding of the way we sense, perceive, and learn about the world would be greatly restricted without the information about the neuron that biopsychologists have acquired.

RECAP

◀ Neurons are the basic elements of the nervous system; they allow the transmission of messages that coordinate the complex activities of the human body.

◀ All neurons have a similar basic structure: They receive messages through the dendrites and transmit them through the axon to other neurons.

◀ Neurons fire according to an all-or-none law; they are either firing or resting.

REVIEW 1

1. The _____ is the fundamental element of the nervous system.
2. Messages are carried through the neuron in what direction?
   a. dendrites ⟶ axon
   b. axon ⟶ dendrites
   c. myelin ⟶ nucleus
   d. terminal button ⟶ brain
3. Just as electrical wires have an outer coating, so axons are insulated by a coating called the _____ _____.
4. The electric nerve impulse which travels down a neuron is called a(n) _____ _____.
5. The _____ law states that a neuron is either firing or resting.
6. The _____ refractory period is a time when the neuron must receive a stronger stimulus than normal in order to fire, while the _____ refractory period is a time when it cannot fire at all.

Ask Yourself

What might the advantage of neurons following the all-or-none law be?

(Answers to review questions are on page 64.)

WHERE NEURON MEETS NEURON: BRIDGING THE GAP

Have you ever put together a child's radio kit? If you have, you probably remember that the manufacturer supplied you with wires that had to be painstakingly connected to one another or to some other component of the radio; every piece had to be physically connected to something else.

The human body is considerably more sophisticated than a radio, or any other manufactured apparatus, for that matter. It has evolved a neural transmission system that at some points has no need for a structural connection between its components. Instead, a chemical connection bridges the gap, known as a **synapse**, between two neurons (see Figure 3-5). When a nerve impulse comes to

Synapse: The gap between neurons through which chemical messages are communicated

FIGURE 3-5

(a) A synapse is the junction between an axon and a dendrite. The gap between the axon and the dendrite is bridged by chemicals called neurotransmitters. (b) Just as the pieces of a jigsaw puzzle can fit in only one specific location in a puzzle, each kind of neurotransmitter has a distinctive configuration that allows it to fit into a specific type of receptor cell.

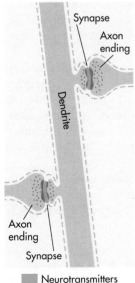

Neurotransmitters

(a)

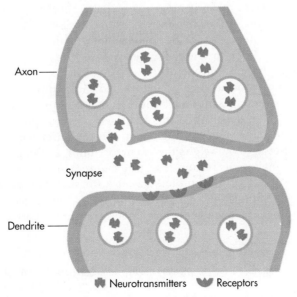

Neurotransmitters   Receptors

(b)

▶ **63**

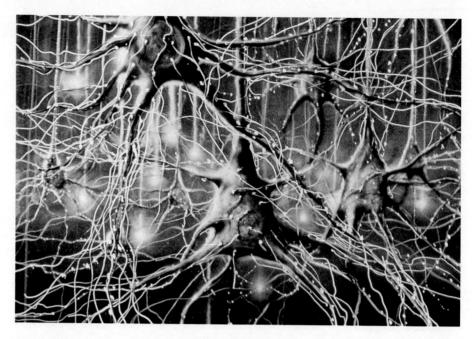

In this electron micrograph, multiple nerve cells are firing, or sending signals through synapses.

Neurotransmitter: A chemical, secreted when a nerve impulse comes to the end of an axon, that carries messages between neurons

Excitatory message: A chemical secretion that makes it more likely that a receiving neuron will fire and an action potential will travel down its axons

Inhibitory message: A chemical secretion that prevents a receiving neuron from firing

the end of the axon and reaches a terminal button, the terminal button releases a chemical called a neurotransmitter. **Neurotransmitters** carry specific chemical messages across the synapse to the dendrite (and sometimes the cell body) of a receiver neuron. Although messages travel in electrical form *within* neurons, they move *between* neurons through a chemical transmission system.

There are several types of neurotransmitters, and not all receiver neurons (also called receptor cells) are capable of receiving the chemical message carried by every neurotransmitter. In the same way that a jigsaw puzzle piece can fit in only one specific location in a puzzle, so each kind of neurotransmitter has a distinctive configuration that allows it to fit into a specific type of receptor cell on the receiving neuron (see Figure 3-5*b*). It is only when a neurotransmitter fits precisely into a receptor cell that successful chemical communication is possible.

If a neurotransmitter does fit into a receiving neuron, the chemical message that arrives with it is basically one of two types: excitatory or inhibitory. **Excitatory messages** make it more likely that a receiving neuron will fire and an action potential will travel down its axons. **Inhibitory messages**, in contrast, do just the opposite; they provide chemical information that prevents or decreases the likelihood that the receiving neuron will fire.

Because the dendrites of a neuron receive many messages simultaneously, some of which are excitatory and some inhibitory, the neuron must integrate the messages in some fashion. It does this through a kind of summation process: If the number of excitatory messages outweighs the number of inhibitory ones, an action potential will occur. On the other hand, if the number of inhibitory messages outweighs the excitatory ones, nothing will happen. The neuron will remain in its resting state (see Figure 3-6).

If neurotransmitters stayed at the site of the synapse, there would be continual stimulation of the receptor cells, and effective communication would no longer be possible. Instead, neurotransmitters are either deactivated by enzymes

---

ANSWERS (REVIEW I):

1. neuron **2.** a **3.** myelin sheath **4.** action potential **5.** all-or-none **6.** relative; absolute

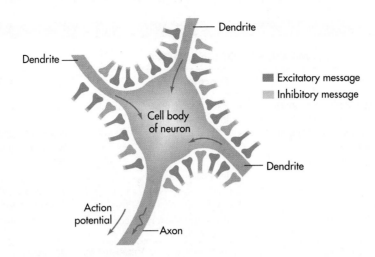

Dendrite

Dendrite

Cell body
of neuron

Dendrite

Action
potential

Axon

■ Excitatory message
■ Inhibitory message

FIGURE 3-6
Because the dendrites of a
neuron receive both excitatory
messages (which stimulate it to
fire) and inhibitory messages
(which tell the neuron not to fire),
it must integrate the messages
through a summation process. In
this case the number of excitatory
messages is greater than the
number of inhibitory messages,
so it is likely to fire.

or—more frequently—reabsorbed by the terminal button in an example of chemical thriftiness called **reuptake**. Certain drugs, such as cocaine, inhibit the reuptake of some kinds of neurotransmitters, thereby prolonging their effects and producing a "high."

Reuptake: The reabsorption of neurotransmitters by a terminal button

Varieties of Neurotransmitters

Neurotransmitters represent a particularly important link between the nervous system and behavior. Not only are they important for maintaining vital body functions, but having a deficiency or an excess of a neurotransmitter can produce brain and behavior disorders.

So far, some fifty chemicals have been found to act as neurotransmitters, and many biopsychologists believe that dozens more may ultimately be identified (Shepherd, 1990). Furthermore, recent, preliminary evidence suggests that at least one neurotransmitter may be produced in the form of nitric oxide, a gas, unlike the others, which are in a liquid state (Hoffman, 1991).

Different neurotransmitters produce the excitation or inhibition of neurons at different rates and in different concentrations. Furthermore, the effects of a given neurotransmitter vary depending on the portion of the nervous system in which it is produced. The same neurotransmitter, then, can cause a neuron to fire when it is secreted in one part of the brain and can inhibit the firing of neurons when it is produced in another part. (The major neurotransmitters are shown in Table 3-1.)

One of the most common neurotransmitters is **acetylcholine** (or **ACh**, its chemical symbol), which produces contractions of skeletal muscles (Blusztajn & Wurtman, 1983; Kasa, 1986). The venom of the deadly black widow spider causes the continuous release of ACh, eventually killing the victim through muscle spasms. ACh is also related to the drug curare, used on the tips of poison darts thrown by South American Indians. Curare keeps ACh from reaching receptor cells, thereby paralyzing the skeletal muscles and ultimately producing death by suffocation because the victim cannot breathe. On the brighter side, the study of ACh has helped provide insights into such medical conditions as myasthenia gravis, a disease in which there is a gradual loss of muscle control. Specifically, treatments have been devised in which drugs can be administered to prevent the destruction of ACh by the body, thereby allowing the normal transmission of impulses across the synapses and restoration of muscle control.

Acetylcholine (a see tul KO leen) **(ACh):** A common neurotransmitter that produces contractions of skeletal muscles

TABLE 3 - 1

MAJOR NEUROTRANSMITTERS

Name	Location	Functions	Associated disorders
Acetylcholine (ACh)	Brain, spinal cord, peripheral nervous system, especially some organs of the parasympathetic nervous system	Excitatory at muscle synopsis; Inhibitory at heart	Deficiency: paralysis (curare and botulism); Alzheimer's disease Excess: violent muscle contraction (black widow-spider venom)
Dopamine (DA)	Brain	Inhibitory	Deficiency: muscular rigidity and uncontrollable tremors (Parkinson's disease)
Enkephalins and endorphins	Brain, spinal cord	Primarily inhibitory, except in hippocampus	None identified
Gramma-amino butyric acid (GABA)	Brain, spinal cord	Main inhibitory neurotransmitter	Deficiency: convulsions, mental deterioration
Norepinephrine (NE)	Brain, some organs of sympathetic nervous system	Excitatory and inhibitory	Deficiency: depression
Serotonin	Brain	Excitatory and inhibitory	Deficiency: depression

Alzheimer's (ALZ high merz) **disease:** A progressively degenerative disorder that ultimately produces loss of memory, confusion, and changes in personality in its victims

Gamma-amino butyric acid (GABA): The nervous system's primary inhibitory neurotransmitter, found in the brain and spinal cord

Dopamine (DA): A common neurotransmitter that inhibits certain neurons and excites others

Some psychologists now suggest that **Alzheimer's disease**, a progressively degenerative disorder that ultimately produces loss of memory, confusion, and changes in personality in its victims, is associated with the production of ACh. Evidence is growing that ACh is closely related to memory capabilities, and some research now shows that Alzheimer's patients have restricted production of ACh in portions of their brains. If this research is corroborated, it may lead to treatments in which production of ACh can be restored (Wolozin, Pruchnicki, Dickson, & Davies, 1986; Rosenzweig & Leiman, 1989).

Gamma-amino butyric acid (GABA) is another important neurotransmitter. GABA, found in both the brain and the spinal cord, appears to be the nervous system's primary inhibitory neurotransmitter. It moderates a variety of behaviors, ranging from eating to aggression.

The deadly poison strychnine produces convulsions by disrupting the transmission of GABA across synapses. Strychnine prevents GABA from carrying out its inhibitory role, permitting neurons to fire wildly, thereby producing convulsions. In contrast, some common substances, such as the tranquilizer Valium and alcohol, are effective because they permit GABA to operate more efficiently.

Another major neurotransmitter is **dopamine (DA)**, which has an inhibitory effect on some neurons and an excitatory effect on others, such as those of the heart. The discovery that certain drugs can have a marked effect on dopamine release has led to the development of effective treatments for a wide variety of physical and mental ailments. For instance, Parkinson's disease, marked by varying degrees of muscular rigidity and shaking, seems to be caused by a deficiency of dopamine in the brain. Drugs have been developed to stimulate the production of dopamine, and in many patients they have proved highly effective in reducing the symptoms of Parkinson's. In patients with severe cases of Parkinson's disease, production of dopamine has been stimulated by implantation of cells into the brain from other parts of the body (Yurek & Sladek, 1990; Weiss, 1990).

Researchers have also hypothesized that schizophrenia and some other mental disturbances are affected or perhaps even caused by the overproduction of dopamine (Wong et al., 1986; Wong et al., 1988). Drugs that block the reception

Logan Tilghman, shown here being helped by his wife, suffers from Parkinson's disease, a condition thought to be caused by a deficiency of dopamine in certain parts of the brain.

of dopamine have been successful in reducing the abnormal behavior displayed by some people diagnosed with schizophrenia—as we will examine further when we consider abnormal behavior and its treatment in Chapters 17 and 18.

In some circumstances, neurotransmitter production can be affected by our routine, daily activities. Consider, for instance, the following case:

> Unless he was jogging, David Bartlett was a quiet, unassuming person. Most people who knew him tended to think of him as an introvert. But when he jogged, a noticeable change seemed to come over David. By the time he finished his daily 5- or 6-mile run he was excited, happy—even euphoric at times—and talkative. Anyone who was with David after a run noticed the change. In fact, some of his friends joked about it, saying that he acted as if he were "high" on something he had taken while he was out running.

What happened to David Bartlett when he was jogging? The most likely explanation is related to a specific neurotransmitter known as endorphin. **Endorphins** are chemicals produced by the body that interact with a particular neuron called an opiate receptor. **Opiate receptors** act to reduce the experience of pain, and in fact many painkilling drugs, such as morphine, are used to activate the opiate receptors. Endorphins are a kind of "natural" morphine produced by the body to reduce pain. For instance, people who are afflicted with diseases that produce long-term, severe pain often develop large concentrations of endorphins in their brains—suggesting an effort by the body to control the pain (Watkins & Mayer, 1982).

Endorphins like morphine and other opiates may go even further than mere pain reduction: They may also produce the kind of euphoric feelings that jogger David Bartlett experienced after running. It is possible that the amount of exercise and perhaps even the pain involved in a long run stimulate the production of endorphins—ultimately resulting in what has been called a "runner's high" (Hathaway, 1984).

Endorphin release may also explain other phenomena that have long puz-

Endorphins: Chemicals produced by the body that interact with an opiate receptor to reduce pain

Opiate receptor: A neuron that acts to reduce the experience of pain

Endorphins, which play a key role in pain reduction, may produce the euphoric feeling that many runners experience after a workout.

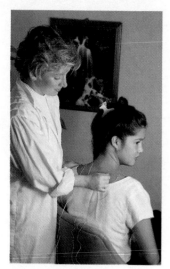

Endorphin release may explain the success of acupuncture in relieving pain.

zled psychologists, such as the reasons that acupuncture and placebos—pills that contain no actual drugs but that patients *believe* will make them better—are sometimes effective in reducing pain. Some biopsychologists speculate that both acupuncture and placebos induce the release of endorphins. In turn, the endorphins produce a positive bodily state (Bolles & Fanselow, 1982; Bandura et al., 1987).

The study of endorphins and other neurotransmitters may also help biopsychologists develop new, more effective painkillers. For instance, researchers studying neurotransmitters have been able to identify the neuronal cell that acts as the receptor for the active ingredient in marijuana. Such a discovery may pave the way for the creation of drugs that yield the positive effects of marijuana—such as relief of pain, asthma, and nausea—without any accompanying intoxication (Matsuda, Lolait, Brownstein, Young, & Bonner, 1990).

THE NERVOUS SYSTEM

Given the complexity of individual neurons and the neurotransmission process, it should come as no surprise that the structures formed by the neurons are likewise complicated in their own right. However, there is both a logic and an elegance to the human nervous system.

Neuronal Architecture

Neural networks: Groups of organized communication links between cells

Neurons are linked to other neurons via **neural networks**, groups of organized communication links between cells. The connections between neurons permit the flow of information over long distances throughout the body. But neural networks do something else: They allow the nervous system to modify, filter, and sift information as it travels to and from the brain (Candill & Butler, 1991).

The study of these neural networks has led to a new scientific enterprise called "computational neuroscience," encompassing aspects of biopsychology and cognitive psychology. Computational neuroscience researchers, whose goal is to identify the patterns of neural networks and to mimic them on computers, have found that the majority of networks fall into one of the simple patterns shown in Figure 3-7 (Gabriel & Moore, 1991; Schwartz, 1990).

Linear circuits: Neurons joined in a single line, receiving and transmitting messages only to the next neuronal link

In **linear circuits**, one neuron transmits to another neuron, which in turn transmits to a third neuron, and so on. Similar to the links of a chain, a neuron

FIGURE 3-7

The major types of neural networks which link groups of neurons together. Each letter represents a different neuron.

Linear circuit

Multiple source/ convergent circuit

Single source/ divergent circuit

joined in a linear circuit receives a message from the neuronal link just next to it in the progression. That neuron in turn transmits the message to the neuronal link just next to it on the other side of the chain.

The advantage of linear circuits is that they permit the transmission of nerve impulses over relatively long distances within the body's nervous system. But like a chain, the linear system is only as strong as its weakest link. Injury or disease at any point in the link can put the entire system in jeopardy.

At a more complex level, neurons are joined together in hierarchies. **Multiple source/convergent circuits** channel information from several neurons into a single neuron. The information that is transmitted to the single recipient neuron may be primarily excitatory, inhibitory, or a combination of the two. As we noted earlier, whether the recipient neuron fires (and consequently transmits the information to yet another neuron) depends on the proportion of excitatory and inhibitory messages it receives.

A second type of hierarchical circuit is the single source/divergent circuit. **Single-source/divergent circuits** consist of networks in which a single neuron transmits messages to a potentially vast number of recipients. Because they often influence many different sorts of neurons simultaneously, single-source/divergent circuits function as the equivalent of an orchestral conductor. Like a conductor, the source neuron directs the coordination and integration of messages traveling across neural pathways.

These basic types of neural networks result in a staggering number of neural connections. Because just one neuron may be connected to 80,000 other neurons, the total number of possible linkages is astounding. Some estimates of the number of neural connections within the brain fall in the neighborhood of 1 quadrillion—a 1 followed by 15 zeros—while some experts put the number even higher (Kolb & Whishaw, 1990).

Numbers of such a magnitude are hard to comprehend. In fact, the ability to precisely map the neuronal architecture of the brain is at a relatively primitive, but rapidly developing, stage (Estes, 1991; McGaugh, Weinberger, & Lynch, 1990).

Central and Peripheral Nervous Systems

As you can see from Figure 3-8, the nervous system is divided into two main parts: the central nervous system and the peripheral nervous system. The **central nervous system (CNS)** is composed of the brain and spinal cord. The **spinal cord** is a bundle of nerves, about the thickness of a pencil, that leaves the brain and runs down the length of the back (see Figure 3-9). It is the main means for transmitting messages between the brain and the body.

Some simple kinds of behaviors are organized entirely within the spinal cord. A common example is the knee jerk, which occurs when the knee is tapped with a rubber hammer. Such behaviors, called **reflexes**, represent an involuntary response to an incoming stimulus which is "reflected" back out of the body, without the involvement of the brain.

For example, when you touch a hot stove and immediately withdraw your hand, a reflex is at work: Although the brain eventually analyzes the pain, the initial withdrawal is directed only by neurons in the spinal cord. Three sorts of neurons are involved in reflexes: **sensory (afferent) neurons**, which transmit information from the perimeter of the body to the central nervous system; **motor (efferent) neurons**, which communicate information from the nervous system to muscles and glands of the body; and **interneurons**, which connect sensory and motor neurons, carrying messages between the two.

Multiple source/convergent circuits: A hierarchical network of neurons in which information from several neurons is channeled into a single neuron

Single-source/divergent circuits: A network of neurons in which a single neuron transmits messages to a potentially vast number of recipients

Central nervous system (CNS): The system that includes the brain and the spinal cord

Spinal cord: A bundle of nerves running along the spine, carrying messages between the brain and the body

Reflexes: Simple movements carried out by the spinal cord without input from the brain

Sensory (afferent) neurons: Neurons that transmit information from the body to the nervous system

Motor (efferent) neurons: Neurons that transmit information from the nervous system to muscles and glands

Interneurons: Neurons that transmit information between sensory and motor neurons

The knee-jerk reflex is one of the best-known reflexes.

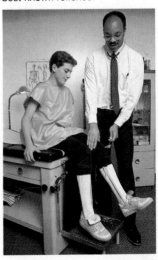

▶ **69**

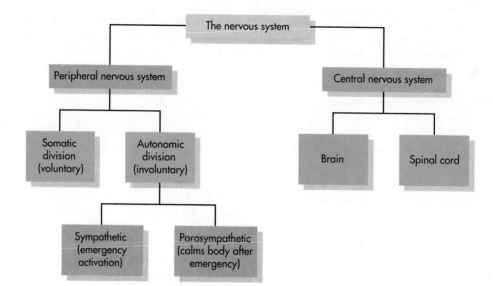

FIGURE 3-8

A schematic diagram of the relationship of the parts of the nervous system.

FIGURE 3-9

The central nervous system consists of the brain and the spinal cord.

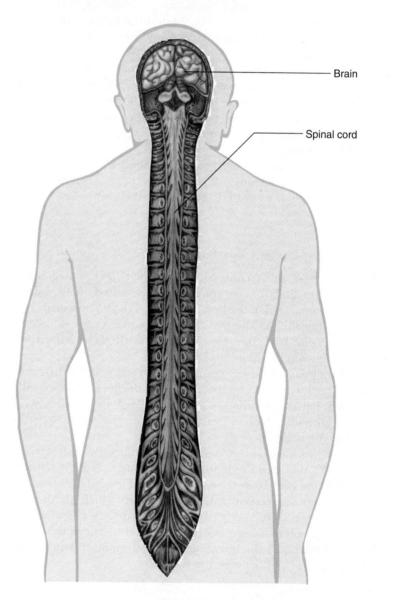

The importance of the spinal cord and reflexes is illustrated by the outcome of accidents in which the cord is injured or severed. In one resulting injury, **paraplegia**, a person is unable to voluntarily move any muscles in the lower half of the body. However, even though the cord is severed, the undamaged area of the spinal cord is still able to produce some simple reflex actions, if stimulated appropriately. For instance, if a paraplegic's knee is tapped lightly, the lower leg will jerk forward slightly. Similarly, in some kinds of spinal cord injuries, people will move their legs in an involuntary response to a pinprick, even though they do not experience the sensation of pain.

The spinal cord is related to other basic biological functions as well. For instance, if a male paraplegic's genitals are stimulated, he is capable of having an erection and ultimately ejaculating. However, with a damaged spinal cord, the paraplegic would not experience the sensations that are normally a part of sexual activity.

As suggested by its name, the **peripheral nervous system** branches out from the spinal cord and brain and reaches the extremities of the body. Made up of long axons and dendrites, the peripheral nervous system encompasses all parts of the nervous system other than the brain and spinal cord. There are two major divisions, the somatic division and the autonomic division, both of which connect the central nervous system with the sense organs, muscles, glands, and other organs. The **somatic division** specializes in the control of voluntary movements—such as the motion of the eyes to read this sentence or of the hand to turn this page—and the communication of information to and from the sense organs. On the other hand, the **autonomic division** is concerned with the parts of the body that keep us alive—the heart, blood vessels, glands, lungs, and other organs that function involuntarily without our awareness. As you read now, the autonomic division of the peripheral nervous system is pumping the blood through your body, pushing your lungs in and out, overseeing the digestion of the meal you had a few hours ago, and so on—all without a thought or care on your part.

Activating the Autonomic Nervous System

The autonomic division plays a particularly crucial role during emergency situations. Suppose as you are reading you suddenly sense that there is a stranger watching you through the window. As you look up, you see the glint of something that just might be a knife. As confusion races through your mind and fear overcomes your attempts to think rationally, what happens to your body? If you are like most people, you react immediately on a physiological level: Your heart rate increases, you begin to sweat, and you develop goose bumps all over your body.

The physiological changes that occur result from the activation of one of the two parts that comprise the autonomic division: the **sympathetic division**. The sympathetic division acts to prepare the body in stressful emergency situations, engaging all the organism's resources to respond to a threat, a response that often takes the form of "fight or flight." In contrast, the **parasympathetic division** acts to calm the body after the emergency situation is resolved. When you find, for instance, that the stranger at the window is actually your roommate who has lost his keys and is climbing in the window to avoid waking you, your parasympathetic division begins to predominate, lowering your heart rate, stopping your sweating, and returning your body to the state it was in prior to your fright. The parasympathetic division also provides a means for the body to maintain storage of energy sources such as nutrients and oxygen. The sympathetic and parasympathetic divisions work together to regulate many functions of the body (see Figure 3-10). For instance, sexual arousal is controlled by the parasympathetic division, while sexual orgasm is a function of the sympathetic division.

Paraplegia: The inability, as a result of injury to the spinal cord, to voluntarily move any muscles in the lower half of the body

Peripheral nervous system: All parts of the nervous system *except* the brain and the spinal cord (includes somatic and autonomic divisions)

Somatic division: The part of the nervous system that controls voluntary movements of the skeletal muscles

Autonomic division: The part of the nervous system that controls involuntary movement (the actions of the heart, glands, lungs, and other organs)

Sympathetic division: The part of the autonomic division of the peripheral nervous system that prepares the body to respond in stressful emergency situations

Parasympathetic division: The part of the autonomic division of the peripheral nervous system that calms the body, bringing functions back to normal after an emergency has passed

▶ **71**

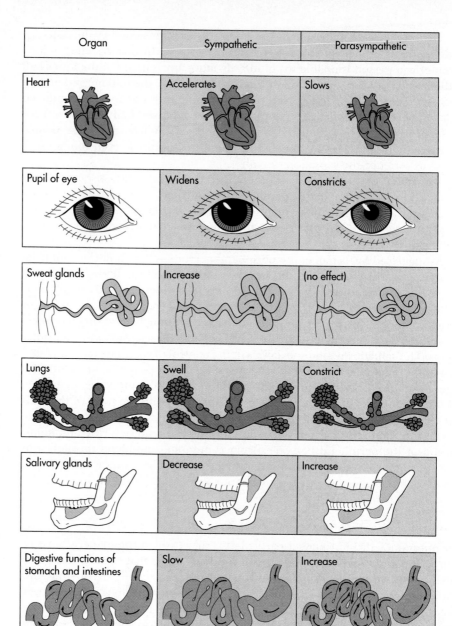

Organ	Sympathetic	Parasympathetic
Heart	Accelerates	Slows
Pupil of eye	Widens	Constricts
Sweat glands	Increase	(no effect)
Lungs	Swell	Constrict
Salivary glands	Decrease	Increase
Digestive functions of stomach and intestines	Slow	Increase

FIGURE 3-10

The major functions of the autonomic nervous system. The sympathetic division acts to prepare certain organs of the body for stressful emergency situations, and the parasympathetic division acts to calm the body after the emergency situation is resolved.

RECAP AND REVIEW II

RECAP

◀ The specific site of transmission of messages from one neuron to another is called the synapse. Messages moving *across* synapses are chemical in nature, although they travel *within* neurons in an electrical form.

◀ Neurotransmitters are the specific chemicals that make the chemical connection at the synapse; these act either to excite other neurons into firing or to inhibit neurons from firing.

◀ Neurons are linked to other neurons via networks, groups of organized communication links between cells.

◀ The central nervous system (CNS) is made up of the brain and spinal cord, a thick bundle of nerves running from the brain down the length of the back. The spinal cord provides the major route for transmission of messages between the brain and the rest of the body.

◀ The peripheral nervous system includes all parts of the nervous system other than the brain and spinal cord. The peripheral nervous system has two major parts: the somatic division (for voluntary movements) and the autonomic division (for involuntary movements).

◄ The autonomic division, which itself has two parts (sympathetic and parasympathetic divisions), plays a major role during emergency situations.

REVIEW

1. The chemical connection between two neurons occurs at a gap known as a(n):
   a. axon.
   b. terminal button.
   c. synapse.
   d. amino acid.
2. _____ are chemical messengers which transmit between neurons.
3. Match the neurotransmitter with its function:
   _____ a. ACh   1. Reduce the experience
   _____ b. GABA   of pain
   _____ c. Endorphins   2. Moderates eating and
                            aggression
                         3. Produces contractions of
                            skeletal muscles
4. Parkinson's disease has been found to be tied to a deficiency of _____ in the brain.
5. Neurons linked in a chainlike structure are said to form a _____ network.
6. A single source/divergent circuit consists of a neuron that transmits information to many other neurons simultaneously. True or false? _____
7. If you should put your hand on a red-hot piece of metal, the immediate response of pulling it away would be an example of a _____.
8. The portion of your nervous system which controls functions such as breathing and digestion is known as the _____ nervous system.
9. The peripheral nervous system includes nerves located in the arms, legs, and spinal cord. True or false?
   _____
10. Maria saw a young boy run into the street and get hit by a car. When she got to the fallen child, she was in a state of panic. She was sweating and her heart was racing. Her physiological state resulted from the activation of what division of the autonomic nervous system?
    a. Parasympathetic
    b. Somatic
    c. Peripheral
    d. Sympathetic

Ask Yourself
How does communication between neurons result in human consciousness?

(Answers to review questions are on page 74.)

THE BRAIN

When you come right down to it, it is not a very pretty sight. Soft, spongy, mottled, and pinkish-gray in color, one could hardly say that it possesses much in the way of physical beauty. Despite its physical appearance, however, it ranks as the greatest natural marvel that we know and possesses a beauty and sophistication all its own.

The object to which this description applies is, as you might guess, the brain. The brain is responsible for our loftiest thoughts—and our most primitive urges. It is the overseer of the intricate workings of the human body. If one were to attempt to design a computer to mimic the capabilities of the brain, the task would be nearly impossible; in fact, it has proved difficult even to come close (Hanson & Olson, 1990). Just the sheer quantity of nerve cells in the brain is enough to daunt even the most ambitious computer engineer. Many billions of nerve cells make up a structure weighing just 3 pounds in the average adult. However, it is not the number of cells that is the most astounding thing about the brain but its ability to allow human intellect to flourish as it guides our behavior and thoughts.

Studying the Structure and Functions of the Brain

The brain has always posed a challenge to those wishing to study it. For most of history, its examination was possible only after an individual was dead. Only then could the skull be opened up and the brain cut into without the risk of causing

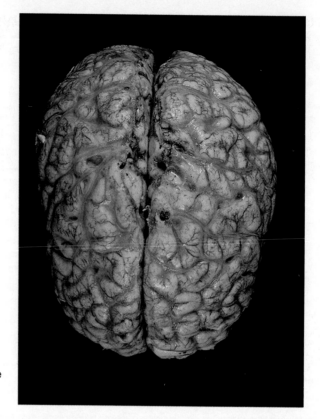

The soft, spongy gray matter of the brain has capabilities far more spectacular than its appearance would lead us to suspect.

Brain scan: A method of "photographing" the brain without opening the skull

Electroencephalogram (ee LEK tro en SEF uh lo gram) **(EEG):** A technique that records the electrical signals being transmitted inside the brain

Computerized axial tomography (CAT) scan: A computerized scanner that constructs an image of the brain by combining thousands of separate x-rays taken at slightly different angles

Magnetic resonance imaging (MRI) scan: A scanner that produces a powerful magnetic field to provide a detailed, computer-generated image of brain structures

serious injury. While informative, such a limited procedure could hardly tell us much about the functioning of the healthy brain.

Today, however, the story is different. Probably the most important advances that have been made in the study of the brain use the **brain scan**, a technique by which a picture of the internal workings of the brain can be taken without having to cut surgically into a patient's skull. The main kinds of scanning techniques are described below and illustrated in Figure 3-11.

■ The **electroencephalogram (EEG)** records the electrical signals being transmitted inside the brain through electrodes placed on the outside of the skull. Although traditionally the EEG could produce only a graph of electrical wave patterns, new techniques now are able to transform the brain's electrical activity into a pictorial representation of the brain that allows the diagnosis of such problems as epilepsy and learning disabilities.

■ The **computerized axial tomography (CAT) scan** uses a computer to construct an image of the brain by combining thousands of separate x-rays taken at slightly different angles. It is extremely useful for showing abnormalities in the structure of the brain, such as swelling and enlargement of certain parts, but does not provide information about brain activity.

■ The **magnetic resonance imaging (MRI) scan** produces a powerful magnetic field to provide a detailed, computer-generated image of brain structures.

ANSWERS (REVIEW II):

1. c **2.** Neurotransmitters **3.** a-3; b-2; c-1 **4.** dopamine **5.** linear circuit **6.** True **7.** reflex **8.** autonomic **9.** False; the spinal cord belongs to the CNS. **10.** d

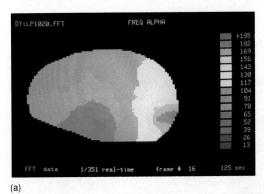

(a)

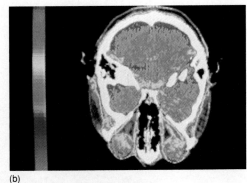

(b)

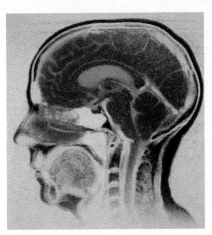

(c)

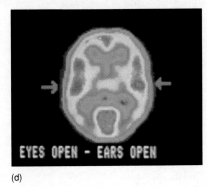

EYES OPEN - EARS OPEN

(d)

FIGURE 3-11

Brain scans produced by different techniques. (*a*) A computer-produced EEG image. (*b*) The CAT scan shows the structures of the brain. (*c*) The MRI scan uses a magnetic field to detail the parts of the brain. (*d*) PET scans display the functioning of the brain at a given moment in time and are sensitive to the person's activities.

■ The **positron emission tomography (PET) scan** indicates actual activity within the brain at a given moment in time. As we explained when discussing the case of Andrea Fyie at the beginning of the chapter, PET scans begin with the injection of radioactive isotopes into the brain. By measuring the location of radiation within the brain, a computer can determine the more active regions, providing a striking picture of the brain at work.

Positron emission tomography (PET) scan: A technique to determine activity within the brain at a given moment in time

Each of these techniques offers exciting possibilities not only for the diagnosis and treatment of brain disease and injuries but also for an increased understanding of the normal functioning of the brain (Gibbons, 1990).

The Central Core: Our "Old Brain"

While the capabilities of the human brain far exceed those of the brain of any other species, it is not surprising that the basic functions, such as breathing, eating, and sleeping, that we share with more primitive animals are directed by a relatively primitive part of the brain. A portion of the brain known as the **central core** (see Figure 3-12) is quite similar to that found in all vertebrates (species with backbones). The central core is often referred to as the "old brain" because it is thought to have evolved relatively early in the development of the human species.

If we were to move up the spinal cord from the base of the skull to locate the structures of the central core of the brain, the first part we would come to would be the **medulla** (see Figure 3-13). The medulla controls a number of im-

Central core: The "old brain," which controls such basic functions as eating and sleeping and is common to all vertebrates

Medulla: The part of the central core of the brain that controls many important body functions, such as breathing and heartbeat

▶ **75**

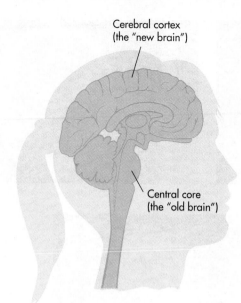

FIGURE 3-12

The major divisions of the brain: the cerebral cortex (the "new" brain) and the central core (the "old" brain).

FIGURE 3-13

(*a*) A three-dimensional view of the structures within the brain. (*b*) In this view, we can see the inside of a brain that has been cut in half; we are viewing the inner surface of the right side.

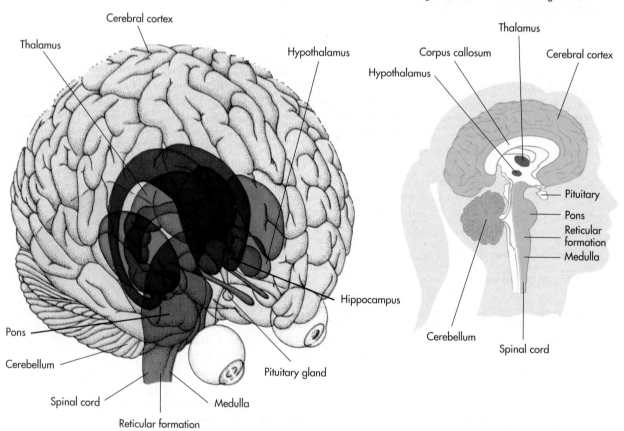

portant body functions, the most important of which are breathing and maintenance of heartbeat. The **pons** comes next, joining the two halves of the cerebellum, which lies adjacent to it. Containing large bundles of nerves, the pons acts as a transmitter of motor information, permitting the coordination of muscles and the integration of movement between the right and left halves of the body.

The **cerebellum** is found just above the medulla and behind the pons. Without the help of the cerebellum we would be unable to walk a straight line without staggering and lurching forward, for it is the job of the cerebellum to control bodily balance. It constantly monitors feedback from the muscles to coordinate their placement, movement, and tension. In fact, drinking too much alcohol seems to depress the activity of the cerebellum, leading to the unsteady gait and movement characteristic of drunkenness.

So far our description of the parts of the brain has suggested that it is made up of a series of individual, well-defined, separate structures. However, some parts of the brain do not simply follow one another in a sequential order; they are found both within and between other structures. An example of this is the reticular formation, which extends from the medulla through the pons. The **reticular formation** is made up of a group of nerve cells that serves as a kind of guard that immediately activates other parts of the brain to cause a general arousal of the body. If, for example, you are startled by a loud noise, your reticular formation is likely to engage your body in immediate vigilance, prompting a heightened state of awareness to determine whether a response is necessary. In addition, it serves a different function when you are sleeping, seeming to screen out background stimuli to allow you to sleep undisturbed.

The final structures that are part of the central core are the thalamus and the hypothalamus. The **thalamus**, located in the middle of the central core, acts primarily as a relay station, mostly for messages concerning sensory information. Messages from the eyes, ears, and skin travel to the thalamus to be communicated upward to higher parts of the brain. The thalamus also integrates information from higher parts of the brain, sorting it out so that it can be sent to the cerebellum and medulla.

The **hypothalamus** is located just below the thalamus. Although tiny—about the size of the tip of a finger—the hypothalamus plays an inordinately important role in the functioning of the body. One of its major functions is to maintain **homeostasis**, a steady internal environment for the body. As we will discuss further in Chapter 11, the hypothalamus helps provide a constant body temperature and monitors the amount of nutrients stored in the cells. A second major function is equally important: It produces and regulates behavior that is critical to the basic survival of the species—eating, drinking, sexual behavior, aggression, and nurturance of offspring. (For a discussion of some recent work on the structure of the brain, see the Cutting Edge box.)

The Limbic System: Beyond the Central Core

In an eerie view of the future, some science fiction writers have suggested that people will someday routinely have electrodes implanted in their brains. These electrodes will permit them to receive tiny shocks that produce the sensation of pleasure by stimulating certain centers of the brain. When they feel upset, people will simply activate their electrodes to achieve an immediate high.

Although farfetched—and ultimately probably unachievable—such a futuristic fantasy is based on fact: The brain does have pleasure centers in an area known as the **limbic system**. Consisting of a series of interrelated structures, the

Pons: The part of the brain that joins the halves of the cerebellum, transmitting motor information to coordinate muscles and integrate movement between the right and left sides of the body

Cerebellum (ser rah BELL um): The part of the brain that controls bodily balance

Reticular formation: A group of nerve cells in the brain that arouses the body to prepare it for appropriate action and screens out background stimuli

Thalamus: The part of the brain's central core that transmits messages from the sense organs to the cerebral cortex and from the cerebral cortex to the cerebellum and medulla

Hypothalamus: Located below the thalamus of the brain, its major function is to maintain homeostasis

Homeostasis: The process by which an organism tries to maintain an internal biological balance or steady state

Limbic system: The part of the brain located outside the "new brain" that controls eating, aggression, and reproduction

Consider the following facts:

- Boys are more likely than girls to have reading problems in elementary school.
- Women recover more quickly from some kinds of brain damage than men do.
- Men often perform better than women on tasks involving spatial abilities.

Why should these assertions all be true? One answer, albeit a controversial one, suggests that there are structural differences between the brains of men and women.

According to this hypothesis, there are subtle differences in the structure of men's and women's brains. These structural differences are viewed as the possible cause of several variations in behavior between males and females.

Several kinds of differences between male and female brains seem to exist. For example, part of the **corpus callosum**, a bundle of fibers that connect one half of the brain to the

ARE MEN'S AND WOMEN'S BRAINS DIFFERENT?

other, is proportionally larger in women than men (Whitelson, 1989).

Studies conducted on animals have also found sex differences. In rats, for example, certain parts of the hypothalamus are larger in males than in females, even though the overall brain size is similar in rats of both sexes. Furthermore, sex differences have been found in the structure of dendrites in rats, hamsters, and monkeys (Allen et al., 1989; Hammer, 1984; Ayoub, 1983).

Although evidence is accumulating that subtle differences exist between male and female brains, the meaning of such differences is far from clear. Consider one possibility related to the part of the corpus callosum that is proportionally larger in women than men: Its increased size may permit stronger connections to develop between those parts of the brain that control speech. This in turn would explain why speech tends to

emerge slightly earlier in girls than in boys.

Before we rush to such a conclusion, though, it is important to consider an alternative hypothesis: It is plausible that the earlier emergence of verbal abilities in girls is due to the greater encouragement being given to them to verbalize as infants than to boys. In turn, this greater early experience may foster growth of certain parts of the brain. Hence, physical brain differences may be a reflection of social and environmental influences, rather than a cause of the differences in men's and women's behavior. (We discuss this issue further when we consider sex and gender differences in Chapter 12.)

It is too early to tell what the causes and consequences of differences in male and female brain structures are. What is clear is that our increasing knowledge of the structure of the brain is pointing to possible new ways of understanding the differences between men's and women's behavior.

Corpus callosum: A bundle of fibers that connects one half of the brain to the other which is thicker in women than in men

limbic system borders the top of the central core and connects with it and with the cerebral cortex (located in Figure 3-12 roughly at the boundaries between the two colors).

The structures of the limbic system jointly control a variety of basic functions relating to self-preservation, such as eating, aggression, and reproduction. Injury to the limbic system can produce striking changes in behavior. It can turn animals that are usually docile and tame into belligerent savages. Conversely, those that are usually wild and uncontrollable may become meek and obedient (Fanelli, Burright, & Donovick, 1983).

Probably the most thought-provoking finding to emerge from the study of the limbic system comes from research that has examined the effects of mild electric shocks to certain parts of the system (Olds & Milner, 1954). In one experiment, rats with an electrode implanted in their limbic systems were given the opportunity to pass an electric current through the electrode by pressing a bar. Even starving rats on their way to food would stop to press the bar as many times as they could. In fact, if allowed to do so, the rats would stimulate their limbic systems literally thousands of times an hour—until they collapsed with fatigue (Routtenberg & Lindy, 1965).

The extraordinarily pleasurable quality of certain kinds of limbic-system stimulation has also been found in humans, who have received electrical stimulation to certain areas of the limbic system, usually as part of some treatment of brain dysfunction. Although at a loss to describe just what it feels like, these people report the experience to be intensely pleasurable, similar in some respects to sexual orgasm.

The limbic system also plays an important role in learning and memory, a finding demonstrated in patients with epilepsy who, in an attempt to stop their seizures, have had portions of the limbic system removed. Such individuals sometimes have difficulty learning and remembering new information. In one case (discussed again when we focus on memory in Chapter 8) a patient who had undergone surgery was unable to remember where he lived, although he had resided at the same address for eight years. Further, even though the patient was able to carry on animated conversations, he was unable, a few minutes later, to recall what had been discussed (Milner, 1966).

The limbic system, then, is involved in several important functions, including self-preservation, learning, memory, and the experience of pleasure. These functions are hardly unique to humans; in fact, the limbic system is sometimes referred to as the "animal brain" because its structures and functions are so similar to those of other mammals. To find that which is uniquely human, we need to turn to another part of the brain, the cerebral cortex.

RECAP AND REVIEW III

RECAP

◀ The central core of the human brain, sometimes referred to as the "old brain," is similar to that found in all vertebrates.

◀ If we trace the CNS from the top of the spinal cord up into the brain, the first structure we find is the medulla, which controls such functions as breathing and heartbeat. Next is the pons, which acts to transmit motor information. The cerebellum is involved in the control of motion.

◀ The reticular formation, extending from the medulla through the pons, arouses and activates the body but also censors outside stimulation during sleep.

◀ The thalamus acts primarily as a sensory-information relay center, whereas the hypothalamus maintains homeostasis, a steady internal environment for the body.

◀ Eating and reproductive behavior are controlled to a large extent by the limbic system, which also produces an extraordinarily pleasurable experience when stimulated electrically.

REVIEW

1. The _____ is a procedure whereby a picture of the brain can be taken without opening the skull.

2. Match the name of each brain scan with the way it is performed:
   _____ a. EEG
   _____ b. CAT
   _____ c. MRI
   _____ d. PET
   1. Magnetic fields produce a computer-generated model of the brain.
   2. Location of radioactive isotopes within the brain determines its active regions.
   3. Electrodes record the electrical signals transmitted through the brain.
   4. Computer image combines thousands of x-ray pictures into one.

3. Control of such functions as breathing and sleep is located in the recently developed "new brain." True or false? _____

4. Match the portion of the brain with its function:
   _____ a. medulla
   _____ b. pons
   _____ c. cerebellum
   _____ d. reticular formation
   1. Maintains breathing and heartbeat
   2. Controls bodily balance
   3. Coordinates and integrates muscle movements
   4. Activates the brain to produce arousal

5. You receive flowers from a friend. The color, smell, and feeling of the flowers are relayed through what part of the brain? _____

6. The _____, a fingertip-sized portion of the brain, is responsible for the maintenance of _____, the regulation of the body's internal environment.

7. The hypothalamus is responsible for the production and regulation of behavior that is critical to the basic survival of the species, such as eating, drinking, sexual behavior, and aggression. True or false? _____

8. It has been proven that women are more verbally adept than men because of the differences inherent in their brains. True or false? _____

9. Starving rats with electrodes planted in the _____ of their brain have been known to turn down food in order to continue stimulating these electrodes, which produce sensations of intense pleasure.

Ask Yourself

How would you answer the argument that ''psychologists should leave the study of neurons and synapses and the nervous system to biologists?''

(Answers to review questions are on page 82.)

The Cerebral Cortex: Up the Evolutionary Ladder

As we have proceeded up the spinal cord and into the brain, our discussion has centered on the brain's areas that control functions similar to those found in less sophisticated organisms. But where, you may be asking, are the portions of the brain that enable humans to do what they do best, and that distinguish humankind from all other animals? Those unique features of the human brain—indeed, the very capabilities that allow you to come up with such a question in the first place—are embodied in the ability to think and remember. The principal location of these abilities, along with many others, is the **cerebral cortex**.

The cerebral cortex, sometimes called the ''new brain'' because of its relatively recent evolution, is a mass of deeply folded, rippled, convoluted tissue. Although it is only about one-twelfth of an inch thick, it would if flattened out cover more than a 2-foot-square area. This physical configuration allows the surface area of the cortex to be considerably greater than if it were more loosely and smoothly packed into the skull. It also allows the neurons within the cortex to be intricately connected to one another, permitting the highest level of integration of neural communication within the brain, and therefore the most sophisticated processing of information.

Cerebral cortex: The ''new brain,'' responsible for the most sophisticated information processing in the brain; contains the lobes

The lobes of the brain.

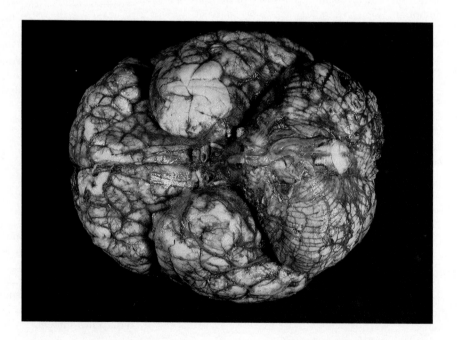

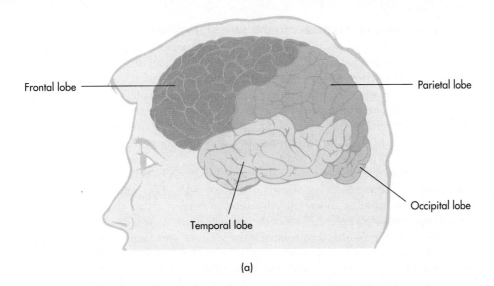

(a)

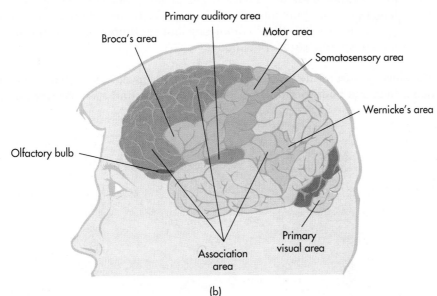

(b)

FIGURE 3-14
The cerebral cortex of the brain.
(*a*) The major physical *structures*
of the cerebral cortex are called
lobes. (*b*) This figure illustrates
the *functions* associated with
particular areas of the cerebral
cortex.

The cortex has four major sections, called **lobes**. If we take a side view of the brain, the **frontal lobes** lie at the front center of the cortex, and the **parietal lobes** lie behind them. The **temporal lobes** are found in the lower center of the brain, with the **occipital lobes** lying behind them. These four sets of lobes are physically separated by deep grooves called sulci. Figure 3-14*a* shows the four areas.

Another way of describing the brain is by considering the functions associated with a given area. Figure 3-14*b* shows the specialized regions within the lobes related to specific functions and areas of the body. Three major areas have been discovered: the motor areas, the sensory areas, and the association areas. Although we will discuss each of these areas as though they were separate and independent entities, keep in mind that this approach represents an oversimplification: In most instances, behavior is influenced simultaneously by several structures and areas within the brain, operating interdependently. Furthermore, even within a given area, additional subdivisions exist (Gibbons, 1990).

Lobes: The four major
sections of the cerebral cortex

Frontal lobes: The brain
structure located at the front
center of the cortex,
containing major motor and
speech and reasoning centers

Occipital lobes: The
structures of the brain lying
behind the temporal lobes;
includes the visual sensory
area

Motor area: One of the major areas of the brain, responsible for voluntary movement of particular parts of the body

The Motor Area of the Brain. If you look at the frontal lobe in Figure 3-14*b*, you will see a shaded portion labeled the **motor area**. This part of the brain is largely responsible for the voluntary movement of particular parts of the body. In fact, every portion of the motor area corresponds to a specific locale within the body. If we were to insert an electrode into a particular part of the motor area of the brain and apply mild electrical stimulation, there would be involuntary movement in the corresponding part of the body (Kertesz, 1983). If we moved to another part of the motor area and stimulated it, a different part of the body would move.

The motor area has been so well mapped that it is possible to devise the kind of schematic representation shown in Figure 3-15. This weird-looking model illustrates the amount and relative location of cortical tissue that is used to produce movement in specific parts of the human body. As you can see, the control of body movements that are relatively large scale and require little precision, such as movement of a knee or a hip, is centered in a very small space in the motor area. On the other hand, movements that must be precise and delicate, such as facial expressions and the use of the fingers, are controlled by a considerably larger portion of the motor area. In sum, the brain's motor area provides a clear guide to the degree of complexity and the importance of the motor capabilities of specific parts of the body.

The Sensory Area of the Brain. Given the one-to-one correspondence between motor area and body location, it is not surprising to find a similar relationship

FIGURE 3-15

The correspondence between the amount and location of tissue in the brain's motor area and the specific body parts where movement is controlled by that tissue. (Penfield & Rasmussen, 1950.)

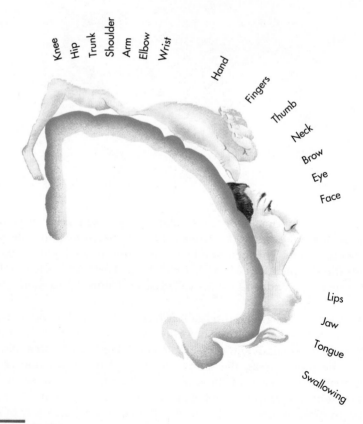

ANSWERS (REVIEW III):

1. brain scan **2.** a-3; b-4; c-1; d-2 **3.** False; it is located in the "old brain" or central core.
4. a-1; b-3; c-2; d-4 **5.** Thalamus **6.** hypothalamus; homeostasis **7.** True **8.** False; it is an interesting hypothesis, but it has not been proven. **9.** limbic system

FIGURE 3-16
The greater the amount of tissue in the somatosensory area of the brain that is related to a specific body part, the more sensitive that body part is. If the size of our body parts reflected the corresponding amount of brain tissue, we would look like this strange creature.

between specific portions of the brain and the senses. The **sensory area** of the cortex includes three regions: one that corresponds primarily to touch, one relating to sight, and a third relating to sound. For instance, the **somatosensory area** encompasses specific locations associated with the ability to perceive touch in a particular area of the body. As with the motor area, the amount of brain tissue related to a particular location on the body determines the degree of sensitivity of that location: The greater the space within the brain, the more sensitive that area of the body. As you can see from Figure 3-16, parts such as the fingers are related to proportionally more space in the somatosensory area and are the most sensitive.

The senses of sound and sight also are represented in specific areas of the cerebral cortex. An auditory area located in the temporal lobe is responsible for the sense of hearing. If the auditory area is stimulated electrically, a person will hear sounds such as clicks or hums. It also appears that particular locations within the auditory area respond to specific pitches.

The visual center in the brain, located in the occipital lobe, operates analogously to the other sensory areas; stimulation by electrodes produces the experience of flashes of light or colors, suggesting that the raw sensory input of images from the eyes is received in this area of the brain and transformed into meaningful stimuli. The visual area also provides another example of how areas of the brain are intimately related to specific areas of the body: Particular areas of the eye are related to a particular part of the brain—with, as you might guess, more space in the brain given to the most sensitive portions of the eye.

Sensory area: The site in the brain of the tissue that corresponds to each of the senses, with the degree of sensitivity relating to the amount of tissue

Somatosensory area: The area within the cortex corresponding to the sense of touch

The Association Area of the Brain.   Consider the following case:

Twenty-five-year-old Phineas Gage, a railroad employee, was blasting rock one day in 1848 when an accidental explosion punched a 3-foot-long spike, about an inch in diameter, completely through his skull. The spike entered just under his left cheek, came out the top of his head, and flew into the air. He immediately suffered a series of convulsions, yet a few minutes later was talking with rescuers. In fact, he was able to walk up a long flight of stairs before receiving any medical attention. Amazingly, after a few weeks his wound healed, and he was physically close to his old self again. Mentally, however, there was a difference: Once a careful and hard-working person, Phineas now became enamored with wild schemes and was flighty and often irresponsible. As one of his physicians put it, "Previous to his injury, though untrained in the schools, he possessed a well-balanced mind, and was looked upon by those who knew him as a shrewd, smart businessman, very energetic and persistent in executing all his plans of operation. In this regard his mind was radically changed, so decidedly that his friends and acquaintances said he was 'no longer Gage' " (Harlow, 1869, p. 14).

What had happened to the old Gage? Although there is no way of knowing for sure—science being what it was in the 1800s—we can speculate that the accident may have injured the association area of Gage's cerebral cortex.

If you return one last time to our diagram of the cerebral cortex (Figure 3-14*b*), you will find that the motor and sensory areas take up a relatively small portion of the cortex; the remainder contains the association area. The **association area** is generally considered to be the site of higher mental processes such as thinking, language, memory, and speech. Most of our understanding of the association area comes from patients who have suffered some brain injury—from natural causes such as a tumor or a stroke, either of which would block certain blood vessels within the cerebral cortex, or, as in the case of Phineas Gage, from accidental causes. Damage to this area can result in unusual behavioral changes, indicating the importance of the association area to normal functioning.

Consider, for instance, the condition known as apraxia. **Apraxia** occurs when a person is unable to integrate activities in a rational or logical manner. For

Association area: One of the major areas of the brain, the site of the higher mental processes, such as thought, language, memory, and speech

Apraxia: The inability to integrate activities in a logical way

As the remarkable case of Phineas Gage demonstrated, damage to the cerebral cortex may cause behavior and personality changes.

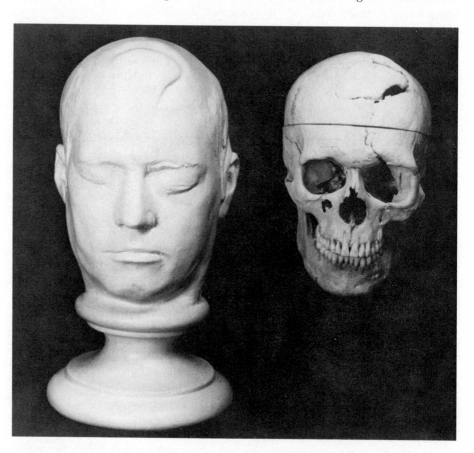

example, a patient asked to get a soda from the refrigerator might go to the refrigerator and open and close the door repeatedly, or might take bottle after bottle of soda out of the refrigerator, dropping each to the floor. Similarly, a person with apraxia who is asked to open a lock with a key may be unable to do so in response to the request—but, if simply left alone in a locked room, wishing to leave, will unlock the door (Lechtenberg, 1982).

Apraxia is clearly not a muscular problem, since the person is capable of carrying out the individual components of the overall behavior. Moreover, if asked to perform the individual components of a larger behavioral pattern one at a time, a patient is often quite successful. It is only when asked to carry out a sequence of behaviors requiring a degree of planning and foresight that the patient shows deficits. It appears, then, that the association area may act as a kind of "master planner," that is, the organizer of actions.

Other difficulties that arise because of injury to the association area of the brain relate to the use of language. Problems with verbal expression, known as **aphasia**, can take many forms. In **Broca's aphasia** (caused by damage to the part of the brain first identified by a French physician, Paul Broca), speech becomes halting and laborious. The speaker is unable to find the right words—in a kind of tip-of-the-tongue phenomenon that we all experience from time to time, except that in the case of the person with aphasia, it happens almost constantly. Patients with aphasia also speak in "verbal telegrams." A phrase like "I put the book on the table" comes out as "I . . . put . . . book . . . table" (Lechtenberg, 1982).

In **Wernicke's aphasia**, named for its discoverer, Carl Wernicke, there are difficulties in understanding the language of others. Found in patients with damage to a particular area of brain first identified by Wernicke, the disorder produces speech that sounds fluent, but makes no sense. For instance, one of Wernicke's patients, Philip Gorgan, was asked what brought him to the hospital. He replied, "Boy, I'm sweating, I'm awful nervous, you know, once in a while I get caught up, I can't mention the tarripoi, a month ago, quite a little, I've done a lot well, I impose a lot, while, on the other hand, you know what I mean, I have to run around, look it over, trebbin and all that sort of stuff" (Gardner, 1975, p. 68).

Aphasia: A disorder resulting in problems with verbal expression due to brain injury

Broca's aphasia: A syndrome in which speech production is disturbed

Wernicke's aphasia: A syndrome involving problems with understanding language, resulting in fluent but nonsensical speech

The Specialization of the Hemispheres: Two Brains or One?

The most recent development, at least in evolutionary terms, in the organization and operation of our brain probably occurred in the last million years: a specialization of the functions controlled by the two sides of the brain, which has symmetrical left and right halves.

Specifically, the brain can be divided into two roughly similar mirror-image halves—just as we have two arms, two legs, and two lungs. Because of the way nerves are connected from the brain to the rest of the body, these two symmetrical left and right halves, called **hemispheres**, control the side of the body opposite to their location. The left hemisphere of the brain, then, generally controls the right side of the body, and the right hemisphere controls the left side of the body. Thus damage to the right side of the brain is typically indicated by functional difficulties in the left side of the body.

Yet the structural similarity between the two hemispheres of the brain is not reflected in all aspects of its functioning; it appears that certain activities are more likely to occur in one hemisphere than in the other. Early evidence for the

Hemispheres: Symmetrical left and right halves of the brain

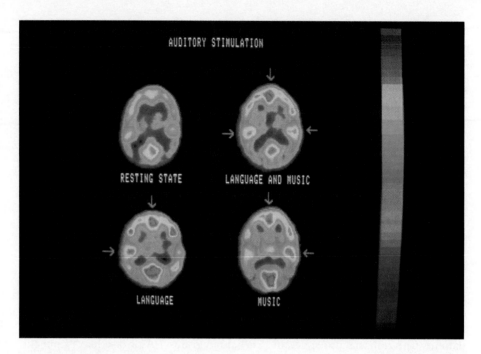

AUDITORY STIMULATION

RESTING STATE   LANGUAGE AND MUSIC

LANGUAGE   MUSIC

FIGURE 3-17

This series of PET scans shows the activity of the left and right hemispheres while the person is performing various activities.

Lateralization: The dominance of one hemisphere of the brain in specific functions

functional differences between halves of the brain came from studies of people with aphasia; researchers found that people with the speech difficulties characteristic of aphasia tended to have physical damage to the left hemisphere of the brain. In contrast, physical abnormalities in the right hemisphere of the brain tended to produce far fewer problems with language (Corballis & Beale, 1983). This finding led researchers to conclude that for most people, language is **lateralized**, or located more in one hemisphere than the other—in this case, in the left side of the brain.

It now seems clear that the two hemispheres of the brain specialize in different functions, although there are individual as well as sex differences in the nature and extent of such specialization, as we will see (Kitterle, 1991). The left hemisphere concentrates on tasks that require verbal strength, such as speaking, reading, thinking, and reasoning. The right hemisphere has its own strengths, particularly in nonverbal areas such as spatial understanding, recognition of patterns and drawings, music, and emotional expression (see Figure 3-17).

In addition, the way in which information is processed seems somewhat different in each hemisphere: The left hemisphere considers information sequentially, one bit at a time, while the right hemisphere tends to process information globally, considering it as a whole (Gazzaniga, 1983; Springer & Deutsch, 1989). Moreover, there is even evidence suggesting that the two hemispheres develop at slightly different rates during the course of people's lives (deSchonen & Mathivet, 1989; Thatcher, Walker, & Giudice, 1987; Hahn, 1987).

Great variation exists in the degree and nature of lateralization from one person to another. If, like most people, you are right-handed, the portion of your brain that controls language is probably concentrated on the left side of your brain. By contrast, if you are among the 10 percent of people who are left-handed or are ambidextrous (you use both hands interchangeably), it is much more likely that the language centers of your brain are located in the right hemisphere or are divided equally between left and right hemispheres (Geschwind & Galaburda, 1987; Gazzaniga, 1985; Springer & Deutsch, 1989).

It also turns out that males and females show some intriguing sex differences in brain lateralization, in addition to the differences in brain structure described earlier in the chapter (Wood, Flowers, & Naylor, 1991). Most males tend to show greater lateralization of language in the left hemisphere: For them, language is clearly relegated largely to the left side of the brain. In contrast, women display less lateralization, with language abilities apt to be more evenly divided between the two hemispheres (Gur et al., 1982). Such differences in brain lateralization may account, in part, for the superiority often displayed by females on some measures of verbal skills, such as the onset and fluency of speech (Kitterle, 1991).

Cultural factors may also account for differences in brain lateralization. For example, native speakers of Japanese seem to process information regarding vowel sounds primarily in the brain's left hemisphere. In contrast, North and South Americans, Europeans, and individuals of Japanese ancestry who learn Japanese later in life handle vowel sounds principally in the right hemisphere.

The reason for this difference may be that certain characteristics of the Japanese language, such as the ability to express complex ideas using only vowel sounds, result in the development of a specific type of brain lateralization in native speakers. Such a difference in lateralization may account for other dissimilarities between the way that native Japanese speakers and Westerners think about the world (Tsunoda, 1985).

Despite examples of hemispheric lateralization and specialization, the two halves of the brain function together and interdependently in almost everyone (Ottoson, 1987). Even people (especially young children) who suffer brain damage to the left side of their brain and lose linguistic capabilities often recover the ability to speak, because the right side of the brain pitches in and takes over some of the functioning of the left side (Weiderhold, 1982). The brain, then, is remarkably adaptable and can modify its functioning, to some extent at least, in response to adverse circumstances (McConnell, 1985; Beaton, 1986; Kucharski & Hall, 1987).

The differences in hemispheric functioning at least suggest the possibility that the characteristics that distinguish us from others may be due in part to the relative strengths of each hemisphere. For example, we might speculate that a talented writer has a brain in which the left side is particularly dominant, while an artist or architect might have more strength in the right hemisphere. What we do best in life, then, may be a function of which side of our brain has the greater strengths. (For some of the practical implications of hemispheric lateralization, see the Psychology at Work box on p. 88.)

The Split Brain: Exploring the Two Hemispheres

When the seizures first started, Cindy Gluccles thought her physician would be able to give her a drug that would prevent their recurrence. Her physician and her neurologist were both optimistic, maintaining that in most cases seizures could be controlled with the proper drugs. But the seizures got worse and more frequent, and no drug treatment seemed to help. Further examination revealed that the seizures were caused by remarkably large bursts of electrical activity that were starting in one hemisphere and moving to the other. Finally, her doctors prescribed a last-ditch measure: surgically cutting the bundle of nerves that connected the two hemispheres to each other. Almost magically, the seizures stopped. The operation was clearly a success—but was Cindy the same person she had been before the operation?

That issue has evoked a great deal of interest on the part of brain researchers and, in fact, has earned a Nobel Prize for Roger Sperry. Sperry, with a group of colleagues, explored the behavior of patients who had had the corpus callosum, the bundle of fibers that link the two hemispheres of the brain, surgically cut.

"You've Got the Right One Baby, Uh-Huh!"

"I Love What You Do For Me"

"WOW! What A Difference"

"A Mind Is a Terrible Thing to Waste"

Sound familiar? They should, for you've probably heard these phrases scores of times. On any given day, the average American is exposed to about 300 advertisements (McCarthy, 1991b). Over the course of a year, that adds up to well over 100,000.

Advertisers, of course, have more than a passing interest in making sure that their ads are the ones that you do remember. To do this, they are turning to a budding new technology which links the practice of advertising with the science of biopsychology.

Early efforts in understanding the biology behind advertising began with instruments that related electrical impulses in the palm of one's hand to the content of commercials.

THE COMMERCIAL VALUE OF THE BRAIN

Using apparatus that measures the conductance of electricity across the palm, advertisers measured moment-by-moment attention levels to commercials. For instance, viewers of an experimental Kodak advertisement showed greatest interest when a smiling, pigtailed girl appeared in it, allowing the ad creators to know that her image was crucial to the success of the advertisement.

More recent innovations in advertising testing have drawn on research on left and right hemisphere brain specialization. Work in one laboratory has shown that commercials that appeal to logic, such as those that show product demonstrations, are processed largely by the left hemisphere of the brain. In contrast, commercials that consist predominately of emotional appeals are processed mainly by the right hemisphere (Weinstein, Drozdenko, & Weinstein,

1984; Price, Rust, & Kumar, 1986).

This knowledge has helped advertisers to anticipate potential problems in commercials. For example, one commercial began with a father and daughter conversing in emotional and affectionate terms, leading to a high amount of right-hemisphere processing. But when the commercial abruptly shifted to presenting product information, thereby leading to more left-hemisphere processing, the impact of the earlier right-hemisphere processing may have interfered with comprehension of the product information (McCarthy, 1991b).

It is important to keep in mind that much of the work done on advertising is experimental and speculative. No conclusive evidence has linked the success of a commercial with right- and left-hemisphere processing. Still, the interest of advertisers in exploring the biological signs of interest in commercials is one interesting example of a practical application growing from work in biopsychology.

The research team found that in most ways there were no major changes in either personality or intelligence.

On the other hand, patients like Cindy Gluccles, called **split-brain patients**, did occasionally display some unusual behavior. For instance, one patient reported pulling his pants down with one hand and simultaneously pulling them up with the other. In addition, he mentioned grabbing his wife with his left hand and shaking her violently, while his right hand tried to help his wife by bringing his left hand under control (Gazzaniga, 1970).

Interest in this occasional curious behavior, however, was peripheral to the rare opportunity that split-brain patients provided for research in the independent functioning of the two hemispheres of the brain, and Sperry developed a number of ingenious techniques for studying how each hemisphere operated (Sperry, 1982). In one experimental procedure, blindfolded subjects were allowed to touch an object with their right hand and were asked to name it. Because the right side of the body is connected to the left side of the brain—the hemisphere that is most responsible for language—the split-brain patient was able to name it. But if the blindfolded subject touched the object with his or her left hand, naming it aloud was not possible. However, the information had registered: When the blindfold was taken off, the subject could choose the object that he or she had touched. Information can be learned and remembered, then, using only the right side of the brain. (By the way, this experiment won't work

Split-brain patient: A person who suffers from independent functioning of the two halves of the brain, as a result of which the sides of the body work in disharmony with you—unless you have had a split-brain operation—since the nerves connecting the two halves of a normal brain immediately transfer the information from one half of the brain to the other.)

It is clear from experiments like this one that the right and left hemispheres of the brain specialize in handling different sorts of information. At the same time, it is important to realize that they are both capable of understanding, knowing, and being aware of the world, albeit in somewhat different ways. The two hemispheres, then, should be seen as different in terms of the efficiency with which they process certain kinds of information, rather than viewed as two entirely separate brains. Moreover, in people with normal, nonsplit brains, the hemispheres work interdependently to allow the full range and richness of thought of which humans are capable.

Brain Modules: The Architecture of the Brain, Revisited

You'll recall that earlier in the chapter we discussed the architecture of the brain as it related to the connections between individual neurons. But there is another way that psychologists consider the architecture of the brain: in terms of the relationship between particular functions and structures of the brain, on the one hand, and complex cognitive processes such as thinking, understanding, perceiving, and awareness, on the other.

According to an emerging view of how the brain operates, the brain is organized into a series of modules. **Brain modules** are separate units that carry out specific tasks. These modules, which are distributed throughout the brain, work interdependently and relatively simultaneously in processing information (Gazzaniga, 1989).

Brain modules: Separate units of the brain that carry out specific tasks

The basic notion behind the modular approach is that abilities that were once thought to be processed in a unitary manner are actually composed of many subtasks. Take, for example, the brain's ability to process information regarding vision. It was once thought that there was a single area within the brain that controlled visual processing. However, as we will discuss when we consider vision in Chapter 4, increasing evidence suggests that there are separate areas of the brain related to specific aspects of vision. For instance, one area of the brain seems to process information about color; another specializes in motion; and still another specializes in depth perception (Goldman-Rakic, 1988). Each of these aspects of vision is simultaneously processed by a separate module, and the information is then integrated to form a whole, intact visual image.

Recent research suggests that the degree of specialization of modules is remarkable. For example, it now seems possible that the brain processes written and spoken language independently due to the existence of separate modules (Caramazza & Hillis, 1991). Instead of one system that learns the rules of a language, it may be that separate modules consider the way words sound, the manner in which words are written, the roots of words, parts of speech, and other aspects of language. Just as with vision, each of these properties of language is processed simultaneously and independently, and then the information is combined.

The growing evidence for the existence of independent, multiple modules within the brain provides a link between individual neurons and the broad consciousness we experience as human beings. Michael Gazzaniga, a well-known biopsychologist, speculates that what provides people with a unified, conscious sense of the world is a module unique to human beings: an "interpreter" located in the left hemisphere of the brain (Gazzaniga, 1989).

According to Gazzaniga, this interpreter module permits us to build our own hypotheses about the meaning of our responses. The interpreter provides us with a means of developing and changing our beliefs about the world, and it gives us a way of understanding what is happening in our environment.

It is too early to tell if Gazzaniga's theory is correct. What is clear is that the human brain and nervous system are increasingly revealing their secrets to an array of biopsychologists, cognitive neuroscientists, and other investigators (Hellige, 1990; Estes, 1991).

THE ENDOCRINE SYSTEM: OF CHEMICALS AND GLANDS

Endocrine system: A chemical communication network that sends messages throughout the nervous system via the bloodstream and secretes hormones that affect body growth and functioning

One aspect of the brain that we have not yet considered is the **endocrine system**, a chemical communication network that sends messages throughout the nervous system via the bloodstream. Although not a structure of the brain itself, the endocrine system is intimately tied to the hypothalamus. The job of the endocrine system is to secrete **hormones**, chemicals that circulate through the blood and affect the functioning or growth of other parts of the body (Crapo, 1985; Kravitz, 1988).

Hormones: Chemicals that circulate throughout the blood and affect the functioning and growth of parts of the body

Like neurons, endocrines transmit messages throughout the body, although the speed and mode of transmission are quite different. Whereas neural messages are measured in thousandths of a second, hormonal communications may take minutes to reach their destination. Furthermore, neural messages move across neurons in specific lines (as with wires strung along telephone poles), whereas hormones travel throughout the entire body, similar to the way radio waves transmit across the entire landscape. Just as radio waves evoke a response only when a radio is tuned to the correct station, so hormones flowing through the bloodstream activate only those cells that are receptive and "tuned" to the appropriate hormonal message.

Pituitary gland: The major component of the endocrine system, which secretes hormones that control growth

The major component of the endocrine system is the **pituitary gland**, found near—and regulated by—the hypothalamus. The pituitary gland sometimes has been called the "master gland," because it controls the functioning of the rest of the endocrine system. But the pituitary gland is more than just the taskmaster of other glands; it has important functions in its own right. For instance, hormones secreted by the pituitary gland control growth. Extremely short people—dwarfs—and unusually tall ones—giants—usually have pituitary gland deficiencies. Other endocrine glands, shown in Figure 3-18, affect emotional reactions, sexual urges, and energy levels.

Despite its designation as the "master gland," the pituitary is actually a servant of the brain, because the brain is ultimately responsible for the endocrine system's functioning. The brain regulates the internal balance of the body, ensuring that homeostasis is maintained through the hypothalamus. Yet the road from brain to endocrine system is not strictly a one-way street: Hormones may permanently modify the way in which brain cells are organized. For example, adult sexual behavior is thought to be affected by the production of hormones that modify cells in the hypothalamus.

Similarly, particular kinds of episodes in our lives can influence the production of hormones. For instance, one experiment in which college students played a computer game against a competitor found that individuals who were winning the game showed a rise in the production of testosterone—a hormone linked to aggressive behavior (Gladue, Boechler, & McCaul, 1989).

Particular hormones are also able to play several roles, depending on cir-

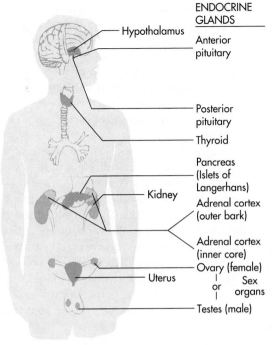

ENDOCRINE GLANDS	FUNCTIONS REGULATED BY SECRETION
Anterior pituitary	Hormones influence secretions of the thyroid, Islets of Langerhans, adrenal cortex, and gonads. Also secretes growth hormones.
Posterior pituitary	Water metabolism, salt metabolism
Thyroid	Metabolic rate
Pancreas (Islets of Langerhans)	Insulin and glucagon control sugar metabolism
Adrenal cortex (outer bark)	Controls salt and carbohydrate metabolism; controls inflammatory reactions
Adrenal cortex (inner core)	Active in emotional arousal and sleep through its hormones epinephrine and norepinephrine
Ovary (female) or Testes (male) — Sex organs	Produce hormones that affect bodily development and that maintain reproductive organs in adults

FIGURE 3-18

Location and function of the major endocrine glands.

cumstances. For example, the hormone oxytocin is at the root of many of life's satisfactions and pleasures. In new mothers, oxytocin produces an urge to nurse newborn offspring. The same hormone also seems to stimulate cuddling between species members. And—at least in rats—it encourages sexually-active males to seek out females more passionately and females to be more receptive to males' sexual advances. One study actually showed that female mice administered oxytocin become 60 to 80 percent more energetic in seeking out males to mount them than a control group of mice who didn't receive any (Angier, 1991).

The Informed Consumer of Psychology: Learning to Control Your Heart—and Brain— through Biofeedback

When her blood pressure rose to unacceptably high levels, Carla Lewitt was first given the option of undergoing a standard treatment with drugs. When she asked whether there was any alternative, her physician suggested an approach that would entail her learning to control her blood pressure voluntarily. Although Carla didn't think she was capable of controlling something she wasn't even aware of, she agreed to give it a try. Within three weeks, her blood pressure had come down to normal levels.

Bill Jackson had experienced excruciatingly painful headaches all his life. No drug seemed to stop them, and they were often accompanied by a loss of appetite and vomiting. When a friend suggested he try a new procedure designed to enable him to voluntarily control the headaches by learning to control the constriction of muscles in his head, he laughed. "I've been trying to learn to stop these headaches all my life," he said, "and it's never worked." Convinced by his friend that it was worth a try, though, he went to a psychologist specializing in biofeedback—and in four weeks had put an end to his headaches.

We typically think of our heart, respiration rate, blood pressure, and other bodily functions as being under the control of parts of the brain over which we

Biofeedback: A technique for learning to control internal physiological processes through conscious thought

have no influence. But, as the cases above illustrate, psychologists are finding that what were once thought of as entirely involuntary biological responses are susceptible to voluntary control—and, in the process, they are learning about important treatment techniques for a variety of ailments.

The technique that both lowered Carla Lewitt's blood pressure and stopped Bill Jackson's headaches was the same: biofeedback. **Biofeedback** is a procedure in which a person learns to control internal physiological processes such as blood pressure, heart rate, respiration speed, skin temperature, sweating, and constriction of certain muscles (Yates, 1980).

How can people learn to control such responses, which are typically considered ''involuntary''? They do so through training with electronic devices that provide continuous feedback on the physiological response in question. For instance, a person interested in controlling her blood pressure might be hooked up to an apparatus that constantly monitors and displays her blood pressure. As she consciously thinks about altering the pressure, she receives immediate feedback on the measure of her success. In this way she can eventually learn to bring her pressure under control. Similarly, if an individual wanted to control headaches through biofeedback, he might have electronic sensors placed on certain muscles in his head and thereby learn to control the constriction and relaxation of those muscles. Then, when he felt a headache coming on, he could relax the relevant muscles and abort the pain.

While the control of physiological processes through the use of biofeedback is not easy to learn, it has been employed with success in a variety of ailments, including emotional problems (such as anxiety, depression, phobias, tension headaches, insomnia, and hyperactivity); medical problems with a psychological component (such as asthma, high blood pressure, ulcers, muscle spasms, and migraine headaches); and physical problems (such as nerve-muscle injuries due to stroke, cerebral palsy, and—as we see in Figure 3-19—curvature of the spine).

Given that biofeedback is still experimental, we cannot assume that treatment is going to be successful in every case. What is certain, however, is that learning through biofeedback has opened up a number of exciting possibilities for treating people with physical and psychological problems (e.g., Kotses et al., 1991; Beckham et al., 1991). Moreover, some psychologists speculate that the use of biofeedback may become a part of everyday life one day in the future.

For instance, one researcher has suggested that students whose minds wander during studying might be hooked up to an apparatus that gives them feedback on whether or not they are paying attention to the information they are studying (Ornstein, 1977). If they stop paying attention, the computer will alert them—putting them back on the right track.

FIGURE 3-19

The traditional treatment for curvature of the spine employs an unsightly, cumbersome brace. In contrast, biofeedback treatment employs an unobtrusive set of straps attached to a small electronic device that produces tonal feedback when the patient is not standing straight. The person learns to maintain a position that gradually decreases the curvature of the spine until the device is no longer needed. (Miller, 1985a.)

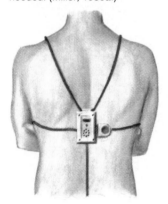

> ### RECAP AND REVIEW IV

RECAP

◀ The cerebral cortex contains three major areas: the motor, sensory, and association areas. These areas control voluntary movement, the senses, and higher mental processes (including thought, language, memory, and speech), respectively.

◀ The two halves, or hemispheres, of the brain are structurally similar, but they seem to specialize in different functions. The left side of the brain is most closely re-

lated to language and verbal skills; the right side, to nonverbal skills such as mathematical and musical ability, emotional expression, pattern recognition, and the processing of visual information.

◀ The endocrine system secretes hormones, chemicals that affect the growth and functioning of the body.

◀ Biofeedback is a procedure by which a person learns to control certain internal physiological processes, thereby bringing relief from a variety of specific ailments.

1. The _____ lobes lie behind the frontal lobes, and the _____ lobes lie behind the temporal lobes.

2. A surgeon places an electrode on a portion of your brain and stimulates it. Immediately, your right wrist involuntarily twitches. The doctor has most likely stimulated a portion of the _____ area of your brain.

3. The motor area of the brain is divided up into segments which control different body parts. The more precise the movements of these parts need to be, the larger the portion of the motor area devoted to that part. True or false? _____

4. The sensory areas of the brain are divided up according to the size of the sensory organ. Thus, since there is more skin on a person's back than on his fingertips, the portion of the sensory area that deals with sensations on the back will be larger than the fingertip section. True or false? _____

5. You see a man who has been asked to sharpen a pencil turn the sharpener for five minutes without putting the pencil into it. The condition that might be responsible for this type of behavior is called _____.

6. Brain hemispheres control the side of the body they are located on; the left hemisphere controls the left side of the body, and the right hemisphere controls the right. True or false? _____

7. Nonverbal realms, such as emotions and music, are controlled primarily by the _____ hemisphere of the brain, while the _____ hemisphere is more responsible for speaking and reading.

8. Current theory suggests that the brain is actually organized into a set of _____, each of which works interdependently on a task.

9. _____, a technique by which people learn to monitor and change physiological phenomena, may someday be used to help students pay attention during studying.

Ask Yourself

Think about two of your acquaintances. Speculate on how they appear to differ in the extent to which their right or left hemispheres dominate.

(Answers to review questions are on page 94.)

LOOKING BACK

■ *Why do psychologists study the brain and nervous system?*

1. A full understanding of human behavior requires knowledge of the biological influences underlying that behavior. This chapter reviews what biopsychologists (psychologists who specialize in studying the effects of biological structures and functions on behavior) have learned about the human nervous system.

■ *What are the basic elements of the nervous system?*

2. Neurons, the most basic elements of the nervous system, allow nerve impulses to pass from one part of the body to another. Information generally enters a neuron through its dendrite, is passed on to other cells via its axon, and finally exits through its terminal buttons.

■ *How does the nervous system communicate electrical and chemical messages from one part to another?*

3. Most neurons are protected by a coating called the myelin sheath. When a neuron receives a message to fire, it releases an action potential, an electric charge that travels through the cell. Neurons operate according to an all-or-none law: They are either at rest or an action potential is moving through them. There is no in-between state.

4. Once a neuron fires, nerve impulses are carried to other neurons through the production of chemical substances, neurotransmitters, which actually bridge the gaps—known as synapses—between neurons. Neurotransmitters may be either excitatory, telling other neurons to fire, or inhibitory, preventing or decreasing the likelihood of other neurons firing. Among the major neurotransmitters are acetylcholine (ACh), which produces contractions of skeletal muscles, and dopamine, which has been linked to Parkinson's disease and certain mental disorders such as schizophrenia.

5. Endorphins, another type of neurotransmitter, are related to the reduction of pain. By interacting with opiate receptors—specialized neurons that reduce the experience of pain—they seem to produce a natural kind of morphine and are probably responsible for creating the kind of euphoria that joggers sometimes experience after running.

■ *In what way are the structures of the nervous system tied together?*

6. Neurons are linked to other neurons via networks, groups of organized communication links between cells. Among the major kinds of networks are linear circuits, multiple source/convergent circuits, and single-source/divergent circuits.

▶ **93**

7. The nervous system is made up of the central nervous system (the brain and spinal cord) and the peripheral nervous system (the remainder of the nervous system). The peripheral nervous system is made up of the somatic division, which controls voluntary movements and the communication of information to and from the sense organs, and the autonomic division, which controls involuntary functions such as those of the heart, blood vessels, and lungs.

8. The autonomic division of the peripheral nervous system is further subdivided into the sympathetic and parasympathetic divisions. The sympathetic division prepares the body in emergency situations, and the parasympathetic division helps the body return to its typical resting state.

■ What are the major parts of the brain, and what are the behaviors for which the parts are responsible?

9. The central core of the brain is made up of the medulla (which controls such functions as breathing and the heartbeat), the pons (which coordinates the muscles and the two sides of the body), the cerebellum (which controls balance), the reticular formation (which acts to heighten awareness in emergencies), the thalamus (which communicates messages to and from the brain), and the hypothalamus (which maintains homeostasis, or body equilibrium, and regulates basic survival behaviors). The functions of the central core structures are similar to those found in other vertebrates; this part of the brain is sometimes referred to as the ''old brain.'' Increasing evidence also suggests that male and female brains may differ in structure in minor ways.

10. The cerebral cortex—the ''new brain''—has areas that control voluntary movement (the motor area); the senses (the sensory area); and thinking, reasoning, speech, and memory (the association area). The limbic system, found on the border of the ''old'' and ''new'' brains, is associated with eating, reproduction, and the experiences of pleasure and pain.

■ How do the parts of the brain operate interdependently?

11. The brain is divided into two halves, or hemispheres, each of which generally controls the opposite side of the body from that in which it is located. However, each hemisphere can be thought of as specialized in the functions it carries out: The left is best at verbal tasks, such as logical reasoning, speaking, and reading; the right is best at nonverbal tasks, such as spatial understanding, pattern recognition, and emotional expression.

12. A growing body of evidence suggests that the brain is organized into a series of modules, separate units that carry out precise, specific functions. These modules, which are distributed throughout the brain, work interdependently and relatively simultaneously in processing information.

13. The endocrine system secretes hormones, allowing the brain to send messages throughout the body. Its major component is the pituitary gland, which affects growth.

■ How can an understanding of the nervous system help us to find ways to relieve disease and pain?

14. Biofeedback is a procedure by which a person learns to control internal physiological processes. By controlling what were previously considered involuntary responses, people are able to relieve anxiety, tension, migraine headaches, and a wide range of other psychological and physical problems.

ANSWERS (REVIEW IV):
1. parietal, occipital **2.** motor **3.** True **4.** False; it is divided according to the degree of sensitivity needed. **5.** apraxia **6.** False; they control opposite sides. **7.** right; left **8.** modules **9.** Biofeedback

KEY TERMS AND CONCEPTS

nervous system (p. 57)
neuroscientists (p. 57)
biopsychologists (p. 57)
neurons (p. 58)
dendrites (p. 58)
axon (p. 58)
terminal buttons (p. 58)
myelin sheath (p. 60)
all-or-none law (p. 61)
resting state (p. 61)
action potential (p. 61)
absolute refractory period (p. 62)
relative refractory period (p. 62)
synapse (p. 63)
neurotransmitter (p. 64)
excitatory message (p. 64)
inhibitory message (p. 64)
reuptake (p. 65)
acetylcholine (p. 65)
Alzheimer's disease (p. 66)
gamma-amino butyric acid
   (GABA) (p. 66)
dopamine (DA) (p. 66)
endorphins (p. 67)
opiate receptor (p. 67)
neural networks (p. 68)
linear circuits (p. 68)
multiple-source/convergent
   circuits (p. 69)

single-source/divergent circuits
   (p. 69)
central nervous system (CNS)
   (p. 69)
spinal cord (p. 69)
reflexes (p. 69)
sensory (afferent) neurons
   (p. 69)
motor (efferent) neurons (p. 69)
interneurons (p. 69)
paraplegia (p. 71)
peripheral nervous system (p. 71)
somatic division (p. 71)
autonomic division (p. 71)
sympathetic division (p. 71)
parasympathetic division (p. 71)
brain scan (p. 74)
electroencephalogram (EEG)
   (p. 74)
computerized axial tomography
   (CAT) scan (p. 74)
magnetic resonance imaging
   (MRI) scan (p. 74)
positron emission tomography
   (PET) scan (p. 75)
central core (p. 75)
medulla (p. 75)
pons (p. 77)
cerebellum (p. 77)

reticular formation (p. 77)
thalamus (p. 77)
hypothalamus (p. 77)
homeostasis (p. 77)
limbic system (p. 77)
corpus callosum (p. 78)
cerebral cortex (p. 80)
lobes (p. 81)
frontal lobes (p. 81)
parietal lobes (p. 81)
temporal lobes (p. 81)
occipital lobes (p. 81)
motor area (p. 82)
sensory area (p. 83)
somatosensory area (p. 83)
association area (p. 84)
apraxia (p. 84)
aphasia (p. 85)
Broca's aphasia (p. 85)
Wernicke's aphasia (p. 85)
hemispheres (p. 85)
lateralization (p. 86)
split-brain patient (p. 88)
brain modules (p. 89)
endocrine system (p. 90)
hormones (p. 90)
pituitary gland (p. 90)
biofeedback (p. 92)

SENSATION

PETE TOWNSHEND

Pete Townshend in performance.

Live Aid. Farm Aid. Hearing Aid.

While the last phrase may seem out of place to you, it probably doesn't to Pete Townshend. The lead guitarist for The Who, Townshend—along with a growing number of rock stars—has found his hearing deteriorating markedly. The cause: prolonged exposure to loud music.

Townshend suffers from tinnitus, a ringing in the ear that rarely ceases. The disease can be a nightmare for its victims. For some, the ringing gets louder and softer. For others, there is a constant ringing, which may become so loud that normal sounds can no longer be heard. As a result of tinnitus, people may feel edgy, be unable to concentrate, and experience anxiety.

For Townshend, the ringing occurred in the same range as the sound of a guitar, disrupting his playing and discouraging him from performing. In his words, "I've shot my hearing. It hurts, and it's painful, and it's frustrating . . ." (Murphy, 1989, p. 93).

The source of the problem lies in the inner ear's tiny hair cells, which contain small hairs projecting from the body of each cell. When sound levels are high, the hairs become bent and flattened. Usually these hairs bounce back to normal, but frequent onslaughts of loud music can make the hairs less elastic. The result may be tinnitus or a permanent loss of hearing, a condition that Pete Townshend must live with.

LOOKING AHEAD

Although a loss of hearing is perhaps the most devastating disorder that can strike a musician, injury to any of our senses can be disastrous. Consider, for instance, what it would be like if we could not see, or taste, or smell the world around us. Obviously, our bodily sensations have a profound effect on our day-to-day behavior.

In this chapter we focus on the area of psychology concerned with the nature of information our body takes in through its senses. Our senses provide us with a tie to the reality of the outside world and permit us to develop our own understanding of what is happening to us. To a psychologist who is interested in the causes of behavior, then, sensation represents an elemental topic, since so much of our behavior is based on our reactions to the stimulation we receive from the world around us.

This chapter discusses how physical stimulation (energy that produces a response in a sense organ) is translated into our own personal sensory experience. We consider issues ranging from such basics as identifying the fundamentals of vision and hearing, to understanding how we know whether ice or fire is colder, how we can tell whether sugar or lemon is sweeter, and how we distinguish a backfiring car from the barking of a dog.

After reading this chapter, then, you will be able to answer questions such as the following:

What is sensation and how do psychologists study it?

What is the relationship between the nature of a physical stimulus and the kinds of sensory responses that result from it?

What are the major senses, and what are the basic mechanisms that underlie their operation?

As we explore these questions, we will see how the senses work together to provide us with an integrated view and understanding of the world.

SENSING THE WORLD AROUND US

To someone lying on the quiet shore of a lake, the environment may seem serene and tranquil, a silent refuge from the sights and sounds of a clamorous world. Yet to members of nonhuman species, more acute in their natural abilities, the same lake may provide a challenge in sorting out the many stimuli that are actually present—stimuli that people, because of the limitations of the human body, cannot detect through their senses.

To a dog wandering by, for instance, the lake may unleash an enticing set of smells, a symphony of random sounds, and a bustling scene of swarming insects and other tiny organisms. Furthermore, the area abounds with other forms of physical energy, of which no person or animal, nor any other living organism, has an awareness: radio waves, ultraviolet light, and tones that are extremely high or low.

To understand how a psychologist might consider such a scene, we first need a basic working vocabulary. In formal terms, if any passing source of physical energy activates a sense organ, the energy is known as a stimulus. A **stimulus**, then, is energy that produces a response in a sense organ. The term **sensation** is used to describe the process by which an organism responds to the stimulus.

Stimuli vary in both kind and intensity. Different kinds of stimuli activate different sense organs. For instance, we can differentiate light stimuli, which activate our sense of sight and allow us to see the colors of a tree in autumn, from sound stimuli, which, through our sense of hearing, permit us to hear the sounds of an orchestra.

Each sort of stimulus that is capable of activating a sense organ can also be considered in terms of its strength, or **intensity**. For instance, such questions as

Stimulus: A source of physical energy that produces a response in a sense organ

Sensation: The process by which an organism responds to a stimulus

Intensity: The strength of a stimulus

Although a human might find this lakeshore a tranquil place to relax, other organisms would perceive it as teeming with arousing stimuli.

how intense a light stimulus needs to be before it is capable of being detected or how much perfume a person must wear before it is noticed by others relate to stimulus intensity.

The issue of how the intensity of a stimulus is related to sensory responses falls into a branch of psychology known as psychophysics. **Psychophysics** is the study of the relationship between the physical nature of stimuli and a person's sensory responses to them. Psychophysics played a central role in the development of the field of psychology; many of the first psychologists studied issues related to psychophysics. It is easy to see why: Psychophysics bridges the physical world outside and the psychological world within (Geissler, Link, & Townsend, 1992).

Psychophysics: The study of the relationship between the physical nature of stimuli and a person's sensory responses to them

Absolute Thresholds

It is obvious that people are not capable of detecting all the physical stimuli that are present in the environment, as noted earlier in our example of the seemingly quiet lake. Just when does a stimulus become strong enough to be detected by our sense organs? The answer to this question requires an understanding of the concept of absolute thresholds. An **absolute threshold** is the smallest intensity of a stimulus that must be present for it to be detected. Although we previously compared the sensory capabilities of humans unfavorably with those of other species, absolute thresholds in human sensory organs are actually quite extraordinary. Consider, for instance, these examples of absolute thresholds for the various senses (Galanter, 1962).

Absolute threshold: The smallest amount of physical intensity by which a stimulus can be detected

- Sight: A candle flame can be seen 30 miles away on a dark, clear night.
- Hearing: The ticking of a watch can be heard 20 feet away under quiet conditions.
- Taste: Sugar can be discerned when 1 teaspoon is dissolved in 2 gallons of water.
- Smell: Perfume can be detected when one drop is present in a three-room apartment.
- Touch: A bee's wing falling from a distance of 1 centimeter can be felt on a cheek.

Such thresholds permit a wide range of sensory stimulation to be detected by the human sensory apparatus. In fact, the capabilities of our senses are so fine-tuned that we might have problems if they were any more sensitive. For instance, if our ears were just slightly more acute, we would be able to hear the sound of air molecules in our ears knocking into our eardrum—a phenomenon that would surely prove distracting and might even prevent us from hearing sounds outside our bodies.

Of course, the absolute thresholds we have been discussing are measured under ideal conditions; normally our senses cannot detect stimulation quite so well because of the presence of noise. **Noise**, as defined by psychophysicists, is background stimulation that interferes with the perception of other stimuli. Hence noise refers not just to auditory stimuli, the most obvious example, but also to those stimuli that affect the other senses. Picture a talkative group of people crammed into a small, crowded, smoke-filled room at a party. The din of the crowd makes it hard to hear individual voices, and the smoke makes it difficult to see, or even taste, the food. In this case, the smoke and crowded con-

Noise: Background stimulation that interferes with the perception of other stimuli

The noise in P. J. Clarke's, in Chicago, is not just auditory; the crowded conditions produce noise that affects the senses of vision, smell, taste, and touch as well.

ditions would be considered "noise," since they are preventing sensation at more discriminating and sensitive levels.

Signal Detection Theory

Noise is not the only factor that influences our sensitivity to stimulation. Consider, for example, what it would be like if you were a physician who is listening to a patient's chest. Your problem is not discerning the sound of the heartbeat—one will clearly be present. Instead, the problem you face is distinguishing a normal heartbeat from one that is unhealthy.

Several factors influence whether you will be able to identify a medical problem, including your expectations about the patient, your knowledge and experience, and your motivation. Clearly, then, your ability to detect and identify a stimulus will not just be a function of properties of the stimulus; it will also be affected by psychological considerations.

Signal detection theory is an outgrowth of psychophysics that seeks to explain the role of psychological factors in our ability to identify stimuli (Green & Swets, 1989; Greig, 1990). The theory acknowledges that observers may miscalculate in one of two ways: in reporting that a stimulus is present when it is not or in reporting that a stimulus is not present when it actually is. By applying statistical procedures, psychologists using signal detection theory are able to obtain an understanding of how different kinds of decisions—which may involve such factors as observer expectations and motivation—relate to judgments about sensory stimuli in different situations. Statistical methods also allow them to increase the reliability of predictions about what conditions will cause observers to be most accurate in their judgments (Commons, Nevin, & Davison, 1991).

Such findings have immense practical importance, such as in the case of radar operators who are charged with identifying and distinguishing incoming enemy missiles from the radar images of passing birds (Getty, Pickett, D'Orsi, & Swets, 1988; Wickens, 1991). Another arena in which signal detection theory has practical implications is the judicial system. Witnesses who are asked to view a lineup find themselves in a classic signal detection situation, in which misiden-

Signal detection theory: The theory that addresses the role of psychological factors in our ability to identify stimuli

Signal detection theory seeks to explain how our responses—such as our ability to identify a criminal from mug shots or in a lineup—are influenced by psychological factors.

tification can have grave consequences for an individual (if an innocent person is incorrectly identified as a perpetrator) and for society (if an actual perpetrator is not detected). However, many witnesses have biases stemming from prior expectations about the socioeconomic status and race of criminals, attitudes toward the police and criminal justice system, and other viewpoints that impede accurate judgment.

Using signal detection theory, psychologists have been able to make suggestions to increase the accuracy of witness identification (Buckhout, 1976). For example, it is helpful to tell witnesses viewing a lineup that the prime suspect just might not be in the lineup at all. Moreover, justice is better served when the people in the lineup appear equally dissimilar from one another, which seems to reduce the chances of witnesses guessing.

Just Noticeable Differences

Suppose a shopkeeper said you could choose six apples from a barrel, and you wanted to compare them in a number of aspects to see which half dozen were best—which were the biggest, which were the reddest, which tasted the sweetest. One approach to this problem would be to systematically compare one apple with another until you were left with a few so similar that you could not tell the difference between them.

Difference threshold: The smallest detectable difference between two stimuli

Just noticeable difference: (See difference threshold)

Psychologists have discussed this comparison problem in terms of the **difference threshold**, the smallest detectable difference between two stimuli, also known as a **just noticeable difference**. They have found that the stimulus value that constitutes a just noticeable difference depends on the initial intensity of the stimulus. For instance, you may have noticed that the light change which comes in a three-way bulb when you switch from 75 to 100 watts appears greater than when you switch from 100 to 125 watts, even though the wattage increase is the same in both cases. Similarly, when the moon is visible during the late afternoon, it appears relatively dim—yet against a dark night sky, it seems quite bright.

The relationship between changes in the original value of a stimulus and the degree to which the change will be noticed forms one of the basic laws of psychophysics: Weber's law. **Weber's law** states that a just noticeable difference is a constant proportion of the intensity of an initial stimulus. Therefore, if a 10-pound increase in a 100-pound weight produces a just noticeable difference, it would take a 1000-pound increase to produce a noticeable difference if the initial weight were 10,000 pounds. In both cases, the same proportional increase is necessary to produce a just noticeable difference—1:10 (10:100 = 1000:10,000). (Actually, Weber found the true proportional increase in weight that produces a just noticeable difference to be between 2 and 3 percent.) Similarly, the just noticeable difference distinguishing changes in loudness between sounds is larger for sounds that are initially loud than for sounds that are initially soft. This principle explains why a person in a quiet room is more apt to be startled by the ringing of a telephone than a person in a room that is already noisy. In order to produce the same amount of reaction in a noisy room, a telephone ring might have to approximate the loudness of cathedral bells.

Weber's law seems to hold up for all sensory stimuli, although its predictions are less accurate at extremely high or extremely low levels of stimulation (Sharpe, Fach, Nordby, & Stockman, 1989). Moreover, the law helps explain psychological phenomena that lie beyond the realm of the senses. For example, imagine that you own a house you would like to sell for $150,000. You might be satisfied if you received an offer of $145,000 from a potential buyer, even though it was $5000 less than the asking price. On the other hand, if you were selling your car and asking $10,000 for it, an offer of $5000 less than your asking price would probably not make you happy. Although the absolute amount of money is the same in both cases, the psychological value of the $5000 is very different.

Weber's law: The principle that states that the just noticeable difference is a constant proportion of the magnitude of an initial stimulus

Sensory Adaptation

As the circus strongman carries a group of five acrobats across the circus tent, someone asks him if they aren't awfully heavy. He replies, "Not if you've just been carrying an elephant."

This story illustrates the phenomenon of **adaptation**, an adjustment in sensory capacity following prolonged exposure to stimuli. Adaptation occurs as people get used to a stimulus and change their frame of reference. Consequently, they do not respond to the stimulus in the way they did earlier.

One example of adaptation is the decrease in sensitivity that occurs after frequent exposure to a stimulus. If, for example, you were to repeatedly hear a loud tone, it would begin to sound softer after a while. This apparent decline in sensitivity to sensory stimuli is due to the inability of the sensory nerve receptors to constantly fire off messages to the brain. Because these receptor cells are most responsive to *changes* in stimulation, constant stimulation is not effective in producing a reaction. In fact, most receptor cells are incapable of constant firing, and their reaction to unvarying stimulation is a steady decline in the rate at which impulses are communicated.

Adaptation occurs with all the senses. For example, if you were able to stare unblinkingly at the exact same spot on this page for a long period of time—something that is impossible to do because of minute, involuntary movements of the eye—the spot would eventually disappear as the visual neurons lost their ability to fire.

Adaptation: An adjustment in sensory capacity following prolonged exposure to stimuli

Judgments of sensory stimuli are also affected by the context in which the judgments are made. Carrying five acrobats seems insignificant to the strongman who has just carted an elephant around the tent. The reason is that judgments are made, not in isolation from other stimuli, but in terms of preceding sensory experience.

You can demonstrate this for yourself by trying a simple experiment. Take two envelopes, one large and one small, and put fifteen nickels in each. Now lift the large envelope, put it down, and lift the small one. Which seems to weigh more?

Most people report that the small one is heavier, although, as you know, the weights are nearly identical. The reason for this misconception is that the physical context of the envelope interferes with the sensory experience of weight; adaptation to the context of one stimulus (the size of the envelope) alters responses to another stimulus (the weight of the envelope) (Coren & Ward, 1989).

Sensory-adaptation phenomena provide another illustration that a person's reaction to sensory stimuli is not always an accurate representation of the physical stimuli that brought it about. This point will become even more apparent as we move from a general consideration of sensation, the direct response of an organism to physical stimuli, to a discussion of the specific senses of the human body.

RECAP AND REVIEW I

RECAP

◀ Sensation occurs when an organism responds to a stimulus, which is any form of energy that activates a sense organ. Psychophysics studies the relationship between the physical nature of stimuli and sensory responses that are made.

◀ An absolute threshold is the smallest amount of physical intensity by which a stimulus can be detected. The level of the absolute threshold is affected by noise—background interference from other stimuli—and by a person's expectations and motivation.

◀ Signal detection theory is used to predict the accuracy of sensory judgments. An observer may err in one of two ways: by reporting the presence of a stimulus when there is none or by reporting the absence of a stimulus when there actually is one.

◀ Difference threshold, or just noticeable difference, refers to the smallest detectable difference between two stimuli. According to Weber's law, a just noticeable difference is a constant proportion of the intensity of an initial stimulus.

◀ Sensory adaptation occurs when people are exposed to a stimulus for so long that they become used to it and therefore no longer respond to it.

REVIEW

1. _____ is the study of physical stimuli and a person's sensory responses to them.
2. The term absolute threshold refers to the largest amount of physical intensity of a stimulus that is detectable without being painful. True or false? _____
3. What are the two ways that signal detection theory states that people can err in making judgments?
4. Stimulus thresholds are absolute within each person and do not vary for different stimuli. True or false? _____
5. The proposition stating that a just noticeable difference is a constant proportion of the intensity of an initial stimulus is known as _____ law.
6. After completing a very difficult rock climb in the morning, Rick found the afternoon climb unexpectedly easy. This case illustrates the phenomenon of _____.

Ask Yourself

Why is sensory adaptation essential for everyday psychological functioning?

(Answers to review questions are on page 106.)

As she sat down to Thanksgiving dinner, Rhona reflected on how happy she was to leave dormitory food behind, at least for the long holiday weekend. She was just plain tired of seeing and smelling the same monotonous cafeteria food. Even chewing the stuff was distasteful—it all felt like mush. "In fact," she thought to herself, "if I have to eat toast covered with chipped beef one more time, I may never eat again." But this thought was soon interrupted when she saw her father carry the turkey in on a tray and place it squarely in the center of the table. The noise level, already high from the talking and laughter of the family members, grew still louder. As she picked up her fork, the smell of the turkey reached her and she felt her stomach growl hungrily. With the sight and sound of her family around the table—not to mention the smell and taste of all that food—Rhona felt more relaxed than she had since she had left for college in the fall. "Ah, home, sweet home," she thought.

Put yourself in this setting and consider how different it might be if any one of your senses were not functioning. What if you were blind and unable to see the faces of your family or the welcome shape of the succulent turkey? What if you had no sense of hearing and could not listen to the conversations of family members, or were unable to feel your stomach growl, or smell the dinner, or taste the food? Clearly, an important dimension of the situation would be lacking, and you would experience the dinner very differently than someone whose sensory apparatus was intact.

Moreover, the sensations mentioned above barely scratch the surface of sensory experience. Although most of us have been taught at one time or another that there are just five senses—sight, sound, taste, smell, and touch—this enumeration is far too modest, since human sensory capabilities go well beyond the basic five senses. It is well established, for example, that we are sensitive not merely to touch, but to a considerably wider set of stimuli—pain, pressure, temperature, vibration, and more. In addition, the ear is responsive to information that allows us not only to hear but to keep our balance as well. Psychologists now believe that there are at least a dozen distinct senses, all of which are interrelated.

Although all the senses, alone and in combination, play a critical role in determining how we experience the world, most psychological research has focused on vision and hearing—the two sensory modes that are most conspicuous in allowing us to interact successfully with our environment.

Vision: The Eyes Have It

To understand how our sense of vision allows us to view the world, we must first begin outside the body and consider the nature of the stimulus that produces vision—**light**. Although we are all familiar with light, having all our lives basked in the sun or an artificial equivalent, its underlying physical qualities are less apparent.

Light: The stimulus that produces vision

The stimuli that register as light in our eyes are actually electromagnetic radiation waves to which our bodies' visual apparatus happens to be sensitive and capable of responding. As you can see in Figure 4-1, electromagnetic radiation is measured in wavelengths, with the size of the wavelength corresponding to different sorts of energy. The range of wavelengths that humans are sensitive to—called the **visual spectrum**—is actually relatively small, but the differences among wavelengths within that spectrum are sufficient to allow us to see a range

Visual spectrum: The range of wavelengths to which humans are sensitive

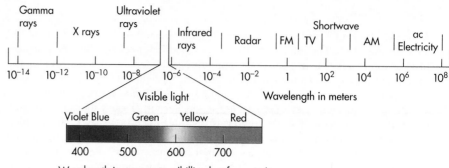

FIGURE 4-1

The visual spectrum—the range of wavelengths to which people are sensitive—represents only a small part of the kinds of wavelengths present in our environment.

of all the colors, running from violet at the low end of the visual spectrum to red at the top. Colors, then, are associated with a particular wavelength within the visual spectrum.

Light waves coming from some object outside the body (imagine the light reflected off George Washington's face in Figure 4-2) first encounter the only organ that is capable of responding to the visual spectrum: the eye. Strangely enough, most of the eye is concerned not with reacting directly to light but with shaping the entering image into a form that can be used by the neurons that will serve as messengers to the brain. The neurons themselves take up a relatively small percentage of the total eye. In other words, most of the eye is a mechanical

FIGURE 4-2

Although human vision is far more complicated than the most sophisticated camera, in some ways basic visual processes are analogous to those used in photography.

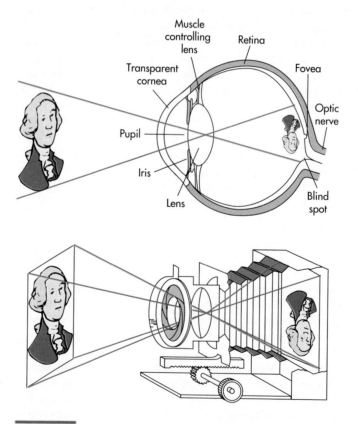

device, analogous in many respects to a camera without film, as you can see in Figure 4-2. It is important to realize, though, the limitations of this analogy: Vision involves processes that are far more complex and sophisticated than any camera is capable of mimicking.

Illuminating the Structure of the Eye.   The ray of light we are tracing as it is reflected off George Washington first travels through the **cornea**, a transparent, protective window that is constantly being washed by tears, keeping it moist and clean. After moving through the cornea, the light traverses the pupil. The **pupil** is a dark hole found in the center of the **iris**, the colored part of the eye, which ranges in humans from a light blue to a dark brown. The size of the pupil opening depends on the amount of light in the environment: The dimmer the surroundings, the more the pupil opens in order to allow more light to enter.

Why shouldn't the pupil be opened all the way all the time, thereby allowing the greatest amount of light into the eye? The answer has to do with the basic physics of light. A small pupil greatly increases the range of distances at which objects are in focus; with a wide-open pupil, the range is relatively small, and details are harder to discern. (Camera buffs know this in terms of the aperture or f-stop setting that they must adjust on their cameras.) The eye takes advantage of bright light by decreasing the size of the pupil and thereby becoming more discerning; in dim light the pupil expands in order to enable us to view the situation better—but at the expense of visual detail. Perhaps one reason that candlelight dinners are often thought of as romantic is that the dimness of the light prevents one from seeing the details of a lover's flaws.

Once light passes through the pupil, it enters the **lens**, which is located directly behind the pupil. The lens acts to bend the rays of light coming from Washington so that they are properly focused on the rear of the eye. The lens focuses the light by changing its own thickness, a process called **accommodation**. The kind of accommodation that occurs depends on the location of the object in relation to the viewer's body. Distant objects require a relatively flat lens; in this case, the muscles controlling the lens relax, allowing the fluid within the eye to flatten the lens. In contrast, close objects are viewed best through a rounded lens. Here, then, the muscles contract, taking tension off the lens—and making it rounder.

Having traveled through the pupil and lens, our image of George Washington is finally able to reach its ultimate destination in the eye—the **retina**—where the electromagnetic energy of light is converted into messages that the brain can use. It is important to note that because of the physical properties of light, the image has reversed itself as it traveled through the lens, and it reaches the retina upside down (relative to its original position). You might think this would cause major difficulties in understanding and moving about the world, but it turns out not to be a problem, because the brain rearranges the image back to its proper position. In fact, if we were ever to put on mirrored glasses that righted the image before it reached the brain, we would have a hard time. Everything would look upside down to us—although eventually we would adjust to the new orientation.

The retina is actually a thin layer of nerve cells at the back of the eyeball (see Figure 4-3). There are two kinds of light-sensitive receptor cells found in the retina, and the names they have been given describe their shapes: **rods**, which are long and cylindrical, and **cones**, which are short, thick, and tapered. The rods and cones are distributed unevenly throughout the retina, with the greatest concentration of cones on the part of the retina called the **fovea** (refer back to Figure 4-2). The fovea is a particularly sensitive region of the retina; if you want

Cornea: A transparent, protective window into the eyeball

Pupil: A dark hole in the center of the eye's iris which changes size as the amount of incoming light changes

Iris: The colored part of the eye

Lens: The part of the eye located behind the pupil that bends rays of light to focus them on the retina

Accommodation: The ability of the lens to vary its shape in order to focus incoming images on the retina

Retina: The part of the eye that converts the electromagnetic energy of light into useful information for the brain

Rods: Long, cylindrical, light-sensitive receptors in the retina that perform well in poor light but are largely insensitive to color and small details

Cones: Cone-shaped, light-sensitive receptor cells in the retina that are responsible for sharp focus and color perception, particularly in bright light

Fovea: A very sensitive region of the retina that aids in focusing

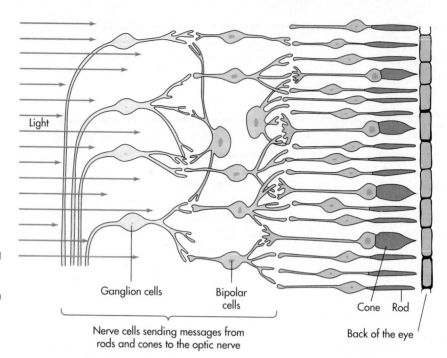

Light

Ganglion cells

Bipolar cells

Cone   Rod

Nerve cells sending messages from
rods and cones to the optic nerve

Back of the eye

FIGURE 4-3

The basic cells of the eye. Light entering the eye travels through the ganglion and bipolar cells and strikes the light-sensitive rods and cones located at the back of the eye. The rods and cones then transmit nerve impulses to the brain via the bipolar and ganglion cells.

to focus in on something of particular interest, you will probably center the image from the lens onto the area of the fovea.

The farther away from the fovea, the fewer the number of cones there are on the retina. Conversely, there are no rods in the fovea—but the number increases rapidly toward the edges of the retina. Because the fovea covers only a small portion of the eye, there are fewer cones (about 7 million) than there are rods (about 125 million).

The rods and cones are not only structurally dissimilar, but they play distinctly different roles in vision (Cohen & Lasley, 1986). Cones are primarily

This microscopic photo of the rods and cones of the eye clearly reveals their distinctive shapes. *(Lennart Nilsson/Behold Man/ Little, Brown & Company)*

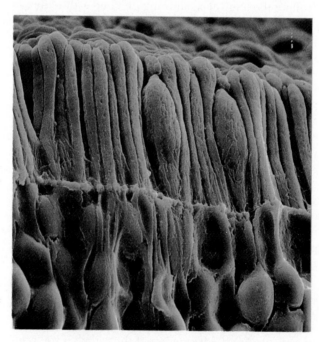

responsible for the sharply focused perception of color, particularly in brightly lit situations, while rods are related to vision in dimly lit situations and are largely insensitive to color and to details as sharp as those the cones are capable of recognizing. The rods are used for **peripheral vision**—seeing objects that are outside the main center of focus—and for night vision. In both cases, the level of detail that can be discerned is far lower when the rods come into play than when the cones are activated, as you know from groping your way across a dark room at night. Although you may just dimly see the outlines of furniture, it is almost impossible to distinguish color and the other details of obstacles in your path. You may also have noticed that you can improve your view of a dim star at night by looking slightly away from it. The reason? If you shift your gaze off-center, the image from the lens falls not on the relatively night-blind foveal cones but on the more light-sensitive rods.

The distinctive abilities of rods and cones make the eye analogous to a camera that is loaded with two kinds of film. One type is a highly sensitive black-and-white film (the rods); the other type is a somewhat less sensitive color film (the cones).

Sending the Message from the Eye to the Brain. When light energy strikes the rods and cones, it starts the first in a chain of events that transforms light into neural impulses that can be communicated to the brain. Before the neural message reaches the brain, however, some initial alteration of the visual information takes place.

What happens when light energy strikes the retina depends in part on whether it encounters a rod or a cone. Rods contain **rhodopsin**, a complex, reddish-purple substance whose composition changes chemically when energized by light and thereby sets off a reaction. The substance found in cone receptors is different, but the principles are similar: Stimulation of the nerve cells in the eye triggers a neural response that is transmitted to other nerve cells, called **bipolar cells** and **ganglion cells**, leading to the brain.

Bipolar cells receive information directly from the rods and cones, and this information is then communicated to the ganglion cells. Ganglion cells collect and summarize visual information, which is gathered and moved out of the back of the eyeball through a bundle of ganglion axons called the **optic nerve**.

Because the opening for the optic nerve pushes through the retina, there are no rods or cones in the area, which creates a blind spot. Normally, however, this absence of nerve cells does not interfere with vision, because you automatically compensate for the missing part of your field of vision. (To find your blind spot, see Figure 4-4.)

Once beyond the eye itself, the neural signals relating to the image of Washington we have been following move through the optic nerve. As the optic nerve leaves the eyeball, its path does not take the most direct route to the part of the brain right behind the eye. Instead, the optic nerves from each eye meet at a point roughly between the two eyes—called the **optic chiasm**—where each optic nerve then splits.

When the optic nerves split, the nerve impulses coming from the right half of each retina are sent to the right side of the brain, and the impulses arriving from the left half of each retina are sent to the left side of the brain. Because the image on the retina is reversed and upside down, however, those images coming from the right half of each retina are actually included in the field of vision to the left of each person, and images coming from the left half of the retina represent the field of vision to the right of the individual (see Figure 4-5).

Peripheral vision: The ability to see objects outside the eyes' main center of focus

Rhodopsin (ro DOP sin): A complex reddish-purple substance that changes when energized by light, causing a chemical reaction

Bipolar cells: Nerve cells leading to the brain that are triggered by nerve cells in the eye

Ganglion cells: Nerve cells that collect and summarize information from rods and carry it to the brain

Optic nerve: A bundle of ganglion axons in the back of the eyeball that carry visual information to the brain

Optic chiasm (ky AZ um): A point between and behind the eyes at which nerve impulses from the optic nerves are reversed and "righted" in the brain

FIGURE 4-4

To find your blind spot, close your right eye and look at the haunted house with your left eye. You will see the ghost on the periphery of your vision. Now, while staring at the house, move the page toward you. When the book is about a foot from your eye, the ghost will disappear. At this moment, the image of the ghost is falling on your blind spot.

But also notice how, when the page is at that distance, not only does the ghost seem to disappear, but also the line seems to run continuously through the area where the ghost used to be. This shows how we automatically compensate for missing information by using nearby material to complete what is unseen. That's the reason you never notice the blind spot: What is missing is replaced by what is seen next to the blind spot.

Glaucoma (glaw KO muh): A dysfunction of the eye in which fluid pressure builds up and causes a decline in visual acuity

Tunnel vision: An advanced stage of glaucoma in which vision is reduced to the narrow circle directly in front of the eye

FIGURE 4-5

Because the optic nerve coming from each eye splits at the optic chiasm, the image to a person's right is sent to the left side of the brain, and the image to the person's left is transmitted to the right side of the brain.

In this way, our nervous system ultimately produces the phenomenon introduced in Chapter 3, in which each half of the brain is associated with the functioning of the opposite side of the body.

One of the most frequent causes of blindness is a restriction of the impulses across the optic nerve. **Glaucoma**, which strikes between 1 and 2 percent of those over age 40, occurs when pressure in the fluid of the eye begins to build up, either because it cannot be properly drained or because it is overproduced. When this first begins to happen, the nerve cells that communicate information about peripheral vision are constricted, leading to a decline in the ability to see anything outside a narrow circle directly ahead. This ensuing problem is called **tunnel vision**. Eventually, the pressure can become so great that all the nerve cells are contracted, leading to total blindness. Fortunately, if detected early enough, glaucoma is highly treatable, either through medication that reduces the pressure in the eye or through surgery.

Processing the Visual Message.　By the time a visual message reaches the brain, it has passed through several stages of processing. One of the initial sites is the ganglion cells. Each ganglion cell gathers information from a group of rods and cones in a particular area of the eye, and compares the amount of light entering the center of that area with the amount of light in the area around it. In some

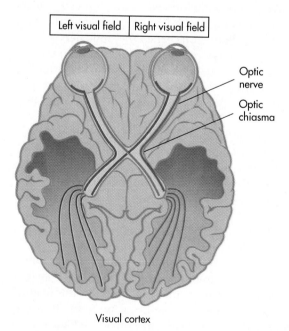

Left visual field | Right visual field

Optic nerve

Optic chiasma

Visual cortex

RECEPTIVE FIELD

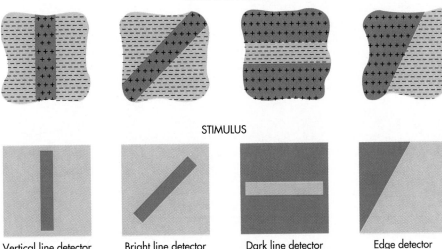

STIMULUS

Vertical line detector   Bright line detector   Dark line detector   Edge detector

FIGURE 4-6

The upper row of the figure shows how certain cells in the visual cortex send an "on" or "off" signal when stimulated by a particular shape. A plus sign indicates a region that makes an "on" response when stimulated by the shape shown in the row below it; a minus sign indicates an "off" response. As the examples illustrate, some cells respond most to vertical lines, others to diagonal lines, some to horizontal lines, and some to edges. (Adapted from Hubel and Wiesel, 1979.)

cases, ganglion cells are activated by light in the center (and darkness in the surrounding area). In other cases, the opposite is true: Some ganglion cells are activated when there is darkness in the center and light in the surrounding areas. The ultimate effect of this process is to maximize the detection of variations in light and darkness. The neural image that is passed on to the brain, then, is an enhanced version of the actual visual stimulus outside the body.

The ultimate processing of visual images takes place in the visual cortex of the brain, of course, and it is here that the most complex kinds of processing occur (Hurlbert & Poggio, 1988). Nobel-prize winners David Hubel and Torsten Wiesel have found that many neurons in the cortex are extraordinarily specialized, being activated only by visual stimuli of a particular shape or pattern—a process known as **feature detection**. For example, some cells are activated only by lines of a particular width, shape, or orientation (see Figure 4-6). Other cells are activated only by moving, as opposed to stationary, stimuli (Hubel & Wiesel, 1979; Logothetis & Schall, 1989). There is evidence from work with monkeys that certain groups of cells are so selective that they seem to respond to stimuli as complex as a face held in a particular orientation (see Figure 4-7; Gross, 1985).

Feature detection: The activation of neurons in the cortex by visual stimuli of specific shapes or patterns

Adaptation: From Light to Dark. Have you ever walked into a movie theater on a bright, sunny day and stumbled into your seat, barely able to see at all? Do you

FIGURE 4-7

The upper row shows the electrical responses of certain neurons in a monkey's brain to the stimuli below it. As you can see, these neurons were stimulated most by intact monkey faces held at particular angles. (*Source:* Gross et al., 1985.)

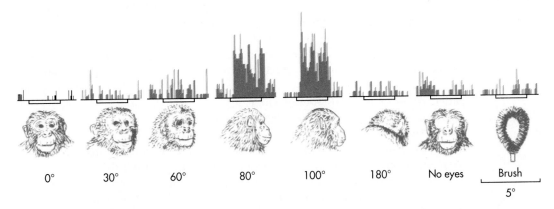

0°   30°   60°   80°   100°   180°   No eyes   Brush

5°

FIGURE 4-8
Dark adaptation—the heightened sensitivity to light that occurs after moving to a dimmer environment—occurs at different rates for rods and cones. As this graph shows, the visual threshold (the lowest amount of light needed to be detected) is lower for rods than for cones after about thirty minutes in a dimly lit environment. (Adapted from Cornsweet, 1970.)

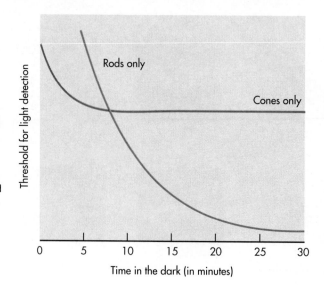

Light adaptation: The eye's temporary insensitivity to light dimmer than that to which it has most recently been exposed

Dark adaptation: A heightened sensitivity to light resulting from being in low-level light

also recall later getting up to buy popcorn and having no trouble navigating your way up the aisle?

Your initial trouble seeing in the dimly lit theater was due to **light adaptation**, a phenomenon in which the eye grows insensitive to light that is dimmer than the level to which it has most recently been exposed. In contrast, the fact that you were later able to see relatively well is due to **dark adaptation**, a heightened sensitivity to light that results from being in relative dimness.

The speed at which both dark and light adaptation occur is a function of the rate at which changes occur in the chemical composition of the rods and cones. As you can see in Figure 4-8, the changes occur at different speeds for the two kinds of cells, with the cones reaching their greatest level of adaptation in just a few minutes, but the rods taking close to thirty minutes to reach the maximum level. On the other hand, the cones never reach the level of sensitivity to light that the rods attain. When rods and cones are considered jointly, though, dark adaptation is complete in a darkened room in about half an hour (Tamura, Nakatani, & Yau, 1989).

Color Vision and Color Blindness: The 7-Million Color Spectrum. Although the range of wavelengths to which humans are sensitive is relatively narrow, at least in comparison to the entire electromagnetic spectrum, the portion to which we are capable of responding still allows us great flexibility in sensing the world. Nowhere is this clearer than in terms of the number of colors we can discern: A person with normal color vision is capable of distinguishing no less than 7 million different colors (Bruce & Green, 1990).

Although the variety of colors that people are generally able to distinguish is vast, there are certain individuals whose ability to perceive color is quite limited—the color-blind. Interestingly, the condition of these individuals has provided some of the most important clues for understanding how color vision operates (Nathans et al., 1986; Nathans et al., 1989).

Before continuing, though, look at the photos shown in Figure 4-9. If you cannot see any difference in the series of photos, you probably are one of the 2 percent of men or 2 out of 10,000 women who are color-blind.

For most people who are color-blind, the world looks quite dull: Red fire engines appear yellow, green grass seems yellow, and the three colors of a traffic light all look yellow. In fact, in the most common form of color blindness, all

(a)   (b)

(c)   (d)

FIGURE 4-9

These hot-air balloons appear as shown in (*a*) to someone with normal vision. (*b*) A person with red-green color blindness would see the scene like this, in hues of blue and yellow. (*c*) A person who is blue-yellow blind, conversely, would see it in hues of red and green. (*d*) To a monochromat, or person with total color blindness, it would look like this. (*Joe Epstein/Design Conceptions*)

red and green objects are seen as yellow. There are other forms of color blindness as well, but they are quite rare. In yellow-blue blindness, people are unable to tell the difference between yellow and blue, and in the most extreme case an individual perceives no color at all: The world to such a person looks something like the picture on a black-and-white television set.

To understand why some of us are color-blind, it is necessary to consider the basics of color vision. There appear to be two processes involved. The first process is based on what has been labeled the **trichromatic theory of color vision**. It suggests that there are three kinds of cones in the retina, each of which responds primarily to a specific range of wavelengths. One is most responsive to blue-violet colors, one to green, and the other to yellow-red (Brown & Wald, 1964). According to trichromatic theory, perception of color is influenced by the relative strength with which each of the three kinds of cones is activated. If, for instance, we see a blue sky, the blue-violet cones are primarily triggered, while the others show less activity. The trichromatic theory provides a straightforward explanation of color blindness: It suggests that one of the three cone systems malfunctions, and colors covered by that range are perceived improperly (Nathans et al., 1989).

However, there are phenomena that the trichromatic theory is less successful at explaining. For instance, it cannot answer why pairs of colors can combine to form gray. The theory also does not explain what happens after you stare at something like the flag shown in Figure 4-10 for about a minute. Try this yourself, and then move your eyes to the white space below. You will see an image of the

Trichromatic theory of color vision: The theory that suggests that the retina has three kinds of cones, each responding to a specific range of wavelengths, perception of color being influenced by the relative strength with which each is activated

FIGURE 4-10

If you stare at the dot in this flag for about a minute and then look at a piece of white paper, the afterimage phenomenon will make a traditional red, white, and blue flag appear.

Afterimage: The image appearing when the eyes shift from a particular image to a blank area

Opponent-process theory of color vision: The theory that suggests that receptor cells are linked in pairs, working in opposition to each other

traditional red, white, and blue American flag. Where there was yellow, you'll see blue, and where there were green and black, you'll see red and white.

The phenomenon you have just experienced is called an **afterimage**, and it occurs because activity in the retina continues even when you are no longer staring at the original picture. However, it also demonstrates that the trichromatic theory does not explain color vision completely. Why should the colors in the afterimage be different from those in the original?

Because trichromatic processes do not provide a full explanation of color vision, vision researchers have developed an alternative explanation. According to the **opponent-process theory of color vision**, receptor cells are linked in pairs, working in opposition to each other. Specifically, there is a blue-yellow pairing, a red-green pairing, and a black-white pairing. If an object reflects light that contains more blue than yellow, it will stimulate the firing of the cells sensitive to blue, simultaneously discouraging or inhibiting the firing of receptor cells sensitive to yellow—and the object will appear blue. If, on the other hand, a light contains more yellow than blue, the cells that respond to yellow will be stimulated to fire while the blue ones are inhibited, and the object will appear yellow.

The opponent-process theory allows us to explain afterimages very directly. When we stare at the yellow in the figure, for instance, our receptor cells for the yellow component of the yellow-blue pairing become fatigued and are less able to respond to yellow stimuli. On the other hand, the blue part of the pair is not tired, since it is not being stimulated. When we look at a white surface, the light reflected off it would normally stimulate both the yellow and the blue receptors equally. But the fatigue of the yellow receptors prevents this; they temporarily do not respond to the yellow, which makes the white light appear to be blue. Because the other colors in the figure do the same thing relative to their specific opponents, the afterimage produces the opponent colors—for a while. The afterimage lasts only a short time, since the fatigue of the yellow receptors is soon overcome, and the white light begins to be perceived more accurately.

Happily, we are not faced with having to choose between opponent-process theory and trichromatic theory, because it is now clear that both opponent processes and trichromatic mechanisms are at work in allowing us to see color. However, they operate in different parts of the visual sensing system. Trichromatic processes work within the retina itself, while opponent mechanisms operate both in the retina and at later stages of neuronal processing (Beck, Hope, & Rosenfeld, 1983; Leibovic, 1990).

It thus appears that the brain's analysis of visual information occurs simultaneously throughout several parts of the eye and brain (Shapley, 1990; Bruce & Green, 1990). Vision does not seem to occur as part of a direct, linear sequence of events in the brain, with one episode of processing following the previous one. Instead, the brain processes visual information coming from the eye using separate systems of structures and neural pathways that are specialized in the analysis of different aspects of vision (Livingstone, 1988; Livingstone & Hubel, 1988).

As the complexity of the brain's processing of visual information becomes progressively evident, psychologists are developing increasingly sophisticated models of the pathways over which visual processing takes place in the brain. In particular, research using animals has permitted the development of extraordinarily detailed "road maps" of the areas of the brain relating to vision. One example is shown in Figure 4-11, on page 116, which illustrates the arrangement of the areas of the cerebral cortex related to vision in macaque monkeys. Researchers have identified thirty-two distinct areas associated with particular aspects of vision and some 305 neuronal circuits connecting those sites. Because the human brain is ten times larger than that of the macaque monkey, the vision system in humans is likely to be even more complex (Gibbons, 1990; Mignard & Malpeli, 1991).

As their knowledge of vision has expanded, psychologists have developed several new approaches for dealing with people with visual deficiencies. For example, some psychologists are attempting to devise traffic signals that the color-blind can distinguish better, permitting a reduction in accidents (Botstein, 1986; Boynton, 1988; Shapley, 1990). Our understanding of vision has also led to significant technological innovations. For instance, the knowledge that there are three types of cones in the eye was put to use in the development of color television: As with the eye, color television screens make use of tiny dots that are either red, green, or blue and are activated to varying degrees.

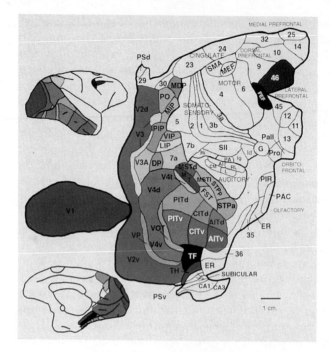

FIGURE 4-11

These are the thirty-two areas of the cerebral cortex of the macaque, a kind of monkey, that are related to vision.

RECAP

◀ Although people have traditionally thought in terms of five senses, psychologists studying sensation have found that the number is actually far greater.

◀ The eyes are sensitive to electromagnetic radiation waves of certain wavelengths; these waves register as the sensation of light.

◀ As light enters the eye, it passes through the cornea, pupil, and lens and ultimately reaches the retina, where the electromagnetic energy of light is converted into nerve impulses usable by the brain. These impulses leave the eye via the optic nerve.

◀ The retina is composed of nerve cells called rods and cones, which play differing roles in vision and are responsible for dark and light adaptation.

◀ Humans are able to distinguish about 7 million colors. Color vision is believed to involve two processes: trichromatic mechanisms and an opponent-processing system.

REVIEW

1. Light entering the eye first passes through the _____, a protective window.
2. The structure that converts light into usable neural messages is called the _____.
3. Light is focused on the rear of the eye by the iris. True or false? _____
4. A woman with blue eyes could be described as having blue pigment in her _____.

RECAP AND REVIEW II

5. What is the name of the process by which the thickness of the lens is changed in order to focus light properly?
6. The proper sequence of structures that light passes through in the eye is the _____, _____, _____, and _____.
7. The greatest number of rods in the retina is located in the area known as the fovea. True or false? _____
8. Match each type of visual receptor with its function.
   _____ a. Rods   1. Used for dim light, largely insensitive to color.
   _____ b. Cones
                      2. Detect color, good in bright light.
9. Choose the correct sequence of structures after light hits the retina.
   a. Ganglion cells, optic nerve, bipolar cells, optic chiasm.
   b. Bipolar cells, ganglion cells, optic chiasm, optic nerve.
   c. Optic chiasm, bipolar cells, ganglion cells, optic nerve.
   d. Bipolar cells, ganglion cells, optic nerve, optic chiasm.
   e. Optic nerve, optic chiasm, ganglion cells, bipolar cells.
10. John was to meet his girlfriend in the movie theater. As was typical, he was late and the movie had begun. He stumbled down the aisle, barely able to see because of _____ adaptation. Unfortunately, the

woman he sat down beside and attempted to put his arm around was not his girlfriend. He sorely wished he had given his eyes a chance and waited for _____ adaptation to occur.

11. _____ theory states that there are three types of cones in the retina, each of which responds primarily to a different color.

(Answers to review questions are on page 118.)

Ask Yourself

Why do you think the eye uses two distinct types of receptor cells, rods and cones? Why would the eye evolve so that the rods, which we rely on in low light, do not provide sharp images? Are there any advantages to this system?

The Sense of Sound and Balance

The blast-off was easy compared with what the astronaut was experiencing now: space sickness. The constant nausea and vomiting were enough to make him consider calling Mission Control and asking to return to base. Even though he had been warned that there was a 50 percent chance that his first experience in space would cause such sickness, he wasn't prepared for how terribly sick he really felt. How could he live and work on the space station for the next three months feeling like this?

Whether or not our mythical astronaut turns his rocket around and heads back to earth, his experience—which is a major problem for space travelers—is related to a basic sensory process that is centered in the ear: the sense of motion and balance, which allows people to navigate their bodies through the world and maintain an upright position without falling. Along with hearing, the process by which sound waves are translated into understandable and meaningful forms, the sensing of motion and balance represent the major functions of the ear.

The Ear: The Site of Sound. Although many of us think primarily of the **outer ear** when we consider hearing, this part functions simply as a reverse megaphone, designed to collect and bring sounds into the internal portions of the ear, illus-

Outer ear: The visible part of the ear that acts as a collector to bring sounds into the internal portions of the ear

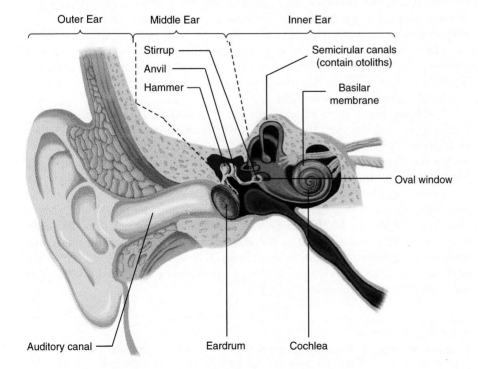

Outer Ear   Middle Ear   Inner Ear

Stirrup
Anvil
Hammer

Semicirular canals (contain otoliths)

Basilar membrane

Oval window

Auditory canal   Eardrum   Cochlea

FIGURE 4-12
The ear.

Like President Lyndon Johnson, many people have distinctively shaped outer ears. This part of the ear operates as a reverse megaphone, funneling sounds into the internal parts of the ear.

Sound: The movement of air molecules brought about by the vibration of an object

Auditory canal: A tubelike passage in the ear through which sound moves to the eardrum

Eardrum: The part of the ear that vibrates when sound waves hit it

Middle ear: A tiny chamber containing three bones—the hammer, the anvil, and the stirrup—which transmit vibrations to the oval window

Hammer: A tiny bone in the middle ear that transfers vibrations to the anvil

Anvil: A minute bone in the middle ear that transfers vibrations to the stirrup

Stirrup: A small bone in the middle ear that transfers vibrations to the oval window

Oval window: A thin membrane between the middle ear and the inner ear that transmits vibrations while increasing their strength

Inner ear: The interior structure that changes sound vibrations into a form that can be transmitted to the brain

trated in Figure 4-12. The outer ear also plays a role in helping to locate the direction from which sounds originate (Middlebrooks & Green, 1991).

Sound is the movement of air molecules brought about by the vibration of an object. Sounds travel through the air in wave patterns similar in shape to those made by a stone thrown into a still pond. When sounds, arriving in the form of wave vibrations, are funneled into the **auditory canal**, a tubelike passage, they reach the eardrum. The **eardrum** is aptly named because it operates like a miniature drum, vibrating when sound waves hit it. The more intense the sound, the more it vibrates. These vibrations are then transmitted into the **middle ear**, a tiny chamber containing just three bones called, because of their shapes, the **hammer**, the **anvil**, and the **stirrup**. These bones have one function: to transmit vibrations to the **oval window**, a thin membrane leading to the inner ear. Because of their shape, the hammer, anvil, and stirrup do a particularly effective job. Because they act as a set of levers, not only do they transmit vibrations but they also actually increase their strength. Moreover, since the opening into the middle ear (the eardrum) is considerably larger than the opening out of it (the oval window), the force of sound waves on the oval window becomes amplified. The middle ear, then, acts as a tiny mechanical amplifier, making us aware of sounds that would otherwise go unnoticed.

The **inner ear** is the portion of the ear that actually changes the sound vibrations into a form that allows them to be transmitted to the brain. It also contains the organs that allow us to locate our position and determine how we are moving through space. When sound enters the inner ear through the oval window, it moves into the **cochlea**, a coiled tube filled with fluid that looks something like a snail. Inside the cochlea is the **basilar membrane**, a structure that runs through the center of the cochlea, dividing it into an upper and a lower chamber (see Figure 4-12). The basilar membrane is covered with **hair cells**. When these hair cells are bent by the vibrations entering the cochlea, a neural message is transmitted to the brain. (These hair cells were the source of the hearing difficulties experienced by Pete Townshend of The Who, discussed at the beginning of this chapter.)

ANSWERS (REVIEW II):

1. cornea 2. retina 3. False; it is focused by the lens. 4. iris 5. Accommodation 6. cornea, pupil, lens, retina 7. False; the fovea has the greatest number of cones. 8. 1-a; 2-b 9. d
10. light; dark 11. Trichromatic

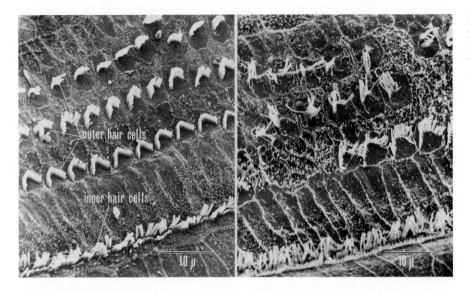

outer hair cells

inner hair cells

10 μ

10 μ

When these hair cells are bent by vibrations entering the cochlea, a neural message is transmitted to the brain. *(Courtesy J. E. Hawkins)*

Although sound typically enters the cochlea via the oval window, there is an additional method of entry: bone conduction. Because the ear rests on a maze of bones within the skull, the cochlea is able to pick up subtle vibrations that travel across the bones from other parts of the head (Lenhardt et al., 1991). For instance, one of the ways you hear your own voice is through bone conduction, which explains why you sound different to yourself than to other people who hear your voice. (Listen to yourself on a tape recorder sometime to hear what you *really* sound like!) The sound of your voice reaches you both through the air and via bone conduction and therefore sounds richer to you than to everyone else.

The Physical Aspects of Sound.   As we mentioned earlier, what we refer to as sound is actually the physical movement of air molecules in regular, wavelike patterns caused by the vibration of an object (see Figure 4-13). Sometimes it is even possible to view these vibrations, as in the case of a stereo speaker that has no enclosure. If you have ever seen one, you know that, at least when the lowest notes are playing, you can see the speaker moving in and out. What is less obvious is what happens next: The speaker pushes air molecules into waves with the same pattern as its movement. These wave patterns soon reach your ear, although their strength has been weakened considerably during their travels. All other stimuli that produce sound work in essentially the same fashion, setting off wave patterns that move through the air to the ear. Air—or some other medium, such as water—is necessary to make the vibrations of objects reach us. This explains why there can be no sound in a vacuum.

Cochlea (KOKE lee uh)**:** A coiled tube filled with fluid that receives sound via the oval window or through bone conduction

Basilar membrane: A structure dividing the cochlea into an upper and a lower chamber

Hair cells: Tiny cells covering the basilar membrane that, when bent by vibrations entering the cochlea, transmit neural messages to the brain

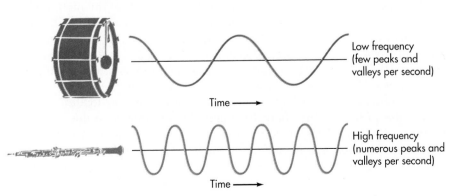

Time ⟶

Low frequency (few peaks and valleys per second)

Time ⟶

High frequency (numerous peaks and valleys per second)

FIGURE 4-13

The waves produced by different stimuli are transmitted—usually through the air—in different patterns, with lower frequencies indicated by fewer peaks and valleys per second.

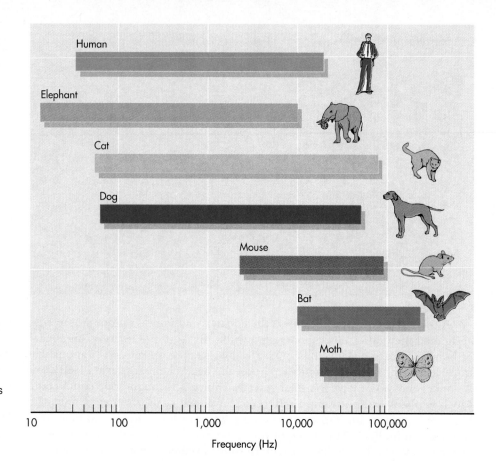

FIGURE 4-14

The range of sound frequencies that can be heard by various species. (Based on data from Fullard & Barclay, 1980, and Heffner & Heffner, 1985.)

Frequency: The number of wave crests occurring each second in any particular sound

Pitch: The characteristic that makes sound "high" or "low"

Intensity: A feature of wave patterns that allow us to distinguish between loud and soft sounds

Decibel: A measure of sound loudness or intensity

We are able to see the speaker moving when low notes are played because of a primary characteristic of sound called frequency. **Frequency** is the number of wave crests that occur in a second. With very low frequencies there are relatively few, and therefore slower, up-and-down wave cycles per second—which are visible to the naked eye as vibrations in the speaker. Low frequencies are translated into a sound that is very low in pitch. (**Pitch** is the characteristic that makes sound "high" or "low.") For example, the lowest frequency that humans are capable of hearing is 20 cycles per second. Higher frequencies translate into higher pitch. At the upper end of the sound spectrum, people can detect sounds with frequencies as high as 20,000 cycles per second. Interestingly, many animals enjoy the capability of hearing sounds over a broader range of frequencies than humans and consequently hear lower or higher sounds than we can (see Figure 4-14; Fay, 1988).

While sound frequency allows us to enjoy the sounds of the high notes of a piccolo and the bass notes of a tuba, **intensity** is a feature of wave patterns that allows us to distinguish between loud and soft sounds. Intensity refers to the difference between the peaks and valleys of air pressure in a sound wave as it travels through the air. Waves with small peaks and valleys produce soft sounds, while those that are relatively large produce loud sounds.

We are sensitive to a broad range of sound intensity: The loudest sounds we are capable of hearing are about 10 million times as intense as the very weakest sound we can hear. This range is measured in **decibels**, which can be used to place everyday sounds along a continuum (see Figure 4-15). When sounds get

Sound level (in decibels)

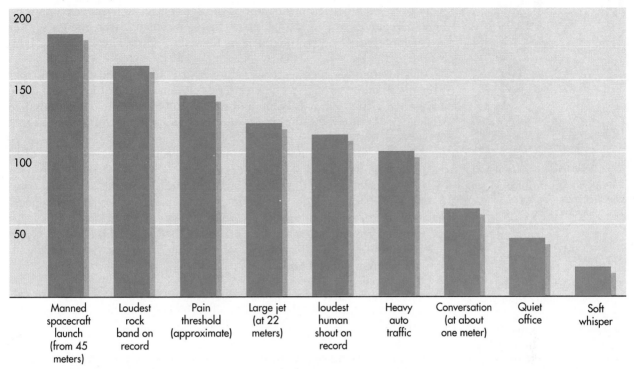

Source of sound

FIGURE 4-15

Illustrations of decibel levels (measures of sound intensity).

higher than 120 decibels, they become painful to the human ear. Exposure to such high levels eventually leads to the kind of hearing problems that befell Pete Townshend of The Who.

How are our brains able to sort out wavelengths of different frequencies and intensities? One clue comes from studies of the basilar membrane, the area within the cochlea that translates physical vibrations into neural impulses. It turns out that sounds affect different areas of the basilar membrane, depending on the frequency of the wave. The part of the basilar membrane nearest the oval window is most sensitive to high-frequency sounds, while the part nearest the cochlea's inner end is most sensitive to low-frequency sounds. This finding has led to the **place theory of hearing**, which says that different areas of the basilar membrane respond to different frequencies.

On the other hand, place theory is not the full story of hearing, since very low frequency sounds trigger neurons across such a wide area of the basilar membrane that no single site is involved. Consequently, an additional explanation for hearing has been proposed: frequency theory. The **frequency theory of hearing** suggests that the entire basilar membrane acts like a microphone, vibrating as a whole in response to a sound. According to this explanation, the nerve receptors send out signals that are tied directly to the frequency (the number of wave crests per second) of the sounds to which we are exposed, with the number of nerve impulses being a direct function of the sound's frequency. Thus, the higher the pitch of a sound (and therefore the greater the frequency of its wave crests), the greater the number of nerve impulses that are transmitted up the auditory nerve to the brain.

Most research points to the conclusion that both place theory and frequency theory provide accurate descriptions of the processes that underlie hearing,

Place theory of hearing: The theory that states that different frequencies are responded to by different areas of the basilar membrane

Frequency theory of hearing: The theory that suggests that the entire basilar membrane acts like a microphone, vibrating in response to sound

This noise inspector, employed to check sound levels in city apartments, is using an instrument that measures sound in decibels.

Vertigo: A disorder of the inner ear resulting from a viral infection or head injury that causes people to feel light-headed and dizzy and to lose their sense of balance

Semicircular canals: Part of the inner ear containing fluid that moves when the body moves to control balance

Otoliths: Crystals in the semicircular canals that sense body acceleration

Baseball star Nick Esasky is undergoing training to compensate for his vertigo, caused by inner ear problems.

although not at every frequency (Levine & Shefner, 1991). Specifically, place theory provides a better explanation of the sensing of high-frequency sounds, whereas frequency theory explains what happens when low-frequency sounds are encountered. Sounds with pitch in between appear to incorporate both processes.

After an auditory message leaves the ear, it is transmitted to the auditory cortex of the brain through a complex series of neural interconnections. As the message is transmitted, it is communicated through neurons that respond to specific types of sounds. Within the auditory cortex itself, there are neurons that respond selectively to very specific sorts of sound features, such as clicks or whistles. Moreover, some neurons respond only to a specific pattern of sounds, such as a steady tone but not an intermittent one.

If we were to analyze the configuration of the cells in the auditory cortex, we would find that neighboring cells are responsive to similar frequencies. The auditory cortex, then, provides us with a "map" of sound frequencies, just as the visual cortex furnishes a representation of the visual field. (To learn about the latest attempts at helping people with hearing, as well as visual, problems, see the Psychology at Work box.)

Balance: The Ups and Downs of Life. Nick Esasky had just signed a $5.7 million baseball contract with the Atlanta Braves when he began to run into trouble. In his words:

I felt great about playing in Atlanta, and I was in the best shape of my whole career. But about a week and a half into spring training, things started falling apart. Suddenly I began feeling weak and tired all the time. At first, I thought it was the flu and that it would go away. Then I began to get headaches and nausea, and I felt light-headed and dizzy. Soon it began to affect the way I was playing. At times it was hard for me to follow the ball. It looked hazy, as if it had a glow. I'd catch some off the end of my glove and miss others completely. Other times, a ball would land in my glove and I'd have no idea how it got there (Esasky, 1991, p. 62).

Esasky's problem would not go away, leading to a round of visits to dozens of specialists. Finally, though, after a variety of misdiagnoses, one doctor identified the source of Esasky's difficulty: his ear. Esasky was suffering from **vertigo**, a disorder of the inner ear resulting from a viral infection or head injury. He is now undergoing a grueling program to bolster his sense of vision and the sense of touch in the soles of the feet, both of which can help compensate for his inner ear problems.

Several structures of the ear are related more to our sense of balance than to our hearing. The **semicircular canals** of the inner ear consist of three tubes containing fluid that sloshes through them when the head moves, signaling rotational or angular movement to the brain. The pull on our bodies caused by the acceleration of forward, backward, or up-and-down motion, as well as the constant pull of gravity, is sensed by the **otoliths**, tiny, motion-sensitive crystals within the semicircular canals. When we move, these crystals shift like sands on a windy beach. The brain's inexperience in interpreting messages from the weightless otoliths is the cause of the space sickness commonly experienced by more than half of all space travelers (Flam, 1991).

Smell, Taste, and the Skin Senses

When Audrey Warner returned home after a day's work, she knew that something was wrong the moment she opened her apartment door. A smell indicative of gas—a strong, sickening odor that immediately made her feel weak—permeated the apart-

What appeared to be science fiction just a few years ago is considerably closer to becoming a reality: the replacement of malfunctioning human sense organs with artificial ones.

The greatest step forward has come in the realm of hearing. Because of technological advances, many partially deaf people in the United States are now able for the first time to hear sounds such as automobile horns and doorbells. Making this advance possible is an electronic ear implant connected directly to the cochlea.

The device works in some cases of deafness in which the hair cells in the cochlea are damaged and unable to convert vibrations into the electrical impulses that the brain is able to use—the root of Pete Townshend's problem discussed at the start of this chapter. A tiny microphone outside the ear is used to pick up sounds, which are then sent to a speech processor worn on a shoulder strap or belt that allows a user to squelch background noise with a button. The electronic signal is then sent from the processor to a transmitter behind the ear and broadcasts a radio wave to a receiver implanted inside the skull. The implanted receiver is directly connected to the cochlea by twenty-two thin wires. The receiver emits electrical signals that stimulate the cochlea, sending a message to the brain that sound is being heard (Molotsky, 1984; Clark, 1987).

Although the device does not allow people to pick up words dis-

IMPROVING THE SENSES WITH TECHNOLOGY

tinctly—users report that the quality of speech heard is like that of Donald Duck—about half the users of state-of-the-art implants are able to understand familiar voices and speak on the phone. Implants also enable users to detect changes in tone of voice and volume. Moreover, as the technology continues to improve, it is likely that sounds will be made more distinct: Perhaps one day the implant will approximate the sensitivity of the ear itself.

Other devices to improve hearing take advantage of the computer. The newest generation of hearing aids includes pocket-sized computers attached to an earpiece. The computer is able to analyze incoming sounds to identify their frequencies, rhythms, and loudness. This information is then used to optimize speech and to squelch background noises, resulting in a vastly improved hearing aid (Kirsch, 1989).

Technological advances are also helping people with vision problems. For example, laser technology promises to be able to correct nearsightedness without the need for glasses or contact lenses (Seligman, 1991). Nearsightedness occurs when the shape of the eye becomes distorted and the retina is unable to correctly focus the image entering the eye onto the retina. By precisely removing a tiny slice of the cornea, the procedure changes the eye's configuration, al-

lowing the image on the retina to be in focus (see Figure 4-16). Eyeglasses and contact lenses, then, may someday be considered relics of the past.

Technological advances are even providing hope to the totally blind. For example, one team of researchers has employed a miniature television camera, which is mounted on spectacle frames worn by a blind person (Bach-Y-Rita, 1982). The picture from the camera is analyzed by a small computer, which translates the picture into 400 dots, varying in darkness. Next, the degree of darkness of each of the spots is transformed into vibrations of varying intensity that are relayed to the blind person's abdomen, with darker spots being represented by more rapid vibrations. With just a small amount of training, blind people are able to "see" and recognize common objects, and eventually they are able to open doors, negotiate their way through halls, and pick up small objects.

The technology is still not as advanced as that employed in ear transplants, since the sensation of sight must be "translated" first into sensations of touch. And neither ear nor eye substitutes have reached the ultimate level of sophistication, in which signals can be fed directly into the brain and perceived as sound or sight. Still, the innovations described here offer real hope to thousands of deaf and blind people now, and there are strong possibilities for future breakthroughs.

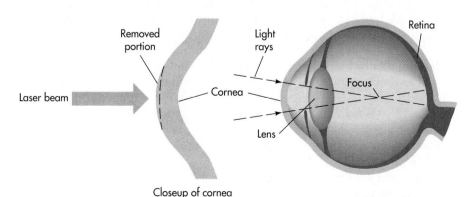

Removed portion — Laser beam — Cornea — Light rays — Lens — Focus — Retina

Closeup of cornea

FIGURE 4-16

Using lasers, eye specialists can remove a tiny slice of the cornea of people who are nearsighted. This procedure permits images entering the eye to be focused precisely on the retina, thereby eliminating the need for glasses or contact lenses. (After Sotoodeh, 1991.)

ment. She left her apartment, ran to the pay phone across the street, and called the gas company. As she was explaining what she smelled, Warner heard a muffled explosion and then saw flames begin to shoot out of her apartment window. Her life had been saved by her ability to smell the gas.

Although there are few instances in which the sense of smell provides such drama, it is clear that our lives would be considerably less interesting if we could not smell freshly mowed hay, sniff a bouquet of flowers, or enjoy the aroma of an apple pie baking. Like our senses of vision and hearing, each of the remaining senses that we now consider—smell, taste, and the skin senses—plays an important role in our lives.

Smell and Taste. Although many animals have keener abilities to detect odors than we do, since a greater proportion of their brains is devoted to the sense of smell than ours is, we are still able to detect more than 10,000 separate smells. We also remember smells well, and long-forgotten events and memories can be brought back with the mere whiff of an odor associated with the memory (Schab, 1990, 1991).

Results of "sniff tests" have shown that women generally have a better sense of smell than men do, as you can see clearly in Figure 4-17. Researchers disagree, though, on why this is the case. Some hypothesize that smell is linked to hormonal differences between men and women because of evidence that women's smelling capabilities change over the course of their menstrual cycles. But other researchers argue that women's superior smelling abilities are more a reflection of their better verbal abilities than anything else. According to this theory, women find it easier than men to identify the name of an odor (Engen, 1987).

The sense of smell also changes with age: Sensitivity to smells is greatest between the ages of 30 and 60, declining from age 60 on. Moreover, a small number of people cannot smell at all. Such a condition may result from a head injury, nasal growths, or sometimes just a bad case of the flu (Doty, 1986; Gilbert & Wysocki, 1987).

Pheromones: Chemicals that produce a reaction in other members of a species

For some animals, smell represents an important mode of communication. By releasing **pheromones**, chemicals that produce a reaction in other members of the species, they are able to send such messages as sexual availability. For instance, certain substances in the vaginal secretions of female monkeys contain a chemical that stimulates sexual interest in male monkeys.

Although it seems reasonable that humans might also communicate through the release of pheromones, the evidence is still scanty. Women's vaginal secretions contain chemicals similar to those found in monkeys, but the smells do not seem to be related to sexual activity in humans. On the other hand, the presence of these substances might explain why women who live together for long periods tend to show similarity in the timing of their menstrual cycles (Engen, 1982, 1987). In addition, women are able to identify their babies solely on the basis of smell just a few hours after birth (Porter, Cernich, & McLaughlin, 1983).

People also seem to have the ability to distinguish males from females on the basis of smell alone. In one experiment, blindfolded students sniffed a sweating hand held one-half inch from their nose. The findings showed that male and female hands could be distinguished from one another with better than 80 percent accuracy (Wallace, 1977). Similarly, unfortunate experimental subjects who were asked to sniff the breath of a male or female volunteer who was hidden from view were able to distinguish the sex of the donor at better than chance levels (Doty et al., 1982).

Our understanding of the mechanisms that underlie the sense of smell is just beginning to emerge. We do know that the sense of smell is sparked when

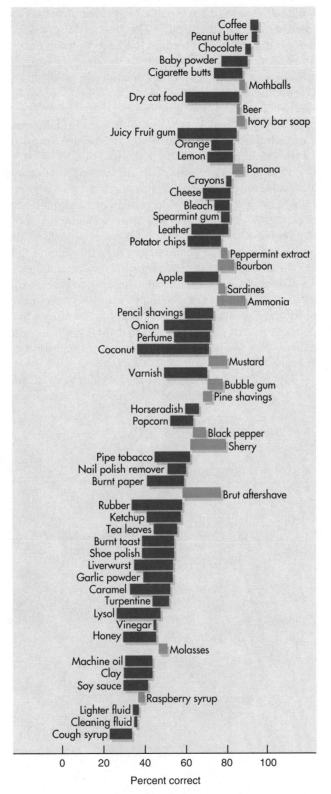

FIGURE 4-17

The performance of men and women in identifying common odors. They are arranged from top to bottom in terms of how easy they were to identify. In addition, the shaded bars indicate better male performance, and the unshaded bars indicate better female performance. (Adapted from Cain, 1982.)

molecules of some substance enter the nasal passages and meet **olfactory cells**, the receptor cells of the nose. At least 1000 separate receptor cells have been identified so far, and each of these cells is so specialized that it only responds to a small band of different odors. Olfactory cells have hairlike structures that stick

Olfactory cells: The receptor cells of the nose that respond to odors

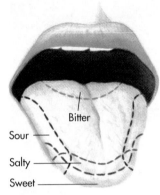

FIGURE 4-18

Particular portions of the tongue are sensitive to tastes that are bitter, sour, sweet, or salty.

Taste buds: The location of the receptor cells for taste, found on the tongue

out into the air and are capable of transforming the passing molecules into nerve impulses that can be used by the brain (Buck & Axel, 1991). Furthermore, although the traditional wisdom has been that the only site of olfactory cells is the nose, recent research has come to the startling conclusion that sperm cells have odor receptors that lead them to swim irresistibly in the direction of fertile eggs (Parmentier et al., 1992).

Unlike smell, which employs more than 1000 separate types of receptor cells, the sense of taste makes do with only four fundamental types of receptors. These four cells react to sweet, sour, salty, and bitter flavors. Every other taste is simply a combination of these four basic qualities.

The receptor cells for taste are located in **taste buds**, which are distributed across the tongue. However, the distribution is uneven, and certain areas of the tongue are more sensitive to particular fundamental tastes than others (Bartoshuk, 1971). As we can see in Figure 4-18, the tip of the tongue is most sensitive to sweetness; in fact, a granule of sugar placed on the rear of the tongue will hardly seem sweet at all. Similarly, only the sides of the tongue are very sensitive to sour tastes, and the rear specializes in bitter tastes.

The different taste areas on the tongue correspond to different locations in the brain. Neurons responding to sour and bitter tastes are located on one end of the area of the cortex corresponding to taste, whereas sweet tastes stimulate neurons on the opposite end of the cortex. In contrast, salty tastes stimulate neurons that are distributed across the entire taste area of the brain (Yamamoto, Yuyama, & Kawamura, 1981).

Of course, the sense of taste does not operate simply through the tongue, as anyone with a stuffy nose can confirm. The smell, temperature, texture, and

FIGURE 4-19

The beer industry has devised the set of descriptive terms in this flavor wheel to help in the production and quality control of beer. Both odors and tastes are included in the wheel. (American Society of Brewing Chemists.)

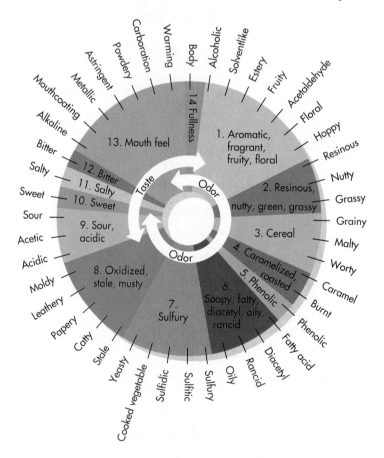

Do you routinely reach for the salt shaker when you're eating certain foods? Do you love to put an extra spoonful of sugar into your coffee?

If you indulge in such behavior—to the dismay of nutritionists—there's someone with whom you can share the blame: the person who prepared your meals when you were growing up. According to recent research, our taste preferences are developed largely through childhood experience. Rather than some of us being born with more of a sweet (or salty) tooth than others, we develop preferences for taste based on the way food was prepared when we were children.

Using a group of preschoolers, psychologists Susan Sullivan and Leann Birch (1990) studied how taste preferences develop. They asked children to taste small samples of one of two unfamiliar foods—tofu or ricotta cheese. For some of the chil-

DISCOVERING THE ORIGINS OF FOOD PREFERENCES

dren, the tofu or ricotta always was plain; for others it always was salted; and for still others it always was sweetened with sugar. The tasting occurred 15 times over nine weeks.

To determine how their taste preferences had been affected by the exposure to a consistently plain, salty, or sweet version of the food, the children were asked how much they liked all of the versions of the foods on three different occasions over a period of several weeks. The results were clear: The children developed a preference for the version of the food to which they had been exposed. If they had been given the salty tofu or ricotta, they preferred the salty version over the plain and sweetened versions; if they had initially been given the sweet tofu or ricotta, they preferred the sweetened version

over the salty and plain versions. Furthermore, not only did their preference for the initial version of the food increase, but their preference for other versions of the same food declined.

It seems, then, that we develop preferences for salty or sweet foods based on our prior experiences. The more we are exposed to a particular food, the more apt we are to like it. Such a finding, of course, is compatible with an old wives' tale about olives, a fruit which many people initially hate. According to this lore, the way to grow to savor olives is to eat nine in a row. By the time you're finished, you'll have developed a lifetime passion for them.

Beyond confirming old wives' tales, of course, the research illustrates the importance of parents' influence on their children's diets. It also shows the practical outcomes of research on the senses.

even appearance of food and drink all affect our sense of taste. Because of this, food and beverage manufacturers continually assess the quality of the taste, odor, and appearance of their products to ensure that quality is maintained. For example, the beer industry has developed a complex set of criteria, indicated in Figure 4-19, to judge the caliber of their product.

People differ greatly in their tasting abilities, with some individuals showing greater sensitivity to certain tastes than others. The ability to taste particular substances also runs in some families. In addition, our own behavior and habits also play a role in our tasting capabilities. Smoking, for example, dulls the flavor of food. We also acquire taste preferences through childhood experience, as we discuss in the Cutting Edge box.

The Skin Senses: Touch, Pressure, Temperature, and Pain. Consider the plight of this boy, born with an extremely rare inherited defect that made him insensitive to pain:

> His arms and legs are deformed and bent, as though he had suffered from rickets. Several fingers are missing. A large open wound covers one knee, and the smiling lips are bitten raw. He looks, to all the world, like a battered child. . . . His fingers were either crushed or burned because he did not pull his hands away from things that were hot or dangerous. His bones and joints were misshapen because he pounded them too hard when he walked or ran. His knee had ulcerated from crawling over sharp objects that he could not feel. Should he break a bone or dislocate a hip, he would not feel enough to cry out for help (Wallis, 1984, pp. 58, 60).

▶ **127**

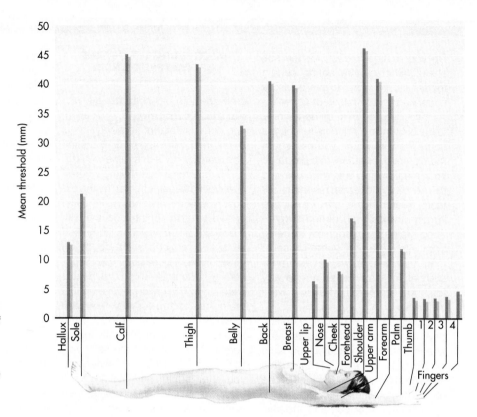

FIGURE 4-20

Skin sensitivity of various parts of the body. The shorter a line, the more sensitive the body part is. The fingers and thumb, lips, nose, cheeks, and big toe are the most sensitive. (After Weinstein, 1968.)

Skin senses: The senses that include touch, pressure, temperature, and pain

Gate-control theory of pain: The theory that suggests that particular nerve receptors lead to specific areas of the brain related to pain; when these receptors are activated by an injury or bodily malfunction, a "gate" to the brain is opened and pain is sensed

Clearly, the consequences of a painfree existence can be devastating. If, for example, you did not experience pain, instead of recoiling when your arm brushed against a hot teapot, you might lean against it, not noticing that you were being severely burned. Similarly, without the warning sign of stomach pain that typically accompanies an inflamed appendix, your appendix might go on to rupture, spreading a fatal infection through your body. Such examples underscore the vital importance of the sense of pain.

In fact, all our **skin senses**—touch, pressure, temperature, and pain—play a critical role in survival, making us aware of potential danger to our bodies. Most of these senses operate through nerve receptor cells located at various depths throughout the skin, although they are not evenly distributed. When we consider receptors sensitive to pressure, for example, some areas, such as the fingertips, have many more cells and as a consequence are notably sensitive to pressure. In contrast, areas with fewer cells, such as the middle of the back, are considerably less sensitive to pressure (see Figure 4-20; Kreuger, 1989).

Probably the most extensively researched skin sense is pain, and with good reason: People consult physicians and take medication for pain more than for any other symptom or condition. Nearly one-third of the population of the United States has problems with persistent or recurrent pain. Many of these individuals are disabled to the point of being unable to function normally in society (Vlaeyen et al., 1990).

Until fairly recently, little was understood about the biology and psychology of pain, and even less about how to treat it (Fordyce, 1988; Flor & Turk, 1989). Today, however, the major theory relating to the experience of pain, called the **gate-control theory of pain**, is providing us with new clues for understanding how we can control pain. The gate-control theory suggests that particular nerve receptors lead to specific areas of the brain related to pain (Melzack & Wall, 1965;

Wall & Melzack, 1989). When these receptors are activated because of some injury or problem with a part of the body, a "gate" to the brain is opened, allowing the sensation of pain to be experienced.

However, another set of neural receptors is able, when stimulated, to close the "gate" to the brain, thereby reducing the experience of pain. The gate may be shut in two different ways. First, other impulses can overwhelm the nerve pathways relating to pain, which are spread throughout the brain (Talbot et al., 1991). In this case, nonpainful stimuli compete with and sometimes displace the neuronal message of pain, thereby shutting off the painful stimulus. This explains why rubbing the skin around an injury helps reduce pain: The competing stimuli from the rubbing may overwhelm the painful ones. Similarly, scratching is able to relieve itching (which is technically classified as a kind of pain stimulus).

A second way in which a gate may be activated is through the brain itself. The brain is able to close a gate by sending a message down the spinal cord to an injured area, producing a reduction in or relief from pain. Thus soldiers who are injured in battle may experience no pain—the surprising situation in more than half of all combat injuries. The lack of pain probably occurs because soldiers experience such relief at still being alive that their brain sends a signal to the injury site to shut down the pain gate (Sternbach, 1987; Willis, 1988; Baker & Kirsch, 1991).

Similarly, gate-control theory may explain cultural differences in the experience of pain. Some of these variations are astounding. For example, people who participate in the "hook-swinging" ritual in India have steel hooks embedded under the skin and muscles of their backs. During the ritual, they swing from a pole, suspended by the hooks. What would seem likely to induce excruciating pain instead produces a state of celebration and near-euphoria. In fact, when the hooks are later removed, the wounds heal quickly, and after two weeks almost no visible marks remain (Kosambi, 1967).

Gate-control theory suggests that the lack of pain is due to a message from the participant's brain, which shuts down the pain pathways. Gate-control theory also may explain the effectiveness of **acupuncture**, an ancient Chinese technique in which sharp needles are inserted into various parts of the body. The sensation from the needles may close the gateway to the brain, reducing the experience

Acupuncture: A Chinese technique of relieving pain through the placement of needles in specific areas of the body

The gate-control theory may explain how some individuals can voluntarily walk over red-hot coals without experiencing pain.

of pain. It is also possible that the body's own painkillers, the endorphins (discussed in Chapter 3), as well as positive and negative emotions, may play a role in opening and closing the gate (Wall & Melzack, 1984; Warga, 1987).

Fighting Pain.   For those who suffer from long-term pain, the causes are less important than the cure. Psychologists and medical specialists have devised several approaches to dealing with pain (Budiansky, 1987; Catalano & Johnson, 1987). Among the most important are the following:

- Drugs: Drugs are the most popular treatment in fighting pain. Drugs range from those that treat the source of the pain—such as reducing swelling in painful joints—to those that work on the symptoms of the pain.
- Hypnosis: For those people who can be hypnotized, hypnosis can produce a major degree of pain relief (Spiegel, 1989; Erickson, Hershman, & Secter, 1990).
- Biofeedback: As we discussed in the previous chapter, biofeedback is a process in which people learn to control such "involuntary" functions as heartbeat and respiration. If the pain involves muscles, such as in tension headaches or back pain, biofeedback can be helpful (Dolce & Raczynski, 1985).
- Relaxation techniques: People can be trained to relax their bodies systematically, as we discuss in Chapter 18. Such relaxation is often effective in decreasing the pain caused by tension.
- Surgery: One of the most extreme methods, surgery can be used to cut certain nerve fibers carrying pain messages to the brain. Still, because there is a danger that other functions of the body will be affected, surgery is a treatment of last resort.
- Nerve and brain stimulation: Pain relief can sometimes occur when a low-voltage electric current is passed through painful parts of the body. This process is known as **transcutaneous electrical nerve stimulation (TENS)**. In the most severe cases, electrodes can be implanted surgically into the brain, and a handheld battery pack can stimulate nerve cells to provide direct relief (Barbaro, 1988).
- Psychological counseling: In cases where pain cannot be successfully treated, psychological counseling is employed to help a patient cope more effectively with the experience of pain. It is possible to change the way that patients perceive pain, making them better able to cope with it (Heyneman et al., 1990).

Transcutaneous electrical nerve stimulation (TENS): A method of providing relief from pain by passing a low-voltage electric current through parts of the body

The Informed Consumer of Psychology: Self-Examination: The Protective Touch

Every year, some 40,000 women die of breast cancer and 6000 men die of testicular cancer. Yet most of these deaths could have been avoided had the victims carried out self-examinations of their breasts or testicles. When tumors are found early, treatment is usually much more effective than when the disease has had a chance to spread. Obviously, this is a case in which a keen sense of touch can be a lifesaver (Sekuler & Blake, 1990; Springer, 1991).

Teaching people to be responsive to changes in their bodies is no simple matter, however. As we discussed when we considered signal detection theory earlier in the chapter, being sensitive to the presence or absence of particular stimuli represents a difficult task. It is dependent on many factors, including knowledge, expectations, and motivation. Even physicians vary greatly in their abilities to distinguish cancerous growths from normal tissue (Fletcher, O'Malley, & Bunce, 1985).

To permit people to be more sensitive and accurate in their self-examinations, some psychologists have devised training programs. For example, one group of psychologists at the University of Florida has developed procedures to increase the sensitivity of women in breast self-examination (Bloom et al., 1982; Springer, 1991). Using silicone models of breasts, they found that people's ability to detect lumps increased significantly with practice. Just reading about the procedure had little effect; it was actual practice that brought about increases in detection skill.

Even without special training, though, self-examination is not that difficult. In fact, consistent, routine practice on our own bodies may be the most effective means of increasing our sensitivity. Such practice permits us to become aware of the normal feel of things, providing a baseline against which to compare any changes. The key, then, is to carry out self-examination regularly. For women, the basic procedure is to repeatedly press or squeeze a breast from the outside to the center while lying with a pillow under the shoulder. It should be done once a month. For men, the technique consists of gently feeling the surface of each testicle to identify any lump or swelling. Such a self-examination should be done weekly. (Complete instructions can be obtained by calling the American Cancer Society at 800-227-2345 or by writing them at 1599 Clifton Road NE, Atlanta, Georgia 30329.)

Women can learn to be more accurate in detecting breast lumps, a possible indication of breast cancer, by practicing with a plastic model like this one.

▷ **RECAP AND REVIEW III**

RECAP

◁ The senses of hearing, motion, and balance are centered in the ear.

◁ The major parts of the ear are the outer ear (which includes the auditory canal and eardrum), the middle ear (with the hammer, anvil, and stirrup), and the oval window leading to the inner ear. The inner ear contains the cochlea, basilar membrane, and hair cells.

◁ The sense of balance is located in the ear's semicircular canals and otoliths.

◁ The physical aspects of sound include frequency and intensity. Both place and frequency processes are believed to operate in the transformation of sound waves into the experience of sound.

◁ Less is known about the senses of smell, taste, and the skin senses (touch, pressure, temperature, and pain) than about vision and hearing. One major research focus has been on understanding the causes of pain and devising ways to alleviate it.

REVIEW

1. The tubelike passage leading from the outer ear is known as the _____ _____.

2. The purpose of the eardrum is to protect the sensitive nerves underneath it. It serves no purpose in actual hearing. True or false? _____

3. To what part of the ear do the three middle ear bones transmit their sound? _____ _____

4. The hair cells that can be damaged by excessively loud noise are located inside the _____ _____.

5. _____ is the feature of sound waves that lets us hear loud or soft sounds, while _____ is the characteristic that makes sounds "high" or "low."

6. What theory of hearing states that the entire basilar membrane responds to a sound, vibrating more or less depending on the nature of the sound?

7. The three fluid-filled tubes in the inner ear which are responsible for our sense of balance are known as the _____ _____.

8. Chemicals that produce a certain reaction in other members of the species are known as _____.

9. Olfactory cells are extremely specialized, each responding to only a narrow range of odor. True or false? _____

10. _____ - _____ the-

ory states that when certain skin receptors are activated as the result of an injury, a ''pathway'' to the brain is opened, allowing pain to be experienced.

Ask Yourself

Much research has been done on repairing faulty sensory organs through such devices as hearing aids, etc. Do you think it would be feasible for science to attempt, via these same methods, to augment already existing senses (such as increasing the range of the human visual or audio spectrum)? What benefits might this bring? What problems could it cause?

(Answers to review questions are on page 133.)

◄ **LOOKING BACK**

■ *What is sensation and how do psychologists study it?*

1. Sensation is our initial contact with stimuli (forms of energy that activate a sense organ). Sensation has traditionally been investigated by the branch of psychology called psychophysics, which studies the relationship between the physical nature of stimuli and a person's sensory responses to them.

■ *What is the relationship between the nature of a physical stimulus and the kinds of sensory responses that result from it?*

2. One major area of psychophysics is the study of the absolute threshold, the smallest amount of physical intensity by which a stimulus can be detected. Although under ideal conditions absolute thresholds are extraordinarily sensitive, the presence of noise (background stimuli that interfere with other stimuli) reduces detection capabilities. Moreover, factors such as an individual's expectations and motivations affect success in detecting stimuli. Signal detection theory is now used to predict the accuracy of judgments by systematically taking into account two kinds of errors made by observers—reporting the presence of a stimulus when there is none and reporting the absence of a stimulus when one is actually present.

3. Difference thresholds relate to the smallest detectable difference between two stimuli, known as a just noticeable difference. According to Weber's law, a just noticeable difference is a constant proportion of the intensity of an initial stimulus.

4. Sensory adaptation occurs when we become accustomed to a constant stimulus and change our evaluation of it. Repeated exposure to a stimulus results in an apparent decline in sensitivity to it.

■ *What are the major senses, and what are the basic mechanisms that underlie their operation?*

5. Human sensory experience goes well beyond the traditional five senses, although most is known about just two: vision and hearing. Vision depends on sensitivity to light, electromagnetic waves that are reflected off objects outside the body. The eye shapes the light into an image that is transformed into nerve impulses and interpreted by the brain.

6. When light first enters the eye, it travels through the cornea and then traverses the pupil, a dark hole in the center of the iris. The size of the pupil opening adjusts according to the amount of light entering the eye. Light then enters the lens, which, by a process called accommodation, acts to focus light rays onto the rear of the eye. On the rear of the eye is the retina, which is composed of light-sensitive nerve cells called rods and cones. The rods and cones are unevenly spaced over the retina, with the greatest concentration of cones occurring in an area called the fovea.

7. The visual information gathered by the rods and cones is transferred via bipolar and ganglion cells through the optic nerve, which leads to the optic chiasm—the point where the optic nerve splits. Because the image on the retina is reversed and upside down, images from the right half of the retina are actually from the field of vision to the left of the person, and vice versa. Moreover, because of the phenomenon of adaptation, it takes time to adjust to situations that are either measurably lighter or measurably darker than the previous environment.

8. Color vision seems to be based on two processes described by the trichromatic theory and the opponent-process theory. The trichromatic theory suggests that there are three kinds of cones in the retina, each of which is responsive to a certain range of colors. The opponent-process theory presumes pairs of different types of cells in the eye. These cells work in opposition to each other.

9. Sound, motion, and balance are centered in the ear. Sounds, in the form of vibrating air waves, enter through the outer ear and travel through the canal until they reach the eardrum. The vibrations of the eardrum are transmitted into the middle ear, which consists of three bones: the hammer, the anvil, and the stirrup. These bones transmit vibrations to the oval window, a thin membrane leading to the inner ear. In the inner ear, vibrations move into the cochlea, which encloses the basilar membrane. Hair cells on the basilar membrane change the mechanical energy of sound waves into nerve impulses which are transmitted to the brain. In addition to processing sound, the ear is involved in the sense of balance and motion through the semicircular canals and otoliths.

10. Sound has a number of important characteristics. One is frequency, the number of wave crests that occur in a second. Differences in the frequency of sound waves create different pitches. Another aspect of sound is intensity, the variations in pressure produced by a wave as it travels through the air. Intensity is measured in decibels. The place theory of hearing and the frequency theory of hearing explain the processes by which we distinguish sounds of varying frequency and intensity.

11. Considerably less is known about smell, taste, and the skin senses than about vision and hearing. Still, it is clear that smell employs olfactory cells (the receptor cells of the nose) and that taste is centered in the tongue's taste buds, which are capable of sensing combinations of sweet, sour, salty, and bitter flavors.

12. The skin senses are responsible for the experiences of touch, pressure, temperature, and pain. We know the most about pain, which can be explained by the gate-control theory. The theory suggests that particular nerve receptors lead to specific areas of the brain related to pain. When these receptors are activated, a "gate" to the brain is opened, allowing the sensation of pain to be experienced. In addition, there is another set of receptors which, when stimulated, close the gate, thereby reducing the experience of pain. Endorphins, internal painkillers, may also affect the operation of the gate.

13. Among the techniques used most frequently to alleviate pain are administration of drugs, hypnosis, biofeedback, relaxation techniques, surgery, nerve and brain stimulation, and psychotherapy.

KEY TERMS AND CONCEPTS

stimulus (p. 99)
sensation (p. 99)
intensity (p. 99)
psychophysics (p. 100)
absolute threshold (p. 100)
noise (p. 100)
signal detection theory (p. 101)
difference threshold (p. 102)
just noticeable difference
  (p. 102)
Weber's law (p. 103)
adaptation (p. 103)
light (p. 105)
visual spectrum (p. 105)
cornea (p. 107)
pupil (p. 107)
iris (p. 107)
lens (p. 107)
accommodation (p. 107)
retina (p. 107)
rods (p. 107)
cones (p. 107)
fovea (p. 107)
peripheral vision (p. 109)

rhodopsin (p. 109)
bipolar cells (p. 109)
ganglion cells (p. 109)
optic nerve (p. 109)
optic chiasm (p. 109)
glaucoma (p. 110)
tunnel vision (p. 110)
feature detection (p. 111)
light adaptation (p. 112)
dark adaptation (p. 112)
trichromatic theory of color
  vision (p. 113)
afterimage (p. 114)
opponent-process theory of color
  vision (p. 114)
outer ear (p. 117)
sound (p. 118)
auditory canal (p. 118)
eardrum (p. 118)
middle ear (p. 118)
hammer (p. 118)
anvil (p. 118)
stirrup (p. 118)
oval window (p. 118)

inner ear (p. 118)
cochlea (p. 119)
basilar membrane (p. 119)
hair cells (p. 119)
frequency (p. 120)
pitch (p. 120)
intensity (p. 120)
decibel (p. 120)
place theory of hearing (p. 121)
frequency theory of hearing
  (p. 121)
vertigo (p. 122)
semicircular canals (p. 122)
otoliths (p. 122)
pheromones (p. 124)
olfactory cells (p. 125)
taste buds (p. 126)
skin senses (p. 128)
gate-control theory of pain
  (p. 128)
acupuncture (p. 129)
transcutaneous electrical nerve
  stimulation (TENS) (p. 130)

ANSWERS (REVIEW III):

1. auditory canal **2.** False; it vibrates when sound waves hit it, and transmits the sound. **3.** Oval window **4.** basilar membrane **5.** Intensity; pitch **6.** Frequency theory **7.** semicircular canals **8.** Pheromones **9.** True **10.** Gate-control.

FLIGHT 901

Wreckage of the Air New Zealand plane on Mount Erebus. The crash was caused by a visual illusion.

The weather was clear as the Air New Zealand DC-10 descended for a closer look at the Antarctic ice cap. The pilot on this routine sightseeing flight was highly experienced, with thousands of hours of flying to his credit.

Yet this was to be his last flight—as well as the last one for the 256 other passengers and crew on board. Sometime after 2 P.M., the plane flew directly into the side of Mount Erebus, a 12,000-foot volcano. The captain, crew, and passengers were all killed in one of the deadliest—and most puzzling—air crashes ever to occur.

Why did an experienced pilot fly directly into the towering Mount Erebus? After months of investigation, it became clear that the pilot and his crew were the victims of several visual illusions. For one thing, their experience that objects seen from a distance look smaller than they really are caused them inadvertently to misjudge the size and distance of the few navigational landmarks found on the barren Antarctic landscape. Furthermore, the crew was misled by a phenomenon in which the lack of texture on a colorless, featureless horizon causes observers to estimate the actual slope of the ground incorrectly. Because they were unable to tell how quickly the ground was actually rising, they failed to increase their altitude sufficiently—with deadly results (O'Hare & Roscoe, 1990).

LOOKING AHEAD

Some 700 people die in airline crashes each year, and human perceptual errors play a central role in many of these accidents. The reason is straightforward: Despite the sophistication of our sensory system, our ultimate understanding of the world is not based on a complete and perfectly accurate reproduction of the information provided by our senses. Instead, we *interpret* the information that our senses supply—and such interpretation is open to error.

On the other hand, our knowledge of the world's extensive and varied stimuli is surprisingly accurate much of the time. For example, we can recognize the face of an old friend whom we have not seen in twenty years, even though he or she may have aged considerably, and we can perceive the tiny shapes on this page as letters and turn them into meaningful words and sentences.

The processes underlying our ability to give meaning to stimuli have been explored by psychologists who study perception. **Perception** is the sorting out, interpretation, analysis, and integration of stimuli from our sensory organs. The study of perception is directed at finding out how we take stimuli and form conscious representations of the environment.

Perception is clearly an outgrowth of sensation, and it is sometimes difficult to distinguish between the two. (Indeed, psychologists—and philosophers, as well—have argued for years over the distinction.) The primary difference is that sensation can be thought of as an organism's first encounter with a raw sensory stimulus, while perception is the process by which it is interpreted, analyzed, and integrated with other sensory information. For instance, if we were considering sensation, we might ask how bright a stimulus appears; if we were considering perception, we might ask whether someone recognizes the stimulus and what it means to that person.

Perception: The sorting out, interpretation, analysis, and integration of stimuli from our sensory organs

To understand the importance of perception, consider for a moment what the world would be like if we responded only to the raw sensory stimuli presented to us. Because of the vast number of stimuli to which we are constantly exposed, the world would be filled with an overwhelming array of sights, sounds, and other sensations, and we would be unable to respond coherently to them. Perception, however, enables us to take those different stimuli and place them in a context that provides us with meaning and understanding.

After reading this chapter, you will be able to answer the following questions relating to perception:

■ What principles underlie our organization of the stimuli to which our sense organs are exposed, allowing us to make sense of our environment?

■ How are we able to perceive the world in three dimensions when our retinas are capable of sensing only two-dimensional images?

■ How do we sort out auditory stimuli, paying attention to particular stimuli and ignoring others?

■ What clues do visual illusions give us about our understanding of general perceptual mechanisms?

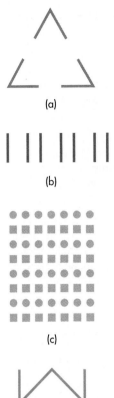

(a)

(b)

(c)

(d)

FIGURE 5-1
Perceptual organization at work. Although the figure in (a) can be seen as three angles, (b) as eight lines, (c) as columns of alternating circles and squares, and (d) as the letter "w" on top of an "m," most of us see in (a) a triangle, in (b) four tubes, in (c) rows of circles and squares, and in (d) a diamond inside two columns.

PERCEPTUAL ORGANIZATION: OUR VIEW OF THE WORLD

Look, for a moment, at the shapes in Figure 5-1. Most of us would report that we saw an incomplete triangle in 5-1(a), four tubes in Figure 5-1(b), rows of circles and squares in Figure 5-1(c), and a square inside two columns in Figure 5-1(d). But are these the only interpretations that could be given? A reasonable person could argue that there are three angles in Figure 5-1(a), eight vertical lines in Figure 5-1(b), seven columns of alternating circles and squares in Figure 5-1(c), and a printed block "W" on top of a block "M" in Figure 5-1(d).

The fact that most of us are apt to interpret the shapes as meaningful wholes illustrates one of the basic processes of perception at work: We try to simplify the complex stimuli presented to us by the environment. If we did not reduce the complex into something understandable, the world would present too much of a challenge for us to function, and—unless we lived as hermits in drab, colorless, silent caves—we would spend all our time just sorting through its extensive stimuli. Ironically, psychologists have found that the process of simplifying the world requires an impressive amount of perceptual effort.

The Gestalt Laws of Organization

The basic perceptual processes operate according to a series of principles that describe how we organize bits and pieces of information into meaningful wholes. These are known as **gestalt laws of organization**, set forth in the early 1900s by a group of German psychologists who studied patterns, or **gestalts** (Wertheimer, 1923). They discovered a number of important principles which are valid for visual and auditory stimuli:

■ *Closure.* Groupings are usually made in terms of enclosed or complete figures rather than open ones. We tend to ignore the breaks, then, in Figure 5-1(a) and concentrate on the overall form.

Gestalt (geh SHTALLT) **laws of organization:** A series of principles that describe how we organize pieces of information into meaningful wholes; they include closure, proximity, similarity, and simplicity

Gestalts: Patterns studied by the gestalt psychologists

Closure: The tendency to group according to enclosed or complete figures rather than open or incomplete ones

Proximity: The tendency to group together those elements that are close together

Similarity: The tendency to group together those elements that are similar in appearance

Simplicity: The tendency to perceive a pattern in the most basic, straightforward, organized manner possible—the overriding gestalt principle

Figure/ground: Figure refers to the object being perceived, whereas ground refers to the background or spaces within the object

FIGURE 5-2

When the usual cues we use to distinguish figure from ground are absent, we may shift back and forth between seeing a pair of faces or a vase. An ingenious designer utilized the figure-ground principle to create this object commemorating the Silver Jubilee of Great Britain's Queen Elizabeth, whose profile appears opposite that of Prince Philip.

- *Proximity.* Elements that are closer together are grouped together. Because of this, we tend to see pairs of dots rather than a row of single dots in the following, just as we see tubes in Figure 5-1(*b*) and not vertical lines:

. . . .

- *Similarity.* Elements that are similar in appearance are grouped together. We see, then, horizontal rows of circles and squares in Figure 5-1(*c*) instead of vertical mixed columns.
- *Simplicity.* In a general sense, the overriding gestalt principle is one of simplicity: When we observe a pattern, we perceive it in the most basic, straightforward manner that we can (Hochberg, 1978). For example, Figure 5-1(*d*) is seen as a square surrounded by two lines, rather than as block letters on top of one another. If we have a choice in interpretations, we generally opt for the simpler one.

Figure and Ground: Half Full or Half Empty?   Consider Figure 5-2 for a moment. Do you see a vase or the profile of two people (who just happen to be Queen Elizabeth and Prince Philip of Great Britain)?

Chances are that now you will shift back and forth between the two interpretations. The reason for the shifting back and forth is this: Because the figure is two-dimensional, the usual means we employ for distinguishing the **figure** (the object being perceived) from the **ground** (the background or spaces within the object) do not work.

The fact that we can look at the same figure in either of two ways illustrates an important point first emphasized by the gestalt psychologists: We do not just passively respond to visual stimuli that happen to fall on our retinas. Instead, we actively try to organize and make sense of what we see. Perception, then, is typically a constructive process by which we go beyond the stimuli that are presented to us and attempt to construct a meaningful situation (Haber, 1983; Kienker et al., 1986).

The Whole is Greater Than Its Parts: Where One Plus One Equals More Than Two.   If someone were to try to convince you that one plus one equals more than two, you would think that person needed to brush up on some basic arithmetic. Yet the idea that two objects considered together form a whole that is greater than the simple combination of the objects was a fundamental principle of the gestalt psychologists. They argued—quite convincingly—that perception of stimuli in our environment goes well beyond the individual elements that we sense and represents an active, constructive process carried out within the brain, where bits and pieces of sensations are put together to make something greater—and more meaningful—than the separate elements.

Consider, for instance, Figure 5-3. As you examine the black patches, it is likely that you will perceive the form of a dog. The dog represents a gestalt, or perceptual whole. Although you can see the individual parts that make up the figure, putting each of them together forms something greater than these individual parts. The whole, then, is greater than the sum of the individual elements.

Feature Analysis: Focusing on the Parts of the Whole

The gestalt view of perception emphasizes how we interpret the individual elements in a scene as a unified, complete whole—as an organized shape or pattern.

FIGURE 5-3

Although at first it is difficult to distinguish anything in this drawing, you probably will eventually be able to discern the figure of a dog. (Ronald C. James, from Carraher, R. G., and Thurston, J. B. [1966]. *Optical Illusions in the Visual Arts.* New York: Von Nostrand Reinhold.)

This view rests on the assumption that the organized whole is somehow different, and in fact greater, than the sum of the individual elements.

A more recent approach to perception takes a different route. **Feature analysis** considers how we perceive a shape, pattern, object, or scene by reacting first to the individual elements that make it up. These individual components are then used to understand the overall nature of what we are perceiving.

Feature analysis begins with the evidence that individual neurons in the brain are sensitive to specific spatial configurations, such as angles, curves, shapes, and edges, as we discussed in Chapter 4. The presence of these neurons suggests that

Feature analysis: Perception of a shape, pattern, object, or scene by responding to the individual elements that make it up

Although a pointillistic painting resembles a jumble of multi-colored dots when viewed at close range (*a*), our eyes resolve the dots into an orderly scene reminiscent of what we see in real life (*b*).

How many human faces can you see in the rocks and trees depicted here?

any stimulus can be broken down into a series of component features. For example, the letter "R" is a combination of a vertical line, a diagonal line, and a half circle.

According to the feature analysis approach to perception, when we encounter a stimulus—such as a letter—our brain's perceptual processing system initially responds to its component parts. Each of these parts is compared with information about components that is stored in memory. When the specific components we perceive match up with a particular set of components that we have encountered previously, we are able to identify the stimulus (Spillman & Werner, 1990; see Figure 5-4).

According to psychologist Irving Biederman (1987), we perceive complex objects in a manner similar to the way in which we perceive simple letters. He suggests that we view an object in terms of its component elements. Biederman

FIGURE 5-4

According to feature analysis approaches to perception, we break down stimuli into their component parts and then compare these parts to information that is stored in memory. When we find a match, we are able to identify the stimulus. In this example, the process by which we recognize the letter "R" is illustrated.

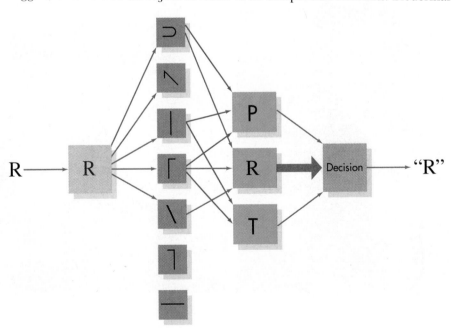

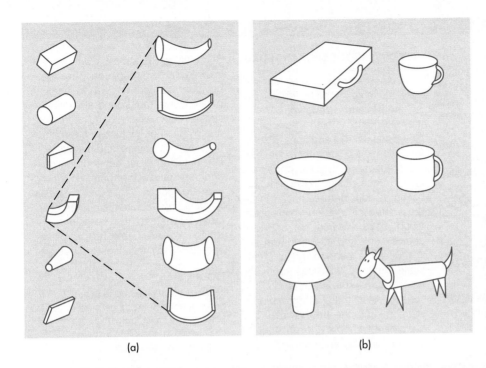

(a)   (b)

FIGURE 5-5

Six geons are illustrated in the left part of (*a*). The various related shapes that come from the fourth geon are shown in the right part of (*a*). Part (*b*) of the figure shows a few of the objects that can be created, using geons as ingredients. (Adapted from Biederman, 1987.)

has demonstrated that just thirty-six fundamental components, called **geons**, can produce over 150 million objects—more than enough to describe the 30,000 separate objects that the average person can recognize. (Some geons are shown in Figure 5-5.)

In sum, feature analysis takes place in a three-step sequence. In the first stage, we identify the component features of the object based on the image of the object on our retina. Next, we combine these component features into a representation of the whole object in the brain. Finally, in the third stage, we compare this combination of features to existing memories, thereby permitting us to identify the object (Biederman, 1987; Coren & Ward, 1989).

Although we have been discussing feature analysis in terms of the perception of visual stimuli, analysis of sounds may occur in an analogous fashion. For example, all of the English language can be perceived in terms of around forty different sounds—a number, you'll note, that is similar to the number of geons related to visual feature analysis (thirty-six). But speech perception is also in some ways more complicated than the analysis of visual stimuli, since it involves both auditory and visual cues. (We consider speech perception further in the Cutting Edge box on pages 142–143.)

Geons: The thirty-six fundamental component elements that when combined can produce more than 150 million objects

Top-Down and Bottom-Up Processing

Ca- yo- re-d t-is -en-en-e, w-ic- ha- ev-ry -hi-d l-tt-r m-ss-ng? After a bit of thought, you'll probably be able to figure out that it says, "Can you read this sentence, which has every third letter missing?"

If perception were based primarily on breaking down a stimulus into its most basic elements, understanding the sentence, as well as other ambiguous stimuli, would not be possible. The fact that you probably were able to recognize such an imprecise stimulus illustrates that perception proceeds along two different avenues, called top-down processing and bottom-up processing.

In **top-down processing**, perception is guided by higher-level knowledge,

Top-down processing: Perception guided by knowledge, experience, expectations, and motivations

We do not often reflect on how sophisticated our speech perception abilities are. Yet our proficiency in perceiving speech is quite remarkable. For instance, we can understand as many as fifty separate sounds per *second* in our native language. What makes this speed particularly extraordinary is that we can perceive nonspeech sounds only at an average rate of two-thirds of a sound per second (Foulke & Sticht, 1969; Miller, 1990).

Several factors enter into our ability to perceive speech. Consider, for a moment, the following:

> Marzi doats n doze edoats n lidul lamzey divey . . . (Lyrics to a 1940s song, quoted in Sekuler & Blake, 1990, p. 354.)

PERCEIVING THE SPOKEN WORD

If these words, spelled phonetically, make no sense to you, try saying them aloud a few times. And if they still mean nothing—as is probable—consider this additional bit of information: the lyrics refer to the feeding practices of mares, does, and lambs. Once you know the context, it becomes considerably easier to figure out that this phrase, when spoken aloud, says, "Mares eat oats and does eat oats and little lambs eat ivy."

Our enhanced ability to understand the lyrics illustrates the importance of context when understanding speech. As with the interpretation of visual stimuli, the other stimuli that are present when a spoken stimulus is produced play an important role in determining the success with which speech will be understood. The most obvious example is seen in homonyms, words that sound alike when spoken but which have different meanings. For instance, bear and bare are homonyms, and the distinction between them depends on our understanding of the context in which they are spoken.

Of course, context is not the only factor related to the success with which we are able to perceive speech. Many investigators believe

FIGURE 5-6

The facial configurations in this computer-generated model change as it shifts from an initial "ba" sound on the left to a "da" sound on the right.

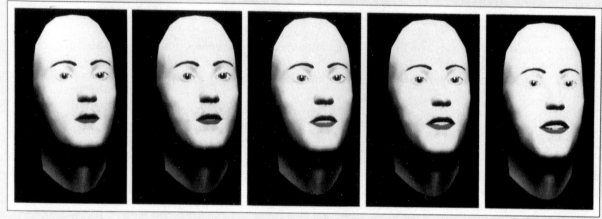

(continued on next page)

experience, expectations, and motivations. You were able to figure out the meaning of the sentence with the missing letters because of your prior reading experience, and because written English contains redundancies: Not every letter of each word is necessary to decode its meaning. Moreover, your expectations played a role in your being able to read the sentence. You were probably expecting a statement that had *something* to do with psychology, and not the lyrics to a Grateful Dead song.

Top-down processing is illustrated by the importance of context in determining our perception of objects (Biederman, 1981). Look, for example, at Fig-

Bottom-up processing:
Recognition and processing of information about the individual components of a stimulus

FIGURE 5-7
The power of context is shown in this figure. Note how the B and the 13 are identical.

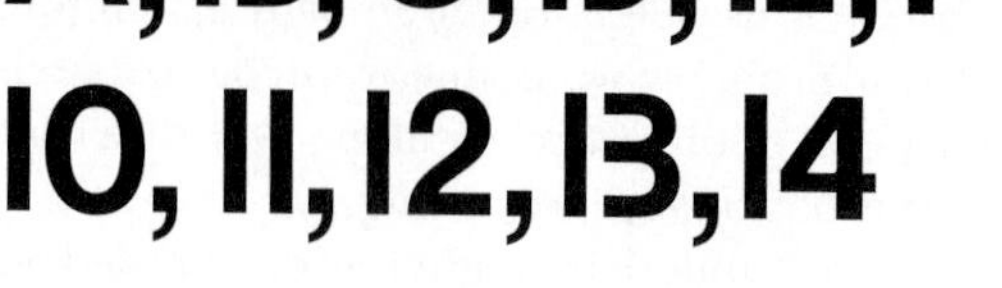

A, B, C, D, E, F
10, 11, 12, 13, 14

that our recognition of speech is so proficient largely because speech involves more than just sound stimuli. We also get information from movements of the mouth involved in speech, and we integrate the auditory and visual information to perceive speech. The ability of hearing-impaired individuals to read lips, for instance, clearly indicates the importance of visual stimuli in the perception of speech.

Although it is clear that both hearing and vision are involved in speech perception, until recently it has been difficult to develop controlled experimental procedures to investigate the relationship between spoken words and observed mouth movements. The problem is that it has been difficult to produce vocal stimuli and visual stimuli that are independent of one another. Consider, for example, how one might produce a stimulus that makes one sound vocally but

produces mouth movements indicative of another sound at the same time.

Fortunately, recent experimental work has been able to overcome this problem through the use of computer-produced sounds and faces. For the past decade, psychologists have had the capability of programming computers with great precision to produce sounds mimicking speech. It is only recently, however, that researchers have been able to provide facial models that show the facial configurations related to spoken sounds.

An example of such facial models is shown in Figure 5-6. In it, the facial model—generated by a computer and presented on a video screen—is shown producing the facial shapes that result when changing from an initial "ba" sound to a "da" sound. The computer can be programmed to produce facial configurations relevant to

a variety of sounds. Because these facial shapes can be produced independently of the sound, which is simultaneously generated by another computer program, it is possible to vary sight and sound stimuli independently of one another and with great precision (Massaro & Cohen, 1990).

Results of this work have shown clearly that we are responsive to both the sound and sight of language production. In fact, one of the reasons that we are so skilled in speech perception is because we have multiple sources of information about the content of speech available to us. Future research, using computer-generated audible and visible speech, should allow us to understand precisely the relative amount of information that comes from speech stimuli that are seen and the amount of information that comes from stimuli that are heard.

---

ure 5-7. Most of us perceive that the first row consists of the letters "A" through "F," while the second contains the numbers 10 through 14. But take a more careful look, and you'll see that the "B" and the "13" are identical. Clearly, our perception is affected by our expectations about the two sequences—even though the two stimuli are exactly the same.

Similarly, when we look at the isolated stimuli shown in Figure 5-8(a) it is almost impossible to tell what they are. But when the same stimuli are placed in the context of a face, they are much easier to identify. Top-down processing, which takes our expectations and understanding of the situation into account, must take place in order for us to understand what we are perceiving.

Of course, top-down processing cannot occur on its own. Even though top-down processing allows us to fill in the gaps in ambiguous and out-of-context stimuli, we would be unable to perceive the meaning of such stimuli without bottom-up processing. **Bottom-up processing** consists of recognizing and processing information about the individual components of the stimuli. We would make no headway in our recognition of the sentence without being able to perceive the individual shapes that make up the letters. Some perception, then, occurs at the level of the patterns and features of each of the separate letters.

It should be apparent that top-down and bottom-up processing occur simultaneously, and interact with each other, in our perception of the world around us. It is bottom-up processing that permits us to process the fundamental characteristics of stimuli, whereas top-down processing allows us to bring our experience to bear on perception. And as we learn more about the complex processes involved in perception, we are developing a better understanding of how our brain continually interprets information from our senses and permits us to make responses appropriate to the environment.

FIGURE 5-8

The odd shapes in (a) become more recognizable when placed on the face in (b). If they had initially appeared as they do in (c), they would have been identified easily. (Based on Palmer, 1975.)

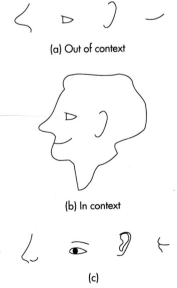

(a) Out of context

(b) In context

(c)

RECAP

◄ Perception refers to the process by which sensory stimuli are interpreted, analyzed, and integrated.

◄ Among the gestalt laws of organization are closure, proximity, and similarity. The overriding principle, however, is simplicity.

◄ People do not respond passively to visual stimuli; rather, they try to separate a given figure from the background.

◄ Feature analysis considers how we perceive a stimulus, break it down into the individual elements that make it up, and then use those elements to understand what we are seeing.

◄ Perception occurs through top-down and bottom-up processing.

REVIEW

1. An organism's initial encounter with a stimulus is referred to as _sensation_; the subsequent interpretation, analysis, and integration of the stimulus is known as _preception_.

2. Match each of the following organizational laws with its meaning:

_3_ a. Closure
_1_ b. Proximity
_4_ c. Similarity
_2_ d. Simplicity

1. Elements close together are grouped together.
2. Patterns are perceived in the most basic, direct manner possible.
3. Groupings are made in terms of complete figures.
4. Elements similar in appearance are grouped together.

3. _Feature_ analysis deals with the way in which we break an object down into its component pieces in order to understand it.

4. Many millions of patterns can be produced by combining only a few basic elements. What is the name of these fundamental components? _Geons_

5. Processing that takes into account higher functions such as expectations and motivations is known as _top down_ processing, while processing that involves recognizing the individual components of a stimulus is known as _bottom up_ processing.

Ask Yourself

Why are both top-down and bottom-up processing necessary to perceive the world?

(Answers to review questions are on page 146.)

Perceptual Constancy

Consider what happens as you finish a conversation with a friend and she begins to walk away from you. As you watch her walk down the street, the image on your retina becomes smaller and smaller. "Hmm," you think to yourself, "I wonder why she is shrinking."

Of course, you don't believe any such thing. Despite the real change in the size of the retinal image, you factor into your thinking the knowledge that your friend is moving further away from you. No matter how far away she moves, and no matter how small the retinal image becomes as a consequence of her distance, you still perceive her as the same size.

Your friend does not appear to shrink, due to perceptual constancy. **Perceptual constancy** is a phenomenon in which physical objects are perceived as unvarying and consistent, despite changes in their appearance or in the physical environment.

One of the most dramatic examples of perceptual constancy involves the rising moon. When the moon first appears at night, close to the horizon, it seems to be huge—considerably larger than when it is high in the sky later in the evening. You may have thought that the apparent size of the moon was caused by the moon's being physically closer to the earth when it first appears. In fact, though, this is not the case at all (Hershenson, 1989).

Instead, the moon appears to be larger when it is close to the horizon primarily because of a misapplication of perceptual constancy (Coren & Aks, 1990). When the moon is near the horizon, the perceptual cues of intervening terrain and objects such as trees on the horizon produce a misleading sense of distance.

Perceptual constancy: The phenomenon by which physical objects are perceived as unvarying despite changes in their appearance or the physical environment

144 ◄

Because perceptual constancy leads us to take that distance into account when we view the moon, we perceive the moon as relatively large. On the other hand, when the moon is high in the sky, we see it by itself, and perceptual constancy leads us to perceive it as relatively small. To prove this, try looking at the moon when it is relatively low on the horizon through a paper-towel tube; the moon will suddenly appear to "shrink" back to normal size.

Although perceptual constancy does not provide a complete explanation for the moon illusion, it is a central component along with several others (Coren, 1989; Coren & Aks, 1990; Suzuki, 1991). Furthermore, perceptual constancy occurs not just with size but with shape and color as well. The image on your retina varies as a plane approaches, flies overhead, and disappears, yet you do not perceive the plane as changing shape. Instead, you perceive it as unchanging, despite the physical variations that occur. Similarly, the soft lighting in a dimly lit restaurant might allow you to notice for the first time that a companion's eyes are an entrancing shade of blue. Yet you probably would not complain the next day when the bright sunlight produced a somewhat different color of blue. In fact, you probably wouldn't even notice the difference: Because of color constancy, you would perceive the blue as the same shade.

Although perceptual constancy aids us in simplifying the world, not all its outcomes are positive ones. For instance, safety experts have found that drivers of small cars have higher accident rates than those of large cars. They suggest that the cause of this is that most people tend to overestimate how distant smaller cars are from them. The reason: at a given distance, a small car produces a smaller retinal image than a larger one. This leads other drivers to assume that the car is farther away than it really is, and makes a collision more likely (Eberts & MacMillan, 1985).

It is clear that perceptual constancy depends in part on our prior experiences. This fact is compellingly illustrated when we examine the behavior of people raised in cultures very different from our own. For example, the Bambuti Pygmies live in a dense rain forest in Zaire, and their vision is consistently limited to short distances. Because of this restriction, they have not had experiences that would permit them to develop size constancy abilities. Anthropologist Colin Turnbull learned this first-hand on a journey he took with one Bambuti, a guide named Kenge, who had never before left the rain forest. On coming to a broad plain, the following incident took place:

> Kenge looked over the plains and down to where a herd of about a hundred buffalo were grazing some miles away. He asked me what kind of insects they were, and I told him they were buffalo, twice as big as the forest buffalo known to him. He laughed loudly and told me not to tell such stupid stories. . . . We got into the car and drove down to where the animals were grazing. He watched them getting larger and larger . . . and muttered that it was witchcraft. . . . Finally, when he realized that they were real buffalo he was no longer afraid, but what puzzled him still was why they had been so small, and whether they really had been small and suddenly grown larger, or whether it had been some kind of trickery. (Turnbull, 1961, pp. 304–308.)

The exact process by which we experience perceptual constancy is not completely understood and has given rise to two competing theories. One explanation—**constructive theory**—suggests that we use our prior experience and expectations about the size of an object to make inferences about its location (Lindsay & Norman, 1977; Rock, 1983). Because we have learned the size of a particular stimulus from earlier experience, we compensate for changes in its size on the retina by inferring its location.

Constructive theory: A theory suggesting that prior experience and expectations about the size of an object are used to make inferences about its location

Differences in texture, such as the ripples in these sand dunes, help us to perceive depth.

Ecological theory: A theory suggesting that the relationship between objects in a scene gives clues about the objects' sizes

In contrast, an alternative view, championed by psychologist James Gibson, suggests that all the information we need to determine distance can be found in the image on our retina. According to this approach, called **ecological theory**, the relationships among different objects in a scene provide us with clues about their sizes. Furthermore, we use the information provided by the nature of the surfaces in the environment to help determine the distance of stimuli. For example, objects that are farther away appear to have different surface textures from those that are closer. These differences in texture help us to make direct judgments about depth (Gibson, 1979; Michaels & Carello, 1981; Landwehr, 1990).

According to ecological theory, then, when a friend walks away from us into the distance, not only is she farther away, but so are the objects she is close to. Therefore, all objects near her are going to produce an image that is proportionally smaller on our retina, with corresponding variations in surface texture. Ecological theory suggests that we consider the scene as a whole and that perceptual constancy is brought about by direct perception of all the stimuli in the scene.

Neither constructive theory nor ecological theory provides an explanation of all instances of perceptual constancy, and it is possible that constructive and ecological processes work in combination (Gogel & DaSilva, 1987; Bruce & Green, 1990). What is clear is that our perceptual abilities develop early in life (Treisman & Gormican, 1988; Gibson, 1988). Indeed, perception is quite sophisticated even at birth (as we discuss in Chapter 13), although learning and experience clearly play a critical role in its development.

Depth Perception: Translating 2-D to 3-D

As sophisticated as the retina is, the images that are projected onto it are flat and two-dimensional. Yet the world around us is three-dimensional, and we perceive it that way. How do we make the transformation from 2-D to 3-D?

ANSWERS (REVIEW I):

1. sensation; perception **2.** a-3; b-1; c-4; d-2 **3.** Feature **4.** Geons **5.** top-down; bottom-up

The ability to view the world in three dimensions and to perceive distance—a skill known as **depth perception**—is due largely to the fact that we have two eyes. Because there is a certain distance between the eyes, a slightly different image reaches each retina. The brain then integrates these two images into one composite view. But it does not ignore the difference in images, which is known as **binocular disparity**; the disparity allows the brain to estimate the distance of an object from us.

You can get a sense of binocular disparity for yourself. Hold a pencil at arm's length and look at it first with one eye and then with the other. There is little difference between the two views relative to the background. Now bring the pencil just 6 inches away from your face, and try the same thing. This time you will perceive a greater difference between the two views.

The fact that the discrepancy between the images in the two eyes varies according to the distance of objects that we view provides us with a means of determining distance: If we view two objects, and one is considerably closer to us than another, the retinal disparity will be relatively large and we will have a greater sense of depth between the two. On the other hand, if the two objects are a similar distance from us, the retinal disparity will be minor, and we will perceive them as being a similar distance from us.

Filmmakers, whose medium compels them to project images in just two dimensions, have tried to create the illusion of depth perception by using two cameras, spaced slightly apart, to produce slightly different images, each destined for a different eye. In a 3-D movie, the two images are projected simultaneously. This produces a double image, unless special glasses are worn to allow each image to be viewed by the eye for which it is intended. The special glasses—familiar to moviegoers since the first 3-D movie, *Bwana Devil*, appeared in 1952—provide a genuine sense of depth. Similar techniques are being developed to show 3-D movies on television (Rogers, 1988a).

Just as binocular disparity is brought about by our two separate eyes, the presence of two ears helps with sound localization, the process by which we identify the origin of a sound. Because the ears are several inches apart, wave patterns in the air enter each ear at a slightly different time, permitting the brain to use the discrepancy to locate the place from which the sound is originating. In addition, the two outer ears delay or amplify sounds of particular frequencies to different degrees (Batteau, 1967; Butler, 1987; Sorkin, Wightman, Kistler, & Elvers, 1989).

Depth perception: The ability to view the world in three dimensions and to perceive distance

Binocular disparity: The difference between the images that reach the retina of each eye; this disparity allows the brain to estimate distance

Moviegoers in the 1950s, such as these people watching *Bwana Devil*, could enjoy a sense of three-dimensionality by wearing specially designed glasses.

It appears that the edges of this road come closer together as they move away from the driver, illustrating the depth cue of linear perspective.

In many Renaissance paintings, such as Raphael's *Marriage of the Virgin* (1502), perspective is used to convey a sense of depth in three-dimensional objects such as human figures and architectural structures.

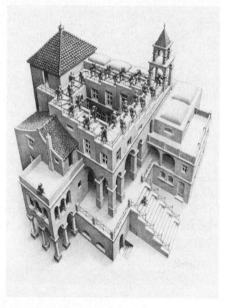

The clever use of linear perspective cues in the M. C. Escher painting creates an impossible scene, as monks walk along a staircase that never ends.

Monocular cues: Signals that allow us to perceive distance and depth with just one eye

Motion parallax: The change in position of the image of an object on the retina as the head moves, providing a monocular cue to distance

However, it is important to realize that depth or location can be perceived even by a single sense organ. For example, it is not always necessary to use two eyes to perceive depth; certain cues permit us to obtain a sense of depth and distance with just one eye (Burnham, 1983). These cues are known as **monocular cues**. One monocular cue—**motion parallax**—is the change in position of an object on the retina as the head moves from side to side. The brain is able to calculate the distance of the object by the amount of change in the retinal image. Similarly, experience has taught us that if two objects are the same size, the one that makes a smaller image on the retina is farther away than the one that provides a larger image—an example of the monocular cue of **relative size**.

Finally, anyone who has ever seen railroad tracks that seem to join together in the distance knows that distant objects appear to be closer together than nearer ones, a phenomenon called linear perspective. People use **linear perspective** as a monocular cue in estimating distance, allowing the two-dimensional retinal image to register the three-dimensional world (Bruce & Green, 1990).

Motion Perception: As the World Turns

When a batter tries to hit a ball that has been pitched, the most important factor is the motion of the ball. How is a batter able to judge the speed and location of a target that is moving at some 90 miles per hour?

The answer rests, in part, on several cues that provide us with relevant information about the perception of motion. For one thing, the perceived movement of an object across the retina is typically made relative to some stable, unmoving background. Moreover, if the stimulus is heading toward us, the image on the retina may expand in size, filling more and more of the visual field. In such cases, we assume that the stimulus is approaching—and not that it is an expanding stimulus viewed at a constant distance.

It is not, however, just the movement of images across the retina that brings about the perception of motion. If it were, we would perceive the world as moving every time we moved our heads. Instead, one of the critical things we learn about perception is to factor information about head and eye movements along with information about changes in the retinal image.

In some cases, movement is so fast that we are unable to follow it. In those instances, we may be able to anticipate where an object will end up on the basis of our prior experience. For example, computer tracking of baseball pitches has shown that most fast balls thrown in major-league games travel too fast for the eye to follow. Indeed, if a batter tried to follow a fast ball from the moment it left a pitcher's hand, he would lose sight of it by the time it got about 5 feet from the plate (Bahill & Laritz, 1984). Research suggests that good hitters take their eyes off the ball during the middle of its trip and shift their vision closer to home plate, waiting for the ball's arrival and (hoped-for) impact with the bat. Thus, instead of relying on the raw sensory input from the traveling ball—the process of sensation—they employ perceptual processes, using what they have learned to expect how balls travel.

Selective Attention: Sorting Out the World

The scene: a crowded, noisy party. As the woman next to you drones on about her new car, you suddenly hear snatches of conversation from behind you about your friend Terry, who seems to have left the party with another guest. Straining to hear what is being said by the person behind you, you lose track of what the woman is saying about her car—until suddenly you realize she has asked a question that requires a response. Brightly you say, "Pardon me—I didn't hear what you said, with all the noise."

Anyone who has been stuck listening to a bore go on and on about something trivial is probably familiar with situations similar to the one described above. Psychologists interested in perception are also familiar with circumstances such as this one, in which there are many stimuli to pay attention to simultaneously. The psychologist's interest lies primarily in the question of how we are able to sort out and make sense of multiple stimuli.

Relative size: The phenomenon by which, if two objects are the same size, the one that makes a smaller image on the retina is perceived to be farther away.

Linear perspective: The phenomenon by which distant objects appear to be closer together than nearer objects.

Selective attention must be used to find the figure of Waldo in the "Where's Waldo?" drawings by Martin Handford.

Selective attention: The perceptual process of choosing a stimulus to attend to

Stroop task: An exercise requiring the division of our attention between two competing stimuli—the meaning of words and the colors in which they are written

Dichotic (dy KOT ik) **listening:** A procedure in which an individual wears earphones through which different messages are sent to each ear at the same time

Selective attention is the perceptual process of choosing which stimulus to pay attention to. We are especially attentive to stimuli that appear exceptionally bright, large, loud, novel, or high in contrast. We also pay greater attention to stimuli that are particularly meaningful or relevant to our own motivations (Whalen & Liberman, 1987; Posner & Presti, 1987). For example, if we feel hungry, we are more apt to be sensitive to food and food-related stimuli.

Advertisers are well aware of the phenomenon of selective attention. For instance, advertisements often include bright contrasts, and television and radio commercials are typically broadcast at higher volumes than the shows they sponsor. Announcers in advertisements speak more rapidly than people usually do. Furthermore, television and radio ads are often run at times of the day when people are particularly sensitive to their content (as when food advertisements are shown at the dinner hour).

In some cases, our attention must be divided between two stimuli. For instance, try the test shown in Figure 5-9, in which you are asked to say aloud the color of the ink used in each of the words—not the color the word spells out. Known as the **Stroop task**, the exercise is a frustratingly difficult one because it encompasses the perception of two powerful stimuli, and you are forced to divide your attention between the color and the meaning of the words. Because both are potent stimuli and because, like most people, you are more experienced with reading than with naming colors, your attention is apt to be drawn away from the color of the ink toward the meaning of the words (Stroop, 1935; Cohen, Dunbar, & McClelland, 1990; MacLeod, 1991).

In order to study selective attention in the auditory realm, psychologists have developed a procedure called **dichotic listening**, whereby a person wears ear-

BLUE   GREEN
GREEN   ORANGE
PURPLE   ORANGE
GREEN   BLUE
RED   RED
GRAY   GRAY
RED   BLUE
BLUE   PURPLE

FIGURE 5-9

To try the Stroop task, name the colors in which each of these words are printed as quickly as you can, ignoring the word that is spelled out. For most people, the task is frustratingly difficult.

phones through which a different message is sent to each ear at the same time. The individual is asked to repeat one of the messages aloud as it comes into one ear—a process known as **shadowing**, since the listener's voice acts as a verbal "shadow" of the message being received.

The question of interest is not so much whether the person is able to shadow the message adequately (most people can do so fairly easily); instead, it revolves around the effects of the message coming into the other ear. It turns out that although the content of the second message typically cannot be recalled, certain characteristics of the message can be remembered (Cherry, 1953). For instance, listeners accurately report whether the speaker was a man or a woman and whether the sex of the speaker changed during the course of the message. About one-third of the time, they can also report hearing whether their names were spoken.

One factor that seems particularly important is the meaningfulness of the message being shadowed. If a message that is being shadowed from one ear suddenly switches to the other, subjects generally "follow" the message to the second ear and begin to shadow from the second ear, even though they have been specifically instructed to shadow only what is being heard in the first ear (see Figure 5-10). Moreover, they are usually not even aware that they have made the switch (Treisman, 1960).

Experiments such as these suggest that although people may fully concentrate on only one message at a time, they still pay attention on some level to other information. This, then, explains our ability to eavesdrop on one conversation at a party but to know when it is time to make a response to someone to whom we are supposedly listening at the same time. Furthermore, these findings

Shadowing: A technique used during dichotic listening in which a subject is asked to repeat one of the messages aloud as it comes into one ear

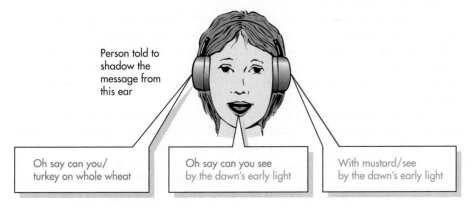

Person told to shadow the message from this ear

Oh say can you/ turkey on whole wheat

Oh say can you see by the dawn's early light

With mustard/see by the dawn's early light

FIGURE 5-10

A shadowing experiment. Subjects are told to shadow—or repeat—only the message being heard in the one ear indicated in the figure, as the two messages shown in the captions are heard simultaneously. Although subjects are unaware that they are doing it, if the message switches to the opposite ear, they will typically begin to shadow that message, despite the experimenter's instructions.

Can you raise your self esteem or improve your memory through hidden, subliminal perception? Probably not—although it may make you *think* you feel better and remember more.

Subliminal perception refers to the perception of messages about which we have no awareness. The stimulus may be a word, a sound, or even a smell that activates the sensory system, but that is not intense enough to be reported as having been experienced by a person. For instance, people may report being unable to perceive a word momentarily flashed on a screen in front of them. Later, though, they may behave in a way that indicates they actually saw it, providing evidence for subliminal perception. Specifically, experiments have shown that people who are exposed so briefly to a descriptive label that they cannot report seeing it later form impressions that are influenced by the label to which they were exposed (Bargh & Pietromonoco, 1982).

Yet does this mean that subliminal messages can actually lead to significant changes in attitudes or behavior? The answer is emphatically no, according to the most recent evidence. In a well-controlled experiment, for example, psychologist Anthony Greenwald and colleagues gave volunteers who wanted to improve either their self-esteem or their

SUBLIMINAL MESSAGES: UNDERCOVER PERCEPTION?

memories audiotapes that had been purchased from three manufacturers (Greenwald, Spangenberg, Pratkanis, & Eskenazi, 1991). The audible content of the tapes consisted of classical music, popular music, or sounds of the surf or woods. However, according to their manufacturers, subliminal audio messages relevant to either improved self-esteem or memory were repeated softly on the tapes.

In order to fully test the effects of the messages, the experimenters manipulated the labels on some of the tapes. Consequently, some participants who thought they were getting a self-esteem–enhancing tape actually were given a memory-improving tape, and some subjects who received a tape labeled as if it were a memory-improving tape actually received one designed to offer self-esteem improvement. Some subjects, of course, received tapes that were correctly labeled.

The results were clear: After a month of use, neither the self-esteem nor the memory tape had any effect on actual self-esteem or memory. What did matter, though, was the label on the tape. Participants who

thought they received a self-esteem tape (whether it was really a self-esteem or a memory tape) tended to report an improvement in their self-esteem; and those who thought they had listened to a memory tape tended to report that their memory had improved, regardless of the true nature of the tape.

In sum, the subliminal messages contained on the tapes seemed to have no real consequences. This conclusion sums up the state of our knowledge about subliminal perception: Although we are able to perceive at least some kinds of information about which we are unaware, such information appears to have little consequential effect.

Still, claims about the effectiveness of subliminal messages continue to be made. For instance, the parents of two boys who committed suicide sued the rock band Judas Priest because of subliminal messages allegedly embedded in their music (Neely, 1990). The parents contended that their sons had killed themselves after listening repeatedly to a subliminal message saying "Do it!" in a song with lyrics discussing the hopelessness of life. The judge and jury disagreed, as would most psychologists who study the issue of subliminal perception.

Subliminal perception: The perception of messages about which a person has no awareness

have raised the possibility that we may perceive information, and even learn it, entirely unawares—a possibility that is not well founded, as we discuss in the Psychology at Work box.

The phenomena involved in selective attention are of particular importance to people whose jobs require the constant monitoring of gauges or dials, such as pilots, air traffic controllers, and nuclear power plant operators. Ironically, however, research has shown that as the importance of accurately attending to deviations from normal readings increases, people are less successfully able to carry out the task (Wickens, 1984).

For example, in the late 1970s the nuclear power plant at Three Mile Island suffered a loss of cooling fluid that ultimately led to the leak of clouds of radioactive steam. At the time, information was available that could have rectified the problem at an early stage. However, the operators on duty attended only to certain portions of the information, which turned out to be erroneous. Had they been attentive to information that was indicated on other instruments, they would have been able to stop the leakage before serious damage had been done.

In order to increase the accuracy with which people are able to scan and selectively attend to many stimuli simultaneously, psychologists have developed several principles for designing instruments that provide important information (Sanders & McCormick, 1987). Among the major ones are minimizing the number of sources of information, simplifying the display of information, and keeping sources of information physically close to one another. These guidelines have helped to improve the accuracy of perception as well as to reduce stress levels among those workers monitoring the instruments (Wiener & Nagel, 1988). Furthermore, they have helped automobile manufacturers to design automobile dashboards that optimize relevant information while keeping distractions to a minimum.

RECAP AND REVIEW II

RECAP

◀ Depth perception occurs because of binocular disparity, motion parallax, and the relative size of images on the retina.

◀ The movement of images across the retina, combined with information about head and eye movements, brings about the perception of motion.

◀ Selective attention is the perceptual process of choosing which stimulus to pay attention to.

REVIEW

1. When a car passes you on the road and appears to shrink as it gets farther away, a perceptual phenomenon allows you to realize that the car does not get smaller, but rather farther away. What is the name of this phenomenon? *linear prospective*

2. Two different theories have been used to describe the phenomenon of perceptual constancy. Match the theory with its definition.

   _b_ 1. Ecological theory   a. Prior experience and expectations are used to infer an object's location.

   _a_ 2. Constructive theory   b. Relationships among different objects in the entire scene provide clues about sizes.

3. _Depth perception_ is the ability to view the world in three dimensions instead of two, while _sound localization_ is the ability to trace the origin of a sound.

4. The eyes use a technique known as _binocular disparity_ which makes use of the differing images each eye sees to give three dimensions to sight.

5. The closer an object is to one's face, the smaller the binocular disparity. True or false? _False - opposite_

6. Match the monocular cues with their definitions.

   _c_ 1. Relative size   a. Straight lines seem to join together as they become more distant.

   _a_ 2. Linear perspective   b. The change in position of an object on the retina as the head moves.

   _b_ 3. Motion parallax   c. If two objects are the same size, the one producing a smaller retinal image is farther away.

Ask Yourself

As your biology professor continues his lecture on the evolution of the fruit fly, you find yourself listening to two people behind you who are talking about a friend of yours. What perceptual phenomenon permits this behavior? How well will you remember what your professor has said?

(Answers to review questions are on page 154.)

PERCEPTION IN EVERYDAY LIFE

For sight follows gracious contours, and unless we flatter its pleasure by proportionate alternations of these parts (so that by adjustment we offset the amount to which it suffers illusions), an uncouth and ungracious aspect will be presented to the spectators.

(a)

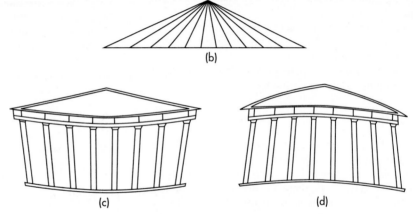

(b)

(c)   (d)

FIGURE 5-11

In building the Parthenon, the Greeks constructed an architectural wonder that looks perfectly straight, with right angles at every corner, as in (*a*). However, if it had been built with completely true right angles, it would have looked as it does in (*b*), due to the visual illusion illustrated in (*c*). To compensate for this illusion, the Parthenon was designed to have a slight upward curvature, as shown in (*d*). (Coren & Ward, 1989, p. 5.)

The phenomenon to which Vitruvius, a Greek architect who lived around 30 B.C., was referring in such elegant language is that people do not always view the world accurately. Consequently, Vitruvius argued that we must consider how people's eyes and brains perceive buildings when designing architectural works.

Consider the Parthenon, one of the most famous buildings of ancient Greece. Although it looks true and straight to the eye, it was actually built with a bulge on one side. This protrusion fools viewers into thinking it is straight. If it didn't have that bulge—and quite a few other "tricks" like it, such as columns that incline inward—it would look as if it were crooked and about to fall down.

The fact that the Parthenon appears to be completely upright, with straight lines and right angles at every corner, is the result of a series of visual illusions. **Visual illusions** are physical stimuli that consistently produce errors in perception. In the case of the Parthenon, the building appears to be completely square, as illustrated in Figure 5-11(*a*). However, had it actually been built that way, it would look to us as it does in Figure 5-11(*b*). The reason for this is the illusion

Visual illusion: A physical stimulus that consistently produces errors in perception (often called an optical illusion)

illustrated in 5-11(*c*), which makes angles placed above a line appear as if they were bent. To offset the illusion, the Parthenon was actually constructed as in Figure 5-11(*d*), with a slight upward curvature.

Such perceptual insights did not stop with the Greeks; modern-day architects and designers also take visual distortions into account in their planning. For example, the New Orleans Superdome makes use of several visual tricks: Its seats vary in color throughout the stadium in order to give the appearance, from a distance, that there is always a full house. The carpeting in some of the sloping halls has perpendicular stripes that make people slow their pace by producing the perception that they are moving faster than they actually are. The same illusion is used at toll booths on superhighways: Stripes painted on the pavement in front of the toll booths make drivers feel that they are moving more rapidly than they actually are and cause them to decelerate quickly.

Visual Illusions: Misperceptions of the Eye

The implications of visual illusions go beyond the attractiveness of buildings. For instance, suppose you were an air traffic controller watching a radar screen like the one shown in Figure 5-12(*a*). You might be tempted to sit back and relax as the two planes, whose flight paths are indicated in the figure, drew closer and closer together. If you did, however, you might end up with an air disaster: Although it looks as if the two planes will miss each other, they are headed for a collision. In fact, investigation has suggested that some 70 to 80 percent of all airplane accidents are caused by pilot errors of one sort or another (O'Hare & Roscoe, 1990).

The flight-path illustration provides an example of a well-known visual illusion called the **Poggendorf illusion**. As you can see in Figure 5-12(*b*), the Poggendorf illusion, when stripped down to its basics, gives the impression that line X would pass *under* line Y if it were extended through the pipelike figure, instead of heading directly toward line Y as it actually does.

The Poggendorf illusion is just one of many that consistently fool the eye (Perkins, 1983; Greist-Bousquet & Schiffman, 1986). Another is the one illustrated in Figure 5-13 called the **Müller-Lyer illusion**. Although the two lines are the same length, the one with the arrow tips pointing inward [Figure 5-13(*a*), top] appears to be longer than the one with the arrow tips pointing outward [Figure 5-13(*b*), bottom].

Although all kinds of explanations for visual illusions have been suggested, most concentrate either on the eye's visual sensory apparatus itself or—as in Figure 5-14—on the interpretation that is given a figure by the brain. Visual

Poggendorf illusion: An illusion involving a line that passes diagonally through two parallel lines

Müller-Lyer illusion: An illusion in which two lines of the same length appear to be of different lengths because of the direction of the arrows at the ends of each line; the line with arrows pointing out appears shorter than the line with arrows pointing in

FIGURE 5-12(*a*)

Put yourself in the shoes of a flight controller and look at the flight paths of the two planes on this radar screen. A first glance suggests that they are headed on different courses and will not hit each other. But now take a ruler and lay it along the two paths. Your career as a flight controller might well be over if you were guiding the two planes and you allowed them to continue without a change in course. (Coren, Porac, & Ward, 1984, p. 7.)

FIGURE 5-12(*b*)

The Poggendorf illusion, in which the two diagonal lines appear (incorrectly) as if they would not meet if extended toward each other.

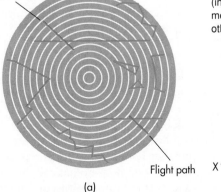

Flight path

Flight path

(a)

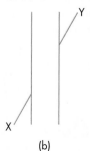

(b)

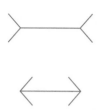

FIGURE 5-13(a)

The Müller-Lyer illusion, in which the upper horizontal line appears longer than the lower one.

FIGURE 5-13(b)

An explanation for the Müller-Lyer illusion suggests that the line with arrow points directed out is interpreted as the relatively close end of a rectangular object extended out toward us (as in the building corner), and the line with arrow points directed inward are viewed as the inside corner of a rectangle extending away from us (as in the room corner). Our previous experience with distance cues leads us to assume that the outside corner is closer than the inside corner and that the inside corner must therefore be longer.

FIGURE 5-14

The right-side-up, upside-down cake. It seems clear that the cake is missing one slice. But now hold the picture upside down; you're looking at just one slice of cake, but one that is right side up. The reason for this illusion is that you have no experience in viewing cake attached to the underside of a plate. When you see it for the first time with the plate on top, your brain reinterprets the situation in a way that seems more reasonable to you. Therefore, no matter how many times you rotate the picture back and forth, it will always appear as if the hands are holding the dish upright.

explanations for the Müller-Lyer illusion suggest, for example, that eye movements are greater when the arrow tips point inward, making us perceive the line as longer than when the arrow tips face outward.

Other evidence suggests that the cause of the illusion rests on the brain's interpretive errors. For instance, one hypothesis assumes that the Müller-Lyer illusion is a result of the meaning we give to each of the lines (Gregory, 1978). When we see the top line in Figure 5-13(a), we tend to perceive it as if it were the inside corner of a room extending away from us, as illustrated on the right in Figure 5-13(b). On the other hand, when we view the bottom line in Figure 5-13(a), we perceive it as the relatively close outside corner of a rectangular object such as the building on the left in Figure 5-13(b). Because previous experience leads us to assume that the outside corner is closer than the inside corner, we make the further assumption that the inside corner must therefore be larger.

Given all the underlying assumptions, it may seem unlikely that this explanation is valid, but there is a good degree of convincing evidence for it. One of the most telling pieces of support comes from cross-cultural studies that show that people raised in areas where there are few right angles—such as the Zulu in Africa—are much less susceptible to the illusion than people who grow up where most structures are built using right angles and rectangles (Segall, Campbell, & Herskovits, 1966).

Several kinds of cultural factors affect the ways in which we perceive the world. Consider, for example, the drawing in Figure 5-15. Sometimes called the "devil's tuning fork," it is likely to produce a mind-boggling effect, as the center tine of the fork alternates between appearing and disappearing.

Now try to reproduce the drawing on a piece of paper. Chances are that the task is nearly impossible for you—unless you are a member of an African tribe with little experience with western cultures. For such individuals, the task is simple; they have no trouble in reproducing the figure. The reason seems to be that western people automatically interpret the drawing as something that cannot exist in three dimensions, and they are therefore inhibited from reproducing it.

The African tribal members, on the other hand, do not make the assumption that the figure is "impossible" and instead view it in two dimensions, which enables them to copy the figure with ease (Deregowski, 1973).

Cultural differences are also reflected in depth perception. A western viewer of Figure 5-16 would interpret the drawing as one in which the hunter is trying to spear the antelope in the foreground while an elephant stands under the tree in the background. A member of an isolated African tribe, however, interprets the scene very differently by assuming that the hunter is aiming at the elephant. Westerners use the difference in sizes between the two animals as a cue that the elephant is farther away than the antelope (Hudson, 1960).

The misinterpretations created by visual illusions are ultimately due, then, to errors in both fundamental visual processing and the way the brain interprets

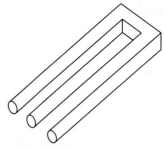

FIGURE 5-15

The "devil's tuning fork" has three prongs . . . or does it have two?

FIGURE 5-16

Is the man about to spear the elephant or the antelope? Westerners assume that the differences in size between the two animals indicate that the elephant is farther away, and therefore the man is aiming for the antelope. On the other hand, members of some African tribes, not used to depth cues in two-dimensional drawings, assume that the man is aiming for the elephant. The same lack of depth cues can be seen in the art of various cultures, such as this manuscript illumination from India. [The drawing is based on Deregowski.]

(a)

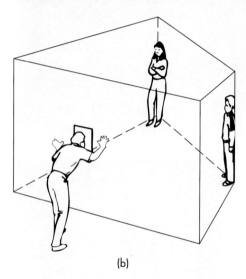

(b)

FIGURE 5-17

Despite the fact that the two people in (a) look like a giant and a dwarf, the woman is actually considerably taller than the child. The reason for their perceived differences in size is that we assume that the room is rectangular, with the back walls at right angles to the side walls. Actually, the room forms a trapezoid, as the floor plan (b) shows, and the woman seen in (a) is standing considerably farther back than the child. Because the images that reach our retina differ—the image of the woman is considerably smaller than that of the child—we make the only logical assumption: There is a size discrepancy. In fact, even when we know the truth about the room, the illusion is compelling and it is hard to dispel the notion of size discrepancy. (Baron Wolman/ Woodfin Camp & Associates.)

the information it receives (see also Figure 5-17). But visual illusions also illustrate something fundamental about perception that makes them more than mere psychological curiosities: There is a basic connection between our prior knowledge, needs, motivations, and expectations about how the world is put together and the way we perceive it. Our view of the world is very much a function, then, of fundamental psychological factors. Furthermore, each of us perceives the environment in a way that is unique and special—a fact that allows each of us to make our own special contribution to the world.

The Informed Consumer of Psychology
Discovering and Treating Dyslexia

At first glance, Chris King seems to represent a model of success. He was president of the senior class at Staples High School in Westport, Connecticut, and he played the lead role in the drama club's production of *Mr. Roberts.* After high school, he graduated from Northwestern University, and he received a graduate degree from Columbia University Teacher's College. Today he is a successful entrepreneur.

However, Chris would be the first to concede that he is far from an ideal model. In his words: "I reverse letters when I read and have trouble taking my thoughts and organizing them on paper," he explained recently. "If I'm rushed, I'll mix words up and come out with something like 'attack-a-heart.' I've learned that I can do just about anything I set out to do, but I have to work a lot harder than other people to do it" [Fiske, 1984, 12(1)].

Chris King suffers from dyslexia. So do perhaps as many as 10 percent of all Americans. **Dyslexia** is a reading disability with a perceptual basis. To a d̲yslexic, every l̲ett̲er t̲hat is u̲nderlin̲ed in t̲his s̲entenc̲e might app̲ear to b̲e r̲ev̲ersed. Dyslexics often have handwriting that is difficult to read, confuse right and left, make unusual and very obvious spelling errors, and appear clumsy in comparison with their peers (Nicolson & Fawcett, 1990; Pavlidis & Fisher, 1986).

The causes of dyslexia are cloaked in mystery, although recent evidence suggests that it involves a brain malfunction relating to the sense of vision. Specifically, researchers have found evidence that some of the major pathways to the brain from the eyes may be out of synch with one another in people with dyslexia. Consequently, visual information does not reach the brain in the proper sequence, leading to the difficulties experienced by dyslexics (Livingston et al., 1991).

However, such evidence is preliminary, and researchers have yet to identify a definitive cause for the disorder. Whatever the cause, it is clear that dyslexia is not related to low intelligence. Many well-known individuals, including inventor Thomas Edison, sculptor Auguste Rodin, President Woodrow Wilson, and actor Tom Cruise, were or are dyslexic.

What should be done if a child is suspected of having dyslexia? Most important, a psychologist who specializes in learning disabilities should be consulted. The psychologist will conduct a series of tests designed to measure the level of perceptual skills that the child has and will also analyze the specific nature of the child's perceptual errors. Most children, at one time or another, make the kinds of mistakes that dyslexics make, and so it is important that a specialist and not just the child's parents or a classroom teacher make the diagnosis.

Over the past few years, many new treatment techniques have been devised. Practice with sounding out words is usually assumed to be the key to successful intervention. Children practice viewing a letter, hearing its sound, pronouncing it, and writing it over and over again. Once they master the basics, they try to create words from the letters and sounds. Building the self-esteem of children with dyslexia is also an important component of any successful treatment program, since such children often experience scholastic failure. To build self-confidence, one should try to emphasize a dyslexic's strengths in other areas, which are often considerable. In addition, older students with dyslexia should make their disability known to their instructors and should try to arrange for alternate test-taking procedures—such as oral tests. (Even standardized tests, such as the SATs, can be taken in an untimed version if prior arrangements are made.)

Although recent research finds that some children may outgrow dyslexia (Shaywitz et al., 1992), for many people dyslexia is a problem that continues throughout life. Consequently, it is possible that an adult suffering from reading problems might be mildly dyslexic (Bruck, 1990). This is especially true because in the past many cases of dyslexia were overlooked or misdiagnosed. If you hold that suspicion—about yourself, a relative, or a friend—the best course of action is to arrange for an examination by a psychologist specializing in perceptual disorders. Dyslexia is no longer the mystery it once was, and the reading difficulties experienced by dyslexics can be overcome with appropriate training.

Dyslexia (dis LEX ee uh): A disability with a perceptual basis that can result in the reversal of letters during reading and writing, confusion between left and right, and difficulties in spelling

Despite his dyslexia, Chris King had an impressive high school record.

RECAP

Visual illusions are physical stimuli that consistently produce errors in perception. Among the most common are the Poggendorf illusion and the Müller-Lyer illusion. Illusions occur both in visual processing and in the way the brain interprets this information.

Dyslexia is a reading disability that is caused by perceptual difficulties. People with dyslexia reverse letters, confuse right and left, and make unusual and obvious spelling errors.

REVIEW

1. Visual illusions have been demonstrated to be a function of the structure of the brain, and are therefore universal across cultures. True or false? _____*False*_____
2. Which of the following has *not* been proposed as an explanation of why we perceive visual illusions?

a. Variations in the eye's visual sensory apparatus
b. Small distance between eyeballs
c. Interpretive errors made by the brain
d. Previous learning experience

3. You ask the person sitting next to you if you can borrow her notes from the previous class. When she hands them to you, you notice that many of the letters are reversed, the handwriting is poor, and there are many spelling errors. What disorder might cause this anomaly? *Dyslexia*

Ask Yourself

As noted in our discussion of visual illusions, people from different cultures are not subject to the same illusions that we are, and we are not subject to some of their visual illusions. Armed with this information, you are asked to guide an Australian aborigine on a walking tour of Manhattan. What problems might occur? How would you overcome them? Do you think you would gain anything from such an experience?

(Answers to review questions are on page 161.)

■ *What principles underlie our organization of the stimuli to which our sense organs are exposed, allowing us to make sense of our environment?*

1. Perception is the process by which we sort out, interpret, analyze, and integrate stimuli to which our senses are exposed. Perception follows the gestalt laws of organization. These laws provide a series of principles by which we organize bits and pieces of information into meaningful wholes, known as gestalts. Among the most important laws are those of closure, proximity, similarity, and simplicity.

2. Work on figure-ground distinctions shows that perception is a constructive process in which people go beyond the stimuli that are physically present and try to construct a meaningful situation. Moreover, the gestalt psychologists demonstrated convincingly that perception follows the general rule: "The whole is greater than the sum of its parts."

3. Feature analysis considers how we consider a shape, pattern, or object in terms of the individual elements that make it up. These component features are then combined into a representation of the whole object in the brain. Finally, this combination of features is compared against existing memories, permitting identification of the object.

4. Processing of perceptual stimuli occurs in both a top-down and a bottom-up fashion. In top-down processing, perception is guided by higher-level knowledge, experience, expectations, and motivations. In bottom-up processing, perception involves recognition and processing of information about the individual components of stimuli.

5. Perceptual constancy permits us to perceive stimuli as unvarying and consistent, despite changes in the environment or the appearance of the objects being perceived. Two competing theories seek to explain constancy effects: constructive theory, which suggests that we use our prior experience about size to make unconscious inferences about location, and ecological theory, which suggests that the relationship between different environmental cues in a scene gives us information about their size. Probably both processes work together to produce perceptual constancy.

■ *How are we able to perceive the world in three dimensions when our retinas are capable of sensing only two-dimensional images?*

6. Depth perception is the ability to perceive distance and to view the world in three dimensions, even though the images projected on our retinas are two-dimensional. We are able to judge depth and distance as a result of binocular disparity (the difference in images as seen by each of the eyes) and monocular cues, such as motion parallax (the apparent movement of objects as one's head moves from side to side), the relative size of images on the retina, and linear perspective.

7. Motion perception depends on several cues. They include the perceived movement of an object across our retina and information about how the head and eyes are moving.

■ *How do we sort out auditory stimuli, paying attention to particular stimuli and ignoring others?*

8. Selective attention is the perceptual process of choosing which stimulus to pay attention to. Psychologists study attention using a dichotic-listening procedure, in which a message is presented in each ear and the person is asked to repeat, or shadow, one of the messages.

■ *What clues do visual illusions give us about our understanding of general perceptual mechanisms?*

9. Visual illusions are physical stimuli that consistently produce errors in perception, causing judgments that do not accurately reflect the physical reality of the stimulus. Among the best-known illusions are the Poggendorf illusion and the Müller-Lyer illusion. Most evidence suggests that visual illusions are a result of errors in the brain's interpretation of visual stimuli.

10. Dyslexia is a reading disability that has a perceptual basis. People with dyslexia often reverse letters, have poor handwriting, make unusual and obvious spelling errors, and may appear clumsy. If dyslexia is properly diagnosed, treatment can be successful.

KEY TERMS AND CONCEPTS

perception (p. 136)
gestalt laws of organization (p. 137)
gestalts (p. 137)
closure (p. 138)
proximity (p. 138)
similarity (p. 138)
simplicity (p. 138)
figure (p. 138)
ground (p. 138)
feature analysis (p. 139)

geons (p. 141)
top-down processing (p. 141)
bottom-up processing (p. 142)
perceptual constancy (p. 144)
constructive theory (p. 145)
ecological theory (p. 146)
depth perception (p. 147)
binocular disparity (p. 147)
monocular cues (p. 148)
motion parallax (p. 148)
relative size (p. 149)

linear perspective (p. 149)
selective attention (p. 150)
Stroop task (p. 150)
dichotic listening (p. 150)
shadowing (p. 151)
subliminal perception (p. 152)
visual illusion (p. 154)
Poggendorf illusion (p. 155)
Müller-Lyer illusion (p. 155)
dyslexia (p. 159)

ANSWERS (REVIEW III):

1. False; visual illusions are in part culturally determined. **2.** b **3.** Dyslexia

STATES OF CONSCIOUSNESS

Ryan Shafer's father mourns his son.

RYAN SHAFER

Like most parents, I had thought of drug use as something you worried about when your kids got to high school. Now I know that, on the average, kids begin using drugs at 11 or 12, but at the time that never crossed our minds. Ryan had just begun attending mixed parties. He was playing Little League. In the eighth grade, Ryan started getting into a little trouble—one time he and another fellow stole a fire extinguisher, but we thought it was just a prank. Then his grades began to deteriorate. He began sneaking out at night. He would become belligerent at the drop of a hat, then sunny and nice again. By then he was pretty heavy into drugs, but we were denying what we saw. You build up this trust with your child, and the last thing you want to do is break it. But looking back, there were signs everywhere. His room was filled with bottles of eye drops, to cover the redness from smoking marijuana. Money was missing from around the house, and he began burning incense in his room.

It wasn't until Ryan fell apart at 14 that we started thinking about drugs. He had just begun McLean High School, and to him, it was like going to drug camp every day. Back then, everything was so available. He began cutting classes, a common tip-off, but we didn't hear from the school until he was flunking everything. It turned out that he was going to school for the first period, getting checked in, then leaving and smoking marijuana all day (Shafer, 1990, p. 82).

LOOKING AHEAD

Ryan's parents were soon to learn that marijuana was not the only drug that he was using. Ryan was what his friends called a "garbage head," someone who would try anything. He used cocaine, PCP, and alcohol, but his drug of choice was LSD. He became abusive and violent, kicking in doors and screaming at his parents.

After discovering the extent of his drug problem, his parents enrolled him in what was to be the first of several drug treatment programs. However, none of the treatments proved to be more than temporarily successful in stopping his drug use. Ultimately, Ryan stumbled onto an interstate highway in a drug-induced panic and was killed by a passing car. He was sixteen years old.

Ryan Shafer is but one of many people whose lives have been shattered by the use of drugs and alcohol. In fact, difficulties with drugs, including alcohol, remain one of western society's most vexing problems.

Ironically, though, the use of some kinds of drugs is viewed with tolerance by society. Social drinking is encouraged by a billion-dollar alcohol industry, drugs for medical and psychological disorders are routinely prescribed, and drinking coffee to decrease sleepiness is certainly a well-accepted practice. Furthermore, in some subcultures drug use is not only tolerated but actively encouraged. For instance, members of the Native American Church regularly smoke peyote, a drug that produces altered perceptions, in religious services.

The use of drugs is just one of the ways in which people change their state of **consciousness**, their awareness of the sensations, thoughts, and feelings being experienced at a given moment. Consciousness is our subjective understanding

Consciousness: A person's awareness of the sensations, thoughts, and feelings that he or she is experiencing at a given moment

"If you ask me, all three of us are in different states of awareness."

Psychologists agree that we may experience different states of consciousness.

of both the environment around us and our private internal world, unobservable to outsiders.

The nature of consciousness spans several dimensions. Consciousness can range from our perceptions while wide awake to the dreams we have during sleep, with wide variation in how aware we are of outside stimuli. In fact, some psychologists argue that "consciousness" is a term that should even be applied to mental experiences which we are not aware of. For example, it does seem that we process certain kinds of information with little or perhaps even no awareness, as we discussed in the last chapter. Consequently, some psychologists argue that the definition of consciousness ought to be expanded to include *all* mental experiences, whether or not we are aware of them. This broader definition, however, has not been widely accepted (Natsoulas, 1983).

It is clear, though, that even while we are awake, consciousness can vary from an active to a passive state (Hilgard, 1980). In more active states, we systematically carry out mental activity, thinking and considering the world around us. In passive waking states, thoughts and images come to us more spontaneously; we daydream or drift from one thought to another. Finally, changes in consciousness can vary in terms of whether they occur naturally, as when we drift from wakefulness into sleep, or are artificially induced, as in a drug "high."

Because consciousness is so personal a phenomenon—who can say that your consciousness is similar to or, for that matter, different from anyone else's?—psychologists have sometimes been reluctant to study it. In fact, some early psychological theoreticians suggested that the study of consciousness was out of bounds for the psychologist, since it could be understood only by relying on the "unscientific" introspections of subjects about what they were experiencing at a given moment. Proponents of this view argued that the study of consciousness was better left to philosophers, who could speculate at their leisure on such knotty issues as whether consciousness is separate from the physical body, how people know they exist, how the body and mind are related to each other, and how we identify what state of consciousness we are in at a given moment in time.

Most contemporary psychologists reject the view that the study of consciousness is unsuitable for the field of psychology. They argue instead that there are several approaches that allow the scientific study of consciousness. For example,

Peyote, a drug that produces an altered state of consciousness, has traditionally been used as part of Native American spiritual practices. Pictured here is the opening prayer of a Cree peyote ceremony in Saskatchewan.

recent insights into the biology of the brain allow measurement of brain-wave patterns under conditions of consciousness ranging from sleep to waking to hypnotic trances. Moreover, new understanding of the chemistry of drugs such as marijuana and alcohol has provided insights into the way they produce their pleasurable—and adverse—effects. Finally, psychologists have come to realize that there are actually several kinds of consciousness that may be studied separately. By concentrating on particular **altered states of consciousness**—those that differ from a normal, waking consciousness—they have been able to study the phenomenon of consciousness scientifically, even if the more difficult questions, such as whether our consciousness exists separately from our physical bodies, remain unanswered.

Although various kinds of altered states of consciousness produce widely disparate effects, all share some characteristics (Ludwig, 1969; Martindale, 1981). One is an alteration in our thinking, which may become shallow, illogical, or impaired in some way. In addition, our sense of time may become disturbed, and our perceptions of the world and of ourselves may be changed. We may experience a loss of self-control, doing things that we would never otherwise do. Finally, we may have a sense of ineffability—the inability to understand an experience rationally or describe it in words.

This chapter considers several states of consciousness, beginning with two that we have all experienced: sleeping and dreaming. Next, we turn to states of consciousness found under conditions of hypnosis and meditation. Finally, we examine drug-induced altered states of consciousness.

After reading this chapter, you will be able to answer questions such as these:

■ What are the different states of consciousness?

■ What happens when we sleep, and what are the meaning and function of dreams?

■ How much do we daydream?

■ What are the major sleep disorders and how can they be treated?

■ Are hypnotized people in an altered state of consciousness, and can they be hypnotized against their will?

■ What are the major classifications of drugs, and what are their effects?

Altered states of consciousness: Experiences of sensation or thought that differ from a normal waking consciousness

Donald J. Dorff, whose sleeping disorder was cured.

SLEEP AND DREAMS

The crowd roared as running back Donald Dorff, age 67, took the pitch from his quarterback and accelerated smoothly across the artificial turf. As Dorff braked and pivoted to cut back over tackle, a huge defensive lineman loomed in his path. One hundred twenty pounds of pluck, Dorff did not hesitate. But let the retired grocery merchandiser from Golden Valley, Minnesota, tell it:

"There was a 280-pound tackle waiting for me, so I decided to give him my shoulder. When I came to, I was on the floor in my bedroom. I had smashed into the dresser and knocked everything off it and broke the mirror and just made one heck of a mess. It was 1:30 A.M." (Long, 1987, p. 787).

Dorff, it turned out, was suffering from a rare condition afflicting some older men. The problem occurs when the mechanism that usually shuts down bodily movement during dreams does not function properly. People suffering from the malady have been known to hit others, smash windows, punch holes in walls—all the while being fast asleep.

Testing Your Knowledge of Sleep and Dreams

Although sleeping is something we all do for a significant part of our lives, many myths and misconceptions about the topic abound. To test your own knowledge of sleep and dreams, try answering the following questions before reading further.

1. Some people never dream. True or false? ____
2. Most dreams are caused by bodily sensations such as an upset stomach. True or false? ____
3. It has been proved that eight hours of sleep is needed to maintain mental health. True or false? ____
4. When people do not recall their dreams, it is probably because they are secretly trying to forget them. True or false? ____
5. Depriving someone of sleep will invariably cause the individual to become mentally unbalanced. True or false? ____
6. If we lose some sleep, we will eventually make up all the lost sleep the next night or another night. True or false? ____
7. No one has been able to go for more than forty-eight hours without sleep. True or false? ____
8. Everyone is able to sleep and breathe at the same time. True or false? ____
9. Sleep enables the brain to rest since there is little brain activity taking place during sleep. True or false? ____
10. Drugs have been proved to provide a long-term cure for sleeping difficulties. True or false? ____

Scoring: This is an easy set of questions to score, for every item is false. But don't lose any sleep if you missed them; they were chosen to represent the most common myths regarding sleep. (Items were drawn from a questionnarie developed by Palladino & Carducci, 1984.)

FIGURE 6-1

Testing your knowledge of sleep and dreams. (Adapted from Palladino & Carducci, 1984.)

Donald Dorff's problem had a happy ending: With the help of clonazepam, a drug that suppresses movement during dreams, his malady vanished. He now sleeps through the night in welcome repose.

The success of Dorff's treatment illustrates just one of the recent advances that has occurred in our understanding of sleep. Yet there are still many unanswered questions, including why we sleep, how much sleep we need, the meaning and function of dreams, and how to avoid insomnia. (Before you read on, you might want to test your knowledge of sleep and dreams by answering the questions in Figure 6-1.)

The Cycles of Sleep

Most of us consider sleep a time of quiet tranquility, as we set aside the tensions of the day and spend the night in uneventful slumber. However, a closer look at sleep shows that a good deal of activity occurs throughout the night, and what at first appears to be an undifferentiated state is, in fact, quite diverse.

Much of our knowledge of what happens during sleep comes from the **electroencephalogram** or **EEG**, which, as discussed in Chapter 3, is a measurement of electrical activity within the brain. When probes from an EEG machine are attached to the surface of a sleeping person's scalp and face, it becomes readily apparent that instead of being dormant, the brain is active throughout the night, producing electrical discharges that form systematic, wavelike patterns that change in height (or amplitude) and speed (or frequency) in regular sequences. Instruments that measure muscle and eye movements also reveal a good deal of physical activity.

Electroencephalogram (ee LEK tro en SEF uh lo gram) **(EEG):** measurement of electrical activity within the brain

People progress through four distinct stages of sleep during a night's rest, moving through cycles lasting about 90 minutes. Each of these four sleep stages is associated with a unique pattern of brain waves, as shown in Figure 6-2. Moreover, there are specific biological indicators of dreaming.

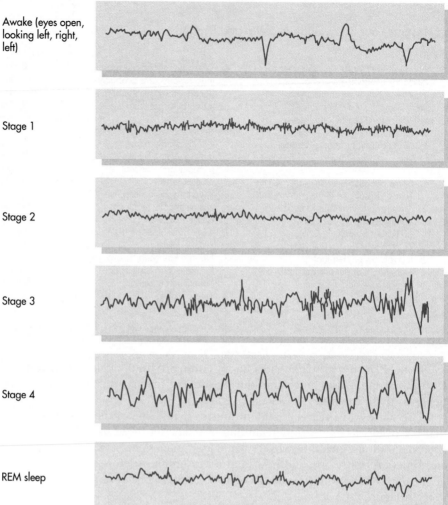

Awake (eyes open, looking left, right, left)

Stage 1

Stage 2

Stage 3

Stage 4

REM sleep

FIGURE 6-2

Brain-wave patterns (measured by an EEG apparatus) and eye movements in the different stages of sleep. (Cohen, 1979.)

Stage 1 sleep: The state of transition between wakefulness and sleep, characterized by relatively rapid, low-voltage brain waves

Stage 2 sleep: A sleep deeper than that of stage 1, characterized by sleep spindles

Stage 3 sleep: A sleep characterized by slow brain waves, with greater peaks and valleys in the wave pattern

Stage 4 sleep: The deepest stage of sleep, during which we are least responsive to outside stimulation

When people first go to sleep, they move from a waking state in which they are relaxed with their eyes closed—sometimes called stage 0 sleep—into **stage 1 sleep**, which is characterized by relatively rapid, low-voltage brain waves. This is actually a stage of transition between wakefulness and sleep. During stage 1 images sometimes appear; it's as if we were viewing still photos. However, true dreaming does not occur during the initial entry into this stage.

As sleep becomes deeper, people enter **stage 2 sleep**, which is characterized by a slower, more regular wave pattern. However, there are also momentary interruptions of sharply pointed waves called, because of their configuration, "sleep spindles." It becomes increasingly difficult to awaken a person from stage 2 sleep, which makes up about half of the total sleep of those in their early 20s.

As people drift into **stage 3 sleep**, the next stage of sleep, the brain waves become slower, with an appearance of higher peaks and lower valleys in the wave pattern. By the time sleepers arrive at *stage 4*, the pattern is even slower and more regular, and people are least responsive to outside stimulation.

As you can see in Figure 6-3, **stage 4 sleep** is most likely to occur during the early part of the night when a person first goes to sleep. In addition to passing through regular transitions between stages of sleep, then, people tend to sleep less and less deeply over the course of the night. In the first half of the evening,

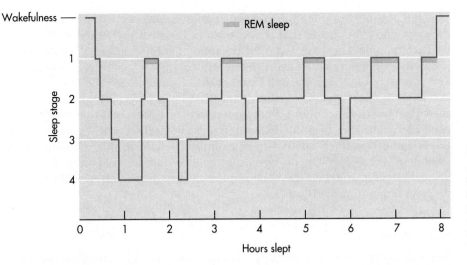

FIGURE 6-3
During the night, the typical sleeper passes through all four stages of sleep and several REM periods. [*Source:* Hartmann, E. (1967). *The biology of dreaming.* Springfield, IL: Charles C Thomas.]

our sleep is dominated by stages 3 and 4. The last half is characterized by lighter stages of sleep—as well as the phase of sleep during which dreams occur, as we discuss next (Dement & Wolpert, 1958).

REM Sleep: The Paradox of Sleep.   Several times a night, after sleepers cycle from higher stages back into stage 1 sleep, something curious happens: Their heart rate increases and becomes irregular, their blood pressure rises, their breathing rate increases, and males—even male infants—have erections. Most characteristic of this period is the back-and-forth movement of their eyes, as if they were watching an action-filled movie. This period of sleep is called **rapid eye movement**, or **REM, sleep.** REM sleep occupies a little over 20 percent of adults' total sleeping time.

Paradoxically, while all this activity is occurring, the major muscles of the body act as if they are paralyzed—except in rare cases such as Donald Dorff's—and it is hard to awaken the sleeper. In addition, REM sleep is usually accompanied by dreams which, whether people remember them or not, are experienced by *everyone* during some part of the night.

Rapid eye movement (REM) sleep: Sleep occupying around 20 percent of an adult's sleeping time, characterized by increased heart rate, blood pressure, and breathing rate; erections; eye movements; and the experience of dreaming

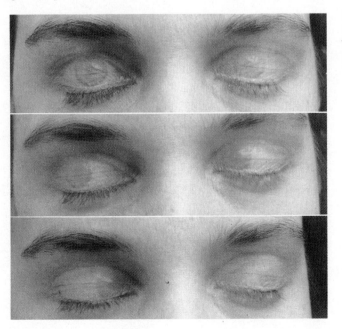

During REM sleep, our eyes move busily as if we were watching the images we see moving in our dreams.

One possible but still unproven explanation for rapid eye movements is that the eyes follow the action that is occurring in the dream (Dement, 1979). For instance, people who have reported dreaming about watching a tennis match just before they were awakened showed regular right-left-right eye movements, as if they were observing the ball flying back and forth across the net.

There is good reason to believe that REM sleep plays an important role in everyday human functioning. People deprived of REM sleep—by being awakened every time they begin to display the physiological signs of the stage—show a **rebound effect** when allowed to rest undisturbed. With this rebound effect, REM-deprived sleepers spend significantly more time in REM sleep than they normally would. It is as if the body requires a certain amount of REM sleep in order to function properly.

Rebound effect: An increase in REM sleep after one has been deprived of it

Is Sleep Necessary?

Sleep, in general, seems necessary for human functioning, although surprisingly enough this fact has not been firmly established. It is reasonable to expect that the body would require a tranquil "rest and relaxation" period in order to re-vitalize itself. However, several arguments suggest this is not the full explanation. For instance, most people sleep between seven and eight hours each night, but there is wide variability among individuals, with some people needing as little as three hours (see Figure 6-4).

Sleep requirements also vary over the course of a person's lifetime; as people age, they generally need less and less sleep. If sleep played a restorative function for the body, it is hard to see why the elderly would need less sleep than those who are younger.

Furthermore, people who have participated in sleep deprivation experiments, in which they were kept awake for stretches as long as 200 hours, have shown no lasting effects. They do experience weariness, lack of concentration, a decline in creativity, irritability, and a tendency toward hand tremors while they are being kept awake. However, after being allowed to sleep normally once again, they bounce back quickly and are able to perform at predeprivation levels after a few days (Dement, 1976).

FIGURE 6-4

Although most people report sleeping between eight and nine hours per night, the amount varies a great deal. (From Borbely, 1986, p. 43, and Kripke et al., 1979.)

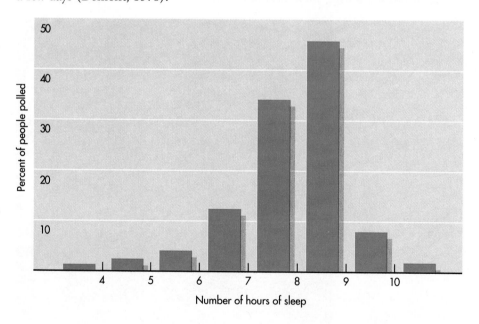

Even severe sleep deprivation—like that depicted in the movie *They Shoot Horses, Don't They?* about dance marathons in the 1930s—does not appear to have lasting effects once the individuals have resumed normal sleep schedules.

If you're worried, then, that long hours of study, work, or perhaps partying are ruining your health, you should feel heartened: As far as anyone can tell, you'll suffer no long-term consequences of such sleep deprivation (Eckholm, 1988). At the same time, though, a lack of sleep may make you feel irritable, slow your reaction time, and even lower your performance on academic tasks. A good night's rest is thus a reasonable goal (Angier, 1990b).

Circadian Rhythms: Life Cycles

The fact that we cycle back and forth between wakefulness and sleep is just one example of our body's circadian rhythms. **Circadian rhythms** (from the Latin *circa dies*, or "around a day,") are biological processes that occur repeatedly on approximately a twenty-four-hour cycle. Sleep and waking, for instance, occur naturally to the beat of an internal pacemaker which works on a cycle of about twenty-five hours. Several other bodily functions, such as body temperature, also work on circadian rhythms.

Circadian rhythms: Biological processes that occur repeatedly on approximately a twenty-four-hour cycle

These circadian cycles can be quite complex. For instance, sleepiness occurs not just in the evening, but throughout the day in regular patterns. As you can see in Figure 6-5, most of us tend to get drowsy in midafternoon—regardless of whether we have eaten a heavy lunch (Dement, 1989). The dip in alertness is due solely to time of day.

Circadian cycles are powerful—as anyone who has worked a night shift knows well. Even after a full night's work, people who work night shifts often have trouble sleeping during the day. Furthermore, they are less productive and more likely to have accidents than day workers. For example, it is probably no coincidence that the near-meltdown at the Three Mile Island nuclear plant occurred

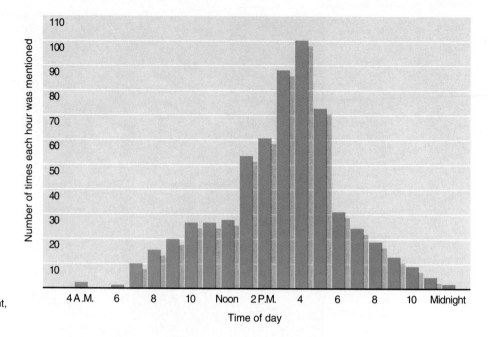

FIGURE 6-5
The hours that people report having the greatest difficulty staying awake. (Source: Dement, 1989.)

at 4:00 A.M. with a crew that had only recently switched to the night shift; that the Chernobyl reactor exploded at 1:23 A.M.; and that the release of deadly chemicals at the Bhopal chemical plant began with a series of errors just after midnight (Mapes, 1990; Moore-Ede, Sulzman, & Fuller, 1982).

Circadian rhythms can be modified, although the process is not easy, as people who have suffered from jet lag will testify. However, psychologists have recently developed at least one promising way of changing circadian rhythms. This work has far-ranging implications, as we discuss in the accompanying Cutting Edge box.

The Function and Meaning of Dreaming

I was sitting at my desk thinking about the movie I was going to see that evening. Suddenly I remembered that this was the day of my chemistry final! I felt awful; I hadn't studied a bit for it. In fact, I couldn't even remember where the class was held, and I had missed every lecture all semester. What could I do? I was in a panic, and began running across campus desperately searching for the classroom so that I could beg the professor to give me another chance. But I had to stop at every classroom building, looking in one room after another, hoping to find the professor and the rest of the class. It was hopeless; I knew I was going to fail and flunk out of college.

If you have had a dream similar to this—one that is common among people involved in academic pursuits—you know how utterly convincing are the panic and fear that events in the dream can bring about. Some dreams could not seem more real.

Nightmares: Unusually frightening dreams

Night terrors: Profoundly frightening nightmares which wake up the dreamer

Nightmares, unusually frightening dreams, occur fairly often: In one survey, almost half of a group of college students who kept records of their dreams over a two-week period reported having at least one nightmare. This works out to some 24 nightmares a year per person, on average (Wood & Bootzin, 1990).

Even more frightening than nightmares are **night terrors**, instances in which a sleeping individual experiences a profoundly frightening emotion and wakes

When the crew of the space shuttle *Columbia* wanted to reset their biological clocks in order to work the night shift in space, their first attempt was a total failure. For the two weeks before their mission was scheduled to depart, they forced themselves to stay up all night, watching old movies, and tried to sleep through the day. They ate breakfast in the evening, and dinner in the morning. The result was disappointing, though: They never acclimated to the new time change, couldn't eat or sleep well, and in general felt miserable (Rosenthal, 1991).

However, the crew got another chance. The mission was postponed for several months, and they tried a new technique. The astronauts were exposed to doses of bright lights over a period of three days. In just that time, their circadian rhythms shifted so radically that they were wide awake at night and craved sleep at dawn.

The astronauts accomplished this shift in sleep-waking cycles through a process pioneered by sleep re-

ILLUMINATING CIRCADIAN RHYTHMS

searcher Charles Czeisler. In his research, Czeisler found that people exposed to five hours of bright lights during the nighttime over a three-day period reset their internal clocks as much as twelve hours (Czeisler et al., 1989). The timing of the light could not be haphazard, however: The exposure had to be synchronized with particular phases of a person's circadian rhythm in order for it to be effective.

In later research, Czeisler confirmed his findings with people attempting to work through the night. He exposed a group of these subjects to five hours of light over a three-night period. The light was bright—as strong as the sunlight produced on a cloudy day. In comparison to the situation in which the same group of people were exposed only to normal light levels, the bright light produced a clear resetting of the subjects' circadian rhythms. When this occurred, the subjects showed significantly

greater alertness and thought more clearly at night. In contrast, when they were exposed to normal lighting, the subjects never succeeded in changing their circadian rhythms and they had great difficulty in sleeping soundly during the day (Czeisler et al., 1990).

It is still too early to know just why bright lights modify circadian rhythms. It does seem likely that the lights trick the part of the brain associated with circadian rhythms into thinking that night is actually day. It is clear, though, that Czeisler's work has enormous practical implications. For example, it may be that factory workers who must alternate between day and night shifts could prepare themselves by spending time under bright lights. Similarly, it is conceivable that airlines could shine bright lights on passengers during long flights to prepare them for the change in time zones at their destination. Better still, people reaching a new destination might spend a few days at the beach, soaking up some rays, in order to reset their internal clocks.

---

up, in some cases screaming in horror. Often the fear is so real that people cannot get back to sleep immediately and need time to regain their emotional composure.

On the other hand, most dreams are much less dramatic, recounting such everyday events as going to the supermarket or preparing a meal. We just seem to remember the more exciting ones more readily (Webb, 1979). The most common dreams are shown in Figure 6-6 on page 174.

Whether dreams have a specific function is a question that scientists have considered for many years. Sigmund Freud, for example, used dreams as a guide to the unconscious (Freud, 1900). In his theory of **unconscious wish fulfillment**, he proposed that dreams represented unconscious wishes that the dreamer wanted to fulfill. However, because these wishes were threatening to the dreamer's conscious awareness, the actual wishes—called the **latent content of dreams**—were disguised. The true subject and meaning of a dream, then, may have little to do with its overt story line, called by Freud the **manifest content of dreams**.

To Freud, it was important to pierce the armor of a dream's manifest content to understand its true meaning. To do this, Freud tried to get people to discuss their dreams, associating symbols in the dreams to events in the past. He also suggested that there were certain common symbols with universal meaning that

Unconscious wish fulfillment: A theory of Sigmund Freud, which proposes that dreams represent unconscious wishes that a dreamer wants to fulfill

Latent content of dreams: According to Freud, the "disguised" meanings of dreams, hidden by more obvious subjects

Manifest content of dreams: According to Freud, the overt story line of dreams

▶ **173**

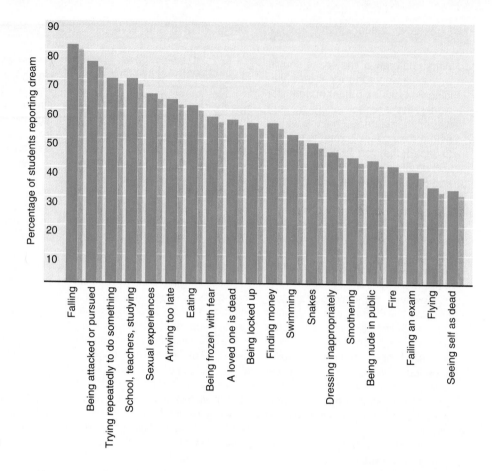

FIGURE 6-6

The twenty most common dreams reported by students. (Griffith, Miyago, & Tago, 1958.)

appeared in dreams. For example, to Freud, dreams in which the person was flying symbolized a wish for sexual intercourse. (See Table 6-1 for other common symbols.)

Today many psychologists reject Freud's view that dreams typically represent unconscious wishes and that particular objects and events in a dream are symbolic. Instead, the direct, overt action of a dream is considered the focal point in understanding its meaning. For example, a dream in which we are walking down a long hallway to take an exam for which we haven't studied does not relate to unconscious, unacceptable wishes; rather, it simply means we are concerned about an impending test. Even more complex dreams can often be interpreted in terms of everyday concerns and stress (Cook, Caplan, & Wolowitz, 1990).

TABLE 6-1

DREAM SYMBOLISM, ACCORDING TO FREUD

Symbol	Interpretation
Climbing up a stairway, crossing a bridge, riding an elevator, flying in an airplane, walking down a long hallway, entering a room, train traveling through a tunnel	Sexual intercourse
Apples, peaches, grapefruits	Breasts
Bullets, fire, snakes, sticks, umbrellas, guns, hoses, knives	Male sex organs
Ovens, boxes, tunnels, closets, caves, bottles, ships	Female sex organs

Moreover, we now know that some dreams reflect events occurring in the dreamer's environment as he or she is sleeping. For example, sleeping subjects in one experiment were sprayed with water while they were dreaming; these unlucky volunteers reported more dreams involving water than a comparison group of subjects who were left to sleep undisturbed (Dement & Wolpert, 1958). Similarly, it is not unusual to wake up to find that the doorbell that was being rung in a dream is actually an alarm clock telling us it is time to get up.

Although the content of dreams clearly can be affected by environmental stimuli, the question of *why* we dream remains unresolved, and several alternatives to Freud's theory have been proposed. According to the **reverse learning theory**, for instance, dreams have no meaning whatsoever. Instead, they represent a kind of reverse learning, in which we flush away unnecessary information that we have accumulated during the day. In this view, dreaming simply represents the reverse learning of material that ultimately would prove to be confusing to us. Dreams, then, are a kind of mental housecleaning of the brain, but have no meaning in and of themselves (Crick & Mitchison, 1983).

The **dreams-for-survival theory** proposes yet another function for dreams. According to this theory, dreams permit information critical for our daily survival to be reconsidered and reprocessed during sleep. Dreaming is seen as an inheritance from our animal ancestors, whose small brains were unable to sift sufficient information during waking hours. Consequently, dreaming provided a mechanism that permitted the processing of information twenty-four hours a day.

In this theory, dreams do have meaning. They represent concerns about our daily lives, illustrating the uncertainties, indecisions, ideas, and desires of our lives. Dreams are seen, then, as consistent with everyday living. Rather than being disguised wishes, as Freud suggests, they represent key concerns growing out of our daily experiences (Pavlides & Winson, 1989; Winson, 1990).

The most influential current explanation for dreaming considers dreams as a by-product of fundamental biological activity. According to psychiatrist J. Allan Hobson, who proposed the **activation-synthesis theory**, the brain produces random electrical energy during REM sleep, possibly due to changes in the production of particular neurotransmitters. This electrical energy randomly stimulates memories lodged in various portions of the brain. Because we have a need to make sense of our world, even while asleep, the brain takes these chaotic memories and weaves them into a logical story line, filling in the gaps to produce a rational scenario. In this view, then, dreams are closer to a self-generated game of Madlibs than to significant, meaningful psychological phenomena (Hobson & McCarley, 1977; Hobson, 1988).

Yet Hobson does not entirely reject the view that dreams reflect unconscious wishes. He suggests that the particular scenario that a dreamer produces is not just random but instead is a clue to the dreamer's fears, emotions, and concerns. Hence, what starts out as a random process culminates in something meaningful.

Evidence that dreaming represents a response to random brain activity comes from work with people who are injected with drugs similar to the neurotransmitter acetylcholine. Under the influence of the drug, people quickly enter REM sleep and have dreams similar in quality to those occurring in natural sleep (Schmeck, 1987). Still, evidence such as this does not confirm that the dreams that are produced have psychological meaning.

The range of theories about dreaming (summarized in Table 6-2) clearly illustrates that dream researchers have yet to agree on the fundamental meaning of dreams. However, it does seem likely that the specific content of our dreams is unique to us and in some way represents meaningful patterns and concerns.

Reverse learning theory: A theory which proposes that dreams have no meaning in themselves, but instead function to rid us of unnecessary information that we have accumulated during the day

Dreams-for-survival theory: A theory which proposes that dreams permit information critical for our daily survival to be reconsidered and reprocessed during sleep

Activation-synthesis theory: Hobson's theory that dreams are a result of random electrical energy stimulating memories lodged in various portions of the brain, which the brain then weaves into a logical story line.

TABLE 6-2

FOUR VIEWS OF DREAMS

Theory	Basic Explanation	Meaning of Dreams	Is Meaning of Dream Disguised?
Unconscious wish fulfillment theory (Freud)	Dreams represent unconscious wishes the dreamer wants to fulfill	Latent content reveals unconscious wishes	Yes, by manifest content of dreams
Reverse learning theory	Unnecessary information is "unlearned" and removed from memory	None	No meaning
Dreams-for-survival theory	Information relevant to daily survival is reconsidered and reprocessed	Clues to everyday concerns about survival	Not necessarily
Activation-synthesis theory	Dreams are the result of random activation of various memories, which are tied together in a logical story line	Dream scenario that is constructed is related to dreamer's concerns	Not necessarily

Ultimately, dreams may provide clues about the things that on some level of consciousness are most important to us.

Daydreams: Dreams without Sleep

It is the stuff of magic: Our past mistakes can be wiped out and the future filled with noteworthy accomplishments. Fame, happiness, and wealth can be ours. In the next moment, though, the most horrible of tragedies can occur, leaving us alone, penniless, a figure of pitiful unhappiness.

Daydreams: Fantasies people construct while awake

The source of these scenarios is **daydreams**, fantasies that people construct while awake. Unlike dreaming that occurs while sleeping, daydreams are more under people's control, and therefore their content is often more closely related to immediate events in the environment than is the content of the dreams that occur during sleep. Although they may, as we will see in Chapter 12, include sexual content, daydreams also pertain to other activities or events that are relevant to a person's life.

Daydreams are a typical part of waking consciousness, but their extent, and the daydreamer's involvement in them, varies from person to person. For example, around 2 to 4 percent of the population spend at least half their free time fantasizing. Although most people daydream much less frequently, almost everyone fantasizes to some degree. Studies that ask people to identify what they are doing at random times during the day have shown that they are daydreaming about 10 percent of the time. As for the content of fantasies, most concern such mundane, ordinary events as paying the telephone bill, picking up the groceries, or solving a romantic problem (Singer, 1975; Lynn & Rhue, 1988).

Although frequent daydreaming might seem to suggest psychological difficulties, there actually appears to be little relationship between psychological disturbance and daydreaming (Rhue & Lynn, 1987; Lynn & Rhue, 1988). Except in those rare cases in which a daydreamer is unable to distinguish a fantasy from reality (a mark of serious problems, as we discuss in Chapter 17), daydreaming seems to be a normal part of waking consciousness. Indeed, fantasy may contribute to the psychological well-being of some people by enhancing their creativity and by permitting them to use their imagination to understand what other people are experiencing.

Lorenzo Lotto painted one of the earliest depictions of daydreaming in *A Maiden's Dream*, around 1500.

Sleep Disturbances: Slumbering Problems

At one time or another, almost all of us have difficulty sleeping—a condition known as **insomnia**. It may be due to a particular situation such as the breakup of a relationship, concern about a test score, or the loss of a job. Some cases of insomnia, however, have no obvious reason or cause. Some people are simply unable to fall asleep easily, or they go to sleep readily but wake up frequently during the night (Hauri, 1991). Insomnia is a problem that afflicts about a quarter of the population of the United States.

Other sleep problems are less common than insomnia, although they are still widespread. For instance, some 20 million people suffer from **sleep apnea**, a condition in which a person has difficulty breathing and sleeping simultaneously. The result is disturbed, fitful sleep, as the person is constantly reawakened when the lack of oxygen becomes great enough to trigger a waking response. In some cases, people with apnea wake as many as 500 times during the course of an evening, although they may not even be aware that they have wakened. Not surprisingly, such disturbed sleep results in complaints of sleepiness the next day. Sleep apnea may account for **sudden infant death syndrome**, a mysterious killer of seemingly normal infants who die while sleeping.

Narcolepsy is an uncontrollable need to sleep for short periods during the day (Dement, 1976). No matter what the activity—holding a heated conversation, exercising, or driving—the narcoleptic will suddenly drift into sleep. People with narcolepsy go directly from wakefulness to REM sleep, skipping the other stages (Siegel et al., 1991). The causes of narcolepsy are not known, although there may be a genetic component, with narcolepsy running in some families.

Insomnia: An inability to get to sleep or stay asleep

Sleep apnea: A sleep disorder characterized by difficulty in breathing and sleeping simultaneously

Sudden infant death syndrome: A disorder in which seemingly healthy infants die in their sleep

Narcolepsy (NARK o lep see): An uncontrollable need to sleep for short periods during the day

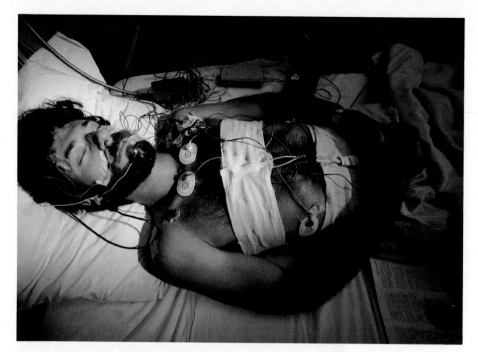

This man's sleep patterns are being studied at the Stanford Sleep Disorders Clinic in California in order to increase our understanding of sleep.

We know relatively little about sleeptalking and sleepwalking, two fairly harmless sleep disturbances. Both occur during stage 4 sleep and are more frequent in children than in adults. In most cases, sleeptalkers and sleepwalkers have a vague consciousness of the world around them, and a sleepwalker may be able to walk around obstructions in a crowded room in an agile fashion. Unless a sleepwalker wanders into a dangerous environment, sleepwalking typically poses little risk. Moreover, the conventional wisdom that one shouldn't awaken sleepwalkers is wrong: No harm will come from waking them, although they will probably be quite confused.

THE INFORMED CONSUMER OF PSYCHOLOGY:
Sleeping Better

Fortunately, the most severe sleep disorder from which most of us suffer is insomnia. Yet the fact that things could be worse provides little solace to weary insomniacs, whose difficulty in sleeping can make them feel exhausted every waking moment.

For those of us who spend hours tossing and turning in bed, psychologists studying sleep disturbances have made a number of suggestions for overcoming insomnia. These include:

- Exercise during the day; not surprisingly, it helps to be tired before going to sleep! Moreover, learning systematic relaxation techniques and biofeedback (see Chapter 3) can help you unwind from the day's stresses and tensions (Woolfolk & McNulty, 1983).

- Choose a regular bedtime, and then stick to it. Adhering to a habitual schedule helps your internal timing mechanisms regulate your body better.

- Don't use your bed as an all-purpose area; leave studying, reading, eating, watching TV, and other recreational activities to some other area of your living quarters. By following this advice, your bed will be a cue for sleeping.

■ Avoid drinks with caffeine (such as coffee, tea, and some soft drinks) after lunch; their effects can linger for as long as eight to twelve hours after they are consumed.

■ Drink a glass of warm milk at bedtime. Your grandmother was right, although she probably didn't know why. (Milk contains the chemical tryptophan, which helps people get to sleep.)

■ Avoid sleeping pills. Although over $100 million a year is spent on sleeping pills in the United States, most of this money is wasted. They can be temporarily effective, but in the long run sleeping pills may cause more harm than good, since they disrupt the normal sleep cycle (McClusky et al., 1991).

■ Try *not* to go to sleep. This advice, which sounds strange at first, actually makes a good deal of sense. Psychologists have found that part of the reason people have difficulty falling asleep is that they are trying so hard. A better strategy is one suggested by Richard P. Bootzin of the University of Arizona, who teaches people to recondition their sleeping habits. He tells them to go to bed only when they feel tired. If they don't get to sleep within ten minutes, they should leave the bedroom and do something else, returning to bed only when they do feel tired. This process should be continued, all night if necessary. But in the morning, the patient must get up at his or her usual hour and must not take a nap during the day. After three to four weeks on this regimen, most people become conditioned to associate their beds with sleep—and fall asleep rapidly at night (Youkilis & Bootzin, 1981; Seltzer, 1986).

Even if these techniques do not work to your satisfaction and you still feel that insomnia is a problem, there is one consolation: Many people who *think* they have sleeping problems may be mistaken. Observers find that patients who enter sleep laboratories for treatment actually sleep much more than they think they do (Trinder, 1988). For example, researchers have found that some people who report being up all night actually fall asleep in thirty minutes and stay that way all night. Furthermore, some people with insomnia can accurately recall sounds that they heard while they were asleep, which gives them the impression that they were actually awake during the night (Engle-Friedman, Baker, & Bootzin, 1985).

The problem with many people with insomnia, then, is not an actual lack of sleep but rather faulty perceptions of their sleeping patterns. In many cases, just becoming aware of how long they really do sleep—and understanding the fact that the older they become the less sleep they need—is enough to "cure" people's perception that they have a sleep disorder.

◀ **RECAP AND REVIEW I**

RECAP

◀ Consciousness refers to a person's awareness of the sensations, thoughts, and feelings being experienced at a given moment.

◀ There are four distinct stages of sleep, as well as REM (rapid eye movement) sleep. These stages recur in cycles during the course of a normal night's sleep.

◀ The four major explanations of dreams are Freud's wish fulfillment theory, reverse learning theory, dreams-for-survival theory, and activation-synthesis theory.

◀ The major sleep disorders include insomnia, narcolepsy, and sleep apnea.

REVIEW

1. _____ is the term used to describe our understanding of the world external to us, as well as our own internal world.
2. Contrary to popular belief, a great deal of neural activity goes on during sleep. True or false? _____
3. Dreams occur in what stage of sleep?
4. _____ _____ are internal bodily processes that occur on a daily cycle.
5. Freud's theory of unconscious _____ _____ states that the actual wishes that an individual expressed in dreams were disguised because they were threatening to the person's conscious awareness.
6. Match the theory of dreaming with its definition.

    _____ 1. Dreams-for-survival theory   a. Dreams permit necessary information to be reprocessed during sleep.

    _____ 2. Reverse learning theory   b. Random energy produced during sleep stimulates the brain, which then weaves the activated

    _____ 3. Activation-synthesis theory   memories into a story line.

     c. Dreams "flush away" excess information gathered during the day.

7. Match the sleep problem with its definition.

    _____ 1. Insomnia   a. Condition which makes breathing while sleeping difficult.

    _____ 2. Narcolepsy   b. Difficulty in sleeping.

    _____ 3. Sleep apnea   c. Uncontrollable need to sleep during the day.

Ask Yourself

A new "miracle pill" has been developed. This pill, once taken, will allow a person to function with only one hour's sleep each night. Because of this short stretch of time, any individual who takes this pill will never dream again. Knowing what you know about the functions of sleep and dreaming, what would some of the advantages and drawbacks of such a pill be from a personal standpoint? What would some of the advantages and drawbacks of such a pill be from a societal standpoint? Would you take such a pill?

(Answers to review questions are on page 182.)

HYPNOSIS AND MEDITATION: ALTERED STATES OF CONSCIOUSNESS

You are feeling relaxed and drowsy. You are getting sleepier and sleepier. Your body is becoming limp. Now you are starting to become warm, at ease, more comfortable. Your eyelids are feeling heavier and heavier. Your eyes are closing; you can't keep them open any more. You are totally relaxed.

Now, as you listen to my voice, do exactly as I say. Place your hands above your head. You will find they are getting heavier and heavier—so heavy you can barely keep them up. In fact, although you are straining as hard as you can, you will be unable to hold them up any longer.

An observer watching the above scene would notice a curious phenomenon occurring: Many of the people listening to the voice would, one by one, drop their arms to their sides, as if they were holding heavy lead weights. The reason for this strange behavior: The people have been hypnotized.

Hypnosis

Hypnosis: A state of heightened susceptibility to the suggestions of others

A person under **hypnosis** is in a state of heightened susceptibility to the suggestions of others. In some respects, it appears that a person in a hypnotic trance is asleep (although measures of brain waves show that this is not the case). Yet other aspects of behavior contradict this appearance of sleep, for the person is attentive to the hypnotist's suggestions and carries out suggestions that may be bizarre or silly.

At the same time, people do not lose all will of their own when hypnotized: They will not perform antisocial behaviors, and they will not carry out self-destructive acts. People will not reveal hidden truths about themselves, and they are capable of lying. Moreover, people cannot be hypnotized against their will—despite popular misconceptions.

There are wide variations in people's susceptibility to hypnosis (Lynn et al., 1991; Sabourin, Cutcomb, Crawford, & Pribram, 1990). About 5 to 20 percent of the population cannot be hypnotized at all, while some 15 percent are very easily hypnotized. Most people fall in between. Moreover, the ease with which a person is hypnotized is related to a number of other characteristics. People who are readily hypnotized are also easily absorbed while reading books or listening to music, becoming unaware of what is happening around them, and they often spend an unusual amount of time in happy daydreaming (Hilgard, 1974; Lynn & Rhue, 1985; Lynn & Snodgrass, 1987; Crawford, 1982). In sum, then, they show a high ability to concentrate and to become completely absorbed in what they are doing.

A Different State of Consciousness?

The issue of whether hypnosis represents a state of consciousness that is qualitatively different from normal waking consciousness has long been controversial among psychologists.

Ernest Hilgard (1975) has argued convincingly that hypnosis does represent a state of consciousness that differs significantly from other states. He contends that particular behavioral characteristics clearly differentiate hypnosis from other states, including higher suggestibility; increased ability to recall and construct images, including visual memories from early childhood; a lack of initiative; and the ability to accept uncritically suggestions that clearly contradict reality. For example, hypnotized people can be told that they are blind, and they subsequently report an inability to see objects shown to them (Bryant & McConkey, 1990). Moreover, research has found changes in electrical activity in the brain that are associated with hypnosis, supporting the position that hypnotic states represent a state of consciousness different from that of normal waking (Spiegel, 1987).

Still, some theorists reject the notion that hypnosis represents an altered state of consciousness (Spanos, 1986; Spanos & Chaves, 1989). They argue that altered brain wave patterns are not sufficient to demonstrate that a hypnotic state is qualitatively different from normal waking consciousness, given that there are no other specific physiological changes that occur when a person is in a trance.

Furthermore, some researchers have shown that people merely pretending to be hypnotized display behaviors that are nearly identical to those of truly hypnotized individuals, and that hypnotic susceptibility can be increased through training procedures (Gfeller, Lynn, & Pribble, 1987; Spanos et al., 1987). There also is little support for the contention that adults can accurately recall memories of childhood events while hypnotized (Nash, 1987). Such converging evidence suggests that there is nothing qualitatively special about the hypnotic trance (Barber, 1975; Lynn, Rhue, & Weekes, 1990).

The jury remains out on whether hypnosis represents a truly unique state of consciousness. On the other hand, although there is disagreement over the true nature of consciousness associated with hypnotic states, few would dispute the tremendous practical value of hypnosis in a variety of settings. Psychologists working in many different areas have found hypnosis to be a reliable, effective tool. Among the range of applications are the following:

■ Control of pain. Patients suffering from chronic pain may be given the suggestion, while hypnotized, that their pain is eliminated or reduced. They can be told to feel that a painful area is hot, cold, or numb. They also may be taught to hypnotize themselves to relieve pain or to gain a sense of control over their symptoms. Hypnosis has proved to be particularly useful during childbirth and dental procedures (Erickson, Hershman, & Secter, 1990).

■ Ending tobacco addiction. Although it hasn't been successful in stopping drug and alcohol abuse, hypnosis is sometimes successful in helping people to stop unwanted behavior such as smoking. In some approaches, hypnotized smokers are given the suggestion that the taste and smell of cigarettes are unpleasant. Other techniques include teaching self-hypnosis to deal with cravings for cigarettes or suggesting during hypnosis that smokers owe their bodies protection from the ravages of smoking (Erickson, Hershman, & Secter, 1990).

■ Psychological therapy. Hypnosis is sometimes used during treatment for psychological disorders. For example, hypnosis may be used to heighten relaxation, increase expectations of success, or modify thoughts that are self-defeating. It can also be used to decrease anxiety (Weitzenhoffer, 1989).

■ Law enforcement uses. Witnesses and victims are sometimes better able to recall details of a crime when hypnotized. In one well-known case, a witness to the kidnapping of a group of California schoolchildren was placed under hypnosis and was able to recall all but one digit of the license number on the kidnapper's vehicle (*Time*, 1976). On the other hand, the evidence regarding the accuracy of recollections obtained under hypnosis is decidedly mixed. In some cases, accurate recall of specific information increases—but so do the number of errors. Moreover, there is an increase in a person's

Hypnosis may aid those suffering from chronic pain, tobacco addiction, and a variety of other conditions.

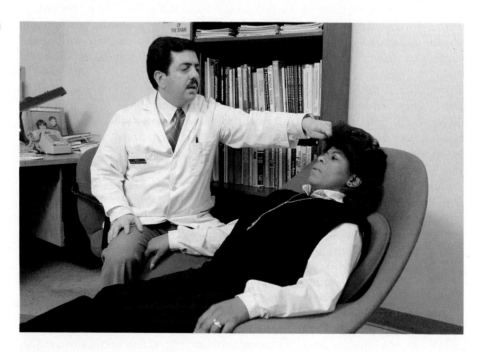

confidence about the recollections obtained during hypnosis, even when the memory is inaccurate. The hypnotic state may simply make people more willing to report whatever they think they remember. Because of these questions about its usefulness, the legal status of hypnosis has yet to be resolved (Dywan & Bowers, 1983; Nogrady, McConkey, & Perry, 1985; Council of Scientific Affairs, 1985).

■ Professional sports. Athletes sometimes turn to hypnosis to improve their performance. For example, championship fighter Ken Norton used hypnosis prior to a bout to prepare himself for the encounter, and baseball star Rod Carew used hypnotism to increase his concentration when batting (Udolf, 1981).

Hypnosis, then, has many potential applications. Of course, it is not invariably effective: For the significant number of people who cannot be hypnotized, it offers little help. But for people who make good hypnotic subjects, hypnosis has the potential for providing significant benefits.

Meditation: Regulating Your Own State of Consciousness

When traditional practitioners of the ancient eastern religion of Zen Buddhism want to achieve greater spiritual insight, they turn to a technique that has been used for centuries to alter their state of consciousness. This technique is called meditation.

Meditation is a learned technique for refocusing attention that brings about an altered state of consciousness. Although there is an exotic sound to it, some form of meditation is found within every major religion—including Christianity and Judaism. In the United States today, some of the major proponents of meditation are followers of Maharishi Mahesh Yogi, who practice a form of meditation called transcendental meditation, or TM, although many other groups teach various forms of meditation.

The specific meditative technique used in TM involves repeating a **mantra**— a sound, word, or syllable—over and over; in other forms of meditation, the focus is on a picture, flame, or specific part of the body (see Figure 6-7). Regardless of the nature of the particular initial stimulus, in most forms of meditation the key to the procedure is concentrating on it so thoroughly that the meditator becomes unaware of any outside stimulation and a different state of consciousness is reached.

Following meditation, people report feeling thoroughly relaxed. They sometimes relate that they have gained new insights into themselves and the problems they are facing. The long-term practice of meditation may even improve health: one study of a group of residents of several old-age homes found higher longevity for those who practiced TM over a three-year period (Alexander et al., 1989).

Several physiological changes occur during meditation. For example, oxygen usage decreases, heart rate and blood pressure decline, and brain-wave patterns may change (Wallace & Benson, 1972). On the other hand, similar changes occur during relaxation of any sort, so whether these changes qualify as indicators of a true alteration in consciousness remains an open question (Holmes, 1985).

It *is* clear that you too can meditate without exotic trappings by using a few simple procedures developed by Herbert Benson, who has studied meditation extensively (Benson, Kotch, Crassweller, & Greenwood, 1977). The basics—

Meditation: A learned technique for refocusing attention that brings about an altered state of consciousness

Mantra: A sound, word, or syllable repeated over and over to take one into a meditative state

FIGURE 6-7
An ancient mandala that can be used to focus one's attention while meditating. A mandala is constructed so that attention is drawn to the center of the figure.

which are similar in several respects to those developed as a part of eastern religions but have no spiritual component—include sitting in a quiet room with your eyes closed, breathing deeply and rhythmically, and repeating a word or sound—such as the word "one"—over and over. Although the procedure is a bit more complicated than this, most people find themselves in a deeply relaxed state after just twenty minutes. Practiced twice a day, Benson's meditative techniques seem to be just as effective in bringing about relaxation as more mystical methods (Benson & Friedman, 1985).

RECAP AND REVIEW II

RECAP

◀ Hypnosis places people in a state of heightened susceptibility to the suggestions of others. People cannot be hypnotized against their will, and they vary in their susceptibility to hypnosis.

◀ One crucial question about hypnosis is whether or not it represents a separate state of consciousness. There is evidence on both sides of the issue.

◀ Meditation is a learned technique for refocusing attention that is meant to bring about an altered state of consciousness.

REVIEW

1. _____ is a state of heightened susceptibility to the suggestions of others.

2. A friend tells you "I once heard of a person who was murdered by being hypnotized and then told to jump from the Golden Gate Bridge!" Could such a statement be true? Why or why not?

3. _____ is a learned technique for refocusing attention to bring about an altered state of consciousness.

4. Leslie repeats a unique sound, known as a _____, when she engages in transcendental meditation.

5. Meditation can be learned only by following procedures which include some spiritual component. True or false?
   _____

Ask Yourself

If meditation has psychological benefits, does this suggest that we are mentally overburdened in our normal state of consciousness?

(Answers to review questions are on page 186.)

As the butane torch flame vaporized the cocaine in the bowl of a glass smoking pipe, Amir Vik-Kiv inhaled deeply, held the smoke in his expanded chest, then exhaled in a breathless rush. Suddenly, his eyes bulged and his hands trembled. Beads of sweat broke out on his forehead, and perspiration stains formed under his arms.

Moments earlier . . . the former television cameraman had "cooked" a gram of refined cocaine in the kitchen of his Northeast Washington apartment. Using a simple recipe of water and baking soda, he had reduced the substance to a potent, insidious form known as "crack."

Within an hour he had "burned" about $100 worth of the drug, but what had happened in his brain just seven seconds after taking the first hit was more like an explosion. Although he had not eaten food in a day or had sex in months, he was no longer hungry for either. . . .

What would happen when the dope ran out was another story. Before long Vik-Kiv would be crawling around the kitchen floor, searching for bits of cocaine that might have spilled. When he found anything white, he would take it—and gag at the taste of what could have been anything from a burning bread crumb to a moldering roach egg (Milloy, 1986, p. 1).

Although few people reach such extremes of behavior, almost all of us are experienced drug users. From infancy on, most people take vitamins, aspirin, cold-relief medicine, and the like. These drugs have little effect on our consciousness, operating instead primarily on our biological functions. When we speak of drugs that affect consciousness, we are referring to **psychoactive drugs**, drugs that influence a person's emotions, perceptions, and behavior. Even these drugs are common in most people's lives; if you have ever had a cup of coffee or sipped a beer, you have taken a psychoactive drug.

A large number of people have used more potent—and dangerous—psychoactive drugs than coffee and beer (see Figure 6-8). On the other hand, drug use among high school students has declined over the last decade. One survey found that 48 percent of high school seniors had used an illegal drug at least once in their lives, and 32 percent had tried one in the last year. These figures represent substantial declines from drug use in the early 1980s, which ranged from 25 to 35 percent higher (National Institute of Drug Abuse, 1991).

Obviously, drugs vary in the nature of the effects they have on users. The most dangerous are those that are addictive. **Addictive drugs** produce a biological

Psychoactive drugs: Drugs that influence a person's emotions, perceptions, and behavior

Addictive drugs: Drugs that produce a physical or psychological dependence in the user

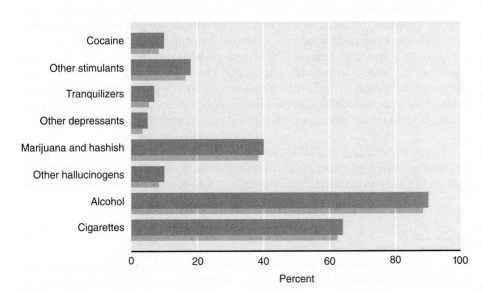

FIGURE 6-8
How many people use drugs? Results of the most recent comprehensive survey of 17,000 high school seniors across the United States shows the percentage of respondents who have used various substances for nonmedical purposes at least once. (*Source:* Johnston, Bachman, & O'Malley, 1991.)

or psychological dependence in the user, and their withdrawal leads to a craving for the drug that, in some cases, may be nearly irresistible. Addictions may be biologically based, in which case the body becomes so accustomed to functioning in the presence of a drug that it cannot function in its absence. Or addictions may be psychological, in which case people believe that they need the drug in order to respond to the stresses of daily living. Although we generally associate addiction with drugs such as heroin, everyday sorts of drugs like caffeine (found in coffee) and nicotine (found in cigarettes) have addictive aspects as well.

We know relatively little about the reasons underlying addiction. One of the problems in identifying the causes is that different drugs (such as alcohol and cocaine) affect the brain in very different ways—and yet may be equally addicting. Furthermore, it takes longer to become addicted to some drugs than to others, even though the ultimate consequences of addiction may be equally grave (Barnes, 1988; Julien, 1991).

Why do people take drugs in the first place? There are many reasons, ranging from the perceived pleasure of the experience itself, to the escape a drug-induced high affords from the everyday pressures of life, to an attempt to achieve a religious or spiritual state. But other factors, ones that have little to do with the nature of the experience itself, also lead people to try drugs. For instance, the alleged drug use of well-known role models such as movie star John Belushi or Washington, D.C., mayor Marion Barry, the easy availability of some illegal drugs, and the pressures of peers play a role in the decision to use drugs (Graham, Marks, & Hansen, 1991; Jarvik, 1990; Stein, Newcomb, & Bentler, 1987). In some cases, the motive is simply the thrill of trying something new and perhaps illegal. Finally, the sense of helplessness experienced by poor unemployed individuals trapped in lives of poverty may lead people to try drugs as a way of escaping the bleakness of their lives. Regardless of the forces that lead a person to begin to use drugs, drug addiction is among the most difficult of all behaviors to modify, even with extensive treatment (Marlatt et al., 1988).

Stimulants: Drug Highs

It's one o'clock in the morning, and you still haven't finished reading the last chapter of the text on which you are being tested in the morning. Feeling exhausted, you turn to the one thing that may help you keep awake for the next two hours: a cup of strong, black coffee.

If you have ever found yourself in such a position, you have been relying on a major **stimulant**, caffeine, to stay awake. **Caffeine** is one of a number of stimulants that affect the central nervous system by causing a rise in heart rate, blood pressure, and muscular tension. Caffeine is present not only in coffee; it is an important ingredient in tea, soft drinks, and chocolate as well (see Figure 6-9). The major behavioral effects of caffeine are an increase in attentiveness and a decrease in reaction time. Caffeine can also bring about an improvement in mood, most likely by mimicking the effects of a natural brain chemical, adenosine.

Too much caffeine, however, can result in nervousness and insomnia. People can build up a biological dependence on the drug: If they suddenly stop drinking coffee, they may experience headaches or depression. Many people who drink

Stimulants: Drugs that affect the central nervous system, causing increased heart rate, blood pressure, and muscle tension

Caffeine: An addictive stimulant found most abundantly in coffee, tea, soda, and chocolate

---

ANSWERS (REVIEW II):

1. Hypnosis 2. No; people who are hypnotized cannot be made to perform self-destructive acts.
3. Meditation 4. mantra 5. False; some meditative techniques have no spiritual component.

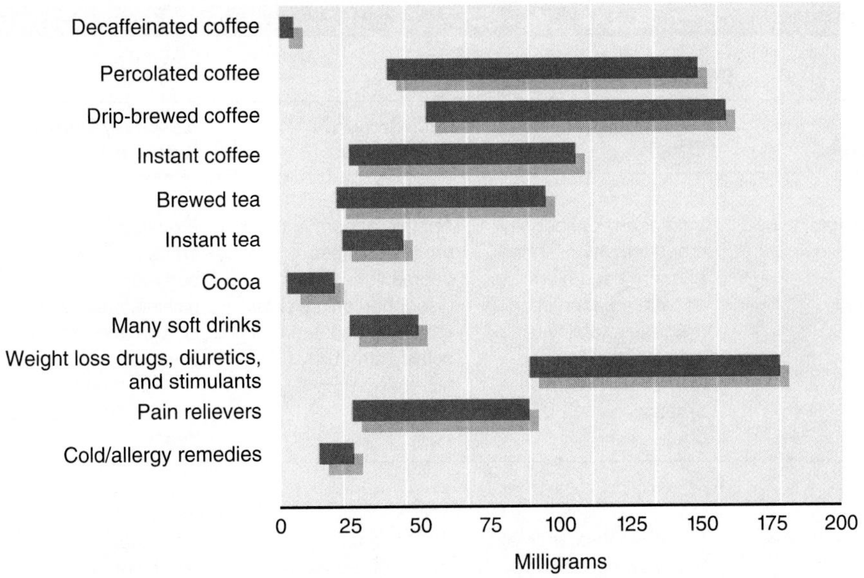
Decaffeinated coffee
Percolated coffee
Drip-brewed coffee
Instant coffee
Brewed tea
Instant tea
Cocoa
Many soft drinks
Weight loss drugs, diuretics, and stimulants
Pain relievers
Cold/allergy remedies
0
25
50
75
100
125
150
175
200
Milligrams

FIGURE 6-9
How much caffeine are you eating and drinking? This chart shows the range of caffeine found in common foods and drinks. The average American drinks about 200 milligrams of caffeine each day. (*Source: Blakeslee, 1991.*)

large amounts of coffee on weekdays have headaches on weekends because of a sudden drop in the amount of caffeine they are consuming (Konner, 1988).

Another common stimulant is **nicotine**, found in cigarettes. The soothing effects of nicotine help explain why cigarette smoking is rewarding for smokers, many of whom continue to smoke despite clear evidence of its long-term health dangers. As we will discuss further in Chapter 16 when we consider health psychology, smoking is addictive; smokers develop a dependence on nicotine, and smokers who suddenly stop develop strong cravings for the drug (Murray, 1990). According to the former U.S. Surgeon General C. Everett Koop, who changed the designation of smoking from a "habit" to an "addiction" in 1988, the use of nicotine is "driven by strong, often irresistible urges and can persist despite . . . repeated efforts to quit" (Koop, 1988).

Nicotine: An addictive stimulant present in cigarettes

Cocaine. There is little doubt that the illegal drug that has posed the most serious problems in the last decade has been the stimulant **cocaine** and its derivative, crack. Cocaine is inhaled or "snorted" through the nose, smoked, or injected directly into the bloodstream. It is rapidly absorbed into the body, making its effects apparent almost immediately.

Cocaine: An addictive stimulant that, when taken in small doses, initially creates feelings of confidence, alertness, and well-being, but eventually causes mental and physical deterioration

When taken in relatively small quantities, cocaine produces feelings of profound psychological well-being, increased confidence, and alertness. (For a summary of the effects of cocaine and other illegal drugs, see Table 6-3.)

Cocaine produces this "high" through the neurotransmitter dopamine. As you'll recall from Chapter 3, dopamine is one of the chemicals that transmits messages between neurons which are related to ordinary feelings of pleasure. Normally, when dopamine is released, excess amounts of the neurotransmitter are reabsorbed by the releasing neuron. However, when cocaine enters the brain, it blocks the reabsorption of leftover dopamine. As a result, the brain is flooded with dopamine-producing pleasurable sensations.

However, the price paid for the pleasurable effects of cocaine is steep. The drug is psychologically and physically addictive, and users may grow obsessed with obtaining it. Cocaine addicts indulge in binges of use, administering the drug every ten to thirty minutes if it is available. During these binges, they think of nothing but cocaine, and eating, sleeping, money, friends, family, and even survival have no importance (Gawin & Ellinwood, 1988). Their lives become tied to the drug; they deteriorate mentally and physically, losing weight and growing

DRUGS AND THEIR EFFECTS

Drug	Street Name	Effects	Withdrawal Symptoms	Adverse/Overdose Reactions
Stimulants				
Cocaine	Coke, blow, toot, snow, lady, crack	Increased confidence, mood elevation, sense of energy and alertness, decreased appetite, anxiety, irritability, insomnia, transient drowsiness, delayed orgasm	Apathy, general fatigue, prolonged sleep, depression, disorientation, suicidal thoughts, agitated motor activity, irritability, bizarre dreams	Elevated blood pressure, increase in body temperature, face-picking, suspiciousness, bizarre and repetitious behavior, vivid hallucinations, convulsions, possible death
Amphetamines				
Benzedrine	Speed			
Dexedrine	Speed			
Caffeine				
Depressants				
Barbiturates		Impulsiveness, dramatic mood swings, bizarre thoughts, suicidal behavior, slurred speech, disorientation, slowed mental and physical functioning, limited attention span	Weakness, restlessness, nausea and vomiting, headaches, nightmares, irritability, depression, acute anxiety, hallucinations, seizures, possible death	Confusion, decreased response to pain, shallow respiration, dilated pupils, weak and rapid pulse, coma, possible death
Nembutal	Yellowjackets, yellows			
Seconal	Reds			
Phenobarbital				
Quaalude	Ludes, 714s			
Alcohol	Booze			
Narcotics				
Heroin	H, hombre, junk, smack, dope, horse, crap	Apathy, difficulty in concentration, slowed speech, decreased physical activity, drooling, itching, euphoria, nausea	Anxiety, vomiting, sneezing, diarrhea, lower back pain, watery eyes, runny nose, yawning, irritability, tremors, panic, chills and sweating, cramps	Depressed levels of consciousness, low blood pressure, rapid heart rate, shallow breathing, convulsions, coma, possible death
Morphine	Drugstore dope, cube, first line, mud			
Hallucinogens				
Cannabis		Euphoria, relaxed inhibitions, increased appetite, disoriented behavior	Hyperactivity, insomnia, decreased appetite, anxiety	Severe reactions are rare but include panic, paranoia, fatigue, bizarre and dangerous behavior, decreased production of testosterone over long term, possibly temporarily; immune-system effects
Marijuana	Bhang, kif, ganja, dope, grass, pot, smoke, hemp, joint, weed, bone, Mary Jane, herb, tea			
Hashish				
Hash oil				

suspicious of others. In extreme cases, cocaine can cause hallucinations; a common one is that insects are crawling over one's body (Fisher, Rashkin, & Uhlenhuth, 1987). Ultimately, an overdose of cocaine can lead to users' deaths.

When cocaine is not available, abusers of the drug go through three distinct phases (see Figure 6-10, page 190). In the first stage, users "crash." They crave cocaine, feel depressed and agitated, and their anxiety intensifies. In the second stage, which begins from nine hours to four days later, heavy users begin the process of "withdrawal." During this period, they initially crave cocaine less, feel bored and unmotivated, and experience little anxiety.

TABLE 6 - 3 (continued)

DRUGS AND THEIR EFFECTS

Drug	Street Name	Effects	Withdrawal Symptoms	Adverse/Overdose Reactions
Hallucinogens (continued)				
LSD	Electricity, acid, quasey, blotter acid, microdot, white lightning, purple barrels	Fascination with ordinary objects; heightened aesthetic responses to color, texture, spatial arrangements, contours, music; vision and depth distortion; hearing colors, seeing music; slowing of time; heightened sensitivity to faces and gestures; magnified feelings of love, lust, hate, joy, despair; paranoia; panic; euphoria; bliss	Not reported	Nausea and chills; increased pulse, temperature, and blood pressure; trembling; slow, deep breathing; loss of appetite; insomnia; longer, more intense "trips"; bizarre, dangerous behavior possibly leading to injury or death
Phencyclidine (PCP)	Angel dust, hog, rocket fuel, superweed, peace pill, elephant tranquilizer, dust, bad pizza	Increased blood pressure and heart rate, sweating, nausea, numbness, floating sensation, slowed reflexes, altered body image, altered perception of time and space, impaired immediate and recent memory, decreased concentration, paranoid thoughts and delusions	Not reported	Highly variable and possibly dose-related: disorientation, loss of recent memory, lethargy/stupor, bizarre and violent behavior, rigidity and immobility, mutism, staring, hallucinations and delusions, coma

Later, though, cocaine abusers are highly sensitive to any cues that remind them of their prior cocaine use—which might be a person, event, location, or drug abuse equipment such as a glass pipe. When this happens, they are susceptible to return to cocaine use if the drug is available. But if addicts are able to pass through the withdrawal stage, they move into the third stage, in which craving for cocaine is further reduced and moods become relatively normal. However, they are still highly sensitive to cues related to cocaine use, and relapses are common. Cocaine abuse, then, has powerful, and lasting, consequences.

Almost one out of every two Americans between the ages of 25 and 30 has tried cocaine, and between 1 and 3 million cocaine abusers are estimated to be in need of treatment. Although its use among high school students has declined over the past few years, the drug still represents a major problem (Gawin, 1991; National Institute of Drug Abuse, 1991).

Amphetamines. The phrase "speed kills" became popular in the late 1970s, when use of **amphetamines**—strong stimulants such as Dexedrine and Benzedrine (popularly known as speed)—soared. Although its use has declined from

Amphetamines: Strong stimulants that cause a temporary feeling of confidence and alertness but may increase anxiety and appetite loss and, taken over a period of time, suspiciousness and feelings of persecution

▶ **189**

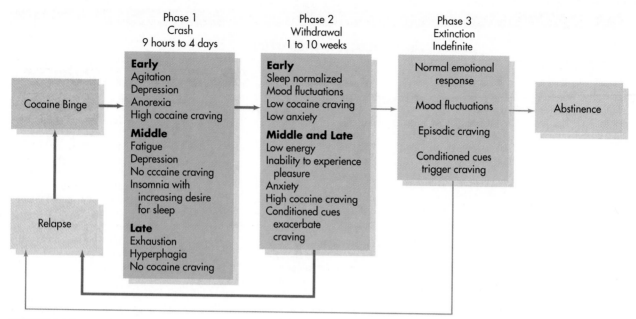

Phase 1
Crash
9 hours to 4 days

Phase 2
Withdrawal
1 to 10 weeks

Phase 3
Extinction
Indefinite

Cocaine Binge

Early
Agitation
Depression
Anorexia
High cocaine craving

Middle
Fatigue
Depression
No cccaine craving
Insomnia with
    increasing desire
    for sleep

Late
Exhaustion
Hyperphagia
No cocaine craving

Early
Sleep normalized
Mood fluctuations
Low cocaine craving
Low anxiety

Middle and Late
Low energy
Inability to experience
    pleasure
Anxiety
High cocaine craving
Conditioned cues
    exacerbate
    craving

Normal emotional
    response

Mood fluctuations

Episodic craving

Conditioned cues
    trigger craving

Abstinence

Relapse

FIGURE 6-10

Phases of cocaine deprivation.
(Based on Gawin, 1991.)

its 1970s peak, many drug experts feel that speed would quickly resurface in large quantities if cocaine supplies were interrupted.

In small quantities, amphetamines bring about a sense of energy and alertness, talkativeness, heightened confidence, and a mood "high." Fatigue is reduced, while concentration is increased. Amphetamines also cause a loss of appetite, increased anxiety, and irritability. When taken over long periods of time, amphetamines can cause feelings of being persecuted by others, as well as a general sense of suspiciousness. People taking amphetamines may lose interest in sex. If taken in too large a quantity, amphetamines cause so much stimulation of the central nervous system that convulsions and death can occur—hence the phrase "speed kills."

Depressants: Drug Lows

In contrast to the initial effect of stimulants, which is an increase in arousal of the central nervous system, the effect of **depressants** is to impede the nervous system by causing the neurons to fire more slowly. Small doses result in at least temporary feelings of **intoxication**—drunkenness—along with a sense of euphoria and joy. When large amounts are taken, however, speech becomes slurred, muscle control becomes disjointed, causing difficulty of motion, and ultimately consciousness may be lost entirely.

The most common depressant is **alcohol**, which is used by more people than any other drug. Based on liquor sales, the average person over the age of 14 drinks two and a half gallons of pure alcohol over the course of the year—which works out to more than 200 drinks per person. Although the amount of alcohol consumption has declined steadily over the last decade, surveys show that more than three-quarters of college students admit to having had a drink within the last thirty days, and close to 42 percent say that they have had five or more drinks within the past two weeks (NIAAA, 1990; Carmody, 1990).

There are wide individual differences in alcohol consumption, as well as gender and cultural variations. For example, women are less likely to be drinkers and tend to be lighter drinkers than men (NIAAA, 1990; Engs, 1990). Ironically, though, women tend to be more susceptible to the effects of alcohol, because

Depressants: Drugs that slow down the nervous system

Intoxication: A state of drunkenness

Alcohol: The most common depressant, which in small doses causes release of tension and feelings of happiness, but in larger amounts can cause emotional and physical instability, memory impairment, and stupor

their stomachs are less able to neutralize the drug and more alcohol goes directly into their bloodstreams (Frezza et al., 1990; Lex, 1991).

There are also pronounced ethnic differences in alcohol consumption. For example, people of East Asian backgrounds who live in the United States tend to drink significantly less than whites or blacks, and their incidence of alcohol-related problems is lower. The reason seems to be that the physical reactions to drinking, which may include sweating, quickened heartbeat, and flushing, are more unpleasant for East Asians than for other groups (Akutsu, Sue, Zane, & Nakamura, 1989).

Although alcohol is a depressant, most people claim that it increases their sense of sociability and well-being. The discrepancy between the actual and the perceived effects of alcohol lies in its initial effects: release of tension, feelings of happiness, and loss of inhibitions (Steele & Southwick, 1985; Steele & Josephs, 1990). As the dose of alcohol increases, however, the depressive effects become clearer (see Figure 6-11). People may feel emotionally and physically unstable; they show poor judgment; their memories are impaired; their speech slurs, and

FIGURE 6-11
The effects of alcohol.

Number of Drinks Consumed in 2 Hours	Alcohol in Blood Percent	Typical Effects, Average-size Adult
2	0.05	Judgment, thought, and restraint weakened; tension released, giving carefree sensation
3	0.08	Tensions and inhibitions of everyday life lessened; cheerfulness
4	0.10	Voluntary motor action affected, making hand and arm movements, walk and speech clumsy
7	0.20	Severe impairment–staggering, loud, incoherent, emotionally unstable; 100 time greater traffic risk; ehuberance and aggressive inclinations magnified
9	0.30	Deeper areas of brain affected, with stimuls response and understanding confused; stuperous; blurred vision
12	0.40	Incapable of voluntary action, sleepy, difficult to arouse; equivalent of surgical anesthesia
15	0.40	Comatose; centers controlling breathing and heartbeat anesthetized; death increasingly probable

Note: A drink refers to a typical 12-ounce bottle of beer, a 1.5-ounce shot of hard liquor, or a 5-ounce glass of wine.

THE SOUND OF INTOXICATION

The grounding of the Exxon Valdez off the Alaska coast was one of the worst environmental disasters ever. Some 11 million gallons of crude oil spilled into Prince William Sound, leading to thousands of animal deaths and fouled shores and water.

When the captain of the tanker, Joseph Hazelwood, was brought to trial, the central allegation against him was that he was legally drunk at the time of the accident. Yet no blood test had been conducted when the mishap occurred, so the amount of alcohol in his body could not be determined.

Still, one source of data did exist: the Coast Guard had tape recordings of Hazelwood's conversations following the accident. Could the recordings provide a clue to his state of intoxication?

According to psychologist David Pisoni, the answer was yes. Pisoni had recently found in a laboratory study that alcohol intoxication produced clear changes in the physical characteristics of speech. Such measures as rate of speech, sound duration, and variability of voice pitch all changed consistently when a person was drunk (Pisoni, 1989). Although most bartenders and state troopers probably would wager that they could tell when patrons and speeders were intoxicated by simply listening to their speech, such judgments are purely subjective and easily biased. On the other hand, Pisoni's research showed that objective changes in speech occurred when individuals were intoxicated and that such variations could be reliably measured by various instruments.

In the Exxon Valdez case, Pisoni judged that the audiotape recordings supported the belief that Hazelwood was intoxicated at the time of the accident. Hazelwood's speech showed both an increase in the duration of speech sounds and a rise in variability. Both changes conform to the pattern shown by people who are legally intoxicated.

Legal technicalities prevented Pisoni's evidence from being presented in court—it was so new a scientific process that there was no precedent for the presentation of this kind of evidence to a jury. Consequently, the tanker captain was acquitted of charges of being impaired due to alcohol intoxication.

However, Pisoni is optimistic that the technique will eventually gain legal acceptance. Meanwhile, automobile manufacturers are providing funds for his research. Their interest lies in systems that would prevent cars from being started if their drivers' voices indicated that they were intoxicated (Kent, 1991).

---

they become incoherent and may eventually fall into a stupor and pass out. If they drink enough alcohol in a short time, they may die of alcohol poisoning (NIAAA, 1990). (See the accompanying Psychology at Work box.)

Although most people fall into the category of casual users, there are some 18 million alcoholics in the United States. **Alcoholics**, people with alcohol abuse problems, come to rely on alcohol and continue to drink even though it causes serious difficulties. In addition, they become increasingly immune to the effects of alcohol. Consequently, alcoholics must drink progressively more in order to experience the initial positive feelings that alcohol brings about.

In some cases of alcoholism, people must drink constantly in order to feel well enough to function in their daily lives. In other cases, though, people drink inconsistently, but occasionally go on sporadic binges in which they consume large quantities of alcohol.

It is not clear why certain people become alcoholic and develop a tolerance for alcohol, while others do not (Rivers, 1986; Gallant, 1987). Some evidence suggests a genetic cause, although the question of whether there is a specific inherited gene that produces alcoholism is quite controversial (Blum et al., 1990; Bolos et al., 1990). What is clear is that the chances of becoming alcoholic are considerably higher if alcoholics are present in earlier generations of a person's family. On the other hand, not all alcoholics have close relatives who are alcoholics; in these cases, environmental stressors are suspected of playing a larger role (Frank, Jacobson, & Tuer, 1990; Holden, 1991).

Alcoholics: People with alcohol abuse problems

Barbiturates. **Barbiturates**, which include such drugs as Nembutal, Seconal, and phenobarbital, are another form of depressant. Frequently prescribed by physicians to induce sleep or to reduce stress, barbiturates produce a sense of relaxation. Yet they too are psychologically and physically addictive and, when combined with alcohol, can be deadly, since such a combination relaxes the muscles of the diaphragm to such an extent that the user suffocates. The street drug known as Quaalude is closely related to the barbiturate family and has similar dangers associated with it.

Narcotics: Relieving Pain and Anxiety

Narcotics are drugs that increase relaxation and relieve pain and anxiety. Two of the most powerful narcotics, **morphine** and **heroin**, are derived from the poppy seed pod. Although morphine is used medically to control severe pain, heroin is illegal in the United States. This has not prevented its widespread use.

Heroin users usually inject the drug directly into their veins with a hypodermic needle. The immediate effect has been described as a ''rush'' of positive feeling, similar in some respects to a sexual orgasm—and just as difficult to describe. After the rush, a heroin user experiences a sense of well-being and peacefulness that lasts three to five hours. When the effects of the drug wear off, however, the user feels extreme anxiety and a desperate desire to repeat the experience. Moreover, larger amounts of heroin are needed each time to produce the same pleasurable effect. This leads to a cycle of biological and psychological addiction: The user is constantly either shooting up or attempting to obtain ever-increasing amounts of the drug. Eventually, the life of the addict becomes centered around heroin.

Because of the powerful positive feelings the drug produces, heroin addiction is particularly difficult to cure. One treatment that has shown some success is the use of methadone. **Methadone** is a chemical that satisfies a heroin user's physiological cravings for the drug without providing the ''high'' that accompanies heroin. When heroin users are placed on regular doses of methadone they may be able to function relatively normally. The use of methadone has one substantial drawback, however: Although it removes the psychological dependence on heroin, it replaces the biological addiction to heroin with a biological addiction to methadone. Researchers, then, are attempting to identify nonaddictive chemical substitutes for heroin, as well as substitutes for other addictive drugs, that do not replace one addiction with another (Waldrop, 1989).

Hallucinogens: Psychedelic Drugs

What do mushrooms, jimsonweed, and morning glories have in common? Besides being fairly common plants, each can be a source of a powerful **hallucinogen**, a drug that is capable of producing hallucinations, or changes in the perceptual process.

The most common hallucinogen in widespread use today is **marijuana**, whose active ingredient—tetrahydrocannabinol (THC)—is found in a common weed, cannabis. Marijuana is typically smoked in cigarettes, although it can be cooked and eaten. At least one-third of all Americans over the age of 12 have tried it at least once, and among 18- to 25-year-olds, the figure is twice as high. Despite its illegality, marijuana use is so prevalent that about 30 percent of those in high

Marijuana is one of the most commonly used hallucinogens.

school say they have used the drug within the past year. Still, use of the drug is down considerably from its peak in 1972, when more than half of all high school students reported using the drug at least once within the prior year (NIDA, 1991).

The effects of marijuana vary from person to person, but they typically consist of feelings of euphoria and general well-being. Sensory experiences seem more vivid and intense, and a person's sense of self-importance seems to grow. Memory may be impaired, causing the user to feel pleasantly "spaced out." On the other hand, the effects are not universally positive: Individuals who take marijuana when feeling depressed can end up even more depressed, since the drug tends to magnify both good and bad feelings.

Marijuana has the reputation of being a "safe" drug when used in moderation, and there seems to be no scientific evidence that its use is addictive or that users "graduate" to more dangerous drugs. In addition, marijuana has some proven medical uses, and in some cases it is legally prescribed for the treatment of the eye disease of glaucoma or in cases of severe asthma.

However, the long-term effects of heavy marijuana use present some potential hazard. For instance, there is some evidence that heavy use at least temporarily decreases the production of the male sex hormone testosterone, potentially affecting sexual activity and sperm count (Miller, 1975). Similarly, heavy use affects the ability of the immune system to fight off germs and increases stress on the heart, although it is unclear how strong these effects are (Turkington, 1986). One negative consequence of smoking large quantities of marijuana is unquestionable, though: The smoke damages the lungs much the way cigarette smoke does, producing an increased likelihood of developing cancer and other lung diseases (Institute of Medicine, 1982).

In sum, the *short-term* effects of marijuana use appear to be relatively minor— if users follow obvious cautions, such as avoiding driving or using machinery.

However, it is less clear whether the long-term consequences are harmful. The case regarding the use of marijuana is far from closed, and more research is necessary before the question of its safety can be settled.

LSD and PCP. Two of the strongest hallucinogens are **lysergic acid diethyl-amide**, or **LSD** (known commonly as acid), and **phencyclidine**, or **PCP** (often referred to as angel dust). Both drugs affect the operation of the neurotransmitter serotonin in the brain, causing an alteration in brain-cell activity and perception (Jacobs, 1987).

LSD, which was the preferred drug of Ryan Shafer, whose case began the chapter, produces vivid hallucinations. Perceptions of colors, sounds, and shapes are altered so much that even the most mundane experience—such as looking at the knots in a wooden table—can seem exciting and moving. Time perception is distorted, and objects and people may be viewed in a new way, with some users reporting that LSD increases their understanding of the world. For others, however, the experience brought on by LSD can be terrifying, particularly if users have had emotional difficulties in the past. Furthermore, people can experience flashbacks, in which they hallucinate long after the initial drug usage.

One of the most recent additions to the drug scene, PCP also causes strong hallucinations. However, the potential side effects associated with its use make the drug even more dangerous than LSD. Large doses may cause paranoid and destructive behavior, and in some cases users become violent toward themselves and others.

Lysergic acid diethylamide (LSD): One of the most powerful hallucinogens, affecting the operation of neurotransmitters in the brain and causing brain cell activity to be altered

Phencyclidine (PCP): A powerful hallucinogen that alters brain-cell activity and can cause paranoid and destructive behavior

The Informed Consumer of Psychology: Identifying Drug and Alcohol Problems

In a society bombarded with commercials for drugs that are guaranteed to do everything from curing the common cold to giving new life to "tired blood," it is no wonder that drug-related problems represent a major social issue. Yet many people with drug and alcohol problems deny they have them, and even close friends and family members may fail to realize when occasional social use of drugs or alcohol has turned into abuse.

Certain signs, however, indicate when use becomes abuse (Brody, 1982; Gelman, 1989; NIAAA, 1990). Among them:

- Always getting high to have a good time
- Being high more often than not
- Getting high to get oneself going
- Going to work or class while high
- Missing or being unprepared for class or work because you were high
- Feeling bad later about something you said or did while high
- Driving a car while high
- Coming in conflict with the law because of drugs
- Doing something while high that you wouldn't otherwise do
- Being high in nonsocial, solitary situations
- Being unable to stop getting high
- Feeling a need for a drink or a drug to get through the day
- Becoming physically unhealthy
- Failing at school or on the job

■ Thinking about liquor or drugs all the time

■ Avoiding family or friends while using liquor or drugs

Any combination of these symptoms should be sufficient to alert you to the potential of a serious drug problem. Because drug and alcohol dependence are almost impossible to cure on one's own, people who suspect that they have a problem should seek immediate attention from a psychologist, physician, or counselor.

You can also get help from one of these national hotlines: For alcohol difficulties, call the National Council on Alcoholism at (800) 622-2255; for drug problems, call the National Institute on Drug Abuse at (800) 662-4357. You can also check your telephone book for a local listing of Alcoholics Anonymous or Narcotics Anonymous. Finally, you can write to the National Council on Alcoholism and Drug Dependence, 12 West 21 Street, New York, NY 10010, for help with alcohol and drug problems.

RECAP AND REVIEW III

RECAP

◀ Psychoactive drugs affect a person's emotions, perceptions, and behavior. The most dangerous drugs are those that are addictive—they produce a biological or psychological dependence.

◀ Stimulants produce an increase in the arousal of the central nervous system.

◀ Depressants decrease arousal in the central nervous system; they can produce intoxication.

◀ Narcotics produce relaxation, and relieve pain and anxiety.

◀ Hallucinogens produce hallucinations and other alterations of perception.

REVIEW

1. What is the technical term for drugs that affect a person's consciousness?

2. Match the type of drug to an example of that type.
   _____ 1. Barbiturate   a. LSD
   _____ 2. Amphetamine   b. Phenobarbitol
   _____ 3. Hallucinogen   c. Dexedrine

3. For each drug listed, classify it as:
   _____ 1. PCP   a. Stimulant
   _____ 2. Nicotine   b. Depressant
   _____ 3. Cocaine   c. Hallucinogen
   _____ 4. Alcohol   d. Narcotic
   _____ 5. Heroin
   _____ 6. Marijuana

4. The effects of LSD may recur long after the drug has been taken. True or false? _____

5. _____ is a drug which has been used to cure people of heroin addictions.

6. What is the problem with the use of methadone treatment?

Ask Yourself

Why is the use of psychoactive drugs and the search for altered states of consciousness found in almost every culture?

(Answers to review questions are on page 198.)

LOOKING BACK

■ *What are the different states of consciousness?*

   1. Consciousness refers to a person's awareness of the sensations, thoughts, and feelings being experienced at a given moment. It can vary in terms of how aware one is of outside stimuli; from an active to a passive state; and in terms of whether it is artificially induced or occurs naturally.

■ *What happens when we sleep, and what is the meaning and function of dreams?*

   2. Using the electroencephalogram, or EEG, to study sleep, scientists have found that the brain is active throughout the night, and that sleep proceeds through a series of stages identified by unique patterns of brain waves. In what is sometimes called stage 0, people move out of a waking state, in which they are relaxed with their eyes closed, into stage 1. Stage 1 is characterized by relatively rapid, low-voltage waves, whereas stage 2 shows more regular, spindle patterns. In stage 3, the brain waves become slower, with higher peaks and lower valleys apparent. Finally, stage 4 sleep includes waves that are even slower and more regular.

3. REM (rapid eye movement) sleep is characterized by an increase in heart rate, a rise in blood pressure, an increase in the rate of breathing and, in males, erections. Most striking is the rapid movement of the eyes, which dart back and forth under closed eyelids. Dreams occur during this stage. REM sleep seems to be critical to human functioning, whereas other stages of sleep are less essential.

4. According to Freud, dreams have both a manifest content (their apparent story line) and a latent content (their true meaning). He suggested that the latent content provides a guide to a dreamer's unconscious, revealing unfulfilled wishes or desires. Many psychologists disagree with this view; they suggest that the manifest content represents the true import of the dream.

5. The reverse learning theory suggests that dreams represent a process in which unnecessary information is "unlearned" and removed from memory. In this view, dreams have no meaning. In contrast, the dreams-as-survival theory suggests that information relevant to daily survival is reconsidered and reprocessed. Finally, the activation-synthesis theory proposes that dreams are a result of random electrical energy. This electrical energy randomly stimulates different memories, which are then woven into a coherent story line.

■ How much do we daydream on average?

6. Daydreaming, which may occur 10 percent of the time, is a typical part of waking consciousness, although wide individual differences exist in the amount of time devoted to it. There is little relationship between psychological disorders and a high incidence of daydreaming.

■ What are the major sleep disorders and how can they be treated?

7. Insomnia is a sleep disorder characterized by difficulty sleeping. Sleep apnea is a condition in which people experience difficulties in sleeping and breathing at the same time. People with narcolepsy have an uncontrollable urge to sleep. Sleepwalking and sleeptalking are relatively harmless.

8. Psychologists and sleep researchers advise people with insomnia to consider the following measures: increasing exercise during the day, avoiding caffeine and sleeping pills, drinking a glass of warm milk before bedtime, and avoiding *trying* to go to sleep.

■ Are hypnotized people in an altered state of consciousness, and can they be hypnotized against their will?

9. Hypnosis produces a state of heightened susceptibility to the suggestions of the hypnotist. Although there are no physiological indicators that distinguish hypnosis from normal waking consciousness, significant behavioral changes occur, including increased concentration and suggestibility, heightened ability to recall and construct images, lack of initiative, and acceptance of suggestions that clearly contradict reality. However, people cannot be hypnotized unwillingly.

10. Meditation is a learned technique for refocusing attention that brings about an altered state of consciousness. In transcendental meditation, the most popular form practiced in the United States, a person repeats a mantra (a sound, word, or syllable) over and over, concentrating until he or she becomes unaware of any outside stimulation and reaches a different state of consciousness.

■ What are the major classifications of drugs, and what are their effects?

11. Drugs can produce an altered state of consciousness. However, they vary in how dangerous they are and in whether or not they are addictive, producing a physical or psychological dependence. People take drugs for several reasons: to perceive the pleasure of the experience itself, to escape from everyday pressures, to attain religious or spiritual states, to follow the model of prestigious users or peers, or to experience the thrill of trying something new and perhaps illegal. Whatever the cause, drug addiction is one of the most difficult behaviors to modify.

12. Stimulants cause arousal in the central nervous system. Two common stimulants are caffeine (found in coffee, tea, and soft drinks) and nicotine (found in cigarettes). More dangerous are cocaine and amphetamines, or "speed." Although in small quantities they bring about increased confidence, a sense of energy and alertness, and a "high," in larger quantities they may overload the central nervous system, leading to convulsions and death.

13. Depressants decrease arousal in the central nervous system, causing the neurons to fire more slowly. They may cause intoxication along with feelings of euphoria. The most common depressants are alcohol and barbiturates.

14. Alcohol is the most frequently used depressant. Although it initially releases tension and produces positive feelings, as the dose of alcohol increases, the depressive effects become more pronounced. Alcoholics develop a tolerance for alcohol, and must drink alcoholic beverages in order to function. Both genetic causes and environmental stressors may lead to alcoholism.

15. Morphine and heroin are narcotics, drugs that produce relaxation and relieve pain and anxiety. Because of their addictive qualities, morphine and heroin are particularly dangerous.

16. Hallucinogens are drugs that produce hallucinations and other changes in perception. The most frequently used hallucinogen is marijuana; its use is common throughout the United States. Although occasional, short-term use of marijuana seems to be of little danger, long-term effects are less clear. The lungs may be damaged; there is the possibility that testosterone levels are lowered in males; and the immune system may be affected. Two other hallucinogens, LSD and PCP, affect the operation of neurotransmitters in the brain, causing an alteration in brain-cell activity and perception.

17. A number of signals indicate when drug use becomes drug abuse. These include frequent usage, getting high in order to get to class or work, driving while high, developing legal problems, and getting high alone. A person who suspects that he or she has a drug problem should get professional help; people are almost never capable of solving drug problems on their own.

ANSWERS (REVIEW III):

1. Psychoactive **2.** 1-b; 2-c; 3-a **3.** 1-c; 2-a; 3-a; 4-b; 5-d; 6-c **4.** True **5.** Methadone
6. People become addicted to the methadone.

KEY TERMS AND CONCEPTS

consciousness (p. 164)

altered states of consciousness (p. 166)

electroencephalogram (EEG) (p. 167)

stage 1 sleep (p. 168)

stage 2 sleep (p. 168)

stage 3 sleep (p. 168)

stage 4 sleep (p. 168)

rapid eye movement (REM) sleep (p. 169)

rebound effect (p. 170)

circadian rhythms (p. 171)

nightmares (p. 172)

night terrors (p. 172)

unconscious wish fulfillment (p. 173)

latent content of dreams (p. 173)

manifest content of dreams (p. 173)

reverse learning theory (p. 175)

dreams-for-survival theory (p. 175)

activation-synthesis theory (p. 175)

daydreams (p. 176)

insomnia (p. 177)

sleep apnea (p. 177)

sudden infant death syndrome (p. 177)

narcolepsy (p. 177)

hypnosis (p. 180)

meditation (p. 183)

mantra (p. 183)

psychoactive drugs (p. 185)

addictive drugs (p. 185)

stimulants (p. 186)

caffeine (p. 186)

nicotine (p. 187)

cocaine (p. 187)

amphetamines (p. 189)

depressants (p. 190)

intoxication (p. 190)

alcohol (p. 190)

alcoholics (p. 192)

barbiturates (p. 193)

narcotics (p. 193)

morphine (p. 193)

heroin (p. 193)

methadone (p. 193)

hallucinogen (p. 193)

marijuana (p. 193)

lysergic acid diethylamide (LSD) (p. 195)

phencyclidine (PCP) (p. 195)

7

LEARNING

BRAD GABRIELSON AND BO

Brad Gabrielson and his dog Bo.

One day a few years ago, Brad Gabrielson, now 30, was moving through his apartment in his wheelchair when he took a spill. He landed on the floor, with the chair on top of him. Gabrielson, of Jamestown, North Dakota, has cerebral palsy, which has robbed him of control of his muscles. "On my own, I would have had to lie there, under the chair, until my fiancee got home six hours later," he says. "I was all alone, except for Bo."

Bo is a wonderful friend, a companion who has stood by Brad faithfully, giving unselfishly of time and affection, asking little in return. But Bo is also a dog, a 5-year-old golden retriever and labrador mix. And without hands to lift his master or words to call for help, what could a dog do in a crisis like this?

"Bo came over and licked my face, to make sure I was all right, that I responded," Brad says. "Then he went to look for help." And Brad, who knew exactly what Bo could do, stopped worrying (Ryan, 1991, p. 14).

Gabrielson was right to stop worrying: Bo did just what he'd been trained to do. He left the apartment and went across the hall to a neighbor's door where he scratched and barked. Unluckily, though, the neighbor was not home.

Fortunately, Bo knew what to do. After coming back for a moment to lick Brad's face, Bo went upstairs to another neighbor's apartment. When that neighbor—who had never met Bo before—came to the door, Bo led him downstairs, carefully tugging his hand. The neighbor helped Brad back into his wheelchair, with Bo standing careful watch at his side.

Bo's success in this instance is just one of a long series of near-miraculous accomplishments. Through careful training, Bo has reduced Brad's dependence on family and friends and has increased his self-reliance. If the doorbell rings, Bo can answer the door. If Brad drops something, Bo will pick it up. If Brad is thirsty, Bo can bring him a drink.

Bo's remarkable capabilities did not just happen, of course. They are the result of meticulous training procedures. But to Brad, the process by which Bo was able to learn so much is less important than the changes that have occurred in his own life. Bo's presence has given Brad the opportunity to maintain a considerable degree of independence, one of the most precious commodities for a disabled person.

LOOKING AHEAD

The same processes that allowed trainers to harness and shape Bo's capabilities to benefit Brad Gabrielson are at work in each of our lives, as we read a book, drive a car, play poker, study for a test, or perform any of the other activities that make up our daily routine. Like Bo, each of us must acquire and then hone our skills and abilities through learning.

A fundamental topic for psychologists, learning underlies many of the diverse areas discussed throughout this book. For example, a psychologist studying perception might ask, "How do we learn that people who look small from a distance are far away and not simply tiny?" A developmental psychologist might inquire, "How do babies learn to distinguish their mothers from other people?" A clinical psychologist might wonder, "Why do some people learn to be afraid when they see a spider?" A social psychologist might ask, "How do we learn to feel that we are in love?" Each of these questions, although drawn from very different fields of psychology, can be answered only with reference to learning processes. In fact, learning plays a central role in almost every topic of interest to psychologists.

What do we mean by learning? Although psychologists have identified a number of different types of learning, a general definition encompasses them all: **Learning** is a relatively permanent change in behavior brought about by experience. What is particularly important about this definition is that it permits us to distinguish between performance changes due to **maturation** (the unfolding of biologically predetermined patterns of behavior due simply to getting older) and those changes brought about by experience. For instance, children become better tennis players as they grow older partially because their strength increases with their size—a maturational phenomenon. Such maturational changes need to be distinguished from improvements due to learning, which are a consequence of practice.

Similarly, we must distinguish between short-term changes in behavior that are due to factors other than learning, such as declines in performance resulting from fatigue or lack of effort, and performance changes that are due to actual learning. For example, if Jennifer Capriati performs poorly in a tennis game because of tension or fatigue, this does not mean that she has not learned to play correctly or has forgotten how to play well.

The distinction between learning and performance is critical, and not always easy to make (Bjork et al., 1991). To some psychologists, learning can only be inferred indirectly, by observing changes in performance. Because there is not always a one-to-one correspondence between learning and performance, understanding when true learning has occurred is difficult. (Those of us who have done poorly on an exam because we were tired and made careless mistakes can well understand this distinction.) Poor performance, then, does not necessarily indicate an absence of learning.

On the other hand, some psychologists have approached learning from a very different route. By considering learning simply as any change in behavior, they maintain that learning and performance are the same thing. Such an approach tends to dismiss the mental components of learning and focus on observable performance. As we will see, the degree to which learning can be understood without considering mental processes represents one of the major areas of disagreement among learning theorists of varying orientations.

In this chapter, we examine basic learning processes in order to answer a number of fundamental questions:

- What is learning?
- How do we learn to form associations between stimuli and responses?
- What is the role of reward and punishment in learning?
- What is the role of cognition and thought in learning?
- What are some practical methods for bringing about behavior change, both in ourselves and in others?

Learning: A relatively permanent change in behavior brought about by experience

Maturation: The unfolding of biologically predetermined patterns of behavior due to aging

Ivan Pavlov is best known for his contributions to the field of classical conditioning.

CLASSICAL CONDITIONING

What happens when you catch a glimpse of the golden arches in front of McDonald's? If the mere sight of them makes your mouth water and your thoughts turn to hamburgers and french fries, you are displaying a rudimentary form of learning called classical conditioning.

The processes that underlie classical conditioning explain such diverse phenomena as crying at the sight of a bride walking down the aisle at a wedding, fearing the dark, and falling in love with the boy or girl next door. To understand classical conditioning, however, it is necessary to move back in time and place to the early part of this century in Russia.

The Basics of Conditioning

Ivan Pavlov, a Russian physiologist, never intended to do psychological research. In 1904 he won the Nobel Prize for his work on digestion, testimony to his contribution to that field. Yet Pavlov is remembered not for his physiological research, but for his experiments on basic learning processes—work that he began quite accidentally.

Pavlov had been studying the secretion of stomach acids and salivation in dogs in response to the ingestion of varying amounts and kinds of food. While doing so, he observed a curious phenomenon: Sometimes stomach secretions and salivation would begin when no food had actually been eaten. The mere sight of a food bowl, the individual who normally brought the food, or even the sound of the footsteps of that individual was enough to produce a physiological response in the dogs. Pavlov's genius was his ability to recognize the implications of this rather basic discovery. He saw that the dogs were responding not only on the basis of a biological need (hunger), but also as a result of learning—or, as it came to be called, classical conditioning. In **classical conditioning**, an organism learns a response to a neutral stimulus that normally does not bring about that response.

Classical conditioning: A kind of learning in which a previously neutral stimulus comes to elicit a response through its association with a stimulus that naturally brings about the response

204 ◀

To demonstrate and analyze classical conditioning, Pavlov ran a series of experiments (Pavlov, 1927). In one, he attached a tube to the salivary gland of a dog, allowing him to measure precisely the amount of salivation that occurred. He then sounded a tuning fork and, just a few seconds later, presented the dog with meat powder. This pairing, carefully planned so that exactly the same amount of time elapsed between the presentation of the sound and the meat, occurred repeatedly. At first the dog would salivate only when the meat powder itself was presented, but soon it began to salivate at the sound of the tuning fork. In fact, even when Pavlov stopped presenting the meat powder, the dog still salivated after hearing the sound. The dog had been classically conditioned to salivate to the tone.

As you can see in Figure 7-1, the basic processes of classical conditioning underlying Pavlov's discovery are straightforward, although the terminology he chose has a technical ring. Consider first the diagram in Figure 7-1(*a*). Prior to conditioning, we have two unrelated stimuli: the sound of a tuning fork and

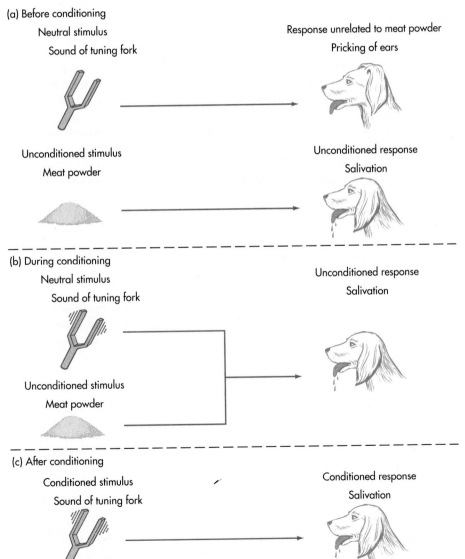

(a) Before conditioning

Neutral stimulus
Sound of tuning fork

Response unrelated to meat powder
Pricking of ears

Unconditioned stimulus
Meat powder

Unconditioned response
Salivation

(b) During conditioning

Neutral stimulus
Sound of tuning fork

Unconditioned response
Salivation

Unconditioned stimulus
Meat powder

(c) After conditioning

Conditioned stimulus
Sound of tuning fork

Conditioned response
Salivation

FIGURE 7-1

The basic process of classical conditioning. (*a*) Prior to conditioning, the sound of a tuning fork does not bring about salivation—making the tuning fork a neutral stimulus. On the other hand, meat powder naturally brings about salivation, making the meat powder an unconditioned stimulus and salivation an unconditioned response. (*b*) During conditioning, the tuning fork is sounded just before the presentation of the meat powder. (*c*) Eventually, the sound of the tuning fork alone brings about salivation. We can now say that conditioning has been accomplished: The previously neutral stimulus of the tuning fork is now considered a conditioned stimulus which brings about the conditioned response of salivation.

Neutral stimulus: A stimulus that, before conditioning, has no effect on the desired response

Unconditioned stimulus (UCS): A stimulus that brings about a response without having been learned

Unconditioned response (UCR): A response that is natural and needs no training (e.g., salivation at the smell of food)

Conditioned stimulus (CS): A once-neutral stimulus that has been paired with an unconditioned stimulus to bring about a response formerly caused only by the unconditioned stimulus

Conditioned response (CR): A response that, after conditioning, follows a previously neutral stimulus (e.g., salivation at the sound of a tuning fork)

meat powder. We know that the sound of a tuning fork leads not to salivation but to some irrelevant response such as perking of the ears or, perhaps, a startle reaction. The sound in this case is therefore called the **neutral stimulus** because it has no effect on the response of interest. We also have meat powder, which, because of the biological makeup of the dog, naturally leads to salivation—the response that we are interested in conditioning. The meat powder is considered an **unconditioned stimulus**, or **UCS**, because food placed in a dog's mouth automatically causes salivation to occur. The response that the meat powder produces is called an **unconditioned response**, or **UCR**—a response that is not associated with previous learning. Unconditioned responses are natural, innate responses that involve no training. They are always brought about by the presence of unconditioned stimuli.

Figure 7-1(*b*) illustrates what happens during conditioning. The tuning fork is repeatedly sounded just before presentation of the meat powder. The goal of conditioning is for the tuning fork to become associated with the unconditioned stimulus (meat powder) and therefore to bring about the same sort of response as the unconditioned stimulus. During this period, salivation gradually increases each time the tuning fork is sounded, until the tuning fork alone causes the dog to salivate.

When conditioning is complete, the tuning fork has evolved from a neutral stimulus to what is now called a **conditioned stimulus**, or **CS**. At this time, salivation that occurs as a response to the conditioned stimulus (tuning fork) is considered a **conditioned response**, or **CR**. This situation is depicted in Figure 7-1(*c*). After conditioning, then, the conditioned stimulus evokes the conditioned response.

The sequence and timing of the presentation of the unconditioned stimulus and the conditioned stimulus are particularly important (Rescorla, 1988). Like a malfunctioning railroad warning light at a street crossing that does not go on until after a train has passed by, a neutral stimulus that follows an unconditioned stimulus has little chance of becoming a conditioned stimulus. On the other hand, just as a warning light works best if it goes on right before a train is about to go by, a neutral stimulus that is presented just before the unconditioned stimulus is most apt to result in successful conditioning. Research has shown that conditioning is most effective if the conditioned stimulus precedes the unconditioned stimulus by between a half second and several seconds, depending on what kind of response is being conditioned.

Although the terminology employed by Pavlov to describe classical conditioning may at first seem confusing, the following rules of thumb can help to make the relationships between stimuli and responses easier to understand and remember:

■ *Un*conditioned stimuli lead to *un*conditioned responses.

■ *Un*conditioned stimulus–*un*conditioned response pairings are *un*learned and *un*trained.

■ During conditioning, previously neutral stimuli are transformed into conditioned stimuli.

■ Conditioned stimuli lead to conditioned responses, and conditioned stimulus–conditioned response pairings are a consequence of learning and training.

■ Unconditioned responses and conditioned responses are similar (such as salivation in the example described above), but the conditioned response is learned, whereas the unconditioned response occurs naturally.

In Watson's work with Albert, the infant's conditioned fear of white rats was generalized to include many furry white objects, including the Santa Claus mask worn by Watson in this photo.

Applying Conditioning Principles to Human Behavior

Although the initial classical conditioning experiments were carried out with animals, the principles that underlie the early work were soon found to explain many aspects of everyday human behavior. Recall, for instance, the earlier illustration of how people's mouths may start to water at the sight of McDonald's golden arches. The cause of this reaction is classical conditioning: The previously neutral arches have come to be associated with the food inside the restaurant (the unconditioned stimulus), causing the arches to become a conditioned stimulus that brings about the conditioned response of salivation.

Emotional responses are particularly apt to be learned through classical conditioning processes. For instance, how do some of us develop fears of mice, spiders, and other creatures that, if we thought about it much, would not seem intrinsically more ferocious or potentially harmful than a pet dog or cat? In a now-famous experiment designed to show that classical conditioning was at the root of such fears, an 11-month-old infant named Albert, who initially showed no fear of rats, was exposed to a loud noise at the same time that a rat was presented to him (Watson & Rayner, 1920). The noise (the UCS) evoked fear (the UCR). After just a few pairings of noise and rat, Albert began to show fear of the rat by itself. The rat, then, had become a CS that brought about the CR, fear. Similarly, the pairing of the appearance of certain species (such as mice or spiders) with the fearful comments of an adult may cause children to develop the same fears their parents have.

In adulthood, learning via classical conditioning occurs a bit more subtly. You may come to know that a professor's mood is particularly menacing when her tone of voice changes; in the past you may have seen that the professor uses that tone only when she is about to criticize someone's work. Likewise, you may not go to a dentist as often as you should because of prior associations with dentists and pain. Or you may have a particular fondness for the color blue because that was the color of your childhood bedroom. Classical conditioning, then, explains many of the reactions we have to stimuli in the world around us (Klein & Mowrer, 1989).

Extinction: Unlearning What You Have Learned

As long as you can remember, you have hated broccoli. The very sight of it makes you queasy. Yet your new boyfriend's parents seem to love it, serving it every time you come to visit. Being polite, you feel you must eat a little of it. The first few times it is torture; you feel as if you are about to embarrass yourself by getting sick at the table, but you steel yourself to keep the broccoli down. After a few weeks it becomes easier. In fact, after a couple of months, you are surprised to realize that you no longer feel sick at the thought of eating broccoli.

Your behavior can be explained by one of the basic phenomena of learning: extinction. **Extinction** occurs when a previously conditioned response decreases in frequency and eventually disappears. To produce extinction, one needs to end the association between conditioned and unconditioned stimuli. If we had trained a dog to salivate at the sound of a bell, we could bring about extinction by ceasing to provide meat after the bell was sounded. At first the dog would continue to salivate when it heard the bell, but after a few such instances, the amount of salivation would probably decline, and the dog would eventually stop responding to the bell altogether. At that point, we could say that the response had been extinguished. In sum, extinction occurs when the conditioned stimulus is repeatedly presented without the unconditioned stimulus.

As we will describe more fully in Chapter 18, psychologists have treated people with irrational fears or phobias using a form of therapy called systematic desensitization. The goal of **systematic desensitization** is to bring about the extinction of the phobia. For example, a therapist using systematic desensitization may repeatedly expose a person to a feared object or situation, starting with its least feared aspects and moving toward more fearful ones. As the negative consequences of exposure to the object or situation do not materialize, the fear eventually becomes extinguished.

Spontaneous Recovery: The Return of the Conditioned Response

Once a conditioned response has been extinguished, has it vanished forever? Not necessarily. Pavlov discovered this fact when he returned to his previously conditioned dog a week after the conditioned behavior had been extinguished. If he sounded a tuning fork, the dog once again salivated. Similarly, consider people who have been addicted to cocaine who manage to break the habit. Even though they are "cured," if they are subsequently confronted by a stimulus with strong connections to the drug—such as a white powder or a pipe used for smoking cocaine—they may suddenly experience an irresistible impulse to use the drug again, even after a long absence from drug use (Gawin, 1991).

This phenomenon is called **spontaneous recovery**—the reappearance of a previously extinguished response after time has elapsed without exposure to the conditioned stimulus. Usually, however, responses that return through spontaneous recovery are weaker than they were initially and can be extinguished more readily than before.

Generalization and Discrimination

Despite differences in color and shape, to most of us a rose is a rose is a rose. The pleasure we experience at the beauty, smell, and grace of the flower is similar for different roses. Pavlov noticed an analogous phenomenon: His dogs often salivated not only at the sound of the tuning fork that was used during their original conditioning but at the sound of a bell or a buzzer as well.

Such behavior is the result of stimulus generalization. **Stimulus generalization** takes place when a conditioned response follows a stimulus that is similar to the original conditioned stimulus. The greater the similarity between the two

Extinction: The weakening and eventual disappearance of a conditioned response

Systematic desensitization: A form of therapy in which fears are minimized through gradual exposure to the source of the fear.

Spontaneous recovery: The reappearance of a previously extinguished response after a period of time during which the conditioned stimulus has been absent

Stimulus generalization: Response to a stimulus that is similar to but different from a conditioned stimulus; the more similar the two stimuli, the more likely generalization is to occur

stimuli, the greater the likelihood of stimulus generalization. Baby Albert, who, as we mentioned earlier, was conditioned to be fearful of rats, was later found to be afraid of other furry white things; he was fearful of white rabbits, white fur coats, and even a white Santa Claus mask. On the other hand, according to the principle of stimulus generalization, it is unlikely that he would be afraid of a black dog, since its color would differentiate it sufficiently from the original fear-evoking stimulus.

The conditioned response evoked by the new stimulus is usually not as intense as the original conditioned response, although the more similar the new stimulus is to the old one, the more similar the new response will be. It is unlikely, then, that Albert's fear of the Santa Claus mask was as great as his learned fear of a rat. Still, stimulus generalization permits us to know, for example, that we ought to brake at all red lights, even if there are minor variations in size, shape, and shade.

If stimuli are sufficiently distinct from one another so that the presence of one evokes a conditioned response but the other does not, we can say that **stimulus discrimination** has occurred. In stimulus discrimination, an organism learns to differentiate among different stimuli and restricts its responding to one stimulus rather than to others. Without the ability to discriminate between a red and a green traffic light, we would be mowed down by oncoming traffic; and if we could not discriminate a cat from a mountain lion, we might find ourselves in uncomfortable straits on a camping trip.

Stimulus discrimination: The process by which an organism learns to differentiate among stimuli, restricting its response to one in particular

Higher-Order Conditioning

Suppose a four-year-old boy is knocked over a few times by his neighbor's large and ill-behaved dog, Rags. After a few such incidents, it would not be surprising that merely hearing the dog's name would produce a reaction of fear of the animal.

The unpleasant emotional reaction the child experiences on hearing "Rags" represents an example of higher-order conditioning. **Higher-order conditioning** occurs when a conditioned stimulus that has been established during earlier conditioning is then paired repeatedly with a neutral stimulus. If this neutral stimulus, by itself, comes to evoke a conditioned response similar to the original conditioned stimulus, higher-order conditioning has occurred. The original conditioned stimulus acts, in effect, as an unconditioned stimulus.

Our example of Rags can illustrate higher-order conditioning. The child has learned to associate the sight of Rags, who originally was a neutral stimulus, with rough behavior. The mere sight of Rags, then, has become a conditioned stimulus, which evokes the conditioned response of fear.

Later, however, the child makes the association that every time he sees Rags, its owner is calling the dog's name, saying, "Here, Rags." Because of this recurring pairing of the name of Rags (which was originally a neutral stimulus) with the sight of Rags (now a conditioned stimulus), the child becomes conditioned to experience a reaction of fear and loathing whenever he hears the name Rags, even though he may be safely inside his house. The name "Rags," then, has become a conditioned stimulus because of its earlier pairing with the conditioned stimulus of the sight of Rags. Higher-order conditioning has occurred: The sound of Rags' name has become a conditioned stimulus evoking a conditioned response.

Some psychologists have suggested that higher-order conditioning may provide an explanation for the acquisition and maintenance of prejudice against

Higher-order conditioning: A form of conditioning that occurs when an already conditioned stimulus is paired with a neutral stimulus until the neutral stimulus evokes the same response as the conditioned stimulus

members of racial and ethnic groups (Staats, 1975). Suppose, for instance, that every time a young girl's parents mentioned a particular racial group, they used such negative words as "stupid" or "filthy." Eventually, the girl might come to associate members of the group with the unpleasant emotional reaction that is evoked by the words "stupid" and "filthy" (reactions learned through prior classical conditioning). Although this is not a complete explanation for prejudice, as we shall see when we discuss it more fully in Chapter 20, it is likely that such higher-order conditioning is part of the process.

Beyond Traditional Classical Conditioning: Challenging Basic Assumptions

Theoretically, it ought to be possible to keep producing unlimited higher-order response chains, associating one conditioned stimulus with another. In fact, Pavlov hypothesized that all learning is nothing more than long strings of conditioned responses. However, this notion has not been supported by subsequent research, and it turns out that classical conditioning provides us with only a partial explanation of how people and animals learn (Rizley & Rescorla, 1972).

Some of the other fundamental assumptions of classical conditioning have also been questioned. For example, according to Pavlov, as well as to many contemporary proponents of classical conditioning, the process of linking stimuli and responses occurs in a mechanistic, unthinking way. In contrast to this perspective, learning theorists influenced by cognitive psychology have argued that there is more to classical conditioning than this mechanical view. They contend that learners develop an understanding and expectancy about what particular unconditioned stimuli are matched with specific conditioned stimuli. In a sense, this view suggests that the learner develops and holds an idea or image about what goes with what in the world (Rescorla, 1988; Turkkan, 1989; Baker & Mercier, 1989).

Evidence regarding the importance of learners' expectancies comes from a classic study done by psychologist Leon Kamin investigating classical conditioning in rats (1969). In the experiment, Kamin first presented repeated pairings of a tone and a shock to a group of rats. As expected, the animals soon demonstrated a classically conditioned response: If the tone alone was presented, the rats would respond with fear.

In phase two of the study, though, both a tone *and* a light were presented together to the same rats, followed each time with a shock. When the rats' learning was assessed, Kamin found that, as would be expected, presentation of the tone alone still brought about a classically conditioned fear response. However, even after repeated presentations of light, tone, and shock, presentation of the light, by itself, caused virtually no response. In effect, the rats seemed incapable of learning the new relationship between light and shock.

What made this result notable was how it compared to the behavior of a group of rats in a control condition. These rats had skipped the first phase of the experiment and had been conditioned with tone, light, and shock presented together from the outset. For these animals, the results were very different: Either a tone *or* a light—by itself—was sufficient to evoke a classically conditioned response to fear (see Figure 7-2).

Blocking: A phenomenon in which the association of one conditioned stimulus with an unconditioned stimulus obstructs the learning of a response to a second stimulus

Kamin argued that his results illustrated a phenomenon he called **blocking**, in which the association of one conditioned stimulus with an unconditioned stimulus obstructs the learning of a response to a second stimulus. The reason, he speculated, was that the presence of the first conditioned stimulus (the tone)

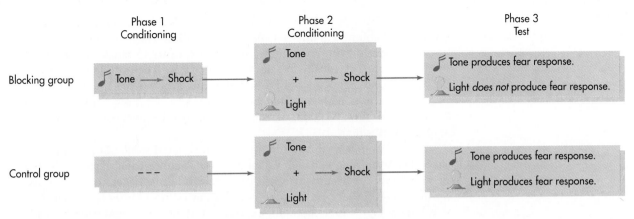

	Phase 1 Conditioning	Phase 2 Conditioning	Phase 3 Test
Blocking group	Tone → Shock	Tone + → Shock Light	Tone produces fear response. Light *does not* produce fear response.
Control group	---	Tone + → Shock Light	Tone produces fear response. Light produces fear response.

caused the organism to ignore the second stimulus (the light) when it was presented in the second phase of the experiment.

Furthermore, Kamin suggested that when the rats first were shocked following presentation of the tone in phase one of the study, they experienced surprise. It was this surprise that caused them to associate tone with shock and produced classical conditioning. In fact, Kamin argued that learning only occurs when surprising, unanticipated events occur. This explains why the light could not produce a conditioned response: The shock no longer came as a surprise to the rats during phase two, because they had already learned that the tone indicated an impending shock. Hence, when the tone, light, and shock were presented together, there was no longer an element of surprise in the situation, and the relationship between the light and shock went unlearned.

Kamin's complex reasoning is certainly a far cry from traditional classical conditioning explanations. Both the notions of ''ignoring'' a stimulus and ''surprise'' suggest that learners build an understanding and representation of the world in their minds. They expect certain events to be associated with one another. Such a view is compatible with cognitive psychology, but less so with traditional approaches to classical conditioning. As a result, Kamin's view remains controversial.

The Interval Between the CS and the UCS. Learning psychologists have raised other concerns about the traditional explanations of how classical conditioning functions. For example, work done by John Garcia, a leading researcher in learning processes, has disputed the supposition that optimum learning occurs only when the unconditioned stimulus immediately follows the conditioned stimulus (Garcia, Brett, & Rusiniak, 1989; Papini & Bitterman, 1990).

Like Pavlov, Garcia made his major contribution while studying a phenomenon unrelated to learning; he was initially concerned with the effects of exposure to nuclear radiation on laboratory animals. In the course of his experiments, he realized that rats in a radiation chamber drank almost no water, while in their home cage they drank it eagerly. The most obvious explanation, that it had something to do with the radiation, was soon ruled out: Garcia found that even when the radiation was not turned on, the rats still drank little or no water in the radiation chamber.

Initially puzzled by the rats' behavior, Garcia was eventually able to put the pieces together and understand what was happening. He noticed that the drinking cups in the radiation chamber were made of plastic, thereby giving the water an unusual, plastic-like taste, whereas those in the home cage were made of glass and left no abnormal taste.

FIGURE 7-2

An experiment illustrating blocking. In the first phase of the study, rats in the blocking group were conditioned to respond with fear to a tone. In the second phase, the tone and light were presented simultaneously, followed by a shock. The result, shown in phase three, was that the tone alone produced a fear response, while the light alone did *not* produce fear. In comparison, rats in the control group (who skipped the first phase of the experiment) were exposed to the tone and light simultaneously. In this condition, either the tone *or* the light, by itself, evoked the fear response.

After a series of experiments to rule out several alternative explanations, only one possibility remained: Apparently, the plastic-tasting water had become repeatedly paired with illness brought on by exposure to radiation, and had led the rats to form a classically conditioned association. The process began with the radiation acting as an unconditioned stimulus evoking the unconditioned response of sickness. With repeated pairings, the plastic-tasting water had become a conditioned stimulus that evoked the conditioned response of sickness (Garcia, Hankins, & Rusiniak, 1974).

The problem with this finding was that it violated some of the basic rules of classical conditioning—that an unconditioned stimulus should *immediately* follow the conditioned stimulus for optimal conditioning to occur. Instead, Garcia's findings showed that conditioning could occur even when there was an interval of as long as eight hours between exposure to the conditioned stimulus and the response of sickness. Furthermore, the conditioning persisted over very long periods and sometimes occurred after just one exposure to water that resulted in illness.

These findings have had important practical implications. In order to prevent coyotes from killing their sheep, some ranchers now routinely lace a sheep carcass with a drug and leave the carcass in a place where coyotes will find it. The drug temporarily makes the coyotes quite ill, but it does not permanently harm them. After just one exposure to a drug-laden sheep carcass, coyotes tend to avoid sheep, which are normally one of their primary natural victims. The sheep, then, have become a conditioned stimulus to the coyotes. This approach is a far more humane one than shooting, the traditional response of ranchers to predators (Gustavson, Garcia, Hankins, & Rusiniak, 1974).

RECAP AND REVIEW I

RECAP

◀ Learning is a relatively permanent change in behavior brought about by experience.

◀ Classical conditioning is a kind of learning in which an initially neutral stimulus, which does not evoke a relevant response, is paired repeatedly with an unconditioned stimulus. Eventually, the previously neutral stimulus evokes a response similar to that brought about by the unconditioned stimulus.

◀ Classical conditioning underlies many sorts of everyday learning, such as the acquisition of emotional responses.

◀ Among the basic phenomena of classical conditioning are extinction, systematic desensitization, spontaneous recovery, stimulus generalization and discrimination, and higher-order conditioning.

REVIEW

1. _____*Learning*_____ involves changes brought about by experience, whereas _____*maturation*_____ describes changes due to biological development.

2. _____*Pavlov*_____ is the name of the scientist responsible for discovering the learning phenomenon

known as _____*classical*_____ conditioning, in which an organism learns a response to a stimulus to which it would not normally respond.

Refer to the passage below to answer questions 3 through 6.

The last three times Theresa visited Dr. Noble for checkups, he administered a painful preventive immunization shot that left her in tears. When her mother takes her for another checkup, Theresa begins to sob as soon as she comes face to face with Dr. Noble, even before he has had a chance to say hello.

3. The painful shot that Theresa received during each visit was a(an) _____*UC*_____ _____*S*_____, which elicited the _____*UC*_____ _____*R*_____, her tears.

4. Dr. Noble is upset because his presence has become a _____*C*_____ _____*S*_____ for Theresa's crying.

5. When elicited by Dr. Noble's presence alone, Theresa's crying is referred to as a(an) _____*C*_____ _____*R*_____.

6. Fortunately, Dr. Noble gave Theresa no more shots for quite some time. Over that time she gradually stopped crying and even came to like him. _____*extinction*_____ had occurred.

7. In order to overcome his fear, a person afraid of spiders

is first taught to relax, then is gradually asked to approach a spider in an aquarium, and then finally handle the spider. What is the name of this technique? *systematic desensitization*

8. _stimulus_ _generalization_ occurs when a stimulus similar to, but not identical to, a conditioned stimulus produces a response. On the other hand, _stimulus_ _discrimination_ occurs when an organism does not produce a response to a stimulus that is distinct from the CS.

(Answers to review questions are on page 214.)

Ask Yourself

Theoretically, it should be possible to build an infinitely long chain of classically conditioned higher-order responses so that stimuli can be paired together indefinitely. What factors might prevent such a possibility from occurring in humans?

OPERANT CONDITIONING

Very good. . . . What a clever idea. . . . Fantastic. . . . I agree. . . . Thank you. . . . Excellent. . . . This is the best paper you've ever written; you get an A. . . . You are really getting the hang of it. . . . I'm impressed. . . . Let me give you a hug. . . . You're getting a raise. . . . Have a cookie. . . . You look great. . . . I love you. . . .

Few of us mind being the recipient of any of the above comments directed at us. But what is especially noteworthy about them is that each of these simple statements can be used to bring about powerful changes in behavior and to teach the most complex tasks through a process known as operant conditioning. Operant conditioning forms the basis for many of the most important kinds of human, and animal, learning.

Operant conditioning describes learning in which a voluntary response is strengthened or weakened, depending on its positive or negative consequences. Unlike classical conditioning, in which the original behaviors are the natural, biological responses to the presence of some stimulus such as food, water, or pain, operant conditioning applies to voluntary responses, which an organism performs deliberately, in order to produce a desirable outcome. The term "operant" emphasizes this point: The organism *operates* on its environment to produce some desirable result. For example, operant conditioning is at work when we learn that working industriously can bring about a raise, or that cleaning our room produces words of praise from our parents, or that studying hard results in good grades.

As with classical conditioning, the basis for understanding operant conditioning was laid by work with animals. We turn now to some of that early research, which began with a simple inquiry into the behavior of cats.

Thorndike's Law of Effect

If you placed a hungry cat in a cage and then put a small piece of food outside, chances are the cat would eagerly search for a way out of the cage. The cat might first claw at the sides or push against an opening. Suppose, though, that you had rigged things so that the cat could escape by stepping on a small paddle that released the latch to the door of the cage (see Figure 7-3). Eventually, as it moved around the cage, the cat would happen to step on the paddle, the door would open, and the cat would eat the food.

What would happen if you then returned the cat to the box? The next time, it would probably take a little less time for the cat to step on the paddle and escape. After a few trials, the cat would deliberately step on the paddle as soon

Operant conditioning: Learning in which a voluntary response is strengthened or weakened, depending on its positive or negative consequences; the organism operates on its environment in order to produce a particular result

FIGURE 7-3

Edward L. Thorndike devised this puzzle box to study the process by which a cat learns to press a paddle to escape the box and receive food (Thorndike, 1932; Sepp Seitz/Woodfin Camp. & Associates).

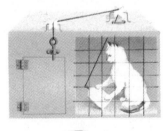

Law of effect: Thorndike's theory that responses that satisfy are more likely to be repeated, whereas those that don't satisfy are less likely to be repeated

as it was placed in the cage. What would have occurred, according to Edward L. Thorndike (1932), who studied this situation extensively, was that the cat would have learned that pressing the paddle was associated with the desirable consequence of getting food. Thorndike summarized that relationship by formulating the **law of effect**, which states that responses that are satisfying are more likely to be repeated, and those that are not satisfying are less likely to be repeated.

Thorndike believed that the law of effect operated as automatically as leaves falling off a tree in autumn. It was not necessary for an organism to understand that there was a link between a response and a reward. Instead, he thought that over time and through experience, the organism would form a direct connection between the stimulus and the response without any awareness that the connection existed.

The Basics of Operant Conditioning

Thorndike's early research formed the foundation for the work of one of the most influential psychologists, B. F. Skinner, who died in 1990. You may have heard of the Skinner box (shown in one form in Figure 7-4), a chamber with a highly controlled environment used to study operant conditioning processes with laboratory animals. Whereas Thorndike's goal was to get his cats to learn to obtain food by leaving the box, animals in a Skinner box learn to obtain food by operating on their environment within the box. Skinner became interested in specifying how behavior varied as a result of alterations in the environment.

Skinner, whose work went far beyond perfecting Thorndike's earlier apparatus, is considered the father of a whole generation of psychologists studying operant conditioning. To illustrate Skinner's contribution, let's consider what happens to a pigeon in the typical Skinner box.

Suppose you want to teach a hungry pigeon to peck a key that is located in its box. At first the pigeon will wander around the box, exploring the environment in a relatively random fashion. At some point, however, it will probably

FIGURE 7-4

A Skinner box, used to study operant conditioning. Laboratory animals learn to press the lever in order to obtain food, which is delivered in the tray (Sepp Seitz/ Woodfin Camp. & Associates).

B. F. Skinner was the major figure of operant conditioning.

peck the key by chance, and when it does, it will receive a food pellet. The first time this happens, the pigeon will not learn the connection between pecking and receiving food and will continue to explore the box. Sooner or later the pigeon will again peck the key and receive a pellet, and in time the frequency of the pecking response will increase. Eventually, the pigeon will peck the key continually until it satisfies its hunger, thereby demonstrating that it has learned that the receipt of food is contingent on the pecking behavior.

Reinforcing Desired Behavior.   In a situation such as this one, the food is called a reinforcer. A **reinforcer** is any stimulus that increases the probability that a preceding behavior will occur again. Here, food is a reinforcer because it increases the probability that the behavior of pecking the key (formally referred to as the "response" of pecking) will take place. Bonuses, toys, and good grades could also serve as reinforcers, if they strengthen a response that comes before their introduction. In each case, it is critical that the organism learn that the delivery of the reinforcer is contingent on the response occurring in the first place.

Of course, we are not born knowing that 75 cents can buy us a candy bar. Rather, through experience we learn that money is a valuable commodity because of its association with stimuli, such as food, drink, and shelter, that are naturally reinforcing. This fact suggests a distinction that can be drawn regarding whether something is a primary reinforcer or a secondary reinforcer. A **primary reinforcer** satisfies some biological need and works naturally, regardless of a person's prior experience; food for the hungry person, warmth for the cold person, and cessation of pain for a person who is hurting would all be classified as primary reinforcers. A **secondary reinforcer**, in contrast, is a stimulus that becomes reinforcing because of its association with a primary reinforcer. For instance, we know that money is valuable because it allows us to obtain other desirable objects, including primary reinforcers such as food and shelter; money thus becomes a secondary reinforcer.

What makes something a reinforcer is very individualistic. While a Hershey bar may act as a reinforcer for one person, an individual who hates chocolate might find 75 cents much more desirable. The only way we can know if a stimulus is a reinforcer for a given organism is to observe whether the rate of response of a previously occurring behavior increases after the presentation of the stimulus.

When an effective reinforcer ultimately is identified, however, the range of behaviors that can be taught is remarkable. As noted in the Psychology at Work box, operant procedures have been employed to teach an extraordinary variety of behaviors.

Reinforcer: Any stimulus that increases the probability that a preceding behavior will be repeated

Primary reinforcer: A reward that satisfies a biological need (e.g., hunger or thirst) and works naturally

Secondary reinforcer: A stimulus that becomes reinforcing by its association with a primary reinforcer (e.g., money, which allows us to obtain food, a primary reinforcer)

An ocean diver is swimming off the coast of the Pacific shore. He's been in the water for a few hours, when suddenly he realizes that he's been separated from his diving companion. Except for an array of passing fish, he's totally alone. He looks around, almost in a panic, unsure of what to do next.

Suddenly, a dolphin comes into view and swims straight at him. The dolphin brushes against him and clamps a small electrical box on his shoulder. The diver's panic abruptly subsides, as he realizes that help is on the way.

The reason for the diver's sudden relief comes from his awareness of the Navy's Marine Mammal Program—and of the capabilities of operant conditioning. The program utilizes ordinary dolphins and trains them to seek out and "tag" divers in the depths of the ocean (Holing, 1988).

The dolphins are trained using basic operant conditioning principles, primarily in the form of the presentation of positive reinforcement following the performance of desired behavior. In the same way that a pigeon learns to tap a key in order to receive a pellet of grain, dolphins learn that

SAVING LIVES WITH OPERANT CONDITIONING: DOLPHIN DEFENSES AND PIGEON POSSES

Operant conditioning is used to train dolphins to carry out complex behavior.

they will receive a reward of food when they locate a diver or other object under the water.

Because their inborn underwater skills far outstrip those of any human or machine, dolphins are uniquely qualified for the job of locating objects underwater. For example, their underwater hearing is very acute—they can hear sounds a quarter of a mile away—and, unlike humans, they can make repeated dives and surfacings over a short time.

Using operant conditioning, Navy psychologists have trained dolphins to carry out a variety of notable feats. Not only can they locate lost divers (or potential saboteurs), but they can

identify submarines and find pieces of rockets that have fallen to the ocean floor. They can even reveal the location of an object to waiting humans by hitting a series of underwater paddles with their snout. Although the information has been kept secret by the Navy, some observers suspect that dolphins were used in the 1991 Gulf War to communicate the location of mines in the Persian Gulf. These mines could then be defused or blown up by Navy personnel.

Dolphins are not the only animals being employed by the Navy. In one program, psychologists trained ordinary pigeons, housed in the belly of an airplane searching for missing sailors in the ocean, to peck a series of keys at the sight of an orange life jacket. Because the pigeons' vision is far more acute than that of humans, they are much better at locating lost sailors than the pilots of search planes (Cusak, 1984).

The use of animals such as dolphins and pigeons is often more effective, more reliable, and ultimately more economical than the utilization of humans or mechanical devices. Consequently, the military—as well as other governmental agencies—is continuing to explore the use and training of animals, based on the principles of operant conditioning.

Positive Reinforcers, Negative Reinforcers, and Punishment

Positive reinforcer: A stimulus added to the environment that brings about an increase in the response that preceded it

Negative reinforcer: A stimulus whose removal is reinforcing, leading to a greater probability that the response bringing about this removal will occur again

In many respects, reinforcers can be thought of in terms of rewards; both a reinforcer and a reward increase the probability that a preceding response will occur again. But the term "reward" is limited to *positive* occurrences, and this is where it differs from a reinforcer—for it turns out that reinforcers can be positive or negative.

A **positive reinforcer** is a stimulus added to the environment that brings about an increase in a preceding response. If food, water, money, or praise is provided following a response, it is more likely that that response will occur again in the future. The paycheck that workers get at the end of the week, for example, increases the likelihood that they will return to their jobs the following week.

In contrast, a **negative reinforcer** refers to a stimulus whose *removal* is reinforcing, leading to an increase in the probability that a preceding response will occur again in the future. For example, if you have cold symptoms that are relieved when you take medicine, you are more likely to take the medicine (a negative reinforcer) when you experience such symptoms again. Similarly, if the radio is too loud and hurts your ears, you are likely to find that turning it down relieves the situation; lowering the volume is negatively reinforcing and you are more apt to repeat the action in the future. Negative reinforcement, then, teaches the individual that taking an action removes a negative condition that exists in the environment.

Negative reinforcement occurs in two major forms of learning: escape conditioning and avoidance conditioning. In **escape conditioning**, an organism learns to make a response that brings about an end to an aversive situation. Escape conditioning is commonplace, and it often occurs quickly. For example, it doesn't take too long for children to learn to withdraw their hands from a hot radiator—an example of escape conditioning. Similarly, busy college students who take a day off to elude the stress of too much work are showing escape conditioning.

In contrast to escape conditioning, **avoidance conditioning** occurs when an organism responds to a signal of an impending unpleasant event in a way that permits its evasion. For example, a rat will readily learn to tap a bar to avoid a shock that is signaled by a tone. Similarly, human automobile drivers learn to fill up their gas tanks in order to avoid running out of fuel.

It is important to note that whether negative reinforcement consists of escape or avoidance conditioning, it is not the same as punishment. **Punishment** refers to unpleasant or painful stimuli—termed **aversive stimuli**—that are *added* to the environment if a certain behavior occurs. The intended result of punishment is a *decrease* in the probability that that behavior will occur again. In contrast, negative reinforcement is associated with the *removal* of an unpleasant or painful stimulus, which produces an *increase* in the behavior that brought an end to the unpleasant stimulus. If we receive a shock after behaving in a particular fashion, then, we are receiving punishment; but if we are already receiving a shock and do something to stop that shock, the behavior that stops the shock is considered to be negatively reinforced. In the first case, a specific behavior is apt to decrease because of the punishment; in the second, we are likely to increase the behavior because of the negative reinforcement (Azrin & Holt, 1966).

While punishment is typically considered in terms of applying some aversive stimulus—a spanking for misbehaving or ten years in jail for committing a crime—it may also consist of the removal of something positive. For instance, when a teenager is told she will no longer be able to use the family car because of her poor grades, or when an employee is informed that he has been demoted with a cut in pay because of poor job evaluations, punishment in the form of the removal of a positive reinforcer is being administered.

The distinctions between the types of punishment, as well as positive and negative reinforcement, may appear confusing at first glance, but the following rules of thumb (and the summary in Table 7-1) can help you to distinguish these concepts from one another:

■ Reinforcement *increases* the behavior preceding it; punishment *decreases* the behavior preceding it.

■ The *application* of a *positive* stimulus brings about an increase in behavior and is referred to as positive reinforcement; the *removal* of a *positive* stimulus decreases behavior and is called punishment by removal.

■ The *application* of a *negative* stimulus decreases or reduces behavior and is called punishment by application; the *removal* of a *negative* stimulus that results in an increase in behavior is termed negative reinforcement.

Escape conditioning: An organism's response, which brings about an end to an aversive situation

Avoidance conditioning: An organism's response to a signal of an impending unpleasant event in a way that permits its evasion

Punishment: An unpleasant or painful stimulus that is added to the environment after a certain behavior occurs, decreasing the likelihood that the behavior will occur again

Aversive stimuli: Unpleasant or painful stimuli

TABLE 7-1

TYPES OF REINFORCEMENT AND PUNISHMENT

Nature of Stimulus	Application	Removal or Termination
Positive	*Positive reinforcement* Example: Giving a raise for good performance Result: Increase in frequency of response (good performance)	*Punishment by removal* Example: Removal of favorite toy after misbehavior Result: Decrease in frequency of response (misbehavior)
Negative	*Punishment by application* Example: Giving a spanking following misbehavior Result: Decrease in frequency of response (misbehavior)	*Negative reinforcement* Example: Terminating a headache by taking aspirin Result: Increase in frequency of response (taking aspirin)

The Pros and Cons of Punishment: Why Reinforcement Beats Punishment

Is punishment an effective means of modifying behavior? Punishment often presents the quickest route to changing behavior that, if allowed to continue, might be dangerous to an individual. For instance, we may not have a second chance to warn a child not to run into a busy street, so punishing the first incidence of this behavior might prove to be wise. Moreover, the use of punishment to suppress behavior, even temporarily, provides the opportunity to reinforce a person for behaving in a more desirable way.

There are some instances in which punishment may be the most humane approach to treating certain deep-seated psychological problems. For example, some children suffer from autism, a rare psychological disorder in which they may abuse themselves, tearing at their skin or banging their heads against the wall, injuring themselves severely in the process. In such cases, punishment in the form of a quick but intense electric shock has been used, sometimes with remarkable results, to prevent self-injurious behavior when all other treatments have failed (Lovaas & Koegel, 1973; Linscheid et al., 1990). Such punishment, however, is used only as a treatment of last resort, keeping the child safe and buying time until positive reinforcement procedures can be initiated.

Several disadvantages make the routine use of punishment questionable. For one thing, it is frequently ineffective, particularly if the punishment is not delivered shortly after the behavior being suppressed or if the individual is able to withdraw from the setting in which the punishment is being given. An employee who is reprimanded by the boss may quit; a teenager who loses the use of the family car may run away from home. In such instances, then, the initial behavior that is being punished may be replaced by one that is even less desirable.

Even worse, physical punishment may convey to the recipient the idea that physical aggression is permissible and perhaps even desirable. A father who yells and hits his son teaches the son that aggression is an appropriate, adult response, and the son may soon copy his father's behavior and act aggressively toward others. In addition, physical punishment is often administered by people who are themselves angry or enraged. It is unlikely that individuals in such an emotional state will be able to think through what they are doing or to carefully control the degree of punishment they are inflicting.

The use of physical punishment produces the risk that the people administering the punishment will grow to be feared. Furthermore, unless people who are being punished can be made to understand the reasons—that the punishment is meant to change behavior and that it is independent of the punishers' view of them as individuals—punishment may lead to lowered self-esteem.

Finally, punishment does not convey any information about what an alternative, more appropriate behavior might be. In order to be useful in bringing about more desirable behavior in the future, punishment must be paired with specific information about what is being punished, along with information about a more desirable behavior. To punish a child for staring out the window in school may lead her to stare at the floor instead. Unless we teach her the appropriate way to respond, we have managed only to substitute one undesirable behavior for another. If punishment is not combined with reinforcement for alternative behavior that is more appropriate, little will be accomplished. In sum, reinforcing desired behavior is a more appropriate technique for modifying behavior than using punishment. Both in and out of the scientific arena, then, reinforcement usually beats punishment (Azaroff & Mayer, 1991).

RECAP AND REVIEW II

RECAP

◀ Operant conditioning is a form of learning in which a voluntary response is strengthened or weakened, depending on its positive or negative consequences.

◀ A reinforcer is any stimulus that increases the probability that a preceding response will occur.

◀ Primary reinforcers are those that satisfy a biological need and therefore are effective without prior experience; secondary reinforcers are stimuli that, because of their previous association with primary reinforcers, begin to elicit the same responses as primary reinforcers.

◀ A positive reinforcer is a stimulus that is added to the environment to increase the likelihood of a response. A negative reinforcer is a stimulus whose removal leads to an increase in the probability that a preceding response will occur in the future.

◀ Punishment is the administration of an unpleasant stimulus, following a response, which is meant to decrease or suppress behavior; it may also consist of the removal of a positive reinforcer.

◀ The distinction between punishment and negative reinforcement is critical: In punishment, the goal is to decrease or suppress undesired behavior by administering a stimulus; in negative reinforcement, the goal is to increase a desired behavior by removing a stimulus.

REVIEW

1. _____ conditioning describes learning that occurs as a result of reinforcement.
2. Thorndike found that behaviors that lead to reward are likely to be repeated, while behaviors that lead to punishment will not be repeated. What did he call this phenomenon?
3. A child who cleans his room is given a cookie. The cookie in this situation acts as a _____.
4. A hungry person would find food to be a _____ reinforcer, while a ten-dollar bill would be a _____ reinforcer, because it would allow him to buy food.
5. Scientists have found a set of about ten basic reinforcers that will be effective on any human. True or false? _____
6. Match the type of operant learning with its definition:

   a. _____ Positive reinforcement

   b. _____ Negative reinforcement

   c. _____ Punishment

   1. An unpleasant stimulus is presented to decrease behavior.
   2. An unpleasant stimulus is removed to increase behavior.
   3. A pleasant stimulus is presented to increase behavior.

7. Punishment should be administered approximately 12-24 hours after unwanted behavior, so that the natural consequences of the behavior have time to sink in. True or false?

   _____

8. Sandy had had a rough day, and his son's noisemaking was not helping him relax. Not wanting to resort to scolding, Sandy lowered his tone of voice and told his son in a serious manner that he was very tired and would like the boy to play quietly for an hour. This approach worked. For Sandy, the change in his son's behavior was

   a. positively reinforcing.

   b. secondarily reinforcing.

c. punishing.

d. negatively reinforcing.

9. Sandy was pleased. He had not been happy with himself a week earlier, when he yelled loudly at his son. On that occasion he had halted his son's excessive noise through

a. removal of a reinforcer.

b. punishment.

c. negative reinforcement.

d. extinction.

Ask Yourself

B. F. Skinner believed that a person's entire life could be structured according to operant conditioning principles. Do you think this is possible? What benefits and problems would result?

(Answers to review questions are on page 222.)

Schedules of reinforcement: The frequency and timing of reinforcement following desired behavior

Continuous reinforcement schedule: The reinforcing of a behavior every time it occurs

Partial reinforcement schedule: The reinforcing of a behavior some, but not all, of the time

Cumulative recorder: A device that automatically records and graphs the pattern of responses made in reaction to a particular reinforcement schedule

Slot machines and other casino games provide reinforcement intermittently. Does this help to explain why many people continue to gamble even though they know their chances of winning are slim?

Schedules of Reinforcement: Timing Life's Rewards

The world would be a different place if poker players folded for good at their first losing hand, fishermen returned to shore as soon as they missed a catch, or door-to-door salespeople stopped selling at the first house at which they were turned away. The fact that such unreinforced behaviors continue, often with great frequency, illustrates that reinforcement need not be received continually in order for behavior to be learned and maintained. In fact, behavior that is reinforced only occasionally may ultimately be learned better than behavior that is always reinforced.

When we refer to the frequency and timing of reinforcement following desired behavior we are talking about **schedules of reinforcement**. Behavior that is reinforced every time it occurs is said to be on a **continuous reinforcement schedule**; if it is reinforced some but not all of the time, it is on a **partial reinforcement schedule**. Although learning occurs more rapidly under a continuous reinforcement schedule, learned behavior lasts longer after reinforcement stops when it is learned under a partial reinforcement schedule.

Why should partial reinforcement schedules result in stronger, longer-lasting learning than continuous reinforcement schedules? We can answer the question by examining how we might behave when using a soda vending machine compared with a Las Vegas slot machine. When we use a vending machine, prior experience has taught us that the schedule of reinforcement is continuous—every time we put in 75 cents, the reinforcement, a soda, ought to be delivered. In comparison, a slot machine offers a partial reinforcement schedule: We have learned that after putting in 75 cents, most of the time we will not receive anything in return. At the same time, though, we know that we will occasionally win something.

Now suppose that, unbeknownst to us, both the soda vending machine and the slot machine are broken, and neither one is able to dispense anything. It will not be very long before we stop depositing coins into the broken soda machine; probably at most we would try only two or three times before leaving the machine in disgust. But the story would be quite different with the broken slot machine. Here, we would drop in money for a considerably longer time, even though no response would be forthcoming.

In formal terms, we can see the difference between the two reinforcement schedules: Partial reinforcement schedules (such as those provided by slot machines) maintain performance longer than continuous reinforcement schedules (such as those established in soda vending machines) before extinction occurs.

Using a **cumulative recorder**, a device that automatically records and graphs the pattern of responses made in reaction to a particular schedule (see Figure 7-5), learning psychologists have found that certain kinds of partial reinforcement schedules produce stronger and lengthier responding before extinction than others do (King & Logue, 1990). Although many different partial reinforce-

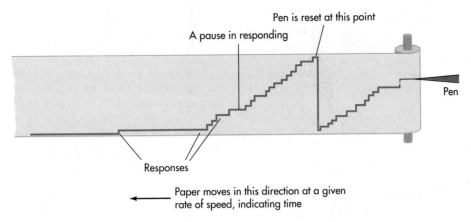

A pause in responding

Pen is reset at this point

Pen

Responses

Paper moves in this direction at a given rate of speed, indicating time

FIGURE 7-5

A cumulative recorder. As the paper slowly unrolls, the pen indicates when a response has been made by moving a notch upward. Pauses in responding are indicated by a lack of upward movement of the line. As is the case in this example, it is typical for the time between initial responses to decrease as the organism learns to make the response.

ment schedules have been examined, they can most readily be put into two categories: schedules that consider the *number of responses* made before reinforcement is given, called fixed-ratio and variable-ratio schedules, and those that consider the *amount of time* that elapses before reinforcement is provided, called fixed-interval and variable-interval schedules.

Fixed- and Variable-Ratio Schedules.   In a **fixed-ratio schedule**, reinforcement is given only after a certain number of responses are made. For instance, a pigeon might receive a food pellet every tenth time it pecked a key; here, the ratio would be 1:10. Similarly, garment workers are generally paid on fixed-ratio schedules: They receive *x* dollars for every ten blouses they sew. Because a greater rate of production means more reinforcement, people on fixed-ratio schedules are apt to work as quickly as possible. Even when rewards are no longer offered, responding comes in bursts—although pauses between bursts become longer and longer until the response peters out entirely (see Figure 7-6, p. 222).

In a **variable-ratio schedule**, reinforcement occurs after a varying number of responses rather than after a fixed number. Although the specific number of responses necessary to receive reinforcement varies, the number of responses usually hovers around a specific average. Probably the best example of a variable-ratio schedule is that encountered by a door-to-door salesperson. She may make a sale at the third, eighth, ninth, and twentieth houses she visits without being successful at any of the houses in between. Although the number of responses that must be made before making a sale varies, it averages out to a 20 percent success rate. Under these circumstances, you might expect that the salesperson would try to make as many calls as possible in as short a time as possible. This is the case with all variable-ratio schedules; they promote a high rate of response and a high resistance to extinction.

Fixed- and Variable-Interval Schedules: The Passage of Time.   In contrast to fixed- and variable-ratio schedules—in which the crucial factor is the number of responses—fixed-*interval* and variable-*interval* schedules focus on the amount of *time* that has elapsed since a person or animal was rewarded. One example of a fixed-interval schedule is a weekly paycheck. For people who receive regular, weekly paychecks, it makes little difference how much they produce in a given week—as long as they show up and do *some* work.

Because a **fixed-interval schedule** provides a reinforcement for a response only if a fixed time period has elapsed, overall rates of response are relatively low. This is especially true in the period just after reinforcement when the time

Fixed-ratio schedule:
A schedule whereby reinforcement is given only after a certain number of responses is made

Variable-ratio schedule:
A schedule whereby reinforcement occurs after a varying number of responses rather than after a fixed number

Fixed-interval schedule:
A schedule whereby reinforcement is given at established time intervals

▶ **221**

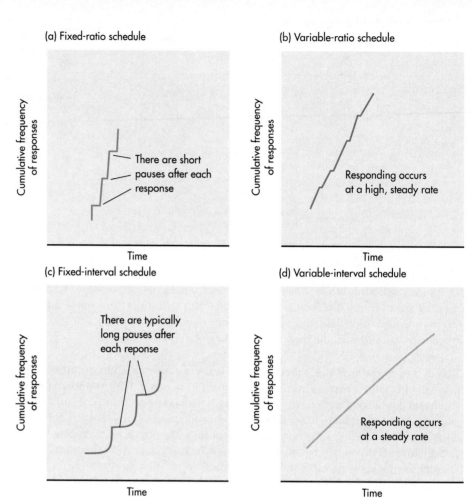

(a) Fixed-ratio schedule

There are short pauses after each response

(b) Variable-ratio schedule

Responding occurs at a high, steady rate

(c) Fixed-interval schedule

There are typically long pauses after each reponse

(d) Variable-interval schedule

Responding occurs at a steady rate

FIGURE 7-6

Typical outcomes of different reinforcement schedules. (*a*) In a fixed-ratio schedule, short pauses occur after each response. Because the more responses, the more reinforcement, fixed-ratio schedules produce a high rate of responding. (*b*) In a variable-ratio schedule, responding also occurs at a high rate. (*c*) A fixed-interval schedule produces lower rates of responding, especially just after reinforcement has been presented, since the organism learns that a specified time period must elapse between reinforcements. (*d*) A variable-interval schedule produces a fairly steady stream of responses.

Variable-interval schedule:
A schedule whereby reinforcement is given at various times, usually causing a behavior to be maintained more consistently

before another reinforcement is relatively great. Students' study habits often exemplify this reality: If the periods between exams are relatively long (meaning that the opportunity for reinforcement for good performance is fairly infrequent), students often study minimally or not at all until the day of the exam draws near. Just before the exam, however, students begin to cram for it, signaling a rapid increase in the rate of their studying response (Mawhinney et al., 1971). As you might expect, just after the exam there is a rapid decline in the rate of responding, with few people opening a book the day after a test.

One way to decrease the delay in responding that occurs just after reinforcement, and to maintain the desired behavior more consistently throughout an interval, is to use a variable-interval schedule. In a **variable-interval schedule**, the time between reinforcements varies around some average rather than being fixed. For example, a professor who gives surprise quizzes that vary from one every three days to one every three weeks, averaging one every two weeks, is using a variable-interval schedule. Students' study habits would most likely be very different as a result of such an unpredictable schedule than those we observed with

ANSWERS (REVIEW II):

1. Operant **2.** Law of effect **3.** reinforcer **4.** primary; secondary **5.** False; reinforcers are highly individualized. **6.** a-3; b-2; c-1 **7.** False; punishment should be presented immediately after the behavior. **8.** d **9.** b

a fixed-interval schedule: Students would be apt to study more regularly since they would never know when the next surprise quiz would be coming. Variable-interval schedules, in general, are more likely to produce relatively steady rates of responding than fixed-interval schedules, with responses that take longer to extinguish after reinforcement ends.

Discrimination and Generalization in Operant Conditioning

It does not take a child long to learn that a red light at an intersection means stop, while a green light indicates that it is permissible to continue. Just as in classical conditioning, then, operant learning involves the phenomena of discrimination and generalization.

The process by which people learn to discriminate stimuli is known as stimulus control training. In **stimulus control training**, a behavior is reinforced in the presence of a specific stimulus, but not in its absence. For example, one of the most difficult discriminations many people face is determining when someone's friendliness is not mere friendliness, but a signal of romantic interest. People learn to make the discrimination by observing the presence of certain subtle nonverbal cues—such as increased eye contact and touching—that indicate romantic interest. When such cues are absent, they learn that no romantic interest is indicated. In this case, the nonverbal cue acts as a discriminative stimulus, one to which an organism learns to respond during stimulus control training. A **discriminative stimulus** signals the likelihood that reinforcement will follow a response. For example, if you wait until your roommate is in a good mood before asking to borrow her favorite compact disc, your behavior can be said to be under stimulus control.

Just as in classical conditioning, the phenomenon of stimulus generalization, in which an organism learns a response to one stimulus and then applies it to other stimuli, is also found in operant conditioning. If you have learned that being polite produces the reinforcement of getting your way in a certain situation, you are likely to generalize your response to other situations. Sometimes, though, generalization can have unfortunate consequences, such as when people behave negatively toward all members of a racial group because they have had an unpleasant experience with one member of the racial group.

Superstitious Behavior

Wade Boggs, the star player of the Boston Red Sox, performs an elaborate set of pregame and midgame rituals throughout the baseball season. According to one news report, "he eats specific foods on specific days, leaves for the ball park at the same time each day, takes the same number of practice grounds from the same coach, runs his sprints at the same time, runs to his position retracing his exact footprints, and draws the Hebrew symbol *chai* ("life") in the dirt each time he steps up to home plate" (Globe Magazine, 1989, p. 44). Boggs believes that he must complete these exacting rituals in order to play a successful game.

While it is easy to dismiss Wade Boggs' elaborate rituals, learning psychologists would consider them as an example of a revealing class of responses called **superstitious behavior** (Zimmer, 1984). In fact, many of us have some superstitions of our own; wearing a special shirt when we take a test or go for a job interview, telling ourselves that if we make all the traffic lights on a certain road we'll have good luck for the rest of the day, or—an old favorite—avoiding a black cat in our path.

Stimulus control training: Training in which an organism is reinforced in the presence of a certain specific stimulus, but not in its absence

Discriminative stimulus: A stimulus to which an organism learns to respond as part of stimulus control training

Superstitious behavior: The mistaken belief that particular ideas, objects, or behavior will cause certain events to occur, as a result of learning based on the coincidental association between the idea, object, or behavior and subsequent reinforcement

Baseball player Wade Boggs is known for engaging in superstitious practices, including drawing the Hebrew symbol for "life" in the dirt with his foot before going up to bat.

Is everyone susceptible to
superstitious beliefs?

Where do such superstitions come from? To learning psychologists, the answer originates from the principles of reinforcement (Justice & Looney, 1990). As we have discussed, behavior that is followed by a reinforcer tends to be strengthened. Occasionally, however, the behavior that occurs prior to the reinforcement is entirely coincidental. Imagine, for instance, that a baseball player hits his bat against the ground three times in a row and then gets a home run. The hit is, of course, coincidental to the batter's hitting the ground, but to the player it may be seen as somehow related. Because the association is made in the player's mind, he may hit the ground three times every time he is at bat in the future. And because he will be at least partially reinforced for this behavior— batters usually get a hit 25 percent of the time—his ground-hitting behavior will probably be maintained.

Do superstitions actually affect subsequent behavior? In fact, they do. According to some psychologists, superstitious behavior allows people to cope with anxiety by providing routines or rituals that can give them a sense of control over a situation (Zimmer, 1984). In this way, wearing a "lucky" shirt helps to calm a person—which, in fact, may lead to better performance when taking a test or during a stressful interview. As you can see, then, your superstitions may shape your subsequent behavior.

Shaping: Reinforcing What Doesn't Come Naturally

Consider the difficulty of using operant conditioning to teach people to repair an automobile transmission. If you had to wait until they fixed it perfectly before you provided them with reinforcement, the Model T might be back in style long before they ever mastered the repair process.

There are many complex behaviors, ranging from auto repair to zebra hunting, which we would not expect to occur naturally as part of anyone's spontaneous behavior. In cases such as these, in which there otherwise might be no opportunity to provide reinforcement for the particular behavior (since it never occurs in the first place), a procedure known as shaping is used. **Shaping** is the process of teaching a complex behavior by rewarding closer and closer approximations of the desired behavior. In shaping, any behavior that is at all similar to the behavior you want the person to learn is reinforced at first. Later, you reinforce only responses that are closer to the behavior you ultimately want to teach. Finally, you reinforce only the desired response. Each step in shaping, then, moves only slightly beyond the previously learned behavior, permitting the person to link the new step to the behavior learned earlier.

Shaping allows even lower animals to learn complex responses that would never occur naturally, ranging from lions trained to jump through hoops to dolphins trained to rescue divers lost at sea (as we saw in the Psychology at Work box earlier). Shaping also underlies the learning of many complex human skills. For instance, the organization of most textbooks is based on the principles of shaping. Typically, information is presented so that new material builds on previously learned concepts or skills. Thus the concept of shaping could not be presented in this chapter until we had discussed the more basic principles of operant learning.

Shaping: The process of teaching a complex behavior by rewarding closer and closer approximations of the desired behavior

Using Programmed Instruction in College Classes: Programs as Professors

Chemistry students can mix chemicals to their hearts' delight without risk of explosion. Medical students can perform simulated operations without endangering a patient's life. Physics students can see the path electrons travel in response to different forces (Pollack, 1987, p. D6).

The opportunity to carry out each of these activities comes not from a resourceful and clever classroom teacher but from an inanimate replacement: a computer. According to proponents of the use of computers to teach college students, the increasingly widespread availability of computers and an increase in computer literacy on many college campuses will lead to a revolution in instruction. In this view, computers may be routinely used to supplement human instruction, or to teach courses entirely, in the not-too-distant future.

The use of computers in classrooms is based on a procedure first developed some sixty years ago (Benjamin, 1988). Called programmed instruction or computer-assisted instruction, it represents one of the most common applications of shaping (Burns, Parlett, & Redfield, 1991; Steinberg, 1990; Skinner, 1986). **Programmed instruction** explicitly uses the principles of learning in the design of instructional material. A student using such material is first asked to type into the computer very simple responses that are printed on the screen; then the student moves on to increasingly complex problems. Correct responses are immediately reinforced, while mistakes evoke a review of previous material. The reinforcement for correct responses may be explicit, in the form of encouragement printed on the screen ("Good," "Great job, Laura," "Keep it up," and the like), or the user may simply be allowed to move on to the next part of the lesson, which in itself can act as a powerful reinforcer. Each correct response shapes the student's behavior to bring him or her closer to the final desired behavior—mastery of a relatively complex body of material.

Programmed instruction: The development of learning by building gradually on basic knowledge, with review and reinforcement when appropriate

The advantages of using programmed instruction are many (Steinberg, 1990). Computers never become fatigued, and they are available whenever the student is. Sophisticated programs can critically analyze students' patterns of

FIGURE 7-7

This example of computerized programmed instruction comes from MacLaboratory, a program that presents psychology experiments. (Courtesy of Douglas L. Chute, MacLaboratory, 1992.)

errors and present material in a manner that is specifically suited to the learning capabilities of each student. In addition, the computer is capable of providing sophisticated simulations that permit students to experience situations that would otherwise be physically impossible or excessively expensive. State-of-the-art computers use optical disks—newer versions of the compact disks used for music—to deliver stereo sound, photos, and moving pictures, along with enough written text to fill a small library (Steinberg, 1991).

The potential of computer-assisted instruction is great. For instance, computers offer the opportunity for a psychology student, who is studying learning, to read a selection on the screen about the principles of classical conditioning. Then, the student could choose to participate in a simulation of conditioning in which a video of Pavlov's apparatus was presented on the screen. Next, the student might choose to learn more about Pavlov, branching to information about nineteenth-century Russia and the environment in which Russian scientists worked. From there, the student might decide to branch to material on scientific methods in the nineteenth century, or might choose to consider the biological bases of dogs' salivation, depending on what was of interest. Clearly, the future holds broad possibilities for programmed instruction (Spiro & Jehng, 1990). (For an example of current programmed instruction, see Figure 7-7.)

Programmed instruction is not without its critics, however. Some people believe that the excessive use of simulations will not provide students with an understanding of what actually happens in the real world, such as when laboratory experiments go awry. Others feel that the inability of students to ask questions beyond those that have been programmed is too restrictive.

Still, most data suggest that carefully designed programmed instruction can be an effective teaching technique (Redfield & Steuck, 1991; Larkin & Chabay, 1991). Computers are also helping to illuminate basic learning processes, as you can see in the accompanying Cutting Edge box.

Discriminating between Classical and Operant Conditioning

Up to now, we have been discussing classical and operant conditioning as though they were two entirely distinct approaches. However, these two types of conditioning share several features.

LEARNING LIKE HUMANS: BUILDING NEURAL NETWORKS VIA COMPUTER

A computer is teaching itself to read out loud. Initially, its attempts sound like gibberish, since it has not been given any rules about what the sounds of particular letters are. However, after electronically receiving corrective feedback following each mistake it makes, it soon begins to produce babylike babbling sounds as it learns to distinguish between vowels and consonants. After an evening of computing, it reads with only minor errors (Pollack, 1987).

A new breed of computer programs, such as this one developed by Terrence Sejnowski of Johns Hopkins University, are demonstrating that they can learn how to learn—and, in the process, are illuminating the manner in which human beings themselves learn. These new programs are based on the rapidly increasing knowledge developed by biopsychologists regarding the structure of the brain.

As you'll recall from our discussion in Chapter 3, groups of neurons in the brain are organized into neural networks that arrange communication links between cells. By mimicking these networks in their computer programs, researchers are attempting to develop computers that in essence program themselves, without requiring a human to produce a set of rules

and procedures for the computer to follow (Roberts, 1989; Commons, Grossberg, & Staddon, 1991).

Computers using neural networks operate in a manner analogous to the way neurons in the brain operate during learning. Instead of working on a problem in a series of sequential steps, one step at a time, the computer's processing units (called nodes) are programmed to operate simultaneously on a problem, as do the billions of neurons in the brain. Each of these computer nodes is connected to many others, again analogous to the way in which the brain's neurons are connected via synapses to other neurons, with the strength of the connections varying.

Each computer node has a particular activation level that determines whether or not it will "fire," thereby sending information to another node. Furthermore, not only does the activation level vary, but the magnitude of the connection between two nodes may differ. Either of these variables can be set by the computer programmer in advance, or the computer itself can, through trial and error, set its own levels, according to the nature of the problem on which it is working (Ackley, Hinton, & Sejnowski, 1985; Gluck & Rumelhart, 1990).

When faced with a problem, the computer network processes information simultaneously on many levels. Unlike traditional computer programs, in which the rules must be completely specified in advance (for example, the letter "t" is pronounced differently when it is followed by an "h" than when it is followed by a vowel), neural network computers can develop their own rules based on the feedback they receive.

What is particularly interesting is how the computer's use of the electronic feedback it is provided mimics the shaping procedures that psychologists have discovered to underlie the learning of complex information. Moreover, neural network computers are helping to unravel the question of how much learning is due to the mere application of rules, and under what conditions classical conditioning and operant conditioning principles are most pertinent.

Still, computers have yet to approach the learning capabilities of human beings. Given the fact that there may be a quadrillion neural connections in the human brain, the likelihood that any computer will soon reach the level of human learning is low. However, the day may come when a computer can be made to learn effectively—helping us in turn to understand the process of human learning better.

For example, generalization and discrimination processes are found in operant conditioning, just as they are in classical conditioning. A pigeon that has learned to peck a red key to receive food will probably do the same thing to a blue key, illustrating that generalization has occurred. Similarly, discrimination processes are also present in operant conditioning. A child who learns from the reinforcers his parents provide that he ought to stay away from strangers, but be polite and friendly to acquaintances, is demonstrating the principle of discrimination.

The fact that generalization and discrimination are present in both classical and operant conditioning suggests that the distinction between these two types of learning is not always clear-cut. Consider, for instance, what happens when you are called into the house for dinner. As you hear the call for dinner, you begin to salivate, and the smells of the food become stronger as you approach the kitchen. You quickly reach the table and receive your reward for coming: a big helping of roast beef, potatoes, and salad.

▶ **227**

Is your behavior the result of classical conditioning or operant conditioning? Actually, it is both. Your salivation reflects classical conditioning. You have learned to associate being called in to dinner with the food that follows it. But the footsteps taking you to the table, which actually allow you to receive the reinforcement of food, reflect a behavioral pattern learned through operant conditioning; you have purposefully responded in a way that gets you a reward.

As you see, the distinction between classical and operant conditioning is not always immediately clear when we consider specific instances of behavior, since both processes are often at work in terms of a particular sequence of behavior. Moreover, even some of the most basic differences between operant and classical conditioning have been called into question. For example, as we discussed in Chapter 3, people are able to learn to control "involuntary" responses, such as blood pressure and heart rate, through biofeedback. What would typically be thought of as a response involving classical conditioning, then, can be viewed in terms of operant conditioning.

Even the essential nature of classical conditioning has been disputed. For example, learning psychologist Robert Rescorla (1988) questions the basic assumption of classical conditioning that learning is the result of a simple, mechanical pairing of stimuli. Instead, he argues that for conditioning to take place, an organism must use the appearance of a conditioned stimulus to *predict* the presence of an unconditioned stimulus. It is the information value of the conditioned stimulus that leads to classical conditioning, in Rescorla's view.

Still, although many questions regarding classical and operant conditioning remain unanswered (Rachlin, 1990; Spear, Miller, & Jagielo, 1990), the two processes are distinct in most of the cases of behavior that psychologists analyze: In classical conditioning, the unconditioned stimulus precedes the response; the response is elicited by the unconditioned stimulus. In operant conditioning, in contrast, the response is emitted prior to the reinforcement and is therefore performed intentionally—that is, the response is made to obtain the reward. In classical conditioning, then, the response is basically involuntary, whereas in operant conditioning the response is voluntary.

Biological Constraints on Learning: You Can't Teach an Old Dog Just Any Trick

Keller and Marian Breland were pleased with their idea. As consultants to professional animal trainers, they came up with the notion of having a pig place a wooden disk into a piggy bank. With their experience in training animals through operant conditioning, they thought the task would be easy to teach, given that it was certainly well within the range of the pig's physical capabilities. Yet every time they tried out the procedure, it failed: Upon viewing the disk, the pigs were willing to do nothing but root the wooden disk along the ground. Apparently, the pigs were biologically programmed to push stimuli in the shape of disks along the ground.

Their lack of swine success led the Brelands to substitute a raccoon. Although the procedure worked fine with one disk, when two disks were used, the raccoon refused to deposit either of them and instead rubbed the two together, as if it were washing them. Once again, it appeared that the disks evoked biologically innate behaviors that were impossible to supplant with even the most exhaustive training (Breland & Breland, 1961).

Biological constraints: Built-in limitations in an organism's ability to learn particular behaviors

The Brelands' difficulties illustrate an important point: Not all behaviors can be trained in all species equally well. Instead, there are **biological constraints**, built-in limitations, in the ability of animals to learn particular behaviors. In some cases, an organism will have a special bent that will aid in its learning a behavior (such as behaviors which involve pecking in pigeons); in other cases, biological constraints will act to prevent or inhibit an organism from learning a behavior. In either instance, it is clear that animals have specialized learning mechanisms which influence how readily both classical and operant conditioning function, and each species is biologically primed to develop particular kinds of associations and to face obstacles in learning others (Hollis, 1984).

RECAP AND REVIEW III

RECAP

◀ Reinforcement need not be constant in order for behavior to be learned and maintained; partial schedules of reinforcement, in fact, lead to greater resistance to extinction than continuous schedules of reinforcement.

◀ In fixed-ratio schedules, reinforcement is given only after a set number of responses is made. In variable-ratio schedules, reinforcement is given after a varying number of responses.

◀ In fixed-interval schedules, reinforcement is given after a desired response only if a specified period of time has elapsed since the last reinforcement. In contrast, in variable-interval schedules, the time between delivery of reinforcement varies around some average period of time.

◀ Generalization, discrimination, and shaping are among the basic phenomena of operant conditioning.

◀ There are biological constraints on learning which aid, inhibit, or prevent learning.

REVIEW

1. In a _____ reinforcement schedule, behavior is reinforced some of the time, while in a _____ reinforcement schedule, behavior is reinforced all the time.

2. Learned behavior lasts longer after reinforcement stops when learned under a partial reinforcement schedule. True or false? _____

3. Match the type of reinforcement schedule with its definition.

a. _____ Fixed-ratio
b. _____ Variable-interval
c. _____ Fixed-interval
d. _____ Variable-ratio

1. Reinforcement occurs after a set time period
2. Reinforcement occurs after a set number of responses
3. Reinforcement occurs after a varying time period
4. Reinforcement occurs after a varying number of responses

4. Fixed reinforcement schedules produce greater resistance to extinction than variable reinforcement schedules. True or false? _____

5. _____ is the act of teaching a complex behavior by rewarding successive approximations of the behavior.

6. Conditioning principles have shown that, given the proper reinforcement, it is possible to train animals to perform any behavior that is within their physical capabilities. True or false? _____

7. Name two distinctions between operant and classical conditioning.

Ask Yourself

If you were asked to "cure" Wade Boggs' superstitious behavior, what techniques might you use?

(Answers to review questions are on page 230.)

COGNITIVE APPROACHES TO LEARNING

The criminal in the television movie hits a police officer's head against a brick wall. By knocking the officer out, the criminal manages to escape. He smiles triumphantly and coolly steps on the body as he runs away.

An 8-year-old boy, who has seen the movie the previous evening, gets into a fight with his brother. Although in the past the fights have rarely involved physical violence, this time the boy knocks his brother into a wall and tries to step on him.

The impetus for the boy's new behavior is clear: It is the television movie. But the underlying process that accounts for his conduct cannot easily be explained by either classical or operant conditioning. Knocking people into a wall would not seem to be either an unconditioned or a conditioned response. Moreover, given the fact that the boy had not had fights of this sort in the past, he would hardly have had the opportunity to be reinforced for such behavior, as operant conditioning would suggest.

Instances such as these imply that some kinds of learning must involve higher-order thinking processes in which people's thoughts and memories and the way they process information account for their responses. Such situations argue against a perspective that looks at learning as the unthinking, mechanical, and automatic acquisition of associations between stimuli and responses, as in classical conditioning, or as a consequence of the presentation of reinforcement, as in operant conditioning.

Instead, some psychologists view learning in terms of the thought processes, or cognitions, that underlie it—an approach known as **cognitive learning theory**. Although psychologists using cognitive learning theory do not deny the importance of classical and operant conditioning, they have developed approaches that focus on the unseen mental processes that occur during learning, rather than concentrating solely on external stimuli, responses, and reinforcements.

In its most basic formulation, cognitive learning theory suggests that it is not enough to say that people make responses because there is an assumed link between a stimulus and a response due to a past history of reinforcement for the response. Instead, according to this point of view, people—and even animals—develop an *expectation* that they will receive a reinforcer upon making a response.

Evidence for this point of view comes from several quarters. For instance, we have already discussed the phenomenon of blocking in the classical conditioning of rats. However, some of the most direct evidence regarding cognitive processes comes from a series of experiments that revealed a type of cognitive learning called latent learning. In **latent learning**, a new behavior is learned but is not demonstrated until reinforcement is provided for displaying it (Tolman & Honzik, 1930). In the studies, the behavior of rats in a maze such as that shown in Figure 7-8(*a*) was examined. In one representative experiment, a group of rats was allowed to wander around the maze once a day for seventeen days without ever receiving any reward; understandably, these rats made many errors and spent a relatively long time reaching the end of the maze. A second group, however, was always given food at the end of the maze, and these rats learned to run quickly and directly to the food box, making few errors.

A third group of rats started out in the same situation as the unrewarded rats, but only for the first ten days. On the eleventh day, a critical experimental manipulation was instituted: From that point on, the rats in this group were given food for completing the maze. The results of this manipulation were dramatic, as you can see from the graph in Figure 7-8(*b*). The previously unrewarded rats, who had earlier seemed to wander about aimlessly, showed reductions in running time and declines in error rates that almost immediately matched those of the group that had received rewards from the start.

To cognitive theorists, it seemed clear that the unrewarded rats had learned the layout of the maze early in their explorations; they just never displayed their latent learning until the reinforcement was offered. Instead, the rats seemed to

Cognitive learning theory: The study of the thought processes that underlie learning

Latent learning: Learning in which a new behavior is acquired but not readily demonstrated until reinforcement is provided

Cognitive map: A mental representation of spacial locations and directions

---

ANSWERS (REVIEW III):

1. partial; continuous **2.** True **3.** a-2; b-3; c-1; d-4 **4.** False; variable ratios are more resistant to extinction. **5.** Shaping **6.** False; there appear to be biological restrictions on what can be learned. **7.** Classical: Unconditioned stimulus occurs before the response; response is involuntary. Operant: Response is made before reinforcement; response is voluntary.

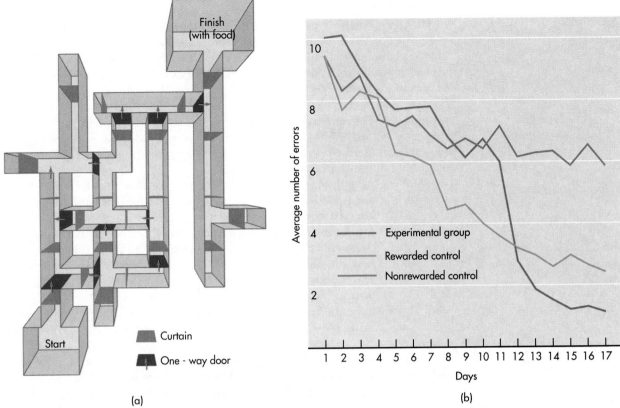

(a)

(b)

FIGURE 7-8

develop a **cognitive map** of the maze—a mental representation of spatial locations and directions.

People, too, develop cognitive maps of their surroundings, based primarily on particular landmarks (Garling, 1989). When they first encounter a new environment, their maps tend to rely on specific paths—such as the directions we might give someone unfamiliar with an area: "Turn right at the stop sign, make a left at the bridge, and then go up the hill." However, as people become more familiar with an area, they develop an overall conception of it, which has been called an abstract cognitive map. Using such a map, they are eventually able to take shortcuts as they develop a broad understanding of the area (Gale, Golledge, Pellegrino, & Doherty, 1990).

Unfortunately, though, our cognitive maps are often riddled with errors, representing simplifications of the actual terrain. We tend to develop maps that ignore curving roads and instead conceive of areas in terms of straight grids of intersecting roadways (Tversky, 1981). Our cognitive maps, then, are imperfect versions of actual maps.

Despite their inadequacies, the possibility that we develop our cognitive maps through latent learning presents something of a problem for strict reinforcement theorists. If we consider the results of Tolman's maze experiment, for instance, it is unclear what the specific reinforcement was that allowed the rats which received no reward to initially learn about the layout of the maze, since there was no obvious reinforcer present. Although we might speculate on the presence of internal reinforcers—such as the fulfillment of the organism's curiosity—such talk makes behavioral psychologists uneasy.

(*a*) In an attempt to demonstrate latent learning, rats were allowed to roam through a maze of this sort once a day for seventeen days. (*b*) Those rats that were never rewarded (the nonrewarded control condition) consistently made the most errors, whereas those that received food at the finish every day (the rewarded control condition) made far fewer errors. But the results also showed latent learning: Rats that were initially unrewarded but began to be rewarded only after the tenth day (the experimental group) showed an immediate reduction in errors and soon matched the error rate of the rats that had been consistently rewarded. According to cognitive learning theorists, the reduction in errors indicates that the rats had developed a cognitive map—a mental representation—of the maze (Tolman & Honzik, 1930).

Rule-Learning in Animals

Psychologists adhering to the cognitive learning approach have produced other challenges to the view that learning represents merely a mechanistic series of linkages between stimuli and responses. Specifically, they point to experiments which they interpret as showing that animals draw inferences about rules. In one such study, for example, a group of pigeons was shown hundreds of photos of outdoor scenes (Herrnstein, Loveland, & Cable, 1976; Herrnstein, 1979). The pigeons received reinforcement if they pecked a bar when a tree was shown in the scene, but no reinforcement if the scene did not include a tree. The pigeons soon showed themselves to be quite discriminating, pecking only in the presence of a photo that included a tree.

The key question was this: How were the pigeons able to determine when a tree was present? It was not a matter of mere memorization, because the pigeons showed accuracy even when viewing a group of entirely new scenes. Furthermore, they weren't just keying into some specific, isolated feature of a tree, such as pecking when leaves were present and not pecking in the absence of leaves. (This was clear because the pigeons responded positively to winter scenes where the trees had no leaves, and they responded negatively when they saw shrubs that had leaves.) Instead, cognitive learning psychologists argue that the pigeons were able to learn the rule stating what particular group of individual components—such as the presence of leaves *and* branches *and* large size—constituted a tree.

Other research suggests that animals can infer such elaborate notions as sequences of numbers, learning that reinforcement is provided in certain patterns. For instance, rats are capable of learning that the number of food pellets provided for running a maze changes in a set pattern or that reinforcement will only be provided after running a certain number of trials (Hulse, Fowler, & Honig, 1978; Capaldi & Miller, 1988; Roitblat, 1987).

The research suggesting that animals may employ rules and develop complex concepts about number sequences runs counter to traditional classical and operant conditioning views of learning. But to psychologists using a cognitive learning theory framework, the evidence is clear that organisms develop, and act upon, a thoughtful, internal representation of the world that is used to make associations about events in the environment.

Observational Learning: Learning through Copying

Let's return for a moment to the case of the boy who imitates a response that he has observed earlier in a television movie. How can we account for instances such as these in which someone with no direct experience in carrying out a particular behavior learns and carries out such behavior? To answer this question, psychologists have proposed another form of cognitive learning: observational learning.

Observational learning: Learning through observations of others (models)

Model: A person serving as an example to an observer; if a model's behavior is rewarded, the observer may imitate that behavior

According to psychologist Albert Bandura and colleagues, a major part of human learning consists of **observational learning**, which they define as learning through observing the behavior of another person, a **model** (Bandura, 1977). Bandura and his colleagues demonstrated rather dramatically the ability of models to stimulate learning. In what is now considered a classic experiment, young children saw a film of an adult wildly hitting a 5-foot-tall inflatable punching toy called a Bobo doll (Bandura, Ross, & Ross, 1963a, 1963b). Later the children were given the opportunity to play with the Bobo doll themselves and, sure enough, they displayed the same kind of behavior, in some cases mimicking the aggressive behavior almost identically.

Research indicates that children acquire both positive and negative behaviors through observation of others.

Not only negative behaviors are acquired through observational learning. In one experiment, for example, children who were afraid of dogs were exposed to a model—dubbed the Fearless Peer—playing with a dog (Bandura, Grusec, & Menlove, 1967). Following exposure, observers were considerably more likely to approach a strange dog than children who had not viewed the Fearless Peer.

According to Bandura, observational learning takes place in four steps: (1) paying attention and perceiving the most critical features of another person's behavior; (2) remembering the behavior; (3) reproducing the action; and (4) being motivated to learn and carry out the behavior. Instead of learning occurring through trial and error, then, with successes being reinforced and failures punished, many important skills are learned through observational processes (Bandura, 1986).

Observational learning is particularly important in acquiring skills in which shaping is inappropriate. Piloting an airplane and performing brain surgery, for example, would hardly be behaviors that could be learned using trial-and-error methods without grave cost—literally—to those involved in the learning.

Not all behavior that we witness is learned or carried out, of course. One crucial factor that determines whether we later imitate a model is the consequences of the model's behavior. If we observe a friend being rewarded for putting more time into her studies by receiving higher grades, we are more likely to model her behavior than if her behavior results in no increase in grades but rather greater fatigue and less of a social life. Models who are rewarded for behaving in a particular way are more apt to be mimicked than models who receive punishment. Interestingly, though, observing the punishment of a model does not necessarily stop observers from learning the behavior. Observers can still recount the model's behavior—they are just less apt to perform it (Bandura, 1977, 1986).

Learned Helplessness: Accepting the Unacceptable

Learned helplessness:
An organism's learned belief
that it has no control over the
environment

Have you ever heard someone say, "You can't fight city hall"; "No matter how hard I study I'll never pass this course"; or "I'll never learn to play tennis, regardless of how much I practice"? According to psychologist Martin Seligman, each of these statements may represent an example of **learned helplessness**, the learned belief of a person or animal that no control can be exerted over the environment (Seligman, 1975).

Learned helplessness was first demonstrated in experiments in which dogs were exposed to a series of moderately painful but not physically damaging shocks that they could not avoid. Although at first the dogs tried desperately to escape, they eventually accepted the shocks, seemingly in a resigned manner. But the next phase of the experiment was the most revealing: The dogs were placed in a box with two compartments, separated by a low barrier that they could easily jump over. By jumping the barrier, they could avoid any shock administered in the first compartment. In comparison with dogs who had not received shocks previously and who quickly learned to jump into the next compartment, the dogs who had received the inescapable shocks earlier tended to give up rapidly, lie down, and wait for the shock to be over. The conclusion drawn by Seligman was that the dogs had learned to be helpless. They expected that nothing they did would be useful in preventing the shocks, and therefore simply accepted them.

People, too, can learn to be helpless (Mineka & Hendersen, 1985). For example, in one experiment, groups of college students were exposed to a loud tone from which they could not escape. When later they were asked to complete a task and were given the opportunity to avoid a loud noise, they made fewer attempts to escape and performed more poorly than a control group of subjects completing the task who had earlier been exposed to a tone from which they could escape. The students had seemingly learned to be helpless in the face of something that, if they had only tried, they could have escaped (Hiroto & Seligman, 1975).

The concept of learned helplessness provides an explanation for several puzzling phenomena. For instance, battered children sometimes do not seek relief even when given the opportunity, and may come to accept their beatings. One explanation is that they have learned helplessness in the face of what they perceive to be inescapable punishment. Similarly, as we will discuss in Chapter 17, learned helplessness may underlie cases of severe human depression in which people come to feel that they are victims of events beyond their control and are helpless in their environment (Abramson, Metalsky, & Alloy, 1989).

The Unresolved Controversy of Cognitive Learning Theory

The degree to which learning is based on unseen internal factors rather than on external factors remains one of the major issues dividing learning theorists today (Amsel, 1988). Both classical conditioning and operant conditioning theories consider learning in terms of external stimuli and responses—a kind of "black box" analysis in which all that matters are the observable features of the environment, not what goes on inside a person's head. To the cognitive learning theorists, such an analysis misses the mark; what is crucial is the mental activity—the thoughts and expectations—that takes place.

Some psychologists argue that neither approach, by itself, is sufficient to explain all learning. Rather than viewing behavioral and cognitive approaches as contradictory, they see them as addressing learning through differing but complementary approaches. Such a theoretical outlook has allowed psychologists to make important advances in such areas as the treatment of certain kinds of abnormal behavior, as we will see in Chapter 18.

Still, while the controversy surrounding different approaches to learning rages on as a major issue of psychology, tremendous advances are taking place in the practical application of principles derived from the various theories, as we shall see in the remainder of this chapter (Glaser, 1990).

The Informed Consumer of Psychology: Using Behavior Analysis and Behavior Modification

A couple who had been living together for three years began to fight more and more frequently. The issues ranged from the seemingly petty, such as who was going to do the dishes, to the more profound, such as the quality of their love life and whether they found each other interesting. Disturbed about this increasingly unpleasant pattern of interaction, they went to a behavior analyst, a psychologist who specialized in behavior-modification techniques. After interviewing each of them alone and then speaking to them together, he asked them to keep a detailed written record of their interactions over the next two weeks—focusing, in particular, on the events that preceded their arguments.

When they returned two weeks later, he carefully went over the records with them. In doing so, he noticed a pattern that the couple themselves had observed after they had started keeping their records: Each of their arguments had occurred just after one or the other had left some household chore undone. For instance, the woman would go into a fury when she came home from work and found that the man, a student, had left his dirty lunch dishes on the table and had not even started dinner preparations. The man would get angry when he found the woman's clothes draped on the only chair in the bedroom; he insisted it was her responsibility to pick up after herself.

Using the data that had been collected, the behavior analyst devised a system for the couple to try out. He asked them to list all of the chores that could possibly arise and assign each one a point value depending on how long it took to complete. Then he had them divide the chores equally and agree in a written contract to fulfill the ones assigned to them. If either failed to carry out one of the assigned chores, he or she would have to place $1 per point in a fund for the other to spend. They also agreed to a program of verbal praise, promising to verbally reward each other for completing a chore.

Although skeptical about the value of such a program, the couple agreed to try it for a month and to keep careful records of the number of arguments they had during this period. To their surprise, the number declined rapidly, and even the more basic issues in their relationship seemed on the way to being resolved.

The case described above provides an illustration of **behavior modification**, a formalized technique for promoting the frequency of desirable behaviors and decreasing the incidence of unwanted ones. Using the basic principles of learning theory, behavior-modification techniques have proved to be helpful in a variety of situations. Severely retarded people have learned the rudiments of language and, for the first time in their lives, have started dressing and feeding themselves. Behavior modification has also helped people to lose weight, give up smoking, and behave more safely (Bellack, Hersen, & Kazdin, 1991; Sulzer-Azaroff & Mayer, 1991).

The techniques used by behavior analysts are as varied as the list of processes that modify behavior—including the use of reinforcement scheduling, shaping, generalization training, discrimination training, and extinction. Behavioral approaches do, however, typically follow a series of similar basic steps in a behavior-change program (Royer & Feldman, 1984). These steps include:

Behavior modification:
A formalized technique for promoting the frequency of desirable behaviors and decreasing the incidence of unwanted ones

One treatment for people who want to stop smoking involves aversive conditioning, in which smoking and cues relating to smoking are repeatedly paired with unpleasant stimuli.

■ Identifying goals and target behaviors. The first step is to define "desired behavior." Is it an increase in time spent studying? A decrease in weight? An increase in the use of language? A reduction in the amount of aggression displayed by a child? The goals must be stated in observable terms and lead to specific targets. For instance, a goal might be "to increase study time," while the target behavior would be "to study at least two hours per day on weekdays and an hour on Saturdays."

■ Designing a data-recording system and recording preliminary data. In order to determine whether behavior has changed, it is necessary to collect data before any changes are made in the situation. This provides a baseline against which future changes can be measured.

■ Selecting a behavior-change strategy. The most crucial step is to select an appropriate strategy. Since all the principles of learning can be employed to bring about behavior change, a "package" of treatments is normally used. This might include the systematic use of positive reinforcement for desired behavior (verbal praise or something more tangible, such as food), as well as a program of extinction for undesirable behavior (ignoring a child who throws a tantrum). Selecting the right reinforcers is critical; you may have to experiment a bit to find out what is important to a given individual. Avoid threats, since they are merely punishing and are not very effective in bringing about long-term changes in behavior.

■ Implementing the program. The next step is to institute the program. Probably the most important aspect of program implementation is consistency. It is also important to make sure that you are reinforcing the behavior you want to reinforce. For example, suppose you want a child to spend more time on her homework, but as soon as she sits down to study, she asks for a snack. If you get one for her, you are likely to be reinforcing her delaying tactic, not her studying. Instead, you might tell her that you will provide her with a snack after a certain time interval has gone by during which she has studied—thereby using the snack as a reinforcement for studying.

■ Keeping careful records after the program is implemented. Another crucial task is record keeping; if the target behaviors are not monitored, there is no way of knowing whether the program has actually been successful. Don't rely on your memory, because it is all too easy for memory lapses to occur.

■ Evaluating and altering the ongoing program. Finally, the results of the program should be compared with preimplementation data to determine its effectiveness. If successful, the procedures employed can gradually be phased out. For instance, if the program called for reinforcing every instance of picking up one's clothes from the bedroom floor, the reinforcement schedule could be modified to a fixed-ratio schedule in which every third instance was reinforced. On the other hand, if the program had not been successful in bringing about the desired behavior change, consideration of other approaches might be advisable.

Behavior-change techniques based on these general principles have had wide success and have proved to be one of the most powerful means of modifying behavior. Clearly, it is possible to employ the basic notions of learning theory to improve our own lives.

RECAP AND REVIEW IV

RECAP

◀ Cognitive learning theory focuses on the unseen, internal mental processes that are occurring within a person.

◀ Modeling consists of learning from the observation of others' behavior. The rewards that a model receives contribute to the imitation of the model.

◀ Learned helplessness is the learned belief of a person or animal that no control can be exerted over the environment.

◀ Behavior modification, a formal technique for promoting desirable behaviors and reducing undesirable ones, has been used successfully in changing both one's own and others' behavior.

REVIEW

1. A distinguished scientist tells you "Learning can best be understood in terms of its underlying thought processes." What theory is being described?

2. In cognitive learning theory, it is assumed that people develop an _____ about receiving a reinforcer instead of basing behavior on past reinforcers.

3. _____ learning describes learning that takes place but is not shown until appropriate reinforcement is presented.

4. Bandura's theory of _____ learning states that people learn through watching a _____,

which is another person displaying the behavior of interest.

5. _____ _____ refers to the theory that people may come to feel as if they have no control over their environment.

6. Cognitive learning theorists are only concerned with overt behavior, not with its internal causes. True or false?

_____

7. A man wishes to quit smoking. Upon the advice of a psychologist, he begins a program where he sets goals for his withdrawal, carefully records his progress, and rewards himself for not smoking during a certain period of time. What type of program is he following?

8. Fill in the key steps missing in the behavior-analysis model:
   a. identifying goals and target behaviors.
   b.
   c. selecting a behavior-change strategy.
   d. implementing the program.
   e. keeping careful records.
   f.

Ask Yourself

What dangers may observational learning pose when considering the content of today's television programs and movies? How could behavior modification techniques be used to combat these problems?

(Answers to review questions are on page 238.)

■ *What is learning?*

1. Learning, a relatively permanent change in behavior due to experience, is a basic topic of psychology. However, it is a process that must be assessed indirectly—we can only assume that learning has occurred by observing performance, which is susceptible to such factors as fatigue and lack of effort.

■ *How do we learn to form associations between stimuli and responses?*

2. One major form of learning is known as classical conditioning. First studied by Ivan Pavlov, classical conditioning occurs when a neutral stimulus—one that brings about no relevant response—is repeatedly paired with a stimulus (called an unconditioned stimulus) that brings about a natural, untrained response. For instance, a neutral stimulus might be a buzzer; an unconditioned stimulus might be a dish of ice cream. The response ice cream might bring about in a hungry person—salivation—is called an unconditioned response; it occurs naturally, owing to the physical makeup of the individual being trained.

3. The actual conditioning occurs when the neutral stimulus is repeatedly presented just before the unconditioned stimulus. After repeated pairings, the neutral stimulus begins to bring about the same response as the unconditioned stimulus. When this occurs, we can say that the neutral stimulus is now a conditioned stimulus, and the response made to it is the conditioned response. For example, after a person has learned to salivate to the sound of the buzzer, we say the buzzer is a conditioned stimulus, and the salivation is a conditioned response.

4. Learning is not always permanent, however. Extinction occurs when a previously learned response decreases in frequency and eventually disappears. Extinction provides the basis for systematic desensitization, a treatment designed to decrease people's strong, irrational fears.

5. Stimulus generalization occurs when a conditioned response follows a stimulus that is similar to the original conditioned stimulus. The greater the similarity between the two stimuli, the greater the likelihood of stimulus generalization; the closer the new stimulus to the old one, the more similar the new response. The converse phenomenon, stimulus discrimination, occurs when an organism learns to respond to one stimulus but not to another.

6. Higher-order conditioning occurs when an established conditioned stimulus is paired with a neutral stimulus, and the new neutral stimulus comes to evoke the same conditioned response as the original conditioned stimulus. The neutral stimulus changes, then, into another conditioned stimulus.

■ *What is the role of reward and punishment in learning?*

7. A second major form of learning is operant conditioning. Moving beyond Edward Thorndike's original work on the law of effect, which states that responses that produce satisfying results are more likely to be repeated than those that do not, B. F. Skinner carried out pioneering work on operant learning.

8. According to Skinner, the major factor underlying learning is the reinforcer—any stimulus that increases the probability that the preceding response will occur again. We can determine whether a stimulus is a reinforcer only by observing its effects upon behavior. If behavior increases, the stimulus is, by definition, a reinforcer. Primary reinforcers involve rewards that are naturally effective without prior exposure because they satisfy a biological need. Secondary reinforcers, in contrast, begin to act as if they were primary reinforcers through frequent pairings with a primary reinforcer.

9. Positive reinforcers are stimuli that are added to the environment and lead to an increase in a preceding response. Negative reinforcers are stimuli whose removal from the environment leads to an increase in the preceding response. Negative reinforcement occurs in two major forms. In escape conditioning, an organism learns to make a response that brings about an end to an aversive situation. In avoidance conditioning, an organism responds to a signal of an impending unpleasant event in a way that permits its evasion.

10. Punishment is the administration of an unpleasant stimulus following a response in order to produce a decrease in the incidence of that response. Punishment can also be characterized by the removal of a positive reinforcer. In contrast to reinforcement, in which the goal is to increase the incidence of behavior, punishment is meant to decrease or suppress behavior. Although there are some benefits to the use of punishment, its disadvantages usually outweigh its positive effects.

11. Schedules and patterns of reinforcement affect the strength and duration of learning. Generally, partial reinforcement schedules—in which reinforcers are not delivered on every trial—produce stronger and longer lasting learning than continuous reinforcement schedules.

12. Among the major categories of reinforcement schedules are fixed- and variable-ratio schedules, which are based on the number of responses made, and fixed- and

---

ANSWERS (REVIEW IV):

1. Cognitive learning theory **2.** expectation **3.** Latent **4.** observational; model **5.** Learned helplessness **6.** False; cognitive learning theorists are primarily concerned with mental processes. **7.** Behavior modification **8.** b—designing a recording system and recording preliminary data; f—evaluating and altering the ongoing program.

variable-interval schedules, which are based on the time interval that elapses before reinforcement is provided. Fixed-ratio schedules provide reinforcement only after a certain number of responses are made; variable-ratio schedules provide reinforcement after a varying number of responses are made—although the specific number typically settles around some average. In contrast, fixed-interval schedules provide reinforcement after a fixed amount of time has elapsed since the last reinforcement; variable-interval schedules provide reinforcement over varying amounts of time, although the times form a specific average.

13. Generalization and discrimination are phenomena that operate in operant conditioning as well as classical conditioning. Generalization occurs when an organism makes the same or a similar response to a new stimulus that it has learned to make in the past to a similar stimulus. Discrimination occurs when the organism responds to one stimulus, but does not respond to a similar (but different) stimulus.

14. Superstitious behavior results from the mistaken belief that particular ideas, objects, or behavior will cause certain events to occur. It occurs as a consequence of learning that is based on the coincidental association between a stimulus and subsequent reinforcement.

15. Shaping is a process for teaching complex behaviors by rewarding closer and closer approximations of the desired final behavior. Shaping forms the basis for learning many everyday skills and is central to presenting complicated information in textbooks and in computerized programmed instruction.

16. There are biological constraints, or built-in limitations, on the ability of an organism to learn. Because of these constraints, certain behaviors will be relatively easy to learn, whereas other behaviors will be either difficult or impossible to learn.

■ *What is the role of cognition and thought in learning?*

17. Cognitive approaches consider learning in terms of thought processes or cognition. Phenomena such as latent learning—in which a new behavior is learned but not performed until reinforcement is provided for its performance—and the apparent development of cognitive maps support cognitive approaches. Learning also occurs through the observation of behavior of others, known as models. The major factor that determines whether an observed behavior will actually be performed is the nature of reinforcement or punishment a model receives. Learned helplessness, the learned belief of a person or animal that it cannot exert control over the environment, also suggests the importance of cognitive processes in learning.

■ *What are some practical methods for bringing about behavior change, both in others and in ourselves?*

18. Behavior modification is a method for formally using the principles of learning theory to promote the frequency of desired behaviors and to decrease or eliminate unwanted ones. The typical steps in a behavior-change program are identifying goals and target behaviors, designing a data-recording system, recording preliminary data, selecting a behavior-change strategy, implementing the strategy, and evaluating and altering the ongoing program.

KEY TERMS AND CONCEPTS

learning (p. 203)
maturation (p. 203)
classical conditioning (p. 204)
neutral stimulus (p. 206)
unconditioned stimulus (UCS)
 (p. 206)
unconditioned response (UCR)
 (p. 206)
conditioned stimulus (CS)
 (p. 206)
conditioned response
 (CR) (p. 206)
extinction (p. 208)
systematic desensitization
 (p. 208)
spontaneous recovery (p. 208)
stimulus generalization (p. 208)
stimulus discrimination (p. 209)
higher-order conditioning
 (p. 209)

blocking (p. 210)
operant conditioning (p. 213)
law of effect (p. 214)
reinforcer (p. 215)
primary reinforcer (p. 215)
secondary reinforcer (p. 215)
positive reinforcer (p. 216)
negative reinforcer (p. 216)
escape conditioning (p. 217)
avoidance conditioning (p. 217)
punishment (p. 217)
aversive stimuli (p. 217)
schedules of reinforcement
 (p. 220)
continuous reinforcement
 schedule (p. 220)
partial reinforcement schedule
 (p. 220)
cumulative recorder (p. 220)

fixed-ratio schedule (p. 221)
variable-ratio schedule (p. 221)
fixed-interval schedule (p. 221)
variable-interval schedule
 (p. 222)
stimulus control training (p. 223)
discriminative stimulus (p. 223)
superstitious behavior (p. 223)
shaping (p. 225)
programmed instruction (p. 225)
biological constraints (p. 228)
cognitive learning theory (p. 230)
latent learning (p. 230)
cognitive map (p. 230)
observational learning (p. 232)
model (p. 232)
learned helplessness (p. 234)
behavior modification (p. 235)

PAMILLA SMITH

If Pamilla Smith were to read this prologue about herself, an hour later she would be unable to recall ever having seen it. Pamilla has a rare memory affliction in which she is unable to remember any recent events in her life.

Pamilla's memory problem began nine years ago, when she fell into a coma following a severe asthma attack. Because part of her brain involved in memory had been deprived of oxygen, she awakened two days later with a strange set of problems. In her words, "My mind is like a tape recorder that keeps erasing itself. I carry around a notebook filled with information that will help me have conversations with people, but I keep forgetting to open it! . . . I've taught myself to memorize key details—my address, my parents' phone number and address, the streets near where I live. That way when I get lost while driving I can ask someone directions.

"I date seldom, because I forget who my date is supposed to be. . . . Reading books is a waste of time, because after every few pages I can't even remember the title" (Mullins, 1990, p. 53). Pamilla is even unable to go to the movies, because by the time the movie is ending she cannot remember how it started.

What is particularly ironic about Pamilla's situation is that although she cannot remember recent events, her memory for things that happened a decade earlier is largely unimpaired. Thus, her basic intelligence is intact—although she'll probably never be able to remember anything new.

LOOKING AHEAD

Memory failures, such as those afflicting Pamilla Smith, are the most dramatic illustrations of how drastically our lives would be altered without the ability to recall information from our past. But most of us do not need to be reminded of the importance of memory—and of the fluctuations in our abilities that occur daily. For instance, we are able to retrieve a vast array of information to which we have been exposed, such as the name of a friend we haven't seen or been in touch with for ten years or a picture that hung in our bedroom as a child. At the same time, it is not uncommon to forget where we left the keys to the car or to be unable to answer an exam question about material that we studied just a few hours before.

In this chapter, we address a number of issues about memory that psychologists are investigating. We examine the ways in which information is stored and retrieved. We discuss evidence showing that there are actually three separate types of memory, and we explain how each type operates in a somewhat different fashion. The problems of retrieving information from memory and the reasons information is sometimes forgotten are examined, and we consider the biological foundations of memory. Finally, we discuss some practical means of increasing memory capacity.

After reading this chapter, then, you will be able to answer the following questions:

- What is memory?
- Are there different kinds of memory?
- What causes difficulties and failures in remembering?

"Well, here I sit, surrounded by my memorabilia, and I can't remember having done a damn thing."

■ What are the biological bases of memory?

■ What are the major memory impairments?

ENCODING, STORAGE, AND RETRIEVAL OF MEMORY

What is memory, and why do we remember certain events and activities and forget others? To illustrate how psychologists answer these questions, consider what might occur if you were asked to name the sea on which Bombay is located during a game of Trivial Pursuit.

If you have trouble answering the question, your difficulty may be related to the initial encoding stage of memory. **Encoding** refers to the process by which information is initially recorded in a form usable to memory. You may never, for instance, have been exposed to information regarding Bombay's location, or it simply may not have registered in a meaningful way if it had been pointed out to you.

On the other hand, even if you had been exposed to the information and originally knew the name of the sea, you may still be unable to recall it because of a failure in the retention process. Memory specialists speak of placing information in **storage**, the location in the memory system in which material is saved. If the material is not stored adequately in the first place, it cannot be recalled later.

Memory also depends on one last process: retrieval. In **retrieval**, material in memory storage is located, brought into awareness, and used. Your inability to recall Bombay's location, then, may rest on your inability to retrieve the information that you learned earlier.

In sum, psychologists consider **memory** as the process by which we encode, store, and retrieve information (see Figure 8-1, p. 244). Each of the three parts of the definition of memory—encoding, storage, and retrieval—represents a different process. And only if all three processes have operated will you be able to recall the sea on which Bombay is located: the Arabian Sea.

Encoding: The process by which information is initially recorded in a form usable to memory

Storage: The location in the memory system in which material is saved.

Retrieval: The process by which material in memory storage is located, brought into awareness, and used

Memory: The capacity to record, retain, and retrieve information

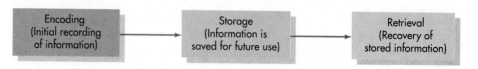

FIGURE 8-1

Memory is built on these three basic processes.

Sensory memory: The initial, short-lived storage of information recorded as a meaningless stimulus

Short-term memory: The storage of information for fifteen to twenty-five seconds

Long-term memory: The storage of information on a relatively permanent basis, although retrieval may be difficult

FIGURE 8-2

In this three-stage model of memory, information initially recorded by the person's sensory system enters sensory memory, which momentarily holds the information. It then moves to short-term memory, which stores the information for fifteen to twenty-five seconds. Finally, the information can move into long-term memory, which is relatively permanent. Whether the information moves from short-term to long-term memory depends on the kind and amount of rehearsal of the material that is carried out. (After Atkinson & Shiffrin, 1968.)

Before continuing our discussion of memory, it is important to note a critical point: Although we typically think of the inability to remember information as a failure of memory, forgetting is essential to the proper functioning of memory. The ability to forget trivial details about experiences and objects allows us to form abstractions and generalizations that summarize similar recollections. For example, it would not be terribly useful to form separate memories of the way friends look each and every time we saw them. Thus, we tend to forget their clothing, facial blemishes, and other transient features that change from one occasion to the next. Instead, our memories are based on a generalization or abstraction of various critical features. Forgetting of unnecessary information, then, is as essential to the proper functioning of memory as remembering material in the first place.

The Three Stages of Memory: Memory Storehouses

Although the processes of encoding, storing, and retrieving information are necessary for memory to operate successfully, they do not describe the specific manner in which material is entered into our storehouse of memories. Many psychologists studying memory suggest that there are different stages through which information must travel if it is to be remembered.

According to one of the most influential theories, three kinds of memory storage systems exist. These types of storehouses vary in terms of their function and the length of time information is retained (Atkinson & Shiffrin, 1968).

As shown in Figure 8-2, **sensory memory** refers to the initial, momentary storage of information, lasting only an instant. It is recorded by the person's sensory system as a raw, nonmeaningful stimulus. **Short-term memory** holds information for fifteen to twenty-five seconds. In this phase, the information is stored in terms of its meaning rather than as mere sensory stimulation. The third type of store is **long-term memory**. Here, information is relatively permanent, although it may be difficult to retrieve.

Although we'll be discussing the three types of memory in terms of separate memory stores, keep in mind that these are not mini-warehouses located in par-

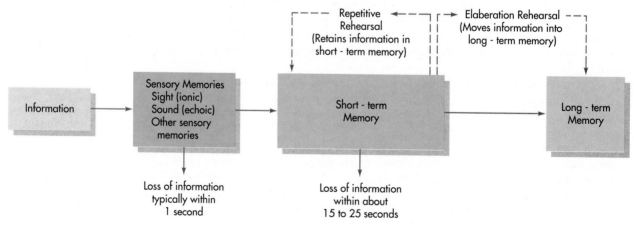

ticular portions of the brain. Instead, they represent three different types of abstract memory systems with different characteristics. Furthermore, not all psychologists agree with this three-part differentiation, viewing memory instead as a more unitary network of recollections (e.g., Cowan, 1988). Still, considering memory in terms of the three major kinds of stores is a useful framework for understanding how information is both recalled and forgotten.

Sensory Memory. A momentary flash of lightning, the sound of a twig snapping, and the sting of a pinprick all represent stimulation of exceedingly brief duration, but they may nonetheless provide important information that can require some response. Such stimuli are initially—and briefly—stored in sensory memory, the first repository of the information that the world presents to us. Actually, the term "sensory memory" encompasses several types of sensory memories, each related to a different source of sensory information. There is **iconic memory**, which reflects information from our visual system; **echoic memory**, which stores information coming from the ears; and corresponding memories for each of the other senses.

Iconic (i KON ik) **memory:** The storage of visual information

Regardless of the individual subtypes, sensory memory in general is able to store information for only a very short time, and if material does not pass to another form of memory, that information is lost for good. For instance, iconic memory seems to last less than a second, although, if the initial stimulus is very bright, the image may last a little longer (Long & Beaton, 1982). Echoic memory fades within three or four seconds (Darwin, Turvey, & Crowder, 1972). However, despite the brief duration of sensory memory, its precision is high: It is able to store an almost exact replica of each stimulus to which it is exposed.

Echoic (eh KO ik) **memory:** The storage of information obtained from the sense of hearing

If the storage capabilities of sensory memory are so limited and information stored within sensory memory so fleeting, it would seem almost impossible to find evidence for its existence; new information would constantly be replacing older information, even before a person could report its presence. Not until psychologist George Sperling (1960) conducted a series of clever and now-classic studies was sensory memory well understood. Sperling briefly exposed people to a series of twelve letters arranged in the following pattern:

F	T	Y	C
K	D	N	L
Y	W	B	M

When exposed to this array for just one-twentieth of a second, most people could accurately recall only four or five of the letters. Although they knew that they had seen more, the memory had faded by the time they reported the first few letters. It was possible, then, that the information had initially been accurately stored in sensory memory, but during the time it took to verbalize the first four or five letters the memory of the other letters faded.

To test that possibility, Sperling conducted an experiment in which a high, medium, or low tone sounded just after a person had been exposed to the full pattern of letters. People were told to report the letters in the highest line if a high tone were sounded, the middle line if the medium tone occurred, or the lowest line at the sound of the low tone. Because the tone occurred after the exposure, people had to rely on their memory to report the correct row.

The results of the study showed very clearly that people had been storing the complete pattern in memory: They were quite accurate in their recollection of the letters in the line that had been indicated by the tone, regardless of whether it was the top, middle, or bottom line. Obviously, *all* the lines they had seen had been stored in sensory memory. Despite its rapid loss, then, the information in sensory memory was an accurate representation of what people had seen.

By gradually lengthening the time between the presentation of the visual pattern and the tone, Sperling was able to determine with some accuracy the length of time that information existed in sensory memory. The ability to recall a particular row of the pattern when a tone was sounded declined progressively as the period between visual exposure and tone increased. This decline continued until the period reached about one second in duration, at which point the row could not be recalled accurately at all. The conclusion: The entire visual image was stored in sensory memory for less than a second.

In sum, sensory memory operates as a kind of snapshot that stores information— which may be of a visual, auditory, or other sensory nature—for a brief moment in time. But it is as if each snapshot, immediately after being taken, is destroyed and replaced with a new one. Unless the information in the snapshot is transferred to some other type of memory, it is lost.

Short-Term Memory: Our Working Memory.   Because the information that is stored briefly in our sensory memory consists of representations of raw sensory stimuli, it is not necessarily meaningful to us. In order for us to make sense of it and to allow for the possibility of long-term retention, the information must be transferred to the next stage of memory, short-term memory. Short-term memory, sometimes referred to as working memory, is the memory in which material initially has meaning, although the maximum length of retention is relatively short.

The specific process by which sensory memories are transformed into short-term memories is not yet clear. Some theorists suggest that the information is first translated into graphical representations or images, and others hypothesize that the transfer occurs when the sensory stimuli are changed to words (Baddeley & Wilson, 1985). What is clear, however, is that unlike sensory memory, which holds a relatively full and detailed—if short-lived—representation of the world, short-term memory has incomplete representational capabilities.

In fact, the specific amount of information that can be held in short-term memory has been identified: seven items, or "chunks," of information, with variations up to plus or minus two chunks. A **chunk** is a meaningful grouping of stimuli that can be stored as a unit in short-term memory. According to George Miller (1956), it could be individual letters, as in the following list:

> C N Q M W N T

Each letter here qualifies as a separate chunk, and—as there are seven of them—they are easily held in short-term memory.

But a chunk might also consist of larger categories, such as words or other meaningful units. For example, consider the following list of twenty-one letters:

> T W A C I A A B C C B S M T V U S A A A A

Clearly, because the list exceeds seven chunks, it is difficult to recall the letters after one exposure. But suppose they were presented to you as follows:

> TWA   CIA   ABC   CBS   MTV   USA   AAA

Chunk: A meaningful grouping of stimuli that can be stored as a unit in short-term memory

Rehearsal: The transfer of material from short- to long-term memory via repetition

In this case, even though there are still twenty-one letters, it would be possible to store them in memory, since they represent only seven chunks.

You can see how chunking works in your own memory process by trying to memorize the shapes in Figure 8-3 after looking at them for just a few moments. Although it may at first seem to be an impossible task, just one hint will guarantee that you can easily memorize all the shapes: Each figure represents part of the letters in the word "PSYCHOLOGY."

The reason the task suddenly became so simple was that the shapes could be grouped together into one chunk—a word that we all recognize. Rather than being nineteen separate symbols with no meaning, they are recoded as just one chunk.

Chunks can vary in size from single letters or numbers to categories that are far more complicated, and the specific nature of what constitutes a chunk varies according to one's past experience. You can see this for yourself by trying an experiment that was first carried out comparing expert and inexperienced chess players (deGroot, 1966).

Examine the chessboard on the top of Figure 8-4 for about five seconds, and then, after covering up the board, try to reproduce the position of the pieces on the blank chessboard on the bottom. Unless you are an experienced chess player, you are likely to have great difficulty carrying out such a task. Yet chess masters—the kind who win tournaments—do quite well: They are able to reproduce correctly 90 percent of the pieces on the board. In comparison, inexperienced chess players typically are able to reproduce only 40 percent of the board properly. The chess masters do not have superior memories in other respects; they generally test normally on other measures of memory. What they can do better than others is to chunk the board into meaningful units and reproduce the chess pieces by using these units. (Also see Figure 8-5, p. 248).

Although it is possible to remember seven or so relatively complicated sets of information entering short-term memory, the information cannot be held there very long. Just how short term is short-term memory? Anyone who has looked up a telephone number at a pay phone, struggled to find coins, and forgotten the number at the sound of the dial tone knows that information in short-term memory does not remain there terribly long. Most psychologists believe that information in short-term memory is lost after fifteen to twenty-five seconds—unless it is transferred to long-term memory.

Rehearsal. The transfer of material from short- to long-term memory proceeds largely on the basis of **rehearsal**, the repetition of information that has entered short-term memory. Rehearsal accomplishes two things. First, as long as the information is repeated, it is kept alive in short-term memory. More important, however, rehearsal allows the material to be transferred into long-term memory.

Whether the transfer is made from short- to long-term memory seems to depend largely on the kind of rehearsal that is carried out. If the material is simply repeated over and over again—as we might do with a telephone number while we rush from the phone book to the telephone—it is kept current in short-term memory but it will not necessarily be placed in long-term memory. Instead, as soon as we stop dialing, the number is likely to be replaced by other information and will be completely forgotten.

On the other hand, if the information in short-term memory is rehearsed using a process called elaborative rehearsal, it is much more likely to be trans-

FIGURE 8-3

Try looking at the shapes in this figure for a few moments, and memorize them in the exact sequence in which they appear. If you consider this an impossible task, here's a hint that will guarantee that you can easily memorize all of them: They are the shapes of each part of the letters in the word "PSYCHOLOGY." The reason the task suddenly becomes so simple is that the shapes can be grouped together into one chunk—a word that we all recognize. Rather than being considered nineteen separate shapes, the symbols are recoded in the memory as just one chunk.

FIGURE 8-4

Look at the top chessboard for about five seconds, and then cover it with your hand. Now try to recreate the chess pieces on the blank board below it. Unless you are an experienced chess player, you will probably have a good deal of difficulty recalling the configuration and types of chess pieces. On the other hand, expert chess players have little difficulty recreating the board on the top. (deGroot, 1966.)

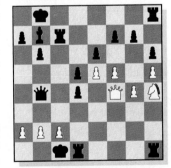

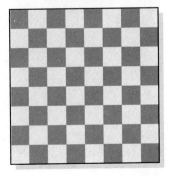

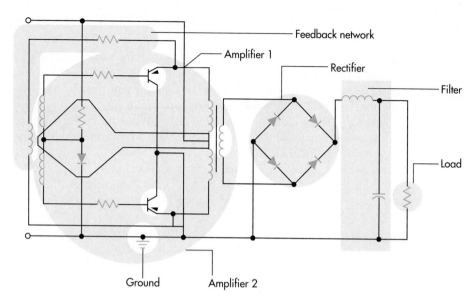

FIGURE 8-5

Although most of us would have difficulty memorizing this circuit schematic, experienced electronics technicians recall it with ease because they are able to view it as a meaningful unit or chunk. (Egan & Schwartz, 1979.)

Elaborative rehearsal:
Organizing information in short-term memory into a logical framework to assist in recalling it

Mnemonics (neh MON ix):
Formal techniques for organizing material to increase the likelihood of its being remembered

Some of these Sun City, Arizona, cyclists may have gone for years without riding a bike; however, motor code in long-term memory enables them to resume riding with little practice.

ferred into long-term memory (Craik & Lockhart, 1972). **Elaborative rehearsal** occurs when the material is considered and organized in some fashion. The organization might include expanding the information to make it fit into a logical framework, linking it to another memory, turning it into an image, or transforming it in some other way. For example, a list of vegetables to be purchased at a store could be woven together in memory as items being used to prepare an elaborate salad; they could be linked to the items bought on an earlier shopping trip; or they could be thought of in terms of the image of a farm with rows of each item.

By using organizational strategies called **mnemonics**, we can vastly improve our retention of information (Higbee & Kunihira, 1985). Mnemonics are formal techniques for organizing material in a way that makes it more likely to be remembered. For instance, when a beginning musician learns that the spaces on the music staff spell the word "FACE" or when we learn the rhyme "Thirty days

hath September, April, June, and November; all the rest have . . . ,'' we are using mnemonics.

Long-Term Memory: The Final Storehouse.   Material that makes its way from short-term memory to long-term memory enters a storehouse of almost unlimited capacity. Like a new book delivered to a library, the information in long-term memory is filed and cataloged so that it can be retrieved when we need it.

Evidence of the existence of long-term memory, as distinct from short-term memory, comes from a number of sources. For example, people with certain kinds of brain damage, like Pamilla Smith (whose case began the chapter), have no lasting recall of new information following the damage, although people and events in memory prior to the injury remain (Milner, 1966). Because short-term memory following the injury appears to be operative—new material can be recalled for a very brief period—and because information from before the injury is recalled, we might infer that there are two distinct memories, one for short-term and one for long-term storage.

Evidence from laboratory experiments is also consistent with the notion of separate short- and long-term memories. For example, in one set of studies people were asked to recall a relatively small amount of information (such as a set of three letters)—but then, to prevent practice of the initial information, were required to recite some extraneous material aloud, such as counting backward by threes (Brown, 1958; Peterson & Peterson, 1959). By varying the amount of time between which the initial material was first presented and its recall was required, investigators found that recall was quite good when the interval was very short, but it declined rapidly thereafter. After fifteen seconds had gone by, recall hovered at around 10 percent of the material initially presented.

Apparently, the distraction of counting backward prevented almost all the initial material from reaching long-term memory. Initial recall was good because it was coming from short-term memory, but these memories were lost at a rapid rate. Eventually, all that could be recalled was the small amount of material that had made its way into long-term storage despite the distractions of counting backward.

Episodic and Semantic Memories.   There are actually two kinds of memories held in long-term memory: episodic and semantic (Tulving, 1983). **Episodic memories** relate to our individual lives, recalling what we have done and the kinds of experiences we have had. When you recall your first date, the time you fell off your bicycle, or what you felt like when you graduated from high school, you are recalling episodic memories. The information in episodic memory is connected with specific times and places. In contrast, **semantic memories** consist of organized knowledge and facts about the world; because of semantic memory, we know that 2 x 2 = 4, the earth is round, and ''memoree'' is misspelled.

Episodic memories can be surprisingly detailed. Consider, for instance, what your response would be if you were asked to identify what you were doing on a specific day two years ago. An impossible task? You might think otherwise as you read the following exchange between a researcher and a subject who was asked, in a memory experiment, what he was doing ''on Monday afternoon in the third week of September two years ago.''

SUBJECT: Come on. How should I know?
EXPERIMENTER: Just try it anyhow.
SUBJECT: OK. Let's see: Two years ago . . . I would be in high school in Pittsburgh. . . .

Episodic memories: Stored information relating to personal experiences

Semantic memories: Stored, organized facts about the world (e.g., mathematical and historical data)

As experienced by this Raleigh, North Carolina, couple, long-term memory can be stimulated by exposure to pictures or objects from the past.

That would be my senior year. Third week in September—that's just after summer—that would be the fall term. . . . Let me see. I think I had chemistry lab on Mondays. I don't know. I was probably in chemistry lab. Wait a minute—that would be the second week of school. I remember he started off with the atomic table—a big fancy chart. I thought he was crazy trying to make us memorize that thing. You know, I think I can remember sitting . . . (Lindsay & Norman, 1977).

Episodic memory, then, can provide information from events that happened long in the past (Reynolds & Takooshian, 1988). But semantic memory is no less impressive: By calling upon it, all of us are able to dredge up thousands of facts ranging from the date of our birthday to the knowledge that $1 is less than $5. Both individual pieces of information and the rules of logic for deducing other facts are stored in semantic memory.

Many psychologists, using **associative models** of memory, argue that semantic memory consists of associations between mental representations of various pieces of information (e.g., Collins & Quillian, 1969; Collins & Loftus, 1975). Consider, for example, Figure 8-6, which shows some of the relationships in memory relating to "animal."

The basic notion of associative models of semantic memory is that when we think about a particular concept, related concepts are activated and more readily brought to mind. For example, thinking about a "robin" leads to the activation of related concepts such as "eats worms" and "has a red breast." As a result, if we are trying to recall some specific bit of information, activating associated material may help us recall it.

In such instances, related information helps prime us to recall information that we are otherwise unable to recollect. In **priming**, prior presentation of information subsequently makes it easier to recall related items, even when we have no conscious memory of the original information (Tulving & Schacter, 1990).

The typical experiment designed to illustrate priming helps clarify the phenomenon. In such an experiment, subjects are first presented with some stimulus. The stimulus might be a particular word, an object, or perhaps a drawing of a face. The second phase of the experiment is held after an interval ranging from several seconds to months later. At that point, subjects are exposed to incomplete

Associative models: A technique of recalling information by thinking about related information

Priming: A technique of recalling information by having been exposed to related information at an earlier time

FIGURE 8-6

Associative models suggest that semantic memory consists of relationships between pieces of information, such as those relating to the concept of "animal," shown in this figure. (After Collins & Quillian, 1969.)

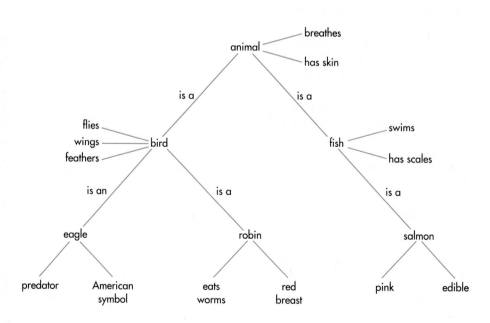

perceptual information that is related to the first stimulus and asked whether they recognize it. For example, it may consist of the first letter of a word that had been presented earlier, or a part of a face that had been shown earlier.

If subjects are able to identify the stimulus more readily than they identify stimuli that have not been presented earlier, priming is said to have occurred. What is interesting about the phenomenon of priming is that it occurs even when subjects report having no conscious awareness of having seen the stimulus earlier.

The discovery that people have memories about which they are not aware has been an important one. It has led to speculation that a form of memory, dubbed "implicit memory," may exist side by side with explicit memory. We discuss this possibility in the accompanying Cutting Edge box.

Explicit memory: Intentional or conscious recollection of information

Implicit memory: Memories of which people are not consciously aware, but which can improve subsequent performance and behavior

---

THE CUTTING EDGE

IMPLICIT MEMORY: RETENTION WITHOUT REMEMBERING

If you have ever had surgery, you may have wondered what the physicians and nurses talked about as they thrust a scalpel deep into your body. Although you may have assumed that you would never know the answer—or perhaps never really cared to know—recent evidence suggests that you may recall more than you think.

According to a study by memory researchers John Kihlstrom, Daniel Schacter, and colleagues, patients undergoing anesthesia may indeed remember information to which they were exposed (Kihlstrom, Schacter, Cork, Hurt, & Behr, 1990). In their study, they presented a group of surgical patients with fifteen pairs of words while they were anesthetized for a variety of types of surgery. The pairs consisted of fifteen stimulus terms, called cues, and responses, called targets. (The targets were words that were most often made by average subjects when hearing the cue.) These pairs of words were played continuously during the entire operation—an average of fifty minutes per patient. Patients heard either one of two sets of paired words.

These patients did show evidence of recall—but only on certain types of measures of memory. When simply asked to recall any words that they had heard during surgery, the patients demonstrated no recall. Similarly, when presented with the cue words from both the list that they had

heard during surgery and the one that they had not, they performed the same on both lists—thus demonstrating no recall for the list they had heard during surgery. Finally, when presented with a series of words and asked if each reminded them of a word they heard under surgery, they could not differentiate words they had heard from those they hadn't.

On the other hand, evidence that memory did exist emerged when subjects were presented with the list of cue words and asked to report the first word that came to mind. Unlike the previous measures of memory, the patients were significantly more likely to come up with words that they had heard than words that they had not heard during surgery. In sum, they did have some recollections for the material to which they had been exposed under anesthesia.

The difference in performance on the different memory tasks provides evidence that two distinct types of memory exist. **Explicit memory** refers to intentional or conscious recollection of information. In contrast, **implicit memory** refers to memories of which people are not consciously aware, but which can improve subsequent performance and behavior.

Great controversy exists regarding the basis of differences between implicit and explicit memory (Roe-

diger, 1990; Lewandowsky, Dunn, & Kirsner, 1989; Schacter, 1990). Some researchers suggest that two distinct memory systems exist, one for implicit and the other for explicit memory (e.g., Weiskrantz, 1989). In contrast, other researchers have proposed that the two kinds of memory systems differ simply in the way that information is processed (e.g., Roediger, Weldon, & Challis, 1989). According to this latter view, different memory tasks encompass several kinds of underlying processes. From this perspective, the differences between various memory test results are due to the fact that different memory tasks require the operation of separate processes.

It is still too early to tell which of these views will prevail in the memory research arena. Studies that support both sides of the argument are continuing to be conducted. In the meantime, research in several areas of psychology is demonstrating that the influence of implicit memories on people's behavior may be consequential. For instance, social psychologists are asking how we remember what others are like and how our implicit memories of people affect the way that we subsequently treat them. Similarly, psychologists specializing in learning are investigating how we can use implicit memory to teach skills more effectively. Such work promises to have important applications.

This young woman is confronted with the limitations of short-term memory, having just looked up a phone number only to forget it as soon as she closed the directory.

Linguistic code: Memory storage relying on language

Imaginal code: Memory storage based on visual images

Motor code: Memory storage based on physical activities

Storage in Long-Term Memory.   Episodic and semantic information are stored in long-term memory in several ways. One of the primary ways is through the **linguistic code**, which relies on language. The linguistic code allows us to store information abstractly without having to rely on a specific image. For instance, we may be able to recall that someone talking about a sloth is discussing an animal, even while we are unable to conjure up a specific image of what it looks like.

An **imaginal code**, in contrast, is memory storage that is based on visual images. If someone asked you to describe the path you take on the way from your psychology class to your home or dormitory, you would be likely to recall the images you have seen when taking the route in the past.

The third type of coding in long-term memory is the **motor code**, storage that is based on memories of physical activities. Your ability to ride a bicycle is based on motor memories; you probably would be hard-pressed to recall in verbal terms how you are able to do it. Motor codes are particularly well remembered. Even after years of never riding a bicycle, you would probably have little trouble remembering how to do it.

Levels of Processing

So far, we have used the notion that the processing of information in memory proceeds along three sequential stages, starting with sensory memory, proceeding to short-term memory, and finally ending with long-term memory. However, not all psychologists specializing in memory agree with such a view. Some suggest that a single process accounts for how well information is remembered: the way in which material is first perceived, considered, and understood.

Levels-of-processing theory: The theory which suggests that the way information is initially perceived and learned determines recall

The **levels-of-processing theory** emphasizes the degree to which new material is mentally analyzed (Craik & Lockhart, 1972). In contrast to the view that there are sensory, short-term, and long-term memories, levels-of-processing theory suggests that the amount of information processing that occurs when material is initially encountered is central in determining how much of the information is ultimately remembered. According to this approach, the depth of processing during exposure to material—meaning the degree to which it is analyzed and considered—is critical; the greater the intensity of its initial processing, the more likely we are to remember it.

Because we do not pay close attention to much of the information to which we are exposed, only scant mental processing takes place, and we forget it almost immediately. However, information to which we pay greater attention is processed more thoroughly. Therefore, it enters memory at a deeper level—and is less apt to be forgotten than information processed at shallower levels.

The theory goes on to suggest that there are considerable differences in the way information is processed at various levels of memory. At shallow levels, information is processed merely in terms of its physical and sensory aspects; for example, we may pay attention only to the shapes that make up the letters in the word "dog." At an intermediate level of processing, the shapes are translated into meaningful units—in this case, letters of the alphabet. These letters are considered in the context of words, and a specific sound of the word may be attached to the letters.

At the deepest level of processing, information is analyzed in terms of its meaning. It may be seen in a wider context, and associations between the meaning of the information and broader networks of knowledge may be drawn. For instance, we may think of dogs not merely as animals with four legs and a tail, but in terms of their relationship to cats and other mammals. We may form an image of our own dog, relating it to our own lives.

According to the levels-of-processing approach, the deeper the initial level of processing of specific information, the longer the information will be retained. The approach suggests, then, that the best way to remember new information is to consider it thoroughly when you are first exposed to it—reflecting on how it relates to information that you currently have (McDaniel, Riegler, & Waddill, 1990).

The levels-of-processing theory considers memory as involving more active mental processes than the three-stage approach to memory. However, research has not been entirely supportive of the levels-of-processing approach. For example, in some cases material that is processed on a shallow level is remembered better than information processed on a deeper level (Baddeley, 1978; Cermak & Craik, 1979).

In sum, neither the levels-of-processing model nor the three-stage model of memory is able to account for all phenomena relating to memory. As a result, other models of memory have been proposed. For example, psychologist Nelson Cowan (1988) has suggested that the most accurate representation of memory comes from a model in which short-term storage is considered a part of long-term storage, rather than representing a separate stage. Still, it is too early to tell—let alone remember—which model gives us the most accurate representation of memory.

RECAP AND REVIEW I

RECAP

◄ Memory is the process by which we encode, store, and retrieve information.

◄ Sensory memory contains a brief but accurate representation of physical stimuli to which a person is exposed. Each representation is constantly being replaced with a new one.

◄ Short-term memory has a capacity of seven (plus or minus two) chunks of information. Memories remain in short-term storage for fifteen to twenty-five seconds and are then either transferred to long-term memory or lost.

◄ Long-term memories are either episodic or semantic, and they enter long-term storage through rehearsal.

◄ Implicit memories refers to memories of which people are not aware consciously, but which can improve subsequent performance and behavior.

◄ An alternative to the three-stage model of memory, the levels-of-processing approach, suggests that information is analyzed at different levels, with material processed at deeper levels being retained the longest.

REVIEW

1. The process by which information is initially stored in memory is known as ___encoding___ . ___Retrieving___ is the process by which elements of memory are brought into awareness and used.

2. Match the type of memory with its definition:
   1. _b_ Long-term memory   a. Holds information fifteen to twenty-five seconds.
   2. _a_ Short-term memory   b. Permanent storage, could be difficult to retrieve.
   3. _c_ Sensory memory   c. Initial storage of information, only lasts a second.

3. Iconic memory refers to sensory input from the ___eyes___, while echoic memory deals with input from the ___ears___.

4. A ___chunking___ is a meaningful group of stimuli that can be stored together in short-term memory.

5. You are going to a party. Your friend calls you up and gives you the address to go to. As you drive there, you repeat the address to yourself over and over so you won't forget it. What term describes this phenomenon? _rehearsal_

6. ___mnemonics___ are organizational strategies used to organize information.

7. Long-term memory seems to be divided into two subdivisions: ___semantic___ memory, which consists of knowledge and facts, and ___episodic___ memory, which consists of personal experiences.

8. ___Associative___ models of memory state that long-term memory is stored as associations between pieces of information.

9. A subject in a psychology experiment hears the word "ice cream" followed by a list of syllables to memorize. One week later, she is unable to recall any syllables on her own, but when the experimenter says "ice cream" to her, she recalls part of the list. What effect explains this phenomenon? _Priming_

10. Match the type of memory storage system with its definition:
    1. _a_ Motor code   a. Storage based on memories of physical activities.
    2. _c_ Imaginal code   b. Stores information without relying on a specific image.
    3. _b_ Linguistic code   c. Code based on concrete images.

11. You read an article stating that the more a person analyzes a statement, the more likely he or she is to remember it later. What theory is this article describing? _Levels of processing theory._

Ask Yourself

Priming seems to occur without conscious awareness in most cases. How might this effect be used by advertisers and others to promote their products? What ethical principles are involved?

(Answers to review questions are on page 256.)

RECALLING LONG-TERM MEMORIES

An hour after his job interview, Rich was sitting in a coffee shop, telling his friend Laura about his apparent success, when the woman who had interviewed him walked in. "Well, hello, Rich. How are you doing?" Trying to make a good impression, Rich began to introduce Laura, but then realized he could not remember the name of the interviewer. Stammering, he desperately searched his memory for her name but couldn't remember. "I *know* her name," he thought to himself, "but here I am, looking like a fool. I can kiss this job goodbye."

Have you ever tried to remember someone's name, absolutely certain that you knew it, but unable to recall it no matter how hard you tried? This not infrequent occurrence—known as the **tip-of-the-tongue phenomenon**—exemplifies the difficulties that can occur in retrieving information stored in long-term memory (Harris & Morris, 1986; A. S. Brown, 1991).

One reason recall is not perfect is the sheer quantity of recollections that are stored in long-term memory. Although the issue is far from settled, many psychologists have suggested that the material that makes its way there is relatively permanent (Tulving & Psotka, 1971). If they are correct, this suggests that the capacity of long-term memory is vast, given the variety of people's experiences and education. For instance, if you are like the average college student, your vocabulary includes some 50,000 words, you know hundreds of mathematical "facts," and you are able to conjure up images—such as the way your childhood home looked—with no trouble at all. In fact, simply cataloging all your memories would probably take years of work.

Tip-of-the-tongue phenomenon: The inability to recall information that one realizes one knows—a result of the difficulty of retrieving information from long-term memory

How do we sort through this vast array of material and retrieve specific information at the appropriate time? One of the major ways is through the use of retrieval cues. A **retrieval cue** is a stimulus that allows us to recall information that is located in long-term memory more easily (Tulving & Thompson, 1973). It may be a word, an emotion, a sound; whatever the specific cue, a memory will suddenly come to mind when the retrieval cue is present. For example, the smell of roasting turkey may evoke memories of Thanksgiving or family gatherings.

Retrieval cues guide people through the information stored in long-term memory in much the same way as the cards in a card catalog guide people through a library. They are particularly important when *recalling* information, as opposed to being asked to *recognize* material stored in memory. In recall, a specific piece of information must be retrieved—such as that needed to fill in the blanks or write an essay on a test. In contrast, recognition occurs when people are presented with a stimulus and asked whether they have been exposed to it previously, or are asked to identify it from a list of alternatives.

As you might guess, recognition is generally much easier than recall. **Recall** is more difficult because it consists of a series of processes: a search through memory, retrieval of potentially relevant information, and then a decision regarding whether or not the information you have found is accurate. If it appears correct, the search is over, but if it does not, the search must continue. On the other hand, **recognition** is simpler since it involves fewer steps (Anderson & Bower, 1972).

Flashbulb Memories

Where were you when you learned that the space shuttle *Challenger* had exploded?

You probably have little trouble recalling your exact location and a variety of other trivial details about occurrences that happened when you heard the news, even though the accident happened years ago. The reason is a phenomenon known as **flashbulb memories**. Flashbulb memories are memories centered around a specific, important, or surprising event that are so vivid it is as if they represented a snapshot of the event.

Several types of flashbulb memories are common among college students. For example, involvement in a car accident, meeting one's roommate for the first time, and the night of high school graduation are all typical flashbulb memories (Rubin, 1985). (See Figure 8-7.)

Of course, flashbulb memories do not contain every detail of an original scene. For instance, I remember vividly that some three decades ago I was sitting in Mr. Sharp's tenth-grade geometry class when I heard that President Kennedy had been shot. Although I recall where I was sitting and how my classmates reacted to the news, I do not recollect what I was wearing or what I had for lunch that day. Flashbulb memories, then, are not complete and unfailingly accurate, and just how much their essential nature differs from everyday memories remains an open question (McCloskey et al., 1988; Cohen, McCloskey, & Wible, 1990; Pillemer, 1990; Christianson & Loftus, 1990).

Still, flashbulb memories are extraordinary because of the details they do include. An analysis of people's recollections of the Kennedy assassination found that their memories tended to have a number of features in common (Brown & Kulik, 1977). Most contained information regarding where the person heard the news, who told him or her about it, what event was interrupted by the news, the emotions of the informant, the person's own emotions, and some personal details of the event (such as seeing a robin fly by while the information was being given).

Retrieval cue: A stimulus such as a word, smell, or sound that allows one to more easily recall information located in long-term memory

Recall: Drawing from memory a specific piece of information for a specific purpose

Recognition: Acknowledging prior exposure to a given stimulus, rather than recalling the information from memory

Flashbulb memories: Memories of a specific event that are so clear they seem like "snapshots" of the event

▶ **255**

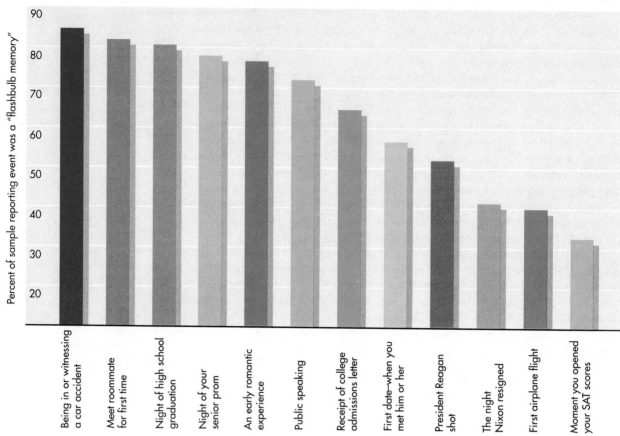

FIGURE 8-7

The most common flashbulb memories of a sample of college students are shown here. (Rubin, 1985.)

Where were you when you first heard that the United States had bombed Baghdad during the Gulf War? Flashbulb memory is the facility that enables you to remember specific, important events.

ANSWERS (REVIEW I):

1. Encoding; retrieval **2.** 1-b; 2-a; 3-c **3.** Eyes; ears **4.** Chunk **5.** Rehearsal **6.** Mnemonics **7.** Semantic; episodic **8.** Associative **9.** Priming **10.** 1-a; 2-c; 3-b **11.** Levels-of-processing theory

On the other hand, we can't be sure that all the details recalled in flashbulb memories are accurate. For example, one day after the *Challenger* accident, psychologists Nicole Harsh and Ulric Neisser asked a group of college students how they had heard the news of the disaster. When they asked the same people the identical question three years later, most responded readily, providing reasonable responses. The trouble was that in about one-third of the cases, their answers were completely wrong (Harsh & Neisser, 1989; Neisser & Harsch, in press).

Flashbulb memories illustrate a more general phenomenon about memory: Memories that are exceptional are more easily retrieved than those relating to events that are commonplace. We are more likely, for example, to recall a particular number if it appears in a group of twenty words than if it appears in a group of twenty other numbers. The more distinctive a stimulus, then, the more likely we are to recall it later. This phenomenon is known as the **von Restorff effect**, named after its discoverer (von Restorff, 1933).

von Restorff effect: The phenomenon by which distinctive stimuli are recalled more readily than less distinctive ones

The von Restorff effect operates in our everyday lives: We are far better at remembering unusual, atypical events that happen to us than the mundane, routine occurrences that take up most of our time. For instance, in one study, a group of college students were equipped with beepers that went off at random intervals, at which time they wrote down what they were doing. When the students' recollections were compared to their written accounts, it was clear that most of them were unable to recall much of what they had been doing. However, distinctive, unusual events, such as a first date, were remembered well (Brewer & Dupree, 1983).

Constructive Processes in Memory: Rebuilding the Past

Although it is clear that we can have detailed recollections of significant and distinctive events, it is difficult to gauge the accuracy of such memories. In fact, it is apparent that our memories reflect, at least in part, **constructive processes**, processes in which memories are influenced by the meaning that we give to events. When we retrieve information, then, the memory that is produced is affected not just by the direct prior experience we have had with the stimulus, but by our guesses and inferences about its meaning as well.

Constructive processes: Processes in which memories are influenced by the interpretation and meaning we give to events

The notion that memory is based on constructive processes was first put forward by Sir Frederic Bartlett, a British psychologist, who suggested that people tend to remember information in terms of **schemas**, general themes that contain relatively little specific detail (Bartlett, 1932). He argued that such schemas were based on the information provided not only by a stimulus but also by our understanding of the situation, our expectations about the situation, and our awareness of the motivation underlying people's behavior.

Schemas: General themes in terms of which we remember a situation

In a demonstration of the operation of schemas, researchers have employed a process known as **serial reproduction**, in which information from memory is passed sequentially from one person to another. For an example of serial reproduction, look briefly at the cartoon in Figure 8-8, p. 258, and then try to describe it to someone else without looking back at it. Then ask that person to describe it to another person, and repeat the process with still one more person.

Serial reproduction: The passage of interpretive information from person to person, often resulting in inaccuracy through personal bias and misinterpretation

If you listen to the last person's report of the contents of the cartoon, you are sure to find that it differs in important respects from the cartoon itself. Many people recall the cartoon as showing a razor in the hand of the black person—obviously an incorrect recollection, given that the razor is held by the white person (Allport & Postman, 1958).

This example, which is drawn from a classic experiment, illustrates the role

FIGURE 8-8

When one person views this cartoon and then describes it from memory to a second person, who in turn describes it to a third, and so on—in a process known as serial reproduction—the last person to repeat the contents of the cartoon typically gives a description that differs in important respects from the original. (Based on Allport & Postman, 1958.)

of expectations in memory. The migration of the razor from the white person's hand to the black person's hand in memory clearly indicates that expectations about the world—reflecting, in this case, the unwarranted prejudice that blacks may be more violent than whites and thus more apt to be holding a razor—have an impact upon how events are recalled.

Bartlett thought that schemas affected recall at the time of retrieval of information, and that the information had originally been entered into memory accurately. However, subsequent work has shown that our expectations and prior knowledge affect the way information is initially entered into memory. For example, read and try to remember the following passage:

> The procedure is actually quite simple. First you arrange items into different groups. Of course, one pile may be sufficient, depending on how much there is to do. If you have to go somewhere else due to lack of facilities, that is the next step; otherwise, you are pretty well set. It is important not to overdo things. That is, it is better to do too few things at once than too many. In the short run this may not seem important but complications can easily arise. A mistake can be expensive as well. At first, the whole procedure will seem complicated. Soon, however, it will become just another facet of life. It is difficult to foresee any end to the necessity for this task in the immediate future, but then one can never tell. After the procedure is completed, one arranges the materials into different groups again. Then they can be put into their appropriate places. Eventually, they will be used once more and the whole cycle will then have to be repeated. However, this is a part of life (Bransford & Johnson, 1972, p. 722).

As the results of a study that used this passage revealed, your ability to recall it—as well as understand it initially—would have been far superior if you had known prior to reading it that it referred to washing laundry (Bransford & Johnson, 1972). Our prior understanding of information, then, can facilitate our ability to remember it.

Furthermore, it is not just our expectations and prior knowledge that have an impact on what we recall. Our understanding of others' motivations also leads to constructive processes in memory. For example, in what has been called the **soap opera effect**, knowledge about what motivates an individual can lead to elaborations in memory of earlier events involving that person.

Soap opera effect: The phenomena by which memory of a prior event involving a person is more reliable when we understand that person's motivations

For William Jackson, the inadequate memories of two people cost him five years of his life. Jackson was the victim of mistaken identity during criminal proceedings. Two witnesses picked him out of a lineup as the perpetrator of a crime. On that basis, he was convicted and sentenced to serve fourteen to fifty years in jail.

It was five years later when the actual criminal was identified, and Jackson was released. For Jackson, though, it was too late. In his words, "They took away part of my life, part of my youth. I spend five years down there, and all they said was 'we're sorry'" (*Time*, 1982).

Unfortunately, Jackson is not the only victim to whom apologies have had to be made; many cases of mistaken identity have occurred (Brandon & Davies, 1973). Research on eyewitness identification of suspects, as well as memory for other details of crimes, has shown that witnesses are apt to make substantial errors when they try to recall details of criminal activity (Bishop, 1988; Wells & Luus, 1990).

One reason is the impact of weapons used in crimes. When a criminal perpetrator displays a gun or knife, it acts like a perceptual magnet, with all witnesses' eyes being drawn to the weapon. As a consequence, less attention is paid to other details of the crime, and witnesses are less able to recall what actually occurred (Loftus, Loftus, & Messo, 1987).

Even when weapons are not involved, eyewitnesses are prone to errors relating to memory. For instance, viewers of a twelve-second film of a mugging that was shown on a New York City television news program were later given the opportunity to pick out the assailant from a six-person lineup. Of some 2000 viewers who called the station after the program, only 15 percent were able to pick out the right person—a figure similar to random guessing (Buckhout, 1975).

MEMORY ON TRIAL: THE FALLIBILITY OF WITNESSES

Other research suggests that the mistakes witnesses make show wide variability. For example, one study found that witnesses of staged crimes disagreed by as much as 2 feet in their estimates of the height of a perpetrator and averaged a difference of 8 inches from his true height. There was a discrepancy from the true age averaging eight years, hair color was recalled incorrectly 83 percent of the time, and about a quarter of all witnesses left out more than half of the details they had actually seen (Gardner, 1933).

Even the specific wording of a question posed to a witness can affect the way in which something is recalled, as a number of experiments illustrate. For example, in one experiment subjects were shown a film of two cars crashing into each other. Some were then asked the question, "About how fast were the cars going when they *smashed* into each other?" They estimated the speed to be an average of 40.8 miles per hour. In contrast, when another group of subjects was asked, "About how fast were the cars going when they *contacted* each other?" the average estimated speed was only 31.8 miles per hour (Loftus & Palmer, 1974).

The problem of memory reliability becomes even more acute when children are witnesses. Recent years have seen a number of instances in which children's recollections of sexual abuse are central to a court case. In one famous trial involving the owners of a preschool in Manhattan Beach, California, for example, children were asked to recall whether they had undergone sexual abuse almost a decade after it had supposedly occurred. The owners were found not guilty, largely due to the apparently cloudy and contradictory memories of the children involved (Schindehette, 1990).

The lack of reliance on the children's memories seems well founded. Most research on the question suggests that children's memories are highly suggestible. For instance, in one experiment, 5- to 7-year-old girls who had just had a routine physical examination were shown an anatomically explicit doll.

Witnesses often make errors in recalling the details of a crime. William Jackson (a) was mistakenly identified as the perpetrator of a crime that was actually committed by the man shown in (b).

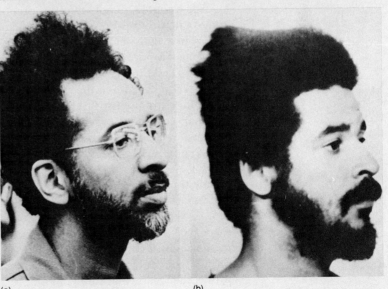

(a)   (b)

The soap opera effect derives its name from soap opera characters who, at least in the eyes of occasional viewers, make seemingly innocent statements. However, to long-term viewers, who are aware of the characters' real motives, the same statements may be fraught with significance. In turn, this information will be remembered differently according to a person's understanding of the motivation behind the statement (Owens, Bower, & Black, 1979).

In sum, it is clear that our understanding of the motivations behind a person's behavior, as well as our expectations and knowledge about the world, affects the reliability of our memories (Katz, 1989). As discussed in the Psychology at Work box, the imperfections of our recollections can have important consequences.

Autobiographical Memory: Where Past Meets Present

Your memory of your own past might well be a fiction—or at least a distortion of what actually occurred. The same constructive processes that act to make us inaccurately recall the behavior of others also reduce the accuracy of autobiographical memories. **Autobiographical memories** refer to our recollections of the facts about our own lives (Bradburn, Rips, & Shevell, 1987).

Autobiographical memories: Recollections of the facts about our own lives

For example, people tend to forget information about their past that is incongruent with the way in which they currently see themselves. One study found that adults who were well adjusted but who had been treated for emotional problems during the early years of their lives tended to forget important but troubling childhood events. For instance, they forget such details as their family's receipt of welfare when they were children, being in foster care, and living in a home for delinquents (Robbins, 1988). Similarly, people who are depressed remember sad events from their past more easily than happy people do, and people who report being happy in adulthood remember more happy events than depressing ones (Bower & Cohen, 1982).

It is not just certain kinds of events that are distorted; particular periods of life are remembered more easily than others (Rubin, 1985). Furthermore, there are remarkable commonalities among people in what periods are remembered best. As you can see in Figure 8-9, 70-year-olds tend to recall details of their lives from their twenties and thirties best, whereas 50-year-olds tend to have more memories of their teenage years and their twenties. In both cases, it is the recollection of details of the more recent decades of people's lives, in comparison with earlier years, that suffers most.

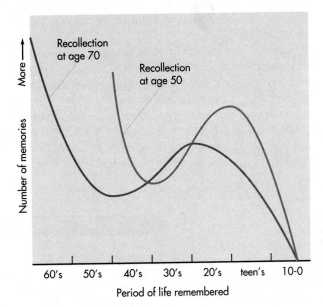

FIGURE 8-9
We selectively recall certain periods of our lives. At age 70, people remember more of their twenties than their forties and fifties, while people age 50 remember more of their teenage years. (Rubin, 1986.)

Everyday Memory: Different in the Laboratory?

The limitations of autobiographical memory suggest the importance of considering memory within the context of people's everyday lives. A number of memory researchers have raised the specter that much of the existing research on memory is deficient because it relies so heavily on research conducted in laboratory settings. Such critics of laboratory research have argued that memory experiments should be carried out in naturalistic settings, using recollections from people's own personal experience (e.g., Neisser, 1982; 1991).

Indeed, some researchers employ the term "everyday memory" to distinguish those memories that have relevance to the lives of subjects from laboratory-induced memories. For example, one memory researcher took a forty-seven-day bicycle tour through Europe with a companion, identified as MVP, who was the subject of the study. During the trip, the experimenter recorded various events, such as the number of postcards MVP mailed, and so on. Three months after the trip ended, the researcher gave MVP a memory test of the frequency of various events. He found—not too surprisingly—that MVP showed better recall for what had happened on the trip than a control group of individuals who simply guessed what events had occurred. More importantly, the researcher investigated the process by which MVP came up with the frequency estimates. He found that the process used to estimate low-frequency events differed from that used to estimate more frequent occurrences (Bruce & Read, 1988).

To supporters of the "everyday memory" approach to research, the bicycle trip study exemplifies the importance of using real-world episodes to study memory. They argue that no laboratory study could ever approximate a forty-seven-day trip, and hence an understanding of memory of actual, engrossing, and important events cannot be ascertained from laboratory studies alone.

On the other hand, many memory researchers are critical of such a view. They suggest that whatever gains are obtained from such naturalistic studies are lost due to our inability to generalize the results to other situations and individuals. They ask just how much can be learned from the experiences of one person. Furthermore, they question why we would expect the results of such naturalistic studies to be any different from those obtained inside the laboratory (Banaji & Crowder, 1989).

Recently, a middle ground between the two camps has emerged. Detractors of naturalistic research have come to recognize that certain kinds of memory research produce misleading results when done within the confines of the laboratory (e.g., Ceci & Bronfenbrenner, 1991). Similarly, "everyday memory" researchers acknowledge the importance of carefully controlled memory studies carried out in laboratory settings (Neisser, 1991). Almost everyone agrees with the point that the critical issue about memory research is not so much *where* it is carried out as how *carefully* it is done.

RECAP AND REVIEW II

RECAP

◀ The tip-of-the-tongue phenomenon refers to the inability to recall something that a person is sure he or she knows.

◀ Retrieval cues are particularly important when recalling information—as opposed to recognizing it.

◀ Flashbulb memories are memories that are centered around a specific, important event and are so clear it is as if they represent a snapshot of the event.

◀ Memories reflect, at least in part, constructive processes, in which they are influenced by the meaning that we give to events. Autobiographical memory, for instance, is distorted.

REVIEW

1. Mary, while with a group of friends at a dance, bumps into a man she dated last month. When she tries to introduce him to her friends, she cannot remember his name, though she is positive she knows it. What is the term for this occurrence? *Tip of the tongue*

2. A person is shown a certain stimulus and asked if he or she has ever seen it before. This person is being asked to use which type of memory test? *recognition*

3. _____*Recall*_____ is used when a person is asked to retrieve a specific item from memory.

4. A friend of your mother's tells you "I know exactly where I was and what I was doing when I heard that Elvis died." What phenomenon explains this type of recollection? *flash bulb*

5. The person described in No. 4 could probably also accurately tell you the exact details of what she was wearing when Elvis passed on, right down to the color of the ribbon on her blue suede shoes. True or false? *False*

6. We are more likely to be able to recall stimuli that are distinctive. What is the name of this phenomenon? *Von Restorff*

7. Retrieval of memories deals not only with objective reality, but also with our constructions of past events. True or false? *True*

8. _____*Schemas*_____ are "themes," containing little specific detail, used to organize information in memory.

9. Research has shown that recall of autobiographical material is best when looking at the most recent times of one's life. True or false? *False*

Ask Yourself

How might courtroom procedure be improved, knowing what you now know about memory errors and biases? Would this necessitate any changes in the legal code as well?

(Answers to review questions are on page 264.)

FORGETTING: WHEN MEMORY FAILS

He could remember, quite literally, nothing—nothing, that is, that had happened since the loss of his brain's temporal lobes and hippocampus during experimental surgery to reduce epileptic seizures. Until that time, his memory had been quite normal. But after the operation he was unable to recall anything for more than a few minutes, and then the memory was seemingly lost forever. He did not remember his address, or the name of the person to whom he was talking. He would read the same magazine over and over again. According to his own description, his life was like waking from a dream and being unable to know where he was or how he got there (Milner, 1966).

The difficulties faced by a person without a normal memory are legion, as exemplified in the case described above and that of Pamilla Smith, which we discussed at the beginning of the chapter. All of us who have experienced even routine instances of forgetting—such as not remembering an acquaintance's name or a fact on a test—understand the serious consequences of memory failure.

The first attempts to study forgetting were made by German psychologist Hermann Ebbinghaus about a hundred years ago. Using himself as his only subject, he memorized lists of three-letter nonsense syllables—meaningless sets of two consonants with a vowel in between, such as FIW and BOZ. By measuring how easy it was to relearn a given list of words after varying periods of time from initial learning had passed, he found that forgetting occurred systematically, as shown in Figure 8-10. As the figure indicates, the most rapid forgetting occurs in the first nine hours, and particularly in the first hour. After nine hours, the rate of forgetting slows and declines little, even after the passage of many days.

Despite his primitive methods, Ebbinghaus's research had an important influence on subsequent research, and his basic conclusions have been upheld (Wixted & Ebbeson, 1991). There is almost always a strong initial decline in memory, followed by a more gradual drop over time. Furthermore, relearning of previously mastered material is almost always faster than starting from scratch, whether the material is academic information or a motor skill such as serving a tennis ball.

Efforts at understanding the problem of *why* we forget have yielded two major solutions. One theory explains forgetting in terms of a process called **decay**, or the loss of information through its nonuse. This explanation assumes that when new material is learned, a **memory trace** or **engram**—an actual physical change in the brain—occurs. In decay, the trace simply fades away with nothing left behind, because of the mere passage of time.

Although there is evidence that decay does occur, it does not seem to be the complete explanation for forgetting. Often there is no relationship between how long ago a person was exposed to information and how well it is recalled. If decay explained all forgetting, we would expect that the longer the time between the initial learning of information and our attempt to recall it, the harder it would be to remember it, since there would be more time for the memory trace to

Hermann Ebbinghaus (1850–1909) was among the first to attempt to study forgetting.

Decay: The loss of information through nonuse

Memory trace or **engram:** A physical change in the brain corresponding to the memory of material

FIGURE 8-10

In his classic work, Ebbinghaus found that the most rapid forgetting occurs in the first nine hours after exposure to new material. However, the rate of forgetting then slows down and declines very little even after many days have passed. (Ebbinghaus, 1885.)

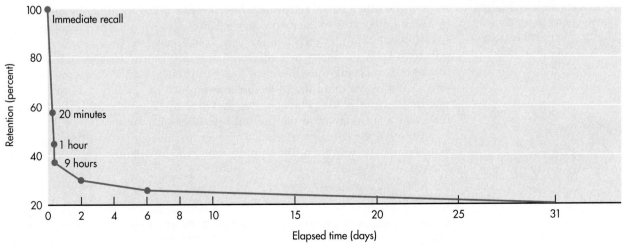

decay. Yet people who take several consecutive tests on the same material often recall more of the initial information when taking later tests than they did on earlier tests. If decay were operating, we would expect the opposite to occur (Payne, 1986).

Because decay is not able to fully account for forgetting, memory specialists have proposed an additional mechanism: **interference**. In interference, information in memory displaces or blocks out other information, preventing its recall.

Interference: The phenomenon by which recall is hindered because of other information in memory which displaces or blocks the information out

To distinguish between decay and interference, think of the two processes in terms of a row of books on a library shelf. In decay, the old books are constantly crumbling and rotting away, leaving room for new arrivals. Interference processes suggest that new books knock the old ones off the shelf, where they become inaccessible.

Most research suggests that interference is the key process in forgetting (Potter, 1990). We mainly forget things not because the memory trace has decayed, but because new memories interfere with the retrieval of old ones.

Although we may view interference negatively, it is important to remember that it may actually enhance our ability to understand and interact with the world around us. Interference assists us in developing general, summary memories of our experiences. For instance, rather than recalling every detail of every encounter with a particular professor, we tend to remember the most important episodes and forget those that are less meaningful. This ability allows us to draw a general, although not necessarily detailed or totally accurate, characterization of what our encounters with the professor have been like in the past. Furthermore, it helps to anticipate the course of future interactions (Potter, 1990).

Proactive and Retroactive Interference: The Before and After of Forgetting

There are actually two sorts of interference that influence forgetting: proactive and retroactive. In **proactive interference**, information learned earlier interferes with recall of newer material. Suppose, as a student of foreign languages, you first learned French in tenth grade, and then in eleventh grade you took Spanish. When it comes time to take a college achievement test in the twelfth grade in Spanish you may find you have difficulty recalling the Spanish translation of a word because all you can think of is its French equivalent.

Proactive interference: The phenomenon by which information stored in memory interferes with recall of material learned later

Retroactive interference: The phenomenon by which new information interferes with the recall of information learned earlier

On the other hand, **retroactive interference** refers to difficulty in recall of information because of later exposure to different material. If, for example, you have difficulty on a French achievement test because of your more recent exposure to Spanish, retroactive interference is the culprit (see Figure 8-11). One way of remembering the difference between proactive and retroactive interference is to keep in mind that *pro*active interference moves forward in time—the past interferes with the present—whereas *retro*active interference retrogresses in time, working backward as the present interferes with the past.

Although the concepts of proactive and retroactive interference suggest why material may be forgotten, they still do not explain whether forgetting due to

ANSWERS (REVIEW II):

1. Tip-of-the-tongue phenomenon **2.** Recognition **3.** Recall **4.** Flashbulb memory **5.** False; small details probably won't be remembered via flashbulb memory. **6.** von Restorff effect **7.** True **8.** Schemas **9.** False; the best recall seems to be for the more distant past.

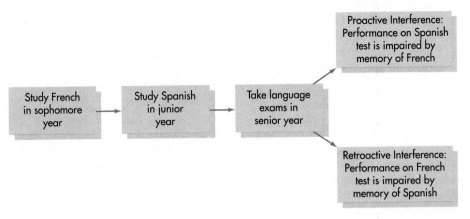

FIGURE 8-11

Proactive interference occurs when material learned earlier interferes with the recall of newer material. In this example, exposure to French prior to learning Spanish interferes with performance on a Spanish test. In contrast, retroactive interference exists when material learned after initial exposure to other material interferes with the recall of the first material. In this case, retroactive interference occurs when the recall of French is impaired because of later exposure to Spanish.

interference is caused by the actual loss or modification of information, or by problems in retrieval of information. Most research suggests that material that has apparently been lost because of interference can eventually be recalled if appropriate stimuli are presented (Anderson, 1981; Tulving & Psotka, 1971), but the question has not been fully answered. In an effort to resolve the issue, some psychologists have begun to study the biological bases of memory in order to better understand what is remembered and what is forgotten—an increasingly important avenue of investigation that we turn to now.

The Biological Bases of Memory: The Search for the Engram

Just where is the engram—the physical, neural trace that represents a memory in the brain—located?

This question has proved to be a major puzzle to psychologists interested in memory and has become the focus of a good deal of ongoing work. The search began in the 1920s, when psychologist Karl Lashley ran a series of experiments in which he removed portions of the cortex of rats. He found that rats who were made to relearn a problem involving running a maze showed learning deficits in proportion to the extent of the damage to their cortex; when more material was removed from the cortex, greater learning difficulties took place.

More intriguing, however, was the finding that the time it took to relearn the problem was unrelated to the specific *location* of the injury. Regardless of the particular portion of the brain that had been removed, the degree of learning deficit was similar, suggesting that memory traces are somewhat evenly distributed across the brain. Results of Lashley's work—summarized in a famous paper titled "In Search of the Engram"—led to the view held for several decades that stored memories are widely and fairly equally distributed across the brain (Lashley, 1950).

Contemporary research, however, seems to be coming to a different conclusion. Such research starts from findings on the physiology of learning that show that separate, distinct areas of the cortex simultaneously process information about particular dimensions of the world, including visual, auditory, and other sensory stimuli. Because different areas of the brain are simultaneously involved in processing information about different aspects of a stimulus, it seems reasonable that information storage might be linked to the sites of processing and therefore located in those particular areas. In sum, the location of an engram depends on the nature of the material that is being learned and the specific neural system that processed the information (Alkon, 1987; Matthies, 1989; Squire, 1987; Miller, Li, & Desimone, 1991).

How can we reconcile the growing contemporary view that memory is related to specific neural processing employed during learning, when we consider Lashley's findings that memory deficits were unrelated to the location of injury to the cortex? One answer is that the contradiction between the two findings is more apparent than real. It is likely, for example, that Lashley's procedure of having rats run through a maze actually involves several kinds of information and learning—including visual information, spatial configuration, smells, and perhaps even sounds. Assuming this to be the case, learning and processing of information must have been occurring in several modalities simultaneously, although presumably in different locations in the brain. If each of these processing modalities resulted in a separate memory trace, then removing any particular portion of the cortex would still leave the other memory traces intact—and produce the same apparent deficit in performance, independent of which area of the cortex was removed.

In sum, it appears that memory is localized to specific areas in that a particular memory trace is related to a particular information processing system in the brain. But in a larger sense, memory traces are distributed, given that several brain processing systems are involved in any learning situation—leading to the distribution of the traces throughout various areas of the brain (Squire, 1987; Bear, Cooper, & Ebner, 1987; Cotman & Lynch, 1989).

Other investigators are following different paths to learn about the biological bases of memory. For instance, recent work suggests that the hippocampus plays a central role in the conversion of new sensory information into a form that ultimately allows it to be stored in the cerebral cortex of the brain (Zola-Morgan & Squire, 1990). Furthermore, certain chemicals and neurotransmitters have been linked to the formation, impairment, and improvement of memory. In one study, for example, a group of chicks who received a drug that inhibited protein synthesis performed more poorly on a memory task than those who didn't receive the drug (Gibbs & Ng, 1977; McGaugh, 1989; Sawaguchi & Goldman-Rakic, 1991).

Finally, even various kinds of foods may be associated with memory. One recent study, for example, suggests that something as simple as a tall glass of lemonade may help us remember better. The results of an experiment by memory researcher Paul Gold and colleagues showed that increasing the level of glucose in the blood—by drinking a glass of highly sweetened lemonade—produced increased performance on some memory tasks in the elderly (Manning, Hall, & Gold, 1990). Although such findings are far from definitive, they do suggest that one day we might choose a diet at least partially on the basis of how well it enhances our ability to remember.

Memory Dysfunctions: Afflictions of Forgetting

To a casual observer, Harold appears to be a brilliant golfer. He seems to have learned the game perfectly; his shots are almost flawless.

Yet anyone accompanying him on the course is bound to notice some startling incongruities. Although he is immediately able to size up a situation and hit the ball exactly where it should go, he cannot remember where the ball has just landed. At the end of each hole, he forgets the score (Blakeslee, 1984, p. C1; Schacter, 1983).

Alzheimer's disease: An illness associated with aging that includes severe memory loss, physical deterioration, and loss of language abilities

Harold's problem: he suffers from **Alzheimer's disease**, the illness that includes severe memory problems among its symptoms. Alzheimer's, discussed first in Chapter 3, is the fourth leading cause of death among U.S. adults. It strikes around 10 percent of people over the age of 65, and almost half of all people who live beyond 85 develop the disease (Gelman, 1989b; Dickinson, 1991).

In its initial stages, Alzheimer's symptoms appear as simple forgetfulness of things like appointments and birthdays. As the disease progresses, memory loss becomes more profound, and even the simplest tasks—such as how to dial a telephone—are forgotten. Ultimately, victims can forget their own names or family members' faces. In addition, physical deterioration sets in, and language abilities may be lost entirely.

Although the causes of Alzheimer's disease are not fully understood, recent evidence suggests that it may be linked to a specific inherited defect. The flaw leads to difficulties in the production of the protein beta amyloid, necessary for the maintenance of nerve cell connections. When the manufacture of beta amyloid goes awry, it leads to the deterioration of nerve cells in the brain—producing the symptoms of Alzheimer's (Hardy et al., 1991).

Alzheimer's disease is just one of several memory dysfunctions that plague their victims. Another is **amnesia**, memory loss that occurs without other mental difficulties. The classic case—immortalized in many a drama—is a victim who receives a blow to the head and is unable to remember anything from his or her past. In reality, amnesia of this type, known as retrograde amnesia, is quite rare. In **retrograde amnesia**, memory is lost for occurrences prior to a certain event. There is usually a gradual reappearance of lost memory, although it may take as long as several years for a full restoration to occur. In certain cases, some memories are lost forever (Baddeley, 1982).

A second type of amnesia is exemplified by the cases of Pamilla Smith and the man we discussed earlier, both of whom could remember nothing of their current activities. In **anterograde amnesia**, loss of memory occurs for events following an injury. Information cannot be transferred from short-term to long-term memory, resulting in the inability to remember anything other than what was in long-term storage prior to the accident.

Amnesia is also displayed by people who suffer from **Korsakoff's syndrome**, a disease that afflicts long-term alcoholics who have also had an impaired diet, resulting in a thiamine deficiency. Although many of their intellectual abilities may be intact, they display a strange array of symptoms, including hallucinations; repeating questions, even after being told the answer; and repeating the same story over and over again.

Fortunately, most of us have memories that are intact, and the occasional failures that we do suffer may actually be preferable to having a perfect memory. Consider, for instance, the case of a man who had total recall. After reading passages of the *Divine Comedy* in Italian—a language he did not speak—he was able to repeat them from memory even some fifteen years later. He could memorize lists of fifty unrelated words and recall them at will more than a decade later. He could even repeat the same list of words backward, if asked (Luria, 1968).

Such a skill might at first seem to have few drawbacks, but it actually presented quite a problem. The man's memory became a jumble of lists of words, numbers, and names, and when he tried to relax, his mind was filled with images. Even reading was difficult, since every word evoked a flood of thoughts from the past that interfered with his ability to understand the meaning of what he was reading. Partially as a consequence of the man's unusual memory, psychologist A. R. Luria, who studied his case, found him to be a "disorganized and rather dull-witted person" (Luria, 1968, p. 65).

We may be grateful, then, that being somewhat forgetful plays a useful role in our lives.

Amnesia: Memory loss unaccompanied by other mental difficulties

Retrograde amnesia: Memory loss of occurrences prior to some event

Anterograde amnesia: Memory loss of events following an injury

Korsakoff's syndrome: A disease among long-term alcoholics involving memory impairment

The Informed Consumer of Psychology: Improving Your Memory

Apart from the advantages of forgetting, say, the details of a gruesome science fiction movie, most of us still would like to find ways of improving our memories. Given our understanding of memory, is it possible to find practical ways of increasing our recall of information? Most definitely. Research has revealed a number of strategies that can be used to help us develop better memories (Cohen, 1989). Among the best:

Keyword technique: The pairing of a foreign word with a common, similar sounding English word to aid in remembering the new word

■ The keyword technique. Suppose you are taking a class in a foreign language and need to learn long lists of vocabulary words. One way of easing this process is to use the **keyword technique**, in which a foreign word is paired with a common English word that has a similar *sound*. This English word is known as the keyword. For example, to learn the Spanish word duck (*pato*, pronounced *pot-o*), the keyword might be "pot"; for the Spanish word for horse (*caballo*, pronounced *cob-eye-yo*), the keyword might be "eye."

Once you have thought of a keyword, you form a mental image of it graphically "interacting" with the English translation of the word. For instance, you might envision a duck taking a bath in a pot to remember the word *pato*, or a horse with a large, bulging eye in the center of its head to recall *caballo*. This technique has produced considerably superior results in learning foreign language vocabulary than more traditional techniques involving memorization of the words themselves (Pressley & Levin, 1983; Pressley, 1987).

Method of loci (LO sy): Assigning words or ideas to places, thereby improving recall of the words by envisioning those places

■ Method of loci. If you have ever had to give a talk in class, you know the difficulty of keeping in mind all the points you want to make. One technique that works quite effectively was developed by the ancient Greeks: When Greek orators sought to memorize long speeches, they used the **method of loci** (*loci* is the Latin word for places) to organize their recollections of what they wanted to say. With this technique, each part of a speech is imagined as "residing" in a different location of a building.

For instance, you might think of the preface of a talk as being in your house's entryway, the first major point being in the living room, the next major point residing in the dining room, and so forth, until the end of the speech is reached at the back bedroom of the house.

This technique can easily be adapted to learning lists of words; each word on the list is imagined as being located in a series of sequential locations. The method works best by using the most outlandish images possible: If you wanted to remember a list of groceries consisting of bananas, ketchup, and milk, for instance, you might think of a banana intertwined in the leaves of your living-room begonia, the ketchup spilled over the end table, and the milk spraying from the top of a table lamp. When you got to the supermarket, you could mentally "walk" through your living room, recalling the items easily.

Encoding specificity: The phenomenon by which memory of information is enhanced when recalled under the same conditions as when it was learned

■ The encoding specificity phenomenon. Some research suggests that we remember information best in an environment that is the same as or similar to where we initially learned it—a phenomenon known as **encoding specificity** (Tulving & Thompson, 1973). You may do better on a test, then, if you study in the same classroom in which the test is going to be given. On the other hand, if you must take tests in a room different from the one in which you studied, don't despair: The features of the test itself, such as the wording of the test questions, are sometimes so powerful that they overwhelm the subtler cues relating to the original encoding of the material (Bjork & Richardson-Klarehn, 1989).

■ Organization of text material. Most of life's more important recall tasks involve not lists of words but rather texts that have been read. How can you facilitate recall of such material? One proven technique for improving recall of written material consists of organizing the material in memory as it is being read for the first time. To do this, you should first identify any advance information about the structure and content of the material—scanning by using the table of contents, chapter outline, headings, and even the end-of-chapter summary—before reading a given chapter. Understanding the structure of the material will enable you to recall it better.

Another technique is to ask yourself questions that integrate the material you have read, and then answer them. Asking questions will enable you to make connections and see relationships between the various specific facts, thereby promoting the processing of the material at a deeper level. As the levels-of-processing approach to memory that we discussed earlier suggests, doing so will aid later recall (Royer & Feldman, 1984). For example, you might at this moment ask yourself, "What are the major techniques for remembering material in textbooks?" and then try to answer the question.

■ Organization of lecture notes. "Less is more" is perhaps the best advice for taking lecture notes that aid in recall. Rather than trying to jot down every detail of a lecture, it is better to listen and think about the material, taking down the main points after you have considered them in a broader context. In effective note taking, thinking about the material initially is more important than writing it down. This is one reason that borrowing someone else's notes is a bad proposition, since you will have no framework in memory to use in understanding them (Peper & Mayer, 1978).

■ Practice and rehearsal. Although practice does not necessarily make perfect, it does help. By studying and rehearsing material past the point of initial mastery—a process called **overlearning**—people are able to show better long-

Overlearning: Rehearsing material beyond the point of mastery to improve long-term recall

These actors in a high school theater program are demonstrating that rehearsal, and overlearning, improves long-term recall.

term recall than if they stop practicing after their initial learning of the material.

Eventually, of course, practice has little or no effect; you probably already know your address so well that no amount of additional practice will make you recall it any better than you already do. But it is safe to say that, given the volume of material covered in most courses, academic material is rarely so securely retained, and you would generally be wise to review material a few times even after you feel you have learned it, in order to reach a true level of overlearning.

Research on the outcomes of elaborative rehearsal, discussed earlier in the chapter, also suggests that it is important that the practice of asking and rehearsing the answers to questions be as active as possible. In this way, the connections between the parts of the material are likely to become explicit, aiding in later recall by providing ample retrieval cues.

Finally, people who cram for tests should note that the best retention comes from practice that is distributed over many sessions, rather than left for one long session. Research clearly demonstrates that fatigue and other factors prevent long practice sessions from being as effective as distributed practice.

RECAP AND REVIEW III

RECAP

◀ Decay and interference are the primary explanations for forgetting.

◀ There are two kinds of interference: proactive interference (when information learned earlier interferes with recall of newer information) and retroactive interference (when new information interferes with recall of information learned earlier).

◀ The major memory dysfunctions include Alzheimer's disease, retrograde amnesia, anterograde amnesia, and Korsakoff's syndrome.

◀ Specific techniques for increasing the recall of information include the keyword technique, the method of loci, the use of encoding specificity, organizing information in textbooks, good note taking, and practice and rehearsal.

REVIEW

1. After learning the history of the Roman Empire for a class two years ago, you now find yourself unable to recall what you had learned. A friend tells you that nonuse had caused you to lose the information. What is the formal name for this process?

2. An _____ is an actual physical change in the brain brought about by learning.

3. Memory which is difficult to access because of the presence of other information illustrates what phenomenon?

4. _____ interference occurs when previous material is difficult to retrieve because of exposure to later material. _____ interference refers to the difficulty in retrieving later material due to the interference of previous material.

5. Memories seem to be generalized within the brain; there do not appear to be any divisions of memory locations. True or false? _____

6. Match the following memory disorders with the correct information:

   a. _____ Alzheimer's disease
   b. _____ Korsakoff's syndrome
   c. _____ Amnesia

   1. Affects alcoholics; thiamine deficiency.
   2. Memory loss occurring without other mental problems.
   3. Beta amyloid defect; progressive forgetting and physical deterioration.

7. _____ _____ is the phenomenon which explains why a person may do better on a test if he or she studies for the test in the same room it is to be given in.

Ask Yourself

How might biopsychology, especially the knowledge gained by the "search for the engram," aid in the treatment of memory disorders such as amnesia?

(Answers to review questions are on page 272.)

What is memory?

1. Memory is the process by which we encode, store, and retrieve information. There are three basic kinds of memory storage: sensory memory, short-term memory, and long-term memory.

Are there different kinds of memory?

2. Sensory memory (made up of memories corresponding to each of the sensory systems) is the first place where information about the world is saved, although the memories are very brief. For instance, iconic memory (made up of visual sensations) lasts less than a second, and echoic memory (corresponding to auditory sensations) lasts less than four seconds. Despite their brevity, sensory memories are very precise, storing almost an exact replica of each stimulus to which a person is exposed. Unless they are transferred to other types of memory, however, sensory memories appear to be lost.

3. Roughly seven (plus or minus two) chunks of information are capable of being transferred and held in short-term memory. A chunk is a meaningful bit of information, ranging in size from a letter or a single digit to more complicated categorizations. Information in short-term memory is held from fifteen to twenty-five seconds and, if not transferred to long-term memory, is lost primarily through interference, as well as through decay. Interference is the loss of material through the displacement of older material by newer information, whereas decay is the loss of information through its nonuse.

4. Memories are transferred into long-term storage through rehearsal. The most effective type is elaborative rehearsal, in which the material to be remembered is organized and expanded. Formal techniques for organizing material are called mnemonics.

5. If memories are transferred into long-term memory, they become relatively permanent. Long-term memories are of two types: episodic and semantic. Episodic memories relate to our individual lives (such as recalling what a grade-school teacher looked like); semantic memories consist of organized knowledge and facts about the world (for example, $4 \times 5 = 20$).

6. Explicit memory refers to intentional or conscious recollection of information. In contrast, implicit memory refers to memories of which people are not consciously aware, but which can improve subsequent performance and behavior. Some researchers suggest that two distinct memory systems exist, one for implicit and the other for explicit memory. In contrast, other researchers have proposed that the two kinds of memory systems differ simply in the way that information is processed.

7. The levels-of-processing approach to memory suggests that the way in which information is initially perceived and analyzed determines the success with which the information is recalled. The deeper the initial processing, the greater the recall of the material.

What causes difficulties and failures in remembering?

8. The tip-of-the-tongue phenomenon refers to the experience of trying in vain to remember information that one is certain one knows. A major way of successfully recalling information is to use retrieval cues, stimuli that permit a search through long-term memory.

9. Flashbulb memories are memories centered around a specific, important event. The memories are so clear that they appear to represent a ''snapshot'' of the event. Flashbulb memories illustrate the broader point that the more distinctive a memory, the more easily it can be retrieved—a phenomenon called the von Restorff effect.

10. Memory is a constructive process in which we relate memories to the meaning, guesses, and expectations that we give to the events the memory represents. Specific information is recalled in terms of schemas, or general themes that contain relatively little detail.

11. Autobiographical memory refers to memories of events in our own lives. Partly because of the systematic inaccuracies found in such memories, some researchers have argued that more attention should be paid to everyday memory and less to the results of artificial laboratory studies.

12. Even with the use of retrieval cues, some information appears irretrievable, owing to decay or interference. Interference seems to be the major cause of forgetting. There are two sorts of interference: proactive interference (when information learned earlier interferes with the recall of material to which one is exposed later) and retroactive interference (when new information interferes with the recall of information to which one has been exposed earlier).

What are the biological bases of memory?

13. Current research on the biology underlying memory is concerned with the site of the engram, or memory trace. Certain drugs impair or aid memory in animals, suggesting that drugs may be used to improve the memory of people in the future.

What are the major memory impairments?

14. There are several memory dysfunctions. Among them are Alzheimer's disease, which leads to a progressive loss of memory, and amnesia, a memory loss that occurs without other mental difficulties and that can take two forms. In retrograde amnesia, there is loss of memory for occurrences prior to some event; in anterograde amnesia, there is loss of memory for events following an injury. Korsakoff's syndrome is a disease that afflicts long-term alcoholics, resulting in memory impairment.

15. Psychologists have developed a number of specific techniques to improve memory. These include using the keyword technique to memorize foreign vocabulary; applying the method of loci to learn lists; using the encoding specificity phenomenon; organizing text material; and practicing enough so that overlearning—studying and rehearsing past the point of initial mastery—occurs.

KEY TERMS AND CONCEPTS

encoding (p. 243)
storage (p. 243)
retrieval (p. 243)
memory (p. 243)
sensory memory (p. 244)
short-term memory (p. 244)
long-term memory (p. 244)
iconic memory (p. 245)
echoic memory (p. 245)
chunk (p. 246)
rehearsal (p. 247)
elaborative rehearsal (p. 248)
mnemonics (p. 248)
episodic memories (p. 249)
semantic memories (p. 249)
associative models (p. 250)
priming (p. 250)
explicit memory (p. 251)

implicit memory (p. 251)
linguistic code (p. 252)
imaginal code (p. 252)
motor code (p. 252)
levels-of-processing theory
 (p. 252)
tip-of-the-tongue phenomenon
 (p. 254)
retrieval cue (p. 255)
recall (p. 255)
recognition (p. 255)
flashbulb memories (p. 255)
von Restorff effect (p. 257)
constructive processes (p. 257)
schemas (p. 257)
serial reproduction (p. 257)
soap opera effect (p. 258)

autobiographical memories
 (p. 260)
decay (p. 263)
memory trace (p. 263)
engram (p. 263)
interference (p. 264)
proactive interference (p. 264)
retroactive interference (p. 264)
Alzheimer's disease (p. 266)
amnesia (p. 267)
retrograde amnesia (p. 267)
anterograde amnesia (p. 267)
Korsakoff's syndrome (p. 267)
keyword technique (p. 268)
method of loci (p. 268)
encoding specificity (p. 268)
overlearning (p. 269)

COGNITION AND LANGUAGE

RESCUE IN SPACE

The capture of the Intelsat VI satellite by NASA astronauts.

Engineers at the National Aeronautics and Space Administration had thought through the problem repeatedly and had spent two years designing, developing, and testing a solution. The target of their efforts: a giant, $157 million Intelsat VI communications satellite that had been placed in the wrong orbit by a malfunctioning rocket. The orbit was so low that the satellite was left useless, and, unless it could be moved to a higher position, it would have to be scrapped.

The owners of the satellite commissioned NASA to devise a way to rescue it. After months of deliberation and reflection, NASA engineers devised a solution, which they felt nearly certain would succeed.

To salvage the satellite, NASA planned a daring recovery mission. An astronaut from the space shuttle Endeavour was to leave the spacecraft and employ a specially designed capture bar during a walk in space. The bar, which itself cost close to a million dollars, was meant to snap shut on the bottom of the satellite, allowing it to be brought back to the Endeavour. From there, it would be attached to a rocket booster and launched from the space shuttle into the proper orbit.

The astronauts had practiced for close to a year on earth at the Johnson Space Center in Houston, Texas. Engineers had constructed three simulators. In one of the simulators, astronauts rehearsed the rescue underwater in an effort to mimic the effects of weightlessness on the procedure that had been devised.

However, once in space, events did not proceed according to plan. Because the engineers could not effectively simulate the weightlessness of space, no one had anticipated that the satellite would spin wildly out of control when an astronaut merely nudged it with the capture bar. Because of the satellite's motion, astronauts were unable to employ the bar.

When an astronaut failed to catch the satellite on two separate occasions, the engineers on earth were in a quandary over how to proceed. They searched frantically for a remedy, considering and rejecting one solution after another while the astronauts waited impatiently aboard the Endeavour.

Eventually, though, the engineers on earth devised a simple, yet effective, solution. Three astronauts were dispatched from the Endeavour, and they simultaneously grabbed the rotating satellite with their hands in order to hold it still. It was a dramatic moment, marking the first time that three U.S. astronauts had worked together on a joint recovery mission outside a spacecraft.

Once the satellite was stabilized, the astronauts maneuvered the capture bar into place. The bar latched onto the satellite, and the three returned to the Endeavour with the satellite in tow. The rescue mission was a total success (Leary, 1992).

LOOKING AHEAD ▶

The rescue of the satellite was a moment of problem-solving triumph for the NASA engineers on the ground, as well as the astronauts in space. Overcoming the obstacles to a solution and working under enormous time constraints, the engineers had succeeded in solving a difficult and risky problem. Their success illustrates how thoughtful and diligent effort can provide solutions in the face of formidable challenges.

In addition, their accomplishment raises a number of issues of interest to psychologists: How do people use and retrieve information to devise innovative solutions to problems? How is such knowledge transformed, elaborated upon, and utilized? More basically, how do people think about, understand, and, using language, describe the world?

In this chapter we consider **cognitive psychology**, the branch of psychology that focuses on the study of cognition. **Cognition** encompasses the higher mental processes of humans, including how people know and understand the world, process information, make judgments and decisions, and describe their knowledge and understanding to others. The realm of cognitive psychology is broad, then, and includes the research on memory examined in the previous chapter and much of the work on intelligence that we discuss in the next chapter (Massaro, 1991; Barsalou, 1992).

In this chapter, we will concentrate on three broad topics that are central to the field of cognitive psychology: thinking and reasoning, problem solving, and language. We first consider concepts, the building blocks of thinking, and various kinds of reasoning. We also examine different ways to approach problems, means of generating solutions, and ways of making judgments about the usefulness and accuracy of solutions. Finally, in our focus on language, we consider how language is developed and acquired, what its basic characteristics are, and whether language is a uniquely human ability.

After reading this chapter, then, you will be able to answer a number of basic questions:

- How do we think, reason, and make decisions?
- How do people approach and solve problems?
- What are the major obstacles to problem solving?
- How do people use language, and how does it develop?

Cognitive psychology: The branch of psychology that specializes in the study of cognition

Cognition: The higher mental processes by which we understand the world, process information, make judgments and decisions, and communicate knowledge to others

THINKING AND REASONING

Thinking

What is thinking?

The mere ability to pose such a question illustrates how distinctive the human ability to think is. No other species can contemplate, analyze, recollect, or plan in the manner that humans can. Yet knowing that we think and understanding what thinking is are two different things. Philosophers, for example, have argued for generations about the meaning of thinking, with some placing it at the core of human beings' understanding of their own existence. (You may be familiar with the philosopher Descartes' famous quote, "I think, therefore I am.")

Psychologists take a broad and scientific approach to thinking. To them, **thinking** is the manipulation of mental representations of information. The representation may be a word, a visual image, a sound, or data in any other modality. What thinking does is to transform the representation of information into a new and different form for the purpose of answering a question, solving a problem, or aiding in reaching a goal.

Although a clear sense of what specifically goes on when we are thinking still remains somewhat elusive, the nature of the fundamental elements we use in thinking is becoming increasingly well understood (Newell, 1990). We begin by considering our ability to use concepts, the building blocks of thinking.

Thinking: The manipulation of mental representations of information

Concepts: Categorizing the World

Concepts: Categorizations of objects, events, or people that share common properties

Artificial concepts: Concepts that are clearly defined by a unique set of properties or features

Natural concepts: Concepts that are defined by a set of general, relatively loose characteristic features, such as prototypes

Prototypes: Typical, highly representative examples of a concept

If someone asked you what was in your kitchen cabinet, you might answer with a detailed list of every item ("a jar of Skippy peanut butter, three packages of macaroni-and-cheese mix, six unmatched dinner plates," and so forth). More likely, though, you would respond by using some broader categories, such as "food" and "dishes."

The use of such categories reflects the operation of concepts. **Concepts** are categorizations of objects, events, or people that share common properties. By employing concepts, we are able to distill the complexities of the world into simpler, and therefore more easily usable, cognitive categories.

Concepts allow us to classify newly encountered objects into a form that is understandable in terms of our past experience. For example, we are able to tell that a small, four-legged creature with a wagging tail is probably a dog—even if we have never encountered that specific breed of dog before. Ultimately, concepts influence behavior; we would assume, for instance, that it might be appropriate to pet the animal, after determining that it is, in fact, a dog.

When cognitive psychologists first studied concepts, they focused on artificial concepts. **Artificial concepts** are concepts that are clearly defined by a unique set of properties or features. For example, an equilateral triangle is a shape that has three sides of equal length. If an object has these characteristics, it is an equilateral triangle; if it does not, then it is not an equilateral triangle.

Other concepts—the ones that have the most relevance to our everyday lives—are much fuzzier and more difficult to define than artificial concepts. For example, how would you formally define "table" or "bird"? Both are examples of **natural concepts**—ones that are familiar and uncomplicated, and represent common objects which share a set of characteristic features. Unlike artificial concepts, natural concepts do not have unvarying, universal defining features. Instead, they are defined by a set of general, relatively loose characteristic features and are exemplified by prototypes. **Prototypes** are typical, highly representative examples of a concept. For instance, a prototype of the concept "bird" is a robin; a prototype of "table" is a coffee table. Relatively high agreement exists among people as to which examples of a natural concept are prototypes, and which examples fit less well with the concept. Cars and trucks, for instance, are viewed by most people as good examples of vehicles, whereas elevators and wheelbarrows are not, thereby making cars and trucks prototypes of the natural concept of vehicle (see Table 9-1).

The importance of concepts lies in their ability to allow us to think about and understand more readily the complex, intricate world in which we live. For example, the judgments we make about the reasons for other people's behavior are based on the way we classify their behavior. Hence, our evaluations of a person who washes her hands twenty times a day could vary, depending on whether we place her behavior within the conceptual framework of health care worker or mental patient. Similarly, the way that physicians make diagnoses is based on concepts and prototypes of symptoms that they learn in medical school. Gaining an understanding of how people classify their knowledge of the world thus represents an important undertaking for cognitive psychologists.

Decision Making

Professors giving their students grades. An employer determining who to hire out of a pool of job applicants. The President deciding whether the United States should go to war.

TABLE 9-1

PROTOTYPES OF SIX NATURAL CONCEPTS

Item	Furniture	Vehicle	Fruit	Weapon	Vegetable	Clothing
1	Chair	Car	Orange	Gun	Peas	Pants
2	Sofa	Truck	Apple	Knife	Carrots	Shirt
3	Table	Bus	Banana	Sword	String beans	Dress
4	Dresser	Motorcycle	Peach	Bomb	Spinach	Skirt
5	Desk	Train	Pear	Hand grenade	Broccoli	Jacket
6	Bed	Trolley car	Apricot	Spear	Asparagus	Coat
7	Bookcase	Bicycle	Plum	Cannon	Corn	Sweater
8	Footstool	Airplane	Grapes	Bow and arrow	Cauliflower	Underpants
9	Lamp	Boat	Strawberry	Club	Brussels sprouts	Socks
10	Piano	Tractor	Grapefruit	Tank	Lettuce	Pajamas
11	Cushion	Cart	Pineapple	Teargas	Beets	Bathing suit
12	Mirror	Wheelchair	Blueberry	Whip	Tomato	Shoes
13	Rug	Tank	Lemon	Icepick	Lima beans	Vest
14	Radio	Raft	Watermelon	Fists	Eggplant	Tie
15	Stove	Sled	Honeydew	Rocket	Onion	Mittens

Source: Rosch & Mervis (1975).

The common thread among these three events: Each represents a form of decision making. We all make decisions constantly, although the consequences of most are fairly trivial. Just starting our daily routine represents a string of decisions: How long can I stay in bed without being late to work? What clothes should I wear? What cereal should I have for breakfast? What route should I follow when commuting? Other decisions are more consequential. What college to attend, what job to take, and what automobile to purchase all represent decisions that we may put off and agonize over for many months.

Decision making is among the most complex forms of thinking. As a consequence, one of the major tasks confronting cognitive psychologists has been the exploration of the primary elements underlying both processes.

Deductive and Inductive Reasoning. One approach taken by cognitive psychologists in their efforts to understand decision making is to examine how people use formal reasoning procedures. Two major forms exist: deductive reasoning and inductive reasoning (Rips, 1990).

In **deductive reasoning**, we draw inferences and implications from a set of assumptions and apply them to specific cases. Deductive reasoning begins with a series of assumptions or premises that are thought to be true, and then derives the implications of these assumptions. If the assumptions are true, then the conclusions must also be true.

A major technique for studying deductive reasoning is the use of syllogisms. A **syllogism** presents a series of two assumptions or premises that are used to derive a conclusion. By definition, the conclusion must be true if the assumptions or premises are true. For example, consider the following syllogism:

Deductive reasoning: A reasoning process whereby inferences and implications are drawn from a set of assumptions and applied to specific cases

Syllogism: A technique in deductive reasoning, in which a series of two assumptions are used to derive a conclusion

▶ **279**

Decision making can have weighty consequences, as these United Nations delegates were aware when they voted in favor of an embargo that prevented supplies from reaching Iraq.

All men are mortal.
Socrates is a man.
Therefore, Socrates is mortal.

Of course, if the premises in a syllogism are not accurate, the conclusion will not be. Suppose, for example, you saw the following:

All people are good.
Hitler is a person.
Therefore Hitler is good.

Even though the conclusion is logically valid, you might well argue with the accuracy of the first premise.

The conclusion drawn from a set of statements, then, is only as justifiable as the trustworthiness of the premises involved. Unfortunately, in many instances the inaccuracy of a premise is not as clear-cut as it was in the example of Hitler, and we may accept a conclusion that is not logically valid. Consider, for instance, the following examples of faulty reasoning:

Many brightly colored snakes are poisonous.
The copperhead snake is not brightly colored.
So the copperhead is not a poisonous snake.

There is no doubt that some drugs are poisonous.
All brands of beer contain the drug alcohol.
Therefore, some brands of beer are poisonous.

All poisonous things are bitter.
Arsenic is not bitter.
Therefore, arsenic is not poisonous.

Although each of the conclusions is logically unsound, you may find yourself thinking that the stated conclusion is valid—if you happen to agree with it. Experimental evidence suggests that people are more apt to believe that arguments are logical when they agree with a conclusion than when they disagree with it (Janis & Frick, 1943; Solso, 1991).

Similarly, people's cultural backgrounds have an impact on their ability to think logically. For instance, consider the following sequence, presented to a group of students in Russia:

Ivan and Boris always eat together.

Boris is eating.

What is Ivan doing?

Only one-fifth of the Russian students gave the correct answer to this simple question, with the most frequent answer being, "I don't know, I didn't see him." Although it would be easy to conclude that the students had less reasoning skill than their American counterparts—who rarely get the answer wrong—such a conclusion is unlikely to be the best explanation. A more plausible explanation is one that takes into account the influence of the cultural backgrounds of the students. It seems reasonable that people living in highly industrialized western society learn, through experience, to use abstract logic to form conclusions about the world. On the other hand, people in less industrialized societies may be apt to rely on more concrete modes of reasoning. Therefore, they are more likely to use direct sensory experience to draw conclusions, and are less comfortable using abstract logic alone (Solso, 1991).

Ultimately, then, people's use of formal deductive reasoning may fail for several reasons. They may use inaccurate premises, draw erroneous conclusions, or simply fail to use formal logic in the first place. Using deductive reasoning, then, does not ensure that everyone will draw the same conclusions.

The conceptual complement of deductive reasoning is inductive reasoning. In **inductive reasoning**, *we infer a general rule from specific cases.* Using our observations, knowledge, experiences, and beliefs about the world, we develop a summary conclusion. (You can recall the difference between deductive and inductive reasoning in this way: In *de*ductive reasoning, the conclusion is *de*rived through the use of general rules, whereas in *in*ductive reasoning, a conclusion is *in*ferred from specific examples.) For example, if the person in the apartment below you is always playing Bob Dylan songs, you may begin to form an impression of what that individual is like, based on the sample of evidence available to you. You use pieces of evidence to draw a general conclusion.

The limitation of inductive reasoning is that any conclusions that are drawn may be biased if insufficient or invalid evidence is used. Psychologists know this well: The various scientific methods that they may employ in the collection of data to support their hypotheses are prone to many kinds of biases, as we discussed in Chapter 2. Similarly, we may fail to draw appropriate conclusions if our sampling is biased. In the case of your neighbor, for instance, your impression might well change if you knew more about him.

Algorithms and Heuristics. When faced with a decision, we often turn to algorithms and heuristics to help us. An **algorithm** is a rule which, if followed, guarantees a solution to a problem. We can use an algorithm even if we cannot understand the reason why it works. For example, you may know that the length

Inductive reasoning: A reasoning process whereby a general rule is inferred from specific cases, using observation, knowledge, and experience

Algorithm: A set of rules that, if followed, guarantee a solution, though the reason they work may not be understood by the person using them

of the third side of a right triangle can be found using the formula $a^2 + b^2 = c^2$. You may not have the foggiest notion of the math behind the formula, but this algorithm is always accurate and provides a solution to a particular problem.

For many problems and decisions, however, no algorithm is available. In those instances, we may be able to use heuristics to help us. A **heuristic** is a rule of thumb or mental shortcut that may lead to a solution. Unlike algorithms, heuristics enhance the likelihood of success in coming to a solution but cannot ensure it. For example, chess players often follow the heuristic of attempting to gain control of the center of the board in determining what move to make. The tactic doesn't guarantee that they will win, but it does increase their chances of success. Similarly, some students follow the heuristic of preparing for a test by ignoring the assigned textbook reading and only studying their lecture notes— a strategy that may or may not pay off.

Although heuristics may help people solve problems and make decisions, the use of several specific kinds of heuristics may backfire. For example, people may use the **representativeness heuristic** to determine whether a given example is a member of a particular category by evaluating how characteristic it is of that category. Suppose, for instance, you are the owner of a fast-food store and have been robbed many times by teenagers. The representativeness heuristic would lead you to raise your guard each time someone of this age group enters your store (even though, statistically, it is unlikely that a given teenager will rob you).

The **availability heuristic** involves judging the probability of an event by how easily the event can be recalled from memory (Tversky & Kahneman, 1974). According to this heuristic, we assume that events we remember easily are likely to have occurred more frequently in the past than those that are harder to remember. Furthermore, we assume that the same sort of event is more likely to occur in the future. For example, we are more likely to worry about being murdered than dying of diabetes, despite the fact that it is twice as likely that we will die of the disease. The reason we err is due to the ease with which we remember dramatic, highly publicized events like murder, leading us to overestimate the likelihood of their occurring.

Similarly, suppose you were told about a person named Tom who is highly intelligent, neat, and orderly but lacks true creativity. His writing is rather dull, although it is occasionally enlivened by corny puns and flashes of sci-fi imagination. Being rather self-centered, he does not have much feeling and is not sympathetic to others, but he does have a strong moral sense.

If you were asked whether he is a computer science major or a humanities major, what would you guess? To answer such a question, most people employ the heuristic of representativeness, trying to determine how well the person fits their mental image of computer science major or humanities major. On the basis of the description, people usually opt for computer science major.

However, suppose you were to learn that Tom is a member of a class of 100 students, of whom eighty are humanities majors and twenty are computer science majors. Would your guess change on the basis of this new information?

Most likely you would stick with your original choice of computer science major. But if you were to follow the laws of logic and probability more precisely, your answer *should* have changed, despite the representativeness heuristic: Chances are greater that any one person from the class would belong to the group of eighty who are humanities majors, regardless of any personality characteristics that the person may display. In this case, then, the representativeness heuristic leads people's judgments astray (Kahneman & Tversky, 1974).

The availability heuristic, in which judgments of the probability of an event are based on how easily the event can be recalled, is also a potential source of error in decision making. Suppose you were asked to pick up a dictionary and

Heuristic (hyur ISS tik): A rule of thumb that may bring about a solution to a problem but is not guaranteed to do so

Representativeness heuristic: A rule in which people and things are judged by the degree to which they represent a certain category

Availability heuristic: A rule for judging the probability that an event will occur by the ease with which it can be recalled from memory

randomly choose a word with at least three letters. Do you think it is more likely that the first letter or the third letter of the word would be an ''r''?

Most people would conclude that the first letter would be more likely to be an ''r,'' which is erroneous. (The letter ''r'' actually occurs more frequently as the third letter than the first in the English language.) The reason for the mistaken judgment? It is considerably easier to retrieve words from memory that start with a given letter (run, rats, root) than it is to retrieve words on the basis of their third letter (bar, tart, purse).

As you can see, the same heuristics that assist in decision making can also be misapplied and act as hindrances in finding the correct solution. Furthermore, there are other instances in which the process of analysis that we employ can compromise the quality of solutions, as we discuss in the accompanying Cutting Edge box.

THE CUTTING EDGE

Benjamin Franklin had his preferred method for making a difficult choice, as he noted in one letter:

> My way is to divide half a sheet of paper by a line into two columns, writing over the one Pro, and over the other Con. Then, during three or four days consideration, I put down under the different heads short hints of the different motives, that at different times occur to me, for or against each measure. . . . I find at length where the balance lies; and if, after a day or two of further consideration, nothing new that is of importance occurs on either side, I come to a determination accordingly. . . . When each [reason] is thus considered, separately and comparatively, and the whole lies before me, I think I can judge better, and am less likely to make a rash step. (Quoted in Goodman, 1945, p. 746.)

Most experts in decision making would agree with Franklin's approach. For example, psychologist Irving Janis argued that decision makers should produce a "balance sheet" in which the pros and cons of a decision could be listed and weighed against one another (Janis & Mann, 1977). Indeed, in one way or another, most cognitive psychologists have suggested that optimal decisions are made when decision makers objectively and deliberately

THINKING TOO MUCH? WHEN THOUGHT LEADS TO POOR DECISIONS

reflect on the reasons that lie beneath various alternative decisions.

New evidence, however, suggests that such conventional wisdom may be wrong. The results of several studies imply that thinking too much about the reasons for a potential decision ultimately may actually compromise the quality of the decision.

According to psychologist Timothy Wilson and colleagues, many decisions are made without much thought or introspection. We simply develop a position or make a judgment without considering the alternatives in any systematic manner. Happily, the decisions we make are often reasonable ones; they work for us, even if we haven't thought about them all that much (Wilson & Schooler, 1991).

But consider what happens if we are asked to analyze the reasons that lie behind a decision. In this case, the process of analysis may focus our attention on aspects of the decision that are not particularly important. If we tend to exaggerate the importance of these less optimal, trivial, or irrelevant aspects, we may be led astray and make a poorer decision than we would have if we had not spent as much time analyzing the problem.

Wilson found support for this reasoning in an experiment in which students were asked to choose their col-

lege psychology courses for the upcoming term. Some students were simply given a set of course descriptions and told to choose their courses. In contrast, two other groups of students were asked to put considerably more cognitive effort into their decision. One group of students was asked to rate the importance of each piece of information provided to them about the courses. A second group was asked to consider each course description and then write how they felt about each of these courses.

In contrast to the students who simply made choices and were not forced to analyze their decisions in any way, those having to rate or write about each course made less optimal decisions. (Optimal decisions were based on a group of professors' judgments about what the best courses to take would be.) In this case, the students were better off making broad, nonintrospective decisions than focusing on the various details that made up the decision. In sum, forcing students to think actively about the factors involved in their choices led them to make poorer decisions than when they didn't think about them.

Of course, it is not true that thinking about choices will invariably lead to less optimal decisions. Additional research will be required before it is possible to differentiate situations in which introspection is more or less desirable.

RECAP

◄ Cognitive psychologists specialize in the study of the higher mental processes of humans, including problem solving, knowing, reasoning, judging, and decision making.

◄ Thinking is the manipulation of mental representations of information.

◄ Concepts are categorizations of objects, events, or people that share common properties. Natural concepts, consisting of prototypes, represent familiar objects, are simple, and share a set of characteristic features.

◄ When making decisions, people frequently use algorithms (sets of rules that, if followed, guarantee that a solution will be reached) and heuristics (rules of thumb that may lead to a solution).

REVIEW

1. _____ are categorizations of objects that share common properties.

2. _____ concepts are characterized by universal, unvarying features.

3. When you think of the term "chair," you immediately think of a comfortable easy chair. A chair of this type could be thought of as a _____ of the category "chair."

4. Match the type of reasoning with its definition:

   1. ____ Deductive reasoning   a. Deriving the conclusion from a set of premises

   2. ____ Inductive reasoning   b. Inferring a general rule from specific cases

5. Assuming that the conclusion follows logically from the premises, deductive reasoning is an infallible judgment-making tool. True or false? _____

6. An _____ is a problem-solving "formula" that is guaranteed to produce a solution.

7. When you ask your friend how best to study for your psychology final, he tells you "I've always found it best to skim over the notes once, then read the book, then go over the notes again." What decision-making tool might this be an example of?

8. The _____ heuristic is used when one judges how likely an event is to occur by how easily it is retrieved from memory.

Ask Yourself

You are an expert computer programmer. You are given the task of designing a robot that can "learn" (through observation) to play the perfect game of chess and never lose. What knowledge of algorithms and heuristics would you bring to the task? What problems might you foresee?

(Answers to review questions are on page 286.)

PROBLEM SOLVING

According to an old legend, a group of monks in Vietnam devote much of their time to attempting to solve a problem called the Tower of Hanoi puzzle. Should they succeed, the monks expect that it will bring an end to the world as we know it (Raphael, 1976). (Should your preference be that the world remain in its present state, you have no need for immediate concern: according to one estimate, the puzzle is so complex that it will take about a trillion years to reach a solution.)

In a simpler version of the puzzle, illustrated in Figure 9-1, there are three posts on which three disks are to be placed in the order shown. The goal of the puzzle is to move all three disks to the third post and arrange them in the same order, using as few moves as possible. But there are two restrictions: Only one disk can be moved at a time, and no disk can ever cover a smaller one during a move.

Why are cognitive psychologists interested in the Tower of Hanoi problem? The answer is that the way people go about solving this puzzle and simpler ones like it helps illuminate the processes by which people solve more complex problems that they encounter in school and at work. For example, psychologists have found that problem solving typically involves three major steps: preparation for the creation of solutions, production of solutions, and evaluation of solutions that have been generated (Sternberg & Frensch, 1991).

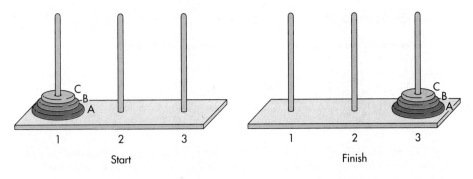

FIGURE 9-1
The goal of the Tower of Hanoi puzzle is to move all three disks from the first post to the last and still preserve the original order of the disks, using the least number of moves possible while following the rules that only one disk at a time can be moved and no disk can cover a smaller one during a move. Try it yourself before you look at the solution, which is listed according to the sequence of moves. (Solution: Move C to 3, B to 2, C to 2, A to 3, C to 1, B to 3, and C to 3.)

Preparation: Understanding and Diagnosing Problems

When encountering a problem like the Tower of Hanoi, most people begin by trying to ensure that they thoroughly understand the problem. If the problem is a novel one, they are likely to pay particular attention to any restrictions placed on coming to a solution and the initial status of the components of the problem. If the problem is familiar, they are apt to spend considerably less time in this stage than if it is completely new to them.

Problems vary from well-defined to ill-defined (Reitman, 1965). For a **well-defined problem**—such as a mathematical equation or the solution to a jigsaw puzzle in which no pieces have been lost—both the nature of the problem itself and the information needed to solve the problem are available and clear. Thus, straightforward judgments can be made about whether a potential solution is appropriate. With an **ill-defined problem**, such as how to increase morale on an assembly line or bring peace to the Middle East, not only may the specific nature of the problem be unclear, but the information required to solve the problem may be even less obvious.

For example, consider the following problem, first devised by Karl Duncker (1945):

> Suppose you are a doctor faced with a patient who has a malignant tumor in his stomach. To operate on the patient is impossible, but unless the tumor is destroyed, the patient will die. A kind of ray, at a sufficiently high intensity, can destroy the tumor. Unfortunately, at this intensity the healthy tissue that the rays pass through on the way to the tumor will also be destroyed. At lower intensities the rays are harmless to healthy tissue but will not affect the tumor, either. How can the rays be used to destroy the tumor without injuring the healthy tissue? (Holyoak, 1990, p. 134.)

Most people have a great deal of difficulty in thinking of even one solution to this problem. The major barrier is that the ill-defined nature of the problem, which involves some vague sort of "rays," doesn't suggest any immediate solutions. However, there is an ingenious solution to the problem: aiming weak rays at the tumor from several different entry points. In this way, no one portion of healthy tissue is damaged, while the tumor receives a full dosage.

Kinds of Problems. Problems typically fall into one of the three categories exemplified in Figure 9-2 (page 286): arrangement, inducing structure, and transformation (Greeno, 1978). Each requires somewhat different kinds of psychological skills and knowledge to solve.

Arrangement problems require that a group of elements be rearranged or recombined in a way that will satisfy a certain criterion. There are usually several

Well-defined problem:
A problem whose nature is clear, and the information needed to solve it is available

Ill-defined problem:
A problem whose specific nature is unclear, and the information required to solve it is not obvious

Arrangement problems:
Problems whose solution requires the rearrangement of a group of elements in order to satisfy a certain criterion

▶ **285**

A. ARRANGEMENT PROBLEMS

1. Anagrams: Rearrange the letters in each set to make an English word:

EFCTA
IAENV
BODUT
LIVAN
IKCTH

2. Two strings hang from a ceiling but are too far apart to allow a person to hold one and walk to the other. On the floor are a book of matches, a screwdriver, and a few pieces of cotton. How could the strings be tied together?

B. PROBLEMS OF INDUCING STRUCTURE

1. What number comes next in the series:

1 4 2 4 3 4 4 4 5 4 6 4

2. Complete these analogies:

baseball is to bat as tennis is to _____

merchant is to sell as customer is to _____

C. TRANSFORMATION PROBLEMS

1. Missionaries and cannibals: Three cannibals and three missionaries want to cross a river. However, they only have one boat, which will hold just two people. There is no other way to cross the river. If more cannibals than missionaries are left on either bank, the cannibals will eat the missionaries. What is the most efficient way that the six people can get to the other side of the river without harm?

2. Water jars: A person has three jars having the following capacities:

Jar A: 28 ounces
Jar B: 7 ounces
Jar C: 5 ounces

How can the person measure exactly 11 ounces of water?

FIGURE 9-2

The major categories of problems: (a) arrangement, (b) inducing structure, and (c) transformation. Solutions appear on p. 288. (Sources: Bourne et al., 1986; missionary problem: Solso, 1991, p. 448.)

different possible arrangements that can be made, but only one or a few of the arrangements produce a solution. Anagram problems and jigsaw puzzles represent arrangement problems.

In **problems of inducing structure**, a person must identify the relationships that exist among the elements presented and construct a new relationship among them. In such a problem, it is necessary to determine not only the relationships among the elements, but the structure and size of the elements involved. In the example shown in Figure 9-2, a person must first determine that the solution requires the numbers to be considered in pairs (14-24-34-44-54-64). It is only after that part of the problem is identified that the solution rule (the first number of each pair increases by one, while the second number remains the same) can be determined.

Problems of inducing structure: Problems whose solution requires the identification of existing relationships among elements presented so as to construct a new relationship among them

ANSWERS (REVIEW I):

1. Concepts **2.** Artificial **3.** prototype **4.** 1-a; 2-b **5.** False; there are many potential problems, such as failure to use abstract reasoning or invalid premises. **6.** algorithm **7.** Heuristic **8.** availability

The Tower of Hanoi puzzle represents a third kind of problem. **Transformation problems** consist of an initial state, a goal state, and a series of methods for changing the initial state into the goal state. In the Tower of Hanoi problem, the initial state is the original configuration; the goal state consists of the three disks on the third peg; and the method consists of the rules for moving the disks.

Whether the problem is one of arrangement, inducing structure, or transformation, the initial stage of understanding and diagnosing is critical in problem solving because it allows us to develop our own cognitive representation of the problem and to place it within a personal framework. The problem may be divided into subparts or some information may be ignored as we try to simplify the task. Winnowing out the unessential information is often a critical step in problem solving.

Representing and Organizing the Problem.   A crucial aspect of the initial encounter with a problem is the way in which we represent it to ourselves and organize the information presented to us (Brown & Walter, 1990). Consider the following problem:

> A man climbs a mountain on Saturday, leaving at daybreak and arriving at the top near sundown. He spends the night at the top. The next day, Sunday, he leaves at daybreak and heads down the mountain, following the same path that he climbed the day before. The question is this: Will there be any time during the second day when he will be at exactly the same point on the mountain as he was at that time on the first day?

If you try to solve this problem by using algebraic or verbal representations, you will have a good deal of trouble. However, if you represent the problem with the kind of simple diagram illustrated in Figure 9-3, the solution becomes apparent.

Successful problem solving, then, requires that a person form an appropriate representation and organization of the problem. However, there is no one optimal way of representing and organizing material, since that depends on the nature of the problem. Sometimes simply restructuring a problem, from a verbal form to a pictorial or mathematical form for instance, can help point out a direct solution (Mayer, 1982).

Production: Generating Solutions

If a problem is relatively simple, a direct solution may already be stored in long-term memory, and all that is necessary is to retrieve the appropriate information. If the solution cannot be retrieved or is not known, we must instigate a process by which possible solutions can be generated and compared with information in long- and short-term memory.

At the most primitive level, solutions to problems can be obtained through trial and error. Thomas Edison was able to invent the light bulb only because he tried thousands of different kinds of materials for a filament before he found one that worked (carbon). The difficulty with trial and error, of course, is that some problems are so complicated it would take a lifetime to try out every possibility. For example, according to one estimate, there are some 10^{120} possible sequences of chess moves.

In place of trial and error, complex problem solving often involves the use of heuristics—rules of thumb that lead the way to solutions. Probably the most frequently applied heuristic in problem solving is a means-ends analysis. In a

Transformation problems: Problems to be solved using a series of methods to change an initial state into a goal state

FIGURE 9-3

Using a graph, it is easy to solve the problem posed in the text. Remember, the goal is not to determine the specific time, but to indicate whether an exact time exists. (Anderson, 1980.)

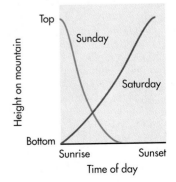

Solutions to problems in Figure 9-2 on page 286.

A. ARRANGEMENT PROBLEMS
1. FACET, NAIVE, DOUBT, ANVIL, THICK
2. The screwdriver is tied to one of the strings. This makes a pendulum that can be swung to reach the other string.

B. PROBLEMS OF INDUCING STRUCTURE
1. 7
2. racket; buy

C TRANSFORMATION PROBLEMS
1.

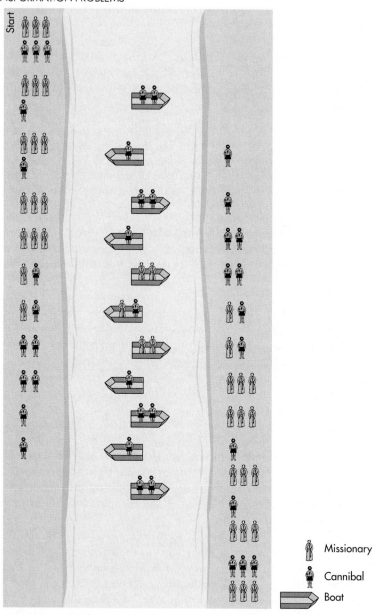

2. Fill jar A, empty into jar B once and into jar C twice. What remains in Jar A is 11 ounces.

(Source of missionary/cannibal solution figure: Solso, 1991, p. 448.)

means-ends analysis, a person repeatedly tests for differences between the desired outcome and what currently exists, trying each time to reduce the difference between the possible solution and the desired outcome. For example, people using a means-ends analysis to search for the correct sequence of roads to get to a city that they can see in the distance would analyze their solutions in terms of how much closer each individual choice of roadway brings them to the ultimate goal of arriving at the city. Such a strategy is only effective, though, if there is a direct solution to the problem. If the problem is such that indirect steps have to be taken which appear to *increase* the discrepancy between the current state and the solution, means-ends analyses can be counterproductive. In our example, if roadways are laid out in such a way that a person must temporarily move *away* from the city in order to reach it eventually, a means-ends analysis will keep the person from reaching the goal.

For some problems, the converse of a means-ends approach is the most effective: working backward by beginning with the goal and moving toward the starting state. Instead of altering the elements of a problem in a series of steps that move closer and closer to the solution, people can work in the opposite direction, moving away from the goal and aiming to reach the beginning point (Bourne et al., 1986; Malin, 1979).

Subgoals. Another commonly used heuristic is to divide a problem into intermediate steps, or **subgoals**, and to solve each of those steps. For instance, if you return to the Tower of Hanoi problem, there are several obvious subgoals that could be chosen, such as moving the largest disk to the third post.

If solving a subgoal is part of the ultimate solution to a problem, then identifying subgoals is an appropriate strategy. There are cases, however, in which the formation of subgoals is not all that helpful and may actually take the problem solver longer to find a solution (Reed, 1988; Hayes, 1966). For example, some problems cannot be subdivided. Others are so difficult to subdivide that it takes longer to identify the appropriate subdivisions than to solve the problem by other means. Finally, even when a problem is divided into subgoals, it may be unclear what to do after a given subgoal has been reached.

Insight. Some approaches to problem solving focus less on step-by-step processes than on the sudden bursts of comprehension that may come when solving a problem. Just after World War I, German psychologist Wolfgang Köhler examined learning and problem-solving processes in chimps (Köhler, 1927). In his studies, Köhler exposed chimps to challenging situations in which the elements of the solution were all present; what was necessary was for the chimps to put them together.

For example, in one series of studies, chimps were kept in a cage in which boxes and sticks were strewn about, with a bunch of tantalizing bananas hanging high in the cage out of their reach. Initially, the chimps engaged in a variety of trial-and-error attempts at getting to the bananas: They would throw the stick at the bananas, jump from one of the boxes, or leap wildly from the ground. Frequently, they would seem to give up in frustration, leaving the bananas dangling temptingly overhead. But then, in what seemed like a sudden revelation, they would leave whatever activity they were involved in and stand on a box in order to be able to reach the bananas with a stick. Köhler called the cognitive processes underlying the chimps' behavior **insight**, a sudden awareness of the relationships among various elements that had previously appeared to be independent of one another.

Means-ends analysis: Repeated testing to determine and reduce the distance between the desired outcome and what currently exists in problem solving

Subgoals: A commonly used heuristic to divide a problem into intermediate steps and to solve each one of them

Insight: Sudden awareness of the relationships among various elements that had previously appeared to be independent of one another

(a) (b) (c)

In a remarkable display of problem solving, Köhler's chimp Sultan sees a bunch of bananas out of his reach (*a*). He then retrieves several crates sitting in the room (*b*), and stacks them up so that he can reach the bananas (*c*).

Although Köhler emphasized the apparent suddenness with which solutions were revealed, subsequent research has shown that prior experience and initial trial-and-error practice in problem solving are prerequisites for producing the appearance of insight (Metcalfe, 1986). One study demonstrated that only chimps who had experience in playing with sticks could successfully solve the problem; inexperienced chimps never made the connection between standing on the box and reaching the bananas (Birch, 1945). Some researchers have suggested that the behavior of the apes represented little more than the chaining together of previously learned responses, no different from the way a pigeon learns, by trial and error, to peck a key (Epstein, 1987; Epstein et al., 1984). It is clear that insight depends on previous experience with the elements involved in a problem.

Judgment: Evaluating the Solutions

The final step in problem solving consists of judging the adequacy of a solution. Often, this is a simple matter: If there is a clear solution—as in the Tower of Hanoi problem—we will know immediately whether we have been successful. On the other hand, if the solution is less concrete, or if there is no single correct solution, evaluating solutions becomes more difficult.

If there is more than one solution to a problem, or if the solution criteria are vague, we must decide which solution alternative is best. Unfortunately, we are sometimes quite inaccurate in estimating the quality of our own ideas. There is often little relationship between our judgments of the value of our ideas and more objective criteria (Johnson, Parrott, & Stratton, 1968).

Theoretically, if the heuristics and information we rely on to make decisions are appropriate and valid, we can make accurate choices among problem solutions. However, as we see next, there are several kinds of obstacles and biases in problem solving that affect the quality of the decisions and judgments we make.

Impediments to Problem Solving

Consider the following problem-solving test (Duncker, 1945): You are presented with a set of tacks, candles, and matches in small boxes, and told your goal is to place three candles at eye level on a nearby door, so that wax will not drip on the floor as the candles burn (see Figure 9-4). How would you approach this challenge?

If you have difficulty solving the problem, you are not alone. Most people are unable to solve it when it is presented in the manner illustrated in the figure, in which the objects are located *inside* the boxes. On the other hand, if the objects were presented *beside* the boxes, just resting on the table, chances are you would solve the problem much more readily—which, in case you are wondering, requires tacking up the boxes and then placing the candles in the boxes (see Figure 9-6 on p. 292).

The difficulty you probably had in solving the problem stems from its presentation and relates to the fact that you were misled at the initial preparation stage. Actually, significant obstacles to problem solving exist at each of the three major stages. Although cognitive approaches to problem solving suggest that thinking proceeds along fairly rational, logical lines as a person confronts a problem and considers various solutions, there are a number of factors acting to hinder the development of creative, appropriate, and accurate solutions.

Functional Fixedness and Mental Set. The reason that most people experience difficulty with the candle problem rests on a phenomenon known as **functional fixedness**, the tendency to think of an object only in terms of its typical use. Functional fixedness occurs because the objects are first presented inside the boxes, which are then seen simply as containers for the objects they hold rather than as a potential part of the solution.

Functional fixedness is an example of a broader phenomenon known as **mental set**, the tendency for old patterns of problem solving to persist. This phenomenon was demonstrated in a classic experiment carried out by Abraham Luchins (1946). As you can see in Figure 9-5, the object of the task is to use the jars in each row to measure out the designated amount of liquid. (Try it yourself to get a sense of the importance of mental set before moving on.)

If you have tried the problem, you know that the first five parts are all solved in the same way: Fill the largest jar (B) and from it fill the middle-size jar (A) once and the smallest jar (C) two times. What is left in B is the designated amount. (Stated as a formula, it is B - A - 2C.) The demonstration of mental set comes with the sixth part of the problem, a point at which you probably encountered some difficulty. If you are like most people, you tried the formula and were perplexed when it failed. Chances are, in fact, that you missed the simple (but different) solution to the problem, which simply involves subtracting C from A. Interestingly, those people who were given problem six *first* had no difficulty with it at all.

Mental set can affect perceptions. It can prevent you from seeing your way beyond the apparent constraints of a problem. For example, try to draw four straight lines so that they pass through all nine dots in the grid at the top of p. 292—without lifting your pencil from the page.

FIGURE 9-4

The problem here is to place three candles at eye level on a nearby door so that the wax will not drip on the floor as the candles burn—using only materials in the figure (tacks, candles, and matches in boxes). For a solution, turn to p. 292, Figure 9-6.

Functional fixedness: The tendency to think of an object in terms of its most typical use

Mental set: The tendency for old patterns of problem solving to persist

FIGURE 9-5

Try this classic demonstration, which illustrates the importance of mental set in problem solving. The object is to use the jars in each row to measure out the designated amount of liquid. After you figure out the solution for the first five rows, you'll probably have trouble with the sixth row—even though the solution is actually easier. In fact, if you had tried to solve the problem in the sixth row first, you probably would have had no difficulty at all.

Given jars with these capacities (in quarts)

	A	B	C	Obtain
1.	21	127	3	100
2.	14	163	25	99
3.	18	43	10	5
4.	9	42	6	21
5.	20	59	4	31
6.	28	76	3	25

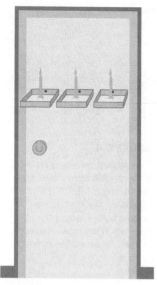

FIGURE 9-6

A solution to the problem posed in Figure 9-4 is to tack the boxes to the wall and place the candles on the boxes.

Confirmation bias: A bias in problem solving favoring an initial hypothesis and disregarding contradictory information suggesting alternative solutions

Creativity: The combining of responses or ideas in novel ways

. . .
. . .
. . .

If you had difficulty with the problem, it was probably because you felt compelled to keep your lines within the grid. If you had gone outside the boundaries, however, you would have succeeded with solutions such as those shown in Figure 9-7 on p. 294.

Inaccurate Evaluation of Solutions. When the nuclear power plant at Three Mile Island in Pennsylvania suffered its initial malfunction in 1979, a disaster that almost led to a nuclear meltdown, the plant operators were faced immediately with solving a problem of the most serious kind. Several monitors indicated contradictory information about the source of the problem: One suggested that the pressure was too high, leading to the danger of an explosion; others indicated that the pressure was too low, which could lead to a meltdown. Although the pressure was in fact too low, the supervisors on duty relied on the one monitor—which was faulty—that suggested the pressure was too high. Once they had made their decision and acted upon it, they ignored the contradictory evidence from the other monitors (Wickens, 1984).

One reason for the operators' mistake is the **confirmation bias**, in which initial hypotheses are favored and contradictory information supporting alternative hypotheses or solutions is ignored. Even when we find evidence that contradicts a solution we have chosen, we are apt to stick with our original hypothesis.

There are several reasons for the confirmation bias. One is that it takes cognitive effort to rethink a problem that appears to be solved already, so we are apt to stick with our first solution. Another is that evidence contradicting an initial solution may present something of a threat to our self-esteem, leading us to hold to the solutions that we have come up with first (Rasmussen, 1981; Fischoff, 1977).

Creativity and Problem Solving

Despite obstacles to problem solving, many people are adept at coming up with creative solutions to problems. One of the enduring questions that cognitive psychologists have tried to answer is what factors underlie **creativity**, which is usually defined as the combining of responses or ideas in novel ways (Glover, Ronning, & Reynolds, 1989).

Although being able to identify the stages of problem solving helps us to understand how people approach and solve problems, it does little to explain why some people come up with better solutions than others. Solutions to even the simplest of problems often show wide discrepancies. Consider, for example, how you might respond to the question "How many uses can you think of for a newspaper?" Compare your own solution with this one proposed by a 10-year-old boy:

> You can read it, write on it, lay it down and paint a picture on it. . . . You could put it in your door for decoration, put it in the garbage can, put it on a chair if the chair is messy. If you have a puppy, you put newspaper in its box or put it in your backyard for the dog to play with. When you build something and you don't want anyone to see it, put newspaper around it. Put newspaper on the floor if you have no mattress, use it to pick up something hot, use it to stop bleeding, or to catch the drips from

drying clothes. You can use a newspaper for curtains, put it in your shoe to cover what is hurting your foot, make a kite out of it, shade a light that is too bright. You can wrap fish in it, wipe windows, or wrap money in it. . . . You put washed shoes in newspaper, wipe eyeglasses with it, put it under a dripping sink, put a plant on it, make a paper bowl out of it, use it for a hat if it is raining, tie it on your feet for slippers. You can put it on the sand if you had no towel, use it for bases in baseball, make paper airplanes with it, use it as a dustpan when you sweep, ball it up for the cat to play with, wrap your hands in it if it is cold (Ward, Kogan, & Pankove, 1972).

It is obvious that this list shows extraordinary creativity. Unfortunately, it has proved to be considerably easier to identify *examples* of creativity than to determine its causes. There are several factors, however, that seem to be associated with creativity (Richards et al., 1988).

One factor closely related to creativity is divergent thinking. **Divergent thinking** refers to the ability to generate unusual, yet still appropriate, responses to problems or questions. This type of thinking contrasts with **convergent thinking**, which produces responses that are based primarily on knowledge and logic. For instance, someone relying on convergent thinking answers "You read it" to the query "What do you do with a newspaper?" In contrast, "You use it as a dustpan" is a more divergent—and creative—response (Runco, 1991).

> **Divergent thinking:** The ability to generate unusual but appropriate responses to problems or questions

> **Convergent thinking:** A type of thinking which produces responses based on knowledge and logic

Another ingredient of creativity is **cognitive complexity**, the use of and preference for elaborate, intricate, and complex stimuli and thinking patterns. Similarly, creative people often have a wider range of interests and are more independent and more interested in philosophical or abstract problems than less creative individuals are (F. Barron, 1990).

> **Cognitive complexity:** The use of and preference for elaborate, intricate, and complex stimuli and thinking patterns

Certain transitory factors also seem to be able to enhance creativity, at least temporarily. Humor, for instance, is useful. In a recent experiment, psychologist Alice Isen and colleagues found that people who had just watched a humorous film of television "bloopers" were more likely to come to a creative (and appropriate) solution to the candle problem discussed earlier (Figures 9-4 and 9-5) than people who had not viewed the film. Also, people who watched the comedy sequence seemed to think more generally, perceiving relationships among different sorts of information. Being in a good mood, then, may help us to be more creative and to think more broadly (Isen, Daubman, & Nowicki, 1987).

One factor that is *not* closely related to creativity is intelligence. Most tests of intelligence focus on convergent thinking skills in that their problems are well defined and have only one acceptable answer. Creative people who are divergent thinkers may therefore find themselves at a disadvantage. This may explain why researchers consistently find that creativity is only slightly related to intelligence or school grades, particularly when intelligence is measured using typical intelligence tests (Barron & Harrington, 1981; Sternberg, 1988; Alber, 1992).

The Informed Consumer of Psychology: Thinking Critically and Creatively

Can people be taught to be better thinkers? A growing body of evidence supports the notion that people can learn to perform better on decision-making and problem-solving tasks (Baron & Brown, 1991; Holyoak, 1990; Brown & Walter, 1990; Hayes, 1989). Abstract rules of logic and reasoning may be taught, and such training improves the way in which people are able to reason about the underlying causes of everyday life events (Larrick, Morgan, & Nisbett, 1990).

Ultimately, cognitive psychologists may routinely teach students not only to increase the skill with which they are able to solve problems, but to think more critically as well.

On the basis of the research we have discussed on problem solving, thinking, and creativity, there are several strategies that can help you think more critically and evaluate problems more creatively—whether they be the challenges of everyday life or more academically oriented problems such as determining the correct answer to a question on a test. Suggestions for increasing critical thinking and creativity include the following (Baron & Sternberg, 1987; Feldman & Schwartzberg, 1990; Hayes, 1989; Whimbey & Lochhead, 1991):

■ Redefine problems. The boundaries and assumptions you hold can be modified. For example, a problem can be rephrased at a more abstract or more concrete level, depending on how it is initially presented (Brown & Walter, 1990).

■ Use "fractionation," in which an idea or concept is broken down into the parts that make it up. Through fractionation, each part can be examined for new potentials and approaches, leading to a novel solution for the problem as a whole (deBono, 1967).

■ Adopt a critical perspective. Rather than passively accepting assumptions or arguments, critically evaluate material by considering its implications and thinking about possible exceptions and contradictions.

■ Use analogies. Analogies not only help us uncover new understanding, they provide alternative frameworks for interpreting facts. One particularly effective means of coming up with analogies is to look for them in the animal kingdom when the problem concerns people, and in physics or chemistry when the problem concerns inanimate objects.

■ Think divergently. Instead of thinking in terms of the most logical or most common use for an object, consider how it might be of help if you were forbidden to use it in its usual way.

■ Take the perspective of another person, one who is either involved in the situation or is a disinterested bystander. In doing so, you may gain a fresh view of the situation.

■ Use heuristics. As mentioned earlier, heuristics are rules of thumb that can help bring about a solution to a problem. If the nature of the problem is such that it has a single, correct answer, and a heuristic is available or can be constructed, using the heuristic frequently helps you to develop a solution more rapidly and effectively.

■ Experiment with various solutions. Don't be afraid to use different routes to find solutions for problems (verbal, mathematical, graphic, even acting out a situation). Try coming up with every conceivable idea you can, no matter how wild or bizarre it may seem at first. After you have come up with a list of solutions, you can go back over each and try to think of ways of making what at first appeared impractical seem more feasible (Sinnott, 1989).

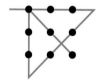

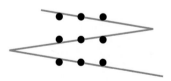

FIGURE 9-7

Solutions to the nine-dot problem, presented on p. 292, require the use of lines drawn beyond the boundaries of the figure—something that our mental set may prevent us from seeing easily.

RECAP

◀ In solving problems, people typically pass through a series of three steps: preparation, production, and judgment.

◀ Insight is a sudden awareness of the relationships among various elements that had earlier seemed independent of one another.

◀ Among the obstacles to successful problem solving are mental set and functional fixedness; the faulty application of algorithms and heuristics; and the confirmation bias.

◀ Creativity is related to divergent thinking and cognitive complexity.

◀ Some methods of enhancing critical thinking and creative problem solving include redefining a problem, using analogies, using divergent thinking, taking another perspective, using heuristics, and experimenting with different solutions.

REVIEW

1. Three steps of problem solving studied by psychologists are _____, _____, and _____.

2. Match the type of problem with its definition:

   1. _____ Inducing structure
   2. _____ Arrangement
   3. _____ Transformation

   a. Changing the initial state to the goal state.
   b. Rearranging elements to fit certain criteria.
   c. Constructing a new relationship between elements.

3. Solving a problem by trying to reduce the difference between the current state and the goal state is known as a _____.

4. _____ is the term used to describe the sudden "flash" of revelation that often accompanies the solution to a problem.

5. Thinking of an object only in terms of its typical use is known as _____ _____. A broader, related tendency for old problem-solving patterns to persist is known as a _____ _____.

6. _____ _____ describes the phenomenon favoring an initial hypothesis and ignoring subsequent competing hypotheses.

7. Generating unusual but still appropriate responses to a question is known as _____ _____.

8. Intelligence, as measured on standard intelligence tests, is highly correlated with measures of creativity. True or false? _____

Ask Yourself

If certain strategies that enhance creativity can indeed be taught, what potential benefits could this bring in the realms of: Business? Science? Working with the handicapped?

(Answers to review questions are on page 296.)

LANGUAGE

> 'Twas brillig, and the slithy toves
>   Did gyre and gimble in the wabe:
> All mimsy were the borogoves,
>   And the mome raths outgrabe.

Although few of us have ever come face to face with a tove, we have little difficulty in discerning that in Lewis Carroll's (1872) poem "Jabberwocky," the expression "slithy toves" represents an adjective, "slithy," and the noun it modifies, "toves."

Our ability to make sense out of nonsense, if the nonsense follows typical rules of language, illustrates both the sophistication of human language capabilities and the complexity of the processes that underlie the development and use of language. The way in which people are able to use **language**—the systematic, meaningful arrangement of symbols—clearly represents an important cognitive ability, one that is indispensable for communicating with others. But language is not only central to communication, it is also closely tied to the very way in which we think about and understand the world, for there is a crucial link between thought and language. It is not surprising, then, that psychologists have devoted considerable attention to studying the topic of language.

Language: The systematic, meaningful arrangement of symbols

Language is central to communication and our ability to understand the world.

Grammar: Language's Language

In order to understand how language develops, and what its relationship to thought is, we first need to review some of the formal elements that constitute language. The basic structure of language rests on grammar. **Grammar** is the framework of rules that determine how our thoughts can be expressed.

Grammar deals with three major components of language: phonology, syntax, and semantics. **Phonology** refers to the smallest unit of sounds, called **phonemes**, that affect the meaning of speech and to the way we use those sounds to produce meaning by placing them into the form of words. For instance, the "a" in "fat" and the "a" in "fate" represent two different phonemes in English (Halle, 1990).

Although English-speakers use just forty-two basic phonemes to produce words, the basic phonemes of other languages range from as few as fifteen to as many as eighty-five (Akmajian, Demers, & Harnish, 1984). Differences in phonemes are one reason people have difficulty in learning other languages: For example, to the Japanese-speaker, whose native language does not have an "r" phoneme, English words such as "roar" present some difficulty.

Syntax refers to the rules that indicate how words and phrases can be combined to form sentences. Every language has intricate rules that guide the order in which words may be strung together to communicate meaning. English-speakers have no difficulty in knowing that "Radio down the turn" is not an appropriate sequence, while "Turn down the radio" is. The importance of appropriate syntax is demonstrated by the changes in meaning that come from the differing order of words in the following three sequences: "John kidnapped the boy," "John, the kidnapped boy," and, "The boy kidnapped John" (Lasnik, 1990).

The third major component of language is semantics. **Semantics** refers to the rules governing the meaning of words and sentences (Larson, 1990). Se-

Grammar: The framework of rules that determine how our thoughts can be expressed

Phonology: The study of the sounds we make when we speak and of how we use those sounds to produce meaning by forming them into words

Phonemes (FONE eems): The smallest units of sound used to form words

Syntax: The rules that indicate how words are joined to form sentences

Semantics: The rules governing the meaning of words and sentences

mantic rules allow us to use words to convey the subtlest of nuances. For instance, we are able to make the distinction between "The truck hit Laura" (which we would be likely to say if we had just seen the vehicle hitting Laura) and "Laura was hit by a truck" (which we would probably say if asked why Laura was missing class while she recuperated).

Despite the complexities of language, most of us acquire the basics of grammar without even being aware that we have learned its rules (Rice, 1989). Moreover, even though we might have difficulty explicitly stating the rules of grammar that we employ, our linguistic abilities are so sophisticated that they enable us to utter an infinite number of different statements. We turn now to how such abilities are acquired.

Language Development: Developing a Way with Words

To parents, the sounds of their infant babbling and cooing are music to the ears (except, perhaps, at three o'clock in the morning). These sounds also serve an important function: They mark the first step on the road to the development of language.

Children **babble**—making speechlike but meaningless sounds—from around the ages of 3 months through 1 year. While babbling they may produce, at one time or another, any of the sounds found in all languages, not just the one to which they are exposed. Even deaf children display their own form of babbling: Infants who are unable to hear and who are exposed to sign language from birth "babble," but they do it with their hands (see Figure 9-8; Petitto & Marentette, 1991).

Babbling increasingly begins to reflect the specific language that is being spoken in the environment, initially in terms of pitch and tone, and eventually in terms of specific sounds (Reich, 1986; Kuhl et al., 1992). By the time the child is approximately 1 year old, sounds that are not in the language disappear. It is then a short step to the production of actual words. In English, these are typically

Babble: Speechlike but meaningless sounds

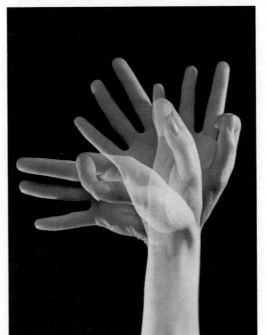

FIGURE 9-8
A syllable in signed language, similar to this, is found in the manual babbling of deaf infants and in the spoken babbling of hearing infants. The similarities in language structure suggest that language has biological roots.

The ability to comprehend language occurs early in infancy, before the child has learned to speak.

short words that start with a consonant such as "b," "d," "m," "p," or "t"— helping to explain why "mama" and "dada" are so often among babies' first words. Of course, even before they produce their first words, children are capable of understanding a fair amount of the language they hear. Language comprehension precedes language production.

After the age of 1 year, children begin to learn more complicated forms of language. They produce two-word combinations, which become the building blocks of sentences, and there is an acceleration in the number of different words they are capable of using. By the age of 2 years, the average child has a vocabulary of more than fifty words. Just six months later, that vocabulary has grown to several hundred words. At that time, children can produce short sentences, although they use **telegraphic speech**—sentences that sound as if they were part of a telegram, in which words not critical to the message are left out. Rather than saying, "I showed you the book," a child using telegraphic speech might say, "I show book"; and "I am drawing a dog" might become "Drawing dog." As the child gets older, of course, the use of telegraphic speech declines and sentences become increasingly complex.

Telegraphic speech: Sentences containing only the most essential words

By the time children are 3 years of age, they learn to make plurals by adding "s" to nouns, and they are able to form the past tense by adding "ed" to verbs. This ability also leads to errors, since children tend to apply rules too inflexibly. This phenomenon is known as **overregularization**, whereby children apply rules even when the application results in an error. Thus, although it is correct to say "he walked" for the past tense of "walk," the "ed" rule doesn't work quite so well when children say "he runned" for the past tense of "run."

Overregularization: Applying rules of speech in instances in which they are inappropriate

Toddlers' acquisition of language is assisted by the kind of language that their parents use with them. When speaking with children, adults use a form of language that is atypical of their everyday speech but promotes language development. They speak more slowly, use a more primitive vocabulary, substitute nouns for pronouns, and in general simplify sentence structure (deVilliers & deVilliers, 1978).

Much of children's acquisition of the basic rules of language is complete by the time they are five. However, a full vocabulary and the ability to comprehend and use subtle grammatical rules are not attained until later. For example, if you showed a 5-year-old boy a blindfolded doll and asked, "Is the doll easy or hard to see?" he would have great difficulty answering the question. In fact, if he were asked to make the doll easier to see, he would probably try to take off the doll's blindfold. On the other hand, 9-year-olds have little difficulty understanding the question, realizing that the doll's blindfold has nothing to do with an observer's ability to see the doll (Chomsky, 1969).

Understanding Language Acquisition: Identifying the Roots of Language

While anyone who is around children will notice the enormous strides that are made in language development throughout childhood, the reasons for this rapid growth are less obvious. Two major explanations have been put forward: one based on learning theory and the other on innate processes.

The **learning-theory approach** suggests that language acquisition follows the principles of reinforcement and conditioning discussed in Chapter 7. For example, a child who utters the word "mama" is hugged and praised by her mother, thereby reinforcing the behavior and making its repetition more likely. This view suggests that children first learn to speak by being rewarded for making sounds that approximate speech. Ultimately, through a process of shaping, language becomes more and more like adult speech (Skinner, 1957).

The learning theory approach is less successful when it comes to explaining the acquisition of language rules. Children are reinforced not only when they use proper language, but also when they respond incorrectly. For example, parents answer the child's "Why the dog won't eat?" as readily as they do the correctly phrased question "Why won't the dog eat?" Both sentences are understood equally well. Learning theory, then, does not seem to provide the full story of language acquisition.

An alternative model is provided by Noam Chomsky (1968, 1978), who argues that an **innate mechanism** plays an important role in learning a language. He suggests that humans are born with an innate linguistic capability that emerges primarily as a function of maturation. According to his analysis, all the world's languages share a similar underlying structure called a **universal grammar**. Chomsky suggests that the human brain has a neural system, the **language-acquisition device**, which both permits the understanding of the structure of language and provides strategies and techniques for learning the unique characteristics of a given native language. According to this view, then, language is a uniquely human phenomenon brought about by the presence of the language-acquisition device.

Chomsky's view, as you might suspect, is not without its critics. For instance, learning theorists contend that the apparent ability of animals such as chimpanzees to learn the fundamentals of human language (as we discuss next) argues against the innate view. The issue of how humans acquire language thus remains hotly contested (Rice, 1989; Pinker, 1990).

Do Animals Use Language?

One of the enduring questions that has long puzzled psychologists is whether language is uniquely human or other animals are able to acquire it as well. It is clear that many animals communicate with one another in some rudimentary forms, such as fiddler crabs that wave their claws to signal, bees whose dance

Learning-theory approach: Language acquisition follows the principles of reinforcement and conditioning (see Chapter 7)

Innate mechanism: According to Chomsky, the innate linguistic capability in humans that emerges as a function of maturation

Universal grammar: An underlying structure shared by all languages, the basis of Chomsky's theory that certain language characteristics are based in the brain's structure and are therefore common to all people

Language-acquisition device: A neural system of the brain hypothesized to permit understanding of language

Psychologist Sue Savage-Rumbaugh signs the word for "trailer" as she and chimp Kanzi confer about the day's plans.

indicates the direction in which food will be found, or certain birds that say "zick, zick" during courtship and "kia" when they are about to fly away. But researchers have yet to demonstrate conclusively that these animals use true language, which is characterized in part by the ability to produce and communicate new and unique meanings following a formal grammar.

Psychologists have, however, been able to teach chimps to communicate at surprisingly high levels. For instance, Kanzi, a 9-year-old pygmy chimpanzee, has linguistic skills that some psychologists claim are close to those of a 2-year-old human being. Psychologist Sue Savage-Rumbaugh and colleagues, who have worked extensively with Kanzi, suggest that he can create sentences that are grammatically sophisticated and can even concoct new rules of syntax (Savage-Rumbaugh et al., 1986).

Despite the skills displayed by primates such as Kanzi, critics contend that the language they use still lacks a grammar and sufficiently complex and novel constructions to approach the realm of human capabilities (Seidenberg & Petitto, 1987). Instead, they maintain that the chimps are displaying a skill no different from that of a dog which learns to lie down on command in order to get a reward.

Most evidence supports the contention that humans are better equipped than animals to produce and organize language in the form of meaningful sentences. But the issue of whether animals are capable of being taught to communicate in a way that resembles human language remains a controversial one (Seidenberg & Petitto, 1987; Savage-Rumbaugh, 1987; Gibbons, 1991).

Does Thought Determine Language—Or Does Language Determine Thought?

When an Eskimo woman peers outside her igloo and sees that it is snowing, she doesn't simply announce, "It's snowing." For Eskimos have at their disposal some twenty individual words to describe different types of snow. This linguistic prowess raises an important question: Do Eskimos *think* about snow differently than English-speakers do?

The possible answers to that question have sparked controversy. According to the **linguistic-relativity hypothesis**, language shapes and, in fact, may determine the way people of a particular culture perceive and understand the world (Whorf, 1956). According to this view, Eskimos think about snow in a way that is qualitatively different from the way English-speakers think about it, since the range of linguistic categories provided by the Eskimo language permits finer discriminations than the more limited English language. Actually English is not entirely impoverished when it comes to considering snow, if we include such terms as "blizzard," "dusting," and "avalanche" (Martin & Pullum, 1991).

Let us consider another possibility, however. Suppose that, instead of language being the *cause* of certain ways of thinking about the world, language is a *result* of thinking about and experiencing relevant stimuli in the environment. In this view, thought *produces* language. The only reason Eskimos have more words for "snow" than we do is that snow is considerably more relevant to them than it is to people in most other cultures. In accordance with this viewpoint, if we were to move to the Arctic Circle (or become ski bums), we would be perfectly capable of differentiating various types of snow. Our language usage might not be particularly eloquent (we might say "deep, crunchy, hard-packing snow that is going to be on the ground all winter"), but we would have no trouble perceiving and thinking about the differences in snow.

In an effort to determine which of the two descriptions (language produces thought versus thought produces language) provides the more accurate account, investigators have carried out a significant amount of research. In one study, Eleanor Rosch (1974) compared the perception of colors by Americans and by members of the Dani tribe of New Guinea. The Dani have only two names for color: one for cold, dark colors and one for warm, lighter colors. In English, of course, there are hundreds of color names, but eleven of them represent major color categories (red, yellow, green, blue, black, gray, white, purple, orange, pink, and brown). Rosch argued that if the linguistic-relativity hypothesis were accurate, English-speakers should be more efficient at recognizing and distinguishing colors that represent the major categories than colors that were not members of major categories. In contrast, she reasoned that the Dani tribe members should show no difference in recognition between colors that were members of major or nonmajor categories, since there were no words in their vocabulary to describe any of them.

However, the results did not support this hypothesis. There was no difference in the way that either English-speakers or Dani perceived the colors; both perceived colors in the major categories more efficiently than colors in the nonmajor categories. According to these results, then, language differences do not produce affect perception.

Subsequent research is congruent with Rosch's study and, by and large, has not supported the linguistic-relativity hypothesis (Brown, 1986; Pinker, 1990). It seems most appropriate to conclude that, in general, cognition influences language and not the other way around.

On the other hand, language *does* affect thinking and cognition in some ways. For instance, the manner in which information is stored in memory—and how well such information can subsequently be retrieved—is related to language (Cairns & Cairns, 1976). Likewise, the words and categorizations available in a given language affect the way that concepts, which we discussed at the beginning of the chapter, are formed.

Linguistic-relativity hypothesis: The theory claiming that language shapes and may even determine the way people perceive and understand the world

Finally, our impressions and memories of others' personality and behavior are affected by the linguistic categories provided us by the language we speak (Hoffman, Lau, & Johnson, 1986). Although language does not determine thought, then, it certainly influences it. And, as we discuss in the Psychology at Work box, language has come to represent an important social issue related to education.

P S Y C H O L O G Y   A T   W O R K

For picture day at New York's P.S. 217, a neighborhood elementary school in Brooklyn, the notice to parents was translated into five languages. That was a nice gesture, but insufficient: More than 40 percent of the children are immigrants whose families speak any one of twenty-six languages, ranging from Armenian to Urdu.

At the Leroy D. Feinberg Elementary School in Miami, a science teacher starts a lesson by holding up an ice cube and asking "Is it hot?" The point here is vocabulary. Only after the students who come from homes where English is not spoken learn the very basics will they move onto the question of just what an ice cube might be.

The first grade of Magnolia Elementary School in Lanham, Maryland, is a study in cooperation. A Korean boy who has been in the United States for almost a year quizzes two mainland Chinese girls who arrived ten days ago. Nearby, a Colombian named Julio is learning to read with the help of an American-born boy. (Leslie, 1991, p. 56.)

From the biggest cities to the most rural areas, the face—and voice—of education in the United States is changing. Children with names like Thong, Kim, and Karachnicoff are becoming increasingly common as the wave of immigration of the 1980s, larger than that of the early 1900s, hits the country's schools. In seven

CLASSROOMS OF BABEL: BILINGUAL EDUCATION

states, including Texas, New York, and Colorado, more that one-quarter of the students are not native English-speakers.

How to deal appropriately and effectively with the increasing number of children who are not native English-speakers represents an important educational issue. Most educators suggest that a bilingual approach is best, in which students are taught some subjects in their native language while they simultaneously learn English. They hold that it is necessary for students to develop a sound footing in basic subject areas and that, initially at least, only instruction in their native language will provide them with that foundation. At the same time they are learning English, and the eventual goal is to shift all their instruction into that language.

In contrast, some educators suggest that all instruction ought to be in English from the very moment non-native English speakers enroll in school. To these educators, teaching students in a language other than English simply hinders nonnative English-speakers' integration into the society in which they live and ultimately does them a disservice.

While the question is a controversial and highly political one, psychological research has provided several insights relevant to the issue. A central question relates to the relationship between bilingualism and cognition, and a growing body of research suggests that people who speak more than one language may

well have some cognitive advantages over those who only speak one language.

For example, speakers of two languages show more cognitive flexibility. They have more linguistic possibilities available for contemplating situations they encounter because of their multiple-language abilities. In turn, this permits them to solve problems with greater creativity and flexibility.

Bilingual students also are more aware of the rules of language, and they may understand concepts more readily (Hakuta & Garcia, 1989). They even may score higher on intelligence tests. For example, one survey that studied French- and English-speaking schoolchildren in Canada found that bilingual students scored significantly higher on both verbal and nonverbal tests of intelligence than those who were monolingual (Lambert & Peal, 1972).

Finally, evidence exists that there are common principles of language acquisition. Therefore, initial instruction in the native language may actually enhance the learning of English as a second language. There certainly is no evidence that children will be cognitively overwhelmed by instruction in both their native language and English (Lindholm, 1991).

In sum, research suggests that bilingual students actually have an advantage over students who speak just one language. Therefore, rather than urging those for whom English is not a native language to speak only English, the best course might be to enhance their skills in both their original language *and* English.

RECAP

◀ Language is characterized by grammar, a framework of rules that determine how our thoughts can be expressed.

◀ Language acquisition proceeds rapidly from birth and is largely complete by the age of 5, although there are subsequent increases in vocabulary and sophistication.

◀ The learning-theory view suggests that language is learned through the principles of reinforcement and conditioning. In contrast, Chomsky's view suggests that language capabilities are innate, a result of the existence of a language-acquisition device in the brain.

◀ The question of whether language determines thought (the linguistic-relativity hypothesis) or thought determines language remains controversial.

REVIEW

1. Match the component of grammar with its definition:
   1. _____ Syntax
   2. _____ Phonology
   3. _____ Semantics

   a. Rules showing how words can be combined into sentences.
   b. Rules governing the meaning of words and sentences.
   c. Relates to sound units that affect speech.

2. Language production and language comprehension develop in infants at approximately similar times. True or false? _____

3. _____ _____ refers to the phenomenon in which young children omit nonessential portions of sentences.

4. A child knows that adding "ed" to certain words puts them in the past tense. As a result, instead of saying "He came," the child says "He comed." This is an example of _____.

5. _____ theory assumes that language acquisition is based on operant learning principles.

6. Chomsky argues that language acquisition is an innate ability tied to the structure of the brain. True or false? _____

7. Thought has been proven to influence language, but language does not seem to have an influence on thought. True or false? _____

Ask Yourself

Scientists have studied language acquisition in animals for many years with no clear results. Suppose that you hear on the news tomorrow that a pair of chimpanzees have mastered English (via a computer console) at an eighth-grade level. What effect will this have on current theories of language acquisition? How can this knowledge be applied to humans?

(Answers to review questions are on page 304.)

■ *How do we think, reason, and make decisions?*

1. Cognitive psychologists study cognition, which encompasses the higher mental processes. These processes include the way people know and understand the world, process information, make decisions and judgments, and describe their knowledge and understanding to others.

2. Thinking is the manipulation of mental representations of information. Thinking transforms such representations into novel and different forms, permitting people to answer questions, solve problems, or reach goals.

3. Concepts, one of the building blocks of thinking, are categorizations of objects, events, or people that share common properties. Natural concepts (which are concepts that are simple, and represent familiar objects which share a set of characteristic features) include prototypes, representative examples of the concept.

4. In deductive reasoning, people derive the implications of a set of assumptions that they know to be true. In inductive reasoning, in contrast, people infer a general rule from specific cases. Inductive reasoning allows people to use their observations, knowledge, experiences, and beliefs about the world to develop summary conclusions.

5. Decisions may be improved through the use of algorithms and heuristics. Algorithms are rules which, if followed, guarantee a solution, while heuristics are rules of thumb that may lead to a solution but are not guaranteed to do so.

6. There are several kinds of heuristics. In the representativeness heuristic, people decide whether a given example is a member of a particular category by evaluating how representative of that category the example is. The availability heuristic consists of judging the probability of an event by how easily other instances of the event can be recalled from memory.

■ *How do people approach and solve problems?*

7. Problem solving typically involves three major steps:

preparation, production of solutions, and evaluation of solutions that have been generated. Preparation begins when people try to understand the problem. Some problems are well defined, with clear solution requirements; other problems are ill defined, with ambiguities in both the information required for a solution and the solution itself.

8. In arrangement problems, a group of elements must be rearranged or recombined in a way that will satisfy a certain criterion. In problems of inducing structure, a person must identify the relationships among the elements presented and construct a new relationship among them. Finally, transformation problems consist of an initial state, a goal state, and a series of methods for changing the initial state into the goal state.

9. A crucial aspect of the preparation stage is the representation and organization of the problem. Sometimes restructuring a problem from a verbal form to a pictorial or mathematical form can help point the way to the solution.

10. In the production stage, people try to generate solutions. The solutions to some problems may already be in long-term memory and can be directly retrieved. Alternatively, some problems may be solved through simple trial and error. More complex problems, however, require the use of algorithms and heuristics.

11. In a means-ends analysis, a person will repeatedly test for differences between the desired outcome and what currently exists, trying each time to come closer to the goal. Another heuristic is to divide a problem into intermediate steps or subgoals and solve each of those steps.

12. One approach to problem solving is exemplified by Köhler's research with chimps, in which the elements of the situation had to be manipulated in a novel fashion in order for the chimps to solve the problem. Köhler called the cognitive processes underlying the chimps' behavior insight, a sudden awareness of the relationships among elements that had previously seemed independent.

■ *What are the major obstacles to problem solving?*

13. Several factors hinder effective problem solving. Functional fixedness (the tendency to think of an object only in terms of its most typical use), is an example of a broader phenomenon known as mental set. Mental set is the tendency for old patterns of problem solving to persist. The inappropriate use of algorithms and heuristics can also act as an obstacle to the production of solutions to problems. Finally, the confirmation bias, in which initial hypotheses are favored, can hinder the accurate evaluation of solutions to problems.

14. Creativity is the combining of responses or ideas in novel ways. Divergent thinking is the ability to respond with unusual, but still appropriate, responses to problems or questions and is associated with creativity. Cognitive complexity, the use of and preference for elaborate, intricate, and complex stimuli and thinking patterns, is also related to creativity.

15. A growing body of evidence supports the idea that people can learn to perform better in problem-solving situations. By learning abstract rules of logic and reasoning, people are able to think critically about the underlying causes of everyday events.

16. Suggestions for solving problems creatively include redefining the problem, using analogies, thinking divergently, taking the perspective of another person, using heuristics, and experimenting with different solutions.

■ *How do people use language, and how does it develop?*

17. Language is the systematic, meaningful arrangement of symbols. All languages have a grammar—a framework of rules that determine how our thoughts can be expressed—which encompasses the three major components of language: phonology, syntax, and semantics. Phonology refers to the sounds (called phonemes) we make when we speak and the use of those sounds to produce meaning; syntax refers to the rules that indicate how words are joined together to form sentences; and semantics refers to the rules governing the meaning of words and sentences of language.

18. Language production, preceded by language comprehension, develops out of babbling (speechlike but meaningless sounds), which leads to the production of actual words. After a year, children use two-word combinations and their vocabulary increases. They first use telegraphic speech, in which words not critical to the message are dropped. By the age of 5, acquisition of language rules is relatively complete.

19. There are two major theories of language acquisition. Learning theorists suggest that language is acquired through reinforcement and conditioning. In contrast, Chomsky suggests that there is an innate language acquisition device which guides the development of language. The degree to which language is a uniquely human skill remains controversial.

20. The linguistic-relativity hypothesis suggests that language shapes and may determine the way people think about the world. Most evidence suggests that although language does not determine thought, it does affect the way information is stored in memory and how well it can be retrieved.

ANSWERS (REVIEW III):

1. 1-a; 2-c; 3-b **2.** False; language comprehension precedes language acquisition. **3.** Telegraphic speech **4.** overregularization **5.** Learning **6.** True **7.** False; language and thought seem to interact with each other in a variety of ways.

KEY TERMS AND CONCEPTS

cognitive psychology (p. 277)
cognition (p. 277)
thinking (p. 277)
concepts (p. 278)
artificial concepts (p. 278)
natural concepts (p. 278)
prototypes (p. 278)
deductive reasoning (p. 279)
syllogism (p. 279)
inductive reasoning (p. 281)
algorithm (p. 281)
heuristic (p. 282)
representativeness heuristic
    (p. 282)
availability heuristic (p. 282)
well-defined problem (p. 285)

ill-defined problem (p. 285)
arrangement problems (p. 285)
problems of inducing structure
    (p. 286)
transformation problems (p. 288)
means-ends analysis (p. 289)
subgoals (p. 289)
insight (p. 289)
functional fixedness (p. 291)
mental set (p. 291)
confirmation bias (p. 292)
creativity (p. 292)
divergent thinking (p. 293)
convergent thinking (p. 293)
cognitive complexity (p. 293)
language (p. 295)

grammar (p. 296)
phonology (p. 296)
phonemes (p. 296)
syntax (p. 296)
semantics (p. 296)
babble (p. 297)
telegraphic speech (p. 298)
overregularization (p. 298)
learning-theory approach
    (p. 299)
innate mechanism (p. 299)
universal grammar (p. 299)
language-acquisition device
    (p. 299)
linguistic-relativity hypothesis
    (p. 301)

10

INTELLIGENCE

LESLIE LEMKE

Leslie Lemke.

The concert began with a polished version of Gershwin's "Rhapsody in Blue." The entertainer then belted out a rendition of "Hello, Dolly!" and "I Believe." After several other songs, he ended with "Amazing Grace" and "He Touched Me." The music was beautiful, and many in the audience had to fight back tears.

There was little out of the ordinary at the concert, except for one thing: the musician, 32-year-old Leslie Lemke, was blind, crippled by cerebral palsy, and severely retarded. He can hold only the simplest of conversations and has the mental capabilities of a young child. Yet despite his multiple handicaps—and the fact that by most standards he lacks so much—his contributions to the musical world are extraordinary, far beyond the capabilities of most people with "normal" intelligence.

Lemke's condition, called the "savant syndrome," occurs when an individual, despite being mentally retarded, demonstrates spectacular talent in a specific area. Although the savant syndrome, which was made famous in the movie *Rain Man*, is very rare, the skills displayed by savants are quite extraordinary. In one case, for example, a severely retarded savant, who could not do the simplest arithmetic problem, could name the months in which the eighteenth day fell on a Saturday for each year during the 1900s. Another could compute square roots in his head, and still another could accurately reproduce in sculpture any animal that he saw just once.

If you asked Leslie to explain his extraordinary talents, he probably would not even be able to understand the question. Yet, he is able to respond to the question of how he feels when he sits down at the piano: He says, simply, "I feel happy" (Breu, 1984, p. 30).

LOOKING AHEAD

Although the capabilities of Leslie Lemke and other savants have yet to be explained satisfactorily, one thing is clear: Intelligence is an unusually complex phenomenon. It is also a major focal point for psychologists intent on understanding how people are able to adapt their behavior to the environment in which they live, and how individuals differ from one another in the way in which they learn about and understand the world.

In this chapter, we consider the challenges involved in defining and measuring intelligence. If you are like most people, you have probably wondered how smart you are. Psychologists, too, have pondered the nature of intelligence. We will examine some of their conceptions of intelligence as well as efforts to develop and use standardized tests as a means of measuring intelligence. We will also consider the two groups displaying extremes of individual differences in intelligence: the mentally retarded and the gifted. The special challenges of each population will be discussed along with special programs that have been developed to help individuals from both groups reach their full potential. Finally, we will discuss what are probably the two most controversial issues surrounding intelligence: the degree to which intelligence is influenced by heredity and by the environment, and whether traditional tests of intelligence are biased toward the dominant cultural groups in society.

After reading this chapter, then, you will be able to answer the following questions:

■ How do psychologists conceptualize and define intelligence?

■ What are the major approaches to measuring intelligence?

■ How can the extremes of intelligence be differentiated, and what are some of the special programs designed to help people maximize their full potential?

■ Are traditional IQ tests culturally biased?

■ Are there racial differences in intelligence, and to what degree is intelligence influenced by the environment and to what degree by heredity?

DEFINING INTELLIGENT BEHAVIOR

It is typical for members of the Trukese, a small tribe in the South Pacific, to sail a hundred miles in open ocean waters. Although their destination may be just a small dot of land less than a mile wide, the Trukese are able to sail unerringly toward it without the aid of compass, chronometer, sextant, or any of the other sailing tools that are indispensable to modern western navigation. They are able to sail accurately, even when prevailing winds do not allow a direct approach to the island and they must take a zigzag course (Gladwin, 1964).

How are the Trukese able to navigate so effectively? If you ask them, they could not explain it. They might tell you that they use a process that takes into account the rising and setting of the stars and the appearance, sound, and feel of the waves against the side of the boat. But at any given moment as they are sailing along, they could not identify their position or say why they are doing what they are doing. Nor could they explain the navigational theory underlying their sailing technique.

Some might say the inability of the Trukese to explain how their sailing technique works in western terms is a sign of primitive and even unintelligent behavior. In fact, if we made Trukese sailors take a standardized western test of

Intelligence takes many forms. The skills needed to survive as a hunter in the Amazon region of Peru (*a*) are different from but at least as crucial as those required by a career in architecture (*b*).

(a)　　　　(b)

navigational knowledge and theory, or, for that matter, a traditional test of intelligence, they very well might do poorly on it. Yet, as a practical matter, it is hard to accuse the Trukese of being unintelligent: Despite their inability to explain how they do so, they are able to navigate successfully through the open ocean waters.

The way in which the Trukese navigate points out the difficulty in coming to grips with what is meant by intelligence. To a westerner, traveling in a straight line along the most direct and quickest route using a sextant and other navigational tools is likely to represent the most "intelligent" kind of behavior; a zigzag course, based on the "feel" of the waves, would not seem very reasonable. To the Trukese, however, who are used to their own system of navigation, the use of complicated navigational tools might well seem so overly complex and unnecessary that they might think of western navigators as lacking in intelligence.

It is clear that the term "intelligence" can take on many different meanings (Lohman, 1989; Davidson, 1990). If, for instance, you lived in a remote African village, the way you differentiate between more intelligent and less intelligent people might be very different from the way that someone living in the middle of New York City would distinguish individual differences. To the African, high intelligence might be represented by exceptional hunting or other survival skills; to the New Yorker, it might be exemplified by dealing effectively with a mass-transit system, by achieving success as a member of a high-salaried, prestigious profession, or by getting good grades at a rigorous private school.

In fact, each of these conceptions of intelligence is reasonable, for each represents an instance in which more intelligent people are better able to use the resources of their environment than less intelligent people are, a distinction that we would assume to be basic to any definition of intelligence. Yet it is also clear that these conceptions represent very different views of intelligence.

That two such different sets of behavior can exemplify the same psychological concept has long posed a challenge to psychologists. For years, they have grappled with the issue of devising a general definition of intelligence that would remain independent of a person's specific culture and other environmental factors. Interestingly, untrained laypersons have fairly clear conceptions of intelligence (Sternberg, 1985b). For example, in one survey that asked a group of people to define what they meant by intelligence, three major components of intelligence emerged (Sternberg, Conway, Ketron, & Bernstein, 1981). First, there was problem-solving ability: Survey respondents maintained that people who reason logically and identify more solutions to problems are intelligent. Second, the respondents thought that verbal abilities exemplified intelligence. Finally, they assumed that intelligence was indicated by social competence: the ability to show interest in others and interact effectively with them.

Intelligence: The capacity to understand the world, think rationally, and use resources effectively when faced with challenges

The definition of intelligence that psychologists employ contains some of the same elements found in the layperson's conception. To psychologists, **intelligence** is the capacity to understand the world, think rationally, and use resources effectively when faced with challenges (Wechsler, 1975).

Intelligence tests: A battery of measures to determine a person's level of intelligence

Unfortunately, neither the layperson's nor the psychologist's conception of intelligence is much help when it comes to distinguishing, with any degree of precision, more intelligent people from less intelligent ones. To overcome this problem, psychologists who study intelligence have focused much of their attention on the development of batteries of tests, known, quite obviously, as **intelligence tests**, and have relied on such tests to identify a person's level of intelligence. These tests have proved to be of great benefit in identifying students in need of special attention in school, in diagnosing cognitive difficulties, and in helping people make optimal educational and vocational choices. At the same time, their use has proved quite controversial.

Measuring Intelligence

The first intelligence tests followed a simple premise: If performance on certain tasks or test items improved with age, then performance could be used to distinguish more intelligent people from less intelligent ones within a particular age group. Using this principle, Alfred Binet, a French psychologist, devised the first formal intelligence test, which was designed to identify the "dullest" students in the Paris school system in order to provide them with remedial aid.

Binet began by presenting tasks to same-age students who had been labeled "bright" or "dull" by their teachers. If a task could be completed by the bright students but not by the dull ones, he retained the task as a proper test item; otherwise it was discarded. In the end he came up with a test that distinguished between the bright and dull groups, and—with further work—one that distinguished among children in different age groups (Binet & Simon, 1916).

On the basis of the Binet test, children were assigned a score that corresponded to their **mental age**, the average age of children taking the test who achieved the same score. For example, if a 10-year-old boy received a score of 45 on the test and this was the average score received by 8-year-olds, his mental age would be considered to be 8 years. Similarly, a 14-year-old girl who scored an 88 on the test—matching the mean score for 16-year-olds—would be assigned a mental age of 16 years.

Assigning a mental age to students provided an indication of whether they were performing at the same level as their peers. However, it did not allow for adequate comparisons among people of different **chronological**, or physical, **ages**. By using mental age alone, for instance, we might assume that an 18-year-old responding at a 16-year-old's level would be as bright as a 5-year-old answering at a 3-year-old's level, when actually the 5-year-old would be displaying a much greater *relative* degree of slowness.

A solution to the problem came in the form of the **intelligence quotient**, or **IQ score**, a measure of intelligence that takes into account an individual's mental *and* chronological ages. To calculate an IQ score, the following formula is used, in which MA stands for mental age and CA for chronological age:

$$IQ \text{ score} = MA/CA \times 100$$

Using this formula, we can return to the earlier example of an 18-year-old performing at a mental age of 16 and calculate an IQ score of $(16/18) \times 100 = 88.9$. In contrast, the 5-year-old performing at a mental age of 3 comes out with a considerably lower IQ score: $(3/5) \times 100 = 60$.

As a bit of trial and error with the formula will show you, anyone who has a mental age equal to his or her chronological age will have an IQ equal to 100. Moreover, people with a mental age that is greater than their chronological age will have IQs that exceed 100.

Although the basic principles behind the calculation of an IQ score still hold, IQ scores are figured in a somewhat different manner today and are known as **deviation IQ scores**. First, the average test score for everyone of the same age who takes the test is determined, and this average score is assigned an IQ of 100. Then, with the aid of sophisticated mathematical techniques that calculate the differences (or "deviations") between each score and the average, IQ values are assigned to all the other test scores for this age group.

Alfred Binet devised the first formal IQ test.

Mental age: The typical intelligence level found for people at a given chronological age

Chronological age: A person's physical age

Intelligence quotient (IQ) score: A measure of intelligence that takes into account an individual's mental and chronological ages

Deviation IQ score: A calculation of an IQ score that allows one person's performance to be measured in relation to those of others

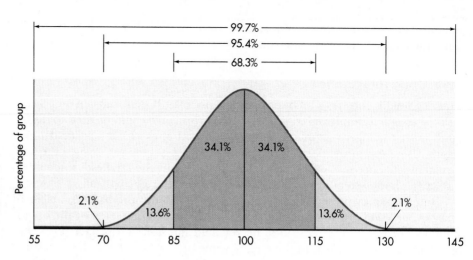

FIGURE 10-1

The average and most frequent IQ score is 100, and 68.3 percent of all people are within a thirty-point range centered on 100. Some 95.7 percent of the population have scores that are within thirty points above or below 100, and 99.7 percent have scores that are between 55 and 145.

As you can see in Figure 10-1, approximately two-thirds of all individuals fall within fifteen IQ points of the average score of 100. As scores increase or fall beyond that range, the percentage of people in a category falls considerably.

Measuring IQ

Just what is an IQ test like? It is probable that sometime during your academic career you have taken one; almost all of us are given IQ tests at one time or another.

The original test is still with us, although it has been revised many times and in its modern incarnation bears little resemblance to the original version. Now called the **Stanford-Binet test** Fourth Edition, the measure was last revised in 1985 (Hagen, Sattler, & Thorndike, 1985; Thorndike, Hagan, & Sattler, 1986). It consists of a series of items which vary in nature according to the age of the person being tested. For example, young children are asked to copy figures or answer questions about everyday activities. Older people are asked to solve analogies, explain proverbs, and describe similarities that underlie sets of words.

Stanford-Binet test: A test of intelligence that includes a series of items varying in nature according to the age of the person being tested

The test is administered orally. An examiner begins by finding a mental age level at which the person is able to answer all questions correctly, and then moves on to successively difficult problems. When a mental age level is reached at which no items can be answered, the test is over. By examining the pattern of correct and incorrect responses, the examiner is able to compute an IQ score for the person being tested.

The other IQ test frequently used in America was devised by psychologist David Wechsler and is known as the **Wechsler Adult Intelligence Scale—Revised**, or, more commonly, the **WAIS-R**. There is also a children's version, the **Wechsler Intelligence Scale for Children—III**, or **WISC-III**. Both the WAIS-R and the WISC-III have two major parts: a verbal scale and a performance—or nonverbal—scale. As you can see from the sample questions in Figure 10-2, the two scales include questions of very different types. Whereas verbal tasks consist of more traditional kinds of problems, including vocabulary definition and comprehension of various concepts, the nonverbal part consists of assembling small objects and arranging pictures in a logical order. Although an individual's scores on the verbal and performance sections of the test are generally close to each other, the scores of a person with a language deficiency or a background of severe environmental deprivation may show a relatively large discrepancy. By providing separate scores, the WAIS-R and WISC-III give a more precise picture of a person's specific abilities.

Wechsler Adult-Intelligence Scale—Revised (WAIS-R): A test of intelligence consisting of verbal and nonverbal performance sections, providing a relatively precise picture of a person's specific abilities

Wechsler Intelligence Scale for Children—III (WISC-III): An intelligence test for children; see Wechsler Adult Intelligence Scale—Revised

Verbal scale

Information	Where does milk come from?
Comprehension	Why do we put food in the refrigerator?
Arithmetic	Stacey had two crayons and the teacher gave her two more. How many did she have all together?
Similarities	In what way are cows and horses alike?

Performance scale

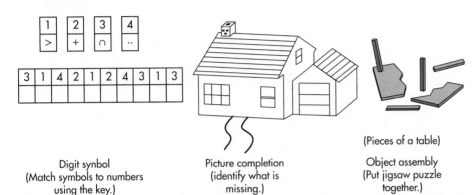

Digit synbol
(Match symbols to numbers
using the key.)

Picture completion
(identify what is
missing.)

(Pieces of a table)

Object assembly
(Put jigsaw puzzle
together.)

FIGURE 10-2

Typical kinds of items found on the verbal and performance scales of the Wechsler Intelligence Scales for Children (WISC-III).

Because the Stanford-Binet, WAIS-R, and WISC-III all require individualized administration, it is relatively difficult and time-consuming to administer and score them on a wide-scale basis. Consequently, there are now a number of IQ tests that allow for group administration (Anastasi, 1988). Rather than having one examiner ask one person at a time to respond to individual items, group IQ tests are strictly paper-and-pencil measures, in which those taking the tests read the questions and provide their answers in writing. The primary advantage of group tests is their ease of administration.

There are, however, sacrifices made in group testing which, in some cases, may outweigh the benefits. For instance, group tests generally sample a more restricted range of questions than tests administered individually. Furthermore, people may be more motivated to perform at their highest ability level when working on a one-to-one basis with a test administrator. Finally, in some cases, it is simply impossible to employ group tests, particularly with young children or people with unusually low IQs.

Achievement and Aptitude Tests

IQ tests are not the only kind of tests that you have taken during the course of your schooling. Two other kinds of tests, related to intelligence but designed to measure somewhat different phenomena, are achievement tests and aptitude tests. An **achievement test** is a test meant to ascertain a person's level of knowledge in a given subject area: Rather than measuring general ability as an intelligence test does, an achievement test concentrates on the specific material that a person has learned.

An **aptitude test** is designed to predict a person's ability in a particular area or line of work. You may already have taken the most famous aptitude test of them all: the Scholastic Aptitude Test, or SAT. The SAT is meant to predict how well people will do in college and has proved over the years to correlate moderately well with college grades.

Achievement test: A test intended to determine a person's level of knowledge in a given subject

Aptitude test: A test designed to predict ability in a particular line of work

Although in theory the distinction between intelligence, aptitude, and achievement tests can be precisely drawn, as a practical matter there is a good deal of overlap between them. For example, the SAT has been roundly criticized for being less of an aptitude test than one that actually measures achievement. It is difficult, then, to devise tests that predict future performance but do not rely on past achievement.

Alternative Formulations of Intelligence

Although Binet's procedure for measuring intelligence, exemplified by the modern Stanford-Binet and WAIS-R intelligence tests, remains one of the most frequently employed, some theorists argue that it lacks an underlying conception of what intelligence is. To Binet and his followers, intelligence was generally conceived of as a direct reflection of what score a person received on his test. That was an eminently practical approach, but it depends not on an understanding of the nature of intelligence but primarily on comparing one person's performance with that of others. For this reason, the intelligence tests of Binet and his successors do little to increase our understanding of what intelligence is all about; they merely measure behavior assumed to exemplify intelligence.

This does not mean, however, that researchers and theoreticians have ignored the question of what intelligence really is. One important issue for them is whether intelligence is a single, unitary factor, or whether it is made up of particular subdivisions (Weinberg, 1989; Brophy, 1992). The earliest psychologists interested in intelligence made the assumption that there was a general factor for mental ability, called **g**, or **g-factor** (Spearman, 1927). This factor was thought to underlie performance on every aspect of intelligence, and it was the g-factor that was presumably being measured on tests of intelligence.

More contemporary theoreticians have suggested that there are really two different kinds of intelligence: fluid intelligence and crystallized intelligence (Cattell, 1967, 1987). **Fluid intelligence** is the ability to deal with new problems and situations. If you were asked to group a series of letters according to some criterion or to remember a set of numbers, you would be using fluid intelligence. **Crystallized intelligence** is the store of information, skills, and strategies that people have acquired through their experience and use of fluid intelligence. You would be likely to rely on crystallized intelligence, for instance, if you were asked to argue about the causes of a social problem or to deduce the solution to a mystery, drawing upon your past unique experiences. The differences between fluid and crystallized intelligence become particularly evident in the elderly, who—as we will discuss further in Chapter 14—show declines in fluid, but not crystallized, intelligence (Horn, 1985).

Other theoreticians conceive of intelligence as encompassing even more subdivisions. For instance, by examining the talents of people who display unusual ability in certain areas (like Leslie Lemke, discussed at the start of the chapter) psychologist Howard Gardner has suggested that we have seven multiple intelligences, each relatively independent of the others (Gardner, 1983; Walters & Gardner, 1986; Krechevsky & Gardner, 1990). Specifically, he considers intelligence to include the seven spheres illustrated in Table 10-1.

Although Gardner illustrates the individual intelligences with descriptions of well-known people, it is important to remember that each of us theoretically harbors the same kinds of intelligence. Moreover, although the seven are presented individually, Gardner suggests that these separate intelligences do not operate in isolation. Normally, any activity encompasses several kinds of intelligence working together.

G or g-factor: A theoretical single general factor accounting for mental ability

Fluid intelligence: The ability to deal with new problems and encounters

Crystallized intelligence: The store of specific information, skills, and strategies that people have acquired through experience

Crystallized intelligence—the accumulation of information, skills, and strategies through experience—may be a particular advantage for this older woman attending college.

GARDNER'S SEVEN INTELLIGENCES

1. Musical intelligence (skills in tasks involving music). Case example:

   When he was 3, Yehudi Menuhin was smuggled into the San Francisco Orchestra concerts by his parents. The sound of Louis Persinger's violin so entranced the youngster that he insisted on a violin for his birthday and Louis Persinger as his teacher. He got both. By the time he was 10 years old, Menuhin was an international performer.

2. Bodily kinesthetic intelligence (skills in using the whole body or various portions of it in the solution of problems or in the construction of products or displays, exemplified by dancers, athletes, actors, and surgeons). Case example:

   Fifteen-year-old Babe Ruth played third base. During one game, his team's pitcher was doing very poorly and Babe loudly criticized him from third base. Brother Mathias, the coach, called out, "Ruth, if you know so much about it, *you* pitch!" Babe was surprised and embarrassed because he had never pitched before, but Brother Mathias insisted. Ruth said later that at the very moment he took the pitcher's mound, he *knew* he was supposed to be a pitcher.

3. Logical-mathematical intelligence (skills in problem-solving and scientific thinking). Case example:

   Barbara McClintock won the Nobel Prize in medicine for her work in microbiology. She describes one of her breakthroughs, which came after thinking about a problem for half an hour . . . : "Suddenly I jumped and ran back to the [corn] field. At the top of the field (the others were still at the bottom) I shouted, 'Eureka, I have it!' "

4. Linguistic intelligence (skills involved in the production and use of language). Case example:

   At the age of 10, T. S. Eliot created a magazine called *Fireside*, to which he was the sole contributor. In a three-day period during his winter vacation, he created eight complete issues.

5. Spatial intelligence (skills involving spatial configurations, such as those used by artists and architects). Case example:

   Navigation around the Caroline Islands . . . is accomplished without instruments. . . . During the actual trip, the navigator must envision mentally a reference island as it passes under a particular star and from that he computes the number of segments completed, the proportion of the trip remaining, and any corrections in heading.

6. Interpersonal intelligence (skills in interacting with others, such as sensitivity to the moods, temperaments, motivations, and intentions of others). Case example:

   When Anne Sullivan began instructing the deaf and blind Helen Keller, her task was one that had eluded others for years. Yet, just two weeks after beginning her work with Keller, Sullivan achieved a great success. In her words, "My heart is singing with joy this morning. A miracle has happened! The wild little creature of two weeks ago has been transformed into a gentle child."

7. Intrapersonal intelligence (knowledge of the internal aspects of oneself; access to one's own feelings and emotions). Case example:

   In her essay "A Sketch of the Past," Virginia Woolf displays deep insight into her own inner life through these lines, describing her reaction to several specific memories from her childhood that still, in adulthood, shock her: "Though I still have the peculiarity that I receive these sudden shocks, they are now always welcome; after the first surprise, I always feel instantly that they are particularly valuable. And so I go on to suppose that the shock-receiving capacity is what makes me a writer."

Source: Adapted from Walters & Gardner (1986).

Two men, involved for years in deep, romantic liaisons with their lovers, find that their relationships have suddenly ended. One says this:

> I felt empty, sad, confused, like my life had no meaning. It was as though a part of me were missing. But, after a while, I tried to put it in perspective. I used it as an opportunity to learn something about myself. In the depths of my depression, I felt miserable, but gradually thoughts about both the positive things I had done and the mistakes I had made came to me clear as a bell (Salovey & Mayer, 1991, p. 3)

The other has a very different reaction to the end of his relationship:

> So we broke up after six years. I don't know what got into her. The things she said! It was terrible, everything hurt—headaches, stomach aches, but who cares anyway? I don't even think about it anymore. That's life, I guess. Now I feel fine, really (Salovey & Mayer, 1991, p. 3).

These two individuals obviously view the end of their relationships from different perspectives. The first is able to discuss what he was feeling, and he seemed to discover

EMOTIONAL INTELLIGENCE: GETTING SMART ABOUT EMOTIONS

things about himself as a consequence of the experience. On the other hand, the second does not seem to have learned much. He explains his emotions in terms of ambiguous physical feelings, and he has little insight into the way in which his emotions have had an impact on his life.

To psychologists Peter Salovey and John Mayer, the two people differ in what they refer to as "emotional intelligence." Emotional intelligence is a set of skills that underlie the accurate assessment, evaluation, expression, and regulation of emotions (Salovey & Mayer, 1990).

Emotional intelligence allows people to actively employ their emotions to achieve desired goals. For example, rather than unproductively mulling over stressful events, reliving negative emotions, and speculating about causes, people with high emotional intelligence react differently. They are able to regulate and communicate their feelings in a way that results in fewer physical symptoms as a result of the stress (Goldman et al., 1991).

The concept of emotional intelligence fits with research that shows a relationship between people's general social competence and their skills at "reading" the meaning of nonverbal displays of emotions in others. Specifically, people who are adept at decoding the emotional content of others' facial expressions often show high social competence in terms of getting along well with others and of being likable themselves (Feldman, Philippot, & Custrini, 1991).

It is not yet clear how distinct emotional intelligence is from traditional conceptions of intelligence. However, it is likely that the two concepts tap abilities that are quite different. For example, it is not hard to think of people who are unusually bright but who lack sensitivity and skill in emotional realms. Conversely, one can imagine people who are quite sensitive to their own emotions, yet who are not extraordinarily intelligent in the traditional sense.

We are still far from the time when tests of emotional intelligence will be routinely employed. Indeed, no such tests have even been developed. Yet it is reasonable to assume that a person's emotional intelligence might be considered for certain kinds of jobs that require the ability to get along well with others.

Gardner's model has led to a number of advances in our understanding of the nature of intelligence. For example, one outgrowth of the model is the development of test items in which more than one answer can be correct, providing the opportunity for the demonstration of creative thinking. According to these approaches, then, different kinds of intelligence may produce different—but equally valid—responses to the same question. (For more on different kinds of intelligence, see the Cutting Edge box on emotional intelligence).

Is Information Processing Intelligence? Contemporary Approaches

The most recent contribution to understanding intelligence comes from the work of cognitive psychologists. Drawing on the research and theory that we discussed in Chapter 9, cognitive psychologists use an information-processing approach. They assert that the way people store material in memory and use the material to solve intellectual tasks provides the most accurate measure of intelligence (Sternberg, 1990). Rather than focusing on the structure of intelligence in the form of its underlying content or dimensions, cognitive approaches have examined the *processes* underlying intelligent behavior.

By breaking tasks and problems into their component parts and identifying the nature and speed of problem-solving processes, researchers have noted distinct differences between those who score high on traditional IQ tests and those who score lower. Take, for example, a college student who is asked to solve the following analogy problem (Sternberg, 1982):

lawyer is to *client* as *doctor* is to:

(a) *patient* or (b) *medicine*

According to Sternberg's theory, a student presented with this analogy tends to move through a series of stages in attempting to reach a solution (see Figure 10-3). First she will *encode* the initial information, which means providing each item with identifying cues that help retrieve relevant information buried in long-term memory. For instance, she may think of lawyer in terms of law school, the Supreme Court, "L.A. Law," and a courtroom. Each of the other terms will be similarly encoded. Next, she will *infer* any possible relationship between lawyer and client. She may infer that the relevant relationship is that a client employs a lawyer, or, alternatively, that a lawyer gives services to a client.

Once she has inferred the relationship, she must *map* the higher-order relationship between the first half of the analogy and the second half—both deal with people who provide professional services for a fee. The crucial stage that follows is one of *application*, in which she tries out each answer option with the relationship she has inferred. She will presumably decide that a doctor provides professional services to a patient, not to medicine. Finally, the last component of solving the problem is responding.

By breaking problems into component parts in this manner, it is possible to identify systematic differences in both quantitative and qualitative aspects of problem solving, and to demonstrate that people with higher intelligence levels differ not only in the number of correct solutions they come up with, but in their method of solving problems. For instance, high scorers are apt to spend more time on the initial encoding stages of a problem, identifying the parts of the problem and retrieving relevant information from long-term memory. This initial emphasis on recalling relevant information pays off in the end; those who spend relatively less time on the initial stages tend to be less able to find a solution. People's use of such information-processing strategies, therefore, may underlie differences in intelligence.

Applying this cognitive approach to intelligence, psychologist Robert Sternberg (1985a; 1991) developed what he calls a triarchic theory of intelligence. The **triarchic theory of intelligence** suggests that there are three major aspects to intelligence: componential, experiential, and contextual. The componential aspect focuses on the mental components involved in analyzing information to solve problems, particularly those processes operating when a person displays rational behavior. In contrast, the experiential aspect focuses on how a person's prior experiences affect intelligence, and how those experiences are brought to bear on problem-solving situations. Finally, the contextual aspect of intelligence takes into account how successful people are in facing the demands of their everyday environment.

Recent approaches to intelligence have focused most heavily on Sternberg's third aspect of intelligence (Sternberg & Detterman, 1986). Several new theories emphasize **practical intelligence**—intelligence related to overall success in living, rather than to intellectual and academic performance, as we discuss in the Psychology at Work box.

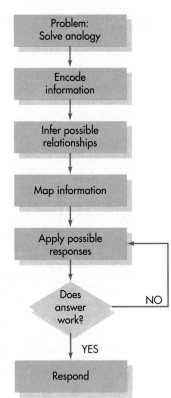

FIGURE 10-3
Information-processing stages in solving analogies (Sternberg, 1982.)

Triarchic theory of intelligence: A theory suggesting three major aspects of intelligence: componential, experiential, and contextual

Practical intelligence: Intelligence related to overall success in living, rather than to intellectual and academic performance

▶ **317**

Your year on the job has been generally favorable. Performance ratings for your department are at least as good as they were before you took over, and perhaps even a little better. You have two assistants. One is quite capable. The other just seems to go through the motions and is of little real help. Even though you are well liked, you believe that there is little that would distinguish you in the eyes of your superiors from the nine other managers at a comparable level in the company. Your goal is rapid promotion to an executive position. The following is a list of things you are considering doing. Rank the importance of each of these actions toward reaching your goal:

1. Find a way to get rid of the "deadwood"—namely, the less helpful assistant and three or four other employees in your department.
2. Participate in a series of panel discussions to be shown on the local public television station.
3. Find ways to make sure that your superiors are aware of your important accomplishments.
4. Accept a friend's invitation to join the exclusive country club that many higher-level executives belong to.
5. When making decisions, give a great deal of weight to the way your superiors like things done. (Based on Wagner & Sternberg, 1985, p. 447.)

The way in which you would answer this question may have a lot to do with your future success in a business career, at least according to its author, psychologist Robert J. Sternberg. (The optimal order of choices is

IS PRACTICAL INTELLIGENCE DIFFERENT FROM SCHOOL INTELLIGENCE?

given below.) In fact, the question is one of a series designed to help give an indication of your intelligence. It is not traditional intelligence that the question is designed to tap, but rather intelligence of a particular kind: practical intelligence for business (Sternberg & Wagner, 1986; Wagner & Sternberg, 1991).

The test that Sternberg has devised is one of several new intelligence measures now taking form. Each is designed to overcome one of the most glaring limitations of traditional IQ tests: Although literally hundreds of studies have shown that students with high IQs tend to get high grades and those with low IQs tend to be less successful in school, the fact remains that IQ does not relate to *career* success. For example, while it is clear that successful business executives usually score at least moderately well on IQ tests, the rate at which they advance and their ultimate business achievements are only minimally associated with their specific IQ scores.

A more significant influence, according to psychologist Siegfried Streufert (1984), is the way in which people approach problems and their style of thinking. This kind of intelligence is manifested in successful business leaders through a kind of cognitive complexity in decision making. Instead of being locked into a simple pattern of thinking, successful managers are able to acquire and integrate complex sets of information and to see with clarity the interrelationships among events. Rather than viewing problems in terms of a single goal or factor—such as profit making—leaders with high practical intelligence are able to coordinate differing goals simultaneously when devising solutions to problems.

Business is hardly the sole sphere in which this kind of practical intelligence is crucial, and some psychologists are working to develop tests that identify it in various domains of everyday life. For example, Seymour Epstein has developed a test of what he terms "constructive thinking," in which life success can be predicted. Here are some of the kinds of items found on the test (Epstein & Meier, 1989, p. 350):

1. I am the kind of person who takes action rather than just thinks or complains about a situation. Agree or disagree?
2. I don't let little things bother me. Agree or disagree?
3. I tend to take things personally. Agree or disagree?
4. I get so distressed when I notice that I am doing poorly in something that it makes me do worse. Agree or disagree?

According to Epstein, his test assesses such attributes as happiness with social relationships, job success, and even physical and emotional health. His data indicate that the test is far more predictive of actual success in life than traditional IQ tests are.

In sum, it is clear that there are many ways to demonstrate—and measure—intelligence. A high IQ does not guarantee success in life, especially if it accompanies low practical intelligence.

(By the way, the optimum order of choices for Sternberg's test of practical intelligence for business is 5, 1, 3, 2, 4. In Epstein's test of constructive thinking, the ideal choices are (1) agree, (2) agree, (3) disagree, and (4) disagree. Keep in mind that because these items represent such a small sample of Sternberg's and Epstein's measures, it is impossible to infer how you might score on the complete tests.)

Students at Southern Connecticut State University labor over a standardized test.

The Informed Consumer of Psychology: Can You Do Better on Standardized Tests?

Even though psychologists disagree about the nature of intelligence, intelligence tests—as well as many other kinds of tests—are still widely used in a variety of situations. In school or on the job, almost all of us have had to cope with these widely used, formal, standardized tests—tests that have been formulated and verified with large representative samples. And most of us can probably understand the concern of students taking college entrance exams, such as the Scholastic Aptitude Test (SAT), who worry that success in their future lives hangs on one morning's test results.

One outcome of the prevalence of tests in our society is the development of numerous coaching services that purport to train people to raise their scores by reviewing basic skills and teaching test-taking strategies. But do they work?

Although the Educational Testing Service (ETS), the creators of the SAT, at one time suggested that coaching for the test was useless, today it holds a more positive attitude regarding the practice. While still suggesting that the SAT measures underlying competencies so fundamental that a course of a few weeks' duration will provide little advantage, ETS concedes that the practice in test taking provided during the course may have a slightly beneficial effect. But ETS goes on to point out that the coaching required to bring about average score increases of more than twenty to thirty points is so extensive that it would be the equivalent of going to school full time (Messick & Jungeblut, 1981).

Most research carried out by psychologists verifies that coaching for the SAT exams produces small effects—usually in the range of fifteen-point increases in verbal and math scores (Kulik, Bangert-Drowns, & Kulik, 1984). On the other hand, research also shows that coaching on other sorts of aptitude and intelligence tests can result in more substantial increases in test scores.

Since some kinds of coaching do help raise the scores people receive on tests, one crucial concern is to determine what kind of coaching is most likely to be effective. Among the points to consider when deciding whether coaching will be an effective and useful strategy for raising your score on an upcoming test are whether the instruction addresses the basic areas covered by the test, particularly those in which you are rusty and may need drill and practice; whether the course is geared to the specific test; whether the instructor has recent public versions of the test that can be used for practice with the mechanics of the test itself; and whether there are data to show that this particular coaching service has previously produced significant gains in scores. Finally, you must ask yourself whether it is worth the cost in time and money to end up with only a small gain on the test—particularly in view of the fact that most people have higher test scores the second time they take a test whether they are coached or not.

Only careful research can answer these questions, and it is wise to be skeptical of the claims of coaches. At the same time, there are certain steps you can take, without the benefit of coaching, to maximize your opportunity to score well on standardized tests. For example, these four points provide good advice for anyone taking standardized tests—as well as any other test, for that matter (Crocetti, 1983):

■ Preview each section. Not only will it give you a chance to take a deep breath and prevent you from frantically rushing through the section, it will also alert you to any unexpected changes in the test format. Previewing will give you a sense of what to expect as you work through each problem.

■ Time yourself carefully. The computer that scores your test will not care how deeply you have thought out and considered each answer; all it notes is whether or not you have answered a problem correctly. Therefore, it is important not to spend too much time on initial problems at the expense of later ones. If you are unsure of an answer, try to narrow down the options, then guess and go on to the next problem. Perfection is not your goal; maximizing the number of correct responses is.

■ Check the test-scoring policy to determine whether guessing is appropriate. On the Scholastic Aptitude Test, wrong answers are subtracted from your score, making blind guessing a bad strategy. In comparison, the Graduate Record Exam and many other tests do not penalize you for wrong answers. On tests with penalties for wrong answers, guess only if you can narrow the choices down to two or three. On the other hand, for tests in which wrong answers do not lower your score, it pays to guess, even if you have no idea of the correct response.

■ Complete answer sheets accurately. Obviously, it makes sense to check your answer sheet when you have finished the test. It is also a good idea to write your answers in the test booklet itself, so that when you go back to review your answers you won't have to refer to the answer sheet.

These tips won't ensure a high score on the next test you take, but they will help to maximize your opportunity for better performance.

RECAP AND REVIEW I

RECAP

◄ Intelligence is the capacity to understand the world, think rationally, and use resources effectively when faced with challenges.

◄ The measure of intelligence used in tests is the intelligence quotient, or IQ.

◄ There are a number of alternative formulations of intelligence, including models which look at the components of intelligence and models which suggest that information-processing strategies provide the most useful understanding of intelligence.

◄ Coaching has some impact on improving test scores, although there is wide variability in its effectiveness.

1. _____ is a measure of intelligence that takes into account both a person's chronological and mental ages.
2. Group intelligence testing has been found to be generally superior to individual testing. True or false?

_____

3. _____ tests predict a person's ability in a specific area, while _____ tests determine the specific level of knowledge in an area.
4. Some psychologists make the distinction between _____ intelligence, which deals with information and skill storage, and _____

intelligence, which is the ability to deal with novel problems.
5. Cognitive psychologists use an _____ _____ approach to measure intelligence.
6. _____ intelligence is that type of intelligence related to success in everyday living.
7. IQ is not related to success in one's career. True or false?

_____

Ask Yourself

If such concepts as fluid and crystallized intelligence do exist, how might they be tested? What applications would each of these types of intelligence have?

(Answers to review questions are on page 322.)

VARIATIONS IN INTELLECTUAL ABILITY

Bill never liked school much. For the first few years he managed to get by, although his parents had to push hard to get him to do a minimally acceptable level of first- and second-grade work. He seemed slower at learning things that the other kids had no trouble with, and—although he wasn't exactly a poorly behaved child—his attention span was short and he had trouble following what was going on in class. He also seemed tired much of the time, but a physical examination ruled out any medical problems. His teachers began to suspect he was simply lazy and unmotivated, though he did, on occasion, show great interest in lessons that involved working with his hands. Finally, out of desperation, his teachers and parents arranged for him to be evaluated by a psychologist. To their surprise, they found out he had an IQ of 63— so far below average that it fell into the range of IQ scores classified as mentally retarded.

Bill is one of more than 7 million people in the United States who have been identified as having intelligence far enough below average for it to be regarded as a serious deficit. Both those people with low IQs, known as the mentally retarded, and those with unusually high IQs, referred to as the intellectually gifted, make up groups of individuals who require special attention to reach their full potential.

Mental Retardation

Although sometimes thought of as a rare phenomenon, mental retardation occurs in 1 to 3 percent of the population. There is wide variation among those labeled as mentally retarded, in large part because of the inclusiveness of the definition developed by the American Association on Mental Deficiency. The association suggests that **mental retardation** exists when there is "significantly subaverage general intellectual functioning existing concurrently with deficits in adaptive behavior and manifested during the developmental period" (Grossman, 1983). What this means is that people classified as mentally retarded can range from individuals whose performance differs little in a qualitative sense from those with higher IQs, to those who virtually cannot be trained and who must receive institutional treatment throughout their lives (Matson & Mulick, 1991).

Most mentally retarded people have relatively minor deficits and are classified as having **mild retardation**. These individuals have IQ scores ranging from 55 to 69, and they constitute some 90 percent of all retarded individuals. Although their development is typically slower than that of their peers, they can

Mental retardation: A significantly subaverage level of intellectual functioning accompanying deficits in adaptive behavior

Mild retardation: Mental retardation characterized by an IQ between 55 and 69 and the ability to function independently

▶ **321**

These Mill Valley, California, teenagers are brother and sister. The girl suffers from Down syndrome, a disorder associated with mental retardation and a cluster of physical characteristics.

Moderate retardation: Mental retardation characterized by an IQ between 40 and 54

Severe retardation: Mental retardation characterized by an IQ between 25 and 39 and difficulty in functioning independently

Profound retardation: Mental retardation characterized by an IQ below 25 and an inability to function independently

Down syndrome: A common cause of mental retardation, brought about by the presence of an extra chromosome

Familial retardation: Mental retardation in which there is a history of retardation in a family but no evidence of biological causes

function quite independently by adulthood and are able to hold jobs and have families of their own.

At greater levels of retardation—**moderate retardation** (IQs of 40 to 54), **severe retardation** (IQs of 25 to 39), and **profound retardation** (IQs below 25)— the difficulties are more pronounced. With the moderately retarded, deficits are obvious early, with language and motor skills lagging behind those of peers. Although these people can hold simple jobs, they need to have a moderate degree of supervision throughout their lives. The severely and profoundly retarded are generally unable to function independently. Often they have no language skills, poor motor control, and even an inability to be toilet-trained. These people are typically institutionalized for their entire lives.

What are the causes of mental retardation? In nearly one-third of the cases there is a known biological cause, the most common being Down syndrome. **Down syndrome**, which was once referred to as mongolism (because those with the disorder were viewed as having an Asian facial configuration) is caused by the presence of an extra chromosome (Cicchetti & Beeghly, 1990). In other cases of mental retardation, an abnormality occurs in the structure of a chromosome (Oberle et al., 1991; Yu et al., 1991). Birth complications, such as a temporary lack of oxygen, may also cause retardation.

The majority of cases of mental retardation are classified as familial retardation. In **familial retardation**, retarded people have no known biological defect, but do have a history of retardation within their families. Whether their families' backgrounds of retardation are caused by environmental factors, such as extreme continuous poverty leading to malnutrition, or by some underlying genetic factor is usually impossible to determine for certain. What is characteristic of familial retardation is the presence of more than one retarded person in the immediate family.

Regardless of the cause of mental retardation, important advances in the care and treatment of the mentally retarded have been made in the last fifteen

ANSWERS (REVIEW I):

1. IQ **2.** False; individual testing is generally more accurate than group tests. **3.** Aptitude; achievement **4.** crystallized; fluid **5.** information processing **6.** Practical **7.** True

years (Turkington, 1987; Garber, 1988; Landesman & Ramey, 1989). Much of this change was instigated by the Education for All Handicapped Children Act of 1975 (Public Law 94-142). In this federal law, Congress ruled that the mentally retarded are entitled to a full education and that they must be educated and trained in the **least-restrictive environment**. The law increased the educational opportunities for the retarded, facilitating their integration into regular classrooms as much as possible—a process known as **mainstreaming**.

The philosophy behind mainstreaming suggests that the interaction of retarded and nonretarded students in regular classrooms will improve the educational opportunities for the mentally retarded, increase their social acceptance, and facilitate their integration into society as a whole. The philosophy was once to segregate the retarded into special-education classes where they could learn at their own pace along with other handicapped students. Mainstreaming attempts to prevent the isolation inherent in special-education classes and to reduce the social stigma of retardation by allowing the handicapped to interact with their age peers as much as possible (Mastropieri & Scruggs, 1987).

Of course, there are still special-education classes; some retarded individuals function at too low a level to benefit from placement in regular classrooms. Moreover, retarded children mainstreamed into regular classes typically attend special classes for at least part of the day. Still, mainstreaming holds the promise of increasing the integration of the mentally retarded into society and allowing them to make their own contributions to the world at large.

The Intellectually Gifted

While the uniqueness of the mentally retarded is readily apparent, members of another group differ equally from the norm. Instead of having low intelligence, the **intellectually gifted** have substantially higher-than-average intelligence.

Comprising 2 to 4 percent of the population, the intellectually gifted have IQ scores greater than 130. The stereotype associated with the gifted suggests that they are awkward, shy, social misfits unable to get along well with peers, but most research suggests just the opposite: The intellectually gifted are outgoing, well-adjusted, popular people who are able to do most things better than the average person (Stanley, 1980; Horowitz & O'Brien, 1987).

Least-restrictive environment: The official phrase from PL94-142 that guarantees the right of full education for retarded people in an environment that is most similar to the educational environment of typical children

Mainstreaming: The integration of retarded people into regular classroom situations

Intellectually gifted: Individuals characterized by higher-than-average intelligence, with IQ scores above 130

Children who display high intelligence are sometimes placed in special classes or programs to help them develop their potential.

▶ **323**

For example, in a long-term study by Lewis Terman that started in the early 1920s and is still going on, 1500 children who had IQ scores above 140 were followed and examined periodically through the next sixty years (Sears, 1977; Terman & Oden, 1947). From the very start, members of this group were physically, academically, and socially more able than their nongifted peers. They were generally healthier, taller, heavier, and stronger than average. Not surprisingly, they did better in school as well. They also showed better social adjustment than average. And all these advantages paid off in terms of career success: As a group, the gifted received more awards and distinctions, earned higher incomes, and made more contributions in art and literature than typical individuals. For example, by the time the members of the group were 40 years old, they had collectively written more than ninety books, 375 plays and short stories, and 2000 articles, and had registered more than 200 patents. Perhaps most important, they reported greater satisfaction in life than the nongifted.

On the other hand, the picture of these intellectually gifted people was not unvaryingly positive. Not every member of the group Terman studied was successful, and in fact there were some notable failures. Moreover, other research suggests that high intelligence is not a homogeneous quality; a person with a high overall IQ is not necessarily gifted in every academic subject but may excel in just one or two (Stanley, 1980; Sternberg & Davidson, 1986). A high IQ, then, does not guarantee success in everything.

Although special programs attempting to overcome the deficits of the mentally retarded abound, only recently have ways of encouraging the talents of the intellectually gifted been developed. This lack of special attention has been due in part to the persistent view that the gifted ought to be able to "make it on their own"; if they can't, then they really weren't gifted in the first place (Maeroff, 1977; Berger, 1988). More enlightened approaches, however, have acknowledged that without some form of special attention, the gifted may become bored and frustrated with the pace of their schooling and may never reach their full potential (Reis, 1989; Borland, 1989).

One particularly successful program for the intellectually gifted is a project called the Study of the Mathematically Precocious Youth (SMPY). In the program, seventh-graders who have shown unusual mathematical ability are enrolled in summer classes in which they are rapidly taught complex mathematical skills, culminating in college-level calculus (Stanley, 1980). In addition, they receive instruction in a variety of other subjects, including the sciences and languages. The ultimate goal of the program, and others like it, is to provide sufficient enrichment and acceleration to the gifted to allow their talents to flourish and to increase the likelihood that they will reach their maximum potential. Although it is too early to tell whether enrichment programs such as SMPY are effective—since the graduates of these programs have yet to reach adulthood—such special programs are rated highly by participants.

RECAP AND REVIEW II

RECAP

◀ Mental retardation is defined by significantly subaverage general intellectual functioning along with deficits in adaptive behavior.

◀ The levels of retardation include mildly retarded (IQ of 55 to 69), moderately retarded (IQ of 40 to 54), severely retarded (IQ of 25 to 39), and profoundly retarded (IQ below 25).

◀ The most frequent causes of mental retardation are Down syndrome and familial influences.

◀ The intellectually gifted have IQs above 130 and comprise 2 to 4 percent of the population.

1. Mental retardation refers specifically to those people with an IQ below 60. True or false? _____
2. _____ _____ is a disorder caused by an extra chromosome that is responsible for some cases of mental retardation.
3. _____ is the process by which mentally retarded students are placed in normal classrooms to facilitate learning and reduce isolation.
4. Retardation can have a genetic base, and can be passed through entire families. True or false? _____
5. _____ is the term used to describe those people with an IQ of 130 or more.
6. People with high intelligence are generally shy and socially withdrawn. True or false? _____

Ask Yourself

The federal government today announced a $10 billion program designed to give aid to special schools in which gifted students can be enrolled. These schools will be designed to help gifted students achieve their maximum potential in specific areas in which they are the strongest. The schools will be offered free to such students, with a special tax being levied to pay for this project. The assumption behind these schools is that the productivity of such students in later years will more than make up for the loss of money in the present. What benefits could come from such a program? What drawbacks might occur?

(Answers to review questions are on page 326.)

INDIVIDUAL DIFFERENCES IN INTELLIGENCE: HEREDITY, ENVIRONMENT—OR BOTH?

Kwang is often washed with a pleck tied to a _____.
- (a) rundel
- (b) flink
- (c) pove
- (d) quirj

If you found this kind of item on an intelligence test, you would probably complain that the test was totally absurd and had nothing to do with your intelligence or anyone else's. How could anyone be expected to respond to items presented in a language that was so unfamiliar?

But suppose you found the following item, which at first glance might look equally foreign:

Which word is most out of place here?
- (a) splib
- (b) blood
- (c) gray
- (d) spook

Just as absurd, you say? On the contrary, there is considerably more reason to use this second item on an intelligence test than the first example, which was made up of nonsense syllables. Although this second item may appear as meaningless as the first to most of the white population of the United States, to urban African-Americans the question might be a reasonable test of their knowledge.

The second item is drawn from a test created by sociologist Adrian Dove, who tried to illustrate a problem that has plagued the developers of IQ tests from the beginning. By using terminology that would be familiar to urban African-Americans with inner-city backgrounds, but typically unfamiliar to whites (and to African-Americans raised within the dominant white culture), he dramatized the fact that cultural experience could play a critical role in determining intelligence test scores. (The answer to the item presented above, by the way, is *c*. To try your hand at other items drawn from Dove's test, see Table 10-2.)

▶ **325**

A CULTURE-*UNFAIR* INTELLIGENCE TEST

If you have been raised within the dominant white culture, particularly in a suburban or rural environment, you may have difficulty in answering the following questions, which are designed to illustrate the importance of devising culture-fair intelligence tests.

1. Bird, or Yardbird, was the jacket that jazz lovers from coast to coast hung on
   (a) Lester Young
   (b) Peggy Lee
   (c) Benny Goodman
   (d) Charlie Parker
   (e) Birdman of Alcatraz

2. The opposite of square is
   (a) Round
   (b) Up
   (c) Down
   (d) Hip
   (e) Lame

3. If you throw the dice and 7 is showing on the top, what is facing down?
   (a) 7
   (b) Snake eyes
   (c) Boxcars
   (d) Little Joes
   (e) 11

4. Jazz pianist Ahmad Jamal took an Arabic name after becoming really famous. Previously he had what he called his "slave name." What was his previous name?
   (a) Willie Lee Jackson
   (b) LeRoi Jones
   (c) Wilbur McDougal
   (d) Fritz Jones
   (e) Andy Johnson

5. In C. C. Rider, what does "C. C." stand for?
   (a) Civil Service
   (b) Church Council
   (c) County Circuit Preacher
   (d) Country Club
   (e) Cheating Charley (the "Boxcar Gunsel")

Answers It is obvious how this test illustrates, in an exaggerated reverse fashion, the difficulties that an African-American from an inner-city background might have in responding to items on the typical intelligence test, which mirrors the dominant middle- and upper-class white culture. The correct answers are **1.** *d;* **2.** *d;* **3.** *a;* **4.** *d;* **5.** *c.* (Dove, 1968)

The issue of devising fair intelligence tests that measure knowledge unrelated to cultural and family background and experience would be minor if it were not for one important and persistent finding: Members of certain racial and cultural groups consistently score lower on intelligence tests than members of other groups (MacKenzie, 1984). For example, as a group, African-Americans tend to average fifteen IQ points lower than whites. Does this reflect a true

ANSWERS (REVIEW II):

1. False; the term is used to describe a wide range of people with various degrees of mental impairment. **2.** Down syndrome **3.** Mainstreaming **4.** True **5.** Gifted **6.** False; the gifted are generally more socially adept than those of lower IQ.

difference in intelligence, or are the questions biased in the kinds of knowledge they test? Clearly, if whites perform better because of their greater familiarity with the kind of information that is being tested, their higher IQ scores are not necessarily an indication that they are more intelligent than members of other groups.

There is good reason to believe that some standardized IQ tests contain elements that discriminate against minority-group members whose experiences differ from those of the white majority. Consider the question "What would you do if another child grabbed your hat and ran with it?" Most white middle-class children answer that they would tell an adult, and this response is scored as "correct." On the other hand, a reasonable response might be to chase the person and fight to get the hat back, the answer that is chosen by many urban African-American children—but one that is scored as incorrect (Albee, 1978; Miller-Jones, 1989).

The possibility of bias and discrimination against minority-group members in traditional IQ tests has led some jurisdictions to ban their use. For example, the state of California does not permit public schools to give African-American students IQ tests to decide whether they should be placed in special-education classes—regardless of the students' academic background or socioeconomic status, or even following parental request—unless express permission is obtained from the courts (Baker, 1987). (Ironically, because the ban pertains only to African-American students, and not to whites, Hispanics, and other racial and ethnic groups, some people have argued that the ban itself is discriminatory.)

The Basic Controversy: The Relative Influence of Heredity and of Environment

In an attempt to produce what has come to be called a **culture-fair IQ test**, one that does not discriminate against members of any minority group, psychologists have tried to devise test items which assess experiences common to all cultures or which emphasize questions that do not require language usage. However, test makers have found this difficult to do, and some culture-fair tests have produced even larger discrepancies between majority and minority groups than traditional tests which rely more heavily on verbal skills (Anastasi, 1988).

The efforts of psychologists to produce culture-fair measures of intelligence relate to a lingering controversy over differences in intelligence between members of minority and majority groups. In attempting to identify whether there are differences between such groups, psychologists have had to confront the broader issue of determining the relative contribution to intelligence of genetic factors (heredity) and experience (environment).

Arthur Jensen, an educational psychologist, fueled the fires of the debate with a 1969 article. He argued that an analysis of IQ differences between whites and African-Americans demonstrated that, although environmental factors played a role, there were also basic genetic differences between the two races. Jensen based his argument on a number of findings. For instance, on average, whites score fifteen points higher than African-Americans on traditional IQ tests even when socioeconomic class is taken into account. According to Jensen, middle- and upper-class African-Americans score lower than middle- and upper-class whites, just as lower-class African-Americans score lower on average than lower-class whites. Intelligence differences between African-Americans and whites, Jensen concluded, could not be attributed to environmental differences alone.

Moreover, intelligence in general shows a high degree of **heritability**, a measure of the degree to which a characteristic is related to genetic, inherited factors

Culture-fair IQ test: A test that does not discriminate against members of any minority culture group

Heritability: A measure of the degree to which a characteristic is related to genetic, inherited factors as opposed to environmental factors

FIGURE 10-4

Summary findings on IQ and closeness of genetic relationship. The length of the line indicates the range of correlations found in different studies, and the arrows show the average correlation. Note, for example, that the average correlation for unrelated people reared apart is quite low, while the correlation for identical twins reared together is substantially higher. The more similar the genetic and environmental background of two people, the greater the correlation. (Jencks et al., 1972; Kamin, 1979; Walker & Emory, 1985; Scarr & Carter-Saltzmann, 1985; Bouchard et al., 1990.)

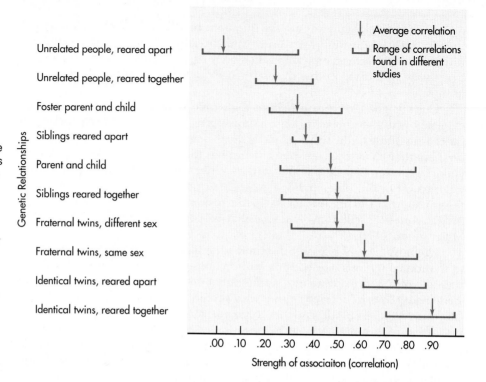

(e.g., Bouchard, 1990). As can be seen in Figure 10-4, the closer the genetic link between two people, the greater the correspondence of IQ scores. Using data such as these, Jensen argued that fully 75 to 80 percent of the variability in IQ scores could be attributed solely to genetic factors. On the basis of such evidence, Jensen claimed that differences between races in IQ scores were caused by genetically based differences in intelligence.

The psychology community reacted quickly to Jensen's contentions and convincingly refuted many of his claims. For one thing, even when socioeconomic conditions are supposedly held constant, wide variations remain among individual households, and no one can convincingly assert that living conditions of African-Americans and whites are identical even when their socioeconomic status is similar. Second, as we discussed earlier, there is reason to believe that traditional IQ tests may discriminate against lower-class urban African-Americans by asking for information pertaining to experiences they are unlikely to have had.

Moreover, there is direct evidence that African-Americans who are raised in enriched environments do not tend, as a group, to have lower IQ scores than whites in similar environments. For example, a study by Sandra Scarr and Richard Weinberg examined African-American children who were adopted at an early age by white middle-class families of above-average intelligence (Scarr & Weinberg, 1976). The IQ scores of the children averaged 106—about fifteen points above the average IQ scores of unadopted African-American children reared in their own homes, and above the average in scores of the general population. In addition, the younger a child's age at adoption, the higher his or her IQ score tended to be. The evidence that genetic factors play the major role in determining racial differences in IQ, then, is not compelling, although the question still evokes controversy (MacKenzie, 1984).

Ultimately, it is crucial to remember that IQ scores and intelligence have greatest relevance in terms of individuals, not groups, and that by far the greatest

The gap which existed in scholarly achievement between African-American and white students appears to be narrowing. These graduates are about to receive diplomas from the UCLA School of Social Welfare.

discrepancies in IQ occur not among mean *group* IQ scores but among the IQ scores of *individuals*. There are African-Americans who score high on IQ tests and whites who score low, just as there are whites who score high and African-Americans who score low. For the concept of intelligence to aid in the betterment of society, we must examine how *individuals* perform, not the groups to which they belong, as well as the degree to which intelligence can be enhanced in a given person (Angoff, 1988).

Other issues make the heredity-versus-environment debate somewhat irrelevant to practical concerns. For example, as we discussed earlier, there are multiple kinds of intelligence, and traditional IQ scores do not tap many of them. Furthermore, some psychologists argue that IQ scores are only weakly linked to intelligence, and IQ scores are often inadequate predictors of ultimate work and academic success (Flynn, 1987). Finally, actual school achievement differences between whites and African-Americans appear to be narrowing (Jones, 1984). In sum, questions concerning differences in white and African-American intelligence levels may prove to be less pertinent than those relating to understanding individual differences in IQ, without regard to race.

Placing the Heredity/Environment Question in Perspective

There is no absolute resolution to the question of the degree to which intelligence is influenced by heredity and by environment. We are dealing with an issue for which experiments to determine cause and effect unambiguously cannot be devised. (A moment's thought about how we might experimentally assign infants to enriched or deprived environments will reveal the impossibility of devising ethically reasonable experiments!)

The more critical question to ask, then, is not whether it is primarily heredity or environment that underlies intelligence but whether there is anything we can do to maximize the intellectual development of each individual (Scarr & Carter-Saltzman, 1982; Angoff, 1988). We then will be able to make changes in the environment—which may take the form of enriched home and school environments—that can lead each person to reach his or her highest potential.

RECAP

◄ The issue of whether IQ tests are biased in favor of dominant groups in society arises because African-Americans tend to average fifteen IQ points lower than whites on standardized tests.

◄ Culture-fair IQ tests have been developed in an attempt to avoid discriminating against minority groups.

◄ Probably the most important issue concerning IQ is not the degree to which it is influenced by heredity or the environment, but what we can do to nurture and maximize the development of intelligence in all individuals.

REVIEW

1. Intelligence tests may be biased toward the prevailing culture in such a way that minorities are put at a disadvantage when taking these tests. True or false? _____

2. A _____-_____ test tries to use only questions appropriate to all people taking the test.

3. IQ tests can accurately determine the intelligence of entire groups of people. True or false? _____

4. Intelligence can be seen as a combination of _____ and _____ factors.

Ask Yourself

Industrial psychologists use a variety of tests to determine job hirings, promotions, etc. Armed with what you know about intelligence testing, you are asked to oversee the testing program for promotion to management positions at IBM. What recommendations would you make for this program?

(Answers to review questions are on page 331.)

■ *How do psychologists conceptualize and define intelligence?*

1. Because intelligence can take many forms, defining it presents a challenge to psychologists. One commonly accepted view is that intelligence is the capacity to understand the world, think rationally, and use resources effectively when faced with challenges.

■ *What are the major approaches to measuring intelligence?*

2. Intelligence tests are used to measure intelligence. They provide a mental age which, when divided by a person's chronological age and then multiplied by 100, gives an IQ, or intelligence quotient, score. Specific tests of intelligence include the Stanford-Binet test, the Wechsler Adult Intelligence Scale—Revised (WAIS-R), and the Wechsler Intelligence Scale for Children—III (WISC-III). In addition to intelligence tests, other standardized tests take the form of achievement tests (which measure level of knowledge in a given area) and aptitude tests (which predict ability in a given area).

3. Although intelligence tests are able to identify individual differences in intelligence, they do not provide us with an understanding of the underlying nature of intelligence. One of the major issues here is whether there is a single, unitary factor underlying intelligence or whether intelligence is made up of particular components.

4. The earliest psychologists interested in intelligence made the assumption that there was a general factor for mental ability called *g*. However, later psychologists disputed the view that intelligence was unidimensional.

5. Some researchers suggest that there are two kinds of intelligence: fluid intelligence and crystallized intelligence. Gardner's theory of multiple intelligences proposes that there are seven spheres of intelligence: musical, bodily kinesthetic, logical-mathematical, linguistic, spatial, interpersonal, and intrapersonal.

6. Information-processing approaches suggest that intelligence should be conceptualized as the way in which people represent and use material cognitively. Rather than focusing on the structure of intelligence, they examine the processes underlying intelligent behavior. One example of an information- processing approach is Sternberg's triarchic theory of intelligence, which suggests three major aspects to intelligence: componential, experiential, and contextual.

■ *How can the extremes of intelligence be differentiated, and what are some of the special programs designed to help people maximize their full potential?*

7. At the two extremes of intelligence are the mentally retarded and the intellectually gifted. The levels of mental retardation include mild retardation (IQ of 55 to 69), moderate retardation (IQ of 40 to 54), severe retardation (IQ of 25 to 39), and profound retardation (IQ below 25). About one-third of the cases of retardation have a known biological cause; Down syndrome is the most common. Most cases, however, are classified as ones of familial retardation, in which there is no known biological cause.

8. There have been a number of recent advances in the treatment of both the mentally retarded and the intellectually gifted, particularly after federal law mandated that the mentally retarded be educated in the least-restrictive environment. In mainstreaming, the mentally retarded are integrated into regular education classrooms as much as possible.

■ *Are traditional IQ tests culturally biased?*

9. Traditional intelligence tests have frequently been criticized for being biased in favor of the white middle-class population majority. That controversy has led to attempts to devise culture-fair tests, IQ measures which avoid questions that depend on a particular cultural background.

■ *Are there racial differences in intelligence, and to what degree is intelligence influenced by the environment and by heredity?*

10. Issues of race and environmental and genetic influences on intelligence represent major controversies. Because individual IQ scores vary far more than group IQ scores, it is most critical to ask what we can do to maximize the intellectual development of each individual.

KEY TERMS AND CONCEPTS

intelligence (p. 310)
intelligence tests (p. 310)
mental age (p. 311)
chronological age (p. 311)
intelligence quotient (IQ) score (p. 311)
deviation IQ score (p. 311)
Stanford-Binet test (p. 312)
Wechsler Adult Intelligence Scale—Revised (WAIS-R) (p. 312)
Wechsler Intelligence Scale for Children—III (WISC-III) (p. 312)

achievement test (p. 313)
aptitude test (p. 313)
g or g-factor (p. 314)
fluid intelligence (p. 314)
crystallized intelligence (p. 314)
triarchic theory of intelligence (p. 317)
practical intelligence (p. 317)
mental retardation (p. 321)
mild retardation (p. 321)
moderate retardation (p. 322)

severe retardation (p. 322)
profound retardation (p. 322)
Down syndrome (p. 322)
familial retardation (p. 322)
least-restrictive environment (p. 323)
mainstreaming (p. 323)
intellectually gifted (p. 323)
culture-fair IQ test (p. 327)
heritability (p. 327)

ANSWERS (REVIEW III):

1. True **2.** culture-fair **3.** False; IQ tests are used to measure individual intelligence. Within any group there are wide variations in individual intelligence. **4.** hereditary; environmental

MOTIVATION AND EMOTION

Peter Potterfield.

PETER POTTERFIELD

I'll never forget that bottle, the look of it, the magic weight of it. I unscrewed the lid and began drinking. Never had anything tasted so sweet, been so quenching, provided so much relief. I drank in long gulps, stopping halfway through to breathe before finishing it off in another series of gulps.

"Got any more?" I asked. He handed me another bottle, which I drank in one chug-a-lug, leaving just a little to pour on my overheated head. I felt like a new man. (Potterfield, 1991, p. 193.)

For Peter Potterfield, that drink of water represented life itself. An experienced rock climber, Potterfield had suffered an agonizing fall onto a narrow crest of Chimney Rock in the Cascade Mountains. Near death, with broken bones protruding from his body, Potterfield struggled to remain conscious while his climbing partner sought help. Potterfield knew that water was crucial to his survival, and he hoarded his meager supplies for hours. Eventually, though, his water ran out, and he lay on his small perch, baking in the unblinking sunlight.

As day turned into night, Potterfield's thoughts were consumed by his thirst. As he later wrote, "For the first time, I knew what thirst really was, and it was a deranging agony. Imagining beverages I might be having at home—cranberry juice with club soda, or large glasses of ice water with lime—I conjured up in detail how they would look and taste. Each time I swallowed, the parched tissues of my mouth and throat rasped, and sometimes I gagged" (p. 186).

It was almost twenty-four hours after his accident that Potterfield finally received the liquid he craved so strongly, as rescuers, dropped by helicopter, reached him at last. He downed a gallon of water in just a half-hour. And just in time: His kidneys were on the verge of shutting down.

LOOKING AHEAD

What was it that made Potterfield crave the water that he needed after his accident? Why did he pursue rock climbing as a hobby in the first place? And what produced his tremendous will to live, enabling him to survive under such inhospitable conditions?

In this chapter, we consider the processes that underlie motivation, as well as the related topic of emotion. **Motivation** looks at the factors that direct and energize the behavior of humans and other organisms.

Psychologists who study motivation seek to discover the **motives**, or desired goals, that underlie behavior. Such motives may be represented by behavior as basic as drinking to satisfy thirst or as inconsequential as taking a walk to obtain exercise. To the psychologist specializing in the study of motivation, underlying motives are assumed to steer the choice of activities.

The study of motivation, then, consists of identifying why people do the things they do. Psychologists studying motivation ask questions such as these: "Why do people choose particular goals for which to strive?" "What specific motives direct behavior?" "What are the individual differences in motivation that account for the variability in people's behavior?"

Motivation: The factors that direct and energize behavior

Motives: Desired goals that prompt behavior

Whereas motivation is concerned with the forces that direct future behavior, emotion pertains to the feelings we experience throughout the course of our lives. The study of emotions focuses on our internal experiences at any given moment. Most of us have felt a variety of emotions: happiness at getting an A on a difficult exam, sadness brought about by the death of a loved one, anger at being unfairly treated. Because emotions not only can motivate our behavior but also can reflect our underlying motivation, they play a broad role in our lives, and the study of emotions has been a critical area for psychologists.

In this chapter, we consider motivation and emotion. We begin by focusing on the major conceptions of motivation, discussing how the different motives and needs people experience jointly affect behavior. We consider both primary motives—those that are biologically based and universal, such as hunger—and motives that are unique to humans—the need for achievement, the need for affiliation, and the need for power. We then turn to the nature of emotional experience on both a physiological and a cognitive level. We consider the roles and functions that emotions play in people's lives, discussing a number of theories meant to explain how people understand what emotion they are experiencing at a given moment. Finally, the chapter ends with a discussion of how emotions are communicated to others through nonverbal behavior.

After you finish this chapter, then, you will be able to answer questions such as these:

- How does motivation direct and energize behavior?
- What are the biological and social factors that underlie thirst and hunger?
- How are needs relating to achievement, affiliation, and power motivation exhibited?
- What are emotions, how do we experience them, and what are their functions?
- How does nonverbal behavior relate to the expression of emotions?

EXPLANATIONS OF MOTIVATION

What kept Peter Potterfield striving to stay alive? Like most questions revolving around motivation, this one has several answers. Clearly, biological aspects of motivation were at work: The need for water, food, and warmth affected Potterfield's attempts to save himself. But cognitive factors were also apparent in his belief that he was too young to die. Finally, social factors—his desire to see family and friends—helped keep his will to survive intact.

The complexity of motivation has led to the development of a variety of conceptual approaches to it. Although they vary in the degree to which they encompass biological, cognitive, and social factors, all seek to explain the energy that guides people's behavior in particular directions.

Instincts: Born to Be Motivated

Psychologists first sought to explain motivation in terms of **instincts**, inborn patterns of behavior that are biologically determined. According to instinct theories of motivation, people and animals are born with preprogrammed sets of behaviors essential to their survival. These instincts provide the energy that channels

Instinct: An inborn pattern of behavior that is biologically determined

behavior in appropriate directions. Hence, sex might be explained as a response to an instinct for reproduction, and exploratory behavior might be viewed as motivated by an instinct to examine one's territory.

There are several difficulties with such a conception, however. For one thing, psychologists have been unable to agree on what the primary instincts are. One early psychologist, William McDougall (1908), suggested that there are eighteen instincts, including pugnacity and gregariousness. Others found even more—with one sociologist claiming that there are exactly 5,759. Clearly, such an extensive enumeration provides little more than labels for behavior.

No explanation based on the concept of instincts goes very far in explaining *why* a specific pattern of behavior, and not some other, has appeared in a given species. Furthermore, the variety and complexity of human behavior, much of which is clearly learned, are difficult to explain if instincts are the primary motivational force. Therefore, conceptions of motivation based on instincts have been supplanted by newer explanations, although instinct approaches still play a role in certain theories. For example, in later chapters we will discuss Freud's work, which suggests that instinctual drives of sex and aggression motivate behavior. Moreover, many animal behaviors clearly have an instinctual basis.

Drive-Reduction Theories of Motivation

Drive-reduction theory: The theory which claims that drives are produced to obtain our basic biological requirements

In rejecting instinct theory, psychologists first proposed simple drive-reduction theories of motivation in its place (Hull, 1943). **Drive-reduction theories** suggest that when people lack some basic biological requirement such as water, a drive to obtain that requirement (in this case, the thirst drive) is produced.

Drive: A motivational tension or arousal that energizes behavior in order to fulfill a need

To understand this approach, we need to begin with the concept of drive. A **drive** is motivational tension, or arousal, that energizes behavior in order to fulfill some need. Many basic kinds of drives, such as hunger, thirst, sleepiness, and sex, are related to biological requirements of the body or of the species as a whole. These are called **primary drives**. Primary drives contrast with **secondary drives**, in which no obvious biological need is being fulfilled. In secondary drives, needs are brought about by prior experience and learning. As we will discuss later, some people have strong needs to achieve academically and in their careers. We can say that their achievement need is a secondary drive motivating their behavior.

Primary drives: Biological needs such as hunger, thirst, fatigue, and sex

Secondary drives: Drives in which no biological need is fulfilled (e.g., need for achievement)

We usually try to resolve a primary drive by reducing the need underlying it. For example, we become hungry after not eating for a few hours and may raid the refrigerator if our next scheduled meal is too far away. If the weather turns cold, we put on extra clothing or raise the setting on the thermostat in order to keep warm. If, like Peter Potterfield, our body needs liquids in order to function properly, we experience thirst and seek out water.

Homeostasis: Maintenance of an internal biological balance, or "steady state"

The reason for such behavior is homeostasis, a basic motivational phenomenon underlying primary drives. **Homeostasis** is the maintenance of some optimal level of internal biological functioning by compensating for deviations from an organism's usual, balanced, internal state. Although not all basic biological behaviors related to motivation fit a homeostatic model—sexual behavior is one example, as we will see in the next chapter—most of the fundamental needs of life, including hunger, thirst, and the need for sleep, can be explained reasonably well by such an approach.

Unfortunately, although drive-reduction theories provide a good explanation of how primary drives motivate behavior, they are inadequate when it comes to explaining behaviors in which the goal is not to reduce a drive, but rather to maintain or even to increase a particular level of excitement or arousal. For example, many of us go out of our way to seek thrills through such activities as riding a roller coaster and steering a raft down the rapids of a river.

Other behaviors seem to be motivated by nothing more than curiosity. Anyone who has rushed to pick up newly delivered mail, who avidly follows gossip columns in the newspaper, or who yearns to travel to exotic places, knows the importance of curiosity in directing behavior. And it is not just human beings who display behavior indicative of curiosity: monkeys will learn to press a bar just to be able to peer into another room, especially if something interesting (such as a toy train moving along a track) can be glimpsed (Butler, 1954). Monkeys will also expend considerable energy solving simple mechanical puzzles, even though their behavior produces no obvious reward (Harlow, Harlow, & Meyer, 1950; Mineka & Hendersen, 1985).

Thrill seeking and curiosity are just two kinds of behavior that shed doubt on drive-reduction theories of motivation as all-encompassing explanations. In both cases, rather than seeking to reduce an underlying drive, people and animals appear to be motivated to increase their overall level of stimulation and activity. In order to explain this phenomenon, psychologists have suggested several alternatives to drive reduction.

Arousal Theory: The Search for Stimulation

Arousal theories seek to explain behavior in which the goal is the maintenance of or an increase in excitement (Berlyne, 1967; Brehm & Self, 1989). According to **arousal theory**, each of us tries to maintain a certain level of stimulation and activity. As with the drive-reduction model, if our stimulation and activity levels become too high, we try to reduce them. But the arousal model also suggests something quite different from the drive-reduction model: If the levels

Arousal theory: The belief that we try to maintain certain levels of stimulation and activity, increasing or reducing them as necessary

The inventive play of children may be motivated by a desire to maintain a particular level of arousal or curiosity.

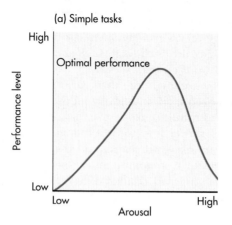

(a) Simple tasks

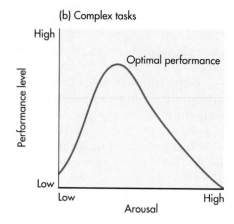

(b) Complex tasks

FIGURE 11-1

The Yerkes-Dodson law states that the optimal performance on a task will come from different levels of arousal, depending on whether the task is simple, as seen in (*a*), or complex, as seen in (*b*).

Yerkes-Dodson law: The theory that a particular level of motivational arousal produces optimal performance of a task

of stimulation and activity are too low, we will try to *increase* them by seeking stimulation.

Arousal theory provides an explanation for one of the oldest principles of psychology, devised by two psychologists in 1908: the **Yerkes-Dodson law.** According to this law and its later revisions, a particular level of motivational arousal produces optimal performance on a task. More specifically, performance on simple tasks usually benefits from higher levels of arousal than performance on more complex tasks does (Hebb, 1955). It seems as if high arousal gets in the way of successful responses to complex tasks while promoting better performance on simpler tasks (see Figure 11-1).

On the other hand, both complex and simple tasks suffer when the level of arousal is *too* high. In this case, the arousal is distracting and anxiety-producing, decreasing performance regardless of the difficulty of the task. In sum, consistent with arousal theory, there is an optimal level of arousal for task performance; arousal that is either too high or too low will result in poorer performance (Covington & Omelich, 1987; Sarason, Sarason, & Pierce, 1990).

People vary widely in the optimal level of arousal that they seek out (Mineka & Henderson, 1985; Babbitt, Rowland, & Franken, 1990; Stacy, Newcomb, & Bentler, 1991). For example, people as diverse as comic John Belushi, DNA researcher Sir Francis Crick, daredevil Evel Knievel, and bank robbers Bonnie and Clyde have been hypothesized to exhibit a high need for arousal (Farley, 1986). But it is not just the celebrated who pursue arousal; many of us characteristically seek out relatively high levels of stimulation. For a sense of your own characteristic level of stimulation, try the questionnaire in Table 11-1.

Arousal theory has significant applications to a variety of fields. For example, students who are highly anxious while taking tests on complex material may perform well below their ability because of their high level of arousal. In a completely different realm—the baseball field—research has shown that batting performance, a complex task, also suffers under conditions of high arousal but is enhanced under conditions of low arousal (Jackson, Buglione, & Glenwick, 1988).

Incentive Theory: The Pull of Motivation

Incentive: An external stimulus anticipated as a reward which directs and energizes behavior

When a luscious dessert is brought to the table after a filling meal, the attraction we feel has little or nothing to do with internal drives or with the maintenance of arousal. Rather, if we choose to eat the dessert, such behavior is motivated by the external stimulus of the dessert itself, which acts as an anticipated reward. This reward, in motivational terms, is an **incentive.**

TABLE 11-1

DO YOU SEEK OUT SENSATION?

How much stimulation do you crave in your everyday life? You will have an idea after you complete the following questionnaire, which lists some items from a scale designed to assess your sensation-seeking tendencies. Circle either *A* or *B* in each pair of statements.

1. *A* I would like a job that requires a lot of traveling.
   B I would prefer a job in one location.
2. *A* I am invigorated by a brisk, cold day.
   B I can't wait to get indoors on a cold day.
3. *A* I get bored seeing the same old faces.
   B I like the comfortable familiarity of everyday friends.
4. *A* I would prefer living in an ideal society in which everyone was safe, secure, and happy.
   B I would have preferred living in the unsettled days of our history.
5. *A* I sometimes like to do things that are a little frightening.
   B A sensible person avoids activities that are dangerous.
6. *A* I would not like to be hypnotized.
   B I would like to have the experience of being hypnotized.
7. *A* The most important goal of life is to live it to the fullest and to experience as much as possible.
   B The most important goal of life is to find peace and happiness.
8. *A* I would like to try parachute jumping.
   B I would never want to try jumping out of a plane, with or without a parachute.
9. *A* I enter cold water gradually, giving myself time to get used to it.
   B I like to dive or jump right into the ocean or a cold pool.
10. *A* When I go on a vacation, I prefer the comfort of a good room and bed.
    B When I go on a vacation, I prefer the change of camping out.
11. *A* I prefer people who are emotionally expressive, even if they are a bit unstable.
    B I prefer people who are calm and even-tempered.
12. *A* A good painting should shock or jolt the senses.
    B A good painting should give one a feeling of peace and security.
13. *A* People who ride motorcycles must have some kind of unconscious need to hurt themselves.
    B I would like to drive or ride a motorcycle.

Scoring Give yourself one point for each of the following responses: 1*A*, 2*A*, 3*A*, 4*B*, 5*A*, 6*B*, 7*A*, 8*A*, 9*B*, 10*B*, 11*A*, 12*A*, 13*B*. Find your total score by adding up the number of points and then use the following scoring key:

0–3 very low sensation seeking
4–5 low
6–9 average
10–11 high
12–13 very high

Keep in mind, of course, that this short questionnaire, for which the scoring is based on the results of college students who have taken it, provides only a rough estimate of your sensation-seeking tendencies. Moreover, as people get older, their sensation-seeking scores tend to decrease. Still, the questionnaire will at least give you an indication of how your sensation-seeking tendencies compare with those of others.

Source: Zuckerman, 1978.

Incentive theory attempts to explain why behavior is not always motivated by an internal need, such as the desire to reduce drives or to maintain an optimum level of arousal. Instead of focusing on internal factors, incentive theory explains motivation in terms of the nature of the external stimuli, the incentives that

Incentive theory: The theory explaining motivation in terms of external stimuli direct and energize behavior. In this view, properties of external stimuli largely account for a person's motivation.

Although the theory explains why we may succumb to an incentive (like an attractive dessert) even though internal cues (like hunger) are lacking, it seems insufficient to provide a complete explanation of motivation, since organisms seek to fulfill needs even when incentives are not apparent. Because of this, many psychologists believe that the internal drives proposed by drive-reduction theory work in tandem with the external incentives of incentive theory to "push" and "pull" behavior, respectively. Rather than contradicting each other, then, drives and incentives may work together in motivating behavior (Petri, 1991).

Opponent-Process Theory: The Yin and Yang of Motivation

Opponent-process theory of motivation: The theory which postulates that increases in arousal ultimately produce a calming reaction in the nervous system, and vice versa

When Chinese philosophers suggested long ago that there were two opposing forces in the universe—the yin and the yang—which influenced human behavior, they were foreshadowing the development of one further model of motivation, called opponent-process theory (Solomon & Corbit, 1974). **Opponent-process theory of motivation** seeks to explain the motivation behind such phenomena as drug addiction and the physiological and emotional reactions that occur as a result of extremes of physical danger, as in skydiving.

According to opponent-process theory, stimuli that first produce increases in arousal later produce an opposite, calming reaction in the nervous system, whereas stimuli that first produce decreases in arousal later produce an increase in arousal. Moreover, with each exposure to a stimulus, the original response to the stimulus remains fairly stable or perhaps even declines, while the opponent process—the reaction to the original response—tends to grow in strength.

Let's look at some concrete examples. Suppose a man takes a drug that produces feelings of unusual happiness. According to the theory, after these initial positive feelings subside, an opponent process will follow, swinging the man toward an opposite of happiness, or depression. In addition, the theory suggests that the opponent process (depression) tends to strengthen each time the drug is taken, whereas the initial process (happiness) tends to weaken. Consequently, the negative reaction will increase after each drug use, whereas the pleasure derived from the drug will decline. Ultimately, the man's motivation to increase the positive process (and avoid the eventual unpleasant opponent process) will lead him to take a larger quantity of the drug—the likely result being a pattern of addiction.

Opponent processes work in the reverse way when the initial experience is negative. Consider a woman about to make her first skydiving jump from an airplane. Her initial reaction is likely to be one of terror. But there will also be an opponent process at work: a feeling of euphoria after the jump is over. Opponent-process theory suggests that each time she jumps, the original process resulting in terror will grow no stronger and in fact may even weaken, whereas the opponent process resulting in euphoria is likely to increase. Ultimately, then, skydiving may become almost addictive to a skydiver.

In sum, opponent-process theory helps explain why people hold strong motivation for behavior that on the surface has few benefits. It is frequently the opponent process, not the initial reaction, that maintains the motivation to carry out such behavior.

High-sensation seekers may enjoy the physical risk of sky diving.

Cognitive Theory

Cognitive theories of motivation focus on the role of our thoughts, expectations, and understanding of the world. For instance, according to one kind of cognitive theory, **expectancy-value theory**, two kinds of cognitions underlie our behavior. The first is our expectation that a behavior will cause us to reach a particular goal, and the second is our understanding of the value of that goal to us (Tolman, 1959). For example, the degree to which students will be motivated to study for a test will be based jointly on their expectation of how well their studying will pay off (in terms of a good grade) and the value they place on getting a good grade. If both expectation and value are high, students will be motivated to study diligently; but if either one is low, their motivation to study will be relatively lower.

Cognitive theories of motivation make a key distinction between intrinsic and extrinsic motivation. **Intrinsic motivation** causes us to participate in an activity for our own enjoyment, not for any tangible reward that it will bring us. In contrast, **extrinsic motivation** causes us to do something for a tangible reward.

According to research on the two types of motivation, we are more apt to persevere, work harder, and produce work of higher quality when motivation for a task is intrinsic rather than extrinsic (Lepper, 1983; Deci & Ryan, 1985). Furthermore, some psychologists suggest that providing rewards for desirable behavior may cause intrinsic motivation to decline and extrinsic motivation to increase. In one demonstration of this phenomenon, a group of nursery school students were promised a reward for drawing with magic markers (an activity for

Cognitive theories of motivation: Theories explaining motivation by focusing on the role of an individual's thoughts, expectations, and understanding of the world

Expectancy-value theory: A cognitive theory that suggests that people are motivated by expectations that certain behaviors will accomplish a goal and their understanding of the importance of the goal

Intrinsic motivation: Motivation causing people to participate in an activity for their own enjoyment, not for the reward it will get them

Extrinsic motivation: Motivation causing people to participate in an activity for a tangible reward

which they had previously shown high motivation). The reward served to reduce their enthusiasm for the task, for they later showed considerably less zeal for drawing (Lepper & Greene, 1978). It was as if the promise of reward undermined their intrinsic interest in drawing, turning what had been play into work.

Such research suggests the importance of promoting intrinsic motivation and indicates that providing extrinsic rewards (or, as in this case, simply calling attention to them) may actually undermine the effort and quality of performance. Teachers might think twice, then, about offering their students an A for a good work. Instead, the research on intrinsic motivation suggests that better results would come from reminding students about the intrinsic reasons for their efforts to perform well—such as the joys of producing a carefully crafted paper.

Maslow's Hierarchy: Ordering Motivational Needs

What do Eleanor Roosevelt, Abraham Lincoln, and Albert Einstein have in common? Quite a bit, according to a model of motivation devised by psychologist Abraham Maslow: Each of them reached and fulfilled the highest levels of motivational needs underlying human behavior.

Maslow's model considers different motivational needs to be ordered in a hierarchy, and it suggests that before more sophisticated, higher-order needs can be met, certain primary needs must be satisfied (Maslow, 1970; 1987). The model can be conceptualized as a pyramid (see Figure 11-2) in which the more basic needs are at the bottom and the higher-level needs are at the top. In order for a particular need to be activated and thereby guide a person's behavior, the more basic needs in the hierarchy must be met first.

The most basic needs are those described earlier as primary drives: needs for water, food, sleep, sex, and the like. In order to move up the hierarchy, a person must have these basic physiological needs met. Safety needs come next in the hierarchy; Maslow suggests that people need a safe, secure environment in order to function effectively. Physiological and safety needs compose the lower-order needs.

Only when the basic lower-order needs are met can a person consider fulfilling higher-order needs, consisting of love and belongingness, esteem, and self-actualization. Love and belongingness needs include the need to obtain and give affection and to be a contributing member of some group or society. After these needs are fulfilled, the person strives for esteem. In Maslow's thinking, esteem relates to the need to develop a sense of self-worth by knowing that others are aware of one's competence and value.

Self-actualization: In Maslow's theory, a state of self-fulfillment in which people realize their highest potential

Once these four sets of needs are fulfilled—no easy task—the person is ready to strive for the highest-level need, self-actualization. **Self-actualization** is a state of self-fulfillment in which people realize their highest potential. When Maslow first discussed the concept, he used it to describe just a few well-known individuals such as Eleanor Roosevelt, Lincoln, and Einstein. But self-actualization is not limited to the famous. A parent with excellent nurturing skills who raises a family, a teacher who year after year creates an environment that maximizes students' success, and an artist who realizes her creative potential might all be self-actualized. The important thing is that people feel at ease with themselves and satisfied that they are using their talents to the fullest. In a sense, reaching self-actualization produces a decline in the striving and yearning for greater fulfillment that marks most people's lives and instead provides a sense of satisfaction with the current state of affairs (Jones & Crandall, 1991).

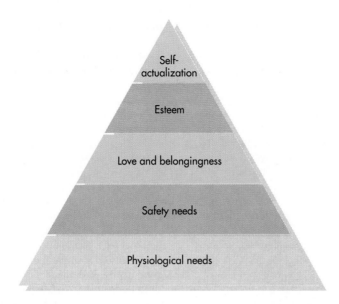

FIGURE 11-2
Maslow's hierarchy illustrates how our motivation progresses up the pyramid from a basis in the broadest, most fundamental biological needs to higher-order ones. (After Maslow, 1970.)

Unfortunately, research has not been able to validate the specific ordering of the stages of Maslow's theory, and it has proven difficult to measure self-actualization objectively (Haymes, Green, & Quinto, 1984; Weiss, 1991; Neher, 1991). However, Maslow's model is important in two ways: It highlights the complexity of human needs, and it emphasizes the fact that until more basic biological needs are met, people are going to be relatively unconcerned with higher-order needs. If people are hungry, their first interest will be in obtaining food; they will not be concerned with such things as love and self-esteem. The model helps explain why victims of such disasters as famine and war may suffer the breakdown of normal family ties and be unconcerned with the welfare of anyone other than themselves.

A Final Word About the Theories of Motivation

Now that we have examined several different theoretical approaches to motivation, it is natural to wonder which provides the fullest account of motivational phenomena. In fact, many of the conceptual approaches are complementary, rather than contradictory, and it is often useful to employ several theories simultaneously in order to understand a particular motivational system. Thus, as we proceed to consider specific motives, such as the needs for food, water, achievement, affiliation, and power, we will draw upon several of the theories in order to gain a better understanding of motivation.

RECAP AND REVIEW I

RECAP

◀ The study of motivation looks at the factors that energize and direct people's behavior.

◀ A drive is a motivational tension that energizes behavior to fulfill some need. Primary drives typically operate according to the principle of homeostasis, in which an organism strives to restore any deviations from a balanced, preferred internal state.

◀ Drive-reduction theory proposes that behavior is motivated by drives to reduce biological needs. However, it does not explain why people sometimes seek out stimulation.

- Arousal theory suggests that we try to maintain a certain level of stimulation and activity. Arousal theory is consistent with the Yerkes-Dodson law, which demonstrates that too much or too little arousal will result in inferior performance on a task.
- Opponent-process theory suggests that changes in arousal level in one direction lead to a reaction in the nervous system in the opposite direction.
- Cognitive theories of motivation, exemplified by expectancy-value theory, suggest that people's thoughts, understanding, and interpretation of the world underlie their motivation.
- According to Maslow's motivational model, motivational needs progress in a hierarchy from the most basic to higher-order needs. The specific categories include physiological, safety, love and belongingness, esteem, and self-actualization needs.

REVIEW

1. _Motivation_ are forces that guide a person's behavior in a certain direction.
2. Biologically determined, inborn patterns of behavior are known as _instincts_.
3. Your psychology professor tells you, "Explaining behavior is easy! When we lack something we are motivated to get it." What theory of motivation does your professor ascribe to? _Drive-reduction_
4. In this theory, food would be considered a _primary_ _drive_, while aca-

demic success would be considered a _secondary drive_.

5. By drinking water after running a marathon, a runner tries to keep his or her body at an optimal level of functioning. What is the name of this process? _homeostasis_
6. _Arousal_ theory states that we will either screen ourselves from or seek out stimulation, depending on the level of activity which is optimal for us.
7. According to the Yerkes-Dodson law, the more stimulation that is present in a given situation, the better a person's performance. True or false? _False_
8. Even though I am not thirsty, I am offered and accept a mug of beer. Assuming that I like beer very much, what theory of motivation would predict this behavior? _Incentive_
9. The expectancy-value theory of motivation has two components to it. Name and describe them. _____
10. I help an old woman across the street because doing a good deed makes me feel good. What type of motivation is at work here? What type of motivation would be at work if I were to help an old lady across the street because she paid me $20? _Intrinsic, extrinsic_
11. According to Maslow, a person with no job, no home and no friends can become self-actualized. True or false? _False - satisfy basic need 1st._

Ask Yourself

You have just been hired as a consultant at a large automobile plant. How might each of the theories of motivation discussed in this section be put to use in the workplace to motivate workers?

(Answers to review questions are on page 346.)

HUMAN NEEDS AND MOTIVATION: EAT, DRINK, AND BE DARING

To Bob, doing well in college meant that he would get into a good law school, which he saw as a stepping-stone to a successful future. Consequently, he never let up academically and always tried his best to do well in his courses. But his constant academic striving went well beyond the desire to get into law school; he tried not only to get good grades, but to get *better* grades than his classmates.

In fact, Bob was always trying to be the best at everything he did. He could turn the simplest activity into a competition. Bob couldn't even play poker without acting as if his success at the game were essential. There were, however, some areas in which he didn't compete. He was interested only if he thought he had a fighting chance to succeed; he ignored challenges that were too difficult as well as those that were too easy for him.

What is the motivation behind Bob's consistent striving to achieve? To answer that question, we must begin to consider some of the specific kinds of needs that underlie behavior.

We will examine several of the most important human needs. Because human beings are in a fundamental sense biological creatures, we first consider the primary drives that have received the most attention among psychologists: thirst and hunger. But because much of human behavior has no clear biological basis, we will also examine the secondary drives—those uniquely human strivings, based on learned needs and past experience, that help explain behavior such as Bob's.

Thirst

More than 75 percent of our weight is accounted for by water, and maintenance and regulation of that amount of liquid is no easy task for our bodies. The significance of thirst is underlined by the fact that although we could live for more than a month without food, we would die within several days if deprived of water. Given that we lose a significant amount of water through sweating and urination, thirst represents an important motivational drive.

The stimuli that motivate us to drink are mainly internal; the dry mouth that accompanies thirst is a symptom of the need for water rather than the cause. Actually, three primary internal mechanisms produce thirst. First, the salt concentration of the cells of the body varies according to the amount of internal fluid. When that concentration reaches a certain level, it triggers the hypothalamus to act, thereby resulting in the experience of thirst.

The second mechanism that induces thirst is a decrease in the total volume of fluid in the circulatory system (Fitzsimons, 1961). For instance, a person who loses a significant amount of blood through an injury subsequently experiences a powerful sense of thirst.

Finally, a third factor that produces thirst is a rise in body temperature or a significant energy expenditure. The thirst is probably due to a rise in the salt concentration in the body, which occurs as a consequence of increased sweating. It is likely that this mechanism accounted for Peter Potterfield's all-consuming sense of thirst when he tumbled down the mountain during his rock-climbing excursion.

The complexity of the mechanisms involved in thirst are illustrated by the fact that people deprived of water for twenty-four hours will drink eagerly, consuming two-thirds of the water they need in the first two and a half minutes. They then taper off, and drink more slowly until they ingest enough to replenish almost the exact amount of the water they lacked.

What is noteworthy about this rapid and accurate process is its speed. Water replenishment occurs so rapidly that it is not possible for the water that is being consumed to reach the body's water-starved tissues immediately. How, then, does the body know when it has drunk enough water? The answer is that the body seems to have a kind of water-meter of the mouth and stomach, which monitors the amount of water that has been ingested and immediately informs drinkers when they have drunk sufficient amounts of liquid to meet their needs (Rolls, Wood, & Rolls, 1980). Hence, our body's ability to regulate its intake of fluids is based not just upon the quantity of liquid in its cells at a given moment, but also on the amount of liquid that passes through the mouth and stomach on the way to the individual cells.

Hunger

About a quarter of the United States population suffers from **obesity**, defined as being more than 20 percent above the average weight for a person of a given height (see Table 11-2), and losing unwanted weight has become an American obsession. Many people spend untold time, energy, and money attempting to regulate the amount and type of food they eat in order to decrease their weight. Others, with a problem many of us would envy, are concerned with trying to *gain* weight.

Obesity: The state of being more than 20 percent above the average weight for a person of a particular height

TABLE 11-2

HOW MUCH SHOULD YOU WEIGH?[1]

Height	Recommended weight (Metropolitan Life)		Obesity[2] (NIH panel)		Age-adjusted recommended weight[3] (Gerontology Research Center)				
	Men	Women	Men	Women	20–29 yr.	30–39 yr.	40–49 yr.	50–59 yr.	60–69 yr.
4'10"	—	100–131	—	137	84–111	92–119	99–127	107–135	115–142
5'0"	—	103–137	—	143	90–119	98–127	106–135	114–143	123–152
5'2"	125–148	108–144	160	150	96–127	105–136	113–144	122–153	131–163
5'4"	129–155	114–152	164	157	102–135	112–145	121–154	130–163	140–173
5'6"	133–163	120–160	172	164	109–144	119–154	129–164	138–174	148–184
5'8"	137–171	126–167	179	172	116–153	126–163	137–174	147–184	158–196
5'10"	141–179	132–173	186	179	122–162	134–173	145–184	156–195	167–207
6'0"	147–187	—	194	—	129–171	141–183	153–195	165–207	177–219
6'2"	153–197	—	203	—	137–181	149–194	162–206	174–219	187–232
6'4"	—	—	—	—	144–191	157–205	171–218	184–231	197–244

[1] Values in this table are for height without shoes and weight without clothes.
[2] Based on 20 percent more than midpoint of Metropolitan Life recommended weight range.
[3] Recommended weight ranges apply to both men and women.
Source: Consumer Report Health Letter, February 1990.

Surprisingly, in the majority of instances, people who are not monitoring their weight show only minor weight fluctuations in spite of substantial variations in how much they eat and exercise over time. Clearly, then, eating is subject to some form of homeostasis.

Psychologists began their search for an understanding of eating motivation with animals, which are relatively free of the problems of obesity that beset human beings. Most nonhumans, when left in an environment in which food is readily available, do a good job of regulating their intake—as anyone knows who makes sure that a dish of food is always available for a pet. Cats, for instance, will eat only until their immediate hunger is satisfied; they leave the remainder, returning to it only when internal cues tell them to eat.

Furthermore, there appear to be internal mechanisms that regulate not only the quantity of food intake, but also the kind of food that an animal desires. Hungry rats that have been deprived of particular foods tend to seek out alternatives that contain the specific nutrients their diet is lacking, and laboratory experiments show that animals given the choice of a wide variety of foods in cafeteria-like settings choose a fairly well-balanced diet (Rozin, 1977).

ANSWERS (REVIEW I):

1. Motives **2.** instincts **3.** Drive reduction **4.** primary drive; secondary drive **5.** Homeostasis **6.** Arousal **7.** False; the optimal level of arousal is determined by the difficulty of the task. **8.** Incentive **9.** Expectation that a behavior will lead to a goal; value of that goal. **10.** Intrinsic; Extrinsic **11.** False; lower-order needs must be fulfilled before self-actualization can occur.

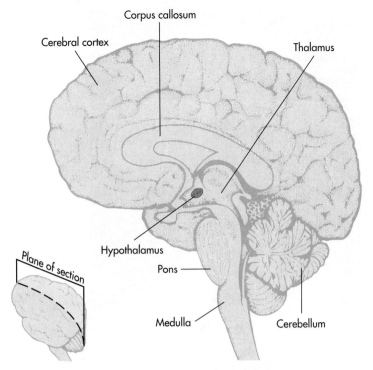

FIGURE 11-3

The hypothalamus acts as the brain's "feeding center," being primarily responsible for food intake.

The mechanisms by which organisms know whether they require food or should stop eating are complex ones (Keesey & Powley, 1986). It is not just a matter of an empty stomach causing hunger pangs and a full one alleviating hunger, since people who have had their stomachs removed still experience the sensation of hunger (Inglefinger, 1944). Similarly, laboratory animals tend to eat larger quantities when their food is low in nutrients; in contrast, when given a high-nutrient diet, they lower their food intake—despite the degree to which their stomach is empty or full or the amount of time it takes to eat the food (Harte, Travers, & Savich, 1948).

It appears, then, that animals, as well as people, are sensitive to both the amount and the nutritional value of the foods they eat (Barker, Best, & Domjan, 1977; Logue, 1991). One mechanism that helps to regulate food intake is a change in the chemical composition of the blood. For instance, experiments show that when glucose, a kind of sugar, is injected into the blood, hunger decreases and animals will refuse to eat. On the other hand, when insulin, a hormone that is involved in the conversion of glucose into stored fat, is introduced into the bloodstream, hunger increases (Rodin, 1985).

But what part of the body monitors changes in the blood chemistry relating to eating behavior? One particular structure of the brain, the **hypothalamus** (see Figure 11-3), appears to be primarily responsible for food intake. Injury to the hypothalamus has been shown to cause radical changes in eating behavior, depending upon the site of the injury. For example, rats whose **lateral hypothalamus** is damaged may literally starve to death; they refuse food when offered, and unless they are force-fed they eventually die. Rats with an injury to the **ventromedial hypothalamus** display the opposite problem: extreme overeating. Rats with this injury can increase in weight by as much as 400 percent. Similar phenomena occur in humans who have tumors of the hypothalamus.

Although it is clear that the hypothalamus plays an important role in regu-

Hypothalamus: The structure in the brain that is primarily responsible for regulating food intake

Lateral hypothalamus: The part of the brain which, when damaged, results in an organism's starving to death

Ventromedial hypothalamus: The part of the brain which, when injured, results in extreme overeating

Following an operation in which its ventromedial hypothalamus was cut, this obviously obese rat tipped the scales at something on the order of four times its normal weight.

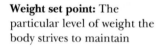

Weight set point: The particular level of weight the body strives to maintain

lating food intake, the exact mechanism by which it operates is uncertain. Some researchers think it affects an organism's sense or perception of hunger; others hypothesize that it directly regulates the neural connections that control the muscles involved in eating behavior (Stricker & Zigmond, 1976).

One theory suggests that injury to the hypothalamus affects the weight set point by which food intake is regulated (Nisbett, 1972). The **weight set point** is the particular level of weight that the body strives to maintain. Acting as a kind of internal weight thermostat, the hypothalamus calls for either greater or less food intake. According to this explanation, injury to the hypothalamus drastically raises or lowers the set point, and the organism strives to meet its internal goal by increasing or decreasing its food consumption.

Social Factors in Eating. You have just finished a full meal and are completely stuffed. Suddenly, your host announces with great fanfare that he will be serving his "house specialty" dessert, bananas flambé, and that he has spent the better part of the afternoon preparing it. Even though you are full and don't even like bananas, you accept a serving of his dessert and eat all of it.

Clearly, internal biological factors are not the full story when it comes to explaining our eating behavior. External social factors, based on societal rules and conventions and on what we have learned about appropriate eating behavior from our prior experience, also play an important role.

Take, for example, the simple fact that people customarily eat breakfast, lunch, and dinner at approximately the same times every day. Because we are accustomed to eating on schedule every day, we tend to feel hungry as the usual hour approaches—sometimes quite independently of what our internal cues are telling us. Similarly, we tend to take roughly the same amount of food on our plates every day—even though the amount of exercise we may have had, and consequently our need for energy replenishment, varies from day to day. We also tend to prefer particular foods over others; rats may be a delicacy in certain cultures, but few people in western cultures find them greatly appealing—despite their potentially high nutritional value. In sum, cultural influences and our own

Even though most campus meal plans allow students to eat unlimited quantities, the majority do not eat significantly more than they would at home.

individual habits play an important role in determining when, what, and how much we eat (Polivy & Herman, 1985; Boaks, Popplewell, & Burton, 1987).

An oversensitivity to external eating cues based on social convention, and a parallel insensitivity to internal hunger cues, is related to obesity in some individuals. Research has shown, for example, that obese people who are placed in a room next to an inviting bowl of crackers are apt to eat considerably more than nonobese people—even though they may have just finished a filling sandwich (Schachter, Goldman, & Gordon, 1968). In addition, obese individuals are more apt to scorn and avoid unpleasant-tasting food—even if they have been deprived of food for a period of time—than nonobese people, who tend to be less concerned with the taste of the food. Finally, the obese are less apt to eat if doing so involves any sort of work: In one experiment obese subjects were less likely to eat nuts that had to be shelled, but ate copious amounts of nuts that already had their shells removed. Nonobese people, in contrast, ate the same amount of nuts, regardless of whether or not the nuts had to be shelled (Schachter, 1971).

In addition, there is essentially no correspondence between reports of hunger in obese individuals and the amount of time they have been deprived of food, in contrast to a significant correlation for people of normal weight (Nisbett, 1968). It thus appears that many obese people give undue attention to external cues and are less aware of the internal cues that help nonobese people regulate their eating behavior.

On the other hand, many individuals who are highly reliant on external cues never become obese, and there are quite a few obese people who are relatively unresponsive to external cues (Herman, 1987; Rodin, 1981). Other factors, then, are clearly at work in determining why some people become obese.

The Weight Set Point, Metabolism, and Obesity.   One plausible suspect as the cause of obesity is the weight set point. Specifically, it is possible that overweight people have higher set points than people of normal weight. Because their set points are unusually high, their attempts to lose weight by eating less may make them especially sensitive to external, food-related cues and therefore more apt to eat, perpetuating their obesity.

But why may some people's weight set points be higher than others? One factor may be the size and number of fat cells in the body, which rise as a function of weight increase. Because the set-point level may reflect the number of fat cells a person has, any increase in weight, which raises the number of fat cells, may raise the set point. Moreover, any loss of weight after the age of two does not decrease the number of fat cells in the body, although it may cause them to shrink in size (Knittle, 1975). Hence, although fat babies are sometimes considered cute, obese children may have acquired so many fat cells that their weight set point is too high—long after they have reached the age at which being chubby or fat is still appealing.

In sum, according to weight-set-point theory, the presence of too many fat cells may result in the set point becoming "stuck" at a higher level than is desirable. Under such circumstances, losing weight becomes a difficult proposition, since one is constantly at odds with one's own internal set point.

Metabolism: The rate at which energy is produced and expended by the body

Other factors also work against people's efforts to lose weight. For example, there are large differences in people's **metabolism**, the rate at which energy is produced and expended by the body. Some people, with a high metabolism rate, seem to be able to eat as much as they want without gaining weight, while others, with low metabolism, may eat only half as much and yet gain weight readily. Actually, those who gain weight easily are biologically more efficient: They have the dubious advantage of easily converting food into body tissue. In contrast, those who are able to eat large quantities without gaining weight are inefficient in using the foods they eat; much gets wasted—and they stay thin.

Finally, there is growing evidence that some people may be genetically born to be fat. Several studies indicate that people who are prone to obesity may gain weight mainly because they inherit low rates of metabolism—and not because they overeat. In one experiment, for example, the metabolism rates of members of an Arizona Indian tribe which is prone to obesity—some 80 percent of the tribe members are obese by their early twenties—were carefully studied (Ravussin et al., 1988). As part of the study, metabolism rates were measured over several twenty-four-hour periods, during which the subjects stayed virtually immobile. Over the two years of the study, the subjects who gained the most weight were the ones who initially had the slowest metabolism. Although we cannot rule out the possibility that Indians who gained the most weight were also eating more, the data are clear in suggesting that most of the weight gain was due to slower metabolism.

Still other factors may lead to obesity. Children who are given food after becoming upset may learn, through the basic mechanisms of classical and operant conditioning, that eating is associated with consolation, so they may eat whenever they experience difficulties as adults. When parents provide food as the "treatment" for their child's stress, anxiety, and depression, eating may become a learned response to any emotional difficulty, leading to eating behavior that has little or nothing to do with internal hunger cues (Davis, 1986; Herman & Polivy, 1975).

Anorexia nervosa: An eating disorder usually striking young women in which symptoms include various degrees of self-starvation in an attempt to avoid obesity

Eating Disorders. In the most extreme cases, eating behavior can be so disordered that it becomes life threatening. In one major disorder, **anorexia nervosa**, people may refuse to eat, while denying that their behavior and appearance—which can become skeletonlike—are unusual. Some 15 to 20 percent of anorexics literally starve themselves to death.

Anorexia nervosa afflicts mainly females between the ages of 12 and the early

She could be the girl next door. Bright, hard-working, successful, and good-looking, 20-year-old Christine Bergel was a standard against whom others compared themselves.

The trouble was that Christine never saw herself the way others did. She hated how she looked and grew preoccupied with her appearance and weight. To cope with her feelings, Christine secretly began repeated cycles of binging on huge quantities of food, and then eliminating the food by vomiting. During her worst times, she would stuff herself and then force herself to throw up three times a day. Obsessed by the thought that she was too fat, she exercised three hours daily. Her constant binging-and-purging cycles were accompanied by deep feelings of guilt and depression over what she recognized as self-destructive behavior.

Christine's problem is bulimia, and it is shared by between 1 and 2 percent of college-age women. It is one of a number of eating disorders that afflict mainly women of college age, although it can be found in others as well. The habitual binging-and-purging cycles of bulimia can lead to digestive-tract problems, rotted teeth, and even heart failure (Fichter, 1990).

Christine's story, however, has a happy ending. Realizing the seriousness of her problem, Christine checked herself into a residential treatment facility for people with eating disorders. After six weeks of treatment, which included individual and group therapy, Christine was able to

TREATING EATING DISORDERS

get her eating behavior, and her obsession with her appearance, under control (Kohn, 1987).

The kind of treatment that Christine received was typical of that used for people with eating disorders. For people with bulimia, treatment usually consists of therapy to gain an understanding of the causes for their eating behavior. In addition, patients are taught to eat foods that they enjoy, but are prevented from vomiting afterward. One goal of such a procedure is to teach bulimics that they have control over their eating habits (Schneider et al., 1987).

In cases of anorexia, the first aim of treatment is to get the patient to gain weight, which must be done in order to prevent the shriveling of muscles and chemical imbalances. In extreme cases, feeding tubes are inserted through the nose. Long-term weight gains are promoted through

treatments that reinforce weight gains. For example, by eating, patients may obtain the privilege of watching television or receiving mail. The goal for patients is typically to gain as much as one pound per day.

After anorexics have gained enough weight, they begin psychological counseling. Often such therapy involves the entire family, since anorexia has sometimes been linked to family difficulties (Strober et al., 1990).

Through treatments such as these, about half of all anorexics bounce back completely, reaching a normal weight. In addition, some 30 to 40 percent gain some weight, although they still remain underweight (Anderson, Hedblom, & Hubbard, 1983; Hsu, 1990).

Prior to being photographed, Christine Bergel said she was afraid she would appear too fat. Having her body outline traced gave her an opportunity to view her own silhouette more objectively.

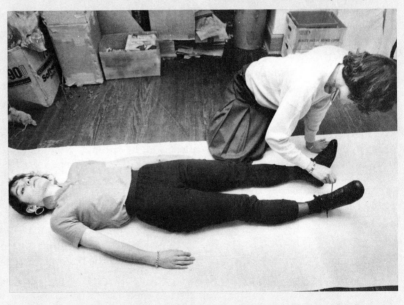

twenties, although both men and women of any age may develop it. People with the disorder typically come from stable homes, and they often are successful, attractive, and relatively affluent. Their lives revolve around food: Although they eat little themselves, they may cook for others, go shopping for food frequently, or collect cookbooks (Bruch, 1973; Hsu, 1990).

Bulimia: An eating disorder characterized by vast intake of food that may be followed by self-induced vomiting

A related problem, **bulimia**, is a disorder in which a person binges on incredibly large quantities of food (as we discuss in the accompanying Psychology at Work box.) An entire gallon of ice cream and a whole pie may easily be consumed in a single sitting. Following such a binge, sufferers feel guilt and depression and typically induce vomiting or take laxatives to rid themselves of the food—behavior known as purging (Hinz & Williamson, 1987). Constant binging-and-purging cycles and the use of drugs to induce vomiting or diarrhea may create a chemical imbalance that can lead to heart failure. Typically, though, the weight of a person suffering from bulimia remains normal.

What causes anorexia nervosa or bulimia? Some researchers suspect there is a physiological cause such as a chemical imbalance in the hypothalamus or pituitary gland (Gold et al., 1986). Other psychologists believe that the cause is rooted in societal expectations about the value of slenderness and the parallel notion that being obese is undesirable (Crandall & Biernat, 1990; Rothblum, 1990). In this view, people with anorexia nervosa and bulimia take to heart the societal view that one can never be too thin and become preoccupied with their weight. Consistent with such an explanation, clear standards exist on certain college campuses about "appropriate" binging behavior, and the amount of binging is associated with a woman's popularity (Crandall, 1988). Finally, some psychologists suggest that the disorders occur as a consequence of overdemanding parents or other family problems (Logue, 1991).

At this time, no full explanation exists for either anorexia nervosa or bulimia. It would not be surprising if anorexia nervosa and bulimia were found to stem from both physiological and social causes, just as eating behavior in general is influenced by a variety of factors (Fichter, 1990).

The Informed Consumer of Psychology: Dieting and Losing Weight Successfully

For many people, dieting represents a losing battle: Most people who diet eventually regain the weight they have lost, so they try again and get caught in a seemingly endless cycle of weight loss and gain. Given what we know about the causes of obesity this is not entirely surprising, since so many factors appear to affect eating behavior and weight.

According to diet experts, there are several things to keep in mind when trying to lose weight (Kolata, 1988; CRHL, 1990; Gurin, 1989; Brownell, 1989):

■ There is no easy route to weight control; you will have to make permanent changes in your life in order to lose weight and to keep from gaining it back. The most obvious step, cutting down on the amount of food you eat, is just the beginning of a lifetime commitment to changing your eating habits. You must begin to consider the energy value of the food as well as the overall quantity and the balance in different kinds of nutrients (Webb, 1990).

■ Set reasonable goals. Know how much weight you want to lose before you start to diet. Don't try to lose too much weight too quickly or you may doom yourself to failure.

■ Exercise. When you exercise, you burn fat stored in your body, which is used as fuel for muscles. As this fat is used, you will probably lose weight. Weight-set-point theory suggests another advantage to moderate exercise: It may lower your set point. Although there is some dispute about just how much exercise is sufficient to actually lower weight (Pi-Sunyer, 1987), most experts recommend at least thirty consecutive minutes of moderate exercise at least three times a week. (If nothing else, the release of endorphins following exercise—discussed in Chapter 3—will make you feel better, even if you don't lose weight.)

■ Decrease the influence of external, social stimuli on your eating behavior. There are a number of things you can do to lower your susceptibility to external food cues. For example, you can give yourself smaller portions of food, or you can leave the table before you see what is available for dessert. Don't even buy snack foods such as peanuts or potato chips; if they're not readily available in the kitchen cupboard, you're not apt to eat them. Wrap foods in the refrigerator in aluminum foil so you cannot see the contents. That way, you won't be tantalized by the sight of food every time you open the refrigerator.

■ Avoid fad diets. No matter how popular they are at a given time, extreme diets, including liquid diets, usually don't work in the long run and can be dangerous to your health (CRHL, 1990; O'Neil, 1990).

■ When you have reached your desired weight, you must maintain the habits you built up while dieting in order to avoid gaining back the weight you have lost. Consider revamping the role that food and eating play in your life, as well as your general values (Schwartz & Inbar-Saban, 1988; Westover & Lanyon, 1990).

Above all, don't feel guilty if you don't succeed in losing weight. Given the evidence that obesity may be genetically determined, the inability to lose weight should not be seen as a major failure in life. Indeed, you are in good company, for some 90 percent of dieters put back the weight they have lost (Bennett & Gurin, 1982). And even a relatively small weight loss is better than none: just a 10 percent drop in body weight may lower the major health risks that are associated with obesity (Brody, 1987a).

The Need for Achievement: Striving for Success

While hunger and thirst may represent two of the most potent drives in our day-to-day lives, we are also motivated by powerful secondary drives that have no clear biological basis (McClelland, 1985; Geen, 1984). Among the most prominent of these is the need for achievement.

The **need for achievement** is a stable, learned characteristic in which satisfaction is obtained by striving for and attaining a level of excellence (McClelland, Atkinson, Clark, & Lowell, 1953). People with a high need for achievement seek out situations in which they can compete against some standard—be it grades, money, or winning at a game—and prove themselves successful. But they are not indiscriminate when it comes to picking their challenges: They tend to avoid situations in which success will come too easily (which would be unchallenging) or those in which success is unlikely. Instead, people high in achievement motivation are apt to choose tasks that are of intermediate difficulty.

In contrast, people with low achievement motivation tend mainly to be motivated by a desire to avoid failure. As a result, they seek out easy tasks, being sure to avoid failure, or they seek out very difficult tasks for which failure has no negative implications, since almost anyone would fail at them. People with a high fear of failure will stay away from tasks of intermediate difficulty, since they may fail where others have been successful (Atkinson & Feather, 1966).

The outcomes of a high need for achievement are generally positive, at least in a success-oriented society such as our own (Heckhausen, Schmalt, & Schnei-

Need for achievement: A stable, learned characteristic in which satisfaction comes from striving for and achieving a level of excellence

FIGURE 11-4

This ambiguous picture is similar to those used in the Thematic Apperception Test to determine people's underlying motivation.

Thematic Apperception Test (TAT): A test consisting of a series of ambiguous pictures about which a person is asked to write a story. The story is taken to be a reflection of the writer's personality

der, 1985; Spence, 1985). For instance, people motivated by a high need for achievement are more likely to attend college than their low-achievement counterparts, and once in college they tend to receive higher grades in classes that are related to their future careers (Atkinson & Raynor, 1974). Furthermore, high achievement motivation is associated with future economic and occupational success (McClelland, 1985a).

Measuring Achievement Motivation.   How can we measure a person's need for achievement? The technique used most frequently is to administer a **Thematic Apperception Test (TAT)**. In the TAT, people are shown a series of ambiguous pictures, such as the one in Figure 11-4. They are told to write a story that describes what is happening, who the people are, what led to the situation, what the people are thinking or wanting, and what will happen next. A standard scoring system is then used to determine the amount of achievement imagery in people's stories. For example, someone who writes a story in which the main character is striving to beat an opponent, studying in order to do well at some task, or working hard in order to get a promotion shows clear signs of an achievement orientation. It is assumed that the inclusion of such achievement-related imagery in their stories indicates an unusually high degree of concern with—and therefore a relatively strong need for—achievement.

Other techniques have been developed for assessing achievement motivation on a societal level (Reuman, Alwin, & Veroff, 1984). For example, a good indication of the overall level of achievement motivation in a particular society can be found by assessing achievement imagery in children's stories or folk tales. Researchers who have examined children's reading books for achievement imagery over long periods have found correlations between the amount of imagery in the books and the economic activity in the society over the next few decades (DeCharms & Moeller, 1962). Whether stories incorporating achievement imagery actually influence children or simply reflect growing economic trends cannot be determined, of course. It is clear, though, that children might be learning more from their books than how to read—they may be acquiring an understanding of the level of achievement motivation that society expects from them.

Learning to Achieve: The Development of Achievement Motivation.   How do people come to be high in the need for achievement? Several factors seem to be at work, beginning at a very early age. For instance, parents who set high standards (even when it comes to everyday tasks such as dressing), who are relatively demanding, and who strongly encourage independence produce children high in need for achievement. Although parental directiveness may make parents seem rather unpleasant, this is not the case: Such parents are also usually quick to praise their children's success, and they warmly encourage their children in all areas of endeavor. Even if their children fail, these parents do not complain; instead, they urge their children to find areas in which they will be able to succeed (McClelland, 1985a).

Training Achievement Motivation in Adults.   Can we teach people to have higher achievement motivation? Such a question is hardly academic, since we know that a high need for achievement is associated with ultimate economic success.

To answer the question, psychologists David McClelland and David Winter (1971) went to India, a less technologically developed country in which economic needs are profound, and implemented a training program consisting of several components. First, they taught participants—who were all owners of small businesses—such things as the importance of setting moderate goals and taking personal responsibility for meeting them. After reviewing biographies of successful entrepreneurs, participants were told to imagine themselves being successful. They were asked to make concrete, step-by-step plans, and to keep track of their progress toward their goals.

The results of the program were impressive. Compared with a control group made up of business owners who did not receive training, participants increased their level of business activity significantly. They created new jobs, and they expanded their businesses. Even more important was the fact that the gains lasted. The economic achievements of the participants were significantly greater ten years after the program than were those in the control group (McClelland & Winter, 1971; McClelland, 1978). It is never too late, then, to learn higher achievement motivation. Even adults can increase their achievement strivings— and consequent success.

The Need for Affiliation: Striving for Friendship

Few of us choose to lead our lives as hermits. Why?

One reason is that most people have a **need for affiliation**, a concern with establishing and maintaining relationships with other people. Individuals with a high need for affiliation write TAT stories that emphasize the desire to maintain or reinstate friendships and show concern over being rejected by friends.

People who are higher in affiliation needs are particularly sensitive to relationships with others. They desire to be with their friends more of the time, and they want to be alone, less often than people who are lower in affiliation. At the same time, affiliation motivation may be less important than gender in deter-

Need for affiliation: A need to establish and maintain relationships with other people

The need for power may have motivated these students to participate in a legislative workshop at the Texas state capitol.

mining how much time is actually spent with friends. According to the results of one study, regardless of their affiliative orientation, female students spend significantly more time with their friends and less time alone than male students do (Wong & Csikszentmihalyi, 1991).

The Need for Power: Striving for Impact on Others

Need for power: A tendency to want to seek impact, control, or influence on others in order to be seen as a powerful individual

If your fantasies include being elected President of the United States or running General Motors, they may be reflecting a high need for power. The **need for power**, a tendency to seek impact, control, or influence over others, and to be seen as a powerful individual, represents an additional type of motivation (Winter, 1973; 1987).

As you might expect, people with a strong need for power are more apt to belong to organizations and seek office than those low in the need for power. They also are apt to be in professions in which their power needs may be fulfilled (such as business management and—you may or may not be surprised—teaching). In addition, they try to show the trappings of power: even in college, they are more apt to collect prestigious possessions, such as stereos and sports cars.

There are some significant sex differences in the display of need for power. Men who are high in power needs tend to show unusually high levels of aggression, drink heavily, act sexually exploitative, and participate more frequently in competitive sports—behaviors that collectively represent somewhat extravagant, flamboyant behavior (Winter, 1973). In contrast, women display their power needs in a more restrained manner, congruent with traditional societal restraints on women's behavior. Women high in a need for power are more apt than men to channel their power needs in a socially responsible manner (such as by showing concern for others or through highly nurturant behavior) (Winter, 1988).

Clearly, needs for power can be fulfilled in several sorts of ways (Spangler & House, 1991). As with all motives, the way in which a need is manifested reflects a combination of people's skills, values, and the specific situation in which they find themselves.

RECAP

◄ Thirst, a primary drive, operates according to the principles of homeostasis.

◄ Hunger is affected by internal cues that regulate the amount and kind of food eaten. The hypothalamus plays a particularly important role in determining food intake.

◄ People's weight set point, their sensitivity to external social cues, the number of fat cells they have, their metabolism, and genetic factors all affect eating patterns.

◄ Among the major secondary drives are needs for achievement, affiliation, and power.

REVIEW

1. The three mechanisms primarily responsible for thirst are: _____, _____, and _____.

2. Laboratory animals, when deprived of certain nutrients, have been found to instinctively choose foods that contain the nutrients they are lacking. True or false?

_____

3. Match the following terms with their definitions:
   1. __b__ Hypothalamus
   2. __a__ Lateral hypothalamic damage
   3. __c__ Ventromedial hypothalamic damage

   a. Leads to refusal of food and starvation.
   b. Responsible for monitoring food intake.
   c. Causes extreme overeating.

4. The ____weight____ ____set____ ____point____ is the particular level of weight the body strives to maintain.

5. Research by Schachter has shown that some obese people may be overly sensitive to cues that are internal in origin. True or false? ____False____

6. ____metabolism____ is the rate at which energy is produced and expended by the body.

7. ____Bulimia____ is an eating disorder characterized by binge eating, then purging the body by inducing vomiting. A person with the disorder of ____anorexia nervosa____ refuses to eat and denies that his or her behavior and appearance are unusual.

8. Jake is the type of person who constantly strives for excellence. He feels intense satisfaction when he is able to master a new task. Jake most likely has a high need for ____achievement____.

9. Debbie's Thematic Apperception Test (TAT) story depicts a young girl who had been rejected by one of her peers and sought to regain her friendship. What major type of motivation is Debbie displaying in her story?
   a. Need for achievement
   b. Need for motivation
   c. Need for affiliation ✓
   d. Need for power

Ask Yourself

Can traits such as need for achievement, need for power, and need for affiliation be used to select workers for jobs? What other criteria, both motivational and personal, would need to be considered when making such a selection?

(Answers to review questions are on page 358.)

UNDERSTANDING EMOTIONAL EXPERIENCES

Karl Andrews held in his hands the envelope he had been waiting for. It could be his ticket to his future: an offer of admission to his first-choice college. But what was it going to say? He knew it could go either way; his grades were pretty good, and he had been involved in some extracurricular activities; but his SAT scores had been, to put it bluntly, lousy. He felt so nervous that his hands shook as he opened the thin envelope (not a good sign, he thought). Here it comes. "Dear Mr. Andrews," it read. "The President and Trustees of the University are pleased to admit you. . . ." That was all he needed to see. With a whoop of excitement, Karl found himself jumping up and down gleefully. A rush of emotion overcame him as it sank in that he had, in fact, been accepted. He was on his way.

At one time or another, all of us have experienced the strong feelings that accompany both very pleasant and very negative experiences. Perhaps it was the thrill of being accepted into college, the joy of being in love, the sorrow over someone's death, or the anguish of inadvertently hurting someone. Moreover, we experience such reactions on a less intense level throughout our daily lives: the pleasure of a friendship, the enjoyment of a movie, or the embarrassment of breaking a borrowed item.

Despite the varied nature of these feelings, they all represent emotions. As we discussed earlier, such emotions are an important component in motivating our behavior, and the behavior that results from motivational needs in turn influences our emotions.

While we all know what it is like to experience an emotion, finding a definition acceptable to psychologists has proven to be an elusive task. One reason is that different theories of emotion—which we will discuss later—emphasize different aspects of emotions, and therefore each theory ultimately produces its own definition. Despite these difficulties, though, we can use a general definition: **Emotions** are feelings that generally have both physiological and cognitive elements and that influence behavior.

Consider, for example, how it feels to be happy. First, you obviously experience a feeling that you can differentiate from other emotions. It is likely that you also experience some identifiable physical changes in your body: Perhaps your heart rate increases, or—as in our example earlier—you find yourself "jumping for joy." Finally, the emotion probably encompasses cognitive elements; your understanding and evaluation of the meaning of what is happening in your environment prompts your feelings of happiness.

It is also possible, however, to experience an emotion without the presence of cognitive elements. For instance, we may react with fear to an unusual or novel situation (such as coming into contact with an erratic, unpredictable individual), or we may experience pleasure over sexual excitation without having cognitive awareness or understanding of what it is about the situation that is exciting.

In fact, some psychologists argue that there are entirely separate systems that govern cognitive responses and emotional responses. One current controversy is whether the emotional response takes predominance over the cognitive response or vice versa. Some theorists suggest that we first respond to a situation with an emotional reaction, and later try to understand it (Zajonc, 1985). For

Emotions: Feelings (such as happiness, despair, and sorrow) that generally have both physiological and cognitive elements and that influence behavior

---

ANSWERS (REVIEW II):

1. salt concentration of cells; total fluid volume in circulatory system; rise in body temperature or energy expenditure **2.** True **3.** 1-b; 2-a; 3-c **4.** weight set point **5.** False; these cues tend to be primarily external. **6.** Metabolism **7.** Bulimia; anorexia nervosa **8.** achievement **9.** c.

example, we may enjoy a complex modern symphony without understanding it or knowing why we like it.

In contrast, other theorists propose that people first develop cognitions about a situation and then react emotionally. This school of thought suggests that it is necessary for us to first think about and understand a stimulus or situation, relating it to what we already know, before we can react on an emotional level (Lazarus, 1984; 1991a; 1991b).

Both sides of this debate are supported by research, and the question is far from being resolved (Scheff, 1985; Frijda, 1987, 1988). It is possible that the sequence varies from situation to situation, with emotions predominating in some instances and cognitive processes occurring first in others. Whatever the ultimate sequence, however, it is clear that our emotions play a major role in influencing our behavior.

The Functions of Emotions

Imagine what it would be like if you had no emotions—no depths of despair, no depression, no remorse, but at the same time no happiness, joy, or love. Obviously life would be much less interesting, even dull, without the experience of emotion.

But do emotions serve any purpose beyond making life interesting? Psychologists have identified a number of important functions that emotions play in our daily lives (Scherer, 1984). Among the most important of those functions are the following:

■ Preparing us for action. Emotions act as a link between events in the external environment and behavioral responses that an individual makes. For example, if we saw an angry dog charging toward us, the emotional reaction (fear) would be associated with physiological arousal of the sympathetic division of the autonomic nervous system (see Chapter 3). The role of the sympathetic division is to prepare us for emergency action, which presumably would get us moving out of the dog's way—quickly. Emotions, then, are stimuli that aid in the development of effective responses to various situations.

■ Shaping our future behavior. Emotions serve to promote learning of information that will assist us in making appropriate responses in the future. For example, the emotional response that occurs when a person experiences something unpleasant—such as the threatening dog—teaches that person to avoid similar circumstances in the future. Similarly, pleasant emotions act as reinforcement for prior behavior and therefore are apt to lead an individual to seek out similar situations in the future. Thus, the feeling of satisfaction that follows giving to a charity is likely to reinforce charitable behavior and make it more likely to occur in the future.

■ Helping us to regulate social interaction. As we shall discuss in detail later, the emotions we experience are frequently obvious to observers, as they are communicated through our verbal and nonverbal behaviors. These behaviors can act as a signal to observers, allowing them to better understand what we are experiencing and predict our future behavior. In turn, this promotes more effective and appropriate social interaction. For instance, a mother who sees the terror on her 2-year-old son's face when he sees a frightening picture in a book is able to comfort and reassure him, thereby helping him to deal with his environment more effectively in the future.

Determining the Range of Emotions: Labeling our Feelings

If we were to try to list the words in the English language that have been used to describe emotions, we would end up with at least 500 different examples (Averill, 1975). The list would range from such obvious emotions as "happiness" and "fear" to less common ones, such as "adventurousness" and "pensiveness."

One challenge for psychologists has been to try to sort through this list in order to identify the most important, fundamental emotions in our everyday lives, as well as to try to determine how our emotions are related to one another (Russell, 1991). One of the most comprehensive efforts has been carried out by Robert Plutchik (1984), who asked people to rate each of a large set of emotions along thirty-four different rating scales. Then, by mathematically combining the ratings, he was able to determine the relationship among the various emotions, as well as which emotions were most fundamental.

The results were clear: Eight different fundamental emotions (joy, acceptance, fear, surprise, sadness, disgust, anger, and anticipation) emerged, and they formed the pattern within the wheel shown in Figure 11-5. Furthermore, these primary emotions could be consolidated into the two-emotion combinations shown on the outside of the wheel. Emotions nearer one another in the circle are more closely related, while those opposite each other are conceptual opposites. For instance, sadness is opposite joy, and anticipation is opposite surprise.

While Plutchik's configuration of the basic emotions is reasonable, it is not the only plausible one. Other psychologists have come up with somewhat different lists, as we shall see when we discuss the communication of emotion and nonverbal behavior later in this chapter. Furthermore, some theorists reject entirely the notion that a small number of basic emotions exist. Instead, they suggest that emotions are best understood by breaking them down into their component parts (Ortony & Turner, 1990).

Still, while it has proven challenging for psychologists to produce a definitive

FIGURE 11-5

Plutchik's emotion wheel demonstrates how eight primary emotions are related to one another. (Plutchik, 1980.)

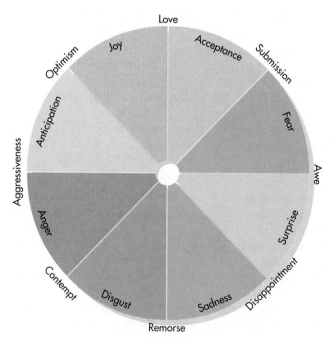

list of the primary emotions, each of us has little difficulty in identifying what we are experiencing at any given moment. The process by which we come to this understanding forms the basis of a number of theories of emotion, which we will discuss next.

DECIPHERING OUR OWN EMOTIONS

I've never been so angry before; I feel my heart pounding, and I'm trembling all over. . . . I don't know how I'll get through the performance. I feel like my stomach is filled with butterflies. . . . That was quite a mistake I made! My face must be incredibly red. . . . When I heard the footsteps in the night I was so frightened that I couldn't catch my breath.

If you examine our language, you will find that there are literally dozens of ways to describe how we feel when we are experiencing an emotion, and that the language we use to describe emotions is, for the most part, based on the physical symptoms that are associated with a particular emotional experience (Koveces, 1987).

Consider, for instance, the experience of fear. Pretend that it is late one New Year's Eve. You are walking down a dark road, and you hear a stranger approaching behind you. It is clear that he is not trying to hurry by but is coming directly toward you. You think of what you will do if the stranger attempts to rob you—or worse, hurt you in some way.

While these thoughts are running through your head, it is almost certain that something rather dramatic will be happening to your body. Among the most likely physiological reactions that may occur, which are associated with activation of the autonomic nervous system (see Chapter 3), are those listed here:

- The rate and depth of your breathing will increase.
- Your heart will speed up, pumping more blood through your circulatory system.
- The pupils of your eyes will open wider, allowing more light to enter and thereby increasing your visual sensitivity.
- Your mouth will become dry as your salivary glands, and in fact your entire digestive system, stop functioning. At the same time, though, your sweat glands may increase their activity, since increased sweating will help you rid yourself of excess heat developed by any emergency activity in which you engage.
- As the muscles just below the surface of your skin contract, your hair may literally stand on end.

Of course, all these physiological changes are likely to occur without your awareness. At the same time, though, the emotional experience accompanying them will be obvious to you: You would most surely report being fearful.

Although it is a relatively straightforward matter to describe the general physical reactions that accompany emotions, the specific role that these physiological responses play in the experience of emotions has proved to be a major puzzle for psychologists. As we shall see, some theorists suggest that there are specific bodily reactions that *cause* us to experience a particular emotion—we experience fear, for instance, *because* our heart is pounding and we are breathing deeply. In contrast, other theorists suggest that the physiological reaction is the *result* of the experience of an emotion. In this view, we experience fear, and this emotional experience causes our heart to pound and our breathing to deepen.

The James-Lange Theory: Do Gut Reactions Equal Emotions?

To William James and Carl Lange, who were among the first researchers to explore the nature of emotions, emotional experience is, very simply, a reaction to instinctive bodily events that occurred as a response to some situation or event in the environment. This view is summarized in James's statement, "... we feel sorry because we cry, angry because we strike, afraid because we tremble" (James, 1890).

James and Lange took the view that the instinctive response of crying at a loss leads us to feel sorrow; that striking out at someone who frustrates us results in our feeling anger; that trembling at a menacing threat causes us to feel afraid. They suggested that every major emotion has a particular physiological "gut" reaction of internal organs—called a **visceral experience**—attached to it, and it is this specific pattern of visceral response that leads us to label the emotional experience.

In sum, James and Lange proposed that we experience emotions as a result of physiological changes that produce specific sensations. In turn, these sensations are interpreted by the brain as particular kinds of emotional experiences (see Figure 11-6). This view has come to be called the **James-Lange theory of emotion** (Izard, 1990a; Laird & Bresler, 1990).

The James-Lange theory has some serious drawbacks, however. In order for the theory to be correct, visceral changes would have to occur at a relatively rapid pace, since we experience some emotions—such as fear upon hearing a stranger rapidly approaching on a dark night—almost instantaneously. Yet emotional experiences frequently happen even before many physiological changes have time to be set into motion. Because of the slowness with which some visceral changes

Visceral (VIS er al) **experience:** The "gut" reaction experienced internally, triggering an emotion (see James-Lange theory)

James-Lange theory of emotion: The belief that emotional experience is a reaction to bodily events occurring as a result of an external situation ("I feel sad because I am crying")

FIGURE 11-6

A comparison of three models of emotion.

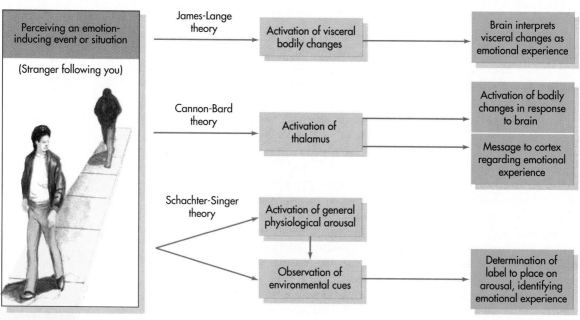

take place, it is hard to see how they could be the source of immediate emotional experience.

The James-Lange theory poses another difficulty: Physiological arousal does not invariably produce emotional experience. For example, a person who is jogging has an increased heartbeat and respiration rate, as well as many of the other physiological changes associated with certain emotions. Yet joggers do not typically think of such changes in terms of emotions. There cannot be a one-to-one correspondence, then, between visceral changes and emotional experience. Visceral changes by themselves may not be sufficient to produce emotion.

Finally, our internal organs produce relatively limited sensations. It is difficult to imagine how the range of emotions that people are capable of experiencing could be the result of unique visceral changes. Many emotions are actually correlated with relatively similar sorts of visceral changes, a fact that contradicts the James-Lange theory.

The Cannon-Bard Theory: Physiological Reactions as the Result of Emotions

In response to the difficulties inherent in the James-Lange theory, Walter Cannon—and later Philip Bard—suggested an alternative view. In what has come to be known as the **Cannon-Bard theory of emotion**, they proposed the model illustrated in the second part of Figure 11-6 (Cannon, 1929). The major thrust of the theory is to reject the view that physiological arousal alone leads to the perception of emotion. Instead, the theory assumes that both physiological arousal *and* the emotional experience are produced simultaneously by the same nerve impulse, which Cannon and Bard suggested emanates from the brain's thalamus.

According to the theory, after an emotion-inducing stimulus is perceived, the thalamus is the initial site of the emotional response. In turn, the thalamus sends a signal to the viscera, which are then activated, and at the same time communicates a message to the cerebral cortex regarding the nature of the emotion being experienced. Hence, it is not necessary for different emotions to have unique physiological patterns associated with them—as long as the message sent to the cerebral cortex differs according to the specific emotion.

The Cannon-Bard theory seems to have been accurate in its rejection of the view that physiological arousal alone accounts for emotions. However, recent research has led to some important modifications to the theory. As you may recall from Chapter 3, it is now understood that the hypothalamus and the limbic system—not the thalamus—play a major role in emotional experience. In addition, the simultaneity of the physiological and emotional responses—a fundamental assumption of the theory—has yet to be conclusively demonstrated (Pribram, 1984). This ambiguity has allowed room for yet another theory of emotions: the Schachter-Singer theory.

Cannon-Bard theory of emotion: The belief that both physiological and emotional arousal are produced simultaneously by the same nerve impulse

The Schachter-Singer Theory: Emotions as Labels

Suppose, as you were being followed down a dark street on New Year's Eve, you noticed a man being followed by a shady figure on the other side of the street. Now assume that instead of reacting with fear, the man begins to laugh and act gleeful. Might the reactions of this other individual be sufficient to lay your fears to rest? Might you, in fact, decide there is nothing to fear, and get into the spirit of the evening by beginning to feel happiness and glee yourself?

Schachter-Singer theory of emotion: The belief that emotions are determined jointly by a nonspecific kind of physiological arousal and its interpretation, based on environmental cues

According to an explanation that focuses on the role of cognition, the **Schachter-Singer theory of emotion**, this might very well happen. This final approach to explaining emotions emphasizes that we identify the emotion we are experiencing by observing our environment and comparing ourselves with others (Schachter & Singer, 1962).

A classic experiment found evidence for this hypothesis. In the study, subjects were told that they would receive an injection of a vitamin called Suproxin. In reality, they were given epinephrine, a drug that causes an increase in physiological arousal, including higher heart and respiration rates and a reddening of the face, responses that typically occur during strong emotional reactions. Although one group of subjects was informed of the actual effects of the drug, another was kept in the dark.

Subjects in both groups were then individually placed in a situation where a confederate of the experimenter acted in one of two ways. In one condition, he acted angry and hostile, complaining that he would refuse to answer the personal questions on a questionnaire that the experimenter had asked him to complete. In the other condition, his behavior was quite the opposite. He behaved euphorically, flying paper airplanes and tossing wads of paper, in general acting quite happy with the situation.

The key purpose of the experiment was to determine how the subjects would react emotionally to the confederate's behavior. When they were asked to describe their own emotional state at the end of the experiment, subjects who had been told of the effects of the drug were relatively unaffected by the behavior of the confederate. They thought their physiological arousal was due to the drug and therefore were not faced with the need to find a reason for their arousal. Hence, they reported experiencing relatively little emotion.

On the other hand, subjects who had not been told of the drug's real effects were influenced by the confederate's behavior. Those subjects exposed to the angry confederate reported that they felt angry, while those exposed to the euphoric confederate reported feeling happy. In sum, the results suggest that uninformed subjects turned to the environment and the behavior of others for an explanation of the physiological arousal they were experiencing.

The results of the Schachter-Singer experiment, then, support a cognitive view of emotions, in which emotions are determined jointly by a relatively nonspecific kind of physiological arousal *and* the labeling of the arousal based on cues from the environment (refer back to the third part of Figure 11-6).

The Schachter-Singer theory of emotion has led to some interesting psychological experiments in many areas of psychology. For example, psychologists studying the determinants of interpersonal attraction have drawn applications from the theory. In one intriguing and imaginative experiment, an attractive, college-aged woman stood at the end of a swaying 450-foot suspension bridge that spanned a deep canyon. The woman was ostensibly conducting a survey, and she asked men who made it across the bridge a series of questions. She then gave them her telephone number, telling them that if they were interested in the results of the experiment they could contact her in the upcoming week.

In comparison to members of a control group who had completed the questionnaire after strolling across a stable bridge spanning a shallow stream ten feet below, the men who had come across the dangerous bridge showed significant differences in their questionnaire results: Sexual imagery was considerably higher. Furthermore, those crossing the dangerous span were significantly more likely to call the woman in the upcoming week, suggesting that their attraction to her was higher. The men whose arousal was increased by the dangerous bridge

This bridge was used to increase the arousal of men in an experiment carried out by Donald Dutton.

seemed to have searched for a reason for their physiological arousal—and ended up attributing the cause to the attractive woman (Dutton & Aron, 1974). Consistent with the Schachter-Singer theory, then, the men's emotional response was based on a labeling of their arousal.

Unfortunately, evidence gathered to confirm the Schachter-Singer theory has not always been supportive (Reisenzein, 1983; Leventhal & Tomarken, 1986). Even the original experiment has been criticized on methodological grounds and for certain ambiguities in the results. Furthermore, there is evidence both that physiological arousal is not essential for emotional experience to occur in some cases, and that physiological factors *by themselves* can account for one's emotional state in other instances (Marshall & Zimbardo, 1979; Chwalisz, Diener, & Gallagher, 1988). For example, some drugs invariably produce depression as a side effect no matter what the nature of the situation or the environmental cues present.

On the whole, however, the Schachter-Singer theory of emotions is important because it suggests that, at least under some circumstances, emotional experiences are a joint function of physiological arousal and the labeling of that arousal. When the source of physiological arousal is unclear to us, we may look to our environment to determine just what it is we are experiencing.

Summing Up the Theories of Emotion

At this point, you have good reason to ask why there are so many theories of emotion and, perhaps even more important, which is most accurate. Actually, we have only scratched the surface; there are even more explanatory theories of emotion (e.g., Izard, Kagan, & Zajonc, 1989; Kemper, 1990; Frijda, Kuipers, & terSchure, 1989; Lazarus, 1991b).

The explanation as to why there are so many theories and which is the most accurate is actually the same: Emotions are such complex phenomena that no single theory has been able to explain all facets of emotional experience completely satisfactorily. For each of the three major theories there is contradictory evidence of one sort or another, and therefore no theory has proven invariably accurate in its predictions. On the other hand, this is not a cause for despair—or unhappiness, fear, or any other negative emotion. It simply reflects the fact that psychology is an evolving, developing science. Presumably, as more evidence is gathered, the specific answers to questions about the nature of emotions will become clearer. Moreover, the lack of definitive knowledge about the nature of emotions has not stopped people from applying what we now know about emotional responses to some practical problems, as we discuss next.

The Truth About Lies: Using Emotional Responses to Separate the Dishonest from the Honest

> An accused rapist wants to prove his innocence and asks to take a lie detector test. . . . In order to receive their top-secret clearance, the President's cabinet members had to take a lie detector test. . . . To determine if potential employees are taking drugs, a defense contractor requires all prospective employees to take a lie detector test.

Polygraph: An electronic device that measures bodily changes which may signal that a person is lying; often called a lie detector

The common element in these situations is the use of the lie detector, or polygraph, to determine if people are telling the truth. A **polygraph** is an electronic device designed to expose people who are telling lies. The basic assumption behind the apparatus is straightforward: The sympathetic nervous system of a person who is not being truthful becomes aroused as his or her emotionality increases, and the physiological changes that are indicative of this arousal can be detected by the polygraph.

Actually, a number of separate physiological changes are measured simultaneously by a lie detector, including an irregularity in breathing pattern, an increase in heart rate and blood pressure, and an increase in sweating. In theory, the polygraph operator asks a series of questions, some of which he knows will elicit verifiable, truthful responses—such as what a person's name and address are. Then, when more critical questions are answered, the operator can observe the nature of the physiological changes that occur. Answers whose accompanying physiological responses deviate significantly from those accompanying truthful responses are assumed to be false (Patrick & Iacono, 1991).

Unfortunately, there is no foolproof technique for assessing the extent of the physiological changes that may indicate a lie. Even truthful responses may elicit physiological arousal, if the question is emotion-laden (Waid & Orne, 1982). How many innocent people accused of a murder, for instance, would *not* respond emotionally when asked whether they committed the crime, since they know that their future may hang in the balance?

One further drawback of lie detector tests is that people are occasionally capable of fooling the polygraph (Barland & Raskin, 1973; Honts, Raskin, & Kircher, 1987). For instance, biofeedback techniques (see Chapter 3) can be employed to produce emotional responses to accompany even truthful statements, meaning that the polygraph operator will be unable to differentiate between honest and dishonest responses. Even biting one's tongue or hiding a tack in a shoe and pressing on it as each question is answered may be sufficient to produce physiological arousal during each response, making truthful and deceptive responses indistinguishable (Honts, Hodes, & Raskin, 1985).

Because of these sources of error, lie detector operators often make mistakes when trying to judge another person's honesty (Saxe, Dougherty, & Cross, 1985; Iacono, 1991), and the American Psychological Association has adopted a resolution stating that the evidence for the effectiveness of polygraphs "is still unsatisfactory'' (*APA Monitor*, 1986). Even the major proponent of the use of polygraphs—the American Polygraph Association—admits an error rate between 4 and 13 percent, and critics suggest that research has shown that the actual rate is closer to 30 percent (Meyer, 1989). Using such evidence, U.S. federal law bars employers from using polygraphs as screening devices for most jobs (Bales, 1988).

In sum, good reason exists to doubt that polygraph tests can determine accurately whether someone is lying. Because of skepticism about the validity of lie detectors, many employers have turned instead to written ''honesty tests.'' Such tests are designed to winnow out potentially honest employees from dishonest ones, and we will discuss these in Chapter 15. For now, the major point to keep in mind is that no one has yet identified a foolproof way to distinguish people who are telling the truth from those who are lying.

RECAP AND REVIEW III

RECAP

◀ Emotions are feelings that generally have both a physiological component and a cognitive component.

◀ Emotions have a number of functions, including preparing us for action, shaping our future behavior, and regulating social interaction.

◀ A number of physiological changes accompany strong emotion, including rapid breathing and increased heart rate, opening of the pupils, dryness in the mouth, increase in sweating, and the sensation of hair ''standing on end.''

◀ The major theories of emotion are the James-Lange, Cannon-Bard, and Schachter-Singer theories.

◀ Polygraphs, designed to identify people who are lying on the basis of their physiological reactions, are not dependable.

REVIEW

1. Emotions are always accompanied by a cognitive response. True or false? ___*False*___
2. The __*James*-*Lange*__ theory of emotions states that emotions are a response to instinctive bodily events.
3. The bodily events described in No. 2 are known as ___*visceral*___ or ___*gut*___ reactions.

4. Each emotion is accompanied by a unique set of physiological responses, thus proving the James-Lange emotion theory. True or false? ___*False*___
5. According to the __*Cannon-Bard*__ theory of emotion, both an emotional response and physiological arousal are produced simultaneously by nerve impulses. These nerve impulses were originally thought to emanate from the __*thalamus*__.
6. Your friend tells you, ''I was at a party last night. During the course of the evening, my general level of arousal increased. Since I was at a party where people were enjoying themselves, I assumed I must have felt happy.'' What theory of emotion does your friend ascribe to? *Schachter-Singer*
7. The __*polygraph*__ or ''lie detector'' is a machine used to measure physiological responses associated with answers to questions.

Ask Yourself

Knowing what you do about physiological responses associated with emotions, do you think polygraphs should be used in criminal situations in order to determine a person's guilt or innocence? Should they be used in business to verify the truth of employees' statements on such topics as drug use, or as a means to decide hirings and firings?

(Answers to review questions are on page 368.)

NONVERBAL BEHAVIOR AND THE EXPRESSION OF EMOTIONS

Ancient Sanskrit writings speak of someone who, on making an evasive answer, ''rubs the great toe along the ground, and shivers.'' Shakespeare writes of Macbeth's face as ''a place where men may read strange matters.'' Old torch songs

Channels: Paths along which verbal and nonverbal behavioral messages are communicated (e.g., facial expressions, eye contact, body movements)

claim "your eyes are the eyes of a woman in love." Such examples demonstrate how nonverbal behavior has long had the reputation of revealing people's emotions. Only recently, though, have psychologists demonstrated the validity of such speculation, finding that nonverbal behavior does represent a major means by which we communicate our emotions.

We now know that nonverbal behavior communicates messages simultaneously across several **channels**, paths along which communications flow. For example, facial expressions, eye contact, body movements, tone of voice, and even less obvious behaviors such as the positioning of the eyebrows can each be conceptualized as separate nonverbal channels of communication. Furthermore, each individual channel is capable of carrying a particular message—which may or may not be related to the message being carried by the other channels. Because facial expressions represent the primary means of communicating emotional states, we will concentrate on them, examining their role in the experience of emotions.

Universality in Emotional Expressivity

Consider, for a moment, the six photos displayed in Figure 11-7. Can you identify the emotions being expressed by the person in each of the photos?

If you are a good judge of facial expressions, you will conclude that six of the basic emotions are displayed: happiness, anger, sadness, surprise, disgust, and fear. These categories are the emotions that emerge in literally hundreds of studies of nonverbal behavior as being consistently distinct and identifiable, even by untrained observers (Ekman & O'Sullivan, 1991).

What is particularly interesting about these six categories is that they are not limited to members of western cultures but rather appear to represent the basic emotions expressed universally by members of the human race, regardless of where they have been raised and what learning experiences they have had. This point was demonstrated convincingly by psychologist Paul Ekman, who traveled to New Guinea to study members of an isolated jungle tribe having had almost no contact with westerners (Ekman, 1972). The people of the tribe did not speak or understand English, they had never seen a movie, and they had had very limited experience with Caucasians before Ekman's arrival.

To learn about how the New Guineans used nonverbal behavior in emotional expression, Ekman told them a story involving an emotion and then showed them a set of three faces of westerners, one of which was displaying an emotion appropriate for the story. The task was to choose the face showing the most reasonable expression. The results showed that the New Guineans' responses were quite similar to those of western subjects, and New Guinean children showed even greater skill in identifying the appropriate emotion than the New Guinean adults did. Interestingly, the only difference occurred in identifying fearful faces, which were often confused with surprise by the tribespeople.

In addition to learning whether the New Guinean natives interpreted emotional expression in the same way as westerners did, it was important to find out whether both groups showed similar nonverbal responses. To do this, other natives were told the stories that Ekman had used earlier and were asked to provide a facial expression appropriate to the subject of the story. These expressions

---

ANSWERS (REVIEW III):

1. False; emotions may occur without a cognitive response **2.** James-Lange **3.** visceral; "gut" **4.** False; a wide number of emotions are related to similar bodily reactions. **5.** Cannon-Bard; thalamus **6.** Schachter-Singer **7.** polygraph

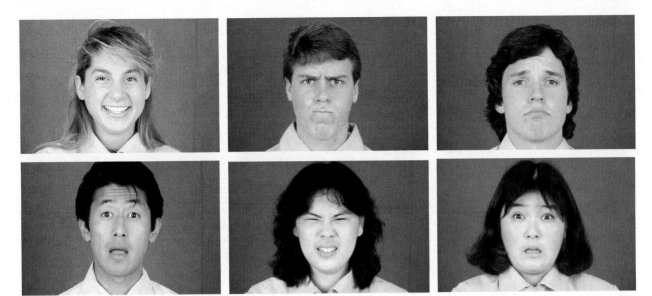

FIGURE 11-7
These photos demonstrate six of the primary emotions: happiness, anger, sadness, surprise, disgust, and fear.

were videotaped, and a group of subjects in the United States were asked to look at the faces and identify the emotion being expressed. The results were clear: The western viewers—who had never before seen any New Guineans—were surprisingly accurate in their judgments, with the exception of expressions of fear and surprise.

In sum, convincing evidence exists for universality across cultures in the way basic emotions are displayed and interpreted (Ekman & O'Sullivan, 1991; Aronoff, Barclay, & Stevenson, 1988). Because the New Guineans were so isolated, they could not have learned from westerners to recognize or produce similar facial expressions. Instead, their similar abilities and manner of responding emotionally appear to have been present innately. Of course, it is possible to argue that similar experiences in both cultures led to learning of similar types of nonverbal behavior, but this appears unlikely, since the two cultures are so very different. The expression of basic emotions, then, seems to be universal (Ekman, 1989).

Why is there similarity in the expression of basic emotions across cultures? One explanation is based on a hypothesis known as the **facial-affect program** (Ekman, 1972). The facial-affect program—which is assumed to be universally present at birth—is analogous to a computer program that is turned on when a particular emotion is experienced. When set in motion, the "program" activates a set of nerve impulses that make the face display an appropriate expression. Each primary emotion produces a unique set of muscular movements, forming the kinds of expressions seen in Figure 11-7. For example, the emotion of happiness is universally displayed by movement of the zygomatic major, a muscle that raises the corners of the mouth—forming what we would call a smile (Ekman, Davidson, & Friesen, 1990).

Facial-affect program: The activation of a set of nerve impulses that make the face display the appropriate expression

The Facial-Feedback Hypothesis: Smile, Though You're Feeling Blue

If you want to feel happy, try smiling.

That is the implication of an intriguing notion known as the **facial-feedback hypothesis**. According to this hypothesis, facial expressions not only *reflect* emotional experience, they also help *determine* how people experience and label emotions (Izard, 1990). The basic idea is that "wearing" an emotional expression

Facial-feedback hypothesis: The notion that facial expressions not only reflect, but also determine and help people identify, the experience of emotions

(a)

(b)

(c)

FIGURE 11-8

This actor was told to (a) "raise your brows and pull them together," (b) "now raise your upper eyelids," and (c) "now also stretch your lips horizontally, back toward your ears." If you follow these directions yourself, it may well result in your experiencing fear.

provides muscular feedback to the brain which helps produce an emotion congruent with the expression. For instance, the muscles activated when we smile may send a message to the brain indicating the experience of happiness—even if there is nothing in the environment that would produce that particular emotion. Some theoreticians have gone further, suggesting that facial expressions are *necessary* for an emotion to be experienced (Rinn, 1984, 1991). According to this view, if there is no facial expression present, the emotion cannot be felt.

Support for the facial-feedback hypothesis comes from what has become a classic experiment carried out by psychologist Paul Ekman and colleagues (Ekman, Levenson, & Friesen, 1983). In the study, professional actors were asked to follow very explicit instructions regarding movements of muscles in their faces (see Figure 11-8). You might try this example yourself:

> Raise your brows and pull them together; raise your upper eyelids; now stretch your lips horizontally back toward your ears.

FIGURE 11-9

According to the controversial vascular theory of emotion, facial expressions affect emotional experience by regulating the flow of blood within the brain. (Source: Robert Zajonc.)

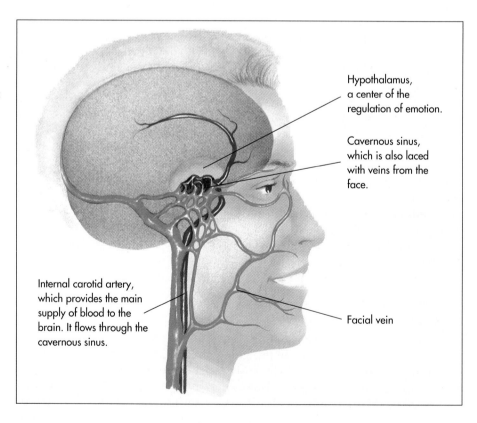

Hypothalamus, a center of the regulation of emotion.

Cavernous sinus, which is also laced with veins from the face.

Internal carotid artery, which provides the main supply of blood to the brain. It flows through the cavernous sinus.

Facial vein

Although ample evidence demonstrates the existence of a close link between facial expressions and emotional states, neither the facial-affect program nor the facial-feedback hypothesis explains *why* a specific expression is linked to a particular emotion. Is it just chance that people smile when they are happy and frown when they are sad?

Not at all, in the opinion of psychologist Robert Zajonc. In his controversial **vascular theory of emotions**, he argues that there is a logical reason why, for example, we don't smile when we are sad or frown when we are happy. According to Zajonc (pronounced Zi-onz), the configuration of the face during displays of particular emotions affects the temperature of blood flowing to the brain and in particular the hypothalamus. Because the hypothalamus is involved in the regulation of behavior such as aggression, eating, and sex (as we discussed earlier in the chapter), it is closely related to emotional experience. Furthermore, if the blood flow-

WHY DON'T WE SMILE WHEN WE'RE SAD? THE BLOODLINES OF EMOTIONS

ing to the hypothalamus is cooled, people report being in a better mood; and if it is warmer, people say they feel more unhappy (see Figure 11-9).

Zajonc contends that facial expressions affect the temperature of the blood reaching the hypothalamus. For example, smiling tightens certain muscles within the cheeks, and the wider the smile, the tighter the muscles constrict. In turn, this brings about a decrease in the temperature of the blood supply leading to the brain's hypothalamus, resulting in the experience of positive emotions. Expressions such as a frown or a scowl, in contrast, tighten a different set of muscles that tend to raise the temperature of the blood reaching the brain. In this case, the temperature of the blood to the brain increases, and people feel bleak (Zajonc, Murphy, & Inglehart, 1989; Zajonc, 1990).

Pursuing this line of reasoning, Zajonc comes up with some interesting hypotheses. For example, he suggests that breathing through one's nose also cools the blood supply leading to the brain. As a result, people feel more positive. Speculating further, Zajonc suggests that the positive moods that result from meditation and biofeedback may result from changes in breathing patterns. As more air is inhaled through the nose, people's blood and hypothalamus are cooled, and they experience more positive emotions.

The intriguing hypothesis that links the temperature of the blood flow to the brain and the experience of particular emotions remains just that: an intriguing hypothesis. For instance, it is not clear that changes in brain blood flow are directly associated with specific emotional experiences. Nevertheless, evidence is mounting that the link between specific facial configurations and emotion may be an important one (Zajonc, 1990; Izard, 1990a).

After carrying out these directions—which, as you may have guessed, are meant to produce an expression of fear—the actors showed a rise in heart rate and a decline in body temperature, physiological reactions that are characteristic of fear. Overall, facial expressions representative of the primary emotions produced physiological effects similar to those accompanying the emotions under other circumstances.

Although support for the facial-feedback hypothesis is not firm (Matsumoto, 1987), there is sufficient evidence in its favor to suggest that the old lyric "Smile, though you're feeling blue" may not be far from the mark in its suggestion that you will feel better by putting a smile on your face (Izard, 1990a; Levenson, Ekman, & Friesen, 1990). (For more on the relationship between facial expression and emotion, see the Cutting Edge box.)

Vascular theory of emotions: The theory that there is a link between particular facial expressions and the temperature of the blood flow to the brain, which in turn affects the experience of emotions

RECAP AND REVIEW IV

RECAP

◄ Six primary emotions are displayed through facial expressions and understood similarly across different cultures.

◄ The facial-feedback hypothesis maintains that facial expressions not only reflect emotional experience, but

they may also determine how people experience and label emotions.

◄ One theory suggests that there is an association between specific facial configuration and blood flow to the brain, leading to emotional experience.

1. What are the six primary emotions that can be identified from facial expressions?
2. Viewed as similar to a computer program, the _____facial_____-_____affect_____ program provides a possible explanation for the universality in the expression of emotions.
3. According to the ___facial___ - ___feedback___ hypothesis, an emotion cannot be felt without an accompanying facial response.

4. According to Robert Zajonc, blood temperature can affect a person's mood state. True or false? ____True____

Ask Yourself

If basic emotions are displayed similarly across cultures, why do we sometimes have difficulty in interpreting the meaning of the nonverbal behavior of individuals from cultures different than our own?

(Answers to review questions are on page 373.)

LOOKING BACK

■ *How does motivation direct and energize behavior?*

1. The topic of motivation considers the factors that direct and energize behavior. Drive is the motivational tension that energizes behavior in order to fulfill a need. Primary drives relate to basic biological needs. Secondary drives are those in which no obvious biological need is fulfilled. Motivational drives often operate under the principle of homeostasis, by which an organism tries to maintain an optimal level of internal biological functioning by making up for any deviations from its usual state.

2. A number of broad theories of motivation move beyond explanations that rely on instincts. Drive-reduction theories, though useful for primary drives, are inadequate for explaining behavior in which the goal is not to reduce a drive but to maintain or even increase excitement or arousal. Arousal theory suggests that we try to maintain a particular level of stimulation and activity. The Yerkes-Dodson law, dealing with the relationship between task difficulty and the optimal level of motivation, is consistent with arousal theory.

3. An alternative explanation of motivation—incentive theory—focuses on the positive aspects of the environment that direct and energize behavior. In contrast, opponent-process theory suggests that opponent forces in the nervous system arise when initial arousal results from some stimulus. If the initial arousal is positive, the opponent forces are negative, and vice versa.

4. Cognitive theories of motivation focus on the role of thoughts, expectations, and understanding of the world. Expectancy-value theory, a kind of cognitive theory, suggests that expectations that a behavior will accomplish a particular goal and our understanding of the value of that goal underlie behavior.

5. Maslow's hierarchy of needs suggests that there are five needs (physiological, safety, love and belongingness, esteem, and self-actualization). Only after the more basic needs are fulfilled is a person able to move toward higher-order needs.

■ *What are the biological and social factors that underlie thirst and hunger?*

6. The stimuli that motivate drinking are mainly internal. Salt concentration of the body's cells varies as a function of the amount of internal fluid. Furthermore, a decrease in the total volume of fluid in the circulatory system can cause thirst. A rise in body temperature or an energy expenditure can increase thirst.

7. Eating behavior is subject to homeostasis, since most people's weight stays within a relatively stable range. Organisms tend to be sensitive to the nutritional value of the food they eat, with the hypothalamus being closely related to food intake. In addition to the biological factors that affect eating behavior, social factors also play a role. For instance, mealtimes, cultural food preferences, the attractiveness of food, and other learned habits determine when and how much one eats. An oversensitivity to social cues and an insensitivity to internal cues may also be related to obesity. In addition, obesity may be caused by an unusually high weight set point—the weight at which the body attempts to maintain homeostasis—or by the rate of metabolism.

■ *How are needs relating to achievement, affiliation, and power motivation exhibited?*

8. Need for achievement refers to the stable, learned characteristic in which a person strives to attain a level of excellence. People high in the need for achievement tend to seek out tasks that are of moderate difficulty, while those low in the need for achievement seek out only very easy and very difficult tasks. Need for achievement is usually measured through the Thematic Apperception Test (TAT), a series of pictures about which a person writes a story.

9. The need for affiliation is a concern with establishing and maintaining relationships with others, whereas the need for power is a tendency to seek to exert an impact on others.

■ What are emotions, how do we experience them, and what are their functions?

10. One broad definition of emotions views them as feelings that may affect behavior and generally have both a physiological and a cognitive component. What this definition does not do is address the issue of whether there are separate systems that govern cognitive and emotional responses, and whether one has primacy over the other.

11. Among the functions of emotions are to prepare us for action, shape future behavior through learning, and help to regulate social interaction. Although the range of emotions is wide, according to one category system there are only eight primary emotions: joy, acceptance, fear, surprise, sadness, disgust, anger, and anticipation.

12. Among the general physiological responses to strong emotion are opening of the pupils, dryness of the mouth, and increases in sweating, rate of breathing, heart rate, and blood pressure. Because these physiological changes are not the full explanation of emotional experience, a number of distinct theories of emotion have been developed.

13. The James-Lange theory suggests that emotional experience is a reaction to bodily, or visceral, changes that occur as a response to an environmental event. These visceral experiences are interpreted as an emotional response. In contrast to the James-Lange theory, the Cannon-Bard theory contends that visceral movements are too slow to explain rapid shifts of emotion and visceral changes do not always produce emotion. Instead, the Cannon-Bard theory suggests that both physiological arousal *and* an emotional experience are produced simultaneously by the same nerve impulse. Therefore, the visceral experience itself does not necessarily differ among differing emotions.

14. The third explanation, the Schachter-Singer theory, rejects the view that the physiological and emotional responses are simultaneous. Instead, it suggests that emotions are determined jointly by a relatively nonspecific physiological arousal and the subsequent labeling of that arousal. This labeling process uses cues from the environment to determine how others are behaving in the same situation.

■ How does nonverbal behavior relate to the expression of emotions?

15. Emotions can be revealed through a person's facial expression. In fact, there is universality in emotional expressivity, at least for the basic emotions, across members of different cultures. In addition, there are similarities in the way members of different cultures understand the emotional expressions of others. One explanation for this similarity rests on the existence of an innate facial-affect program which activates a set of muscle movements representing the emotion being experienced.

16. The facial-feedback hypothesis suggests that facial expressions not only are a reflection of emotions but also can help determine and produce emotional experience. The vascular theory of emotions suggests a link between a particular facial configuration and the temperature of the blood flow to the brain, which in turn affects the experience of emotions.

KEY TERMS AND CONCEPTS

motivation (p. 334)
motives (p. 334)
instinct (p. 335)
drive-reduction theory (p. 336)
drive (p. 336)
primary drives (p. 336)
secondary drives (p. 336)
homeostasis (p. 336)
arousal theory (p. 337)
Yerkes-Dodson law (p. 338)
incentive (p. 338)
incentive theory (p. 339)
opponent-process theory of
  motivation (p. 340)
cognitive theories of motivation
  (p. 341)
expectancy-value theory (p. 341)

intrinsic motivation (p. 341)
extrinsic motivation (p. 341)
self-actualization (p. 342)
obesity (p. 345)
hypothalamus (p. 347)
lateral hypothalamus (p. 347)
ventromedial hypothalamus
  (p. 347)
weight set point (p. 348)
metabolism (p. 350)
anorexia nervosa (p. 350)
bulimia (p. 352)
need for achievement (p. 353)
Thematic Apperception Test
  (TAT) (p. 354)
need for affiliation (p. 355)
need for power (p. 356)

emotions (p. 358)
visceral experience (p. 362)
James-Lange theory of emotion
  (p. 362)
Cannon-Bard theory of emotion
  (p. 363)
Schachter-Singer theory of
  emotion (p. 364)
polygraph (p. 366)
channels (p. 368)
facial-affect program (p. 369)
facial-feedback hypothesis
  (p. 369)
vascular theory of emotions
  (p. 371)

ANSWERS (REVIEW IV):
1. Surprise, sadness, happiness, anger, disgust, and fear **2.** facial-affect **3.** facial-feedback
4. True

12

SEXUALITY AND GENDER

CASEY LETVIN

Casey Letvin, who hopes that her public discussion of date rape will reduce its incidence.

It was a warm Friday evening in autumn, the kind of night that makes a college campus seem a magical place, full of excitement and promise. Exhilarated by her new independence, Casey Letvin, like hundreds of other recently arrived University of Colorado freshmen, was looking for a party. The students milling about the streets of Boulder seemed convivial, and Casey and her roommate thought nothing of stopping four upperclassmen to ask where the parties were. "We just wanted to meet new people and have fun," says Casey, now 20. The four young men offered to take them to a nearby off-campus house where about twenty students were gathered. But approximately four hours later, the evening ended in a brutal breach of trust. At 12:30 A.M., Casey Letvin was taken back to her dormitory and raped on her own narrow bed by a man she might never have spoken to if he hadn't been a fellow student (Freeman, 1990, p. 94).

LOOKING AHEAD

Casey Letvin was the victim of a crime that just a decade ago lacked a specific title. Today, however, few people are unaware of the term that describes what happened to her: date rape. Surveys of college women now make clear that the greatest danger of rape comes not from some unknown assailant but from a fellow classmate.

Date rape is just one of many important issues pertaining to sex and gender which are central to our lives. Questions about sexual behavior, AIDS, and gender roles all represent major personal, as well as societal, concerns.

Human sexuality is also a key topic for psychologists. Representing an interplay between human biology and psychology, sexuality provides a rich area of study for psychologists in a variety of specialties. For example, psychologists interested in motivation view sexuality in terms of sexual needs, drives, and gratification; biopsychologists consider it from the perspective of the functioning of the sexual organs and their underlying physiology; and social psychologists focus on society's rules of sexual conduct and the role that sexual behavior plays in interpersonal behavior. In this chapter, we consider sex from several of these vantage points.

Gender: The sense of being male or female

We first consider **gender**, the sense of being male or female. We examine the ways in which expectations about how a man and woman should behave differ, and the impact that those expectations have on our lives. Next we turn to sexual behavior, describing the biological aspects of sexual excitement and arousal, and then examining the variations in sexual activities in which people engage. We conclude the chapter with a discussion of nonconsenting sex, sexually transmitted diseases, and the psychological aspects of sexual difficulties.

After reading this chapter, then, you will be able to answer questions such as these:

- ■ What are the major differences between male and female gender roles?
- ■ Why, and under what circumstances, do we become sexually aroused?

■ What is "normal" sexual behavior, and how do most people behave sexually?

■ Why is rape not a crime of sex, and how prevalent is it and other forms of nonconsenting sex?

■ What are the major sexually transmitted diseases and sexual difficulties that people encounter?

GENDER AND SEX

"It's a boy!" "It's a girl!"

The first words uttered upon the birth of the child are almost always these or some equivalent. The ways that we think about others, and even the ways in which we view ourselves, are based to a large extent on whether we are male or female. But the effects of gender go well beyond the mere biological fact of a body which harbors male or female sex organs. Our conclusions about what is or is not "appropriate" behavior for others and ourselves are based on **gender roles**—the set of expectations, defined by society, that indicate what is appropriate behavior for men and women.

Were the expectations associated with men and women's gender roles to be equivalent, they would have only minor impact upon our lives. However, not only do the expectations differ, but in many cases they result in favoritism toward one sex or the other, leading to stereotyping. **Stereotyping** refers to beliefs and expectations about members of a group based on their membership in that group. Stereotypes about gender roles produce **sexism**, negative attitudes and behavior toward a person based on that individual's sex.

Our society holds particularly well-defined stereotypes about men and women, and they prevail regardless of age, economic status, and social and educational background. For example, in an examination of traditional stereotypes about men and women, one study carried out in the early 1970s asked a group of college students (seventy-four men and eighty women) to examine a list of traits and specify which of them were more characteristic of men than women and which were more characteristic of women than men.

Table 12-1 shows the traits seen as applicable to one sex more than the other by at least 75 percent of the subjects (Broverman et al., 1972). From the way in which the traits cluster, you can see that men were more apt to be viewed as having traits involving competence; women, on the other hand, were seen as having traits involving warmth and expressiveness. Because our society traditionally holds competence in higher esteem than warmth and expressiveness, the perceived differences between men and women are biased in favor of men.

Of course, given that Broverman's study was carried out two decades ago, one could argue that times—and stereotypes—have changed. Unfortunately, this does not seem to be the case; males are still viewed as holding more competence-related traits, whereas women continue to be seen in terms of their warmth and expressiveness (Deaux & Lewis, 1984; C. L. Martin, 1987; Signorella & Frieze, 1989). Because society still tends to hold competence in higher esteem than warmth and expressiveness, this perceived difference—and keep in mind that we are talking about people's perceptions, not necessarily factual differences—may have sexist implications (O'Leary & Smith, 1988).

Furthermore, important differences remain about which occupations are seen as appropriate for men and for women, with members of each sex expecting greater success when they enter a profession viewed as appropriate for their sex (Eccles, 1987; Bridges, 1988). Although more women are entering the work

Gender roles: Societal expectations about appropriate behavior for women and men

Stereotyping: Beliefs and expectations about members of a group based on their membership in that group

Sexism: Negative attitudes toward a person based on that person's sex

TABLE 12-1

COMMON STEREOTYPES ABOUT MEN AND WOMEN

Traits perceived as characteristic of men	Traits perceived as characteristic of women
Aggressive	Talkative
Independent	Tactful
Unemotional	Gentle
Self-confident	Religious
Very objective	Aware of feelings of others
Likes math and science	Interested in own appearance
Ambitious	Neat
Active	Quiet
Competitive	Strong need for security
Logical	Enjoys art and literature
Worldly	Easily expresses tender feelings
Direct	Does not use harsh language
Adventurous	Dependent

Source: Adapted from Broverman et al., 1972.

force, they continue to be seen as suited to traditionally female jobs: secretaries, nurses, bookkeepers, cashiers, and other female-dominated professions that feature low pay and low status. Even when women enter high-status professions, they may face discrimination from their colleagues (Barinaga, 1991). For instance, many women encounter sexual harassment on the job, as we discuss in the accompanying Cutting Edge box.

The extent of different gender stereotyping is also illustrated by the findings of several surveys. For example, when first-year college students are asked to name a probable career choice, women are much less likely to choose careers that have been traditionally male-dominated, such as engineering or computer programming, than men (Glick, Zion, & Nelson, 1988; CIRE, 1990). Finally, women hold significantly lower expectations than men about their entering and peak salaries (Major & Konar, 1984; Martin, 1989).

In sum, gender stereotypes seem more positive for men than women. Of course, such stereotypes reflect people's perceptions and not the reality of the world. But because people often act upon their expectations, gender stereotypes can lead to the unfortunate consequence of more favorable behavior toward men than toward women.

Gender and Sex Differences: More Similar than Different

Although the prevalence and clarity of gender stereotypes might lead us to expect that actual differences between men's and women's behavior are large, the reality is quite different. In considering the differences between men and women that have been well documented, it is important to remember that in most respects men and women are more similar to one another than they are different. Moreover, when differences have been found, their magnitude is usually small. When we compare men and women, then, keep in mind that there is more

We'll probably never know the truth about Supreme Court Justice Clarence Thomas and attorney Anita Hill. You probably recall that Hill accused Justice Thomas of sexual harassment when she worked for him in two high U.S. government positions. Thomas denied all charges, and he was ultimately confirmed to his Supreme Court position.

Although no one can claim to know the actual story, the charges and countercharges brought the issue of sexual harassment into the public's eye as it had never been before. For many people, the issue was hardly academic: one-fifth of women in a national poll said that they had been sexually harassed at work. Furthermore, 42 percent of the women and 37 percent of the men polled said they knew someone who had been the victim of sexual harassment (Kantrowitz, 1991).

What constitutes harassment? The courts have ruled that several different kinds of conduct can be considered harassment (Lublin, 1991):

- Unwanted sexual advances, in which an employee is asked repeatedly to participate in a sexual relationship.
- Coercion, in which an employee is asked to participate in a relationship with the implication that the employee will receive favoritism for establishing the relationship or will be punished for not participating.
- Physical conduct, where an employee is touched or is the recipient of threatening or vulgar gestures.

SEXUAL HARASSMENT

- Visual harassment, in which pornographic materials are displayed or graffiti about particular employees are written on the walls.

Of course, sexual harassment is not found only in the workplace. One study showed that 30 percent of women who had graduated from the University of California in Berkeley reported being the recipient of some form of harassment. The type of harassment ranged from invitations for dates and leering to sexual bribery, in which a professor offered a grade in exchange for an affair (Benson & Thomson, 1982).

Some psychologists believe that sexual harassment has less to do with sex than with power (similar to the motivation behind many cases of rape, as we will see later in the chapter). In this view, higher-status persons who engage in harassment may be less concerned with receiving sexual fulfillment than with demonstrating their power over the victim (Goleman, 1991).

Whatever the motivation that lies behind the behavior of sexual harassers, the consequences for the victim are clear. Feelings of shame and embarrassment are standard. Because typically they are in a lower-status position, targets of harassment also may experience a sense of helplessness and powerlessness. They often suffer emotional and physical consequences, and the quality of their work may decline (Gutek, 1985).

Sexual harassment goes well beyond being a minor irritant. It may affect professional advancement, and in some cases it can result in the loss of a job. For those who have experienced it, sexual harassment is devastating.

Clarence Thomas.

Anita Hill.

overlap in behavior and psychological characteristics than there are differences between the sexes. Those differences that have been found reflect average male and female group differences and tell us nothing about any individual male or female. Even if we find that males, on the whole, tend to be more aggressive than females (as they are), there are going to be many men who are less aggressive than most women, just as there will be many women who act more aggressively than most men.

Personality Differences.   As already mentioned, one of the most pronounced differences between men and women is their degree of aggressive behavior. By the time they are 2 years old, boys tend to show more aggression than girls, and this higher level of aggression persists throughout the lifespan (Hyde, 1991; Maccoby & Jacklin, 1974). Although the difference is greatest in terms of physical aggression, there are also differences in terms of aggression that produce psychological harm to others. Furthermore, women feel greater anxiety and guilt about their aggressiveness and are more concerned about its effects on their victims than men are (Eagly & Steffen, 1986).

Men and women also differ in average levels of self-esteem (Block, 1983). Women, on the average, have lower self-esteem than men. Furthermore, not only do women tend to downgrade themselves relative to men; but their self-denigration translates into lower confidence in their estimates of how well they will succeed on future tasks. For example, one recent survey of first-year college students compared men's and women's views of whether they were above or below average on a variety of traits. As you can see in Figure 12-1, more men than women thought that they were above average on a variety of traits, including academic and mathematical ability, competitiveness, and emotional health. Furthermore, other research shows that women evaluate themselves more harshly than men (Beyer, 1990).

Of course, women's lower self-esteem is not especially surprising, given the message of incompetence that society's stereotypes are communicating. In fact, when considered in light of their tendency to be less aggressive, women's lower self-esteem may help explain their reluctance to enter high-prestige professions dominated by men, in which aggressiveness and self-confidence may be prerequisites for success (Roberts, 1991).

Men and women also differ in both their verbal and nonverbal communication styles. For starters, there is a difference in the amount of talking—but not

"We're a great team, Sash—you with your small and large motor skills, me with my spatial awareness and hand-eye coördination."

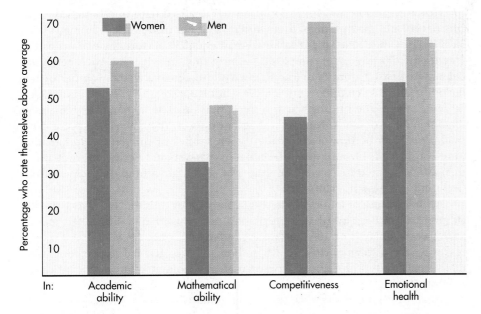

FIGURE 12-1

Male first-year college students are much more likely than female first-year college students to rate themselves as above average in academic ability, mathematical ability, competitiveness, and emotional health. (Source: *The American Freshman: National Norms for Fall 1990*, Astin, Korn, & Berz. Higher Education Research Institute, UCLA.)

what the stereotype would have us believe: Men tend to talk more than women (McMillan et al., 1977).

The content of men's and women's speech also differs, with women's speech being more precise. At the same time, women's speech patterns lead others to view them as more tentative and less assertive; they more often raise their pitch at the end of sentences, and they more often add "tags" at the end of an opinion, rather than stating the opinion outright: Instead of saying "It's awfully warm today," a female speaker might say instead "It's awfully warm today, *isn't it?*," thereby appearing less certain of her opinion (Matlin, 1987). When females use such tentative language, they are judged to be less competent and knowledgeable than when they speak assertively (Carli, 1990).

Women's and men's nonverbal behavior also differs in several significant respects. In mixed-sex conversations, women look at a partner significantly more while listening than while speaking, whereas men display more equivalent levels of looking while speaking and looking while listening. The effect of the male's pattern is to communicate power and dominance, while the woman's pattern is associated with lower levels of power. Men also are more likely to touch others, while women are more likely to be touched. Women, on the other hand, are better than men at decoding the facial expressions of others. In addition, smiling women are judged more competent than nonsmiling women, while there is no difference for men (Hall, 1978; Dovidio & Ellyson, 1985; Dovidio et al., 1988; Shaw, 1991).

Cognitive Abilities. Although there are no differences between men and women in overall IQ scores, learning, memory, problem solving, and concept-formation tasks, a few differences in more specific cognitive areas have been identified. However, the true nature of these differences—and even their existence—has been called into question by recent research.

When Eleanor Maccoby and Carol Jacklin carried out a pioneering review of sex differences in 1974, they concluded that girls outperformed boys in verbal abilities, and that there was a gender difference favoring boys over girls in quantitative and spatial abilities. This conclusion was widely accepted as one of the truisms of the psychological literature.

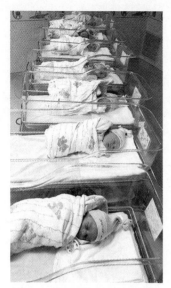
Starting from birth, girls and boys are often treated differently by adults.

However, recent and more sophisticated analyses have questioned the specific nature and magnitude of these differences. For instance, psychologist Janet Shibley Hyde and colleagues examined mathematical performance of males and females on 100 studies, encompassing some 4 million subjects (Hyde, Fennema, & Lamon, 1990). Contrary to traditional wisdom, females actually outperformed males in math in elementary and middle schools, although by only a tiny amount. By high school, the finding was reversed: Males scored higher than females in mathematics problem solving. At all ages, however, the differences were quite small, and they became even smaller when studies of the general population were considered. In sum, the differences in mathematics performance between men and women are relatively insignificant, and, if anything, they appear to be declining (Friedman, 1989).

A similar state of affairs exists regarding gender differences in verbal skills. Despite the earlier view that women show greater verbal abilities than men, a more recent analysis of 165 studies of gender differences in verbal ability, representing the testing of close to 1.5 million subjects, has led to the conclusion that verbal gender differences between men and women are insignificant (Hyde & Linn, 1988).

Current evidence suggests, then, that gender differences in cognitive skills are minimal. This does not mean, however, that no differences exist between performance on particular tests of mathematical and verbal skills. For example, high scorers on the mathematics part of the Scholastic Aptitude Test are predominately male. Specifying the nature of cognitive gender differences, then, is not simple and requires additional research.

Sources of Gender and Sex Differences

If the identification of gender differences has posed a thorny and complex problem for researchers, the search for their causes has proved to be even more elusive and controversial. Given the indisputable fact that sex is a biological variable, it would seem reasonable to look at factors involving biological differences between men and women. But environmental factors can hardly be ruled out, given the obvious importance of growing up in a world in which people are treated differently on the basis of their sex from the time they are born.

Before considering both the biological and environmental factors that help explain sex and gender differences, we should note that it is unlikely that either biological or environmental factors alone are capable of providing a full explanation. Rather, it is probable that some combination of the two, interacting with each other, will ultimately provide us with an understanding of the causes of sex and gender differences.

Biological Causes.   Do differences between male and female brains underlie sex and gender differences? This intriguing suggestion, first discussed in Chapter 3, has been put forward in recent years by psychologists studying brain structure and functioning. For example, Julian Stanley and Camilla Benbow (1983) found that children with exceptional talent in mathematics were characterized by an unusual assortment of physical attributes, such as an overrepresentation of left-handedness and a high incidence of allergies and nearsightedness. Such seemingly unrelated characteristics, it turns out, may be associated with the degree of prenatal exposure to **androgens**, male sex hormones, which may slow the growth of the left hemisphere of the brain. According to one theory, the right hemisphere of the brain—which specializes in mathematical problems—then com-

Androgens: Male sex hormones

pensates for the deficiencies of the left hemisphere by becoming strengthened, thereby leading to the increased performance of men in certain mathematical spheres (Gerschwind, 1985). Similarly, evidence from at least one study suggests that women perform better on tasks involving verbal skill and muscular coordination during periods when their production of the female sex hormone, **estrogen**, is relatively high than when it is low. In contrast, they perform better on tasks involving spatial relationships when their estrogen level is relatively low (Kimura & Sampson, 1988).

We don't yet know the extent to which biological causes may underlie sex differences, but the evidence is growing that such factors may explain, at least in part, behavioral differences between men and women (Kimura & Sampson, 1988; Witelson, 1989a; Gur et al., 1982). However, it is also clear that environmental factors play a critical role in producing sex and gender differences. Moreover, because environmental factors can be changed, such influences offer us the opportunity to decrease the detrimental effects of sex stereotyping.

Environmental Causes. Starting from the moment of birth, with blue blankets for boys and pink ones for girls, most parents and other adults provide environments that differ in important respects according to gender. For example, the kinds of toys that are given to boys and girls vary, and fathers play more roughly with their infant sons than with their daughters. Middle-class mothers tend to talk more to their daughters than to their sons. Although the extent of behavioral differences between parents of boys and girls may not be great (Lytton & Romney, 1991), it is clear that adults frequently treat children differently on the basis of their gender (Houston, 1983; Maccoby & Jacklin, 1974; Eccles, Jacobs, & Harold, 1990).

Such differences in behavior, and there are many more, produce different socialization experiences for men and women. **Socialization** is the process by which an individual learns the rules and norms of appropriate behavior. In this case, it refers to learning what society calls appropriate behavior for men and women. According to the processes of social-learning theory (discussed in Chapter 7) boys and girls are taught and rewarded for performing behaviors that are perceived by society as being appropriate for men or for women, respectively.

It is not just parents, of course, who provide socialization experiences for children. Society as a whole communicates clear messages to children as they are growing up. Children's reading books have traditionally portrayed girls in stereotypically-nurturant roles, while the boys were more physical and action-oriented (McDonald, 1989). Television, too, acts as a particularly potent source of socialization. Despite programs like *L.A. Law, Designing Women,* and *Murphy Brown,* which feature women in key roles, men still outnumber women on television and women are often cast in such stereotypic roles as housewife, secretary, and mother. The potency of television as a socialization force is indicated by the fact that some data suggest that the more television children watch, the more sexist they become (Morgan, 1982; Liebert & Sprafkin, 1988; Carter, 1991).

Our educational system also provides differential treatment of boys and girls. For example, boys are five times more likely to receive more attention from classroom teachers than girls. Boys receive significantly more praise, criticism, and remedial help than girls do. Even in college classes, male students receive more eye contact from their professors than female students, men are called upon more in class, and they are more apt to receive extra help from their professors (Epperson, 1988).

According to Sandra Bem (1987), socialization produces a **gender schema**,

Estrogen: The female sex hormone

Socialization: The process by which individuals learn what society deems appropriate behavior, including gender roles

Gender schema: A cognitive framework that organizes and guides a child's understanding of gender

▶ **383**

a cognitive framework that organizes and guides a child's understanding of information relevant to gender. On the basis of what their schemas are regarding what is or is not appropriate for being a male or a female, children begin to behave in ways that reflect society's gender roles. Hence, a child who goes to summer camp and is offered the opportunity to sew a costume may evaluate the activity, not in terms of the intrinsic components of the process (such as the mechanics of using a needle and thread), but in terms of whether the activity is compatible with his or her gender schema.

Androgynous: A state in which gender roles encompass characteristics thought typical of both sexes

According to Bem, one way in which gender schemas can be circumvented is by encouraging children to be **androgynous**, a state in which gender roles encompass characteristics thought typical of both sexes. Specifically, an androgynous male may not only be aggressive and forceful (typically viewed by society as masculine characteristics) under certain circumstances, but may be compassionate and gentle (typically thought of as feminine characteristics) when the situation calls for such behavior. Conversely, an androgynous female may be affectionate and soft-spoken, while also being assertive and self-reliant.

The concept of androgyny does not suggest that there should be no differences between men and women. Instead, it proposes that differences should be based on choices, freely made, of the best *human* characteristics, and not on an artificially restricted inventory of characteristics deemed by society to be appropriate only for men or only for women.

RECAP AND REVIEW I

RECAP

◀ Gender roles, society's expectations about what is appropriate behavior for men and women, lead to sex stereotyping and sexism.

◀ Although there are both personality and cognitive gender differences, the magnitude of the differences tends to be small, and the specific differences can change over time.

◀ Sex and gender differences are caused by the interaction of biological and environmental factors.

REVIEW

1. _____ _____ are sets of societal expectations about what is appropriate behavior for men and women.

2. Gender stereotypes seem to be much less prevalent today than they were several decades ago. True or false? _____

3. Which of the following statements is true about male/female differences in aggressiveness?
   a. Males are only more aggressive physically than females during childhood.
   b. Male/female differences in aggressiveness first become evident during adolescence.
   c. Males are more aggressive than females throughout the lifespan.
   d. Females and males feel equally anxious about their aggressive acts.

4. Although Lee typically acts in a gentle and compassionate manner, he sometimes acts in an aggressive manner. In terms of gender roles, Lee might be considered to be _____.

5. _____ _____ are frameworks that organize understanding of gender-specific information.

Ask Yourself

You are asked to participate in an experiment in child-rearing. You are given a child and are asked to raise the child in as androgynous a manner as possible. How would you do it? What problems might such a child encounter in the real world? Do you think this is the best way to raise a child in today's society?

(Answers to review questions are on page 386.)

When I started "tuning out," teachers thought I was sick—physically sick that is. They kept sending me to the school nurse to have my temperature taken. If I'd told them I was carrying on with Cindy Crawford in their classes, while supposedly learning my Caesar and my Latin vocabulary, they'd have thought I was—well, delirious. I *was!* I'd even think of Cindy while jogging; I'd have to stop because it'd hurt down there! You can't run and have sex—or can you? (Based on Coles & Stokes, 1985, pp. 18–19.)

Not everyone's sexual fantasies are as consuming as those reported by this teenage boy. Yet sex is an important consideration in most people's lives, for although the physical aspects of human sex are not all that different from those of other species, the meaning, values, and feelings that humans place on sexual behavior elevate it to a special plane. To fully appreciate this difference, however, it is first necessary to understand the basic biology underlying sexual responses.

Basic Biology: The Underlying Sex Drive

Anyone who has seen two dogs mating knows that sexual behavior has a biological basis. Their sexual behavior appears to occur spontaneously, without much prompting on the part of others. A number of genetically controlled factors influence the sexual behavior of animals. For instance, animal behavior is affected by the presence of certain hormones in the blood. Moreover, females are receptive to sexual advances only at certain, relatively limited periods of time during the year.

Human sexual behavior, by comparison, is more complicated, although the underlying biology is not all that different from that of related species. In males, for example, the **testes** secrete androgen, the male sex hormone, beginning at puberty (see Figure 12-2 for the basic anatomy of the male and female **genitals**, or sex organs). Not only does androgen produce secondary sex characteristics, such as the development of body hair and a deepening of the voice; it also increases the sex drive. Although there are long-term changes in the amount of androgen that is produced—with the greatest production occurring just after sexual maturity—its short-term production is fairly constant. Men, therefore, are capable of (and interested in) sexual activities without any regard to biological cycles. Given the proper stimuli leading to arousal, male sexual behavior can occur.

Testes: The male reproductive organs responsible for secreting androgens

Genitals: The male and female sex organs

Women show a different, and more complex, pattern. When they reach maturity at puberty, the two **ovaries**, the female reproductive organs, begin to produce estrogen—the female sex hormone. Estrogen, however, is not produced consistently; instead, its production follows a cyclical pattern. The greatest output occurs during **ovulation**, when an egg is released from the ovaries, making the chances of fertilization by a male sperm cell highest. While in nonhumans the period around ovulation is the only time that the female is receptive to sex, people are different. Although there are variations in reported sex drive, women are receptive to sex throughout their cycles, depending on the external stimuli they encounter in their environment (Hoon, Bruce, & Kinchloe, 1982).

Ovaries: The female reproductive organs

Ovulation: The monthly release of an egg from an ovary

Though biological factors "prime" people for sex, it takes more than hormones to motivate and produce sexual behavior. In animals it is the presence of a partner who provides arousing stimuli that leads to sexual activity. Humans are

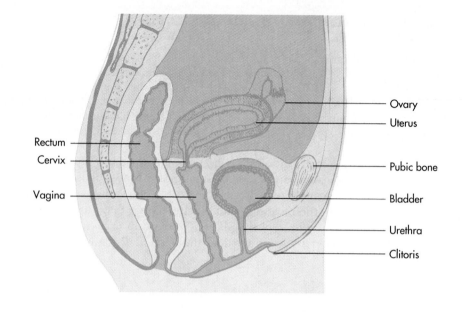

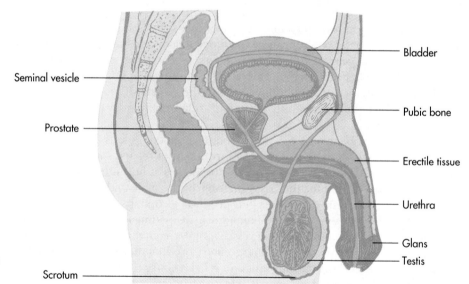

FIGURE 12-2

Cutaway side views of the female and male sex organs.

considerably more versatile; not only other people, but nearly any object, sight, smell, sound, or other stimulus can lead to sexual excitement. Because of prior associations, then, people may be turned on sexually by the smell of Chanel No. 5 or Brut, the sight of a bikini brief, or the sound of a favorite song, hummed softly in their ear. The reaction to a specific, potentially arousing stimulus, as we shall see, is a very individual one—what turns one person on may do just the opposite for another.

ANSWERS (REVIEW I):

1. Gender roles   **2.** False; they are still quite prevalent.   **3.** c   **4.** androgynous   **5.** Gender schemas

The Psychological Aspects of Sexual Excitement: What Turns People On?

▶ **387**
SEXUALITY AND GENDER

If you were to argue that the major sex organ is the brain, in a sense you would be right. Much of what is considered sexually arousing in our society has little or nothing to do with our genitals but instead is related to external stimuli which, through a process of learning, have come to be labeled as **erotic**, or sexually stimulating.

Erotic: Sexually stimulating

For example, there are no areas of the body that when touched automatically produce sexual arousal. What are called **erogenous zones**—areas of the body that are particularly sensitive because of the presence of an unusually rich array of nerve receptors—are sensitive not just to sexual touch, but to any kind of touch. When a physician touches a breast or a penis, the information sent to the brain by the nerve cells is essentially the same as that sent when a lover touches the same area. What differs is the interpretation given to the touch. Only when a certain part of the body is touched in what people define as a sexual manner is sexual arousal likely to follow (Gagnon, 1977).

Erogenous (eh RAH jun us) **zones:** Areas of the body that are particularly sensitive because of an unusually rich array of nerve receptors

Although people can learn to respond sexually to almost any stimulus, there is a good deal of agreement within a society or culture about what usually represents an erotic stimulus. In western society, large, full breasts represent a standard against which many males measure female appeal, but in many other cultures breast size is irrelevant. For instance, in some cultures plumpness is viewed as arousing, and in others the female thigh is viewed as very erotic—if sporting a tattoo (Rothblum, 1990).

In our own culture, most women prefer men with small buttocks and a moderately large chest. They also see the chest as most sexually stimulating—more so than buttocks, legs, or the penis (Wildman, Wildman, Brown, & Trice, 1976). These preferences have led to the development of entire industries that promise consumers enhanced sexual desirability.

Sexual fantasies also play an important role in producing sexual arousal. Not only do people have fantasies of a sexual nature during their everyday activities, but about 60 percent of all people have fantasies during sexual intercourse. Interestingly, such fantasies often include having sex with someone other than one's partner of the moment.

Men's and women's fantasies differ little from each other in terms of content or quantity (Jones & Barlow, 1990). As you can see in Figure 12-3, thoughts of being sexually irresistible and of engaging in oral-genital sex are most common in both sexes (Sue, 1979; McCauley & Swann, 1980). It is important to note that fantasies are just that—fantasies—and do not represent a desire to fulfill them in the real world. We should not assume from such data that females want to be sexually overpowered, nor should we assume that in every male lurks a potential rapist desirous of forcing sexual overtures on a submissive victim.

The Phases of Sexual Response

Although the kinds of stimuli that produce sexual arousal are to some degree unique to each of us, there are some basic aspects of sexual responsiveness that we all share. According to pioneering work done by William Masters and Virginia Johnson (1966), who studied sexual behavior in carefully controlled laboratory settings, sexual responses follow a regular pattern consisting of four phases: excitement, plateau, orgasm, and resolution. Although other researchers argue

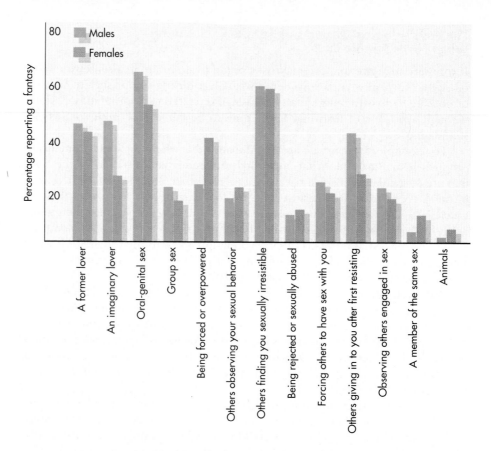

FIGURE 12-3

Men and women have similar fantasies during sexual intercourse. (Sue, 1979.)

Excitement phase: A period during which the body prepares for sexual intercourse

Penis: The primary male sex organ

Clitoris: The small and very sensitive organ in the female's external genitals

Vagina: The female canal into which the penis enters during sexual intercourse

Plateau phase: A period in which the maximum level of arousal is attained, the penis and clitoris swell with blood, and the body prepares for orgasm

Orgasm: The peak of sexual excitement during which time rhythmic muscular contractions occur in the genitals

Semen: A fluid containing sperm that is ejaculated through the penis during orgasm

that sexual responses follow a somewhat different form (e.g., Kaplan, 1974; Zilbergeld & Ellison, 1980), Masters and Johnson's research is the most widely accepted account of what happens when people become sexually excited.

In the **excitement phase**, which can last from just a few minutes to over an hour, an arousing stimulus begins a sequence that prepares the genitals for sexual intercourse. In the male, the **penis** becomes erect when blood flows into it; for females, the **clitoris** swells because of an increase in the blood supply to the area, and the **vagina** becomes lubricated. Women may also experience a "sex flush," a measles-like coloration that typically spreads over the chest and throat.

Next comes the **plateau phase**, the body's preparation for orgasm. During this stage, the maximum level of sexual arousal is attained as the penis and clitoris swell with blood. The size of women's breasts and vagina increases. Heartbeat and blood pressure rise, and the breathing rate increases. Muscle tension becomes greater as the body prepares itself for the next stage, orgasm.

Although it is difficult to explain the sensation of **orgasm** beyond saying that it is an intense, highly pleasurable experience, the biological events that accompany the feeling are fairly straightforward. When the orgasm stage is reached, rhythmic muscular contractions occur in the genitals every eight-tenths of a second. In the male, the contractions expel **semen**, a fluid containing sperm, from the penis—a process known as **ejaculation**. Breathing and heart rates reach their maximum.

Although we can't be sure, the subjective experience of orgasm seems identical for males and females, despite the differences in the organs that are involved. In one experiment, a group of men and women wrote down their descriptions of how an orgasm felt to them. These descriptions were given to a group of experts, who were asked to identify the sex of the writer. The results showed that the experts were correct at no better than chance levels, suggesting

WINMOR SERIES

Committed to Design, Quality and Service

The societal preference for men with muscular upper bodies has contributed to the development of a thriving fitness industry.

that there was little means to distinguish the descriptions of orgasms on the basis of gender (Vance & Wagner, 1976). To get a sense of how people describe orgasms, see Table 12-2.

Following orgasm, people move into the last stage of sexual arousal, the **resolution stage**. The body returns to its normal state, reversing the changes brought about by arousal. The genitals resume their normal size and shape, and blood pressure, breathing, and heart rate return to normal.

Male and female responses differ significantly during the resolution stage; these differences are depicted in Figure 12-4. Women are able to cycle back to

Ejaculation: The expulsion of semen through the penis

Resolution stage: The final stage of sexual arousal during which the body returns to its normal state

TABLE 12-2

ORGASM, MALE AND FEMALE

What does it feel like to have an orgasm? The following ten descriptions were written by men and women in an introductory psychology class. As you read through them, see if you can tell which were written by men and which by women.

1. Your heart pounds more than 100 miles per hour, your body tenses up, you feel an overwhelming sensation of pleasure and joy.
2. An orgasm feels like blood pulsating through my body, rushing essentially to the genital area, a surge of contraction-like waves paired with a rapidly beating heart and strong pulse; my heart feels like someone is squeezing it, painful, and I have trouble breathing deeply.
3. Feels like being plugged into an electrical socket, but pleasurable rather than painful. Nearly indescribable!
4. It's as if every muscle in your body is being charged with intense electricity; your mind is incapable of thinking about anything, and you become totally incoherent. All the nerves in your body tremble, and you have trouble breathing, and get the urge to scream, or yell, or do something wild.
5. An orgasm to me is like the sensations of hot and cold coming together in one throbbing, thrusting, prolonged moment. It is the ultimate excitement of my passion.
6. Like exquisite torture. The sudden release of all the primal urges in the body. The gladness and yet the sadness that the fun is over.
7. An orgasm is that point when you don't care if anyone hears you screaming out your pleasures of ecstasy.
8. It's like all the cells in my brain popping at once and whirling around, while all the muscles in my body heave upward till I reach ultimate sensory bliss.
9. Tingling, throbbing, pleasurable feeling. Breathing is very fast and not rhythmic. Tend to hold my breath at peak. Possible shaking afterward and tightening/contraction of muscles.
10. An orgasm is a heavenly experience. It can be compared to nothing.

If you thought that men and women experience orgasm differently, you may be surprised at how hard it is to tell the difference from these descriptions. The correct answers:

1. Male 2. Female 3. Male 4. Female 5. Female 6. Male 7. Female 8. Male
9. Female 10. Male

FIGURE 12-4

A four-stage model of the sexual response cycle for males and females based on the findings of Masters and Johnson (1966). Note how the male pattern (on the left) includes a refractory period. The figure on the right shows three possible female patterns. In (a), the pattern is closest to the male cycle, except that the woman has two orgasms in a row. In (b), there is no orgasm, whereas in (c) orgasm is reached quickly and the woman rapidly returns to an unaroused state. (After Masters & Johnson, 1966.)

the orgasm phase and experience repeated orgasms. Ultimately, of course, females enter the final resolution stage, and they return to their prestimulation state. In contrast, it is generally thought that men enter a refractory period during the resolution stage. During the **refractory period**, men are not able to be aroused and are therefore unable to have another orgasm and ejaculate. The refractory period may last from a few minutes to several hours, although in the elderly it may continue for several days.

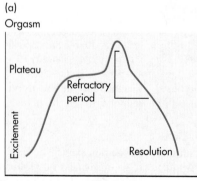

(a)

Male pattern

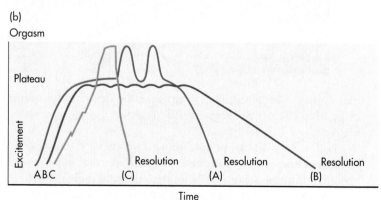

(b)

Female patterns

Interestingly, some evidence suggests that the traditional view that males are unable to have multiple orgasms without an intervening refractory period may be in error. In one study, for example, 12 percent of a group of 282 males reported experiencing multiple orgasms before they ejaculated (Hartman & Fithian, 1984; Robbins & Jensen, 1978). Moreover, measures of physiological responses that accompany orgasm confirmed the validity of the subjects' reports. From such research, and from the fact that orgasm and ejaculation are controlled by separate parts of the nervous system, it appears that orgasm and ejaculation may occur independently—a fact that is typically hidden, since they almost always happen together. Although further research is needed, what we now know suggests that it is possible that all men have the ability to have repeated orgasms without ejaculating; it is just that most have not learned the proper technique.

Refractory period: Entered by a male after the resolution stage, a temporary period during which he cannot be sexually aroused again

RECAP

◀ Although biological factors prime people for sex, other stimuli are necessary for sexual excitement to occur.

◀ Erogenous zones are areas of the body that are particularly sensitive to touch because of the presence of a rich array of nerve receptors. However, what makes a touch sexual is the context and interpretation given it.

◀ Fantasies, thoughts, and images in people's minds play an important role in producing sexual arousal.

◀ Although there are differences in detail, both men's and women's sexual response follows a regular pattern consisting of four phases: excitement, plateau, orgasm, and resolution.

REVIEW

1. Match the phase of sexual arousal with its characteristics
   1. _____ Excitement phase   a. Maximum level of sexual arousal occurs here
   2. _____ Plateau phase   b. Erection, lubrication, sex flush
   3. _____ Orgasm phase   c. Ejaculation; intense pleasurable experience
   4. _____ Resolution phase   d. Body returns to resting state

2. Men are generally thought to enter a _____ period after sex, in which orgasm is impossible for a period of time.

3. Whereas men are interested in sexual activity regardless of their biological cycles, women are truly receptive to sex only during ovulation, when the production of their sex hormones is greatest. True or false? _____

4. Men's and women's sexual fantasies are essentially similar to each other. True or false? _____

Ask Yourself

How do people learn to be aroused by the stimuli which their society considers erotic? When do they learn this, and where does the message come from?

(Answers to review questions are on page 392.)

THE VARIETIES OF SEXUAL BEHAVIOR: DIFFERENT STROKES FOR DIFFERENT FOLKS

A boy will not feel so vigorous and springy; he will be more easily tired. . . . He will probably look pale and pasty, and he is lucky if he escapes indigestion and getting his bowels confined, both of which will probably give him spots and pimples on his face. . . . The results on the mind are the more severe. . . . A boy who practices this habit can never be the best that Nature intended him to be. His wits are not so sharp. His memory is not so good. His power of fixing his attention on whatever he is doing is lessened. . . . A boy like this is a poor thing to look at. . . . [He is] untrustworthy, unreliable, untruthful, and probably even dishonest'' (Schofield & Vaughan-Jackson, 1913, pp. 30–42).

The source of this condition: masturbation—at least according to the authors of the early twentieth-century sex manual, *What Every Boy Should Know.*

▶ **391**

Though such a view may seem bizarre and farfetched to you—a notion with which experts on human sexual behavior would certainly agree—it was, at one time, considered perfectly sound and accurate by people who were otherwise quite reasonable. Indeed, trivia buffs might be interested to learn that one nineteenth-century physician, J. W. Kellogg, felt that because some foods produced sexual excitation, an alternative of "unstimulating" grains was needed, thereby leading to the first bowl of corn flakes.

Clearly, sex and sex-related behavior are influenced by expectations, attitudes, beliefs, and the state of medical and biological knowledge of a given period. Today we know that sexual behavior may take a variety of forms, and what was once seen as "unnatural" and "lewd" is readily accepted in contemporary society. In fact, as we shall see, distinctions between normal and abnormal sexual behavior are not easily drawn.

Approaches to Sexual Normality

If we were to develop a scale for "sexual normality," it would not be hard to define the end points. Most people would agree, for instance, that male-female sexual intercourse involving consenting members of a married couple would fit comfortably at one end of the scale, while a person who becomes sexually aroused only while spiders are crawling over his or her body might reasonably be placed at the other end. It is when we consider behaviors that fall in between that defining normality poses difficulties.

One approach—which we will discuss further in the context of defining abnormal behavior (see Chapter 17)—is to define abnormal sexual behavior in terms of deviation from the average, or typical, behavior. In order to determine abnormality, we simply observe what behaviors are rare and infrequent in a society and label these deviations from the norm as abnormal. The difficulty with such an approach, however, is that some behaviors that are statistically unusual hardly seem worthy of concern. Even though most people have sexual intercourse in the bedroom, does the fact that someone prefers sex in the dining room imply abnormality? If some people prefer fat sexual partners, are they abnormal in a society that holds slimness in high esteem? Clearly, the answer to both these questions is "no," and so the deviation-from-the-average definition is inappropriate for determining sexual abnormality.

An alternative approach would be to compare sexual behavior against some standard or ideal. But there is a problem here: What standard should be used? Some might suggest the Bible, some might turn to philosophy, and some might consider psychology the ultimate determinant. The trouble is that none of these potential sources of standards is universally acceptable, and since standards change radically with shifts in societal attitudes and new knowledge, such an approach is undesirable. For instance, until 1973 the American Psychiatric Association listed homosexuality as a mental illness, but then voted to change its official mind and said that homosexuality was no longer a signal of mental disorder. Obviously the behavior had not changed—only the label placed on it by the psychiatric profession had.

Given the difficulties with other approaches, it seems that the most reasonable definition of sexual normality is one that considers the psychological consequences of the behavior. In this approach, sexual behavior is considered abnormal if it produces a sense of distress, anxiety, or guilt—or if it is harmful to some other person. According to this view, then, sexual behaviors can be viewed as abnormal only when they have a negative impact on a person's sense of well-being or on others.

It is important to recognize that what is seen as normal and what is seen as abnormal in sexual behavior are very much matters of value, resting largely in the eye of the beholder, and that there have been dramatic shifts from one generation to another in definitions of what constitutes appropriate sexual behavior. While people can, and should, make their own personal value judgments about what is appropriate in their own sex lives, there are few universal rights and wrongs when it comes to sexual behavior in general.

The vast variety of sexual behavior in which people engage was largely a mystery shrouded in ignorance until the late 1930s, when Albert Kinsey, a biologist by training, began a series of surveys on the sexual behavior of Americans that was to span eighteen years. The result was the first comprehensive look at sexual practices, highlighted by the publication of his landmark volumes, *Sexual Behavior in the Human Male* (Kinsey et al., 1948) and *Sexual Behavior in the Human Female* (Kinsey et al., 1953).

Prior to Kinsey's efforts, there was little systematic attempt at learning about human sexual behavior. What knowledge existed was based on unsystematic case histories, and no large-scale surveys had ever been attempted. In contrast, Kinsey adopted the goal of collecting 100,000 sexual histories. Although he never reached that ambitious total, he and his colleagues did manage to interview tens of thousands of individuals. Kinsey's interview techniques are still regarded as exemplary because of his sensitivity and ability to learn sensitive information without causing embarrassment. However, his sampling techniques are open to criticism. By and large, Kinsey's interviews overrepresented college students, young people, well-educated individuals, urban dwellers, and people living in Indiana and the northeast; his interviews underrepresented manual laborers, people of low education, Roman Catholics and Jews, members of racial minorities, and people who lived in rural areas (Kirby, 1977).

Furthermore, as with all surveys of sexual behavior made up of volunteers, it is unclear how representative his data are of people who refused to participate in the study. Similarly, because no survey observes behavior directly, it is not simple to assess how accurately people's descriptions of what they do in private match their actual sexual practices. People may be ashamed to admit to certain behaviors, or they may feel embarrassed that they have *not* engaged in practices that they think everyone else has engaged in, such as a virgin who is concerned about ''lagging behind'' his or her peer group.

Kinsey's work set the stage for later surveys, although it is surprising how few comprehensive national surveys have been carried out since Kinsey did his initial work some forty years ago (Booth, 1988b, 1989; McDonald, 1988). However, by examining the common results gleaned from different samples of subjects, we now have a reasonably complete picture of contemporary sexual practices—to which we turn next.

Masturbation: Solitary Sex

If you were to listen to physicians even fifty years ago, you would have been told that **masturbation**, sexual self-stimulation, often using the hand to rub the genitals, would lead to a wide variety of physical and mental disorders, ranging from hairy palms to insanity. Had they been correct, however, most of us would be

Masturbation: Sexual self-stimulation

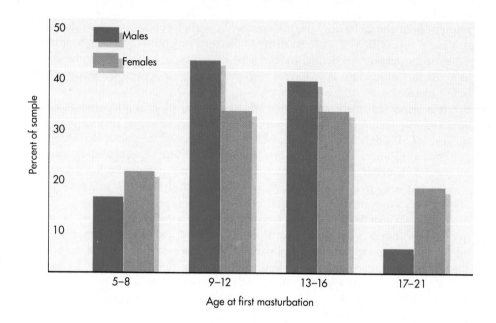

FIGURE 12-5

The age at which a sample of college students first masturbated. The percentages are based on only those people who have masturbation experience. (Arafat & Cotton, 1974.)

wearing gloves to hide the sight of our hair-covered palms—for masturbation is one of the most frequently practiced sexual activities. Some 94 percent of all males and 63 percent of all females have masturbated at least once, and among college students, the frequency ranges from ''never'' to ''several times a day'' (Houston, 1981; Hunt, 1974).

Men and women typically begin to masturbate for the first time at different ages, as you can see in Figure 12-5. Furthermore, males masturbate more often than women, although there are differences in frequency according to age. For instance, male masturbation is most frequent in the early teens and then declines, whereas females both begin and reach a maximum frequency later.

Although masturbation is often considered an activity to engage in only if no other sexual outlets are available, this view bears little relationship to reality. Close to three-quarters of married men (age 20 to 40) report masturbating an average of twenty-four times a year, and 68 percent of the married women in the same age group masturbate an average of ten times each year (Hunt, 1974).

Despite the high incidence of masturbation, attitudes toward it still reflect some of the negative views of yesteryear. For instance, one survey found that around 10 percent of the people who masturbated experienced feelings of guilt, and 5 percent of the males and 1 percent of the females considered their behavior perverted (Arafat & Cotton, 1974). Despite these negative attitudes, however, most experts on sex view masturbation not only as a healthy, legitimate—and harmless—sexual activity, but also as a means of learning about one's own sexuality.

Heterosexuality

Heterosexuality: Sexual behavior between a man and a woman

People often believe that the first time they have sexual intercourse they have achieved one of life's major milestones. However, **heterosexuality**—sexual behavior between men and women—goes well beyond sexual intercourse between men and women, encompassing kissing, petting, caressing, massaging, and other forms of sex play. Still, the focus of sex researchers has been on the act of intercourse, particularly in terms of its first occurrence and its frequency.

Although some behaviors relevant to sexuality are readily labeled as "normal," others present more difficult definitional problems.

Premarital Sex.   Until fairly recently, premarital sex, at least for women, was considered one of the major taboos of our society. Traditionally, women have been warned by society that "nice girls don't do it"; men have been told that although premarital sex is OK for them, they should make sure they marry virgins. This view, that premarital sex is permissible for males but not for females, is called the **double standard**.

Although as recently as the 1960s the majority of adult Americans believed that premarital sex was always wrong, since that time there has been a dramatic shift in public opinion. For example, as you can see in Table 12-3, in 1969 the majority of people thought it was wrong for a man and woman to have sexual intercourse before marriage. However, by 1987, the figures had shifted; at that point, more people thought it was permissible than those who thought it was wrong.

Changes in approval of premarital sex were matched by actual rates of premarital sexual activity during the same period. For instance, the most recent figures show that just over one-half of women between the ages of 15 and 19

Double standard: The view that premarital sex is permissible for males but not for females

TABLE 12-3

ATTITUDES TOWARD PREMARITAL SEXUAL INTERCOURSE

Percentage of people responding to question, "Do you think it is wrong for a man and woman to have sex relations before marriage or not?"

	1969	1978	1987
Yes, it is wrong	68%	50%	46%
No, it is not wrong	21%	41%	48%
Don't know	11%	9%	6%

Source: Gallup Poll, 1969; Gallup Poll, 1978; Gallup Poll, 1987.

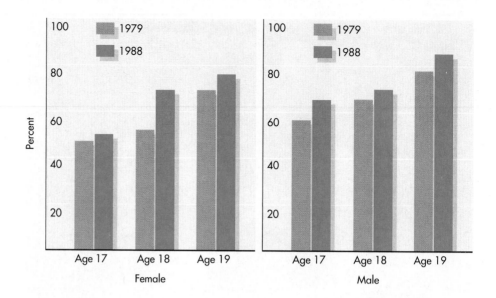

FIGURE 12-6

The percentage of both males and females who have had premarital sexual intercourse increased from 1979 to 1988. (CDC, 1991.)

have had premarital sexual intercourse. These figures are close to double the number of women in the same age range who reported having sex in 1970 (CDC, 1991b, 1992). Clearly, the trend over the last several decades has been toward more women engaging in premarital sexual activity (Gerrard, 1988; Hofferth, Kahn, & Baldwin, 1987; CDC, 1991b, 1992). (See Figure 12-6.)

Males, too, have shown an increase in the incidence of premarital sexual intercourse, although the increase has not been as dramatic as it has for females—probably because the rates for males were higher to begin with. For instance, the first surveys carried out in the 1940s showed an incidence of 84 percent across males of all ages; recent figures put the figure at closer to 95 percent. Moreover, the average age of males' first sexual experience has also been declining steadily. Some 60 percent of male high school students have had sexual intercourse; and, by the time they reach the age of 20, 80 percent have had sex (Arena, 1984; CDC, 1992).

What may be most interesting about these patterns is that they show a convergence of male and female attitudes and behavior in regard to premarital sex. But is the change sufficient to signal an end to the double standard?

The answer appears to be affirmative. Particularly among younger individuals, the double standard appears to have been replaced by a new standard: "permissiveness with affection" (Hyde, 1990). In the standard of **permissiveness with affection**, premarital intercourse is viewed as permissible for both men and women if it occurs within a long-term, committed, or loving relationship (Reiss, 1960).

Still, the double standard has not disappeared completely. Where differing standards remain, the attitudes are almost always more lenient toward the male than the female (Peplau, Rubin & Hill, 1977; Sullivan, 1985). Furthermore, there are substantial cultural differences regarding the incidence and acceptability of premarital intercourse. In Japan, for example, the incidence of premarital sex is very low for both males and females, while in Mexico, where strict standards exist regarding the virginity of adolescent females, males are considerably more likely to have premarital sex than females (Liskin, 1985). Even within the United States, subcultural differences emerge: On the average, African-Americans begin to have sex about two years earlier than whites or Asians (Moore & Erickson, 1985).

Permissiveness with affection:
The view that premarital sex is permissible for both men and women if it occurs within a long-term or loving relationship

Although the appearance of many Japanese weddings is influenced by Western trends, research indicates that most couples adhere to the Asian tradition of abstaining from intercourse before marriage.

Marital Sex. To judge by the number of articles about sex in marriage, one would think that sexual behavior was the number-one standard by which marital bliss is measured. Married couples are often concerned that they are having too little sex, too much sex, or the wrong kind of sex.

Although there are many different dimensions against which sex in marriage is measured, one is certainly the frequency of sexual intercourse. What is typical? As with most other types of sexual activities, there is no easy answer to the question, since there are such wide variations in patterns between individuals. We do know that the average frequency for married couples is approximately six times per month (Smith, 1991). In addition, there are differences according to the number of years a couple have been together: the longer the marriage, the lower the frequency of sex (see Figure 12-7).

The frequency of marital sexual intercourse also appears to be higher at this point in time than in other recent historical periods. A number of factors account for this increase. Increased availability of birth-control methods (including birth-control pills) and abortion have led couples to be less concerned about unwanted pregnancies. Moreover, several social changes are likely to have had an impact. As sex becomes more openly discussed in magazines, books, and even television shows, many married couples have come to believe that the frequency of sex is a critical index of the success of their marriage. Furthermore, as women's roles have changed, and the popular media have reinforced the notion that female sexuality is OK, the likelihood that a wife may initiate sex, rather than waiting for her husband's overture as in the more traditional scenario, has increased (Westoff, 1974).

The consequences of the increase in marital intercourse are difficult to assess. It is clear that the degree of sexual satisfaction is related to overall satisfaction with a marriage (Tavris & Sadd, 1977). Yet the *frequency* of sexual intercourse does not appear to be associated with happiness in marriage (Goleman, 1985). The rise in frequency of sexual intercourse does not suggest, then, that there will be an accompanying increase in marital satisfaction.

FIGURE 12-7

The longer a couple has been married, the less frequently it has sexual intercourse. (Blumstein & Schwartz, 1983.)

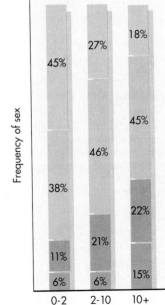

Three times a week or more

One to three times a week

Once a month to once a week

Once per month or less

Frequency of sex

	0-2	2-10	10+
18%		27%	18%
45%	45%	46%	45%
38%	38%	21%	22%
11%	11%		15%
6%	6%	6%	

Years the couple have been together

▶ **397**

Extramarital sex: Sexual activity between a married person and someone who is not his or her spouse

The increase in the frequency of sexual intercourse in marriage has been accompanied by an increase in the frequency of **extramarital sex**, sexual activity that occurs between a married person and someone who is not his or her spouse. In the 1940s, some 50 percent of all married men and 25 percent of all married women admitted to having had sex at least once with a partner other than their husband or wife. More recent surveys have shown a slight increase for men, but a more significant rise for women. What has not changed at all are people's attitudes toward extramarital sex: There is a high, consistent degree of disapproval, with more than three-quarters of those surveyed saying the practice is wrong (Hunt, 1974). (You'll note that if the statistics are correct, they suggest that some of the people who feel it is wrong must be the same ones who are having extramarital sex!)

Homosexuality and Bisexuality

Just as there seems to be no genetic or biological reason for heterosexual women to find men's buttocks particularly erotic, humans are not born with an innate attraction to the special characteristics of the opposite sex. We should not find it surprising, then, that some people, **homosexuals**, are sexually attracted to members of their own sex, while others, **bisexuals**, are sexually attracted to people of the same *and* the opposite sex.

Homosexuality: A sexual attraction to a member of one's own sex

Bisexuality: A sexual attraction to members of both sexes

The number of people who choose same-sex sexual partners at one time or another is considerable. Estimates suggest that about 20 to 25 percent of males and about 15 percent of females have had at least one homosexual experience during adulthood, and between 5 and 10 percent of both men and women are estimated to be exclusively homosexual during extended periods of their lives (Hunt, 1974; Kinsey, Pomeroy, & Martin, 1948; Fay et al., 1989; McWhirter, Sanders, & Reinisch, 1990).

Although people often view homosexuality and heterosexuality as two completely distinct sexual orientations, the issue is not that simple. Pioneering sex researcher Alfred Kinsey acknowledged this when he considered sexual orientation along a scale, with exclusively homosexual at one end and exclusively heterosexual at the other. Updated by sociologist Martin S. Weinberg and colleagues (Weinberg, Williams, & Pryor, 1991), Kinsey's approach suggests that sexual orientation is dependent on a person's sexual feelings, sexual behaviors, and romantic feelings (see Figure 12-8).

What determines people's sexual orientation? Although there are a number

FIGURE 12-8

Sexual orientation can vary on three dimensions: sexual feelings, sexual behaviors, and romantic feelings. (Weinberg, Williams, & Pryor, 1991.)

	Sexual Feelings	Sexual Behaviors	Romantic Feelings
Exclusively homosexual	6	6	6
Mainly homosexual with a small degree of heterosexuality	5	5	5
Mainly homosexual with a significant degree of heterosexuality	4	4	4
Equally heterosexual and homosexual	3	3	3
Mainly heterosexual with a significant degree of homosexuality	2	2	2
Mainly heterosexual with a small degree of homosexuality	1	1	1
Exclusively heterosexual	0	0	0

Although the precise factors that determine sexual orientation have not been identified, it is clear that heterosexuals, homosexuals, and bisexuals enjoy the same degree of psychological adjustment. This family is attending a picnic sponsored by Center Kids, an organization for homosexual parents and their children.

of theories, none has proved completely satisfactory. Some approaches are biological in nature, suggesting that there may be a genetic or hormonal reason for the development of homosexuality (Gladue, 1984; Hutchinson, 1978; Bailey & Pillard, 1991). For example, recent evidence has found a difference in the structure of the anterior hypothalamus, an area of the brain that governs sexual behavior, between male homosexuals and heterosexuals (LeVay, 1991).

However, research suggesting that biological causes are at the root of homosexuality is far from conclusive, given that most findings are based on only small samples of individuals. Still, the possibility is real that some genetic or biological factor exists that predisposes a person toward homosexuality, if certain environmental conditions are met (Gartell, 1982; Money, 1987).

Other theories of homosexuality have focused on the childhood and family background of homosexuals. For instance, Freud believed that homosexuality occurred as a result of inappropriate identification with the opposite-sex parent during development (Freud, 1922/1959). Similarly, other psychoanalysts suggest that the nature of the parent-child relationship can lead to homosexuality, and that male homosexuals frequently have overprotective, dominant mothers and passive, ineffective fathers (Bieber, 1962).

The problem with such theories is that there are probably as many homosexuals who were not subjected to the influence of such family dynamics as who were. The evidence does not support explanations which rely on child-rearing practices or on the nature of the family structure (Bell & Weinberg, 1978; Isay, 1990).

Another explanation for homosexuality rests on learning theory (Masters & Johnson, 1979). According to this view, sexual orientation is learned through rewards and punishments in much the same way that we might learn to prefer swimming over tennis. For example, a young adolescent who had a heterosexual experience whose outcome was unpleasant might learn to link unpleasant associations with the opposite sex. If that same person had a rewarding, pleasant homosexual experience, homosexuality might be incorporated into his or her sexual fantasies. If such fantasies are then used during later sexual activities—

such as masturbation—they may be positively reinforced through orgasm, and the association of homosexual behavior and sexual pleasure might eventually cause homosexuality to become the preferred form of sexual behavior.

Although the learning theory explanation is plausible, there are several difficulties which rule out its being seen as a definitive one. Because our society tends to hold homosexuality in low esteem, one ought to expect that the punishments involved in homosexual behavior would outweigh the rewards attached to it (Whitam, 1977). Furthermore, children growing up with a homosexual parent are statistically unlikely to become homosexual, thus contradicting the notion that homosexual behavior might be learned from others (Green, 1978).

Given the difficulty in finding a consistent explanation, the majority of researchers reject the notion that any single factor orients a person toward homosexuality, and most suspect that a combination of biological and environmental factors are at work (Money, 1987; McWhirter, Sanders, & Reinisch, 1990). Although we don't know at this point exactly why people develop a particular sexual orientation, one thing is clear: There is no relationship between psychological adjustment and sexual preference. Bisexuals and homosexuals enjoy the same overall degree of mental and physical health as heterosexuals do, and they hold equivalent ranges and types of attitudes about themselves, independent of sexual orientation (Reiss, 1980; Herek, 1990).

RECAP AND REVIEW III

RECAP

◀ Definitions of what is sexually normal behavior are influenced by the expectations, attitudes, beliefs, and state of medical knowledge of a given period.

◀ Masturbation (sexual self-stimulation) is common among both men and women, although it is still viewed negatively by many people.

◀ The double standard has declined over the last decade; tolerance for and actual acts of premarital sex have increased greatly over the last decades.

◀ Homosexuals are attracted to members of their own sex, and bisexuals are attracted both to people of the same and of the opposite sex. No theory fully explains why people develop a particular sexual orientation.

REVIEW

1. The work carried out by _____ in the 1930s was the first systematic study of sexual behavior ever undertaken.

2. Although the incidence of masturbation among young adults is high, once men and women become involved in intimate relationships, they typically cease masturbating. True or false? _____

3. The increase in premarital sex in recent years has been greater for women than for men. True or false? _____

4. _____ _____ _____ refers to the new societal standard that premarital sex is acceptable within a loving, long-term relationship.

5. Research comparing homosexuals and heterosexuals clearly demonstrates that there is no difference in the level of adjustment or psychological functioning between the two groups. True or false? _____

Ask Yourself

If two (or more) consenting adults willingly agree to perform a particular sexual behavior, should it be labeled as wrong? Is there any sexual practice so deviant that it should not be allowed even under these circumstances?

(Answers to review questions are on page 402.)

SEXUAL DIFFICULTIES AND TREATMENT: WHEN SEX GOES WRONG

When sex—an activity that should be pleasurable, joyful, and intimate—is forced on someone, it becomes one of the ultimate acts of aggression and brutality that people are capable of inflicting on one another, and few crimes produce such profound and long-lasting consequences. Similarly, few personal difficulties produce as much anxiety, embarrassment and even shame as those resulting from sexually transmitted diseases or sexual dysfunctions. We turn now to the major types of problems related to sex.

Rape

When one person forces another to submit to sexual activity such as intercourse or oral-genital sex, **rape** has occurred. Although it usually applies to a male forcing a female, rape can be said to occur when members of either sex are forced into sexual activities against their will.

Rape: The act whereby one person forces another to submit to sexual activity

Most people think of rape as a rare crime and one committed by strangers. Unfortunately, they are wrong on both counts. In fact, it occurs far more frequently than is commonly thought, and rapists are typically acquaintances of their victims. For instance, a national survey conducted at thirty-five universities revealed the startling finding that one out of eight women reported having been raped, and of that group, about half said the rapists were first dates, casual dates, or romantic acquaintances—a phenomenon called **date rape**, discussed first at the beginning of the chapter (Sweet, 1985; Koss et al., 1988).

Date rape: Rape in which rapist is either a date or an acquaintance

Statistically, then, a woman is far more likely to be raped on a date than by a stranger jumping out of the bushes. But whether on a date or alone, a woman's chances of being raped are shockingly high. According to one researcher, there is a 26 percent chance that a woman will be the victim of a rape during her lifetime (Russell & Howell, 1983).

Although on the surface it might appear that rape is primarily a crime of sex, other kinds of motivations also underlie the behavior (Lisak & Roth, 1988; Gelman, 1990; Hamilton & Yee, 1990). In some cases, the rapist uses sex as a means of demonstrating power and control over the victim. As such, there is little that is sexually satisfying about rape to the rapist; instead, the pleasure comes in forcing someone else to be submissive.

In other cases of rape, the primary motivation is anger. Sexual behavior is used to show the male rapist's rage at women in general, usually because of some perceived rejection or hurt that he has suffered in the past. Such rapes are likely to include physical violence and degrading acts against the victim.

Finally, some rapes *are* based on a desire for sexual gratification. Some men hold the attitude that it is appropriate and desirable for them to actively seek out sex. To them, sexual encounters represent a form of "war" between the sexes —with winners and losers—and violence is sometimes an appropriate way to obtain what they want. They reason accordingly that using force to obtain sexual gratification is permissible (Mosher & Anderson, 1986; Hamilton & Yee, 1990).

In addition, there is a common, although unfounded, societal belief that many women offer token resistance to sex, saying "no" to sex when they mean "yes," and that their protests need not be taken seriously (Muehlenhard & Hollabaugh, 1988). For example, consider the following two descriptions of a case of date rape:

> Bob: Patty and I were in the same statistics class together. She usually sat near me and was always very friendly. I liked her and thought maybe she liked me, too. Last Thursday I decided to find out. After class I suggested that she come to my place to study for midterms together. She agreed immediately, which was a good sign. That night everything seemed to go perfectly. We studied for a while and then took a break. I could tell that she liked me, and I was attracted to her. I was getting excited. I started kissing her. I could tell that she really liked it. We started touching each

other and it felt really good. All of a sudden she pulled away and said "Stop." I figured she didn't want me to think that she was "easy" or "loose." A lot of girls think they have to say "no" at first. I knew once I showed her what a good time she could have, and that I would respect her in the morning, it would be OK. I just ignored her protests and eventually she stopped struggling. I think she liked it but afterwards she acted bummed out and cold. Who knows what her problem was?

* * * * *

Patty: I knew Bob from my statistics class. He's cute and we are both good at statistics, so when a tough midterm was scheduled, I was glad that he suggested we study together. It never occurred to me that it was anything except a study date. That night everything went fine at first, we got a lot of studying done in a short amount of time, so when he suggested we take a break I thought we deserved it. Well, all of a sudden he started acting really romantic and started kissing me. I liked the kissing but then he started touching me below the waist. I pulled away and tried to stop him but he didn't listen. After a while I stopped struggling; he was hurting me and I was scared. He was so much bigger and stronger than me. I couldn't believe it was happening to me. I didn't know what to do. He actually forced me to have sex with him. I guess looking back on it I should have screamed or done something besides trying to reason with him but it was so unexpected. I couldn't believe it was happening. I still can't believe it did (Hughes & Sandler, 1987, p. 1).

Clearly, the two views of the identical situation are quite divergent, reflecting very different interpretations of the meaning of the other person's behavior. However, psychologists have devised ways of reducing the risk of date rape, as we discuss in the Psychology at Work box.

Childhood Sexual Abuse

One form of sexual behavior that is surprisingly common, yet about which the least is known, is the sexual abuse of children. Although reported cases are low in number and firm data are hard to come by, the frequency of child sexual abuse—instances in which an older person engages in sexual activity with a child—is thought to be relatively high. The reason, of course, is that only the most extreme cases are apt to be reported to authorities (Darnton, 1991). Child abuse is a secret crime, where participants are often motivated—although for different reasons—to keep their activities from being discovered. One nationwide survey, however, found that a startling 22 percent of adult Americans who were polled reported having been the victims of some form of child sexual abuse (Timnick, 1985). Sexual intercourse was involved in 55 percent of the molestations, while 36 percent involved fondling.

Who commits child sexual abuse? In most cases it is a relative (23 percent) or acquaintance (42 percent); in only about one-quarter of the cases was the abuse carried out by a stranger. The most vulnerable age for being molested is around 10 years old, and the abusers tend to be about twenty years older than their victims. In almost all instances, the abuser is a male (Finkelhor, 1984).

Both the short- and long-term consequences of childhood sexual abuse are most typically negative. In terms of initial effects, victims report increased fear, anxiety, depression, anger, hostility, and aggression, and their sexual behavior frequently shows signs of disorder. Long-term effects may include depression and self-destructive behavior, anxiety, feelings of isolation and stigma, poor self-

---

ANSWERS (REVIEW III):

1. Kinsey **2.** False; even people in married relationships show a continued incidence of masturbation. **3.** True **4.** Permissiveness with affection **5.** True

In order to decrease the incidence of date rape, it is important for both men and women to change their understanding of what appropriate sexual behavior is. The following suggestions provide some guidance (American College Health Association, 1989; Goleman, 1989; Warshaw, 1988):

- Women should clearly believe in their rights to set limits and to communicate those limits clearly, firmly, and early on. They should say "no" when they mean "no."

- Women should be assertive when someone is pressuring them to engage in an activity in which they don't want to engage. They should keep in mind that men may interpret passivity as permission.

- Women should be aware of situations in which they are at risk.

LOWERING THE RISKS OF DATE RAPE

They should keep in mind that some men interpret certain kinds of dress as sexually provocative, and that not all men subscribe to the same standards of sex as they do.

- Men should be aware of their dates' views of sexual behavior.

- Men should not hold the view that the goal of dating is to "score."

- The word "no" should be understood to mean "no" and not an invitation to continue. Men should know that a woman who says "no" is not rejecting them, but is rejecting a specific act at a specific time.

- Men should not assume that certain kinds of dress or flirtatious behavior is an invitation to sex.

Both women and men need to keep in mind that accepting a date is not an invitation to have sex.

- Both men and women should understand that alcohol and drugs cloud judgment and hinder communication between men and women.

esteem, difficulty in trusting others, substance abuse, and sexual maladjustment. The exact consequences of childhood sexual abuse are related to the specific nature of the abuse. For example, it is known that experiences involving fathers, genital contact, and force are the most damaging (Browne & Finkelhor, 1986; Finkelhor, 1979).

Unlike this girl, most victims of sexual abuse do not have the opportunity to deal with the experience in therapy during childhood. Therapists who treat children for sexual abuse may use dolls to facilitate communication.

The announcement that basketball star Magic Johnson carries the AIDS virus served to make many people aware of the risk of contracting the virus through sexual contact.

Acquired immune deficiency syndrome (AIDS): A fatal, sexually transmitted disease that is caused by a virus that destroys the body's immune system and has no known cure

Sexually transmitted disease (STD): A disease spread primarily through sexual contact

Sexually Transmitted Diseases (STDs): The Case of AIDS

No factor has had a greater effect on sexual behavior in the last decade than **acquired immune deficiency syndrome (AIDS)**. Transmitted only through sexual contact or by exposure to infected blood, AIDS has no cure and is ultimately fatal to those afflicted with it. Because it is primarily spread sexually, AIDS is classified as a **sexually transmitted disease (STD)**.

Although in the United States AIDS began largely as a disease affecting homosexuals, it has spread to other populations, and in some parts of the world, such as Africa, it primarily affects heterosexuals. In the United States, experts estimate that 435,000 people will have AIDS in 1993, and that by the year 2000 there will be well over 1 million reported cases (McLaughlin, 1991; Cowley, 1990; Brookmeyer, 1991). The worldwide figures are even more daunting: As of 1991, around 10 million people were estimated to carry the AIDS virus, leading to an epidemic of massive proportions (Palca, 1991; see Figure 12-9).

The threat of contracting AIDS has led to large-scale changes in sexual behavior. People are less likely to engage in "casual" sex with new acquaintances, and the use of condoms during sexual intercourse has increased (McKusick, Horstman, & Coates, 1985; Bauman & Siegel, 1987; Kolata, 1991).

The only foolproof method of avoiding AIDS is celibacy—a drastic step that most people find an unrealistic alternative. However, as you can see in Table 12-4, there are ways of reducing the risk of contracting AIDS through what have come to be called "safer sex" practices.

AIDS presents several profound psychological issues. First, there is the question of how to treat the psychological distress of victims of the disease, who must face the knowledge that the disease is incurable and invariably fatal—and that society is fearful that they will spread the disease. Second, because a blood test can detect whether a person who does not have the disease yet is a carrier of the virus (and therefore at risk to actually contract AIDS in the future), there is the issue of how to deal with the concerns of people who stand a chance of eventually coming down with the disease (Jacobsen, Perry, & Hirsch, 1990). Third, psy-

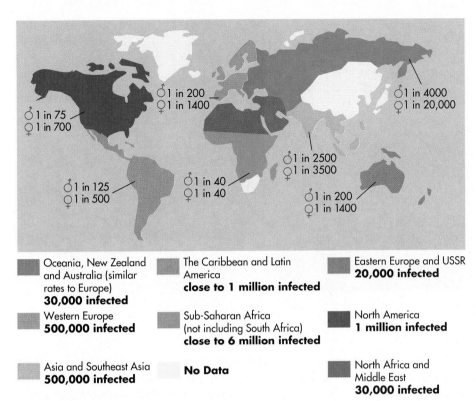

FIGURE 12-9

The incidence of AIDS infections varies dramatically from one geographical area to another. These figures represent estimates for adults aged 15 to 49. (World Health Organization, 1991.)

Oceania, New Zealand and Australia (similar rates to Europe) **30,000 infected**

The Caribbean and Latin America **close to 1 million infected**

Eastern Europe and USSR **20,000 infected**

Western Europe **500,000 infected**

Sub-Saharan Africa (not including South Africa) **close to 6 million infected**

North America **1 million infected**

Asia and Southeast Asia **500,000 infected**

No Data

North Africa and Middle East **30,000 infected**

chologists need to devise methods of reducing the anxiety of people whose fears of catching AIDS lead them to demand that extreme measures be taken against the victims of the disease (going so far, for instance, as calling for a quarantine for those with AIDS).

Finally and, in the long run, probably most important, psychologists need to develop ways to help prevent the spread of AIDS by changing people's sexual behavior. Until a cure is found for the disease, AIDS will continue to present difficult problems that are likely to have a major impact on sexual behavior (O'Keefe, Nesselhof-Kendall, & Baum, 1990; Coates, 1990; Pryor, Reeder, & McManus, 1991).

T A B L E   1 2 - 4

SAFER SEX: SEXUAL PRACTICES THAT HELP PREVENT THE TRANSMISSION OF AIDS

Despite the specter of AIDS and other sexually transmitted diseases, most people will not choose to become celibate. In the face of this reality, experts have suggested several practices to minimize the risks of contracting AIDS and other sexually transmitted diseases (Voeller, Reinisch, & Gottlieb, 1991; Paalman, 1990):

■ *Know your sexual partner—well.* Sexual activities are risky with someone whose sexual history is unfamiliar to you. Before entering into a sexual relationship with someone, be aware of his or her background.

■ *Avoid the exchange of bodily fluids, particularly semen.* In particular, most experts recommend the avoidance of anal intercourse. The AIDS virus can spread through small tears in the rectum, making anal intercourse without using condoms particularly dangerous.

■ *Use condoms.* For those in sexual relationships, condoms are the most reliable means of preventing transmission of the AIDS virus.

■ *Consider the benefits of monogamy.* People in long-term, monogamous relationships with partners who have been faithful are at a lower risk of contracting AIDS.

Psychologists are working to develop ways of preventing the spread of AIDS by changing individuals' behavior.

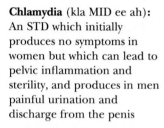

Chlamydia (kla MID ee ah): An STD which initially produces no symptoms in women but which can lead to pelvic inflammation and sterility, and produces in men painful urination and discharge from the penis

Genital herpes: A noncurable virus producing small blisters or sores around the genitals; symptoms disappear but often recur

Gonorrhea: An STD which leads to infertility and infection

Syphilis: An STD which, if untreated, may affect the brain, heart, and developing fetus, and can be fatal

Genital warts: An STD that causes small lumpy warts to form on or near the penis or vagina

Other STDs

Although AIDS is the best-known STD, others are considerably more prevalent (see Figure 12-10). For instance, the most widespread is **chlamydia**, an STD which initially produces no symptoms in women but which, if left untreated, can lead to pelvic inflammation and even sterility. In men, there is burning on urination and discharge from the penis. Chlamydia affects some 4.5 million women and men and is treated with antibiotics.

Genital herpes is a virus related to the cold sores that sometimes appear around the mouth. Herpes first appears as small blisters or sores around the genitals which later break open, causing severe pain. These sores heal after a few weeks, but the disease can and often does reappear after an indeterminate interval, and the cycle repeats itself. There is no cure for genital herpes, and during the active phases of the disease it can be transmitted to sexual partners.

Gonorrhea and **syphilis** are the two STDs that have been recognized the longest. Gonorrhea can lead to fertility problems and infection. Syphilis, if untreated, may affect the brain, heart, and a developing fetus, and can even be fatal. Syphilis reveals itself first through a small sore at the point of sexual contact. In its secondary stage, it may include a rash. Both gonorrhea and syphilis can be treated successfully with antibiotics if diagnosed early enough.

Another common STD is **genital warts**, small, lumpy warts that form on or near the penis or vagina. The warts are easily diagnosed because of their distinctive appearance: they look like small cauliflower bulbs. They usually form about two months after exposure, and they can be treated with an application of a drug or, in a more recent innovation, through the use of a laser treatment.

Sexual Problems

While few of us would feel embarrassed by a case of appendicitis or a broken leg, most of us would have to admit that sexual difficulties are a cause for major concern, given the importance that society places on "appropriate" sexual conduct. Interest in their own sexuality leads many people to consider and reconsider its every nuance.

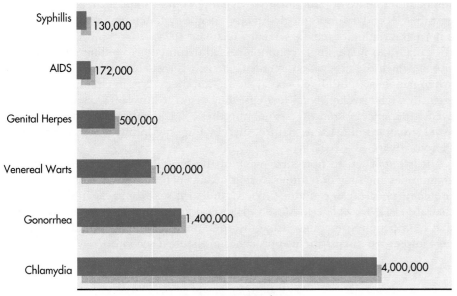

FIGURE 12-10

Estimates of the number of new cases annually of sexually transmitted diseases. (Center for Disease Control, 1991.)

While for most people sexual activity proceeds relatively smoothly, there are times in almost everyone's life when sexual problems arise. Among the most common are some of the disorders we discuss below.

Erectile failure is the inability of a male to achieve or maintain an erection (Segraves & Schoenberg, 1985). In one rare manifestation, **primary erectile failure**, the male has never been able to have an erection. But in the more common case, **secondary erectile failure**, the male, though now unable to have an erection, has had at least one in the past. Erectile failure is not an uncommon problem, and it is the rare man who has never experienced it at least once during his lifetime. This is hardly surprising, since the ability to achieve and hold an erection is sensitive to alcohol, drugs, performance fears, anxiety, and a host of other factors. It becomes a more serious problem when it occurs more than occasionally.

In **premature ejaculation**, a male is unable to delay orgasm as long as he wishes. Because "as long as he wishes" is dependent on a man's—and his partner's—attitudes and opinions about how long is appropriate, this is a difficult disorder to define, and sometimes the problem can be resolved simply by having a male redefine how long he wants to delay ejaculation.

Premature ejaculation is most often a psychological problem, since there are rarely physical reasons for it. One cause may be early sexual learning: Because sexual experiences during adolescence are often accompanied by a fear of being caught, some men learn early in their lives to reach orgasm as quickly as possible.

Inhibited ejaculation is the opposite problem. In this case, the male is unable to ejaculate when he wants to, if at all. Sometimes learning general relaxation techniques is sufficient to allow men to overcome the difficulty.

Some women experience **anorgasmia**, or a lack of orgasm. In **primary orgasmic dysfunction**, women have never experienced orgasm, while in **secondary orgasmic dysfunction**, a woman is capable of experiencing orgasm only under certain conditions—such as during masturbation but not during sexual intercourse. Because the inability to have orgasm during sexual intercourse is so common, with some one-third of all women reporting they do not receive sufficient

Erectile failure: A male's inability to achieve or maintain an erection

Primary erectile failure: A long-term inability to achieve or maintain an erection

Secondary erectile failure: A male's temporary inability to achieve or maintain an erection

Premature ejaculation: A male's inability to delay ejaculation

Inhibited ejaculation: A male's inability to ejaculate when he wants to, if at all

Anorgasmia (an or GAZ mee uh)**:** A female's lack of orgasm

Primary orgasmic dysfunction: A female's long-term inability to achieve orgasm

Secondary orgasmic dysfunction: A female's temporary inability to achieve orgasm or her ability to achieve orgasm only under certain conditions (such as masturbation)

Inhibited sexual desire: A condition in which the motivation for sexual activity is restrained or lacking

stimulation to have orgasm during sexual intercourse, some sex researchers suggest that secondary orgasmic dysfunction is not dysfunctional at all, but merely a normal variation of female sexuality (Kaplan, 1974).

Finally, an increasingly common sexual dysfunction is **inhibited sexual desire**, in which the motivation for sexual activity is restrained or lacking entirely. When people with inhibited sexual desire find themselves in circumstances that typically would evoke sexual feelings, they begin to turn off sexually and may even experience a kind of "sexual anesthesia." Ultimately they may begin to avoid situations of a sexual nature, thereby forgoing intimacy with others (Lo-Piccolo, 1980).

It is important to note that many of the problems we have discussed are common at one time or another during sexual encounters. It is only when these problems persist, cause undue anxiety, and turn sex from play into work that they are cause for concern. Moreover, several techniques have been developed that help people overcome sexual disorders that in the past would have gone unresolved. We discuss these approaches in the next section.

The Informed Consumer of Psychology: Recognizing the Promises and Pitfalls of Sex Therapy

Given the importance of sex, both in terms of our society and for each of us as individuals, it is not surprising that problems and concerns with sexuality have become a big business. Clinics for treating sexual problems have sprung up all over the country, and therapists concentrating on the treatment of sexual problems have become more and more common.

Unfortunately, not all sexual problems respond to treatment equally well. Moreover, sex therapy does not operate in the same way that medical treatment for a disease would. A person cannot take a pill or receive an injection and suddenly become "cured." Sexual problems are complex, having as they do both physical and psychological components.

There are certain factors that informed consumers of sex therapy ought to consider when seeking help for sexual problems. Among those are the following:

■ The sex therapist should have credentials indicating that he or she has been specially trained in sex therapy. For instance, the American Association of Sex Educators, Counselors, and Therapists (AASECT) has an active certification program.

■ Sex therapy should *never* involve sexual activity with the therapist. This does not mean that a physical examination is not a typical part of sex therapy, since some sexual problems have physical causes. But it does mean that therapists who suggest that sexual interaction with them is necessary are guilty of incompetent and highly unethical behavior.

■ Remember that not all sexual "problems" are problems. Holding up your sexual behavior to some standard—such as frequency of sexual intercourse—is not necessarily appropriate. You and your partner are individuals, and if your sex life works for you, don't worry about how it compares to other peoples' sex lives.

■ A good sex life won't cure a bad relationship. Improving sexual functioning is not a cure-all for helping a relationship. Even if a couple's sex life gets better, their relationship may still be in trouble.

■ Sexual problems do not lie in the genitals alone but reflect the whole person and his or her interactions with others. As we have seen, sexual arousal and satisfaction are complex phenomena, involving physical, cognitive, emotional, social, and societal factors. All must be taken into account when sexual problems are being treated.

RECAP AND REVIEW IV

RECAP

◀ Rape occurs when one person forces another to submit to sexual activity. It is most often motivated by power or anger, rather than by desire for sexual gratification.

◀ Child sexual abuse is a surprisingly frequent phenomenon.

◀ The major sexually transmitted diseases (STDs) include AIDS, chlamydia, genital herpes, gonorrhea, syphilis, and genital warts.

◀ Among the major sexual problems are erectile failure, premature ejaculation, anorgasmia, and inhibited sexual desire.

REVIEW

1. A college woman is more likely to be raped by an acquaintance than by a stranger. True or false?

_____

2. Which of the following is unlikely to be a motivation for the act of rape?
   a. Need for power
   b. Desire for sexual intimacy
   c. Desire for sexual gratification

d. Anger against women in general

3. Which of the following STDs is the most widespread?
   a. Genital herpes
   b. Gonorrhea
   c. Chlamydia
   d. Syphilis

4. An increasingly common sexual dysfunction is _____ sexual desire.

5. Which of the following is *not* true about changes in sexual behavior as a result of the AIDS epidemic?
   a. The use of condoms has increased.
   b. People are less likely to engage in casual sex.
   c. Many people have found celibacy to be a realistic alternative.
   d. The risk of contracting AIDS may be reduced by engaging in safer-sex practices.

6. Sexual dysfunctions, even if they occur only once, are cause for considerable concern and should be treated immediately. True or false? _____

Ask Yourself

Because of the possibility of transmitting AIDS, should physicians, dentists, and other public health workers be tested for the AIDS virus and their test results made public?

(Answers to review questions are on page 410.)

LOOKING BACK

■ *What are the major differences between male and female gender roles?*

1. Our sense of the way in which we think about ourselves is partly determined by gender, the sense of being male or female. Gender roles are the expectations, defined by society, that indicate what is appropriate behavior for men and women. When gender roles reflect favoritism toward one particular sex, they lead to stereotyping and produce sexism, negative attitudes and behavior based on an individual's sex.

2. The gender-role stereotype for men suggests that they are endowed with competence-related traits, whereas women are seen in terms of their capacity for warmth and expressiveness. Actual sex differences are much less clear, and of smaller magnitude, than the stereotypes would suggest. There are differences in levels of aggression, self-esteem, communication styles, and perhaps cognitive abilities, but the magnitude of the differences is not great. The differences that do exist are produced by a combination of biological and environmental factors.

3. Biological causes of sex difference are reflected by evidence suggesting a possible difference in brain structure and functioning between men and women and may be associated with differential exposure to hormones prior to birth. In terms of environmental causes, socialization experiences produce gender schemas, cognitive frameworks that organize and guide a child's understanding of information relevant to gender.

■ Why, and under what circumstances, do we become sexually aroused?

4. Although biological factors, such as the presence of androgens (the male sex hormone) and estrogens (the female sex hormone) prime people for sex, almost any kind of stimulus can produce sexual arousal, depending on a person's prior experience. Erogenous zones are areas of the body that are particularly sensitive to touch and that have become associated with sexual arousal. Fantasies, thoughts, and images are also important in producing arousal.

5. People's sexual responses follow a regular pattern consisting of four phases: excitement, plateau, orgasm, and resolution. Women can experience multiple orgasms, whereas men may enter a refractory period, during which more sex is impossible until a sufficient amount of time has passed. Recent evidence, though, suggests that men may actually be capable of multiple orgasms but not multiple ejaculations.

■ What is "normal" sexual behavior, and how do most people behave sexually?

6. There are a number of approaches to determining normality: deviation from the average, comparison of sexual behavior with some standard or ideal, or—in the approach used most often—consideration of the psychological and physical consequences of the behavior to the person and whether it is harmful to others.

7. Masturbation is sexual self-stimulation. The frequency of masturbation is high, particularly for males. Although attitudes toward masturbation have become more liberal, they are still somewhat negative—even though no negative consequences have been detected.

8. Heterosexuality, or the sexual attraction to members of the opposite sex, is the most common sexual orientation. In terms of premarital sex, the double standard, in which premarital sex is thought to be more permissible for men than for women, has declined, particularly among young people. It has been replaced by the standard of permissiveness with affection, which suggests that premarital intercourse is permissible if it occurs in the context of a loving and committed relationship.

9. The frequency of marital sex varies widely. However, younger couples tend to have sexual intercourse more frequently than older ones. In addition, extramarital sex, of which most people disapprove, occurs with more than half of all married men and one-quarter of married women.

10. Homosexuals are sexually attracted to members of their own sex; bisexuals are sexually attracted to people of the same and the opposite sex. About one-quarter of males and 15 percent of females have had at least one homosexual experience, and around 5 to 10 percent of all men and women are exclusively homosexual during extended periods of their lives. No explanation for why people become homosexual has been confirmed; among the possibilities are genetic or biological factors, childhood and family influences, and prior learning experiences and conditioning. What is clear is that there is no relationship between psychological adjustment and sexual preference.

■ Why is rape not a crime of sex, and how prevalent is it and other forms of nonconsenting sex?

11. Rape occurs when one person forces another to submit to sexual activity. Rape does not occur only between strangers; often the victim is acquainted with the rapist. The motivation for rape is only sometimes sexual gratification. More frequently, though, it is power, aggression, or anger.

12. Childhood sexual abuse is widespread; some 22 percent of all Americans report some form of sexual abuse as children. Most often the perpetrator is an acquaintance or a family member. Lingering negative effects, which may even continue into adulthood, can be experienced by victims of sexual abuse.

■ What are the major sexually transmitted diseases and sexual difficulties that people encounter?

13. Acquired immune deficiency syndrome, or AIDS, represents a health problem that is having profound effects on sexual behavior. First limited largely to homosexuals, AIDS is now found in the heterosexual population and is bringing about changes in casual sex and in people's sexual practices. The disease raises a number of psychological issues that are difficult to resolve. Other sexually transmitted diseases include chlamydia, genital herpes, gonorrhea, syphilis, and genital warts.

14. Among the major sexual problems reported by males are erectile failure (primary, for males who have never had an erection, or secondary, for males who have had erections in the past); premature ejaculation, in which orgasm cannot be delayed; and inhibited ejaculation, in which the male cannot ejaculate during sexual intercourse. For females, the major problem is anorgasmia, or a lack of orgasm. Here, too, the problem may be primary (in women having never experienced an orgasm) or secondary (in women capable of experiencing orgasm, but doing so only under certain conditions). Both men and women may suffer from inhibited sexual desire.

15. Because of the prevalence of sexual therapists and different forms of treatment, it is important to keep several considerations in mind when seeking therapy. Among them are the credentials of the sex therapist, the fact that there should be no sexual contact between therapist and client, and the realization that not all so-called sexual problems may really be problems, that bad relationships won't be fully resolved by good sex, and that sexual problems affect the whole person.

ANSWERS (REVIEW IV):

1. True **2.** b **3.** c **4.** inhibited **5.** c **6.** False; sexual dysfunction occurs to almost everyone at one time or another.

KEY TERMS AND CONCEPTS

gender (p. 376)
gender roles (p. 377)
stereotyping (p. 377)
sexism (p. 377)
androgens (p. 382)
estrogen (p. 383)
socialization (p. 383)
gender schema (p. 383)
androgynous (p. 384)
testes (p. 385)
genitals (p. 385)
ovaries (p. 385)
ovulation (p. 385)
erotic (p. 387)
erogenous zones (p. 387)
excitement phase (p. 388)
penis (p. 388)
clitoris (p. 388)
vagina (p. 388)
plateau phase (p. 388)

orgasm (p. 388)
semen (p. 388)
ejaculation (p. 389)
resolution stage (p. 389)
refractory period (p. 391)
masturbation (p. 393)
heterosexuality (p. 394)
double standard (p. 395)
permissiveness with affection
    (p. 396)
extramarital sex (p. 398)
homosexuality (p. 398)
bisexuality (p. 398)
rape (p. 401)
date rape (p. 401)
acquired immune deficiency
    syndrome (AIDS) (p. 404)
sexually transmitted disease
    (STD) (p. 404)

chlamydia (p. 406)
genital herpes (p. 406)
gonorrhea (p. 406)
syphilis (p. 406)
genital warts (p. 406)
erectile failure (p. 407)
primary erectile failure (p. 407)
secondary erectile failure
    (p. 407)
premature ejaculation (p. 407)
inhibited ejaculation (p. 407)
anorgasmia (p. 407)
primary orgasmic dysfunction
    (p. 407)
secondary orgasmic dysfunction
    (p. 407)
inhibited sexual desire (p. 408)

13

DEVELOPMENT:
THE BEGINNINGS OF LIFE

THE TWIN CONNECTION

Gerald Levey and Mark Newman.

How many bald, six-foot-six, 250-pound volunteer fire fighters are there in New Jersey who have droopy mustaches and aviator-style eyeglasses and wear a key ring on his belt on the right side?

The answer is: two. Gerald Levey and Mark Newman are twins, separated at birth, who did not even know the other existed until they were reunited—in a fire station—by a fellow fire fighter who knew Newman and was startled to see Levey at a fire fighters' convention.

Their lives, although separate, took remarkably similar paths. Levey went to college, studying forestry; Newman planned to study forestry in college but instead took a job trimming trees. Both had jobs in supermarkets. One has a job installing sprinkler systems; the other installed fire alarms.

Both men are unmarried and find the same kind of woman attractive: "tall, slender, long hair." They share similar hobbies, enjoying hunting, fishing, going to the beach, and watching old John Wayne movies and professional wrestling. Both like Chinese food and they drink the same brand of beer. Their mannerisms are also similar—for example, they both throw their heads back when they laugh. And, of course, there is one more thing: They share a passion for fighting fires.

* * *

Music lies at the core of Joan Gardiner's life. An accomplished concert pianist, Gardiner has performed with the Minnesota Orchestra. Her musical talent seemed inborn; her parents never prompted her to play or even practice.

Joan Gardiner and Jean Nelson.

Jean Nelson, however, doesn't play the piano, even though her mother was a piano teacher. Her disinterest in music is particularly striking, given the daily hours of practicing she was encouraged to do as a child.

The inconsistency in musical interests between the two women would hardly be noteworthy were it not for the fact that, like Gerald Levey and Mark Newman, Jean Nelson and Joan Gardiner are identical twins, separated a few months after birth. The question concerning these women is why they differ so much in their musical interests—a domain that is so pivotal to one of them (Lang, 1987).

LOOKING AHEAD

We know of the similarities—and differences—within each set of twins because of their participation in a large-scale, national study of twins being conducted at the Minnesota Center for Twin and Adoption Research. In the study, researchers are finding many pairs of twins that mirror the amazing degree of similarity between Levey and Newman. At the same time, however, they are also finding pairs of twins in which crucial characteristics are quite different. Such similarities and differences are being studied not as mere curiosities, but because they provide us with important clues about one of the most fundamental questions facing psychologists: how the environment and the natural endowment with which the human being is born interact to produce a unique individual.

This question, and others, falls within the domain of developmental psychology. **Developmental psychology** is the branch of psychology that studies the patterns of growth and change occurring throughout life. In large part, devel-

Developmental psychology: The branch of psychology that studies patterns of growth and change occurring throughout life

opmental psychologists study the interaction between the unfolding of biologically predetermined patterns of behavior and a constantly changing, dynamic environment. They ask how our genetic background affects our behavior throughout our lives, whether our potential is limited by heredity, and how our built-in biological programming affects our day-to-day development. Similarly, they are committed to understanding the way in which the environment works with—or against—our genetic capabilities, how the world we live in affects our development, and how we can be encouraged to develop our full potential.

More than other psychologists, developmental psychologists consider the day-to-day patterns and changes in behavior that occur across the lifespan. This chapter focuses on the early part of the life cycle, beginning with birth, moving through infancy, and ending with childhood. The following chapter explores aspects of development during the remainder of the life cycle from adolescence to adulthood, and finally to old age and death.

We begin our discussion of development by examining the approaches that have been used to understand and delineate the environmental and genetic factors that direct a person's development. Then we consider the very start of development, beginning with conception and the nine months of life prior to birth. We describe both genetic and environmental influences on the unborn individual, and how these can affect behavior throughout the remainder of the life cycle.

Next, we examine the physical and perceptual developments that occur after birth, witnessing the enormous and rapid growth that takes place during the early stages of life. We also focus on the developing child's social world, indicating what draws the child into relationships with others and membership in society. Finally, we discuss cognitive growth during infancy and childhood, tracing changes in the way that children think about the world.

After reading this chapter, you will have the answers to several fundamental questions about development:

- How do psychologists study the degree to which development is a joint function of heredity and environmental factors?
- What is the nature of development prior to birth, and what factors affect a child during the mother's pregnancy?
- What are the major milestones of physical, perceptual, and social growth after birth?
- How can we best describe cognitive development, and what can parents appropriately do to promote the cognitive development of their children?

NATURE AND NURTURE: A FUNDAMENTAL DEVELOPMENTAL ISSUE

The similarities we saw earlier between twins Gerald Levey and Mark Newman are as striking as the differences between twins Jean Nelson and Joan Gardiner. Cases such as these vividly illustrate one of the fundamental questions posed by developmental psychologists: How can we distinguish between the causes of behavior that are **environmental** (the influence of parents, siblings, family, friends, schooling, nutrition, and all the other experiences to which a child is exposed), and those causes that are **hereditary** (those based on the genetic makeup of an individual that influence growth throughout life)? This question, which we first explored considering the determinants of intelligence in Chapter 10, is also

Environment: Influences on behavior that occur in the world around us—in family, friends, school, nutrition, and many other factors

Heredity: Influences on behavior that are transmitted genetically from parents to a child

Nature-nurture issue: The issue of the degree to which environment and heredity influence behavior

known as the **nature-nurture issue**, where nature refers to heredity and nurture to environmental influences.

The nature-nurture issue has deep philosophical roots. English philosopher John Locke argued in the 1600s that a newborn was, in effect, a blank slate, a *tabula rasa*, on which the story of his or her individual experience could be written from scratch. In other words, he believed that the environment acted as the sole influence on development. In contrast, the French philosopher Jean Jacques Rousseau suggested a very different conception of development in the 1700s. He believed that people's ''natural'' characteristics (namely, genetic factors) were most influential, although subject to what Rousseau considered to be the corrupting influence of the environment.

Although the question was first posed as the nature-*versus*-nurture question, developmental psychologists today agree that *both* nature and nurture interact to produce specific developmental patterns. The question has changed from *which* influences behavior to *how* and to what degree environment and heredity produce their effects. No one grows up without being influenced by the environment, nor does anyone develop without being affected by his or her inherited, or **genetic makeup**. However, the debate over the relative influence of the two factors remains an ongoing one, with different approaches and theories of development emphasizing the environment or heredity to a greater or lesser degree.

Genetic makeup: The inherited biological factors that transmit hereditary information

For example, some developmental theories stress the role of learning in producing changes in behavior in the developing child, relying on the basic principles of learning discussed in Chapter 7. Such theories emphasize the role of environment in accounting for development. In contrast, other approaches emphasize the influence of one's physiological makeup and functioning on development. Such theories stress the role of heredity and **maturation**—the unfolding of biologically predetermined patterns of behavior—in producing developmental change. Maturation can be seen, for instance, in the development of sex characteristics (such as breasts or body hair) that occur at the start of adolescence.

Maturation: The unfolding of biologically predetermined behavior patterns

On some points, however, agreement exists among developmental psychologists of different theoretical persuasions (Loehlin, 1989; Plomin, 1989). It seems clear that genetic factors not only provide the potential for particular behaviors or traits to emerge, but they also place limitations on the emergence of such behavior or traits. For instance, heredity defines people's general level of intelligence, setting an upper limit which—regardless of the quality of the environment—people cannot exceed. Heredity also provides limits on physical abilities; humans simply cannot run at a speed of 60 miles an hour, nor are they going to grow as tall as 10 feet, no matter what the quality of their environment (Plomin, 1990).

Table 13-1 lists some of the characteristics that are most affected by heredity. As you consider these items, it is important to keep in mind that these characteristics are not *entirely* determined by heredity—merely that the best evidence suggests that variations in these factors are due to a relatively large extent to the genetic makeup of an individual.

In most instances, environmental factors play a critical role in enabling people to reach the potential capabilities provided by their genetic background. Had Albert Einstein received no intellectual stimulation as a child and not been sent to school, it is unlikely that he would have reached his genetic potential. Similarly, a great athlete like basketball star Michael Jordan would have been unlikely to display much physical skill had he not been raised in an environment that

TABLE 13-1

CHARACTERISTICS WITH STRONG COMPONENTS

Physical characteristics	Intellectual characteristics	Emotional characteristics and disorders
Height	Memory	Shyness
Weight	Ability as measured on intelligence tests	Extraversion
Obesity		Emotionality
Tone of voice	Age of language acquisition	Neuroticism
Blood pressure	Reading disability	Schizophrenia
Tooth decay	Mental retardation	Anxiety
Athletic ability		Alcoholism
Firmness of handshake		
Age of death		
Activity level		

Source: Papalia & Olds, 1988; Plomin, 1989.

nurtured his innate talent and gave him the opportunity to train and perfect his natural abilities.

In sum, developmental psychologists take an **interactionist** position on the nature-nurture issue, suggesting that a combination of genetic predisposition and environmental influences produces development. The challenge facing developmental psychologists is to identify the specific kind and relative strength of each of these influences on the individual. (For an example of current work showing how genetic and environmental factors are related, see the Cutting Edge box on p. 418.)

The search to understand the relative influences of nature and nurture is not merely an academic exercise. Important advances in our understanding of the optimal way to raise children have been made as a result of research findings on heredity and the environment. For instance, the way in which we educate children, how children in institutions such as orphanages are raised, and the kinds of day-care that are considered optimal have all been influenced by our understanding of the interaction of heredity and environment.

Interactionist: Someone who believes that a combination of genetic predisposition and environmental influences determines the course of development

Addressing the Nature-Nuture Question

Developmental psychologists have tried to determine the relative influence of genetic and environmental factors on behavior in several different ways, although no technique is foolproof. We can, for example, experimentally control the genetic makeup of laboratory animals, carefully breeding them for specific traits. Just as the people who raise Butterball turkeys have learned to produce a breed that grows particularly quickly (so they can be brought to the marketplace less expensively), psychologists are able to breed strains of laboratory animals who share a similar genetic makeup. Observing animals with a similar genetic background in varied environments allows researchers to ascertain the effects of particular kinds of environmental stimulation. Ultimately, of course, we do have the problem of generalizing the findings of research with animals to a human

Standing apart from the other children, 8-year-old Sondra kept a watchful eye on the exuberant game of kickball that was taking place on the school playground. She never joined in, though. Instead, she played jump-rope by herself, counting out each successful jump quietly aloud. When the playground monitor approached her and tried to coax her into the game, she avoided the teacher's gaze and said softly that she would rather play by herself.

It does not take an expert to characterize Sondra as a shy child. What is noteworthy about her behavior, however, is that it is fully consistent with the way Sondra appeared as an infant. As early as 2 months of age, she would spontaneously frown, even while resting quietly—something that is unusual in young infants. At 9 months, she became remarkably fearful at the sight of an unfamiliar adult and even fretted when confronted with unfamiliar objects or new settings. By the time she was 4 years old, her parents and teachers had labeled her as shy.

To developmental psychologist Jerome Kagan, Sondra's behavior is characteristic of the "inhibited" child. Inhibited children, who make up about 10 percent of Caucasian children, are consistently shy and emotionally restrained in unfamiliar situations. When placed in a novel environment or when meeting people for the first time, they become notice-

BORN TO BE SHY? INHIBITED AND UNINHIBITED CHILDREN

ably quiet. When they are asked questions of just moderate difficulty by an unfamiliar adult in experiments, they become anxious, which has the effect of hindering their performance. They are more likely than other children to show unusual fears, such as going into their bedrooms by themselves at night or speaking aloud in class. In contrast, uninhibited children show little fear of strangers or of new situations, acting sociable and relaxed when encountering novelty (Kagan, 1989b).

Kagan's ongoing research has found that inhibited children also differ from uninhibited ones on a physiological level. Inhibited children show higher muscle tension at age five, particularly in the vocal cords and larynx. They tend to have more rapid resting heartbeats, and their heartbeats increase more when confronted with a new situation. There are also hormonal differences and variations in the excitability of the limbic system of the brain between inhibited and uninhibited children (Kagan & Snidman, 1991).

Based on this evidence, Kagan has suggested that the differences between inhibited and uninhibited children rest in the inhibited children's greater physiological reactivity—an inborn characteristic. According to his hypothesis, some infants, due to their genetic endowment, are more reactive to novel stimuli than others. Even the mildest stress raises their

heartbeat, increases muscle tension, and causes changes in hormonal levels. It is this characteristic reactivity that ultimately leads most of the infants who show this pattern to later display shy social behavior.

On the other hand, not all infants born with easily aroused nervous systems later become shy: About one-quarter overcome their biological predisposition and do not exhibit shyness in later years. It appears that certain kinds of environmental stress, such as parental marital strife or a chronic illness in the family, increase the likelihood of the later appearance of shyness. It is the interaction of heredity and environment, then, that determine whether a child will or won't become shy.

Furthermore, even people who are shy during childhood can overcome their genetic predisposition and change their behavior. For example, Kagan provides the following case:

> I recall a man in one of our studies who was extremely inhibited as a boy. He told me that as an adolescent he had been very shy with girls, but decided to overcome this fear by inviting the most attractive girl in the school to the senior high school dance. She accepted, and he regarded that as the beginning of a change in his personality. Sometimes human behavior is the result of deliberation and will imposed on the invisible forces of biology and personal history (Kagan, 1990, p. 5).

population, but the animal findings provide fundamental information that could not be obtained by using human subjects, for ethical reasons.

Human twins also provide us with an important source of information about the relative effects of genetic and environmental factors. If **identical twins** (those who are genetically identical) display different patterns of development, we have to attribute such differences to variations in the environment in which they were raised. The most useful data come from identical twins (such as Gerald Levey and Mark Newman) who are adopted at birth by different sets of foster parents and raised apart from each other in different environments. Studies of nontwin siblings who are raised in different environments also shed some light on the

Identical twins: Twins with identical genetic makeup

issue. Because they share relatively similar genetic backgrounds, siblings who show similarities as adults provide strong evidence for the importance of heredity.

It is also possible to take the opposite tack. Instead of concentrating on people with similar genetic backgrounds who are raised in different environments, we may consider people raised in similar environments who have totally dissimilar genetic backgrounds. If we find, for example, that two adopted children—who have dissimilar genetic backgrounds—raised in the same family develop similarly, we have evidence for the importance of environmental influences on development. Moreover, it is possible to carry out research with animals with dissimilar genetic backgrounds; by experimentally varying the environment in which they are raised, we can determine the influence of environmental factors, independent of heredity, on development.

Studying Development

The specific research methods used by developmental psychologists to consider the nature-nurture issue, as well as other questions of a developmental nature, tend to fall into two categories: cross-sectional and longitudinal (Cohen & Reese, 1991). In **cross-sectional research**, people of different ages are compared at the same point in time. Suppose, for instance, you were interested in the development of intellectual ability in adulthood. To carry out a cross-sectional study, you might compare a sample of 25-, 45-, and 65-year olds on an IQ test, seeing how the average scores differ.

Cross-sectional research: A research method in which people of different ages are compared at the same point in time

Cross-sectional research has pitfalls, however. In our example, for instance, it is possible that any differences you found in IQ scores were due not to age differences per se but to the fact that the average educational level attained by the older subjects was lower than that of the younger sample, since far fewer people went to college forty years ago.

One way around the problem is to conduct **longitudinal research**, in which the behavior of one or more subjects is traced as the subjects age. By examining changes over several points in time, we can clearly see how individuals develop. Unfortunately, though, there are also drawbacks to longitudinal research: It requires an enormous expenditure of time (as the researcher waits for the subjects to get older), and subjects who participate at an early stage may drop out, move away, or even die as the research continues. Moreover, subjects who take the same test at several points in time may become "testwise" and perform better each time they take it, just because they are becoming more familiar with the test.

Longitudinal research: A research method which investigates behavior through time as subjects age

To make up for the drawbacks in cross-sectional and longitudinal research, investigators have devised an alternative method. Known as **cross-sequential research**, it combines cross-sectional and longitudinal approaches by taking a number of different age groups and examining them over several points in time. For example, investigators might use a group of 3-, 5-, and 7-year-olds, examining them every six months for a period of several years. This technique allows the developmental psychologist to tease out the effects of age changes themselves from other possibly influential factors.

Cross-sequential research: A research method which combines cross-sectional and longitudinal research

The Start of Life: Conception and Beyond

Our understanding of the biology of the start of life—when a male's sperm cell penetrates a female's egg cell, marking the moment of **conception**—makes it no less of a miracle. At that single moment, an individual's genetic endowment is established for the rest of his or her life.

Conception: The process by which an egg cell is fertilized by a sperm cell

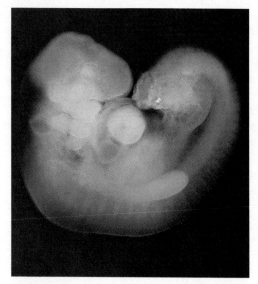 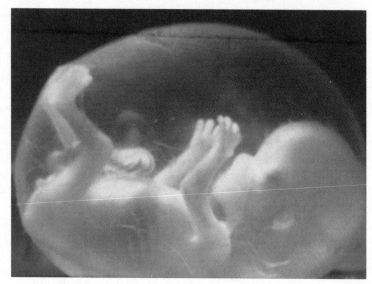

FIGURE 13-1

These remarkable photos of a live embryo and fetus display the degree of physical development at 4 and 15 weeks. (*Left*, Lennart Nilsson, *A Child Is Born*/Dell Publishing, Inc. *Right*, Petit Format/Science Source/Photo Researchers.)

Zygote: The one-celled product of fertilization

Chromosomes: Rod-shaped structures that contain basic hereditary information

Genes: The parts of a chromosome through which genetic information is transmitted

Embryo: A developed zygote that has a heart, a brain, and other organs

Critical period: The first of several stages of development in which specific kinds of growth must occur to enable further normal development

When the egg becomes fertilized by the sperm, the result is a one-celled entity called a **zygote** that immediately begins to develop. The zygote contains twenty-three pairs of **chromosomes**, rod-shaped structures that contain the basic hereditary information. One member of each pair is from the mother and the other is from the father. Each chromosome contains thousands of **genes**—smaller units through which genetic information is transmitted—that, either individually or in combination, produce particular characteristics in the individual.

While some genes are responsible for the development of systems common to all members of the human species—the heart, circulatory system, brain, lungs, and so forth—others control the characteristics that make each human unique, such as facial configuration, height, eye color, and the like. The child's sex is also determined by a particular combination of genes. Specifically, a child inherits an X chromosome from its mother, and either an X or Y chromosome from its father. With an XX combination, it is a female; with an XY combination, it develops as a male. Recent findings suggest that male development is triggered by a single gene on the Y chromosome, and without the presence of that specific gene, the individual will develop as a female (Roberts, 1988a).

The zygote starts out as a microscopic speck. As it divides through an intricate preprogrammed system of cell division, it grows 10,000 times larger in just four weeks, to about one-fifth of an inch long. At that point it is called an **embryo** and has developed a rudimentary heart (that beats), a brain, an intestinal tract, and a number of other organs. Although all these organs are at a primitive stage of development, they are clearly recognizable. Moreover, by the eighth week, the embryo is about an inch long, and has arms, legs, and a face that are discernible (see Figure 13-1).

Following the eighth week, the embryo faces what is known as a **critical period**, the first of several stages in prenatal development in which specific kinds of growth must occur if the individual is to develop normally. For example, if the eyes and ears do not develop during this stage, they will never form later on, and if they form abnormally, they are permanently damaged. During critical periods, organisms are particularly sensitive to environmental influences such as the presence of certain kinds of drugs, which, as we will see later, can have a devastating effect on subsequent development (Bornstein & Krasnegor, 1989; Bornstein & Bruner, 1989).

Beginning in the ninth week and continuing until birth, the developing individual is called a **fetus**. At the start of this period, it begins to be responsive to touch; it bends its fingers when touched on the hand. At 16 to 18 weeks, its movements become strong enough for the mother to sense the baby. At the same time, hair may begin to grow on the baby's head, and the facial features become similar to those the child will display at birth. The major organs begin to function, although the fetus could not be kept alive outside the mother. In addition, a lifetime's worth of brain neurons have been produced—although it is unclear whether the brain is capable of thinking in any real sense at this early stage.

By the twenty-fourth week, a fetus has many of the characteristics it will display as a newborn. In fact, when an infant is born prematurely at this age, it can open and close its eyes; suck; cry; look up, down, and around; and even grasp objects placed in its hands, although it is still unable to survive for long outside the mother.

The fetus continues to develop prior to birth. It begins to grow fatty deposits under the skin and it gains weight. The fetus reaches the **age of viability**, the point at which it can survive if born prematurely, at about 28 weeks, although through advances in medical technology this crucial age is getting earlier. At 28 weeks, the fetus weighs about 3 pounds and is about 16 inches long. It may be capable of learning: One study found that the infants of mothers who repeatedly had read aloud the Dr. Seuss story "The Cat in the Hat" prior to birth preferred the sound of that particular story over other stories after they were born (Spence & DeCasper, 1982).

In the final weeks of pregnancy, the fetus continues to gain weight and grow, becoming increasingly fit. At the end of the normal thirty-eight weeks of pregnancy the fetus typically weighs around 7 pounds and is about 20 inches in length.

Genetic Influences on the Fetus. The process of fetal growth that we have just described reflects normal development, which occurs in 95 to 98 percent of all pregnancies. Some people are less fortunate, for in the remaining 2 to 5 percent of cases, children are delivered with serious birth defects. A major cause of such defects is genetic: The information in the chromosomes inherited from one or both of the parents causes a problem. Here are some of the most common genetic difficulties.

■ *Phenylketonuria (PKU).* A child born with the inherited disease phenylketonuria (PKU) cannot produce an enzyme that is required for normal development. This results in an accumulation of poisons that eventually cause profound mental retardation. The disease is treatable, however, if it is caught early enough. Most infants today are routinely tested for PKU, and children with the disorder can be placed on a special diet that allows them to develop normally.

■ *Sickle-cell anemia.* About 10 percent of the American black population has the possibility of passing on sickle-cell anemia, a disease that gets its name from the abnormal shape of the red blood cells. Children with the disease may have poor appetites, swollen stomachs, and yellowish eyes; they rarely live beyond childhood.

■ *Tay-Sachs disease.* Children born with Tay-Sachs disease, a disorder found most often in Jews of eastern European ancestry, usually die by the age of 3 or 4 because of the body's inability to break down fat. If both parents carry the genetic defect producing the fatal illness, their child has a one in four chance of being born with the disease (Navon & Proia, 1989).

Fetus: A developing child, from nine weeks after conception until birth

Age of viability: The point at which a fetus can survive if born prematurely

Phenylketonuria (FEEN ul kee toe NYUR ee uh) **(PKU):** An inherited disease that prevents its victims from being able to produce an enzyme that resists certain poisons, resulting in profound mental retardation

Sickle-cell anemia: A disease of the blood that affects about 10 percent of America's black population

Tay-Sachs (TAY SAKS) **disease:** A genetic defect preventing the body from breaking down fat and typically causing death by the age of 3 or 4

Down syndrome: A disorder caused by the presence of an extra chromosome, resulting in mental retardation

■ *Down syndrome.* In Chapter 10, we discussed Down syndrome as a cause of mental retardation. Down syndrome is brought about not by an inherited trait passed on by the parents, but by a malfunction whereby the zygote receives an extra chromosome at the moment of conception, causing retardation and an unusual physical appearance (which led to an earlier label for the disease: mongolism). Down syndrome is related to the mother's and father's age; mothers over 35, in particular, stand a higher risk of having a child with the problem.

Prenatal Environmental Influences. Genetic factors are *not* the only causes of difficulties in fetal development; a number of environmental factors also have an effect on the course of development. The major prenatal environmental influences include:

■ *Mother's nutrition and emotional state.* What a mother eats during her pregnancy can have important implications for the health of her baby. Mothers who are seriously undernourished cannot provide adequate nutrition to the growing baby, and they are likely to give birth to underweight babies or to babies that are more susceptible to disease (Wyden, 1971). Moreover, there is some evidence that the mother's emotional state affects the baby. Mothers who are anxious and tense during the end of their pregnancies are more apt to have infants who are irritable and who sleep and eat poorly. The reason? One hypothesis is that the autonomic nervous system of the fetus becomes especially sensitive as a result of the chemical changes produced by the mother's emotional state (Kagan, Kearsley, & Zelazo, 1978).

Rubella: German measles; when contracted by pregnant women, it can cause severe birth defects

■ *Illness of mother.* During 1964 and 1965 an epidemic of **rubella**, or German measles, in the United States resulted in the prenatal death or malformation of close to 50,000 children. Although the disease has relatively minor effects on the mother, it is one of a number of illnesses that can have devastating results on the developing fetus when contracted during the early part of a woman's pregnancy. Other maternal diseases that may produce a permanent effect on the fetus include syphilis, diabetes, and high blood pressure.

AIDS—acquired immune deficiency syndrome—can be passed from mother to child prior to birth. Sadly, in many cases mothers may not even know they carry the disease and inadvertently transmit it to their children. According to some evidence, the AIDS virus can also be passed on through breast feeding after birth (Heyward & Curran, 1988).

Fetal alcohol syndrome: An ailment producing mental and physical retardation in a baby as a result of the mother's alcohol intake while pregnant

■ *Mother's use of drugs.* Drugs taken by a pregnant woman can have a tragic effect on the unborn child. Probably the most dramatic example was the use of thalidomide, a tranquilizer that was widely prescribed during the 1960s—until it was discovered that it caused such severe birth defects as the absence of arms and legs. The hormone diethylstilbestrol (DES), prescribed until the 1950s to prevent miscarriages, is now known to have placed children of mothers who took it at risk for abnormalities of the cervix and vagina and for developing cancer of the uterus in the case of daughters, and for infertility and reproductive problems in the case of sons.

Alcohol and nicotine are also dangerous to fetal development. For example, **fetal alcohol syndrome**, a condition resulting in mental and growth retardation, has been found in the children of mothers who consumed heavy

Although smoking and drinking are not advisable at any time during pregnancy, the period when most fetal damage can occur is during the first few weeks after conception, when the woman herself may not know she is pregnant.

or sometimes even moderate amounts of alcohol during pregnancy. Moreover, mothers who take physically addictive drugs such as cocaine run the risk of giving birth to babies similarly addicted. Their newborns suffer painful withdrawal symptoms after birth as well as sometimes showing permanent physical and mental impairment (Chavez et al., 1979; Miller, 1986; Waterson & Murray-Lyon, 1990).

■ **Birth complications.** Although most births are unexceptional, the process sometimes goes awry, resulting in injury to the infant. For example, the umbilical cord connecting the baby to the mother may become compressed, withholding oxygen from the child. If this occurs for too long, the child may suffer permanent brain damage.

A number of other environmental factors have an impact upon the child prior to and during birth (see Table 13-2, p. 424). It is important to keep in mind, however, that development represents the interaction of environmental and genetic influences, and that although we have been discussing the influences of genetics and environment separately, neither factor works alone. Moreover, while we have been flagging some of the points at which development can go awry, the vast majority of births occur without difficulty, and development follows normal patterns—which we discuss next.

TABLE 13-2

ENVIRONMENTAL FACTORS AFFECTING PRENATAL DEVELOPMENT

Factor	Possible effect
Rubella (German measles)	Blindness, deafness, heart abnormalities, stillbirth
Syphilis	Mental retardation, physical deformities, maternal miscarriage
Addictive drugs	Low birth weight, addiction of infant to drug, with possible death, after birth, from withdrawal
Smoking	Premature birth, low birth weight and length
Alcohol	Mental retardation, lower-than-average birth weight, small head, limb deformities
Radiation from x-rays	Physical deformities, mental retardation
Inadequate diet	Reduction in growth of brain, smaller-than-average weight and length at birth
Mother's age—younger than 18 at birth of child	Premature birth, increased incidence of Down syndrome
Mother's age—older than 35 at birth of child	Increased incidence of Down syndrome
DES (diethylstilbestrol)	Reproductive difficulties and increased incidence of genital cancer in children of mothers who were given DES during pregnancy to prevent miscarriage

Source: Adapted from Schikendanz, Schikendanz & Forsyth, 1982, p. 95.

RECAP AND REVIEW I

RECAP

◀ A fundamental issue of developmental psychology is the nature-nurture question, which seeks to determine the relative influence of environmental and genetic factors on development.

◀ During the course of prenatal development, the one-cell zygote evolves into an embryo and subsequently a fetus. Birth typically occurs thirty-eight weeks after conception.

◀ The major difficulties caused by genetic factors are sickle-cell anemia, phenylketonuria (PKU), Tay-Sachs disease, and Down syndrome. Among the primary environmental influences on prenatal development and newborn health are the mother's nutrition, state of health, and drug intake, and the nature of the baby's delivery.

REVIEW

1. Developmental psychologists are interested in the effects of both _____ and _____ on development.

2. Locke believed that children were a _____ _____ or "blank slate" which was written on through experience.

3. Environment and heredity both influence development, with genetic potentials generally establishing limits on environmental influences. True or false? _____

4. By observing genetically similar animals in differing environments, we can increase our understanding of the influences of hereditary and environmental factors in humans. True or false? _____

5. _____ research studies the same individuals over a period of time, while _____ research studies people of different ages at the same time.

6. Match the following terms with their definition:
   1. _____ Zygote
   2. _____ Gene
   3. _____ Chromosome

   a. Smallest unit through which genetic information is passed
   b. Fertilized egg
   c. Rod-shaped structure containing genetic information

7. Specific kinds of growth must take place during a _____ _____ if the embryo is to develop normally.

8. An embryo past the ninth week of development is known as a _____.

Ask Yourself

Given the possible effects of the environment on the developing child, do you think expectant mothers should be subject to legal prosecution for their use of alcohol and other drugs which may seriously harm their unborn children? Defend your position.

(Answers to review questions are on page 426.)

HOW WE DEVELOP PHYSICALLY AND SOCIALLY

His head was molded into a long melon shape and came to a point at the back. . . . He was covered with a thick greasy white material known as "vernix," which made him slippery to hold, and also allowed him to slip easily through the birth canal. In addition to a shock of black hair on his head, his body was covered with dark, fine hair known as "lanugo." His ears, his back, his shoulders, and even his cheeks were furry. . . . His skin was wrinkled and quite loose, ready to scale in creased places such as his feet and hands. . . . His ears were pressed to his head in unusual positions— one ear was matted firmly forward on his cheek. His nose was flattened and pushed to one side by the squeeze as he came through the pelvis (Brazelton, 1969, p. 3).

Neonate: A newborn child

Vernix: A white lubricant that covers a fetus, protecting it during birth

What kind of creature is this? Although the description hardly fits that of the Gerber baby seen in commercials, we are in fact talking about a normal, completely developed child just after the moment of birth. Called a **neonate**, the newborn presents itself to the world in a form that hardly meets the typical standards of beauty against which we normally measure babies. Yet ask any parents: No sight is more beautiful or exciting than the first glimpse of their newborn.

The neonate's flawed appearance is brought about by a number of factors. Its travels through its mother's birth canal may have squeezed the incompletely formed bones of the skull together and squashed the nose into the head. It is covered with **vernix**, a white, greasy material that is secreted to protect its skin prior to birth, and it may have **lanugo**, a soft fuzz, over its entire body. Its eyelids may be puffy with an accumulation of fluids because of its upside-down position during birth.

Lanugo (lan OO go): A soft fuzz covering the body of a newborn

Reflexes: Unlearned, involuntary responses to certain stimuli

All this changes during the first two weeks of life, as the neonate takes on a more familiar appearance. Even more impressive are the capabilities that the neonate begins to display from the time it is born—capabilities that grow at an astounding rate over the ensuing months and years.

The neonate is born with a number of **reflexes**—unlearned, involuntary responses that occur automatically in the presence of certain stimuli. Many of these reflexes are critical for survival and unfold naturally as a part of an infant's ongoing maturation. The **rooting reflex**, for instance, causes neonates to turn their heads toward things that touch their cheeks—such as a nipple of a mother's breast or a bottle. Similarly, a **sucking reflex** prompts the infant to suck at things that touch its lips. Among the other reflexes are a **gag reflex** (to clear its throat); the **startle reflex** (a series of movements in which the infant flings out its arms, fans its fingers, and arches its back in response to a sudden noise); and the **Babinski reflex** (the baby's toes fan out when the outer edge of the sole of its foot is stroked).

These primitive reflexes are lost after the first few months of life and re-

Rooting reflex: A neonate's tendency to turn its head toward things that touch its cheek

Sucking reflex: A reflex that prompts an infant to suck at things that touch its lips

Gag reflex: An infant's reflex to clear its throat

Startle reflex: The reflex action in which an infant, in response to a sudden noise, flings its arms, arches its back, and spreads its fingers

Babinski reflex: The reflex action in which an infant fans out its toes in response to a stroke on the outside of its foot

▶ **425**

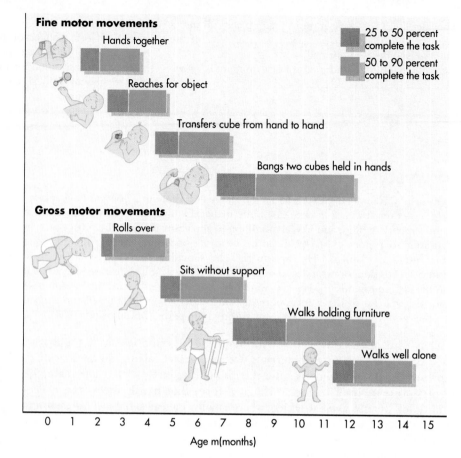

FIGURE 13-2

These landmarks of physical development illustrate the range of ages at which most infants learn various physical tasks. (Frankenburg & Dodds, 1967.)

placed by more complex and organized behaviors. Although at birth the neonate is capable of only jerky, limited voluntary movement, during the first year of life the ability to move independently grows enormously. The typical baby is able to roll over by the age of 3 months; it can sit without support at 6 months; stand alone at about 11½ months; and walk by the time it is just over a year old. Not only does the ability to make large-scale movements improve during this time, but fine-muscle movements also become increasingly sophisticated (as illustrated in Figure 13-2).

Growth After Birth

Perhaps the most obvious sign of development is the physical growth of the child. During the first year of life, children typically triple their birth weight, and their height increases by about half. This rapid growth slows down as the child gets older—think how gigantic adults would be if that rate of growth were constant—and the average rate of growth from age 3 to the beginning of adolescence, around age 13, is a gain of about 5 pounds and 3 inches a year.

The physical changes that occur as children develop are not just a matter of increasing growth; the relationship of the size of the various body parts to one another changes dramatically as children age. As you can see in Figure 13-3, the

ANSWERS (REVIEW I):

1. heredity; environment **2.** tabula rasa **3.** True **4.** True **5.** Longitudinal; cross-sectional
6. 1-b; 2-a; 3-c **7.** critical period **8.** fetus

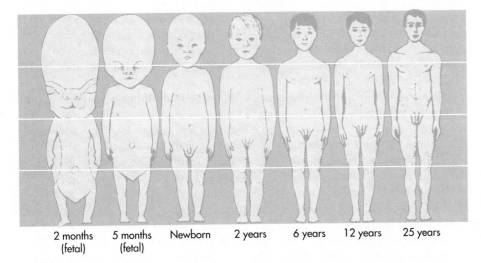

2 months   5 months   Newborn   2 years   6 years   12 years   25 years
(fetal)   (fetal)

FIGURE 13-3

As development progresses, the size of the head—in relation to the rest of the body—decreases until adulthood is reached. (Adopted from Robbins, 1929.)

head of the fetus (and the newborn) is disproportionally large. However, the head soon becomes more proportional in size to the rest of the body as growth occurs mainly in the trunk and legs.

Development of Perception: Taking in the World

When proud parents pick up their neonate and peer into its eyes, is the child able to return their gaze? Although it was thought for some time that newborns could see only a hazy blur, most current findings indicate that the capabilities of neonates are far more impressive (Horowitz & Colombo, 1990). Their eyes have limited capacity to modify the shape of the lens, making it difficult to focus on objects that are not within a 7- to 8-inch distance from the face, yet neonates are able to follow objects moving within their field of vision. They also show the rudiments of depth perception, as they react by raising their hands when an object appears to be moving rapidly toward their face (Aslin & Smith, 1988; Bornstein, 1988; Colombo & Mitchell, 1990).

You might think that it would be hard to figure out just how well neonates are able to see, since their lack of both language and reading ability clearly prevents them from saying what direction the "E" on a vision chart is facing. However, a number of ingenious methods, which rely on the physiological responses and innate reflexes of the newborn, have been devised to test their perceptual skills.

One important technique measures changes in an infant's heart rate, for heart rate is closely correlated with the baby's reaction to a stimulus that he or she is looking at—a phenomenon known as habituation. **Habituation** is a decrease in responding to repeated presentations of the same stimulus. For example, infants who are shown a novel stimulus will pay close attention to it, and their heart rates will show a change in speed. But if the infant is repeatedly shown the same stimulus, his or her attention to it will decrease, as indicated by the return to a normal heart rate—showing that habituation has occurred.

Then, when a new stimulus is subsequently presented, the baby will again experience a discernible change in heart rate as long as he or she is able to detect that the new stimulus is different from the old one. Using this technique, then, developmental psychologists can tell when a stimulus can be detected and discriminated by a child too young to speak (Bornstein & Lamb, 1992).

Researchers have developed a number of other methods of measuring neonate and infant perception. One technique, for instance, involves babies sucking

Habituation: A decrease in responding to repeated presentations of the same stimulus

on a nipple attached to a computer. A change in the rate and vigor with which they suck is used to infer that they can perceive variations in stimuli. Other study approaches include examining babies' eye movements and observing which way babies move their heads when presented with a visual stimulus (Milewski, 1976; Kolata, 1987a; Bronson, 1990).

Using such research techniques, we now know that infants' visual perception is remarkably sophisticated from the start of life. At birth, babies show preferences for patterns with contours and edges over less distinct patterns, indicating that they are capable of responding to the configuration of stimuli. Furthermore, even newborns are aware of size constancy, apparently being sensitive to the fact that objects stay the same size even though the image on the retina may vary as their distance changes (Slater, Mattock, & Brown, 1990).

In fact, neonates have the ability to discriminate facial expressions—and even to imitate them (Field, 1982). As you can see in Figure 13-4, newborns exposed to an adult with a happy, sad, or surprised facial expression are able to produce a good imitation of the adult's expression. Even very young infants, then, can respond to the emotions and moods that their caregivers' facial expressions reveal. This capability provides the foundations of social interactional skills in children (Phillips et al., 1990).

Other visual abilities grow rapidly after birth. By the end of their first month, babies can distinguish some colors from others, and after four months they can readily focus on near or far objects. By 4 or 5 months, they are able to recognize two- and three-dimensional objects, and they can make use of the gestalt patterns that we discussed in relation to adult perception in Chapter 5. Furthermore, there are rapid improvements in perceptual abilities: Sensitivity to visual stimuli, for instance, becomes three to four times greater at 1 year of age than it was at birth (Aslin & Smith, 1988; Bower, 1989; Atkinson & Braddick, 1989).

In addition to vision, infants' other sensory capabilities are quite impressive (e.g., Trehub et al., 1991). Newborns can distinguish different sounds to the point of being able to recognize their own mothers' voices at the age of 3 days (DeCasper & Fifer, 1980). They are also capable of making subtle linguistic distinctions that underlie the language abilities we discussed in Chapter 9: At 4 days of age babies can discriminate between such closely related sounds as *ba* and *pa*, and they are soon able to distinguish between their native tongue and foreign languages (Jusczyk & Derrah, 1987; Jusczyk, 1986). By 6 months of age, they are capable of discriminating virtually any difference in sound that is relevant to the production of language (Aslin, 1987). Moreover, they are capable of discriminating different tastes and smells at a very early age (Steiner, 1979). There even seems to be something of a built-in sweet tooth: Neonates prefer liquids that have been sweetened with sugar over their unsweetened counterparts.

Development of Social Behavior

As anyone who has seen an infant smiling at the sight of its mother can guess, at the same time infants are growing physically and perceptually, they are also developing socially. The nature of a child's early social development provides the foundation for social relationships that will last a lifetime.

Attachment: The positive emotional bond that develops between a child and a particular individual

Attachment, the positive emotional bond that develops between a child and a particular individual, is the most important form of social development that occurs during infancy (Greeberg, Cicchetti, & Cummings, 1990). One of the first investigators to demonstrate the importance and nature of attachment was psychologist Harry Harlow. Harlow found that infant monkeys who were given the choice of a wire "monkey" that provided food or a soft, terry-cloth "monkey" that was warm but did not provide food, clearly preferred the cloth one, although

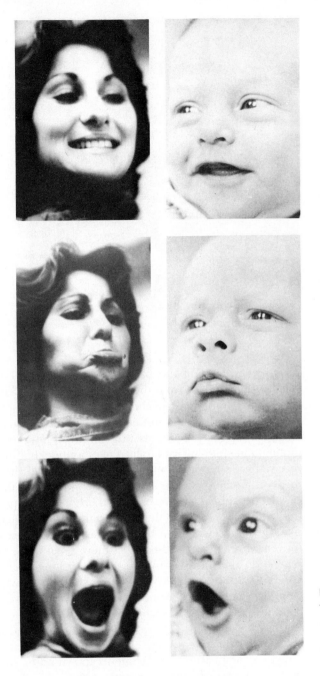

FIGURE 13-4
This newborn infant is clearly imitating the happy, sad, and surprised expressions of the adult model in these amazing photos.

they made occasional forays to the wire monkey to nurse (Harlow & Zimmerman, 1959). Clearly, the cloth monkey provided greater comfort to the infants; food alone was insufficient to create attachment (see Figure 13-5, p. 430).

Building on this initial work, other researchers have suggested that attachment grows through the responsiveness of infants' caregivers to the signals the babies provide, such as cries, smiles, reaching, and clinging. The greater the responsiveness of the caregiver to the child's signals, the more likely it is that the child will become securely attached. Full attachment eventually develops as a result of a complex series of interactions between caregiver and child known as the Attachment Behavioral System. (Bell & Ainsworth, 1972.) It is important to note that the infant plays as critical and active a role in the formation of a bond as the caregiver. Infants who respond positively to a caregiver promote more

FIGURE 13-5

Although the wire "mother" dispensed milk to the hungry infant monkey, the soft, terry-cloth "mother" was preferred.

positive behavior on the part of the caregiver, which in turn elicits an even stronger attachment from the child. (See Figure 13-6.)

At what point does attachment begin? According to a hypothesis put forward by Marshall Klaus and John Kennell (1976), a critical period takes place just after birth. During this juncture, lasting only a few hours, skin-to-skin contact between mother and child was said to lead to emotional bonding. Because the hypothesis received wide publicity, many hospitals changed their procedures to allow immediate contact between newly born children and their parents.

It now appears, however, that there is little support for the hypothesis. Although it does seem that the mothers in Klaus and Kennell's study who had early physical contact with their babies were more responsive to them, the effect lasted for only three days. Furthermore, there seem to be no lasting consequences of separation after birth, even when it lasts as long as several days (Goldberg, 1983; Lamb, 1982b). For parents who adopt children, or who, because of illness of the child or some other reason, miss out on the opportunity for contact with their child just after its birth, such news is reassuring.

Measuring Attachment.   Developmental psychologists have devised a quick and direct way of measuring attachment, known as the strange situation. Developed by Mary Ainsworth, the **Ainsworth strange situation** consists of a sequence of events involving a child and (typically) his or her mother. Initially, the mother and baby enter an unfamiliar room, and the mother permits the baby to explore while she sits down. An adult stranger then enters the room, after which the mother leaves. The mother then returns, and the stranger leaves. The mother then once again leaves the baby alone, and the stranger returns. Finally, the stranger leaves, and the mother returns (Ainsworth et al., 1978).

Babies' reactions to the strange situation vary drastically, depending, according to Ainsworth, on their degree of attachment to the mother. One-year-old children who are labeled ''securely attached'' employ the mother as a kind of

Ainsworth strange situation: A sequence of events involving a child and his or her mother that provides a measurement of attachment

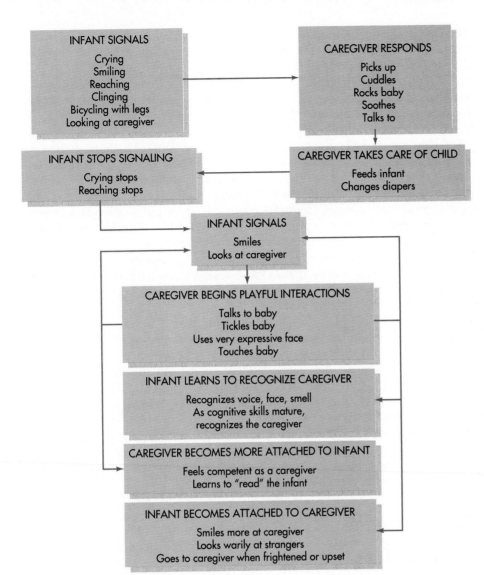

FIGURE 13-6

The Attachment Behavioral System shows the sequence of activities that infants employ to keep their primary caregivers physically close and to bring about attachment. Early in life, crying is the most effective behavior. Later, though, infants are able to keep the caregiver near through other, more socially appropriate behaviors such as smiling, looking, and reaching. After they are able to walk, children are able to play a more active role in staying close to the caregiver. At the same time, the caregiver's behavior interacts with the baby's activities to promote attachment. (Tomlinson, 1985.)

home base, exploring independently but returning to her occasionally. When she leaves, they exhibit distress, and they go to her when she returns. Children termed "avoidant" do not cry when the mother leaves, but they seem to avoid her when she returns, appearing to be angry with her. Finally, "ambivalent" children display anxiety before they are separated and are upset when the mother leaves, but they may show ambivalent reactions to her return such as seeking close contact but simultaneously hitting and kicking her.

The nature of attachment between children and their mothers has far-reaching consequences on later development. For example, one study found that boys who were securely attached at age 1 showed fewer psychological difficulties when they were older than did avoidant or ambivalent youngsters (Lewis et al., 1984). Moreover, children who are securely attached to their mothers tend to be more socially and emotionally competent than their less securely attached peers, and they are viewed as more cooperative, capable, and playful (Sroufe, Fox, & Pancake, 1983; Ainsworth, 1989; Ainsworth & Bowlby, 1991).

The Father's Role.   For many years, the father stood in the shadows behind the mother—at least as far as developmental research was concerned. Because traditionally it was thought that the mother-infant bond was the most crucial in a child's life, researchers in earlier decades focused on the mother's relationship with her children. However, the last ten years have seen a host of studies which focus on fathers and their interactions with their children (Lamb, 1987).

Even in households in which both parents are employed full time, by and large fathers spend less time caring for and playing with their children than do mothers. However, the strength of attachment between fathers and their children can be as great as between mothers and their children. Although children can be simultaneously attached to both their parents (Lamb, 1982b), the nature of attachment is not always identical between children and mothers and fathers. For instance, infants tend to prefer to be soothed by their mothers, even though fathers are just as adept at comforting and nurturing babies.

The reason for differences in attachment between mothers and children and fathers and children may be that mothers spend a greater proportion of their time feeding and directly nurturing their children, whereas fathers spend more time, proportionally, playing with them (Parke, 1981). Moreover, the quality of fathers' play is often different from that of mothers. Fathers engage in more physical, rough-and-tumble sorts of activities, whereas mothers play more verbally oriented games and traditional ones such as peekaboo. Such differences in play style are typically very pronounced, and occur even in the small minority of families in which the mother works to support the family and the father stays at home with the children (Field, 1978; Power & Parke, 1982).

Despite the differences between the behavior of fathers and mothers, each parent is an important attachment figure and plays a major role in the social development of a child. Furthermore, it is becoming increasingly apparent that the amount of time an adult spends with a child is less important than the quality of that time (Hetherington & Parke, 1986).

Social Relationships with Peers

Watching a preschooler rush off to play with a neighborhood friend, you know the enjoyment that children derive from being with their peers. Such friendships are crucial to a child's social development (Lewis & Feinman, 1991). According to developmental psychologist Willard Hartup, experience is necessary both in "vertical" relationships (those with people of greater knowledge and social power, such as parents) *and* in "horizontal" relationships (those with people who have the same amount of knowledge and social power) in order for effective social competence to develop (Hartup, 1989; Ladd, 1990; Collins & Gunnar, 1990).

From the age of 2 years, children become less dependent on their parents and more self-reliant, increasingly preferring to play with friends. Initially, play is relatively independent: Two-year-olds pay more attention to toys than to one another when playing. Later, however, children actively interact, modifying one another's behavior and later exchanging roles during play.

As children reach school age, their social interactions become increasingly formalized, as well as more frequent. They may engage in elaborate games involving complex scenarios. Play also becomes more structured, involving teams and games with rigid rules (Mueller & Lucas, 1975).

It is important to realize that children's play serves other purposes than mere enjoyment. It allows them to become increasingly competent in their social in-

This Orinda, California, girl is participating in a game with formal, complex rules—a typical activity for older children.

teractions with others, learning to take the perspective of other people and to infer others' thoughts and feelings, even when they are not being directly expressed. Furthermore, they learn self-control: They avoid hitting an adversary who bests them, they learn to be polite, and they learn to control their emotional displays and facial expressions, smiling even when receiving a disappointing gift (Selman et al., 1983; Feldman, 1982). Situations that provide children with opportunities for social interaction, then, may enhance their social development—a point illustrated in the Psychology at Work box, pp. 434–435, which considers the effects of day-care on children.

Although many advances in social development are prompted by peer interaction, parents' child-rearing patterns also shape their children's social competence. Psychologist Diana Baumrind (1971, 1980) found that parental styles fall into three main categories. **Authoritarian parents** are rigid and punitive and value unquestioning obedience from their children. They have strict standards and discourage expressions of disagreement. **Permissive parents** give their children lax or inconsistent direction and, although warm, require little of them. Finally, **authoritative parents** are firm, setting limits for their children. As the children get older, these parents try to reason and explain things to them. They also set clear goals and encourage their children's independence.

As you might expect, the three kinds of child-rearing styles were associated with very different kinds of behavior in their children (although there were, of course, many exceptions). Children of authoritarian parents tend to be unsociable, unfriendly, and relatively withdrawn. In contrast, permissive parents' children are immature, moody, and dependent and have low self-control. The children of authoritative parents fare best: Their social skills are high—they are likable, self-reliant, independent, and cooperative.

Authoritarian parents: Parents who are rigid and punitive, and who value unquestioning obedience from their children

Permissive parents: Parents who are lax, inconsistent, and undemanding, yet warm toward their children

Authoritative parents: Parents who are firm, set clear limits, and reason with and explain things to their children

A mother and her 3-year-old son head off together at the start of the day. But they are not out for a day's excursion; instead, they head for a day-care center near the mother's office. She says goodbye to her son and leaves for work for the day, knowing that she will not see him again until she picks him up some nine hours later. It is a scene that she and her son repeat five days a week, every week of the year—except during the mother's two weeks of vacation.

One of the biggest societal changes to occur over the last two decades is the upsurge in the number of children enrolled in day-care centers. Roughly a million children, some still in their infancy, are looked after by paid child-care workers, generally in centers outside the home, from a couple of hours a day to all day long. To parents contemplating enrolling their children in such a center, certain questions are critical: What are the effects of day-care on children? How early can children start? What separates good day-care from bad? Because day-care is a necessity in many families with two working parents or in single-parent families, such questions take on particular urgency.

Fortunately, answers to these questions have begun to emerge as a result of research conducted during the last two decades, and—although the long-term consequences of child care have yet to be determined definitively—the results are encouraging: Children who attend high-quality child care centers may not only do as well as children who stay at home with their parents but in some respects may actually do better (Clarke-Stewart, 1991; Scarr, 1986; Scarr, Phillips, & McCartney, 1990; Howes, 1990). Among the specific findings that support this suggestion are the following:

WHO'S CARING FOR THE CHILDREN? DETERMINING THE EFFECTS OF DAY-CARE

- Social development. Researchers have found several kinds of positive results from child care center experiences. Children in child care are generally more considerate and sociable than other children, and they interact more positively with teachers (e.g., Phillips, McCartney, & Scarr, 1987). They may also be more compliant and regulate their own behavior more effectively. Although some research suggests that children in child care situations are more aggressive and assertive than their peers (e.g., Haskins, 1985), these outcomes may well fade as the children get older (Finkelstein, 1982).

- Intellectual development. For children from poor or disadvantaged homes, child care in specially enriched environments—those with many toys, books, a variety of children , and high-quality care providers—often proves to be more intellectually stimulating than the children's home en-

vironment. Such child care can lead to increased intellectual achievement in terms of higher IQ scores and better language development (Lee, Brooks-Gunn, Schnur, & Liaw, 1990). On the other hand, we don't know how long such improvements last; the intellectual benefits of early child care have yet to be demonstrated in adults who received such care as children.

It is also less than clear that child care experiences bolster intellectual development in children who are from more affluent backgrounds. However, some recent research suggests that children in child care centers score higher on tests of cognitive abilities than those who are cared for by their mothers or by sitters or day-care home providers (Clark-Stewart, 1991).

- Relationship with parents. Are children less attached to their mothers and fathers when they spend part of the day being

Most research has found little difference between children who have been in high-quality day-care and those who have been cared for at home.

cared for by others? This question—raised by many critics of day-care—is a difficult one to answer, and the research on the issue is contradictory. Some evidence suggests that infants who are involved in outside care more than twenty hours a week in their first year show less attachment to their mothers than those who have not been in day-care (Belsky & Rovine, 1988). On the other hand, most other research finds little or no difference in the strength of parental attachment bonds of infants and toddlers who have been in day-care and those raised solely by their parents, regardless of how long they have been in day-care. Moreover, there is no evidence that children in day-care centers are more attached to the day-care workers than to their parents; in fact, they almost always appear to be more attached to their parents (Rutter, 1982; Ragozin, 1980). In sum, evidence is lacking that children who are in day-care are less attached to their parents than those who are not in day-care.

Summing Up. Overall, most research has found little difference between children who have been in high-quality day-care and those who have not—a comforting state of affairs for parents concerned about the effects of day-care on their children. Furthermore, long-term follow-up research shows that first-, third-, and fifth-graders whose mothers worked performed better academically, were more socially adjusted, and were more self-reliant than children whose mothers did not work. They were also more involved in school activities and scored higher on IQ tests (Scarr, 1986).

Yet there are many unanswered questions: Is there an age before which day-care should be avoided? How do the effects of good day-care centers differ from the effects of less optimal centers? Does it matter what kind of day-care curriculum is used? What are the critical characteristics to consider when choosing a day-care center? Given the necessity of employment for a significant proportion of the parent population, these questions must be addressed. For many people, then, the significant issue is not whether to choose day-care, but how to make their child's experience in day-care as positive as possible (Clarke-Stewart, 1989; Zaslow, 1991; Zigler & Lang, 1991).

Before we rush to congratulate authoritative parents and condemn authoritarian and permissive ones, it is important to note that in many cases authoritarian and permissive parents produce children who are perfectly well adjusted. Moreover, as discussed in the Cutting Edge box on shy children, we are born with particular **temperaments**—basic, innate dispositions (Goldsmith et al., 1987). Some children are naturally warm and cuddly, whereas others are irritable and fussy. The kind of temperament a baby is born with may in part elicit particular kinds of parental child-rearing styles.

Temperament: Basic, innate disposition

Furthermore, the findings regarding child-rearing styles are chiefly applicable to American society, in which a dominant value is that children should learn to be independent and not rely too heavily on their parents. In contrast, Japanese parents encourage dependence in order to promote the values of cooperation and community life. These differences in cultural values result in very different philosophies of child rearing. For example, Japanese mothers believe it is a punishment to make a young child sleep alone, so many children sleep next to their mothers throughout infancy and toddlerhood (Kagan, Kearsley, & Zelazo, 1978; Miyake, Chen, & Campos, 1985).

In sum, a child's upbringing is a consequence of the child-rearing philosophy parents hold and employ, as well as the nature of their child's personality. As is the case with almost all development, then, behavior is a function of a complex interaction of environmental and genetic factors (Kagan, 1989a, 1989b; Kagan & Snidman, 1991; Thomas & Chess, 1980).

Erikson's Theory of Psychosocial Development

Psychosocial development:
Development of individuals'
interactions and
understanding of each other
and their knowledge and
understanding of themselves
as members of society

Trust-versus-mistrust stage:
According to Erikson, the
first stage of psychosocial
development, occurring from
birth to 18 months of age,
during which time infants
develop feelings of trust or
lack of trust

Autonomy-versus-shame-and-doubt stage: The period
during which, according to
Erikson, toddlers (ages 18
months to 3 years) develop
independence and autonomy
if exploration and freedom
are encouraged, or shame
and self-doubt if they are
restricted and overprotected

Initiative-versus-guilt stage:
According to Erikson,
the period during which
children aged 3 to 6 years
experience conflict between
independence of action and
the sometimes negative results
of that action

**Industry-versus-inferiority
stage:** According to Erikson,
the period during which
children aged 6 to 12 years
may develop positive social
interactions with others or
may feel inadequate and
become less sociable

In trying to trace the course of social development, some theorists have considered how society and culture present challenges that change as the individual matures. Following this path, psychoanalyst Erik Erikson developed the most comprehensive theory of social development. According to Erikson (1963), the developmental changes occurring throughout our lives can be viewed as a series of eight stages of psychosocial development. **Psychosocial development** encompasses changes in our interactions and understanding of one another as well as in our knowledge and understanding of ourselves as members of society.

Erikson suggests that passage through each of the stages necessitates resolution of a crisis or conflict. Accordingly, each of Erikson's eight stages is represented as a pairing of the most positive and most negative aspects of the crisis of the period. Although each crisis is never resolved entirely—life becomes increasingly complicated as we grow older—it needs to be resolved sufficiently so that we are equipped to deal with demands made during the following stage of development.

In the first stage of psychosocial development, the **trust-versus-mistrust stage** (birth to 1½ years), infants develop feelings of trust if their physical requirements and psychological needs for attachment are consistently met and their interactions with the world are generally positive. On the other hand, inconsistent care and unpleasant interactions with others can lead to the development of mistrust and leave the infant unable to meet the challenges required in the next stage of development.

In the second stage, the **autonomy-versus-shame-and-doubt stage** (1½ to 3 years), toddlers develop independence and autonomy if exploration and freedom are encouraged, or they experience shame, self-doubt, and unhappiness if they are overly restricted and protected. According to Erikson, the key to the development of autonomy during this period is for the child's caregivers to provide the appropriate amount of control. If parents provide too much control, children will be unable to assert themselves and develop their own sense of control over their environment; if parents provide too little control, children themselves become overly demanding and controlling.

The next crisis that children face is that of the **initiative-versus-guilt stage** (ages 3 to 6). In this stage, the major conflict is between a child's desire to initiate activities independently and the guilt that comes from the unwanted and unexpected consequences of such activities. If parents react positively to the child's attempts at independence, they help to resolve the initiative-versus-guilt crisis positively.

The fourth and last stage of childhood is the **industry-versus-inferiority stage** (ages 6 to 12). During this period, successful psychosocial development is characterized by increasing competency across all tasks, be they social interactions or academic skills. In contrast, difficulties in this stage lead to feelings of failure and inadequacy.

Erikson's theory suggests that psychosocial development continues throughout life, and he proposes that there are four more crises to face past childhood (which we discuss in the next chapter). Although his theory has been criticized on several grounds—such as the imprecision of the concepts he employs and a greater emphasis on male development than female development—it remains influential and is one of the few that encompasses the entire lifespan.

RECAP

◀ The neonate is born with a number of reflexes, including the rooting, sucking, startle, and Babinski reflexes.

◀ Physical growth is initially rapid: During the first year, children typically triple their birth weight, and height increases by 50 percent. Rate of growth declines after age 3, averaging about 5 pounds and 3 inches a year until adolescence.

◀ The perceptual abilities of infants grow rapidly, although they are remarkably sophisticated at birth.

◀ Social development is demonstrated through the growth of attachment, the positive emotional bond that develops between a child and a particular individual. As a child ages, relationships with friends become increasingly important.

◀ Erikson's theory suggests that there are four stages of psychosocial development within childhood, with four other stages spanning the rest of life.

REVIEW

1. Match the name of each reflex with its definition:
   1. _____ Startle
   2. _____ Rooting
   3. _____ Babinski
   a. Toes fan out when sole of the foot is stroked
   b. Infant fans out arms and arches back in response to sudden noise
   c. Turns head toward something brushed along the cheek

2. Researchers studying newborns use _____, or decreased response to a stimulus, as an indicator of the baby's interest.

3. The emotional bond that develops between a child and its caregiver is known as _____.

4. Children develop an attachment to their mothers only; the father's role is important, but children do not become attached per se to their fathers. True or false? _____

5. Day-care, when it is of high quality, has been shown to have few if any detrimental effects on children and their relationship with parents. True or false? _____

6. Match the parenting style with its definition:
   1. _____ Permissive
   2. _____ Authoritative
   3. _____ Authoritarian
   a. Rigid; highly punitive; demand obedience
   b. Give little direction; lax on obedience
   c. Firm but fair; try to explain their decisions

7. Similar child-rearing styles have been documented around the world. True or false? _____

8. Erikson's theory of _____ development involves a series of _____ stages, each of which must be resolved in order for a person to develop optimally.

Ask Yourself

You are given a child to raise in an environment that you can shape totally to your liking. What would your optimal child-rearing environment be? What style of child-rearing would you use? How do you think the child's temperamental style would influence or modify your choices?

(Answers to review questions are on page 438.)

COGNITIVE DEVELOPMENT

Suppose you had two drinking glasses of different shapes—one short and broad and one tall and skinny. Now imagine that you filled the short, broad one with soda about halfway and then poured the liquid from that glass into the tall one. The soda appears to fill about three-quarters of the second glass. If someone asked you whether there was more soda in the second glass than there had been in the first, what would you say?

You might think that such a simple question hardly deserves an answer; of course there is no difference in the amount of soda in the two glasses.

However, most 4-year-olds would be likely to say that there is more soda in the second glass. If you then poured the soda back into the short glass, they would say there is now less soda than there was in the taller glass.

Why are young children confused by this problem? The reason is not readily apparent. Anyone who has observed preschoolers must be impressed at how far

When equal amounts of liquid are poured into containers of different sizes, 3-year-old children believe that the amount of liquid differs because of variation in the containers' shape.

they have progressed from the early stages of development. They speak with ease, know the alphabet, count, play complex games, use a tape player, tell stories, and communicate quite ably.

Yet, despite this outward sophistication, there are profound gaps in children's understanding of the world. Some theorists have suggested that children are incapable of understanding certain ideas about the world until they reach a particular stage of **cognitive development**—the process by which a child's understanding of the world changes as a function of age and experience. In contrast to theories of physical and social development that were discussed earlier (such as those of Erikson), theories of cognitive development seek to explain the quantitative and qualitative intellectual advances that occur during development.

Piaget's Theory of Cognitive Development

No theory of cognitive development has had more impact than that of Swiss psychologist Jean Piaget. Piaget (1970) suggested that children proceed through a series of four separate stages in a fixed order that is universal across all children. He maintained that these stages differ not only in the *quantity* of information acquired at each stage, but in the *quality* of knowledge and understanding as well. Taking an interactionist point of view, he suggested that movement from one stage to the next occurred when the child reached an appropriate level of maturation *and* was exposed to relevant types of experiences. Without such experiences, children were assumed to be incapable of reaching their highest level of cognitive growth.

Piaget's four stages are known as the sensorimotor, preoperational, concrete operational, and formal operational stages (see Table 13-3). Let's examine each of them and the approximate ages that they span.

Sensorimotor Stage: Birth to Two Years.   During the initial part of the **sensorimotor stage** the child has relatively little competence in representing the environment using images, language, or other kinds of symbols. Consequently, the infant has no awareness of objects or people who are not immediately present at a given moment, lacking what Piaget calls **object permanence**. Object permanence is the awareness that objects—and people—continue to exist even if they are out of sight.

How can we know that children lack object permanence? Although we cannot ask infants, we can watch their reaction when a toy that they are playing with is hidden under a blanket. Until the age of about 9 months, children will make no attempt to locate the toy. However, soon after this age they will begin to actively search for the object when it is hidden, indicating that they have developed a mental representation of the toy. Object permanence, then, is a critical development during the sensorimotor stage.

Cognitive development: The process by which a child's understanding of the world changes as a function of age and experience

Sensorimotor stage: According to Piaget, the stage from birth to 2 years during which a child has little competence in representing the environment using images, language, or other symbols

Object permanence: The awareness that objects do not cease to exist when they are out of sight

	TABLE 13-3	
	A SUMMARY OF PIAGET'S STAGES	

Approximate age range	Stage	Major characteristics
Birth–2 years	Sensorimotor	Development of object permanence, development of motor skills, little or no capacity for symbolic representation
2–7 years	Preoperational	Development of language and symbolic thinking, egocentric thinking
7–12 years	Concrete operational	Development of conservation, mastery of concept of reversibility
12–adulthood	Formal operational	Development of logical and abstract thinking

Preoperational Stage: Two to Seven Years. The most important development during the **preoperational stage** is in the use of language, described in more detail in Chapter 9. Children develop internal representational systems of the world that allow them to describe people, events, and feelings. They even use symbols in play, pretending, for example, that a book pushed across the floor is a car.

Although children's thinking is more advanced in this stage than in the earlier sensorimotor stage, it still is qualitatively inferior to that of adults. One example of this is seen in the preoperational child's **egocentric thought**, in which the world is viewed entirely from the child's own perspective. Preoperational children think that everyone shares their own perspective and knowledge. Thus, children's stories and explanations to adults can be maddeningly uninformative, as they are described without any context. For example, a preoperational child may start a story with "He wouldn't let me go," neglecting to mention who "he" is or where the storyteller wanted to go. Egocentric thinking is also seen when children at the preoperational stage play hiding games. For instance, 3-year-olds frequently hide with their faces against a wall, covering their eyes—although they are still in plain view. It seems to them that if *they* cannot see, no one else will be able to see them, since they assume that others share their view.

Another deficiency of the preoperational child is demonstrated by the **principle of conservation**, which is the knowledge that quantity is unrelated to the arrangement and physical appearance of objects. Children who have not mastered this principle do not know that the amount, volume, or length of an object does not change when its shape or configuration is changed. The question about the two glasses—one short and broad, the other tall and thin—with which we began our discussion of cognitive development illustrates this point quite clearly. Children who do not understand the principle of conservation invariably state that the amount of liquid changes as it is poured back and forth; they cannot comprehend that a transformation in appearance does not imply a transformation in amount. Instead, it seems just as reasonable to the child that there is a change in quantity as it does to the adult that there is no change.

There are a number of other ways, some quite startling, in which the lack of understanding of the principle of conservation affects children's responses. Research demonstrates that principles that are obvious and unquestioned by adults may be completely misunderstood by children during the preoperational period,

Preoperational stage: According to Piaget, the period from 2 to 7 years of age that is characterized by language development

Egocentric thought: Viewing the world entirely from one's own perspective

Principle of conservation: The knowledge that quantity is unrelated to the arrangement and physical appearance of objects

Type of conservation	Modality	Change in physical appearance	Average age at which invariance is grasped
Number	Number of elements in a collection	Rearranging or dislocating elements	6–7
Substance (mass)	Amount of a malleable substance (e.g., clay or liquid)	Altering shape	7–8
Length	Length of a line or object	Altering shape or configuration	7–8
Area	Amount of surface covered by a set of plane figures	Rearranging the figures	8–9
Weight	Weight of an object	Altering shape	9–10
Volume	Volume of an object (in terms of water displacement)	Altering shape	14–15

FIGURE 13-7

These tests are among those used most frequently to assess whether children have learned the principle of conservation across a variety of dimensions.

and it is not until the next stage of cognitive development that children grasp the concept of conservation. (Several examples of conservation are illustrated in Figure 13-7.)

Concrete operational stage:
According to Piaget, the period from 7 to 12 years of age that is characterized by logical thought and a loss of egocentrism

Concrete Operational Stage: Seven to Twelve Years. The beginning of the **concrete operational stage** is marked by mastery of the principle of conservation. However, there are still some aspects of conservation—such as conservation of weight and volume—that are not fully understood for a number of years.

During the concrete operational stage, children develop the ability to think in a more logical manner, and they begin to overcome some of the egocentrism characteristic of the preoperational period. One of the major principles that children learn during this stage is reversibility, the idea that some changes can be undone by reversing an earlier action. For example, children in the concrete operational stage can understand that when a ball of clay is rolled into a long sausage shape, it is possible to recreate the original ball by reversing the action. They can even conceptualize this principle in their heads, without having to see the action performed before them.

Although children make important advances in their logical capabilities during the concrete operational stage, there is still one major limitation to their thinking: They are largely bound to the concrete, physical reality of the world. For the most part, they have difficulty understanding questions of an abstract, hypothetical nature.

Formal Operational Stage: Twelve Years to Adulthood.   The **formal operational stage** produces a new kind of thinking—that which is abstract, formal, and logical. Thinking is no longer tied to events that are observed in the environment but makes use of logical techniques to resolve problems.

Formal operational stage: According to Piaget, the period from age 12 to adulthood that is characterized by abstract thought

The emergence of formal operational thinking is illustrated by the way in which the "pendulum problem," devised by Piaget, is attacked (Piaget & Inhelder, 1958). The problem solver is asked to figure out what determines how fast a pendulum swings. Is it the length of the string, or the weight of the pendulum, or the force with which the pendulum is pushed? (For the record, the answer is the length of the string.)

Children in the concrete operational stage approach the problem haphazardly, without a logical or rational plan of action. For example, they may simultaneously change the length of the string *and* the weight on the string *and* the force with which they push the pendulum. Since they are varying all factors at once, they are unable to tell which factor is the critical one. In contrast, people in the formal operational stage approach the problem systematically. Acting as if they were scientists conducting an experiment, they examine the effects of changes in just one variable at a time. This ability to rule out competing possibilities is characteristic of formal operational thought.

Although formal operational thought emerges during the teenage years, this type of thinking is, in some cases, used only infrequently (Burbules & Linn, 1988). Moreover, it appears that many individuals never reach this stage at all; most studies show that only 40 to 60 percent of college students and adults fully reach it, with some estimates running as low as 25 percent in the general population (Keating & Clark, 1980). In addition, in certain cultures—particularly those that are less technologically sophisticated than western societies—almost no one reaches the formal operational stage (Chandler, 1976; Super, 1980).

Stages versus Continuous Development: Is Piaget Right?   No other theorist has provided us with as comprehensive a theory of cognitive development as Piaget. Still, some contemporary theorists suggest that a better description of how children develop cognitively can be provided by approaches that do not employ a series of stages. For instance, children are not always consistent in their performance of tasks that—if Piaget's theory were accurate—ought to be performed equally well at a given stage. Similarly, Piaget in some ways underestimated the age at which infants and children are able to understand the world; they seem to be more sophisticated in their cognitive abilities than he believed (Tomlinson-Keasey et al., 1979; Bornstein & Sigman, 1986).

Furthermore, some developmental psychologists suggest that cognitive development proceeds in a more continuous fashion than Piaget's stage theory implies. Instead, they propose that cognitive developmental growth is primarily quantitative, rather than qualitative. They argue that although there are differences in when, how, and to what extent a child is capable of using given cognitive abilities—thereby reflecting quantitative changes—the underlying cognitive processes change relatively little with age (Gelman & Baillargeon, 1983; Case, 1991).

On the other hand, most developmental psychologists agree that, although the processes that underlie changes in cognitive abilities may not be those suggested by his theory, Piaget generally has provided us with an accurate account of age-related changes in cognitive development. Moreover, the influence of the theory has been enormous (Ginsburg & Opper, 1988; Gholson & Rosenthal, 1984). For example, Piaget suggests that increases in cognitive performance cannot be attained unless both cognitive readiness brought about by maturation *and* appropriate environmental stimulation are present. This view has been influential in determining the nature and structure of educational curricula and how children are taught. Piaget's theory and methods have also been used to investigate issues surrounding animal cognition, such as whether primates show object permanence (they seem to; Dore & Dumas, 1987).

Information-Processing Approaches

Information processing: The way in which people take in, use, and store information

If cognitive development does not proceed in the stagelike fashion suggested by Piaget, what *does* underlie the enormous growth in children's cognitive abilities that is apparent to even the most untutored eye? To many developmental psychologists, the answer can be found in changes in **information processing**, the way in which people take in, use, and store information.

According to this approach, which reflects the cognitive aspects of behavior that we discussed in Chapter 9, quantitative changes occur in children's ability to organize and manipulate information about the world. From this perspective, children are seen as becoming increasingly adept at information processing, analogous to the way a computer program might become more sophisticated as a programmer modifies it on the basis of experience. Information-processing approaches consider the kinds of "mental programs" that children invoke when approaching problems (Siegler, 1989).

Several significant changes occur in children's information processing capabilities. For one thing, speed of processing increases with age as some abilities become more automatic. The speed at which stimuli can be scanned, recognized, and compared with other stimuli increases with age. Attention span also lengthens; with increasing age, children can pay attention to stimuli longer and are less easily distracted (Kail, 1991).

Memory also improves dramatically with age. You may recall from Chapter 8 that adults are able to keep seven, plus or minus two, chunks of information in short-term memory. In contrast, preschoolers can hold only two or three chunks; 5-year-olds can hold four; and 7-year-olds can hold five. The size of chunks also grows with age, as does the sophistication and organization of knowledge stored in memory (Bjorkland, 1985; Ornstein & Naus, 1988).

Metacognition: An awareness and understanding of one's own cognitive processes

Finally, improvement in information processing is tied to advances in **metacognition**, an awareness and understanding of one's own cognitive processes. Metacognition involves the planning, monitoring, and revising of cognitive strategies. Younger children, who lack knowledge of their own cognitive processes, are often unaware of their incapabilities, causing them to misunderstand others and not even to recognize their errors. It is only later, when metacognitive abilities become more sophisticated, that children are able to know when they *don't* understand (Astington, Harris, & Olson, 1988; Flavell, Green, & Flavell, 1990).

The growth in metacognitive abilities is but one of the many advances that occurs as part of our continuing development. We have seen in this chapter the enormous strides youngsters make as they move from relatively helpless infants to competent, able children. In the next chapter, we consider the challenges presented by adolescence and adulthood and the ways in which people continue to grow and change throughout their lives.

The Informed Consumer of Psychology: Maximizing Cognitive Development

Are there ways of maximizing a child's cognitive development? Although our examination of the nature-nurture issue makes clear that genetic background plays a critical role in defining the limits that we can ultimately achieve, it is also apparent that environmental factors can enhance the probability of achieving our potential. Research carried out by developmental psychologists has identified several child-rearing practices that are important in maximizing cognitive development (Meyerhoff & White, 1986; Schwebel, Maher, & Fagley, 1990; Schulman, 1991). Among the most crucial:

■ Be responsive to children, both emotionally and intellectually. Parents with high-achieving children are interested in their children's lives and encourage and reinforce their efforts. They are warm and supportive, and act as children's "personal consultants." They allow children to make mistakes, providing consistent support.

■ Provide children with the maximum opportunity to explore and investigate their environments. For instance, if a room can be made safe, toddlers should not be restricted to playpens.

■ Use language that is highly descriptive and accurate when speaking with children. Avoid "baby talk" and speak *with* children, not *at* them. Ask questions, listen to babies' responses, and provide further feedback.

■ Don't push children too hard. Despite the rigors and demands of modern life, childhood should be a time of enjoyment and not viewed merely as a prelude to adulthood. Some psychologists believe that we are producing a society of "hurried children" whose lives revolve around rigid schedules and who are so pressed to succeed that their childhood is filled with stress (Elkind, 1981). Remember that—as in the rest of the lifespan—it is important to step back and set priorities regarding what is and is not most important.

RECAP AND REVIEW III

RECAP

◀ The major theory of cognitive development—the way in which children's understanding of the world changes as a function of age and experience—is Piaget's theory. Piaget proposes four major states: sensorimotor, preoperational, concrete operational, and formal operational.

◀ Although Piaget's description of what happens within the various stages of cognitive development has largely been upheld, some theorists argue that development is more gradual and continuous and due more to quantitative than to qualitative changes in cognition.

◀ Information-processing approaches to cognitive development focus on the quantitative changes that occur in the way in which people take in, use, and store infor-

mation. Major changes occur with age in the speed of processing, length of attention span, memory, and metacognitive abilities.

REVIEW

1. _____ suggested four stages of cognitive development, each of which is dependent on maturational and environmental factors.
2. Match the stage of development with the thinking style characteristic of the stage:
   1. ____ Egocentric thought
   2. ____ Object permanence

   a. Sensorimotor
   b. Formal operational
   c. Preoperational
   d. Concrete operational

3. _____ Abstract
   reasoning
4. _____ Conservation;
   reversibility
3. Current research suggests that child development may proceed in a continuous fashion, rather than in stages as suggested by Piaget. True or false? _____
4. _____ _____ theories of development suggest that the way a child handles information is critical to his or her development.

Ask Yourself

According to Piaget's theory, a child must have reached a certain level of maturity before particular kinds of information can be learned. Do you think that there could be any advantages to exposing a child to more complex material at an early age? What might information-processing theory have to say about this?

(Answers to review questions are on page 445.)

LOOKING BACK

■ *How do psychologists study the degree to which development is a joint function of hereditary and environmental factors?*

1. Developmental psychology is the branch of psychology that studies growth and change throughout life. One fundamental question is how much developmental change is due to nature—hereditary factors—and how much to nurture—environmental factors. Most developmental psychologists believe that heredity defines the upper limits of our growth and change, whereas the environment affects the degree to which the upper limits are reached.

2. Cross-sectional research compares people of different ages with one another at the same point in time. In contrast, longitudinal research traces the behavior of one or more subjects as the subjects become older. Finally, cross-sequential research combines the two methods by taking several different age groups and examining them over several points in time.

■ *What is the nature of development prior to birth, and what factors affect a child during the mother's pregnancy?*

3. At the moment of conception, a male's sperm cell and a female's egg cell unite, with each contributing to the new individual's genetic makeup. The new cell, a zygote, immediately begins to grow, becoming an embryo measuring about one-fifth of an inch long at four weeks. By the ninth week, the embryo is called a fetus and is responsive to touch and other stimulation. At about twenty-eight weeks it reaches the age of viability: It may survive if born prematurely. A fetus is normally born after thirty-eight weeks of pregnancy, weighing around 7 pounds and measuring about 20 inches in length.

4. Genetic abnormalities produce birth defects such as phenylketonuria (PKU), sickle-cell anemia, Tay-Sachs disease, and Down syndrome. Among the prenatal environmental influences on fetal growth are the mother's nutritional status, illnesses, drug intake, and birth complications.

■ *What are the major milestones of physical, perceptual, and social development after birth?*

5. The newborn, or neonate, has many capabilities. Among them are the rooting reflex, the startle reflex, and the Babinski reflex. After birth, physical development is rapid; children typically triple their birth weights in a year. Perceptual abilities also increase rapidly; infants can distinguish color and depth after just one month. Other sensory capabilities are also impressive at birth; infants can distinguish sounds and discriminate tastes and smells. However, the development of more sophisticated perceptual abilities depends on increased cognitive abilities.

6. Social development in infancy is marked by the phenomenon of attachment—the positive emotional bond between a child and a particular individual. Attachment is measured in the laboratory using the Ainsworth strange situation and is related to later social and emotional adjustment.

7. As children become older, the nature of their social interactions with peers changes. Initially play occurs relatively independently but it becomes increasingly cooperative. Play helps increase social competence and self-control.

8. Different styles of child rearing result in differing outcomes. Authoritarian parents are firm, punitive, and strict. Their children tend to be unsociable and withdrawn. Permissive parents provide lax or inconsistent discipline, although they are warm. Their children tend to be immature, moody, dependent, and low in self-control. Finally, authoritative parents are firm, setting limits, but using reasoning and explanations. Their children tend to be likable, self-reliant, independent, and high in social skills. Of course, there are many exceptions, depending in part on the children's temperament and on the culture in which they are raised.

9. According to Erikson, eight stages of psychosocial development encompass people's changing interactions and understanding of themselves and others. During childhood, there are four stages, each of which relates to a crisis that requires resolution. These stages are labeled trust-versus-mistrust (birth to 18 months), autonomy versus shame and doubt (18 months to 3 years), initiative versus guilt (3 to 6 years), and industry versus inferiority (6 to 12 years).

■ *How can we best describe cognitive development, and what can parents appropriately do to promote the cognitive development of their children?*

10. Piaget's theory suggests that cognitive development proceeds through four stages in which qualitative changes occur in thinking. In the sensorimotor stage (birth to 2 years), children develop object permanence, the awareness that objects and people continue to exist even if they are out of sight. In the preoperational stage (2 to 7 years), children display egocentric thought, and by the end of the stage they begin to understand the principle of conservation—the knowledge that quantity is unrelated to the arrangement and physical appearance of an object. The conservation principle is not fully grasped until the concrete operational stage (7 to 12 years), in which children begin to think more logically, and to understand the concept of reversibility. In the final stage, the formal operational period (12 years to adulthood), thinking becomes abstract, formal, and fully logical.

11. Although Piaget's theory has had an enormous influence, some theorists suggest that the notion of developmental stages is inaccurate. They say that development is more continuous and that the changes occurring within and between stages are reflective of quantitative advances in cognitive development rather than in the quality of thought.

12. Information-processing approaches suggest that quantitative changes occur in children's ability to organize and manipulate information about the world, such as significant increases in speed of processing, attention span, and memory. In addition, there are advances in metacognition, the awareness and understanding of one's own cognitive processes.

13. Because environmental factors play such an important role in cognitive development, child-rearing practices can have an important effect on the degree to which a child realizes his or her genetic potential. Parents can help by giving children the opportunity to explore their environment, being emotionally responsive and involved with their children, being verbally interactive, providing appropriate play materials, giving children a chance to make and learn from mistakes, and holding high expectations.

KEY TERMS AND CONCEPTS

developmental psychology (p. 414)
environment (p. 415)
heredity (p. 415)
nature-nurture issue (p. 416)
genetic makeup (p. 416)
maturation (p. 416)
interactionist (p. 417)
identical twins (p. 418)
cross-sectional research (p. 419)
longitudinal research (p. 419)
cross-sequential research (p. 419)
conception (p. 419)
zygote (p. 420)
chromosomes (p. 420)
genes (p. 420)
embryo (p. 420)
critical period (p. 420)
fetus (p. 421)
age of viability (p. 421)
phenylketonuria (PKU) (p. 421)
sickle-cell anemia (p. 421)

Tay-Sachs disease (p. 421)
Down syndrome (p. 422)
rubella (p. 422)
fetal alcohol syndrome (p. 422)
neonate (p. 425)
vernix (p. 425)
lanugo (p. 425)
reflexes (p. 425)
rooting reflex (p. 425)
sucking reflex (p. 425)
gag reflex (p. 425)
startle reflex (p. 425)
Babinski reflex (p. 425)
habituation (p. 427)
attachment (p. 428)
Ainsworth strange situation (p. 430)
authoritarian parents (p. 433)
permissive parents (p. 433)
authoritative parents (p. 433)
temperament (p. 435)

psychosocial development (p. 436)
trust-versus-mistrust stage (p. 436)
autonomy-versus-shame-and-doubt stage (p. 436)
initiative-versus-guilt stage (p. 436)
industry-versus-inferiority stage (p. 436)
cognitive development (p. 438)
sensorimotor stage (p. 438)
object permanence (p. 438)
preoperational stage (p. 439)
egocentric thought (p. 439)
principle of conservation (p. 439)
concrete operational stage (p. 440)
formal operational stage (p. 441)
information processing (p. 442)
metacognition (p. 442)

ANSWERS (REVIEW III):

1. Piaget   **2.** 1-c; 2-a; 3-b; 4-d   **3.** True   **4.** Information-processing

14

DEVELOPMENT: ADOLESCENCE TO THE END OF LIFE

RICHARD COHEN

Richard Cohen.

Several years ago, my family gathered on Cape Cod for a weekend. My parents were there, my sister and her daughter, too, two cousins and, of course, my wife, my son and me. We ate at one of those restaurants where the menu is scrawled on a blackboard held by a chummy waiter and had a wonderful time. With dinner concluded, the waiter set the check down in the middle of the table. That's when it happened. My father did not reach for the check.

In fact, my father did nothing. Conversation continued. Finally, it dawned on me. Me! I was supposed to pick up the check. After all these years, after hundreds of restaurant meals with my parents, after a lifetime of thinking of my father as the one with the bucks, it had all changed. I reached for the check and whipped out my American Express card. My view of myself was suddenly altered. With a stroke of the pen, I was suddenly an adult (Cohen, 1987, p. 70).

LOOKING AHEAD

At some point in our lives, each of us comes to the realization that we have grown up. No longer children, we become aware that it is up to us to face and adapt to the challenges that continually present themselves in the course of our lives. Development, then, extends throughout life, and adolescence and beyond—the greater part of most people's lives—is a period marked by crucial changes that progress until the very end of life.

In this chapter, we examine development from adolescence through young adulthood, middle age, and old age. Our discussion of adolescence focuses on some of the major physical, emotional, and cognitive changes that occur during people's entry into adulthood. Next, we consider early and middle adulthood, stages in which people are at the peak of their physical and intellectual abilities. We discuss the developmental changes that people undergo during these periods and their relationship to work, families, and living patterns.

Finally, in our discussion of old age, we examine the kinds of physical, intellectual, and social changes that occur as a consequence of the aging process, and see that aging may bring about both improvements and declines in various kinds of functioning. We end with a discussion of the ways people prepare themselves for death and mourn for those who have died.

In sum, this chapter provides you with the answers to these fundamental questions about development:

■ What major physical, social, and emotional transitions characterize adolescence?

■ What are the principal kinds of physical, social, and intellectual changes that occur in early and middle adulthood, and what are their causes?

■ How does the reality of old age differ from the stereotypes about the period?

■ How can we adjust to death and mourning?

It is not easy to be a male adolescent in the Awa tribe: First come the beatings. Seated around a fire, the boys are hit with sticks and prickly branches, both for their own past misdeeds and in honor of those tribesmen who were killed in warfare.

But the beatings—which last for two or three days—are just the beginning. In the next phase of the ritual, adults jab sharpened sticks into the boys' nostrils until copious bleeding takes place. Then they force a 5-foot length of vine deep into the boys' throats, until they gag and vomit.

Finally, tribesmen make deep cuts in the boys' genitals, and severe bleeding occurs. The boys are then released to bleed into a stream, while adult onlookers laugh, jeer, and poke at the cuts to make them bleed even more.

Although the rites that mark the coming-of-age of boys in the Awa tribe in New Guinea sound horrifying to us, they are comparable to those in other cultures, in which it may be necessary to endure public circumcision and kneeling on hot coals without displaying pain. And it is not just males who must participate in such trials: In some tribes, girls must toss wads of burning cotton from hand to hand and allow themselves to be bitten by hundreds of ants.

While western society has no rituals as physically and psychologically taxing to represent the entry into adulthood—for which most of us will heave a sigh of relief—adolescence, the period that follows childhood, is still an important time in our lives. For most people, adolescence is marked by profound changes and, sometimes, turmoil. Considerable biological change marks the adolescent's attainment of sexual and physical maturity, rivaled by important social, emotional, and cognitive changes that occur as adolescents strive for independence and move toward adulthood.

Adolescence, which is generally thought of as a developmental stage between childhood and adulthood, represents a critical period in people's development. Given the many years of schooling that precede one's entry into the workforce in our society, the stage is a fairly lengthy one, beginning just before the teenage years and ending just after them. No longer children, but considered by society to be not quite adults, adolescents face a period of rapid physical and social change that affects them for the rest of their lives.

Adolescence: The developmental stage between childhood and adulthood during which many physical, cognitive, and social changes take place

Physical Development: The Changing Adolescent

If you think back to the start of your own adolescence, it is likely that the most dramatic changes you remember are of a physical nature. A spurt in height, the growth of breasts in girls, deepening voices in boys, the development of body hair, and intense sexual feelings are a source of curiosity, interest, and sometimes embarrassment for individuals entering adolescence.

The physical changes that occur at the start of adolescence, which are largely a result of the secretion of various hormones (see Chapter 3), affect virtually every aspect of the adolescent's life; not since infancy has development been so dramatic (see Figure 14-1, p. 450). Weight and height increase rapidly; a growth spurt begins at around age 10 for girls and age 12 for boys, and adolescents may grow as much as 5 inches in one year.

Puberty, the period at which maturation of the sexual organs occurs, begins at about age 11 or 12 for girls and 13 or 14 for boys. However, there are wide variations, and it is not too rare for a girl to begin to menstruate—the first sign of sexual maturity in females—as early as age 8 or 9 or as late as age 16. Furthermore, there are cultural variations in the timing of first menstruation. For

Puberty: The period during which maturation of the sexual organs occurs

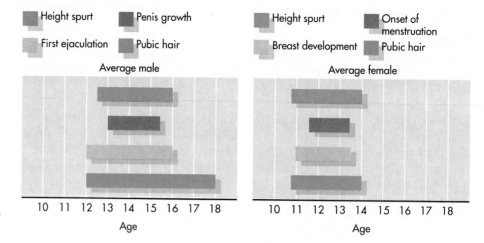

FIGURE 14-1

The bars illustrate the range of ages during which major sexual changes occur during adolescence. (Based on Tanner, 1978.)

example, the average Lumi girl in New Guinea does not begin menstruating until she is 18 (Eveleth & Tanner, 1976).

In western cultures, the average age at which adolescents reach sexual maturity has been steadily decreasing over the last century, most likely a result of better nutrition and medical care (Dreyer, 1982). This change in the onset of puberty provides a good illustration of how changes in the environment interact with heredity to affect development.

The age at which puberty begins has important implications for the way adolescents feel about themselves—as well as how others treat them. Early-maturing boys have a distinct advantage over later-maturing boys; they do better in athletics and they are generally more popular and have more positive self-concepts. On the other hand, they are more likely to have difficulties at school and become involved in minor delinquency. The reason seems to be that early-maturing boys are more likely to become friends with older, and therefore more influential, boys, who may lead them into age-inappropriate activities. On balance, though, the results of early maturing for boys are basically positive; early maturers are typically more responsible and cooperative in later life (Livson & Peskin, 1980; Duncan et al., 1985).

The picture is different for girls. Although early-maturing girls are more sought after as dates and have higher self-concepts than later-maturing girls, some of the consequences of their early physical maturation may be less positive. For example, the development of such obvious characteristics as breasts may set them apart from their peers and be a source of ridicule (Simmons & Blyth, 1987).

Late maturers, in contrast, may suffer psychological consequences as a result of the delay. Boys who are smaller and less coordinated than their more mature peers tend to be ridiculed and seen as less attractive, and may come to view themselves in the same way. The consequences of late maturation may extend well into a male's thirties (Mussen & Jones, 1957). Similarly, late-maturing girls are at a disadvantage in junior high and high school. They hold a relatively low social status, and they may be overlooked in dating and other male-female activities (Apter et al., 1981; Clarke-Stewart & Friedman, 1987).

Clearly, the rate at which physical changes occur during adolescence can have significant effects on the way people are viewed by others and the way they view themselves. Just as important as physical changes, however, are the psychological and social changes that evolve during adolescence.

The differences in height and physical maturity among high school boys are often striking. Because of the social importance of athletic success, early-maturing boys have an advantage when it comes to popularity.

Moral and Cognitive Development: Distinguishing Right from Wrong

In Europe, a woman is near death from a special kind of cancer. The one drug that the doctors think might save her is a form of radium that a druggist in the same town has recently discovered. The drug is expensive to make, and the druggist is charging ten times the cost, or $2000, for a small dose. The sick woman's husband, Heinz, goes to everyone he knows to borrow the money, but he can get together only about $1000. He tells the druggist that his wife is dying and asks him to sell the drug cheaper or let him pay later. The druggist says, "No, I discovered the drug and I'm going to make money from it." Heinz is desperate and considers breaking into the man's store to steal the drug for his wife.

What would you tell Heinz he should do?

In the view of psychologist Lawrence Kohlberg, the advice you give Heinz is a reflection of your level of moral development. According to Kohlberg, people pass through a series of stages in the evolution of their sense of justice and in the kind of reasoning they use to make moral judgments (Kohlberg, 1984). Largely because of the various cognitive deficits that Piaget described (see Chapter 13), preadolescent children tend to think either in terms of concrete, unvarying rules ("It is always wrong to steal" or "I'll be punished if I steal") or in terms of the rules of society ("Good people don't steal" or "What if everyone stole?").

Adolescents, however, are capable of reasoning on a higher plane, typically having reached Piaget's formal operational stage of cognitive development. Because they are able to comprehend broad moral principles, they can understand that morality is not always black and white and that conflict can exist between two sets of socially accepted standards.

Kohlberg (1984) suggests that the changes occurring in moral reasoning can be understood best as a three-level sequence, which, in turn, is divided into six stages. These levels and stages, along with samples of subjects' reasoning at each

TABLE 14-1

KOHLBERG'S SEQUENCE OF MORAL REASONING

Level	Stage	Sample moral reasoning of subjects	
		In favor of stealing	Against stealing
Level 1 Preconventional morality: At this level, the concrete interests of the individual are considered in terms of rewards and punishments.	*Stage 1* Obedience and punishment orientation: At this stage, people stick to rules in order to avoid punishment, and obedience occurs for its own sake.	"If you let your wife die, you will get in trouble. You'll be blamed for not spending the money to save her, and there'll be an investigation of you and the druggist for your wife's death."	"You shouldn't steal the drug because you'll be caught and sent to jail if you do. If you do get away, your conscience will bother you thinking how the police will catch up with you at any minute."
	Stage 2 Reward orientation: At this stage, rules are followed only for a person's own benefit. Obedience occurs because of rewards that are received.	"If you do happen to get caught, you could give the drug back and you wouldn't get much of a sentence. It wouldn't bother you much to serve a little jail term, if you have your wife when you get out."	"You may not get much of a jail term if you steal the drug, but your wife will probably die before you get out, so it won't do much good. If your wife dies, you shouldn't blame yourself; it isn't your fault she has cancer."
Level 2 Conventional morality: At this level, people approach moral problems as members of society. They are interested in pleasing others by acting as good members of society.	*Stage 3* "Good boy" morality: Individuals at this stage show an interest in maintaining the respect of others and doing what is expected of them.	"No one will think you're bad if you steal the drug, but your family will think you're an inhuman husband if you don't. If you let your wife die, you'll never be able to look anybody in the face again."	"It isn't just the druggist who will think you're a criminal; everyone else will too. After you steal the drug, you'll feel bad thinking how you've brought dishonor on your family and yourself; you won't be able to face anyone again."
	Stage 4 Authority and social-order-maintaining morality: People at this stage conform to society's rules and consider that "right" is what society defines as right.	"If you have any sense of honor, you won't let your wife die just because you're afraid to do the only thing that will save her. You'll always feel guilty that you caused her death if you don't do your duty to her."	"You're desperate and you may not know you're doing wrong when you steal the drug. But you'll know you did wrong after you're sent to jail. You'll always feel guilty for your dishonesty and lawbreaking."
Level 3 Postconventional morality: At this level, people use moral principles which are seen as broader than those of any particular society.	*Stage 5* Morality of contract, individual rights, and democratically accepted law: People at this stage do what is right because of a sense of obligation to laws which are agreed upon within society. They perceive that laws can be modified as part of changes in an implicit social contract.	"You'll lose other people's respect, not gain it, if you don't steal. If you let your wife die, it will be out of fear, not out of reasoning. So you'll just lose self-respect and probably the respect of others too."	"You'll lost your standing and respect in the community and violate the law. You'll lose respect for yourself if you're carried away by emotion and forget the long-range point of view."
	Stage 6 Morality of individual principles and conscience: At this final stage, a person follows laws because they are based on universal ethical principles. Laws that violate the principles are disobeyed.	"If you don't steal the drug, and if you let your wife die, you'll always condemn yourself for it afterward. You won't be blamed and you'll have lived up to the outside rule of the law but you won't have lived up to your own standards of conscience."	"If you steal the drug, you won't be blamed by other people, but you'll condemn yourself because you won't have lived up to your own conscience and standards of honesty."

Source: Adapted from Kohlberg, 1969.

stage, are described in Table 14-1. Note that the arguments either in favor of or against stealing the drug can be categorized into the same stage of moral reasoning. It is the nature and sophistication of the argument that determine into what category it falls.

Kohlberg's category system assumes that people move through the six stages in a fixed order, and that they are not capable of reaching the highest stage until about the age of 13—primarily because of deficits in cognitive development that are not overcome until that age. However, many people never reach the highest level of moral reasoning. In fact, Kohlberg suggests that only about 25 percent of all adults rise above stage 4 of his model.

Extensive research has shown that the stages identified by Kohlberg generally provide a valid representation of moral development. Yet the research also raises several methodological issues. One major problem is that Kohlberg's procedure measures moral *judgments,* not *behavior.* Although Kohlberg's theory seems to be a generally accurate account of how moral judgments develop, some research finds that such judgments are not always related to moral behavior (Snarey, 1985; Malinowski & Smith, 1985; Damon, 1988). On the other hand, other investigators suggest that a relationship between moral judgments and behavior does exist. For example, one study found that students who were most likely to commit acts of civil disobedience were those whose moral judgments were at the highest levels (Candee & Kohlberg, 1987). Still, the evidence is mixed on this question; knowing right from wrong does not mean that we will always act in accordance with our judgments (Darley & Shultz, 1990; Denton & Krebs, 1990; Thoma, Rest, & Davison, 1991).

Moral Development in Women.   Psychologist Carol Gilligan (1982; 1987) has pointed out an important shortcoming in Kohlberg's original research: It was carried out using only male subjects and is thus more applicable to them than to women. Furthermore, she convincingly argues that because of differing socialization experiences, a fundamental difference exists in the manner in which men and women view moral behavior. According to her, men view morality primarily in terms of broad principles such as justice and fairness, whereas women see it in terms of responsibility toward individuals and willingness to sacrifice to help a specific individual within the context of a particular relationship. Compassion for individuals is a more salient factor in moral behavior for women than it is for men (Gilligan, Ward, & Taylor, 1988; Gilligan, Lyons, & Hanmer, 1990).

Thus, because Kohlberg's model conceives of moral behavior largely in terms of principles of justice, it is inadequate in describing the moral development of females. This factor accounts for the surprising finding that women typically score at a lower level than men on tests of moral judgment using Kohlberg's stage sequence. In Gilligan's view, women's morality is centered on individual well-being rather than moral abstractions, and the highest levels of morality are represented by compassionate concern for others' welfare.

According to Gilligan's research, women's moral development proceeds in three stages. In the first stage, termed "orientation toward individual survival," a woman concentrates on what is practical and best for her. During this stage, there is a transition from selfishness to responsibility, in which the woman thinks about what would be best for others.

At the second stage of moral development, termed "goodness as self-sacrifice," a woman begins to think that she must sacrifice her own wishes to what other people want. Ultimately, though, she makes the transition from "goodness" to "truth," in which she takes into account her own needs plus those of others.

In the third stage, "morality of nonviolence," a woman comes to see that hurting anyone is immoral—including hurting herself. This realization establishes a moral equality between herself and others and represents, according to Gilligan, the most sophisticated level of moral reasoning.

As you can see, Gilligan's sequence of stages is very different from that presented by Kohlberg, and some psychologists have suggested that her rejection of Kohlberg's work is too sweeping (Colby & Damon, 1987). It is clear, though, that gender plays an important role in determining what is seen as moral, and that men and women have differing conceptions of what constitutes moral behavior (McGraw & Bloomfield, 1987; Handler, Franz, & Guerra, 1992).

Psychosocial Development: The Search for Identity

To most adolescents, answering the questions "Who am I?" and "How do I fit into the world?" is one of life's major challenges. Although these questions continue to be posed throughout a person's lifetime, they take on particular significance during the adolescent years.

Erikson's theory of psychosocial development, which we first discussed in Chapter 13, places particular importance on this search for identity during the adolescent years. As noted earlier, psychosocial development encompasses how people's understanding of themselves, one another, and the world around them changes as a part of development (Erikson, 1963).

Identity-versus-role-confusion stage: According to Erikson, a time in adolescence of testing to determine one's own unique qualities

Identity: The distinguishing character of the individual: who each of us is, what our roles are, and what we are capable of

The fifth stage of Erikson's theory (summarized, with the other stages, in Table 14-2) is labeled the **identity-versus-role-confusion stage** and encompasses adolescence. This stage is a time of major testing, as people try to determine what is unique and special about themselves. They attempt to discover who they are, what their skills are, and what kinds of roles they are best suited to play for the rest of their lives—in short, their **identity.** Confusion over the most appropriate role to follow in life can lead to lack of a stable identity, adoption of a socially unacceptable role such as that of a social deviant, or difficulty in maintaining close personal relationships later in life (Kahn et al., 1985).

During the identity-versus-role-confusion period, pressures to identify what one wants to do with one's life are acutely felt. Because these pressures come at a time of major physical changes and important changes in what society expects of them, adolescents can find the period a particularly difficult one. The identity-versus-role-confusion stage has another important characteristic: a decline in reliance on adults for information, with a shift toward using the peer group as a source of social judgments. The peer group becomes increasingly important, enabling adolescents to form close, adultlike relationships and helping them clarify their personal identities.

Intimacy-versus-isolation stage: According to Erikson, a period during early adulthood that focuses on developing close relationships with others

Generativity-versus-stagnation stage: According to Erikson, a period in middle adulthood during which we take stock of our contributions to family and society

During the college years, most students enter the **intimacy-versus-isolation stage** (spanning the period of early adulthood, from around age 18 to age 30), in which the focus is on developing close relationships with others. Difficulties during this stage result in feelings of loneliness and a fear of relationships with others, while successful resolution of the crises of the stage results in the possibility of forming relationships that are intimate on a physical, intellectual, and emotional level.

Erikson goes on to describe the last stages of adulthood, in which development continues. During middle adulthood, people are in the **generativity-versus-stagnation stage.** Generativity refers to a person's contribution to his or her fam-

A SUMMARY OF ERIKSON'S STAGES

Stage	Approximate age	Positive outcomes	Negative outcomes
1. Trust vs. mistrust	Birth–1½ years	Feelings of trust from environmental support	Fear and concern regarding others
2. Autonomy vs. shame and doubt	1½–3 years	Self-sufficiency if exploration is encouraged	Doubts about self, lack of independence
3. Initiative vs. guilt	3–6 years	Discovery of ways to initiate actions	Guilt from actions and thoughts
4. Industry vs. inferiority	6–12 years	Development of sense of competence	Feelings of inferiority, no sense of mastery
5. Identity vs. role confusion	Adolescence	Awareness of uniqueness of self, knowledge of role to be followed	Inability to identify appropriate roles in life
6. Intimacy vs. isolation	Early adulthood	Development of loving, sexual relationships and close friendships	Fear of relationships with others
7. Generativity vs. stagnation	Middle adulthood	Sense of contribution to continuity of life	Trivialization of one's activities
8. Ego-integrity vs. despair	Late adulthood	Sense of unity in life's accomplishments	Regret over lost opportunities of life

Ego-integrity-versus-despair stage: According to Erikson, a period from late adulthood until death during which we review life's accomplishments and failures

ily, community, work, and society as a whole. Success in this stage results in positive feelings about the continuity of life, while difficulties lead to feelings of triviality regarding one's activities and a sense of stagnation or of having done nothing for upcoming generations. In fact, if a person has not successfully resolved the identity crisis of adolescence, he or she may still be floundering toward identifying an appropriate career.

Finally, the last stage of psychosocial development, the period of **ego-integrity-versus-despair**, comprises later adulthood and continues until death. Success in resolving the difficulties presented by this stage of life is signified by a sense of accomplishment; difficulties result in regret over what might have been achieved, but was not.

One of the most noteworthy aspects of Erikson's theory is its suggestion that development does not stop at adolescence but continues throughout adulthood. Prior to Erikson, the prevailing view was that psychosocial development was largely complete after adolescence. He helped to establish that considerable development continues throughout our lives.

Stormy Adolescence: Myth or Reality?

Does puberty invariably foreshadow a stormy, rebellious period of adolescence?

At one time most children entering adolescence were thought to enter a period fraught with stress and unhappiness, but psychologists are now finding that such a characterization is largely a myth. Most young people, it seems, pass through adolescence without appreciable turmoil in their lives (Steinberg, Belsky, & Meyer, 1991; Peterson, 1988).

This is not to say that adolescence is completely tranquil (Rowlison & Felner,

Although adolescents typically experience some conflict with their parents, the degree of discord is usually not all that great.

1988; Buchanan, Eccles, & Becker, 1992). There is clearly a rise in the amount of arguing and bickering in most families. Young teenagers, as part of their search for identity, tend to experience a tension between their attempts to become independent from their parents and their actual dependence on them. They may experiment with a range of behaviors, flirting with a variety of activities that their parents, and even society as a whole, find objectionable (as we discuss in the accompanying Cutting Edge box.) Happily, though, for the majority of families such tensions tend to stabilize during middle adolescence—around age 15 or 16—and eventually decline around age 18 (Montemayor, 1983).

One of the reasons for the increase in discord in adolescence appears to be the protracted period in which children stay at home with their parents. In prior historical periods—and in some nonwestern cultures today—children leave home immediately after puberty. Today, however, sexually mature adolescents may spend as many as seven or eight years with their parents (Steinberg, 1989). Current statistics even foreshadow an extension of the conflicts of adolescence beyond the teenage years for a significant number of people. Some one-third of all unmarried men and one-fifth of unmarried women between the ages of 25 and 34 continue to reside with their parents (Gross, 1991).

Adolescence also introduces a variety of stresses outside the home. Typically, adolescents change schools at least twice (from elementary to middle or junior high, then to senior high school), and relationships with friends and peers are particularly volatile. Many adolescents hold part-time jobs, increasing the demands of school, work, and social activities on their time. Such stressors can lead to tensions at home (Steinberg & Dornbusch, 1991).

Teenage Suicide

Although the vast majority of teenagers pass through adolescence without major psychological difficulties, some experience unusually severe psychological tension. Sometimes the problems become extreme—such as in the case of teenage suicide, the third leading cause of death for adolescents in the United States. Current statistics show that a teenager commits suicide every ninety minutes.

PSYCHOLOGICAL HEALTH AND DRUG USE IN ADOLESCENCE

People who experiment with drugs are maladjusted. People who just say no are well adjusted. Right?

Not quite—at least according to the results of a comprehensive longitudinal study conducted by psychologist Jack Block and colleagues. Using a group of subjects who were tested at ages 3, 4, 5, 7, 11, 14, and 18, Block, along with colleague Jonathan Shedler, looked at the association between the amount and nature of drug use and psychological health during late adolescence (Shedler & Block, 1990). He came up with a surprising conclusion: Adolescents who had experimented with drugs, mainly marijuana, were the best adjusted in the sample of subjects.

In contrast, subjects who were regular, frequent drug users were clearly maladjusted, showing alienation from others, poor self-control, and emotional distress and anxiety. Interestingly, subjects who had never experimented with drugs also showed signs of being somewhat maladjusted. They tended to have high anxiety levels and were emotionally restrained and overly self-controlled.

Two factors seem to account for the high levels of adjustment in the experimenters. First, marijuana use was commonplace during the time the subjects were teenagers (during the late 1970s and early 1980s); some two-thirds of all teenagers reported trying drugs at least once. Consequently, drug use can be viewed as following adolescent standards of that time. In a statistical sense, use of marijuana was not deviant; in fact, *not* trying marijuana was statistically rarer than trying it. Adolescents tuned into the culture of their peers, then, were apt to be enticed toward trying marijuana.

A second reason for the high adjustment of the experimenters rests on the fact that adolescence is a time of forging new identities and trying out new roles, values, and beliefs. In this context, drug use can be viewed as a means of experimentation and a testing of parental and societal limits.

In sum, the twin factors that societal use of marijuana was relatively frequent and that adolescence is a time of experimentation help explain why sociable, psychologically healthy adolescents might well be tempted to try drugs. But keep in mind these very important limitations to the study: These findings do *not* mean that using drugs made adolescents psychologically healthy; they were psychologically healthy to begin with. Nor should the results be seen as giving license or encouragement to experiment with drugs, because both societal standards about drugs and the actual incidence of drug use have undergone major changes in the last few years. It will take future developmental studies to identify what alternate types of experimentation adolescents are engaging in today.

Over the last two decades, the occurrence of teenage suicide has tripled, due perhaps to increasing pressure on teenagers or other societal changes. Actually, the reported rate of suicide may underestimate its true incidence, as medical personnel are reluctant to report suicide as a cause of death. Instead, they often prefer to label a death as an accident in order to "protect" the survivors.

Adolescent suicide has several causes. According to some studies, one major factor that underlies suicide is depression, characterized by unhappiness, extreme fatigue, and—a variable that seems particularly important—a profound sense of hopelessness. In other cases, adolescents who commit suicide are perfectionists, inhibited socially and prone to extreme anxiety when faced with any social or academic challenge (Schneidman, 1987; Cimbolic & Jobes, 1990; Lester, 1990; Leenaars, 1991).

Family background and adjustment difficulties are also related to suicide (Jacobs, 1971). There may be a long-standing history of conflicts between the parents and children. These conflicts may lead to adolescent behavior problems, such as delinquency, dropping out of school, and aggressive tendencies. In addition, teenage alcoholics and abusers of other drugs have a relatively high rate of suicide. (Figure 14-2, p. 458, identifies the problems cited by first-time callers to one suicide-prevention telephone hotline.)

Several warning signs indicate when a teenager's problems may be severe enough to warrant concern about the possibility of a suicide attempt (Dunne, McIntosh, & Dunne-Maxim, 1987; Berman, 1990; Davis & Sandoval, 1991). They include:

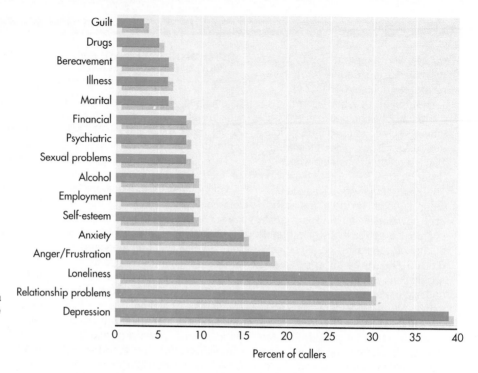

FIGURE 14-2

The problems cited by callers to a suicide-prevention hotline that are leading to their consideration of suicide. (Boston Samaritans, 1991.)

 School problems, such as missing classes, truancy, and a sudden change in grades

 Running away from home

 Frequent incidents of self-destructive behavior, such as careless accidents

 Loss of appetite or excessive eating

 Withdrawal from friends and peers

 Sleeping problems

 Signs of depression, tearfulness, or overt indications of psychological difficulties, such as hallucinations

 A preoccupation with death, an afterlife, or what would happen "if I died"

Signs of depression or indications that a loved one is contemplating suicide should always be taken seriously.

■ Putting affairs in order, such as giving away prized possessions, making arrangements for the care of a pet, and drawing up a will

■ An explicit announcement that the person is thinking about suicide

Of course, in some cases of teenage suicide none of these signs appears, and in some teenagers, some of the symptoms are present and suicide is never attempted. Yet if an adolescent shows indications that suicide is a possibility, it is unreasonable to ignore them, and it is wise to urge the person to seek professional help. Because suicidal people feel such a profound sense of hopelessness and believe that they cannot be helped, assertive action may be needed, such as enlisting the assistance of family members or friends. Talk of suicide is a signal for help, not a confidence to be kept. As yet, no sure way of predicting the likelihood of suicide exists, and it is better to be safe than sorry. (For immediate help with a suicide problem, call 800-882-3386.)

RECAP AND REVIEW I

RECAP

◀ Adolescence is the developmental stage between childhood and adulthood.

◀ Several critical physical changes occur during puberty. Early maturing is generally socially beneficial, whereas late maturing is usually disadvantageous.

◀ According to Kohlberg, moral development passes through a series of increasingly sophisticated levels. In Gilligan's contrasting view of moral development, women, more than men, focus on principles involving compassion toward the individual rather than on abstract principles of justice or fairness.

◀ During adolescence, people enter the crucial identity-versus-role-confusion stage, which may include an identity crisis.

◀ Although adolescence was once thought of as a stormy, rebellious period, psychologists now believe that such a view reflects more myth than reality.

◀ The rate of teenage suicide has tripled over the last two decades.

REVIEW

1. _____ is the period during which the sexual organs begin to mature.

2. Delayed maturation typically provides both males and females with a social advantage. True or false? _____

3. _____ proposed a set of six stages of moral development ranging from reasoning based on rewards and punishments, to abstract thinking involving concepts of justice.

4. Match each of Gilligan's stages of women's moral development with its definition:

1. ____ Morality of nonviolence
2. ____ Orientation toward individual survival
3. ____ Goodness as self-sacrifice

   a. Centered on what is best for the woman in particular
   b. Woman must sacrifice her wants to what others want
   c. Hurting anyone, including the self, is immoral

5. During adolescence, Erikson believed that people must search for _____, while during the college years, the major task is _____.

6. Adolescent suicide is generally unexpected and cannot be detected before it happens. True or false? _____

Ask Yourself

Many cultures have "rites of passage" (like those described in the beginning of this section) whereby a person is officially recognized as an adult. Do you think there could be any benefit to them? Given that adolescence is such a confusing time, might an official designation to "adult" status be a good thing even in our culture?

(Answers to review questions are on page 460.)

EARLY AND MIDDLE ADULTHOOD: THE MIDDLE YEARS OF LIFE

Psychologists generally consider early adulthood to begin around age 20 and last until about age 40 to 45, and middle adulthood to last from about age 40 to 45 to around age 65. Despite the enormous importance of these periods of life—

in terms of both the accomplishments that occur within them and their overall length (together they span some forty years)—they have been studied less than any other stages by developmental psychologists. One reason is that the physical changes during these periods are less apparent and occur more gradually than do those at other times during the life span. In addition, the social changes are so diverse that they prevent simple categorization. Still, there has been a recent upsurge of interest in adulthood among developmental psychologists, with a special focus on the social changes that occur in terms of the family, marriage, divorce, and careers for women.

Physical Development: The Peak of Health

For most people, early adulthood marks the peak of physical health. From about 18 to 25 years of age, people's strength is greatest, their reflexes are quickest, and their chances of dying from disease are quite slim. Moreover, reproductive capabilities are at their highest level.

The changes that begin at age 25 are largely of a quantitative rather than a qualitative nature. The body begins to operate slightly less efficiently and becomes somewhat more prone to disease. Overall, however, ill health remains the exception; most people stay remarkably healthy. (Can you think of any machine other than the body that can operate without pause for so long a period?)

Menopause: The point at which women stop menstruating, generally at around age 45

The major biological change that does occur pertains to reproductive capabilities during middle adulthood. On average, during their late forties or early fifties, women begin **menopause**, the point at which they stop menstruating and are no longer fertile. Because menopause is accompanied by a reduction in estrogen, a female hormone, women sometimes experience symptoms such as hot flashes, or sudden sensations of heat. Most symptoms of menopause, though, are successfully treated with artificial estrogen.

Menopause was once blamed for a host of psychological symptoms, including depression, but most research now suggests that such problems, if they do occur, are caused more by women's perceived reactions to reaching an "old" age in a society that values youth so highly than by menopause itself. Society's attitudes, then, more than the physiological changes of menopause, may produce psychological difficulties (Ballinger, 1981).

For men, the aging process during middle adulthood is somewhat subtler, since there are no physiological signals of increasing age equivalent to the end of menstruation in women. Moreover, men remain fertile and are capable of fathering children until well into old age. However, some gradual physical declines appear: Sperm production decreases and the frequency of orgasm tends to decline. Once again, though, any psychological difficulties that do occur are usually brought about not so much by physical deterioration, but by the inability of the aging individual to meet the exaggerated standards of youthfulness held in high regard by our society.

ANSWERS (REVIEW I):

1. Puberty   **2.** False; both male and female adolescents suffer from delayed maturation. **3.** Kohlberg   **4.** 1-c; 2-a; 3-b   **5.** identity; intimacy   **6.** False; there are often warning signs of a possible suicide attempt.

Social Development: Working at Life

Whereas physical changes during adulthood reflect development of a quantitative nature, social developmental transitions are more profound. It is during this period that people typically launch themselves into careers, marriage, and families.

Psychologist Daniel Levinson (1986) has proposed a model of adult development based on a comprehensive study of major events in the lives of a group of forty men. Although his initial sample was small and consisted only of white middle-class males, the study is important because it provided one of the first comprehensive descriptions of the stages through which people pass following adolescence. According to Levinson, six major stages occur from the entry into early adulthood through the end of middle adulthood (see Figure 14-3).

After a transitional period at around age 20, the stages in early adulthood relate to leaving one's family and entering the adult world. An individual envisions what Levinson calls "The Dream"—an all-encompassing vision about what goals are desired from life, be it writing the great American novel or becoming a physician. Career choices are made, and perhaps discarded, during early adulthood, until eventually long-term decisions are reached. This leads to a period of settling down in the late thirties, during which people establish themselves in a particular set of roles and begin to develop and work toward a vision of their own future.

Around the age of 40 or 45, people generally begin to question their lives as they enter a period called the **midlife transition**, and the idea that life is finite becomes paramount in their thinking. Rather than maintaining a future-oriented view of life, people begin to ask questions about their past accomplish-

Midlife transition: Beginning around the age of 40, a period during which we come to the realization that life is finite

FIGURE 14-3

Developmental periods over the course of adulthood. (Source: Levinson, 1986.)

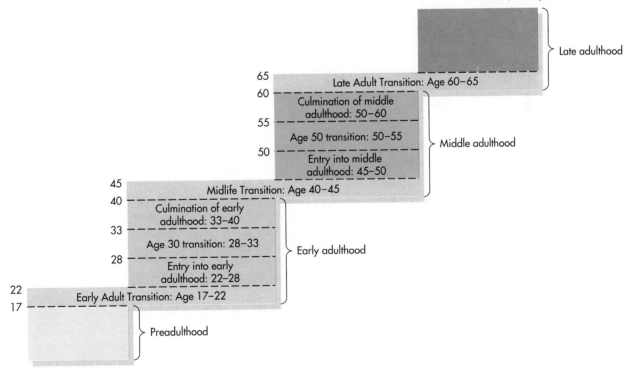

THE TERRIBLE FORTY-TWOS

People entering middle age may find themselves questioning the values they held in early adulthood.

ments, assessing what they have done and how satisfying it has been to them (Gould, 1978). They realize that not all they had wanted to accomplish will be completed before their life ends.

In some cases, people's assessments of their lives are negative, and they may enter what has been popularly labeled a **midlife crisis**. At the same time that they face signs of physical aging, they become aware that their careers are not going to progress considerably further. Even if they have attained the heights to which they aspired—be it company president or well-respected community leader—they find that the satisfaction derived from their accomplishments is not all that they had hoped it would be. As they look at their past, they may also be motivated to try to define what went wrong and how they can remedy previous dissatisfaction.

Midlife crisis: The negative feelings that accompany the realization that we have not accomplished in life all that we had hoped

In most cases, though, the passage into middle age is relatively placid, and some developmental psychologists even question whether most people experience a midlife crisis (Whitbourne, 1986). Most 40-year-olds view their lives and accomplishments positively enough to have their midlife transition proceed relatively smoothly, and the forties and fifties are a particularly rewarding period of life. Rather than looking to the future, people at this stage concentrate on the present, and their involvement with their families, friends, and other social groups takes on new importance. A major developmental thrust of this period of life is learning to accept that the die has been cast, and that one must come to terms with one's circumstances.

Finally, during the last stages of middle adulthood—the fifties—people generally become more accepting of others and their lives and less concerned about issues or problems which once bothered them. Rather than being driven to achieve as they were in their thirties, they come to accept the realization that death is inevitable, and they try to understand their accomplishments in terms of the broader meaning of life (Gould, 1978). Although people may begin, for the first time, to label themselves as "old," many also develop a sense of wisdom and feel freer to enjoy life (Karp, 1988).

Because most work on the phases of social development in adulthood has been based on the study of men's lives, it is important to consider whether women's lives follow the same patterns. We might expect significant gender differences on several grounds. For one thing, women often play different roles in society than men, either by choice or because of societal expectations. Moreover, women's roles have undergone rapid social change in the last decade, as we shall discuss next, making generalizations about women's development during early and middle adulthood difficult (Gilligan, 1982; Gilligan, Lyons, & Manmer, 1990; Mercer, Nichols, & Doyle, 1989).

Unfortunately, there is as yet no clear answer to the question of how women's social development differs from men's, since researchers have only begun to accumulate a large enough body of data focusing directly on women. Some recent research suggests, however, that there are both similarities and differences between men and women. Levinson (1992), for example, argues that women generally go through the same stages at the same ages as men, although disparities exist in the specific details of some of the stages. For instance, important differences appear during "The Dream," the stage in which people develop a vision of what their future life will encompass. Women often have greater difficulty than men in forming a clear dream, for they may experience conflict between the goals of working and of raising a family. For men, this conflict tends to be much less important, since a man who wishes to marry and have a family usually views working as the means of taking care of his family.

Marriage, Children, and Divorce: Family Ties

In many a fairy tale, the typical ending has a dashing young man and a beautiful woman marrying, having children, and living happily ever after. Unfortunately, such a scenario is just that—a fairy tale. In most cases, it does not match the realities of love and marriage in the 1990s. Today, it is just as likely that the man and woman would first live together, then get married and have children—but ultimately end up getting divorced.

According to census figures, the percentage of unmarried couples in U.S. households has increased dramatically over the last two decades, and the average age at which marriage takes place is higher than at any time since the turn of the century (Barringer, 1989). When people do marry, the probability of divorce is high, particularly for younger couples. Even though divorce rates appear to be declining since they peaked in 1981, 60 percent of all first marriages still end in divorce, and two-fifths of children will experience the breakup of their parents' marriage before they are 18 years old (Scott, 1990; Cherlin et al., 1991).

Because of these matrimonial and divorce trends, society has witnessed more than a doubling of single-parent households over the past two decades. In 1990, some 28 percent of all family households had one parent, compared with just 13 percent in 1970. Some racial and ethnic groups have been particularly hard-hit by the phenomenon: more than half of all black children and almost one-third of Hispanic children lived in homes with only one parent in 1990. Furthermore, in most single-parent families, it is the mother, rather than the father, with whom the children reside—a phenomenon that is consistent across racial and ethnic groups (U.S. Census Bureau, 1991). (See Figure 14-4.)

Divorce and subsequent life in a single-parent household presents the potential for the development of several kinds of psychological difficulties, for both parents and children. Children initially may be exposed to high levels of parental

Composition of Family Groups with Children, by Race: 1970 to 1990

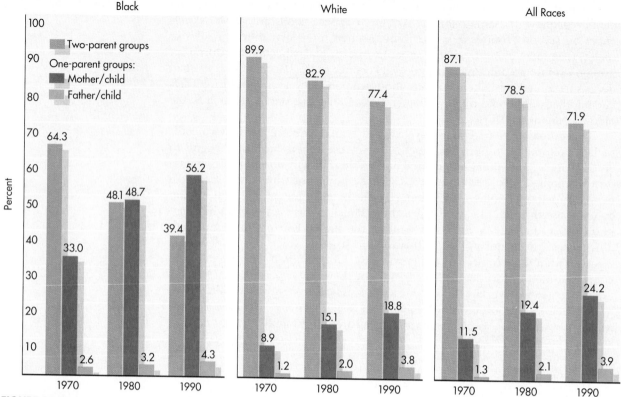

FIGURE 14-4

The number of single-parent families has increased dramatically over the past two decades. (U.S. Census Bureau, 1991.)

conflict, leading to heightened anxiety and aggressive behavior. Later separation from one or the other parent is a painful experience and may result in obstacles to establishing close relationships throughout life. In many cases, good child-care is hard to find, producing psychological stress and sometimes guilt over the arrangements working parents must, for economic reasons, make. Time is always at a premium in single-parent families.

On the other hand, little evidence suggests that children from single-parent families are less well adjusted than those from two-parent families (Barber & Eccles, 1992). Moreover, it is clear that children are more successful growing up in a relatively tranquil single-parent family than in a two-parent family in which the parents are engaged in continuous conflict with one another. In fact, the emotional and behavioral problems displayed by some children of divorced parents may stem more from family problems that existed prior to the divorce than from the divorce itself (Cherlin et al., 1991).

Do current statistics suggest that marriage is as obsolete as the horse and buggy? At first they may seem to, but a closer look reveals that this is not the case. For one thing, survey data show that most people want to get married at some time in their lives, and close to 95 percent eventually do. Even people who divorce are more likely than not to get remarried, some for three or more times—a phenomenon known as serial marriage. Finally, individuals who are married report being happier than those who are not (Brody, Neubaum, & Fore-hand, 1988; Strong, 1978; Glenn, 1987).

Although marriage thus remains an important institution in our culture, the roles that men and women play within a marriage are changing. More women

Most evidence suggests that
children raised by a single parent
are as well adjusted as those
from two-parent families.

than ever before either want, or are forced by their economic situation, to act simultaneously as wives, mothers, and wage earners—in contrast to the traditional marriage, in which the husband was the sole wage earner and the wife took primary responsibility for caring for the home and children (Gottfried & Gottfried, 1988).

Close to three-quarters of all married women with school-aged children are employed outside the home, and 56 percent of mothers with children under six are working. Statistical projections suggest that by the mid-1990s, almost 70 percent of mothers with infants and young children will be employed (Scarr, Phillips, & McCartney, 1989; U.S. Bureau of Labor Statistics, 1988; Darnton, 1990).

Although married women are more likely than they once were to be out of the house working, they are not out of the kitchen, for the distribution of household tasks between husbands and wives has not changed substantially. Even in marriages in which the spouses hold jobs of similar status, working wives are still more likely to view themselves as responsible for the traditional homemaking tasks such as cooking and cleaning, whereas husbands of working wives still view themselves as responsible primarily for such household tasks as repairing broken appliances, putting up screens in the summer, and doing yard work (Schellhardt, 1990; Biernat & Wortman, 1991).

In addition, the way in which time is spent by married men and women during the average week is quite different. As you can see in Figure 14-5, page 466, although married men average slightly more work hours per week than married women, they spend considerably less time on household chores and child-care. Overall, working women spend much more time than working men on combined job and family demands. In fact, the number of hours put in by working mothers can be staggering; one survey found employed mothers of children under 3 years of age worked an average of ninety hours per week (Googans & Burden, 1987; Rexroat & Shehan, 1987)!

Families in which both parents work still tend to view the mother as holding primary responsibility for child rearing. Consequently, rather than careers supplanting what women do at home, they often exist in addition to the role of

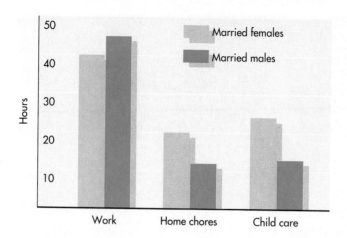

FIGURE 14-5

The number of hours per week devoted to home chores and child-care differs considerably for men and women, even though they spend almost the same number of hours on the job. (Googans & Burden, 1987.)

homemaker. This factor sometimes leads to resentment toward husbands who spend less time than wives may have expected on child-care and housework (Ruble et al., 1988; Williams & McCullers, 1983). For women, the competing demands of family and work make social development during early adulthood particularly arduous.

On the other hand, the benefits of work may outweigh the disadvantages of having major responsibilities in multiple roles. For instance, women who work, particularly those in high-prestige occupations, report feeling a greater sense of mastery, pride, and competence than women who stay at home. The value of work, then, goes beyond merely earning a salary and extends to providing self-satisfaction and a sense of contributing to society (Hoffman, 1989; Crosby, 1991).

It is clear that success at work has important psychological consequences for both men and women. People report feeling happier and more in control of their lives; have higher self-esteem; and even feel that they have better marriages when they are successful at their jobs. Conversely, work failures—such as being fired—can lead to depression, impotence, and a host of other psychological symptoms (Gruenberg, 1980). In sum, for men and women in the middle years of life, job-related achievement represents an important aspect of continued growth and development.

RECAP AND REVIEW II

RECAP

◀ The peak of physical strength occurs from about age 18 to age 25, after which there are declines in strength and general health.

◀ According to a model developed by Levinson, social development during early and middle adulthood proceeds through a series of stages.

◀ Although many marriages end in divorce, marriage is still highly valued by society, with most people saying that they want to get married and ultimately doing so.

◀ The proportion of working women has increased, although the division of household roles between husband and wife has not changed radically.

REVIEW

1. Emotional and psychological changes that sometimes accompany menopause are probably not due to menopause itself. True or false? _____

2. Forty-year-old Rob recently found himself surveying his goals and accomplishments to date. Although he has accomplished a lot, he realizes that many of his goals will not be met in his lifetime. Levinson would term this stage in Rob's life as _____ _____.

3. It is typically in the best interests of children for their parents to remain in a stormy marriage until the children move away from home. True or false? _____

4. In households where both partners have similar jobs, the division of labor that generally occurs is the same as in "traditional" households where the husband works and the wife stays at home. True or false? _____

5. A decrease in the hormone of _____ is responsible for the onset of menopause.

Ask Yourself

Given the current divorce rate and the number of households in which both parents work, do you think it is reasonable to talk in terms of a "traditional" household in which the father is the breadwinner while the wife is a homemaker? What problems might such a definition cause for children whose homes do not match this definition?

(Answers to review questions are on page 468.)

THE LATER YEARS OF LIFE: GROWING OLD

I've always enjoyed doing things in the mountains—hiking or, more recently, active cliff-climbing. When climbing a route of any difficulty at all, it's absolutely necessary to become entirely absorbed in what you're doing. You look for a crack that you can put your hand in. You have to think about whether the foothold over there will leave you in balance or not. Otherwise you can get trapped in a difficult situation. And if you don't remember where you put your hand or feet a few minutes before, then it's very difficult to climb down.

The more difficult the climb, the more absorbing it is. The climbs I really remember are the ones I had to work on. Maybe a particular section where it took two or three tries before I found the right combination of moves that got me up easily—and, preferably, elegantly. It's a wonderful exhilaration to get to the top and sit down and perhaps have lunch and look out over the landscape and be so grateful that it's still possible for me to do that sort of thing (Lyman Spitzer, quoted in Kotre & Hall, 1990, pp. 358–359.)

Lyman Spitzer. Age: 74.

If you can't quite picture a 74-year-old climbing rocks, some rethinking of your view of old age might well be in order. In spite of the societal stereotype of old age as a time of inactivity and physical and mental decline, **gerontologists**, specialists who study aging, are beginning to paint quite a different portrait of the elderly. By focusing on the period of life that starts at around age 65, gerontologists are making important contributions in clarifying the capabilities of the elderly and demonstrating that significant developmental processes continue even during old age.

Gerontologists: Specialists who study aging

Physical Changes in the Elderly: The Old Body

Napping, eating, walking, conversing. It probably doesn't surprise you that these relatively unvigorous activities represent the typical pastimes of the elderly. But what is striking about this list is that these activities are identical to the most common leisure activities reported in a survey of college students. Although the students cited more active pursuits—such as sailing and playing basketball—as their favorite activities, in actuality they engaged in such sports relatively infrequently, spending most of their free time napping, eating, walking, and conversing (Harper, 1978).

Although the leisure activities in which the elderly engage may not differ all that much from those that younger people pursue, many physical changes are, of course, brought about by the aging process. The most obvious are those of appearance—hair thinning and turning gray, skin wrinkling and folding, and sometimes a slight loss of height as the size of the disks between vertebrae in the spine decreases—but there are also subtler changes in the body's biological functioning (Munnichs, Mussen, Olbrich, & Coleman, 1985).

For example, sensory acuity decreases as a result of aging; vision and hearing are less sharp, and smell and taste are not as sensitive. Reaction time slows. There are changes in physical stamina. Because oxygen intake and heart-pumping ability decline, the body is unable to replenish lost nutrients as quickly—and therefore the rebound from physical activity is slower (Shock, 1962). Of course, none of these changes begins suddenly at age 65; gradual declines in some kinds of functioning start earlier. It is in old age, however, that these changes become more apparent.

What are the reasons for these physical declines? There are two major explanations: genetic preprogramming theories and wear-and-tear theories (Bergener, Ermini, & Stahelin, 1985; Whitbourne, 1986). **Genetic preprogramming theories of aging** suggest that there is a built-in time limit to the reproduction of human cells, and that after a certain time they are no longer able to divide (Hayflick, 1974). A variant of this idea is that some cells are genetically preprogrammed to become harmful to the body after a certain amount of time has gone by, causing the internal biology of the body to "self-destruct" (Pereira-Smith et al., 1988).

The second approach for understanding physical declines due to aging is based on the same factors that force people to buy new cars every so often: mechanical devices wear out. According to **wear-and-tear theories of aging**, the mechanical functions of the body simply stop working efficiently. Moreover, waste by-products of energy production eventually accumulate, and mistakes are made when cells reproduce. Eventually the body, in effect, wears out.

We do not know which of these theories provides a better explanation of the physical aging process; it may be that both contribute. It is important to realize, however, that physical aging is not a disease, but rather a natural biological process. Many physical functions do not decline with age. For example, sex remains pleasurable well into old age (although the frequency of sexual activity decreases), and some elderly people even report that the pleasure they derive from sex increases (Lobsenz, 1975; Rowe & Kahn, 1987; Olshansky, Carnes, & Cassel, 1990).

Furthermore, neither genetic preprogramming theories nor wear-and-tear theories successfully explain a fact that is immediately apparent to anyone studying aging: Women live longer than men. Throughout the industrialized world, women outlive men by a margin of four to ten years (Holden, 1987b). The female advantage begins just after conception. Although more males are conceived than females, males have a higher rate of prenatal, infant, and childhood death, and by age 30 there are equal numbers of males and females. By age 65, 84 percent of females and 70 percent of males are still alive.

Largely because of positive changes in men's health habits, including decreased smoking and consumption of cholesterol and greater exercise, the gender gap is not increasing. But health habits do not provide the complete explanation for the gap, and a full explanation of why women live longer than men remains to be found. What is clear is that women, more often than men,

Genetic preprogramming theories of aging: Theories that suggest a built-in time limit to the reproduction of human cells

Wear-and-tear theories of aging: Theories that suggest that the body's mechanical functions cease efficient activity and, in effect, wear out

---

ANSWERS (REVIEW II):

1. True **2.** Midlife transition. **3.** False; a stable one-parent home is generally preferable to a two-parent home filled with conflict. **4.** True **5.** Estrogen

must make the profound adjustments needed following the death of a spouse. Women's longer lives are something of a mixed blessing: The end of life must frequently be faced without a partner.

Cognitive Changes: Thinking About—and During—Old Age

> Three women were talking about the inconveniences of growing old.
>
> "Sometimes," one of them confessed, "when I go to my refrigerator, I can't remember if I'm putting something in or taking something out."
>
> "Oh, that's nothing," said the second woman. "There are times when I find myself at the foot of the stairs wondering if I'm going up or if I've just come down."
>
> "Well, my goodness!" exclaimed the third woman. "I'm certainly glad I don't have any problems like that"—and she knocked on wood. "Oh," she said, starting up out of her chair, "there's someone at the door" (Dent, 1984, p. 38).

At one time, many gerontologists would have agreed with the view—suggested by the story above—that the elderly are forgetful and confused. Today, however, most research tells us that this is far from an accurate assessment of elderly people's capabilities.

One reason for the change in view is the use of more sophisticated research techniques. For example, if we were to give a group of elderly people an IQ test, we might find that the average score was lower than for a group of younger people. We might conclude that this signifies a decline in intelligence. But if we looked a little closer at the specific test, we might find that such a conclusion was unwarranted. For instance, many IQ tests include portions based on physical performance (such as arranging a group of blocks) or on speed. In such a case, poorer performance on the IQ test may be due to increases in reaction time—a physical decline that accompanies old age—and have little or nothing to do with the intellectual capabilities of the elderly (Schaie, 1991).

Other difficulties hamper research into the cognitive functioning of the elderly. For example, the elderly are more likely than younger people to suffer from physical ill health. Some studies of IQ in the past inadvertently compared a group of physically healthy younger people with a group of elderly people who

(a)

(b)

Setting new goals can continue through old age. Los Angeles resident Luba Kahan (*a*), shown here with a samovar brought from Russia when she and her family immigrated in the early 1900s, gave up smoking at the age of 89. Scott O'Dell (*b*) of Waccabuc, New York, wrote a book every year from 1966 until his death in 1988. He is shown here at age 89.

were generally less healthy, with the finding of significantly lower scores for the elderly group. However, when only *healthy* elderly people are observed, intellectual declines are markedly less evident (Riegel & Riegel, 1972; Avorn, 1983). Furthermore, it is unfair to compare the test results of an elderly group with those of a younger group of subjects when the mean level of education is probably lower in the older group (for historical reasons) than in the younger one.

Similarly, declines in the IQ scores of the elderly may be caused by their having lower motivation to perform well on intelligence tests than younger people. Finally, traditional IQ tests may not be the most appropriate measures of intelligence in the elderly. For example, as we discussed in Chapter 10, some researchers contend that several kinds of intelligence exist, and others have found that the elderly perform better on tests of everyday problems and social competence than do younger individuals (Cornelius & Caspi, 1987).

On the other hand, some declines in the intellectual functioning of the elderly have been found, even when using more sophisticated research methods (Cerella, 1985; Schaie & Willis, 1985). If you recall from Chapter 10, intelligence can be conceptualized in terms of **fluid intelligence** (the ability to deal with new problems and situations) and **crystallized intelligence** (intelligence based on the accumulation of particular kinds of knowledge and experience as well as on strategies that have been acquired through the use of fluid intelligence). Tests show clear, although not substantial, declines in fluid intelligence in old age. It is noteworthy, however, that such changes actually begin to appear in early adulthood, as indicated in Figure 14-6 (Baltes & Schaie, 1974; Schaie, 1985).

Crystallized intelligence, in contrast, does not decline; it actually improves with age, as shown in Figure 14-6. For example, an elderly woman asked to solve a geometry problem (which taps fluid intelligence) might have greater difficulty than she once did, but she might be better at solving verbal problems that require reasoned conclusions.

One possible reason for the developmental differences between fluid and crystallized intelligence during old age is that fluid intelligence may be more sensitive to changes in the nervous system than crystallized intelligence. Another factor may be the degree to which the two kinds of intelligence are used during a person's lifetime. Whatever the reason, people compensate for the decline. They can still learn what they want to; it just may take more time (Storandt, et al., 1984).

Furthermore, recent evidence suggests that cognitive declines might be remedied by increasing the amount of blood in the brains of the elderly. In support of this reasoning, in one experiment the drug Nimodipine—which increases blood flow—was given to a group of elderly rabbits. The rabbits that

Fluid intelligence: The ability to deal with new problems and situations

Crystallized intelligence: Intelligence based on the store of specific information, skills, and strategies that people have acquired through experience

FIGURE 14-6

Although crystallized intelligence remains steady and even seems to increase slightly with age, fluid intelligence does show a decline. (Horn & Donaldson, 1980.)

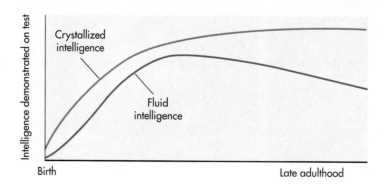

- Winston Churchill is reelected to the House of Commons as a member of the British Parliament. Age: 84.
- Grandma Moses, who began to paint only ten years earlier, has her first one-person exhibit. Age: 80.
- Cellist Pablo Casals' performance in a concert is highly acclaimed. Age: 88.

The stereotype of old age suggests that senility and declining awareness of what is happening in the world are inevitable. Yet the accomplishments of many elderly people—like the three noted above—clearly rebut this mistaken notion. Certainly, for some people, the stereotype becomes reality, and a decline in cognitive abilities occurs as they age, but others maintain and even increase their intellectual capabilities well into their eighties and nineties.

The fact that some elderly do perform so well cognitively raises the question of whether intellectual declines are truly inevitable. Some ger-

OLDER *AND* WISER: LONG-TERM RESULTS OF TRAINING THE ELDERLY

ontologists have argued that with appropriate environmental stimulation, cognitive deterioration might largely be prevented.

In clear support of this hypothesis, psychologist Sherry L. Willis and colleagues of the Pennsylvania State University conducted a seven-year longitudinal study of elderly men and women when they were at three ages: 69 years, 71, and 77 years. At each of these ages, the subjects participated in several one-hour intensive training sessions relating to spatial skills. Participants in the program were taught general strategies for dealing with spatial problems and completed practice test items typical of those used to measure spatial skills. Then, following the training, they were given a battery of spatial skill tests (Willis & Nesselroade, 1990).

The training program was a success at each of the age levels. Com-

pared with a control group of same-age subjects who had not received the training, the elderly participants in the training program scored significantly better on the spatial skills tests. Furthermore, the gains continued throughout the age range included in the study; even the oldest subjects benefited from the training.

In sum, the results demonstrated quite clearly that teaching the elderly strategies for dealing with spatial cognitive problems is an effective means of preventing declines in performance. Even brief educational experiences can be effective in improving performance.

The results argue quite clearly that declines in cognitive functioning in old age should not be considered unavoidable and that the intellectual abilities of the elderly are resilient. They also suggest, though, that providing some degree of intellectual stimulation may be the key to maintaining cognitive skills. Like the rest of us, elderly people need a stimulating environment in order to hone and maintain their skills.

received the drug learned a classically conditioned response significantly faster than a control group of rabbits that did not receive the drug. In fact, the rabbits that received the drug learned as rapidly as a group of young rabbits (Deyo, Straube, & Disterhoft, 1989). (Other ways of increasing intellectual functioning are explored in the Psychology at Work box.)

Memory Changes in Old Age: Are the Elderly Forgetful?

One of the characteristics most frequently attributed to the elderly is forgetfulness. How accurate is this assumption?

Most evidence suggests that memory change is *not* an inevitable part of the aging process. Even when elderly people do show memory declines, their deficits tend to be limited to particular types of memory. For example, short-term memory capabilities rarely deteriorate, except in cases of illness. Instead, when memory loss occurs, it is typically restricted to long-term memory (Craik, 1977).

In addition, the losses that do occur in long-term memory tend to be limited to episodic memories, which relate to specific experiences about our lives. Other types of memories, such as semantic memories (which refer to knowledge and facts) and implicit memories (which are memories about which we are not consciously aware) are largely unaffected by age (Graf, 1990).

Declines in episodic memories can often be traced to changes in the lives of the elderly. For instance, it is not surprising that a retired person, who may no longer face the same kind of consistent intellectual challenges encountered on the job, might well be less practiced in using memory or even be less motivated to remember things, leading to an apparent decline in memory. Even in cases in which long-term memory declines, the elderly person can usually profit from compensatory efforts. Training the elderly to use the kinds of mnemonic strategies described in Chapter 8 may not only prevent their long-term memory from deteriorating, but may actually improve it (Perlmutter & Mitchell, 1986; Brody, 1987c; Ratner et al., 1987).

In the past, elderly people with severe cases of memory decline, accompanied by other cognitive difficulties, were viewed as suffering from senility. *Senility* is a broad, imprecise term typically applied to elderly people who experience progressive deterioration of mental abilities, including memory loss, disorientation to time and place, and general confusion.

Alzheimer's disease: A progressive brain disease leading to an irreversible decline in mental and physical abilities

Once thought to be an inevitable state that accompanies aging, senility is now viewed by most gerontologists as a label that has outlived its usefulness. Rather than senility being the cause of certain symptoms, the symptoms are deemed to be caused by some other factor. In some cases there is an actual disease, such as **Alzheimer's disease**, the progressive brain disorder discussed in Chapter 8 which leads to a gradual and irreversible decline in mental abilities. In other cases, the symptoms of senility are caused by temporary anxiety and depression, which may be successfully treated, or may even be due to overmedication. The danger is that people suffering such symptoms may be labeled senile and left untreated, thereby continuing their decline—even though treatment would have been beneficial.

The Social World of the Elderly: Old but Not Alone

Just as the view that senility is an inevitable outcome of old age has proved to be wrong, so has the view that old age inevitably brings loneliness. The elderly most often see themselves as functioning members of society, with one representative poll showing that just 12 percent of people 65 and over view loneliness as a serious problem (Harris Poll, 1975).

Still, the social patterns and behaviors of the elderly are different in some respects from those of younger individuals. Two major approaches have been suggested to explain elderly people's social environment: disengagement theory and activity theory.

Disengagement theory of aging: A theory that suggests that aging is a gradual withdrawal from the world on physical, psychological, and social levels

The **disengagement theory of aging** sees aging as a gradual withdrawal from the world on physical, psychological, and social levels (Cummings & Henry, 1961). Physically, lower energy levels produce less activity; psychologically, the focus shifts from others to the self; and socially, there is less interaction with others and a reduction in the level of participation in society at large. But rather than viewing this disengagement in a negative light, theorists suggest that it should be seen positively, since it provides for increased reflectiveness and decreased emotional investment in others at a time of life when social relationships will inevitably be ended by death.

Disengagement theory has been criticized because of its suggestion that disengagement is an automatic process, marking a sharp departure from earlier behavior patterns. Even more important are data showing that the elderly who report being the happiest are those who remain the most active (Havighurst, 1973).

Activity theory suggests that the elderly continue doing things they enjoyed when younger and add more activities to replace those lost through changes such as retirement. These Harlem women are members of a seniors' water ballet team.

Such criticisms have led to the development of an alternative approach describing social adjustment to aging. The **activity theory of aging** suggests that the elderly who age most successfully are those who maintain the interests and activities they pursued during middle age and who resist any decline in the amount and kind of social interaction they have with others (Blau, 1973). According to activity theory, old age should reflect a continuation, as much as possible, of the activities in which people participated during the earlier part of their lives, as well as activities to replace those lost through changes such as retirement.

Activity theory of aging: A theory that suggests that the elderly who age most successfully are those who maintain the interests and activities they had during middle age

Activity theory is not without its critics. For instance, activity alone does not guarantee happiness. Rather, the *nature* of activities in which people engage is probably more critical (Gubrium, 1973). Furthermore, not all elderly people need a life filled with activities and social interaction to be happy; as in every stage of life, there are those who are just as satisfied leading a relatively inactive, solitary existence as a life filled with activity and social relationships.

We cannot say whether disengagement theory or activity theory presents a more accurate view of the elderly, probably because there are vast individual differences in how people cope with becoming old. Clearly, however, the elderly are not just marking time until death. Rather, old age is a time of continued growth and development, as important as any other period of life.

The Informed Consumer of Psychology: Adjusting to Death

At some time in your life, you will face death—certainly your own, as well as the deaths of friends and loved ones. Although there is nothing more inevitable in life than death, it remains a frightening, emotion-laden topic. There may be little more stressful than the death of a loved one or the contemplation of your own imminent death, and preparing for death is likely to represent one of your most crucial developmental tasks.

Not too long ago, talk of death was taboo. The topic was never mentioned to dying people, and gerontologists had little to say about it. That changed, however, with the pioneering work of Elisabeth Kübler-Ross (1969), who brought the subject out into the open with her observation that those facing death move through five stages.

- Denial. In this first stage, people resist the idea that they are dying. Even if told that their chances for survival are small, they refuse to admit that they are facing death.

- Anger. After moving beyond the denial stage, dying people are angry—angry at people around them who are in good health, angry at medical professionals for being ineffective, angry at God. They ask the question "Why me?" and are unable to answer it without feeling anger.

- Bargaining. Anger leads to bargaining, in which the dying try to think of ways to postpone death. They may decide to dedicate their lives to religion if God saves them; they may say, "If only I can live to see my son married, I will accept death then." Such bargains are rarely kept, most often because the dying person's illness keeps progressing and invalidates any "agreements."

- Depression. When dying people come to feel that bargaining is of no use, they move to the next stage: depression. They realize that the die is cast, that they are losing their loved ones and their lives really are coming to an end. They are experiencing what Kübler-Ross calls "preparatory grief" for their own death.

- Acceptance. In this last stage, people are past mourning for the loss of their own lives, and they accept impending death. Usually, they are unemotional and uncommunicative; it is as if they have made peace with themselves and are expecting death without rancor.

Although not everyone experiences each of these stages in the same way, if at all, Kübler-Ross's theory remains our best description of people's reactions to their approaching death. There are, however, vast individual differences, depending on the specific cause and duration of dying as well as the person's sex, age, and personality and the type of support received from family and friends (Kastenbaum, 1975; Zautra, Reich, & Guarnaccia, 1990).

Mourning

For the survivors of a loved one's death, there remains a painful period of mourning and coming to terms with death. Most adults pass through four major stages of grief, not altogether unrelated to what the dying person experienced prior to death (Greenblatt, 1978; Malinak, Hoyt, & Patterson, 1979; Sanders, 1989).

The first stage is one of shock, denial, and disbelief, usually lasting a few days, although sometimes extending over a period of weeks or even months. This phase is followed by a period of depression, of yearning for the dead person, and wishing he or she could somehow return. Crying, anger, fear, sleeplessness, and other symptoms of grief are common during this period, which peaks within five days to two weeks. In some cases, these symptons last much longer—up to a year or more.

In the second and third stages, the person comes to terms with the death. After a period of mourning, people pick up the pieces of their lives, turning to others and beginning to free themselves from some of the bonds that held them to the loved one. Finally, in the fourth stage, they begin to construct a new identity, one that is independent of the lost loved one. They form new relation-

The experience of attending a loved one's funeral may facilitate the transition from the first stages of mourning into later ones.

ships and may come to understand themselves better. In fact, around half of all people who reach this stage report that the death of a loved one helped them grow as human beings, forcing them to be more self-reliant and more appreciative of life.

As with the stages of dying, not everyone moves through the same stages of mourning in the same manner; people will experience grief in their own way, partly dependent on the nature of their relationship with the deceased. Furthermore, some deaths are particularly difficult to deal with, such as a sudden, untimely death or the death of one's child. When grief is so profound that the person is immobilized, when mourning continues for extraordinarily long periods, when physical symptoms develop, or when there are general, long-lasting changes in personality, the mourner may require some professional guidance for dealing with his or her grief (Sanders, 1988; Weiss, 1988; Horowitz, 1990).

Few of us enjoy the contemplation of death. Yet awareness of its psychological effects and consequences can make its inevitable coming less anxiety-producing and perhaps more understandable.

◀ RECAP AND REVIEW III

RECAP

◀ The leisure activities of the elderly do not differ substantially from those of younger people, but a number of physical declines do occur with age. These declines are explained by two classes of theories: genetic preprogramming theories and wear-and-tear theories.

◀ Fluid intelligence and memory are affected by aging.

◀ Disengagement theory and activity theory seek to explain changes in social activity during old age.

◀ People approaching death move through a series of stages, as do people mourning another's death.

REVIEW

1. _____ _____ theories suggest that there is a maximum time limit in which cells are able to reproduce. This time limit explains the eventual breakdown of the body during old age.

2. In contrast to the above theories, _____-_____-_____ theories state that the body simply becomes less efficient as time passes.

3. Lower IQ test scores by the elderly do not necessarily mean a decrease in intelligence. True or false? _____

4. During old age, a person's _____ intelligence continues to increase, while _____ intelligence may decline.

5. Lois feels that, in her old age, she has gradually decreased her social contacts and has become more self-oriented. A proponent of _____ theory interprets the situation as a result of Lois's not maintaining her past interests. A supporter of _____ theory views her behavior in a more positive light, suggesting that it is a natural process accompanied by enhanced reflectiveness and declining emotional investment.

6. In Kubler-Ross's _____ stage, people resist the idea of death. In the _____ stage, they attempt to make deals to avoid death, while in the _____ stage, they passively await death.

Ask Yourself

Many people today suffer from misconceptions about the elderly, thinking of them as senile, slow, lonely, and so forth. How might you go about proving these stereotypes wrong? What advantages might a change in our misconceptions have in terms of utilizing the elderly as a valuable resource?

(Answers to review questions are on page 477.)

> **LOOKING BACK**

■ *What major physical, social, and emotional transitions characterize adolescence?*

1. Adolescence, the developmental stage between childhood and adulthood, is marked by the onset of puberty, the point at which sexual maturity occurs. The age at which puberty begins has implications for the way people view themselves and the way they are seen by others.

2. Moral judgments during adolescence increase in sophistication, according to Kohlberg's three-level, six-stage model. Although Kohlberg's stages are an adequate description of males' moral judgments, they do not seem to be as applicable in describing females' judgments. Specifically, Gilligan suggests that women view morality in terms of concern for individuals rather than in terms of broad, general principles of justice or fairness; in her view, moral development in women proceeds in three stages.

3. According to Erikson's model of psychosocial development, adolescence may be accompanied by an identity crisis, although this is by no means universal. Adolescence is followed by three stages of psychosocial development which cover the remainder of the life span.

■ *What are the principal kinds of physical, social, and intellectual changes that occur in early and middle adulthood, and what are their causes?*

4. Early adulthood marks the peak of physical health. Physical changes occur relatively gradually in men and women during adulthood, although one major change occurs at the end of middle adulthood for women: They begin menopause, after which they are no longer fertile. For men, the aging process is subtler, since they remain fertile.

5. Levinson's model of adult development suggests that six major stages occur, beginning with entry into early adulthood at around age 20 and ending at around age 60 or 65. One of the most critical transitions—at least for men—occurs during midlife (around age 40 to 45), when people typ-

ically experience a midlife transition in which the notion that life is not infinite becomes more important. In some cases this can lead to a midlife crisis; usually, however, the passage into middle age is relatively calm. Although Levinson suggests that women's lives follow basically the same pattern as men's, several gender differences are likely to occur.

6. As aging continues during middle adulthood, people realize in their fifties that their lives and accomplishments are fairly well set, and they try to come to terms with them.

7. Among the most important developmental milestones during adulthood are marriage, family changes, and divorce. Although divorce is more prevalent than ever before, most people still view marriage as important and desirable. Another important determinant of adult development is work. Recently, single and married women have joined the work force in historically high numbers.

■ *How does the reality of old age differ from the stereotypes about the period?*

8. Old age may bring marked physical declines. Although the activities of the elderly are not all that different from those of younger people, elderly people do experience reaction-time increases, as well as sensory declines and a decrease in physical stamina. These declines might be caused by genetic preprogramming, which sets a time limit on the reproduction of human cells, or they may simply be due to wear and tear on the mechanical parts of the body.

9. Although intellectual declines were once thought to be an inevitable part of aging, most research suggests that this is not necessarily the case. Fluid intelligence does decline with age, and long-term memory abilities are sometimes impaired. In contrast, crystallized intelligence shows slight increases with age, and short-term memory remains at about the same levels. Senility, then, is no longer seen as a universal outcome of old age.

10. Disengagement theory sees successful aging as a

process accompanied by gradual withdrawal from the physical, psychological, and social worlds. In contrast, activity theory suggests that the maintenance of interests and activities from earlier years leads to successful aging. Because there are vast individual differences, it is unclear whether either of the two theories is completely accurate.

■ *How can we adjust to death and mourning?*

11. According to Kübler-Ross, dying people move through five stages as they face death: denial, anger, bargaining, depression, and acceptance. Following the death of a loved one, mourners also appear to move through a series of stages in coming to terms with death.

KEY TERMS AND CONCEPTS

adolescence (p. 449)
puberty (p. 449)
identity-versus-role-confusion
    stage (p. 454)
identity (p. 454)
intimacy-versus-isolation stage
    (p. 454)
generativity-versus-stagnation
    stage (p. 454)

ego-integrity-versus-despair stage
    (p. 455)
menopause (p. 460)
midlife transition (p. 461)
midlife crisis (p. 462)
gerontologists (p. 467)
genetic preprogramming theories
    of aging (p. 468)

wear-and-tear theories of aging
    (p. 468)
fluid intelligence (p. 470)
crystallized intelligence (p. 470)
Alzheimer's disease (p. 472)
disengagement theory of aging
    (p. 472)
activity theory of aging (p. 473)

15

PERSONALITY

John Gotti.

JOHN GOTTI

In many ways, John Gotti appears to be an ordinary enough fellow. He describes himself as a salesman who merchandises plumbing and heating supplies to builders and zippers to dressmakers. The paychecks from his business go right into his bank account each week. He lives in a modest home with a satellite dish on the roof. His friends say he's just an ordinary guy, and it wouldn't be at all surprising to find him at a local bar, drinking a few beers.

There's another side to Gotti, though. He frequents posh, expensive restaurants, wearing custom-made suits and designer socks. His hair is always freshly barbered, and his nails are meticulously manicured. If you met him at such a nightspot, you would probably view him as a rich, highly successful businessman. You might approach him for a contribution to your favorite charity, and you wouldn't be surprised to receive a generous donation.

But there may be yet another side to John Gotti. United States prosecutors, who have indicted him four times, see him as the head of a crime family similar to the one portrayed in *The Godfather.* They consider him to be an heir of gangster Albert Anastasia, who was the brains behind "Murder Inc." These prosecutors claim that Gotti is guilty of racketeering, assault, conspiracy, and robbery. To them and a jury that found him guilty of murder, he is a ruthless, immoral mobster (Barron, 1990).

LOOKING AHEAD

Will the real John Gotti please stand up?

Many people, like Gotti, have different sides to their personalities, appearing one way in certain situations and quite differently in others. At the same time, you probably know people whose behavior is so predictable that you can tell, almost without thinking, what they are going to do in a particular situation. These are people whose behavior is almost entirely consistent from one setting to the next.

Psychologists whose primary focus is seeking to understand the characteristic ways in which people behave specialize in the field of psychology known as **personality**. The term itself is used in two different, but related, ways. On the one hand, personality refers to the characteristics that differentiate people—those behaviors that make an individual unique. On the other hand, personality is used as a means of explaining the stability in people's behavior that leads them to act uniformly both in different situations and over extended periods of time.

In this chapter we consider a number of personality theories. We begin with the broadest and most comprehensive approach: Freud's psychoanalytic theory. Next, we turn to more recent theories of personality. We consider approaches that concentrate on identifying the most fundamental personality traits that differentiate one person from another; on theories that emphasize how personality is a set of learned behaviors; and on approaches, known as humanistic theories, that highlight the uniquely human aspects of personality. The chapter ends with a discussion of the ways in which personality is measured and the ways personality tests can be used.

Personality: The sum total of characteristics that differentiate people, or the stability in a person's behavior across different situations

After reading this chapter, you will have the answers to questions such as these:

- How do psychologists define and use the concept of personality?
- What is the structure and development of personality according to Freud and his successors?
- What are the major aspects of trait, learning, and humanistic theories of personality?
- How can we most accurately assess personality, and what are the major types of personality measures?

PSYCHOANALYTIC THEORIES OF PERSONALITY

Oscar Madison: sloppy, disheveled, unkempt.

Felix Unger: neat, precise, controlled.

As anyone who has seen the play or the old television series *The Odd Couple* can attest, Oscar and Felix are two people who could hardly seem to possess more dissimilar personalities. Yet to one group of personality theorists, psychoanalysts, the two men might actually be quite similar—at least in terms of the underlying part of personality that motivates their behavior. According to **psychoanalysts**, our behavior is triggered largely by powerful forces within personality of which we are not aware. These hidden forces, shaped by childhood experiences, play an important role in energizing and directing our everyday behavior.

The most important theorist to hold such a view, and indeed one of the best-known figures in all psychology, is Sigmund Freud. An Austrian physician, Freud was the originator of **psychoanalytic theory** in the early 1900s.

Psychoanalysts: Physicians or psychologists who specialize in psychoanalysis

Freud's Psychoanalytic Theory

The college student was intent on sounding smooth and making a good first impression with an attractive woman he had spotted across a crowded room at a party. As he walked toward her, he mulled over a line he had heard in an old movie the night before: "I don't believe we've been properly introduced yet." To his horror, what came out was a bit different. After threading his way through the crowded room, he finally reached the woman and blurted out, "I don't believe we've been properly seduced yet."

Although this may seem to be merely an embarrassing slip of the tongue, according to psychoanalytic theory such a mistake is not an error at all (Motley, 1987). Rather, it is an indication of deeply felt emotions and thoughts that are harbored in the **unconscious**, a part of the personality of which a person is not aware. Many of life's experiences are painful, and the unconscious provides a "safe" haven for our recollection of such events, a place where they can remain without continually disturbing us. Similarly, the unconscious contains **instinctual drives**: infantile wishes, desires, demands, and needs that are hidden from conscious awareness because of the conflicts and pain they would cause us if they were part of our everyday lives.

To Freud, conscious experience is just the tip of the iceberg; like the unseen mass of a floating iceberg, the material found in the unconscious dwarfs the information about which we are aware. Much of people's everyday behavior is viewed as being motivated by unconscious forces about which they know little.

Psychoanalytic theory: Freud's theory that unconscious forces act as determinants of personality

Unconscious: A part of the personality of which a person is unaware and which is a potential determinant of behavior

Instinctual drives: Infantile wishes, desires, demands, and needs hidden from conscious awareness

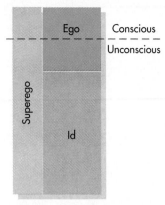

FIGURE 15-1

In Freud's model of personality, there are three major components: the id, the ego, and the superego. As the schematic shows, only a small portion of personality is conscious. This figure should not be thought of as an actual, physical structure, but rather as a model of the interrelationships between the parts of personality.

Id: The raw, unorganized, inherited part of personality whose purpose is to reduce tension created by biological drives and irrational impulses

Libido: Freud's term for the instinctive drives, or energies, that motivate behavior; the sexual energy underlying biological urges

Pleasure principle: The principle by which the id operates, in which the person seeks the immediate reduction of tension and the maximization of satisfaction

Ego: The part of personality that provides a buffer between the id and the outside world

Reality principle: The principle by which the ego operates, in which instinctual energy is retained in order to maintain an individual's safety and integration into society

For example, a child's concern over being unable to please his strict and demanding parents may lead him to have low self-esteem as an adult, although he may never understand why his accomplishments—which may be considerable—seem insufficient. Indeed, consciously the adult may recall his childhood with great pleasure; it is his unconscious, which holds the painful memories, that provokes the low self-evaluation.

According to Freud, to fully understand personality, it is necessary to illuminate and expose what is in the unconscious. But because the unconscious disguises the meaning of material it holds, it cannot be observed directly. It is therefore necessary to interpret clues to the unconscious—slips of the tongue, fantasies, and dreams—in order to understand the unconscious processes directing behavior. A slip of the tongue, such as the one quoted earlier, might be interpreted as revealing the speaker's underlying unconscious sexual desires.

If the notion of an unconscious does not seem so farfetched to most of us, it is only because Freudian theory has had such a widespread influence, with applications ranging from literature to religion. In Freud's day, however, the idea that the unconscious could harbor painful material from which people were protecting themselves was revolutionary, and the best minds of the time summarily rejected his ideas as being without basis and even laughable. That it is now so easy to accept the existence of a portion of personality about which people are unaware—and one that is responsible for much of our behavior—is a tribute to the influence of Freud's theory (Moore & Fine, 1990; Westen, 1990).

Structuring Personality: Id, Ego, and Superego.   To describe the structure of personality, Freud developed a comprehensive theory which held that personality consisted of three separate but interacting components: the id, the ego, and the superego. Although Freud described these in very concrete terms, it is important to realize that they are not actual physical structures found in a certain part of the brain. Instead, they represent aspects of a general *model* of personality that describes the interaction of various processes and forces within one's personality that motivate behavior. Yet Freud suggested that the three structures can be depicted diagrammatically to show how they are related to the conscious and the unconscious (see Figure 15-1).

If personality consisted only of primitive, instinctual cravings and longings, it would have but one component: the id. The **id** is the raw, unorganized, inherited part of personality whose sole purpose is to reduce tension created by primitive drives related to hunger, sex, aggression, and irrational impulses. These drives are fueled by "psychic energy" or **libido**, as Freud called it. The id operates according to the **pleasure principle**, in which the goal is the immediate reduction of tension and the maximization of satisfaction.

Unfortunately for the id—but luckily for people and society—reality prevents the demands of the pleasure principle from being fulfilled in most cases. Instead, the world produces constraints: We cannot always eat when we are hungry, and we can discharge our sexual drives only when time, place—and partner—are willing. To account for this fact of life, Freud suggested a second part of personality, which he called the ego.

The **ego** provides a buffer between the id and the realities of the objective, outside world. In contrast to the pleasure-seeking nature of the id, the ego operates according to the **reality principle**, in which instinctual energy is restrained in order to maintain the safety of the individual and help integrate the person into society. In a sense, then, the ego is the "executive" of personality: It makes decisions, controls actions, and allows thinking and problem solving of a higher

"We have to go now. Robert's façade is beginning to crumble."

Freud's theory suggests that an important part of personality lies under the surface.

order than the id is capable of. The ego is also the seat of higher cognitive abilities such as intelligence, thoughtfulness, reasoning, and learning.

The **superego**, the final personality structure to develop, represents the rights and wrongs of society as handed down by a person's parents, teachers, and other important figures. It becomes a part of personality when children learn right from wrong and continues to develop as people begin to incorporate into their own standards the broad moral principles of the society in which they live.

The superego actually has two parts, the **conscience** and the **ego-ideal**. The conscience *prevents* us from doing morally bad things, while the ego-ideal *motivates* us to do what is morally proper. The superego helps to control impulses coming from the id, making them less selfish and more virtuous.

Although on the surface the superego appears to be the opposite of the id, the two share an important feature: Both are unrealistic in that they do not consider the practical realities imposed by society. Thus the superego pushes the person toward greater virtue and, if left unchecked, it would create perfectionists who were unable to make the compromises that life requires. Similarly, an unrestrained id would create a primitive, pleasure-seeking, thoughtless individual, seeking to fulfill every desire without delay. The ego, then, must compromise between the demands of the superego and the id, permitting a person to obtain some of the gratification sought by the id while keeping the moralistic superego from preventing the gratification.

Developing Personality: A Stage Approach. Freud did not stop after describing the components of adult personality; his theory also provides a view of how personality develops throughout a series of stages during childhood.

What is especially noteworthy about the sequence is that it suggests how experiences and difficulties during a particular childhood stage may predict specific sorts of idiosyncrasies in adult personality. The theory is also unique in focusing each stage on a major biological function, which is assumed to be the focus of pleasure in a given period.

Superego: The part of personality that represents the morality of society as presented by parents, teachers, and others

Conscience: The part of the superego that prevents us from doing what is morally wrong

Ego-ideal: The part of the superego that motivates us to do what is morally proper

TABLE 15-1

THE STAGES OF PERSONALITY DEVELOPMENT ACCORDING TO FREUD'S PSYCHOANALYTIC THEORY

Stage	Age	Major characteristics
Oral	Birth to 12–18 months	Interest in oral gratification from sucking, eating, mouthing, biting
Anal	12–18 months to 3 years	Gratification from expelling and withholding feces; coming to terms with society's controls relating to toilet training
Phallic	3 to 5–6 years	Interest in the genitals; coming to terms with Oedipal conflict, leading to identification with same-sex parent
Latency	5–6 years to adolescence	Sexual concerns largely unimportant
Genital	Adolescence to adulthood	Reemergence of sexual interests and establishment of mature sexual relationships

This baby is going through a period that Freud would label the oral stage. An adult who has a fixation at this stage might eat or smoke excessively.

Oral stage: According to Freud, a stage from birth to from 12 to 18 months, in which an infant's center of pleasure is the mouth

Fixation: Behavior reflecting an earlier stage of development

Anal stage: According to Freud, a stage, from 12 to 18 months to 3 years of age, in which a child's pleasure is centered on the anus

Phallic stage: According to Freud, a period beginning around age 3 during which a child's interest focuses on the genitals

Oedipal (ED ih pul) **conflict:** A child's sexual interest in his or her opposite-sex parent, typically resolved through identification with the same-sex parent

Identification: A child's attempt to be similar to his or her same-sex parent

In the first period of development, called the **oral stage**, the baby's mouth is the focal point of pleasure (see Table 15-1 for a summary of the stages). During the first 12 to 18 months of life, children suck, mouth, and bite anything that will fit into their mouths. To Freud, this behavior suggested that the mouth was the primary site of a kind of sexual pleasure, and if infants were either overly indulged (perhaps by being fed every time they cried) or frustrated in their search for oral gratification, they might become fixated at this stage. Displaying **fixation** means that an adult shows personality characteristics that are related to an earlier stage of development. For example, fixation at the oral stage might produce an adult who was unusually interested in overtly oral activities—eating, talking, smoking—or who showed symbolic sorts of oral interests: being "bitingly" sarcastic or being very gullible ("swallowing" anything).

From around 12 to 18 months until 3 years of age—where the emphasis in most cultures is on toilet training—the child enters the **anal stage**. At this point, the major source of pleasure changes from the mouth to the anal region, and children derive considerable pleasure from both retention and expulsion of feces. If toilet training is particularly demanding, the result may be fixation. If fixation occurs during the anal stage, Freud suggested that adults might show unusual rigidity, orderliness, punctuality—or extreme disorderliness or sloppiness, as in our earlier examples of Oscar and Felix.

At about age 3, the **phallic stage** begins, at which point there is another major shift in the primary source of pleasure for the child. This time, interest focuses on the genitals and the pleasures derived from fondling them. This is also the stage of one of the most important points of personality development, according to Freudian theory: the **Oedipal conflict**. As children focus their attention on their genitals, the differences between male and female anatomy become more salient. Furthermore, at this time Freud believed that the male begins to develop sexual interests in his mother, starts to see his father as a rival, and harbors a wish to kill his father—as Oedipus did in the ancient Greek tragedy. But because he views his father as too powerful, he develops a fear of retaliation in the form of "castration anxiety." Ultimately, this fear becomes so powerful that the child represses his desires for his mother and instead chooses **identification** with his father, trying to be as much like him as possible.

For girls, the process is different. Freud reasoned that girls begin to feel sexual arousal toward their fathers and—in a suggestion that was later to bring serious, and not unreasonable, accusations that he viewed women as inferior to men—that they begin to experience **penis envy**. They wish they had the anatomical part that, at least to Freud, seemed most clearly "missing" in girls. Blaming their mothers for their lack of a penis, they come to believe that their mothers are responsible for their "castration." As with males, though, they find that in order to resolve such unacceptable feelings, they must identify with the same-sex parent by behaving like her and adopting her attitudes and values. In this way, a girl's identification with her mother is completed.

At this point, the Oedipal conflict is said to be resolved, and, if things have gone smoothly, Freudian theory assumes that both males and females move on to the next stage of development. If difficulties arise during this period, however, all sorts of problems are thought to occur, which include improper sex-role behavior and the failure to develop a conscience.

Following the resolution of the Oedipal conflict, typically at around age 5 or 6, children move into the **latency period**, which lasts until puberty. During this period, little of interest is occurring, according to Freud; sexual concerns are more or less put to rest, even in the unconscious. Then, during adolescence, sexual feelings reemerge, marking the start of the final period, the **genital stage**, which extends until death. The focus in the genital stage is on mature, adult sexuality, which Freud defined as sexual intercourse.

Defense Mechanisms. Freud's efforts to describe and theorize about the underlying dynamics of personality and its development were motivated by very practical problems that his patients faced in dealing with **anxiety**, an intense, negative emotional experience. According to Freud, anxiety is a danger signal to the ego. Although anxiety may arise from realistic fears—such as seeing a poisonous snake about to strike—it may also occur in the form of **neurotic anxiety**, in which irrational impulses emanating from the id threaten to burst through and become uncontrollable. Because anxiety, naturally, is unpleasant, Freud believed that people develop a range of defense mechanisms to deal with it. **Defense mechanisms** are unconscious strategies people use to reduce anxiety by concealing the source from themselves and others (Cramer, 1987; Cooper, 1989).

The primary defense mechanism is **repression**, in which unacceptable or unpleasant id impulses are pushed back into the unconscious. Repression is the most direct method of dealing with anxiety; instead of handling an anxiety-producing impulse on a conscious level, one simply ignores it. For example, a college student who feels hatred for her mother might repress these personally and socially unacceptable feelings. They remain lodged within the id, since acknowledging them would be so anxiety-provoking. This does not mean, however, that they have no effect: True feelings might be revealed through dreams, slips of the tongue, or symbolically in some other fashion. The student might, for instance, have difficulty with authority figures such as teachers and do poorly in school. Alternatively, she might join the military, where she could give harsh orders to others without having them questioned.

If repression is ineffective in keeping anxiety at bay, other defense mechanisms may be called upon. For example, **regression** might be used, whereby people behave as if they were at an earlier stage of development. By retreating to a younger age—for instance by complaining and throwing tantrums—they might succeed in having fewer demands put upon them.

Penis envy: According to Freud, a girl's wish, developing around age 3, that she had a penis

Latency period: According to Freud, the period, between the phallic stage and puberty, during which children's sexual concerns are temporarily put aside

Genital stage: According to Freud, a period, from puberty until death, marked by mature sexual behavior (i.e., sexual intercourse)

Anxiety: A feeling of apprehension or tension

Neurotic anxiety: Anxiety caused when irrational impulses from the id threaten to become uncontrollable

Defense mechanisms: Unconscious strategies people use to reduce anxiety by concealing its source from themselves and others

Repression: The primary defense mechanism, in which unacceptable or unpleasant id impulses are pushed back into the unconscious

Regression: Behavior reminiscent of an earlier stage of development, carried out as a defense mechanism in order to have fewer demands put upon oneself

Displacement: The expression of an unwanted feeling or thought, directed toward a weaker person

Rationalization: A defense mechanism whereby people justify a negative situation in a way that protects their self-esteem

Denial: A defense mechanism through which people refuse to accept or acknowledge anxiety-producing information

Projection: A defense mechanism in which people attribute their own inadequacies or faults to someone else

Sublimation: A defense mechanism, considered healthy by Freud, in which a person diverts unwanted impulses into socially acceptable thoughts, feelings, or behaviors

Anyone who has ever been angered by the unfairness of a professor and then returned to the dorm and yelled at his or her roommate knows what displacement is all about. In **displacement**, the expression of an unwanted feeling or thought is redirected from a more threatening, powerful person to a weaker one. A classic case is yelling at one's secretary after being criticized by the boss.

Rationalization, another defense mechanism, occurs when we distort reality by justifying what happens to us. We develop explanations that allow us to protect our self-esteem. If you've ever heard someone say that he didn't mind being stood up for a date because he really had a lot of work to do that evening, you have probably seen rationalization at work.

In **denial**, a person simply refuses to accept or acknowledge an anxiety-producing piece of information. For example, when told that his wife has died in an automobile crash, a husband may at first deny the tragedy, saying that there must be some mistake, and only gradually come to conscious acceptance that she actually has been killed. In extreme cases, denial may linger; the husband may continue to expect that his wife will return home.

Projection is a means of protecting oneself by attributing unwanted impulses and feelings to someone else. For example, a man who feels sexually inadequate may complain to his wife that *she* is sexually inept.

Finally, one defense mechanism that Freud considered to be particularly healthy and socially acceptable is sublimation. In **sublimation**, people divert unwanted impulses into socially approved thoughts, feelings, or behaviors. For example, a person with strong feelings of aggression may become a butcher—and hack away at meat instead of people. Sublimation allows the butcher the opportunity not only to release psychic tension but to do so in a way that is socially acceptable.

All of us employ defense mechanisms to some degree, according to Freudian theory. Yet some people use them so much that a large amount of psychic energy must constantly be directed toward hiding and rechanneling unacceptable impulses, making everyday living difficult. In this case, the result is "neurosis," Freud's term for mental disorders produced by anxiety.

Evaluating Freudian Theory.   More than almost any other psychological theory we have discussed, Freud's personality theory presents an elaborate and complicated set of propositions—some of which are so removed from everyday explanations of behavior that they may appear difficult to accept. But laypeople are not the only ones to be concerned about the validity of Freud's theory; personality psychologists, too, have criticized its inadequacies.

Among the most compelling criticisms is the lack of scientific data to support the theory. Although there are a wealth of individual assessments of particular people that *seem* to support the theory, we lack definitive evidence showing that the personality is structured and operates along the lines Freud laid out—due, in part, to the fact that Freud's conception of personality is built on unobservable abstractions. Moreover, while we can readily employ Freudian theory in after-the-fact explanations, it is extremely difficult to predict how certain developmental difficulties will be displayed in the adult. For instance, if a person is fixated at the anal stage, he might, according to Freud, be unusually messy—or he might be unusually neat. Freud's theory offers no guidance for predicting which manifestations of the difficulty will occur. It produces good history, then, but not such good science. Finally, Freud made his observations—albeit insightful ones—and derived his theory from a limited population: primarily upper-class Austrian women living in the strict, puritanical era of the early 1900s. How far one can generalize beyond this population is a matter of considerable question.

Despite these criticisms, which cannot be dismissed, Freud's theory has had an enormous impact on the field of psychology—and indeed on all of western thinking. The ideas of the unconscious, anxiety, defense mechanisms, and the childhood causes of adult psychological difficulties have permeated people's views of the world and their understanding of the causes of their own behavior and that of others.

Furthermore, Freud's emphasis on the unconscious has been partially supported by some of the current research findings of cognitive psychologists. This work has revealed that mental processes about which people are unaware have an important impact on thinking and actions. In addition, new experimental techniques have been developed that allow the unconscious to be studied in a more scientifically sophisticated manner, overcoming the reliance of traditional Freudian approaches on single-subject case studies and unconfirmable theoretical interpretations of dreams and slips of the tongue for support (Kihlstrom, 1987; Kline, 1987; Westen, 1990).

The importance of psychoanalytic theory is underscored by the fact that it spawned a significant—and enduring—method of treating psychological disturbances, as we will discuss further in Chapter 18. For a variety of reasons, then, Freud's psychoanalytic theory remains a significant contribution to our understanding of personality.

The Neo-Freudian Psychoanalysts

One particularly important outgrowth of Freud's theorizing was the work done by a series of successors who were trained in traditional Freudian theory but who later strayed from some of its major points. These theorists are known as **neo-Freudian psychoanalysts**.

The neo-Freudians placed greater emphasis than Freud did on the functions of the ego, suggesting that it had more control than the id over day-to-day activities. They also paid greater attention to social factors and the effects of society and culture on personality development. Carl Jung (pronounced "yoong"), for example, who initially adhered closely to Freud's thinking, later rejected the notion of the primary importance of unconscious sexual urges—a key notion of Freudian theory—and instead looked at the primitive urges of the unconscious more positively. He suggested that people had a **collective unconscious**, a set of influences we inherit from our own particular ancestors, the whole human race, and even animal ancestors from the distant past. This collective unconscious is shared by everyone and is displayed by behavior that is common across diverse cultures—such as love of mother, belief in a supreme being, and even behavior as specific as fear of snakes.

Jung went on to propose that the collective unconscious contained **archetypes**, universal symbolic representations of a particular person, object, or experience. For instance, a mother archetype, which contains reflections of our ancestors' relationships with mother figures, is suggested by the prevalence of mothers in art, religion, literature, and mythology. (Think of the Virgin Mary, Earth Mother, wicked stepmothers of fairy tales, Mother's Day, and so forth!)

To Jung, archetypes play an important role in determining our day-to-day reactions, attitudes, and values. For instance, Jung might explain the popularity of a movie such as *Batman* as being due to its use of broad archetypes of good (Batman), evil (the Joker), and innocence (Vicki Vail).

Neo-Freudian psychoanalysts (neo-Freudians): Theorists who place greater emphasis than Freud did on the functions of the ego and its influence on our daily activities

Collective unconscious: A concept developed by Jung proposing that we inherit certain personality characteristics from our ancestors and the human race as a whole

Archetypes: According to Jung, universal, symbolic representations of a particular person, object, or experience

In Jungian terms, Batman and The Joker represent the archetypes of good and evil.

Inferiority complex: A phenomenon whereby adults have continuing feelings of weakness and insecurity

Alfred Adler, another important neo-Freudian psychoanalyst, also considered Freudian theory's emphasis on sexual needs as misplaced. Instead, Adler proposed that the primary human motivation was a striving for superiority, not in terms of superiority over others, but as a quest to achieve self-improvement and perfection. Adler used the term **inferiority complex** to describe situations in which adults have not been able to overcome the feelings of inferiority that they developed as children, when they were small and limited in their knowledge about the world. Early social relationships with parents have an important effect on how well children are able to outgrow feelings of personal inferiority and instead orient themselves toward attaining more socially useful goals such as improving society.

Other neo-Freudians, such as Erik Erikson (whose theory we discussed in Chapters 13 and 14) and Karen Horney (1937), also focused less than Freud on inborn sexual and aggressive motivation and more on the social and cultural factors behind personality. Horney, for example, suggested that personality develops in terms of social relationships and depends particularly on the relationship between parents and child and how well the child's needs were met. She rejected Freud's suggestion that women had penis envy, asserting that what women envied most in men was not their anatomy but the independence, success, and freedom that women were often denied. Horney was one of the first feminist psychologists.

RECAP AND REVIEW I

RECAP

◄ Freud's psychoanalytic theory proposes that many deeply felt emotions, feelings, and thoughts are found in the unconscious, the part of personality of which a person is unaware. Personality consists of three components: the id, the ego, and the superego.

◄ According to psychoanalytic theory, personality develops during a series of stages in which the focus of pleasure is on a particular part of the body. The stages are the oral, anal, phallic (which leads to the Oedipal conflict), latency, and genital stages.

- Defense mechanisms are unconscious strategies that people use to reduce anxiety by concealing its source. Among the most important are repression, regression, displacement, rationalization, projection, and sublimation.
- Although Freud's theory may be criticized on a number of grounds—including its inability to be scientifically tested and its failure to permit clear-cut predictions rather than after-the-fact explanations—it has been enormously influential.
- Among the neo-Freudian psychoanalysts who built and modified psychoanalytic theory are Jung, who developed the concepts of the collective unconscious and archetypes, Adler, who coined the term "inferiority complex," and Horney, who viewed personality development in terms of social relationships.

REVIEW

1. _____ theory states that behavior is motivated primarily by unconscious forces.
2. According to Freud's theory, the best means to determine the underlying causes of behavior is to directly examine the unconscious. True or false?

_____

3. Match each section of the personality (according to Freud) with its description:

   1. _____ Ego
   2. _____ Id
   3. _____ Superego

   a. Determines right from wrong on the basis of cultural standards
   b. Operates according to the "reality principle"; energy is redirected to integrate the person into society
   c. Seeks to reduce tension brought on by primitive drives

4. Within the superego, the _____ - _____ motivates us to do what is right, while the _____ prevents us from doing what is unacceptable.
5. Which of the following represents the proper order of personality development according to Freud?
   a. Oral, phallic, latency, anal, genital
   b. Anal, oral, phallic, genital, latency
   c. Oral, anal, phallic, latency, genital
   d. Latency, phallic, anal, genital, oral
6. In the resolution of the _____ complex, Freud believed that boys learn to repress their desire for their mother and identify with their father.
7. _____ _____ is the term Freud used to describe unconscious strategies used to reduce anxiety.
8. _____ occurs when unacceptable impulses are pushed into the unconscious, where they do not have to be dealt with. In _____, a person may simply not accept that a traumatic event has occurred. Finally, in _____, a person may retreat to an earlier stage of development in order to avoid current problems.
9. Your friend tells you that whenever he gets really angry, he goes to the gym and works out very strenuously until he feels better. Which of Freud's defense mechanisms might this behavior represent?
10. According to Jung, sexual urges are less important than the urges of the _____ _____, a vast set of influences inherited from our ancestors.

Ask Yourself
How might we be able to prevent fixation from occurring during childhood?

(Answers to review questions are on page 490.)

TRAIT, LEARNING, AND HUMANISTIC APPROACHES: IN SEARCH OF PERSONALITY

"Tell me about Lee," said Sue.

"Oh, he's just terrific. He's the friendliest guy I know—goes out of his way to be nice to everyone. He hardly ever gets mad. He's just so even-tempered, no matter what's happening. And he's really smart, too. About the only thing I don't like is that he's always in such a hurry to get things done; he seems to have boundless energy, much more than I have."

"He sounds great to me, especially in comparison to Richard," replied Sue. "He is so self-centered and arrogant it drives me crazy. I sometimes wonder why I ever started going out with him."

Friendly. Even-tempered. Smart. Energetic. Self-centered. Arrogant.

If we were to analyze the conversation printed above, the first thing we would notice is that it is made up of a series of trait characterizations of the two people being discussed. In fact, most of our understanding of the reasons behind others' behavior is based on the premise that people possess certain traits that are assumed to be consistent across different situations. A number of formal theories of personality employ variants of this approach. We turn now to a discussion of these and other personality theories, all of which provide alternatives to the psychoanalytic emphasis on unconscious processes in determining behavior.

Trait Theories: Labeling Personality

If someone were to ask you to characterize another person, it is probable that—like the two people in the conversation just presented—you would come up with a list of that individual's personal qualities, as you see them. But how would you know which of these qualities were most important in determining the person's behavior?

Personality psychologists have asked similar questions themselves. In order to answer them, they have developed a sophisticated model of personality known as **trait theory**. **Traits** are enduring dimensions of personality characteristics along which people differ.

Trait theorists do not assume that some people have a trait and others do not; rather, they propose that all people have certain traits, but that the degree to which the trait applies to a specific person varies and can be quantified. For instance, you might be relatively friendly, whereas I might be relatively unfriendly. But we both have a "friendliness" trait, although you would be quantified with a higher score and I with a lower one. The major challenge for trait theorists taking this approach has been to identify the specific primary traits necessary to describe personality. As we shall see, different theorists have come up with surprisingly different sets.

Trait theory: A model that seeks to identify the basic traits necessary to describe personality

Traits: Enduring dimensions of personality characteristics differentiating people from one another

Allport's Trait Theory: Identifying the Basics.   When personality psychologist Gordon Allport carefully leafed through an unabridged dictionary, he came up with some 18,000 separate terms that could be used to describe personality. Although he was able to pare down the list to a mere 4500 descriptors after eliminating synonyms, he obviously was still left with a problem crucial to all trait theories: Which of these were the most basic?

Allport answered this question by suggesting that there are three basic categories of traits: cardinal, central, and secondary (Allport, 1961, 1966). A **cardinal trait** is a single characteristic that directs most of a person's activities. For example, a totally selfless woman might direct all her energy toward humanitarian activities; an intensely power-hungry person might be driven by an all-consuming need for control.

Most people, however, do not develop all-encompassing cardinal traits; instead, they possess a handful of central traits that make up the core of personality. **Central traits**, such as honesty and sociability, are the major characteristics of the individual; they usually number from five to ten in any one person. Finally, **secondary traits** are characteristics that affect behavior in fewer situations and are less influential than central or cardinal traits. For instance, a preference for ice cream or a dislike of modern art would be considered a secondary trait.

Cardinal trait: A single personality trait that directs most of a person's activities (e.g., greed, lust, kindness)

Central traits: A set of major characteristics that make up the core of a person's personality

Secondary traits: Less important personality traits (e.g., preferences for certain clothes or movies) that do not affect behavior as much as central and cardinal traits do

The Theories of Cattell and Eysenck: Factoring Out Personality.   More recent attempts at discovering primary traits have centered on a statistical technique

---

ANSWERS (REVIEW I):
1. Psychoanalytic   **2.** False; the unconscious cannot be directly observed.   **3.** 1-b; 2-c; 3-a   **4.** ego-ideal; conscience   **5.** c   **6.** Oedipal   **7.** Defense mechanisms   **8.** Repression; denial; regression   **9.** Sublimation   **10.** collective unconscious

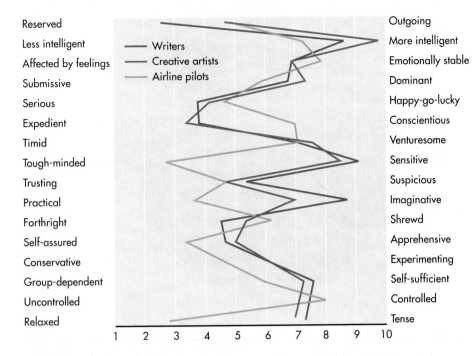

	Reserved											Outgoing
	Less intelligent											More intelligent
	Affected by feelings											Emotionally stable
	Submissive											Dominant
	Serious											Happy-go-lucky
	Expedient											Conscientious
	Timid											Venturesome
	Tough-minded											Sensitive
	Trusting											Suspicious
	Practical											Imaginative
	Forthright											Shrewd
	Self-assured											Apprehensive
	Conservative											Experimenting
	Group-dependent											Self-sufficient
	Uncontrolled											Controlled
	Relaxed											Tense

— Writers
— Creative artists
— Airline pilots

1 2 3 4 5 6 7 8 9 10

FIGURE 15-2
Personality profiles for source traits developed by Cattell for three groups of subjects: airline pilots, creative artists, and writers. The average score for the general population is between 4.5 and 6.5 on each scale. (Adapted from *Handbook for the 16PF*. Copyright 1970 by the Institute for Personality and Ability Testing. Reproduced by permission.)

known as factor analysis. **Factor analysis** is a method of summarizing the relationships among a large number of variables into fewer, more general patterns. For example, a personality researcher might administer a questionnaire to many subjects, asking them to describe themselves along an extensive list of traits. By statistically combining responses and computing which traits are associated with one another in the same person, a researcher can identify the most fundamental patterns or combinations of traits—called factors—that underlie subjects' responses.

Using factor analysis, personality psychologist Raymond Cattell (1965) suggested that the characteristics that can be observed in a given situation represent forty-six **surface traits**, or clusters of related behaviors. For example, you might encounter a friendly, gregarious librarian who goes out of his way to be helpful to you, and from your interactions with him decide that he possesses the trait of sociability—in Cattell's terms, a surface trait.

However, such surface traits are based on people's perceptions and representations of personality; they do not necessarily provide the best description of the underlying personality dimensions that are at the root of all behavior. Carrying out further factor analysis, Cattell found that sixteen **source traits** represented the basic dimensions of personality. Using these source traits, he developed the Sixteen Personality Factor Questionnaire, or 16 PF, a measure that provides scores for each of the source traits. Figure 15-2 shows the pattern of average scores on each of the source traits for three different groups of subjects—airplane pilots, creative artists, and writers.

Another trait theorist, psychologist Hans Eysenck (1975; Eysenck & Eysenck, 1985), also used factor analysis to identify patterns within traits, but he came to a very different conclusion about the nature of personality. He found that personality could best be described in terms of just two major dimensions: **introversion-extroversion** and **neuroticism-stability**. On the one extreme of the introversion-extroversion dimension are people who are quiet, careful, thoughtful, and restrained (the introverts), and on the other are those who are outgoing,

Factor analysis: A statistical technique for combining traits into broader, more general patterns of consistency

Surface traits: According to Cattell, clusters of a person's related behaviors that can be observed in a given situation

Source traits: The sixteen basic dimensions of personality that Cattell identified as the root of all behavior

Introversion-extroversion: According to Eysenck, a dimension of personality traits encompassing shyness to sociability

Neuroticism-stability: Eysenck's personality spectrum of traits encompassing moodiness to even-temperedness

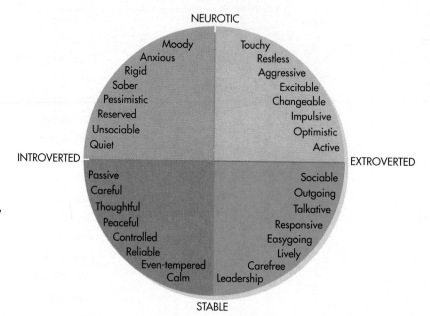

FIGURE 15-3

According to Eysenck, personality can be viewed as lying along two major dimensions: introversion-extroversion and neuroticism-stability. Other personality characteristics can be ordered along the circular figure depicted here. (Eysenck, 1973.)

sociable, and active (the extroverts). Independent of that, people can be rated as neurotic (moody, touchy, sensitive) versus stable (calm, reliable, even-tempered). By evaluating people along these two dimensions, Eysenck has been able to predict behavior accurately in a variety of types of situations (see Figure 15-3).

The most recent research on traits suggests that five broad trait factors lie at the core of personality. The five are surgency (extraversion and sociability), neuroticism (emotional stability), intellect, agreeableness, and conscientiousness (Digman, 1990; Funder, 1991; Goldberg, 1990). Still, despite a growing consensus among trait theorists on the importance of these five factors, the evidence is far from conclusive. Consequently, the specific number and kinds of traits remain a source of debate (and investigation) among trait theorists.

Evaluating Trait Theories of Personality.   Trait theories have several virtues. They provide a clear, straightforward explanation of people's behavioral consistencies. Furthermore, traits allow us to readily compare one person with another. Because of these advantages, trait conceptions of personality have had an important practical influence on the development of several personality measures that we discuss later in the chapter (Buss, 1989; Funder, 1991).

On the other hand, trait theories have several drawbacks. For example, we have seen that various trait theories describing personality come to quite different conclusions about which traits are the most fundamental and descriptive. The difficulty in determining which of the theories is most accurate has led some personality psychologists to question the validity of trait conceptions of personality in general.

Actually, there is an even more fundamental difficulty with trait approaches. Even if we are able to identify a set of primary traits, we are left with little more than a label or description of personality—rather than an explanation of behavior. If we say that someone donates money to charity because he or she has the trait of generosity, we still do not know *why* the person became generous in the first place, or the reasons for displaying generosity in a given situation. In the view of some critics, then, traits do not provide explanations for behavior; they merely describe it.

Is Personality a Myth? Personality Versus Situational Factors. The objections to trait theories of personality have led some psychologists to pose a question that is fundamental to the entire area of personality: Is behavior really consistent over different situations, as trait conceptions would imply? How, for instance, would a trait theorist explain John Gotti's behavior described at the beginning of this chapter? Trying to answer this question has provided personality psychologists with one of its most vexing and controversial problems.

When personality psychologist Walter Mischel began to review the literature on the strength of the relationship between people's personality traits and their behavior in the late 1960s, he found a curious situation: Broad personality traits could be used to explain only a minor, insignificant portion of behavior. Instead, it seemed to Mischel that most behavior could be explained primarily by the nature of the situation in which people found themselves—not by their personalities (Mischel, 1968).

Mischel's views fanned the flames of a raging controversy that continues to be one of the major issues dividing personality theorists: the degree to which people's behavior is caused by personality versus situational factors. On one side of the controversy are traditional personality theorists who argue that traits, if measured appropriately, provide a valid explanation of behavior across diverse situations. For instance, Seymour Epstein (Epstein & O'Brien, 1985) argued that it is necessary to consider behavior over repeated settings and times to get a true picture of the degree of consistency displayed. When this was done—a group of subjects were repeatedly assessed over a period of months—there were strong indications of consistency, contrary to Mischel's suggestions.

In response, Mischel has argued that even though his critics may have demonstrated consistency over time, they have not shown consistency over situations. For instance, an office supervisor may be verbally aggressive toward her staff day in and day out, thereby showing consistency over time, but may not be verbally aggressive toward her boss—demonstrating *in*consistency over situations. It is this inconsistency across situations that makes personality-trait approaches suspect to Mischel (Mischel & Peake, 1982a, 1982b; Mischel, 1990).

Although the controversy shows little indication of abating, several important facts have emerged as a result of it (Kenrick & Funder, 1988; Funder & Colvin, 1991). Trait ratings are most accurate when they are done by raters who are thoroughly familiar with the person being rated; when multiple ratings and multiple raters are used; and when the observed behavior is directly relevant to the trait in question. On the other hand, lower accuracy is apt to be achieved in situations in which only one sample of behavior is observed or in which powerful forces are pushing an individual toward certain behavior. Thus, when a sergeant orders a private to peel potatoes, the subsequent behavior could hardly be viewed as an indication of a trait relating to the private's culinary interest.

The controversy has also led personality theorists to focus more directly on the nature of person-situation interactions—how the characteristics of a situation will influence the behavior of an individual with a specific type of personality. By considering such person-situation interactions, personality psychologists are developing a more accurate portrait of the role of personality in the particular situations and environments that are part of people's everyday lives (Kenrick & Funder, 1988; Funder & Colvin, 1991).

Finally, the person-situation debate has persuaded some researchers of the importance of focusing on the factors that produce specific traits in the first place. In particular, some researchers are examining the relative contributions of heredity and environment in forming traits.

When observing behavior, we need to consider the extent to which the behavior is voluntary. A student's enrollment in Introductory Psychology, for example, would not necessarily indicate an interest in psychology if this course were required for the completion of a degree.

For example, personality psychologists Auke Tellegen and colleagues at the University of Minnesota have been examining the personality traits of some 350 pairs of twins (Tellegen et al., 1988). Forty-four of the pairs were genetically identical but raised apart from each other, providing the opportunity to determine the influence of genetic factors on personality. Each of the twins was given a battery of personality tests, including one that measured eleven key personality traits. The results of the tests indicated that in major respects the twins were quite similar in personality. Moreover, certain traits were more influenced by heredity than others. For example, social potency (the degree to which a person takes mastery and leadership roles in social situations) and traditionalism (the following of authority) had particularly strong genetic components, whereas achievement and social closeness had relatively weak genetic components (see Figure 15-4).

Other studies support Tellegen's findings and suggest that the expression of both altruism and aggression is affected by heredity (Rushton, Fulker, Neale, Nias & Eysenck, 1986). Even human sexuality, political attitudes (at least in terms of basic conservatism and authoritarianism), and religious interests and values have strong genetic components (Eysenck, 1976; Eaves & Eysenck, 1974; Waller et al., 1990).

It seems, then, that heredity plays an important role in determining an individual's personality. Does this mean that parental influence and other environmental factors are of only minor importance? The answer is a clear no, since parents and other figures in the child's environment shape the extent to which traits produced by heredity assert themselves (Loehlin, Willerman & Horn, 1987; Rose et al., 1988). It is possible, for instance, to reduce the degree to which children high in self-absorption display that trait by exposing them to experiences with other children. Similarly, highly assertive children might be helped to temper their assertiveness through experiences that make them more aware of the feelings of others.

It is important to keep in mind that the final chapter in the controversies regarding the importance of traits and the consistency of behavior across situa-

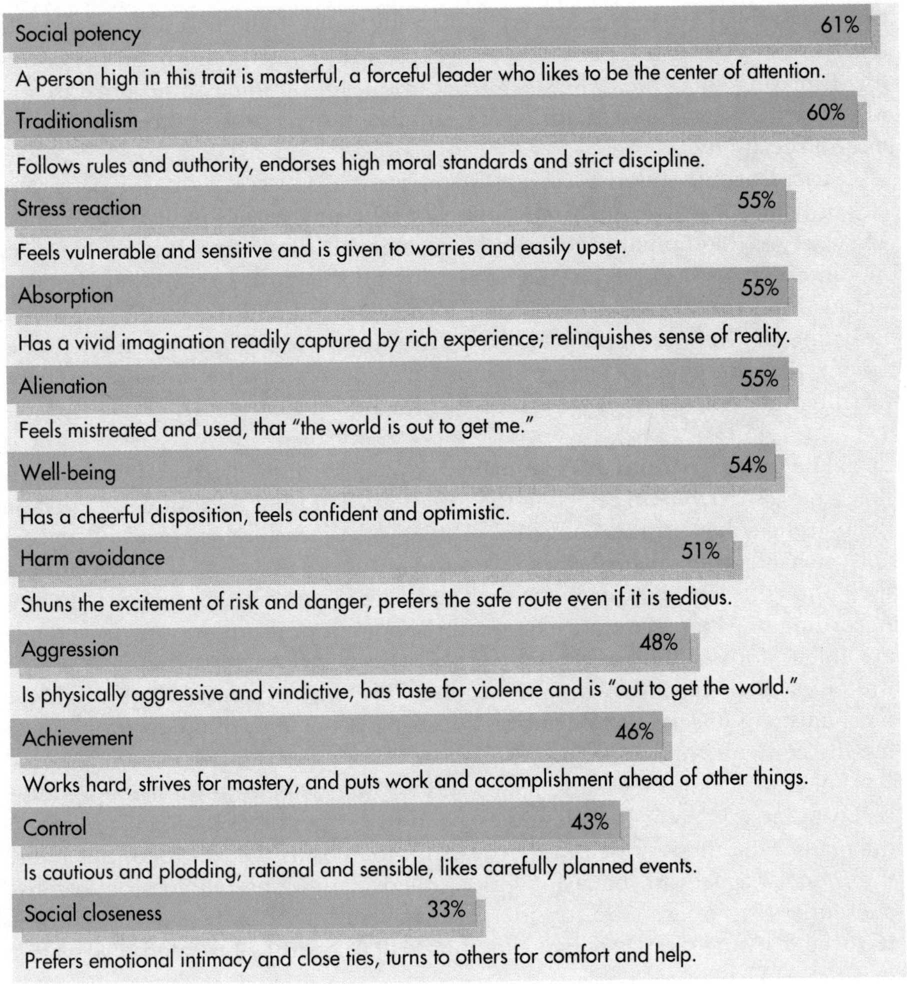

Social potency	61%

A person high in this trait is masterful, a forceful leader who likes to be the center of attention.

Traditionalism	60%

Follows rules and authority, endorses high moral standards and strict discipline.

Stress reaction	55%

Feels vulnerable and sensitive and is given to worries and easily upset.

Absorption	55%

Has a vivid imagination readily captured by rich experience; relinquishes sense of reality.

Alienation	55%

Feels mistreated and used, that "the world is out to get me."

Well-being	54%

Has a cheerful disposition, feels confident and optimistic.

Harm avoidance	51%

Shuns the excitement of risk and danger, prefers the safe route even if it is tedious.

Aggression	48%

Is physically aggressive and vindictive, has taste for violence and is "out to get the world."

Achievement	46%

Works hard, strives for mastery, and puts work and accomplishment ahead of other things.

Control	43%

Is cautious and plodding, rational and sensible, likes carefully planned events.

Social closeness	33%

Prefers emotional intimacy and close ties, turns to others for comfort and help.

FIGURE 15-4

The roots of personality. The percentages indicate the degree to which eleven major personality characteristics reflect the influence of heredity. (Tellegen et al., 1988.)

tions has yet to be written. Furthermore, some personality psychologists, such as the learning theorists whose work we turn to next, find the debate largely irrelevant. Rejecting the notion that a concept of traits is even necessary, they turn to the basic principles of learning to explain personality.

Learning Theories of Personality

Whereas psychoanalytic and trait theories concentrate on the inner person—the stormy fury of an unobservable but powerful id or a hypothetical but critical set of traits—learning theories of personality focus on the outer person. In fact, to a strict learning theorist, personality is simply the sum of learned responses to the external environment. Internal events such as thoughts, feelings, and motivations are ignored; though their existence is not denied, learning theorists say that personality is best understood by looking at features of a person's environment.

According to the most influential of the learning theorists, B. F. Skinner (whom we discussed first in terms of operant conditioning in Chapter 7), personality is a collection of learned behavior patterns (Skinner, 1975). Similarities in responses across different situations are caused by similar patterns of reinforcement that have been received in such situations in the past. If I am sociable both at parties and at meetings, it is because I have been reinforced previously for displaying social behaviors—not because I am fulfilling some unconscious wish based on experiences during my childhood or because I have an internal trait of sociability.

Strict learning theorists such as Skinner are less interested in the consistencies in behavior across situations, however, than in ways of modifying behavior. Their view is that humans are infinitely changeable. If one is able to control and modify the patterns of reinforcers in a situation, behavior that other theorists would view as stable and unyielding can be changed and ultimately improved. Learning theorists are optimistic in their attitudes about the potential for resolving personal and societal problems through treatment strategies based on learning theory—methods we will discuss further in Chapter 18.

Social Learning Theories of Personality. Not all learning theories of personality take such a strict view in rejecting the importance of what is "inside" the person by focusing solely on the "outside." Unlike other learning theories of personality, **social learning theory** emphasizes the influence of a person's cognitions—their thoughts, feelings, expectations, and values—in determining personality. According to Albert Bandura, the main proponent of this point of view, people are able to foresee the possible outcomes of certain behaviors in a given setting without actually having to carry them out. This takes place mainly through the mechanism of **observational learning**—viewing the actions of others and observing the consequences (Bandura, 1977).

For instance, as we first discussed in Chapter 7, children who view a model behaving in, say, an aggressive manner tend to copy the behavior if the consequences of the model's behavior are seen to be positive. If, on the other hand, the model's aggressive behavior has resulted in no consequences or negative consequences, children are considerably less likely to act aggressively. According to social learning theory, personality thus is developed by repeated observation of others' behavior.

Bandura places particular emphasis on the role played by **self-efficacy**, learned expectations regarding success, in determining the behavior we display. Self-efficacy underlies people's faith in their ability to carry out a behavior, regardless of how successful they have been in the past or what barriers currently lie in their paths. The greater a person's sense of self-efficacy, the more likely it is that success will take place. For instance, people with a high sense of self-efficacy regarding academic accomplishments will be more likely to achieve academic success.

Compared with other learning explanations of personality, social learning theories are distinctive in the emphasis they place on the reciprocity between individuals and their environment. Not only is the environment assumed to affect personality, but people's behavior and personalities are assumed to "feed back" and modify the environment—which in turn affects behavior in a web of reciprocity.

In fact, Bandura has suggested that reciprocal determinism is the key to understanding behavior. In **reciprocal determinism**, it is the interaction of environment, behavior, and individual that ultimately causes people to behave in the ways that they do (Bandura, 1981, 1986). For instance, a man with aggressive needs may get into a fight at a hockey game. He may later seek out hockey games in order to fulfill his enjoyment of fighting. At the same time, the drive to be aggressive may increase because of his fighting. In sum, the environment of the

Social learning theory: The theory that suggests that personality develops through observational learning

Observational learning: Learning that is the result of viewing the actions of others and observing the consequences

Self-efficacy: The theory that people's learned expectations regarding success determine their behavior

Reciprocal determinism: The view that the interaction of environment, behavior, and the individual causes people to behave the way that they do

hockey game, the behavior of fighting, and the individual's characteristics interact with one another in a reciprocal fashion.

Evaluating Learning Theories of Personality. By ignoring the internal processes that are uniquely human, traditional learning theorists such as Skinner have been accused of oversimplifying personality so much that the concept becomes meaningless. In fact, reducing behavior to a series of stimuli and responses, and excluding thoughts and feelings from the realm of personality, leaves behaviorists practicing an unrealistic and inadequate form of science, in the eyes of their critics.

Of course, some of these criticisms are blunted by social learning theory, which explicitly considers the role of cognitive processes in personality. Still, all learning theories share a highly **deterministic** view of human behavior, a view maintaining that behavior is shaped primarily by forces outside the control of the individual. In the eyes of some critics, determinism disregards the ability of people to pilot their own course through life.

On the other hand, learning approaches have had a major impact in a variety of ways. For one thing, they have helped make the study of personality an objective, scientific venture by focusing on observable features of people and the environments in which they live. Beyond this, learning theories have produced important, successful means of treating personality disorders. The degree of success these treatments have enjoyed provides confidence that learning theory approaches have merit.

Determinism: The view suggesting that people's behavior is shaped primarily by factors outside their control

Humanistic Theories of Personality

Where, in all these theories of personality, is an explanation for the saintliness of a Mother Teresa, the creativity of a Michelangelo, the brilliance and perseverance of an Einstein? An understanding of such unique individuals—as well as more ordinary sorts of people who share some of the same attributes—comes from humanistic theory.

According to humanistic theorists, all of the theories of personality that we have previously discussed share a fundamental misperception in their views of human nature. Instead of seeing people as controlled by unconscious, unseen forces (as does psychoanalytic theory), a set of stable traits (trait theory), or situational reinforcements and punishments (learning theory), **humanistic theory** emphasizes people's basic goodness and their tendency to grow to higher levels of functioning. It is this conscious, self-motivated ability to change and improve, along with people's unique creative impulses, that make up the core of personality.

The major representative of the humanistic point of view is Carl Rogers (1971). Rogers suggests that people have a need for positive regard that reflects a universal requirement to be loved and respected. Because others provide this positive regard, we grow dependent on them. We begin to see and judge ourselves through the eyes of other people, relying on their values.

According to Rogers, one outgrowth of placing import on the values of others is that there is often some degree of mismatch between a person's experiences and his or her **self-concept**, or self-impression. If the discrepancy is minor, so are the consequences. But if it is great, it will lead to psychological disturbances in daily functioning, such as the experience of frequent anxiety.

Rogers suggests that one way of overcoming the discrepancy between experience and self-concept is through the receipt of unconditional positive regard

Humanistic theory: The theory that emphasizes people's basic goodness and their natural tendency to rise to higher levels of functioning

Self-concept: The impression one holds of oneself

According to Carl Rogers, people have a need for love and respect. The interaction between this volunteer English teacher and her students may fulfill such needs.

Unconditional positive regard: Supportive behavior from another individual, regardless of one's words or actions

from another person—a friend, a spouse, or a therapist. As we will discuss further in Chapter 18, **unconditional positive regard** refers to an attitude of acceptance and respect on the part of an observer, no matter what a person says or does. This acceptance, says Rogers, allows people the opportunity to evolve and grow both cognitively and emotionally as they are able to develop more realistic self-concepts.

Self-actualization: A state of self-fulfillment in which people realize their highest potential

To Rogers and other humanistic personality theorists (such as Abraham Maslow, whose theory of motivation we discussed in Chapter 11), an ultimate goal of personality growth is self-actualization. **Self-actualization** is a state of self-fulfillment in which people realize their highest potential. This, Rogers would argue, occurs when their experience with the world and their self-concept are closely matched. People who are self-actualized accept themselves as they are in reality, which enables them to achieve happiness and fulfillment (Ford, 1991).

Evaluating Humanistic Theories. Although humanistic theories suggest the value of providing unconditional positive regard toward people, unconditional positive regard toward humanistic theories has been less forthcoming from many personality theorists. The criticisms have centered on the difficulty of verifying the basic assumptions of the theory, as well as on the question of whether unconditional positive regard does, in fact, lead to greater personality adjustment.

Humanistic approaches have also been criticized for making the assumption that people are basically "good"—a notion which is unverifiable and, equally important, one in which nonscientific values are used to build supposedly scientific theories. Still, humanistic theories have been important in highlighting the uniqueness of human beings and in guiding the development of a significant form of therapy designed to alleviate psychological difficulties.

Comparing Approaches to Personality

Given the multiple theories of personality that we have discussed, you may be wondering which of the theories provides the most accurate representation of personality. Unfortunately, it is a question that cannot be answered with confidence. Each theory looks at somewhat different aspects of personality and holds distinct premises about it. Furthermore, in many cases personality is most reasonably viewed from a number of perspectives simultaneously. Of course, the potential exists that someday there will be a unified theory of personality, but the field has not yet reached that point, and it is unlikely to happen in the near future.

In the meantime, it is possible to highlight and compare the major differences between each of the theories. Listed below are the most important dimensions along which the theories differ:

■ The unconscious versus the conscious. Psychoanalytic theory emphasizes the importance of the unconscious; humanistic theory stresses the conscious; and trait and learning theories largely disregard both.

■ Nature (genetic factors) versus nurture (environmental factors). Psychoanalytic theory stresses the innate, genetically produced structure of personality; learning theory focuses on the environment; trait theory varies; and humanistic theory stresses the interaction between both in the development of personality.

■ Freedom versus determinism. Humanistic theories stress the freedom of individuals to make choices in their lives; other theories stress determinism, the view that behavior is directed and caused by factors outside people's willful control. Determinism is particularly evident in psychoanalytic and learning theories, as well as in most trait theories.

■ Stability versus modifiability of personality characteristics. Psychoanalytic and trait theories emphasize the stability of characteristics across a person's life. Learning and humanistic theories stress that personality remains flexible and resilient throughout the life span.

■ Nomothetic versus idiographic approaches. **Nomothetic approaches to personality** accentuate the broad uniformities across behavior, whereas **idiographic approaches to personality** emphasize what makes one person unique—different from all others. Although each of the theories contains nomothetic and idiographic aspects, psychoanalytic theory, which posits broad developmental stages, and trait theory, which searches for universal characteristics, are more closely allied to nomothetic approaches than the others. Learning theory and humanistic theory are more idiographic, stressing the consequences of a person's particular background and environment on personality.

Nomothetic approaches to personality: The study of personality accentuating the broad uniformities across behavior

Idiographic approaches to personality: The study of personality emphasizing what makes one person different from others

---

RECAP AND REVIEW II

RECAP

◄ Traits are relatively enduring dimensions along which people's personalities differ. Trait theorists have tried to identify the major traits that characterize personality.

◄ Allport divided traits into cardinal, central, and secondary traits. Using a statistical technique called factor analysis, Cattell identified forty-six surface traits and sixteen basic source traits, whereas Eysenck found just two major dimensions: introversion-extroversion and neuroticism-stability.

◄ Learning theories of personality concentrate on how environmental factors shape personality. Among the most

important approaches are Skinner's reinforcement theory and social learning theories.

◄ Humanistic theories view the core of personality as the ability to change, improve, and be creative in a uniquely human fashion.

◄ The major characteristics along which personality theories differ include the role of the unconscious versus the conscious, nature (genetic factors) versus nurture (environmental factors), freedom versus determinism, stability versus modifiability of personality characteristics, and nomothetic versus idiographic approaches to personality.

1. a. Carl's determination to succeed is the dominant force in all his activities and relationships. According to Gordon Allport's theory, this is an example of a _____ trait.

   b. In contrast, Cindy's fondness for old Western movies is an example of a _____ trait.

2. Which trait theorist used surface traits and source traits to explain behavior on the basis of sixteen personality dimensions?

   a. Hans Eysenck
   b. Walter Mischel
   c. Gordon Allport
   d. Raymond Cattell

3. What broad factors did Eysenck propose to describe personality?

4. The statistical approach known as _____ _____ analysis is used to summarize large batches of information into several homogeneous groups.

5. A person who enjoys such activities as parties and hang gliding might be described by Eysenck as high on what trait?

6. What is the major problem with trait theories of personality, according to Walter Mischel?

   a. Too many traits are being used.
   b. People do not show consistency within traits.
   c. No one knows how to accurately measure certain traits.

   d. Each person has a completely different set of cardinal traits.

7. Which theorist would be most likely to agree with the statement "Personality can be thought of as the sum total of a person's patterns of behavior"?

   a. Seymour Epstein
   b. Carl Jung
   c. B. F. Skinner
   d. Hans Eysenck

8. _____ learning occurs when one watches another person performing a behavior and observes the consequence of that behavior.

9. A person who would make the statement "I know I can't do it" would be rated by Bandura as low on _____-_____.

10. Which type of personality theory emphasizes the innate goodness of people and their desire to grow?

    a. Humanistic
    b. Psychoanalytic
    c. Learning
    d. Growth

Ask Yourself

Which of these theories of personality is most appealing to you? Which seems to make the most sense? If you were asked to write an essay describing the answer to "the definitive definition of personality," how would you use the information on personality we've been discussing to do it?

(Answers to review questions are on page 502.)

ASSESSING PERSONALITY: DETERMINING WHAT MAKES US SPECIAL

You have a need for other people to like and admire you.

You have a tendency to be critical of yourself.

You have a great deal of unused potential that you have not turned to your advantage.

Although you have some personality weaknesses, you are generally able to compensate for them.

Your adjustment to the opposite sex has presented problems to you.

More disciplined and self-controlled outside, you tend to be worrisome and insecure inside.

At times you have serious doubts as to whether you have made the right decision or done the right thing.

You prefer a certain amount of change and variety and become dissatisfied when hemmed in by restrictions and limitations.

You do not accept others' statements without satisfactory proof.

You have found it unwise to be too frank in revealing yourself to others.

If you think these statements provide a surprisingly accurate account of your personality, you are not alone: Most college students think that the descriptions are tailored just to them. In fact, though, the statements are intentionally de-signed to be so vague as to be applicable to just about anyone (Forer, 1949; Russo, 1981).

The ease with which we can agree with such imprecise statements under-scores the difficulty in coming up with accurate and meaningful assessments of people's personalities (Johnson, Cain, Falke, Hayman, & Perillo, 1985; Prince & Guastello, 1990). Just as trait theorists were faced with the problem of determin-ing the most critical and important traits, psychologists interested in assessing personality must be able to define the most meaningful ways of discriminating between one person's personality and another's. To do this, they use **psycholog-ical tests**, standard measures devised to assess behavior objectively. Such tests are used by psychologists to help people make decisions about their lives and un-derstand more about themselves. They are also employed by researchers inter-ested in the causes and consequences of personality (Groth-Marnat, 1990).

Psychological tests: Standard measures devised to objectively assess behavior

Reliability and Validity

When we use a ruler, we expect to find that it measures an inch in the same way as the last time we used it. When we weigh ourselves on the bathroom scale, we hope that the variations we see on the scale are due to changes in our weight and are not errors on the part of the scale (unless the change in weight is in an unwanted direction!).

In the same way, we hope that psychological tests have **reliability**—that they measure what they are trying to measure consistently. We need to be sure that each time we administer the test, a person taking the test will achieve the same results—assuming that nothing about the person has changed relevant to what is being measured.

Reliability: Consistency in the measurements made by a test

Suppose, for instance, that when you first took the College Board exams you scored a 400 on the verbal section of the test. Then, when taking the test again a few months later, you scored a 700. Upon receiving your new score, you might well stop celebrating for a moment to question whether the test is reliable, since it is unlikely that your abilities could have changed enough to raise your score by 300 points.

But suppose your score changed hardly at all, and both times you received a score of about 400. Though you couldn't complain about a lack of reliability, if you knew your verbal skills were above average you might be concerned that the test did not adequately measure what it was supposed to measure. The ques-tion has now become one of validity rather than of reliability. A test has **validity** when it actually measures what it is supposed to measure.

Validity: The ability of a test to measure what it is supposed to measure

Knowing that a test is reliable is no guarantee that it is also valid. For instance, we could devise a very reliable means for measuring trustworthiness, if we de-cided that trustworthiness is related to skull size. But there is certainly no guar-antee that the test is valid, since one can assume with little danger of being contradicted that skull size has nothing to do with trustworthiness. In this case, then, we have reliability without validity.

On the other hand, if a test is unreliable, it cannot be valid. Assuming that all other factors—a person's motivation, knowledge of the material, health, and so forth—are similar, if someone scores high the first time she takes a specific test and low the second time, the test cannot be measuring what it is supposed to measure, and is therefore both unreliable and not valid.

Test validity and reliability are prerequisites for accurate personality assess-ment—as well as for any other measurement task carried out by psychologists.

Thus the intelligence tests that we discussed in Chapter 10; clinical psychologists' assessment of psychological disorders that we will consider in Chapters 17 and 18; and social psychologists' measures of attitudes must meet the tests of validity and reliability in order for the results to be meaningful.

Assuming that a test is both valid and reliable, one further step is necessary in order to interpret the meaning of a particular test-taker's score: the establishment of norms. **Norms** are standards of test performance that permit the comparison of one person's score on the test to the scores of others who have taken the same test. For example, a norm permits test-takers to know that they have scored in the top 15 percent of those who have taken the test.

Norms: Standards of test performance

The basic scheme for developing norms is for test designers to calculate the average score for a particular group of people to whom the test is designed to be given. They can then determine the extent to which each person's score differs from those of the others who have taken the test in the past. Test-takers are then able to consider the meaning of their raw scores relative to the scores of others who have taken the test, giving them a qualitative sense of their performance.

Obviously, the subjects who are employed in the establishment of norms are critical to the norming process. Those people used to determine norms must be representative of the individuals to whom the test is directed—a requirement that may lead away from psychology and into politics, as we discuss in the Psychology at Work box.

We turn now to some of the specific sorts of measures used by psychologists in their study of personality.

Self-Report Measures of Personality

If someone wanted to assess your personality, one useful method would be to carry out an extensive interview with you in order to determine the most important events of your childhood, your social relationships, and your successes and failures. Obviously, though, such a technique would be extraordinarily costly in terms of time and effort.

Self-report measures: A method of gathering data about people by asking them questions about a sample of their behavior

It is also unnecessary. Just as physicians do not need to drain your entire blood supply in order to test it, psychologists can utilize **self-report measures** that ask people about a relatively small sample of their behavior. This sampling of self-reports is then used to infer the presence of particular personality characteristics.

Minnesota Multiphasic Personality Inventory-2 (MMPI-2): A test used to identify people with psychological difficulties

One of the best examples of a self-report measure, and the most frequently used personality test, is the **Minnesota Multiphasic Personality Inventory-2 (MMPI-2)**, developed by a group of researchers in the 1940s and revised several times (Hathaway & McKinley, 1989; Butcher, 1990). Although the original purpose of the measure was to differentiate people with specific sorts of psychological difficulties from those without disturbances, it has been found to predict a variety of other behaviors. For instance, MMPI scores have been shown to be good predictors of whether college students will marry within ten years and

---

ANSWERS (REVIEW II):

1. a—cardinal; b—secondary **2.** d **3.** Eysenck's theory proposed that personality can best be described in terms of two dimensions: introversion-extroversion, and neuroticism-stability. **4.** factor analysis **5.** Extroversion **6.** b **7.** c **8.** Observational **9.** self-efficacy **10.** a

The passions of politics meet the objectivity of science head on when test norms must be established, at least in the realm of tests that are meant to predict future job performance. In fact, a national controversy has developed regarding whether different norms should be established for members of various racial and ethnic groups (Kilborn, 1991).

At issue is the U.S. government's 50-year-old General Aptitude Test Battery, a test that measures a broad span of abilities ranging from eye-hand coordination to reading proficiency. The problem that started the controversy is that African-Americans and Hispanics tend to score lower on the test, on average, than members of other groups, often due to a lack of relevant experience and prior job opportunities caused by prejudice and discrimination.

In order to promote the employment of minority racial groups, the government developed a separate set of norms for African-Americans and Hispanics. Rather than using the pool of all people who took the test to develop norms, the scores of African-American and Hispanic applicants were compared just with other African-Americans and Hispanics taking

"RACE NORMING": WHERE PSYCHOLOGY AND POLITICS MEET

The General Aptitude Test Battery has been used for decades to screen applicants for a broad range of government positions, including data entry jobs in the Census Bureau. Critics have argued that the practice of interpreting test results differently according to the racial and ethnic background of the applicant is suspect.

the test. Consequently, a Hispanic who scored in the top 20 percent of other Hispanics taking the test was considered to have received an equivalent score to a white job applicant who scored in the top 20 percent of the whites who took the test, even though the absolute score of the Hispanic might be lower than that of the white.

Critics of the adjusted norming system suggest that such a procedure is riddled with problems. According to them, not only is such a system unfair to white job applicants, but it fans the flames of racial bigotry. On the other hand, proponents of the system suggest that the norming procedure is an affirmative action tool that simply permits minority job-seekers to be placed on an equal footing with white job-seekers. A panel of the National Academy of Sciences concurred with the practice of adjusting test norms, suggesting that the unadjusted test norms are not terribly useful in predicting job performance, and that they would tend to screen out otherwise-qualified minority group members.

Job-testing is not the only area in which issues arise regarding norms and the meaning of test scores. As we saw in Chapter 10, when we discussed racial differences in IQ scores, the issue of how to treat racial differences in test scores is both a controversial and a divisive one. Clearly, profound and intense political issues are sometimes intertwined with the supposed dispassion of science.

---

whether they will get an advanced degree (Dworkin & Widom, 1977). Police departments use the test to measure whether police officers are prone to use their weapons. Psychologists in the former Soviet Union even administered a modified form of the MMPI to their cosmonauts and Olympic athletes (Holden, 1986).

The test itself consists of a series of 567 items to which a person responds "true," "false," or "cannot say." The questions cover a variety of issues, ranging from mood ("I feel useless at times") to opinions ("people should try to understand their dreams") to physical and psychological health ("I am bothered by an upset stomach several times a week" and "I have strange and peculiar thoughts"). There are no right or wrong answers, of course. Instead, interpretation of the results rests on the pattern of responses. The test yields scores on ten separate scales, plus three scales meant to measure the validity of the respondent's answers. For example, there is a "lie scale" that indicates (from items such as "I can't remember ever having a bad night's sleep") when people are falsifying their responses in order to present themselves more favorably (Butcher, Graham, Dahlstrom, & Bowman, 1990; Graham, 1990).

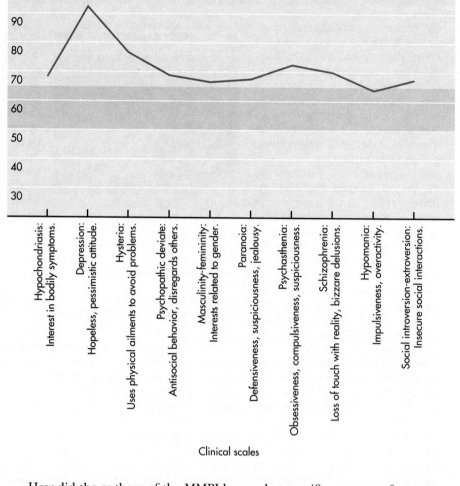

FIGURE 15-5

A sample profile on the MMPI-2 of a person with severe depression.

Clinical scales

Test standardization: A technique used to validate questions in personality tests by studying the responses of people with known diagnoses

How did the authors of the MMPI know what specific patterns of responses indicate? The procedure they used is typical of personality test construction—a process known as **test standardization**. To devise the test, groups of psychiatric patients with a specific diagnosis, such as depression or schizophrenia, were asked to complete a large number of items. The test authors then determined which items best differentiated members of these groups from a comparison group of normal subjects, and these specific items were included in the final version of the test. By systematically carrying out this procedure on groups with different diagnoses, the test authors were able to devise a number of subscales which identified different forms of abnormal behavior (see Figure 15-5).

When the MMPI is used for the purposes for which it was devised—identification of personality disorders—it has proved to do a reasonably good job (Graham, 1990). However, like other personality tests, it presents the opportunity for abuse. For instance, employers who use it as a screening tool for job applicants may interpret the results improperly, relying too heavily on the results of individual scales instead of taking into account the overall patterns of results, which require skilled interpretation. Other tests, such as the California Psychological Inventory and the Edwards Personal Preference Schedule, are more appropriately used for screening job applicants, as well as for providing people with information about their personalities to help them make informed career choices and to identify their strengths and weaknesses.

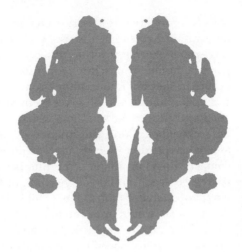

Projective Methods

If you were shown the kind of inkblot presented in Figure 15-6 and asked what it represented to you, you might not think that your impressions would mean very much. But to a psychoanalytic theoretician, your responses to such an ambiguous figure would provide valuable clues to the state of your unconscious, and ultimately to your general personality characteristics.

The inkblot in the figure is representative of **projective personality tests**, in which a person is shown an ambiguous stimulus and asked to describe it or tell a story about it. The responses are then considered to be "projections" of what the person is like.

Projective personality test: An ambiguous stimulus presented to a person for the purpose of determining personality characteristics

The best-known projective test is the **Rorschach test**. Devised by Swiss psychiatrist Hermann Rorschach (1924), the test consists of showing a series of symmetrical stimuli, similar to the one in Figure 15-6, to people who are then asked what the figures represent to them. Their responses are recorded, and through a complex set of clinical judgments on the part of the examiner, people are classified into different personality types. For instance, respondents who see a bear in one inkblot are thought to have a strong degree of emotional control, according to the rules developed by Rorschach.

Rorschach (ROAR shock) **test:** A test consisting of inkblots of indefinite shapes, the interpretation of which is used to assess personality characteristics

The **Thematic Apperception Test (TAT)** is another well-known projective test. As noted when we discussed achievement motivation in Chapter 11, the TAT consists of a series of pictures about which a person is asked to write a story. The stories are then used to draw inferences about the writer's personality characteristics.

Thematic Apperception Test (TAT): A test consisting of a series of ambiguous pictures about which a person is asked to write a story, which is then taken to be a reflection of the writer's personality

By definition, tests with stimuli as ambiguous as the Rorschach and TAT require particular skill and care in their interpretation. They are often criticized as requiring too much inference on the part of the examiner. However, they are widely used, particularly in clinical settings, and their proponents suggest that their reliability and validity are high.

Behavioral Assessment

If you were a psychologist subscribing to a learning approach to personality, you would be likely to object to the indirect nature of projective tests. Instead, you would be more apt to use **behavioral assessment**—direct measures of an individ-

Behavioral assessment: Direct measures of an individual's behavior used to describe characteristics indicative of personality

ual's behavior used to describe characteristics indicative of personality. As with observational research (discussed in Chapter 2), behavioral assessment may be carried out naturalistically by observing people in their own settings: in the workplace, at home, or in school, for instance. In other cases, behavioral assessment occurs in the laboratory, under controlled conditions in which a psychologist sets up a situation and observes an individual's behavior.

Regardless of the setting in which behavior is observed, an effort is made to ensure that behavioral assessment is carried out objectively, quantifying behavior as much as possible. For instance, an observer might record the number of social contacts a person initiates, the number of questions asked, or the number of aggressive acts. Another method might be to measure duration of events: the length of a temper tantrum in a child, the length of a conversation, the amount of time spent working, or the time spent in cooperative behavior.

Behavioral assessment is particularly appropriate for observing—and eventually remedying—specific behavioral difficulties, such as increasing socialization in shy children. It provides a means of assessing the specific nature and incidence of a problem and subsequently allows psychologists to determine whether intervention techniques have been successful.

Techniques based on behavioral assessment and learning theories of personality have also made important contributions to the treatment of certain kinds of psychological difficulties. Indeed, the knowledge of normal personality provided by the theories we have discussed throughout this chapter has led to significant advances in our understanding and treatment of both physical and psychological disorders.

The Informed Consumer of Psychology: Assessing Personality Assessments

> *Wanted:* People with "kinetic energy," "emotional maturity," and the ability to "deal with large numbers of people in a fairly chaotic situation."

Although this job description may seem most appropriate for the job of co-host of *Wheel of Fortune,* in actuality it is part of an advertisement for managers for American MultiCinema's theaters (Dentzer, 1986). To find people with such qualities, AMC has developed a battery of personality measures for job applicants to complete. In developing its own tests, AMC joined scores of companies, ranging from General Motors to J. C. Penney, which employ personality tests to help determine who gets hired and, once on the job, who gets promoted or even who gets fired. (For another aspect of employment testing, see the accompanying Cutting Edge box.)

Individuals, too, have come to depend on personality testing. Many organizations will—for a hefty fee—administer a battery of personality tests that purport to steer people toward a career for which their personality is particularly suited.

Before relying too heavily on the results of such personality testing, either in the role of potential employee, employer, or consumer of testing services, several points should be kept in mind:

■ Understand what the test purports to measure. Standard personality measures are accompanied by information that discusses how the test was developed, to whom it is most applicable, and how the results should be interpreted. If possible, you should read the accompanying literature; it will help you understand the meaning of any results.

■ No decision should be based solely on the results of any one test. Test results should be interpreted in the context of other information—academic

Have you ever been tempted to steal?

Do you believe everyone breaks rules occasionally?

If you can answer both questions honestly, you may be well on your way to being identified as a person of integrity. Maybe.

In large numbers, employers are turning to a new form of personality test known as "integrity tests." Designed to identify individuals who are honest, the integrity tests ask a series of questions designed to predict the honesty of employees, weeding out those who are likely to steal goods or cheat their employer in some manner.

The problem with the tests is that between 40 and 60 percent of people who are identified by such tests as likely to be dishonest are, in fact, honest employees (Office of Technology

TO TELL THE TRUTH: CAN INTEGRITY TESTS IDENTIFY HONEST PEOPLE?

Assessment, 1990). Consequently, substantial numbers of honest workers may be unable to get jobs, or actually lose an existing job, due to the tests' deficiencies.

In order to determine the validity of integrity testing, a recent task force of the American Psychological Association conducted a thorough assessment of existing integrity tests (Goldberg, 1991). Although the study found that integrity tests were the best available alternatives for employers seeking to screen job applicants and employees for honesty, there were many unanswered questions regarding their validity.

For example, quite a few publishers of such tests refuse to disseminate reports of research involving

their tests, and users are consequently forced to rely on the assurances of the publishers that the tests actually work as advertised. Furthermore, although integrity tests may be good at predicting the abilities of large numbers of people, any one individual—particularly someone who has difficulties performing well on standardized tests—may not receive an adequate assessment of his or her honesty. For reasons such as these, several states are considering banning their use.

Despite their potential shortcomings, the use of integrity tests is on the rise in employment settings (De Angelis, 1991b). Given their increasing use, you should not be surprised if one day an employer asks you to spend a few minutes answering a few questions. No matter how honest you are, you should answer with caution.

records, social interests, and home and community activities. Without these data, individual scores are relatively uninformative at best and may even be harmful.

■ Tests are not infallible. The results may be in error; the test may be unreliable or invalid. You may, for example, have had a "bad day" when you took the test, or the person scoring and interpreting the test may have made a mistake. You should not place undue stock in the results of the single administration of any test.

In sum, it is important to keep in mind the complexity of human behavior—particularly your own. No one test can provide an understanding of the intricacies of someone's personality without considering a good deal more information than can be provided in a single testing session.

RECAP AND REVIEW III

RECAP

◄ Psychological tests are standard measures used to measure behavior objectively. They must be reliable, measuring with consistency what they are trying to measure, and valid, measuring what is supposed to be measured.

◄ Self-report measures of personality ask people about a sample range of their behaviors. The results are then used to infer personality characteristics.

◄ Projective personality tests present ambiguous stimuli which the person is asked to describe or tell a story

about. Responses are used as an indication of information about the individual's personality.

◄ Behavioral assessment employs direct measures of an individual's behavior to describe characteristics indicative of personality.

REVIEW

1. _____ is the consistency of a measuring instrument, while _____ is the abil-

ity of an instrument to actually measure what it is designed to measure.

2. _____ are standards used to compare scores of different people taking the same test.

3. Tests such as the MMPI-2, in which a small sample of behavior is assessed to determine larger trends, are examples of
   a. cross-sectional tests
   b. projective tests
   c. achievement tests
   d. self-report tests

4. A person shown a picture and asked to make up a story about it would be taking a _____ personality test.

5. The Rorschach personality test is an objective measure requiring little decision-making on the part of the person administering the test. True or false? _____

Ask Yourself

Should personality tests be used for personnel decisions? If you were asked to take such a test, what questions concerning test construction and validation would be important to you? If you were designing such a test, how would these concerns affect you?

(Answers to review questions are on page 509.)

■ *How do psychologists define and use the concept of personality?*

1. In this chapter, we have examined characteristics and behaviors that make people different from one another—those behaviors that psychologists consider to be at the root of personality. More formally, personality is thought of in two different, but related, ways: First, it refers to the characteristics that differentiate one person from another. Second, it provides a means of explaining the stability in people's behavior that leads them to act uniformly both in different situations and over extended periods of time.

■ *What is the structure and development of personality according to Freud and his successors?*

2. According to psychoanalysts, much of behavior is caused by parts of personality which are found in the unconscious and of which we are unaware. Freud's theory suggests that personality is composed of the id, the ego, and the superego. The id is the unorganized, inherited part of personality whose purpose is to immediately reduce tensions relating to hunger, sex, aggression, and other primitive impulses. The ego restrains instinctual energy in order to maintain the safety of the individual and to help the person to be a member of society. The superego represents the rights and wrongs of society and consists of the conscience and the ego-ideal.

3. Freud's psychoanalytic theory suggests that personality develops through a series of stages, each of which is associated with a major biological function. The oral stage is the first period, occurring during the first year of life. Next comes the anal stage, lasting from approximately age 1 to age 3. The phallic stage follows, with interest focusing on the genitals. At age 5 or 6, near the end of the phallic stage, children experience the Oedipal conflict, a process through which they learn to identify with the same-sex parent by acting as much like that parent as possible. Then follows a latency period lasting until puberty, after which people move into the genital stage, a period of mature sexuality.

4. Defense mechanisms, used for dealing with anxiety relating to impulses from the id, provide people with unconscious strategies to reduce anxiety. The most common defense mechanisms are repression, regression, displacement, rationalization, denial, projection, and sublimation.

5. Freud's psychoanalytic theory has provoked a number of criticisms. These include a lack of supportive scientific data, the theory's inadequacy in making predictions, and its limitations owing to the restricted population on which it is based. Still, the theory remains a pivotal one. For instance, the neo-Freudian psychoanalytic theorists built on Freud's work, although they placed greater emphasis on the role of the ego and paid greater attention to social factors in determining behavior.

■ *What are the major aspects of trait, learning, and humanistic theories of personality?*

6. Trait theories have tried to identify the most basic and relatively enduring dimensions along which people differ from one another—dimensions known as traits. For example, Allport suggested that there are three kinds of traits—cardinal, central, and secondary. Later theorists employed a statistical technique called factor analysis to identify the most crucial traits. Using this method, Cattell identified sixteen basic traits, while Eysenck found two major dimensions: introversion-extroversion and neuroticism-stability.

7. Learning theories of personality concentrate on observable behavior. To the strict learning theorist, personality is the sum of learned responses to the external environment. In contrast, social learning theory concentrates on the role of cognitions in determining personality. Social learning theory pays particular attention to self-efficacy and reciprocal determinism in determining behavior.

8. Humanistic theory emphasizes the basic goodness of people. It considers as the core of personality a person's ability to change and improve. Rogers' concept of the need for positive regard suggests that a universal requirement to be loved and respected underlies personality.

9. The major personality theories differ along a number of important dimensions, including the role of the unconscious versus the conscious, nature versus nurture, freedom versus determinism, stability versus modifiability of personality characteristics, and nomothetic (focusing on the broad uniformities across behavior) versus idiographic (emphasizing the differentiation between people) approaches.

■ *How can we most accurately assess personality, and what are the major types of personality measures?*

10. Psychological tests are standard assessment tools that objectively measure behavior. They must be reliable, measuring what they are trying to measure consistently, and valid, measuring what they are supposed to measure.

11. Self-report measures ask people about a sample range of their behaviors. These reports are used to infer the presence of particular personality characteristics. The most commonly used self-report measure is the Minnesota Multiphasic Personality Inventory-2 (MMPI-2), designed to differentiate people with specific sorts of psychological difficulties from normal individuals.

12. Projective personality tests present an ambiguous stimulus; the observer's responses are then used to infer information about the observer. The two most frequently used projective tests are the Rorschach, in which reactions to inkblots are employed to classify personality types, and the Thematic Apperception Test (TAT), in which stories about ambiguous pictures are used to draw inferences about the storyteller's personality.

13. Behavioral assessment is based on the principles of learning theory. It employs direct measurement of an individual's behavior to determine characteristics related to personality.

KEY TERMS AND CONCEPTS

personality (p. 480)
psychoanalysts (p. 481)
psychoanalytic theory (p. 481)
unconscious (p. 481)
instinctual drives (p. 481)
id (p. 482)
libido (p. 482)
pleasure principle (p. 482)
ego (p. 482)
reality principle (p. 482)
superego (p. 483)
conscience (p. 483)
ego-ideal (p. 483)
oral stage (p. 484)
fixation (p. 484)
anal stage (p. 484)
phallic stage (p. 484)
Oedipal conflict (p. 484)
identification (p. 484)
penis envy (p. 485)
latency period (p. 485)
genital stage (p. 485)
anxiety (p. 485)
neurotic anxiety (p. 485)
defense mechanisms (p. 485)

repression (p. 485)
regression (p. 485)
displacement (p. 486)
rationalization (p. 486)
denial (p. 486)
projection (p. 486)
sublimation (p. 486)
neo-Freudian psychoanalysts (p. 487)
collective unconscious (p. 487)
archetypes (p. 487)
inferiority complex (p. 488)
trait theory (p. 490)
traits (p. 490)
cardinal trait (p. 490)
central traits (p. 490)
secondary traits (p. 490)
factor analysis (p. 491)
surface traits (p. 491)
source traits (p. 491)
introversion-extroversion (p. 491)
neuroticism-stability (p. 491)
social learning theory (p. 496)
observational learning (p. 496)
self-efficacy (p. 496)

reciprocal determinism (p. 496)
determinism (p. 497)
humanistic theory (p. 497)
self-concept (p. 497)
unconditional positive regard (p. 498)
self-actualization (p. 498)
nomothetic approaches to personality (p. 499)
idiographic approaches to personality (p. 499)
psychological tests (p. 501)
reliability (p. 501)
validity (p. 501)
norms (p. 502)
self-report measures (p. 502)
Minnesota Multiphasic Personality Inventory-2 (MMPI-2) (p. 502)
test standardization (p. 504)
projective personality test (p. 505)
Rorschach test (p. 505)
Thematic Apperception Test (TAT) (p. 505)
behavioral assessment (p. 505)

ANSWERS (REVIEW III):
1. Reliability, validity   **2.** Norms   **3.** d   **4.** projective   **5.** False; the test has been criticized for being overly subjective.

▶ **509**

HEALTH PSYCHOLOGY: STRESS, COPING, AND HEALTH

WAR IN THE PERSIAN GULF

A "Patriot" anti-missile missile is launched in Israel to intercept an Iraqi SCUD missile.

First came the missiles, aimed with deadly accuracy at the heart of the country. These were quickly followed by a huge convoy of planes, making their way northward and westward toward targets determined long in advance. In a scene that was to become eerily familiar, reporters perched on the tops of hotels described sudden explosions and the sound of anti-aircraft artillery filling the air.

It was the beginning of the Gulf War, an occasion that brought a collective trauma to the United States. Viewers sat frozen in front of their television screens, watching as alarms over incoming SCUD missiles were sounded and trying to make sense out of happenings occurring far away. It all had an air of unreality.

LOOKING AHEAD

To those actually in the Gulf, however, the war was all too real. In addition to the large-scale physical destruction, thousands of people were maimed and killed as the war raged. But the consequences of the war were not just physical: Even those who escaped bodily harm received psychological scars that would long have an impact on their lives. Few of those involved will probably be fully free of one of the war's major aftermaths: stress.

Stress has long been a major topic of study for psychologists as they have attempted to develop an understanding of its causes and devise ways to help people cope with it. In recent years, however, psychologists have begun to consider stress and coping within the broader context of a new field of study known as health psychology.

Health psychology: The branch of psychology that explores the relationship between physical and psychological factors

Health psychology is the area of psychology applied to the prevention, diagnosis, and treatment of medical problems. It considers questions about the way in which illness is influenced and in some cases caused by psychological factors and how treatments for disease and illness can be based on psychological principles and findings. It is also concerned with issues of prevention: how health problems such as heart disease and stress can be avoided by more healthful behavior.

Health psychologists take a strong stand on the perennial mind-body issue that philosophers, and later psychologists, have debated since the time of the ancient Greeks (a debate that we first raised in Chapter 1). They suggest that rather than the mind and body being two distinct systems, they are clearly linked. Consequently, physical health and psychological factors are interwoven.

It is now clear that good health and the ability to cope with illness when it does occur are affected by psychological factors such as the ability to manage stress and an individual's health habits. Even our attitudes and emotions appear to have a significant influence on our health. For example, evidence suggests that the **immune system**, the complex of organs, glands, and cells that comprise our body's natural line of defense in fighting disease, is affected by our attitudes and emotional state. Health psychologists thus view the mind and the body as two parts of a whole human being that cannot be considered independently.

Immune system: The body's natural defenses that fight disease

Just two decades ago, the marriage of the fields of psychology and medicine that health psychology represents was in the prenuptial stage. Disease was viewed as a purely biological phenomenon, and psychological factors were of little interest to most health-care workers. Furthermore, in earlier parts of the century, the primary causes of death were short-term infections, from which one was either rapidly cured—or died. Now, however, the major causes of death, such as heart disease, cancer, and diabetes, are chronic illnesses that often cannot be cured and that may linger for years, posing significant psychological issues. (Sarafino, 1990; Taylor, 1991.)

In this chapter we discuss ways in which psychological factors affect health, focusing first on the causes and consequences of stress, as well as on the means of coping with it. Next, we explore the psychological aspects of several major health problems, including heart disease, cancer, and smoking. Finally, we examine the ways in which patient-doctor interactions influence our health, and offer suggestions for increasing people's compliance with behavior that will improve their well-being.

In sum, after reading this chapter, you will be able to answer questions such as these:

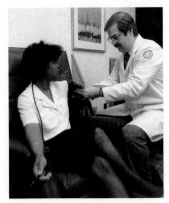

Cathy Collins being outfitted with the apparatus to measure her stress level during the workday.

■ How does health psychology represent a union between medicine and psychology?

■ What is stress, how does it affect us, and how can we best cope with it?

■ How do psychological factors affect such health-related problems as coronary heart disease, cancer, and smoking?

■ How does the nature of our interactions with physicians affect our health and compliance to medical treatment?

STRESS AND COPING

It is now 10:26 a.m. Cathy Collins, a Teaneck, New Jersey, wife, mother, and administrative aide in a metropolitan hospital, has already been up for five hours, having left breakfast for her children and taken two buses to reach her tiny, windowless office.

She is standing with a phone cradled on her shoulder, contending with: a patient sitting at her desk, waiting to ask her some questions; a secretary with a question about another patient's chart; two calls on hold, and her intercom buzzing; several forms to be completed on her desk, which she attempts to fill out between calls; a stack of paperwork three inches high in her "in" box; and a boss who has just walked out of his office and asked for something to be copied.

At this moment, a mechanism strapped to Cathy's waist and arm measures her blood pressure and heartbeat, finding that both are elevated 25 and 15 percent, respectively, over earlier readings. As it happened, this was not the biggest increase of the day for Collins (Tierney, 1988).

Because Cathy Collins was participating in a hospital study of stress in the workplace, we know about her hidden physiological reactions to the events of the moment. And although no measurements were taken of her emotional reactions, few of us would have difficulty in guessing what she would report experiencing during this same period: stress.

Most of us need little introduction to the phenomenon of **stress**, formally defined as the response to events that threaten or challenge a person. Whether it be a paper or exam deadline, a family problem, or even a cumulative series of small events such as those faced by Cathy Collins on the job, life is full of circumstances—known as **stressors**—that produce threats to our well-being. Even pleasant events—such as planning a party or beginning a sought-after job—can produce stress, although negative events result in greater detrimental conse-

Stress: The response to events that are threatening or challenging

Stressors: Circumstances that produce threats to our well-being

▶ **513**

quences than positive ones (Sarason, Johnson, & Siegel, 1978; Brown & McGill, 1989).

All of us face stress in our lives. Some health psychologists believe that daily life actually involves a series of repeated sequences of perceiving a threat, considering ways of coping with it, and ultimately adapting to the threat, with greater or lesser success (Gatchel & Baum, 1983). Although adaptation is often minor and occurs without our being aware of it, in those cases in which the stress is more severe or longer lasting, adaptation requires major effort and may produce physiological and psychological responses that result in health problems.

The High Cost of Stress

Stress can take its toll in many ways, producing both physiological and psychological consequences. Often the most immediate reaction to stress is a physiological one, for exposure to stress induces a rise in certain hormones secreted by the adrenal glands, an increase in heart rate and blood pressure, and changes in how well the skin conducts electrical impulses (Mason, 1975; Selye, 1976). On a short-term basis, these responses may be adaptive because they produce an "emergency reaction"—the response of the sympathetic nervous system discussed in Chapter 3—and may allow more effective coping with the stressful situation.

However, continued exposure to stress results in a decline in the body's overall level of biological functioning because of the continued secretion of the stress-related hormones. Over time stressful reactions can promote actual deterioration of body tissues such as the blood vessels and the heart. Ultimately, we become more susceptible to disease as our ability to fight off germs is lowered (Kiecolt-Glaser & Glaser, 1986; Schneiderman, 1983; Cohen, Tyrrell, & Smith, 1991).

In addition to major health difficulties, many of the minor aches and pains that we experience may be caused or worsened by stress. These include headaches, backaches, skin rashes, indigestion, fatigue, and constipation (Brown, 1984). Moreover, a whole class of medical problems, known as **psychosomatic disorders**, often result from stress. These medical problems are caused by an interaction of psychological, emotional, and physical difficulties. Among the most common psychosomatic disorders are ulcers, asthma, arthritis, high blood pressure, and eczema. In fact, the likelihood of onset of any major illness seems to be related to the number of stressful events a person experiences (see Table 16-1).

On a psychological level, high levels of stress prevent people from coping with life adequately. Their view of the environment can become clouded (a minor criticism made by a friend is blown out of proportion), and—at the greatest levels of stress—emotional responses may be so severe that people are unable to act at all. Moreover, people under a lot of stress become less able to deal with new stressors. The ability to contend with future stress, then, declines as a result of past stress (Eckenrode, 1984).

The General Adaptation Syndrome Model: The Course of Stress

The effects of stress are best illustrated by a model developed by Hans Selye (pronounced "sell-yea"), a major stress theorist (Selye, 1976). This model, the

Psychosomatic (sy ko so MAT ik) **disorders:** Medical problems caused by an interaction of psychological, emotional, and physical difficulties

TABLE 16-1

PREDICTING THE ILLNESS OF THE FUTURE FROM THE STRESS OF THE PAST

Is there a stress-related illness in your future? Survey research has shown that the number of stressors in a person's life is associated with the experience of a major illness (Rahe & Arthur, 1978).

To find out the degree of stress in your life, take the stressor value given beside each event you have experienced and multiply it by the number of occurrences over the past year (up to a maximum of four), then add up these scores.

87 Experienced the death of a spouse

77 Married

77 Experienced the death of a close family member

76 Were divorced

74 Experienced a marital separation

68 Experienced the death of a close friend

68 Experienced pregnancy or fathered a pregnancy

65 Had a major personal injury or illness

62 Were fired from work

60 Ended a marital engagement or a steady relationship

58 Had sexual difficulties

58 Experienced a marital reconciliation

57 Had a major change in self-concept or self-awareness

56 Experienced a major change in the health or behavior of a family member

54 Became engaged to be married

53 Had a major change in financial status

52 Took on a mortgage or loan of less than $10,000

52 Had a major change in use of drugs

50 Had a major conflict or change in values

50 Had a major change in the number of arguments with your spouse

50 Gained a new family member

50 Entered college

50 Changed to a new school

50 Changed to a different line of work

49 Had a major change in amount of independence and responsibility

47 Had a major change in responsibilities at work

46 Experienced a major change in use of alcohol

45 Revised personal habits

44 Had trouble with school administration

43 Held a job while attending school

43 Had a major change in social activities

42 Had trouble with in-laws

42 Had a major change in working hours or conditions

42 Changed residence or living conditions

41 Had your spouse begin or cease work outside the home

41 Changed your choice of major field of study

41 Changed dating habits

40 Had an outstanding personal achievement

38 Had trouble with your boss

(continued on next page)

38 Had a major change in amount of participation in school activities

37 Had a major change in type and/or amount of recreation

36 Had a major change in church activities

34 Had a major change of sleeping habits

33 Took a trip or vacation

30 Had a major change in eating habits

26 Had a major change in the number of family get-togethers

22 Were found guilty of minor violations of the law

Scoring   If your total score is above 1435, you are in a high-stress category, which, according to Marx, Garrity, & Bowers (1975), puts you at risk for experiencing a stress-related illness in the future. On the other hand, you should not assume that a high score destines you to a future illness. Because the research on stress and illness is correlational, major stressful events cannot be viewed as necessarily causing illness (Dohrenwend et al., 1984; Lakey & Heller, 1985). Moreover, some research suggests that future illness is better predicted by the daily, ongoing hassles of life, rather than by the major events depicted in the questionnaire (Lazarus, DeLoungis, Folkman, & Gruen, 1985). Still, a high level of stressful events in one's life is a cause for concern, and so it makes sense to take measures to reduce stress (Marx, Garrity, & Bowers, 1975, p. 97; Maddi, Bartone, & Puccetti, 1987).

General adaptation syndrome (GAS): A theory developed by Selye that suggests that a person's response to stress consists of three stages: alarm and mobilization, resistance, and exhaustion

Alarm and mobilization stage: In Selye's general adaptation syndrome, a person's initial awareness of the presence of a stressor

Resistance stage: The second stage of Selye's general adaptation syndrome: coping with the stressor

FIGURE 16-1

The general adaptation syndrome (GAS) suggests that there are three major stages in people's response to stress. (Selye, 1976.)

general adaptation syndrome (GAS), suggests that the same set of physiological reactions to stress occurs regardless of the particular cause of stress.

As shown in Figure 16-1, the model has three phases. The first stage, the **alarm and mobilization stage**, occurs when people become aware of the presence of a stressor. Suppose, for instance, you learned at the end of the first term of college that you were on academic probation because of your low grades. You would be likely to respond first with alarm, feeling concerned and upset. Subsequently, though, you would probably begin to mobilize your efforts, making plans and promises to yourself to study harder for the rest of the school year.

On a physiological level, the sympathetic nervous system is energized during the alarm and mobilization phase. Prolonged activation of this system may lead to problems of the blood circulatory system or stomach ulcers, and the body may become vulnerable to a host of diseases.

In the next stage of the model, the **resistance stage**, you would prepare yourself to fight the stressor. During resistance, a person uses various means to cope with the stressor—sometimes successfully—but at a cost of some degree of physical or psychological general well-being. For instance, your resistance might take the form of devoting long hours to studying. You may ultimately be successful in raising your grades, but it may be at the expense of a loss of sleep and hours of worry.

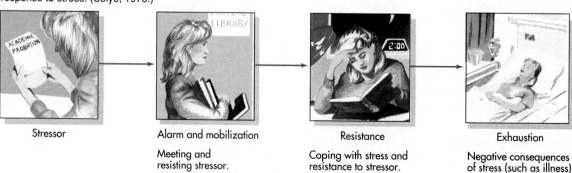

Stressor

Alarm and mobilization

Meeting and resisting stressor.

Resistance

Coping with stress and resistance to stressor.

Exhaustion

Negative consequences of stress (such as illness) occur when coping is inadequate.

If resistance is not adequate, the last stage of the model, the **exhaustion stage**, is reached. During the exhaustion stage, a person's ability to adapt to the stressor declines to the point where negative consequences of stress appear: physical illness, psychological symptoms in the form of an inability to concentrate, heightened irritability, or, in severe instances, disorientation and a loss of touch with reality. In a sense, people wear out. For instance, if you become overwhelmed by pressure to perform well in your courses, you may become sick or find it impossible to study altogether.

Of course, not everyone reaches the exhaustion stage. If people can resist a stressor in the second stage, their physical resources are not drained and they can bounce back, thereby avoiding exhaustion.

How do people get beyond the third stage after they have entered it? In some cases, the exhaustion means that people can avoid the stressor. For example, people who become ill from overwork may be excused from their duties for a time, thereby giving them a temporary respite from their responsibilities. At least for a time, then, the immediate stress is reduced.

The GAS model has had a substantial impact on our understanding of stress. For instance, by suggesting that the exhaustion of resources in the third stage of the model produces physiological damage, it has provided a specific explanation of how stress can lead to illness. Furthermore, the model can be applied to both humans and animals.

On the other hand, some aspects of the GAS model have been questioned. One of the most important criticisms is directed at the theory's supposition about the sympathetic division's emergency reaction that is activated during the alarm and mobilization phase. The theory proposes that the reaction is basically the same, regardless of the kind of stressor to which a person is exposed. However, some critics argue that certain stressors produce distinct physiological reactions, such as the secretion of specific hormones. Hence, stress reactions may well be less similar to one another than the GAS implies (Mason, 1974; Hobfoll, 1989).

Furthermore, the model's reliance on physiological factors leaves little room for attention to psychological factors, particularly in terms of the way in which stressors are appraised differently by different people (Mikhail, 1981). Still, the model provides a basis for our understanding of stress.

Exhaustion stage: The third stage of Selye's general adaptation syndrome: failure to adapt to a stressor, leading to physical, psychological, and emotional problems

The Nature of Stressors: My Stress Is Your Pleasure

As noted above, the general adaptation syndrome model is useful in explaining how people respond to stress, but it is not specific about what constitutes a stressor for a given person. Although it is clear that certain kinds of events, such as the death of a loved one or participation in combat during a war, are almost universally stressful, other situations may or may not be stressful to a particular person (Fleming, Baum, & Singer, 1984; Lazarus & Cohen, 1977). Consider, for instance, automobile racing. Some of us would find driving cars at breakneck speeds to be a very stressful activity, one that would be likely to provoke reactions similar to those of other stressful occurrences. However, there are those for whom car racing is a challenging and fun-filled activity. Instead of experiencing stress, they look forward to driving around a track at 200 miles per hour. Whether or not car racing is stressful depends in part, then, on individual perceptions of the activity.

For people to consider an event to be stressful, they must perceive it as threatening and must lack the resources to deal with it effectively (Folkman et al., 1986). Consequently, the same event may at times be stressful and at other

Although for many people car racing would be a stressful activity, those who choose to participate in it find it exciting and enjoyable.

times provoke no stressful reaction at all. For instance, a young man might experience stress when he is turned down for a date—if he attributes the refusal to his unattractiveness or unworthiness. But if he attributes it to some factor unrelated to his self-esteem, such as a previous commitment of the woman he asked, the experience of being refused might create no stress at all. Hence, cognitive factors relating to our interpretation of events play an important role in the determination of what is stressful.

A number of other factors also influence the severity of stress. For example, stress is greater when the importance and number of goals that are threatened are high, when the threat is immediate, or when the anticipation of the threatening event extends over a long period (Paterson & Neufeld, 1987).

Categorizing Stressors. What kinds of events tend to be seen as stressful? There are three general classes of events: cataclysmic events, personal stressors, and background stressors (Gatchel & Baum, 1983; Lazarus & Cohen, 1977). **Cataclysmic events** are strong stressors that occur suddenly and affect many people simultaneously. Disasters such as tornadoes and plane crashes are examples of cataclysmic events that can affect hundreds or thousands of people simultaneously. Curiously, however, cataclysmic events may sometimes be less stressful in the long run than events that are initially less intense. One reason is that such events have a clear resolution: Once they are over and done with, people can look forward to the future knowing that the worst is behind them. Moreover, the stress induced by cataclysmic events is shared by others who have also experienced the disaster (Cummings, 1987). This permits people to provide one another with social support and a firsthand understanding of the difficulties the others are going through.

On the other hand, some victims of major catastrophes can experience a **posttraumatic stress disorder**, in which the original events and the feelings associated with them are reexperienced in vivid flashbacks or dreams. As we discuss in the Psychology at Work box, certain kinds of profound stress can cause lasting emotional harm.

Cataclysmic events: Strong stressors that occur suddenly, affecting many people at once (e.g., natural disasters)

Posttraumatic stress disorder: A phenomenon in which victims of major incidents reexperience the original stress event and associated feelings in flashbacks or dreams

The patient is a Vietnam veteran seen in the late 1970s, ten years after combat duty. During his year in the army his platoon was repeatedly ambushed, and in one of those ambushes his closest friend was killed while he stood a few feet away. He himself hit a boy who was a Vietcong fighter with a rifle butt and killed him. He admits that his mind keeps returning to these events, and he still has nightmares about them, but he insists that he does not want to talk about any of that. He is constantly anxious and agitated, and he jumps at the sound of a firecracker or backfiring automobile. He becomes enraged at anything he regards as a mistake or misdeed by a person in authority, and he thinks that neighbors who trespass on his property "deserve to be wasted." He says that he feels constantly bored and depressed and is "only going through the motions" at work and at home. He hardly talks to his family and has alienated most of his friends. He often carries a gun, and in moments of sudden anger he strikes his wife or starts fights with strangers over trivial annoyances (HMHL, 1991, p. 1).

Depending upon what statistics one employs, between 5 and 60 percent of the veterans of the Vietnam War suffer from posttraumatic stress disorder, or PTSD. For people with the disorder, the war that ended decades earlier is still very much a part

POSTTRAUMATIC STRESS DISORDER: RELIVING CATASTROPHE

These Gulf War veterans, like anyone who has lived through a violent, life-threatening experience, are at risk for posttraumatic stress disorder.

of their lives, leading to symptoms such as sleep difficulties, problems in relating to others, and—in some cases—alcohol and drug abuse. The suicide rate for Vietnam veterans is as much as 25 percent higher than for the general population (Pollock et al., 1990; Peterson, Prout, & Schwarz, 1991).

But it is not just veterans of the Vietnam war who suffer from posttraumatic stress syndrome; even the Persian Gulf War, which was over swiftly, produced the condition (Hobfoll et al., 1991). Furthermore, victims of child abuse, rape, or any sudden natural disaster or accident that leaves one feeling helpless and terrified may suffer from the same disorder.

Regardless of the cause, people who experience posttraumatic stress disorder share a similar set of symptoms. These include involuntarily

reexperiencing the event in repeated dreams or flashbacks. Any stimulus that resembles the original event may trigger a memory. At the same time, though, other, contradictory symptoms of the disorder may appear. For instance, a person may experience a general numbing of emotional response, feeling strong emotion only in relation to the trauma.

Some of the more recent cases of PTSD arose following the massive San Francisco earthquake of 1989, although quick action by local psychologists probably prevented many cases from becoming critical. For example, on the day following the earthquake, hundreds of local psychologists "debriefed" people especially at risk for PTSD. Fire fighters or paramedics, for instance, were urged to talk about how it felt to crawl through wreckage looking for victims. Debriefing of this sort helped prevent the emotional numbing that may occur as a result of PTSD (Buie, 1989).

Still, some psychologists predicted that most survivors would experience some form of PTSD following the quake, although the majority would return to normal after a few weeks. The people who were most susceptible were those who had relatively impaired psychological health prior to the quake and people who had been exposed to particularly dangerous or difficult situations relating to the earthquake (Nolen-Hoeksema & Morrow, 1991). For this latter group, psychological treatment was recommended to help alleviate their stress.

Personal stressors include major life events such as the death of a parent or spouse, the loss of one's job, a major personal failure, or diagnosis of a life-threatening illness. Typically, personal stressors produce an immediate major reaction that soon tapers off. For example, stress arising from the death of a loved one tends to be greatest just after the time of death, but people begin to feel less stress and are better able to cope with the loss after the passage of time.

Personal stressors: Major life events, such as the death of a family member, that have immediate negative consequences which generally fade with time

▶ **519**

In some cases, though, the effects of stress are lingering. Victims of rape sometimes suffer lasting consequences long after the event, facing major difficulties in adjustment. Similarly, the malfunction of the Three Mile Island nuclear plant in Pennsylvania in the early 1980s, which exposed people to the stressor of a potential nuclear meltdown, produced emotional, behavioral, and physiological consequences that lasted more than a year and a half (Baum, Gatchel, & Schaeffer, 1983).

Background stressors or **daily hassles:** Daily hassles, such as being stuck in traffic, that cause minor irritations but have no long-term ill effects, unless they continue or are compounded by other stressful events

Standing in a long line at a bank and getting stuck in a traffic jam are examples of **background stressors** or, more informally, **daily hassles** (Lazarus & Cohen, 1977). These stressors represent the minor irritations of life that we all face time and time again: delays, noisy cars and trucks, broken appliances, other people's irritating behavior, and so on. Background stressors also consist of long-term, chronic problems such as dissatisfaction with school or job, unhappy relationships, or living in crowded quarters without privacy.

By themselves, daily hassles do not require much coping or even response on the part of the individual, although they certainly do produce unpleasant emotions and moods (Clark & Watson, 1988). Yet daily hassles add up—and ultimately they may produce as great a toll as a single, more stressful incident. In fact, there is an association between the number of daily hassles that people face and the number of psychological symptoms they report (Kanner et al., 1981; Zika & Chamberlain, 1987; Chamberlain & Zika, 1990). Even health problems (such as flu, sore throat, headaches, and backaches) have been linked to daily hassles (DeLongis, Folkman, & Lazarus, 1988; Jones, Brantley, & Gilchrist, 1988; Kohn, Lafreniere, & Genrevich, 1991).

Although the nature of daily hassles differs from day to day and from person to person, background stressors do have certain characteristics in common. One critical factor is related to the degree of control people have over aversive, unpleasant stimuli in the environment (Folkman, 1984; Rodin, 1986). When people feel that they can control a situation and determine its outcome, stress reactions are reduced considerably. For instance, people exposed to high levels of noise suffer fewer adverse effects if they know they are able to control the noise than those exposed to the same amount of noise who are unable to control its intensity and duration (Glass & Singer, 1972).

Uplifts: Minor positive events that make one feel good

The flip side of hassles are **uplifts**, those minor positive events that make one feel good—even if only temporarily. As indicated in Figure 16-2, uplifts range from relating well to a companion to finding one's surroundings pleasing. What is especially intriguing about these uplifts is that they are associated with people's psychological health in just the opposite way that hassles are: The greater the number of uplifts experienced, the fewer the psychological symptoms people later report.

Learned Helplessness

You've probably heard someone complaining about an intolerable situation that he couldn't seem to resolve, heard him say that he was tired of "hitting his head against the wall," and was giving up and accepting things the way they were. This example illustrates one of the possible consequences of being in an environment in which control over a situation is not possible—a state that produces learned helplessness. According to psychologist Martin Seligman, **learned helplessness**, as discussed first in Chapter 7, occurs when people conclude that unpleasant or aversive stimuli cannot be controlled—a pattern that becomes so ingrained that they do not try to remedy the aversive circumstances, even if they actually can

Learned helplessness: A learned belief that one has no control over the environment

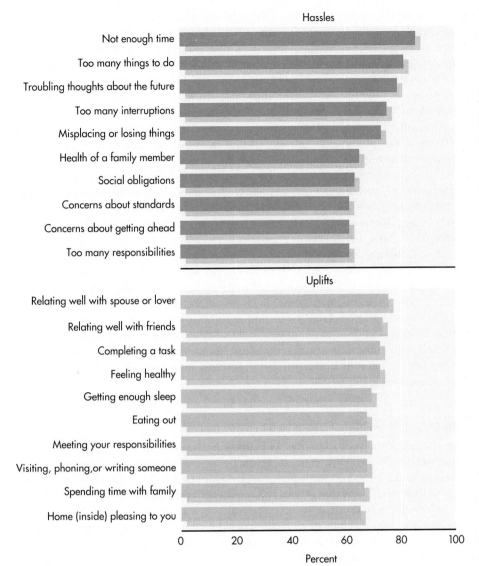

FIGURE 16-2

The most common everyday
hassles and uplifts. (Sources:
hassles: Chamberlin & Zika,
1990; uplifts: Kanner, Coyne,
Schaefer, & Lazarus, 1981.)

exert some influence (Seligman, 1975). Victims of the phenomenon of learned helplessness have decided that there is no link between the responses they make and the outcomes that occur.

Take, for example, what often happens to elderly people when they are placed in nursing homes or hospitals. One of the most striking features of their new environment is that they are no longer independent: They do not have control over the most basic activities. They are told what and when to eat, their sleeping schedules are arranged by someone else, and they are told when they may watch TV or participate in recreational activities. It is not hard to see how this loss of control can have negative effects upon people suddenly placed, often reluctantly, in such a situation.

The results of this loss of control and the ensuing stress are frequently poorer health and even a likelihood of earlier death. These outcomes were confirmed in an experiment conducted in a nursing home where elderly residents in one

Nursing home residents who are allowed to decide what to eat and which daily activities to engage in may live longer and enjoy better health than those who are not given such choices.

group were encouraged to make more choices and take greater control of their day-to-day activities (Langer & Janis, 1979). As a result, members of the group were more active and happier than a comparison group of residents who were encouraged to let the nursing home staff care for them. Moreover, an analysis of the residents' medical records revealed that six months after the experiment, the group encouraged to be self-sufficient showed significantly greater health improvement than the comparison group. Even more startling was an examination of the death rate: Eighteen months after the experiment began, only 15 percent of the "independent" group had died—compared with 30 percent of the comparison group.

Other research confirms that learned feelings of helplessness have negative consequences, and not just for the elderly. People of all ages report more physical symptoms and depression when they have little or no control than when they feel control over a situation (Pennebaker, Burnam, Schaeffer, & Harper, 1977; Peterson & Raps, 1984; Rodin, 1986).

Not everyone experiences learned helplessness, even in situations in which they have little control. One reason has to do with people's attributions, or explanations, for the lack of control (Abramson, Garber, & Seligman, 1980). People are most apt to experience helplessness when they perceive the causes of the lack of control to be related to something about their own personal characteristics (as opposed to outside, environmental forces); when they view the causes as stable and enduring (rather than just temporary); and when they see the causes are global and universal (cutting across many situations, rather than in just one sphere of life).

Coping with Stress

Stress is a normal part of living. As Hans Selye has noted, to avoid stress totally, a person would probably have to cease living. Yet, as we have seen, too much stress can take its toll on both physical and psychological health. How do people deal with stress? Is there a way to reduce its negative effects?

Coping: The efforts to control, reduce, or learn to tolerate the threats that lead to stress

The efforts to control, reduce, or learn to tolerate the threats that lead to stress are known as **coping**. We habitually use certain coping responses to help ourselves deal with stress. Most of the time, we're not aware of these responses— just as we may be unaware of the minor stressors of life until they build up to sufficiently aversive levels.

Defense mechanisms: Unconscious strategies people use to reduce anxiety by concealing its source from themselves and others

One means of dealing with stress that occurs on an unconscious level is the use of defense mechanisms. As we discussed in Chapter 15, **defense mechanisms** are reactions that maintain a person's sense of control and self-worth by distorting or denying the actual nature of the situation. For example, one study showed that California students who live close to a geological fault in dormitories which are rated as being unlikely to withstand an earthquake were significantly more likely to deny the seriousness of the situation and to doubt experts' predictions of an impending earthquake than those who lived in safer structures (Lehman & Taylor, 1988).

Another defense mechanism sometimes used to cope with stress is emotional insulation, in which a person stops experiencing any emotions at all, thereby remaining unaffected and unmoved by both positive and negative experiences. The problem with defense mechanisms, of course, is that they do not deal with reality but merely hide the problem.

People use other, more direct and potentially more positive means for coping with stress, as shown in several studies (Aldwin & Revenson, 1987; Compas,

1987; Miller, Brody, & Summerton, 1988). For instance, one thorough review suggested that coping strategies fall into three categories: (1) problem solving, (2) avoidance, and (3) the seeking out of social support. Specifically, problem solving consisted of trying to resolve a problem causing stress or setting goals to deal with the situation. In contrast, avoidance techniques involved avoiding the presence of others, daydreaming about better times, or watching television more than usual. Finally, some people sought out others, attempting to confide in a friend or relative or seeking reassurance from people who knew them well (Amirkhan, 1990).

Other psychologists interested in methods of classifying coping strategies find that people employ two major techniques for dealing with stress: the conscious regulation of emotions, called **emotion-focused coping**, and the management of the stressful problem or stimulus, called **problem-focused coping**. Examples of emotion-focused coping include such strategies as "accepted sympathy and understanding from someone" and "tried to look on the bright side," whereas examples of problem-focused strategies include "got the person responsible to change his or her mind" and "made a plan of action and followed it." In most stressful incidents, people employ *both* emotion-focused and problem-focused strategies. However, they use emotion-focused strategies more frequently when they perceive circumstances as being unchangeable, and problem-focused approaches more often in situations they see as relatively modifiable (Folkman and Lazarus, 1980; 1988a).

Emotion-focused coping: The conscious regulation of emotion as a means of dealing with stress

Problem-focused coping: The management of a stressful stimulus as a way of dealing with stress

Coping Style: The Hardy Personality. Most of us cope with stress in a characteristic manner, employing a "coping style" that represents our general tendency to deal with stress in a specific way. For example, you may know people who habitually react to even the smallest amount of stress with hysteria, and others who calmly confront even the greatest stress in an unflappable manner. These kinds of people clearly have quite different coping styles (Taylor, 1991).

Among those who cope with stress most successfully are people with a coping style that has come to be called "hardiness." **Hardiness** is a personality characteristic associated with a lower rate of stress-related illness. It consists of three components: commitment, challenge, and control (Kobasa, 1979; Gentry & Kobasa, 1984).

Commitment is a tendency to throw ourselves into whatever we are doing with a sense that our activities are important and meaningful. Hardy people are also high in a sense of challenge, the second component; they believe that change, rather than stability, is the standard condition of life. To them, the anticipation of change acts as an incentive rather than a threat to their security. Finally, hardiness is marked by a sense of their control—the perception that people can influence the events in their lives.

Hardiness seems to act as a buffer against stress-related illness. The hardy individual approaches stress in an optimistic manner and is apt to take direct action to learn about and deal with stressors, thereby changing stressful events into less threatening ones. As a consequence, a person with a hardy personality style is less likely to suffer the negative outcomes of high stress (Wiebe, 1991).

Although the concept of hardiness is a useful one, researchers disagree about whether it is a single phenomenon, or if actually just one or two of its three underlying components account for the positive effects on health that are typically found (Hull, Von Treuren, & Virnelli, 1987). What is clear is that people with hardier personality styles are better able to cope with stress than those with less hardy styles (Allred & Smith, 1989).

Hardiness: A personality characteristic associated with a lower rate of stress-related illness, consisting of three components: commitment, challenge, and control

Social support: Knowledge of being part of a mutual network of caring, interested people

Social Support: Turning to Others.   Our relationships with others may also help us to cope with stress. Researchers have found that **social support**, the knowledge that we are part of a mutual network of caring, interested others, enables people to experience lower levels of stress and to be better able to cope with the stress they do undergo (Dunkel-Schetter, Folkman, & Lazarus, 1987; Sarason, Sarason, & Pierce, 1990; Lepore, Evans, & Schneider, 1991).

The social and emotional support that people provide each other helps in dealing with stress in several ways. For instance, such support demonstrates that a person is an important and valued member of a social network. Similarly, other people can provide information and advice about appropriate ways of dealing with stress—as well as being available as sounding boards.

Finally, people who are part of a social support network can provide actual goods and services to help others in stressful situations. For instance, they can supply a person whose house has burned down with temporary living quarters, or they can help a student study for a test who is experiencing stress due to poor academic performance (House, Landis, & Umberson, 1989; Taylor, Buunk, & Aspinwall, 1990; Croyle & Hunt, 1991).

Surprisingly, the benefits of social support occur not just from the comfort of other humans. One study found that owners of pets were less likely to require medical care following exposure to stressors than those without pets! Dogs, in particular, helped diminish the effects of stress (Siegel, 1990).

The Informed Consumer of Psychology: Coping Strategies That Work

How does one cope most effectively with stress? Researchers have made a number of recommendations for dealing with the problem. There is no universal solution, of course, since effective coping depends on the nature of the stressor and the degree to which control is possible. Still, some general guidelines can be followed (Folkman, 1984; Everly, 1989; Holahan & Moos, 1987, 1990):

Turning Threat into Challenge.   When a stressful situation might be controllable, the best coping approach is to treat the situation as a challenge, focusing on ways to control it. For instance, if you experience stress because your car is always breaking down, you might take an evening course in auto mechanics and learn to deal directly with the car's problems. Even if the repairs prove too difficult to do yourself, at least you'll be in a better position to understand what's wrong.

Making a Threatening Situation Less Threatening.   When a stressful situation seems to be uncontrollable, a different approach must be taken. It is possible to change one's appraisal of the situation, to view it in a different light, and to modify one's attitudes toward it (Smith & Ellsworth, 1987). The old truism "Look for the silver lining in every cloud" seems to be supported by research findings that show that people who discover something good in negative situations show less distress and better coping ability than those who do not (Silver & Wortman, 1980).

Changing One's Goals.   When a person is faced with an uncontrollable situation, another reasonable strategy is to adopt new goals that are practical in view of the particular situation. For example, a dancer who has been in an automobile accident and has lost full use of her legs may no longer aspire to a career in dance, but might modify her goals and try to become a dance instructor. Similarly, an executive who has lost his job may change his goal of becoming wealthy to that of obtaining a more modest, but secure, source of income.

Taking Physical Action. Another approach to coping with stress is to bring about changes in one's physiological reactions to it. For example, biofeedback, discussed in Chapter 3, can alter basic physiological processes, allowing people to reduce blood pressure, heart rate, and other consequences of heightened stress. In addition, exercise can be effective in reducing stress in several ways. For one thing, regular exercise reduces heart rate, respiration rate, and blood pressure (although these responses temporarily increase during exercise periods). Furthermore, exercise gives people a sense of control over their bodies, plus a feeling of accomplishment. It even provides a temporary respite from the environment that is causing the stress in the first place, and it helps people to sleep better at night (Brown, 1991).

Finally, sometimes a change in diet is helpful in coping with stress. For instance, people who drink large quantities of caffeine are susceptible to feeling jittery and anxious; simply decreasing the amount they consume may be sufficient to reduce the experience of stress. Similarly, being overweight may itself be a stressor, and losing excess weight may be an effective measure for reducing stress—unless dieting is so tension-filled that it becomes stressful.

Preparing for Stress Before It Happens. A final strategy for coping with stress is **inoculation**: preparing for stress *before* it is encountered. First developed as a means of preventing postsurgical emotional problems among hospital patients, inoculation methods prepare people for stressful experiences—of either a physical or an emotional nature—by explaining, in as much detail as possible, the difficult events they are likely to encounter. As part of the process, people are asked to imagine how they will feel about the circumstances and to consider various ways of dealing with their reactions—all before the experience has ac-

Inoculation: Preparation for stress before it is encountered

Regular exercise reduces stress in several ways.

tually occurred. Probably the most crucial element, however, is providing individuals with clear, objective strategies for handling the situation, rather than simply telling them what to expect (Janis, 1984).

When carried out properly, inoculation works. Coping is greater for people who have received inoculation treatments prior to facing a stressful event than for those who have not (Ludwick-Rosenthal & Neufeld, 1988; Register et al., 1991).

RECAP AND REVIEW I

RECAP

◄ Stress is the process by which events threaten an individual's ability to deal adequately with the situation.

◄ According to Selye's general adaptation model, stress follows three stages: alarm and mobilization, resistance, and exhaustion.

◄ The specific nature of stressors varies from person to person; what is stressful for one person may be invigorating to another. There are, however, three general categories of stressors: cataclysmic events, personal stressors, and background stressors (or daily hassles).

◄ Perceptions of control typically reduce stress. In some instances, though, learned helplessness occurs—people perceive that aversive stimuli cannot be controlled.

◄ Coping devices may take the form of adopting defense mechanisms, turning threat into challenge, reducing the perception of threat, changing goals, or preparing for stress through inoculation.

REVIEW

1. _____ is defined as a response to challenging or threatening events.
2. Match each portion of the GAS with its definition
   1. _____ Alarm
   2. _____ Exhaustion
   3. _____ Resistance

   a. Ability to adapt to stress diminishes; symptoms appear
   b. Activation of sympathetic nervous system
   c. Various strategies used to cope with a stressor

3. _____ _____ _____ occurs when the feelings associated with stressful events are relived after the event is over.
4. Stressors that affect a single person and produce an immediate major reaction are known as
   a. Personal stressors
   b. Psychic stressors
   c. Cataclysmic stressors
   d. Daily stressors
5. The converse of stressors are _____. Like stressors, these tend to accumulate, but they may alleviate stress-related symptoms.
6. Efforts to reduce or eliminate stress are known as _____.
7. In situations that are changeable, which of the following coping styles is used most frequently and effectively:
   a. Problem-focused
   b. Stressor-focused
   c. Emotion-focused
   d. Action-focused
8. People with the personality characteristic of _____ seem to be more able to successfully combat stressors.

Ask Yourself

Given what you know about coping strategies related to stress, how would you go about training people to successfully avoid stress in their everyday lives? How would you use this information with a group of Gulf War veterans suffering from posttraumatic stress disorder?

(Answers to review questions are on page 528.)

PSYCHOLOGICAL ASPECTS OF MAJOR HEALTH PROBLEMS

The process starts off silently in childhood. There is no symptom, no pain, no warning. A small globule of fat attaches itself to a wall in an artery leading to the heart. Slowly, as the years pass by, other fat cells join the first, building up a lingering deposit that eventually clogs the passageway through which oxygen-rich blood must pass.

Then, one day, a blood clot breaks off in the bloodstream. As it reaches the small passageway in the artery that is already obstructed with fat, so much of the blood flow is cut off that a part of the heart dies from lack of oxygen. The result: a heart attack.

Twenty years ago, a recounting of the processes that bring about coronary heart disease—the leading cause of death in the United States—would have been largely complete with the description above, which focuses on the biological aspects of the problem. Today, however, a growing body of research demonstrates the importance of psychological factors in problems that were once seen in purely physiological terms. We focus now on the major health problems of heart disease, cancer, and smoking.

The A's and B's of Coronary Heart Disease

Have you ever seethed impatiently at being caught behind a slow-moving vehicle, felt anger and frustration at not finding material you needed at the library, or experienced a sense of competitiveness with almost all your classmates?

Many of us experience these sorts of feelings at one time or another, but for some people they represent a pervasive, characteristic set of personality traits known as the **Type A behavior pattern**. Type A individuals are competitive, show a continual sense of urgency about time, are aggressive, exhibit a driven quality regarding their work, and are hostile, both verbally and nonverbally—especially when interrupted while trying to complete a task. On the other hand, individuals who show what is called the **Type B behavior pattern** display essentially the opposite set of behaviors. They are far less competitive, not especially time-oriented, and not usually aggressive, driven, or hostile. Although people are typically not "pure" Type A's or Type B's, showing instead a combination of both behavior types, they generally do fall into one or the other category (Rosenman, 1990; Strube, 1990).

Type A people lead fast-paced, driven lives. They put in longer hours at work than Type B's and are impatient with other people's performance, which they typically perceive as too slow. They also engage in what is known as polyphasic thinking; concentrating on several activities simultaneously. Consider, for example, the actual case of a man who built a desk onto the front of his exercise bike. When seated on the bike, which he positioned in front of the television, he was able to get his daily exercise, sign letters, read, and view television—all at the same time. He noted that his wife could always tell when there had been an exciting football play: He pumped the pedals so quickly that she could hear the bike in the next room.

Type A behaviors would be of little more than passing interest to health psychologists were it not for the fact that the Type A behavior pattern has repeatedly been linked to coronary heart disease. For example, in a major eight-year study of some 3000 men who were initially diagnosed as being free of heart disease and as having the Type A pattern, it was found that they developed coronary heart disease twice as often, suffered significantly more fatal heart attacks, and reported five times as many coronary problems as those classified as having the Type B pattern (Roseman, Brand, Sholtz, & Friedman, 1976). Moreover, the Type A pattern predicted who was going to develop heart disease at least as well as—and independently of—any other single factor, including age, blood pressure, smoking habits, and cholesterol levels in the body. The Type A behavior pattern is generally associated, then, with a heightened risk of coronary heart disease (Williams et al., 1988).

Type A behavior pattern: A pattern of behavior characterized by competitiveness, impatience, a tendency toward frustration, and hostility

Type B behavior pattern: A pattern of behavior characterized by noncompetitiveness, nonaggression, and patience in times of potential stress

Why should Type A behavior be linked to coronary heart disease? The most convincing theory is that Type A's tend to become excessively aroused physiologically whenever they are placed in stressful situations. This arousal, in turn, results in increased production of the hormones epinephrine and norepinephrine, as well as increased heart rate and blood pressure. Such exaggerated physiological responsivity seems to be tied to an increased incidence of cardiovascular disease, ultimately leading to the increased incidence of coronary heart disease (Matthews, 1982).

Paradoxically, not all research evidence consistently shows a strong, clear link between Type A behavior and coronary heart disease. For example, the results of one study suggest that men who fit the Type A pattern may be more likely to survive a second heart attack than men fitting the Type B pattern—even though the Type A men are more likely to have an initial heart attack (Ragland et al., 1988). In light of such puzzling evidence, a small minority of researchers go so far as to claim that the relationship between Type A behavior and coronary heart disease is illusory (Fischman, 1987).

However, the most definitive research reviews find that there is at least a modest relationship between the two factors, although certain components of Type A behavior seem to be more closely associated with coronary heart disease than others. For example, the hard-driving and competitive aspects of the Type A personality are major factors in coronary heart disease; impatience in completing tasks seems less important (Booth-Kewley & Friedman, 1987; Wright, 1988; Evans, 1990).

Overall, the most important concept to emerge from recent research is that people who experience frequent negative emotions—whether aggressive competitiveness, frustration, anger, depression, or some combination—are most prone to coronary heart disease. Because Type A people are more likely than Type B's to experience such negative emotions, then, they may be more apt to experience coronary heart disease.

If you display Type A behaviors, you may be worrying about whether you are destined to have coronary heart disease. The answer is no, particularly if you are female. The great majority of research has been carried out on men, since the rates of coronary heart disease are significantly higher for males than for females. (Still, some preliminary research suggests that some behaviors associated with Type A, including time urgency and impatient behavior, are linked to coronary heart disease in women; Thoresen & Low, 1990).

In addition, the evidence relating Type A behavior and coronary heart disease is correlational. We cannot say for sure whether Type A behavior *causes* heart disease or whether, instead, some other factor causes both heart disease and Type A behavior. Indeed, some evidence suggests that rather than focusing on Type A behavior as the cause of heart disease, we should concentrate on Type B behavior, which appears to be critical in the *prevention* of heart disease (Krantz, Glass, Schaeffer, & Davia, 1982).

More important, even if a causal link between Type A behavior and coronary heart disease exists, people may be able to learn to change from their A behaviors to B behaviors and, as a consequence, decrease their risk of heart disease. For example, in one extensive program carried out in the San Francisco Bay area, 600 Type A men were trained to act more like Type B's (Friedman et al., 1984).

ANSWERS (REVIEW I):

1. Stress **2.** 1-b; 2-a; 3-c **3.** Posttraumatic stress disorder **4.** a **5.** uplifts **6.** coping **7.** a **8.** hardiness.

If having to stand in line upsets you, you might benefit from the techniques used to modify Type A attitudes.

In the study, the subjects—all of whom had previously suffered heart attacks and, therefore, were at a relatively high risk for future heart disease—were taught specific techniques to modify their reactions to stressful situations.

Several training techniques were used (Friedman et al., 1984). One strategy was intended to change the way Type A's interpreted situations that had in the past produced stress. For example, suppose a Type A were in a long, slow-moving line at a bank. This person's characteristic reaction would be to fume, feel anxious, think about where he or she had to go and how much was not being accomplished because of the delay. Type B's, on the other hand, would tend to take a more leisurely view of the situation, possibly even welcoming the delay as an opportunity to pause and reflect. The training suggested that program participants should consider how a Type B would view the situation, and react similarly—thereby lowering their level of anxiety. To learn to do so, Type A's were told to look for lines and practice patiently standing and waiting.

Other techniques were directed toward the participants' physiological reactions to stress. Participants were trained in muscle relaxation procedures and in moderating their general physical activity level. Finally, they were urged to make changes in their lifestyles, including the renewal of old friendships and the adoption of hobbies unrelated to their careers.

The results of the program were highly encouraging. Compared with a control group of heart attack victims who received traditional medical treatment and information about heart attacks, those enrolled in the program fared significantly better—with a dramatically lower incidence of repeat heart attacks (Friedman et al., 1984).

However, we cannot say for sure that a reduction in Type A behavior led directly to a reduced risk of coronary heart disease, since a variety of treatment procedures were used in the program and since it is unclear what specific Type A factor might account for the reduction in heart attacks (Roskies, 1990).

There is something else to consider: Type A behaviors are associated with many of the highly esteemed cultural norms of our society, including achievement, competitiveness, and the importance of the work ethic (Carver & Humphries, 1982). Furthermore, there is even some evidence showing that people with the Type A behavior pattern feel more vigorous, self-confident, and happier. Ironically, then, if the incidence of Type A behavior is reduced, the result may be physically healthier individuals, but not necessarily more productive and happier ones (Carver & Humphries, 1982; Bryant & Yarnold, 1990).

Psychological Aspects of Cancer: Mind over Tumor?

Hardly any disease is more feared than cancer. Most people think of cancer in terms of lingering pain, and being diagnosed with the disease is typically viewed as receiving a death sentence.

Although a diagnosis of cancer is not as grim as you might at first suspect—several kinds of cancer have a high cure rate if detected early enough—cancer remains the second leading cause of death after coronary heart disease. The precise trigger for the disease is not well understood, but the process by which cancer spreads is straightforward. Certain cells in the body become altered and multiply rapidly and in an uncontrolled fashion. As these cells grow, they form tumors, which, if left unchecked, suck nutrients from healthy cells and body tissue, ultimately destroying the body's ability to function properly.

While the process involved in the spread of cancer is basically physiological in nature, accumulating evidence suggests that the emotional response of cancer patients to their disease may have a critical effect on its course. For example, one experiment found that people who adopt a fighting spirit ("I don't care what the odds are, I'm going to lick this disease") are more likely to recover than those who pessimistically suffer and resign themselves to death ("I'm a goner"). The study analyzed the survival rates of women who had undergone the removal of a breast because of cancer (Pettingale, Morris, Greer, & Haybittle, 1985). The results suggested that the survival rates were related to the psychological response of the women three months after surgery (see Figure 16-3). Women who stoically accepted their fate, trying not to complain, and those who felt the situation was hopeless and that nothing could be done, showed the lowest survival rates; most of these women were dead after ten years. On the other hand,

FIGURE 16-3

The relationship between women's psychological response to breast cancer three months after surgery and their survival ten years after the operation. (Pettingale, Morris, Greer, & Haybittle, 1985.)

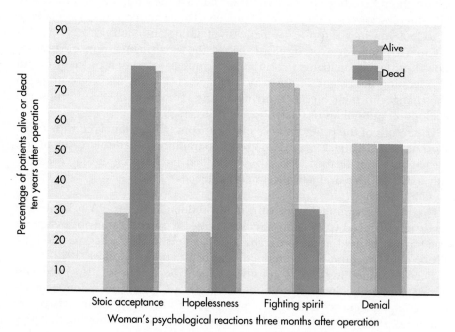

the survival rates of women who showed a fighting spirit (predicting that they would overcome the disease and planning to take steps to prevent its recurrence) and the survival rates of women who (erroneously) denied that they had ever had cancer (saying that the breast removal was merely a preventative step) were significantly higher. In sum, according to this study, cancer patients with a positive attitude were more likely to survive than those with a more negative one.

Studies such as these suggest that patients' emotional responses may partially determine the course of their disease. Although the exact mechanism by which the process could occur is not well understood, accumulating evidence suggests that a patient's emotional state may affect the immune system, the body's natural defenses that fight disease. In the case of cancer, for instance, it is possible that positive emotional responses may produce natural "killer" cells that help to control the size and spread of cancerous tumors. Conversely, negative emotions may suppress the ability of the same kinds of cells to fight tumors (Glaser et al., 1986).

The notion that a positive mental state increases longevity is supported by other studies. Psychologists Sandra Levy and colleagues, for example, found that a factor they labeled "joy"—referring to mental resilience and vigor—was the strongest predictor of survival times for a group of patients with recurrent breast cancer (Levy et al., 1988). Similarly, cancer patients who are characteristically optimistic report less distress throughout the course of their treatment (Carver, 1990; also see the Cutting Edge box below).

Other research has examined the relationship between social support and the development of cancer. For instance, one fifteen-year-long study found that people who developed cancer reported little closeness in their families (Thomas, Duszynski, & Schaffer, 1979). Moreover, researchers have tried to find whether a particular personality type is linked to cancer. Some findings suggest that cancer patients are less emotionally reactive, suppress anger, and lack outlets for emotional release. However, the data are still too tentative and inconsistent to

---

THE CUTTING EDGE

CAN PSYCHOLOGICAL THERAPY EXTEND THE LIVES OF CANCER PATIENTS?

Women with breast cancer who received psychological treatment lived at least a year and a half longer, and experienced less anxiety and pain, than women who did not participate in therapy.

That is the conclusion of a careful study done by David Spiegel of Stanford University. In the study, subjects in the advanced stages of breast cancer were randomly assigned either to psychological group therapy or to be part of a no-treatment control group in which they did not get therapy (Spiegel et al., 1989). The therapy consisted of open discussions with others in a group setting, led by a trained group leader.

The short-term effects of the treatment were clear: Patients participat-

ing in the therapy felt less fearful and depressed, reported experiencing less anxiety, and learned to reduce their pain through self-hypnosis. But the long-term consequences of participation in therapy were most surprising. Those in the control group lived an average of about one and a half years after starting the study, while those who had been in the group therapy lived an average of almost three years—twice as long. And the three women who were still alive ten years later all had been in the group receiving psychological treatment.

While Siegel's results regarding the benefits of psychological therapy are persuasive, it is premature to say definitively that therapy prolongs life. According to a study by the U.S. government, the question of whether psychological methods influence the onset and progression of cancer is still an open one (Office of Technology Assessment, 1990). Still, the results are promising. Spiegel is replicating his study, and he has received funding from the American Cancer Society to distribute a manual to other researchers interested in conducting similar studies. One day, perhaps, psychological therapy will become a standard part of the treatment for cancer.

suggest firm conclusions about a link between personality characteristics and cancer. Furthermore, it is certainly not reasonable to assume that people who develop cancer would not have done so if their personality had been of a different sort or if their attitudes had been more positive (Smith, 1988; Zevon & Corn, 1990).

While it is still too early to draw conclusions about the relationship between personality and cancer, increasing evidence clearly demonstrates that the immune system is affected by people's attitudes in several other medical realms. For instance, research has shown that patients with genital herpes are more likely to report outbreaks of the disease when they feel depressed than when they are not depressed—and that such outbreaks have a physiological basis associated with a decline in the cells that play an important role in controlling the virus (Kemeny, 1985). Furthermore, it is clear that stress, in general, alters functioning of the immune system and increases susceptibility to disease (Jemmott & Locke, 1984).

If stress and negative attitudes lead to suppression of the immune system, do positive attitudes help it function more effectively? The question is far from answered, but certainly the possibility is a real one. In sum, although this area of research remains controversial, most psychologists believe that there are significant links between people's emotional states and their illnesses.

Smoking

Would you go into a supermarket and buy an item with a label warning you that its consumption was considered dangerous by the U.S. Surgeon General? Although most of us would probably answer no, millions make such a purchase every day: a pack of cigarettes. Moreover, we do this despite clear, well-publicized evidence that smoking is linked to cancer, heart attacks, strokes, bronchitis, emphysema, and a host of other serious illnesses. According to government reports and the U.S. Surgeon General, smoking is the greatest preventable cause of death in America.

Why do people smoke, despite all the evidence showing that it is bad for their health? It is not that they are somehow unaware of the association between smoking and disease; surveys show that 71 percent of *smokers* agree with the statement "Cigarette smoking frequently causes disease and death" (U.S. Department of Health and Human Services, 1981).

Although some evidence suggests that there is at least a partial genetic influence on smoking, most research suggests that environmental factors are primarily to blame (Epstein et al., 1989). It seems that smokers tend to drift into a pattern of smoking, only gradually becoming hooked on the behavior as they move through a series of four basic stages that culminate in the smoking habit (Hirschman, Leventhal, & Glynn, 1984; Leventhal & Cleary, 1980):

■ Preparation. Old movie buffs ought to recall that many of the movie characters in the 1940s were avid smokers. In fact, female leads often used the skillful manipulation of their cigarettes in suggestive poses, thereby communicating the idea that smoking was sexy. Although movies today are less apt to use this ploy, powerful images are still conveyed by the media and other sources which promote the view that smoking is socially desirable. This view sets the first stage of smoking: a relatively positive attitude about it, generally gleaned from the media, peers, and advertising, and expressed in one of three guises: Smoking is "cool" or sophisticated; smoking is a rebel-

These children are playing "dress-up" and pretending to smoke. Did they learn from the media that smoking is a sophisticated adult behavior?

lious act; smoking helps one perform calmly under stressful situations (Grube, Rokeach, & Getzlaf, 1990).

■ Initiation. Smoking a cigarette is often a "rite of passage" for adolescents, tried at the urging of friends and viewed as a sign of growing up. One or two cigarettes do not usually make a lifetime smoker, but if people go on to smoke even ten cigarettes at some early age, they stand an 80 percent chance of becoming regular smokers (Salber, Freeman, & Abelin, 1966; Bowen, Dahl, Mann, & Peterson, 1991).

■ Becoming a smoker. In this crucial stage, smoking becomes a habit. Probably the most important hallmark of this stage is that people begin to consider themselves smokers, and smoking becomes part of their self-concept. Moreover, they become tolerant of, and potentially dependent on, the physiological effects of smoking, since nicotine, a primary ingredient of tobacco, is highly addictive (Russell, 1979; U.S. Surgeon General, 1988).

■ Maintaining the smoking habit. In this final stage there is an interaction of both psychological and biological factors that makes smoking a routine behavior. The most important psychological mechanisms include the establishment of a learned habit, positive emotional reactions such as stimulation and relaxation, a decrease in negative emotional reactions such as tension and anxiety, and social factors such as peer-group approval and support from other smokers (Oskamp, 1984). But it is also clear that apart from the purely psychological factors, there are biological reasons for maintenance of smoking: People develop a physiological dependence on the nicotine content of cigarettes. Ultimately, a complex relationship develops between smoking, nicotine levels, and the smoker's emotional state. Specifically, it seems that smoking tends to affect and regulate people's emotions. Because smoking raises the nicotine level in the blood, a certain nicotine level eventually becomes associated with a positive emotional state. People smoke, then, in an effort to regulate *both* emotional states and nicotine levels in the blood (Leventhal & Cleary, 1980; Pomerleau & Pomerleau, 1989).

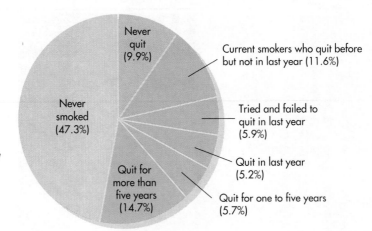

FIGURE 16-4

Quitting smoking—and failing. Results of a national survey show that many smokers have tried unsuccessfully to quit. (Source: Office on Smoking and Health, Centers for Disease Control, 1989.)

Quitting Smoking. Because smoking has both psychological and biological causes, few habits are as difficult to break. Long-term successful treatment typically occurs in just 15 percent of those trying to stop smoking, and once it becomes a habit, it is as hard to stop as an addiction to cocaine or heroin (U.S. Surgeon General, 1988). Many people try to quit and fail, as you can see in Figure 16-4.

Behavioral strategies, which view smoking as a learned habit and concentrate on changing the smoking response, have been most effective. Initial "cure" rates of 60 percent have been reported, and one year after treatment more than half of those who quit have not resumed smoking (Lictenstein, 1982; Pomerleau, Adkins, & Pertschuk, 1978).

Yet what may prove to be the most effective means of reducing smoking are the broad changes that are now occurring in societal norms and attitudes about smoking and the kinds of people who smoke. For instance, many cities and towns have made smoking in public places illegal, and other legislation restricting smoking in such places as college classrooms and buildings—based on strong popular sentiment—is being passed with increasing frequency.

The long-term effect of the constant barrage of information regarding the negative consequences of smoking on people's health has been substantial; overall, smoking has declined over the last two decades, particularly for males (Schelling, 1992). Still, 31 percent of men and 26 percent of women identify themselves as current smokers, and those who smoke are starting at a younger age (CDC, 1991a). Clearly, the threat to public health represented by smoking is far from over.

RECAP AND REVIEW II

RECAP

◀ Among the major problems studied by health psychologists are coronary heart disease, cancer, and smoking.

◀ The Type A behavior pattern is associated with a higher incidence of coronary heart disease. Type A's are competitive, show a sense of time urgency, appear to be unduly driven, and are relatively aggressive and hostile,

especially when interrupted. Type B's tend to display the opposite sorts of behaviors.

◀ The success of cancer treatment may be affected by patients' attitudes.

◀ Smokers pass through four basic stages: preparation, initiation, becoming a smoker, and maintaining the smoking habit.

PSYCHOLOGICAL FACTORS RELATED TO PHYSICAL ILLNESS: GOING TO THE DOCTOR

When Stuart Grinnel first noticed the small lump in his arm, he assumed that it was just a bruise from the touch-football game he had played last week. But as he thought about it, he envisioned more serious possibilities and decided that he better get it checked out by a physician at the university health service. The visit—like most of his encounters with physicians—was less than satisfactory. A shy and inarticulate person, Stuart felt embarrassed and inept about communicating his medical problems. Then, after answering all the questions he was asked, he couldn't even understand the doctor's list of possible problems. All he heard was medical jargon that meant little to him. Why couldn't the physician just have carried out a physical examination to find out what was wrong? After all, hadn't the doctor gone to medical school in order to be able to make a diagnosis on the basis of physical symptoms?

Stuart Grinnel's attitudes toward doctors and his view of a physician's role are shared by many of us. Yet not everything of importance *can* be discerned from a physical examination alone; several critical psychological factors, such as the nature of physician-patient communication, influence a health-care practitioner's effectiveness in diagnosing and treating medical problems.

Physician-Patient Communication

It may surprise you that many patients are reluctant to describe their symptoms to their physicians. But the situation is a common one. Many individuals believe that physicians are so skilled that they can easily identify a patient's problems through a thorough physical examination, the way a good mechanic can diagnose car problems (Leigh & Reiser, 1980; Mentzer & Snyder, 1982). Moreover, physicians' relatively high social prestige and power may intimidate patients by making them feel that their problems are trivial and unimportant, or making them reluctant to volunteer information that might cast them in a bad light (Taylor, 1982).

Conversely, physicians may have difficulties encouraging their patients to provide the proper information. In many cases, physicians dominate an interview with questions of a technical nature, while patients attempt to communicate a personal sense of their illness and the impact it is having on their lives (Goleman, 1988a).

▶ **535**

TABLE 16-2

A PATIENT TALKS TO HER PHYSICIAN

The following excerpt from a case study used at the Harvard Medical School is an example of poor interviewing technique on the part of the physician.

Patient: I can hardly drink water.

Doctor: Um hum.

Patient: Remember when it started? . . . It was pains in my head. It must have been then.

Doctor: Um hum.

Patient: I don't know what it is. The doctor looked at it . . . said something about glands.

Doctor: OK. Um hum, aside from this, how have you been feeling?

Patient: Terrible.

Doctor: Yeah.

Patient: Tired . . . there's pains. . . . I don't know what it is.

Doctor: OK. . . . Fevers or chills?

Patient: No.

Doctor: OK. . . . Have you been sick to your stomach or anything?

Patient: (Sniffles, crying) I don't know what's going on. I get up in the morning tired. The only time I feel good . . . maybe like around suppertime . . . and everything (crying) and still the same thing.

Doctor: Um hum. You're getting the nausea before you eat or after (Goleman, 1988a, p. B16)?

Although the frequent "um hums" suggest that the physician is listening to the patient, in fact they do not encourage the patient to disclose more pertinent details. Even more, late in the interview, the physician ignores the patient's emotional distress and coldly continues through the list of questions.

The reluctance of patients to reveal medical information fully to health-care providers, and the difficulties that providers experience in eliciting information, may prevent providers from understanding the extent of the difficulties that led the patients to seek medical care in the first place (see Table 16-2). Furthermore, the view held by many patients that physicians are "all-knowing" can result in serious communication problems. For instance, many patients do not understand their treatment yet fail to ask their doctors for clearer explanations of a prescribed course of action. Research has shown that about half of all patients cannot accurately report how long they are to continue taking a medication prescribed for them, and about a quarter do not even know the purpose of the drug (Svarstad, 1976). In fact, some patients are not even sure, as they are about to be rolled into the operating room, why they are having surgery!

One reason for patient-physician communication difficulties is that frequently the material that needs to be communicated is too difficult or too technical for patients, who may lack fundamental knowledge about the body and basic medical practices (Ley & Spelman, 1967). Moreover, the use of professional jargon can be confusing. Suppose, for instance, you were told that you had "essential hypertension" and that you had to "take hydrochlorathiazide twice a day and reduce sodium intake.'' These instructions obviously would have been a lot easier to comprehend if you had been told you had high blood pressure, should take a drug that eliminates fluids, and should reduce the amount of salt in your diet (DiMatteo & DiNicola, 1982).

Sometimes medical practitioners take the opposite tack and use baby talk or overly simplistic explanations. A physician who said, ''Nurse, would you just pop off her things for me? I want to examine her,'' elicited the following comments from a patient:

> In the hospital, everything is ''popped'' on or off, ''slipped'' in or out. I don't think I met a single doctor who, in dealing with patients, didn't resort to this sort of nursery talk. I once heard one saying to a patient, an elderly man, ''We're just going to pop you into the operating theater to have a little peep into your tummy'' (Toynbee, 1977).

Obviously, there is a middle ground between the extremes of technical jargon and baby talk. Unfortunately, because they deal with so many patients, health practitioners often have difficulty determining just how much individuals actually do understand about their conditions. As a consequence, practitioners routinely underestimate what patients understand (McKinley, 1975).

Another difficulty in patient-physician communication is that patients typically construct their own theories about their illnesses—theories which may have little basis in reality (Leventhal, Nerenz, & Leventhal, 1985). For example, a patient who has been prescribed medication for high blood pressure may think (erroneously) that headaches are a symptom of the high blood pressure. Because of this false assumption, she may think it necessary to take her medicine only when she has a headache—even if she has been told to take it every day. Her mistake is reinforced because she measures her blood pressure only when she has a headache—and then finds that it is high. Of course, if she were to take her blood pressure at other times, she would find it high then, too, and the inaccuracy of her theory would become apparent. But this is unlikely to happen, so the woman will continue to resist appropriate treatment because of her own misunderstanding of her medical problem.

Still, there are ways of combating physician-patient communication problems. For example, when patients are taught to ask forthright questions, they receive better medical care and ultimately feel better. Similarly, physicians who are taught to follow simple rules of courtesy—such as saying hello, addressing patients by name, explaining the purpose of a procedure while they are treating the patient, and saying goodbye—are perceived as warmer and more supportive than physicians who do not follow such rules (DiMatteo & DiNicola, 1982; Thompson, 1988; Thompson, Nanni, & Schwankovsky, 1990).

Complying with Physicians' Orders

One major consequence of patient-physician communication difficulties is a lack of compliance with medical advice. The problem is a serious one: Surveys show that only 40 to 70 percent of patients follow a physician's advice or take their prescribed medicine (Gatchel & Baum, 1983). Such noncompliance can take many forms—for example, failing to show up for scheduled appointments, not following diets or not giving up smoking, discontinuing medication during treatment, and failing to take prescribed medicine at all.

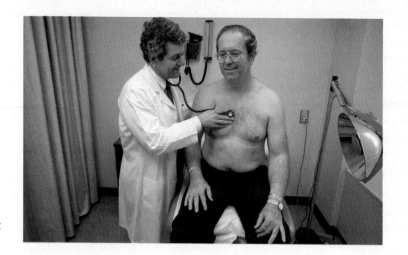

When a doctor does a thorough job of informing a patient about diagnosis and treatment, the chances of successful treatment are enhanced.

Compliance with medical advice is also linked to the degree of satisfaction patients have with their physicians. Patients who are satisfied with their physicians and view them as friendly and interested in their care are more apt to comply with their advice than patients reporting a lower level of satisfaction with their physician (Korsch & Negret, 1972).

Although compliance with a physician's advice does not guarantee that the patient's medical problems will go away, it does optimize the possibility that the patient's condition will improve. What, then, can physicians do to produce greater compliance on the part of their patients? One approach is for physicians to demonstrate greater warmth toward their patients. Patients who are comfortable with their physicians may be able to process information (and therefore comply with their advice) better than patients who experience stress due to an aloof or unpleasant physician.

It is also reasonable to assume that patients who view their physicians positively may feel an enhanced sense of control over their own care. Rather than perceiving themselves as merely following the advice of a powerful physician, they perceive that they are part of a partnership, jointly determining their medical care. Feelings of patient control have been directly linked to increased compliance (Rodin & Janis, 1979; Langer, 1983).

Of course, patient compliance is a complex process involving both physician and patient, and powerful psychological forces can operate to prevent both partners from modifying their behavior. For instance, consider the suggestion that physicians communicate with their patients in a warmer and more open manner and offer clear advice and information. Some would argue that in many cases it is better for physicians to maintain emotional distance between themselves and their patients (Parsons, 1975). According to proponents of this view, physicians can thereby diagnose and treat patients in a more objective manner.

Furthermore, evidence suggests that in many cases physicians themselves may be motivated by psychological factors to keep patients in the dark about the true nature of their illnesses, about what to expect in terms of the difficulties and pain involved in treatment, and about the potential for a disease to lead to a patient's death. Surveys show that physicians typically want to avoid telling dying patients that their illnesses are terminal. The experience that produces the greatest amount of anxiety for first-year medical students is discussing a fatal illness with a patient (Feifel, 1963; Saul & Kass, 1969).

However, almost every survey on the issue reveals that most people say that they want to be informed of the details of their illnesses—even if it means they learn that they are dying (Blumenfield, Levy, & Kaplan, 1979; Miller & Mangan, 1983). In fact, the strongest predictor of how satisfied patients are with their doctors is the amount of information the doctor gives about their condition and its treatment (Hall, Roter, & Katz, 1988b).

In sum, patients generally prefer to be well informed, and their degree of satisfaction with their medical care is linked to how well and how accurately physicians are able to convey the nature of their medical problems and treatment. The ultimate result of enhanced patient satisfaction is not just increased compliance with a physician's advice but more positive treatment outcomes as well. Patients who like their physicians tend to have greater confidence in the physician's technical expertise, which, in turn, leads to a reduction in patient anxiety (Ben-Sira, 1976). In addition, an increase in patient satisfaction is likely to have a positive influence on the recuperation process of patients who have had surgery, since the level of anxiety patients experience—related in part to their confidence in their physician—is itself related to postoperative recovery (Langer, Janis, & Wolfer, 1975).

RECAP AND REVIEW III

RECAP

◀ Problems in communication affect the success with which a physician can diagnose and treat medical problems.

◀ Patients often construct their own—sometimes inaccurate—theories or explanations of their illness.

◀ Patient compliance can be increased when patients are persuaded that they are in a partnership with their physician and have some control over their medical condition, as well as when physicians are warmer and friendlier and keep patients well informed.

REVIEW

1. Many health psychologists believe that the biggest problem in health-care is:
   a. Incompetent health-care providers
   b. Rising health-care costs
   c. Lack of communication between doctor and patient
   d. Scarcity of medical research funding
2. Patients are more likely to comply with a doctor's advice if:
   a. They are satisfied with and friendly toward their doctor.
   b. The doctor is female.
   c. They have a critical illness.
   d. The doctor is a specialist as opposed to a general practitioner.
3. Patients typically do not want to be informed when their illness is terminal. True or false? _____
4. A good physician should be able to
   a. make an accurate diagnosis on the basis of a physical examination alone
   b. provide information and advice in technical terms
   c. explain to the patient every decision that is made in his or her care, without considering patient input
   d. provide good medical skills and sufficient information to the patient

Ask Yourself

You are given the job of instructing a group of medical school students on "Doctor/Patient Interactions." How would you set up your class, and what kind of information would you give them?

(Answers to review questions are on page 540.)

■ *How does health psychology represent a union between medicine and psychology?*

1. The field of health psychology considers how psychology can be applied to the prevention, diagnosis, and treatment of medical problems.

■ *What is stress, how does it affect us, and how can we best cope with it?*

2. Stress is a response to threatening or challenging environmental conditions. People's lives are filled with stressors—the circumstances that produce stress—of both a positive and negative nature.

3. Stress produces immediate physiological reactions, including a rise in hormonal secretions, heart-rate and blood-pressure elevations, and changes in the electrical conductance of the skin. In the short term, these reactions may be adaptive, but in the long term they may have negative consequences, including the development of psychosomatic disorders. The consequences of stress can be explained in part by Selye's general adaptation syndrome (GAS), which suggests there are three stages to stress responses: alarm and mobilization, resistance, and exhaustion.

4. Stress factors are not universal—the way an environmental circumstance is interpreted affects whether it will be considered stressful. Still, there are general classes of events that tend to provoke stress: cataclysmic events, personal stressors, and background stressors or daily hassles. Stress is reduced by the presence of uplifts, minor positive events that make people feel good— even if only temporarily.

5. Stress can be reduced by developing a sense of control over one's circumstances. In some cases, however, people develop a state of learned helplessness—a response to uncontrollable situations that produce the feeling that no behavior will be effective in changing the situation; therefore no response is even attempted. Coping with stress can take a number of forms, including the unconscious use of defense mechanisms and the use of emotion-focused or problem-focused coping strategies.

■ *How do psychological factors affect such health-related problems as coronary heart disease, cancer, and smoking?*

6. Coronary heart disease, cancer, and smoking are major health problems studied by health psychologists. Research has shown that coronary heart disease is linked to a specific type of behavior pattern known as Type A. In contrast to Type B people, Type A individuals tend to be competitive, show a sense of time urgency and hurriedness, are hostile and aggressive, and seem to be driven.

7. There is increasing evidence that people's attitudes and emotional responses affect the course of a disease. Although the exact mechanism underlying this link is not well understood, it appears that people's emotional responses affect their immune system, the body's natural defenses that attack disease.

8. Smoking, the leading preventable cause of health problems, has proved to be difficult to control, even though most smokers are aware of the dangerous consequences of the behavior. People go through four stages in becoming habitual smokers: preparation, initiation, becoming a smoker, and maintaining the habit.

■ *Does the nature of our interactions with physicians affect our health and compliance to medical treatment?*

9. Although patients often expect physicians to make a diagnosis from only a physical examination, communicating one's problem to the physician is equally critical. Among the reasons that patients may find it difficult to communicate openly with their doctors are the high social prestige of physicians and the technical nature of medical information.

10. Problems in communication can be attributed to the behavior of physicians and other health-care workers as well. These professionals may fail to communicate treatment requirements adequately to their patients, thereby lowering patient compliance. Compliance is also related to satisfaction with medical care and to the kinds of theories patients may develop to explain their medical conditions.

ANSWERS (REVIEW III):

1. c **2.** a **3.** False; patients generally want all the information they can get about their illness. **4.** d

KEY TERMS AND CONCEPTS

health psychology (p. 512)
immune system (p. 512)
stress (p. 513)
stressors (p. 513)
psychosomatic disorders (p. 514)
general adaptation syndrome
    (GAS) (p. 516)
alarm and mobilization stage
    (p. 516)
resistance stage (p. 516)

exhaustion stage (p. 517)
cataclysmic events (p. 518)
posttraumatic stress disorder
    (p. 518)
personal stressors (p. 519)
background stressors (p. 520)
daily hassles (p. 520)
uplifts (p. 520)
learned helplessness (p. 520)

coping (p. 522)
defense mechanisms (p. 522)
emotion-focused coping (p. 523)
problem-focused coping (p. 523)
hardiness (p. 523)
social support (p. 524)
inoculation (p. 525)
Type A behavior pattern (p. 527)
Type B behavior pattern (p. 527)

17

ABNORMAL BEHAVIOR

JUDY SMITH

Judy Smith.

By day she rests on a black plastic garbage bag placed neatly on the sidewalk, smiling at passers-by who stop and hand her a dollar or two and thanking them warmly in a pleasant, husky voice. Many of them live in the surrounding neighborhood of expensive townhouses and antique stores, and have come to feel protective toward her.

At night she gathers her belongings—a large padlocked box on a suitcase cart, a red-and-gray striped carry bag and a black Lancome tote bag—and lugs them three blocks to Second Avenue and 63rd Street. There she puts them carefully in the doorway of a bank, walks to the curb and screams obscenities into the night.

At 41, her face is ruddy from outdoor living, and she has deep brown eyes. When she is docile, she has a sweet, inquiring expression. She wears layers of clothing—a black T-shirt, a loose print cotton dress, a multicolored sweater and, lately, a turquoise Norma Kamali down coat. Her long brown hair is covered by a blue-and-black knit cap worn over a gray knit one. She wears blue leg warmers and pink sneakers.

Conversations range from rational exchanges to total confusion.

"Do you know this neighborhood?" she asked a reporter the other day. "It's a very nice historical neighborhood, and you should really write about it."

A minute later she said that she owned all the land in the neighborhood and that she had been on that corner for centuries. Solemnly she explained that she was tied to the tracks under the ground (Carmody, 1984, p. B1).

Judy Smith[1] did not always act this way. Growing up in the Midwest, her childhood and adolescence were unremarkable. She sang in her church choir and was invited to join the high school honor society. She married the son of a well-known town resident, and they had a daughter.

But eventually Judy's behavior began to take some strange twists. The husband she married soon after high school, who turned out to be the first of three, said she made up facts. She began to talk to herself, although most of the time she behaved normally. She graduated from college and took enough courses for a master's degree. She gave wonderful parties and was an excellent housekeeper, according to her mother.

However, her behavior began to deteriorate further, and after several years her conversations with imaginary individuals became more frequent and vehement. Her mother failed in the first of several attempts to commit her to a mental hospital, because Judy refused. After telling her mother she was ready to enter the hospital, a lawyer met with her in preparation for the commitment hearing and convinced her that she should not be hospitalized. The lawyer then represented her at the hearing, and the judge ruled that she was no threat to herself and others, and thus should not be hospitalized.

Since that time, Judy has lived on the streets. Sometimes she seems totally

[1] Smith is not her actual last name.

rational, arguing with a laundry owner about the price he charges for cleaning her clothes, or mailing packages via United Parcel Service to her family. She is meticulous about cleaning herself, washing daily with bottled Evian water.

Judy has another side, though. She screams for hours on end, shouting obscenities. She has also developed another personality, with whom she argues violently. She is convinced that she has special knowledge of a conspiracy to defraud the United States.

But Judy refuses psychological help. She thinks she doesn't need it.

LOOKING AHEAD ▶

Most of us would disagree with Judy's assessment of her mental health. Yet her case raises a series of perplexing questions. Why did Judy live in the streets? Why did she spurn help which others tried to provide? Why did her behavior approach normalcy during the day and deteriorate into screaming obscenities during the night? What was the cause of her behavior? Could she have been spared a life in the streets through early treatment? More generally, how do we distinguish normal from abnormal behavior, and how can Judy's behavior be categorized and classified and the specific nature of her problem pinpointed?

Although none of these questions can be answered definitively, especially with a case as complex as Judy's, we can start to address some of the issues raised by her atypical behavior in this and the following chapter. We begin by discussing the distinction between normal and abnormal behavior, considering the subtle distinctions that must be made. We examine the various approaches that have been used to explain abnormal behavior, ranging from explanations based on superstition to those based on contemporary, scientific approaches, and apply these approaches to the case of Judy, showing how the various explanations complement one another.

The heart of the chapter consists of a description of the various types of abnormal behaviors. Using a classification system employed by mental health practitioners, we examine the most significant kinds of disorders. The chapter also includes a discussion of the problems and dangers of self-diagnosis, and the signals people might see in themselves that could lead them to consider seeking help from a mental health professional.

In sum, after reading this chapter, you will have the answers to several fundamental questions about mental health:

- ■ How can we distinguish normal from abnormal behavior?
- ■ What are the major models of abnormal behavior used by mental health professionals, and how are they applied to specific cases?
- ■ What is the classification system used to categorize abnormal behavior, and what are the major mental health disorders?
- ■ What are the major indicators that signal a need for the help of a mental health practitioner?

NORMAL VERSUS ABNORMAL: MAKING THE DISTINCTION

Universally that person's acumen is esteemed very little perceptive concerning whatsoever matters are being held as most profitable by mortals with sapience endowed to be studied who is ignorant of that which the most in doctrine erudite and certainly by reason of that in them high mind's ornament deserving of veneration constantly maintain when by general consent they affirm that other circumstances being equal by no exterior splendour is the prosperity of a nation more efficaciously asserted than by the measure of how far forward may have progressed the tribute of its solicitude for that proliferent continuance which of evils the original if it be absent when fortunately present constitutes the certain sign of omnipollent nature's incorrupted benefaction.

It would be easy to conclude that these words were the musings of a madman. The passage does not seem, at least at first consideration, to make any sense at all. But literary scholars would disagree. In actuality this passage is from James Joyce's classic *Ulysses*, which has been hailed as one of the major works of twentieth-century literature (Joyce, 1934, p. 377).

As this example illustrates, making a cursory examination of a person's writing is insufficient to determine the degree to which he or she is "normal." But even when we consider more extensive samples of a person's behavior, we find that there may only be a fine line between behavior that is considered normal and that which is considered abnormal.

Approaches to Abnormality

The difficulty in distinguishing normal from abnormal behavior has led to a diversity of approaches for devising a precise, scientific definition of "abnormal behavior." Over the years, in fact, the definitions of what constitutes normal and abnormal behavior have taken a number of twists. We examine next the four major approaches employed at one time or another.

Deviation from the Average.   The approach that is perhaps the most obvious defines abnormality as deviation from the average—a statistical definition. In order to determine abnormality, we simply observe what behaviors are rare or infrequent in a given society or culture and label these deviations from the norm as abnormal.

Although such a definition may be appropriate in some instances, its drawback is that some behaviors that are statistically rare clearly do not lend themselves to classification as abnormal. If most people prefer to have orange juice with breakfast, but you prefer apple juice, this hardly makes your behavior abnormal. Similarly, such a conception of abnormality would unreasonably label a person who has an unusually high IQ as abnormal, simply because it is statistically rare. A definition of abnormality that rests on deviation from the average, then, is insufficient by itself.

Deviation from the Ideal: Striving for Perfection.   An alternative approach to defining abnormality is one that takes into account not what most people do (the average), but the standard toward which most people are striving—the ideal. Under this sort of definition, behavior is considered abnormal if it deviates enough from some kind of ideal or standard (Jahoda, 1958). Unfortunately, the definition suffers from even more difficulties than the deviation-from-the-average definition, since society has so few standards about which people agree. Moreover, the standards that do arise tend to change over time, making the deviation-from-the-ideal approach inadequate.

Abnormality as a Sense of Subjective Discomfort. Given the drawbacks of both the deviation-from-the-average and deviation-from-the-ideal definitions of normality, we must turn to more subjective approaches. One of the most useful definitions of abnormal behavior concentrates on the psychological consequences of the behavior for the individual. In this approach, behavior is considered abnormal if it produces a sense of distress, anxiety, or guilt in an individual—or if it is harmful to others in some way.

Even a definition that rests on subjective discomfort has its drawbacks, for in some particularly severe forms of mental disturbance, people report feeling euphoric and on top of the world—yet to others, their behavior is bizarre. In this case, then, there is a subjective state of well-being, yet the behavior is within the realm of what most people would consider abnormal. This suggests that a definition of abnormality that does not consider people's ability to function effectively is inadequate. Thus psychologists have developed one final approach to distinguishing between normal and abnormal behavior.

Abnormality as the Inability to Function Effectively. Most people are able to feed themselves, hold a job, get along with others, and in general live as productive members of society. Yet there are those who are unable to adjust to the demands of society or function effectively.

According to this last view of abnormality, people who are unable to function effectively and adapt to the demands of society are considered abnormal. For example, an unemployed, homeless woman living on the street, such as Judy Smith, might be considered unable to function effectively. Therefore her behavior would be considered abnormal, even if she had made the choice to live in this particular fashion. It is her inability to adapt to the requirements of society that makes her "abnormal," according to this approach.

The Continuum of Abnormal and Normal Behavior: Drawing the Line on Abnormality. None of the four definitions alone is broad enough to cover all instances of abnormal behavior, and the division between normal and abnormal behavior often remains indistinct, sometimes even to trained professionals. Furthermore, the label of abnormal behavior is highly affected by cultural expectations relating to what happens to be typical in a society.

Probably the best way to deal with this imprecision is not to consider abnormal and normal behavior as absolute states. Rather, they should be viewed as marking the two ends of a continuum (or scale) of behavior, with completely normal functioning at one end and totally abnormal behavior at the other. Obviously, behavior typically falls somewhere between these two extremes.

Because the difference between normal and abnormal behavior is indistinct, the issue of when society should intervene and require treatment for people displaying abnormal behavior is also ambiguous. For example, should mental health officials have stepped in and forced Judy, whose case began the chapter, to seek psychological treatment?

There is no clear-cut answer to the question, both in Judy's case and in those of other homeless people who suffer from psychological disturbances. However, lawyers and forensic psychologists—psychologists who specialize in the law— have attempted to define the circumstances under which legal intervention in cases of abnormal behavior is appropriate. In most states, a person must meet

HOMELESSNESS

A woman pushing a cart loaded with a ragtag collection of clothing, bags, and others' trash. A man lying on a subway grate on a snowy evening, talking to himself. A scruffy man, sitting on a bus terminal bench, who keeps swatting at a fly that only he can see.

The images are haunting and unforgettable. They also represent one of the most conspicuous social and mental health problems facing the United States today.

Assessments vary widely regarding just how many homeless people there are, with estimates ranging from a low of several hundred thousand to a high of 3 million (Breakey & Fischer, 1990). Most surveys suggest a significant minority of the homeless suffer from some psychological disorder, with some 10 to 40 percent of the homeless having serious, chronic psychological disorders. Perhaps 20 to 30 percent have drug or alcohol problems, and between 10 and 20 percent exhibit signs of severe difficulties, such as hearing voices or feeling persecuted by unknown forces. Between one-fourth and one-third have been hospitalized for psychological disorders at some previous time in their lives. Of course, it is also important to note that the majority of homeless do *not* have serious psychological difficulties (Fisher & Breakey, 1991; Drake, Osher, & Wallach, 1991; Rossi, 1990).

For those with psychological disorders, becoming homeless repre-

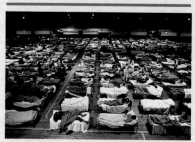

A study of adults in homeless shelters showed that many had been in foster care as children.

sents the last step of a lengthy process of psychological deterioration. For many, such a decline begins in childhood. For example, one study found that almost half of those entering a public shelter who had been hospitalized previously had also been institutionalized or been in foster care as children. Regardless of whether their homelessness was brought about by an immediate economic setback such as the loss of a job or by being evicted from other housing, most homeless people with psychological problems have experienced psychological difficulties for an extended period (HMHL, 1991; Weitzman, Knickman, & Shinn, 1990).

In some cases, homeless people choose to remain homeless. For instance, Judy Smith, whose case began this chapter, rejected entreaties made by her family and residents of the neighborhood in which she lives to spend her nights in homeless shelters. (According to her mother, Smith

refuses to go to shelters because she doesn't like to interact with the kind of people she might find there!)

One of the major issues relating to homelessness is the degree to which governmental welfare agencies should intervene and force people with mental disorders off the street. As was the case with Smith, many in the legal system resist efforts to involuntarily hospitalize the homeless. If homeless individuals such as Smith commit no crime and appear to be in no danger to themselves or others, some legal experts find no reason to limit their freedom and to force them into shelters or treatment. Such logic dictates that the homeless be allowed to stay on the streets, even if their behavior appears disturbed, not to say distasteful, to others. On the other hand, some psychologists argue that people who live outside throughout a winter's freezing temperatures and a summer's sweltering heat are in clear danger of harming themselves. To these experts, it is the responsibility of society to impel such people into a situation which is less potentially injurious.

Clearly, the issues are not easily resolved, as they pit the civil liberties of individuals against the rights of society as a whole. What is clear is that homelessness will continue to be a major societal issue for some time, and that a significant minority of the people living on the streets of our cities and towns have profound psychological disorders.

four criteria prior to intervention (Schwitzgabel & Schwitzgabel, 1980): The person must be (1) dangerous to himself or herself; (2) incapable of providing for basic physical needs; (3) unable to make reasonable decisions about whether treatment is required; and (4) require treatment or care. Of course, these four criteria still do not clearly answer the question of when treatment should be provided to an individual since the criteria are fraught with ambiguity. The determination, then, of when society should intervene in the presence of abnormal behavior is clearly a difficult one to make. (Also see the Cutting Edge box.)

The Prevalence of Mental Disorders: The Mental State of the Union

Given the difficulties in satisfactorily defining abnormality, it should come as no surprise that determining the number of people showing signs of abnormal behavior is no simple task. But a survey conducted by the U.S. government in the mid-1980s does provide a sense of how many Americans show signs of mental disorder (Regier et al., 1984; Regier et al., 1988; Robins & Regier, 1991).

The survey was conducted in five communities and included about 18,000 Americans. In individual interviews that lasted two hours, each interviewee answered 200 questions about particular kinds of problems, such as feeling panicky when leaving the house or losing interest in normally pleasant activities. By using standard categories of mental disturbance that we will explore later in the chapter, the researchers were able to produce a statistical profile of the "mental state of the union."

The survey showed that close to 20 percent of the adults queried currently had a mental disorder, and that close to one-third had experienced a disorder at some time in their lives. The current rates of disorder were about the same for men and women, although more men than women had experienced a disorder at some point in their lifetime (Robins, Locke, & Regier, 1991).

Projecting the results to the nation as a whole indicates that more than 29 million Americans have one or more mental disorders or have suffered from one within the past six months. For example, 13 million have difficulties related to anxiety, 10 million abuse alcohol or some other drug, and some 11 million have irrational fears. (Because subjects could report more than one problem, there is overlap in these statistics.) Surprisingly, just one in five of those with a problem seek help.

It is not just adults who have a high rate of psychological disorder. For instance, one major survey suggests that 20 percent of American children have a developmental, learning, or emotional problem at some point. Moreover, problems such as these are twice as likely to occur in families in which disruption has occurred (such as divorce or single-parent households) than in those that are two-parent, intact households (Zill & Schoenborn, 1990).

These survey results suggest that abnormal behavior is far from rare. Moreover, in further surveys now under way, researchers are obtaining information about which mental disorders benefit most from treatment and which ones simply go away on their own, as well as information on how major life events (such as marriage and death in the family) influence mental disorders. This work offers the promise of identifying specific events that trigger abnormal behavior and of finding ways to prevent their occurrence (Robins & Regier, 1991).

> **RECAP AND REVIEW I**

RECAP

◄ Distinctions between normal and abnormal behavior are not always readily apparent.

◄ Definitions of abnormality include those based on deviation from the average, deviation from the ideal, the psychological consequences of the behavior for the individual, and the individual's ability to function effectively and adapt as a member of society.

◄ Abnormal and normal behavior may best be viewed as marking the two ends of a continuum or scale.

1. A problem in defining abnormal behavior is:
   a. Statistically rare behavior may not be abnormal.
   b. Not all abnormalities are accompanied by feelings of discomfort.
   c. Cultural standards are too general to use as a measuring tool.
   d. All of the above
2. According to community surveys, while a significant number of Americans have shown at least some form of psychological abnormality, relatively few ever seek treatment for their problem. True or false? _____
3. According to the definition of abnormality as experiencing subjective discomfort or causing harm to others, which of the following people is most likely to need treatment?
   a. An executive is afraid to accept a promotion because it would require moving from his ground-floor office to the top floor of a tall office building.
   b. A woman quits her job and chooses to live on the street.
   c. A man believes that friendly spacemen visit his house every Thursday.
   d. A photographer lives with nineteen cats in a small apartment.
4. Karl's family is worried about his decision to live in a tree house—unheard-of behavior in their wealthy neighborhood. What approach to defining abnormality is Karl's family using? _____
5. A scale of behavior ranging from "most abnormal" to "most normal" is an example of a(n) _____.
6. Virginia's mother thinks that Virginia's behavior is clearly abnormal because, despite being offered admission to medical school, she decides to become a waitress. What approach is Virginia's mother using to define abnormal behavior? _____

Ask Yourself

If you were asked to develop a new legal definition of mental illness, what would it be? How would it differ from the definitions proposed in this chapter? What problems could you foresee?

(Answers to review questions are on page 552.)

MODELS OF ABNORMALITY: FROM SUPERSTITION TO SCIENCE

The disease occurred at the height of the summer heat. People, asleep or awake, would suddenly jump up, feeling an acute pain like the sting of a bee. Some saw the spider, others did not, but they knew that it must be the tarantula. They ran out of the house into the street, to the marketplace, dancing in great excitement. Soon they were joined by others who like them had been bitten, or by people who had been stung in previous years. . . .

Thus groups of patients would gather, dancing wildly in the queerest attire. . . . Others would tear their clothes and show their nakedness, losing all sense of modesty. . . . Some called for swords and acted like fencers, others for whips and beat each other. . . . Some of them had still stranger fancies, liked to be tossed in the air, dug holes in the ground, and rolled themselves into the dirt like swine. They all drank wine plentifully and sang and talked like drunken people . . . (Sigerist, 1943, pp. 103, 106–107).

This description of a peculiar form of abnormal behavior that occurred during the thirteenth century—behavior attributed, at the time, to the imagined bite of a tarantula spider—indicates that mental disturbance and theories about its causes are nothing new. Yet our understanding of the causes of such behavior has become considerably more sophisticated.

For much of the past, abnormal behavior was linked to superstition and witchcraft. People displaying abnormal behavior were accused of being possessed by the devil or some sort of demonic god (Howells & Osborn, 1984). Authorities felt justified in "treating" abnormal behavior by attempting to drive out the source of the problem. This typically involved whipping, immersion in hot water, starvation, or other forms of torture in which the cure was often worse than the affliction.

Contemporary approaches to abnormal behavior take a more enlightened

This "spinning chair," invented by physician Benjamin Rush, was one of a number of torture-based treatments for psychological disorder commonly used in the eighteenth century.

view, and six major perspectives on abnormal behavior predominate: the medical model, the psychoanalytic model, the behavioral model, the cognitive model, the humanistic model, and the sociocultural model. These models suggest not only different causes of abnormal behavior but—as we shall see in the next chapter—different treatment approaches as well.

The Medical Model

When a person displays the symptoms of tuberculosis, we generally find the tuberculin germ in his or her body tissue. In the same way, the **medical model of abnormality** suggests that when an individual displays the symptoms of abnormal behavior, the root cause will be found in an examination of some physical aspect of the individual, such as a hormonal imbalance, a chemical deficiency, or an injury to part of the body. Indeed, when we speak of mental "illness," the "symptoms" of abnormal behavior, and mental "hospitals," we are using terminology related to the medical model.

Medical model of abnormality: The model that suggests that when an individual displays symptoms of abnormal behavior, the cause is physiological

As we will discuss later, because many sorts of abnormal behaviors have been linked to physiological causes, the medical model would seem to be a reasonable approach. In fact, the medical model does represent a major advance over explanations of abnormal behavior based on superstitions. Yet serious criticisms have been leveled against it. For one thing, there are many instances in which no physiological cause has been identified for abnormal behavior, thus negating the basic assumption of the medical model. Other criticisms have equally important, though less obvious, implications. For instance, some critics have argued that the use of the term "illness" implies that there is something "wrong" with a person, something that is in need of a cure (Szasz, 1982, 1990). Using such terms suggests that people displaying abnormal behavior hold little control over their actions and have no responsibility for them—and that any "cure" is entirely in the hands of someone else (who, given the assumptions of the medical model, would presumably be a physician).

The Psychoanalytic Model

On the surface, Judy's background shows little difference from that of anyone else. Yet could certain aspects of her past, of which she was unaware, have brought about her unusual behavior? Such a possibility is suggested by the psychoanalytic model of abnormal behavior.

Psychoanalytic model of abnormality: The model that suggests that abnormality stems from childhood conflicts over opposing desires regarding sex and aggression

Whereas the medical model suggests that physiological causes are at the root of abnormal behavior, the **psychoanalytic model of abnormality** holds that abnormal behavior stems from childhood conflicts over opposing wishes regarding sex and aggression. As we discussed in Chapter 15, Freud believed that children pass through a series of stages in which sexual and aggressive impulses take different forms that require resolution. If the conflicts of childhood are not successfully dealt with, they remain unresolved in the unconscious and eventually bring about abnormal behavior during adulthood.

In order to understand the roots of a person's disordered behavior, the psychoanalytic model scrutinizes his or her early life history. For example, if we knew more details of Judy Smith's childhood, we might discover experiences that produced unresolved insecurities and conflicts in adulthood. Of course, it would be difficult to prove a direct link between her childhood experiences and later abnormal behavior—pointing to one of the major objections that critics have raised regarding psychoanalytic theorizing. Because there is no conclusive way of linking people's childhood experiences with the abnormal behaviors they display as adults, we can never be sure that the mechanisms suggested by psychoanalytic theory are accurate. Moreover, psychoanalytic theory, like the medical model, paints a picture of people as having little control over their behavior and of behavior as being guided by unconscious impulses, implying that the treatment of abnormal behavior is dependent on people other than those exhibiting the behavior.

On the other hand, the contributions of psychoanalytic theory have been significant. More than any other approach to abnormal behavior, this model highlights the fact that people can have a rich, involved inner life and that prior experiences can have a profound effect on current psychological functioning.

The Behavioral Model

Behavioral model of abnormality: The model that suggests that abnormal behavior itself is the problem to be treated, rather than viewing behavior as a symptom of some underlying medical or psychological problem

The medical model and the psychoanalytic model display a common approach to behavior disorders: They both look at abnormal behaviors as *symptoms* of some underlying problem. In contrast, the **behavioral model of abnormality** looks at the behavior itself as the problem. According to theorists using this approach, one need not look beyond a person's display of abnormal behavior or past the environment to be able to understand and ultimately change that behavior.

Using the principles of learning we discussed in Chapter 7, behavioral theorists can thus explain why people behave abnormally—or normally. Both normal and abnormal behaviors are seen as responses to a set of stimuli, responses that have been learned through past experience and are guided in the present by the stimuli that one finds in one's environment. Indeed, in its most extreme form, the behavioral model rejects the notion that it is important to understand what a person is thinking. What is critical is analyzing how an abnormal behavior has been learned and observing the circumstances in which it is displayed in order to explain why such behavior is occurring. For example, a behavioral approach would explain a person's avoidance of new people as being due to a lack of effective social skills. This could be remedied by teaching the individual techniques for initiating conversations, using appropriate facial expressions, and acting as an effective listener. Other approaches, in contrast, would try to determine the underlying causes of the person's avoidance of others.

ANSWERS (REVIEW I):

1. d **2.** True **3.** a **4.** Deviation from the average **5.** continuum **6.** Deviation from the ideal

The emphasis on overt observable behavior represents both the greatest strength and the greatest weakness of the behavioral approach to abnormal behavior. Because of its emphasis on the present, the behavioral approach is the most precise and objective in examining manifestations of abnormal behavior. Rather than hypothesizing elaborate, underlying, unobservable mechanisms to explain abnormal behavior, behavioral theorists concentrate on immediate behavior. They have developed many techniques (discussed in the next chapter) to modify such behavior successfully.

The Cognitive Model

Like medical and psychoanalytic explanations, behavioral theories view people's behavior as being caused by factors largely outside of their own control. To many critics, however, the very real fact that people have complex, unobservable thoughts that influence their behavior cannot be ignored.

In response to such concerns, some psychologists now employ a **cognitive model of abnormality**. Rather than considering only external behavior, as in traditional behavioral approaches, the cognitive approach assumes that **cognitions** (people's thoughts and beliefs) are central to a person's abnormal behavior. A primary goal of treatment using the cognitive model is to explicitly teach new cognitions. Because the approach involves learning as a central component, it is often referred to as a **cognitive-behavioral approach**.

Consider, for instance, a student who holds the erroneous cognition, "This exam is crucial to my future," whenever she takes an exam and who consequently is so filled with anxiety that she is unable to perform adequately. According to the cognitive approach, the student should be taught to develop more realistic cognitions. For example, she might be taught to hold the alternative (and more realistic) thought: "My entire future is not dependent on this one exam." Although the basic principles of learning theory are used, the target of behavior change is a modification of cognitions. The melding of behavioral and cognitive approaches has led to important treatment advances, as we will see in Chapter 18.

The Humanistic Model

You might wonder if there is any model of abnormal behavior that considers a person to be in full control of her or his behavior, a reasonable question in light of the four models we have discussed. In each of these approaches the individual is seen, to a greater or lesser degree, as something of a pawn, beset by physiological difficulties, unconscious conflicts, environmental stimuli, or cognitive misapprehensions that direct and motivate behavior.

Psychologists who subscribe to the **humanistic model of abnormality**, in contrast, emphasize the control and responsibility that people have for their own behavior, even when such behavior is abnormal. The humanistic model of abnormality concentrates on what is uniquely human, viewing people as basically rational, oriented toward a social world, and motivated to get along with others (Rogers, 1980).

Although diverse in many ways, humanistic approaches to abnormal behavior all focus on the relationship of the individual to the world, on the ways in which people view themselves in relation to others and see their place in the world in a philosophical sense. People have an awareness of life and of themselves that leads them to search for meaning and self-worth. So-called abnormal be-

Pointing out that his entire future does not hinge on this one test would be a cognitive-behavioral technique for helping this student overcome test anxiety.

Cognitive model of abnormality: The model that suggests that people's thoughts and beliefs are a central component to abnormal behavior

Cognitions: People's thoughts and beliefs

Cognitive-behavioral approach: A process by which people's faulty cognitions about themselves and the world are changed to more accurate ones

Humanistic model of abnormality: The model that suggests that people are basically rational, and that abnormal behavior results from an inability to fulfill human needs and capabilities

havior is basically a sign of a person's inability to fulfill his or her human needs and capabilities. Moreover, humanistic approaches take a much less judgmental view of atypical behavior than other models. Rather than assuming that a "cure" is required, the humanistic model suggests that individuals can, by and large, set their own limits of what is acceptable behavior. As long as they are not hurting others and do not feel personal distress, people should be free to choose the behaviors they engage in. It is only if *they* feel that their behavior needs some correction that they ought to consider taking responsibility for modifying it. The way to bring about such modification is by exploring ways to reach higher levels of self-fulfillment.

Humanistic models consider abnormal behavior, then, in a more positive light than the models we discussed earlier. Rather than assuming there is something wrong with an individual, humanistic theorists view abnormal behavior as an understandable reaction to circumstances arising in the person's daily life. Moreover, the humanistic model suggests that people have a relatively high degree of control over their lives and can make informed and rational choices to overcome their difficulties.

The humanistic model is not without its detractors. It has been criticized for its reliance on unscientific, unverifiable information, as well as for its vague, almost philosophical formulation related to such concepts as "human striving" and "fulfillment of human needs." Despite these criticisms, the humanistic model offers a view of abnormal behavior that stresses the unique aspects of being human and provides a number of important suggestions for helping those with psychological problems.

The Sociocultural Model

Sociocultural model of abnormality: The model that suggests that people's behavior, both normal and abnormal, is shaped by family, society, and cultural influences

The **sociocultural model of abnormality** makes the assumption that people's behavior—both normal and abnormal—is shaped by the kind of family group, society, and culture in which they live. We all are part of a social network of family, friends, acquaintances, and even strangers, and the kinds of relationships that evolve with others may support abnormal behaviors and even cause them to occur. According to the sociocultural model of abnormality, then, the kinds of stresses and conflicts people experience—not in terms of unconscious processes, but as part of their daily interactions with the environment—can promote and maintain abnormal behavior.

Some proponents of this view take the extreme position that there really is no such thing as abnormal behavior. Although people who violate social rules may be labeled by society as showing abnormal behavior, in reality there is nothing wrong with such individuals. Rather, there is something wrong with a society that is unwilling to tolerate deviant behavior.

To support the position that sociocultural factors shape abnormal behavior, theorists say statistics show that certain kinds of abnormal behavior are far more prevalent among certain social classes than others, and poor economic times tend to be linked to general declines in psychological functioning (Pines, 1982).

For instance, diagnoses of schizophrenia tend to be higher among members of lower socioeconomic classes than among members of more affluent groups, and proportionally more black individuals are involuntarily hospitalized for psychological disorders than are whites (Hollingshead & Redich, 1958; Keith, Regier, & Rae, 1991). The reason may relate to the way in which abnormal behavior is interpreted by diagnosticians, who tend to be psychiatrists and psychologists who are Caucasian and from upper socioeconomic classes (Lopez, 1989). Alternatively, it may be that stresses on members of lower socioeconomic classes are greater than those on people in higher classes. Whatever the reason, there is frequently a link between sociocultural factors and abnormal behavior, suggesting the possibility of a cause-and-effect relationship.

As with the other theories, the sociocultural model does not have unequivocal support. Alternative explanations abound for the association between abnormal behavior and social factors. For example, people of lower classes may be less likely than those of higher classes to seek help until their symptoms become relatively severe and warrant a more serious diagnosis (Gove, 1982). Moreover, sociocultural explanations provide relatively little in the way of direct guidance for the treatment of individuals showing mental disturbance, since the focus is on broader societal factors.

Could the stress of living in poverty be a cause of the higher rate of schizophrenia among poor people?

Applying the Models: The Case of Judy Smith

We began this chapter by discussing Judy Smith's case. Perhaps you are wondering which of these models brings us closest to understanding the reasons for her behavior. Indeed, you may be looking for the answer to a more encompassing question: Which of these approaches provides the best model for explaining abnormal behavior in general?

The most appropriate answer to both questions is, in fact, that *all* of them can be reasonably and profitably used. As in other branches of their field, psychologists have found that there is more than one workable approach to the problems of abnormal behavior. As we shall see, effective and worthwhile approaches to resolving psychological problems have been made using each of the different models. Indeed, it is possible to address various parts of a given problem simultaneously using each model.

Consider the case of Judy Smith. A proponent of the medical model might recommend that Smith be examined to determine if she had any physical problems—such as dependence on cocaine or heroin, a brain tumor, a chemical imbalance in the brain, or some type of disease—that could possibly account for her unusual behavior.

A psychoanalytic theorist would take a very different approach, seeking out information about Smith's past, concentrating on her childhood and probing her memories to determine the nature of conflicts residing in her unconscious. A behavioral theorist would take still another approach, concentrating on the nature of the rewards and punishments that Smith received for behaving in the way she did, as well as the stimuli in the environment that maintained or reinforced her behavior. For instance, Smith's street life made her a center of attention in the neighborhood in which she lived.

Advocates of the cognitive model, in contrast, would focus on Smith's cognitions about the world. They would examine her perceptions of the world and seek to understand how she came to hold such misguided cognitions. Finally, humanistic and sociocultural approaches would concentrate on Smith's view of herself, in relation to other people and to the world in general.

Humanistic theories might suggest that, by living on the streets and refusing to stay in the mental hospital, Smith had made a series of choices—although unconventional ones—about the way she wanted to lead her life. Sociocultural approaches, in contrast, would focus on the ways in which society contributed to Smith's problems, looking at how her relationships with others, possible economic difficulties, family structure, and cultural background influenced her behavior. Taking an extreme view, a sociocultural theorist might suggest that homelessness was a legitimate alternative lifestyle and that society should not intervene in Smith's preferences.

As you can see, finding support for one or another of these approaches does not automatically make the others wrong. Each focuses on somewhat different aspects of Smith's behavior and life. Of course, if her background were analyzed in depth, one approach might ultimately provide a better explanation than the others. But because the theories consider abnormal behavior at different levels, and because people's lives are multifaceted, a single approach may be insufficient to provide a full explanation for a person's abnormal behavior.

The Informed Consumer of Psychology: Do You Feel Abnormal?

Medical student's disease: The feeling that symptoms and illnesses one studies are characteristic of oneself

As we conclude this introduction to abnormal behavior and begin to consider its specific classifications and treatment, it is important to note a phenomenon that has long been known to medical students, and one that you, too, may find yourself susceptible to—a phenomenon called **medical student's disease**. Although in the present case it might more aptly be labeled "psychology student's disease," the basic symptoms are the same: deciding that you suffer from the same sorts of problems you are studying.

Most often, of course, your concerns will be unwarranted. As we have discussed, the differences between normal and abnormal behavior are often so fuzzy that it is easy to jump to the conclusion that one has the same symptoms that are involved in serious forms of mental disturbance.

Before coming to such a conclusion, though, it is important to keep in mind that from time to time we all experience a wide range of emotions and subjective experiences, and it is not unusual to feel deeply unhappy, to fantasize about bizarre situations, or to feel anxiety about life's circumstances. It is the persistence, depth, and consistency of such behavior that sets normal reactions apart from abnormal ones. If you have not previously had serious doubts about the normality of your behavior, it is unlikely that reading about others' abnormality should prompt you to reevaluate your earlier conclusion.

RECAP AND REVIEW II

RECAP

◀ Historically, abnormal behavior was first linked to superstition and witchcraft.

◀ Current theories view abnormality in terms of six major models: the medical, psychoanalytic, behavioral, cognitive, humanistic, and sociocultural models.

◀ The question of which model provides the best explanation of abnormal behavior can be answered most reasonably by noting that each model can be profitably used.

REVIEW

1. Which of the following is a strong argument against the medical model?
   a. Physiological abnormalities are almost impossible to identify.
   b. There is no conclusive way to link past experience and behavior.
   c. The medical model rests too heavily on the effects of nutrition.
   d. Assigning behavior to a physical problem takes responsibility away from the individual.

2. Which model suggests that behavior is shaped by a person's interactions with others? _____

3. What model are we using if we say that someone's lingering depression is due to his inability to find meaning in his life? _____

4. Cheryl is painfully shy. According to the behavioral model, the best way to help her "abnormal" behavior is to
   a. treat the underlying physical problem
   b. use the principles of learning theory to modify her shy behavior
   c. express a great deal of caring
   d. uncover her negative past experiences through hypnosis

5. Sigmund Freud is most closely associated with the
   a. medical model
   b. psychoanalytic model
   c. behavioral model

d. humanistic model

6. Imagine that an acquaintance of yours was recently arrested for shoplifting a $10.95 necktie. Briefly explain this behavior in terms of *each* of the following:
   a. The medical model
   b. The psychoanalytic model
   c. The behavioral model
   d. The cognitive model
   e. The humanistic model
   f. The sociocultural model

7. Experiencing another person's problems as a result of reading about them is called _____.

Ask Yourself

If none of the models we've considered is correct in and of itself, can each of them still be useful in diagnosis? What problems might there be in integrating these models into a unified theory of abnormal behavior?

(Answers to review questions are on page 558.)

CLASSIFYING ABNORMAL BEHAVIOR: THE ABCS OF DSM

Crazy. Nutty as a fruitcake. Loony. Insane. Neurotic. Strange. Demented. Odd. Possessed.

Society has long placed labels on people displaying abnormal behavior. Unfortunately, most of the time these labels have reflected intolerance, and they have been used with little thought to what the label signifies.

Providing appropriate and specific names and classifications for abnormal behavior has presented a major challenge to psychologists. It is not too hard to understand why, given the difficulties we discussed earlier in simply distinguishing normal from abnormal behavior. Yet classification systems are necessary in order to be able to describe and ultimately understand abnormal behavior.

Over the years many different classification systems have been used, varying in terms of their utility and how universally they have been accepted by mental health workers. Today, however, one standard system, devised by the American Psychiatric Association, has emerged and is employed by most professionals to classify abnormal behavior. The classification system is known as the ***Diagnostic and Statistical Manual of Mental Disorders, Third Edition—Revised (DSM-III-R)***.

Published in 1987, *DSM-III-R* presents comprehensive and relatively precise definitions for more than 230 separate diagnostic categories. By following the criteria presented in the system, diagnosticians can provide a clear description of the specific problem an individual is experiencing. (Table 17-1 provides a brief outline of the major diagnostic categories.)

DSM-III-R evaluates a person's behavior according to five dimensions, or axes. The first three axes assess the person's present condition according to the particular maladaptive behaviors being exhibited; the nature of any long-standing personality problems in adults or any specific developmental problems in children and adolescents that may be relevant to treatment; and any physical

Diagnostic and Statistical Manual of Mental Disorders, Third Edition—Revised (DSM-III-R): A manual that presents comprehensive definitions of more than 230 separate diagnostic categories for identifying problems and behaviors

▶ **557**

TABLE 17-1

MAJOR *DSM-III-R* DIAGNOSTIC CATEGORIES

The following list of disorders represents the major categories from *DSM-III-R*, presented in the order in which they are discussed in the text. This is only a partial list of the 230 disorders found in *DSM-III-R*.

Anxiety disorders (problems in which anxiety impedes daily functioning)
Subcategories: generalized anxiety disorder, panic disorder, phobic disorder, obsessive-compulsive disorder, posttraumatic stress disorder

Somatoform disorders (psychological difficulties displayed through physical problems)
Subcategories: hypochondriasis, conversion disorder

Dissociative disorders (the splitting apart of crucial parts of personality that are usually integrated)
Subcategories: multiple personality, psychogenic amnesia, psychogenic fugue

Mood disorders (emotions of depression or euphoria that are so strong they intrude on everyday living)
Subcategories: major depression, bipolar disorder

Schizophrenia (declines in functioning and thought, language disturbances, perception disorders, emotional disturbance, and withdrawal from others)
Subcategories: disorganized, paranoid, catatonic, undifferentiated, residual

Personality disorders (problems that create little personal distress but that lead to an inability to function as a normal member of society)
Subcategories: antisocial (sociopathic) personality disorder, narcissistic personality disorder

Sexual disorders (problems related to sexual arousal from unusual objects or problems related to sexual functioning)
Subcategories: paraphilias, sexual dysfunction

Psychoactive substance-use disorders (problems related to drug dependence and abuse)
Subcategories: alcohol, cocaine, hallucinogens, marijuana

Organic mental disorders (problems produced by physical deterioration of the brain)
Subcategories: Alzheimer's disease, delirium, dementia

---

disorders or illnesses that may also be present. The fourth and fifth axes take into account a broader consideration of the person, focusing on the severity of stressors present and the general level of functioning over the past year in social relationships, work, and the use of leisure time.

One noteworthy feature of *DSM-III-R* is that it is designed to be primarily descriptive and devoid of suggestions as to the underlying causes of an individual's behavior and problems (Klerman, 1984). Hence, the term "neurotic"—a label that is commonly used by people in their everyday descriptions of abnormal behavior—is not listed as a *DSM-III-R* category. The reason is that "neurotic" derives directly from Freud's theory of personality (discussed in Chapter 15). Because the term refers to problems associated with a specific cause and theoretical approach, neurosis is no longer listed as a category.

DSM-III-R has the advantage, then, of providing a descriptive system that does not specify the cause or reason behind the problem. Instead, it paints a picture

---

ANSWERS (REVIEW II):

1. d **2.** Sociocultural **3.** Humanistic **4.** b **5.** b **6.** Possible answers, which may vary, include: **a.** A physiological problem may exist which causes him to behave irresponsibly. **b.** Unresolved childhood conflicts led to the behavior. **c.** He had enjoyed the immediate rewards of stealing in the past. **d.** He holds inaccurate cognitions about the acceptability of stealing. **e.** Stealing was an attempt to "discover" himself. **f.** Stealing was caused by economic difficulties. **7.** medical (or psychology) student's disease

of the behavior that is being manifested. Why should this be important? For one thing, it allows communication between mental health professionals of diverse backgrounds and approaches and does not immediately suggest that there is only one appropriate treatment. Another important point is that precise classification enables researchers to go forward and to explore the causes of a problem. If the manifestations of an abnormal behavior cannot be reliably described, researchers will be hard-pressed to find ways of investigating the difficulties. Finally, *DSM-III-R* provides a kind of conceptual shorthand through which professionals can describe the behaviors that tend to occur simultaneously in an individual.

It is also important to note that the *DSM* is designed to be revised periodically. Reflecting the fact that changes in society affect what behaviors are viewed as abnormal, *DSM-IV* is scheduled for publication in the mid-1990s (DeAngelis, 1991a; Widiger, Frances, Pincus, & Davis, 1990).

Of course, *DSM-III-R* has its drawbacks, as does any classification system (Vaillant, 1984). Perhaps the strongest criticism is its possible overreliance on a medical model. Because it was drawn up by psychiatrists—who are physicians—it was criticized as viewing abnormal behaviors primarily in terms of symptoms of some underlying physiological disorder. Moreover, some critics suggest that *DSM-III-R* pigeonholes people into inflexible categories, and that it would be more reasonable to use systems that classify people along some sort of continuum or scale.

Other concerns with *DSM-III-R* are subtler but equally important. For instance, Szasz (1961) argues that labeling an individual as a deviant provides a lifetime stigma that is dehumanizing. Moreover, there is a tendency for a diagnosis itself to be mistaken for an explanation of a problem. Saying, for instance, that a woman with schizophrenia hears voices may make it seem as though schizophrenia is an *explanation* for her behavior—when in fact schizophrenia is simply a label that gives no clue as to *why* the woman hears voices (Rosenhan, 1975). Furthermore, after an initial diagnosis is made, other diagnostic possibilities may be overlooked by mental health professionals, who concentrate on the initial diagnostic category.

The notion that diagnostic categories provide rigid labels was illustrated in a now-classic experiment conducted in the early 1970s (Rosenhan, 1973). In the study, Rosenhan and seven of his colleagues presented themselves at the doors of separate mental hospitals across the United States and sought admission. The reason, they each stated, was that they were hearing voices—"unclear voices" which said "empty," "hollow," and "thud." Aside from changing their names and occupations, *everything* else they did and said was representative of their true behavior, including the responses they gave during extensive admission interviews and answers to the battery of tests they were asked to complete. In fact, as soon as they were admitted, they said they no longer heard any voices. In sum, each of the pseudo-patients acted in a "normal" way.

One would assume that Rosenhan and his colleagues would have been quickly discovered as the impostors they were, but this was not the case. Instead, each of them was diagnosed as severely abnormal on the basis of observed behavior. Most were labeled as schizophrenic, and they were kept in the hospital from three to fifty-two days, with the average stay being nineteen days. In most cases, they were not allowed to leave without the assistance of people outside the hospital. Even when they were discharged, most of the patients left with the label "schizophrenia—in remission," meaning that the abnormal behavior had only temporarily subsided and could recur at any time. Most disturbing of all, none of the pseudo-patients was identified by the staff of the hospitals as impostors. In sum, placing labels on people powerfully influences how their actions are perceived and interpreted.

Despite the drawbacks inherent in any labeling system, *DSM-III-R* has had an important effect on the way in which mental health professionals consider psychological disorders. It has increased both the reliability and validity of diagnostic categorization. In addition, it provides a logical way to organize our examination of the major types of mental disturbance, to which we turn next.

In our discussion of the major disorders, we will consider those that are most common, serious, or debilitating. We begin with disorders in which anxiety plays a predominate role, those in which psychological difficulties take on a physical form, and disorders in which the parts of personality are no longer integrated. Although these disturbances are discussed in a dispassionate manner, it is important to keep in mind that each represents a very human set of difficulties that influence, and in some cases wreak considerable havoc with people's lives.

THE MAJOR DISORDERS

I remember walking up the street, the moon was shining and suddenly everything around me seemed unfamiliar, as it would be in a dream. I felt panic rising inside me, but managed to push it away and carry on. I walked a quarter of a mile or so, with the panic getting worse every minute. . . . By now, I was sweating, yet trembling; my heart was pounding and my legs felt like jelly. . . . Terrified, I stood not knowing what to do. The only bit of sanity left in me told me to get home. Somehow this I did very slowly, holding onto the fence in the road. I cannot remember the actual journey back, until I was going into the house, then I broke down and cried helplessly (Melville, 1977, pp. 1, 14).

Anxiety Disorders

Anxiety: A feeling of apprehension or tension

All of us, at one time or another, experience **anxiety**, a feeling of apprehension or tension, in reaction to stressful situations. There is nothing "wrong" with such anxiety; everyone feels it to some degree, and usually it is a reaction to stress that helps, rather than hinders, our daily functioning. Without anxiety, for instance, most of us would not be terribly motivated to study hard, to undergo physical exams, or to spend long hours at our jobs.

Anxiety disorder: The occurrence of anxiety without obvious external cause, intruding on daily functioning

But some people, such as the person who wrote the passage above, experience anxiety in situations in which there is no external reason or cause. When anxiety occurs without external justification and begins to impede people's daily functioning, it is considered a psychological problem known as an **anxiety disorder**. There are four main types of anxiety disorders: generalized anxiety disorder, panic disorder, phobic disorder, and obsessive-compulsive disorder.

Generalized anxiety disorder: The experience of long-term anxiety with no explanation

Generalized Anxiety Disorder. As the name implies, **generalized anxiety disorder** refers to a disorder in which an individual experiences long-term, consistent anxiety without knowing why. Such people feel afraid of *something*, but are unable to articulate what it is. Because of their anxiety they are unable to function normally. They cannot concentrate, cannot set their fears aside, and their lives become centered around their anxiety. Such anxiety may eventually result in the development of physiological problems. Because of heightened muscle tension and arousal, individuals with generalized anxiety disorder may begin to experience headaches, dizziness, heart palpitations, or insomnia. The most frequent symptoms are given in Figure 17-1.

Panic disorder: Anxiety that manifests itself in the form of panic attacks

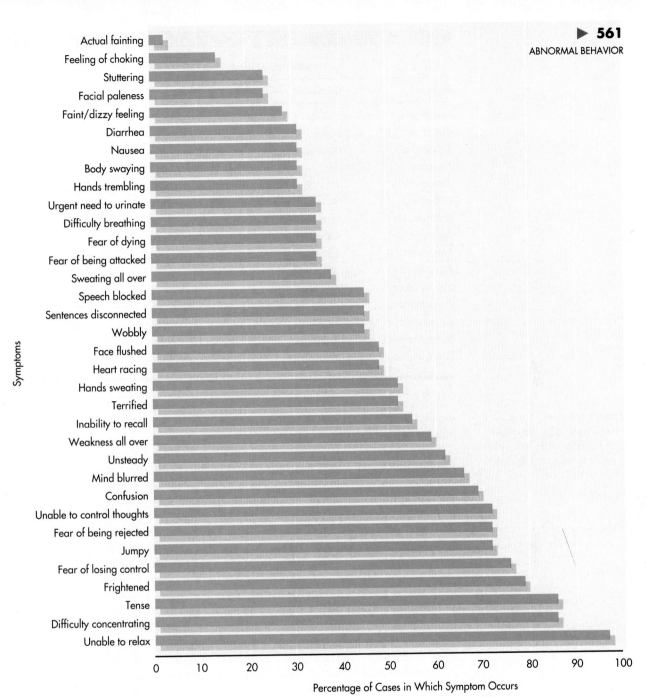

FIGURE 17-1

Frequency of symptoms in cases of generalized anxiety disorder. (Adapted from Beck & Emery, 1985, pp. 87–88.)

Panic Disorder. In another type of anxiety disorder, **panic disorder**, there are instances of **panic attacks** that last from a few seconds to as much as several hours. During an attack, such as the one described at the beginning of this section, the anxiety that a person has been chronically experiencing suddenly rises to a peak, and the individual feels a sense of impending, unavoidable doom. Although symptoms differ from person to person, they may include heart palpitations, shortness of breath, unusual amounts of sweating, faintness and dizziness, an urge to urinate, gastric sensations and—in extreme cases—a sense of imminent

Panic attack: Sudden anxiety characterized by heart palpitations, shortness of breath, sweating, faintness, and great fear

TABLE 17-2

GIVING FEAR A PROPER NAME

Phobia	Stimulus	Phobia	Stimulus
Acrophobia	Heights	Herpetophobia	Reptiles
Aerophobia	Flying	Hydrophobia	Water
Agoraphobia	Open spaces	Mikrophobia	Germs
Ailurophobia	Cats	Murophobia	Mice
Amaxophobia	Vehicles, driving	Mysophobia	Dirt or germs
Anthophobia	Flowers	Numerophobia	Numbers
Anthrophobia	People	Nyctophobia	Darkness
Aquaphobia	Water	Ochlophobia	Crowds
Arachnophobia	Spiders	Ophidiophobia	Snakes
Astraphobia	Lightning	Ornithophobia	Birds
Brontophobia	Thunder	Phonophobia	Speaking out loud
Claustrophobia	Closed spaces	Pyrophobia	Fire
Cynophobia	Dogs	Thanatophobia	Death
Dementophobia	Insanity	Trichophobia	Hair
Gephyrophobia	Bridges	Xenophobia	Strangers

Phobic disorder: A disorder characterized by unrealistic fears (phobias) that may keep people from carrying out routine daily behaviors

Phobias: Intense, irrational fears of specific objects or situations

Obsessive-compulsive disorder: A disorder characterized by obsessions or compulsions

Obsession: A thought or idea that keeps recurring

death (Baker, 1989). After such an attack, it is no wonder that people tend to feel exhausted.

Phobic Disorder.   Claustrophobia. Acrophobia. Xenophobia. Although these sound like characters in a Greek tragedy, they are actually members of a class of psychological disorders known as phobias. **Phobias** are intense, irrational fears of specific objects or situations. For example, claustrophobia is a fear of enclosed places, acrophobia a fear of high places, and xenophobia a fear of strangers. Although the objective danger posed by an anxiety-producing stimulus (which can be just about anything, as you can see from the list in Table 17-2) is typically small or nonexistent, to the individual suffering from the phobia it represents great danger, and a full-blown panic attack may follow exposure to the stimulus. Phobic disorders differ from generalized anxiety disorders and panic disorders in that there is a specific, identifiable stimulus that sets off the anxiety reaction.

Phobias may have only a minor impact on people's lives if those who suffer from them can avoid the things they fear. Unless one is a professional fire fighter or tightrope walker, for example, a fear of heights may have little impact on one's daily life. On the other hand, a fear of strangers presents a more debilitating problem. In one extreme case, a Washington housewife left her home just three times in thirty years—once to visit her family, once for an operation, and once to purchase ice cream for a dying companion (Adler, 1984).

Obsessive-Compulsive Disorder.   In **obsessive-compulsive disorder**, people are plagued by unwanted thoughts, called obsessions, or feel that they must carry out some actions, termed compulsions, against their will.

An **obsession** is a thought or idea that keeps recurring in one's mind. For example, a student may not be able to stop feeling that he has neglected to put his name on a test and may think about it constantly for the two weeks it takes to get the paper back. A man may go on vacation and wonder the whole time whether he locked his house. A woman may hear the same tune running through her head over and over again. In each case, the thought or idea is unwanted and difficult to put out of mind. Of course, many of us suffer from mild obsessions from time to time, but usually such thoughts persist for a short period only. For people with serious obsessions, however, the thoughts persist for days or months and may consist of bizarre, troubling images. In one classic case of an obsession, the patient complained of experiencing ''terrible'' thoughts:

> When she thought of her boyfriend she wished he were dead; when her mother went down the stairs, she ''wished she'd fall and break her neck''; when her sister spoke of going to the beach with her infant daughter, the patient ''hoped that they would both drown.'' These thoughts ''make me hysterical. I love them; why should I wish such terrible things to happen? It drives me wild, makes me feel I'm crazy and don't belong to society'' (Kraines, 1948, p. 199).

As part of an obsessive-compulsive disorder, people may also experience **compulsions**, urges to repeatedly carry out some act that seems strange and unreasonable, even to them. Whatever the compulsive behavior, people experience extreme anxiety if they cannot carry it out, even if it is something they want to stop. The acts involved may be relatively trivial, such as repeatedly checking the stove to make sure all the burners are turned off, or more unusual, such as a continuous need to wash oneself (Rachman & Hodgson, 1980). For example, consider this case report of a 27-year-old woman with a cleaning ritual:

Compulsion: An urge to repeatedly carry out an act that even the sufferer realizes is unreasonable

> Bess would first remove all of her clothing in a preestablished sequence. She would lay out each article of clothing at specific spots on her bed, and examine each one for any indications of ''contamination.'' She would then thoroughly scrub her body, starting at her feet and working meticulously up to the top of her head, using certain washcloths for certain areas of her body. Any articles of clothing that appeared to have been ''contaminated'' were thrown into the laundry. Clean clothing was put in the spots that were vacant. She would then dress herself in the opposite order from which she took the clothes off. If there were any deviations from this order, or if Bess began to wonder if she had missed some contamination, she would go through the entire sequence again. It was not rare for her to do this four or five times in a row on certain evenings (Meyer & Osborne, 1982, p. 156).

Unfortunately for people experiencing an obsessive-compulsive disorder, there is no reduction of anxiety from carrying out a compulsive ritual. They tend to lead lives filled with unrelenting tension.

The Causes of Anxiety Disorders. No one mechanism fully explains all cases of anxiety disorders, and each of the models of abnormal behavior that we discussed earlier has something to say about its causes. However, the medical, behavioral, and cognitive models have been particularly influential in psychologists' thinking.

Biological approaches, stemming from the medical model, have shown that genetic factors play an important role in anxiety disorders. For example, if one member of a pair of identical twins has panic disorder, there is a 30 percent chance that the other twin will have it also (Torgersen, 1983). Other evidence suggests that certain chemical deficiencies in the brain may produce some kinds of anxiety disorder. Specifically, low levels of several of the neurotransmitters we discussed in Chapter 3 have been identified in individuals with obsessive-compulsive disorder (Gorman, Liebowitz, Fyer, & Stein, 1989).

Psychologists employing the behavioral model have taken a different approach, emphasizing environmental factors. They consider anxiety to be a learned response to stress. For instance, suppose a young girl is bitten by a dog. When she sees a dog next, she is frightened and runs away—a behavior that relieves her anxiety and thereby reinforces her avoidance behavior. After repeated encounters with dogs in which she is reinforced for her avoidance behavior, she may develop a full-fledged phobia regarding dogs.

Finally, the cognitive model suggests that anxiety disorders are an outgrowth of inappropriate and inaccurate cognitions about circumstances in a person's world. For example, people with anxiety disorders may view a friendly puppy as a ferocious and savage pit bull, or they may see an air disaster looming every moment they are in the vicinity of an airplane. According to the cognitive perspective, it is people's faulty thinking about the world that is at the root of an anxiety disorder.

Somatoform Disorders: When the Psychological Leads to the Physical

Most of us know people who cannot wait to regale us with their latest physical problems; even an innocent "How are you?" brings a long list of complaints in response. People who consistently report physical problems, have a preoccupation with their health, and have unrealistic fears of disease may be experiencing a problem known as hypochondriasis. In **hypochondriasis** there is a constant fear of illness, and physical sensations are misinterpreted as signs of disease. It is not that the "symptoms" are faked; hypochondriacs actually experience the aches and pains that most of us feel as we go through an active existence (Costa & McCrae, 1985). It is the misinterpretation of these sensations as symptoms of some dread disease—often in the face of inarguable medical evidence to the contrary—that characterizes hypochondriasis.

Hypochondriasis is just one example of a class of disorders known as **somatoform disorders**, psychological difficulties that take on a physical (somatic) form of one sort or another. Even though an individual with a somatoform disorder reports physical symptoms, there is no underlying physical problem, or, if a physical problem does exist, the person's reaction greatly exaggerates what would be expected from the medical problem alone. Only when a physical examination rules out actual physiological difficulties can a diagnosis of somatoform disorder be made.

In addition to hypochondriasis, the other major somatoform disorder is **conversion disorder**. In contrast to hypochondriasis, in which there is no actual physical problem, conversion disorders involve an actual physical disturbance such as the inability to use a sensory organ or the complete or partial inability to move an arm or leg. The *cause* of such a physical disturbance is purely psychological. There is no biological reason for the problem. Some of Freud's classic cases involved conversion disorders. For instance, one patient of Freud's was suddenly unable to use her arm, without any apparent physiological cause. Later, just as abruptly, she regained its use.

Conversion disorders are often characterized by their rapid onset. People wake up one morning blind or deaf, or they experience numbness that is restricted to a certain part of the body. A person's hand, for example, might become entirely numb, while an area above the wrist—controlled by the same nerves—remains inexplicably sensitive to touch. Such a condition is referred to

Hypochondriasis (HY po kon DRY a sis): A constant fear of illness and misinterpretation of normal aches and pains

Somatoform disorder: Psychological difficulties that take on physical (somatic) form

Conversion disorder: Psychological disturbances characterized by actual physical disturbances, such as the inability to speak or move one's arms

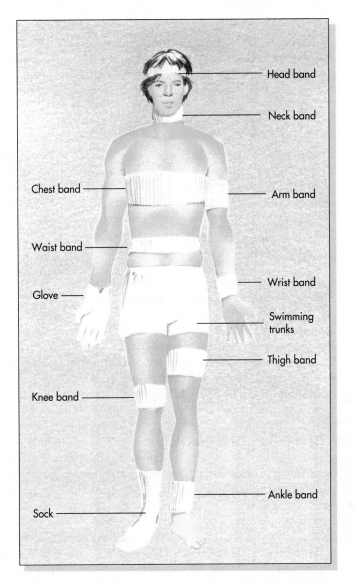

Head band

Neck band

Chest band

Arm band

Waist band

Wrist band

Glove

Swimming trunks

Thigh band

Knee band

Ankle band

Sock

FIGURE 17-2

The shaded areas of the body indicate places where numbness might occur as a result of a psychological disorder rather than actual nerve damage.

as "glove anesthesia," because the area that is numb is the part of the hand covered by a glove, and not a region related to pathways of the nervous system (see Figure 17-2).

One of the most surprising characteristics of conversion disorders is a lack of concern over symptoms that most people would expect to be highly anxiety-producing. For instance, a person in good health who wakes up blind might react in a bland, matter-of-fact way. Considering how most of us would feel if we woke up in this condition, such a reaction hardly seems appropriate.

Conversion disorders occasionally occur on a large scale. In one instance, nearly one out of five student aviators enrolled at the U.S. Naval Aerospace Medical Institute began to suffer symptoms such as blurred vision, double vision, and the development of blind spots and focusing trouble (Mucha & Reinhardt, 1970). However, no underlying physical problem could be identified. Investigation revealed that the students found outright quitting an unacceptable response to the stress they were experiencing and instead developed physical responses that allowed them to avoid the demands of the program. Their stress was thus relieved through a face-saving physical problem.

In general, conversion disorders seem to occur when an individual is under some kind of emotional stress that could be reduced by a physical symptom. The physical condition allows the person to escape or reduce the source of stress. An emotional problem is turned, then, into a physical ailment that acts to relieve the source of the original emotional problem.

Dissociative Disorders

Dissociative disorder:
Psychological dysfunction characterized by the splitting apart of critical personality facets that are normally integrated, allowing stress avoidance by escape

The most dramatic and celebrated cases of psychological dysfunction (although they are actually quite rare) have been **dissociative disorders**. The movie *The Three Faces of Eve*, the book *Sybil* (about a girl with sixteen personalities), and cases of people found wandering the streets with no notion of who they are or where they came from exemplify dissociative disorders. The key factor in such problems is the splitting apart (or dissociation) of critical parts of personality that are normally integrated and work together. This lack of integration acts to allow certain parts of a personality to avoid stress—since another part can be made to face it. By dissociating themselves from key parts of their personality, individuals with the disorder can eliminate anxiety.

Multiple personality: A
disorder in which a person displays characteristics of two or more distinct personalities

Three major types of dissociative disorders have been distinguished: multiple personality, psychogenic amnesia, and psychogenic fugue. A person with a **multiple personality** displays characteristics of two or more distinct personalities. Each personality has a unique set of likes and dislikes and its own reactions to situations. Some people with multiple personalities even carry several pairs of glasses because their vision changes with each personality (Braun, 1985). Moreover, each individual personality can be well adjusted when considered on its own (Ross, 1989).

The problem, of course, is that there is only one body available to the various personalities, forcing the personalities to take turns. Because there can be strong variations in personalities, the person's behavior—considered as a whole—can appear very inconsistent. For instance, in the famous case portrayed in *The Three Faces of Eve*, the meek, bland Eve White provided a stunning contrast to the dominant and carefree Eve Black (Sizemore, 1989).

Psychogenic amnesia: A
failure to remember past experience

Psychogenic amnesia, another dissociative disorder, is a failure or inability to remember past experiences. Psychogenic amnesia is unlike simple amnesia, which, as we discussed in Chapter 8, involves an actual loss of information from memory, typically due to a physiological cause. In contrast, in cases of psychogenic amnesia, the "forgotten" material is still present in memory—it simply cannot be recalled.

In the most severe forms, individuals cannot recall their names, are unable to recognize parents and other relatives, and do not know their addresses. In other respects, though, they may appear quite normal. Apart from an inability to remember certain facts about themselves, they may be able to recall skills and abilities that they developed earlier. For instance, even though a chef may not remember where he grew up and received training, he may still be able to prepare gourmet meals.

In some cases of psychogenic amnesia, the memory loss is quite profound. For example, a woman—dubbed Jane Doe by her rescuers—was found by a Florida park ranger in the early 1980s. Incoherent, thin, and only partially clothed, Doe was unable to recall her name, her past, and even how to read and write. On the basis of her accent, authorities thought the woman was from Illinois, and interviews conducted while she was given tranquilizing drugs revealed that she had had a Catholic education. However, the childhood memories she revealed were so universal that her background could not be further pinpointed. In a

Chris Sizemore, the real "Eve White."

desperate attempt to rediscover her identity, she appeared on the television show *Good Morning America*, and ultimately a couple from Roselle, Illinois, whose daughter had moved to Florida, stepped forward, saying that they were her parents. However, Jane Doe never regained her memory (Carson, Butcher & Coleman, 1988).

A more unusual form of amnesia is a condition known as **psychogenic fugue**. In this state, people take an impulsive, sudden trip, often assuming a new identity. After a period of time—days, months, or sometimes even years—they suddenly realize that they are in a strange place and completely forget the time that they have spent wandering. Their last memories are those just before they entered the fugue state.

What the dissociative disorders have in common is that they allow people to escape from some anxiety-producing situation. Either the person produces a new personality to deal with stress, or the situation that caused the stress is forgotten or left behind as the individual journeys to some new—and perhaps less anxiety-ridden—situation.

Psychogenic fugue: An amnesiac condition in which people take sudden, impulsive trips, sometimes assuming a new identity

◀ **RECAP AND REVIEW III**

RECAP

◀ Although they have their drawbacks, classification systems are necessary to describe and ultimately understand abnormal behavior.

◀ The *Diagnostic and Statistical Manual of Mental Disorders, Third Edition—Revised (DSM-III-R)* provides a description of some 230 separate diagnostic categories of abnormal behavior.

◀ Anxiety disorders occur when anxiety is so great that it impedes people's everyday functioning.

◀ Somatoform disorders are psychological problems that take on a physical form.

◀ Dissociative disorders occur when there is a splitting apart of normally integrated parts of personality.

1. *DSM-III-R* is intended to both describe abnormal behaviors and suggest their underlying causes. True or false? _____

2. The experience of long-term, consistent anxiety without a clear cause is known as _____ _____ _____.

3. Kathy is terrified by elevators. She is likely to be suffering from a(n)
   a. obsessive-compulsive disorder
   b. phobic disorder
   c. panic disorder
   d. generalized anxiety disorder

4. John described an incident in which his anxiety suddenly rose to a peak and he felt a sense of impending doom. He had experienced a(n) _____ _____.

5. Troubling thoughts which persist for days or months are known as
   a. obsessions
   b. compulsions
   c. rituals

   d. panic attacks

6. An overpowering urge to carry out a strange ritual is called a(n) _____.

7. In what major way does conversion disorder differ from hypochondriasis?

8. The splitting apart of the personality, providing escape from stressful situations, is the key factor in _____ disorders.

9. Sue Ann has no memory of the time since she moved to another town and changed her identity. She probably suffers from
   a. psychogenic fugue
   b. psychogenic amnesia
   c. variable personality
   d. multiple personality

Ask Yourself

Do you agree or disagree that *DSM* should be updated every several years? What makes mental illness so variable? Why can't there be one definition of "mental illness" that is unchanging?

(Answers to review questions are on page 570.)

Mood Disorders: The Feeling Is Wrong

> I do not care for anything. I do not care to ride, for the exercise is too violent. I do not care to walk, for walking is too strenuous. I do not care to lie down, for I should either have to remain lying, and I do not care to do that, or I should have to get up again, and I do not care to do that either. . . . I do not care at all.

Did you ever apply for a job you really wanted, and for which you had a terrific interview, only to learn later that you didn't get it? Although the reactions you experienced were probably not as strong as those described by the Danish philosopher Søren Kierkegaard in the passage above, it is likely that you experienced a feeling of depression, an emotional reaction of sadness and melancholy. Unlike Kierkegaard, though, who suffered feelings of depression for extended periods, more than likely you returned to a pleasanter frame of mind relatively quickly. We all experience mood swings. Sometimes we are happy, perhaps even euphoric; at other times we feel upset, saddened, or depressed. Such changes in mood are a normal part of everyday life. In some people, however, moods are so pronounced and so long-lasting that they interfere with the ability to function effectively. In extreme cases a mood may become life-threatening, and in others it may cause the person to lose touch with reality. Situations such as these represent **mood disorders**, disturbances in emotional feelings strong enough to intrude on everyday living.

Mood disorder: Affective disturbance severe enough to interfere with normal living

Major Depression.   Moses. Rousseau. Dostoevsky. Queen Victoria. Lincoln. Tchaikovsky. Freud.

The common link among these people? Each is believed to have suffered from periodic attacks of **major depression**, one of the most common forms of mood disorders. At any one time, some 14 million people in the United States are experiencing major depression, and depression is the most frequent problem

Major depression: A severe form of depression that interferes with concentration, decision making, and sociability

(a)   (b)

Governor Lawton Chiles of Florida (*a*) and novelist William Styron (*b*) have both suffered from depression.

diagnosed in outpatient clinics, affecting about one-third of the patients (Winokur, 1983; McGrath, Keita, Strickland, & Russo, 1990).

Women are twice as likely to experience major depression as men, with one-fourth of all females apt to encounter major depression at some point during their lives. Furthermore, the incidence of depression is on the rise, with many more people experiencing depression now than two generations ago. Even depression during childhood is common. For instance, a sample of 3000 third-, fourth-, and fifth-graders found that around 5 percent were depressed (Lefkowitz & Tesiny, 1985; Seligman, 1988).

When psychologists speak of major depression they do not mean the sadness that comes from experiencing one of life's disappointments. Some depression is normal following the breakup of a long-term relationship, the death of a loved one, or the loss of a job. It is even normal for less serious problems: doing badly in school or not getting into the college of one's choice. (For a list of the most frequent problems of college students, see Table 17-3, p. 570.)

People who suffer from major depression experience similar sorts of feelings, but the severity tends to be considerably greater. They may feel useless, worthless, and lonely and may despair over the future—feelings that may continue for months and years. They may have uncontrollable crying jags and disrupted sleep. The depth of such behavior and the length of time it lasts are the hallmarks of major depression.

Mania and Bipolar Disorders: Ups and Downs. While some people are sinking into the depths of depression, others are soaring high emotionally, experiencing what is called mania. **Mania** refers to an extended state of intense euphoria and elation. People experiencing mania feel intense happiness, power, invulnerability, and energy. They may become involved in wild schemes, believing that they will succeed at anything they attempt. There are many cases on record of people squandering all their money while in a state of mania. Consider, for example, the following description of an individual who experienced a manic episode:

Mania: An extended state of intense euphoria and elation

TABLE 17-3

COLLEGE STUDENTS' PROBLEMS

Among the most prevalent problems of college students are the following (Duke & Nowicki, 1979, 1986; Wechsler, Rohman, & Solomon, 1981):

For male students:
- Grades
- Social life
- Vocational decisions
- The future
- Sexual relationships
- Peer pressures
- Adjusting to a new environment
- Leaving family for the first time
- Competition
- Depression

For female students:
- What to do with their lives
- Developing sexual and emotional relationships
- Strain from too much work
- Grades
- Adjustment
- Gaining independence
- Identity
- Pressure from parents
- Peer pressures
- Morals

How prevalent are these problems? One survey found that 47 percent of the students queried said that they had at least one psychological issue of concern to them (Wechsler, Rohman, & Solomon, 1981). Furthermore, certain subgroups of students showed particular problems. For example, students who were overweight reported a greater frequency of psychological apprehensions, and minority women displayed a higher frequency of motivational problems than white women.

Mr. O'Reilly took a leave of absence from his civil service job. He purchased a large number of cuckoo clocks and then an expensive car, which he planned to use as a mobile showroom for his wares, anticipating that he would make a great deal of money. He proceeded to "tear around town" buying and selling clocks and other merchandise, and when he was not out, he was continuously on the phone making "deals." He rarely slept and, uncharacteristically, spent every evening in neighborhood bars drinking heavily and, according to him, "wheeling and dealing." ... He was $3000 in debt and had driven his family to exhaustion with his excessive activity and talkativeness. He said, however, that he felt "on top of the world" (Spitzer, Skodol, Gibbon, & Williams, 1983, p. 115).

Bipolar disorder: A disorder in which a person alternates between euphoric feelings of mania and bouts of depression

Mania is often found paired with bouts of depression. This alternation of mania and depression is called **bipolar disorder** (or, as it used to be known, manic-depressive disorder). The swings between highs and lows may occur as frequently as a few days apart or they may alternate over a period of years. In addition, the periods of depression tend to be longer in most individuals than the periods of mania, although this pattern is reversed in some.

Interestingly, some of society's most creative individuals may suffer from a mild form of bipolar disorder. The imagination, drive, excitement, and energy that they display during manic stages allow them to make unusually creative contributions. On the other hand, most people who display mania go beyond the bounds of what would generally be considered normal, and their behavior clearly causes self-harm (Fieve, 1975; Goodwin & Jamison, 1990).

ANSWERS (REVIEW III):

1. False; *DSM-III-R* is intended to be descriptive only.   **2.** generalized anxiety disorder   **3.** b
4. panic attack   **5.** a   **6.** compulsion   **7.** In conversion disorder, an actual physical disturbance is present.   **8.** dissociative   **9.** a

Causes of Mood Disorders. Because they represent a major mental health problem, mood disorders—and, in particular, depression—have received a good deal of study, and a number of approaches have been used to explain their occurrence. Psychoanalytic approaches, for example, see depression as the result of anger at oneself. In this view, people feel responsible for the bad things that happen to them and direct their anger inward.

On the other hand, there is convincing evidence that both bipolar disorder and major depression may have a biological foundation. For example, heredity plays a role in bipolar disorder; the affliction runs in some families (Egeland et al., 1987). Furthermore, some researchers have found a chemical imbalance in the brains of some depressed patients. Certain abnormalities have been identified in the chemical substances involved in the transmission of electrical charges across the gaps between nerve cells (Wender & Klein, 1981).

Some explanations for mood disorders look to cognitive factors. For instance, psychologist Martin Seligman suggests that depression is largely a response to learned helplessness. As we discussed in Chapters 7 and 16, **learned helplessness** is a state in which people perceive and eventually learn that there is no way to escape from or cope with stress. As a consequence, they simply give up fighting the stress and submit to it, thereby spawning depression (Seligman, 1975, 1988). Building on Seligman's notions, other psychologists suggest that depression may be a result of hopelessness, a combination of learned helplessness and an expectation that negative outcomes in one's life are inevitable (Abramson, Metalsky, & Alloy, 1989).

Learned helplessness: A state in which people believe they cannot escape from or cope with stress, and they give up fighting it, leading to depression

Psychologist Aaron Beck has proposed that people's faulty cognitions underlie their depressed feelings. Specifically, his cognitive theory of depression suggests that depressed individuals typically view themselves as life's losers, blaming themselves whenever anything goes wrong. By focusing on the negative side of situations, they feel inept and unable to act constructively to change their environment. In sum, their negative cognitions lead to feelings of depression (Beck, 1976, 1982).

The various theories of depression have still not provided a complete answer to an elusive question that has dogged researchers: Why is the incidence of depression twice as high for women as for men? One explanation is that the stress experienced by women may be greater than that experienced by men at certain points in their lives—such as when a woman must simultaneously earn a living and be primary caregiver for her children. In addition, women have a higher risk for physical and sexual abuse, typically earn lower wages than men, and report greater unhappiness with their marriages (McGrath, Keita, Strickland, & Russo, 1990).

But biological factors may also explain some women's depression. For example, 25 to 50 percent of women who take oral contraceptives report symptoms of depression, and depression that occurs following the birth of a child is linked to hormonal changes (Strickland, 1988).

It is clear, ultimately, that researchers have discovered no definitive solutions to the puzzle of depression, and there are many alternative explanations. Most likely, mood disorders are caused by a complex interaction of several factors (Ingram, 1990; Wolman & Stricker, 1990).

Schizophrenia: When Reality Is Lost

For many years she has heard voices, which insult her and cast suspicion on her chastity. They mention a number of names she knows, and tell her she will be stripped and abused. The voices are very distinct, and, in her opinion, they must be carried by a telescope or a machine from her home. Her thoughts are dictated to her; she is obliged to think them, and hears them repeated after her. She is interrupted in her work, and has all kinds of uncomfortable sensations in her body, to which something is "done." In particular, her "mother parts" are turned inside out, and people send a pain through her back, lay ice water on her heart, squeeze her neck, injure her spine, and violate her (Kraepelin, 1904).

The label given to the most severe forms of mental disturbance, such as that described in the famous case study above, is schizophrenia. Schizophrenics make up by far the largest percentage of those hospitalized for mental disorders and in most respects are the least likely to recover from their difficulties.

Schizophrenia refers to a class of disorders in which severe distortion of reality occurs. Thinking, perception, and emotion may deteriorate; there may be a withdrawal from social interaction; and there may be displays of bizarre behavior. Although several types of schizophrenia (see Table 17-4) have been observed, the distinctions between them are not always clear-cut (e.g., Zigler & Glick, 1988). Moreover, the symptoms displayed by a schizophrenic person may vary considerably over time, and people with schizophrenia show significant differences in the pattern of symptoms even when they are labeled with the same diagnostic category. Nonetheless, a number of characteristics reliably distinguish schizophrenia from other disorders. They include:

- ■ Decline from a previous level of functioning. An individual can no longer carry out activities he or she was once able to do.

- ■ Disturbances of thought and language. Schizophrenics use logic and language in a peculiar way; their thinking does not make sense and they do not follow conventional linguistic rules. Consider, for example, the following response to the question "Why do you think people believe in God?"

> Uh, let's, I don't know why, let's see, balloon travel. He holds it up for you, the balloon. He don't let you fall out, your little legs sticking down through the clouds. He's down to the smokestack, looking through the smoke trying to get

Schizophrenia: A class of disorders characterized by a severe distortion of reality, resulting in antisocial behavior, silly or obscene behavior, hallucinations, and disturbances in movement

TABLE 17-4

THE MAJOR TYPES OF SCHIZOPHRENIA

Type	Symptoms
Disorganized (hebephrenic) schizophrenia	Inappropriate laughter and giggling, silliness, incoherent speech, infantile behavior, strange and sometimes obscene behavior
Paranoid schizophrenia	Delusions and hallucinations of persecution or of greatness, loss of judgment, erratic and unpredictable behavior
Catatonic schizophrenia	Major disturbances in movement; in some phases, loss of all motion, with patient frozen into a single position, remaining that way for hours and sometimes even days; in other phases, hyperactivity and wild, sometimes violent, movement
Undifferentiated schizophrenia	Variable mixture of major symptoms of schizophrenia; classification used for patients who cannot be typed into any of the more specific categories
Residual schizophrenia	Minor signs of schizophrenia following a more serious episode

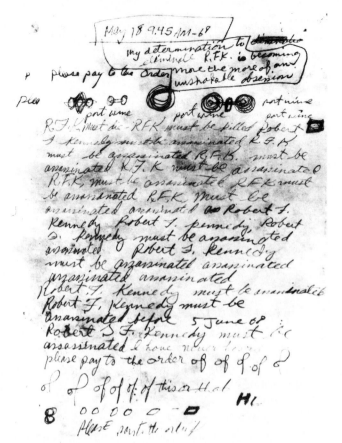

FIGURE 17-3

This excerpt from the diary of Sirhan Sirhan, the killer of Robert F. Kennedy, shows the disturbances of thought and language characteristic of schizophrenia.

the balloon gassed up you know. Way they're flying on top that way, legs sticking out. I don't know, looking down on the ground, heck, that'd make you so dizzy you just stay and sleep you know, hold down and sleep there. I used to be sleep outdoors, you know, sleep outdoors instead of going home (Chapman & Chapman, 1973, p. 3).

As this selection illustrates, although the basic grammatical structure may be intact, the substance of schizophrenics' thinking is often illogical, garbled, and lacking in meaningful content (see Figure 17-3).

■ Delusions. People with schizophrenia often have **delusions**, firmly held, unshakable beliefs with no basis in reality. Among the most frequent ones are the beliefs that they are being controlled by someone else, that they are being persecuted by others, and that their thoughts are being broadcast so that others are able to know what they are thinking.

Delusions: Firmly held beliefs with no basis in reality

■ Perceptual disorders. Schizophrenics do not perceive the world as most other people do. They may see, hear, or smell things differently from others (see Figure 17-4, p. 574) and do not even have a sense of their bodies in the way that others do. Some reports suggest that schizophrenics have difficulty determining where their own bodies stop and the rest of the world begins (Ritzler & Rosenbaum, 1974). They may also have **hallucinations**, the experience of perceiving things that do not actually exist.

Hallucinations: Perceptions of things that do not actually exist

■ Emotional disturbances. People with schizophrenia sometimes show a bland lack of emotion in which even the most dramatic events produce little or no emotional response. Conversely, they may display emotion that is

FIGURE 17-4

This haunting art was created by an individual suffering from severe mental disturbance.

inappropriate to a situation. For example, a schizophrenic might laugh uproariously at a funeral or may react with anger when being helped by someone.

■ Withdrawal. Schizophrenics tend to have little interest in others. They tend not to socialize or hold real conversations with others, although they may talk *at* another person. In the most extreme cases they do not even acknowledge the presence of other people, appearing to be in their own isolated world.

Process schizophrenia: One course of schizophrenia in which symptoms begin early in life and develop slowly and subtly

Reactive schizophrenia: One course of schizophrenia in which the onset of symptoms is sudden and conspicuous

The symptoms of schizophrenia follow two primary courses. In **process schizophrenia**, the symptoms develop relatively early in life, slowly and subtly. There may be a gradual withdrawal from the world, excessive daydreaming, a blunting of emotion, until eventually the disorder reaches the point where others cannot overlook it. In other cases, known as **reactive schizophrenia**, the onset of symptoms is sudden and conspicuous. The treatment outlook for reactive schizophrenia is relatively favorable; process schizophrenia has proved to be much more difficult to treat.

A relatively recent addition to the classifications used in schizophrenia distinguishes positive-symptom from negative-symptom schizophrenia (Opler et al., 1984; Andreasen, 1985). Negative-symptom schizophrenia means an absence or loss of normal functioning, such as social withdrawal or blunted emotions. In contrast, positive-symptom schizophrenia is indicated by the presence of disordered behavior such as hallucinations, delusions, and extremes of emotionality. The distinction, although controversial, is becoming increasingly important because it suggests that two different underlying processes may explain the roots of schizophrenia—which remains one of the greatest mysteries facing psychologists who deal with abnormal behavior.

Solving the Puzzle of Schizophrenia. Although it is clear that schizophrenic behavior departs radically from normal behavior, its causes are less apparent. It does appear, however, that schizophrenia has both biological and psychological components at its roots.

Biological components. Because schizophrenia is more common in some families than in others, genetic factors seem to be involved in producing at least a susceptibility to or readiness for developing schizophrenia. For example, researchers have found evidence of a link between schizophrenia and an abnormally functioning gene (Brynjolfsson et al., 1990; Gurling et al., 1989). In addition, some studies show that people who have been classified as suffering from schizophrenia have about a 25 percent chance of having children with severe psychological problems. Furthermore, if one of a pair of identical twins has schizophrenia, the other has as much as a 42 percent chance of developing it (Gottesman & Schields, 1972; Kringlen, 1978). However, if genetics alone were entirely accountable, the chance of the other identical twin having schizophrenia would be 100 percent, since identical twins share the same genetic makeup. The development of schizophrenia, then, is due to more than just genetic factors (Holzman & Matthysse, 1990).

One of the most intriguing hypotheses to explain schizophrenia is that the brains of victims harbor either a biochemical imbalance or structural abnormality. For example, one hypothesis suggests that schizophrenia occurs when people, under stressful conditions, produce chemicals that cause hallucinations or disorganized thought—similar to the effects of a drug such as LSD—in a sort of self-induced chemical overdose (Carson, 1983). Similarly, the **dopamine hypothesis** suggests that schizophrenia occurs when there is excess activity in those areas of the brain that use the chemical dopamine to transmit impulses across nerve cells (Wong et al., 1988; Snyder, 1978). This hypothesis came to light after the discovery that drugs that block dopamine action in brain pathways can be highly effective in reducing the symptoms of schizophrenia.

Dopamine hypothesis: A theory that suggests that schizophrenia occurs when there is excess activity in those areas of the brain using dopamine to transmit nerve impulses

Unfortunately, the dopamine hypothesis does not provide the whole story. Drugs that block dopamine action produce a biological reaction in just a few hours after they're taken—yet the symptoms of schizophrenia don't subside for weeks. If the hypothesis were entirely correct, we would expect an immediate improvement in schizophrenic symptoms. Moreover, these drugs are effective in reducing symptoms not only in schizophrenics but also in those suffering from very different sorts of psychological problems such as mania and depression (Carson, 1983). Nevertheless, the dopamine hypothesis provides a starting point in understanding biochemical factors in schizophrenia.

Other biological explanations for schizophrenia propose that structural abnormalities exist in the brains of people with the disorder. For example, the hippocampus and ventricles of the brains of those with schizophrenia differ in size from those who do not have the disorder (Suddath et al., 1990). Consistent with such research, the electrical activity of the brain also seems to be disordered in people with schizophrenia, as illustrated in Figure 17-5, p. 576 (John, Prichep, Fridman, & Easton, 1988).

Psychological components. Although biological factors provide some pieces of the puzzle of schizophrenia, we still need to consider past and current experiences found in the environments of people who develop the disturbance. For instance, psychoanalytic approaches suggest that schizophrenia is a form of regression to earlier experiences and stages of life. Freud believed, for instance, that people with schizophrenia lack strong enough egos to cope with their unacceptable impulses. They regress to the oral stage—a time in which the id and ego are not

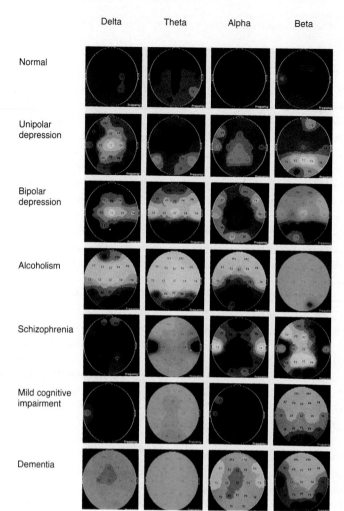

| | Delta | Theta | Alpha | Beta |

Normal

Unipolar depression

Bipolar depression

Alcoholism

Schizophrenia

Mild cognitive impairment

Dementia

FIGURE 17-5

A comparison of electrical activity between normal individuals and those diagnosed with schizophrenia and several other disorders. The color coding corresponds to the degree of deviation from normal activity at each of four different wave patterns (delta, theta, alpha, and beta waves).

yet separated. Therefore, individuals suffering from schizophrenia essentially lack an ego and act out impulses without concern for reality.

Although this reasoning is theoretically plausible, there is little evidence to support psychoanalytic explanations. Only slightly more convincing are theories that look toward the families of people with schizophrenia. For instance, such families often display abnormal communication patterns. These families also may differ on a number of other dimensions, including socioeconomic status, anxiety level, and general degree of stress present (Wynne, Singer, Bartko, & Toohey, 1975; Lidz & Fleck, 1985).

Of course, the faulty communication patterns found in families of a person with schizophrenia may be as much a consequence of the schizophrenia as a cause. Still, theorists taking a behavioral perspective believe such communication problems support a **learned-inattention theory of schizophrenia** (Ullmann & Krasner, 1975). According to the learned-inattention view, schizophrenia is a learned behavior consisting of a set of inappropriate responses to social stimuli. Rather than respond to others, people with schizophrenia have learned to ignore appropriate stimuli. They pay attention instead to stimuli that are not related to normal social interaction. Because this results in bizarre behavior, others re-

Learned-inattention theory of schizophrenia: A theory that suggests that schizophrenia is a learned behavior consisting of a set of inappropriate responses to social stimuli

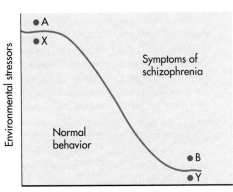

FIGURE 17-6

According to the predisposition model of schizophrenia, schizophrenic behavior occurs when environmental stressors are particularly high, even if the predisposition is relatively low (person A). Similarly, schizophrenic behavior can occur if the predisposition is relatively high, even if stressors are relatively low (person B). On the other hand, even though the stress level is high, person X will not display schizophrenic behavior, because the predisposition is sufficiently low. Similarly, person Y will behave normally despite the strong predisposition, because the stress is low. (Adapted from Zubin & Spring, 1977.)

spond to them in a negative way, leading to social rejection and unpleasant interactions, and, ultimately, to an even less appropriate response by the individual. Eventually, the individual begins to "tune out" appropriate stimuli and develops schizophrenic characteristics.

The Multiple Causes of Schizophrenia. As we have seen, there is research supporting several different biological and psychological causes of schizophrenia. It is likely, then, that not just one but several jointly explain the onset of the problem. The predominant approach used today, the **predisposition model of schizophrenia**, considers a number of factors simultaneously (Zubin & Spring, 1977; Cornblatt & Erlenmeyer-Kimling, 1985; Fowles, 1992). This model suggests that individuals may inherit a predisposition or an inborn sensitivity to schizophrenia which makes them particularly vulnerable to stressful factors in the environment. The stressors may vary—social rejection or dysfunctional family communication patterns—but if they are strong enough and are coupled with a genetic predisposition, the result will be the onset of schizophrenia (see Figure 17-6). Similarly, if the genetic predisposition is strong enough, schizophrenia may occur even when the environmental stressors are relatively weak.

In sum, schizophrenia is associated with several kinds of biological and psychological factors. It is increasingly clear, then, that schizophrenia is not produced by any single factor but by a combination of interrelated variables (Birchwood, Hallett, & Preston, 1989; Fowles, 1992).

Predisposition model of schizophrenia: A model that suggests that individuals may inherit a predisposition toward schizophrenia that makes them particularly vulnerable to stressful factors in the environment

Personality Disorders: Lacking Distress

I had always wanted lots of things; as a child I can remember wanting a bullet that a friend of mine had brought in to show the class. I took it and put it into my school bag and when my friend noticed it was missing, I was the one who stayed after school with him and searched the room, and I was the one who sat with him and bitched about the other kids and how one of them took his bullet. I even went home with him to help him break the news to his uncle, who had brought it home from the war for him.

But that was petty compared with the stuff I did later. I wanted a Ph.D. very badly, but I didn't want to work very hard—just enough to get by. I never did the experiments I reported; hell, I was smart enough to make up the results. I knew enough about statistics to make anything look plausible. I got my master's degree without even spending one hour in a laboratory. I mean, the professors believed anything. I'd stay out all night drinking and being with my friends, and the next day I'd get in just before them and tell 'em I'd been in the lab all night. They'd actually feel sorry for me. I did my doctoral research the same way, except it got published and there was some excitement about my findings. The research helped me get my first college teaching job. There my goal was tenure.

The rules at my university were about the same as at any other. You had to publish and you had to be an effective teacher. "Gathering" data and publishing it was never any problem for me, so that was fine. But teaching was evaluated on the basis of forms completed by students at the end of each semester. I'm a fair-to-good teacher, but I had to be sure that my record showed me as excellent. The task was simple. Each semester, I collected the evaluation forms, took out all the fair-to-bad ones and replaced them with doctored ones. It would take me a whole evening, but I'd sit down with a bunch of different colored pens and pencils and would fill in as many as 300 of the forms. Needless to say, I was awarded tenure (Duke & Nowicki, 1979, pp. 309–310).

Before you leap to the assumption that all college professors are like the one describing himself above, it should be stated that this person represents a clear example of someone with a personality disorder. **Personality disorders** are different from the other problems that we have discussed in this chapter, because there is often little sense of personal distress associated with the psychological maladjustment of those affected. In fact, people with personality disorders frequently lead seemingly normal lives—until one looks just below the surface. There one finds a set of inflexible, maladaptive personality traits that do not permit the individual to function appropriately as a member of society.

The best-known type of personality disorder is the **antisocial or sociopathic personality disorder**. Individuals with this disturbance tend to display no regard for the moral and ethical rules of society or for the rights of others. Although they appear intelligent and are usually likable at first, they can be seen as manipulative and deceptive upon closer examination. Moreover, they tend to share certain other characteristics (Carson, Butcher, & Coleman, 1988):

■ A lack of conscience, guilt, or anxiety over transgressions. When those with an antisocial personality behave in a way that injures someone else, they understand intellectually that they have caused the harm but feel no remorse.

■ Impulsive behavior and an inability to withstand frustration. Antisocial personalities are unable to withstand frustration without reacting in some way—which may include violating the rights of others, if doing so allows them to remove the frustration.

■ Manipulation of others. Antisocial personalities frequently have very good interpersonal skills: They are charming, engaging, and able to convince others to do what they want. Some of the best con men have antisocial personalities. Without a second thought, they are able to get people to hand over their life savings. The misery that follows in the wake of such activities is not cause for concern to the antisocial personality.

What causes such an unusual constellation of problems? A variety of factors have been suggested, ranging from a biological inability to experience emotions to problems in family relationships (e.g., Newman & Kosson, 1986). For example, in many cases of antisocial behavior, the individual has come from a home in which a parent has died or left, or one in which there is a lack of affection, a lack of consistency in discipline, or outright rejection. Other explanations concentrate on sociocultural factors, since an unusually high proportion of antisocial

---

Personality disorder: A mental disorder characterized by a set of inflexible, maladaptive personality traits that keep a person from functioning properly in society

Antisocial or sociopathic personality disorder: A disorder in which individuals display no regard for moral and ethical rules or for the rights of others

personalities come from lower socioeconomic groups. Some researchers have suggested that the breakdown of societal rules, norms, and regulations that may be found in severely deprived economic environments may encourage the development of antisocial personalities (Melges & Bowlby, 1969). Still, no one has been able to pinpoint the specific causes of antisocial personalities, and it is likely that some combination of factors is responsible.

Another example of a personality disturbance is the **narcissistic personality disorder**, characterized by an exaggerated sense of self-importance. Those with the disorder expect special treatment from others, while at the same time they disregard others' feelings. In some ways, in fact, the main attribute of the narcissistic personality is an inability to experience empathy for other people.

Narcissistic personality disorder: A personality disorder characterized by an exaggerated sense of self and an inability to experience empathy for others

There are several other categories of personality disorder, ranging in severity from individuals who may simply be regarded by others as eccentric, obnoxious, or difficult, to people who act in a manner that is criminal and dangerous to others. Although they are not out of touch with reality in the way that schizophrenics are, people with personality disorders lead lives that are on the fringes of society.

Beyond the Major Disorders

The various forms of abnormal behavior described in *DSM-III-R* cover much wider ground than we have been able to discuss in this chapter. Some we have discussed in earlier parts of the book, such as **psychoactive substance-use disorder**, in which problems arise from the abuse of drugs (covered in Chapter 6), and **sexual disorders**, in which one's sexual activity is unsatisfactory (discussed in Chapter 12). Another important class of disorders that we have previously touched on is **organic mental disorders**, problems that have a purely biological basis. Other disorders we have not mentioned at all, and each of the classes we have discussed can be divided into several subcategories. And some forms of psychological disorder are not even included in *DSM-III-R*, as we discuss in the Psychology at Work box on p. 580.

Psychoactive substance-use disorder: Disordered behavior involving drug abuse

Sexual disorders: A form of abnormal behavior in which one's sexual activity is unsatisfactory

Organic mental disorders: Problems having a purely biological basis

In some ways, then, our discussion of psychological disturbances has only touched the surface. The challenge facing psychologists interested in abnormal behavior is to improve their understanding of the nature and causes of these psychological disorders in order to improve the lives of those who suffer from them, as well as to prevent their occurrence in the first place—issues we discuss in the next chapter.

The Informed Consumer of Psychology: Deciding When You Need Help

After you consider the range and variety of psychological disturbances that can afflict people, it would not be surprising if you felt that you were suffering from one (or more) of the problems we have discussed. This is a perfectly natural reaction, for, as we mentioned earlier, people often conclude that they have the same problems they are studying—the classic medical student's disease. Because this is such a common phenomenon, it is important that you be well aware of the pitfalls of self-diagnosis.

One of the truisms of the legal profession is that a lawyer who defends himself has a fool for a client. Similarly, we might say that people who try to categorize their own mental disorders are making a foolish mistake. With categories that are subjective under the best of circumstances, and with problems that can be

In most people's estimation, a person who hears voices of the recently deceased is probably a victim of some psychological disturbance. Yet members of the Plains Indian tribe routinely hear the voices of the dead calling to them from the afterlife.

This is but one example of the role that culture plays in the labeling of behavior as "abnormal." In fact, of all the major adult disorders found within the *DSM* categorization, just four are found across all cultures of the world: schizophrenia, bipolar disorder, major depression, and anxiety disorders (Kleinman, 1991). *All* the rest are particular to North America and western Europe.

Take, for instance, anorexia nervosa, which we first discussed in Chapter 11. Anorexia nervosa is a weight disorder in which people, particularly women, develop inaccurate views of their body appearance, become obsessed with their weight, and refuse to eat, sometimes starving in the process. This disorder occurs only in cultures holding the societal standard that slender female bodies are most desirable. Because for most of the world such a standard does not exist, anorexia nervosa does not occur. Interestingly, there is no anorexia

DSM AND CULTURE—AND THE CULTURE OF DSM

nervosa in all of Asia, with two exceptions: the upper and upper-middle class of Japan and Hong Kong, where western influence tends to be great. It is also interesting that anorexia nervosa is a fairly recent disorder. In the 1600s and 1700s, it did not occur, because the ideal female body in western society at that time was a plump one.

Similarly, multiple-personality disorder only makes sense as a problem in societies in which a sense of self is fairly concrete. In places like India, the self is based more on factors external and relatively independent of the person. There, when an individual displays symptoms of what people in western society would call multiple-personality disorder, it is assumed that that person is possessed either by demons (which is viewed as a malady) or by gods (which is not a cause for treatment).

Similarly, even though such disorders as schizophrenia are found throughout the world, the particular symptoms of the disorder are influenced by cultural factors. Hence, cat-

atonic schizophrenia, in which unmoving patients appear to be frozen into the same position sometimes for days, is rare in North America and western Europe. In contrast, in India, 80 percent of those with schizophrenia are catatonic.

Other cultures have disorders that do not appear in the west. For example, in Malaya, a behavior called "amok" is characterized by a wild outburst in which a person, usually quiet and withdrawn, kills or severely injures another. Another example is "koro," found in southeast Asian males who develop an intense panic that their penis is about to withdraw into their abdomen. Finally, a disorder sometimes found in rural Japan is "kitsunetsuki," in which those afflicted think that they have been possessed by foxes and display facial expressions characteristic of the animals (Carson, Butcher, & Coleman, 1988).

In sum, we should not assume that *DSM* provides the final word on psychological disorders. The disorders it includes are very much a creation and function of western culture at a particular moment in time, and its categories should not be seen as universally applicable.

elusive and fleeting even to well-trained, experienced mental health professionals, it is unreasonable to expect that after reading a chapter in an introductory psychology book anyone could make a valid diagnosis.

On the other hand, there are guidelines you can use to determine when some kind of professional help is warranted. The following signals suggest the possible necessity of outside intervention:

- Long-term feelings of psychological distress that interfere with your sense of well-being, competence, and ability to function effectively in daily activities
- Occasions in which you experience overwhelmingly high stress, accompanied by feelings of inability to cope with the situation
- Prolonged depression or feelings of hopelessness, particularly when they do not have any clear cause (such as the death of someone close)
- Withdrawal from other people

■ A chronic physical problem for which no physical cause can be determined

■ A fear or phobia that prevents you from engaging in normal everyday activities

■ Feelings that other people are out to get you or are talking about and plotting against you

■ The inability to interact effectively with others, preventing the development of friendships and loving relationships

The above criteria can serve as a rough set of guidelines for determining when the normal problems of everyday living are beyond the point that you are capable of dealing with them yourself. In such situations, the least reasonable approach would be to pore over the psychological disorders we have discussed in an attempt to pigeonhole yourself into a specific category. A more reasonable strategy is to consider seeking professional help—a possibility that we discuss in the next chapter.

◀ **RECAP AND REVIEW IV**

RECAP

◀ Mood disorders are characterized by disturbances in affect that are so great they impede daily living.

◀ Schizophrenia represents the most common diagnosis for those hospitalized for mental disturbance.

◀ People with personality disorders do not feel the personal distress associated with other disorders, but they do have maladaptive traits that prevent them from functioning as normal members of society.

◀ Other forms of abnormal behavior include sexual disorders, psychoactive substance-use disorders, and organic mental disorders.

REVIEW

1. Henry's feelings of deep despair, worthlessness, and loneliness have persisted for months. His symptoms are indicative of
   a. an adjustment reaction
   b. normal depression
   c. major depression
   d. affective depression

2. States of extreme euphoria and energy paired with severe depression characterize _____ disorder.

3. Arthur's belief that his thoughts are being controlled by beings from outer space is an example of a _____.

4. _____ schizophrenia shows symptoms that are sudden and of easily identifiable onset, while _____ schizophrenia develops gradually over a person's lifespan.

5. The _____ _____ states that schizophrenia may be caused by an excess of certain neurotransmitters in the brain.

6. Which of the following theories states that schizophrenia is caused by the combination of a genetic predisposition and environmental stressors?
   a. Learned-inattention
   b. Predisposition model
   c. Dopamine hypothesis
   d. Learned-helplessness theory

7. The _____ personality disorder is characterized by a disregard for societal rules or others' rights.

8. A person with a greatly exaggerated sense of self-importance and a disregard for others' feelings may be suffering from a _____ personality disorder.

Ask Yourself

Personality disorders often are characterized by a lack of visibility. Many people with these problems seem to live basically normal lives and are not a threat to others. Since these people can function well in society, why should they be considered "ill"?

(Answers to review questions are on page 582.)

■ *How can we distinguish normal from abnormal behavior?*

1. The most satisfactory definition of abnormal behavior is one based on the psychological consequences of the behavior, which are thought of as abnormal if they produce a sense of distress, anxiety, or guilt, or if they are harmful to others. Another useful definition considers people who cannot adapt to society and who are unable to function effectively to be abnormal.

2. No single definition is totally adequate; therefore it is reasonable to consider abnormal and normal behavior as marking two ends of a continuum, or scale, with completely normal functioning at one end and completely abnormal behavior at the other.

■ *What are the major models of abnormal behavior used by mental health professionals, and how are they applied to specific cases?*

3. The medical model of abnormal behavior views abnormality as a symptom of an underlying disease that requires a cure. Psychoanalytic models suggest that abnormal behavior is caused by conflicts in the unconscious stemming from past experience. In order to resolve psychological problems, people need to resolve the unconscious conflicts.

4. In contrast to the medical and psychoanalytic models, behavioral approaches view abnormal behavior not as a symptom of some underlying problem, but as the problem itself. To resolve the problem, one must change the behavior.

5. The cognitive approach, often referred to as the cognitive behavioral perspective, suggests that abnormal behavior is the result of faulty cognitions. In this view, abnormal behavior can be remedied through a change in cognitions (thoughts and beliefs).

6. Humanistic approaches view people as rational and motivated to get along with others; abnormal behavior is seen as a difficulty in fulfilling one's needs. People are considered to be in control of their lives and able to resolve their own problems.

7. Sociocultural approaches view abnormal behavior in terms of difficulties arising from family and other social relationships. The sociocultural model concentrates on such factors as socioeconomic status and the social rules society creates to define normal and abnormal behavior.

8. Students of psychology are susceptible to the same sort of "disease" that afflicts medical students: the perception that they suffer from the problems they are studying. Unless their psychological difficulties are persistent, have depth, and are consistent, however, it is unlikely that their concerns are valid.

■ *What is the classification system used to categorize abnormal behavior, and what are the major mental health disorders?*

9. The system for classifying abnormal behaviors that is used most widely today is *DSM-III-R—Diagnostic and Statistical Manual of Mental Disorders, Third Edition—Revised.*

10. Anxiety disorders are present when a person experiences so much anxiety that it impedes daily functioning. Specific types of anxiety disorders include generalized anxiety disorder, panic disorder, phobic disorder, and obsessive-compulsive disorder. Generalized anxiety disorder occurs when a person experiences long-term anxiety with no apparent cause. Panic disorders are marked by panic attacks, which are sudden, intense feelings of anxiety. Phobic disorders are characterized by intense, irrational fears of specific objects or situations. People with obsessive-compulsive disorders display obsessions (recurring thoughts or ideas) or compulsions (repetitious, unwanted behaviors).

11. Somatoform disorders are psychological difficulties that are displayed through physical problems. An example is hypochondriasis, in which there is a constant fear of illness and a preoccupation with disease. Another somatoform disorder is conversion disorder, in which there is an actual physical difficulty that occurs without a physiological cause.

12. Dissociative disorders are marked by the splitting apart, or dissociation, of crucial parts of personality that are usually integrated. The three major kinds of dissociative disorders are multiple personality, psychogenic amnesia, and psychogenic fugue.

13. Mood disorders are characterized by emotions of depression or euphoria so strong that they intrude on everyday living. In major depression, people experience sorrow so deep that they may become suicidal. In bipolar disorder, stages of mania, in which there is an extended sense of elation and powerfulness, alternate with depression.

14. Schizophrenia is one of the severest forms of mental illness. The manifestations of schizophrenia include declines in functioning, thought and language disturbances, perceptual disorders, emotional disturbance, and withdrawal from others. There is strong evidence linking schizophrenia to genetic, biochemical, and environmental factors. According to the predisposition model, there is likely to be an interaction among various factors.

15. People with personality disorders experience little or no personal distress, but they do suffer from an inability to function as normal members of society. The best-known type of personality disorder is the antisocial or sociopathic personality disorder, in which the moral and ethical rules of society are ignored. The narcissistic personality is characterized by an exaggerated sense of importance.

ANSWERS (REVIEW IV):

1. c   **2.** bipolar   **3.** delusion   **4.** Reactive; process   **5.** dopamine hypothesis   **6.** b
7. sociopathic   **8.** narcissistic

16. There are many other categories of disorders, including sexual disorders, psychoactive substance-use disorders, and organic mental disorders.

■ *What are the major indicators that signal a need for the help of a mental health practitioner?*

17. A number of signals indicate a need for professional help. These include long-term feelings of psychological distress, feelings of inability to cope with stress, withdrawal from other people, prolonged feelings of hopelessness, chronic physical problems with no apparent causes, phobias and compulsions, paranoia, and an inability to interact with others.

KEY TERMS AND CONCEPTS

medical model of abnormality (p. 551)
psychoanalytic model of abnormality (p. 552)
behavioral model of abnormality (p. 552)
cognitive model of abnormality (p. 553)
cognitions (p. 553)
cognitive-behavioral approach (p. 553)
humanistic model of abnormality (p. 553)
sociocultural model of abnormality (p. 554)
medical student's disease (p. 556)
Diagnostic and Statistical Manual of Mental Disorders, Third Edition—Revised (DSM-III-R) (p. 557)
anxiety (p. 560)

anxiety disorder (p. 560)
generalized anxiety disorder (p. 560)
panic disorder (p. 560)
panic attack (p. 561)
phobic disorder (p. 562)
phobias (p. 562)
obsessive-compulsive disorder (p. 562)
obsession (p. 562)
compulsion (p. 563)
hypochondriasis (p. 564)
somatoform disorder (p. 564)
conversion disorder (p. 564)
dissociative disorder (p. 566)
multiple personality (p. 566)
psychogenic amnesia (p. 566)
psychogenic fugue (p. 567)
mood disorder (p. 568)
major depression (p. 568)
mania (p. 569)

bipolar disorder (p. 570)
learned helplessness (p. 571)
schizophrenia (p. 572)
delusions (p. 573)
hallucinations (p. 573)
process schizophrenia (p. 574)
reactive schizophrenia (p. 574)
dopamine hypothesis (p. 575)
learned-inattention theory of schizophrenia (p. 576)
predisposition model of schizophrenia (p. 577)
personality disorder (p. 578)
antisocial or sociopathic personality disorder (p. 578)
narcissistic personality disorder (p. 579)
psychoactive substance-use disorder (p. 579)
sexual disorders (p. 579)
organic mental disorders (p. 579)

TREATMENT OF ABNORMAL BEHAVIOR

ALICE, MARTHA, AND SANDY

Although most psychotherapy sessions may look similar, their specific content varies greatly according to the orientation of the therapist and the needs of the client.

Alice: I was thinking about this business of standards. I somehow developed a sort of a knack, I guess, of—well—habit—of trying to make people feel at ease around me, or to make things go along smoothly. . . .

Therapist: In other words, what you did was always in the direction of trying to keep things smooth and to make other people feel better and to smooth the situation.

Alice: Yes. I think that's what it was. Now the reason why I did it probably was—I mean, not that I was a good little Samaritan going around making other people happy, but that was probably the role that felt easiest for me to play. I'd been doing it around home so much. I just didn't stand up for my own convictions, until I don't know whether I have any convictions to stand up for.

Therapist: You feel that for a long time you've been playing the role of kind of smoothing out the frictions or differences or what not. . . .

Alice: M-hm.

Therapist: Rather than having any opinion or reaction of your own in the situation. Is that it? (Rogers, 1951, pp. 152–153.)

* * *

Martha: The basic problem is that I'm worried about my family. I'm worried about money. And I never seem to be able to relax.

Therapist: Why are you worried about your family? Let's go into that, first of all. What's to be concerned about? They have certain demands which you don't want to adhere to.

Martha: I was brought up to think that I mustn't be selfish.

Therapist: Oh, we'll have to knock *that* out of your head!

Martha: I think that that is one of my basic problems.

Therapist: That's right. You were brought up to be Florence Nightingale. . . .

Martha: And now I try to break away. For instance, they'll call up and say, "Why don't you come Sunday?" And if I say, "No, I'm busy," rather than saying, "No, I'll come when it's convenient," they get terribly hurt, and my stomach gets all upset.

Therapist: Because you tell yourself, "There I go again. I'm a louse for not devoting myself to them!" As long as you tell yourself that crap, then your stomach or some other part of you will start jumping! But it's your *philosophy*, your *belief*, your *sentence to yourself*—"I'm no goddamned good! How could I do that lousy, stinking thing?" *That's* what's causing your stomach to jump. Now, that is a false sentence. Why are you no goddamned good because you prefer you to them? For that's what it amounts to. *Who* said you're no good—Jesus Christ? Moses? Who said so? The answer is: Your parents said so. And you believe it because they said so. But who the hell are they? (Ellis, 1974, pp. 223–286.)

* * *

Sandy: My father . . . never took any interest in any of us. (Begins to weep.) It was my mother—rest her soul—who loved us, not our father. He worked her to death. Lord, I miss her. (Weeps uncontrollably.)—I must sound angry at my father. Don't you think I have a right to be angry?

> Therapist: Do you think you have a right to be angry?

> Sandy: Of course, I do! Why are you questioning me? You don't believe me, do you?

> Therapist: You want me to believe you.

> Sandy: I don't care whether you believe me or not. As far as I'm concerned, you're just a wall that I'm talking to—I don't know why I pay for this rotten therapy.—Don't you have any thought or feelings at all? I know what you're thinking—you think I'm crazy—you must be laughing at me—I'll probably be a case in your next book! You're just sitting there—smirking—making me feel like a bad person—thinking I'm wrong for being mad, that I have no right to be mad.

> Therapist: Just like your father.

> Sandy: Yes, you're just like my father.—Oh my God! Just now—I—I—thought I was talking to him. (Sue, Sue, & Sue, 1990, pp. 514–515.)

LOOKING AHEAD ▶

Three problems, three therapists.

As these excerpts from actual therapy sessions illustrate, therapy for psychological disorders is far from a uniform process. In the first case, the therapist painstakingly mirrors what Alice has said, reflecting back her observations. In contrast, the therapist in the second excerpt is considerably more active, prodding and inflaming the patient. Finally, the third case shows a therapist who says very little at all; the responses to Sandy's declarations are fundamentally noncommittal.

These three excerpts are just a small sampling of the many styles that are used in the treatment of psychological disorders. Therapists today use over 250 different kinds of treatment, ranging from informal one-session discussions to long-term treatments involving powerful drugs. However, no matter what type of therapy is employed, all have a common goal: the relief of psychological disorder, with the ultimate aim of enabling individuals to achieve richer, more meaningful, and more fulfilling lives.

This chapter explores a number of important issues related to abnormal behavior: How do we treat people with psychological disorders? Who is the most appropriate person to provide treatment? What is the future like for people with severe disturbances? What is the most reasonable therapeutic approach to use? Is one form of therapy better than the others? Does any therapy *really* work? How does a person choose the "right" kind of therapy and therapist?

Most of the chapter focuses on the various approaches used by providers of treatment for psychological disturbances. Despite their diversity, these approaches fall into two main categories: psychologically based and biologically based therapy. Psychologically based therapy, or **psychotherapy**, is the process in which a patient (often referred to as the client) and a professional attempt to remedy psychological difficulties. In psychotherapy, the emphasis is on change as a result of discussions and interactions between therapist and client. In contrast, **biologically based therapy** relies on drugs and other medical procedures to improve psychological functioning.

Psychotherapy: The process in which a patient (client) and a professional attempt to remedy the client's psychological difficulties

Biologically based therapy: An approach to therapy that uses drugs and other medical procedures to improve psychological functioning

TABLE 18-1

GETTING HELP FROM THE RIGHT PERSON

Clinical psychologist
Ph.D. who specializes in assessment and treatment of psychological difficulties

Counseling psychologist
Psychologist with Ph.D. or master's degree who usually treats day-to-day adjustment problems in a counseling setting, such as a university mental health clinic

Psychiatrist
M.D. with postgraduate training in abnormal behavior who can prescribe medication as part of treatment

Psychoanalyst
Either an M.D. or a psychologist who specializes in psychoanalysis, a treatment technique first developed by Freud

Psychiatric social worker
Professional with a master's degree and specialized training in treating people in home and community settings

Each of these trained professionals could be expected to give helpful advice and direction, although the nature of the problem a person is experiencing may make one or another more appropriate. For example, a person who is suffering from severe disturbance and has lost touch with reality will typically require some sort of biologically based drug therapy. In that case, a psychiatrist—who is a physician—would clearly be the professional of choice. On the other hand, those suffering from milder disorders, such as difficulty in adjusting to the death of a family member, have a broader choice that might include any of the professionals listed above. The decision can be made easier by initial consultations with professionals in mental health facilities in communities, colleges, and health organizations who often provide guidance in selecting an appropriate therapist.

Eclectic approach to therapy:
An approach to therapy that uses a variety of treatment methods rather than just one

As we describe the various approaches to therapy, it is important to keep in mind that although the distinctions may seem clear-cut, there is a good deal of overlap in the classifications and procedures employed, and even in the training and titles of various kinds of therapists (see Table 18-1). In fact, many therapists today use a variety of methods with a given person, in what is referred to as an **eclectic approach to therapy** (Karasu, 1982). Assuming that abnormal behavior is often the product of both psychological and biological processes, eclectic therapists may draw from several perspectives simultaneously, in an effort to address both the psychological and the biological aspects of a person's problems.

After reading this chapter, then, you will be able to answer the following questions:

- What are the goals of psychologically and biologically based treatment approaches?

- What are the basic kinds of psychotherapies?

- How effective is therapy, and which kind of therapy works best under a given circumstance?

- How are drug, electroconvulsive, and psychosurgical techniques used today in the treatment of mental disorders?

- What is the best kind of therapy and therapist for a given situation?

Although diverse in many respects, all psychological approaches see treatment as a way of solving psychological problems by modifying people's behavior and helping them gain a better understanding of themselves and their pasts, presents, and futures. We will consider four major kinds of psychotherapies: psychodynamic, behavioral, cognitive, and humanistic, all of which are based on the different models of abnormal behavior we discussed in Chapter 17.

Psychodynamic Treatment: Piercing the Unconscious

Psychodynamic therapy is based on the premise, first suggested by Freud, that the primary sources of abnormal behavior are unresolved past conflicts and anxiety over the possibility that unacceptable unconscious impulses will enter the conscious part of a person's mind. To guard against this undesirable possibility, individuals employ **defense mechanisms**—psychological strategies that protect them from these unconscious impulses (see Chapter 15). Even though repression, the most common defense mechanism (in which threatening conflicts and impulses are pushed back into the unconscious), typically occurs, our unacceptable conflicts and impulses can never be completely buried. Therefore, some of the anxiety associated with them can produce abnormal behavior in the form of what Freud called **neurotic symptoms**.

How does one rid oneself of the anxiety caused by the repression of unconscious, unwanted impulses and drives? To Freud, the answer was to confront the conflicts and impulses by bringing them out of the unconscious part of the mind and into the conscious part. Freud assumed that this technique would reduce anxiety over the past and the patient could then participate in his or her daily life more effectively.

The challenge facing a psychodynamic therapist, then, is how to facilitate patients' attempts to explore and understand their unconscious. The technique that has evolved has a number of components, but basically it consists of leading patients to consider and discuss their past experiences from the time of their first memories, in explicit detail. This process assumes that patients will eventually stumble upon long-hidden crises, traumas, and conflicts that are producing anxiety in their adult lives. They will then be able to "work through"—understand and rectify—these difficulties.

Psychoanalysis: Freud's Therapy.   Classic Freudian psychodynamic therapy, called **psychoanalysis**, tends to be a lengthy and expensive affair. Patients typically meet with their therapists an hour a day, four to six days a week, for several years. In their sessions, they often use a technique developed by Freud called **free association**. Patients are told to say whatever comes to mind, regardless of its apparent irrelevance or senselessness. In fact, they are urged *not* to try to make sense of things or impose logic upon what they are saying, since it is assumed that the ramblings evoked during free association actually represent important clues to the unconscious, which has its own logic. It is the analyst's job to recognize and label the connections between what is being said and the patient's unconscious.

Another important tool of the therapist is **dream interpretation**. As we dis-

Psychodynamic therapy: Therapy based on the notion that the basic sources of abnormal behavior are unresolved past conflicts and anxiety

Defense mechanisms: Psychological strategies that protect people from unconscious impulses

Neurotic symptoms: According to Freud, abnormal behavior brought about by anxiety associated with unwanted conflicts and impulses

Psychoanalysis: Psychodynamic therapy that involves frequent sessions and often lasts for many years

Free association: A Freudian therapeutic technique in which a patient says everything that comes to mind to give the therapist a clue to the workings of the patient's unconscious

Dream interpretation: An examination of a patient's dreams to find clues to the unconscious conflicts and problems being experienced

Manifest content: The surface description and interpretation of dreams

Latent content: The "true" message hidden within dreams

Resistance: An inability or unwillingness to discuss or reveal particular memories, thoughts, or motivations

Transference: A patient's transfer of certain strong feelings for others to the analyst

cussed in Chapter 6, this is an examination of the patients' dreams to find clues to the unconscious conflicts and problems being experienced. According to Freud, dreams provide a close look at the unconscious because people's defenses tend to be lowered when they are asleep. But even in dreaming there is a censoring of thoughts; events and people in dreams are usually represented by symbols. Because of this, one must move beyond the surface description of the dream, the **manifest content** of dreams, and consider its underlying meaning, the **latent content** of dreams, which reveals the true message of the dream.

The processes of free association and dream interpretation do not always move forward easily. The same unconscious forces that initially produced repression may work to keep past difficulties out of the conscious, producing resistance. **Resistance** is an inability or unwillingness to discuss or reveal particular memories, thoughts, or motivations. Resistance can be expressed in a number of ways. For instance, patients may be discussing a childhood memory and suddenly forget what they were saying, or they may completely change the subject. It is the therapist's job to pick up instances of resistance and to interpret their meaning, as well as to ensure that patients return to the subject—which is likely to hold difficult or painful memories for them.

Because of the close, almost intimate interaction between patient and psychoanalyst, the relationship between the two often becomes emotionally charged and takes on a complexity unlike most others. Patients may come to see the analyst as symbolic of significant others in their past, perhaps a parent or a lover, and apply some of their feelings for that person to the analyst—a phenomenon known as **transference**.

Transference can be used by a therapist to help the patient re-create past relationships that were psychologically difficult. For instance, if a patient undergoing transference views his therapist as symbolic of his father—with whom he had a difficult relationship—the patient and therapist may "redo" an earlier interaction, this time including more positive aspects. Through this process, conflicts regarding the real father may be resolved. (Practitioners of psychoanalysis would see transference at work in Sandy's comment at the beginning of this chapter that the therapist is "just like her father.")

Contemporary Alternatives to Psychoanalysis. If time is money, patients in psychoanalysis need a lot of both. As you can imagine, few people have the time, money, or patience that participating in years of traditional psychoanalysis requires. Moreover, there is no conclusive evidence that psychoanalysis, as originally conceived by Freud, works better than other, more contemporary versions of psychodynamic therapy. Today, for instance, psychodynamic therapy tends to be shorter, usually lasting no longer than three months or twenty sessions. The therapist takes a more active role than Freud would have liked, controlling the course of therapy and prodding and advising the patient with considerable directness. Finally, there is less emphasis on a patient's past history and childhood. Instead, a more here-and-now approach is used, in which the therapist concentrates on an individual's current relationships and level of functioning (Strupp, 1981a; Altshuler, 1990; Ursano, Sonnenberg, & Lazar, 1991).

Even with its current modifications, psychodynamic therapy has its critics. It is still relatively time-consuming and expensive, especially in comparison with other forms of psychotherapy that we will discuss later. Moreover, only certain kinds of patients tend to be well suited for this method: those who suffer from anxiety disorders and those who are highly articulate—characteristics enshrined in a (facetious) acronym, YAVIS, for the perfect patient: young, attractive, verbal, intelligent, and successful (Schofield, 1964).

Ultimately, the most important concern about psychodynamic treatment is whether it actually works, and here we find no pat answer. Psychodynamic treatment techniques have been controversial since Freud introduced them. Part of the problem is the difficulty in establishing whether or not patients have improved following psychodynamic therapy. One must depend on reports from the therapist or the patients themselves, reports that are obviously open to bias and subjective interpretation (Luborsky & Spence, 1978; Peterfreund, 1984).

Critics have questioned the entire theoretical basis of psychodynamic theory, maintaining that there is no proof that such constructs as the unconscious exist. Despite the considerable criticism, though, the psychodynamic treatment approach has remained a viable technique. To proponents, it not only provides effective treatment in many cases of psychological disturbance, but also permits the potential development of an unusual degree of insight into one's life (Wallerstein, 1986; Fonagy & Moran, 1990).

Behavioral Approaches to Treatment

Perhaps, as a child, you were rewarded by your parents with an ice cream cone when you were especially good . . . or sent to your room if you misbehaved. As we saw in Chapter 7, the principles behind such a child-rearing strategy are valid: Good behavior is maintained by reinforcement, and unwanted behavior can be eliminated by punishment.

These principles represent the basic underpinnings of **behavioral treatment approaches**. Building upon the fundamental processes of learning—classical and operant conditioning—behavioral treatment approaches make a fundamental assumption: both abnormal and normal behavior is *learned*. People who display abnormal behavior have either failed to learn the skills needed to cope with the problems of everyday living or have acquired faulty skills and patterns that are being maintained through some form of reinforcement. To modify abnormal behavior, then, people must learn new behavior to replace the faulty skills they have developed and unlearn their maladaptive behavior patterns (Bellack, Hersen, & Kazdin, 1990).

To behavioral psychologists, it is not necessary to delve into people's pasts or dig into their psyches. Rather than viewing abnormal behavior as a symptom of some underlying problem, they consider the abnormal behavior itself as the problem in need of modification. Changing people's behavior to allow them to function more effectively solves the problem—with no need for concern about the underlying cause. In this view, then, if you can change abnormal behavior, you've cured the problem.

Classical Conditioning Approaches.   Suppose you bite into your favorite candy bar and find that it is infested with ants and that you've swallowed a bunch of them. You immediately become sick to your stomach and throw up. Your long-term reaction? You never eat that kind of candy bar again, and it may actually be months before you eat any type of candy.

This simple example hints at how classical conditioning might be used to modify behavior. Recall from our discussion in Chapter 7, when a stimulus that naturally evokes a negative response (such as an unpleasant taste or a puff of air in the face) is paired with a previously neutral stimulus (such as the sound of a bell), the neutral stimulus can come to elicit a similar negative reaction by itself.

Behavioral treatment approaches: Approaches to treating abnormal behavior that assume that both normal and abnormal behaviors are learned and that appropriate treatment consists of learning new behavior or unlearning maladaptive behavior

©1986 Universal Press Syndicate

Larson 11-27

**Professor Gallagher and his controversial
technique of simultaneously confronting
the fear of heights, snakes and the dark.**

Systematic desensitization might be a more appropriate treatment technique than that employed in this "Far Side" cartoon by Gary Larson.

Aversive conditioning: A technique used to help people break unwanted habits by associating the habits with very unpleasant stimuli

Using this procedure, first developed by Ivan Pavlov, we may create unpleasant reactions to stimuli that previously were enjoyed—possibly to excess—by an individual. The technique, known as **aversive conditioning**, has been used in cases of alcoholism, drug abuse, and smoking.

The basic procedure in aversive conditioning is relatively straightforward. For example, a person with a drinking problem might be given an alcoholic drink along with a drug that causes severe nausea and vomiting. After these two are paired a few times, the alcohol alone becomes associated with the vomiting and loses its appeal. In fact, what typically happens is that just the sight or smell of alcohol triggers the aversive reaction.

Although aversion therapy works reasonably well to inhibit substance-abuse problems such as alcoholism and certain kinds of sexual deviation, its long-term effectiveness is questionable. Moreover, there are important ethical drawbacks to aversion techniques that employ such potent stimuli as electric shock—used only in the most extreme cases (for example, self-mutilation)—instead of drugs that merely induce gastric discomfort (Russo, Carr, & Lovaas, 1980). It is clear, though, that aversion therapy is an important procedure for eliminating maladaptive responses for some period of time—which provides, even if only temporarily, the opportunity to encourage more adaptive behavior patterns (Harris & Handleman, 1990).

Systematic desensitization: A procedure in which a stimulus that evokes pleasant feelings is repeatedly paired with a stimulus that evokes anxiety in the hope that the anxiety will be alleviated

The most successful treatment based on classical conditioning is known as systematic desensitization. In **systematic desensitization**, a person is taught to relax and then is gradually exposed to an anxiety-producing stimulus in order

One of the most common treatments for phobias involves gradual exposure to the feared object or activity. Here participants in a program to overcome fear of flying go on a test flight.

to extinguish the response of anxiety (Rachman & Hodgson, 1980; Wolpe, 1969; J. Smith, 1990).

Suppose, for instance, you were extremely afraid of flying. The very thought of being in an airplane made you begin to sweat and shake, and you'd never even been able to get yourself near enough to an airport to know how you'd react if you actually had to fly somewhere. Using systematic desensitization to treat your problem, you would first be trained in muscle-relaxation techniques by a behavior therapist (see Table 18-2), learning to relax your body fully—a highly pleasant state, as you might imagine. The next step would involve the construction of a **hierarchy of fears**—a list, in order of increasing severity, of the

Hierarchy of fears: A list, in order of increasing severity, of the things that are associated with one's fears

---

TABLE 18-2

LEARNING TO RELAX

To get a sense of how behavior therapists train people to relax, try this procedure developed by Herbert Benson (1975).

1. Sit quietly in a comfortable position.
2. Close your eyes.
3. Deeply relax all your muscles, beginning at your feet and progressing to your face—keep them relaxed.
4. Breathe through your nose. Become aware of your breathing. As you breathe out, say the word "one" silently to yourself. For example, breathe in . . . out, "one"; in . . . out, "one"; and so on. Breathe easily and naturally.
5. Continue for ten to twenty minutes. You may open your eyes to check the time, but do not use an alarm. When you finish, sit quietly for several minutes, at first with your eyes closed and later with your eyes open. Do not stand up for a few minutes.
6. Do not worry about whether you are successful in achieving a deep level of relaxation. Maintain a passive attitude and permit relaxation to occur at its own pace. When distracting thoughts occur, try to ignore them by not dwelling upon them, and return to repeating "one."

   With practice, the response should come with little effort. Practice the techniques once or twice daily, but not within two hours after any meal, since the digestive processes seem to interfere with the elicitation of the relaxation response (Benson, 1975, pp. 114–115).

things that are associated with your fears. For instance, your hierarchy might resemble this one:

- Watching a plane fly overhead
- Going to an airport
- Buying a ticket
- Stepping into the plane
- Seeing the plane door close
- Having the plane taxi down the runway
- Taking off
- Being in the air

Once this hierarchy had been developed and you had learned relaxation techniques, the two sets of responses would be associated with each other. To do this, your therapist might ask you to put yourself into a relaxed state and then to imagine yourself in the first situation identified in your hierarchy. After you were able to consider that first step while remaining relaxed, you would move on to the next situation, eventually moving up the hierarchy in gradual stages until you could imagine yourself being in the air without experiencing anxiety. In some cases, all this would take place in a psychologist's office, while in others, people would actually be placed in the fear-evoking situation. Thus, it would not be surprising if you were brought, finally, to an airplane to use your relaxation techniques.

Systematic desensitization has proved to be an effective treatment for a number of problems, including phobias, anxiety disorders, and even impotence and fear of sexual contact (Karoly & Kanfer, 1982; Bellack, Hersen, & Kazdin, 1990). As you see, we *can* learn to enjoy the things we once feared.

Observational learning: Learning by watching others' behavior and the consequences of that behavior

Modeling: Imitating the behavior of others (models)

Observational Learning and Modeling.   If we had to be hit by a car in order to learn the importance of looking both ways before we crossed the street, the world would probably suffer from a serious underpopulation problem. Fortunately, this is not necessary, for we learn a significant amount through **observational learning**, by modeling the behavior of other people.

Behavior therapists have used **modeling** to systematically teach people new skills and ways of handling their fears and anxieties. For example, some people have never learned fundamental social skills such as maintaining eye contact with those they are speaking to. A therapist can model the appropriate behavior and thereby teach it to someone deficient in such skills (Sarason, 1976). Children with dog phobias have also been able to lose their fears by watching another child—called the "Fearless Peer"—repeatedly walk up to a dog, touch it, pet it, and finally play with it (Bandura, Grusec, & Menlove, 1967). Modeling, then, can play an effective role in resolving some kinds of behavior difficulties, especially if the model is rewarded for his or her behavior.

Operant Conditioning Approaches.   Consider the A we get for a good paper . . . the raise for fine on-the-job performance . . . the gratitude for helping an elderly person cross the street. Such rewards for our behavior produce a greater likelihood that we will repeat that behavior in the future. Similarly, behavioral approaches using operant conditioning techniques (which demonstrate the effects of rewards and punishments on future behavior) are based on the notion that we should reward people for carrying out desirable behavior, and extinguish behavior that we wish to eliminate either through ignoring or punishing it (Kazdin, 1989).

Probably the best example of the systematic application of operant conditioning principles is the **token system**, whereby a person is rewarded with a token such as a poker chip or some kind of play money for desired behavior. The behavior may range from such simple things as keeping one's room neat to personal grooming to interacting with other people. The tokens that are earned for such behavior can then be exchanged for some desired object or activity, such as snacks, new clothes, or, in extreme cases, being able to sleep in one's own bed (as opposed to on the floor).

Token system: A procedure whereby a person is rewarded for performing certain desired behaviors

Although it is most frequently employed in institutional settings for individuals with relatively serious problems, the system is not unlike what parents do when they give children money for being well behaved—money that they can later exchange for something they want. In fact, contingency contracting, a variant of the more extensive token system, has proved quite effective in producing behavior modification. In **contingency contracting**, a written agreement is drawn up between a therapist and a client (or teacher and student or parent and child). The contract states a series of behavioral goals that the client hopes to attain. It also specifies the consequences for the client if the goals are reached—usually some explicit reward such as money or additional privileges. Contracts frequently state negative consequences if the goals are not met.

Contingency contracting: Acting upon a written contract between a therapist and a client (or parent and child, etc.) that sets behavioral goals, with rewards for achievement

For instance, suppose a person is having difficulty quitting smoking. He and his therapist might devise a contract in which he would pledge that for every day he went without a cigarette he would receive a reward. On the other hand, the contract could include punishments for failure. If the patient smoked on a given day, the therapist might send a check—written out in advance by the patient and given to the therapist to hold—to a cause the patient had no interest in supporting (for instance, to the National Rifle Association if the patient is a staunch advocate of gun control).

How Does Behavior Therapy Stack Up? Behavior therapy is most helpful for certain kinds of problems. Depending on the specific problem being addressed, the success rate can range from 50 percent to as high as 90 percent (Kazdin & Wilson, 1978). For instance, behavior therapy works well for phobias and compulsions, for establishing control over impulses, and for learning complex social skills to replace maladaptive behavior. More than any of the other therapeutic techniques, it has produced methods that can be employed by nonprofessionals to change their own behavior. Moreover, it tends to be economical in terms of time, since it is directed toward the solution of carefully defined problems (Marks, 1982; Wilson et al., 1987).

On the other hand, behavior therapy has been criticized for its emphasis on external behavior, and its consequent devaluation of internal thoughts and expectations. Because of such concerns, some psychologists have turned to cognitive approaches.

Cognitive Approaches to Therapy

If you assumed that faulty, maladaptive cognitions lie at the heart of abnormal behavior, wouldn't the most direct treatment route be to teach people new, more adaptive modes of thinking? The answer is "yes," according to psychologists taking a cognitive approach to treatment.

A self-assertion program for overcoming shyness might involve preparing conversational topics ahead of time so that one is not at a loss for words in a social situation.

Cognitive-behavioral approach: A process by which people's faulty cognitions about themselves and the world are changed to more accurate ones

Rational-emotive therapy: Psychotherapy based on Ellis's suggestion that the goal of therapy should be to restructure one's belief into a more realistic, rational, and logical system

Cognitive approaches to therapy have as their goal a change in faulty cognitions that people hold about the world and themselves. Unlike traditional behavior therapists, who focus on modifying external behavior, cognitive therapists also attempt to change the way people think (Beck, 1991; Kendall, 1991). Because they typically use basic principles of learning, the methods they employ often are referred to as the **cognitive-behavioral approach**.

One of the best examples of cognitive behavioral treatment is rational-emotive therapy. **Rational-emotive therapy** attempts to restructure a person's belief system into a more realistic, rational, and logical set of views. According to psychologist Albert Ellis, many people lead unhappy and sometimes even psychologically disordered lives because they harbor such irrational, unrealistic ideas as these:

■ It is necessary to be loved or approved by virtually every significant other person for everything we do.

■ We should be thoroughly competent, adequate, and successful in all possible respects if we are to consider ourselves worthwhile.

■ It is horrible when things don't turn out the way we want them to.

In order to lead their clients to eliminate such maladaptive cognitions and adopt more effective thinking, rational-emotive therapists take an active, directive role during therapy, openly challenging patterns of thought that appear to be dysfunctional. (Martha's case excerpt at the beginning of the chapter is a good example of the approach.) For instance, a therapist might bluntly dispute the logic employed by a person in treatment by saying, "Why does the fact that your girlfriend left you mean that *you* are a bad person?" or "How does failing an exam indicate that you have *no* good qualities?" By pointing out the problems in clients' logic, therapists employing this form of treatment believe that people can come to adopt a more realistic view of themselves and their circumstances (Ellis & Dryden, 1987; Yankura & Dryden, 1990; Dryden & DiGiuseppe, 1990).

Another form of therapy building on a cognitive perspective is that of Aaron Beck (Beck, 1991). Like rational-emotive therapy, Beck's **cognitive therapy** has the basic goal of changing people's illogical thoughts about themselves and the world.

Cognitive therapy: A procedure in which people are taught to change illogical thoughts about themselves and the world

However, cognitive therapy is considerably less confrontive and challenging than rational-emotive therapy. Instead of the therapist actively arguing with clients regarding their faulty cognitions, therapists are more apt to play the role of teacher. Clients are urged to obtain information on their own that will lead them to discard their inaccurate thinking. During the course of treatment, clients are given specific ''assignments'' designed to help them discover ways of thinking more appropriately about themselves and others.

Cognitive approaches to therapy have proven successful in dealing with a broad range of disorders. Its ability to incorporate additional treatment approaches—such as combining cognitive and behavioral techniques in cognitive behavioral therapy—has made a particularly effective form of treatment.

RECAP AND REVIEW I

RECAP

◄ Psychotherapy is psychologically based therapy in which the emphasis is on producing change through discussion and interaction between client and therapist. Biologically based therapy uses drugs and other medical procedures.

◄ Psychodynamic therapy is based on Freud's notion that abnormal behavior is caused by unconscious conflicts and anxiety. To treat psychological problems, it is necessary to probe the unconscious and bring old difficulties to the surface through free association and dream interpretation.

◄ Behavioral approaches to therapy are built on the premise that people who display abnormal behavior either have failed to acquire appropriate skills or have learned faulty or maladaptive skills. To remedy the problem, it is necessary to learn new, more adaptive behaviors and/or unlearn old, faulty patterns of behavior.

◄ Among the approaches used by behavioral therapists are classical conditioning, including aversive conditioning and systematic desensitization; modeling; and operant conditioning.

◄ Cognitive approaches to treatment include the rational-emotive therapy of Ellis, and Beck's cognitive therapy.

REVIEW

1. Remedies for psychological disorders which are based on discussion and interaction between therapist and client are known as _____.

2. Match the following mental health practitioners with their definition

_____ 1. Psychiatrist
_____ 2. Clinical Psychologist
_____ 3. Counseling psychologist
_____ 4. Psychoanalyst

a. Ph.D. specializing in treatment of psychological disorders
b. Specializes in Freudian therapy techniques
c. M.D. trained in abnormal behavior
d. Ph.D. specializing in adjustments to day-to-day problems

3. According to Freud, people use _____ _____ as a means to ensure that unwanted impulses will not intrude on conscious thought.

4. A technique known as _____ _____, in which people are told to say whatever comes into their mind, is used in psychoanalysis to uncover parts of the unconscious.

5. In dream interpretation, a psychoanalyst must learn to distinguish between the _____ content of a dream, which is what appears on the surface, and the _____ content, its underlying meaning.

6. Which of the following treatments deals with phobias by gradual exposure to the item producing the fear?
a. Systematic desensitization
b. Partial reinforcement
c. Behavioral self-management
d. Ego control

Ask Yourself

In what situations might behavioral therapy be most useful? In what situations might a therapeutic technique that deals with thoughts rather than actions be more suitable?

(Answers to review questions are on page 598.)

Humanistic therapy aims to help clients make better use of their own abilities.

"Of course you have strengths, dear. It's just that you don't communicate them."

Humanistic Approaches to Therapy

As you know from your own experience, it is impossible to master the material covered in a course without some hard work, no matter how good the teacher and the textbook are. It is *you* who must take the time to study, to memorize the vocabulary, to learn the concepts. Nobody else can do it for you. If you choose to put in the effort, you'll succeed; if you don't, you'll fail. The responsibility is primarily yours.

Humanistic therapy draws upon this philosophical perspective of self-responsibility in developing treatment techniques. Although many different types of therapy fit into this category, the ideas that underlie them are the same: We have control of our own behavior; we can make choices about the kinds of lives we want to live; and it is up to us to solve the difficulties that we encounter in our daily lives. Instead of being the directive figures they are in some psychodynamic and behavioral approaches, humanistic therapists view themselves as guides or facilitators, leading people to realizations about themselves and to ways of changing in order to come closer to the ideal they hold for themselves. In this view, abnormal behavior is one result of people's inability to find meaning in life, of feeling lonely and unconnected with others, and of believing that they are pawns in a world that acts upon them without their being able to respond adequately.

Client-Centered Therapy. If you refer back to the case of Alice at the start of the chapter, you'll see that the therapist's comments are not interpretations or answers to questions that the client has raised. Instead, they tend to clarify or reflect back in some way what the client has said (e.g., "In other words, what you did . . ."; "You feel that . . ."; "Is that it?"). This therapeutic technique is

Humanistic therapy: Therapy in which the underlying assumption is that people have control of their behavior, can make choices about their lives, and are essentially responsible for solving their own problems

---

ANSWERS (REVIEW I):

1. psychotherapy **2.** 1-c; 2-a; 3-d; 4-b **3.** defense mechanisms **4.** free association
5. manifest; latent **6.** a

known as **nondirective counseling**, and it is at the heart of client-centered therapy. First practiced by Carl Rogers (1951; 1980), client-centered therapy is the best-known and most frequently used type of humanistic therapy.

The goal of **client-centered therapy** is to enable people to reach their potential for self-actualization. By providing a warm and accepting environment, therapists hope to motivate clients to air their problems and feelings, which, in turn, will enable the clients to make realistic and constructive choices and decisions about the things that bother them in their current lives. Instead of directing the choices clients make, then, the therapist provides what Rogers calls **unconditional positive regard**—expressing acceptance and understanding, regardless of the feelings and attitudes the client expresses. In doing so, the therapist hopes to create an atmosphere in which clients are able to come to decisions that can improve their lives. It does not mean that the therapist must approve of everything the client says or does; rather, it means that the therapist must convey that the client's thoughts and behaviors are seen as genuine reflections of what the client is experiencing (Lietaer, 1984).

It is relatively rare for client-centered therapy to be used today in its purest form. Contemporary approaches are apt to be somewhat more directive, with therapists nudging clients toward insights rather than merely reflecting back their statements. However, clients' insights are still seen as central to the therapeutic process.

Existential Therapy.   What is the meaning of life? We have all probably pondered this thought at one time or another, but for some people it is a central issue in their daily existence. For people who experience psychological problems as a result of difficulty in finding a satisfactory answer, existential therapy is one particularly appropriate place to turn, because this question is central to existential therapeutic techniques.

In contrast to other humanistic approaches that view humans' unique freedom and potential as a positive force, **existential therapy** is based on the premise that the inability to deal with such freedom can produce anguish, fear, and concern (May, 1969). In existential therapy, the goal is to allow individuals to come to grips with the freedom they have, to begin to understand how they fit in with the rest of the world, and to devise a system of values that permits them to give meaning to their lives. Existential therapists try to make their patients aware of the importance of free choice and the fact that they have the ultimate responsibility for making their own choices about their lives.

The specific processes used in existential therapy are more varied than in client-centered approaches. The therapist is considerably more directive in existential therapy, probing and challenging the client's views of the world. In addition, therapists will try to establish a deep and binding relationship with their clients, attempting to be as open with them about their own feelings and points of view as possible. Their objective is to allow clients to see that they share in the difficulties and experiences that arise in trying to deal with the freedom that is part of being human.

Gestalt Therapy.   Have you ever thought back to some childhood incident in which you were treated unfairly and again felt the rage that you had experienced at that time? To therapists working in a gestalt perspective, the healthiest thing for you to do psychologically might be to act out that rage—by hitting a pillow, kicking a chair, or yelling in frustration. This sort of activity represents an important part of what goes on in gestalt therapy sessions, in which the client is encouraged to act out past conflicts and difficulties.

Nondirective counseling: A therapeutic technique in which the therapist creates a warm, supportive environment to allow the client to better understand and work out his or her problems

Client-centered therapy: Therapy in which the therapist reflects back the patient's statements in a way that causes the patient to find his or her own solutions

Unconditional positive regard: Supportive behavior from another individual, regardless of one's words or actions

Existential therapy: A humanistic approach that addresses the meaning of life, allowing a client to devise a system of values that gives purpose to his or her life

In gestalt therapy, people closely examine, and sometimes try to re-create, experiences from their childhoods.

Gestalt therapy: An approach to therapy that attempts to integrate a client's thoughts, feelings, and behavior into a whole

The rationale for this approach to treatment is that it is necessary for people to integrate their thoughts, feelings, and behaviors into a gestalt, the German term for "whole" (as we discussed in reference to perception in Chapter 5). According to Fritz Perls (1967, 1970), who developed **gestalt therapy**, the way to do this is for people to examine their earlier experience and complete any "unfinished business" from their past that still affects and colors present-day relationships. Specifically, Perls assumed that people should reenact the specific conflicts that they experienced earlier. For instance, a client might first play the part of his angry father, and then play himself when his father yelled at him, in order to experience the different parts of a conflict. By increasing their perspectives on a situation, clients are better able to understand their problems and to experience life in a more unified, honest, and complete way (Korb, Gorrell, & VanDeRiet, 1989).

Humanistic Approaches in Perspective. You may be bothered by the lack of specificity of the humanistic treatments, and this is a problem that has also troubled its critics. Humanistic approaches are not very precise and are probably the least scientifically and theoretically developed type of treatment. Moreover, this form of treatment is best suited for the same type of highly verbal client who profits most from psychoanalytic treatment.

On the other hand, the emphasis of humanistic approaches on what is uniquely human and their acknowledgment that the freedom we possess can lead to psychological difficulties provide an unusually supportive environment for therapy. In turn, this atmosphere can aid clients in finding solutions to difficult psychological problems.

Group Therapy

Group therapy: Therapy in which people discuss problems with a group

Although most treatment takes place between a single individual and a therapist, some forms of therapy involve groups of people seeking treatment. In **group therapy**, several unrelated people meet with a therapist to discuss some aspect of their psychological functioning.

Family therapy aims to avoid labeling a single family member as the focus of therapy; instead, it concentrates on the contribution of each person to the way the entire group functions.

People typically discuss their problems with the group, which is often centered around a particular difficulty, such as alcoholism or a lack of social skills. The other members of the group provide emotional support and dispense advice on ways in which they have coped effectively with similar problems (Lewis, 1987; Drum, 1990).

Groups vary a great deal not only in the particular model that is employed (there are psychoanalytic groups, humanistic groups, and groups corresponding to the other therapeutic approaches), but also in the degree of guidance the therapist provides. In some groups, the therapist is quite directive; in others, the members of the group set their own agenda and determine how the group will proceed (Flowers & Booraem, 1990).

Because several people are treated simultaneously in group therapy, it is a much more economical means of treatment than individual psychotherapy. On the other hand, critics argue that group settings do not afford the individual attention inherent in one-to-one therapy, and especially shy and withdrawn individuals may not receive the necessary attention in a group.

Family Therapy.   One specialized form of group therapy is family therapy. As the name implies, **family therapy** involves two or more members of the same family, one (or more) of whose problems led to treatment. But rather than focusing simply on members of the family who present the initial problem, family therapists consider the family as a whole unit, to which each member contributes. By meeting with the entire family simultaneously, family therapists attempt to obtain a sense of how the family members interact with one another.

Family therapy: An approach that focuses on the family as a whole unit

Family therapists view the family as a "system," and they assume that the separate individuals in the family cannot improve without understanding the conflicts that are to be found in the interactions of the family members. Thus each member is expected to contribute to the resolution of individual problems.

Many family therapists assume that family members fall into rigid roles or set patterns of behavior, with one person acting as the scapegoat, another as a bully, and so forth. In their view, family disturbances are perpetuated by this system of roles. One goal of this type of therapy, then, is to get the family members to adopt new, more constructive roles and patterns of behavior (Minuchin, 1974; Kaslow, 1991).

Comparing Psychotherapeutic Approaches

We have seen that there are a variety of forms of psychotherapy. In order to compare them, we can classify them along several dimensions. Among the most important are (Carson, Butcher, & Coleman, 1988):

- ◼ Directive versus nondirective. In some forms of therapy, the therapist takes considerably more responsibility for the person being treated than in others. In directive therapy, the therapist takes an active role, whereas in nondirective therapy, the therapist acts more as a facilitator, helping clients clarify their own feelings. Among the more directive are the behavioral and cognitive approaches. In contrast, psychodynamic and humanistic approaches are considerably less directive.

- ◼ Inner control of behavior versus external control of behavior. In the psychodynamic and humanistic approaches, behavior is seen as largely under the control of the individual, although psychodynamic theorists suggest that the causes of behavior are not necessarily conscious. In contrast, behavioral approaches to therapy view behavior primarily as the result of environmental factors. Cognitive approaches take an intermediate view, seeing behavior determined not only by environmental factors but by internal cognitions as well.

- ◼ Long-term versus short-term therapy. Therapeutic approaches vary widely in terms of the typical length of treatment. Traditional psychoanalysis is the longest lasting, potentially stretching on for years. Today, however, most therapy is considerably shorter and may take as few as two or three sessions, depending on the nature of the problem being addressed.

- ◼ Historical focus versus here-and-now focus. Some kinds of therapy pay primary attention to events from the past that are assumed to be affecting current behavior. Psychodynamic therapies fall into such a category. In contrast, behavioral and cognitive approaches stress the present, minimizing the consequences of early experiences. Other approaches fall in between.

- ◼ Cognitive change versus behavior change. Some kinds of therapy, particularly psychodynamic and cognitive approaches, emphasize the need for changes in attitudes, perceptions, feelings, and cognitions about the world. They assume a change in those characteristics will produce more adaptive behavior. In contrast, behavioral approaches emphasize the change of behavior itself.

It is important to remember that although they are presented in an either/ or fashion, each of these dimensions of therapy marks the end point of a continuum. Most therapeutic approaches will not fall squarely on one or the other end of the continuum but rather will lie somewhere in between.

Evaluating Psychotherapy

Your best friend at school, Ben, comes to you because he just hasn't been feeling right about things lately. He's upset because he and his girlfriend aren't getting along, but his difficulties go beyond that. He can't concentrate on his studies, has a lot of trouble getting to sleep, and—this is what really bothers him—he's begun to think that people are ganging up on him, talking about him behind his back. It just seems that no one really cares about or understands him or makes any effort to see why he's become so miserable.

Ben is aware that he ought to get *some* kind of help, but he is not sure where to turn. He is fairly skeptical of psychologists, thinking that a lot of what they say is just mumbo-jumbo, but he's willing to put his doubts aside and try anything to feel better. He also knows there are many different types of therapy, and he doesn't have a clue as to which would be best for him. He turns to you for advice, because he knows you are taking a psychology course. He asks, "Which kind of therapy works best?"

Such a question requires a complex response, for there is no easy answer. In fact, identifying which form of treatment is most appropriate is a controversial, and still unresolved, task for psychologists specializing in abnormal behavior. For example, even before considering whether any one form of therapy works better than another, we need to determine whether therapy in *any* form is effective in alleviating psychological disturbances.

Until the 1950s most people simply assumed that therapy, on the face of it, was an effective strategy for resolving psychological difficulties. But in 1952 psychologist Hans Eysenck published an influential article reviewing the published literature on the subject, which challenged this widely held assumption. He claimed that people who received psychodynamic treatment and related therapies were no better off at the end of treatment than those people who were placed on a waiting list for treatment—but never received it. According to his analysis, about two-thirds of the people who reported suffering from "neurotic" symptoms believed that those symptoms had disappeared after two years, regardless of whether or not they had been in therapy. Eysenck concluded that people suffering from neurotic symptoms would go into **spontaneous remission**, recovery without treatment, if they were simply left alone—certainly a cheaper and simpler process.

As you can imagine, Eysenck's review was controversial from the start, and its conclusions were quickly challenged. Critics pointed to the inadequacy of the data he reviewed, suggesting that he was basing his conclusions on studies that contained a number of flaws.

Many potential sources of error exist in studies of the effectiveness of psychotherapy. Most often, the data are based on therapist and patient self-reports, which may be biased and unreliable. All the parties involved are motivated to see themselves as successful, so all may report an improvement in psychological functioning when none really exists. Only when independent judges are used to determine how much progress a person has made can we be assured that the patient's report is accurate. Even the use of judges has its drawbacks, however, since no well-agreed-upon set of criteria exists to determine what constitutes good and bad mental health. For all these reasons, then, Eysenck's critics rejected his findings.

Nevertheless, Eysenck's early review did serve to stimulate a continuing stream of better controlled, more carefully crafted studies on the effectiveness of psychotherapy, and today most psychologists agree: Therapy does work. Several recent comprehensive reviews indicate that therapy brings about greater improvement than no treatment at all, with the rate of spontaneous remission (recovery without treatment) fairly low. In most cases, then, the symptoms of abnormal behavior do not go away by themselves if left untreated—although the issue remains a hotly debated one (Goldfried, Greenberg, & Marmar, 1990;

Spontaneous remission:
Recovery without treatment

Landman & Dawes, 1984; Clum & Bowers, 1990; Brody, 1990; Luborsky, 1988; Luborsky, Barber, & Crits-Christoph, 1990).

Which Kind of Therapy Works Best?

Although most psychologists feel confident that psychotherapeutic treatment *in general* is more effective than no treatment at all, the question of whether any specific form of treatment is superior to any other has yet to be answered definitively (Bowers & Clum, 1988; Orwin & Condray, 1984). In part, this is due to methodological issues. For instance, it is difficult to equate the "cures" that various forms of treatment produce, because qualitatively they may be very different. Is the reduction of depression-related anxiety obtained from psychodynamic treatment equivalent to the reduction of phobia-related anxiety brought about by behavior therapy? In both cases the problems are alleviated—but, if we were keeping a tally of cures versus noncures for the two forms of treatment, would they each receive one point? You can see the difficulties involved in comparing types of treatment (Garfield, 1990; Persons, 1991; Jacobson & Truax, 1991).

The problems, however, are not insurmountable. One solution has been to compare the "cure" rate for a particular form of treatment with the "cure" rate for a group of untreated controls. Next, we could do the same thing with another type of treatment and compare this cure rate with its own untreated control. Finally, we could see which of the two forms of therapy produced a higher cure rate. For instance, we could take a sample of people who, because of the nature of their problems, would be "eligible" for psychodynamic treatment, treat half of them, and compare their results to the untreated half. By following the same procedure with a group of people "eligible" for another form of treatment, we could infer which kind of treatment was most successful.

Using this kind of procedure, Smith, Glass, & Miller (1980) came to the conclusions displayed in Figure 18-1. As you can see, although there is some variation among the success rates of the various treatment forms, most are fairly close to one another, ranging from about 70 to 85 percent greater success for treated than for untreated individuals. There is a slight tendency for behavioral approaches and cognitive approaches to be a bit more successful, although this may be due to differences in the severity of cases treated (Orwin & Condray, 1984).

Other research, relying on meta-analytic procedures that we discussed in Chapter 2, in which a large number of studies are statistically combined to draw an overall conclusion, yield similar general conclusions (e.g., Brown, 1987). However, the results of specific studies are not always consistent regarding which specific form of psychotherapy is optimum.

In an effort to produce definitive findings regarding the efficacy of particular types of therapy, the U.S. National Institute of Mental Health is currently conducting an ongoing, large-scale study. In the initial part of the study, which lasted sixteen weeks, depressed patients were randomly assigned to one of two kinds of treatment: cognitive behavioral therapy or "interpersonal therapy," a form of psychotherapy that focuses on patients' interpersonal problems and social functioning. Other subjects were randomly assigned to two control conditions which provided either antidepressant drugs (which we'll discuss later in the chapter) or a placebo pill (a substance with no active ingredients).

The initial findings suggest that the two forms of psychotherapies were about equally effective, although the interpersonal therapy had a slight edge (with a

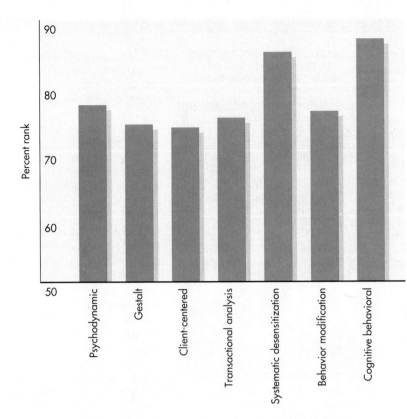

FIGURE 18-1
Estimates of the effectiveness of different types of treatment, in comparison to control groups of untreated people. The percentile score shows how much more effective a particular type of treatment is for the average patient than no treatment. For example, people given psychodynamic treatment score, on average, more positively on outcome measures than about 75 percent of untreated people. (Adapted from Smith, Glass, & Miller, 1980.)

43 percent recovery rate) over cognitive behavioral therapy (36 percent recovery rate). The drug condition was also successful, producing a 42 percent recovery rate, while the placebo condition produced only a 21 percent recovery rate (Elkin et al., 1989). The findings are not definitive, however, and follow-up studies to test the long-term effects of therapy are under way.

To sum up, the preponderance of research indicates only minor differences among the success rates for various types of therapy. However, it is important to keep in mind that not every psychological disorder will be resolved equally well by every sort of therapy. Recall the way that therapy-comparison studies are typically carried out. They initially consider only problems appropriate for a given treatment approach, and then compare treated versus untreated people within that specific approach to see which group of people does better. Such studies say little about whether specific sorts of problems are better treated by one approach or another (Garfield, 1983). Furthermore, in some cases—perhaps as many as 10 percent—psychotherapy *harms* participants. Their disorders actually become worse following therapy, and they would have been better off if they had not undertaken it (Lambert, Shapiro, & Bergin, 1986; Luborsky, 1988).

It is clear, then, that particular kinds of therapies are more appropriate for some problems than for others. For example, consider Ben's concerns, described earlier. If someone is suffering from the kind of general unhappiness and anxiety disclosed by him, psychodynamic or humanistic approaches, which emphasize gaining insight into one's problems, would probably be most appropriate. On the other hand, if Ben's problems had been focused more on a particular set of circumstances that brought about his anxiety—such as a phobia or a lack of good study skills that was preventing him from doing well in school—then a behavioral approach might be more reasonable.

Consider the following description, written by a school counselor about a student:

Jimmy Jones is a 12-year-old Black male student who was referred by Mrs. Peterson because of apathy, indifference, and inattentiveness to classroom activities. Other teachers have reported that Jimmy does not pay attention, daydreams often, and frequently falls asleep during class. There is a strong possibility that Jimmy is harboring repressed rage that needs to be ventilated and dealt with. His inability to directly express his anger had led him to adopt passive aggressive means of expressing hostility, i.e. inattentiveness, daydreaming, falling asleep. It is recommended that Jimmy be seen for intensive counseling to discover the basis of the anger. (Sue & Sue, 1990, p. 44.)

The counselor was wrong, however. After six months of therapy, the true cause of Jimmy's problems became evident: His home environment was extraordinarily poor and disorganized. Because of the overcrowding at his house, he was often kept awake and thus was tired the next day. Frequently, he was also hungry. His problems, then, were due largely to the stress of his impoverished environment and not to any deepseated psychological problem.

This incident points out the impor-

RACIAL AND ETHNIC FACTORS IN TREATMENT: SHOULD THERAPISTS BE COLOR-BLIND?

In order to fully understand the significance even of such simple behavior as daydreaming in class, we need to take a person's cultural, racial, and ethnic backgrounds into account.

tance in taking people's environmental and cultural backgrounds into account during treatment for psychological disorders. In particular, some minority group members, especially those who are also poor, have adopted behaviors that have been helpful in dealing with a society which discriminates against them on the basis of race or ethnic background. For instance, some behaviors that may signal psychological disorder in mid-

dle- and upper-class whites might simply be adaptive. A suspicious and distrustful African-American, then, might be displaying a survival mechanism to protect himself from psychological as well as physical injury (Sue & Sue, 1990).

In fact, some of the most basic assumptions of much of psychotherapy must be questioned when dealing with racial, ethnic, and cultural minority group members. For instance, Asian and Hispanic cultures place much greater emphasis on the group, family, and society on the whole than the dominant culture which focuses on the individual. When critical decisions are to be made, the family helps make them. Consider how different this notion is from that espoused by the therapist in the case in this chapter's Prologue, who urges Martha to develop independence from her family.

Similarly, when traditional Chinese men and women feel depressed or anxious, they are urged by others to avoid thinking about whatever upset them. Consider how this advice contrasts with the view of the treatment approaches that emphasize the value of insight (Sue, 1981).

To answer the question posed in the title of this box, then, therapists *cannot* be "color-blind." Instead, they must take into account the racial, ethnic, cultural, and social class backgrounds of their clients in determining the nature of a psychological disorder and the course of treatment (Greene, 1985; Lopez & Nunez, 1987; Sue & Sue, 1990; Ponterro & Casas, 1991).

Similarly, it might be more appropriate for therapists with certain personal characteristics to work with particular people, and certain kinds of people may be more appropriately treated by one approach than another. (Also see the Psychology at Work box.) For example, a behavioral approach may be more suitable for people who have difficulty expressing themselves verbally or who lack the patience or ability to engage in sustained introspection, qualities that are necessary for a psychodynamic approach (Crits-Christoph & Mintz, 1991).

Finally, there are an increasing number of eclectic approaches to therapy, in which a therapist uses techniques taken from a variety of approaches to treat a person's problems. By using eclectic procedures, the therapist is able to choose the appropriate mix in accordance with the specific needs of the individual (Garfield, 1989; Wells & Giannetti, 1990).

Recent research also suggests that the *process* of therapy may be as important as the particular *outcome* of therapy. Specifically, part of what makes therapy useful and important to people may be related to how the ongoing process affects their everyday lives, feelings, and thinking about the world. By examining what goes on in various types of therapy, it may be possible to come to a better understanding of the therapeutic process (Garfield, 1990; Marmar, 1990).

The question of which therapy works best, then, cannot be answered without consideration of a variety of factors. How appropriate the match is between an individual's problems, therapeutic method, and therapist and client characteristics determines the likelihood of success. Overall, though, it is clear that psychotherapy provides an effective means for solving psychological difficulties.

RECAP AND REVIEW II

RECAP

◀ Humanistic approaches view therapy as a way to help people solve their own problems. The therapist merely acts as a guide or facilitator.

◀ Among the types of humanistic therapies are client-centered therapy, existential therapy, and gestalt therapy.

◀ The major dimensions along which therapies can be evaluated are directive versus nondirective, inner control of behavior versus external control of behavior, long-term versus short-term duration, historical focus versus here-and-now focus, and cognitive change versus behavior change.

◀ A long-standing issue is whether psychotherapy is effective, and, if it is, whether one kind is superior to others.

REVIEW

1. Match the names of the following treatment strategies with the statements you might expect to hear from a therapist.

   _____ 1. Gestalt therapy
   _____ 2. Group therapy
   _____ 3. Unconditional positive regard
   _____ 4. Behavioral therapy
   _____ 5. Nondirective counseling

   a. "In other words, you don't get along with your mother because she hates your girlfriend, is that right?"
   b. "I want you all to take turns talking about why you decided to come, and what you hope to gain in therapy."
   c. "I can understand why you wanted to wreck your friend's car after she hurt your feelings.

   Now, tell me more about the accident."
   d. "That's not appropriate behavior. Let's work on replacing it with something else."
   e. "Remember the anger you felt and scream until you feel better."

2. _____ therapies assume people are responsible for their own lives and the decisions they make.

3. _____ therapy emphasizes the integration of thoughts, feelings, and behaviors.

4. One of the major criticisms against humanistic therapies is that:
   a. They are too imprecise and unstructured
   b. They treat only the symptom of the problem
   c. The therapist dominates the patient-therapist interaction
   d. It works well only on lower-class clients

5. In a controversial study, Eysenck found that some people go into _____ _____, or recovery without treatment, if they are simply left alone instead of treated.

6. Some therapies are more suited for certain types of problems than others. True or false?

7. Treatments that combine techniques from all the theoretical approaches are called _____ procedures.

Ask Yourself

Is group therapy a valid practice? How can people be successfully treated in groups when individuals with the "same" problem are so different? What advantages might group therapy offer over individual therapy?

(Answers to review questions are on page 608.)

BIOLOGICAL TREATMENT APPROACHES: THE MEDICAL MODEL AT WORK

If you get a kidney infection, you're given some penicillin and, with luck, about a week later your kidney is as good as new. If your appendix becomes inflamed, a surgeon removes it and your body functions normally once more. Could an analogous approach, focusing on the body's physiology, be taken with psychological disturbances?

According to biological approaches to treatment, the answer is affirmative. In fact, biologically based treatments are used routinely for certain kinds of problems. The basic model suggests that rather than focusing on a patient's psychological conflicts, past traumas, or environmental factors that may support abnormal behavior, it is more appropriate in certain cases to treat brain chemistry and other neurological factors directly. This can be done through the use of drugs, electric shock, or surgery.

Drug Therapy

Drug therapy: Control of psychological problems through drugs

Are we close to the day when we will take a pill each morning to maintain good psychological health, in the same way that we now take a vitamin pill to help us stay physically healthy? Although that day has not yet arrived, there are quite a few forms of **drug therapy** that successfully alleviate symptoms of a number of psychological disturbances.

Antipsychotic drugs: Drugs that temporarily alleviate psychotic symptoms such as agitation and overactivity

Antipsychotic Drugs. Probably no greater change has occurred in mental hospitals than the successful introduction in the mid-1950s of **antipsychotic drugs**—drugs used to alleviate severe symptoms of disturbance, such as loss of touch with reality, agitation, and overactivity. Previously, mental hospitals typically fulfilled all the stereotypes of the insane asylum, with screaming, moaning, clawing patients displaying the most bizarre behaviors. Suddenly, in just a matter of months, the hospital wards became considerably calmer environments in which professionals could do more than just try to get the patients through the day without causing serious harm to themselves or others.

Chlorpromazine (klor PRO mah zeen): An antipsychotic drug that is used in the treatment of schizophrenia

This dramatic change was brought about by the introduction of a drug from the phenothiazine family called **chlorpromazine**. This drug, and others of similar types, rapidly became the most popular and successful treatment for schizophrenia. Today drug therapy is the preferred treatment for most cases of severely abnormal behavior, used for almost 90 percent of all hospitalized patients.

How do antipsychotic drugs work? They seem to function by blocking the production of dopamine at the sites where electric impulses travel across nerve receptors, a process we discussed in Chapter 17. Unfortunately, they do not produce a "cure" in the same way that, say, penicillin cures an infection. As soon as the drug is withdrawn, the original symptoms tend to reappear. Moreover, such drugs can have long-term side effects, such as dryness of the mouth and throat, dizziness, and even the development of tremors and loss of muscle control that may continue even after drug treatments are stopped (Kane, 1983).

Perhaps even more devastating than these physical side effects are the numb-

---

ANSWERS (REVIEW II):

1. 1-e; 2-b; 3-c; 4-d; 5-a **2.** Humanistic **3.** Gestalt **4.** a **5.** spontaneous remission **6.** True **7.** eclectic

ing effects of antipsychotic drugs on the emotional responses of patients. For example, Mark Vonnegut (son of author Kurt Vonnegut) describes his reactions to the use of the antipsychotic drug Thorazine while he was institutionalized for schizophrenia:

> What the drug is supposed to do is keep away hallucinations. What I think it does is just fog up your mind so badly you don't notice the hallucinations or much else. . . . On Thorazine everything's a bore. Not a bore, exactly. Boredom implies impatience. You can read comic books . . . you can tolerate talking to jerks forever. . . . The weather is dull, the flowers are dull, nothing's very impressive (Vonnegut, 1975, pp. 196–197).

Antidepressant Drugs. As you might guess from the name, **antidepressant drugs** are a class of medications used in cases of severe depression to improve the moods of patients. They were discovered quite by accident: It was found that patients suffering from tuberculosis who were given the drug iproniazid suddenly became happier and more optimistic. When the same drug was tested on people suffering from depression, a similar result occurred, and drugs became an accepted form of treatment for depression (McNeal & Cimbolic, 1986).

Most antidepressant drugs work by allowing an increase in the concentration of certain neurotransmitters in the brain (see Chapter 3). For example, tricyclic drugs modify the amount of norepinephrine and serotonin within the brain. Others, such as bupropion, operate by affecting the neurotransmitter dopamine.

Although antidepressant drugs may produce side effects such as drowsiness and faintness, their overall success rate is quite good (Spiegel, 1989). Unlike antipsychotic drugs, antidepressants can produce lasting, long-term recoveries from depression. In many cases, even after the drugs are no longer being taken, the depression does not return. (For a discussion of one of the newest and already most widely known antidepressants, Prozac, see the Cutting Edge box, p. 610.)

Lithium, a form of simple mineral salts, is a drug that has been used very successfully in cases of bipolar disorders. Although no one knows definitely why it works (it has no known physiological function), it is very effective in reducing manic episodes, ending manic behavior some 70 percent of the time. On the other hand, its effectiveness in resolving depression is not as impressive. It works only in certain cases, and, like other antidepressants, it can produce a number of side effects (Coppen, Metcalfe, & Wood, 1982).

Lithium has a quality that sets it apart from other drug treatments. More than any other drug, it represents a *preventive* treatment. People who have been subject to manic-depressive episodes in the past often can, after returning to a normal state, take a daily dose of lithium that prevents a recurrence of their symptoms. Lithium, then, presents one thought-provoking vision of the future, suggested by medical-model approaches to abnormal behavior: a future in which people take drugs regularly to make them psychologically healthier. The reality, though, is that for better or for worse, such a future is far away.

Antianxiety Drugs. Valium, Miltown, Librium—perhaps you are familiar with these drug names, which are among the most common of all the drugs physicians prescribe. A cure for infection? Relief of the common cold? On the contrary, these drugs have nothing to do with physical symptoms. Instead, they are members of a class of drugs known as antianxiety drugs which are prescribed—often

Antidepressant drugs:
Medication that improves a depressed patient's mood and feeling of well-being

Lithium (LITH ee um): A drug used in the treatment of bipolar disorders

Susan A. has spent most of her adult life fighting with people—her parents, her neighbors, her co-workers, her husband. The 39-year-old Seattle woman has suffered bouts of depression and bulimia, abused drugs and alcohol, and twice tried to kill herself. She once sought relief in an antidepressant called doxepin, but she didn't like the way it made her feel.

Two years ago her therapist, Dr. Michael Norden, suggested she try a new drug called Prozac. She did. Within a month, Susan had given up psychotherapy in favor of school and a full-time job. She had also given up tranquilizers and street drugs. "I feel 1,000%," she said in a written note. "I actually like Mom & Dad now, I'm well liked at work, I don't ruminate on the negatives, I don't have murderous rages, my marriage is five times better." (Cowley, 1990a, p. 39.)

When a drug evokes such strong testimonials from its users that it appears on the cover of *Newsweek*, it is clearly a drug worth pondering. But, media hype aside, is the antidepressant **fluxetine**, sold under the trade name of **Prozac**, truly as revolutionary as its proponents claim?

In some respects, Prozac does merit its accolades. Although it was introduced only in 1987, it is now the most frequently prescribed antidepressant. Despite its high expense, with each daily dose costing close to

PROZAC: MIRACLE DRUG OR MEDIA MADNESS?

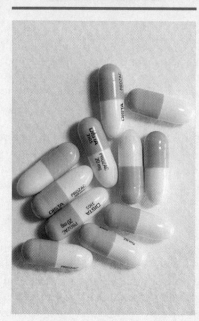

Susan A. claims that Prozac has changed her life, alleviating psychological symptoms that had plagued her for decades.

$2, it has significantly improved the lives of thousands of depressed individuals.

Prozac works by blocking reabsorption of the neurotransmitter serotonin. Unlike other antidepressants, Prozac appears to have few side effects, and the possibility of taking an inadvertent overdose is much smaller. Furthermore, many people who do not respond to other antidepressants do well on Prozac.

On the other hand, the drug has

not been used long enough to know all of its potential side effects, and some reports suggest that Prozac may have a darker side. For example, some Prozac users suffer from intense agitation or tremors, while others seem to become preoccupied with thoughts of suicide. A few patients even maintain that Prozac makes them prone to bouts of violence, and defendants in several murder trials have used a "Prozac defense," claiming that the drug actually induced their homicidal behavior (Marcus, 1991).

Most experts reject these reports, and a U.S. government panel of experts, convened by the Food and Drug Administration, recently found no evidence for the more sensationalistic side effects (FDA, 1991). However, some experts suggest that perhaps as many as 15 percent of users experience side effects of some sort (Angier, 1990a).

Unfortunately, enthusiasm for Prozac on the part of the public presents something of a problem for health care workers. The welter of publicity about the drug raises the likelihood that patients with mild forms of depression or even other disorders will forgo alternate, more suitable types of treatment such as psychotherapy and aggressively seek prescriptions for Prozac. Although Prozac has important benefits, it is not a wonder drug. Like the common cold, no complete cure for depression is on the immediate horizon.

Fluxetine (Prozac): A widely used antidepressant drug

by family physicians—to alleviate the stress and anxiety experienced by patients during particularly difficult periods of their lives. In fact, more than half of all Americans have a family member who has taken such a drug at one time or another.

Antianxiety drugs: Drugs that alleviate stress and anxiety

As the name implies, **antianxiety drugs** reduce the level of anxiety experienced, essentially by reducing excitability and in part by increasing drowsiness. They are used not only to reduce general tension in people who are experiencing temporary difficulties but also to aid in the treatment of more serious anxiety disorders.

Although the popularity of antianxiety drugs suggests that they are relatively risk-free, they can produce a number of potentially serious side effects. For instance, they can cause fatigue, and long-term use can lead to dependence. Moreover, taken in combination with alcohol, some antianxiety drugs can become lethal. But a more important question concerns their use to suppress anxiety. Since almost every theoretical approach to psychological disturbance views continuing anxiety as a symptom of some sort of problem, drugs that mask anxiety may be hiding difficulties that might be more appropriately faced and solved—rather than simply being masked.

Electroconvulsive Therapy (ECT)

The mistaken notion that people with epilepsy (a disorder characterized by seizures and convulsions) were immune to schizophrenia led to the development of electroconvulsive shock therapy (ECT) in the 1930s. A group of psychiatrists reasoned that if a way could be found to actually induce convulsions in schizophrenics, the convulsions might cure them. To test this hypothesis, they administered electric shocks to the heads of patients suffering from schizophrenia to induce convulsions—and experienced some success in alleviating the symptoms of the disorder (Bini, 1938).

The use of **electroconvulsive therapy (ECT)** has continued to the present, although the way in which it is administered has been improved. An electric current of 70 to 150 volts is passed through the head of a patient for about a twenty-fifth of a second, causing the patient to lose consciousness and often experience a seizure. Usually the patient is sedated and receives muscle relaxants prior to administration of the current, helping to prevent violent contractions. The typical patient receives about ten such treatments in the course of a month, but some patients continue with maintenance treatments for months afterward (Breggin, 1979; Weiner, 1982; Fink, 1990).

As you might expect, ECT is a controversial technique. Apart from the obvious distastefulness of a treatment that evokes images of capital punishment, there are frequent side effects. For instance, following treatment, patients often

Electroconvulsive therapy (ECT): Treatment involving the administration of an electric current to a patient's head to treat depression

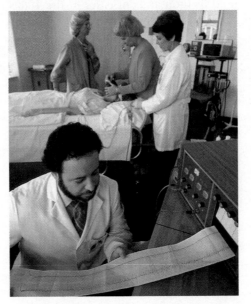

Dr. Richard B. Weiner of Duke University Medical Center reads a patient's EEG as technicians administer electroconvulsive therapy. Although ECT continues to be controversial, it has helped severely depressed patients for whom other treatments have failed.

experience disorientation, confusion, and sometimes memory loss that may remain for months. Moreover, many patients fear ECT, even though they are anesthetized during the actual treatment and thus experience no pain. Finally, we still do not know how or why ECT works, and although it has never been proven, there is the reasonable fear that the treatment may produce permanent neurological damage to the brain (Fisher, 1985).

Given the drawbacks to ECT, why is it used at all? The basic reason is that in many cases it still seems to be an effective treatment for severe cases of depression (Sackheim, 1985; Thienhaus, Margletta, & Bennett, 1990). Indeed, although it is less popular today than it once was, some surveys suggest that the use of ECT rose in the 1980s (Harvard Medical School, 1987). Still, ECT tends to be used only when other treatments have proven ineffective (Sackheim, 1985; APA Task Force, 1990).

Psychosurgery

Psychosurgery: Brain surgery, once used to alleviate symptoms of mental disorder but rarely used today

Prefrontal lobotomy: The surgical destruction of certain areas of a patient's frontal lobes to improve the control of emotionality

If ECT strikes you as a questionable procedure, the use of **psychosurgery**—brain surgery in which the object is to alleviate symptoms of mental disorder—is likely to appear even more so. A technique that has largely disappeared, psychosurgery was first introduced as a treatment of "last resort" in the 1930s. The procedure, a **prefrontal lobotomy**, consists of surgically destroying or removing certain parts of a patient's frontal lobes, which control emotionality. The rationale for this procedure was that destroying the connections between various parts of the brain would make patients less subject to emotional impulses, and their general behavior would improve.

Psychosurgery often did improve a patient's behavior—but not without drastic side effects. For along with remission of symptoms of mental disorder, patients sometimes suffered personality changes, becoming bland, colorless, and unemotional. In other cases, patients became aggressive and unable to control their impulses. In the worst cases, the patients died from treatment.

Despite these problems—and the obvious ethical questions regarding the appropriateness of forever altering someone's personality—psychosurgery was used in thousands of cases in the 1930s and 1940s. The treatment became so routine that in some places fifty patients a day received psychosurgery (Freeman, 1959).

With the advent of effective drug treatments, psychosurgery became practically obsolete. It is still used, in modified form, in very rare cases when all other procedures have failed and the patient's behavior presents a high risk to self and others or when there is severe, uncontrollable pain in terminal cases. When psychosurgery is used today, more precise techniques are employed, and only extremely small areas of brain tissue are destroyed. Still, even in these cases, important ethical issues are raised, and psychosurgery remains a highly controversial treatment (Valenstein, 1986).

Biological Treatment in Perspective: Can Abnormal Behavior Be Cured?

In some respects, there has been no greater revolution in the field of mental health than that represented by the biological approaches to treatment. Mental hospitals have been able to concentrate more on actually helping patients and less on custodial functions as previously violent, uncontrollable patients have been calmed by the use of drugs. Similarly, patients whose lives have been disrupted by depression or manic-depressive episodes have been able to function normally, and other forms of drug therapy have also shown remarkable results.

On the other hand, biological therapies can be criticized. For one thing, in many cases they merely provide relief of the *symptoms* of mental disorder; as soon as the drugs are withdrawn, the symptoms return. Although it is considered a major step in the right direction, biological treatment does not solve the underlying problem that may continue to haunt a patient even while he or she is undergoing treatment. Moreover, biological therapies can have numerous side effects, ranging from physical reactions to the development of *new* symptoms of abnormal behavior (Elkin, 1986). For these reasons, then, biologically based treatment approaches do not represent a cure-all for psychological disorders.

Community Psychology: Focus on Prevention

Each of the treatments that we have reviewed in this chapter has a common element: They are ''restorative'' treatments, aimed at alleviating psychological difficulties that already exist. However, a relatively new movement, dubbed **community psychology**, is geared toward a different aim: to prevent or minimize psychological disorders.

Community psychology came of age in the 1960s, when plans were developed for a nationwide network of community mental-health centers. These centers were meant to provide low-cost mental-health services, including short-term therapy and community educational programs. Moreover, during the last thirty years, the population of mental hospitals has plunged, as drug treatments have made physical restraint of patients unnecessary. The influx of former mental patients into the community, known as **deinstitutionalization**, further spurred the community psychology movement, which was concerned with ensuring not only that the deinstitutionalized received proper treatment but that their civil rights were maintained (Melton & Garrison, 1987).

Unfortunately, the original goals of the field of community psychology have not been met. For instance, the incidence of mental disorders has shown no decline. Many people who need treatment do not get it, and in some cases, care for people with psychological disorders has simply shifted from one form of treatment site to another (Kiesler & Simpkins, 1991).

However, the movement has yielded several encouraging by-products. One of these is the installation of telephone ''hot lines'' in cities throughout the United States. People experiencing acute stress can call a telephone number at any time of day or night and talk to a trained, sympathetic listener who can provide immediate—although obviously limited—treatment.

The college crisis center is another innovation that grew out of the community psychology movement. Modeled after suicide prevention hot-line centers (places for potential suicide victims to call and speak to someone about their difficulties), campus crisis centers provide callers with the opportunity to discuss life crises with a sympathetic listener, who is most often a student volunteer.

Although not professionals, the volunteers receive careful training in telephone counseling. They role-play particular problems and are told how to respond to the difficulties they may confront with callers. The volunteers also hold group meetings to discuss the kinds of problems they are encountering and to share experiences about the kinds of strategies that are most effective.

Community psychology: A movement aimed toward preventing or minimizing psychological disorders in the community

Deinstitutionalization: The transfer of former mental patients from institutions into the community

Initial counseling for crisis situations is sometimes available through trained volunteers, such as this telephone hotline counselor, who can make referrals for longer-term help if needed.

Because they are not professionals, the staff members of college crisis centers do not, of course, offer long-term therapy to those who contact them. But they are able to provide callers with a supportive, constructive response—often when it is most needed. They are also able to refer callers to appropriate agencies on and off campus to get the long-term help they need.

The Informed Consumer of Psychology: Choosing the Right Therapist

Suppose your friend Ben, who sought your advice on the most effective kind of therapy, decides on the general nature of the treatment that he wants and begins therapy. How does he know that he has chosen the right therapist?

Once again, there is no simple answer. There are, however, a number of factors that informed consumers of psychological services can and should take into consideration to determine whether they have made the right choice.

■ The relationship between client and therapist should be a comfortable one. The client should not be afraid or in awe of the therapist but should trust the therapist and feel free to discuss the most personal issues without fearing a negative reaction.

■ The therapist should have appropriate training and credentials for the type of therapy that he or she is conducting and should be licensed by appropriate state and local agencies. Far from being a breach of etiquette to ask a therapist on an initial visit about the kind of training that he or she received, it behooves a wise consumer of psychological services to make such an inquiry.

■ Clients should feel that they are making progress toward resolving their psychological difficulties after therapy has begun, despite occasional setbacks. Although there is no set timetable, the most obvious changes resulting from therapy tend to occur relatively early in the course of treatment (Howard & Zola, 1988). (Later, however, change may take longer, as more deepseated problems are confronted.) If a client has no sense of improvement after repeated visits, this issue should be frankly discussed, with an eye toward the possibility of making a change. Most therapy today is of fairly brief duration, especially that involving college students—who average just five therapy sessions (Nowicki & Duke, 1978).

■ Clients should be aware that they will have to put in a great deal of effort in therapy. Although ours is a culture that promises quick cures for any problem—as anyone who has perused the self-help shelves of bookstores knows—in reality, solving difficult problems is far from easy (Rosen, 1987). People must be committed to making therapy work and should know that it is they, and not the therapist, who must do most of the work to resolve their problems. The potential is there for the effort to pay off handsomely—as people experience more positive, fulfilling, and meaningful lives.

◀ **RECAP AND REVIEW III**

RECAP

◁ Biological treatment approaches encompass drug therapy, electric-shock therapy, and surgical therapy.

◁ Drug therapy has produced dramatic reductions in psychotic behavior. Among the medications used are antipsychotic drugs, antidepressant drugs, and antianxiety drugs.

◁ Electroconvulsive therapy (ECT) consists of passing an electric current through the brain of patients suffering from severe psychological disturbances, particularly schizophrenia and depression.

◁ The most extreme form of biological therapy is psychosurgery, in which patients undergo brain surgery. Although rarely used today, prefrontal lobotomies were once a common form of treatment.

◁ Community psychology aims to prevent or minimize psychological disorders.

REVIEW

1. Like penicillin, antipsychotic drugs have provided effective, long-term, and complete cures for schizophrenia. True or false? _____

2. One of the most effective biological treatments for psychological disorders, used mainly to arrest and prevent manic-depressive episodes, is
   a. chlorpromazine
   b. lithium
   c. Librium
   d. Valium

3. Originally a treatment for schizophrenia, _____ _____ _____ involves administering electric current to a patient's head.

4. Psychosurgery has grown in popularity as a method of treatment as surgical techniques have become more precise. True or false? _____

5. The trend toward releasing more patients from mental hospitals into the community is known as _____.

Ask Yourself

Are the techniques of ECT and psychosurgery ethical? Are there cases in which they should never be used? Does the fact that no one understands why ECT is effective mean that its use should be avoided? In general, should treatments that are seemingly effective, but for unknown reasons, be employed?

(Answers to review questions are on page 616.)

■ *What are the goals of psychologically and biologically based treatment approaches?*

1. Although the specific treatment types are diverse, psychologically based therapy, known as psychotherapy, and biologically based therapy share the goal of resolving psychological problems by modifying people's thoughts, feelings, expectations, evaluations, and ultimately their behavior.

■ *What are the basic kinds of psychotherapies?*

2. Psychoanalytic treatment is based on Freud's psychodynamic theory. It seeks to bring unresolved past conflicts and unacceptable impulses from the unconscious into the conscious, where the problems may be dealt with more effectively. To do this, patients meet frequently with their therapists and use techniques such as free association and dream interpretation. The process can be a difficult one, because of patient resistance and transference, and there is no unquestioned evidence that the process works.

3. Behavioral approaches to treatment view abnormal behavior itself as the problem, rather than viewing the behavior as a symptom of some underlying cause. In order to bring about a "cure," this view suggests that the outward behavior must be changed. In aversive conditioning, unpleasant stimuli are linked to a behavior that the patient enjoys but wants to stop. Systematic desensitization uses the opposite procedure. A stimulus that evokes pleasant feelings is repeatedly paired with a stimulus that evokes anxiety in order to reduce that anxiety. Observational learning is another behavioral treatment used to teach new, more appropriate behavior, as are techniques such as token systems.

4. Cognitive approaches to treatment, which are often referred to as cognitive-behavioral therapy, suggest that the goal of therapy should be a restructuring of a person's belief system into a more realistic, rational, and logical view of the world. Two examples of cognitive treatments are the rational-emotive therapy of Ellis and Beck's cognitive therapy.

5. Humanistic therapy is based on the premise that people have control of their behavior, that they can make choices about their lives, and that it is up to them to solve their own problems. Humanistic therapists take a nondirective approach, acting more as guides who facilitate a client's search for answers. One example of humanistic therapy is Carl Rogers's client-centered therapy, in which the goal is to allow people to reach the potential good assumed to be characteristic of every human being. Existential therapy helps people cope with the unique freedom and potential that human existence offers, whereas gestalt therapy is directed toward aiding people in the integration of their thoughts, feelings, and behavior.

■ *How effective is therapy, and which kind of therapy works best under a given circumstance?*

6. Most research suggests that, in general, therapy is more effective than no therapy, although how much more effective is not known. The answer to the more difficult question of which therapy works best is even less clear, in part because the therapies are so qualitatively different, and in part because the definition of "cure" is so vague. It is indisputable, though, that particular kinds of therapy are more appropriate for some problems than for others.

■ *How are drug, electroconvulsive, and psychosurgical techniques used today in the treatment of mental disorders?*

7. Biological treatment approaches suggest that therapy ought to focus on the physiological causes of abnormal behavior, rather than considering psychological factors. Drug therapy, the best example of biological treatments, has been effective in bringing about dramatic reductions in the appearance of severe signs of mental disturbance.

8. Antipsychotic drugs such as chlorpromazine are very effective in reducing psychotic symptoms, although they can produce serious side effects. Antidepressant drugs reduce depression. The antianxiety drugs, or minor tranquilizers, are among the most frequently prescribed medications of any sort; they act to reduce the experience of anxiety.

9. Electroconvulsive therapy (ECT) consists of passing an electric current of 70 to 150 volts through the head of a patient, who loses consciousness and has a strong seizure. This procedure is an effective treatment for severe cases of schizophrenia and depression. Another biological treatment is psychosurgery. The typical procedure consists of surgically destroying certain parts of a patient's brain in an operation known as a prefrontal lobotomy. Given the grave ethical problems and possible adverse side effects, the procedure is rarely used today.

10. Community psychology aims to prevent or minimize psychological disorders. The movement was spurred in part by deinstitutionalization, in which previously hospitalized mental patients were released into the community. A notable by-product of the movement has been the installation of telephone hot lines and campus crisis centers throughout the country.

ANSWERS (REVIEW III):

1. False; schizophrenia can be controlled, but not cured, by medication. **2.** b
3. electroconvulsive therapy (ECT) **4.** False; psychosurgery is now used only as a treatment of last resort. **5.** deinstitutionalization

KEY TERMS AND CONCEPTS

psychotherapy (p. 587)

biologically based therapy (p. 587)

eclectic approach to therapy (p. 588)

psychodynamic therapy (p. 589)

defense mechanisms (p. 589)

neurotic symptoms (p. 589)

psychoanalysis (p. 589)

free association (p. 589)

dream interpretation (p. 589)

manifest content (of dreams) (p. 590)

latent content (of dreams) (p. 590)

resistance (p. 590)

transference (p. 590)

behavioral treatment approaches (p. 591)

aversive conditioning (p. 592)

systematic desensitization (p. 592)

hierarchy of fears (p. 593)

observational learning (p. 594)

modeling (p. 594)

token system (p. 595)

contingency contracting (p. 595)

cognitive-behavioral approach (p. 596)

rational-emotive therapy (p. 596)

cognitive therapy (p. 597)

humanistic therapy (p. 598)

nondirective counseling (p. 599)

client-centered therapy (p. 599)

unconditional positive regard (p. 599)

existential therapy (p. 599)

gestalt therapy (p. 600)

group therapy (p. 600)

family therapy (p. 601)

spontaneous remission (p. 603)

drug therapy (p. 608)

antipsychotic drugs (p. 608)

chlorpromazine (p. 608)

antidepressant drugs (p. 609)

lithium (p. 609)

fluxetine (Prozac) (p. 610)

antianxiety drugs (p. 610)

electroconvulsive therapy (ECT) (p. 611)

psychosurgery (p. 612)

prefrontal lobotomy (p. 612)

community psychology (p. 613)

deinstitutionalization (p. 613)

SOCIAL PSYCHOLOGY: ATTITUDES AND SOCIAL COGNITION

Los Angeles police officers were videotaped beating Rodney King while arresting him for a traffic violation.

RODNEY KING

If it hadn't been captured on videotape, Rodney King's beating might never have come to light. However, because a resident living close to a Los Angeles freeway had wanted to try out his new videotape camera, King's misfortune made national headlines.

The incident started when Los Angeles police stopped King, who was African-American, after a high-speed car chase in early 1991. According to the police, King resisted arrest, and they were forced to subdue him.

Viewers of the videotape, though, saw something else. In it, policemen are shown repeatedly pummeling King as he lies on the ground, trying to get up. He is hit with nightsticks forty times and kicked over and over by several of the police. The wire of a stun gun is wrapped around him. A large group of police officers and highway patrolmen stand nearby, watching impassively.

According to critics of the police, King's beating was just one in a string of incidents motivated in part by racial bias. An examination of police computer messages gives credence to such a view. For example, in one message sent earlier on the night of the King beating, one of the officers who allegedly beat King alludes to a domestic dispute among an African-American family as "right out of 'Gorillas in the Mist.'" Another police officer responds, "Ha, ha, ha, ha. Let me guess who be the parties" (Baker, 1991).

When a jury found four of the police officers accused of beating King "not guilty," some of the worst rioting in U.S. history occurred. Further legal action will take place in order to assess blame for the beating. Whatever the judicial consequences of the incident involving King, though, one thing is clear: Although it was King who suffered the initial wounds, race relations in Los Angeles also took a beating.

LOOKING AHEAD

Several psychological issues are raised when we think about Rodney King's beating. For example, we might consider the racial prejudice that may have motivated the beating, or question why the police officers behaved so violently, or attempt to explain why no bystanders intervened in the situation.

Issues such as these are central to social psychology. **Social psychology** is the study of how people's thoughts, feelings, and actions are affected by others. Social psychologists consider the nature and causes of individual behavior in social situations.

The broad scope of social psychology is conveyed by the kinds of questions social psychologists ask, such as: How can we convince people to change their attitudes or to adopt new ideas and values? In what ways do we come to understand what others are like? How are we influenced by what others do and think? Why do people display such violence, aggression, and cruelty toward others that people throughout the world live in fear of annihilation? And why, at other times, do people place their own lives at risk to help others?

In this chapter and the next, we explore social psychological approaches to these and other issues. Not only do we examine those processes which underlie social behavior; we also discuss strategies and solutions to a variety of problems and issues that all of us face—ranging from achieving a better understanding of persuasive tactics to forming more accurate impressions of others.

Social psychology: The branch of psychology concerned with how people's thoughts, feelings, and actions are affected by others

We begin with a look at attitudes, our evaluations of people and other stimuli. Next, we discuss how people form judgments about others and the causes of their behavior. Finally, we examine the ways in which we discern the meaning of others' behavior and the kinds of biases that affect our understanding of others. We will see how our interpretation of the causes of other people's behavior affects the way we treat them.

In sum, after reading this chapter you'll have the answers to these questions:

- What are attitudes and how are they formed, maintained, and changed?
- How do we form impressions of what others are like and of the causes of their behavior?
- What are the biases that influence the way in which we view others' behavior?
- How can we make more accurate judgments about others and reduce stereotyping and prejudice?

ATTITUDES, BEHAVIOR, AND PERSUASION

What do Madonna, Joe Montana, and a General Norman Schwarzkopf-lookalike have in common? Each has appeared in a television commercial, exhorting us to purchase some particular product brand.

These commercials were just a few of the thousands that appear on our screens, all designed to persuade us to purchase specific products. These attempts illustrate basic principles that have been articulated by social psychologists who study **attitudes**, learned predispositions to respond in a favorable or unfavorable manner to a particular person or object.

Attitudes, of course, are not restricted to consumer products. They also relate to specific individuals, as well as to more abstract issues. For example, when you think of the various people in your life, you no doubt hold vastly differing attitudes toward them, depending on the nature of your interactions with them. These attitudes may range from highly positive, as in the case of a lover, to extremely negative, as with a despised rival. Attitudes are also likely to vary in importance. Whereas our attitudes toward friends, family, and peers are generally central to our interactions in the social world, our attitudes toward, say, television newscasters may be relatively insignificant.

Social psychologists generally consider attitudes to follow the **ABC model**, which suggests that an attitude has three components: affect, behavior, and cognition (Rajecki, 1989). The **affect component** encompasses our positive or negative emotions about something—how we feel about it. The **behavior component** consists of a predisposition or intention to act in a particular manner that is relevant to our attitude. Finally, the **cognition component** refers to the beliefs and thoughts we hold about the object of our attitude. For example, someone's attitude toward Paula Abdul may consist of a positive emotion (the affect component), an intention to buy her latest recording (the behavior component), and the belief that she is a good singer (the cognition component). (See Figure 19-1, p. 622.)

Every attitude has these three interrelated components, although they vary in terms of which element predominates and in the nature of their relationship. All attitudes, however, develop according to the general principles that social psychologists have discovered about their formation, maintenance, and change—principles that we discuss next.

Attitudes: Learned predispositions to respond in a favorable or unfavorable manner to a particular object

ABC model: The model suggesting that an attitude has three components: affect, behavior, and cognition

Affect component: That part of an attitude encompassing how one feels about the object of one's attitude

Behavior component: A predisposition to act in a way that is relevant to one's attitude

Cognition component: The beliefs and thoughts held about the object of one's attitude

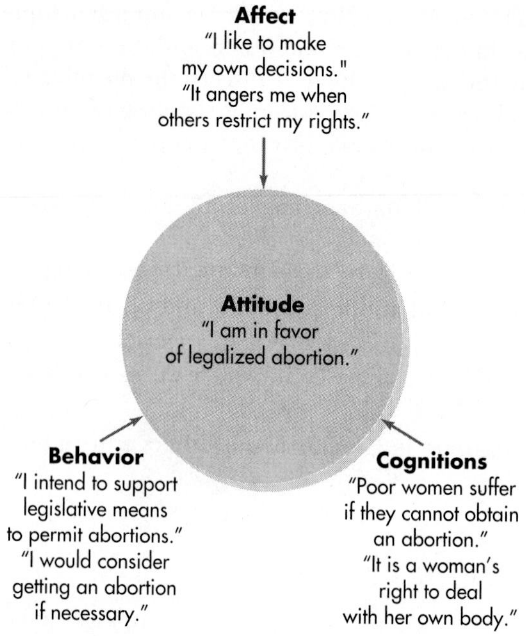

Affect
"I like to make
my own decisions."
"It angers me when
others restrict my rights."

Attitude
"I am in favor
of legalized abortion."

Behavior
"I intend to support
legislative means
to permit abortions."
"I would consider
getting an abortion
if necessary."

Cognitions
"Poor women suffer
if they cannot obtain
an abortion."
"It is a woman's
right to deal
with her own body."

FIGURE 19-1
Like all attitudes, this attitude
on abortion is composed
of an affective, behavioral
predisposition, and a cognitive
component.

Forming and Maintaining Attitudes

Although people do not enter the world holding well-defined attitudes toward any particular person or object, anyone who has seen an infant smile at her parents knows that at least certain attitudes develop quickly. Interestingly, some of the same principles which govern how attitudes are acquired and develop in the youngest of children continue to operate throughout life.

Classical Conditioning and Attitudes. One of the basic processes underlying attitude formation and development can be explained on the basis of learning principles (McGuire, 1985). The same classical conditioning processes that made Pavlov's dogs salivate at the sound of a bell can explain how attitudes are acquired. As we discussed in Chapter 7, people develop associations between various objects and the emotional reactions that accompany them. For example, many soldiers who were stationed in the Persian Gulf during the war with Iraq reported that they never wanted to sit on a sandy beach again. Put another way, the soldiers formed negative attitudes toward sand. Similarly, positive associations can develop through classical conditioning. We may come to hold a positive attitude toward a particular perfume because a favorite aunt wears it.

Advertisers make use of the principles of classical conditioning of attitudes by attempting to link a product they want consumers to buy with a positive feeling or event (Alsop, 1988). For instance, many advertisements feature young, attractive, healthy men and women using a product—even if it is one as uninteresting as toothpaste. The idea behind such advertisements is to create a classically conditioned response to the product, so that just glimpsing a tube of Crest toothpaste evokes a positive feeling.

Operant Conditioning Approaches to Attitude Acquisition. Another basic learning process, operant conditioning, also underlies attitude acquisition. Attitudes that are reinforced, either verbally or nonverbally, tend to be maintained. Conversely, a person who states an attitude that elicits ridicule from others may

Advertising is often designed to appeal to the emotions of the buying public. This engaging photo has been used to sell dozens of products and services including picture frames, wine, real estate, employment counseling, and garden hoses.

modify or abandon the attitude. But it is not only direct reinforcement or punishment that can influence attitudes. **Vicarious learning**, in which a person learns something through the observation of others, can also account for attitude development—particularly when the individual has no direct experience with the object about which the attitude is held. It is through vicarious learning processes that children pick up the prejudices of their parents. For example, even if they have never met a blind person, children whose parents say that "blind people are incompetent" may adopt such attitudes themselves.

Vicarious learning: Learning by observing others

We also learn attitudes vicariously through television, films, and other media. For instance, movies that glorify violence reinforce positive attitudes regarding aggression (as we discuss further in Chapter 20), and portrayals of women as subservient to men shape and bolster sexist attitudes.

Persuasion: Changing Attitudes

What is it about Michael J. Fox, Ray Charles, Fred Savage, and Billy Crystal that leads people to drink more Pepsi?

According to professionals working in the field of advertising, each of these celebrity endorsements is a carefully selected match between the product and the individual chosen to represent it. It is not just a matter of finding a well-known celebrity; the person must also be believable, trustworthy, and representative of the qualities that advertisers want their particular product to project (Alwitt & Mitchell, 1985; Kanner, 1989).

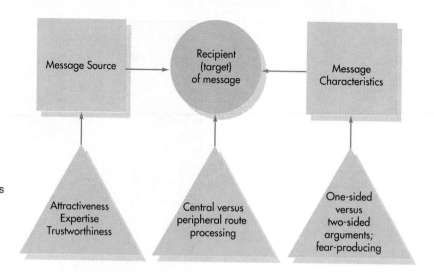

FIGURE 19-2

In this model of the critical factors affecting persuasion, the message source and message characteristics are shown to influence the recipient or target of a persuasive message.

The work of advertisers draws heavily upon findings from social psychology regarding persuasion. This research has identified a number of factors (see Figure 19-2) that promote effective persuasion—many of which you will recognize if you consider for a moment some of the advertisements with which you are most familiar (Johnson, 1991; Tesser & Shaffer, 1990).

Message Source.   The individual who delivers a persuasive message has a major impact on the effectiveness of that message (Wu & Shaffer, 1987). Communicators who are both physically and socially attractive seem to produce greater attitude change (Chaiken, 1979). Moreover, the expertise and trustworthiness of a communicator are related to the impact of a message—except in situations in which the communicator is believed to have an ulterior motive. If a prestigious communicator seems to be benefiting from persuading others, the message may be discounted (Hovland, Janis, & Kelly, 1953; Eagly, Wood, & Chaiken, 1978). For example, a prestigious scientist who argues in favor of opening a nuclear power plant would generally be a particularly influential source, unless it is revealed that the scientist owns stock in the power plant and stands to benefit financially from its opening.

Characteristics of the Message.   As you might expect, it is not just *who* delivers a message but *what* the message is like that affects attitude and behavior change. One-sided arguments—in which only the communicator's side is presented— are probably best if the communicator's message is initially viewed favorably by the audience. But if the audience receives a message presenting an unpopular viewpoint, two-sided messages—which include both the communicator's position and the one he or she is arguing against—are more effective, probably because they are seen as more precise and thoughtful (Karlins & Abelson, 1979). In addition, fear-producing messages ("If you don't practice safer sex, you'll get AIDS") are generally effective, although not always. For instance, if the fear aroused is too strong, messages may evoke people's defense mechanisms and may be ignored. In such cases, fear appeals work best if they include precise recommendations for actions to avoid danger (Leventhal, 1970; Boster & Mongeau, 1985).

Characteristics of the Recipient or Target. Once a message has been communicated, the characteristics of the audience determine whether the message will be accepted. For example, we might expect that recipients' intelligence would be related to their persuasibility—and it is, although the relationship is complex. High intelligence might be expected to both aid and hinder persuasion. Because higher intelligence enables people to understand a message better and later recall it more easily, persuasion would be more likely. On the other hand, higher intelligence is associated with greater knowledge about a subject and more confidence in one's own opinions, and so messages of opposing viewpoints would be more likely to be rejected.

The weight of the research carried out on the question suggests that those who are of high intelligence are more resistant to persuasion than those of lower intelligence. However, the question remains to be fully resolved (Rhodes & Wood, 1992).

Some gender differences in persuasibility also seem to exist. For instance, social psychologist Alice Eagly (1989) has found that women are somewhat more easily persuaded than men, particularly when they have less knowledge of the message topic. However, the magnitude of the differences between men and women is not large.

One factor that is important in determining whether a message is accepted is the type of information processing carried out by the recipient. There are two routes to persuasion: central route and peripheral route processing (Petty & Cacioppo, 1986; Cialdini, 1984; Eagly, 1983). **Central route processing** occurs when the recipient thoughtfully considers the issues and arguments involved in persuasion. **Peripheral route processing**, in contrast, occurs when the recipient uses more easily understood information that requires less thought, such as the nature of the source, or other information less central to the issues involved in the message itself (Mackie, 1987; Petty & Cacioppo, 1986).

In general, central route processing results in the most lasting attitude change. However, if central route processing cannot be employed (for instance, if the target is inattentive, bored, or distracted), then the nature of the message becomes less important, and peripheral factors more critical (Petty & Cacioppo, 1984). Advertising that uses celebrities to sell a product, then, tends to produce change through the peripheral route. In fact, it is possible that well-reasoned, carefully crafted messages will be *less* effective when delivered by a celebrity than by an anonymous source—if the target pays greater attention to the celebrity (leading to peripheral route processing) than to the message (which would have led to central route processing). On the other hand, since recipients of advertising messages are often in a fairly inattentive state, the use of celebrities is probably an excellent strategy. Advertisers are correct, then, in their assumption that well-known individuals can have a significant persuasive impact.

Central route processing:
Message interpretation characterized by thoughtful consideration of the issues and arguments used to persuade

Peripheral route processing:
Message interpretation characterized by consideration of the source and related general information rather than of the message itself

The Link Between Attitudes and Behavior

Not surprisingly, attitudes influence behavior. If you like hamburgers (the affect component), are predisposed to eat at McDonald's or Burger King (the behavior component), and believe hamburgers are a good source of protein (the cognitive component), it is hardly surprising that you will eat hamburgers frequently. The strength of the link between particular attitudes and behavior varies, of course, but generally people strive for consistency between their attitudes and their behavior. Furthermore, people tend to be fairly consistent in the different attitudes they hold. You would probably not hold the attitude that eating meat is immoral and still have a positive attitude toward hamburgers.

Interestingly, the consistency that leads attitudes to influence behavior sometimes works the other way around, for in some cases it is our behavior that shapes our attitudes. Consider, for instance, the following incident:

> You've just spent what you feel is the most boring hour of your life, turning pegs for a psychology experiment. Just as you're finally finished and about to leave, the experimenter asks you to do him a favor. He tells you that he needs a confederate to tell subsequent subjects about the task. All you have to do is tell them that it was interesting. For this, you'll be paid $1.

Cognitive dissonance: The conflict that arises when a person holds contrasting cognitions

Cognitions: Attitudes, thoughts, or beliefs

If you agree to such a request, you may be setting yourself up for a state of psychological tension that is known as cognitive dissonance. According to a major social psychologist, Leon Festinger (1957), **cognitive dissonance** occurs when a person holds two attitudes or thoughts (referred to as **cognitions**) that contradict each other. For example, a smoker who knows that smoking leads to lung cancer holds contradictory cognitions: (1) I smoke; and (2) smoking leads to lung cancer. The theory predicts that these two thoughts will lead to a state of cognitive dissonance. More important, it predicts that the individual will be motivated to reduce such dissonance by one of the following methods: (1) modifying one or both of the cognitions; (2) changing the perceived importance of one cognition; (3) adding cognitions; or (4) denying that the two cognitions are related to each other. Hence the smoker might decide that he really doesn't smoke all that much (modifying the cognition), that the evidence linking smoking to cancer is weak (changing the importance of a cognition), that the amount of exercise he gets compensates for the smoking (adding cognitions), or that there is no evidence linking smoking and cancer (denial). Whatever technique is used, the result is a reduction in dissonance (see Figure 19-3).

Cognitive dissonance arising from the two contradictory cognitions of "I'd like to eat here" and "I can't afford to eat here" may be reduced by deciding that one really does not want to have a meal at the restaurant after all.

"Nothing there appeals to me."

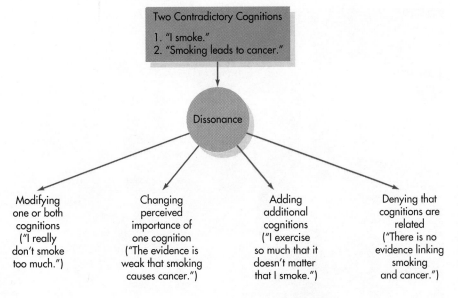

FIGURE 19-3

The presence of two contradictory cognitions ("I smoke" and "Smoking leads to cancer") produces dissonance, which may be reduced through several methods.

If we consider the situation described above, in which a subject in an experiment is paid just $1 to tell someone else that a boring task was interesting, we have set up classic dissonance-producing circumstances. A subject in such a situation is left with two contradictory thoughts: (1) I believe the task is boring; but (2) I said it was interesting with little justification (a dollar's worth).

According to the theory, dissonance should be aroused. But how can such dissonance be reduced? One can't very well deny having said that the task was interesting without making a fairly strong break with reality. But, relatively speaking, it is easy to change one's attitude toward the task—and thus the theory predicts that dissonance will be reduced as the subjects change their attitudes to be more positive.

This prediction was confirmed in a classic experiment (Festinger & Carlsmith, 1959). The experiment followed essentially the same procedure outlined earlier, in which a subject was offered $1 to describe a boring task as interesting. In addition, as a control, a condition was included in which subjects were offered $20 to say that the task was interesting. The reasoning behind this condition was that $20 was so much money that subjects in this condition had a good reason to be telling something that was incorrect; dissonance would *not* be aroused, and *less* attitude change would be expected. The results supported this notion. Subjects who were paid $1 changed their attitudes more (becoming more positive toward the peg-turning task) than subjects who were paid $20.

We now know that dissonance explains a number of everyday occurrences involving attitudes and behavior. For example, consider what happens when you decide to make a major purchase, such as a new car. First you will probably get as much information as possible about a range of models by talking to people and reading about different cars. But after you make your decision, what happens? Most people experience some degree of dissonance because the car they've chosen has some undesirable characteristics, whereas those models that were rejected have some positive features. What typically happens to reduce such dissonance, after a decision has been reached, is that people's attitudes toward the rejected models become *more* negative, while their attitudes toward the chosen model become *more* positive (Converse & Cooper, 1979). Moreover, a **selective exposure** phenomenon occurs. In order to minimize dissonance, people selec-

Selective exposure: An attempt to minimize dissonance by exposing oneself only to information that supports one's choice

When investing in a home computer, this woman may experience cognitive dissonance because the model she has chosen still has some undesirable characteristics. This may lead her to criticize other models in order to reassure herself that she made a good buy.

tively expose themselves to information that supports their own choice and attempt to avoid information that is contrary to their choice (Sears, 1968; Sweeney & Gruber, 1984).

Since its development in the late 1950s, dissonance theory has generated a tremendous amount of research, most of which has supported the theory (Aronson, 1990). However, the theory has not been without its critics. Some psychologists have criticized the methodology used in dissonance experiments, while others have suggested alternative theoretical explanations.

Self-perception theory: Bem's theory that people form attitudes by observing their own behavior and applying the same principles to themselves as they do to others

One of the most plausible alternatives was suggested by Darryl Bem (1967, 1972) in his **self-perception theory.** Bem put forth the idea that people form attitudes by observing their own behavior, using the same principles that they use when they observe others' behavior to draw conclusions about others' attitudes. In other words, people are sometimes unclear about the reasons for which they have just demonstrated a certain behavior. In those instances, they will look at their behavior and try to figure out just why they did what they did.

For example, if I were the subject who received $1 for saying that a task I hated was actually very interesting, I might look at what I said and try to figure out why I said it. The most likely explanation is "Well, if I agreed to say I liked the task for a paltry $1, then I probably didn't dislike it all that much. In fact, I probably liked it." Therefore, when asked by the experimenter to indicate my attitude, I might respond with a relatively positive attitude toward the task. Of course, this is the same result that dissonance theory would predict—more positive attitude change in the lower-incentive condition ($1) than in the higher-incentive condition ($20)—but the underlying reason is different. Whereas the dissonance explanation suggests that attitude change is due to the presence (in the $1 condition) of the unpleasant state of dissonance that a subject tries to overcome, the self-perception theory suggests it is due to an active search for understanding one's behavior.

More recent approaches to dissonance theory have focused on conditions under which dissonance occurs. For example, some research suggests that it is not just discrepancies between cognitions that lead to dissonance—additional factors, such as experiencing feelings of responsibility for unpleasant outcomes or threats to self-concept can produce dissonance as well (e.g., Scher & Cooper, 1989; Steele, 1988).

Although we cannot be sure whether dissonance theory or alternative explanations provide the most accurate description of how people react to inconsistencies between their attitudes and their behavior, it is clear most of us try to make sense of our own attitudes and behavior and maintain consistency between them. When we behave in a way that is inconsistent with our attitudes, we tend to change our attitudes to make them fit better with our behavior.

RECAP AND REVIEW I

RECAP

◀ Attitudes are learned predispositions to respond in a favorable or unfavorable manner to a particular object. They have three components: affect, behavior, and cognition.

◀ Both classical conditioning and operant conditioning underlie attitude acquisition.

◀ The major factors promoting persuasion relate to the message source, characteristics of the message, and characteristics of the recipient or target.

◀ People strive to fit their attitudes and behavior together in a logical framework, and they attempt to overcome any inconsistencies that they perceive.

◀ Cognitive dissonance, a state of psychological tension, occurs when a person holds two attitudes or thoughts (known as cognitions) that contradict each other. Self-perception theory provides an alternative explanation to dissonance theory.

REVIEW

1. A learned predisposition to respond in a favorable or an unfavorable manner to a particular object is called a(n) _____.

2. Match each component of the ABC model of attitudes with its definition:

_____ 1. affect   a. thoughts and beliefs
_____ 2. behavior   b. positive or negative emotions
_____ 3. cognition   c. predisposition to act a particular way

3. One brand of peanut butter advertises its product by describing its taste and nutritional value. It is hoping to persuade customers through _____-route processing. In ads for a competing brand, a popular actor is seen happily eating the product—but does not describe it. This approach is called _____-route processing.

4. Cognitive dissonance theory suggests that we commonly change our behavior to keep it consistent with our attitudes. True or false? _____

5. The theory which suggests that people form attitudes by observing and trying to understand their own behavior is called
   a. operant conditioning
   b. cognitive dissonance
   c. vicarious learning
   d. self-perception

Ask Yourself

Suppose you were assigned to develop a full advertising campaign for a product, including television, radio, and print ads. How might the theories in this chapter guide your strategy to suit the different media?

(Answers to review questions are on page 630.)

SOCIAL COGNITION: UNDERSTANDING OTHERS

Regardless of whether they agreed with his policies and ideology, in spite of how they felt he garbled the facts at news conferences, and irrespective of the trouble his subordinates found themselves in, most Americans genuinely *liked* former President Ronald Reagan. These problems, that might have been expected to reflect unfavorably upon him personally, never seemed to affect Reagan's popularity, and he was dubbed the "Teflon president" by the press. Perceived as a "nice guy," he remained one of the most popular presidents of the century until the end of his second term.

Regardless of whether they agreed or disagreed with President Reagan's specific policies, most people had a positive impression of him as a person during his presidential term.

Situations such as this one illustrate the power of our impressions and attest to the importance of determining how people develop an understanding of others. One of the dominant areas of study in social psychology during the last few years has focused on learning how we come to understand what others are like and how we explain the reasons underlying others' behavior (Fiske & Taylor, 1991).

Understanding What Others Are Like

Consider for a moment the enormous amount of information about other people to which we are exposed. How are we able to decide what is important and what is not, and to make judgments about the characteristics of others? Social psychologists interested in this question study **social cognition**—the processes that underlie our understanding of the social world. They have learned that individuals have highly developed **schemas**, sets of cognitions about people and social experiences. These schemas organize information stored in memory; represent in our minds the way the social world operates; and give us a framework to categorize and interpret information relating to social stimuli.

We typically hold schemas for particular types of people in our environments. Our schema for "teacher," for instance, generally consists of a number of characteristics: knowledge of the subject matter he or she is teaching, a desire to impart that knowledge, and an awareness of the student's need to understand what is being said. Or we may hold a schema for "mother" that includes the characteristics of warmth, nurturance, and caring. Regardless of their accuracy— and, as we shall see, very often their inaccuracy—schemas are important because they organize the way in which we recall, recognize, and categorize information about others. Moreover, they allow us to make predictions of what others are like on the basis of relatively little information, since we tend to fit people into schemas even when there is not much concrete evidence to go on (Smith, 1984; Snyder & Cantor, 1979).

Social cognition: The processes that underlie our understanding of the social world

Schemas: Sets of cognitions about people and social experiences

---

ANSWERS (REVIEW I):

1. attitude **2.** 1-b; 2-c; 3-a **3.** central; peripheral **4.** False; we typically change our attitudes, not our behavior, to reduce cognitive dissonance. **5.** d

Impression Formation.   How do we decide that Gail is a flirt, or Andy is a jerk, or Jon is a really nice guy? The earliest work on social cognition was designed to examine **impression formation**, the process by which an individual organizes information about another person to form an overall impression of that person. In one classic study, for instance, students were told that they were about to hear a guest lecturer (Kelley, 1950). One group of students was told that the lecturer was "a rather warm person, industrious, critical, practical, and determined," while a second group was told that he was "a rather cold person, industrious, critical, practical, and determined."

The simple substitution of "cold" for "warm" was responsible for drastic differences in the way the students in each group perceived the lecturer, even though he gave the same talk in the same style in each condition. Students who had been told he was "warm" rated him considerably more positively than students who had been told he was "cold."

The findings from this experiment led to additional research on impression formation that focused on the way in which people pay particular attention to certain unusually important traits—known as **central traits**—to help them form an overall impression of others. According to this work, the presence of a central trait alters the meaning of other traits (Asch, 1946; Widmeyer & Loy, 1988). Hence the description of the lecturer as "industrious" presumably meant something different according to whether it was associated with the central trait "warm" or "cold."

Other work on impression formation has used information-processing approaches (see Chapter 9) to develop mathematically oriented models of how individual personality traits are combined to create an overall impression (Anderson, 1974). Generally, the results of this research suggest that in forming an overall judgment of a person, we use a psychological "average" of the individual traits we see, in a manner that is analogous to finding the mathematical average of several numbers (Kaplan, 1975; Anderson, 1991).

Of course, as we gain more experience with people and see them exhibiting behavior in a variety of situations, our impressions of them become more complex (Anderson & Klatzky, 1987; Casselden & Hampson, 1990). But, because there usually are gaps in our knowledge of others, we still tend to fit them into personality schemas that represent particular "types" of people. For instance, we might hold a "gregarious person" schema, made up of the traits of friendliness, aggressiveness, and openness. The presence of just one or two of these traits might be sufficient to make us assign a person to a particular schema.

Unfortunately, the schemas that we employ are susceptible to a variety of factors that affect the accuracy of our judgments (Kenny, 1991). For example, our mood affects how we perceive others. People who are happy form more favorable impressions and make more positive judgments than people who are in a bad mood (Forgas & Bower, 1987; Erber, 1991).

Even when schemas are not entirely accurate, they serve an important function. They allow us to develop expectations about how others will behave, permitting us to plan our interactions with others more easily, and serving to simplify a complex social world.

Stereotypes: The Negative Side of Social Cognition

What do you think of when someone says, "He's African-American," or "She's Chinese," or "woman driver"? If you're like most people, you'll probably automatically jump to some sort of impression of what that individual is like (Devine,

Impression formation: The process by which an individual organizes information about another individual to form an overall impression of that person

Central traits: The major traits considered in forming impressions of others

▶ **631**

"I'm surprised, Marty. I thought you were one of us."

Ingroup-outgroup bias is the tendency to hold less favorable opinions of those who belong to groups we are not part of.

Stereotype: A kind of schema in which beliefs and expectations about members of a group are held simply on the basis of their membership in that group

Ingroup-outgroup bias: The tendency to hold less favorable opinions about groups to which we do not belong (outgroups), while holding more favorable opinions about groups to which we do belong (ingroups)

Outgroups: Groups to which an individual does not belong

Ingroups: Groups to which an individual belongs

Discrimination: Negative behavior toward members of a particular group

Self-fulfilling prophecy: An expectation about the occurrence of an event or behavior that increases the likelihood that the event or behavior will happen

1989; Gilbert & Hixon, 1991). This fact illustrates an important point: Although schemas can be helpful in organizing the social world, they also have a negative side—particularly when they promote an oversimplified understanding of other people. **Stereotypes**, beliefs and expectations about members of groups held simply on the basis of their membership in those groups, represent one particularly damaging instance of this approach to impression formation.

Some of the most prevalent stereotypes have to do with racial, religious, and ethnic categorizations. Over the years, various groups have been called, for example, "lazy" or "shrewd" or "cruel" with varying degrees of regularity by nongroup members (Katz & Braly, 1933; Weber & Crocker, 1983; Devine & Baker, 1991). Even today, despite major progress toward the reduction of legally sanctioned discrimination, stereotypes are alive and well, as we discuss in the Cutting Edge box.

But stereotypes are by no means confined to racial and ethnic groups. Sex and age stereotyping—which we discussed in Chapters 12 and 14, respectively—are all too common as well. There is even a general stereotype relating to *any* group, known as the **ingroup-outgroup bias** (Wilder, 1986, 1990; Perdue et al., 1990). We tend to hold less favorable opinions about members of groups of which we are not a part (**outgroups**) and more favorable opinions about members of groups to which we belong (**ingroups**).

Although there is little evidence to support the accuracy of most stereotypes, they often have harmful consequences. When negative stereotypes are acted on, they result in **discrimination**—negative behavior toward members of a particular group. Discrimination can lead to exclusion from jobs, neighborhoods, or educational opportunities, and may result in members of particular groups receiving lower salaries and benefits.

Stereotypes not only produce overt discrimination; they can actually *cause* members of stereotyped groups to behave in ways that reflect the stereotype through a phenomenon known as a **self-fulfilling prophecy** (Archibald, 1974). Self-fulfilling prophecies are expectations about the occurrence of a future event or behavior that act to increase the likelihood that the event or behavior *will* occur. For example, if people think that members of a particular group are lazy, they may treat them in a way that actually brings about their laziness (Skrypnek & Snyder, 1982). Similarly, people holding a stereotype may be "primed" to interpret the behavior of the stereotyped group as representative of the stereo-

STEREOTYPES: ALIVE AND WELL IN THE 1990s

Although it might be comforting to think that prejudice in this country is largely restricted to skinheads, neo-Nazis, and members of the Ku Klux Klan, the reality, alas, is quite different: Racial, ethnic, and religious bigotry are commonplace in the United States.

This fact was brought home in a recent large-scale survey conducted in 300 communities throughout the United States. The results of the survey found that expressions of prejudice were routine (T. W. Smith, 1990).

The study used a careful and innovative measurement technique to assess stereotyping. People are often unwilling to express the prejudice they feel because such sentiments violate societal norms of politeness, so indirect assessments of stereotypes were necessary. To do this, participants in the survey were asked to indicate whether people in each of several groups were closer to one or the other ends of a series of seven-point scales. For example, subjects were asked whether each racial group was closer to the end points of "hard-working" or the opposite end, "lazy." By comparing a particular group's ratings against ratings of other groups, it was possible to determine which groups were the most stereotyped.

As you can see in Figure 19-4, which presents some of the survey results, stereotyping is alive and well. For example, 77 percent of respondents believed that African-Americans were more apt than whites to "pre-fer to live off welfare." In general, African-Americans, Hispanics, and Asians were all assumed to be lazier, more violence-prone, less intelligent, and less patriotic than whites.

Furthermore, members of minority groups even stereotyped themselves. For instance, around one-third of African-Americans and Hispanics thought that members of their own group were less intelligent than whites.

Despite the civil rights advances of the past twenty-five years, stereotyping clearly remains common. Hispanics, Asians, and particularly African-Americans are viewed by whites in a negative manner. Until such stereotypes are dispelled, incidents such as the one that started this chapter are likely to find their way into the nightly news.

type, even when the behavior depicts something entirely different (Slusher & Anderson, 1987).

In addition, knowing that others hold a stereotype about you may induce you to behave in line with the stereotype—even if such behavior is not representative of your typical behavior—if you are striving to make a positive impres-

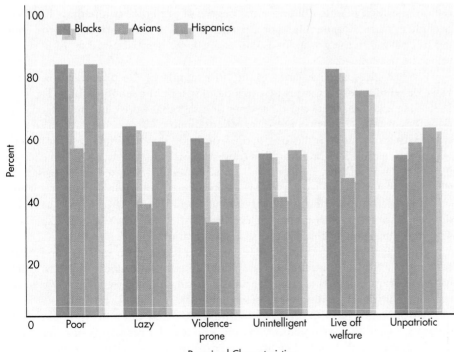

FIGURE 19-4

The percentage of survey respondents holding more negative evaluations for minority group members than they do for whites on each of the characteristics shown. (Source: T. W. Smith, 1990.)

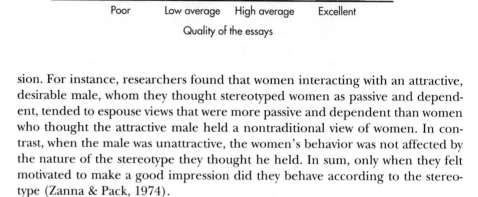

FIGURE 19-5

In an example of reverse discrimination, teachers in an experiment rated essays more positively when they thought they were written by African-American students than when they thought they were written by white students. (Source: Fajardo, 1985.)

Reverse discrimination:
Behavior in which people prejudiced against a group compensate for their prejudice by treating the group's members more favorably than others

sion. For instance, researchers found that women interacting with an attractive, desirable male, whom they thought stereotyped women as passive and dependent, tended to espouse views that were more passive and dependent than women who thought the attractive male held a nontraditional view of women. In contrast, when the male was unattractive, the women's behavior was not affected by the nature of the stereotype they thought he held. In sum, only when they felt motivated to make a good impression did they behave according to the stereotype (Zanna & Pack, 1974).

Reverse Discrimination.   Stereotyping can sometimes lead to reverse discrimination, in which people holding some degree of prejudice compensate for their prejudice by treating members of a particular group *more* favorably than if they did not belong to the group. In a sense, they bend over backward to avoid seeming to be prejudiced.

Psychologist Daniel Fajardo found an example of the phenomenon of **reverse discrimination** in a study he carried out in a public school setting (Fajardo, 1985). He asked teachers to rate a series of essays that were constructed to be of poor, low-average, high-average, or excellent quality. The teachers were also provided with information indicating in one condition that the student authors were white, and in another condition that they were African-American. As you can see in Figure 19-5, at every quality level, the same essay was rated more positively when it was supposedly written by an African-American student than by a white student. In addition, the teachers' tendency to favor the African-American students was strongest with moderate-level essays. In sum, it was average students who were most susceptible to reverse discrimination.

Why was there a discrepancy between the ratings given to "African-American" versus "white" students' essays? When asked, the teachers reported using different grading strategies for African-American students, reading their essays more carefully and grading them more leniently.

As you might imagine, reverse discrimination may often be as damaging as outward, negative discrimination. People who are the recipients of reverse discrimination may feel as if they are "tokens," treated specially, not because of their own talents, but because of their membership in a special group. Furthermore, in academic situations, this special treatment may result in their being passed from grade to grade, without any real effort being made to teach them skills that they might be lacking. Ultimately, such "positive" treatment becomes detrimental.

It is clear from research on stereotyping, then, that the processes of social cognition leading to the creation of schemas both help and hinder social interaction. Although schemas allow us to simplify an otherwise complex social world, they can also lead to oversimplification. We may assume that some people possess certain traits associated with a group just because they are members of that group (Jussim, Coleman, & Lerch, 1987; Hamilton, Sherman, & Ruvolo, 1990).

RECAP AND REVIEW II

RECAP

◀ Social cognition is concerned with the processes that underlie our understanding of the social world. This understanding can be held in the form of schemas—sets of cognitions about people and our social experience.

◀ We often form impressions of others by relying on basic, central traits and combining these individual traits into an overall impression, or by mathematically averaging individual traits into a general impression.

◀ Stereotypes are beliefs and expectations about members of a group formed simply on the basis of their membership in that group.

◀ Stereotypes are frequently held about members of racial, ethnic, sex, and age groups. Although they have little validity, they can produce difficulties in social interaction because of discrimination and self-fulfilling prophecies.

REVIEW

1. A _____ provides a mental framework for us to organize and interpret information about the social world.
2. One theory of impression formation suggests that a few _____ traits shape the way we interpret other characteristics of a person. Another approach, known as _____ _____,

states that we average many individual traits to form an overall impression of a person.
3. Any expectation—positive or negative—about an individual based solely on that person's membership in a group can be a stereotype. True or false? _____
4. The tendency to think most favorably of communities to which we belong is known as:
   a. stereotyping
   b. ingroup-outgroup bias
   c. self-fulfilling prophecy
   d. discrimination
5. Paul is a store manager who does not expect women to succeed in business. He therefore offers important, high-profile responsibilities only to men. If the female employees fail to move up in the company, this could be an example of a _____-_____ prophecy.

Ask Yourself

We have seen that stereotypes can lead to harmful discrimination against a group of people—but that people can go too far in trying to avoid the appearance of bias, resulting in reverse discrimination. How would you try to teach people to recognize and avoid stereotyping, without overcompensating in this way? How might the effects of reverse discrimination be similar to, or different from, other forms of discrimination?

(Answers to review questions are on page 636.)

ATTRIBUTION PROCESSES: UNDERSTANDING THE CAUSES OF BEHAVIOR

When Barbara Washington, a new employee at the Staditron Computer Company, completed a major staffing project two weeks early, her boss, Marian, was delighted. At the next staff meeting, she announced how pleased she was with Barbara and explained that *this* was an example of the kind of performance she was looking for in her staff. The other staff members looked on resentfully, trying to figure out why Barbara had worked night and day to finish the project not just on time, but two weeks early. She must be an awfully compulsive person, they decided.

Attribution theory: The theory that seeks to explain how we decide, on the basis of samples of an individual's behavior, what the specific causes of that behavior are

Situational causes: Causes of behavior that are based on environmental factors

Dispositional causes: Causes of behavior that are based on internal traits or personality factors

Consensus information: The degree to which people behave similarly in the same situation

Consistency information: The degree to which an individual behaves similarly in similar situations

Distinctiveness information: The extent to which a given behavior occurs across different situations

Most of us have, at one time or another, puzzled over the reasons behind someone's behavior. Perhaps it was in a situation similar to the one above, or it may have been under more formal circumstances, such as serving as a judge on a student judiciary board in a cheating case. In contrast to work on social cognition, which describes how people develop an overall impression about others' personality traits, **attribution theory** seeks to explain how we decide, on the basis of samples of an individual's behavior, what the specific causes of that person's behavior are (Weiner, 1985a, 1985b; Jones, 1990).

When trying to understand the causes underlying a given behavior, individuals typically try first to determine whether the cause is situational or dispositional (Heider, 1958). **Situational causes** are those brought about by something in the environment. For instance, someone who knocks over a quart of milk and then cleans it up is probably doing so not because he or she is necessarily a terribly neat person, but because the *situation* is one that requires it. In contrast, a person who spends hours shining the kitchen floor is probably doing so because he or she *is* a neat person—hence, the behavior has a **dispositional cause**, prompted by the person's disposition (his or her internal traits or personality characteristics).

In our example involving Barbara, her fellow employees attributed her behavior to her disposition rather than to the situation. But from a logical standpoint, it is equally plausible that there was something about the situation that caused the behavior. If asked, Barbara might attribute her accomplishment to situational factors, explaining that she had so much other work to do that she just had to get the project out of the way, or that the project was not all that difficult and that it was easy to complete ahead of schedule. To her, then, the reason for her behavior might not be dispositional at all; it could be situational.

How do we determine whether Barbara's behavior is motivated by situational or dispositional factors? Harold Kelley (1967) suggested that people use three types of information to answer this question. First, there is **consensus information**—the degree to which other people behave similarly in the same situation. For instance, if most people would have completed the project two weeks early, Barbara's behavior would be high in consensus, but if most people would have procrastinated, her behavior would be low in consensus. Second, there is **consistency information**—the degree to which the individual would behave similarly in a similar situation. If Barbara always completes her work early, no matter what the project, she is high in consistency. Finally, there is **distinctiveness information**, the extent to which the behavior occurs across other situations. If Barbara gets her work done early only on her job but procrastinates everywhere else, her behavior is high in distinctiveness.

By simultaneously considering all three kinds of information, people are able to make an attribution that is based primarily on dispositional factors or on situational factors. As shown in Figure 19-6, information that is high in consensus, high in consistency, and high in distinctiveness leads to attributions that are situational. In our example, Barbara's behavior would be attributed to the demands of the job. But with situations in which consensus and distinctiveness are low and consistency is high, people tend to make dispositional attributions, assuming the behavior is related to one's personality.

ANSWERS (REVIEW II)

1. schema   **2.** central; information-processing   **3.** True   **4.** b   **5.** self-fulfilling

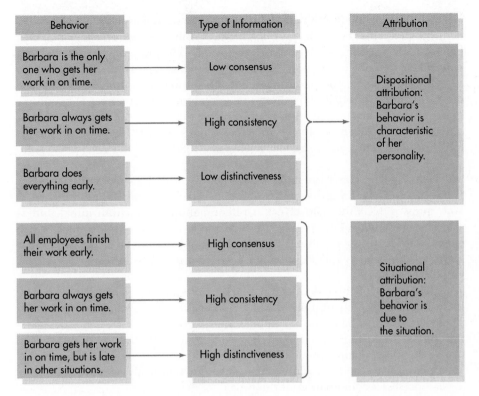

FIGURE 19-6

An illustration of Kelley's model of attribution. Learning that Barbara's behavior represents low consensus, high consistency, and low distinctiveness leads to a dispositional attribution. In contrast, determining that Barbara's behavior represents high consensus, high consistency, and high distinctiveness leads to a situational attribution.

Biases in Attribution: To Err Is Human

If we always processed information in the rational manner that Kelley's model suggests, the world might run a lot more smoothly. Unfortunately, although Kelley's attribution formulation generally makes accurate predictions—at least for cases in which people have concrete, firsthand knowledge of consensus, consistency, and distinctiveness (Hewstone & Jaspars, 1987)—people do not always process information about others in as logical a fashion as the theory seems to suggest (Funder, 1987; Gilbert, Jones, & Pelham, 1987). In fact, research shows that there tend to be consistent biases in the way attributions are made. Among the most typical:

The Fundamental Attribution Bias. One of the most common biases in people's attributions is the tendency to attribute others' behavior to dispositional causes—but one's own behavior to situational causes. Known as the **fundamental attribution bias**, this tendency is quite prevalent (Watson, 1982). For example, an analysis of letters and advice in newspaper columns such as "Dear Abby" and "Ann Landers" showed that writers tended to attribute their own problems to situational factors, while they described the problems of others as due to dispositional causes (Schoeneman & Rubanowitz, 1985). In our own example, we saw how Barbara attributed her behavior to constraints of the environment (situational factors), while Barbara's colleagues thought her behavior was due to her personality characteristics (dispositional factors).

Why should the fundamental attribution bias be so common? One reason has to do with the nature of information that is available to the people making an attribution. When we view the behavior of another person in a particular setting, the information that is most conspicuous is the person's behavior itself.

Fundamental attribution bias:
A tendency to attribute others' behavior to dispositional causes but to attribute one's own behavior to situational causes

Because the individual's immediate surroundings are relatively stable and invariant, the person is the center of our attention. But when we consider our own behavior, changes in the environment are going to be more obvious, and we are more likely to make attributions based on situational factors.

One consequence of the fundamental attribution bias is that we may excuse our own failures by attributing them to extenuating circumstances ("I couldn't finish my paper because the library didn't have the book I needed"), but when others have a problem we blame their personality flaws ("He's just too lazy to finish his paper on time") (Snyder & Higgins, 1988).

The Halo Effect.   Harry is intelligent, kind, and loving. Is he also conscientious?

If you were to hazard a guess, your most likely response would be "yes." Your guess reflects the **halo effect**, a phenomenon in which an initial understanding that a person has positive traits is used to infer other uniformly positive characteristics (Cooper, 1981). The opposite would also hold true. Learning that Harry was unsociable and argumentative would probably lead you to assume he was lazy as well.

Halo effect: A phenomenon in which an initial understanding that a person has positive traits is used to infer other uniformly positive characteristics

The reason for the halo effect is that we hold **implicit personality theories**, theories reflecting our notions of what traits are found together in individuals. These theories are based on a combination of experience and logic. Our perception of the world may be flawed, however, because application of our theory can be singularly inappropriate for a given individual, or it may simply be wrong. Most people have neither uniformly positive nor uniformly negative traits, but instead possess a combination of the two.

Implicit personality theories: Theories reflecting our notions of what traits are found together in individuals

The Pollyanna Effect.   In some respects, people have a blind optimism that is not too different from that of Pollyanna, the heroine of Eleanor Porter's 1913 novel who could see no evil in the world. Because we are typically motivated to view the world as a pleasant, enjoyable place, our perceptions of others are often colored in a positive direction (Sears, 1982). This **Pollyanna effect** produces a tendency to rate others in a generally positive manner.

Pollyanna effect: The tendency to rate others in a generally positive manner

There are several examples of the Pollyanna effect. For instance, the public's evaluation of the U.S. President and other public figures historically is generally positive. Similarly, ratings of other people made by subjects in experiments normally fall in the positive range—even when the people have just met. Humorist Will Rogers may have been reflecting a widespread feeling when he claimed, "I never met a man I didn't like."

Assumed-Similarity Bias.   How similar to you—in terms of attitudes, opinions, and likes and dislikes—are your friends and acquaintances? Most people believe that their friends and acquaintances are fairly similar to themselves. But this feeling goes beyond just people we know; there is a general tendency—known as the **assumed-similarity bias**—to think of people as being similar to oneself, even when meeting them for the first time (Ross, Greene, & House, 1977; Hoch, 1987; Marks & Miller, 1987).

Assumed-similarity bias: The tendency to think of people as being similar to oneself

If other people are, in fact, different from oneself, the assumed-similarity bias reduces the accuracy of the judgments being made. Moreover, it suggests an interesting possibility: It may be that a judgment about another individual better defines the judge's characteristics than those of the person being rated. In some cases, then, the portrait we draw of another person—particularly one about whom we have little information—may in reality be a sketch of the way we view ourselves.

Self-Perception Theory: Understanding Our Own Behavior

The fundamental attribution bias illustrates an important point about attributional processes: People not only make attributions about others; they can sometimes act as observers of their *own* behavior and make attributions on the basis of what they see themselves doing. As we discussed earlier in the chapter in reference to attitudes, Bem's theory of self-perception suggests that people monitor their own behavior and make judgments about themselves on the basis of what they see themselves doing (Bem, 1967). The theory suggests, then, that when situational cues are weak or past experience does not provide relevant information, people will look to their own behavior to make attributions about themselves.

How does the theory work? Suppose you are asked to handle advertising for a play being produced by the campus drama club during the next term. You are pleased to be asked but not too sure you can spare the time, so you tell the person making the request you will get back to her with your decision in a few days. As the days drag on, though, you never seem to have the time to call her back, and you just can't make up your mind. After a few weeks have gone by, you begin to wonder why you can't reach a decision. As you ponder the question, you conclude that your reluctance indicates that you are unenthusiastic and really don't want the job.

Your decision to decline the request is based on self-perception. Using your own behavior as an indication of your underlying motivation, you determine that the hesitancy you observe in yourself is based on a lack of desire to take on the job. Here you are acting much like an outside observer, making an inference on the basis of your behavior. In sum, self-perception theory suggests that we derive knowledge about ourselves by examining our own actions.

Another facet of self-perception is illustrated by the fact that people habitually use a particular style in explaining events in their lives. For example, racial, ethnic, and social-class factors play a role in the kinds of attributions people make. African-Americans, for instance, are less likely than whites to attribute success to internal causes. African-American children tend to feel that the external causes of task difficulty and luck are the major determinants of how well they perform, possibly because societal discrimination has prevented their efforts from yielding success.

In contrast, white children are likely to feel that ability and effort—internal causes—are more important influences on their success (Katz, 1967; Friend & Neale, 1972). Of course, an attributional pattern that overemphasizes the importance of external causes is maladaptive. Attributions to external factors reduce people's sense of personal responsibility for success or failure. But when attributions are based on internal factors, they suggest that a change in behavior—such as increased effort—can bring about a change in success (Graham, 1986; 1990).

Major differences in attributional patterns also exist between members of different nationalities. Students in Japan and China generally tend to attribute their success more to effort (a controllable factor) than to ability (which is fixed and uncontrollable). In comparison, American students tend to overemphasize the importance of ability and play down the relative importance of effort (Holloway, 1988; Hess, Chih-Mei, & McDevitt, 1987).

Such differences in attributional patterns may be the origin of the high achievement of Asian students, who frequently outperform American students in international comparisons of student achievement. Because Japanese and

Asian students tend to believe that academic success is largely the result of effort, whereas Americans tend to attribute it primarily to natural ability.

Chinese students are more likely to assume that academic success results from hard work, they may put greater effort into their academic work than American students, who believe that their inherent ability is a relatively more important determinant of their performance.

The Value of Illusions

The fact that there are psychological benefits to making certain kinds of inaccurate attributions—such as having a consistently optimistic attributional style—tends to fly in the face of much traditional theorizing about the nature of good mental health. A central dictum is that accurate perceptions of the world are a sign of good mental health and that inaccurate or distorted perceptions of reality signify psychological difficulties.

There is, however, increasing evidence to the contrary. Accurate perceptions of reality, at least in terms of oneself, are not always as beneficial as we might first think. Specifically, social psychologist Shelley Taylor concludes that three basic illusions are profitable: holding an unrealistically positive self-evaluation, having an exaggerated perception of control, and being unrealistically optimistic (Taylor & Brown, 1988). Such illusions tend to be associated with better psychological functioning on an everyday basis.

In sum, certain inaccuracies in our perceptions of ourselves may turn out to be beneficial. On the other hand, it is typically better to be precise in our understanding of others. We turn now to ways in which we can learn to form more accurate impressions of others.

The Informed Consumer of Psychology: Forming More Accurate Impressions and Reducing Stereotyping and Prejudice

At one time or another, we've all been guilty of forming an impression of someone and later finding out we were completely off base. For although people try to use the information available to them to construct a meaningful, orderly social world for themselves, there is ample opportunity both in the development of schemas and in attributional processes to make errors, to oversimplify, and thereby to misperceive other people. This would not be of much concern were it not for the fact that once individuals make decisions about others, they act upon these decisions—sometimes with very undesirable consequences. As a result, social psychologists have designed a number of techniques to increase the accuracy with which people can make judgments about others. They have paid particular attention to strategies for reducing the negative effects of stereotyping. Among the most useful of those strategies are the following:

- Increasing contact between the target of stereotyping and the holder of the stereotype. Research has shown that increasing the amount of interaction between people can reduce negative stereotyping (Amir, 1976; Miller & Brewer, 1984). But certain kinds of contact are more likely than others to lead to the development of more accurate schemas. Situations where there is relatively intimate contact, where the individuals are of equal status, or where participants must cooperate with one another or are dependent on one another are most likely to bring about a reduction of stereotyping. Contact seems to be particularly effective, since schemas regarding stereotyped groups become more detailed, individualized, and accurate as the amount of interaction increases. This finding provides part of the basis for such social practices as school integration and fair housing laws (Gaertner et al., 1990; Desforges et al., 1991).

- Making positive values more conspicuous. It is not always necessary to rely on contact to change the nature of schemas and stereotypes. Instead, an alternative approach suggests that people be shown the inconsistencies between values they hold regarding equality and fair treatment of others, on one hand, and negative stereotyping, on the other. For instance, research has shown that people who are made to see that the values they hold regarding equality and freedom are inconsistent with their negative perceptions of minority group members are more likely to work actively against prejudice in the future (Rokeach, 1971).

- Providing information about the objects of stereotyping. Probably the most direct means of changing schemas about the objects of stereotyping is through education, by teaching people to be more aware of the positive characteristics of objects of stereotyping (Langer, Bashner, & Chanowitz, 1985). For instance, once the meaning of puzzling behavior is explained to people holding stereotypes, they may come to appreciate its significance— even though it may still appear foreign and perhaps even threatening (Fiedler, Mitchell, & Triandis, 1971; Landis, Day, McGrew, Thomas, & Miller, 1976).

Each of these strategies for forming more accurate impressions—although not invariably effective—serves to illustrate a major approach taken by social psychologists. In addition, new techniques to stem the tide of prejudice are still being developed, as we discuss in the Psychology at Work box.

The ultimate goal of this work, of course, is to increase the quality of social interaction—something which should follow after people develop a more accurate understanding of one another—and which we discuss further in the next chapter.

One warm spring evening a few years back, an anonymous person—still unidentified—sent notes spewing racial hatred to four African-American students enrolled at Smith College, a small, women's liberal arts college in New England. The incident might well have been written off as just another case of racial bias, which has been on the rise on college campuses (as well as the country as a whole) for the last decade (U.S. Commission on Civil Rights, 1990). However, the college had already gone to some lengths to educate its students about the harmful consequences of prejudice, and the notes indicated that its efforts had not been particularly effective. The incident inspired demonstrations and protests on the college campus.

Ironically, the incident and the protests that followed led to research that spawned the development of a promising new technique for fighting racism. Social psychologist Fletcher Blanchard hired an experimenter to approach students on campus and say that she was conducting an opinion poll for a class (Blanchard, Lilly, & Vaughn, 1991). The purpose of the poll was ostensibly to learn how students felt the college should respond to the racial incident.

At the same time that the experimenter approached a potential subject, a confederate, posing as a student who happened to be passing by, was stopped so that her opinions could also be assessed. The experimenter asked both students how the college should respond to the notes. The confederate responded first and gave one of two prearranged responses. In one condition, she gave an unambiguously extreme antiracist response, endorsing the statement, "The person who is writing these notes should be expelled." In another

FIGHTING PREJUDICE ON CAMPUS

condition, the confederate took a more moderate antiracist point of view, while in a third she took a lukewarm antiracist position.

The outcome was clear: When participants in the experiment heard another individual make strong antiracist responses, they were much more likely to express similar reactions than when hearing another person hold a position that was more accepting of racism. Even when subjects could respond secretly in writing, out of earshot of the confederate, exposure to strong antiracist positions caused participants to espouse more antiracist views themselves.

In sum, hearing another person strongly condemn racism encourages others to denounce prejudice. Why? The primary reason is that public denunciations of racism make public standards, or norms, against racism more prominent. A few outspoken individuals, then, may create an atmosphere in which prejudice is viewed considerably more negatively than one in which others take no stand or take only weak stands.

One important lesson to be learned from the results of the study is that colleges and universities should vigorously promote a climate against racism, and students should be encouraged to publicly state their antiracist views. The research also suggests that institutions of higher learning should have aggressive antiracist policies and respond swiftly to acts of racism. By following such suggestions, norms against prejudice can become more visible, ultimately leading to less tolerance for acts of prejudice and discrimination.

Like many other colleges, Smith College in Northampton, Massachusetts, has been concerned about racism on campus. Research conducted on that campus indicates that attitudes of prejudice can be modified.

RECAP

◄ Attribution theory explains the processes that underlie how we attribute the causes of others' behavior, particularly in terms of situational versus dispositional causes. This is typically done using consensus, consistency, and distinctiveness information.

◄ Attribution processes are affected by a number of biases, including the fundamental attribution bias, the halo effect, the Pollyanna effect, and the assumed-similarity bias.

◄ Self-perception theory suggests that we monitor our own behavior to identify its causes, just as we make attributions about others' behavior, and that people have characteristic attributional styles.

◄ Among the ways of increasing the accuracy of impressions and reducing stereotyping are increasing contact, making positive values conspicuous, and providing information about the targets of stereotyping.

REVIEW

1. Chris is always late for his Monday morning study group. He would be likely to blame his tardiness on the inconvenient time—a _____ factor—while the other members of his group might tend to blame Chris's own irresponsibility or lack of interest, which are _____ factors.

2. You want to determine whether an individual's behavior was motivated by situational or dispositional factors. Match the questions below with the type of information the questions ask for:

_____ 1. Do other people act the same way under similar circumstances?

_____ 2. Has the individual acted the same way under different circumstances?

_____ 3. Has the individual acted the same way under similar circumstances?

a. consensus information
b. consistency information
c. distinctiveness information

3. Monica was happy to lend her textbook to a fellow student who seemed bright and friendly. She was surprised when her classmate did not return it. Her assumption that the bright and friendly student would also be responsible reflects the _____ effect.

4. The tendency to attribute our own failures to extenuating circumstances, but others' behavior to personality flaws, is known as the _____ _____ error.

5. Increased contact with members of a group generally makes our impressions of that group more accurate. True or false? _____

Ask Yourself

We tend to find situational explanations for our own behavior, and dispositional sources for the actions of others. Which of these attributions do you think is more accurate? What are the advantages (and disadvantages) of each attribution style? Could we learn to assess our own behavior more realistically—and should we?

(Answers to review questions are on page 644.)

■ *What are attitudes and how are they formed, maintained, and changed?*

1. In this chapter, we discussed social psychology, the study of the way people's thoughts, feelings, and actions are affected by others, and the nature and causes of individual behavior in social situations.

2. Attitudes, a central topic of study in social psychology, are learned predispositions to respond in a favorable or unfavorable manner to a particular object. The ABC model of attitudes suggests that they have three components: the affect component, the behavior component, and the cognition component. We acquire attitudes through classical conditioning processes, in which a previously neutral object begins to evoke the attitudes associated with another object due to repeated pairings, and through operant conditioning.

3. A number of theories suggest that people try to maintain consistency between attitudes. Cognitive dissonance occurs when two cognitions—attitudes or thoughts—contradict each other and are held simultaneously by an individual. To resolve the contradiction, the person may modify the cognition, change its importance, or deny it, thereby bringing about a reduction in dissonance. However, alternative explanations based on self-perception theory have been proposed to explain dissonance phenomena.

■ *How do we form impressions of what others are like and of the causes of their behavior?*

4. Impressions of others are formed through social cognitions—the processes that underlie our understanding of

▶ **643**

the social world. People develop schemas, which organize information about people and social experiences in memory. Such schemas represent our social life and allow us to interpret and categorize information about others.

5. One of the ways in which people form impressions of others is through the use of central traits, personality characteristics that are given unusually heavy weight when an impression is formed. Information-processing approaches have found that we tend to average sets of traits to form an overall impression.

6. Stereotypes are beliefs and expectations about members of groups held on the basis of membership in those groups. Although they most frequently are used for racial and ethnic groups, stereotypes are also found in categorizations of sex- and age-group membership. Stereotyping can lead not only to discrimination but also to self-fulfilling prophecies, expectations about the occurrence of future events or behaviors that act to increase the likelihood that the event or behavior will actually occur.

7. Attribution theory tries to explain how we understand the causes of behavior, particularly with respect to situational or dispositional factors. To determine causes, people use consensus, consistency, and distinctiveness information.

■ *What are the biases that influence the way in which we view others' behavior?*

8. Even though logical processes are involved, attribution is still prone to error, as the fundamental attribution bias and the prevalence of stereotyping demonstrate. Other biases include the halo effect, in which the initial understanding that a person has positive traits is used to infer other positive characteristics; the Pollyanna effect, the tendency to rate others in a generally positive manner; and the assumed-similarity bias, the tendency to think of people as being similar to oneself.

9. Self-perception theory suggests that attribution processes similar to those we use with others may be used to understand the causes of our own behavior. Furthermore, people have characteristic attributional styles, related to social, ethnic, and social-class factors.

10. An accurate perception of reality, at least in terms of oneself, is not always beneficial. For example, there is increasing evidence that three sorts of illusions—unrealistic positive self-evaluation, exaggerated perceptions of control, and unrealistic optimism—may be adaptive.

■ *How can we make more accurate judgments about others and reduce stereotyping and prejudice?*

11. Among the ways of increasing the accuracy of attributions and impressions are increasing contact, making values apparent, providing information about the target of the attribution or stereotype, and making norms against prejudice conspicuous.

ANSWERS (REVIEW III)
1. situational; dispositional **2.** 1-a; 2-c; 3-b **3.** halo **4.** fundamental attribution **5.** True

KEY TERMS AND CONCEPTS

social psychology (p. 620)

attitudes (p. 621)

ABC model of attitudes (p. 621)

affect component (of attitudes) (p. 621)

behavior component (of attitudes) (p. 621)

cognition component (of attitudes) (p. 621)

vicarious learning (p. 623)

central route processing (p. 625)

peripheral route processing (p. 625)

cognitive dissonance (p. 626)

cognitions (p. 626)

selective exposure (p. 627)

self-perception theory (p. 628)

social cognition (p. 630)

schemas (p. 630)

impression formation (p. 631)

central traits (p. 631)

stereotype (p. 632)

ingroup-outgroup bias (p. 632)

outgroups (p. 632)

ingroups (p. 632)

discrimination (p. 632)

self-fulfilling prophecy (p. 632)

reverse discrimination (p. 634)

attribution theory (p. 636)

situational causes (of behavior) (p. 636)

dispositional causes (of behavior) (p. 636)

consensus information (p. 636)

consistency information (p. 636)

distinctiveness information (p. 636)

fundamental attribution bias (p. 637)

halo effect (p. 638)

implicit personality theories (p. 638)

Pollyanna effect (p. 638)

assumed-similarity bias (p. 638)

20

SOCIAL INFLUENCE AND INTERACTION

GERTRUDE LEWIS AND THE CENTRAL PARK JOGGER

Gertrude Lewis and Kenny.

Fellow runners held a vigil at the site where the 29-year-old Central Park Jogger was attacked.

Kenny spent his first two Christmases in the Harlem hospital where his mother abandoned him, in a roomful of babies with AIDS. His third Christmas he spent in an Albany children's home. There he had the luck to meet his first angel.

Gertrude Lewis spent her days driving a city bus and, every other Saturday, volunteering at the Albany home. "I saw this boy with these beautiful eyes," she recalls, "just looking up and smiling." She was 47 years old, had never married, never had a family of her own. She decided then and there she would become a foster mother.

Now Kenny lies in his crib upstairs in her home, in a house she shares on a tree-lined street. . . . This nursery is merry with orange walls and pictures and 27 watchful stuffed animals. "It's going to be hard to lose him," says Gertrude (Gibbs, 1989, p. 20).

* * *

It was a crime that produced its own special label: "wilding." According to perpetrators of a series of horrific acts that played out one spring evening in New York City's Central Park, wilding referred to the activity of a group running amok, vandalizing, assaulting, and robbing victims at random. It was a practice considered to be "fun" by those engaging in it.

To a jogger who encountered the marauding gang, it was anything but fun. Hit repeatedly with a pipe and a brick, she was sexually assaulted and left for dead. Three-fourths of her blood was lost as a result of the attack, and she suffered permanent brain damage.

LOOKING AHEAD

In these two incidents we see the best and the worst of humanity, examples of some of the extremes of human behavior. Despite their extremity, though, they contain elements that are found in most people's everyday lives, albeit on a considerably less dramatic scale. For instance, we may demonstrate humanitarian behavior by dropping a quarter into a charity collection box. Conversely, we may hurt others by thoughtlessly showing verbal aggression when angered. Both of these behaviors are influenced by social aspects of the world in which we live.

Social influence: The area of social psychology concerned with situations in which the actions of an individual or group affect the behavior of others

This chapter examines people's interactions and social relationships with one another. We begin with a discussion of **social influence**, the area of social psychology that considers situations in which the actions of an individual (or a group) affect the behavior of others. We explore how what others do and say affects our everyday activities, including circumstances in which we submit to, or resist, authority. Next we consider more special and exclusive forms of social relationships: liking and loving. We examine what social psychologists have learned about the ways in which people become attracted to one another, form relationships, and fall in love. The chapter concludes with a look at the factors that underlie some of the most negative and positive social behaviors: aggression and helping.

When you finish reading this chapter, then, you'll be able to answer the following questions about our interactions with others:

■ What are the major sources of social influence and the tactics that are used to bring them about?
■ Why are we attracted to certain people, and what is the progression that social relationships follow?
■ What factors underlie aggression and prosocial behavior?

SOCIAL INFLUENCE

You have just transferred to a new college and are attending your first class. When the professor enters, you find that your fellow classmates all rise, bow down, and then face the back of the room. You do not understand this behavior at all. Is it more likely that you will (1) jump up to join the rest of the class or (2) remain seated?

Based on what research has told us about social influence, the answer to such a question would almost always be the first option. As you undoubtedly know from your own experience, pressures to conform can be painfully strong, and they can bring about changes in behavior that, when considered in perspective, would otherwise never have occurred.

Conformity: Following What Others Do

Conformity is a change in behavior or attitudes brought about by a desire to follow the beliefs or standards of other people. The classic demonstration of pressure to conform comes from a series of studies carried out in the 1950s by Solomon Asch (Asch, 1951). In the experiments, subjects thought they were participating in a test of perceptual skills with a group of six other subjects. The subjects were shown one card with three lines of varying length and a second card which had a fourth line that matched one of the first three (see Figure 20-1). The task was seemingly straightforward: The subjects had to announce aloud which of the first three lines was identical in length to a "standard" line. Because there was always an obvious answer, the task seemed easy to the participants.

Indeed, since the subjects all agreed on the first few trials, the procedure appeared to be quite a simple one. But then something odd began to happen. From the perspective of the subject in the group who got to answer last, all of the first six subjects' answers seemed to be wrong—in fact, unanimously wrong. And this pattern persisted. Over and over again, the first six subjects provided answers that contradicted what the last subject believed to be the correct one. The dilemma that this situation posed for the last subject was whether to follow

Conformity: A change in behavior or attitudes brought about by a desire to follow the beliefs or standards of other people

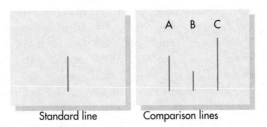

FIGURE 20-1
Subjects in Asch's conformity experiment were first shown a "standard" line and then asked to identify which of the three comparison lines was identical in length. As this example illustrates, there was always an obvious answer.

his or her own perceptions or to follow the group and repeat the answer that everyone else was giving.

As you might have guessed, the situation in the experiment was more contrived than it first appeared. The first six subjects were actually confederates of the experimenter and had been instructed to give unanimously erroneous answers in many of the trials. And the study had nothing to do with perceptual skills. Instead, the issue under investigation was conformity.

What Asch found was that in about one-third of the trials, subjects conformed to the unanimous but erroneous group answer, with about 75 percent of all subjects conforming at least once. However, there were strong individual differences. Some subjects conformed nearly all the time, whereas others never did so.

Since Asch's pioneering work, literally hundreds of studies have examined the factors affecting conformity, and we now know a great deal about the phenomenon (Moscovici, 1985; Tanford & Penrod, 1984). Among the most important variables producing conformity are the following:

Status: The social rank held within a group of an individual

- The characteristics of the group. The more attractive a group is to its members, the greater its ability to produce conformity. The lower the **status**—the social rank held within a group—of a person and the greater the similarity of the individual to the group, the greater is the power of the group over the individual's behavior.

- The nature of the individual's response. Conformity is considerably higher when people must make a response publicly than when they can respond privately, as our founding fathers noted when they authorized secret ballots in voting.

- The kind of task. People working on tasks and questions that are ambiguous (having no clear answer) are more susceptible to social pressure. Giving an opinion, such as on what type of clothing is fashionable, is more likely to produce conformity than answering a question of fact. Moreover, tasks at which an individual is less competent relative to the group create conditions in which conformity is more likely.

Social supporter: A person who shares an unpopular opinion or attitude of another group member, thereby encouraging nonconformity

- Unanimity of the group. Conformity pressures are most pronounced in groups that are unanimous in their support of a position. But what of the case in which people with dissenting views have an ally in the group, known as a **social supporter**, who agrees with them? Having just one person present who shares the unpopular point of view is sufficient to reduce conformity pressures (Allen, 1975; Levine, 1989).

Gender Differences in Conformity: Fact or Fiction? Are women more likely to conform than men? The answer to this question has seesawed back and forth for the last two decades.

For many years, the prevailing wisdom was that women were more easily influenced than men—a view that held until the late 1970s (Allen, 1965). At that time, however, research suggested that the difference was more apparent than real. For example, it seemed that the tasks and topics employed in conformity experiments were often more familiar to men than to women. This unfamiliarity led women to conform more than men because of their feelings that they lacked expertise and not because of any ingrained susceptibility to conformity pressures (Eagly, 1978; Eagly & Carli, 1981).

More recent views, however, have returned to the older conclusion: Women do seem to conform more to others than men, relatively independent of the topic at hand (Eagly, 1989). What causes them to conform are the traditional societal expectations society holds for women, which suggest that women should be concerned more than men in getting along well with others.

Consequently, the best summation of the research on conformity to date is that women are more susceptible to social influence than men, but primarily under public conditions. Still, the topsy-turvy nature of the interpretation of the conformity research suggests that we have not heard the last word on this issue.

Compliance: Submitting to Direct Social Pressure

When we discuss conformity, we are usually talking about a phenomenon in which the social pressure is not in the form of a direct order. But in some situations social pressure is much more obvious, and there is direct, explicit pressure to endorse a particular point of view or to behave in a certain way. Social psychologists call the type of behavior that occurs in response to direct social pressure **compliance**.

Compliance: Behavior that occurs in response to direct social pressure

The Foot in the Door: When a Small Request Leads to a Larger One.
A salesperson comes to your door and asks you to accept a small sample. You agree, thinking you have nothing to lose. A little while later comes a larger request, which, because you have already agreed to the first one, you have a harder time turning down.

The salesperson in this case is employing a tried-and-true strategy that social psychologists call the foot-in-the-door technique. According to the **foot-in-the-door technique**, you first ask that a person agree to a small request and later ask the person to comply with a more important one. It turns out that compliance with the ultimate request increases significantly when the person first agrees to the smaller favor.

Foot-in-the-door technique: A technique in which compliance with an important request is more likely to occur if it follows compliance with a smaller previous request

The foot-in-the-door phenomenon was first demonstrated in a study in which a number of experimenters went door to door asking residents to sign a petition in favor of safe driving (Freedman & Fraser, 1966). Almost everyone complied with this small, benign request. However, a few weeks later, different experimenters contacted the residents again and asked for a much larger request: that they erect a huge sign reading ''Drive Carefully'' on their front lawns. The results were clear: 55 percent of those who had signed the petition agreed to the request, whereas only 17 percent of people in a control group who had not been asked to sign the petition agreed.

Subsequent research has confirmed the effectiveness of the foot-in-the-door technique (Beaman et al., 1983). Why does it work? One reason is that involvement with the small request leads to an interest in an issue, and taking an action—any action—makes the individual more committed to the issue, thereby increasing the likelihood of future compliance. Another explanation revolves around people's self-perceptions. By complying with the initial request, individuals may come to see themselves as the kind of person who provides help when asked. Then, when confronted with the larger request, they agree in order to maintain the kind of consistency in attitudes and behavior that we described in Chapter 19. Although we don't know which of these two explanations is more accurate, it is clear that the foot-in-the-door strategy is effective (Dillard, 1991).

The Door-in-the-Face Technique: Where a Large Request Leads to a Smaller One.
A fund raiser comes to your door and asks for a $500 contribution. You laughingly refuse, telling her that the amount is way out of your league. She then asks for a $10 contribution. What do you do? If you are like most people, you'll

Door-in-the-face technique:
A strategy in which a large
request, refusal of which is
expected, is followed by a
smaller request

probably be a lot more compliant than if she hadn't asked for the huge contribution first. The reason lies in the **door-in-the-face technique**, in which a large request, refusal of which is expected, is followed by a smaller one. Clearly a totally opposite strategy to the foot-in-the-door approach, the door-in-the-face technique has also proved to be effective (Dillard, 1991).

One example of its success was shown in a field experiment in which college students were stopped on the street and asked to agree to a substantial favor—acting as unpaid counselors for juvenile delinquents two hours a week for two years (Cialdini et al., 1975). Not surprisingly, no one agreed to such an enormous commitment. But when they were later asked the considerably smaller favor of taking a group of delinquents on a two-hour trip to the zoo, half the people complied. In comparison, only 17 percent of a control group of subjects who had not first received the larger request agreed.

The use of this technique is widespread in everyday life. You may have used it at some point yourself, perhaps by asking your parents for a very large increase in your allowance and later settling for less. Similarly, television writers sometimes sprinkle their scripts with obscenities that they know will be cut out by network censors, hoping to keep other key phrases intact (Cialdini, 1988).

Reciprocal concessions: A
phenomenon in which
requesters are perceived as
compromising their initial
request, thereby inviting a
compromise from the
individual being asked to
comply

Why is the door-in-the-face procedure effective? One contributing factor is the reciprocal concessions that are occurring between the person making the request and the individual being asked. In **reciprocal concessions**, requesters are seen to make a compromise (reducing their initial request), thereby inviting a compromise on the part of those who initially refused the request. The result is that people are more willing to comply with the smaller request.

The other reason that the door-in-the-face technique works rests in our desire to present ourselves well to others. When we first refuse, we believe we have acted reasonably, but a second refusal can make us feel that we are coming across as uncooperative. We comply, then, to enhance the way we present ourselves to others. (Several other compliance techniques that you might encounter are described in the accompanying Psychology at Work box.)

Obedience: Obeying Direct Orders

Obedience: A change in
behavior due to the
commands of others

Compliance techniques provide a means by which people are gently led toward agreement with another person's request. In some cases, however, requests are geared toward producing **obedience**, a change in behavior that is due to the commands of others. Although obedience is considerably less common than conformity and compliance, it does occur in several specific kinds of relationships. For example, we may show obedience to our boss, teacher, or parent, merely because of the power they hold to reward or punish us.

To acquire an understanding of obedience, consider, for a moment, how you might respond if a stranger said to you:

> I've devised a new way of improving memory. All I need is for you to teach people a list of words and then give them a test. The test procedure requires only that you give learners a shock each time they make a mistake on the test. To administer the shocks you will use a "shock generator" that gives shocks ranging from 30 to 450 volts. You can see that the switches are labeled from "slight shock" through "danger: severe shock" at the top level, where there are three red X's. But don't worry; although the shocks may be painful, they will cause no permanent damage.

Presented with this situation, you would be likely to think that neither you nor anyone else would go along with the stranger's unusual request. Clearly, it lies outside the bounds of what we consider good sense.

You've found the car of your dreams, at a great price. Although it took a bit of dickering, you feel quite successful with your negotiating skills.

After completing a raft of purchase forms, the salesperson goes off to get the manager's signature to finalize the deal. After a few minutes, though, he returns, looking sheepish. "I'm sorry," he says. "My boss won't OK the deal. He says the dealership would lose money." More sheepish looks. "But consider this: If we can just increase the price you've agreed to by $600, he'll OK it." After thinking it over a bit, you decide to bite the bullet, and agree to the price increase. After all, what is $600 in the context of a deal involving tens of thousands of dollars?

You've been had. In this case, you're the victim of a time-honored sales tradition called low-balling. In **low-balling**, an agreement is reached, but then the seller reveals additional costs. The technique works because after committing ourselves to an initial decision, we run through the advantages of the deal in our minds, justifying our own judgment. But just as we've fully convinced ourselves that we've made a good move, the deal comes unglued, and the price goes up. Because we've done such a good job of convincing ourselves of the virtue of our decision, our tendency is to stick with the deal, despite its higher cost (Cialdini, 1988).

Low-balling is just one of several techniques that salespeople use to ensnare customers—techniques

THE PRICE IS RIGHT? THE PRACTICE OF SOCIAL INFLUENCE

A salesperson who made a pitch based on one price and then came back with a higher quote once the customer had decided to buy would be accused of low-balling.

that have been explained by social psychologists studying compliance. Two of the others that you're most apt to encounter are the following:

■ *The that's-not-all technique.* In this procedure, you're offered a deal at an inflated price. But immediately following the initial offer, the salesperson offers an incentive, discount, or bonus to clinch the deal.

Although it sounds transparent, such a practice can be quite effective. In one study, the experimenters set up a booth and sold cupcakes for 75 cents each. In one condition, customers were

told directly that the price was 75 cents. But in another condition, they were told the price was $1.00, but had been reduced to 75 cents. As the that's-not-all technique would predict, more cupcakes were sold at the reduced price—even though it was identical to the cost in the other experimental condition (Burger, 1986).

■ *The not-so-free sample.* If you're ever given a free sample, keep in mind that it comes with a psychological cost. Although they may not couch it in these terms, salespeople who provide samples to potential customers do so in order to instigate the norm of reciprocity. The norm of reciprocity is the well-accepted societal standard dictating that we should treat other people as they treat us. Receipt of a free sample, then, suggests the need for reciprocation—in the form of a sale, of course (Cialdini, 1988).

The three social influence tactics described here (low-balling, the that's-not-all technique, and the not-so-free sample) are ones that you're apt to encounter many times in your life as a consumer. You'll be at an advantage, though: Often the best way to resist them is to be aware of what they are and then to remove yourself from the situation. For example, if you find yourself in a low-ball situation when purchasing a car, the best countercompliance strategy is to get up and walk away. Almost always, the salesperson will figure out a way to return to the original figure. And if not, there's always another car dealership.

Or does it? Suppose the stranger asking for your help were a psychologist conducting an experiment. Or suppose it were your teacher, your employer, or your military commander—all people in authority with some seemingly legitimate reason for their request.

If you still think it unlikely that you would comply, you might reconsider. For the situation represented above describes a now-classic experiment conducted by social psychologist Stanley Milgram in the 1960s (Milgram, 1974). In

Low-balling: A sales strategy in which, after an agreement is reached, the seller reveals additional costs

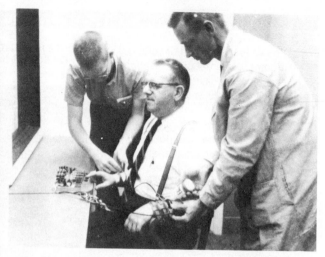

FIGURE 20-2

This impressive-looking "shock generator" was used to lead participants to believe they were administering electric shocks to another person, who was connected to the generator by electrodes that were attached to the skin. (Copyright 1965 by Stanley Milgram. From the film *Obedience*, distributed by the New York University Film Library and Pennsylvania State University, PCR.)

the study, subjects were placed in a situation in which they were told by an experimenter to give increasingly strong shocks to another person as part of a study on learning (see Figure 20-2). In reality, the experiment had nothing to do with learning; the real issue under consideration was the degree to which subjects would comply with the experimenter's requests. In fact, the person supposedly receiving the shocks was actually a confederate who never really received any punishment.

Most people who hear a description of the experiment feel that it is unlikely that *any* subject would give the maximum level of shock—or, for that matter, any shock at all. Even a group of psychiatrists to whom the situation was described predicted that fewer than 2 percent of the subjects would comply completely and administer the strongest shocks. However, the actual results contradicted both experts' and nonexperts' predictions. Almost two-thirds of the subjects eventually used the highest setting on the shock generator to "electrocute" the learner.

Why did so many individuals comply fully with the experimenter's demands? Extensive interviews carried out with subjects following the experiment showed that they were obedient primarily because they believed that the experimenter would be responsible for any potential ill effects that befell the learner. The experimenter's orders were accepted, then, because the subjects thought that they personally could not be held accountable for their actions—they could always blame the experimenter.

Although the Milgram experiment has been criticized for creating an extremely trying set of circumstances for the subjects—thereby raising serious ethical questions—and on methodological grounds (A. G. Miller, 1986; Orne & Holland, 1968), it remains one of the strongest laboratory demonstrations of obedience (Blass, 1991). We need only consider actual instances of obedience to authority to witness some frightening real-life parallels. A major defense of Nazi officers after World War II, for instance, was that they were "only following orders." Milgram's results force each of us to consider how able we would be to withstand the intense power of authority.

The Informed Consumer of Psychology: Strategies for Maintaining Your Own Position

We have seen how susceptible people are to the influence of others, whether it be relatively indirect, as with subtle conformity pressure, or direct, as with a straightforward order. How can one remain independent in the face of these sorts of pressures? Social psychological theory and research have suggested a number of techniques for helping one to remain faithful to one's own point of view:

■ *Inoculation.* To avoid smallpox, people receive a shot containing a small dose of smallpox germs. This injection produces antibodies in the body that can repel a major invasion of smallpox germs if the individual should be exposed to the disease in the future. Similarly, one procedure for helping people remain independent of future attempts at persuasion is for them to expose themselves to a sample of counterarguments to which they might be subjected in the future. In an example of this technique, William McGuire (1964) demonstrated that subjects could be made more resistant to persuasion if they were first exposed to a sample of opposing arguments along with information that refuted those arguments. Exposure to the opposing arguments—**inoculation**, as he called it—led to less subsequent change in beliefs than exposing subjects to information that bolstered their own initial views.

Inoculation: Exposure to arguments opposing one's beliefs, making the subject more resistant to later attempts to change those beliefs

■ *Forewarning.* Telling people that a persuasive message is coming and what that message involves, a strategy called **forewarning**, is sometimes sufficient to reduce social influence, even if counterarguments are not provided. This is particularly true if the issues are important and the target of influence has a large amount of information available (Cacioppo & Petty, 1979; Petty & Cacioppo, 1977). Simply knowing that a persuasive message is likely to be received without knowing the specific content of the upcoming message can reduce subsequent attitude change. The reason? When people are aware that they are going to receive information counter to their attitudes, they tend to develop their own arguments in support of their original attitudes. Forewarned is thus forearmed.

Forewarning: A procedure in which a subject is told in advance that a persuasive message is forthcoming, sometimes reducing the effects of social influence

■ *Consistency.* One technique that is not only effective in reducing persuasibility but that can actually change the attitude of the persuader is **consistency**. Under certain conditions, particularly in group settings where a majority is attempting to influence a minority, the unyielding persistence of the minority in its point of view can actually bring about a change in the majority's attitudes (Moscovici & Mugny, 1983; Clark & Maass, 1990). Apparently, the unyielding repetition of one's own point of view can cause others to rethink their position and, ultimately, to be persuaded by the minority's opinion.

Consistency: The persistence of those holding an unpopular view, eventually bringing about a change in the attitude of the majority

On the other hand, some evidence suggests that a slightly different approach is more effective. Social psychologist Edwin Hollander (1980) has addressed situations in which a minority is attempting to remain independent of a majority position. He suggests a strategy in which individuals conform initially to the views of the source of influence. After doing so, which establishes them as competent and reasonable group members, they can behave more independently and espouse views that are contrary to the majority's views. According to Hollander's theory, instead of remaining consistently firm in a deviant position, as Moscovici's consistency approach suggests, people should first conform—but after establishing their "credentials," they should then press their minority views.

Experimental evidence supports both approaches (Lortie-Lussier, 1987; Maas & Clark, 1984; Clark & Maas, 1988). Such research makes it clear that social influence is not a one-way street; when we are the targets of social influence, we have a fighting chance to remain independent.

RECAP

◄ Social influence encompasses situations in which the actions of one individual or group affect the behavior of another.

◄ Conformity is a change in attitude or behavior brought about by a desire to follow the beliefs or standards of others.

◄ Compliance is a change in behavior made in response to more explicit social pressure. Obedience, in contrast, is a change in behavior resulting from a direct command.

◄ Among the primary techniques for remaining independent of group pressure are inoculation, forewarning, and consistency.

REVIEW

1. A _____ _____, or person who agrees with the dissenting viewpoint, is likely to reduce conformity.

2. Who pioneered the study of conformity?
   a. Skinner   c. Milgram
   b. Asch   d. Fiala

3. Which of the following techniques asks a person to comply with a small initial request which later makes a larger request more likely to be complied with?
   a. Door-in-the-face   c. Small favor paradigm
   b. Foot-in-the-door   d. Low-balling

4. The _____ - _____ - _____ - _____ technique begins with an outrageous request which then makes a smaller request seem reasonable.

5. The technique described in the previous question works in part due to _____ _____, a compromise made by a person that invites a compromise in return.

6. _____ is a change in behavior that is due to another person's orders.

7. Match the technique used to guard against attitude change with its definition:
   _____ 1. Forewarning
   _____ 2. Inoculation
   _____ 3. Consistency

   a. Maintaining a minority position; may cause majority to rethink its position
   b. Telling people a persuasive communication is coming
   c. Giving people samples of counterattitudinal arguments

Ask Yourself

Given that persuasive techniques like those described in this section are so powerful, should there be laws against the use of such techniques? Should people be taught defenses against such techniques? Is the use of such techniques ethically and morally defensible?

(Answers to review questions are on page 658.)

LIKING AND LOVING: INTERPERSONAL ATTRACTION AND THE DEVELOPMENT OF RELATIONSHIPS

When nineteenth-century poet Elizabeth Barrett Browning wrote "How do I love thee? Let me count the ways," she was expressing feelings about a topic that is central to most people's lives—and one that has developed into a major subject of investigation by social psychologists: loving and liking. Known more formally as the study of **interpersonal attraction** or close relationships, this topic encompasses the factors that lead to positive feelings for others.

Interpersonal attraction: Positive feelings for others; liking and loving

How Do I Like Thee? Let Me Count the Ways

By far the greatest amount of research has focused on liking, probably because it has always proved easier for investigators conducting short-term experiments to produce states of liking in strangers who have just met than to promote and observe loving relationships over long periods of time. Hence traditional studies have given us a good deal of knowledge about the factors that initially attract two people to each other (Berscheid, 1985). Among the most important factors considered by social psychologists are the following:

- *Proximity.* If you live in a dormitory or an apartment, consider the friends you made when you first moved in. Chances are you became friendliest with those who lived geographically closest to you. In fact, this is one of the most well-established findings in the interpersonal attraction literature: **Proximity** leads to liking (Festinger, Schachter, & Back, 1950; Nahome & Lawton, 1976).

- *Mere exposure.* Repeated exposure to a person is often sufficient to produce attraction. Interestingly, repeated exposure to *any* stimulus—be it a person, picture, record, or what have you—most frequently makes us like the stimulus more (Zajonc, 1968; M. Bornstein, 1989). Becoming familiar with a stimulus can evoke positive feelings; these positive feelings stemming from familiarity are then transferred to the stimulus itself. There are exceptions, though. In cases in which the initial interactions are strongly negative, repeated exposure is unlikely to cause us to like another person more; instead, the more we are exposed to him or her, the more we may dislike such an individual.

- *Similarity.* Folk wisdom tells us that birds of a feather flock together. Unfortunately, it also maintains that opposites attract.

  Social psychologists have come up with a clear verdict regarding which of the two statements is correct: We tend to like those who are similar to us. Discovering that others are similar in terms of attitudes, values, or traits promotes liking for them. Furthermore, the more similar others are, the more we like them (Byrne, 1969; Hill & Stull, 1981; Carli, Ganley, & Pierce-Otay, 1991).

  One reason similarity increases the likelihood of interpersonal attraction is that we assume that people with similar attitudes will evaluate us positively (Condon & Crano, 1988). Because there is a strong **reciprocity-of-liking effect** (a tendency to like those who like us), knowing that someone evaluates us positively will promote attraction to that person. In addition, we assume that when we like someone else, that person likes us in return (Metee & Aronson, 1974; Tagiuri, 1958).

- *Need complementarity.* We all know exceptions to the general rule that similarity is related to attraction. Some couples seem totally mismatched in terms of personality, interests, and attitudes, yet are clearly quite captivated with one another.

  Social psychologists have explained instances in which people are attracted to dissimilar others by considering the needs that their partners fulfill. According to this reasoning, we may be attracted to those people who fulfill the greatest number of needs for us. Thus a dominant person may seek out someone who is submissive; at the same time, the submissive individual may be seeking someone who is dominant. Although their dissimilarity often makes others expect them to be incompatible, by forming a relationship they are able to fulfill each other's complementary needs.

  The hypothesis that people are attracted to others who fulfill their needs—dubbed the **need-complementarity hypothesis**—was first proposed in the late 1950s in a classic study which found that a sample of married couples appeared to have complementary needs (Winch, 1958). Although research attempting to support the concept since that time has been wildly inconsistent, it does seem that in some realms the hypothesis holds. For example, people with complementary abilities may be attracted to one another. In one study, schoolchildren developed friendships with others whose

The proximity of neighbors is one factor that leads us to like them: We tend to be attracted to those who are geographically close to us.

Proximity: Nearness to another, one cause for liking

Reciprocity-of-liking effect: The tendency to like those who like us

Need-complementarity hypothesis: The hypothesis that people are attracted to others who fulfill their needs

academic skills were in areas distinct from those in which they felt particularly competent, thereby allowing them to stand out in different subjects from their friends. A good mathematics student, then, might form a friendship with someone particularly good in English (Tesser, 1988).

In general, though, most evidence suggests that attraction is related more to similarity than to complementarity (e.g., Meyer & Pepper, 1977). Whether in the area of attitudes, values, or personality traits, then, similarity remains one of the best predictors of whether two people will be attracted to each other.

■ *Physical attractiveness.* For most people, the equation *beautiful = good* is a very real one. As a result, people who are physically attractive are more popular than those who are physically unattractive, if all other factors are equal. This finding, which contradicts the values that most people would profess, is apparent even in childhood—with nursery-school-age children rating popularity on the basis of attractiveness (Dion & Berscheid, 1974)—and continues into adulthood. Indeed, physical attractiveness may be the single most important element promoting initial liking in college dating situations, although its influence eventually decreases when people get to know each other better (Berscheid & Walster, 1974; Hatfield & Sprecher, 1986).

One of the remarkable things about physical attractiveness is the degree of consensus about what constitutes beauty. People have clear and similar preferences regarding the specific dimensions of facial configuration which make a face attractive (Cunningham, 1986; Cunningham, Barbee, & Pike, 1990).

ANSWERS (REVIEW I):

1. social supporter **2.** b **3.** b **4.** door-in-the-face **5.** reciprocal concession **6.** Obedience
7. 1-b; 2-c; 3-a

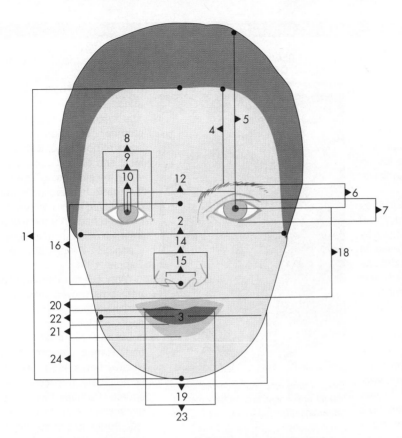

FIGURE 20-3

In order to determine the facial configuration that was seen as most attractive, researchers measured each of the numbered distances on a series of photos that had been previously rated by a group of judges according to how physically and socially attractive they appeared. The results showed that there was surprising uniformity across judges and that several common proportions existed. For example, the "ideal" female face had a chin length that was one-fifth the height of the face. (Cunningham, 1986.)

In research investigating the question of what constitutes beauty, groups of males and females rated the attractiveness and social attributes of women and men from pictures of their faces. From the ratings of the faces, the characteristics of the perceived ideal female and male face could be quantified. For example, the ideal female face had large eyes, small nose, high cheekbones and narrow cheeks. For men, the ideal included prominent cheekbones and a large chin, along with large eyes and a small nose. It was even possible to calculate precise configurations of facial features, using the different measures illustrated in Figure 20-3. For example, the ideal female face had an eye width (No. 12 in the figure) that was three-tenths the width of the face at the level of the eyes (No. 2). Similarly, the distance from the center of the eye to the bottom of the eyebrow (No. 6) was one-tenth the height of the face (No. 1).

It is important to understand, of course, that such proportions represent composite ideals, not those dimensions found in any particular individual. Furthermore, the emphasis on facial configuration discounts the influence of personality traits on the way in which individuals are perceived. Still, the influence of beauty is clearly an important one in everyday interactions, and its influence may even start at the time of birth, as we discuss in the Cutting Edge box, p. 660.

Although physical attractiveness provides many advantages, it also has its downside. While good looks lead to more positive impressions of men in job-related situations, beauty can work against women in managerial positions. The reason is a common (although totally unfounded) stereotype that

Julia Roberts. Kevin Costner. Michelle Pfeiffer. Richard Gere.

Most people would have little trouble agreeing that each of these individuals is clearly attractive. But few of us would be able to express how we know what an attractive person is or where we get our yardsticks for determining how attractive particular people are.

For many years, it was assumed that standards of beauty were gradually learned from the standards set by a particular society. Most research evidence suggested that standards of beauty were not particularly well understood until children became 3 or 4 years of age (Adams & Crane, 1980).

Recent evidence, however, suggests otherwise. According to this work, even very young infants are able to differentiate between attractive and unattractive faces. In one study, for example, 6- to 8-month-old infants were shown pairs of photos—one of a woman judged attractive by adults, and the other of a woman judged unattractive (Langlois et al., 1987). The infants spent significantly more time looking at the attractive faces than the unattractive faces,

IS BEAUTY IN THE EYE OF THE BABY?

Even among very young children, physical attractiveness is a primary factor in determining popularity.

suggesting that the attractive faces were more interesting to them.

But attractiveness produces more than just higher levels of attention; it also seems to lead babies to show greater social responsivity. In one

study, for example, 1-year-olds encountered a stranger wearing a professionally built mask that was either attractive or unattractive. The infants meeting the attractive-stranger condition showed more signs of positive emotions, withdrew less, and played more actively than when the stranger wore the unattractive mask. In a second study, 1-year-olds played significantly longer with a doll who had an attractive face than a similar doll with an unattractive face (Langlois, Roggman, & Rieser-Danner, 1990).

Why did the infants in these experiments show a preference for the attractive faces? Not much learning about societal standards of beauty could have occurred prior to the age of 1. Rather, the preference for attractive faces seems likely to have some innate, genetically determined source. Perhaps faces of particular dimensions and configurations provide some sort of socially useful information. We don't know yet why some kinds of faces are preferred over others, but it is clear that faces judged attractive elicit greater positive responses from all age groups, beginning with infants.

successful, attractive women attain their positions as a result of their looks rather than their abilities (Heilman & Stopek, 1985; Schellhardt, 1991).

In general, though, physical attractiveness is an asset in social situations. It is a powerful factor in determining to whom people are attracted and the kind of social life people have (Reis et al., 1982; Hatfield & Sprecher, 1986).

The factors that we have discussed are not, of course, the only constituents of liking. For example, survey research has sought to identify the factors critical in friendships. In a questionnaire answered by some 40,000 respondents, the qualities that were most valued in a friend were identified as the ability to keep confidences, loyalty, and warmth and affection, followed closely by supportiveness, frankness, and a sense of humor (Parlee, 1979). The results are summarized in Figure 20-4.

How Do I Love Thee? Let Me Count the Ways

Whereas our knowledge of what makes people like one another is extensive, our understanding of love is a more limited and relatively recent phenomenon. For some time, many social psychologists believed that love represented a phenom-

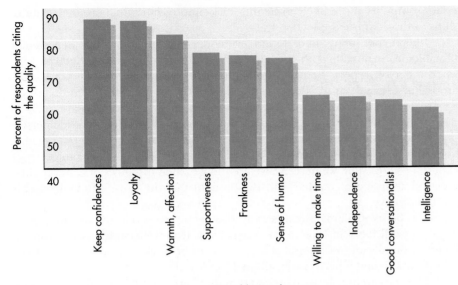

FIGURE 20-4

These are the key qualities looked for in a friend, according to some 40,000 respondents to a questionnaire.

enon too difficult to observe and study in a controlled, scientific way. However, love is such a central issue in most people's lives that, in time, social psychologists could not resist its allure and became infatuated with the topic.

As a first step, researchers tried to identify the distinguishing characteristics between mere liking and full-blown love (Sternberg, 1987). Using this approach, they discovered that love is not simply liking of a greater quantity, but a qualitatively different psychological state (Walster & Walster, 1978). For instance, at least in its early stages, love includes relatively intense physiological arousal, an all-encompassing interest in another individual, fantasizing about the other, and relatively rapid swings of emotion. Similarly, love, unlike liking, includes elements of passion, closeness, fascination, exclusiveness, sexual desire, and intense caring (Davis, 1985; Hendrick & Hendrick, 1989).

Several social psychologists have tried to capture the elusive nature of love using paper-and-pencil measures. For example, Zick Rubin (1970, 1973) tried to differentiate between love and liking using a paper-and-pencil scale. Keep a particular individual in mind as you answer these questions from his scale:

- ■ I feel I can confide in _____ about virtually everything.
- ■ I would do almost anything for _____.
- ■ I feel responsible for _____'s well-being.

A positive response to each question provides an indication of love for the individual you have in mind. Now answer these questions, also drawn from Rubin's scale:

- ■ I think that _____ is unusually well adjusted.
- ■ I think that _____ is one of those people who quickly wins respect.
- ■ _____ is one of the most likable people I know.

These three questions are designed to measure liking, as opposed to loving. Researchers have found that couples scoring high on the love scale differ considerably from those with low scores. They gaze at each other more, and their

Passionate (or romantic) love:
A state of intense absorption
in someone that is
characterized by physiological
arousal, psychological interest,
and caring for another's
needs

Companionate love: The
strong affection we have for
those with whom our lives are
deeply involved

Intimacy component: In
Sternberg's classification
of types of love, feelings of
closeness and connectedness

Passion component: In
Sternberg's classification of
types of love, the motivational
drives relating to sex, physical
closeness, and romance

**Decision/commitment
component:** In Sternberg's
classification of types of love,
the initial cognition that one
loves someone, and the
longer-term feelings of
commitment

relationships are more likely to be intact six months later than are the relation-ships of those who score low on the scale.

Other experiments have found evidence suggesting that the heightened physiological arousal hypothesized to be characteristic of loving is indeed present when a person reports being in love. Interestingly, though, it may not be just arousal of a sexual nature. Berscheid & Walster (1974) have theorized that when we are exposed to *any* stimulus that increases physiological arousal—such as danger, fear, or anger—we may label our feelings as love for another person present at the time of the arousal. This is most likely to occur if there are situa-tional cues that suggest that "love" is an appropriate label for the feelings being experienced. In sum, we perceive we are in love when instances of general phys-iological arousal are coupled with the thought that the cause of the arousal is most likely love.

This theory explains why a person who keeps being rejected or hurt by an-other can still feel "in love" with that person. If the rejection leads to physio-logical arousal, but the arousal still happens to be attributed to love—and not to rejection—then a person will still feel "in love."

Other researchers have theorized that there are actually several kinds of love (Hendrick, Hendrick, & Adler, 1988; Hendrick & Hendrick, 1988; Fehr & Rus-sell, 1991). Some distinguish between two main types of love: passionate love and companionate love. **Passionate (or romantic) love** represents a state of intense absorption in someone. It includes intense physiological arousal, psychological interest, and caring for the needs of another. In contrast, **companionate love** is the strong affection that we have for those with whom our lives are deeply in-volved. The love we feel for our parents, other family members, and even some close friends falls into the category of companionate love.

According to psychologist Robert Sternberg (1986), an even finer differen-tiation between types of love is in order. He proposes that love is made up of three components: an **intimacy component**, encompassing feelings of closeness and connectedness; a **passion component**, made up of the motivational drives relating to sex, physical closeness, and romance; and a **decision/commitment component**, encompassing the initial cognition that one loves someone, and the longer-term feelings of commitment to maintain love. As seen in Table 20-1, particular combinations of the three components produce eight kinds of love.

TABLE 20-1

THE KINDS OF LOVE

	Component*		
	Intimacy	Passion	Decision/Commitment
Nonlove	−	−	−
Liking	+	−	−
Infatuated love	−	+	−
Empty love	−	−	+
Romantic love	+	+	−
Companionate love	+	−	+
Fatuous love	−	+	+
Consummate love	+	+	+

* + = component present; − = component absent.
Source: Sternberg, 1986, Table 2.

With more than one out of two marriages ending in divorce, and broken love affairs a common phenomenon, it is not surprising that social psychologists have begun to turn their attention increasingly toward understanding how relationships develop, are maintained—and, in some cases, dissolve (Clark & Reis, 1988; Hendrick, 1989; Duck, 1990).

The behavior of couples in developing relationships changes in fairly predictable patterns (Berscheid, 1985; Burgess & Huston, 1979). The most frequent pattern follows this course:

- People interact more often, for longer periods of time, and in a widening array of settings.
- They seek each other's company.
- They increasingly "open up" to each other, disclosing secrets and sharing physical intimacies. They are more willing to share both positive and negative feelings and are increasingly willing to provide praise and criticism.
- They begin to understand each other's point of view and way of looking at the world.
- Their goals and behavior become more in tune, and they begin to share greater similarity in attitudes and values.
- Their investment in the relationship—in terms of time, energy, and commitment—increases.
- They begin to feel that their psychological well-being is tied to the well-being of the relationship. They come to see the relationship as unique and irreplaceable.
- They start behaving like a couple, rather than like two separate individuals.

Although this sequence of transitions is typical, it is difficult to predict the exact point in a relationship when each will occur. One important reason is that at the same time the relationship is evolving, the two individuals may be going through personal growth and change themselves. In addition, the people in the relationship may have differing goals for its outcome; one partner may be interested in marriage, while the other may only be looking for a relatively short-term relationship.

Finally, even if both partners have an underlying concern about finding a marriage partner, the kind of mate for whom one is looking may be very different from that sought by the other. For instance, a survey of close to 10,000 individuals across the world found that people had considerably differing preferences regarding qualities in a mate, depending both on their culture and their sex. For example, for people in the United States, mutual attraction and love were the most important characteristics. In contrast, men in China rated good health as most important, and women rated emotional stability and maturity as most important. In Zulu South Africa, males rated emotional stability first and females rated dependable character first. (See Table 20-2, p. 664.)

Once a relationship has evolved, how can we distinguish successful ones from those that will ultimately fail? One answer comes by examining the rate at which the various components of love develop. According to Sternberg's theory of love, the three individual components of love—intimacy, passion, and decision/commitment—vary in their influence over time and follow distinct courses. In strong loving relationships, for instance, the level of commitment peaks and then re-

TABLE 20-2

RANK ORDERING OF DESIRED CHARACTERISTICS IN A MATE

	China		South Africa Zulu		United States	
	Males	Females	Males	Females	Males	Females
Mutual Attraction—Love	4	8	10	5	1	1
Dependable Character	6	7	3	1	3	3
Emotional Stability and Maturity	5	1	1	2	2	2
Pleasing Disposition	13	16	4	3	4	4
Education and Intelligence	8	4	6	6	5	5
Good Health	1	3	5	4	6	9
Sociability	12	9	11	8	8	8
Desire for Home and Children	2	2	9	9	9	7
Refinement, Neatness	7	10	7	10	10	12
Ambition and Industriousness	10	5	8	7	11	6
Good Looks	11	15	14	16	7	13
Similar Education	15	12	12	12	12	10
Good Financial Prospect	16	14	18	13	16	11
Good Cook and Housekeeper	9	11	2	15	13	16
Favorable Social Status or Rating	14	13	17	14	14	14
Similar Religious Background	18	18	16	11	15	15
Chastity (no prior sexual intercourse)	3	6	13	18	17	18
Similar Political Background	17	17	15	17	18	17

Source: Buss et al., 1990.

mains stable, while intimacy continues to grow over the course of a relationship (see Figure 20-5). Passion, on the other hand, shows a marked decline over time, reaching a plateau fairly early in a relationship. Still, it remains an important component of loving relationships.

The Decline of a Relationship

What is it that causes some relationships to flounder? Social psychologist George Levinger (1983) has speculated on the reasons behind the deterioration of relationships. One important factor appears to be a change in judgments about the meaning of a partner's behavior. Behavior that was once viewed as "charming forgetfulness" becomes seen as "boorish indifference," and the partner be-

FIGURE 20-5

The changing ingredients of love. The three components of love vary in strength over the course of a relationship. (Sternberg, 1986.)

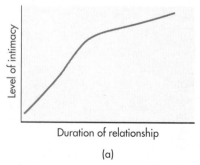
(a)

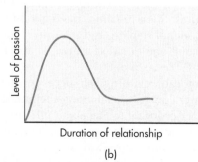
(b)

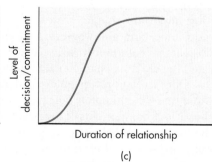
(c)

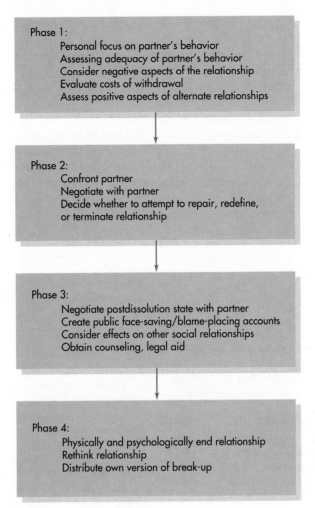

Phase 1:
Personal focus on partner's behavior
Assessing adequacy of partner's behavior
Consider negative aspects of the relationship
Evaluate costs of withdrawal
Assess positive aspects of alternate relationships

Phase 2:
Confront partner
Negotiate with partner
Decide whether to attempt to repair, redefine,
or terminate relationship

Phase 3:
Negotiate postdissolution state with partner
Create public face-saving/blame-placing accounts
Consider effects on other social relationships
Obtain counseling, legal aid

Phase 4:
Physically and psychologically end relationship
Rethink relationship
Distribute own version of break-up

FIGURE 20-6

Endings: the stages of relationship dissolution. (Based on Duck, 1984, p. 16.)

comes less valued. In addition, communications may be disrupted. Rather than listening to what the other person is saying, each partner becomes bent on justifying himself or herself, and communication deteriorates. Eventually, a partner may begin to invite and agree with criticism of the other partner from people outside the relationship, and look to others for the fulfillment of basic needs that were previously met by the partner.

Just as developing relationships tend to follow a common pattern, relationships that are on the decline conform to a pattern of stages (Duck, 1988; see Figure 20-6). The first phase occurs when a person decides that he or she can no longer tolerate being in a relationship. During this stage, the focus is on the other person's behavior and an evaluation of the extent to which this behavior provides a basis for terminating the relationship.

In the next phase, a person decides to confront the partner and determines whether to attempt to repair, redefine, or terminate the relationship. For example, a redefinition might encompass a qualitative change in the level of the relationship. ("We can still be friends" might replace "I'll love you forever.")

If the decision is made to terminate the relationship, the person then enters a period in which there is public acknowledgment that the relationship is being dissolved and an accounting is made to others regarding the events that led to the termination of the relationship. The last stage is a "grave-dressing" phase, in which the major activity is to physically and psychologically end the relationship. One of the major concerns of this period is to rethink the entire relationship, making what happened seem reasonable and in keeping with one's self-perceptions.

Just how much distress do people experience when a relationship ends? The degree of anguish depends on what the relationship was like prior to its end. In the case of undergraduate dating couples who break up, partners who report the most distress are those who had been especially close to one another over a long period and had spent a considerable amount of time exclusively together. They had participated in many activities with their partners and report having been influenced strongly by them. Finally, the degree of distress is related to holding the expectation that it will be difficult to find a new, replacement partner. If no alternatives are on the horizon, people are apt to look more longingly at what they once had (Simpson, 1987).

RECAP AND REVIEW II

RECAP

◀ Studies of interpersonal attraction and close relationships consider liking and loving.

◀ Among the most important elements that affect liking are proximity, mere exposure, similarity, and physical attractiveness.

◀ Love is assumed to be differentiated from liking in qualitative, as well as quantitative, respects. In addition, several different kinds of love can be distinguished.

◀ Social psychologists have begun to pay increasing attention to the factors relating to the maintenance and decline of relationships.

REVIEW

1. We tend to like those people who are similar to us. True or false? _____

2. _____ _____ predicts that we will be attracted to those people with needs different from our own.

3. Preference for attractive people seems to begin around the age of 3 or 4. True or false? _____

4. According to Berscheid, a person can still feel in love with another even when constantly rejected if _____ is present and is misinterpreted as "love."

5. Which of the following three components of love were proposed by Sternberg?
   a. Passion, closeness, sexuality
   b. Attraction, desire, complementarity
   c. Passion, intimacy, commitment
   d. Commitment, caring, sexuality

6. According to survey research, people have similar preferences for a mate, relatively independent of their sex and cultural background. True or false? _____

7. Which of the following is a reason cited by Levinger for couple breakup?
   a. Decline in lovemaking and affection
   b. Change in meaning of partner's behaviors
   c. Financial distress
   d. Advent of the two-paycheck family

Ask Yourself

Can love be adequately studied? Is there an "intangible" quality to love that renders it at least partially unknowable? How would you define "falling in love"? How would you study it?

(Answers to review questions are on page 668.)

AGGRESSION AND PROSOCIAL BEHAVIOR: HURTING AND HELPING OTHERS

The two episodes recounted at the start of this chapter provide very different perspectives on the nature of human behavior. In one, we see the considerate, unselfish side of humanity. In the other, we encounter unthinking, reckless violence.

Such incidents raise fundamental questions regarding the nature of human behavior. Psychologists have long pondered the issues of what motivates helping behavior and its counterpart, aggression. Much of the work was inspired by an incident—described in Chapter 2—that occurred more than twenty years ago when a young woman named Kitty Genovese was heard screaming, "Oh, my God, he stabbed me," and "Please help me," by no fewer than thirty-eight of her neighbors. Not one witness came forward to help, and it was not until thirty minutes had gone by that even one person bothered to call the police. Genovese subsequently died in an alleyway before the police arrived—the victim of a vicious attack by a mugger.

If events such as these foster only a negative, pessimistic interpretation of human capacities, other, equally dramatic incidents promote a more optimistic view of humankind. Consider, for example, the cases of people like Raoul Wallenberg, who risked death to help Jews escape from the Nazis in German-occupied countries during World War II. Or consider the simple kindnesses of life: lending a valued cassette, stopping to help a child who has fallen off her bicycle, or merely sharing a candy bar with a friend. Such instances of helping are no less characteristic of human behavior than the more distasteful examples. In this part of the chapter we explore the work that social psychologists have done in an effort to explain instances of both aggressive and helping behavior.

Hurting Others: Aggression

We need look no further than our daily paper or the nightly news to be bombarded with examples of aggression, both on a societal level (war, invasion, assassination) and on an individual level (crime, child abuse, and the many petty cruelties that humans are capable of inflicting on one another). Is such aggression an inevitable part of the human condition? Or is aggression primarily a product of particular circumstances that, if changed, could lead to its reduction?

The difficulty of answering such knotty questions becomes quickly apparent as soon as we consider how best to define the term "aggression." Depending on the way we define the word, many examples of inflicted pain or injury may or may not qualify as aggression (see Table 20-3, p. 668). Although it is clear, for instance, that a rapist is acting aggressively toward his victim, it is less certain that a physician carrying out an emergency medical procedure without an anesthetic, thereby causing incredible pain to the patient, should be considered aggressive.

Most social psychologists define aggression in terms of the intent and purpose behind the behavior. **Aggression** is intentional injury of or harm to another person (Berkowitz, 1974; Carlson, Marcus-Newhall, & Miller, 1989). Under this definition, it is clear that the rapist in our example is acting aggressively, whereas the physician causing pain during a medical procedure is not.

Aggression: Intentional injury or harm to another person

Instinct Approaches: Aggression as a Release. If you have ever punched an adversary in the nose, you may have experienced a certain satisfaction, despite your better judgment. Instinct theories, noting the prevalence of aggression not only in humans but in animals as well, propose that aggression is primarily the outcome of innate—or inborn—urges.

The major proponent of the instinct approach is Konrad Lorenz, an ethologist (a scientist who studies animal behavior) who suggested that humans, along with members of other species, have a fighting instinct, which in earlier times ensured protection of food supplies and weeded out the weaker of the species (Lorenz, 1966, 1974). The controversial notion arising from Lorenz's instinct

T A B L E   2 0 - 3

IS THIS AGGRESSION?

To see for yourself the difficulties involved in defining aggression, consider each of the following acts and determine whether it represents aggressive behavior—according to your own definition of aggression.

1. A spider eats a fly.
2. Two wolves fight for the leadership of the pack.
3. A soldier shoots an enemy at the front line.
4. The warden of a prison executes a convicted criminal.
5. A juvenile gang attacks members of another gang.
6. Two men fight for a piece of bread.
7. A man viciously kicks a cat.
8. A man, while cleaning a window, knocks over a flower pot, which, in falling, injures a pedestrian.
9. A girl kicks a wastebasket.
10. Mr. X, a notorious gossip, speaks disparagingly of many people of his acquaintance.
11. A man mentally rehearses a murder he is about to commit.
12. An angry son purposely fails to write to his mother, who is expecting a letter and will be hurt if none arrives.
13. An enraged boy tries with all his might to inflict injury on his antagonist, a bigger boy, but is not successful in doing so. His efforts simply amuse the bigger boy.
14. A woman daydreams of harming her antagonist but has no hope of doing so.
15. A senator does not protest the escalation of bombing to which she is morally opposed.
16. A farmer beheads a chicken and prepares it for supper.
17. A hunter kills an animal and mounts it as a trophy.
18. A dog snarls at a mail carrier but does not bite.
19. A physician gives a flu shot to a screaming child.
20. A boxer gives his opponent a bloody nose.
21. A Girl Scout tries to assist an elderly woman but trips her by accident.
22. A bank robber is shot in the back while trying to escape.
23. A tennis player smashes her racket after missing a volley.
24. A person commits suicide.
25. A cat kills a mouse, parades around with it, and then discards it.

Source: Benjamin, 1985, p. 41.

Catharsis: The notion that aggression is built up and must be discharged

approach is the idea that aggressive energy is constantly being built up within an individual until it is finally discharged in a process called **catharsis**. The longer the energy is built up, says Lorenz, the greater will be the magnitude of the aggression displayed when it is discharged.

Probably the most controversial idea to come out of instinct theories of aggression is Lorenz's proposal that society ought to provide acceptable means of catharsis through, for instance, participation in sports and games, in order to prevent its discharge in less socially desirable ways. Although the notion makes logical sense, there is no possible way to devise an adequate experiment to test it. In fact, relatively little support exists for instinct theories in general, because of the difficulty in finding evidence for any kind of pent-up reservoir of aggression (Berkowitz, 1974; Geen & Donnerstein, 1983). Most social psychologists suggest that we should look to other approaches to explain aggression.

Frustration-Aggression Approaches: Aggression as a Reaction to Frustration. Suppose you've been working on a paper that is due for a class early the next morning, and your word processor printer runs out of ink just before you can

ANSWERS (REVIEW II):

1. True **2.** Need complementarity **3.** False; it seems to begin as early as infancy. **4.** arousal
5. c **6.** False; they have distinct patterns of preferences **7.** b

Although Lorenz theorized that pent-up aggression could be vented through acceptable means such as sports, little evidence has been found to support this view.

print out the paper. You rush to the store to buy more ink, only to find the salesclerk locking the door for the day. Even though the clerk can see you gesturing and literally begging him to open the door, he refuses, shrugging his shoulders and pointing to a sign that says when the store will open the next day. At that moment, the feelings you experience toward the salesclerk probably place you on the verge of real aggression, and you probably are seething inside.

Frustration-aggression theory tries to explain aggression in terms of events such as this. When first put forward, the theory said flatly that frustration *always* led to aggression of some sort, and that aggression was *always* the result of some frustration, where **frustration** is defined as the thwarting or blocking of some ongoing, goal-directed behavior (Dollard, Doob, Miller, Mowrer, & Sears, 1939). More recent formulations, however, have modified the original one, suggesting instead that frustration produces anger, leading to a *readiness* to act aggressively. Whether or not actual aggression occurs depends on the presence of **aggressive cues**, stimuli that have been associated in the past with actual aggression or violence and that will trigger aggression again (Berkowitz, 1984; Josephson, 1987). In addition, frustration is assumed to produce aggression only to the extent that the frustration produces negative feelings (Berkowitz, 1989, 1990).

What kinds of stimuli act as aggressive cues? They can range from the most overt, such as the presence of weapons, to the subtlest, such as the mere mention of the name of an individual who has behaved violently in the past. For example, in one experiment, angered subjects behaved significantly more aggressively when in the presence of a rifle and revolver than in a comparable situation in which the guns were not present (Berkowitz & LePage, 1967). Similarly, frustrated subjects in an experiment who had viewed a violent movie were more physically aggressive toward a confederate with the same name as the star of the movie than to a confederate with a different name (Berkowitz & Geen, 1966). It appears, then, that frustration does lead to aggression, at least when aggressive cues are present (Carlson, Marcus-Newhall, & Miller, 1990).

Observational Learning Approaches: Learning to Hurt Others. Do we learn to be aggressive? The observational learning (sometimes called social learning) approach to aggression says we do. Taking an almost opposite view from the instinct

Frustration: A state produced by the thwarting or blocking of some ongoing, goal-directed behavior

Aggressive cues: Stimuli that have been associated with aggression in the past

theories, which focus on the innate aspects of aggression, observational learning theory (which we discussed first in Chapter 7) emphasizes how social and environmental conditions can teach individuals to be aggressive. Aggression is seen not as inevitable, but rather as a learned response that can be understood in terms of rewards and punishments (Bandura, 1973; Zillman, 1978).

Suppose, for instance, that a girl hits her younger brother when he damages one of her new toys. Whereas instinct theory would suggest that the aggression had been pent up and was now being discharged, and frustration-aggression theory would examine the girl's frustration at no longer being able to use her new toy, observational learning theory would look for a previous reinforcement that the girl had received for being aggressive. Perhaps she had learned that aggression resulted in her getting attention from her parents, or perhaps in the past her brother had apologized after being hit. In either case, observational learning theory views the aggression as a result of past rewards the girl had obtained for such behavior.

Observational learning theory pays particular attention not only to direct rewards and punishments that individuals themselves receive, but to the rewards and punishments that models—individuals who provide a guide to appropriate behavior—receive for their aggressive behavior. According to observational learning theory, people observe the behavior of models and the subsequent consequences of the behavior. If the consequences are positive, the behavior is likely to be imitated when the observer finds himself or herself in a similar situation.

In this classic "Bobo doll" experiment, children observed an adult model behaving aggressively. Later, after being angered, the children carried out behaviors remarkably similar to those they had seen earlier.

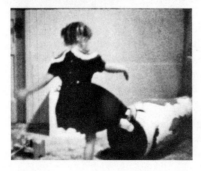

This basic formulation of observational learning theory has received wide support. For example, nursery-school-age children who have watched an adult behave aggressively display the same behavior themselves if they have been previously angered (Bandura, Ross, & Ross, 1963a, 1963b). It turns out, though, that exposure to models typically leads to spontaneous aggression only if the observer has been angered, insulted, or frustrated after exposure (Bandura, 1973). This finding has important implications for understanding the effects of aggression observed in the media.

Media Aggression: Does It Hurt to Watch TV?   The average American child, during the ages of 5 and 15, is exposed to no fewer than 13,000 violent deaths on television; the number of fights and aggressive sequences that children view is still higher. Even Saturday mornings, once filled with relatively peaceful fare, now include cartoons sporting titles such as "Teenage Mutant Ninja Turtles" and "Robo Cop," which include long sequences of aggressive action (Gerbner et al., 1978; Freedman, 1984; Liebert & Sprafkin, 1988).

Does observation of this kind of violence on television, as well as observation of aggression in other forms of media, suggest that our world is destined to become even more violent than it already is? Because observational learning research on modeling shows that people frequently learn and imitate the aggression that they observe, this question is one of the most important being addressed by social psychologists.

Most research suggests that there is a significant association between watching violent television programs and displaying aggressive behavior (Eron, 1982; Huesmann & Eron, 1986). For example, one experiment showed that subjects who watched a lot of television as third-graders became more aggressive adults than those who didn't watch so much TV (Eron, Huesmann, Lefkowitz, & Walden, 1972). Of course, these results cannot prove that viewing television was the *cause* of the adult aggression. Some additional factor, such as socioeconomic status, may have led both to higher levels of television viewing and to increased aggression.

Still, most experts agree that watching media violence can lead to a greater readiness to act aggressively (if not invariably to acting overtly with direct aggression) and to an insensitivity to the suffering of victims of violence (Linz, Don-

Did the violence depicted in the film *The Fisher King* lead to violence in real life? Although cause and effect cannot be established, a ticket stub from the movie was found in the pocket of the gunman in a Texas restaurant massacre.

nerstein, & Penrod, 1988; Bushman & Geen, 1990). Several reasons, beyond mere modeling, help explain why the observation of media violence may provoke aggression. For one thing, viewing violence seems to lower inhibitions against the performance of aggression—watching television portrayals of violence makes aggression seem a legitimate response to particular situations. Furthermore, viewing violence may make our understanding of the meaning of others' behavior shift: We may be predisposed to view even nonaggressive acts of others as aggressive after watching media aggression, and subsequently may act upon these new interpretations by responding aggressively. Finally, a continual diet of aggression may leave us desensitized to violence, and what previously would have repelled us now produces little emotional response. A sense of the pain and suffering brought about by aggression may be lost, and we may find it easier to act aggressively ourselves (Geen & Donnerstein, 1983).

The Link Between Aggressive Pornography and Violence Toward Women. Does viewing pornography that includes violence against women lead to subsequent actual violence toward women? This question is a complex one, but recent evidence suggests that there may, in fact, be a link between certain kinds of erotic material and aggression.

In one experiment examining this issue, angered male subjects who viewed an erotic movie that contained violence toward a woman showed significantly more subsequent aggression toward a female than those who viewed an erotic movie that contained no violence (Donnerstein & Berkowitz, 1981). Other experiments have found that long-term exposure to violent and sexually degrading depictions of women leads to emotional and physiological desensitization. For example, subjects who were shown a series of R-rated violent "slasher" movies later showed less anxiety and depression when exposed to violence against women, and they were less sympathetic toward rape victims than subjects who saw nonviolent films (Linz, Donnerstein, & Penrod, 1987; Linz, Donnerstein, & Adams, 1989).

Overall, research in this area suggests that viewing pornography that contains violence toward women leads to emotional and physiological desensitization regarding aggression directed at women and an increased likelihood of actual aggression toward women (Linz, Donnerstein, & Penrod, 1987). What appears to be particularly critical is whether the pornography contains violence toward women. Aggressive content in erotic materials clearly raises the level of aggression subsequently displayed by those exposed to it.

Whether these findings mean that pornography should be banned is a debatable question—such a move would certainly infringe on First Amendment rights to free speech. Furthermore, it may be that hard-core pornography represents less of a problem than more common R-rated movies, often shown on cable TV. An analysis comparing the content of R-rated movies (restricted to those 17 or older unless accompanied by a parent) with X- and XXX-rated (those under 18 not admitted) provides some pertinent data. Although the percentage of sexual behaviors was far greater in the X-rated movies than in the R-rated movies, violence was proportionally much higher in the R-rated movies (see Figure 20-7).

Most important, the percentage of sexual violence was virtually identical in R-, X-, and XXX-rated movies. A fine-grained analysis of the movies showed that although sexually violent episodes lasted longer in X-rated movies, the proportion of sexual violence directed specifically toward women was higher in R- than in X-rated movies. Surprisingly, then, the negative impact of viewing sexual violence against women in R-rated movies may be greater than in X-rated films (Yang & Linz, 1990).

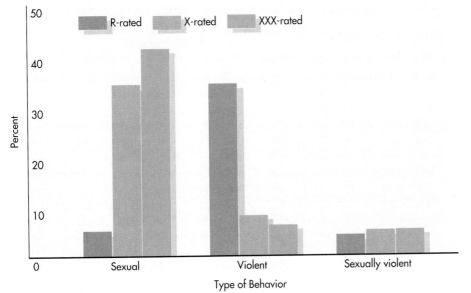

FIGURE 20-7
Proportions of sex, violence, and sexually violent episodes depicted in R-rated, X-rated, and XXX-rated movies. While the proportion of sexual behaviors was far greater in the X-rated movies than in the R-rated movies, violence was proportionally much higher in the R-rated movies. At the same time, the percentage of sexual violence was similar regardless of movie rating. (Based on Yang & Linz, 1990.)

Helping Others: The Brighter Side of Human Nature

Turning away from aggression, we move now to the opposite—and brighter—side of the coin of human nature: helping behavior. Helping behavior, or **prosocial behavior** as it is more formally known, has been investigated under many different approaches, but the question that psychologists have looked at most closely relates to bystander intervention in emergency situations. What are the factors that lead someone to help a person in need?

As we noted in Chapter 2, one critical factor is the number of others present. When more than one person bears witness to an emergency situation, there can be a sense of diffusion of responsibility among bystanders. **Diffusion of responsibility** is the tendency for people to feel that responsibility for acting is shared, or diffused, among those present. The more people that are present in an emergency, then, the less personally responsible each individual feels—and therefore the less help is provided (Latané & Nida, 1981).

Although the majority of research on helping behavior supports the diffusion-of-responsibility formulation, other factors clearly are involved in helping behavior. According to a model developed by Latané and Darley (1970), the process of helping involves four basic steps:

■ Noticing a person, event, or situation that may require help.

■ Interpreting the event as one that requires help. Even if an event is noticed, it may be sufficiently ambiguous to be interpreted as a nonemergency situation (Shotland, 1985). It is here that the presence of others first affects helping behavior. The presence of inactive others may indicate to the observer that a situation does not require help—a judgment not necessarily made if the observer is alone.

■ Assuming responsibility for taking action. It is at this point that diffusion of responsibility is likely to occur if others are present. Moreover, a bystander's particular expertise is apt to play a role in whether helping occurs. For instance, if people with training in medical aid or lifesaving techniques are present, untrained bystanders are less apt to intervene because they feel they have less expertise. This point was well illustrated in a study by Jane and Irving Piliavin (1972), who conducted a field experiment in which an indi-

Prosocial behavior: Helping behavior

Diffusion of responsibility: The tendency for people to feel that responsibility for helping is shared among those present

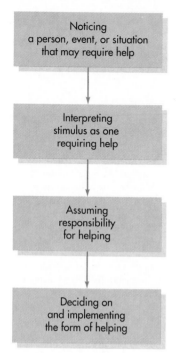

FIGURE 20-8

The basic steps of helping. (Based on Latané & Darley, 1970.)

Rewards-costs approach: The notion that, in a situation requiring help, a bystander's perceived rewards must outweigh the costs if helping is to occur

Altruism: Helping behavior that is beneficial to others while requiring sacrifice on the part of the helper

Empathy: One person's experiencing of another's emotions, leading to an increased likelihood of responding to the other's needs

Studies indicate that people who have recently observed others helping someone in trouble are more likely to lend a hand themselves.

vidual seemed to collapse in a subway car with blood trickling out of the corner of his mouth. The results of the experiment showed that bystanders were less likely to help when a person (actually a confederate) appearing to be an intern was present than when the "intern" was not present.

■ Deciding on and implementing the form of assistance. After an individual assumes responsibility for helping, the decision must be made as to how assistance will be provided. Helping can range from very indirect forms of intervention, such as calling the police, to more direct forms, such as giving first aid or taking the victim to a hospital. Most social psychologists use a **rewards-costs approach** for helping to predict the nature of assistance that a bystander will choose to provide. The general notion is that the rewards of helping, as perceived by the bystander, must outweigh the costs if helping is to occur (Lynch & Cohen, 1978), and most research tends to support this notion.

After the nature of assistance is determined, one step remains: the actual implementation of the assistance. A rewards-costs analysis suggests that the least costly form of implementation is the most likely to be used. However, this is not the whole story: In some cases, people behave altruistically. **Altruism** is helping behavior that is beneficial to others but clearly requires self-sacrifice. For example, an instance in which a person runs into a burning house to rescue a stranger's child might be considered altruistic, particularly when compared with the alternative of simply calling the fire department (Batson, 1990, 1991; Dovidio, Allen, & Schroeder, 1990). (Figure 20-8 summarizes the basic steps of helping.)

Some research suggests that people who intervene in emergency situations tend to have certain personality characteristics that differentiate them from non-helpers. For example, Shotland (1984) suggests that helpers tend to be more self-assured. Other research has found that individuals who are characteristically high in **empathy**—a personality trait in which someone observing another person experiences the emotions of that person—are more likely to respond to others' needs (Cialdini et al., 1987; Eisenberg & Fabes, 1991; Batson et al., 1991).

Still, most social psychologists agree that there is no single set of attributes that differentiates helpers from nonhelpers. Temporary, situational factors play the predominant role in determining whether an individual intervenes in a situation requiring aid (e.g., Carlson, Charlin, & Miller, 1988).

For instance, our transient mood helps determine how helpful we are (Salovey, Mayer, & Rosenhan, 1991). It is not too surprising that being in a good mood encourages helping (Carlson, Charlin, & Miller, 1988). What doesn't make as much sense, at least at first, is the finding that bad moods, too, seem to encourage helping behavior (Eisenberg, 1991). There are some reasonable explanations, however, for this finding. For one thing, we may think that helping will enable us to view ourselves more positively, thereby raising our spirits and getting us out of our bad mood (Cialdini & Fultz, 1990). Similarly, if a bad mood leads us to focus on ourselves, the values we hold about helping may become more conspicuous—leading us to help more (Berkowitz, 1987).

RECAP AND REVIEW III

RECAP

◀ Aggression refers to intentional injury of or harm to another person. Some theories view aggression as instinctual, whereas others view it as a reaction to frustration. Another approach, based on observational learning theory, focuses on the way in which aggression is learned and modeled from others.

◀ Strong evidence links aggression viewed in the media—both in television programs and in pornographic materials—to subsequent aggression, although a cause-and-effect relationship has yet to be established.

◀ Helping in emergencies involves four steps: (1) noticing a person, event, or situation that may require help; (2) interpreting the event as one that requires help; (3) assuming responsibility for taking action; and (4) deciding on and implementing the form of assistance.

REVIEW

1. According to Lorenz, aggression is due primarily to _____. Aggression is released in a process called _____.

2. Which hypothesis states that frustration produces anger, which in turn produces a readiness to act aggressively?
   a. Frustration-aggression
   b. Observational learning
   c. Catharsis
   d. Instinctual aggression

3. According to the above theory, the amount of aggression produced in a given situation depends on the presence of _____ _____.

4. _____ _____ theory would predict that children watching aggressive television programs are more likely to display aggression themselves.

5. It is the combination of sex and violence, rather than graphic sexual content alone, which leads to possible increases in violence against women. True or false? _____

6. Which of the following might be the best way to reduce the amount of fighting a young boy does?
   a. Take him to the gym and let him work out on the boxing equipment
   b. Take him to see *Terminator 2* several times in the hopes that it will provide catharsis
   c. Reward him if he doesn't fight during a certain period
   d. Ignore it and let it die out naturally

7. List the four steps involved in helping in an emergency.

8. If a person in a crowd does not help in an apparent emergency situation because of the other people present, that person is falling victim to the phenomenon of _____ _____.

Ask Yourself

Knowing what you now know about helping behavior, how might it be possible to increase altruistic behavior in people? If you were asked to lecture on this topic, what would you tell your audience?

(Answers to review questions are on page 676.)

■ **What are the major sources of social influence and the tactics that are used to bring them about?**

1. Social influence is the area of social psychology concerned with situations in which the actions of an individual or group affect the behavior of others.

2. Conformity refers to changes in behavior or attitudes that occur as the result of a desire to follow the beliefs or standards of others. Among the factors affecting conformity are the nature of the group, the nature of the response required, the kind of task, and the unanimity of the group.

3. Compliance is behavior that occurs as a result of direct social pressure. Two means of eliciting compliance are the foot-in-the-door technique, in which people are initially asked to agree to a small request but later asked to respond to a larger one, and the door-in-the-face procedure, in which a large request, designed to be refused, is followed by a smaller one. In contrast to compliance, obedience is a change in behavior that results from the commands of others. Among the ways to remain independent of group pressure are inoculation, forewarning, and consistency.

■ **Why are we attracted to certain people, and what is the progression that social relationships follow?**

4. The study of interpersonal attraction, or close relationships, considers liking and loving. Among the primary determinants of liking are proximity, mere exposure, similarity, and physical attractiveness.

5. Loving is distinguished from liking by the presence of intense physiological arousal, an all-encompassing interest in another, fantasies about the other, rapid swings of emotion, fascination, sexual desire, exclusiveness, and strong

feelings of caring. According to one approach, love can be categorized into two types: passionate and romantic. Sternberg's theory further subdivides love into eight kinds.

6. Recent work has examined the development, maintenance, and deterioration of relationships. Relationships tend to move through stages, and the various components of love—intimacy, passion, and decision/commitment—vary in their influence over time.

■ **What factors underlie aggression and prosocial behavior?**

7. Aggression is intentional injury of or harm to another person. Instinct approaches suggest that humans have an innate drive to behave aggressively and that if aggression is not released in socially desirable ways, it will be discharged in some other form—a point for which there is relatively little research support. Frustration-aggression theory suggests that frustration produces a readiness to be aggressive—if aggressive cues are present. Finally, observational learning theory hypothesizes that aggression is learned through reinforcement—particularly reinforcement that is given to models.

8. Helping behavior in emergencies is determined in part by the phenomenon of diffusion of responsibility, which results in a lower likelihood of helping when more people are present. Deciding to help is the outcome of a four-stage process consisting of noticing a possible need for help, interpreting the situation as requiring aid, assuming responsibility for taking action, and deciding on and implementing a form of assistance.

ANSWERS (REVIEW III):

1. instinct; catharsis **2.** a **3.** aggressive cues **4.** Observational learning **5.** True **6.** c **7.** Noticing an event; interpreting the event; assuming responsibility; deciding on and implementing assistance **8.** diffusion of responsibility

KEY TERMS AND CONCEPTS

social influence (p. 648)
conformity (p. 649)
status (p. 650)
social supporter (p. 650)
compliance (p. 651)
foot-in-the-door technique
  (p. 651)
door-in-the-face technique
  (p. 652)
reciprocal concessions (p. 652)
obedience (p. 652)
low-balling (p. 653)
inoculation (p. 655)

forewarning (p. 655)
consistency (p. 655)
interpersonal attraction (p. 656)
proximity (p. 657)
reciprocity-of-liking effect
  (p. 657)
need-complementarity hypothesis
  (p. 657)
passionate (or romantic) love
  (p. 662)
companionate love (p. 662)
intimacy component (of love)
  (p. 662)

passion component (of love)
  (p. 662)
decision/commitment
  component (of love) (p. 662)
aggression (p. 667)
catharsis (p. 668)
frustration (p. 669)
aggressive cues (p. 669)
prosocial behavior (p. 673)
diffusion of responsibility
  (p. 673)
rewards-costs approach (p. 674)
altruism (p. 674)
empathy (p. 674)

CONSUMER AND INDUSTRIAL-ORGANIZATIONAL PSYCHOLOGY

Lee Iacocca came to personify the Chrysler Corporation.

LEE IACOCCA

He's probably the best known business leader in the United States, so trusted that he was repeatedly featured in advertisements for the Chrysler Corporation. When he told consumers that Chrysler autos were better than the competition, he seemed believable. He appeared honest. He seemed to know what he was talking about.

But Iacocca was more than the trusted, grandfatherly figure that consumers perceived him to be as the head of Chrysler. To employees, prior to his retirement he was a sharp, tough-minded leader. A black book perched on his office bookshelf was a constant reminder of just how demanding he was. In the book was a list of each of his senior managers' goals for the upcoming quarter. At the end of each quarter, Iacocca compared their goals with actual performance. The success of his subordinates was thus measured in a clear, direct, and sometimes ruthless way.

LOOKING AHEAD

When Lee Iacocca took over as president of the Chrysler Corporation in 1979, the company was on the brink of bankruptcy. Iacocca managed to turn the company around, and he himself began to personify its success. Iacocca achieved his success in the twin areas of the marketplace and the workplace, areas that are reflected in two applied branches of psychology: consumer psychology and industrial-organizational psychology.

Consumer psychologists: Psychologists who specialize in understanding buying habits and the effects of advertising on buyer behavior

Consumer psychologists specialize in understanding buying habits and the effects of advertising on buyer behavior. Often working with manufacturers or advertising companies, they consider how potential purchasers react to the strategies employed by sellers and manufacturers of products (such as automobiles) and services (like the overnight delivery provided by Federal Express). Lee Iacocca was apt to turn to consumer psychologists to help him develop ways to increase sales and to maintain a positive image of Chrysler in the minds of consumers.

Industrial-organizational (I/O) psychology: The branch of psychology concerned with the workplace

Industrial-organizational (I/O) psychologists focus on another facet of the business realm. **Industrial-organizational (I/O) psychology** is concerned with the workplace, considering such issues as worker motivation, satisfaction, and productivity. I/O psychologists also focus on the operation and design of organizations, asking such questions as how decision making can be improved in large organizations. Iacocca's "black book," used in measuring performance against goals, originated from the ideas developed by I/O psychologists.

In sum, after reading this chapter you'll be able to answer these questions:

- What roles do consumer psychologists and industrial/organizational (I/O) psychologists play in the marketplace and the workplace?
- How do advertisers develop and target advertisements to particular individuals?
- What are the major factors considered by consumers when they make purchase decisions?
- What accounts for people's work motivation and job satisfaction?
- How are decisions made by groups?

It's late December, and for the last few weeks you've been subjected to a media blitz of Ed McMahon telling you about the American Family Publishers Sweepstakes. You've seen friendly, trustworthy Ed introducing a past winner of $1 million. You've seen the letter on TV. Finally, it arrives, your "LAST CHANCE! Million Dollar Document" warning you, "Don't Throw Away! This is the letter you just saw on TV!" . . .

You now open the big envelope. On the large, official-looking document, you find your name printed throughout the text at least twenty times in various sizes of type. The first set of large print catches your eye: there's your name before ". . . SHALL BE PAID A FULL ONE MILLION DOLLARS." In contrasting color in the upper margin is the constant reminder, "LAST CHANCE!" A little farther down, there's your name again with nine—count 'em—*nine* Personal Prize Claim Numbers. . . .

After extensive reading you finally figure out what to paste where to enter the contest. You also have a big page of colorful, perforated, sticky stamps that can be pasted on the entry blank to purchase any of a variety of magazines. Another full-color sheet from Ed tells you, "You can take it from me—THERE ARE NO LOWER PRICES AVAILABLE ANYWHERE TO THE GENERAL PUBLIC. American Family values are GUARANTEED UNBEATABLE!" There is also a list of selected magazines that offer Free Bonus Gifts, such as watches and desk clocks. You decide a Money-Manager Calculator would be useful—so you order *Newsweek*, which will keep you better informed for school. Besides the good price, you don't have to pay now, because you'll be billed in the future. Also there's a money-back guarantee if you don't like the subscription—and, as it says, "You risk nothing!" So, you get the calculator, *Newsweek* at a great price, and maybe . . . just maybe . . . BIG, BIG BUCKS!!! (Peter & Olson, 1987, pp. 305–306.)

If this sales pitch sounds familiar, it ought to: The post-Christmas mails abound with similar ones every year. The timing is no coincidence; after purchasing their presents, most consumers are particularly receptive to the possibility of easy money.

Understanding the reasons particular kinds of advertising strategies are effective is one of the jobs of consumer psychologists. We'll begin our discussion of consumer psychology by examining how advertisers develop and target their ads to particular kinds of individuals. Then we'll talk about how consumer psychologists explain and evaluate the effectiveness of various advertising strategies, taking basic psychological principles into account.

Advertising Appeals: Soft Sell Versus Hard Sell

You probably agree with the makers of Close-up toothpaste that "tartar isn't sexy." Chances are, of course, that before seeing an advertisement stating such an argument you never linked sex and tartar (although you probably have given at least one of the concepts a fair amount of thought). But that's not the point: What is important, according to the philosophy behind the advertisement, is that you develop a positive image regarding the toothpaste because of its link to sexiness.

The Close-up toothpaste advertisement exemplifies one of two major strategies used in advertisements (Fox, 1984; Snyder & DeBono, 1989). In the **soft sell** approach employed by Close-up, the advertiser seeks to associate a product with an image related to the product's use. The soft sell suggests that potential buyers of a product can obtain or radiate a desirable image through the use of the product.

For example, one of the most enduring advertisements embodying a soft sell

Soft sell: An approach to selling in which a product is associated with an image related to the product's use

Hard sell: An approach to selling that focuses on the qualities of the product itself

Self-monitoring: The tendency to change our behavior in order to present ourselves well in particular social situations

approach is that of the Marlboro man, whose robust, masculine image is meant to suggest that people who smoke Marlboro cigarettes will have similar qualities. Similarly, the advertisements of Virginia Slims cigarettes are targeted at women who wish to project a sophisticated, cosmopolitan image.

In contrast to the soft sell approach, the **hard sell** approach focuses on the qualities of the product itself. In the hard sell, advertisers tout the function of the product, how well it works, how good it tastes, or how much improved consumers' lives will be after using the product. When a company talks about the quality of its product or the nutritional benefits of its use, it is employing a hard sell approach. Zenith's slogan that "the quality goes in before the name goes on" is an example of a hard sell technique.

Sometimes both a soft sell and a hard sell approach are combined in advertisements. For instance, a BMW ad headlined with the phrase, "BMW meets the demands of the 90s with its spirit intact," uses both kinds of appeals. The ad goes on to claim that the automobile meets rigid safety standards, but is not stodgy ("A safe car needn't be a boring one").

Is the soft sell or the hard sell more persuasive? Most recent evidence suggests that the answer depends on certain personality characteristics of the consumer. According to consumer psychologists, one important factor is the consumer's characteristic level of self-monitoring. **Self-monitoring** is the tendency to change our behavior in order to present ourselves well in particular social situations. High self-monitors adjust their behavior from one situation to the next in an attempt to present themselves well. They are concerned about the image they project and are apt to show conspicuous variations in their behavior from one social context to the next. In contrast, low self-monitors are relatively insensitive to the demands of different social settings, and their behavior is more indicative of their own attitudes, values, and beliefs. The behavior of low self-monitors is considerably more consistent across situations, then, than that of high self-monitors (Snyder, 1987).

As you might expect, the disparities between high and low self-monitors lead them to be susceptible to different kinds of advertising appeals. Because high self-monitors are concerned with the image they project, they are more likely to be affected by soft-sell advertisements which emphasize the positive image that will come from use of a particular product. In contrast, low self-monitors are likely to be persuaded more by advertising appeals that speak to a product's quality. As a consequence, low self-monitors are more willing to pay more for products whose advertising messages stress high quality. They are also more likely to try products that are advertised with high-quality appeals (Snyder & DeBono, 1985).

Psychologists Kenneth DeBono and Michelle Packer demonstrated the importance of consumers' self-monitoring behavior in determining reactions to advertising in a recent experiment (DeBono & Packer, 1991). In the study, high and low self-monitors were exposed to either an image-oriented advertisement (the soft sell) or a quality-oriented advertisement (the hard sell) for a cola or cassette tape. For example, in the cola advertisement, the image-oriented advertisement showed two cola cans shaking hands in front of an office conference room and a cola can on a mountain, under a headline reading, "In the office . . . or great outdoors, Brand X cola helps you climb to the top." In the advertisement stressing quality, a picture of a can of the cola was displayed followed by an equal sign and then a dollar sign, stressing the value of the drink. After seeing one of the ads, participants consumed a sample of the cola (which was actually a brand sold by a supermarket chain).

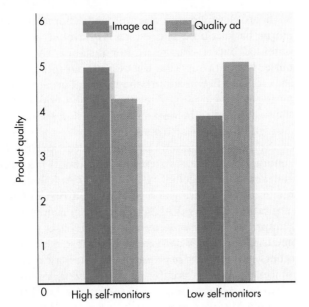

FIGURE 21-1
Judgments of product quality. High self-monitors believed that a product was of higher quality after viewing an image-oriented advertisement than after seeing a quality-oriented ad. In contrast, low self-monitors felt that the product was of higher quality after viewing a quality-oriented ad than after viewing an image-oriented ad. (DeBono & Packer, 1991.)

The results of the experiment were clear: As shown in Figure 21-1, high self-monitors thought that the product was of higher quality when they had seen an image-oriented advertisement than when they viewed a quality-oriented ad. In contrast, the low self-monitors believed that the product was of higher quality when they had seen the quality-oriented advertisement than when they had viewed the image-oriented advertisement.

In sum, advertisements employing a particular strategy are not universally effective with all consumers. High self-monitors are more likely to be influenced by advertisements relating to soft sell, image-oriented aspects of products, while low self-monitors are more apt to be persuaded by quality-oriented sales pitches.

The findings regarding self-monitoring suggest the importance of zeroing in on particular qualities of consumers—a point that has not been lost on product manufacturers. As we see next, they have become expert at targeting customers for particular products.

Psychographics: The Psychology of the Consumer

Does the world really need the dozens of different walking shoes made by various manufacturers? Although you might think not, the manufacturers of such sneakers do, based on their research into the walking shoe market. For example, people walk for many different reasons. Some people walk for enjoyment, others for exercise, others to walk the dog. Some really want to exercise, while others just want to look like they're exercising. Each one of these underlying motivations represents an opportunity for sneaker manufacturers to produce a separate shoe (Rice, 1988).

Traditionally, manufacturers have considered such basic characteristics as gender, age, race, ethnicity, religion, income, marital status, and number of children of potential buyers when they target products and related advertising. More recently, however, producers of many products have begun to use a procedure known as psychographics to analyze consumers' needs, values, attitudes, and motivation in purchasing various consumer goods. **Psychographics** is a technique for dividing people into lifestyle profiles that are related to purchasing patterns.

Psychographics: A technique for dividing people into lifestyle profiles that are related to purchasing patterns

Such profiles take into account such characteristics as marital status, race and ethnic background, and education level, as well as the kinds of activities that potential buyers engage in. For instance, the producers of Peter Pan peanut butter know through the use of psychographics that heavy users in the New York area tend to live in suburban and rural area households with children, headed by 18- to 54-year-olds. They tend to be frequent renters of home videos, go to theme parks, are below-average television viewers, and listen to radio at above-average rates (McCarthy, 1991a).

Some psychographic profiles are less specific. One of the most widely used general classification systems for consumers is known as VALS (short for Values and Lifestyles; Mitchell, 1983). The VALS system was derived from Maslow's hierarchy of needs, which we discussed first in Chapter 11 in terms of general motivation. In the VALS approach, consumers are divided into four major groups. *Need-driven consumers* make purchases primarily to satisfy basic, elemental needs. *Outer-directed consumers*, in contrast, are motivated by the desire to impress others. *Inner-directed consumers* make purchases in order to increase their own self-awareness. Finally, combined *outer- and inner-directed consumers* mesh social and self-needs. (The segments are summarized in Table 21-1.)

Like Maslow's hierarchy, the first few levels in the VALS hierarchy classify groups of individuals whose needs are largely related to two lifestyles, the Survivors and the Sustainers. Both of these are small, impoverished groups whose basic preoccupation is simply eking out a living. Of more interest to sellers are groups that have the financial means to purchase the products they wish to sell. For example, the largest VALS group are the Belongers, who are stable, hard-working blue-collar or service industry workers. They tend to be rather conservative politically, and they conform fairly consistently to societal norms. They make up approximately one-third of the population.

The Achievers, making up 20 percent of the population, tend to be successful managers or professionals. They are competent and rely on themselves to make things happen. They also want the symbols of success, such as expensive houses, cars, and vacations.

Other categories include the I-Am-Me's (young, egocentric people confused about their goals in life), the Experientials (former I-Am-Me's who become surer of their goals and more outward looking), and the Societally Conscious (mature, well-informed individuals with a strong interest in social issues such as the environment). Just as in Maslow's hierarchy, the pinnacle of consumer needs is left for just a few, the Integrateds, who are analogous to individuals falling into Maslow's category of self-actualization. The Integrateds are a cross between the best of the Achievers and the Societally Conscious.

The specific purchases that consumers make are in line with their VALS classification (Mitchell, 1983). For example, Achievers are apt to purchase luxury cars, Belongers buy family-sized cars, the Societally Conscious tend to buy small economy cars, and the Experientials are most likely to buy powerful sports cars.

Subcultural Differences in Consumer Behavior. While VALS and other psychographic systems consider consumers in terms of psychological variables, other means exist for understanding how subgroups within the general population make decisions regarding purchases. Some sellers, for instance, examine subcultural differences in consumer behavior, finding that clear differences emerge between different racial and ethnic groups.

T A B L E 2 1 - 1

VALS NINE AMERICAN LIFESTYLES

Need-Driven Consumers

Survivors (4 percent of the U.S. adult population) These consumers are elderly and intensely poor. They are often widowed and living only on Social Security income. Some have been born into poverty and never escape it; others have slipped to this lifestyle because of bad luck, lack of enterprise, or the onslaughts of old age. Entertainment consists of watching television; basic staples are purchased with an emphasis on low price.

Sustainers (7 percent of the U.S. adult population) These consumers are angry, distrustful, anxious, combative, and live on the edge of poverty. Unlike Survivors, Sustainers have not given up hope; they try for a better life. They are careful shoppers and cautious buyers for their large families.

Outer-Directed Consumers

Belongers (38 percent of the U.S. adult population) These consumers typify what is generally regarded as middle-class America. Traditional, conservative, and old-fashioned, these consumers prefer the status quo or the ways of the past and do not like change. These consumers want to fit in rather than stand out, and they follow the rules of society. They value their home and family and seek security.

Emulators (10 percent of the U.S. adult population) These consumers are intensely striving people, seeking to be like those they consider richer and more successful. They are more influenced by others than any other lifestyle group and are ambitious, competitive, and ostentatious. Many have attended technical school; few have college degrees. Emulators are in a turbulent transition stage; most of them will not make it to Achiever status. They are conspicuous consumers.

Achievers (20 percent of the U.S. adult population) These consumers are the driving and driven people who have built "the system" and are now at the helm. They are effective corporate executives, skilled professionals such as doctors, lawyers, and scientists, adroit politicians, money-oriented athletes and entertainers, and successful artists. They live comfortable, affluent lives and in so doing they have set the standard for much of the nation. They are major consumers of luxury and top-of-the-line products.

Inner-Directed Consumers

I-Am-Me (3 percent of the U.S. adult population) These consumers are young and in a transition period from an outer-directed to an inner-directed way of life. Many have come from Achiever parents and the transition to new values is full of turmoil and confusion of personal identity. Most are students in their 20s and have very energetic, active lives. Clothes and other purchases may be made to differentiate these consumers from their parents and Establishment values.

Experientials (5 percent of the U.S. adult population) Many of these consumers passed through the I-Am-Me stage a few years earlier. They tend to be artistic, liberal, and to seek vivid, direct experiences with other persons, things, and events. They are highly educated, very energetic, and engage in social activities ranging from outdoor sports to wine tasting. Most are in their late 20s and prefer natural products.

Societally Conscious (11 percent of the U.S. adult population) These consumers are well educated, prosperous, politically liberal, and deeply concerned with social issues. They are approaching 40 years of age and are the leaders of movements for improving consumer rights, reducing environmental pollution, and protecting wildlife. Many ride a bike or drive an economy car, insulate their home or install solar heating, and eat only foods grown without pesticides and prepared without additives.

Combined Outer- and Inner-Directed Group

Integrateds (2 percent of the U.S. adult population) These consumers are psychologically mature and find both outer direction and inner direction good, powerful, and useful. They have an unusual ability to weigh consequences and to solve difficult problems. They tend to be open, self-assured, self-expressive, keenly aware of nuance, and command respect and admiration. They tend to be middle-aged or older.

Source: Adapted from Arnold Mitchell (1983), *The Nine American Lifestyles: Who We Are & Where We're Going*, New York: Macmillan Publishing Company; and The Values and Lifestyles Program, SRI International, Menlo Park, California.

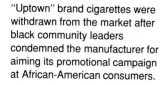

"Uptown" brand cigarettes were withdrawn from the market after black community leaders condemned the manufacturer for aiming its promotional campaign at African-American consumers.

For instance, African-Americans and whites show differing patterns in their purchasing decisions (Engel & Blackwell, 1982). African-Americans are more loyal to national brands than whites; they spend less on food, housing, and automobile transportation than whites; and they buy more milk and soft drinks than whites, but purchase less tea and coffee.

Hispanics also have specific consumption patterns (Boone & Krutz, 1986). For instance, they purchase 50 percent more beer than other groups in the population. They also purchase more juice, three times as many cans of spaghetti, and more shampoo than members of other subcultures.

It is hardly surprising that members of particular subcultures will have distinct purchasing patterns, given that they have significant differences in values and interests, in addition to socioeconomic variations. These differences have led sellers to attempt to target products and advertisements toward certain groups—sometimes with unintended results. In one case a telephone company developed ads directed toward Hispanics. The ad depicts a Puerto Rican actress, playing the role of wife, telling her husband to "run downstairs and phone Mary. Tell her we'll be a little tardy." However, the ad was not successful because it did not take into account two features of Hispanic culture. First, it is a relatively male-oriented culture, so showing a wife telling her husband what to do in such a direct manner does not ring true. Second, the content of the call would not make much sense to many Hispanics, who would not be concerned about running a little late, given that being tardy is not necessarily considered inappropriate within that culture.

In other cases, attempts to target products and advertising to specific subcultural groups has led to ethically questionable results. For instance, the tobacco company RJ Reynolds developed a new cigarette brand it named "Uptown" in the early 1990s. Because of the nature of the advertising that initiated the distribution of the cigarette, it soon became apparent that the product was targeted to African-Americans (Quinn, 1990). Given the dubious ethics of targeting a potentially life-threatening product to a minority population, the product introduction caused considerable controversy and resulted in a condemnation from the Secretary of the U.S. Department of Health and Human Services. The manufacturer stopped distributing the brand soon thereafter. (For more on the targeting of advertisements to specific individuals, see the Cutting Edge box.)

Shoppers in a big Midwestern city early last year found extra rows of strawberry-flavored cream cheese at one supermarket. Just miles away, another store had almost no strawberry but lots of the diet version. Still another had mostly large, 12-ounce cartons of Philadelphia Cream Cheese.

Staged by Kraft USA, the experiment combined a demographic profile of cream cheese buyers with data showing which supermarkets drew most of those shoppers. After that, Kraft pinpointed 30 stores where people frequently bought items from special displays and installed coolers in them, tailoring the types of cream cheese in each to the tastes of the store's shoppers. The result? Sales jumped 147% over the previous year. (McCarthy, 1991a, p. B1.)

The Philadelphia cream cheese experiment illustrates the newest technique in targeting products to particular buyers. Instead of identifying potential purchasers in a general geographical location or according to broad racial- or ethnic-group membership, the method targets particular neighborhoods or even shoppers at a particular store.

The method is called **micromarketing**, and it is made possible by the checkout scanners now in operation in many supermarkets. The scanners are attached to computers that permit a moment-by-moment analysis of what stores are selling. Because information about buyer characteristics from census data is also available,

WE ARE WHAT WE BUY: THE PHILADELPHIA CREAM CHEESE EXPERIMENT

A bar-code scanner can be attached to a computer with the capability to give a moment-by-moment analysis of which goods consumers are purchasing in which stores.

food companies have the opportunity to tailor their sales techniques directly to the consumers found shopping in a particular supermarket.

For example, the makers of Classico pasta sauce found that their best customers tend to earn at least $35,000 per year, have two-income households, live in metropolitan areas, and are more apt to live on the West Coast of the United States. This information allowed them to identify particular locations with shoppers who match these characteristics, and

then to focus their advertising in those areas.

In another instance of micromarketing, supermarkets use buyer profiles to allocate shelf space to various products. Using information regarding buyers of breakfast foods, a group of five supermarkets in St. Louis found that they were providing the wrong mix of products for their predominately lower-income shoppers. Using these data, the stores increased the space devoted to hot cereals and waffle and pancake mixes, and decreased it for toaster products, breakfast snacks, and nutritional bars (McCarthy, 1991a).

Micromarketing is likely to become even more precise in the future. For instance, stores using electronic scanners may begin to collect and use information regarding the purchases of individual buyers. This would provide them with an exact accounting of what specific individuals buy in a given month. Although such information can be used to increase our understanding of people's purchasing behavior, it also raises concerns about privacy and confidentiality.

There's an additional side to these kinds of data collection capabilities. They open the possibility of stores sending consumers advertisements targeted directly toward their own specific buying habits. Dog owners might receive coupons for dogfood, while frequent purchasers of sprouts and tofu could receive ads for health foods. Of course, whether this will improve the quality of life for most of us is a question that has yet to be answered.

Consumer Cognitive Processing: Decision Making in the Marketplace

Micromarketing: A technique of targeting marketing efforts to particular buyers on a neighborhood or even individual store level

Your stereo, which you've had for four years, is giving you some trouble. The cassette player slows down occasionally, and there is some static in the speakers. It's not a terrible problem, but at the same time you begin to think about replacing the stereo with a new one. How do you decide whether to take the plunge and buy a new one, and which one you will choose if you do determine to go ahead with the purchase?

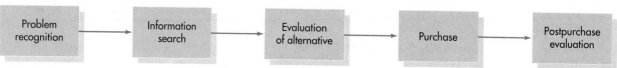

FIGURE 21-2

The five steps in consumer decision making. (Pride & Ferrell, 1987.)

Marketing experts have spent decades attempting to answer these questions, for billions of dollars ride on the collective decisions made by consumers every day. Most sellers employ the model shown in Figure 21-2 to describe the decision sequence, which involves many of the cognitive processes we first discussed in Chapter 9 (Pride & Ferrell, 1987).

Problem Recognition.   According to the model, the first step in the process is to recognize that some type of need exists. In the case of a car that continually breaks down, the need is obvious. In other cases, such as the stereo example described above, the need is more ambiguous, and a certain amount of cognitive effort is required before one can make a decision.

In some cases, no problem exists initially—but salespeople, advertising, or product packaging is used to produce a need. People passing by a bakery and smelling freshly baked bread may suddenly decide that they ought to purchase bread for dinner, or a woman seeing an advertisement for a fast, terrific-looking car might decide that her old automobile is beginning to look a little shabby.

Information Search.   Recognizing a problem, consumers then are poised to move to the next stage: information search. In this stage, consumers may simply be in a state of heightened attention, in which they pay greater attention to the comments of friends, read magazine articles, or even look at advertising more carefully. They may also be more involved in the search for information, actively seeking out data on the potential purchase. A person who has decided to purchase a new stereo may call a knowledgeable friend and ask what brand offers the best quality and what store the best price.

Generally, one or more of the following four sources of information is used in this stage (Kotler, 1986):

- Personal sources include family, friends, neighbors, and acquaintances.
- Commercial sources encompass salespersons, advertisements, and packaging displays.
- Public sources include articles in newspapers and magazines, television shows, and consumer-rating organizations such as Consumers Union.
- Experiential sources comprise trying out samples of a product or behavior such as taking a test drive in an automobile.

Which of these sources of influence is most important depends on several factors. Consumers typically receive the most information from commercial sources. But this does not mean that they are the most influential. As we noted in Chapter 19, when self-interest is seen to underlie an information source, it is relatively unpersuasive. On the other hand, information that is provided by sources that have nothing to gain is seen as more believable. Hence, personal, public, and experiential sources of information are most influential.

Evaluation of Alternatives.   You've decided that it is time to purchase a new stereo. How do you choose between all the brands on the market?

To consumer psychologists, the evaluation of alternatives represents a crucial stage in the decision process. It is at this point that a potential buyer makes a decision to purchase one brand instead of another. Actually, several judgments are involved in the evaluation of alternatives. One relates to consideration of the **product attributes**, the characteristics of the product that are relevant to the decision. For example, the attributes of mouthwash might be its strength, its safety, how long its effects linger, its color, its taste, and so forth. For a stereo, it might be its power, the clarity of the sound, or its size.

Consumers also make decisions regarding their **brand beliefs**. By taking brand into account when evaluating products, buyers consider their prior experiences and perceptions about particular product manufacturers. For instance, a stereo buyer might assume that a Sony product is inherently superior because of its reputation as well as its advertising, which stresses the quality of its product line.

Ultimately, consumers place cognitive weights on each of the attributes that are relevant while also considering their brand beliefs. Finally, potential buyers form an overall summary of judgment of each alternative product and then rank order them.

Purchase. The bottom line for product manufacturers is the actual purchase of a particular product. Typically, the product that has been judged the best during the evaluation stage will be the one that is bought. However, this is not always the case, due to two intervening factors. First, the attitudes of others are relevant. For example, if one's spouse has strong feelings about a purchase, his or her attitudes may override the earlier evaluation process.

The second factor relates to unanticipated situational factors. For example, a person's economic position may suddenly change, leading to a change in decision. Similarly, a store might be holding a sale on a nonchosen alternative, leading to a modification in the decision made in the earlier evaluation process.

Major purchases also involve some degree of risk. For example, in the purchase of a car, consumers typically commit to making relatively large loan payments over a period that may be as long as four or five years. Because none of us can see that far into the future with certainty, a decision to buy a car may rest on how willing we are to take financial risks.

Postpurchase Evaluation. You've gone ahead and bought your new stereo. It's already set up, and you're happily listening to it. Like most people who have made a major purchase, you've probably mulled over the reasons you bought the stereo, and are now even more convinced than before you purchased the stereo that it is a wise choice.

There is a good reason for the increasing confidence in the wisdom of your choice, and it has to do with the last stage in the buying decision process: postpurchase evaluation. In the postpurchase evaluation stage, we assess the choice we have made, appraising the advantages and features of the purchase.

If the purchase is an expensive one, consumers often experience cognitive dissonance. As we noted in Chapter 19, **cognitive dissonance** occurs when we hold two cognitions that are contradictory. In the case of a major purchase, we may initially feel, for example, that (1) we made an expensive investment in a product that (2) really isn't all that exciting. Obviously, such cognitions do not fit together well, and we experience cognitive dissonance.

Dissonance theory suggests that to reduce dissonance, we can change either of the two cognitions. Because it is hard to deny the reality of the purchase, the

Product attributes:
Characteristics of a product relevant to a decision

Brand beliefs: The assumptions held by consumers of a product, based on their knowledge of the manufacturer

Cognitive dissonance: The simultaneous holding of two cognitions that are contradictory

second cognition is the one that we are apt to modify. To reduce the dissonance, then, we are apt to convince ourselves that the purchase is, in fact, an excellent one. We can do this in several ways. We may seek out information supportive of our choice and avoid information that favors the unchosen alternative. We may talk to friends and acquaintances, seeking reassurance about the wisdom of our purchase. We may spend time with the product, learning about and using its features.

In some cases, dissonance reduction techniques are impossible. The product may be obviously inadequate or defective, and no cognitive machinations will permit us to see our way around the problem. In this case, we are likely to take some action to improve the situation, such as returning the product or writing a scathing letter to the manufacturer.

Ultimately, the postpurchase evaluation of a product provides us with information that is used in future purchases. In some ways, then, our lives as consumers revolve in a repeating—and seemingly never-ending—cycle.

The Informed Consumer of Psychology: The Informed Consumer of Psychology Meets the Informed Consumer

In our discussion of consumer psychology, we have looked at consumer psychology largely from the perspective of the sellers of products: How can specific advertising techniques lead to higher sales? What is the best method for getting consumers to purchase a particular brand or item? How does a knowledge of psychographics permit sellers to target items to people's personal needs?

Now it's time to turn the tables, and discuss a few strategies, based on psychological principles, that can help us to evade the barrage of selling techniques that are directed at us. Many of these strategies, it should be noted, are closely related to the principles we discussed in the first few chapters of this book, when we considered ways of evaluating psychology's data, research, and theory.

■ Before purchasing an item, consider your needs objectively. Do you need an expensive watch, or will a cheaper model keep time just as well? This does not mean that you should not buy an expensive, high-status brand, but it does mean that you should objectively factor your wishes for the status value of the watch into your purchasing plans.

■ Remember that salespeople and advertisers have their own self-interest in mind in their sales pitches. Their goal is for you to purchase their product, and they are unlikely to provide any information that might cause any other outcome. They are presenting the best-case scenario, and it is up to you to uncover information that may contradict what they are telling you.

■ Use objective research to determine which brand is best. Magazines such as *Consumer Reports* provide ratings of various products and allow you to take advantage of objective comparisons of different brands. Asking friends about their success with products is also useful, but keep in mind that cognitive dissonance processes may make them less than objective sources of information after they have purchased a product.

■ Do your own research. For example, the Federal government publishes "crash ratings" of various automobiles, ranking them in terms of safety. Libraries often contain material that can be helpful in sorting out selling claims.

■ Be systematic. Don't let emotional appeals sway your decision. List product attributes and weight them according to their importance to you prior to making a major purchase.

■ Above all, keep the phases of purchasing in mind. By knowing the stages that consumers pass through as they make their decisions about what to purchase, you are in a considerably better position to make the optimum choice.

RECAP

◀ Consumer psychologists specialize in the marketplace, while industrial-organizational (I/O) psychologists focus on the workplace.

◀ Two major strategies used by advertisers are the soft sell, which concentrates on a product's image, and the hard sell, which focuses on a product's specific qualities.

◀ Psychographics is a technique for understanding purchasing decisions by dividing people into profiles based on differences in their lifestyles.

◀ The decision to make a purchase proceeds in five steps: problem recognition, information search, evaluation of alternatives, purchase, and postpurchase evaluation.

REVIEW

1. _____ psychologists study such topics as motivation and job satisfaction, while _____ psychologists study advertising and buying habits.

2. A television commercial tries to link Mint-Fresh mouthwash with the image of a suave, debonair gentleman. What marketing technique is the company using?
   a. Hard sell
   b. Image-relevant
   c. Soft sell
   d. the "Marlboro Man" technique.

3. The _____ _____ technique of advertising focuses on the qualities of the product instead of promoting an image.

4. _____, or tendencies to change behavior depending on the social situation, determine which type of advertisement will be most effective on a given person.

5. Dividing people into different lifestyle profiles related to buying habits is known as:
   a. Demographics
   b. Psychographics
   c. Market cluster analysis
   d. Psychodynamics

6. Match each of the groups in the VALS™ system with its definition:
   _____ 1. Need-driven
   _____ 2. Outer-directed
   _____ 3. Inner-directed
   _____ 4. Combined

   a. Purchase to increase their own self-awareness
   b. Purchase to satisfy elemental needs
   c. Combine social and self needs
   d. Purchase in order to impress others

7. _____ allows companies to tailor sales techniques to specific neighborhoods and stores.

8. When evaluating alternative products, consumers take into account the _____ _____ and the _____ _____ in a weighted average model.

9. _____ _____ predicts that after buying a purchase, you will tend to feel even more strongly that you made the correct choice.

Ask Yourself

If manufacturers and salespeople become aware of the effects of cognitive dissonance on consumers, how might they use this knowledge when trying to sell a product? Would it matter what type of product it was? How could a shrewd consumer combat this phenomenon?

(Answers to review questions are on page 692.)

INDUSTRIAL-ORGANIZATIONAL PSYCHOLOGY: WORK MOTIVATION AND SATISFACTION

Now and then, Harriette Ternipsede stands up, defying the stream of calls pouring into her telephone. When she does, she said, her supervisors at the Trans World Airlines reservations office here call across the rows of sales agents and tell her to sit down.

Although standing up slows production, it gives her relief from two-hour stretches of sitting at a computer terminal, and, she says, "It's a way to show I'm a person."

But it is not just the supervisors across the room who are watching Ms. Ternipsede. Through her telephone and video display terminal, Ms. Ternipsede's employers constantly monitor the speed and efficiency with which she makes plane reservations and sells tickets. (Kilborn, 1990, p. A1.)

Ms. Ternipsede's comment that standing up is "a way to show I'm a person" is telling. Like most workers, she sees work as something more than simply earning a living: Employment is potentially a means of demonstrating competence, achieving success and status, and fulfilling one's unique potential.

Examining the role of work in people's lives is one of the major focal points for industrial-organizational (I/O) psychology. I/O psychologists consider the role that work plays in people's lives, examining how jobs can be designed so that they are both motivating and satisfying. We turn now to some of their findings.

The Motivation to Work

If you were Harriette Ternipsede, how motivated would you be to perform well? Most of us would agree that her motivation to give her best is probably not particularly high, given the conditions under which she works. Industrial-organizational psychologists are likely to concur, although the reasons behind their answers would vary according to the theoretical approach that they employ. To account for employee motivation, I/O psychologists have developed three broad types of explanations: need theories, cognitive theories, and reinforcement theory.

Need theories of work motivation grow out of Maslow's theory, first discussed in Chapter 11, which proposes that a hierarchy of needs underlies motivation (Maslow, 1987). Maslow suggests that until people's most basic needs are met, more complex and sophisticated needs will go unfulfilled.

In terms of work situations, the theory proposes that workers initially are most concerned with basic job issues such as pay and job security. But as these needs are met, they begin to consider needs relating to more sophisticated and complex issues, more central to their psychological lives. For instance, people may use work as a way to fulfill their need for social contact or to obtain praise. Ultimately, though, workers aspire to the state analogous to the concept of self-actualization, striving to fulfill their unique potential and abilities through their work (Smither, 1988).

In contrast to need theories of motivation, **cognitive theories of work motivation** focus on our cognitions about work. Cognitive theories consider how people understand and think about various aspects of their jobs and the workplace. For instance, one of the major cognitive explanations highlights the role of setting goals (Locke & Latham, 1990).

According to the goal-setting approach, work performance is determined by the goals that people set for themselves. Not just any goal, however, is effective in producing optimum performance; specific, easy goals, or vague goals such as

---

Need theories of work motivation: Theories, based on work of Maslow, that propose that a hierarchy of needs underlies the motivation to work, and that until people's most basic needs are met, more complex needs will go unfulfilled

Cognitive theories of work motivation: Theories that focus on people's cognitions about their jobs and the workplace as the motivations for work

---

ANSWERS (REVIEW I):

1. I/O, consumer   **2.** c   **3.** hard sell   **4.** Self-monitoring   **5.** b   **6.** 1-b; 2-d; 3-a; 4-c   **7.** Micromarketing   **8.** product attributes; brand beliefs   **9.** Cognitive dissonance

According to need theory, workers may initially be satisfied with any job that provides reasonable pay and job security. Once these needs are met, however, they may feel dissatisfied because the job fails to fulfill other needs such as social contact or a sense of achievement.

"do your best" do little to increase performance. The type of goals that do lead to optimum performance is one that is both specific *and* difficult. For instance, we are more motivated to work toward a goal that states "sales will increase by $10,000" than by one saying "sales will increase substantially." (Applying this principle to the academic realm suggests that the goal of "my grade-point average will go from 3.0 to 3.5" is more likely to become a reality than a goal of "getting better grades.")

Reinforcement theories of work motivation rely on the behavioral principles that we first discussed in Chapter 7. According to this approach, employee motivation can be increased through the judicious administration of positive reinforcement. By providing reinforcement for desired behavior and by using dif-

Reinforcement theories of work motivation: Theories that propose that people are motivated to work based on behavioral principles such as positive reinforcement

Whether at work or in volunteer activities, setting a concrete goal is a more effective motivator than stating a general wish to "do better" or "raise funds."

ferent schedules of reinforcement, employers can produce an environment that elicits desired behavior.

In their simplest form, reinforcement approaches govern work settings in which workers are paid for each product they produce (known as "piecework.") For example, in some factories, the more zippers dressmakers sew, the more money they earn. More sophisticated versions of reinforcement theory can be seen in financial incentive plans, in which employees are rewarded with salary increases, bonuses, or even additional vacation time for achieving certain levels of performance (Katzell & Thompson, 1990).

Returning to Harriette Ternipsede's circumstances in the airline reservations office, we can see how each of these approaches provides a useful perspective. Need theories would focus on her need for recognition and her craving for her employers to acknowledge her unique skills and individualism. Cognitive theories might concentrate on the degree to which she is able to set goals for herself, the precision and difficulty of those goals, and whether she feels she is meeting them. Finally, reinforcement theory would examine the reinforcements available in the situation and whether she feels sufficiently rewarded from her employment. Each of the three theories, then, provides a differing, and complementary, perspective on motivation.

Job Satisfaction

What makes for a satisfied worker?

Industrial-organizational psychologists point to several factors that are central to answering this question. For example, one of the most important influences on how satisfied people are with their jobs is the nature of decision making that occurs within the organization for which they work. Employees who believe that there is **decentralized decision making**, meaning that authority extends throughout the organization, experience greater job satisfaction than those in organizations that have **centralized decision making**, meaning that power and authority rest in the hands of just a few people at the top of the organization (Cummings & Berger, 1976).

In one example of decentralization, for instance, certain manufacturing plants permit any employee to shut down the assembly line on which they work if they have a problem that they cannot otherwise resolve. Such authority is particularly significant because it provides workers with the power to stop the entire plant's production. Even though they rarely exercise this power, having the authority to shut down production (which is a very costly possibility) results in workers who feel particularly satisfied with their jobs (Holden, 1986a).

Supervision and Satisfaction: It Is Better to Give Than to Receive.   The supervisory style of a worker's boss represents another important factor affecting job satisfaction. Employees who perceive their boss as being considerate of their own needs tend to be more satisfied with their work than those who view their supervisor as insensitive (Stogdill, 1974).

Conversely, the job satisfaction of supervisors is affected by the behavior and attitudes of the people they are supervising. As a supervisor, one must constantly balance the demands of the organization for both high productivity and high quality of output against the task of motivating and meeting the needs of employees. Under some conditions, this balancing act can prove to be difficult. Employees who are not well qualified for their jobs may need to receive on-the-job training that the supervisor is poorly equipped to provide. Furthermore,

Decentralized decision making: An organizational model in which authority extends throughout the organization

Centralized decision making: An organizational model in which authority rests in the hands of a few people at the top of the organization

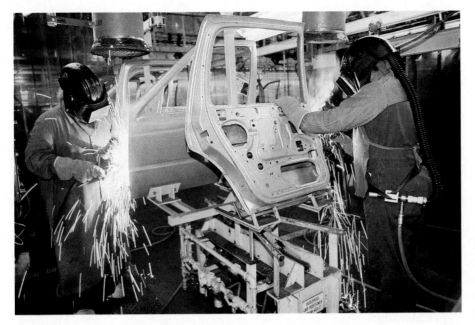

Knowing that they have the power to shut down the entire assembly line if a problem arises that cannot otherwise be solved gives workers a sense of control and participation in decision making.

employees may hold the supervisor personally responsible for the problems they face—even when those problems are not under the supervisor's control. In some situations, then, supervisory responsibilities can lead to lower job satisfaction.

In most cases, however, holding a supervisory position results in a higher level of job satisfaction than being supervised by others. For one thing, bosses tend to have greater responsibility and control over their day-to-day activities than the people under them, and—as we have seen several times before—a sense of control provides important psychological benefits. Furthermore, supervisors have higher status and greater prestige than their subordinates. Finally, bosses have greater power than subordinates to make decisions and to reward and punish others. For all these reasons, it is better to give supervision than to receive it—at least in terms of job satisfaction.

Back to the Future?: Electronic Supervision.   For some workers, the issue is not *who* their supervisor is but *what* it is, for their every keystroke is monitored by the computer terminal at which they work. Consider, for example, the situation of Patricia Alford. When she reports to work each day as a health claims processor for the Equitable Life Assurance Company of New York, she knows exactly what she will do for the next nine hours: sit in front of a computer terminal. Except for two fifteen-minute breaks and an hour off for lunch, Ms. Alford is tied to her terminal—making for a workday filled with tedium, loneliness, and stress. In fact, she doesn't even know how much she will be paid in a given week because her salary depends on how many claims she processes. The pay standards are so complicated that her pay can vary from between $217 to $400 per week, giving her a surprise each time she opens her pay envelope. Moreover, she is closely scrutinized by supervisors. If she stops working, one immediately comes over and asks why (*New York Times*, 1984).

Today's technology has brought an unheard-of degree of sophistication to the tools that managers have to oversee worker productivity, and some experts estimate that between 4 and 6 million clerical workers are currently being monitored electronically at least part of the day (Booth, 1987). In addition to being able to monitor the rate of computer keyboard use—and the specific nature of what is being entered into the computer at a given moment—managers can use the telephone to check on workers. For instance, most telephone operators in the United States are subject to "service observation," which means that a supervisor can listen in on them at any time (Kilborn, 1990).

Ironically, electronic monitoring marks a return to a **classical (or bureaucratic) model of management**, a largely discredited management theory in which explicit rules, regulations, and procedures govern every task. In such a system, a rigid division of labor exists in which people have well-specified and defined jobs that can be carried out with a maximum degree of competence and efficiency. Careful monitoring of an employee's every move is seen as the key to increased productivity (Weber, 1952).

The drawback to such a view of supervision is that it ignores the social nature of the workplace. In settings that follow the classical model, workers easily experience alienation and a loss of a sense of control. They may also develop informal norms that are contrary to management's wishes, such as setting production goals lower than those set by the company. The ultimate result is a decline in efficiency and organizational dysfunction (Katz & Kahn, 1978).

Because of these difficulties with the classical model, then, most organizations today follow a **human relations model of management**, a view of management that places greater emphasis on the social context of work and people's interactions with one another. For example, rather than seeking to control employees, supervisors in many work organizations are taught to act as facilitators, helping workers to carry out their jobs with a sense of independence and control. Proponents of the human relations model recognize the importance of work in people's lives and seek to enhance employee job satisfaction.

The practice of electronic monitoring of employees is difficult to reconcile with the human relations view of management. The clash between the growing technological capabilities of management to monitor employees and employee satisfaction represents one of the newest, and most important, issues for industrial-organizational psychologists. (For another issue related to management styles and job satisfaction, see the Psychology at Work box.)

Satisfaction and the Nature of the Job. Consider what it would be like to walk into a large corporation your first day on the job and be told that your boss is out of town for the next three weeks, and that you should use the time for deciding what you will do and how you are going to get it done. Although some might relish the challenge, most of us would find such a situation difficult, at best.

The degree of explicitness of the rules that determine what is expected of a worker is called **job clarity**. Jobs that have very well-defined expectations have a high degree of clarity, while those that lack clear-cut definitions tend to be low in clarity. The greater the clarity, the more satisfied employees tend to be.

A lack of job clarity is most frequently found in managerial jobs in which there are many different ways to meet a goal—and often no clear-cut goals for which to strive (Kahn et al., 1964). But even relatively low-status positions can produce low clarity, such as the example of an administrative assistant who is not told by his boss what it is he is supposed to do.

Role Conflict. Another factor that has an important impact on job satisfaction is **role conflict**, which arises when job expectations are defined in a way that makes it impossible to carry out the job properly. An individual faced with role

Classical (or bureaucratic) model of management: A largely discredited management theory in which explicit rules govern every task and a rigid division of labor occurs

Human relations model of management: A view of management that places greater emphasis on the social context of work

Job clarity: The degree of explicitness of the rules that determine what is expected of a worker

Role conflict: A problem that occurs when job expectations are defined in a way that makes it impossible to perform the job properly

"What we're looking for is good *kaizens.*"

"Watch that *muda.*"

"We have to *nemawashi* this." (Michaels, 1988, p. 14.)

This is the way that American auto workers chat these days—at least the ones that work at a car production plant in Fremont, California. The auto workers pepper their conversations with Japanese words and phrases because they work under a system developed by the Japanese car manufacturer, Toyota, and their *nemawashi* (discussions) reflect their concern in making *kaizens* (improvements) and preventing *muda* (waste).

It is not just in the linguistic domain that the Japanese are making inroads into American industry. The success of Japanese business organizations has led industrial-organizational psychologists to study Japanese companies, and they have found several factors that make Japanese management styles distinct from those found in the United States. For example, consider the following (Hatvany & Pucik, 1981; Holden, 1986; Imai, 1986a):

- Many Japanese workers are guaranteed lifetime positions. Consequently, employees are less fearful of technological innovations and changes in management than their American counterparts, because they know they will not be replaced. Similarly, advancement in a Japanese company is typically based more on seniority and less on skill. If employees quit their jobs, they must start at the bottom of the status ladder—which makes it less likely that employees will quit. The ultimate result is that Japanese employees tend to stay with the same company and develop tremendous loyalty to it.
- "Quality circles" are used to ensure the quality of goods pro-

IMPORTING JAPAN TO AMERICA

A number of American companies are experimenting with Japanese management techniques. Here workers sing a hymn to productivity in Malibu, California.

duced. Quality circles are small groups of employees who regularly discuss ways of solving work problems. Although the concept of quality circles was a western one—it developed out of humanistic psychological theories such as Maslow's—they have been adopted enthusiastically by the Japanese. Using participative methods of decision making, the workers make decisions that can have a meaningful impact on the workplace.

- Work is done according to the principle of *kaizen.* The Japanese term *kaizen* refers to the constant search for improvement, a norm that is at the heart of Japanese management models. One goal is to produce as much as possible in as little time as possible, but an equally important objective is to produce a high-quality product that can be continually improved. And it is not just products that are expected to progress; employees, too, are constantly striving to improve themselves.
- Companies develop unique philosophies. A conscious effort is made to create a cohesive, familylike atmosphere among employees. Workers are encour-

aged to live together in company housing, to take vacations together, and to socialize during their spare time. Such group activity fosters a strong sense of group cohesiveness and motivates workers to adopt the formal norms of the organization. Rather than giving allegiance to informal groups within the organization, a worker will adopt the norms of the company as a whole. The high cohesiveness serves in this case to increase the influence of the organization over the individual.

- Collective responsibility is stressed. In contrast to the typical American philosophy of individualism, Japanese companies emphasize how success or failure is shared by every worker. If a company is successful in meeting quotas, everyone shares in the accomplishment. Similarly, if the company stumbles, all share in the blame.

Can the Japanese philosophy be successful in the American workplace? If the success of the automobile plant in Fremont is an indication, the answer is yes. Operating as a joint venture between Toyota and General Motors, the plant is producing Chevrolets and Toyotas with fewer defects and higher efficiency than any other GM plant.

The Japanese management philosophy is not without its flaws. Some critics suggest that the emphasis on teamwork and the group stifles individual creativity. Similarly, detractors claim that lifetime employment guarantees and promotion based on seniority make workers less motivated to be successful. Despite these criticisms, though, the success of the Japanese economy makes its organizational philosophy worthy of close examination—something being done by industrial-organizational psychologists.

conflict must respond to two or more sets of pressures or demands that contradict one another—so that if one set of requirements is followed, the other cannot be complied with (Kahn et al., 1964). For example, consider the job of foreman in a manufacturing plant. Suppose one of the foreman's responsibilities is to increase the productivity of his workers. At the same time, he may be told that he must keep the employees happy in order to prevent them from wanting to unionize. This can clearly be a no-win situation. If he forces an increase in productivity he is likely to upset the workers, leading them closer to unionization, but if he tolerates lower productivity, which might prevent the initiation of a unionization drive, he will not be meeting his production goals.

There are other kinds of role conflicts as well. In some cases, the role a person holds outside an organization can produce conflict. A classic example is that of a woman who is simultaneously a mother, a homemaker, and a professional. The job conflicts can create powerful dilemmas. For example, a woman whose child is ill and must be left at home while she makes a business trip experiences conflict no matter what she chooses to do. If she cancels the trip her career and salary may suffer, but if she chooses to go, her child may be resentful (Hammond & Fong, 1988).

As you might expect, role conflict produces a number of serious consequences for individuals and the organizations that employ them (VanSell, Brief, & Schuler, 1981). Not only is job satisfaction generally lower for people in such situations, but they report feeling tense and anxious. They also report low confidence in supervisors and managers above them in the organizational hierarchy. There are also concrete behavioral consequences: Job turnover is higher and productivity lower when people experience role conflict.

Increasing Employee Satisfaction: Fitting the Person to the Job or the Job to the Person. Because job satisfaction has been viewed as so important to employees as well as the organizations for which they work, organizational and industrial psychologists have looked for ways in which it can be promoted. They have identified three main approaches: changing the nature of the job, changing people so they are better matched to the requirements of a particular job, and changing both the jobs and the people that fill them in order to produce a more appropriate match between person and job.

Changing the job. Obviously, if one wants to increase job satisfaction, a logical starting point is the job itself. Role ambiguity and conflict can be reduced by providing carefully delineated job descriptions that describe the specific duties and responsibilities of a given position.

Job enrichment: Techniques for improving the quality of the activities involved in a job

Another strategy relates to the concept of **job enrichment** techniques for improving the quality of the activities involved in a job (Hackman & Oldham, 1976; Katzell & Guzzo, 1983). Job enrichment techniques include:

- Increasing the variety of skills that must be used in a given position
- Modifying what a job entails in order to allow each person to complete a specific, whole, identifiable product
- Increasing the degree to which a person has influence over others
- Increasing the precision with which an individual receives feedback about his or her performance.

When jobs are redesigned to take these dimensions into account, it is possible to increase the meaningfulness of work and the degree to which workers

Employers can promote more positive attitudes toward work by sponsoring enrichment activities such as this English skills class.

feel responsibility for what they have produced. Ultimately, this results not only in higher satisfaction but in increased worker motivation, higher-quality work, lower absenteeism and turnover, and a decrease in job-related stress. These effects can be dramatic. For example, one division of Monsanto found that productivity increased by 75 percent after it started a job-enrichment program (Mares & Simmons, 1985; Umstot, Bell, & Mitchell, 1976).

Changing the person in the job.   In some cases it is impossible to change the nature of a job. Assembly lines, for instance, tend to require people to carry out repetitive activities under unrelenting time constraints, and the job by its very nature cannot be changed very much without revamping the whole assembly-line concept. In situations such as these, an alternative solution is to change people's reactions to the job characteristics that cause low satisfaction (Latham, 1988).

One approach has been the introduction of sensitivity training in organizations to teach members to be more aware of their own feelings and values, as well as those of others. During such training, participants engage in face-to-face interactions in which they discuss their feelings and emotions about themselves and the other members of a group in a ''safe'' setting.

The goals of sensitivity training are to promote greater understanding about others' perspectives and to explore different varieties of social interaction. Advocates assume that the increase in understanding brought about by this process will enable people to be more at ease with the restraints of their jobs—although the evidence supporting such an assumption is decidedly mixed. It is unclear whether the insights gained from participation in sensitivity training generalize to work settings, and, even if they do, whether they ultimately enhance workers' lives (Goldstein, 1986).

Some organizations also use role-playing exercises for employees, in which an incident is described and an individual is assigned to play the role of one of the participants in it. Through this activity, role players come to a better understanding of how *they* might react to being in a similar situation. For example, the role player might have to act out the firing of an employee and would get a chance to see what the reactions of the person receiving the news might be. In this way, he or she might be better able to cope with a similar—and real—incident in the future, ultimately relieving some of the stress that the job entails.

Matching the person to the job.   Rather than expecting to change either the job or the individual who fills it, the most reasonable approach to enhancing job satisfaction is to produce as close a fit as possible between the person in a given position and the position itself. People differ in the degree to which they can tolerate ambiguity and conflict in their jobs. Some people thrive in supervisory roles, whereas others work best under the close supervision of others, without having supervisory responsibilities themselves. As we mentioned in Chapter 14 when discussing the use of personality measures in employee selection, it is at least theoretically possible to keep stress at manageable levels by examining worker personality characteristics and attitudes and by precisely defining the nature of a given job.

Satisfaction May Not Equal Productivity: A Final Note.   Implicit in much of the research that I/O psychologists have carried out in studying job satisfaction is the assumption that there is a link between job satisfaction and worker performance (Petty, McGee, & Cavender, 1984; Druckman & Swets, 1988). Shouldn't a happy worker be a more productive worker?

In fact, the answer seems to be "not necessarily." Only a small and insubstantial relationship exists between workers' satisfaction and their productivity (Iaffaldano & Muchinsky, 1985). What this suggests is that employers seeking to increase both worker productivity and worker satisfaction—two worthy goals—must use different means to achieve the two ends.

Despite the lack of association between productivity and satisfaction, the solutions that have been suggested to increase job satisfaction—changing the job, changing the person, and optimizing the job-person match—still make sense. Indeed, it is reasonable to say that any technique that produces an increase in employee satisfaction is likely to produce a better workplace—one in which the goal of having a motivated, satisfied, and psychologically well-adjusted workforce can be met.

RECAP AND REVIEW II

RECAP

◄ The three major explanations for work motivation are need theories, cognitive theories, and reinforcement theories.

◄ Organizations with more decentralized decision making generally have higher worker satisfaction than those with more centralized decision making.

◄ Job satisfaction is related to the kind of supervisor one has, the nature of the work situation, job clarity, and role conflict.

◄ Approaches to increasing satisfaction in the workplace include changing the nature of the job, changing the person who fills the job, or changing both.

◄ Productivity is only minimally related to job satisfaction.

REVIEW

1. Match the motivational theory of work with its definition:

_____ 1. Need theory

_____ 2. Reinforcement theory

_____ 3. Cognitive theory

a. Work is used as a means to fulfill unsatisfied wants.

b. Motivation is determined by the way people think about work.

c. Motivation is achieved through reward and punishment.

2. Greater job satisfaction occurs when decision making is

_____.

3. A _____ _____ model of management emphasizes the social aspects of work and human interactions. In contrast, a _____ model places importance on rules, regulations, and division of labor.

4. _____ _____ are small employee groups who meet to discuss ways to improve their product.

5. Administrative and managerial jobs generally have a lower level of job clarity than lower-level positions. True or false? _____

6. A worker who is told both to increase the speed at which he works and to increase the quality of his product at the same time may be suffering from what dilemma?

7. _____ _____ describes techniques for improving the quality of a job and giving workers more influence over the task itself and the finished product.

8. I/O psychologists have found that most people can function fairly well within any given job scenario. True or false? _____

Ask Yourself

You are assigned the task of increasing job satisfaction on the floor of an automobile plant without sacrificing a great deal of productivity. What techniques would you use? How would you approach the same problem with a group of managers?

(Answers to review questions are on page 702.)

INDUSTRIAL-ORGANIZATIONAL PSYCHOLOGY: MAKING DECISIONS ON THE JOB

It seemed like a good idea at the time. When Coca-Cola decided, with much fanfare and millions of dollars in costs, to reformulate the ingredients in its popular soft drink, it was banking on the assumption that the public's tastes had changed and that people would prefer the sweeter, less tangy taste of "New Coke." Instead, the public outcry at the change was far greater than the company ever thought possible, and within a few months the original formulation was reintroduced as "Classic Coke." In a news conference, the company chair admitted that Coke had completely miscalculated the public's loyalty to its original formula.

As the above example illustrates, business organizations, like individuals, are not immune from making bad decisions. Even though decisions in organizations tend to be carefully scrutinized and are often made only after months of deliberation, sometimes they still are based on erroneous assumptions and faulty logic—and the results, as noted above, can be disastrous.

Organizational and industrial psychologists have sought to answer a number of questions regarding decision making, including who is best equipped to make a decision, whether decisions ought to be made by individuals or groups, and whether those people who have to implement the decisions should be involved in the decision-making process (Lorsch, 1987). We explore some of their findings next.

Who Makes Decisions: One or Many?

Consider how you might feel if you were told by the president of your company that you must reduce your staff by 20 percent in order to reduce expenses. "Sure," you say to yourself, "it's easy for her to make a decision like this. *She* doesn't have to carry it out. Anyway, why wasn't I included when the decision was made? How can one person determine the best way to cut costs? Everybody knows that group decisions are better: Groups have more facts and information at their disposal, they have a broader perspective, and they can suggest more solutions."

Would your criticisms of the company president be justified?

Answering this question is not a simple task. Consider, for example, the question of whether **participative decision making**, in which the people involved in implementing a decision are involved in making it, is superior to nonpartici-

Participative decision making: A decision-making model in which the people involved in implementing a decision are also involved in making it

pative decision making. Most research suggests that the specifics of each situation must be taken into account. For example, one review of literature on the question found that participative decision making had a positive effect on productivity about as often as it had a negative effect—and more than half of the studies reviewed showed no effect at all (Locke & Schweiger, 1979). On the other hand, research does support the notion that people have higher levels of satisfaction and morale when they implement decisions that they were involved in making than decisions in which they didn't participate. If one is concerned with worker morale, then, participative decision making seems superior.

Clearly, it is not possible to say that participative decision making is invariably effective. Before one can determine whether participative decision making does work, it is necessary to specify the nature of the problem to be decided (Vroom, 1976; Vroom & Yetton, 1973). Highly structured problems—those having clear issues and questions and solutions that will be readily accepted by the people carrying them out—may call for very different decision-making procedures than unstructured problems having solutions that subordinates will have difficulty accepting.

Moreover, participation can take many forms. It can involve a group coming to a joint decision, an advisory group making a recommendation to a manager who then makes the ultimate decision, or someone providing information and potential solutions to a manager, without making a specific recommendation. In sum, the question of whether decisions should be made with the input of those who must implement them is not easily resolved.

Equally complex is the answer to the question of whether decisions are, in general, better made in groups or by individuals. As we suggested in the hypothetical situation in which the company president decides to reduce staff size by 20 percent, group decisions *can* have certain, clear advantages. Groups generally have greater knowledge and information as well as a broader perspective, and they generally produce a greater quantity of solutions (Maier, 1967).

At the same time, group decision making has several disadvantages. Groups are less efficient at making decisions, they have a tendency to adopt compromises that may ultimately lead to poor decisions, and they may be unduly influenced by one or a few powerful individuals. Moreover, they may act too slowly to be able to respond effectively in situations that require immediate action.

We see, then, that group decision making has both advantages and drawbacks. However, several principles provide guidance on whether group or individual decision making is best to accomplish a particular task (Harrison, 1975):

■ For establishing objectives, groups are generally better than individuals because of their collective knowledge.

■ For identifying the greatest number of alternative solutions to a problem, a set of individuals working alone is superior to a group working together—to ensure that nothing is overlooked.

■ For evaluating alternatives, group judgments are superior, since a wider range of information is brought into play.

■ For choosing an alternative, involvement of group members helps ensure a greater stake in the outcome—and greater acceptance of it.

ANSWERS (REVIEW II):

1. 1-a; 2-c; 3-b **2.** decentralized **3.** human relations; bureaucratic **4.** Quality circles **5.** True
6. role conflict **7.** Job enrichment **8.** False; people need to be matched with appropriate jobs to maximize satisfaction.

■ For implementing the choice, individuals tend to be superior to groups. Decisions are usually carried out more effectively when a single person is responsible than when a group is.

Although these guidelines provide general guidance regarding optimum decision making, poor decisions can be made even under the best of circumstances. We turn now to a phenomenon that provides one explanation for why people may make poor decisions: groupthink.

Groupthink

The Bay of Pigs in Cuba marks the site of one of the U.S. government's most embarrassing fiascoes: an abortive attempt to overthrow the government of Fidel Castro. In what he later labeled a "stupid" decision, President John F. Kennedy and a group of advisors decided to support a small group of men with funds and arms to attack Cuba. The 1400 invaders were expected to draw support from the Cuban people and easily defeat the much larger Cuban military forces. The reality was quite different: Within three days of the start of the invasion, most of the attackers were captured.

With the clarity of hindsight that some thirty years affords us, it is clear that Kennedy's decision to allow an ill-equipped group of Cuban refugees to invade a neighboring country that had been well armed by the Soviet Union was the height of folly. How could such a poor decision have been made?

A phenomenon known as groupthink provides an explanation. **Groupthink** is a type of thinking in which group members share such strong motivation to achieve consensus that they lose the ability to critically evaluate alternative points of view (Janis, 1972). Groupthink is most likely to occur when there is a popular or powerful leader who is surrounded by people of lower status—obviously the case with any U.S. President and his advisors, but also true in a variety of other organizations.

The phenomenon of groupthink is apt to occur in several types of situations (McCauley, 1989):

■ There is an illusion that the group is invulnerable and cannot make major errors in judgment.

■ Information that is contradictory to the dominant group view tends to be ignored, discounted, or minimized.

A leader who wants to avoid groupthink should encourage individuality and dissenting opinions among subordinates.

Groupthink: A type of thinking in which group members share such strong motivation to achieve consensus that they lose the ability to critically evaluate alternative points of view

■ Pressures are placed on group members to conform to the majority view—although the pressures may be relatively subtle (such as those discussed in Chapter 20 in reference to conformity).

■ The pressure to conform discourages minority viewpoints from being brought before the group. Consequently, there *appears* to be unanimity in the group, even if this is not really the case.

■ There is an illusion of morality. Because the group views itself as representing something just and moral (in the case of the Bay of Pigs invasion, it was the American cause), members assume that any judgment that is reached by the group will be just and moral as well.

The consequences of groupthink are numerous, and nearly always negative. Groups tend to limit their list of possible solutions to just a few, and they spend relatively little time considering any alternatives once the leader seems to be leaning toward a particular solution. In fact, they may completely ignore information that challenges a developing consensus.

RECAP AND REVIEW III

RECAP

◀ In order to determine whether participative or nonparticipative decision making is superior, the nature of the specific situation must be considered, as well as the type of participation.

◀ In general, group decision making is better for establishing objectives and evaluating and choosing alternatives. Individuals are generally better at identifying alternatives and implementing decisions—all other factors being equal.

◀ Groupthink is a type of thinking in which group members share such strong motivation to achieve consensus that they lose the ability to critically evaluate alternative points of view.

REVIEW

1. Scientific research has proven that group decision making is always superior to individual decision making because of the differing opinions within the group. True or false? _____

2. State whether individuals or groups are generally better at each of the following tasks:
   a. Evaluating alternatives
   b. Implementing decisions
   c. Establishing objectives

3. _____ occurs when a group's desire to achieve consensus is so strong its ability to make effective decisions is compromised.

4. Groupthink is most likely to occur when
   a. the leader is weak.
   b. the group is composed of high-status individuals.
   c. the leader is strong and surrounded by lower-status group members.
   d. the group is considering trivial questions.

Ask Yourself

Can groupthink ever be completely eliminated? How could you as a group member go about minimizing groupthink?

(Answers to review questions are on page 705.)

LOOKING BACK

■ *What roles do consumer psychologists and industrial/organizational (I/O) psychologists play in the marketplace and the workplace?*

1. Consumer psychologists specialize in understanding consumers' buying habits and the effects of advertising on buyer behavior. Industrial/organizational (I/O) psychologists are concerned with the psychology of the workplace, considering worker motivation, satisfaction, and productivity, as well as issues concerning the operation and design of organizations.

■ *How do advertisers develop and target advertisements to particular individuals?*

2. Two major strategies are used in advertising. In the soft sell, advertisers seek to associate a product with a desirable image. In the hard sell, advertisers focus on the specific qualities of the product. The degree to which hard- and soft-sell strategies are effective depends in part on the consumer's level of self-monitoring. Self-monitoring is the tendency people have to change their behavior in order to present themselves well in particular social situations.

3. Psychographics is a technique for dividing people into lifestyle profiles that are related to purchasing patterns. These profiles take into account such characteristics as marital status, race and ethnic background, and education level, as well as the kinds of activities that potential buyers engage in.

4. One of the major psychographic systems is VALS™, derived from Maslow's hierarchy of needs. It suggests that consumers can be divided into four major categories. There are also important subcultural differences in consumer behavior.

■ *What are the major factors considered by consumers when they make a purchase decision?*

5. Five major steps occur in a purchase decision: problem recognition, information search, evaluation of alternatives, purchase, and postpurchase evaluation. Awareness of these stages allows people to make more knowledgeable decisions as consumers.

■ *What accounts for people's work motivation and job satisfaction?*

6. There are three main types of motivational explanations for why people work. Need theories suggests that work satisfies various levels of needs. Cognitive theories focus on cognitions about work, with one explanation focusing particularly on goal-setting behavior. Finally, reinforcement theories suggest that positive reinforcement underlies the motivation to work.

7. One aspect of job satisfaction is the degree to which decisions are decentralized, meaning that authority to make decisions extends throughout an organization. Another aspect is supervision. Generally, people who are in supervisory roles are more satisfied than those who are supervised by others.

8. Electronic supervision via computer leads to worker dissatisfaction. Such supervision is indicative of a classical or bureaucratic model of management, in which explicit rules, regulations, and procedures govern every task. In contrast, human relations management models place greater emphasis on the social context of work and people's interactions with one another.

9. Several approaches produce an increase in job satisfaction. They include changing the nature of the job (through, for example, job enrichment), changing the people who fill the jobs (through sensitivity training or role playing), and matching specific people to specific jobs more effectively.

10. Only a modest relationship exists between job satisfaction and productivity. However, increasing worker satisfaction is likely to have a beneficial impact on work organizations.

■ *How are decisions made by groups?*

11. Research has sought to determine whether participative or nonparticipative decision making is superior. Although the results in terms of productivity are mixed, it is clear that participative decision making is better for worker morale. The question of whether individuals or groups make better decisions is also unresolved; in part, it depends on the nature of the decision being made.

12. One factor working against good group decisions is groupthink, a type of thinking in which group members share such strong motivation to achieve consensus that they lose the ability to critically evaluate alternative points of view. Groupthink is most likely to occur in situations in which there is a popular or powerful leader who is surrounded by individuals who are of lower status.

KEY TERMS AND CONCEPTS

consumer psychologists (p. 680)
industrial-organizational (I/O) psychology (p. 680)
soft sell (p. 681)
hard sell (p. 682)
self-monitoring (p. 682)
psychographics (p. 683)
micromarketing (p. 687)
product attributes (p. 689)
brand beliefs (p. 689)
cognitive dissonance (p. 689)

need theories of work motivation (p. 692)
cognitive theories of work motivation (p. 692)
reinforcement theories of work motivation (p. 693)
decentralized decision making (p. 694)
centralized decision making (p. 694)
classical (or bureaucratic) model of management (p. 696)

human relations model of management (p. 696)
job clarity (p. 696)
role conflict (p. 696)
job enrichment (p. 698)
participative decision making (p. 701)
groupthink (p. 703)

ANSWERS (REVIEW III):

1. False; it depends on the situation.   **2.** a - Groups; b - Individuals; c - Groups   **3.** Groupthink
4. c

GOING BY THE NUMBERS: STATISTICS IN PSYCHOLOGY

SELMA VORWERK

Selma Vorwerk, shortly after her immigration to the United States.

As the boat moved closer to shore, the outline of the Statue of Liberty was plainly visible in the distance. Closer and closer it came, sending a chill down the spine of Selma Vorwerk. A symbol of America, the statue represented the hopes she carried from her native Europe in the early 1900s—hopes of liberty, of success, of a life free of economic and social strain.

Yet as the boat moved closer to Ellis Island, the first point of arrival in the United States, Vorwerk did not realize that her very presence—and that of the other thousands of immigrants seeking their fortune in a land of opportunity—was threatened. A strong political movement was growing in the country on which she was pinning her hopes. This movement sought, by using information collected by psychologists, to stem the flow of immigrants through "scientific" analysis of data.

The major assertion of this group was that a flood of mentally deficient immigrants was poisoning the intellectual capacity of the United States. To proponents of this view, unless drastic measures were taken, it would not be too many years before western civilization collapsed from a lack of collective intelligence.

To support this assertion, Lathrop Stoddard, a member of the anti-immigration movement, reported the results of a study of intelligence in which tests were administered to a group of 82 children and 400 adults. On the basis of these test results, he concluded that the average mental age of Americans was only 14 years—proof to him that unlimited immigration had already seriously eroded American mental capacity.

LOOKING AHEAD

Fortunately for immigrants such as Selma Vorwerk, observers in favor of immigration pointed out the fallacy of using data from a relatively small sample—when a considerably larger set of intelligence test data was available. Specifically, the Army had been collecting intelligence data for years and had the test scores of 1.7 million men available. When these scores were analyzed, it was immediately apparent that the claim that the average mental age of American adults was 14 years was completely without merit.

A debate reminiscent of this earlier one rages today, as some observers suggest that an unrestrained flow of immigrants—this time from Latin America and Asia—would seriously damage the United States. This time, though, the debate is based more on analyses of social and economic statistics, with opponents of immigration suggesting that the social fabric of the country will be changed and that jobs are being taken away from longer-term residents because of the influx of immigrants. Equally vehement proponents of immigration suggest that the relevant statistics are being misinterpreted, and that *their* analyses of the situation result in a quite different conclusion.

Statistics: The branch of mathematics concerned with collecting, organizing, analyzing, and drawing conclusions from numerical data

Statistics, the branch of mathematics concerned with collecting, organizing, analyzing, and drawing conclusions from numerical data, is a part of all our lives. For instance, all of us are familiar with the claims and counterclaims regarding the effects of smoking. The U.S. government requires that cigarette manufacturers include a warning that smoking is dangerous to people's health on every package of cigarettes and in their advertisements; the government's data show clear statistical links between smoking and disease. At the same time, the American Tobacco Institute questions in its advertisements that there is any scientific validity to the claim that smoking is dangerous, for, according to its statistics, the data are inconclusive.

Statistics also lie at the heart of a considerable number of debates within the field of psychology. How do we determine the nature and strength of the effects of heredity on behavior? What is the relationship between learning and schedules of reinforcement? How do we know if the "double standard" of male and female sexual practices has shifted over time? These questions, and most others of interest to psychologists, cannot be answered without a reliance on statistics.

In this appendix, we consider the basic approaches to statistical measurement. We first discuss approaches to summarizing data that allow us to describe sets of observations. Next, we consider techniques for deciding how different one set of scores is from another. Finally, we examine approaches to measuring the relationship between two sets of scores.

After reading this material, then, you will be able to answer these questions:

■ What measures can we use to summarize sets of data?

■ What are the strengths and weaknesses of basic statistical procedures?

■ How can we determine the nature of a relationship and the significance of differences between two sets of scores?

DESCRIPTIVE STATISTICS

Suppose, as a teacher of college psychology, you wanted to evaluate your class's performance on its initial exam. Where might you begin?

You would probably start by using **descriptive statistics**, the branch of statistics that provides a means of summarizing data. For instance, you might first simply list the scores the pupils had received on the test:

72	78	78	92	69	73
85	49	86	86	72	59
58	85	89	80	83	69
78	90	90	96	83	

Viewed in this way, the scores are a jumble of numbers that are difficult to make any sense of. However, there are several methods by which you could begin to organize the scores in a more meaningful way. For example, you might sort them in order of highest to lowest score, as is done in Table A-1. By indicating the number of people who obtained each score, you would have produced what is called a **frequency distribution**, an arrangement of scores from a sample that indicates how often a particular score is present.

Another way of summarizing the scores is to consider them visually. For example, you could construct a **histogram** or bar graph, shown in Figure A-1, page 710. In the histogram, the number of people obtaining a given score is represented pictorially. The scores are ordered along one dimension of the graph, and the number of people obtaining each score along the other dimension.

Arranging the scores from the highest to the lowest allows us to visually interpret the data. Most often, however, visual inspection is insufficient. For one thing, there may be so many scores in a sample that it is impossible to construct a meaningful visual representation. For another, as the research that we dis-

Descriptive statistics: The branch of statistics that provides a means of summarizing data

Frequency distribution: An arrangement of scores from a sample that indicates how often a particular score is present

Histogram: A bar graph used to represent data graphically

TABLE A-1

A SAMPLE FREQUENCY DISTRIBUTION

Score	Number of people attaining that score
96	1
92	1
90	2
89	1
86	2
85	2
83	2
80	1
78	3
73	1
72	2
69	2
59	1
58	1
49	1

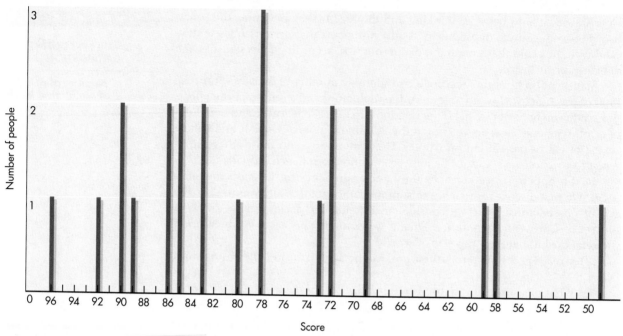

FIGURE A-1

In this histogram, the number of people obtaining each score is represented by a bar.

Central tendency: The most representative score in a distribution of scores (the mean, median, and mode are measures of central tendency)

Mean: The average of all scores, arrived at by adding scores together and dividing by the number of scores

cussed in Chapter 4 suggests, our perceptions of the meaning of stimuli are often biased and inaccurate; more precise, mathematically based measures would seem to be preferable. In cases in which a precise means of summarizing the data is desirable, then, psychologists turn to measures of **central tendency**, the most representative score in a distribution of scores. There are three major measures of central tendency: the mean, the median, and the mode.

The Mean: Finding the Average

The most familiar measure of central tendency is the mean. A **mean** is the technical term for an average, which is simply the sum of all the scores in a set, divided by the number of scores making up the set. For example, to calculate the mean of the sample we have been using, begin by adding each of the numbers $(96 + 92 + 90 + 90 + 89 + \cdots$ and so forth). When you have the total, divide this sum by the number of cases, which is 23. This calculation, $1800 \div 23 = 78.26$, produces a mean score, or average, for our sample, then, of 78.26.

In general, the mean is an accurate reflection of the central score in a set of scores; as you can see from the histogram in Figure A-1, our mean of 78.26 falls roughly in the center of the distribution of scores. Yet the mean does not always provide the best measure of central tendency. For one thing, the mean is very sensitive to extreme scores. As an example, imagine that we added two scores of 20 and 22 to our sample scores. The mean would now become $1842 \div 25$, or 73.68, a drop of almost five points. Because of its sensitivity to extreme scores, then, the mean can sometimes present a deceptive picture of a set of scores, especially where the mean is based on a relatively small number of scores.

Median: The point in a distribution of scores that divides the distribution exactly in half when the scores are listed in numerical order

The Median: Finding the Middle

A measure of central tendency that is less sensitive to extreme scores than the mean is the median. The **median** is the point in a distribution of scores that divides the distribution exactly in half. For example, consider a distribution of five scores 10, 8, 7, 4, and 3. The point that divides the distribution exactly in half is the score 7: Two scores in the distribution lie above the 7 score, while two scores lie below it. If there are an even number of scores in a distribution—in which case there would be no score lying in the middle—the two middle scores would be averaged. If our distribution consisted of scores of 10, 8, 7, 6, 4, and 3, then, we would average the two middle scores of 7 and 6 to form a median of 7 + 6 divided by 2, or 13 ÷ 2 = 6.5.

In our original sample test scores, there are twenty-three scores. The score that divides the distribution exactly in half will be the twelfth score in the frequency distribution of scores, since the twelfth score has eleven scores above it and eleven below it. If you count down to the twelfth score in the distribution depicted in Table A-1 you will see the score is 80. Therefore, the median of the distribution is 80.

One advantage of the median as a measure of central tendency is that it is insensitive to extreme scores. For example, adding the scores of 20 and 22 to our distribution would change the median no more than adding scores of 48 and 47 to the distribution. The reason is clear: The median divides a set of scores in half, and the magnitude of the scores is of no consequence in this process.

The median is often used instead of the mean when extreme scores might be misleading. For example, government statistics on income are typically presented using the median as the measure of central tendency, since the median corrects for the small number of extreme cases of very wealthy individuals, whose high incomes might otherwise inflate the mean income.

The Mode: Finding What Is Most Frequent

The final measure of central tendency is the mode. The **mode** is the most frequently occurring score in a set of scores. If you return to the distribution in Table A-1, you can see that three people scored 78, and the frequency of all of the other scores is either 2 or 1. The mode for the distribution, then, is 78.

Mode: The most frequently occurring score in a set of scores

Some distributions, of course, might have more than one score occurring most frequently. For instance, we could imagine that if the distribution had an additional score of 86 added to the two that are already there, there would be two most frequently occurring categories: 78 and now 86. In this instance, we would say there are two modes—a case known as a **bimodal distribution**.

Bimodal distribution: Cases in which a frequency distribution includes two modes

The mode is often used as a measure of preference or popularity. For instance, if teachers wanted to know who was the most popular child in their elementary school classrooms, they might develop a questionnaire which asked the students to choose someone with whom they would like to participate in some activity. After the choices were tallied, the mode would probably provide the best indication of which child was most popular.

Comparing the Three M's: Mean Versus Median Versus Mode

If a sample is sufficiently large, there is generally little difference between the mean, median, and mode. The reason is that with large samples, scores typically form what is called a normal distribution. A **normal distribution** is a distribution of scores that produces the bell-shaped curve displayed in Figure A-2, page 712, in which the right half mirrors the left half.

Normal distribution: A distribution of scores that produces a bell-shaped, symmetrical curve

Most large distributions, those containing many scores, produce a normal curve. For instance, if you asked a large number of students how many hours a week they studied, you might expect to find that most studied within a similar

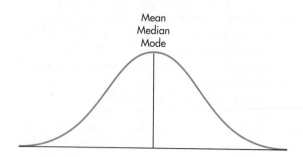

Mean
Median
Mode

FIGURE A-2

In a normal distribution, the mean, median, and mode are identical, falling at the center of the distribution.

range of hours, while there would be a few who studied many, many hours, and some very few who studied not at all. There would be many scores in the center of the distribution of scores, then, and only a few at the extremes—producing a normal distribution. Many phenomena of interest to psychologists produce a normal curve when graphed. For example, if you turn to Figure 10-1 in Chapter 10, where the distribution of intelligence scores is given, you can see the pattern of scores falls into a normal distribution.

The mean, median, and mode fall at exactly the same point in a normal distribution. This means that in a normal distribution of scores, the mean score will divide the distribution exactly in half (the median), and it will be the most frequently occurring score in the distribution (the mode).

The mean, median, and mode differ, however, when distributions are not normal. In cases in which the distributions are **skewed**, or not symmetrical, there is a "hump" at one end or the other (see Figures A-3 and A-4). For instance, if we gave a calculus exam to a group of students enrolled in an elementary algebra class, we would expect that most students would fail the test, leading to low scores being overrepresented in the distribution, as in Figure A-3. On the other hand, if we gave the same students a test of elementary addition problems, the scores would probably form a distribution in which high scores predominated, such as in Figure A-4. Both distributions are skewed, although in opposite directions, and the mean, median, and mode are different from one another.

Skewed distribution: A distribution that is not normal and therefore creates a curve that is not symmetrical

> **RECAP AND REVIEW I**

RECAP

◀ Statistics is the branch of mathematics concerned with collecting, organizing, analyzing, and drawing conclusions from numerical data.

◀ Descriptive statistics is the branch of statistics that provides a means of summarizing data.

◀ Measures of central tendency provide an index of where the centermost point in a distribution of scores lies. The most common measures of central tendency are the mean, median, and mode.

REVIEW

1. A frequency distribution of numbers could be dis-

played pictorially by constructing a bar graph, or _____.

2. Match each item in the left-hand column with the corresponding item in the right-hand column.

   _____ 1. Mean = 10.0   a. 2, 8, 10, 12, 13, 18
   _____ 2. Median = 11   b. 4, 5, 10, 10, 15, 16
   _____ 3. Mode = 12   c. 4, 5, 12, 12, 12, 16

3. The mean, median, and mode are measures of _____ _____.

4. Professor Peters explains to the class that most of the forty exam scores fell within a B range, but there were two extremely high scores. Should she report the median or the mean as a measure of central tendency?

5. The mean, median, and mode will differ in a normal distribution. True or false? _____

(Answers to review questions are on page 714.)

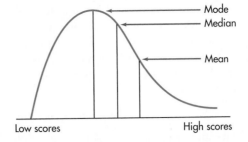

FIGURE A-3

In this skewed distribution, most scores are low.

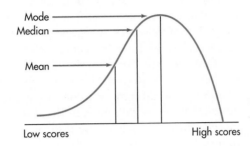

FIGURE A-4

In this example of a skewed distribution, there tend to be more high scores than low ones.

MEASURES OF VARIABILITY

Although measures of central tendency provide us with information about where the center of a distribution lies, often this information is insufficient. For example, suppose a psychologist was interested in determining the nature of people's eye movements while they were reading in order to perfect a new method of teaching reading. It would not be enough to know how *most* people moved their eyes (information that a measure of central tendency would provide); it would also be important to know how much individual people's eye movements differed or varied from one another.

A second important characteristic of a set of scores provides this information: variability. **Variability** is a term that refers to the spread of scores in a distribution. Figure A-5 contains two distributions of scores that have identical means, but which differ in variability. Measures of variability provide a means of describing the spread of scores in a distribution.

Variability: The spread, or dispersion, of scores in a distribution

The Range: Highest to Lowest

The simplest measure of variability is the range. A **range** is the highest score in a distribution minus the lowest score. In the set of scores presented in Table A-1 the distribution has a range of 47 (96 − 49 = 47).

The fact that a range is simple to calculate is about the only virtue it has. The problem with this particular measure of variability is that it is based entirely

Range: The highest score in a distribution minus the lowest score

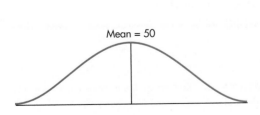

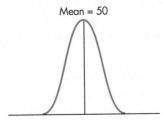

FIGURE A-5

Although the mean is identical in these two distributions, the variability, or spread of scores, is very different.

on extreme scores, and a single score that is very different from the others in a distribution can distort the picture of the distribution as a whole. For example, the addition of a score of 20 to the test score distribution in Table A-1 would almost double the range measure, even though the variability of the remaining scores in the distribution has not changed at all.

The Standard Deviation: Differences from the Mean

Standard deviation: An index of the average deviation of a set of scores from the center of the distribution

The most frequently used method of characterizing the variability of a distribution of scores is the **standard deviation**. The standard deviation bears a conceptual relationship to a mean. You will recall that the mean is the average score in a distribution of scores. A standard deviation is an index of the average deviation of a set of scores from the center of the distribution.

Consider, for instance, the distributions in Figure A-5. The distribution on the left is widely dispersed and on the average an individual score in the distribution can be thought of as deviating quite a bit from the center of the distribution. Certainly the scores in the distribution on the left are going to deviate more from the center of the distribution than those in the distribution on the right.

On the other hand, in the distribution on the right, the scores are closely

TABLE A-2

CALCULATING A STANDARD DEVIATION

1. The calculation of a standard deviation begins with the calculation of the mean of distribution. In the following distribution of scores on a psychology student's weekly quizzes, the mean is 84.5: 82, 88, 71, 86, 96, 84. (As you recall, the mean is the sum of the scores divided by the number of scores in the distribution, or 507 ÷ 6 = 84.5.)
2. The next step is to produce a deviation score for each score in the distribution. A deviation score is simply an original score minus the mean of all the scores in a distribution. This has been done in the second column below:

Original score	Deviation score*	Deviation score squared
82	−2.5	6.25
88	3.5	12.25
71	−13.5	182.25
86	1.5	2.25
96	11.5	132.25
84	−.5	.25

* Original score minus the mean of 84.5.

3. In the third step, the deviation scores are squared (multiplied by themselves) to eliminate negative numbers. This has been carried out in the third column above.
4. The squared deviation scores are then added together, and this sum is divided by the number of scores. In the example above, the sum of the deviation score is 6.25 + 12.25 + 182.25 + 2.25 + 132.25 + .25 = 335.50, and 335.50 ÷ 6 = 55.916.
5. The final step is to take the square root of the resulting number. The square root of 55.916 is 7.4777—which is the standard deviation of the distribution of scores.

ANSWERS (REVIEW I):

1. histogram   **2.** 1-b; 2-a; 3-c   **3.** central tendency   **4.** The median; the mean is too sensitive to extreme scores.   **5.** False; they will be equal.

packed together and there is little deviation of a typical score from the center of the distribution. Based on this analysis, then, it would be expected that a good measure of variability would yield a larger value for the distribution on the left than it would for the one on the right—and, in fact, a standard deviation would do exactly this by indicating how far away a typical score lies from the center of the distribution.

The calculation of the standard deviation follows the logic of calculating the difference of individual scores from the mean of the distribution, and the exact technique is presented in Table A-2. It provides an excellent indicator of the variability of a set of scores because it is based on all of the scores within a set and because it is not highly sensitive to extreme scores. Moreover, the standard deviation provides a means for converting initial scores on standardized tests such as the Scholastic Aptitude Test (SAT) into the scales used to report results. In this way, it is possible to make a score of 585 on the verbal section of the SAT exam, for example, equivalent from one year to the next, even though the specific test items differ from year to year.

RECAP AND REVIEW II

RECAP

◄ Measures of variability provide an index of the dispersion, or spread, of a distribution of scores.
◄ The range and standard deviation are the most commonly used measures of variability.

REVIEW

1. A measure of variability based solely on the distance between the most extreme scores is the
   a. Spread
   b. Standard deviation
   c. Deviation score
   d. Range
2. By simply eyeing the following sets of numbers, predict which will have a higher standard deviation:
   a. 6, 8, 10, 10, 11, 12, 13
   b. 2, 5, 8, 11, 16, 17, 18
3. Calculate the mean and standard deviation for set **a** and **b** in the previous question.
4. The standard deviation is highly sensitive to extreme scores. True or false? _____

(Answers to review questions are on page 716.)

USING STATISTICS TO ANSWER QUESTIONS: INFERENTIAL STATISTICS AND CORRELATION

Suppose you were a psychologist who was interested in whether there was a relationship between smoking and anxiety. Would it be reasonable to simply look at a group of smokers and measure their anxiety using some rating scale? Probably not, since—as we discussed in Chapter 2—it would clearly be more informative if you compared their anxiety to the anxiety exhibited by a group of nonsmokers.

Once you had decided to observe anxiety in two groups of people, you would have to determine just who would be your subjects. In an ideal world with unlimited resources, you might contact *every* smoker and nonsmoker, since these are the two populations with which you are concerned. A **population** consists of all the members of a group of interest. Obviously, however, this would be impossible, given the all-encompassing size of the two groups; instead, you would limit your subjects to a sample of smokers and nonsmokers. A **sample**, in formal statistical terms, is a subgroup of a population of interest that is representative of

Population: All the members of the group being studied

Sample: A subgroup of a population of interest

the larger population. Once you had identified samples representative of the population of interest to you, it would be possible to carry out your study, yielding two distributions of scores—one from the smokers and one from the non-smokers.

The obvious question is whether the two samples differ in the degree of anxiety displayed by their members. The statistical procedures that we discussed earlier are helpful in answering this question, since each of the two samples can be examined in terms of central tendency and variability. The more important question, though, is whether the magnitude of difference between the two distributions is sufficient to conclude that the distributions truly differ from one another, or if, instead, the differences are attributable merely to chance.

To answer the question of whether samples are truly different from one another, psychologists use **inferential statistics**, the branch of statistics that uses data from samples to make predictions about a larger population. To take a simple example, suppose you had two coins that were each flipped 100 times. Suppose further that one coin came up heads forty-one times and the other came up heads sixty-five times. Are both coins fair? We know that a fair coin should come up heads about fifty times in 100 flips. But a little thought would also suggest that it is unlikely that even a fair coin would come up heads exactly fifty times in 100 flips. The question is, then, how far a coin could deviate from fifty heads before the coin would be considered unfair.

Questions such as this—as well as whether the results found are due to chance or represent unexpected, nonchance findings—revolve around how "probable" certain events are. Using coin flipping as an example, fifty-three heads in 100 flips would be a highly probable outcome since it departs only slightly from the expected outcome of fifty heads. In contrast, if a coin was flipped 100 times and ninety of those times it came up heads, it would be a highly improbable outcome. In fact, ninety heads out of 100 flips should occur by chance only once in 2 million trials of 100 flips of a fair coin. Ninety heads in 100 flips, then, is an extremely improbable outcome; if ninety heads did appear, the odds would be that the coin or the flipping process was rigged.

Inferential statistics are used to mathematically determine the probability of observed events. Using inferential statistics to evaluate the result of an experiment, psychologists are able to calculate the likelihood of whether the difference is a reflection of a true difference between populations. For example, suppose we find that the mean on an anxiety scale is 68 for smokers, and 48 for non-smokers. Inferential statistical procedures allow us to determine whether this difference is really meaningful, or whether we might expect the same difference to occur merely because of chance factors.

Results of inferential statistical procedures are described in terms of measures of significance. To a psychologist, a **significant outcome** is one in which the observed outcome would be expected to occur by chance less than five times out of 100. Put another way, a significant difference between two means says that there is a 95 percent or better probability that the difference an experimenter has found is due to real differences between two groups rather than to chance.

Inferential statistics: The branch of statistics that uses data from samples to make predictions about the larger population from which the sample is drawn

Significant outcome: An outcome expected to occur by chance less than 5 percent of the time

---

ANSWERS (REVIEW II):

1. d   **2.** b, because the numbers are more widely dispersed.   **3.** Mean = 10; standard deviation = 2.20; mean = 11, standard deviation = 5.80.   **4.** False; because it is based on all scores; it is not sensitive to extremes.

The Correlation Coefficient: Measuring Relationships

How do we know if television viewing is related to aggression, if reading romance novels is related to sexual behavior, or if mothers' IQs are related to their daughters' IQs?

Each of these questions revolves around the issue of the degree of relationship between two variables. One way of answering them is to draw a **scatterplot**, a means of graphically illustrating the relationship between two variables. We would first collect two sets of paired measures and assign one score to the horizontal axis (variable X) and the other score to the vertical axis (variable Y). Then we would draw a dot at the place where the two scores meet on the graph. The three scatterplots illustrated in Figure A-6 present typical situations. In the first, there is a **positive relationship**, in which high values of variable X are associated with high values of variable Y and low values of X are associated with low values of Y. In the second, there is a **negative relationship**: As values of variable X increase, the values of variable Y decrease. The third panel of the figure illustrates a situation in which no clear relationship between variable X and variable Y exists.

It is also possible to consider scores in terms of their mathematical relationship to one another, rather than simply the way they appear on a scatterplot. Suppose, for example, a psychologist was interested in the degree to which a daughter's IQ was related to the mother's IQ—specifically, if a mother with a high IQ tended to have a daughter who also had a high IQ, and whether a mother with a low IQ tended to have a daughter with a low IQ. To examine the issue, suppose the psychologist measured the IQs of ten mothers and daughters and arranged their IQs as presented in Table A-3, page 718.

An inspection of the data present in the table indicates that the mothers and daughters obviously do not have the same IQs. Moreover, they do not even have IQs that are rank-ordered the same in the two columns. For example, the mother with the highest IQ does not have the daughter with the highest IQ, and the mother with the lowest IQ does not have the daughter with the lowest IQ. It is apparent, then, that there is not a *perfect* relationship between the IQ of the mother and the IQ of the daughter. However, it would be a mistake to conclude that there is a *zero*, or no, relationship between the IQs of the mothers and daughters, since it is clear that there is a tendency for mothers who have high IQs to have daughters with high IQs, and that mothers with low IQs tend to have daughters with low IQs.

Scatterplot: A means of graphically illustrating the relationship between two variables

Positive relationship: A relationship established by data that shows high values of one variable corresponding with high values of another, and low values of the first variable corresponding with low values of the other

Negative relationship: A relationship established by data that shows high values of one variable corresponding with low values of the other

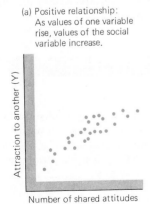

(a) Positive relationship: As values of one variable rise, values of the social variable increase.

Attraction to another (Y)

Number of shared attitudes with another (X)

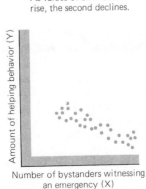

(b) Negative relationship: As values of one variable rise, the second declines.

Amount of helping behavior (Y)

Number of bystanders witnessing an emergency (X)

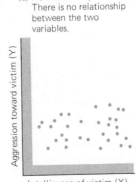

(c) No relationship: There is no relationship between the two variables.

Aggression toward victim (Y)

Intelligence of victim (X)

FIGURE A-6

Scatterplots representing (a) a positive relationship between two variables, (b) a negative relationship, and (c) no clear relationship between two variables.

TABLE A-3

IQ SCORES OF MOTHERS AND DAUGHTERS

Mother's IQ	Daughter's IQ
135	122
128	130
125	110
120	132
114	100
110	116
102	108
96	89
90	84
86	92

Correlation coefficient: A number that indicates the relationship between two variables

The statistic that provides a precise mathematical index of the degree to which two variables are related is the correlation coefficient. A **correlation coefficient** is a number that indicates the extent of the relationship between two variables. It ranges in value from $+1.00$ to -1.00. A value of $+1.00$ would indicate that two variables had a perfect positive relationship with one another, meaning that the highest score on one variable would be associated with the highest score on the other variable, the second highest score on the first variable would be associated with the second highest score on the second variable, and so on. A value of -1.00 would indicate that there was a perfect negative relationship between the two variables; the highest score on the first variable would be associated with the lowest score on the second variable, the second highest score would be associated with the second lowest score, and so forth.

Correlation coefficients around zero indicate that there is no relationship between the two variables. In such cases, there is no tendency for high values on one variable to be associated with either high or low values on the second variable.

Correlation coefficients that range between zero and ± 1.00 reflect varying degrees of relationship between the two variables. For instance, a value of $+.20$ or $-.20$ would indicate that there was a slight relationship between the two variables, a value of around $+.50$ or $-.50$ would indicate a moderate relationship, and a value of $+.80$ or $-.80$ would indicate a relatively strong relationship between the variables. As an example, if we were to calculate the correlation of the two sets of variables in Table A-3, we would find a correlation which is quite strong: The coefficient is $+.86$.

It is important to note that finding a strong correlation between two variables does *not* in any way indicate that one variable *causes* changes in another—only that they are associated with one another. While it might seem plausible to us, for example, that it is the mother's intelligence that causes higher intelligence in a daughter, it is just as possible that a daughter's intelligence affects how the mother performs on an IQ test. (Perhaps the daughter's behavior affects the general home environment, affecting the mother's performance on IQ tests.) It is even plausible that some other unmeasured—and previously unconsidered—third variable is causing both mother's and daughter's IQs to increase or decrease simultaneously. In a clear example of this possibility, even if we found that ice cream sales and violent crimes are correlated with one another (as they happen to be), we would not presume that they were causally related. In this case, it is likely they are both influenced by a third factor—the weather.

The crucial point is that even if we find a perfect correlation between two sets of variables, we would not be able to say that the two variables were linked causally—only that they were strongly related to one another.

RECAP AND REVIEW III

RECAP

◀ Inferential statistical analysis is a technique that uses data from samples to make predictions about a larger population.

◀ Statistical significance occurs when the probability that a difference between means is due to chance is less than 5 in 100.

◀ Measures of relationship provide an index of the degree to which two variables are related. The most frequently used measure is the correlation coefficient.

REVIEW

1. Researchers would like to estimate the level of stress for college freshmen for a given year at a large university. A stress index is given to a randomly assigned group of 500 freshmen. The class size is 6000 for that year. In this example the group of 500 is known as a _____, and the entire class of freshmen is known as the _____.

2. Dr. Sanders states that the results of his experiment show a difference between the two groups, and that there is a

90 percent probability that the results are due to a true difference between the groups and not to chance. Are his results statistically significant?

3. A hypothetical set of data for college freshmen at a university might indicate that as rate of caffeine consumption increases, amount of sleep decreases. The scatterplot for these data is apt to show a _____ relationship.

4. What would the value of the correlation coefficient be for
   a. A perfect negative relationship?
   b. A perfect positive relationship?
   c. No relationship?

5. If we observed a correlation coefficient of −.90 in item 3, we would probably be safe in saying that caffeine consumption *causes* lack of sleep in college students. True or false? _____

6. The researchers in item 3 want to extend their findings to include all college students. As an informed consumer, would you accept their generalization? Why or why not?

(Answers to review questions are given below.)

1. Statistics is concerned with collecting, organizing, analyzing, and drawing conclusions from numerical data. One branch of statistics, descriptive statistics, provides a means of summarizing data.

2. A frequency distribution arranges scores from a sample by indicating how often a particular score is presented. A histogram, or bar graph, presents the same data pictorially.

3. There are three major measures of central tendency, which is the most representative score in a distribution of scores. The mean (or average) is generally the best measure of central tendency. It is calculated by summing the scores in a distribution and dividing by the number of scores. The median is the point or score in a distribution that divides the distribution in half, so that half the scores are higher and half are lower. The third measure of central tendency is the mode. The mode is the most frequently occurring score in a distribution of scores. Distributions sometimes have more than one mode.

4. The range and standard deviation are two measures of variability, which is the spread of scores in a distribution. The range is the highest score in a distribution minus the lowest score. The standard deviation is an index of the extent to which the average score in a distribution deviates from the center of the distribution. The range is a very limited measure of variability because of its sensitivity to extreme scores. The standard deviation, however, is an excellent measure of variability.

5. Inferential statistics, techniques that use data from samples to make predictions about a larger population, are useful in deciding whether differences between distributions of data are attributable to real differences or to chance variation. Usually, if a difference would occur by chance more than 5 times in 100, the difference is attributed to chance. On the other hand, if the difference would occur by chance fewer than 5 times in 100, it is attributed to a true difference brought about by an experimental manipulation.

6. Measures of relationship provide a numerical index of the extent to which two variables are related. The correlation coefficient ranges in value from +1.00 to −1.00, with a +1.00 indicating a perfect positive relationship and −1.00 a perfect negative relationship. Correlations close to or at zero indicate there is little or no relationship between two variables. It is critical to realize that even when correlations are close to perfect one cannot assume that two variables are related in a causal sense.

KEY TERMS AND CONCEPTS

statistics (p. 708)
descriptive statistics (p. 709)
frequency distribution (p. 709)
histogram (p. 709)
central tendency (p. 710)
mean (p. 710)
median (p. 710)
mode (p. 711)

bimodal distribution (p. 711)
normal distribution (p. 711)
skewed distribution (p. 712)
variability (p. 713)
range (p. 713)
standard deviation (p. 714)
population (p. 715)

sample (p. 715)
inferential statistics (p. 716)
significant outcome (p. 716)
scatterplot (p. 717)
positive relationship (p. 717)
negative relationship (p. 717)
correlation coefficient (p. 718)

ANSWERS (REVIEW III):
1. sample; population **2.** No, at least not at the .05 level. **3.** negative **4.** a. −1.00; b. +1.00; c. 0 **5**. False; we cannot assume a causal relation, only an association. **6.** No, the sample (freshmen) does not represent the population (all college students).

ABC model: The model suggesting that an attitude has three components: affect, behavior, and cognition (Ch. 19)

Absolute refractory period: The period following the triggering of a neuron in which the neuron recovers and prepares for another impulse (Ch. 3)

Absolute threshold: The smallest amount of physical intensity by which a stimulus can be detected (Ch. 4)

Accommodation: The ability of the lens to vary its shape in order to focus incoming images on the retina (Ch. 4)

Acetylcholine (a see tul KO leen) **(ACh):** A common neurotransmitter that produces contractions of skeletal muscles (Ch. 3)

Achievement test: A test intended to determine a person's level of knowledge in a given subject (Ch. 10)

Acquired immune deficiency syndrome (AIDS): A fatal, sexually transmitted disease that is caused by a virus that destroys the body's immune system and has no known cure (Ch. 12)

Action potential: An electric nerve impulse that travels through a neuron when it is set off by a "trigger," changing the cell's charge from negative to positive (Ch. 3)

Activation-synthesis theory: Hobson's theory, that dreams are a result of random electrical energy stimulating memories lodged in various portions of the brain, which the brain then weaves into a logical story line (Ch. 6)

Activity theory of aging: A theory that suggests that the elderly who age most successfully are those who maintain the interests and activities they had during middle age (Ch. 14)

Acupuncture: A Chinese technique of relieving pain through the placement of needles in specific areas of the body (Ch. 4)

Adaptation: An adjustment in sensory capacity following prolonged exposure to stimuli (Ch. 4)

Addictive drugs: Drugs that produce a physical or psychological dependence in the user (Ch. 6)

Adolescence: The developmental stage between childhood and adulthood during which many physical, cognitive, and social changes take place (Ch. 14)

Affect component: That part of an attitude encompassing how one feels about the object of one's attitude (Ch. 19)

Afterimage: The image appearing when the eyes shift from a particular image to a blank area (Ch. 4)

Age of viability: The point at which a fetus can survive if born prematurely (Ch. 13)

Aggression: Intentional injury or harm to another person (Ch. 20)

Aggressive cues: Stimuli that have been associated with aggression in the past (Ch. 20)

Ainsworth strange situation: A sequence of events involving a child and his or her mother that provides a measurement of attachment (Ch. 13)

Alarm and mobilization stage: In Selye's general adaptation syndrome, a person's initial awareness of the presence of a stressor (Ch. 16)

Alcohol: The most common depressant, which in small doses causes release of tension and feelings of happiness, but in larger amounts can cause emotional and physical instability, memory impairment, and stupor (Ch. 6)

Alcoholics: People with alcohol abuse problems (Ch. 6)

Algorithm: A set of rules that, if followed, guarantee a solution, though the reason they work may not be understood by the person using them (Ch. 9)

All-or-none law: The principle governing the state of neurons, which are either on (firing) or off (resting) (Ch. 3)

Altered states of consciousness: Experiences of sensation or thought that differ from a normal waking consciousness (Ch. 6)

Altruism: Helping behavior that is beneficial to others while requiring sacrifice on the part of the helper (Ch. 20)

Alzheimer's (ALZ high merz) **disease:** A progressively degenerative disorder associated with aging that includes severe memory loss, physical deterioration, and loss of language abilities (Chs. 3, 8, 14)

Amnesia: Memory loss unaccompanied by other mental difficulties (Ch. 8)

Amphetamines: Strong stimulants that cause a temporary feeling of confidence and alertness but may increase anxiety and appetite loss and, taken over a period of time, suspiciousness and feelings of persecution (Ch. 6)

Anal stage: According to Freud, a stage, from between 12 and 18 months to 3 years of age, in which a child's pleasure is centered on the anus (Ch. 15)

Androgens: Male sex hormones (Ch. 12)

Androgynous: A state in which gender roles encompass characteristics thought typical of both sexes (Ch. 12)

Anorexia nervosa: An eating disorder usually striking young women in which symptoms include self-starvation or near self-starvation in an attempt to avoid obesity (Ch. 11)

Anorgasmia (an or GAZ mee uh): A female's lack of orgasm (Ch. 12)

Anterograde amnesia: Memory loss of events following an injury (Ch. 8)

Antianxiety drugs: Drugs that alleviate stress and anxiety (Ch. 18)

Antidepressant drugs: Medication that improves a depressed patient's mood and feeling of well-being (Ch. 18)

Antipsychotic drugs: Drugs that temporarily alleviate psychotic symptoms such as agitation and over-activity (Ch. 18)

Antisocial or sociopathic personality disorder: A disorder in which individuals display no regard for moral and ethical rules or for the rights of others (Ch. 17)

Anvil: A tiny bone in the middle ear that transfers vibrations to the stirrup (Ch. 4)

Anxiety: A feeling of apprehension or tension (Chs. 15, 17)

Anxiety disorder: The occurrence of anxiety without obvious external cause, intruding on daily functioning (Ch. 17)

Aphasia: A disorder resulting in problems with verbal expression due to brain injury (Ch. 3)

Apraxia: The inability to integrate activities in a logical way (Ch. 3)

Aptitude test: A test designed to predict ability in a particular line of work (Ch. 10)

Archetypes: According to Jung, universal, symbolic representations of a particular person, object, or experience (Ch. 15)

Archival research: The examination of existing records for the purpose of confirming a hypothesis (Ch. 2)

Arousal theory: The belief that we try to maintain certain levels of stimulation and activity, increasing or reducing them as necessary (Ch. 11)

Arrangement problems: Problems whose solution requires the rearrangement of a group of elements in order to satisfy a certain criterion (Ch. 9)

Artificial concepts: Concepts that are clearly defined by a unique set of properties or features (Ch. 9)

Association area: One of the major areas of the brain, the site of the higher mental processes such as thought, language, memory, and speech (Ch. 3)

Associative models: A technique of recalling information by thinking about related information (Ch. 8)

Assumed-similarity bias: The tendency to think of people as being similar to oneself (Ch. 19)

Attachment: The positive emotional bond that develops between parents and their children (Ch. 13)

Attitudes: Learned predispositions to respond in a favorable or unfavorable manner to a particular object (Ch. 19)

Attribution theory: The theory that seeks to explain how we decide, on the basis of samples of an individual's behavior, what the specific causes of that behavior are (Ch. 19)

Auditory canal: A tubelike passage in the ear through which sound moves to the eardrum (Ch. 4)

Authoritarian parents: Parents who are firm and punitive, and who value unquestioning obedience from their children (Ch. 13)

Authoritative parents: Parents who are firm, set clear limits, and reason with and explain things to their children (Ch. 13)

Autobiographical memory: Recollections of the facts about our own lives (Ch. 8)

Autonomic division: The part of the nervous system that controls involuntary movement (the actions of the heart, glands, lungs, and other organs) (Ch. 3)

Autonomy-versus-shame-and-doubt stage: The period during which, according to Erikson, toddlers (ages 18 months to 3 years) develop independence and autonomy if exploration and freedom are en-

couraged, or shame and self-doubt if they are restricted and overprotected (Ch. 13)

Availability heuristic: A rule for judging the probability that an event will occur by the ease with which it can be recalled from memory (Ch. 9)

Aversive conditioning: A technique used to help people break unwanted habits by associating the habits with very unpleasant stimuli (Ch. 18)

Aversive stimuli: Unpleasant or painful stimuli (Ch. 7)

Avoidance conditioning: An organism's response to a signal of an impending unpleasant event in a way that permits its evasion (Ch. 7)

Axon: A long extension from the end of a neuron that carries messages to other cells through the neuron (Ch. 3)

Babble: Speechlike but meaningless sounds (Ch. 9)

Babinski reflex: The reflex action in which an infant fans out its toes in response to a stroke on the outside of its foot (Ch. 13)

Background stressors: Daily hassles, such as being stuck in traffic, that cause minor irritations but have no long-term ill effects, unless they continue or are compounded by other stressful events (Ch. 16)

Barbiturates: Addictive depressants used to induce sleep and reduce stress, the abuse of which, especially when combined with alcohol, can be deadly (Ch. 6)

Basilar membrane: A structure dividing the cochlea into an upper and a lower chamber (Ch. 4)

Behavior component: A predisposition to act in a way that is relevant to one's attitude (Ch. 19)

Behavior modification: A formalized technique for promoting the frequency of desirable behaviors and decreasing the incidence of unwanted ones (Ch. 7)

Behavioral assessment: Direct measures of an individual's behavior used to describe characteristics indicative of personality (Ch. 15)

Behavioral model: The psychological model that suggests that observable behavior should be the focus of study (Ch. 1)

Behavioral model of abnormality: The model that suggests that abnormal behavior itself is the problem to be treated, rather than viewing behavior as a symptom of some underlying medical or psychological problem (Ch. 17)

Behavioral self-management: A procedure in which people learn to identify and resolve their problems using techniques based on learning theory (Ch. 18)

Behavioral treatment approaches: Approaches to treating abnormal behavior that assume that both normal and abnormal behaviors are learned and that appropriate treatment consists of learning new behavior or unlearning maladaptive behavior (Ch. 18)

Bimodal distribution: Cases in which a frequency distribution includes two modes (Appendix)

Biocular disparity: The difference between the images that reach the retina of each eye; this disparity allows the brain to estimate distance (Ch. 5)

Biofeedback: A technique for learning to control internal physiological processes through conscious thought (Ch. 3)

Biological constraints: Built-in limitations in an organism's ability to learn particular behaviors (Ch. 7)

Biological model: The psychological model that views behavior from the perspective of biological functioning (Ch. 1)

Biologically based therapy: An approach to therapy that uses drugs and other medical procedures to improve psychological functioning (Ch. 18)

Biopsychologists: Psychologists who study the ways biological structures and body functions affect behavior (Chs. 1, 3)

Bipolar cells: Nerve cells leading to the brain that are triggered by nerve cells in the eye (Ch. 4)

Bipolar disorder: A disorder in which a person alternates between euphoric feelings of mania and bouts of depression (Ch. 17)

Bisexuality: A sexual attraction to members of both sexes (Ch. 12)

Blocking: A phenomenon in which the association of one conditioned stimulus with an unconditioned stimulus obstructs the learning of a response to a second stimulus (Ch. 7)

Bottom-up processing: Recognition and processing information about the individual components of a stimulus (Ch. 5)

Brain modules: Separate units of the brain that carry out specific tasks (Ch. 3)

Brain scan: A method of "photographing" the brain without opening the skull (Ch. 3)

Brand beliefs: The assumptions held by consumers of a product, based on their knowledge of the manufacturer (Ch. 21)

Broca's aphasia: A syndrome in which speech production is disturbed (Ch. 3)

Bulimia: An eating disorder characterized by a vast intake of food that may be followed by self-induced vomiting (Ch. 11)

Caffeine: An addictive stimulant found most abundantly in coffee, tea, soda, and chocolate (Ch. 6)

Cannon-Bard theory of emotion: The belief that both physiological and emotional arousal are produced simultaneously by the same nerve impulse (Ch. 11)

Cardinal trait: A single personality trait that directs most of a person's activities (e.g., greed, lust, kindness) (Ch. 15)

Case study: An in-depth interview of an individual in order to better understand that individual and to make inferences about people in general (Ch. 2)

Cataclysmic events: Strong stressors that occur suddenly, affecting many people at once (e.g., natural disasters) (Ch. 16)

Catharsis: The notion that aggression is built up and must be discharged through violent acts (Ch. 20)

Central core: The "old brain," which controls such basic functions as eating and sleeping and is common to all vertebrates (Ch. 3)

Central nervous system (CNS): The system that includes the brain and the spinal cord (Ch. 3)

Central route processing: Message interpretation characterized by thoughtful consideration of the issues and arguments used to persuade (Ch. 19)

Central tendency: The most representative score in a distribution of scores (the mean, median, and mode are measures of central tendency) (Appendix)

Central traits: A set of major characteristics that make up the core of a person's personality (Ch. 15) or are the major traits considered in forming impressions of others (Ch. 19)

Centralized decision making: An organizational model in which authority rests in the hands of a few people at the top of the organization (Ch. 21)

Cerebellum (ser rah BELL um): The part of the brain that controls bodily balance (Ch. 3)

Cerebral cortex: The "new brain," responsible for the most sophisticated information processing in the brain; contains the lobes (Ch. 3)

Channels: Paths along which verbal and nonverbal behavioral messages are communicated (e.g., facial expressions, eye contact, body movements) (Ch. 11)

Chlamydia (kla MID ee ah): An STD which initially produces no symptoms in women but which can lead to pelvic inflammation and sterility, and produces in men painful urination and discharge from the penis (Ch. 12)

Chlorpromazine (klor PRO mah zeen): An antipsychotic drug that is used in the treatment of schizophrenia (Ch. 18)

Chromosomes: Rod-shaped structures that contain basic hereditary information (Ch. 13)

Chronological age: A person's physical age (Ch. 10)

Chunk: A meaningful grouping of stimuli that can be stored as a unit in short-term memory (Ch. 8)

Circadian rhythms: Biological processes that occur repeatedly on approximately a twenty-four-hour cycle (Ch. 6)

Classical conditioning: A kind of learning in which a previously neutral stimulus comes to elicit a response through its association with a stimulus that naturally brings about the response (Ch. 7)

Classical (or bureaucratic) model of management: A largely discredited management theory in which explicit rules govern every task and a rigid division of labor occurs (Ch. 21)

Client-centered therapy: Therapy in which the therapist reflects back the patient's statements in a way that causes the patient to find his or her own solutions (Ch. 18)

Clinical psychology: The branch of psychology that deals with the study, diagnosis, and treatment of abnormal behavior (Ch. 1)

Clitoris: The small and very sensitive organ in the female's external genitals (Ch. 12)

Closure: The tendency to group according to enclosed or complete figures rather than open or incomplete ones (Ch. 5)

Cocaine: An addictive stimulant that, when taken in small doses, initially creates feelings of confidence, alertness, and well-being, but eventually causes mental and physical deterioration (Ch. 6)

Cochlea (KOKE lee uh)**:** A coiled tube filled with fluid that receives sound via the oval window or through bone conduction (Ch. 4)

Cognition: The higher mental processes by which we understand the world, process information, make judgments and decisions, and communicate knowledge to others (Ch. 9)

Cognition component: The beliefs and thoughts held about the object of one's attitude (Ch. 19)

Cognitions: People's thoughts, attitudes, and beliefs (Chs. 17, 19)

Cognitive-behavioral approach: A process by which people's faulty cognitions about themselves and the world are changed to more accurate ones (Chs. 17, 18)

Cognitive complexity: The use of and preference for elaborate, intricate, and complex stimuli and thinking patterns (Ch. 9)

Cognitive development: The process by which a child's understanding of the world changes as a function of age and experience (Ch. 13)

Cognitive dissonance: The conflict that arises when a person simultaneously holds cognitions that are contradictory (Chs. 19, 21)

Cognitive learning theory: The study of the thought processes that underlie learning (Ch. 7)

Cognitive map: A mental representation of spatial locations and directions (Ch. 7)

Cognitive model: The psychological model that focuses on how people know, understand, and think about the world (Ch. 1)

Cognitive model of abnormality: The model that suggests that people's thoughts and beliefs are a central component to abnormal behavior (Ch. 17)

Cognitive psychology: The branch of psychology that focuses on the study of higher mental processes, including thinking, language, memory, problem solving, knowing, reasoning, judging, and decision making (Chs. 1, 9)

Cognitive theories of motivation: Theories explaining motivation by focusing on the role of an individual's thoughts, expectations, and understanding of the world (Ch. 11)

Cognitive theories of work motivation: Theories that focus on people's cognitions about their jobs and the workplace as the motivations for work (Ch. 21)

Cognitive therapy: A procedure in which people learn to identify and resolve their problems using techniques based on learning theory (Ch. 18)

Collective unconscious: A concept developed by Jung proposing that we inherit certain personality characteristics from our ancestors and the human race as a whole (Ch. 15)

Community psychology: A movement aimed toward preventing or minimizing psychological disorders in the community (Ch. 18)

Companionate love: The strong affection we have for those with whom our lives are deeply involved (Ch. 20)

Compliance: Behavior that occurs in response to direct social pressure (Ch. 20)

Compulsion: An urge to repeatedly carry out an act that even the sufferer realizes is unreasonable (Ch. 17)

Computerized axial tomography (CAT): A computerized scanner that constructs an image of the brain by combining thousands of separate x-rays taken at slightly different angles (Ch. 3)

Conception: The process by which an egg cell is fertilized by a sperm cell (Ch. 13)

Concepts: Categorizations of objects, events, or people that share common properties (Ch. 9)

Concrete operational stage: According to Piaget, the period from 7 to 12 years of age that is characterized by logical thought and a loss of egocentrism (Ch. 13)

Conditioned response (CR): A response that, after conditioning, follows a previously neutral stimulus (e.g., salivation at the sound of a tuning fork) (Ch. 7)

Conditioned stimulus (CS): A once-neutral stimulus that has been paired with an unconditioned stimulus to bring about a response formerly caused only by the unconditioned stimulus (Ch. 7)

Cones: Cone-shaped, light-sensitive receptor cells in the retina that are responsible for sharp focus and color perception, particularly in bright light (Ch. 4)

Confederate: A participant in an experiment who has been instructed to behave in ways that will affect the responses of other subjects (Ch. 2)

Confirmation bias: A bias in problem solving favoring an initial hypothesis and disregarding contradictory information suggesting alternative solutions (Ch. 9)

Conformity: A change in behavior or attitudes brought about by a desire to follow the beliefs or standards of other people (Ch. 20)

Conscience: The part of the superego that prevents us from doing what is morally wrong (Ch. 15)

Consciousness: A person's awareness of the sensations, thoughts, and feelings that he or she is experiencing at a given moment (Ch. 6)

Consensus information: The degree to which people behave similarly in the same situation (Ch. 19)

Consistency: The persistence of those holding an unpopular view, eventually bringing about a change in the attitude of the majority (Ch. 20)

Consistency information: The degree to which an individual behaves similarly in similar situations (Ch. 19)

Constructive processes: Processes in which memories are influenced by the interpretation and meaning we give to events (Ch. 8)

Constructive theory: A theory suggesting that prior experience and expectations about the size of an object are used to make inferences about its location (Ch. 5)

Consumer psychologists: Psychologists who specialize in understanding buying habits and the effects of advertising on buyer behavior (Ch. 21)

Consumer psychology: The branch of psychology that considers our buying habits and the effects of advertising on buyer behavior (Ch. 1)

Contingency contracting: Acting upon a written contract between a therapist and a client (or parent and child, etc.) that sets behavioral goals, with rewards for achievement (Ch. 18)

Continuous reinforcement schedule: The reinforcing of a behavior every time it occurs (Ch. 7)

Control group: The experimental group receiving no treatment (Ch. 2)

Convergent thinking: A type of thinking which produces responses based on knowledge and logic (Ch. 9)

Conversion disorder: Psychological disturbances characterized by actual physical disturbances, such as the inability to speak or move one's arms (Ch. 17)

Coping: The efforts to control, reduce, or learn to tolerate the threats that lead to stress (Ch. 16)

Cornea: A transparent, protective window into the eyeball (Ch. 4)

Corpus callosum: A bundle of fibers that connects one half of the brain to the other which is thicker in women than in men (Ch. 3)

Correlation coefficient: A number that indicates the relationship between two variables (Appendix)

Correlational research: Research to determine whether there is a relationship between two sets of factors, such as certain behaviors and responses (Ch. 2)

Counseling psychology: The branch of psychology that focuses on educational, social, and career adjustment problems (Ch. 1)

Creativity: The combining of responses or ideas in novel ways (Ch. 9)

Critical period: The first of several stages of development in which specific kinds of growth must occur to enable further normal development (Ch. 13)

Cross-cultural psychology: The branch of psychology that investigates the similarities and differences in psychological functioning in various cultures and ethnic groups (Ch. 1)

Cross-sectional research: A research method in which people of different ages are compared at the same point in time (Ch. 13)

Cross-sequential research: A research method which combines cross-sectional and longitudinal research (Ch. 13)

Crystallized intelligence: Intelligence based on the store of specific information, skills, and strategies that people have acquired through experience (Chs. 10, 14)

Culture-fair IQ test: A test that does not discriminate against members of any minority culture group (Ch. 10)

Cumulative recorder: A device that automatically records and graphs the pattern of responses made in reaction to a particular reinforcement schedule (Ch. 7)

Daily hassles: See *background stressors* (Ch. 16)

Dark adaptation: A heightened sensitivity to light resulting from being in low-level light (Ch. 4)

Date rape: Rape in which the rapist is either a date or an acquaintance (Ch. 12)

Daydreams: Fantasies people construct while awake (Ch. 6)

Decay: The loss of information through nonuse (Ch. 8)

Decentralized decision making: An organizational model in which authority extends throughout the organization (Ch. 21)

Decibel: A measure of sound loudness or intensity (Ch. 4)

Decision/commitment component: In Sternberg's classification of types of love, the initial cognition that one loves someone, and the longer-term feelings of commitment (Ch. 20)

Deductive reasoning: A reasoning process whereby inferences and implications are drawn from a set of assumptions and applied to specific cases (Ch. 9)

Defense mechanisms: Unconscious strategies people use to reduce anxiety by concealing its source from themselves and others (Chs. 15, 16, 18)

Deinstitutionalization: The transfer of former mental patients from institutions into the community (Ch. 18)

Delusions: Firmly held beliefs with no basis in reality (Ch. 17)

Dendrites: Clusters of fibers at one end of a neuron that receive messages from other neurons (Ch. 3)

Denial: A refusal to accept or acknowledge anxiety-producing information (Ch. 15)

Dependent variable: The variable that is measured and is expected to change as a result of experimenter manipulation (Ch. 2)

Depressants: Drugs that slow down the nervous system (Ch. 6)

Depth perception: The ability to view the world in three dimensions and to perceive distance (Ch. 5)

Descriptive statistics: The branch of statistics that provides a means of summarizing data (Appendix)

Determinism: The view suggesting that people's behavior is shaped primarily by factors outside their control (Chs. 1, 15)

Developmental psychology: The branch of psychology that studies how people grow and change throughout the course of their lives (Chs. 1, 13)

Deviation IQ score: A calculation of an IQ score that allows one person's performance to be measured in relation to others (Ch. 10)

Diagnostic and Statistical Manual of Mental Disorders, Third Edition—Revised (DSM-III-R): A manual that presents comprehensive definitions of more than 230 separate diagnostic categories for identifying problems and behaviors (Ch. 17)

Dichotic (dy KOT ik) **listening:** A procedure in which an individual wears earphones through which different messages are sent to each ear at the same time (Ch. 5)

Difference threshold: The smallest detectable difference between two stimuli (Ch. 4)

Diffusion of responsibility: The tendency for people to feel that responsibility for helping is shared among those present in an emergency situation, resulting in the finding that the more people present, the less likely it is that any single person will help (Chs. 2, 20)

Discrimination: Negative behavior toward members of a particular group (Ch. 19)

Discriminative stimulus: A stimulus to which an organism learns to respond as part of stimulus control training (Ch. 7)

Disengagement theory of aging: A theory that suggests that aging is a gradual withdrawal from the world

on physical, psychological, and social levels (Ch. 14)

Displacement: The expression of an unwanted feeling or thought, directed toward a weaker person instead of a more powerful one (Ch. 15)

Display rules: Learned rules that inform us about the appropriateness of showing emotions nonverbally (Ch. 11)

Dispositional causes of behavior: Causes of behavior that are based on internal traits or personality factors (Ch. 19)

Dissociative disorder: Psychological dysfunction characterized by the splitting apart of critical personality facets that are normally integrated, allowing stress avoidance by escape (Ch. 17)

Distinctiveness information: The extent to which a given behavior occurs across different situations (Ch. 19)

Divergent thinking: The ability to generate unusual but appropriate responses to problems or questions (Ch. 9)

Door-in-the-face technique: A strategy in which a large request, refusal of which is expected, is followed by a smaller request (Ch. 20)

Dopamine (DA): A common neurotransmitter that inhibits certain neurons and excites others (Ch. 3)

Dopamine hypothesis: A theory that suggests that schizophrenia occurs when there is excess activity in those areas of the brain using dopamine to transmit nerve impulses (Ch. 17)

Double-blind procedure: The technique by which both the experimenter and the subject are kept from knowing which subjects received a drug, making any observed behavior variations more reliable (Ch. 2)

Double standard: The view that premarital sex is permissible for males but not for females (Ch. 12)

Down syndrome: A disorder caused by the presence of an extra chromosome, resulting in mental retardation (Chs. 10, 13)

Dream interpretation: An examination of a patient's dreams to find clues to the unconscious conflicts and problems being experienced (Ch. 18)

Dreams-for-survival theory: A theory which proposes that dreams permit information critical for our daily survival to be reconsidered and reprocessed during sleep (Ch. 6)

Drive: A motivational tension or arousal that energizes behavior in order to fulfill a need (Ch. 11)

Drive-reduction theory: The theory which claims that drives are produced to obtain our basic biological requirements (Ch. 11)

Drug therapy: Control of psychological problems through drugs (Ch. 18)

Dyslexia (dis LEX ee uh)**:** A disability with a perceptual basis that can result in the reversal of letters during reading and writing, confusion between left and right, and difficulties in spelling (Ch. 5)

Eardrum: The part of the ear that vibrates when sound waves hit it (Ch. 4)

Echoic (eh KO ik) **memory:** The storage of information obtained from the sense of hearing (Ch. 8)

Eclectic approach to therapy: An approach to therapy that uses a variety of treatment methods rather than just one (Ch. 18)

Ecological theory: A theory suggesting that the relationship between objects in a scene gives clues about the objects' sizes (Ch. 5)

Educational psychology: The branch of psychology that considers how the educational process affects students (Ch. 1)

Ego: The part of personality that provides a buffer between the id and the outside world (Ch. 15)

Ego-ideal: The part of the superego that motivates us to do what is morally proper (Ch. 15)

Ego-integrity-versus-despair stage: According to Erikson, a period from late adulthood until death during which we review life's accomplishments and failures (Ch. 14)

Egocentric thought: Viewing the world entirely from one's own perspective (Ch. 13)

Ejaculation: The expulsion of semen through the penis (Ch. 12)

Elaborative rehearsal: Organizing information in short-term memory into a logical framework to assist in recalling it (Ch. 8)

Electroconvulsive therapy (ECT): Treatment involving the administration of an electric current to a patient's head to treat depression (Ch. 18)

Electroencephalogram (ee LEK tro en SEF uh lo gram) **(EEG):** A technique that records electrical activity within the brain (Chs. 3, 6)

Embryo: A developed zygote that has a heart, a brain, and other organs (Ch. 13)

Emotion-focused coping: The conscious regulation of emotion as a means of dealing with stress (Ch. 16)

Emotions: Feelings (such as happiness, despair, and sorrow) that generally have both physiological and cognitive elements and that influence behavior (Ch. 11)

Empathy: One person's experiencing of another's emotions, leading to an increased likelihood of responding to the other's needs (Ch. 20)

Encoding: The process by which information is initially recorded in a form usable to memory (Ch. 8)

Encoding specificity: The phenomenon by which memory of information is enhanced when recalled under the same conditions as when it was learned (Ch. 8)

Endocrine system: A chemical communication network that sends messages throughout the nervous system via the bloodstream and secretes hormones that affect body growth and functioning (Ch. 3)

Endorphins: Chemicals produced by the body that interact with an opiate receptor to reduce pain (Ch. 3)

Engram: See *memory trace* (Ch. 8)

Environment: Influences on behavior that occur in the world around us—in family, friends, school, nu-

trition, and many other factors (Ch. 13)

Environmental psychology: The branch of psychology that considers the relationship between people and their physical environment (Ch. 1)

Episodic memories: Stored information relating to personal experiences (Ch. 8)

Erectile failure: A male's inability to achieve or maintain an erection (Ch. 12)

Erogenous (eh RAH jun us) **zones:** Areas of the body that are particularly sensitive because of an unusually rich array of nerve receptors (Ch. 12)

Erotic: Sexually stimulating (Ch. 12)

Escape conditioning: An organism's response, which brings about an end to an aversive situation (Ch. 7)

Estrogen: The female sex hormone (Ch. 12)

Excitatory message: A chemical secretion that makes it more likely that a receiving neuron will fire and an action potential will travel down its axons (Ch. 3)

Excitement phase: A period during which the body prepares for sexual intercourse (Ch. 12)

Exhaustion stage: The third stage of Selye's general adaptation syndrome: failure to adapt to a stressor, leading to physical, psychological, and emotional problems (Ch. 16)

Existential therapy: A humanistic approach that addresses the meaning of life, allowing a client to devise a system of values that gives purpose to his or her life (Ch. 18)

Expectancy-value theory: A cognitive theory that suggests that people are motivated by expectations that certain behaviors will accomplish a goal and their understanding of the importance of the goal (Ch. 11)

Experiment: A study carried out to investigate the relationship between two or more factors by deliberately producing a change in one factor and observing the effect that change has upon other factors (Ch. 2)

Experimental bias: Factors that could lead an experimenter to an erroneous conclusion about the effect of the independent variable on the dependent variable (Ch. 2)

Experimental manipulation: The change deliberately produced in an experiment (Ch. 2)

Experimental psychology: The branch of psychology that studies the processes of sensing, perceiving, learning, and thinking about the world (Ch. 1)

Experimenter expectations: An experimenter's unintentional message to a subject about results expected from the experiment (Ch. 2)

Explicit memory: Intentional or conscious recollection of information (Ch. 8)

Extinction: The weakening and eventual disappearance of a conditioned response (Ch. 7)

Extramarital sex: Sexual activity between a married person and someone who is not his or her spouse (Ch. 12)

Extrinsic motivation: Motivation by which people participate in an activity for a tangible reward (Ch. 11)

Facial-affect program: The activation of a set of nerve impulses that make the face display the appropriate expression (Ch. 11)

Facial-feedback hypothesis: The notion that facial expressions are involved in determining the experience of emotions and in labeling them (Ch. 11)

Factor analysis: A statistical technique for combining traits into broader, more general patterns of consistency (Ch. 15)

Familial retardation: Mental retardation in which there is a history of retardation in a family but no evidence of biological causes (Ch. 10)

Family therapy: An approach that focuses on the family as a whole unit to which each member contributes (Ch. 18)

Fear of success: A fear that being successful will have a negative influence on the way one is perceived (Ch. 11)

Feature analysis: Perception of a shape, pattern, object, or scene by responding to the individual elements that make it up (Ch. 5)

Feature detection: The activation of neurons in the cortex by visual stimuli of specific shapes or patterns (Ch. 4)

Fetal alcohol syndrome: An ailment producing mental and physical retardation in a baby as a result of the mother's high alcohol intake while pregnant (Ch. 13)

Fetus: A developing child, from nine weeks after conception until birth (Ch. 13)

Figure/ground: Figure refers to the object being perceived, whereas ground refers to the background or spaces within the object (Ch. 5)

Fixation: Behavior reflecting an earlier stage of development (Ch. 15)

Fixed-interval schedule: A schedule whereby reinforcement is given at established time intervals (Ch. 7)

Fixed-ratio schedule: A schedule whereby reinforcement is given only after a certain number of responses is made (Ch. 7)

Flashbulb memories: Memories of a specific event that are so clear they seem like "snapshots" of the event (Ch. 8)

Fluid intelligence: The ability to deal with new problems and situations (Chs. 10, 14)

Fluxetine (Prozac): A widely used antidepressant drug (Ch. 18)

Foot-in-the-door technique: A technique in which compliance with an important request is more likely to occur if it follows compliance with a smaller, previous request (Ch. 20)

Forensic psychology: The branch of psychology that focuses on legal issues, such as deciding what criteria indicate that a person is legally insane and whether larger or smaller juries make fairer decisions (Ch. 1)

Forewarning: A procedure in which a subject is told in advance that a persuasive message is forthcoming, sometimes reducing the effects of social influence (Ch. 20)

Formal operational stage: According to Piaget, the period from age 12 to adulthood that is characterized by abstract thought (Ch. 13)

Fovea: A very sensitive region of the retina that aids in focusing (Ch. 4)

Free association: A Freudian therapeutic technique in which a patient says everything that comes to mind to give the therapist a clue to the workings of the patient's unconscious (Ch. 18)

Free will: The human ability to make decisions about one's life (Ch. 1)

Frequency: The number of wave crests occurring each second in any particular sound (Ch. 4)

Frequency distribution: An arrangement of scores from a sample that indicates how often a particular score is present (Appendix)

Frequency theory of hearing: The theory that suggests that the entire basilar membrane acts like a microphone, vibrating in response to sound (Ch. 4)

Frontal lobes: The brain structure located at the front center of the cortex containing major motor and speech and reasoning centers (Ch. 3)

Frustration: A state produced by the thwarting or blocking of some ongoing, goal-directed behavior (Ch. 20)

Functional fixedness: The tendency to think of an object in terms of its most typical use (Ch. 9)

Functionalism: An early approach to psychology that concentrated on what the mind does—the functions of mental activity—and the role of behavior in allowing people to adapt to their environments (Ch. 1)

Fundamental attribution bias: A tendency to attribute others' behavior to dispositional causes but to attribute one's own behavior to situational causes (Ch. 19)

G or g-factor: A theoretical single general factor accounting for mental ability (Ch. 10)

Gag reflex: An infant's reflex to clear its throat (Ch. 13)

Gamma-amino butyric acid (GABA): The nervous system's primary inhibitory neurotransmitter, found in the brain and spinal cord (Ch. 3)

Ganglion cells: Nerve cells that collect and summarize information from rods and carry it to the brain (Ch. 4)

Gate-control theory of pain: The theory that suggests that particular nerve receptors lead to specific areas of the brain related to pain; when these receptors are activated by an injury or bodily malfunction, a "gate" to the brain is opened and pain is sensed (Ch. 4)

Gender: The sense of being male or female (Ch. 12)

Gender roles: Societal expectations about appropriate behavior for women and men (Ch. 12)

Gender schema: A cognitive framework that organizes and guides a child's understanding of gender (Ch. 12)

General adaptation syndrome (GAS): A theory developed by Selye that suggests that a person's response to stress consists of three stages: alarm and mobilization, resistance, and exhaustion (Ch. 16)

Generalized anxiety disorder: The experience of long-term anxiety with no explanation (Ch. 17)

Generativity-versus-stagnation stage: According to Erikson, a period in middle adulthood during which we take stock of our contributions to family and society (Ch. 14)

Genes: The parts of a chromosome through which genetic information is transmitted (Ch. 13)

Genetic makeup: Pertaining to the biological factors that transmit hereditary information (Ch. 13)

Genetic preprogramming theories of aging: Theories that suggest a built-in time limit to the reproduction of human cells (Ch. 14)

Genital herpes: A noncurable virus producing small blisters or sores around the genitals; symptoms disappear but often recur (Ch. 12)

Genital stage: According to Freud, a period from puberty until death marked by mature sexual behavior (i.e., sexual intercourse) (Ch. 15)

Genital warts: An STD that causes small lumpy warts to form on or near the penis or vagina (Ch. 12)

Genitals: The male and female sex organs (Ch. 12)

Geons: The thirty-six fundamental component elements identified by Biederman that when combined in different ways can produce over 150 million objects (Ch. 5)

Gerontologists: Specialists who study aging (Ch. 14)

Gestalt (geh SHTALLT) **laws of organization:** A series of principles that describe how we organize pieces of information into meaningful wholes; they include closure, proximity, similarity, and simplicity (Ch. 5)

Gestalt (geh SHTALLT) **psychology:** An approach to psychology that focuses on the organization of perception and thinking in a ''whole'' sense, rather than on the individual elements of perception (Ch. 1)

Gestalt therapy: An approach to therapy that attempts to integrate a client's thoughts, feelings, and behavior into a whole (Ch. 18)

Gestalts: Patterns studied by the gestalt psychologists (Ch. 5)

Glaucoma (glaw KO muh): A dysfunction of the eye in which fluid pressure builds up and causes a decline in visual acuity (Ch. 4)

Gonorrhea: An STD which leads to infertility and infection (Ch. 12)

Grammar: The framework of rules that determine how our thoughts can be expressed (Ch. 9)

Group therapy: Therapy in which people discuss problems with a group (Ch. 18)

Groupthink: A type of thinking in which group members share such strong motivation to achieve consensus that they lose the ability to critically evaluate alternative points of view (Ch. 21)

Habituation: A decrease in responding to repeated presentations of the same stimulus (Ch. 13)

Hair cells: Tiny cells covering the basilar membrane that, when bent

by vibrations entering the cochlea, transmit neural messages to the brain (Ch. 4)

Hallucinations: Perceptions of things that do not actually exist (Ch. 17)

Hallucinogen (ha LOOS en o jen): A drug that is capable of producing changes in the perceptual process, or hallucinations (Ch. 6)

Halo effect: A phenomenon in which an initial understanding that a person has positive traits is used to infer other uniformly positive characteristics (Ch. 19)

Hammer: A tiny bone in the middle ear that transfers vibrations to the anvil (Ch. 4)

Hard sell: An approach to selling that focuses on the qualities of the product itself (Ch. 21)

Hardiness: A personality characteristic associated with a lower rate of stress-related illness, consisting of three components: commitment, challenge, and control (Ch. 16)

Health psychology: The branch of psychology that explores the relationship of psychological factors and physical ailments or disease (Chs. 1, 16)

Hemispheres: Symmetrical left and right halves of the brain (Ch. 3)

Heredity: Influences on behavior that are transmitted biologically from parents to a child (Ch. 13)

Heritability: A measure of the degree to which a characteristic is related to genetic, inherited factors, as opposed to environmental factors (Ch. 10)

Heroin: A powerful depressant, usually injected, that gives an initial rush of good feeling but leads eventually to anxiety and depression; extremely addictive (Ch. 6)

Heterosexuality: Sexual attraction to members of the opposite sex (Ch. 12)

Heuristic (hyur ISS tik): A rule of thumb that may bring about a solution to a problem but is not guaranteed to do so (Ch. 9)

Hierarchy of fears: A list, in order of increasing severity, of the things that are associated with one's fears (Ch. 18)

Higher-order conditioning: A form of conditioning that occurs when an already conditioned stimulus is paired with a neutral stimulus until the neutral stimulus evokes the same response as the conditioned stimulus (Ch. 7)

Histogram: A bar graph used to represent data graphically (Appendix)

Homeostasis: An organism's maintenance of an internal biological balance or steady state (Chs. 3, 5, 11)

Homosexuality: A sexual attraction to a member of one's own sex (Ch. 12)

Hormones: Chemicals that circulate throughout the blood and affect the functioning and growth of parts of the body (Ch. 3)

Human relations model of management: A view of management that places greater emphasis on the social context of work (Ch. 21)

Humanistic model: The psychological model that suggests that people are in control of their lives (Ch. 1)

Humanistic model of abnormality: The model that suggests that people are basically rational, and that abnormal behavior results from an inability to fulfill human needs and capabilities (Ch. 17)

Humanistic theory (of personality): The theory that emphasizes people's basic goodness and their natural tendency to rise to higher levels of functioning (Ch. 15)

Humanistic therapy: Therapy in which the underlying assumption is that people have control of their behavior, can make choices about their lives, and are essentially responsible for solving their own problems (Ch. 18)

Hypnosis: A state of heightened susceptibility to the suggestions of others (Ch. 6)

Hypochondriasis (HY po kon DRY a sis): A constant fear of illness and misinterpretation of normal aches and pains (Ch. 17)

Hypothalamus: Located below the thalamus of the brain, its major function is to maintain homeostasis, including the regulation of food intake (Chs. 3, 11)

Hypothesis (hy POTH eh sis): A prediction stated in a way that allows it to be tested (Ch. 2)

Iconic (i KON ik) **memory:** The storage of visual information (Ch. 8)

Id: The raw, unorganized, inherited part of personality whose purpose is to reduce tension created by biological drives and irrational impulses (Ch. 15)

Identical twins: Twins with identical genetic makeup (Ch. 13)

Identification: A child's attempt to be similar to his or her same-sex parent (Ch. 15)

Identity: The distinguishing character of the individual: who each of us is, what our roles are, and what we are capable of (Ch. 14)

Identity-versus-role-confusion stage: According to Erikson, a time in adolescence of testing to determine one's own unique qualities (Ch. 14)

Idiographic approaches to personality: A study of personality emphasizing what makes one person different from others and unique (Ch. 15)

Ill-defined problem: A problem whose specific nature is unclear, and the information required to solve it is not obvious (Ch. 9)

Imaginal code: Memory storage based on visual images (Ch. 8)

Immune system: The body's natural defenses that fight disease (Ch. 16)

Implicit memory: Memories of which people are not consciously aware, but which can improve subsequent performance and behavior (Ch. 8)

Implicit personality theories: Theories reflecting our notions of what traits are found together in individuals (Ch. 19)

Impression formation: The process by which an individual organizes information about another individual to form an overall impression of that person (Ch. 19)

Incentive: An external stimulus anticipated as a reward which directs and energizes behavior (Ch. 11)

Incentive theory: The theory explaining motivation in terms of external stimuli (Ch. 11)

Independent variable: The variable that is manipulated in an experiment (Ch. 2)

Inductive reasoning: A reasoning process whereby a general rule is inferred from specific cases, using observation, knowledge, and experience (Ch. 9)

Industrial-organizational (I/O) psychology: The branch of psychology that studies the psychology of the workplace, considering productivity, job satisfaction, and decision making (Chs. 1, 21)

Industry-versus-inferiority stage: According to Erikson, the period during which children aged 6 to 12 years may develop positive social interactions with others or may feel inadequate and become less sociable (Ch. 13)

Inferential statistics: The branch of statistics that uses data from samples to make predictions about the larger populations from which the samples are drawn (Appendix)

Inferiority complex: A phenomenon whereby adults have continuing feelings of weakness and insecurity (Ch. 15)

Information processing: The way in which people take in, use, and store information (Ch. 13)

Informed consent: A document signed by subjects prior to an experiment in which the study and conditions and risks of participation are explained (Ch. 2)

Ingroup-outgroup bias: The tendency to hold less favorable opinions about groups to which we do not belong (outgroups), while holding more favorable opinions about groups to which we do belong (ingroups) (Ch. 19)

Ingroups: Groups to which an individual belongs (Ch. 19)

Inhibited ejaculation: A male's inability to ejaculate when he wants to, if at all (Ch. 12)

Inhibited sexual desire: A condition in which the motivation for sexual activity is restrained or lacking (Ch. 12)

Inhibitory message: A chemical secretion that prevents a receiving neuron from firing (Ch. 3)

Initiative-versus-guilt stage: According to Erikson, the period during which children aged 3 to 6 years experience conflict between independence of action and the sometimes negative results of that action (Ch. 13)

Innate mechanism: According to Chomsky, the innate linguistic capability in humans that emerges as a function of maturation (Ch. 9)

Inner ear: The interior structure that changes sound vibrations into a form that can be transmitted to the brain (Ch. 4)

Inoculation (regarding attitude change): Exposure to arguments opposing one's beliefs, making the subject more resistant to later attempts to change those beliefs (Ch. 20)

Inoculation (regarding stress): Preparation for stress before it is encountered (Ch. 16)

Insight: Sudden awareness of the relationships among various elements that had previously appeared to be independent of one another (Ch. 9)

Insomnia: An inability to get to sleep or stay asleep (Ch. 6)

Instinct: An inborn pattern of behavior that is biologically determined (Ch. 11)

Instinctual drives: Infantile wishes, desires, demands, and needs hidden from conscious awareness (Ch. 15)

Intellectually gifted: Individuals characterized by higher-than-average intelligence, with IQ scores above 130 (Ch. 10)

Intelligence: The capacity to understand the world, think rationally, and use resources effectively when faced with challenges (Ch. 10)

Intelligence quotient (IQ) score: A measure of intelligence that takes into account an individual's mental and chronological ages (Ch. 10)

Intelligence tests: A battery of measures to determine a person's level of intelligence (Ch. 10)

Intensity: (a) A feature of wave patterns that allows us to distinguish between loud and soft sounds

(b) The strength of a stimulus (Ch. 4)

Interactionist: One who believes that a combination of genetic predisposition and environmental influences determines the course of development (Ch. 13)

Interference: The phenomenon by which recall is hindered because of other information in memory which displaces or blocks it out (Ch. 8)

Interneurons: Neurons that transmit information between sensory and motor neurons (Ch. 3)

Interpersonal attraction: Positive feelings for others; liking and loving (Ch. 20)

Intimacy component: In Sternberg's classification of types of love, feelings of closeness and connectedness (Ch. 20)

Intimacy-versus-isolation stage: According to Erikson, a period during early adulthood that focuses on developing close relationships (Ch. 14)

Intoxication: A state of drunkenness (Ch. 6)

Intrinsic motivation: Motivation by which people participate in an activity for their own enjoyment, not for the reward it will get them (Ch. 11)

Introspection: A procedure used to study the structure of the mind, in which subjects are asked to describe in detail what they are experiencing when they are exposed to a stimulus (Ch. 1)

Introversion-extroversion: According to Eysenck, a dimension of personality traits encompassing the shyest to the most sociable people (Ch. 15)

Iris: The colored part of the eye (Ch. 4)

James-Lange theory of emotion: The belief that emotional experience is a reaction to bodily events occurring as a result of an external situation ("I feel sad because I am crying") (Ch. 11)

Job clarity: The degree of explicitness of the rules that determine what is expected of a worker (Ch. 21)

Job enrichment: Techniques for improving the quality of the activities involved in a job (Ch. 21)

Just noticeable difference: See *difference threshold* (Ch. 4)

Keyword technique: The pairing of a foreign word with a common, similar sounding English word to aid in remembering the new word (Ch. 8)

Korsakoff's syndrome: A disease among long-term alcoholics involving memory impairment (Ch. 8)

Language: The systematic, meaningful arrangement of symbols (Ch. 9)

Language-acquisition device: A neural system of the brain hypothesized to permit understanding of language (Ch. 9)

Lanugo (lan OO go)**:** A soft fuzz covering the body of a newborn (Ch. 13)

Latency period: According to Freud, the period between the phallic stage and puberty, during which children's sexual concerns are temporarily put aside (Ch. 15)

Latent content of dreams: According to Freud, the "disguised" meanings of dreams, hidden by more obvious subjects (Chs. 6, 18)

Latent learning: Learning in which a new behavior is acquired but not readily demonstrated until reinforcement is provided (Ch. 7)

Lateral hypothalamus: The part of the brain which, when damaged, results in an organism's starving to death (Ch. 11)

Lateralization: The dominance of one hemisphere of the brain in specific functions (Ch. 3)

Law of effect: Thorndike's theory that responses that satisfy are more likely to be repeated, whereas those that don't satisfy are less likely to be repeated (Ch. 7)

Learned helplessness: A learned belief that one has no control of the environment, or cannot escape from or cope with stress (Chs. 7, 16, 17)

Learned-inattention theory of schizophrenia: A theory that suggests that schizophrenia is a learned behavior consisting of a set of inappropriate responses to social stimuli (Ch. 17)

Learning: A relatively permanent change in behavior brought about by experience (Ch. 7)

Learning theory approach (to language acquisition): Language acquisition follows the principles of reinforcement and conditioning (Ch. 9)

Least-restrictive environment: The official phrase from PL94-142 that guarantees the right of full education for retarded people in an environment that is most similar to the educational environment of typical children (Ch. 10)

Lens: The part of the eye located behind the pupil that bends rays of light to focus them on the retina (Ch. 4)

Levels-of-processing theory: The theory which suggests that the way information is initially perceived and learned determines recall (Ch. 8)

Libido: Freud's term for the psychic energy that fuels the id's drives (Ch. 15)

Light: The stimulus that produces vision (Ch. 4)

Light adaptation: The eye's temporary insensitivity to light dimmer than that to which it has been most recently exposed (Ch. 4)

Limbic system: The part of the brain located outside the "new brain" that controls eating, aggression, and reproduction (Ch. 3)

Linear circuits: Neurons joined in a single line, receiving and transmitting messages only to the next neuronal link (Ch. 3)

Linear perspective: The phenomenon by which distant objects appear to be closer together than nearer objects, a monocular cue (Ch. 5)

Linguistic code: Memory storage relying on language (Ch. 8)

Linguistic-relativity hypothesis: The theory claiming that language shapes and may even determine the way people perceive and understand the world (Ch. 10)

Lithium (LITH ee um)**:** A drug used in the treatment of bipolar disorders (Ch. 18)

Lobes: The four major sections of the cerebral cortex (Ch. 3)

Longitudinal research: A research method which investigates behavior as subjects age (Ch. 13)

Long-term memory: The storage of information on a relatively permanent basis, although retrieval may be difficult (Ch. 8)

Low-balling: A sales strategy in which after an agreement is reached, the seller reveals additional costs and the buyer complies (Ch. 20)

Lysergic acid diethylamide (LSD): One of the most powerful hallucinogens, affecting the operation of neurotransmitters in the brain and causing brain cell activity to be altered (Ch. 6)

Magnetic resonance imaging (MRI): A scanner that produces a powerful magnetic field to provide a detailed, computer-generated image of brain structures (Ch. 3)

Mainstreaming: The integration of retarded people into regular classroom situations (Ch. 10)

Major depression: A severe form of depression that interferes with concentration, decision making, and sociability (Ch. 17)

Mania: An extended state of intense euphoria and elation (Ch. 17)

Manifest content of dreams: According to Freud, the surface story line of dreams (Chs. 6, 18)

Mantra: A sound, word, or syllable repeated over and over to take one into a meditative state (Ch. 6)

Marijuana: A common hallucinogen, usually smoked (Ch. 6)

Masturbation: Sexual self-stimulation (Ch. 12)

Maturation: The unfolding of biologically predetermined patterns of behavior due to aging (Chs. 7, 13)

Mean: The average of all scores, arrived at by adding scores together and dividing by the number of scores (Appendix)

Means-ends analysis: Repeated testing to determine and reduce the distance between the desired outcome and what currently exists in problem solving (Ch. 9)

Median: The point in a distribution of scores that divides the distribution exactly in half when the scores are listed in numerical order (Appendix)

Medical model of abnormality: The model that suggests that when an individual displays symptoms of abnormal behavior, the cause is physiological (Ch. 17)

Medical student's disease: The feeling that symptoms and illnesses about which one studies are characteristic of oneself (Ch. 17)

Meditation: A learned technique for refocusing attention that brings about an altered state of consciousness (Ch. 6)

Medulla: The part of the central core of the brain that controls many important body functions such as breathing and heartbeat (Ch. 3)

Memory: The capacity to record, retain, and retrieve information (Ch. 8)

Memory trace: A physical change in the brain corresponding to the memory of material (Ch. 8)

Menopause: The point at which women stop menstruating, generally at around age 45 (Ch. 14)

Mental age: The typical intelligence level found for people at a given chronological age (Ch. 10)

Mental retardation: A significantly subaverage level of intellectual functioning accompanying deficits in adaptive behavior (Ch. 10)

Mental set: The tendency for old patterns of problem solving to persist (Ch. 9)

Meta-analysis: A procedure in which the outcomes of different studies are quantified so that they may be compared and summarized (Ch. 2)

Metabolism: The rate at which energy is produced and expended by the body (Ch. 11)

Metacognition: An awareness and understanding of one's own cognitive processes (Ch. 13)

Methadone: A chemical used to detoxify heroin addicts (Ch. 6)

Method of loci (LO sy): Assigning words or ideas to places, thereby improving recall of the words by envisioning those places (Ch. 8)

Micromarketing: A technique of targeting marketing efforts to particular buyers in a neighborhood or even individual store level (Ch. 21)

Middle ear: A tiny chamber containing three bones—the hammer, the anvil, and the stirrup—which transmit vibrations to the oval window (Ch. 4)

Midlife crisis: The negative feelings that accompany the realization that we have not accomplished in life what we had hoped to (Ch. 14)

Midlife transition: Beginning around the age of 40, a period during which we come to the realization that life is finite (Ch. 14)

Mild retardation: Mental retardation characterized by an IQ of between 55 and 69 and the ability to function independently (Ch. 10)

Minnesota Multiphasic Personality Inventory-2 (MMPI-2): A test used to identify people with psychological difficulties (Ch. 15)

Mnemonics (neh MON ix): Formal techniques for organizing material to increase the likelihood of its being remembered (Ch. 8)

Mode: The most frequently occurring score in a set of scores (Appendix)

Model: A person serving as an example to an observer; if a model's behavior is rewarded, the observer may imitate that behavior (Ch. 7)

Modeling: Imitating the behavior of others (models) (Ch. 18)

Models: Systems of interrelated ideas and concepts used to explain phenomena (Ch. 1)

Moderate retardation: Mental retardation characterized by an IQ of between 40 and 54 (Ch. 10)

Monocular cues: Signals that allow us to perceive distance and depth with just one eye (Ch. 5)

Mood disorder: Affective disturbance severe enough to interfere with normal living (Ch. 17)

Morphine: Derived from the poppy

flower, a powerful depressant that reduces pain and induces sleep (Ch. 6)

Motion parallax: The change in position of the image of an object on the retina as the head moves, providing a monocular cue to distance (Ch. 5)

Motivation: The factors that direct and energize behavior (Ch. 11)

Motives: Desired goals that prompt behavior (Ch. 11)

Motor area: One of the major areas of the brain, responsible for voluntary movement of particular parts of the body (Ch. 3)

Motor code: Memory storage based on physical activities (Ch. 8)

Motor (efferent) neurons: Neurons that transmit information from the nervous system to muscles and glands (Ch. 3)

Muller-Lyer illusion: An illusion in which two lines of the same length appear to be of different lengths because of the direction of the arrows at the ends of each line; the line with arrows pointing out appears shorter than the line with arrows pointing in (Ch. 5)

Multiple personality: A disorder in which a person displays characteristics of two or more distinct personalities (Ch. 17)

Multiple source/convergent circuits: A hierarchical network of neurons in which information from several neurons is channeled into a single neuron (Ch. 3)

Myelin sheath: An axon's protective coating, made of fat and protein (Ch. 3)

Narcissistic personality disorder: A personality disorder characterized by an exaggerated sense of self and an inability to experience empathy for others (Ch. 17)

Narcolepsy (NARK o lep see): An uncontrollable need to sleep for short periods during the day (Ch. 6)

Narcotics: Drugs that increase relaxation and relieve pain and anxiety (Ch. 6)

Natural concepts: Concepts that are defined by a set of general, relatively loose characteristic features (Ch. 9)

Naturalistic observation: Observation without intervention, in which the investigator records information about a naturally occurring situation and does not intervene in the situation (Ch. 2)

Nature-nurture issue: The issue of the degree to which environment and heredity influence behavior (Ch. 13)

Need-complementarity hypothesis: The hypothesis that people are attracted to others who fulfill their needs (Ch. 20)

Need for achievement: A stable, learned characteristic in which satisfaction comes from striving for and achieving a level of excellence (Ch. 11)

Need for affiliation: A need to establish and maintain relationships with other people (Ch. 11)

Need for power: A tendency to want to make an impression or have an impact on others in order to be seen as a powerful individual (Ch. 11)

Need theories of work motivation: Theories, based on work of Maslow, that propose that a hierarchy of needs underlies the motivation to work, and that until people's most basic needs are met, more complex needs will go unfulfilled (Ch. 21)

Negative reinforcer: A stimulus whose removal is reinforcing, leading to a greater probability that the response bringing about this removal will occur again (Ch. 7)

Negative relationship: A relationship established by data that show high values of one variable corresponding with low values of the other (Appendix)

Neo-Freudian psychoanalysts (neo-Freudians): Theorists who place greater emphasis than Freud did on the functions of the ego and its influence on our daily activities (Ch. 15)

Neonate: A newborn child (Ch. 13)

Nervous system: The brain and its pathways extending throughout the body (Ch. 3)

Neural networks: Groups of organized communication links between cells (Ch. 3)

Neurons: Specialized cells that are the basic elements of the nervous system that carry messages (Ch. 3)

Neuroscientists: Psychologists and researchers from diverse fields who study the nervous system (Ch. 3)

Neurotic anxiety: Anxiety caused when irrational impulses from the id threaten to become uncontrollable (Ch. 15)

Neurotic symptoms: According to Freud, abnormal behavior brought about by anxiety associated with unwanted conflicts and impulses (Ch. 18)

Neuroticism-stability: Eysenck's personality spectrum encompassing people from the moodiest to the most even-tempered (Ch. 15)

Neurotransmitter: A chemical, secreted when a nerve impulse comes to the end of an axon, that carries messages between neurons (Ch. 3)

Neutral stimulus: A stimulus that, before conditioning, has no effect on the desired response (Ch. 7)

Nicotine: An addictive stimulant present in cigarettes (Ch. 6)

Night terrors: Profoundly frightening nightmares which wake up the dreamer (Ch. 6)

Nightmares: Unusually frightening dreams (Ch. 6)

Noise: Background stimulation that interferes with the perception of other stimuli (Ch. 4)

Nominal group technique: A method of decision making in which group members carefully evaluate all ideas and then hold a secret ballot to rate them all (Ch. 21)

Nomothetic approaches to personality: A study of personality accentuating the broad uniformities across behavior (Ch. 15)

Nondirective counseling: A therapeutic technique in which the therapist creates a warm, supportive environment to allow the client to better understand and work out his or her problems (Ch. 18)

Normal distribution: A distribution

of scores that produces a bell-shaped, symmetrical curve (Appendix)

Norms (for tests): Standards of test performance (Ch. 15)

Norms (of behavior): Public standards and attitudes reflecting what is considered to be appropriate social behavior (Ch. 19)

Obedience: A change in behavior due to the commands of others (Ch. 20)

Obesity: The state of being more than 20 percent above the average weight for a person of a particular height (Ch. 11)

Object permanence: The awareness that objects do not cease to exist when they are out of sight (Ch. 13)

Observational learning: Learning through observation of others (models) and observation of the consequences of their behavior (Chs. 7, 15, 18)

Obsession: A thought or idea that keeps recurring (Ch. 17)

Obsessive-compulsive disorder: A disorder characterized by obsessions or compulsions (Ch. 17)

Occipital lobes: The structure of the brain lying behind the temporal lobes; the site of the brain's visual center (Ch. 3)

Oedipal (ED ih pul) **conflict:** A child's sexual interest in his or her opposite-sex parent, typically resolved through identification with the same-sex parent (Ch. 15)

Olfactory cells: The receptor cells of the nose that respond to odors (Ch. 4)

Operant conditioning: Learning in which a voluntary response is strengthened or weakened, depending on its positive or negative consequences; the organism operates on its environment in order to produce a particular result (Ch. 7)

Operationalization: The process of translating a hypothesis into specific testable procedures that can be measured and observed (Ch. 2)

Opiate receptor: A neuron that acts to reduce the experience of pain (Ch. 3)

Opponent-process theory of color vision: The theory that suggests that receptor cells are linked in pairs, working in opposition to each other (Ch. 4)

Opponent-process theory of motivation: The theory that suggests that increases in arousal produce a calming reaction in the nervous system, and vice versa (Ch. 11)

Optic chiasma (ky AZ muh): A point between and behind the eyes at which nerve impulses from the optic nerves are reversed and "righted" in the brain (Ch. 4)

Optic nerve: A bundle of ganglion axons in the back of the eyeball that carry visual information to the brain (Ch. 4)

Oral stage: According to Freud, a stage from birth to 12–18 months in which an infant's center of pleasure is the mouth (Ch. 15)

Organic mental disorders: Problems having a purely biological basis (Ch. 17)

Orgasm: The peak of sexual excitement during which time rhythmic muscular contractions occur in the genitals (Ch. 12)

Otoliths: Crystals in the semicircular canals that sense body acceleration (Ch. 4)

Outer ear: The visible part of the ear that acts as a collector to bring sounds into the internal portions of the ear (Ch. 4)

Outgroups: Groups to which an individual does not belong (Ch. 19)

Oval window: A thin membrane between the middle ear and the inner ear that transmits vibrations while increasing their strength (Ch. 4)

Ovaries: The female reproductive organs (Ch. 12)

Overlearning: Rehearsing material beyond the point of mastery to improve long-term recall (Ch. 8)

Overregularization: Applying rules of speech in instances in which they are inappropriate (Ch. 9)

Ovulation: The monthly release of an egg from an ovary (Ch. 12)

Panic attack: Sudden anxiety characterized by heart palpitations, short-ness of breath, sweating, faintness, and great fear (Ch. 17)

Panic disorder: Anxiety that manifests itself in the form of panic attacks (Ch. 17)

Paraplegia: The inability, as a result of injury to the spinal cord, to voluntarily move any muscles in the lower half of the body (Ch. 3)

Parasympathetic division: The part of the autonomic division of the peripheral nervous system that calms the body, bringing functions back to normal after an emergency has passed (Ch. 3)

Parietal lobes: The brain structure to the rear of the frontal lobes; the center for bodily sensations (Ch. 3)

Partial reinforcement schedule: The reinforcing of a behavior some, but not all, of the time (Ch. 7)

Participative decision making: A decision-making model in which the people who will implement a decision are also involved in making it (Ch. 21)

Passion component: In Sternberg's classification of types of love, the motivational drives relating to sex, physical closeness, and romance (Ch. 20)

Passionate (or romantic) love: A state of intense absorption in someone that is characterized by physiological arousal, psychological interest, and caring for another's needs (Ch. 20)

Penis: The primary male sex organ (Ch. 12)

Penis envy: According to Freud, a girl's wish, developing around age 3, that she had a penis (Ch. 15)

Perception: The sorting out, interpretation, analysis, and integration of stimuli from our sensory organs (Ch. 5)

Perceptual constancy: The phenomenon by which physical objects are perceived as unvarying despite changes in their appearance or the physical environment (Ch. 5)

Peripheral nervous system: All parts of the nervous system *except* the brain and the spinal cord (includes somatic and autonomic divisions) (Ch. 3)

Peripheral route processing: Message interpretation characterized by consideration of the source and related general information rather than of the message itself (Ch. 19)

Peripheral vision: The ability to see objects outside the eyes' main center of focus (Ch. 4)

Permissive parents: Parents who are lax, inconsistent, and undemanding, yet warm toward their children (Ch. 13)

Permissiveness with affection: The view that premarital sex is permissible for both men and women if it occurs within a long-term or loving relationship (Ch. 12)

Personal stressors: Major life events, such as the death of a family member, that have immediate negative consequences which generally fade with time (Ch. 16)

Personality: The sum total of characteristics that differentiate people, or the stability in a person's behavior across different situations (Ch. 15)

Personality disorder: A mental disorder characterized by a set of inflexible, maladaptive personality traits that keep a person from functioning properly in society (Ch. 17)

Personality psychology: The branch of psychology that studies consistency and change in a person's behavior over time, as well as the individual traits that differentiate the behavior of one person from another when each confronts the same situation (Ch. 1)

Phallic stage: According to Freud, a period beginning around age 3 during which a child's interest focuses on the genitals (Ch. 15)

Phencyclidine (PCP): A powerful hallucinogen that alters brain-cell activity and can cause paranoid and destructive behavior (Ch. 6)

Phenylketonuria (FEEN ul kee toe NYUR ee uh) (PKU): The inability to produce an enzyme that resists certain poisons, causing profound mental retardation (Ch. 13)

Pheromones: Chemicals that produce a reaction in other members of a species (Ch. 4)

Phobias: Intense, irrational fears of specific objects or situations (Ch. 17)

Phobic disorder: A disorder characterized by unrealistic fears (phobias) that may keep people from carrying out routine daily behaviors (Ch. 17)

Phonemes (FONE eems): The smallest units of sound used to form words (Ch. 9)

Phonology: The study of the sounds we make when we speak and of how we use those sounds to produce meaning by forming them into words (Ch. 9)

Pitch: The characteristic that makes sound "high" or "low" (Ch. 4)

Pituitary gland: The "master gland," the major component of the endocrine system, which secretes hormones that control growth (Ch. 3)

Place theory of hearing: The theory that states that different frequencies are responded to by different areas of the basilar membrane (Ch. 4)

Placebo (pla SEE bo): A biologically ineffective pill used in an experiment to keep subjects, and sometimes experimenters, from knowing whether or not the subjects have received a behavior-altering drug (Ch. 2)

Plateau phase: A period in which the maximum level of arousal is attained, the penis and clitoris swell with blood, and the body prepares for orgasm (Ch. 12)

Pleasure principle: The principle by which the id operates, in which the person seeks the immediate reduction of tension and the maximization of satisfaction (Ch. 15)

Poggendorf illusion: An illusion involving a line that passes diagonally through two parallel lines (Ch. 5)

Pollyanna effect: The tendency to rate others in a generally positive manner (Ch. 19)

Polygraph: An electronic device that measures bodily changes which may signal that a person is lying; often called a lie detector (Ch. 11)

Pons: The part of the brain that joins the halves of the cerebellum, transmitting motor information to coordinate muscles and integrating movement between the right and left sides of the body (Ch. 3)

Population: All the members of the group being studied (Appendix)

Positive reinforcer: A stimulus added to the environment that brings about an increase in the response that preceded it (Ch. 7)

Positive relationship: A relationship established by data that shows high values of one variable corresponding with high values of another, and low values of the first variable corresponding with low values of the other (Appendix)

Positron emission tomography (PET): A technique to determine activity within the brain at a given moment in time (Ch. 3)

Posttraumatic stress disorder: A phenomenon in which victims of major catastrophes reexperience the original stress event and associated feelings in flashbacks or dreams (Ch. 16)

Practical intelligence: Intelligence related to overall success in living, rather than to intellectual and academic performance (Ch. 10)

Predisposition model of schizophrenia: A model that suggests that individuals may inherit a predisposition toward schizophrenia that makes them particularly vulnerable to stressful factors in the environment (Ch. 17)

Prefrontal lobotomy: The surgical destruction of certain areas of a patient's frontal lobes to improve the control of emotionality (Ch. 18)

Premature ejaculation: A male's inability to delay ejaculation (Ch. 12)

Preoperational stage: According to Piaget, the period from 2 to 7 years of age that is characterized by language development (Ch. 13)

Primary drives: Biological needs such as hunger, thirst, fatigue, and sex (Ch. 11)

Primary erectile failure: A long-term inability to achieve or maintain an erection (Ch. 12)

Primary orgasmic dysfunction: A female's long-term inability to achieve orgasm (Ch. 12)

Primary reinforcer: A reward that satisfies a biological need (e.g., hunger or thirst) and works naturally (Ch. 7)

Priming: Recall of information after having been exposed to related information at an earlier time (Ch. 8)

Principle of conservation: The knowledge that quantity is unrelated to the arrangement and physical appearance of objects (Ch. 13)

Proactive interference: The phenomenon by which information stored in memory interferes with the recall of material learned later (Ch. 8)

Problem-focused coping: The management of a stressful stimulus as a way of dealing with stress (Ch. 16)

Problems of inducing structure: Problems whose solution requires identifying existing relationships among elements presented so as to construct a new relationship among them (Ch. 9)

Process schizophrenia: One course of schizophrenia in which symptoms begin early in life and develop slowly and subtly (Ch. 17)

Product attributes: Characteristics of a product (Ch. 21)

Profound retardation: Mental retardation characterized by an IQ below 25 and an inability to function independently (Ch. 10)

Program evaluation: The assessment of large-scale programs to determine whether they are effective in meeting their goals (Ch. 1)

Programmed instruction: The development of learning by building gradually on basic knowledge, with review and reinforcement when appropriate (Ch. 7)

Projection: A defense mechanism in which people attribute their own inadequacies or faults to someone else (Ch. 15)

Projective personality test: An ambiguous stimulus presented to a person for the purpose of determining personality characteristics (Ch. 15)

Prosocial behavior: Helping behavior (Ch. 20)

Prototypes: Typical, highly representative examples of a concept (Ch. 9)

Proximity: (a) The tendency to group together those elements that are close together (Ch. 5) (b) Nearness to another, one cause for liking (Ch. 20)

Psychoactive drugs: Drugs that influence a person's emotions, perceptions, and behavior (Ch. 6)

Psychoactive substance-use disorder: Disordered behavior involving drug abuse (Ch. 17)

Psychoanalysis: Psychodynamic therapy that involves frequent sessions and often lasts for many years (Ch. 18)

Psychoanalysts: Physicians or psychologists who specialize in psychoanalysis (Ch. 15)

Psychoanalytic model of abnormality: The model that suggests that abnormality stems from childhood conflicts over opposing desires regarding sex and aggression (Ch. 17)

Psychoanalytic theory: Freud's theory that unconscious forces act as determinants of personality (Ch. 15)

Psychodynamic model: The psychological model based on the belief that behavior is motivated by inner forces over which the individual has little control (Ch. 1)

Psychodynamic therapy: Therapy based on the notion that the basic sources of abnormal behavior are unresolved past conflicts and anxiety (Ch. 18)

Psychogenic amnesia: A failure to remember past experience (Ch. 17)

Psychogenic fugue: An amnesiac condition in which people take sudden, impulsive trips, sometimes assuming a new identity (Ch. 17)

Psychographics: A technique for dividing people into lifestyle profiles that are related to purchasing patterns (Ch. 21)

Psychological tests: Standard measures devised to assess behavior objectively (Ch. 15)

Psychology: The scientific study of behavior and mental processes (Ch. 1)

Psychophysics: The study of the relationship between the physical nature of stimuli and a person's sensory responses to them (Ch. 4)

Psychosocial development: Development of individuals' interactions and understanding of each other and of their knowledge and understanding of themselves as members of society (Ch. 13)

Psychosomatic (sy ko so MAT ik) **disorders:** Medical problems caused by an interaction of psychological, emotional, and physical difficulties (Ch. 16)

Psychosurgery: Brain surgery, once used to alleviate symptoms of mental disorder but rarely used today (Ch. 18)

Psychotherapy: The process in which a patient (client) and a professional attempt to remedy the client's psychological difficulties (Ch. 18)

Puberty: The period during which maturation of the sexual organs occurs (Ch. 14)

Punishment: An unpleasant or painful stimulus that is added to the environment after a certain behavior occurs, decreasing the likelihood that the behavior will occur again (Ch. 7)

Pupil: A dark hole in the center of the eye's iris which changes size as the amount of incoming light changes (Ch. 4)

Random assignment to condition: The assignment of subjects to given groups on a chance basis alone (Ch. 2)

Range: The highest score in a distribution minus the lowest score (Appendix)

Rape: The act whereby one person forces another to submit to sexual activity (Ch. 12)

Rapid eye movement (REM) sleep: Sleep occupying around 20 percent of an adult's sleeping time, characterized by increased heart rate, blood pressure, and breathing rate; erections; eye movements; and the experience of dreaming (Ch. 6)

Rational-emotive therapy: Psychotherapy based on Ellis's suggestion that the goal of therapy should be to restructure one's belief into a more realistic, rational, and logical system (Ch. 18)

Rationalization: A defense mechanism whereby people justify a negative situation in a way that protects their self-esteem (Ch. 15)

Reactive schizophrenia: One course of schizophrenia in which the onset of symptoms is sudden and conspicuous (Ch. 17)

Reality principle: The principle by which the ego operates, in which instinctual energy is restrained in order to maintain an individual's safety and integration into society (Ch. 15)

Rebound effect: An increase in REM sleep after one has been deprived of it (Ch. 6)

Recall: Drawing from memory a specific piece of information for a specific purpose (Ch. 8)

Reciprocal concessions: A phenomenon in which requesters are perceived as compromising their initial request, thereby inviting a compromise from the individual being asked to comply (Ch. 20)

Reciprocal determinism: The view that the interaction of environment, behavior, and the individual causes people to behave the way that they do (Ch. 15)

Reciprocity-of-liking effect: The tendency to like those who like us (Ch. 20)

Recognition: Acknowledging prior exposure to a given stimulus, rather than recalling the information from memory (Ch. 8)

Reflexes: Unlearned, involuntary responses to certain stimuli (Ch. 13)

Refractory period: Entered by a male after the resolution stage, a temporary period during which he cannot be sexually aroused again (Ch. 12)

Regression: Behavior reminiscent of an earlier stage of development, carried out in order to have fewer demands put upon oneself (Ch. 15)

Rehearsal: The transfer of material from short- to long-term memory via repetition (Ch. 8)

Reinforcement theories of work motivation: Theories that propose that people are motivated to work based on behavioral principles such as positive reinforcement (Ch. 21)

Reinforcer: Any stimulus that increases the probability that a preceding behavior will be repeated (Ch. 7)

Relative refractory period: The period during which a neuron, not yet having returned to its resting state, requires more than the normal stimulus to be set off (Ch. 3)

Relative size: The phenomenon by which, if two objects are the same size, the one that makes a smaller image on the retina is perceived to be farther away, a monocular cue (Ch. 5)

Reliability: Consistency in the measurements made by a test (Ch. 15)

Replication: The repetition of an experiment in order to verify the results of the original experiment (Ch. 2)

Representativeness heuristic: A rule in which people and things are judged by the degree to which they represent a certain category (Ch. 9)

Repression: The primary defense mechanism, in which unacceptable or unpleasant id impulses are pushed back into the unconscious (Ch. 15)

Research: Systematic inquiry aimed at discovering new knowledge (Ch. 2)

Resistance: An inability or unwillingness to discuss or reveal particular memories, thoughts, or motivations (Ch. 18)

Resistance stage: The second stage of Selye's general adaptation syndrome: coping with the stressor (Ch. 16)

Resolution stage: The final stage of sexual arousal during which the body returns to its normal state (Ch. 12)

Resting state: The nonfiring state of a neuron when the charge equals about −70 millivolts (Ch. 3)

Reticular formation: A group of nerve cells in the brain that arouses the body to prepare it for appropriate action and screens out background stimuli (Ch. 3)

Retina: The part of the eye that converts the electromagnetic energy of light into useful information for the brain (Ch. 4)

Retrieval: The process by which material in memory storage is located, brought into awareness, and used (Ch. 8)

Retrieval cue: A stimulus such as a word, smell, or sound that allows one to more easily recall information located in long-term memory (Ch. 8)

Retroactive interference: The phenomenon by which new information interferes with the recall of information learned earlier (Ch. 8)

Retrograde amnesia: Memory loss of occurrences prior to some event (Ch. 8)

Reuptake: The reabsorption of neurotransmitters by a terminal button (Ch. 3)

Reverse discrimination: Behavior in which people prejudiced against a group compensate for their prejudice by treating the group's members more favorably than others (Ch. 19)

Reverse learning theory: A theory which proposes that dreams have no meaning in themselves, but instead function to rid us of unnecessary information that we have accumulated during the day (Ch. 6)

Rewards-costs approach: The notion that in a situation requiring help, a bystander's perceived rewards must outweigh the costs if helping is to occur (Ch. 20)

Rhodopsin (ro DOP sin)**:** A complex reddish-purple substance that changes when energized by light, causing a chemical reaction (Ch. 4)

Rods: Long, cylindrical, light-sensitive receptors in the retina that perform well in poor light but are largely insensitive to color and small details (Ch. 4)

Role conflict: A problem that occurs when job expectations are defined in a way that makes it impossible to perform the job properly (Ch. 21)

Rooting reflex: A neonate's tendency to turn its head toward things that touch its cheek (Ch. 13)

Rorschach (ROAR shock) **test:** A test consisting of inkblots of indefinite shapes, the interpretation of which is used to assess personality characteristics (Ch. 15)

Rubella: German measles; when contracted by pregnant women, it can cause severe birth defects. (Ch. 13)

Sample: A subgroup of a population of interest (Appendix)

Scatterplot: A means of graphically illustrating the relationship between two variables (Appendix)

Schachter-Singer theory of emotion: The belief that emotions are determined jointly by a nonspecific kind of physiological arousal and its interpretation, based on environmental cues (Ch. 11)

Schedules of reinforcement: The frequency and timing of reinforcement following desired behavior (Ch. 7)

Schemas: Sets of cognitions about people and social experiences (Ch. 19)

Schemas (in memory): General themes in terms of which we remember a situation (Ch. 8)

Schizophrenia: A class of disorders characterized by a severe distortion of reality, resulting in antisocial behavior, silly or obscene behavior, hallucinations, and disturbances in movement (Ch. 17)

School psychology: The branch of psychology devoted to assessing children in elementary and secondary schools who have academic

or emotional problems and to developing solutions to such problems (Ch. 1)

Scientific method: The process of appropriately framing and properly answering questions, used by practitioners of psychology and those engaged in other scientific disciplines, to come to an understanding about the world (Ch. 2)

Secondary drives: Drives in which no biological need is fulfilled (e.g., need for achievement) (Ch. 11)

Secondary erectile failure: A male's temporary inability to achieve or maintain an erection (Ch. 12)

Secondary orgasmic dysfunction: A female's temporary inability to achieve orgasm or her ability to achieve orgasm only under certain conditions (such as masturbation) (Ch. 12)

Secondary reinforcer: A stimulus that becomes reinforcing by its association with a primary reinforcer (e.g., money, which allows us to obtain food, a primary reinforcer) (Ch. 7)

Secondary traits: Less important personality traits (e.g., preferences for certain clothes or movies) that do not affect behavior as much as central and cardinal traits do (Ch. 15)

Selective attention: The perceptual process of choosing a stimulus to attend to (Ch. 5)

Selective exposure: An attempt to minimize dissonance by exposing oneself only to information that supports one's choice (Ch. 19)

Self-actualization: A state of self-fulfillment in which people realize their highest potential (Chs. 11, 15)

Self-concept: The impression one holds of oneself (Ch. 15)

Self-efficacy: The theory that people's learned expectations regarding success determines their behavior (Ch. 15)

Self-fulfilling prophecy: An expectation about the occurrence of an event or behavior that increases the likelihood that the event or behavior will happen (Ch. 19)

Self-monitoring: The tendency to change our behavior in order to present ourselves well in particular social situations (Ch. 21)

Self-perception theory: Bem's theory that people form attitudes by observing their own behavior and applying the same principles to themselves as they do to others (Ch. 19)

Self-report measures: A method of gathering data about people by asking them questions about a sample of their behavior (Ch. 15)

Semantic memories: Stored, organized facts about the world (e.g., mathematical and historical data) (Ch. 8)

Semantics: The rules governing the meaning of words and sentences (Ch. 9)

Semen: A fluid containing sperm that is ejaculated through the penis during orgasm (Ch. 12)

Semicircular canals: Part of the inner ear containing fluid that moves when the body moves to control balance (Ch. 4)

Senility: A broad, imprecise term used in reference to elderly people who experience progressive deterioration of mental abilities, including memory loss, confusion of time and place, and general disorientation (Ch. 14)

Sensate focus: A method of sexual therapy in which attention is directed away from intercourse and toward other pleasurable behaviors (Ch. 12)

Sensation: The process by which an organism responds to a stimulus (Ch. 4)

Sensorimotor stage: According to Piaget, the stage from birth to 2 years during which a child has little competence in representing the environment using images, language, or other symbols (Ch. 13)

Sensory area: The site in the brain of the tissue that corresponds to each of the senses, with the degree of sensitivity relating to the amount of tissue (Ch. 3)

Sensory memory: The initial, short-lived storage of information recorded as a meaningless stimulus (Ch. 8)

Sensory (afferent) neurons: Neurons that transmit information from the body to the nervous system (Ch. 3)

Serial reproduction: The passage of interpretive information from person to person, often resulting in inaccuracy through personal bias and misinterpretation (Ch. 8)

Severe retardation: Mental retardation characterized by an IQ of between 25 and 39 and difficulty in functioning independently (Ch. 10)

Sexism: Negative attitudes toward a person based on that person's sex (Ch. 12)

Sexual disorders: A form of abnormal behavior in which one's sexual activity is unsatisfactory (Ch. 17)

Sexually transmitted disease (STD): A disease spread primarily through sexual contact (Ch. 12)

Shadowing: A technique used during dichotic listening in which a subject is asked to repeat one of the messages aloud as it comes into one ear (Ch. 5)

Shaping: The process of teaching a complex behavior by rewarding closer and closer approximations of the desired behavior (Ch. 7)

Short-term memory: The storage of information for fifteen to twenty-five seconds (Ch. 8)

Sickle-cell anemia: A disease of the blood that affects about 10 percent of America's black population (Ch. 13)

Signal detection theory: The theory that addresses the role of psychological factors in our ability to identify stimuli (Ch. 4)

Significant outcome: Statistically meaningful results from an experiment that confirm a hypothesis (Ch. 2, Appendix)

Similarity: The tendency to group together those elements that are similar in appearance (Ch. 5)

Simplicity: The tendency to perceive a pattern in the most basic, straightforward, organized manner

possible—the overriding gestalt principle (Ch. 5)

Single-source/divergent circuits: A network of neurons in which a single neuron transmits messages to a potentially vast number of recipients (Ch. 3)

Situational causes of behavior: Causes of behavior that are based on environmental factors (Ch. 19)

Skewed distribution: A distribution that is not normal and therefore creates a curve that is not symmetrical (Appendix)

Skin senses: The senses that include touch, pressure, temperature, and pain (Ch. 4)

Sleep apnea: A sleep disorder characterized by difficulty in breathing and sleeping simultaneously (Ch. 6)

Soap opera effect: The phenomenon by which memory of a prior event involving a person is more reliable when we understand that person's motivations (Ch. 8)

Social cognition: The processes that underlie our understanding of the social world (Ch. 19)

Social influence: The area of social psychology concerned with situations in which the actions of an individual or group affect the behavior of others (Ch. 20)

Social learning theory (of personality): The theory that suggests that personality develops through observational learning (Ch. 15)

Social psychology: The branch of psychology that studies how people's thoughts, feelings, and actions are affected by others (Chs. 1, 19)

Social support: Knowledge of being part of a mutual network of caring, interested others (Ch. 16)

Social supporter: A person who shares an unpopular opinion or attitude of another group member, thereby encouraging nonconformity (Ch. 20)

Socialization: The process by which individuals learn what society deems appropriate behavior, including gender roles (Ch. 12)

Sociocultural model of abnormality: The model that suggests that peo-

ple's behavior, both normal and abnormal, is shaped by family, society, and cultural influences (Ch. 17)

Soft sell: An approach to selling in which a product is associated with an image related to the product's use (Ch. 21)

Somatic division: The part of the nervous system that controls voluntary movements of the skeletal muscles (Ch. 3)

Somatoform disorder: Psychological difficulties that take on physical (somatic) form (Ch. 17)

Somatosensory area: The area within the cortex corresponding to the sense of touch (Ch. 3)

Sound: The movement of air molecules brought about by the vibration of an object (Ch. 4)

Source traits: The sixteen basic dimensions of personality that Cattell identified as the root of all behavior (Ch. 15)

Spinal cord: A bundle of nerves running along the spine, carrying messages between the brain and the body (Ch. 3)

Split-brain patient: A person who suffers from independent functioning of the two halves of the brain, as a result of which the sides of the body work in disharmony (Ch. 3)

Spontaneous recovery: The reappearance of a previously extinguished response after a period of time during which the conditioned stimulus has been absent (Ch. 7)

Spontaneous remission: Recovery without treatment (Ch. 18)

Stage 1 sleep: The state of transition between wakefulness and sleep, characterized by relatively rapid, low-voltage brain waves (Ch. 6)

Stage 2 sleep: A sleep deeper than that of stage 1, characterized by sleep spindles (Ch. 6)

Stage 3 sleep: A sleep characterized by slow brain waves, with greater peaks and valleys in the wave pattern (Ch. 6)

Stage 4 sleep: The deepest stage of sleep, during which we are least responsive to outside stimulation (Ch. 6)

Standard deviation: An index of the average deviation of a set of scores from the center of the distribution (Appendix)

Stanford-Binet test: A test of intelligence that includes a series of items varying in nature according to the age of the person being tested (Ch. 10)

Startle reflex: The reflex action in which an infant, in response to a sudden noise, flings its arms, arches its back, and spreads its fingers (Ch. 13)

Statistics: The branch of mathematics concerned with collecting, organizing, analyzing, and drawing conclusions from numerical data (Appendix)

Status: The social rank held within a group of an individual (Ch. 20)

Stereotype: A kind of schema in which beliefs and expectations about members of a group are held simply on the basis of their membership in that group (Ch. 19)

Stereotyping: Beliefs and expectations about members of a group based on their membership in that group (Ch. 12)

Stimulants: Drugs that affect the central nervous system, causing increased heart rate, blood pressure, and muscle tension (Ch. 6)

Stimulus: A source of physical energy that produces a response in a sense organ (Ch. 4)

Stimulus control training: Training in which an organism is reinforced in the presence of a certain specific stimulus, but not in its absence (Ch. 7)

Stimulus discrimination: The process by which an organism learns to differentiate among stimuli, restricting its response to one in particular (Ch. 7)

Stimulus generalization: Response to a stimulus that is similar to but different from a conditioned stimulus; the more similar the two stimuli, the more likely generalization is to occur (Ch. 7)

Stirrup: A tiny bone in the middle ear that transfers vibrations to the oval window (Ch. 4)

Storage: The location in the memory system in which material is saved (Ch. 8)

Stress: The response to events that are threatening or challenging (Ch. 16)

Stressors: Circumstances that produce threats to our well-being (Ch. 16)

Stroop task: An exercise requiring the division of our attention between two competing stimuli—the meaning of words and the colors in which they are written (Ch. 5)

Structuralism: An early approach to psychology which focused on the fundamental elements that form the foundation of thinking, consciousness, emotions, and other kinds of mental states and activities (Ch. 1)

Subgoals: A commonly used heuristic to divide a problem into intermediate steps and to solve each one of them (Ch. 9)

Subject: A participant in research (Ch. 2)

Subject expectations: A subject's interpretation of what behaviors or responses are expected in an experiment (Ch. 2)

Sublimation: A defense mechanism, considered healthy by Freud, in which a person diverts unwanted impulses into socially acceptable thoughts, feelings, or behaviors (Ch. 15)

Subliminal perception: The perception of messages about which a person has no awareness (Ch. 5)

Sucking reflex: A reflex that prompts an infant to suck at things that touch its lips (Ch. 13)

Sudden infant death syndrome: A disorder in which seemingly healthy infants die in their sleep (Ch. 6)

Superego: The part of personality that represents the morality of society as presented by parents, teachers, and others (Ch. 15)

Superstitious behavior: The mistaken belief that particular ideas, objects, or behavior will cause certain events to occur, as a result of learning based on the coincidental association between the idea, object, or behavior and subsequent reinforcement (Ch. 7)

Surface traits: According to Cattell, clusters of a person's related behaviors that can be observed in a given situation (Ch. 15)

Survey research: Sampling a group of people by assessing their behavior, thoughts, or attitudes, then generalizing the findings to a larger population (Ch. 2)

Syllogisms: A major technique for studying deductive reasoning, in which a series of two assumptions are used to derive a conclusion (Ch. 9)

Sympathetic division: The part of the autonomic division of the peripheral nervous system that prepares the body to respond in stressful emergency situations (Ch. 3)

Synapse: The gap between neurons through which chemical messages are communicated (Ch. 3)

Syntax: The rules that indicate how words are joined to form sentences (Ch. 9)

Syphilis: An STD which, if untreated, may affect brain, heart, and developing fetus, and can be fatal (Ch. 12)

Systematic desensitization: A form of therapy in which fears are minimized through different degrees of exposure, with the patient eventually learning to feel comfortable in the presence of the object of his or her former fears (Chs. 7, 18)

Taste buds: The location of the receptor cells for taste, found on the tongue (Ch. 4)

Tay-Sachs (TAY SAKS) disease: A genetic defect preventing the body from breaking down fat and typically causing death by the age of 3 or 4 (Ch. 13)

Telegraphic speech: Sentences containing only the most essential words (Ch. 9)

Temperament: Basic, innate disposition (Ch. 13)

Temporal lobes: The portion of the brain located beneath the frontal and parietal lobes (Ch. 3)

Terminal buttons: Small branches at the end of an axon that relay messages to other cells (Ch. 3)

Test standardization: A technique used to validate questions in personality tests by studying the responses of people with known diagnoses (Ch. 15)

Testes: The male reproductive organs responsible for secreting androgens (Ch. 12)

Thalamus: The part of the brain's central core that transmits messages from the sense organs to the cerebral cortex and from the cerebral cortex to the cerebellum and medulla (Ch. 3)

Thematic Apperception Test (TAT): A test consisting of a series of ambiguous pictures about which a person is asked to write a story. The story is taken to be a reflection of the writer's personality (Chs. 11, 15)

Theories: Broad explanations and predictions concerning phenomena of interest (Ch. 2)

Thinking: The manipulation of mental representations of information (Ch. 9)

Tip-of-the-tongue phenomenon: The inability to recall information that one realizes one knows—a result of the difficulty of retrieving information from long-term memory (Ch. 8)

Token system: A procedure whereby a person is rewarded for performing certain desired behaviors (Ch. 18)

Top-down processing: Perception guided by knowledge, experience, expectations, and motivations (Ch. 5)

Trait theory: A model that seeks to identify the basic traits necessary to describe personality (Ch. 15)

Traits: Enduring dimensions of personality characteristics differentiating people from one another (Ch. 15)

Transcutaneous electrical nerve stimulation (TENS): A method of providing relief from pain by passing a low-voltage electric current through parts of the body (Ch. 4)

Transference: A patient's transfer of certain strong feelings for others to the analyst (Ch. 18)

Transformation problems: Problems to be solved using a series of methods to change an initial state into a goal state (Ch. 9)

Treatment: The manipulation implemented by the experimenter to influence results in a segment of the experimental population (Ch. 2)

Treatment group: The experimental group receiving the treatment, or manipulation (Ch. 2)

Triarchic theory of intelligence: A theory suggesting three major aspects of intelligence: componential, experiential, and contextual (Ch. 10)

Trichromatic theory of color vision: The theory that suggests that the retina has three kinds of cones, each responding to a specific range of wavelengths, perception of color being influenced by the relative strength with which each is activated (Ch. 4)

Trust-versus-mistrust stage: According to Erikson, the first stage of psychosocial development, occurring from birth to 18 months of age, during which time infants develop feelings of trust or lack of trust (Ch. 13)

Tunnel vision: An advanced stage of glaucoma in which vision is reduced to the narrow circle directly in front of the eye (Ch. 4)

Type A behavior pattern: A pattern of behavior characterized by competitiveness, impatience, tendency toward frustration, and hostility (Ch. 16)

Type B behavior pattern: A pattern of behavior characterized by noncompetitiveness, nonaggression, and patience in times of potential stress (Ch. 16)

Unconditional positive regard: Supportive behavior from another individual, regardless of one's words or actions (Chs. 15, 18)

Unconditioned response (UCR): A response that is natural and needs no training (e.g., salivation at the smell of food) (Ch. 7)

Unconditioned stimulus (UCS): A stimulus that brings about a response without having been learned (Ch. 7)

Unconscious: A part of the personality of which a person is unaware and which is a potential determinant of behavior (Ch. 15)

Unconscious wish fulfillment: A theory of Sigmund Freud which proposes that dreams represent unconscious wishes that a dreamer wants to fulfill (Ch. 6)

Universal grammar: An underlying structure shared by all languages, the basis of Chomsky's theory that certain language characteristics are based in the brain's structure and are therefore common to all people (Ch. 9)

Uplifts: Minor positive events that make one feel good (Ch. 16)

Vagina: The female canal into which the penis enters during sexual intercourse (Ch. 12)

Validity: The ability of a test to measure what it is supposed to measure (Ch. 15)

Variability: The spread, or dispersion, of scores in a distribution (Appendix)

Variable: A behavior or event that can be changed (Ch. 2)

Variable-interval schedule: A schedule whereby reinforcement is given at various times, usually causing a behavior to be maintained more consistently (Ch. 7)

Variable-ratio schedule: A schedule whereby reinforcement occurs after a varying number of responses rather than after a fixed number (Ch. 7)

Vascular theory of emotions: The theory that there is a link between particular facial expressions and the temperature of the blood flow to the brain, which in turn affects the experience of emotions (Ch. 11)

Ventromedial hypothalamus: The part of the brain which, when injured, results in extreme over-eating (Ch. 11)

Vernix: A white lubricant that covers a fetus, protecting it during birth (Ch. 13)

Vertigo: A disorder of the inner ear resulting from a viral infection or head injury that causes people to feel light-headed, and dizzy and to lose their sense of balance (Ch. 4)

Vicarious learning: Learning by observing others (Ch. 19)

Visceral (VIS er al) **experience:** The "gut" reaction experienced internally, triggering an emotion (see James-Lange theory) (Ch. 11)

Visual illusion: A physical stimulus that consistently produces errors in perception (often called an optical illusion) (Ch. 5)

Visual spectrum: The range of wavelengths to which humans are sensitive (Ch. 4)

von Restorff effect: The phenomenon by which distinctive stimuli are recalled more readily than less distinctive ones (Ch. 8)

Wear-and-tear theories of aging: Theories that suggest that the body's mechanical functions cease efficient activity and, in effect, wear out (Ch. 14)

Weber's law: The principle that states that the just noticeable difference is a constant proportion of the magnitude of an initial stimulus (Ch. 4)

Wechsler Adult Intelligence Scale—Revised (WAIS-R): A test of intelligence consisting of verbal and nonverbal performance sections, providing a relatively precise picture of a person's specific abilities (Ch. 10)

Wechsler Intelligence Scale for Children—Revised (WISC-R): An intelligence test for children; see Wechsler Adult Intelligence Scale—Revised (Ch. 10)

Weight set point: The particular level of weight the body strives to maintain (Ch. 11)

Well-defined problem: A problem whose nature is clear and the information needed to solve it is available (Ch. 9)

Wernicke's aphasia: A syndrome involving problems with understanding language, resulting in fluent but nonsensical speech (Ch. 3)

Yerkes-Dodson law: The theory that a particular level of motivational arousal produces optimal performance of a task (Ch. 11)

Zygote: The one-celled product of fertilization (Ch. 13)

Abramson, L. Y., Garber, J., & Seligman, M. E. P. (1980). Learned helplessness in humans: An attributional analysis. In J. Garber and M. E. P. Seligman (Eds.), *Human helplessness: Theory and applications.* New York: Academic.

Abramson, L. Y., Metalsky, G. I., & Alloy, L. B. (1989). Hopelessness depression: A theory-based subtype. *Psychological Review, 96,* 358–372.

Ackley, D. H., Hinton, G. E., & Sejnowski, T. J. (1985). A learning algorithm for Boltzmann machines. *Cognitive Science, 9,* 147–169.

Adams, G. R., & Crane, P. (1980). An assessment of parents' and teachers' expectations of preschool children's social preference for attractive or unattractive children and adults. *Child Development, 51,* 224–231.

Adelmann, P. K., & Zajonc, R. B. (1989). Facial efference and the experience of emotion. *Annual Review of Psychology, 40,* 249–280.

Adler, J. (1984, April 23). The fight to conquer fear. *Newsweek,* pp. 66–72.

Adler, N. E., David, H. P., Major, B. N., Roth, S. H., Russo, N. F., & Wyatt, G. E. (1990, April 6). Psychological responses after abortion. *Science, 248,* 41–43.

Adler, T. (1990, October). NASA boosts behavioral research. *APA Monitor, 10,* 1.

Adler, T. (1991, June). Primate rules focus on mental well-being. *APA Monitor, 6.*

Afari, N. (1989, July). Psychology in space. *APS Observer, 11.*

Aiello, J. R., Baum, A., & Gormley, F. P. (1980). *Social determinants of residential crowding.* Unpublished manuscript, Rutgers University, New Brunswick, NJ.

Ainsworth, M. D. S. (1989). Attachments beyond infancy. *American Psychologist, 44,* 709–716.

Ainsworth, M. D. S., Blehar, M. C., Waters, E., & Wall, S. (1978). *Patterns of attachment: A psychological study of the strange situation.* Hillsdale, NJ: Erlbaum.

Ainsworth, M. D. S., & Bowlby, J. (1991). An ethological approach to personality development. *American Psychologist, 46,* 333–341.

Ajzen, I. (1988). *Attitudes, personality, and behavior.* Stratford, England: Open University Press.

Akmajian, A., Demers, R. A., & Harnish, R. M. (1984). *Linguistics.* Cambridge, MA: MIT Press.

Akutsu, P. D., Sue, S., Zane, N. W. S., & Nakamura, C. Y. (1989). Ethnic differences in alcohol consumption among Asians and Caucasians in the United States: An investigation of cultural and physiological factors. *Journal of Studies on Alcohol, 50,* 261–267.

Albee, G. W. (1978, February 12). I.Q. tests on trial. *The New York Times,* p. E-13.

Albert, R. S. (Ed.) (1992). *The social psychology of creativity and exceptional achievement* (2nd ed.). New York: Pergamon Press.

Aldwin, C. M., & Revenson, T. A. (1987). Does coping help? A reexamination of the relation between coping and mental health. *Journal of Personality and Social Psychology, 53,* 337–348.

Alexander, C. N., Langer, E. J., Newman, R. I., Chandler, H. M., & Davies, J. L. (1989). Transcendental meditation, mindfulness, and longevity: An experimental study with the elderly. *Journal of Personality and Social Psychology, 57,* 950–964.

Alkon, D. L. (1987). *Memory traces in the brain.* New York: Cambridge University Press.

Allen, L. S., Hines, M., Shryne, J. E., & Gorski, R. A. (1989). Two sexually dimorphic cell groups in the human brain. *Journal of Neuroscience, 9,* 497–506.

Allen, L. S., Richey, M. F., Chai, Y. M., & Gorski, R. A. (1991). Sex differences in the corpus callosum of the living human being. *Journal of Neuroscience, 11,* 933–942.

Allen, M. (1988, January 25). When jurors are ordered to ignore testimony, they ignore the order. *The Wall Street Journal,* p. 33.

Allen, V. L. (1965). Situational factors in conformity. In L. Berkowitz (Ed.), *Advances in experimental social psychology* (Vol. 1). New York: Academic.

Allen, V. L. (1975). Social support for nonconformity. In L. Berkowitz (Ed.), *Advances in experimental and social psychology* (Vol. 8). New York: Academic.

Allen Gutmacher Institute (1988). *Report on family planning practices.* New York: Allen Gutmacher Institute.

Allore, R., O'Hanlon, D., Price, R., Neilson, K., Willard, H. F., Cox, D. R., Marks, A., & Dunn, R. J. (1988, March 11). Gene encoding of the B-subunit of S100 protein is on chromosome 21: Implications for Down's syndrome. *Science, 239,* 1311–1313.

Allport, G. W. (1961). *Pattern and growth in personality.* New York: Holt.

Allport, G. W. (1966). Traits revisited. *American Psychologist, 21,* 1–10.

Allport, G. W., & Postman, L. J. (1958). The basic psychology of rumor. In E. D. Maccoby, T. M. Newcomb, & E. L. Hartley (Eds.), *Readings in social psychology* (3rd ed.). New York: Holt.

Allred, K. D., & Smith T. W. (1989). The hardy personality: Cognitive and physiological responses to evaluative threat. *Journal of Personality and Social Psychology, 56,* 257–266.

Alsop, R. (1988, May 13). Advertisers put consumers on the couch. *The Wall Street Journal,* p. 21.

Altshuler, K. Z. (1990). Whatever happened to intensive psychotherapy? *American Journal of Psychiatry, 147,* 428–430.

Altshuler, L. L., Conrad, A., Kovelman, J. A., & Scheibel, A. (1987). Hippocampal pyramidal cell orientation in schizophrenia. *Archives of General Psychiatry, 44,* 1094–1096.

Alumnus. (1989, August–September). AIDS study indicates 1 in 500 carries virus. Amherst: Univ. of Massachusetts

Alwitt, L., & Mitchell, A. A. (1985). *Psychological processes and advertising effects: Theory, research, and applications.* Hillsdale, NJ: Erlbaum.

Amabile, T. M. (1985). Motivation and creativity: Effects of motivational orientation on creative writers. *Journal of Personality and Social Psychology, 48,* 393–399.

Amabile, T. M., Hennessey, B. A., & Grossman, B. S. (1986). Social influences on creativity: The effects of contracted-for reward. *Journal of Personality and Social Psychology, 50,* 14–23.

American College Health Association. (1989). *Guidelines on acquaintance rape.* Washington, DC: American College Health Association.

American Psychological Association. (1980). *Careers in psychology.* Washington, DC: American Psychological Association.

American Psychological Association. (1986a, March). Council resolution on polygraph tests. *APA Monitor.*

American Psychological Association. (1986b). *Guidelines for ethical conduct in the care and use of animals.* Washington, DC: American Psychological Association.

American Psychological Association. (1987). *PsychINFO training manual.* Washington, DC: American Psychological Association.

American Psychological Association. (1988). *Behavioral research with animals.* Washington, DC: American Psychological Association.

American Psychological Association. (1990). Ethical principles of psychologists. *American Psychologist, 45,* 390–395.

Amir, Y. (1976). The role of intergroup contact in change of prejudice and ethnic relations. In P. Katz (Ed.), *Towards the elimination of racism.* New York: Pergamon.

Amirkhan, J. H. (1990). A factor analytically derived measure of coping: The coping strategy indicator. *Journal of Personality and Social Psychology, 59,* 1066–1074.

Amsel, A. (1988). *Behaviorism, neobehaviorism, and cognitivism in learning theory.* Hillsdale, NJ: Erlbaum.

Anastasi, A. (1982). *Psychological testing* (5th ed.). New York: Macmillan.

Anderson, A., Hedblom, J., & Hubbard, F. (1983). A multidisciplinary team treatment for patients with anorexia nervosa and their families. *International Journal of Eating Disorders, 2,* 181–192.

Anderson, B. F. (1980). *The complete thinker: A handbook of techniques for creative and critical problem solving.* Englewood Cliffs, NJ: Prentice-Hall.

Anderson, E. (1987). Preoperative preparation for cardiac surgery facilitates recovery, reduces psychological distress, and reduces the incidence of acute postoperative hypertension. *Journal of Consulting and Clinical Psychology, 55,* 513–520.

Anderson, J. R. (1981). Interference: The relationship between response latency and response accuracy. *Journal of Experimental Psychology: Human Learning and Memory, 7,* 311–325.

Anderson, J. R., & Bower, G. H. (1972). Recognition and retrieval processes in free recall. *Psychological Review, 79,* 97–123.

Anderson, J. R., & Bower, G. H. (1973). *Human associative memory.* Washington, DC: Winston.

Anderson, N. H. (1974). Cognitive algebra integration theory applied to social attribution. In L. Berkowitz (Ed.), *Advances in experimental social psychology* (Vol. 7, pp. 1–101). New York: Academic.

Anderson, N. H. (Ed.). (1991). *Contributions to information integration theory: Vol. 2. Social.* Hillsdale, NJ: Erlbaum.

Anderson, S. M., & Klatzky, R. L. (1987). Traits and social stereotypes: Levels of categorization in person perception. *Journal of Personality and Social Psychology, 53,* 235–246.

Andreasen, N. C. (1985). Positive vs. negative schizophrenia: A critical evaluation. *Schizophrenia, 11,* 380–389.

Angell, M. (1985). Disease as a reflection of the psyche [Editorial]. *New England Journal of Medicine, 312,* 1570–1572.

Angier, N. (1990a, March 29). New antidepressant is acclaimed but not perfect. *The New York Times.*

Angier, N. (1990b, May 15). Cheating on sleep: Modern life turns America into the land of the drowsy. *The New York Times,* C1, C8.

Angier, N. (1991, January 22). A potent peptide prompts an urge to cuddle. *The New York Times,* C1.

Angoff, W. H. (1988). The nature-nurture debate, aptitudes, and group differences. *American Psychologist, 43,* 713–720.

APA (American Psychiatric Association) Task Force on Electroconvulsive Therapy. (1990). *The practice of electroconvulsive therapy: Recommendations for treatment, training, and privileging.* Washington, DC: American Psychiatric Association.

Apter, A., Galatzer, A., Beth-Halachmi, N., & Laron, Z. (1981). Self-image in adolescents with delayed puberty and growth retardation. *Journal of Youth and Adolescence, 10,* 501–505.

Arafat, I., & Cotton, W. L. (1974). Masturbation practices of males and females. *Journal of Sex Research, 10,* 293–307.

Archibald, W. P. (1974). Alternative explanations for the self-fulfilling prophecy. *Psychological Bulletin, 81,* 74–84.

Arena, J. M. (1984, April). A look at the opposite sex. *Newsweek on Campus,* p. 21.

Aronoff, J., Barclay, A. M., & Stevenson, L. A. (1988). The recognition of threatening facial stimuli. *Journal of Personality and Social Psychology, 54,* 647–655.

Aronson, E. (1988). *The social animal* (3rd ed.). San Francisco: Freeman.

Aronson, E. (1990, April). *Cognitive dissonance.* Address presented at the annual meeting of the Wester Psychological Association, Los Angeles.

Aronson, E., Ellsworth, P. C., Carlsmith, J. M., & Gonzales, M. H. (1990). *Methods of research in social psychology* (2nd ed.). New York: McGraw-Hill.

Asch, S. E. (1946). Forming impressions of personality. *Journal of Abnormal and Social Psychology, 41,* 258–290.

Asch, S. E. (1951). Effects of group pressure upon the modification and distortion of judgments. In H. Guetzkow (Ed.), *Groups, leadership, and men.* Pittsburgh: Carnegie Press.

Aslin, R. N. (1987). Visual and auditory development in infancy. In J. Osofsky (Ed.), *Handbook of infant development* (2nd ed.). New York: Wiley.

Aslin, R. N., & Smith, L. B. (1988). Perceptual development. *Annual Review of Psychology, 39,* 435–473.

Asnis, G., & Ryan, N. D. (1983). The psychoneuroendocrinology of schizophrenia. In A. Rifkin (Ed.), *Schizophrenia and effective disorders: Biology and drug treatment* (pp. 205–236). Boston: John Wright.

Astington, J. W., Harris, P. L., & Olson, D. R. (1988). *Developing theories of mind.* Cambridge, England: Cambridge University Press.

Atkinson, J. W., & Braddick, O. (1989). Development of basic visual functions. In A. M. Slater & J. G. Bremner (Eds.), *Infant Development.* Hillsdale, NJ: Erlbaum.

Atkinson, J. W., & Feather, N. T. (1966). *Theory of achievement motivation.* New York: Krieger.

Atkinson, J. W., & Raynor, J. O. (Eds.). (1974). *Motivation and achievement.* Washington, DC: Winston.

Atkinson, R. C., & Shiffrin, R. M. (1968). Human memory: A proposed system and its control processes. In K. W. Spence & J. T. Spence (Eds.), *The psychology of learning and motivation: Advances in research and theory* (Vol. 2, pp. 80–195). New York: Academic.

Atwell, P., & Rule, J. (1984). Computing and organizations: What we know and what we don't know. *Communications of the ACM, 27,* 1184–1192.

Averill, J. R. (1975). A semantic atlas of emotional concepts. *Catalog of Selected Documents in Psychology, 5,* 330.

Avorn, J. (1983). Biomedical and social determinants of cognitive impairment in the elderly. *Journal of the American Geriatrics Society, 31,* 137–143.

Axel, R., & Buck, L. (1991, April 5). A novel multigene family may encode odorant receptors: A molecular basis for odor recognition. *Cell, 65,* 175–187.

Ayoub, D. M., Greenough, W. T., & Juraska, J. M. (1983). Sex differences in dendritic structure in the preoptic area of the juvenile macaque monkey brain. *Science, 219,* 197–198.

Azrin, N. H., & Holt, N. C. (1966). Punishment. In W. A. Honig (Ed.), *Operant behavior: Areas of research and application* (pp. 380–447). New York: Appleton.

Babbitt, T., Rowland, G., & Franken, R. (1990). Sensation seeking and participation in aerobic exercise classes. *Personality and Individual Differences, 11,* 181–184.

Bach-Y-Rita, P. (1982). Sensory substitution in rehabilitation. In L. Illis, M. Sedwick, & H. Granville (Eds.), *Rehabilitation of the neurological patient* (pp. 361–382). Oxford, England: Blackwell.

Backer, T. E., Batchelor, W. F., Jones, J. M., & Mays, V. M. (1988). Introduction to the special issue: Psychology and AIDS. *American Psychologist, 43,* 835–836.

Baddeley, A. (1982). *Your memory: A user's guide.* New York: Macmillan.

Baddeley, A., & Wilson, B. (1985). Phonological coding and short-term memory in patients without speech. *Journal of Memory and Language, 24,* 490–502.

Baddeley, A. D. (1978). The trouble with levels: A reexamination of Craik and Lockhart's framework for memory research. *Psychological Review, 85,* 139–152.

Bahill, T. A., & Laritz, T. (1984). Why can't batters keep their eyes on the ball? *American Scientist, 72,* 249–253.

Bailey, J. M., & Pillard, R. C. (1991). A genetic study of male sexual orientation. *Archives of General Psychiatry, 48,* 1089–1096.

Baker, A. G., & Mercier, P. (1989). Attention, retrospective processing and evolution of a structured connectionist model of Pavlovian conditioning (AESOP). In S. B. Klein & R. R. Mowrer (Eds.), *Contemporary learning theories: Vol. I. Pavlovian conditioning and the status of traditional learning theory.* Hillsdale, NJ: Erlbaum.

Baker, J. N. (1987, July 27). Battling the IQ-test ban. *Newsweek,* p. 53.

Baker, J. N. (1991, April 1). Los Angeles aftershocks. *Newsweek,* pp. 18–19.

Baker, R. (Ed.). (1989). *Panic disorder: Theory, research and therapy.* New York: Wiley.

Baker, S. L., & Kirshc, I. (1991). Cognitive mediators of pain perception and tolerance. *Journal of Personality and Social Psychology, 61,* 504–510.

Bales, J. (1988, April). Polygraph screening banned in Senate bill. *APA Monitor,* p. 10.

Ballinger, C. B. (1981). The menopause and its syndromes. In J. G. Howells (Ed.), *Modern perspectives in the psychiatry of middle age* (pp. 279–303). New York: Brunner/Mazel.

Baltes, P. B., & Schaie, K. W. (1974, March). The myth of the twilight years. *Psychology Today,* pp. 35–38ff.

Banaji, M. R., & Crowder, R. G. (1989). The bankruptcy of everyday memory. *American Psychologist, 44,* 1185–1193.

Bandura, A. (1973). *Aggression: A social learning analysis.* Englewood Cliffs, NJ: Prentice-Hall.

Bandura, A. (1977). *Social learning theory.* Englewood Cliffs, NJ: Prentice-Hall.

Bandura, A. (1981). In search of pure unidirectional determinants. *Behavior Therapy, 12,* 30–40.

Bandura, A. (1986). *Social foundations of thought and action: A social cognitive theory.* Englewood Cliffs, NJ: Prentice-Hall.

Bandura, A., Grusec, J. E., & Menlove, F. L. (1967). Vicarious extinction of avoidance behavior. *Journal of Personality and Social Psychology, 5,* 16–23.

Bandura, A., O'Leary, A., Taylor, C. B., Gauthier, J., & Gossard, D. (1987). Perceived self-efficacy and pain control: Opioid and non-opioid mechanism. *Journal of Personality and Social Psychology, 53,* 563–571.

Bandura, A., Ross, D., & Ross, S. (1963a). Imitation of film-mediated aggressive models. *Journals of Abnormal and Social Psychology, 66,* 3–11.

Bandura, A., Ross, D., & Ross, S. (1963b). Vicarious reinforcement and imitative learning. *Journal of Abnormal and Social Psychology, 67,* 601–607.

Barbaro, N. M. (1988). Studies of PAG/PVG stimulation for pain relief in humans. *Progress in Brain Research, 77,* 165–173.

Barber, B. L., & Eccles, J. S. (1992). Long-term influence of divorce and single parenting on adolescent family- and work-related values, behaviors, and aspirations. *Psychological Bulletin, 111,* 108–126.

Barber, T. X. (1970). Who believes in hypnosis? *Psychology Today, 4,* 20, 24–27, 84.

Barber, T. X. (1975). Responding to "hypnotic" suggestions: An introspective report. *American Journal of Clinical Hypnosis, 18,* 6–22.

Bargh, J., & Pietromonoco, P. (1982). Automatic information processing and social perception: The influence of trait information presented outside of conscious awareness on impression formation. *Journal of Personality and Social Psychology, 43,* 437–449.

Barinaga, M. (1990, February 2). Neuroscience models the brain. *Science, 247,* 524–526.

Barinaga, M. (1991, June 14). Sexism charged by Stanford physician. *Science, 252,* 1484.

Barinaga, M. (1992). Priming the brain's language pump. *Science, 255,* 535.

Barker, L. M., Best, M. E., & Domjan, M. (Eds.). (1977). *Learning mechanisms in food selection.* Waco, TX: Baylor University Press.

Barland, G. H., & Raskin, D. C. (1975). An evaluation of field techniques in detection of deception. *Psychophysiology, 12,* 321–330.

Barnes, D. M. (1988). The biological tangle of drug addiction. *Science, 24,* 415–417.

Baron, J., & Brown, R. V. (Eds.). (1991). *Teaching decision making to adolescents.* Hillsdale, NJ: Erlbaum.

Baron, J. B., & Sternberg, R. J. (1986). *Teaching thinking skills.* New York: Freeman.

Baron, R. A. (1987). Effects of negative air ions on interpersonal attraction: Evidence for intensification. *Journal of Personality and Social Psychology, 52,* 547–553.

Baron, R. A., & Kepner, C. R. (1970). Model's behavior and attraction toward the model as determinants of adult aggressive behavior. *Journal of Personality and Social Psychology, 14,* 335–344.

Barringer, F. (1989, June 9). Doubt on "trial marriage" raised by divorce rates. *The New York Times,* pp. 1, 28.

Barron, F. (1990). *Creativity and psychological health: Origins of personal vitality and creative freedom.* Buffalo, NY: Creative Education Foundation.

Barron, F., & Harrington, D. M. (1981). Creativity, intelligence, and personality. *Annual Review of Psychology, 32,* 439–476.

Barron, J. (1990, December 13). Gotti: A "good fellow" from Queens. *The New York Times,* p. B2.

Barsalou, L. W. (1992). *Cognitive psychology: An overview for cognitive scientists.* Hillsdale, NJ: Lawrence Erlbaum Associates.

Bartlett, F. (1932). *Remembering: A study in experimental and social psychology.* Cambridge, England: Cambridge University Press.

Bartoshuk, L. M. (1971). The chemical senses: I. Taste. In J. N. Kling & L. A. Riggs (Eds.), *Experimental psychology* (3rd ed.). New York: Holt.

Bateson, G. (1960). Minimal requirements for a theory of schizophrenia. *Archives of General Psychiatry, 2,* 477–491.

Batson, C. D. (1990). How social an animal? The human capacity for caring. *American Psychologist, 45,* 336–346.

Batson, C. D. (1991). *The altruism question: Toward a social-psychological answer.* Hillsdale, NJ: Erlbaum.

Batson, C. D., Batson, J. G., Slingsby, J. K., Harrell, K. L., Peekna, H. M., & Todd, R. M. (1991). Empathic joy and the empathy-altruism hypothesis. *Journal of Personality and Social Psychology, 61,* 413–426.

Batteau, D. W. (1967). The role of the pinna in human localization. *Proceedings of the Royal Society of London, Series B, 168,* 158–180.

Baum, A., Gatchel, R. J., & Schaeffer, M. A. (1983). Emotional, behavioral, and physiological effects of chronic stress at Three Mile Island. *Journal of Consulting and Clinical Psychology, 51,* 565–572.

Bauman, L. J., & Siegel, K. (1987). Misperception among gay men of the risk for AIDS associated with their sexual behavior. *Journal of Applied Social Psychology, 17,* 329–350.

Baumrind, D. (1971). Current patterns of parental authority. *Developmental Psychology Monographs, 4* (1, Pt. 2).

Baumrind, D. (1980). New directions in socialization research. *Psychological Bulletin, 35,* 639–652.

Beaman, A. L. (1991). An empirical comparison of meta-analytic and traditional reviews. *Personality and Social Psychology Bulletin, 17,* 252–257.

Beaman, A. L., Cole, C. M., Preston, M., Klentz, B., & Steblay, N. M. (1983). Fifteen years of foot-in-the-door research: A meta-analysis. *Personality and Social Psychology Bulletin, 9,* 181–196.

Bear, M. F., Cooper, L. N., & Ebner, F. F. (1987). A physiological basis for a theory of synapse modification. *Science, 237,* 42–48.

Beaton, A. (1986). *Left side, right side: A review of laterality research.* New Haven: Yale University Press.

Beck, A. T. (1976). *Cognitive therapy and emotional disorders.* New York: International Universities Press.

Beck, A. T. (1982). Cognitive theory of depression: New perspectives. In P. Clayton & J. Barrett (Eds.), *Treatment of depression: Old controversies and new approaches.* New York: Raven Books.

Beck, A. T. (1991). Cognitive therapy: A 30-year perspective. *American Psychologist, 46,* 368–375.

Beck, A. T., & Emery, G., with Greenberg, R. L. (1985). *Anxiety disorders and phobias: A cognitive perspective.* New York: Basic Books.

Beck, J., Hope, B., & Rosenfeld, A. (Eds.). (1983). *Human and machine vision.* New York: Academic.

Beckman, J. C., Keefe, F. J., Caldwell, D. S., & Brown, C. J. (1991). Biofeedback as a means to alter electromyographic activity in a total knee replacement patient. *Biofeedback and Self Regulation, 16,* 23–35.

Belkin, L. (1992, June 4). In lessons on empathy, doctors become patients. *The New York Times,* pp. A1, B5.

Bell, A., & Weinberg, M. S. (1978). *Homosexuality: A study of diversities among men and women.* New York: Simon & Schuster.

Bell, S. M., & Ainsworth, M. D. S. (1972). Infant crying and maternal responsiveness. *Child Development, 43,* 1171–1190.

Bellack, A. S., Hersen, M., & Kazdin, A. E. (1990). *International handbook of behavior modification and therapy.* New York: Plenum Press.

Belliveau, J. W., Dennedy, D. N., McKinstry, R. C., Buchbinder, B. R., Weisskoff, R. M., Cohen, M. S., Vevea, J. M., Brady, T. J., & Rosen, B. R. (1991, November 1). Functional mapping of the human visual cortex by magnetic resonance imaging. *Science, 254,* 716–719.

Belsky, J., & Rovine, M. (1988). Nonmaternal care in the first year of life and infant-parent attachment security. *Child Development, 59,* 157–167.

Bem, D. J. (1967). Self-perception: An alternative interpretation of cognitive dissonance phenomena. *Psychological Review, 74,* 183–200.

Bem, D. J. (1972). Self-perception theory. In L. Berkowitz (Ed.), *Advances in experimental social psychology* (Vol. 6, pp. 1–62). New York: Academic.

Bem, S. (1987). Gender schema theory and its implications for child development: Raising gender-aschematic children in a gender-schematic society. In M. R. Walsh (Ed.), *The Psychology of Women: Ongoing Debates.* New Haven: Yale University Press.

Ben-Sira, Z. (1976). The function of the professional's affective behavior in client satisfaction: A revised approach to social interaction theory. *Journal of Health and Social Behavior, 17,* 3–11.

Benbow, C. P., & Stanley, J. C. (1982). Intellectually talented boys and girls: Educational profiles. *Gifted Child Quarterly, 26,* 82–88.

Benjamin, L. T., Jr. (1985, February). Defining aggression: An exercise for classroom discussion. *Teaching of Psychology, 12*(1), 40–42.

Benjamin, L. T., Jr. (1988). A history of teaching machines. *American Psychologist, 43,* 703–712.

Benjamin, L. T., Jr., & Shields, S. A. (1990). Foreword. In H. Hollingworth, *Leta Stetter Hollingworth: A biography.* Bolton, MA: Anker.

Bennett, W., & Gurin, J. (1982). *The dieter's dilemma: Eating less and weighing more.* New York: Basic Books.

Benson, D. J., & Thomson, G. E. (1982). Sexual harassment on a university campus: The confluence of authority relations, sexual interest and gender stratification. *Social Problems, 29,* 236–251.

Benson, H. (1975). *The relaxation response.* New York: Morrow.

Benson, H., & Friedman, R. (1985). A rebuttal to the conclusions of Davis S. Holme's article, "Meditation and somatic arousal reduction." *American Psychologist,* pp. 725–726.

Benson, H., Kotch, J. B., Crassweller, K. D., & Greenwood, M. (1977). Historical and clinical considerations of the relaxation response. *American Scientist, 65,* 441–445.

Bergener, M., Ermini, M., & Stahelin, H. B. (Eds.). (1985, February). *Thresholds in aging.* The 1984 Sandoz Lectures in Gerontology, Basel, Switzerland.

Berger, J. (1988, March 16). Teachers of the gifted fight accusations of elitism. *The New York Times,* p. 36.

Berkowitz, L. (1974). Some determinants of impulsive aggression: The role of mediated associations with reinforcements for aggression. *Psychological Review, 81,* 165–176.

Berkowitz, L. (1984). Aversive conditioning as stimuli to aggression. In R. J. Blanchard & C. Blanchard (Eds.), *Advances in the study of aggression* (Vol. 1). New York: Academic.

Berkowitz, L. (1987). Mood, self-awareness, and willingness to help. *Journal of Personality and Social Psychology, 52,* 721–729.

Berkowitz, L. (1989). Frustration-aggression hypothesis. *Psychological Bulletin, 106,* 59–73.

Berkowitz, L. (1990). On the formation and regulation of anger and aggression: A cognitive-neoassociationistic analysis. *American Psychologist, 45,* 494–503.

Berkowitz, L., & Geen, R. G. (1966). Film violence and the cue properties of available targets. *Journal of Personality and Social Psychology, 3,* 525–530.

Berkowitz, L., & LePage, A. (1967). Weapons as aggression-eliciting stimuli. *Journal of Personality and Social Psychology, 7,* 202–207.

Berlyne, D. (1967). Arousal and reinforcement. In D. Levine (Ed.), *Nebraska symposium on motivation.* Lincoln, NE: University of Nebraska Press.

Berman, A. L. (Ed.). (1990). *Suicide prevention: Case consultations.* New York: Springer.

Bernard, M. (Ed.). (1991). *Using rational-emotive therapy effectively.* New York: Plenum.

Berscheid, E. (1985). Interpersonal attraction. In G. Lindzey & E. Aronson (Eds.), *Handbook of social psychology* (3rd ed.). New York: Random House.

Berscheid, E., & Walster, E. (1974). Physical attractiveness. In L. Berkowitz (Ed.), *Advances in experimental social psychology* (Vol. 7, pp. 157–215). New York: Academic.

Beyer, S. (1990). Gender differences in the accuracy of self-evaluations of performance. *Journal of Personality and Social Psychology, 59,* 960–970.

Bieber, I., et al. (1962). *Homosexuality: A psychoanalytic study.* New York: Basic Books.

Biederman, I. (1981). On the semantics of a glance at a scene. In M. Kubovy & J. R. Pomerangtz (Eds.), *Perceptual organization.* Hillsdale, NJ: Erlbaum.

Biederman, I. (1987). Recognition-by-components: A theory of human image understanding. *Psychological Review, 94,* 115–147.

Biernat, M., & Wortman, C. B. (1991). Sharing of home responsibilities between professionally employed women and their husbands. *Journal of Personality and Social Psychology, 60,* 844–860.

Binet, A., & Simon, T. (1916). *The development of intelligence in children* (The Binet-Simon Scale). Baltimore, MD: Williams & Wilkins.

Bini, L. (1938). Experimental research on epileptic attacks induced by the electric current. *American Journal of Psychiatry* (Suppl. 94), pp. 172–183.

Birch, H. G. (1945). The role of motivation factors in insightful problem solving: *Journal of Comparative Psychology, 38,* 295–317.

Birchwood, M., Hallett, & Preston (1989). In Birchwood, M., et al. *Schizophrenia: An integrated approach to research and treatment.* New York: New York University Press.

Bishop, J. E. (1988, March 2). Memory on trial: Witnesses of crimes are being challenged as frequently fallible. *The Wall Street Journal,* pp. 1, 18.

Bjork, R. A., & Richardson-Klarehn, A. (1989). On the puzzling relationship between environmental context and human memory. In C. Izawa (Ed.), *Current issues in cognitive processes: The Tulane-Floweree symposium on cognition.* Hillsdale, NJ: Erlbaum.

Bjorklund, D. F. (1985). The role of conceptual knowledge in the development of organization in children's memory. In C. J. Brainerd & M. Pressley (Eds.), *Basic process in memory development.* New York: Springer-Verlag.

Blakeslee, S. (1984, August 14). Scientists find key biological causes of alcoholism. *The New York Times,* p. C-1.

Blakeslee, S. (1991, September 12). Fetal cell transplants show early promise in Parkinson patients. *The New York Times,* p. C3.

Blakeslee, S. (1992, February 4). Babies learn sounds of language by 6 months. *New York Times,* p. C3.

Blanchard, F. A., Lilly, R., & Vaughn, L. A. (1991). Reducing the expression of racial prejudice. *Psychological Science, 2,* 101–105.

Blau, Z. S. (1973). *Old age in a changing society.* New York: New Viewpoints.

Block, J. H. (1983). Differential premises arising from differential socialization of the sexes: Some conjectures. *Child Development, 54,* 1335–1354.

Bloom, H. S., Criswell, E. L., Pennypacker, H. S., Catania, A. C., & Adams, C. K. (1982). Major stimulus dimensions determining detection of simulated breast lesions. *Perception and Psychophysics, 32,* 251–260.

Blum, K., Noble, E. P., Sheridan, P. J., Montgomery, A., Ritchie, T., Jagadees-waran, P., Nogami, H., Briggs, A. H., & Cohn, J. B. (1990, April 18). Allelic association of human dopamine D2 receptor gene in alcoholism. *Journal of the American Medical Association, 263,* 2055–2059.

Blumenfield, M., Levy, N. B., & Kaplan, D. (1979). The wish to be informed of a fatal illness. *Omega, 9,* 323–326.

Blumstein, P. W., & Schwartz, P. (1983). *American couples.* New York: Morrow.

Blusztajn, J. K., & Wurtman, R. J. (1983). Choline and cholinergic neurons. *Science, 221,* 614–620.

Boakes, R. A., Popplewell, D. A., & Burton, M. J. (Eds.). (1987). *Eating habits: Food, physiology, and learned behaviour.* New York: Wiley.

Body, J. (1989). The benefits of physiological psychology. *British Journal of Psychology, 80,* 479–498.

Bolles, R. C., & Fanselow, M. S. (1982). Endorphins and behavior. *Annual Review of Psychology, 33,* 87–101.

Bolos, A. M., Dean, M., Lucas-Deuse, L., Ransburg, M., Brown, A. L., & Goldman, D. (1990, December 26). Population and pedigree studies reveal a lack of association between the dopamine D2 receptor gene and alcoholism. *Journal of the American Medical Association,* 3156.

Boone, L. E., & Krutz, D. L. (1986). *Contemporary marketing* (5th ed.). Chicago: Dryden.

Booth, W. (1987, October 2). Big brother is counting your keystrokes. *Science, 238,* 17.

Booth, W. (1988a, January 15). CDC paints a picture of HIV infection in U.S., *Science, 239,* 253.

Booth, W. (1988b, March 4). The long, lost survey on sex. *Science, 239,* 1084–1085.

Booth, W. (1989). Asking America about its sex life. *Science, 243,* 304.

Borbely, A. (1986). *Secrets of sleep.* New York: Basic Books.

Borland, J. H. (1989). *Planning and implementing programs for the gifted.* New York: Teachers College Press.

Bornstein, M. H. (1989). Sensitive periods in development: Structural characteristics and causal interpretations. *Psychological Bulletin, 105,* 179–197.

Bornstein, M. H., & Bruner, J. S. (Eds.). (1989). *Interaction on human development: Crosscurrents in contemporary psychology services.* Hillsdale, NJ: Lawrence Erlbaum Associates.

Bornstein, M. H., & Krasnegor, N. A. (Eds.). (1989). *Stability and continuity in mental development: Behavioral and biological perspectives.* Hillsdale, NJ: Erlbaum.

Bornstein, M. H., & Lamb, M. E. (1992). *Development in infancy* (3rd ed.). New York: McGraw-Hill.

Bornstein, M. H., & Sigman, M. D. (1986). Continuity in mental development from infancy. *Child Development, 57,* 251–274.

Bornstein, R. F. (1989). Exposure and affect: Overview and meta-analysis of research, 1968–1987. *Psychological Bulletin, 106,* 265–289.

Boster, F. J., & Mongeau, P. (1985). Fear-arousing persuasive messages. In R. N. Bostrom (Ed.), *Communication yearbook (Vol. 8).* Beverly Hills, CA: Sage.

Botstein, D. (1986, April 11). The molecular biology of color vision. *Science, 232,* 142–143.

Bouchard, T. J., Jr., Lykken, D. T., McGue, M., Segal, N. L., & Tellegen, A. (1990, October 12). Sources of human psychological differences: The Minnesota Study of twins reared apart. *Science, 250,* 223–228.

Bourne, L. E., Dominowski, R. L., Loftus, E. F., & Healy, A. F. (1986). *Cognitive processes* (2nd ed.). Englewood Cliffs, NJ: Prentice-Hall.

Bowen, D. J., Kahl, K., Mann, S. L., & Peterson, A. V. (1991). Descriptions of early triers. *Addictive Behaviors, 16,* 95–101.

Bower, G., & Cohen, P. R. (1982). Emotional influences in memory and thinking: Data and theory. In M. S. Clark & S. T. Fiske (Eds.), *Affect and cognition.* Hillsdale, NJ: Erlbaum.

Bower, T. (1989). The perceptual world of the newborn child. In A. M. Slater & J. G. Bremner (Eds.), *Infant Development.* Hillsdale, NJ: Erlbaum.

Bowers, T. G., & Clum, G. A. (1988). Relative contribution of specific and nonspecific treatment effects: Meta-analysis of placebo-controlled behavior therapy research. *Psychological Bulletin, 103,* 315–323.

Boynton, R. M. (1988). Color vision. *Annual Review of Psychology, 39,* 69–100.

Bradburn, N. M., Rips, L. J., & Shevell, S. K. (1987). Answering autobiographical questions: The impact of memory and inference on surveys. *Science, 236,* 157–161.

Branndon, R., & Davies, C. (1973). *Wrongful imprisonment: Mistaken convictions and their consequences.* Hamden, CT: Archon Books.

Bransford, J. D., & Johnson, M. K. (1972). Contextual prerequisites for understanding: Some investigations of comprehension and recall. *Journal of Verbal Learning and Verbal Behavior, 11,* 717–721.

Braun, B. (1985, May 21). Interview by D. Goleman: New focus on multiple personality. *The New York Times,* p. C-1.

Brazelton, T. B. (1969). *Infants and mothers: Differences in development.* New York: Dell.

Breakey, R. B., & Fischer, P. J. (1990). Homelessness: The extent of the problem. *Journal of Social Issues, 46,* 31–47.

Breggin, P. R. (1979). *Electroshock: Its brain-disabling effects.* New York: Springer-Verlag.

Brehm, J. W., & Self, E. A. (1989). The intensity of motivation. *Annual Review of Psychology, 40,* 109–131.

Breland, K., & Breland, M. (1961). Misbehavior of organisms. *American Psychologist, 16,* 681–684.

Breu, G. (1984, July 2). Sing a song of courage. *People Weekly,* pp. 28–30.

Brewer, W. F., & Dupree, D. A. (1983). Use of plan schemata in the recall and . . . recognition of goal-directed actions. *Journal of Experimental Psychology: Learning, Memory, and Cognition, 9,* 117–129.

Bridges, J. S. (1988). Sex differences in occupational performance expectations. *Psychology of Women Quarterly, 12,* 75–90.

Broad, W. J. (1992, February 11). Recipe for love: A boy, a girl, a spacecraft. *The New York Times,* pp. C1, C9.

Brody, G. H., Neubaum, E., & Forehand, R. (1988). Serial marriage: A heuristic analysis of an emerging family form. *Journal of Personality and Social Psychology, 103,* 211–222.

Brody, J. (1982). *New York Times guide to personal health.* New York: New York Times Books.

Brody, J. E. (1987a, March 24). Research lifts blame from many of the obese. *The New York Times,* pp. C-1, C-6.

Brody, J. E. (1987b, May 5). Talking to the baby: Some expert advice. *The New York Times,* p. C-11.

Brody, J. E. (1987c, November 19). Encouraging news for the absent-minded: Memory can be improved, with practice. *The New York Times,* p. C-1.

Brody, N. (1990). Behavior therapy versus placebo: Comment on Bowers and Clum's meta-analysis. *Psychological Bulletin, 107,* 106–109.

Brody, N. (1992). *Intelligence* (2nd ed.). New York: Academic Press.

Bronson, G. W. (1990). The accurate calibration in infants' scanning records. *Journal of Experimental Child Psychology, 49,* 79–100.

Brookmeyer, R. (1991, July 5). Reconstruction and future trends of the AIDS epidemic in the United States. *Science, 253,* 37–42.

Broota, K. D. (1990). *Experimental design in behavioral research.* New York: Wiley.

Broverman, I. K., Vogel, S. R., Broverman, D. M., Clarkson, F. E., & Rosenkrantz, P. S. (1972). Sex-role stereotypes: A current appraisal. *Journal of Social Issues, 28,* 59–78.

Brown, A. S. (1991). A review of the tip-of-the-tongue experience. *Psychological Bulletin, 109,* 204–223.

Brown, B. B. (1984). *Between health and illness.* Boston: Houghton Mifflin.

Brown, J. D. (1987). A review of meta-analyses conducted on psychotherapy outcome research. *Clinical Psychology Review, 7,* 1–23.

Brown, J. D. (1991). Staying fit and staying well: Physical fitness as a moderator of life stress. *Journal of Personality and Social Psychology, 60,* 555–561.

Brown, J. D., & McGill, K. L. (1989). The cost of good fortune: When positive life events produce negative health consequences. *Journal of Personality and Social Psychology, 57,* 1103–1110.

Brown, M. S., & Tanner, C. (1988, May–June). Type A behavior and cardiovascular responsivity in preschoolers. *Nursing Research, 37,* 152.

Brown, P. K., & Wald, G. (1964). Visual pigments in single rod and cones of the human retina. *Science, 144,* 45–52.

Brown, R. (1958). How shall a thing be called? *Psychological Review, 65,* 14–21.

Brown, R. (1986). *Social psychology* (2nd ed.). New York: Macmillan.

Brown, R., & Kulik, J. (1977). Flashbulb memories. *Cognition, 5,* 73–99.

Brown, S. I., & Walter, M. I. (Eds.). (1990). *The art of problem posing* (2nd ed.). Hillsdale, NJ: Lawrence Erlbaum Associates.

Browne, A., & Finkelhor, D. (1986). Impact of child sexual abuse: A review of the research. *Psychological Bulletin, 99,* 66–77.

Brownell, K. D. (1989, June). When and how to diet. *Psychology Today,* pp. 40–89.

Bruce, D., & Read, J. D. (1988). The how and why of memory for frequency. In M. M. Gruneberg, P. E. Morris, & R. N. Sykes (Eds.), *Practical aspects of memory: Current research and issues.* New York: Wiley.

Bruce, V., & Green, P. R. (1990). *Visual perception: Physiology, psychology and ecology* (2nd ed.). Hillsdale, NJ: Erlbaum.

Bruch, H. (1973). *Eating disorders.* New York: Basic Books.

Bruch, H. (1973). Psychiatric aspects of obesity. *Psychiatric Annals, 3,* 6–10.

Bruck, M. (1990). Word-recognition skills of adults with childhood diagnoses of dyslexia. *Developmental Psychology, 26,* 439–454.

Bryant, F. B., & Yarnold, P. R. (1990). The impact of type A behavior on subjective life quality: Bad for the heart, good for the soul? *Journal of Social Behavior and Personality, 5,* 369–404.

Bryant, R. A., & McConkey, K. M. (1990). Hypnotic blindness and the relevance of cognitive style. *Journal of Personality and Social Psychology, 59,* 756–761.

Brynjolfsson, J., Petursson, H., Gurling, H., & Sherrington, R. (1990). Diagnostic issues in the study of schizophrenic genetics. *Nordisk Psykiatrisk Tidsskrift, 44,* 499–505.

Buchanan, C. M., & Eccles, J. S. (1992). Are adolescents the victims of raging hormones: Evidence for activational effects of hormones on moods and behavior at adolescence. *Psychological Bulletin, 62*–107.

Buck, L., & Axel, R. (1991, April 5). A novel multigene family may encode odorant receptors: A molecular basis for odor recognition. *Cell, 65,* 175–167.

Buckhout, R. (1975). Eyewitness testimony. *Scientific American,* pp. 23–31.

Budiansky, S. (1987, June 29). Taking the pain out of pain. *U.S. News and World Report,* pp. 50–57.

Buie, J. (1989, December). *APA Monitor,* p. 20.

Burbules, N. C., & Linn, M. C. (1988). Response to contradiction: Scientific reasoning during adolescence. *Journal of Educational Psychology, 80,* 67–75.

Burck, M. (1990). Word-recognition skills of adults with childhood diagnoses of dyslexia. *Developmental Psychology, 26,* 439–454.

Burger, J. M. (1986). Increasing compliance by improving the deal: The that's-not-all technique. *Journal of Personality and Social Psychology, 51,* 277–283.

Burgess, A. W., & Holmstrom, L. L. (1979). *Rape: Crisis and recovery.* Bowie, MD: Robert J. Brady.

Burnham, D. K. (1983). Apparent relative size in the judgment of apparent distance. *Perception, 12,* 683–700.

Burns, H., Parlett, J. W., & Redfield, C. L. (Eds.). (1991). *Intelligent tutoring systems: Evolutions in design.* Hillsdale, NJ: Erlbaum.

Bushman, B. J., & Geen, R. G. (1990). Role of cognitive-emotional mediators and individual differences in the effects of media violence on aggression. *Journal of Personality and Social Psychology, 58,* 156–163.

Buss, A. H. (1989). Personality as traits. *American Psychologist, 44,* 1378–1388.

Buss, D. M. et al. (1990). International preferences in selecting mates: A study of 37 cultures. *Journal of Cross-Cultural Psychology, 21,* 5–47.

Butcher, J. N. (1990). *The MMPI-2 in psychological treatment.* New York: Oxford University Press.

Butcher, J. N., Graham, J. R., Dahlstrom, W. G., & Bowman, E. (1990). The MMPI-2 with college students. *Journal of Personality Assessment, 54,* 1–15.

Butler, R. A. (1954). Incentive conditions which influence visual exploration. *Journal of Experimental Psychology, 48,* 19–23.

Butler, R. A. (1987). An analysis of the monaural displacement of sound in space. *Perception and Psychophysics, 41,* 1–7.

Byrne, D. (1969). Attitudes and attraction. In L. Berkowitz (Ed.), *Advances in experimental social psychology* (Vol. 4, pp. 35–89). New York: Academic.

Cacioppo, J. T., & Petty, R. E. (1979). Attitudes and cognitive response: An electrophysiological approach. *Journal of Personality and Social Psychology, 37,* 2181–2199.

Cacioppo, J. T., & Tassinary, L. G. (1990). Inferring psychological significance from physiological signals. *American Psychologist, 45,* 16–28.

Cain, W. S. (1982). Odor identification by males and females: Predictions versus performance. *Chemical Senses, 7,* 129–142.

Cairns, H. S., & Cairns, C. E. (1976). *Psycholinguistics: A cognitive view of language.* New York: Holt.

Candee, D., & Kohlberg, L. (1987). Moral judgment and moral action: A reanalysis of Haan, Smith, and Block's (1968) free-speech data. *Journal of Personality and Social Psychology, 52,* 554–564.

Cannon, W. B. (1929). Organization for physiological homeostatics. *Physiological Review, 9,* 280–289.

Caramazza, A., & Hillis, A. E. (1991, February 28). Lexical organization of nouns and verbs in the brain. *Nature, 349,* 788–790.

Carli, L. L. (1990). Gender, language, and influence. *Journal of Personality and Social Psychology, 59,* 941–951.

Carli, L. L., Ganley, R., & Pierce-Otay, A. (1991). Similarity and satisfaction in roommate relationships. *Personality and Social Psychology Bulletin, 17,* 419–426.

Carlson, M., Charlin, V., & Miller, N. (1988). Positive mood and helping behavior: A test of six hypotheses. *Psychological Bulletin, 55,* 211–229.

Carlson, M., Charlin, V., & Miller, N. (1988). Positive mood and helping behavior: A test of six hypotheses. *Journal of Personality and Social Psychology, 55,* 211–229.

Carlson, M., Marcus-Newhall, A., & Miller, N. (1989). Evidence for a general construct of aggression. *Personality and Social Psychology Bulletin, 15,* 377–389.

Carlson, M., Marcus-Newhall, A., & Miller, N. (1990). Effects of situational aggression cues: A quantitative review. *Journal of Personality and Social Psychology, 58,* 622–633.

Carmody, D. (1984, December 17). The tangled life and mind of Judy, whose home is the street. *The New York Times,* p. B1.

Carmody, D. (1990, March 7). College drinking: Changes in attitude and habit. *The New York Times.*

Carson, R. C. (1983). The schizophrenias. In H. E. Adams & P. B. Sutker (Eds.), *Handbook of clinical behavior therapy.* New York: Plenum.

Carson, R. C., Butcher, J. N., & Coleman, J. C. (1988). *Abnormal psychology and modern life* (8th ed.). Glenview, IL: Scott, Foresman.

Carter, B. (1991, May 1). Children's TV, where boys are king. *The New York Times,* pp. A1, C18.

Carver, C. (1990). *Optimism and coping with cancer.* Paper presented at the Conference on "Hostility, Coping and Health," Lake Arrowhead, CA.

Case, R. (1985). *Intellectual development: Birth to adulthood.* New York: Academic.

Case, R. (Ed.). (1991). *The mind's staircase: Exploring the conceptual underpinnings of children's thought and knowledge.* Hillsdale, NJ: Erlbaum.

Casselden, P. A., & Hampson, S. E. (1990). Forming impressions from incongruent traits. *Journal of Personality and Social Psychology, 59,* 353–362.

Catalano, E. M., & Johnson, K. (Eds.). (1987a). *The chronic pain control workbook: A step-by-step guide for coping with and overcoming your pain.* Oakland, CA: New Harbinger.

Catalano, E. M., & Johnson, K. (Eds.). (1987b). *A patient's guide to the management of chronic pain.* Oakland, CA: New Harbinger.

Cattell, R. B. (1963). Theory of fluid and crystallized intelligence: A critical experiment. *Journal of Educational Psychology, 54,* 1–22.

Cattell, R. B. (1967). *The scientific analysis of personality.* Baltimore: Penguin.

Cattell, R. B. (1987). *Intelligence: Its structure, growth, and action.* Amsterdam: North-Holland.

Caudill, M., & Butler, C. (Eds.). (1991). *Understanding neural networks.* Cambridge, MA: Bradford.

CDC (Centers for Disease Control). (1991a). *1988 smoking survey.* Atlanta: Centers for Disease Control.

CDC (Centers for Disease Control). (1991b). *Incidence of sexually transmitted diseases.* Atlanta: Centers for Disease Control.

Ceci, S. J., & Bronfenbrenner, U. (1991). On the demise of everyday memory. *American Psychologist, 46,* 27–31.

Ceci, S. J., Peters, D., & Plotkin, J. (1985). Human subjects review: Personal values and the regulation of social science research. *American Psychologist, 40,* 994–1002.

Center for Disease Control. (1992, January). Most students sexually active: Survey of sexual activity. Atlanta, GA: Center for Disease Control.

Cerella, J. (1985). Information-processing rates in the elderly. *Psychological Bulletin, 98,* 67–83.

Cermak, L. S., & Craik, F. I. M. (Eds.). (1979). *Levels of processing in human memory.* Hillsdale, NJ: Erlbaum.

Chaiken, S. (1979). Communicator physical attractiveness and persuasion. *Journal of Personality and Social Psychology, 37,* 1387–1397.

Chamberlain, K., & Zika, S. (1990). The minor events approach to stress: Support for the use of daily hassles. *British Journal of Psychology, 81,* 469–481.

Chandler, M. J. (1976). Social cognition and life-span approaches to the study of child development. In H. W. Reese & L. P. Lipsitt (Eds.), *Advances in child development and behavior* (Vol. 11). New York: Academic Press.

Chapman, L. J., & Chapman, J. P. (1973). *Disordered thought in schizophrenia.* New York: Appleton-Century-Crofts.

Charlier, M. (1988, February 24). Fasting plans are fast becoming a popular way to combat obesity. *The Wall Street Journal,* p. 28.

Chase, P., & Schulze, A. (1984). *Study guide.* New York: Knopf.

Chavez, C. J., Ostrea, E. M., Stryker, J. C., & Smialek, Z. (1979). Sudden infant death syndrome among infants of drug-dependent mothers. *Journal of Pediatrics, 95,* 407–409.

Cherlin, A. J., Furstenberg, F. F., Jr., Chase-Lansdale, P. L., Kiernan, K. E., Robins, P. K., Morrison, D. R., & Teitler, J. O. (1991, June 7). Longitudinal studies of effects of divorce on children in Great Britain and the United States. *Science, 252,* 1386–1389.

Cherry, E. C. (1953). Some experiments on the recognition of speech with one and two ears. *Journal of the Acoustical Society of America, 25,* 975–979.

Chomsky, N. (1968). *Language and mind.* New York: Harcourt, Brace, Jovanovich.

Chomsky, N. (1969). *The acquisition of syntax in children from five to ten.* Cambridge, MA: MIT Press.

Chomsky, N. (1978). On the biological basis of language capacities. In G. A. Miller & E. Lennenberg (Eds.), *Psychology and biology of language and thought* (pp. 199–220). New York: Academic Press.

Christianson, S. A., & Loftus, E. F. (1990). Some characteristics of people's traumatic memories. *Bulletin of the Psychonomic Society, 28,* 195–198.

Chwalisz, K., Diener, E., & Gallagher, D. (1988). Autonomic arousal feedback and emotional experience: Evidence from the spinal-cord injured. *Journal of Personality and Social Psychology, 54,* 820–828.

Cialdini, R. B. (1984). *Social influence.* New York: Morrow.

Cialdini, R. B. (1988). *Influence: Science and practice* (2nd ed.). Glenview, IL: Scott, Foresman.

Cialdini, R. B., & Fultz, J. (1990). Interpreting the negative. In D. Cicchetti & M. Beeghly (Eds.), *Children with Down Syndrome.* Cambridge, England: Cambridge University Press.

Cialdini, R. B., Schaller, M., Houlihan, D., Arps, K., Fultz, J., & Beaman, A. L. (1987). Empathy-based helping: Is it selflessly or selfishly motivated? *Journal of Personality and Social Psychology, 52,* 749–758.

Cialdini, R. B., Vincent, J. E., Lewis, S. K., Catalan, J., Wheeler, D., & Darby, B. L. (1975). Reciprocal concessions procedure for inducing compliance: The door-in-the-face technique. *Journal of Personality and Social Psychology, 31,* 206–215.

Cimbolic, P., & Jobes, D. A. (Eds.). (1990). *Youth suicide: Issues, assessment, and intervention.* Springfield, IL: Charles C Thomas.

CIRE (Cooperative Institutional Research Program of the American Council on Education). (1990). *The American Freshman: National Norms for Fall 1990.* Los Angeles: American Council on Education.

Clark, M. S. (1987, November 9). Sweet music for the deaf. *Newsweek,* p. 73.

Clark, M. S. (Ed.). (1991). *Prosocial behavior.* Newbury Park, CA: Sage.

Clark, M. S., & Reis, H. T. (1988). Interpersonal processes in close relationships. *Annual Review of Psychology, 39,* 609–672.

Clark, R. D., III, & Maass, A. (1988). Social categorization in minority influence: The case of homosexuality. *European Journal of Social Psychology, 18,* 347–364.

Clark, R. D., III, & Maass, A. (1990). The effects of majority size on minority influence. *European Journal of Social Psychology, 20,* 99–117.

Clarke-Stewart, A., & Friedman, S. (1987). *Child development: Infancy through adolescence.* New York: Wiley.

Clarke-Stewart, K. A. (1989). Infant day care: Maligned or malignant? *American Psychologist, 44,* 266–273.

Clarke-Stewart, K. A. (1991). A home is not a school: The effects of child care on children's development. *Journal of Social Issues, 47,* 105–123.

Clearwater, Y. (1985, July). A human place in outer space. *Psychology Today,* 34–43.

Clum, G. A., & Bowers, T. G. (1990). Behavior therapy better than placebo treatments: Fact or artifact? *Psychological Bulletin, 107,* 110–113.

Coates, T. J. (1990). Strategies for modifying sexual behavior for primary and secondary prevention of HIV disease. *Journal of Consulting and Clinical Psychology, 58,* 57–69.

Coates, T. J. (1990). Strategies of modifying sexual behavior for primary and secondary prevention of HIV disease. *Journal of Consulting and Clinical Psychology, 58,* 57–69.

Cohen, A. G., & Gutek, B. A. (1991). Sex differences in the career experiences of members of two APA divisions. *American Psychologist, 46,* 1292–1298.

Cohen, D. B. (1979). *Sleep and dreaming: Origins, nature, and functioning.* New York: Pergamon.

Cohen, G. (1989). *Memory in the real world.* Hillsdale, NJ: Erlbaum.

Cohen, J. D., Dunbar, K., & McClelland, J. L. (1990). On the control of automatic processes: A parallel distributed processing account of the Stroop effect. *Psychological Review, 97,* 332–361.

Cohen, N. J., McCloskey, M., & Wible, C. G. (1990). Flashbulb memories and underlying cognitive mechanisms: Reply to Pillemer. *Journal of Experimental Psychology: General, 119,* 97–100.

Cohen, R. (1978, May). Suddenly I'm the adult? *Psychology Today,* 70.

Cohen, S., Tyrrell, D. A., & Smith, A. P. (1991). Psychological stress and susceptibility to the common cold. *New England Journal of Medicine, 325,* 606–612.

Cohen, S. H., & Reese, H. W. (Eds.). (1991). *Life-span developmental psychology: Methodological innovations.* Hillsdale, NJ: Erlbaum.

Cohen, T. E., & Lasley, D. J. (1986). Visual sensitivity. In Rosenzweig & Porter (Eds.), *Annual Review of Psychology, 37.* Palo Alto, CA: Annual Reviews.

Colby, A., & Damon, W. (1987). Listening to a different voice: A review of Gilligan's *In a different voice.* In M. R. Walsh (Ed.), *The psychology of women.* New Haven, CT: Yale University Press.

Coleman, J. C., Butcher, J. N., & Carson, R. C. (1984). *Abnormal psychology and modern life.* Glenview, IL: Scott, Foresman.

Coles, R., & Stokes, G. (1985). *Sex and the American teenager.* New York: Harper & Row.

Collins, A. M., & Loftus, E. F. (1975). A spreading-activation theory of semantic processing. *Psychological Review, 82,* 407–428.

Collins, A. M., & Quillian, M. R. (1969). Retrieval times from semantic memory. *Journal of Verbal Learning and Verbal Behavior, 8,* 240–247.

Collins, W. A., & Gunnar, M. R. (1990). Social and personality development. *Annual Review of Psychology, 41,* 387–416.

Colombo, J., & Mitchell, D. W. (1990). Individual differences in early visual attention. In J. Colombo & J. W. Fagen (Eds.), *Individual differences in infancy: Reliability, stability, and prediction.* Hillsdale, NJ: Erlbaum.

Commons, M. L., Grossberg, S., & Staddon, J. E. R. (Eds.). (1991). *Neural network models of conditioning and action.* Hillsdale, NJ: Erlbaum.

Commons, M. L., Nevin, J. A., & Davison, M. C. (Eds.). (1991). *Signal detection: Mechanism, models and applications.* Hillsdale, NJ: Erlbaum.

Compas, B. E. (1987). Coping with stress during childhood and adolescence. *Psychological Bulletin, 101,* 393–403.

Comstock, G., & Paik, H. (1991). *Television and the American child.* New York: Academic Press.

Condon, J. W., & Crano, W. D. (1988). Inferred evaluation and the relation between attitude similarity and interpersonal attraction. *Journal of Personality and Social Psychology, 54,* 789–797.

Consumer Reports Health Letter (see CRHL)

Converse, J., Jr., & Cooper, J. (1979). The importance of decisions and free-choice attitude change: A curvilinear finding. *Journal of Experimental Social Psychology, 15,* 48–61.

Cook, C. A. L., Caplan, R. D., & Wolowitz, H. (1990). Nonwaking responses to waking stressors: Dreams and nightmares. *Journal of Applied Social Psychology, 20,* 199–226.

Cooper, S. H. (1989). Recent contributions to the theory of defense mechanism: A comparative view. *Journal of the American Psychoanalytic Association, 37,* 865–892.

Cooper, W. H. (1981). Ubiquitous halo. *Psychological Bulletin, 90,* 218–244.

Cooperative Institutional Research Program of the American Council on Education (see CIRE)

Coppen, A., Metcalfe, M., & Wood, K. (1982). Lithium. In E. S. Paykel (Ed.), *Handbook of affective disorders.* New York: Guilford Press.

Corballis, M. C., & Beale, I. L. (1983). *The ambivalent mind: The neuro-psychology of left and right.* Chicago: Nelson-Hall.

Coren, S. (1989). The many moon illusions: An integration through analysis. In M. Hershenson (Ed.), *The moon illusion.* Hillsdale, NJ: Erlbaum.

Coren, S., & Aks, D. J. (1990). Moon illusion in pictures: A multi-mechanism approach. *Journal of Experimental Psychology: Human Perception and Performance, 16,* 365–380.

Coren, S., Porac, C., & Ward, L. M. (1979). *Sensation and perception.* New York: Academic.

Coren, S., Porac, C., & Ward, L. M. (1984). *Sensation and perception* (2nd ed.). New York: Academic.

Coren, S., & Ward, L. M. (1989). *Sensation and perception* (3rd ed.). San Diego: Harcourt, Brace, Jovanovich.

Cornblatt, B., & Erlenmeyer-Kimling, L. E. (1985). Global attentional deviance in children at risk for schizophrenia: Specificity and predictive validity. *Journal of Abnormal Psychology, 94,* 470–486.

Cornelius, S. W., & Caspi, A. (1987). Everyday problem solving in adulthood and old age. *Psychology and Aging, 2,* 144–153.

Cornsweet, T. N. (1970). *Visual perception.* New York: Academic.

Costa, P. T., Jr., & McCrae, R. R. (1985).

Hypochondriasis, neuroticism, and aging. *American Psychologist, 40,* 19–28.

Cotman, C. W., & Lynch, G. S. (1989). The neurobiology of learning and memory. *Cognition, 33,* 201–241.

Covington, M. V., & Omelich, C. L. (1987). ''I knew it cold before the exam'': A test of the anxiety-blockage hypothesis. *Journal of Educational Psychology, 79,* 393–400.

Cowan, N. (1988). Evolving conceptions of memory storage, selective attention, and their mutual constraints within the human information-processing system. *Psychological Bulletin, 104,* 163–191.

Cowley, G. (1990a, March 26). The promise of Prozac. *Newsweek,* 38–41.

Cowley, G. (1990b, June 25). AIDS: The next ten years. *Newsweek,* pp. 20–27.

Cowley, G. (1991). The bold and the bashful. *Newsweek, 117,* 24–27.

Craik, F. I., & Lockhart, R. S. (1972). Levels of processing: A framework for memory research. *Journal of Verbal Behavior, 11,* 671–684.

Craik, F. I. M. (1977). Age differences in human memory. In J. E. Birren & K. W. Schaie (Eds.), *Handbook of the psychology of aging.* New York: Van Nostrand Reinhold.

Cramer, P. (1987). The development of defense mechanisms. *Journal of Personality, 55,* 597–614.

Crandall, C., & Biernat, M. (1990). The ideology of anti-fat attitudes. *Journal of Applied Social Psychology, 20,* 227–243.

Crandall, C. S. (1988). Social contagion of binge eating. *Journal of Personality and Social Psychology, 55,* 588–598.

Crawford, H. J. (1982). Hypnotizability, daydreaming styles, imagery vividness, and absorption: A multidimensional study. *Journal of Personality and Social Psychology, 42,* 915–926.

CRHL (Consumer Reports Health Letter). (1990, February). How much should you weigh?

CRHL (Consumer Reports Health Letter). (1990, February). How to lose weight and keep it off, pp. 2, 9–11.

Crick, F., & Mitchison, G. (1983). The function of dream sleep. *Nature, 304,* 111–114.

Crits-Christoph, P., & Mintz, J. (1991). Implications of therapist effects for the design and analysis of comparative studies of psychotherapies. *Journal of Consulting and Clinical Psychology, 59,* 20–26.

Crocetti, G. (1983). *GRE: Graduate record examination general aptitude test.* New York: Arco.

Crosby, F. J. (1991). *Juggling: The unexpected advantages of balancing career and home for women, their families, and society.* New York: Free Press.

Croyle, R. T., & Hunt, J. R. (1991). Coping with health threat: Social influence processes in reactions to medical test

results. *Journal of Personality and Social Psychology, 60,* 382–389.

Cummings, E., & Henry, W. E. (1961). *Growing old.* New York: Basic Books.

Cummings, J. (1987, October 6). An earthquake aftershock: Calls to mental health triple. *The New York Times,* p. A-1.

Cummings, L. L., & Berger, C. J. (1976). Organization structure: How does it influence attitudes and performance? *Organizational Dynamics, 5,* 34–49.

Cunningham, M. R. (1986). Measuring the physical in physical attractiveness: Quasi-experiments on the sociobiology of female facial beauty. *Journal of Personality and Social Psychology, 50,* 925–935.

Cunningham, M. R., Barbee, A. P., & Pike, C. L. (1990). What do women want? Facialmetric assessment of multiple motives in the perception of male facial physical attractiveness. *Journal of Personality and Social Psychology, 59,* 61–72.

Cusack, O. (1984, April). Pigeon posses. *Omni,* p. 34.

Czeisler, C. A., Kronauer, R. E., Allan, J. S., Duffy, J. F., Jewett, M. E., Brown, E. N., & Ronda, J. M. (1989, June 16). Bright light induction of strong (type O) resetting of the human circadian pacemaker. *Science, 244,* 1328–1333.

Czeisler, C. A., Johnson, M. P., Duffy, J. F., Brown, E. N., Rondu, J. M., & Kronanes, R. E. (1990, May 3). Exposure to bright light and darkness to treat physiologic maladaptation to night work. *New England Journal of Medicine, 322,* 1253–1259.

Daehler, M., & Bukato, D. (1985). *Cognitive development.* New York: Random House.

Damon, W. (1988). *The moral child.* New York: Free Press.

Darley, J. M., & Latan, B. (1968). Bystander intervention in emergencies: Diffusion of responsibility. *Journal of Personality and Social Psychology, 8,* 377–383.

Darley, J. M., & Schultz, T. R. (1990). Moral rules: Their content and acquisition. *Annual Review of Psychology, 25,* 525–556.

Darnton, N. (1990, June 4). Mommy vs. Mommy. *Newsweek,* pp. 64–67.

Darnton, N. (1991, October 7). The pain of the last taboo. *Newsweek,* pp. 70–72.

Darwin, C. J., Turvey, M. T., & Crowder, R. G. (1972). An auditory analogue of the Sperling partial-report procedure: Evidence for brief auditory storage. *Cognitive Psychology, 3,* 255–267.

Davidson, J. E. (1990). Intelligence recreated. *Educational Psychologist, 25,* 337–354.

Davis, J. M., & Sandoval, J. (1991). *Suicidal youth.* San Francisco: Jossey-Bass.

Davis, R. (1986). Assessing the eating

disorders. *The Clinical Psychologist, 39,* 33–36.

Dawes, R. M., Faust, D., & Meehl, P. E. (1989, March 31). Clinical versus actuarial judgment. *Science,* 243, 1668–1674.

DeAngelis, T. (1991a, June). DSM being revised, but problems remain. *APA Monitor,* pp. 12–13.

DeAngelis, T. (1991b, June). Honesty tests weigh in with improved ratings. *APA Monitor,* p. 7.

Deaux, K., & Lewis, L. L. (1984). The structure of gender stereotypes: Interrelationships among components and gender label. *Journal of Personality and Social Psychology, 46,* 991–1004.

deBono, E. (1967). *The five day course in thinking.* New York: Basic Books.

DeBono, K. G., & Packer, M. (1991). The effects of advertising appeal on perceptions of product quality. *Personality and Social Psychology Bulletin, 17,* 194–200.

DeCasper, A. J., & Fifer, W. D. (1980). Of human bonding: Newborns prefer their mothers' voices. *Science, 208,* 1174–1176.

DeCharms, R., & Moeller, G. H. (1962). Values expressed in American children's readers, 1800–1950. *Journal of Abnormal and Social Psychology, 64,* 136–142.

Deci, E. L., & Ryan, R. M. (1985). *Intrinsic motivation and self-determination in human behavior.* New York: Plenum.

deGroot, A. D. (1966). Perception and memory versus thought: Some old ideas and recent findings. In B. Kleinmuntz (Ed.), *Problem solving: Research, method, and theory.* New York: Wiley.

Delbeckq, A., Van DeVen, A., & Gustafson, D. (1975). *Group techniques for program planning.* Glenview, IL: Scott, Foresman.

DeLeon, P. H. (1988). Public policy and public service: Our professional duty. *American Psychologist, 43,* 309–315.

DeLongis, A., Folkman, S., & Lazarus, R. S. (1988). The impact of daily stress on health and mood: Psychological social resources as mediators. *Journal of Personality and Social Psychology, 54,* 486–495.

Dement, W. C. (1976). *Some must watch while some must sleep.* New York: Norton.

Dement, W. C. (1979). Two kinds of sleep. In D. Goleman & R. J. Davidson (Eds.), *Consciousness: Brain, states of awareness, and mysticism* (pp. 72–75). New York: Harper & Row.

Dement, W. C. (1989). *Sleep and alertness: Chrono-biological, behavioral and medical aspects of napping.* New York: Raven Press.

Dement, W. C., & Wolpert, E. A. (1958). The relation of eye movements, body mobility, and external stimuli to dream content. *Journal of Experimental Psychology, 55,* 543–553.

Dent, J. (1984, March). *Readers Digest, 124,* 38.

Denton, K., & Krebs, D. (1990). From the scene of the crime: The effect of alcohol and social context on moral judgment. *Journal of Personality and Social Psychology, 59,* 242–248.

Dentzer, S. (1986, May 5). Can you pass the job test? *Newsweek,* pp. 46–53.

Deregowski, J. B. (1973). Illusion and culture. In R. L. Gregory & G. H. Combrich (Eds.), *Illusion in nature and art* (pp. 161–192). New York: Scribner.

deSchonen, S., & Mathivet, E. (1989). First come, first served: A scenario about the development of hemispheric specialization in face recognition during infancy. *European Bulletin of Cognitive Psychology, 9,* 3–44.

Desforges, D. M., Lord, C. G., Ramsey, S. L., Mason, J. A., VanLeeuwen, M. D., West, S. C., & Lepper, M. R. (1991). Effects of structured cooperative contact on changing negative attitudes toward stigmatized social groups. *Journal of Personality and Social Psychology, 60,* 531–544.

Devenport, L. D., & Devenport, J. A. (1990). The laboratory animal dilemma: A solution in our backyards. *Psychological Science, 1,* 215–216.

deVilliers, J. G., & deVilliers, P. A. (1978). *Language acquisition.* Cambridge, MA: MIT Press.

Devine, P. G. (1989). Stereotypes and prejudice: Their automatic and controlled components. *Journal of Personality and Social Psychology, 56,* 5–18.

Devine, P. G., & Baker, S. M. (1991). Measurement of racial stereotype subtyping. *Personality and Social Psychology Bulletin, 17,* 44–50.

Deyo, R. A., Straube, K. T., & Disterhoft, J. F. (1989, February 10). Nimodipine facilitates associative learning in aging rabbits. *Science, 243,* 809–811.

Dickinson, A. (1990, Nov. 12). Helpless to save her sister from Alzheimer's, an anguished actress provides what comfort she can. *People,* pp. 75–78.

Diehl, M., & Stroebe, W. (1987). Productivity loss in brainstorming groups: Toward the solution of a riddle. *Journal of Personality and Social Psychology, 53,* 497–509.

Digman, J. M. (1990). Personality structure: Emergence of the five-factor model. *Annual Review of Psychology, 41,* 417–440.

Dillard, J. P. (1991). The current status of research on sequential-request compliance techniques. *Personality and Social Psychology Bulletin, 17,* 283–288.

DiMatteo, M. R., & DiNicola, D. D. (1982). *Achieving patient compliance: The psychology of the medical practitioner's role.* New York: Pergamon.

Dion, K. K., & Berscheid, E. (1974). Physical attractiveness and peer perception among children. *Sociometry, 37,* 1–12.

Dolce, J. J., & Raczynski, J. M. (1985). Neuromuscular activity and electromyography in painful backs: Psychological and biomechanical models in assessment and treatment. *Psychological Bulletin, 97,* 502–520.

Dollard, J., Doob, L., Miller, N., Mower, O. H., & Sears, R. R. (1939). *Frustration and aggression.* New Haven, CT: Yale University Press.

Donnerstein, E., & Berkowitz, L. (1981). Victim reactions in aggressive erotic films as a factor in violence against women. *Journal of Personality and Social Psychology, 41,* 710–724.

Donnerstein, E., Linz, D., & Penrod, S. (1987). *The question of pornography: Research findings and policy implications.* New York: Free Press.

Doob, A. N., & Wood, L. (1972). Catharsis and aggression: The effects of annoyance and retaliation on aggressive behavior. *Journal of Personality and Social Psychology, 22,* 156–162.

Dore, F. Y., & Dumas, C. (1987). Psychology of animal cognition: Piagetian studies. *Psychological Bulletin, 102,* 219–233.

Doris, J. (Ed.). (1991). *The suggestibility of children's recollections: Implications for eyewitness testimony.* Hyattsville, MD: American Psychological Association.

Dorr, A. (Ed.). (1992). *Television and affect.* Hillsdale, NJ: Erlbaum.

Doty, R. L. (1986). Development and age-related changes in human olfactory function. In W. Breipohl & R. Apfelbach (Eds.), *Ontogeny of olfaction in vertebrates.* Berlin: Springer-Verlag.

Doty, R. L., Green, P. A., Ram, C., & Yankell, S. L. (1982). Communication of gender from human breath odors: Relationship to perceived intensity and pleasantness. *Hormones and Behavior, 16,* 13–22.

Dove, A. (1968, July 15). Taking the chitling test. *Newsweek.*

Dovidio, J. F., Allen, J. L., & Schroeder, D. A. (1990). Specificity of empathy-induced helping: Evidence for altruistic motivation. *Journal of Personality and Social Psychology, 59,* 249–260.

Dovidio, J. F., & Ellyson, S. L. (Eds.). (1985). *Power, dominance, and nonverbal behavior.* New York: Springer-Verlag.

Dovidio, J. F., Ellyson, S. L., Keating, C. F., Heltman, K., & Brown, C. E. (1988). The relationship of social power to visual displays of dominance between men and women. *Journal of Personality and Social Psychology, 54,* 233–242.

Drake, R. E., Osher, F. C., & Wallach, M. A. (1991). Homelessness and dual diagnosis. *American Psychologist, 46,* 1149–1158.

Dreyer, P. H. (1982). Sexuality during adolescence. In B. B. Wolman (Ed.), *Handbook of developmental psychology.* Englewood Cliffs, NJ: Prentice-Hall.

Druckman, D., & Bjork, R. A. (Eds.). (1991). *In the mind's eye.* Washington, DC: National Research Council.

Druckman, D., & Swets, J. A. (Eds.). (1988). *Enhancing human performance: Issues, theories, and techniques.* Washington, DC: National Academy Press.

Drum, D. J. (1990). Group therapy review. *Counseling Psychologist, 18,* 131–138.

Dryden, W., & DiGiuseppe, R. (1990). *A primer on rational-emotive therapy.* Champaign, IL: Research Press.

Duck, S. (1988). *Relating to others.* Chicago: Dorsey Press.

Duck, S. (1990). *Personal relationships and social support.* Newbury Park, CA: Sage.

Duck, S. W. (Ed.). (1982a). *Personal relationships: Vol. 4. Dissolving personal relationships.* New York: Academic Press.

Duck, S. W. (1982b). A topography of relationship disengagement and dissolution. In S. W. Duck (Ed.), *Personal relationships: Vol. 4. Dissolving Personal Relationships.* New York: Academic Press.

Duck, S. W. (Ed.). (1983). *Personal relationships: Repairing personal relationships.* New York: Academic Press.

Duke, M. P., & Nowicki, S., Jr. (1979). *Abnormal psychology: Perspectives on being different.* Monterey, CA: Brooks/Cole.

Duke, M. P., & Nowicki, S., Jr. (1986). *Abnormal psychology: A new look.* New York: Holt.

Duncan, P. D., et al. (1985). The effects of pubertal timing on body image, school behavior, and deviance. Special Issue: Time of maturation and psychosocial functioning in adolescence. *Journal of Youth and Adolescence, 14,* 227–235.

Duncker, K. (1945). On problem solving. *Psychological Monographs, 58,* (5, whole no. 270.)

Dunkel-Schetter, C., Folkman, S., & Lazarus, R. S. (1987). Correlates of social support receipt. *Journal of Personality and Social Psychology, 53,* 71–80.

Dunne, E. J., McIntosh, J. L., & Dunne-Maxim, K. (Eds.). (1987). *Suicide and its aftermath: Understanding and counseling the survivors.* New York: Norton.

Dutton, D. G., & Aron, A. P. (1974). Some evidence for heightened sexual attraction under conditions of high anxiety. *Journal of Personality and Social Psychology, 30,* 510–517.

Dworkin, R. H., & Widom, C. S. (1977). Undergraduate MMPI profiles and the longitudinal prediction of adult social outcome. *Journal of Consulting and Clinical Psychology, 45,* 620–625.

Dykman, J., & Abramson, L. Y. (1990). Contributions of basic research to the cognitive theories of depression. *Personality and Social Psychology Bulletin, 16,* 42–57.

Dywan, J., & Bowers, K. (1983). The use of hypnosis to enhance recall. *Science, 222*, 184–185.

Eagly, A. H. (1978). Sex differences in influenceability. *Psychological Bulletin, 85*, 86–116.

Eagly, A. H. (1983). Gender and social influence: A social psychological analysis. *American Psychologist, 38*, 971–981.

Eagly, A. H. (1989, May). *Meta-analysis of sex differences.* Annual conference on adversity, University of Massachusetts, Amherst, MA.

Eagly, A. H., & Carlie, L. L. (1981). Sex of researchers and sex-typed communications as determinants of sex differences in influenceability: A meta-analysis of social influence studies. *Psychological Bulletin, 90*, 1–20.

Eagly, A. H., & Steffen, V. J. (1986). Gender and aggressive behavior: A meta-analytic review of the social psychological literature. *Psychological Bulletin, 100*, 309–330.

Eagly, A. H., Wood, W., & Chaiken, S. (1978). Causal inferences about communicators and their effect on opinion change. *Journal of Personality and Social Psychology, 36*, 424–435.

Ebbesen, E. B., Duncan, B., & Konecni, V. J. (1975). Effects of content of verbal aggression on future verbal aggression: A field experiment. *Journal of Experimental Social Psychology, 11*, 192–204.

Ebbinghaus, H. (1913). *Memory: A contribution to experimental psychology* (H. A. Roger & C. E. Bussenius, Trans.). New York: Columbia University Press. (Original work published 1885.)

Eberts, R., & MacMillan, A. C. (1985). Misperception of small cars. In R. Eberts & C. Eberts (Eds.), *Trends in ergonomics/human factors, III.* Amsterdam: Elsevier.

Eccles, J. S., Jacobs, J. E., & Harold, R. D. (1990). Gender role stereotypes, expectancy effects, and parents' socialization of gender differences. *Journal of Social Issues, 46*, 183–201.

Eckenrode, J. (1984). Impact of chronic and acute stressors on daily reports of mood. *Journal of Personality and Social Psychology, 46*, 907–918.

Eckholm, E. (1988, April 17). Exploring the forces of sleep. *The New York Times Magazine*, pp. 26–34.

Edidin, M., Kuo, S. C. & Scheetz, M. P. (1991, November 29). Lateral movements of membrane glycoproteins restricted by dynamic cytoplasmic barriers. *Science, 254*, 1379–1380.

Egan, D. E., & Schwartz, B. J. (1979). Chunking in recall of symbolic drawings. *Memory and Cognition, 7*, 149–158.

Egeland, J. A., Gerhard, D. S., Pauls, D. L., Sussex, J. N., Kidd, K. K., Allen, C. R., Hostetter, A. M., & Housman, D. E. (1987). Bipolar effective disorders linked to DNA markers on chromosome 11. *Nature, 325*, 783–787.

Eisenberg, N. (1991). Meta-analytic contributions to the literature on prosocial behavior. *Personality and Social Psychology Bulletin, 17*, 273–282.

Eisenberg, N., & Fabes, R. A. (1991). Prosocial behavior and empathy: A multimethod developmental perspective. In M. S. Clark (Ed.), *Prosocial behavior.* Newbury Park, CA: Sage.

Ekman, P. (1972). Universals and cultural differences in facial expressions of emotion. In J. Cole (Ed.), *Darwin and facial expression: A century of research in review* (pp. 169–222). New York: Academic Press.

Ekman, P. (1984). Expression and the nature of emotion. In K. Scherer & P. Ekman (Eds.), *Approaches to emotion.* Hillsdale, NJ: Erlbaum.

Ekman, P. (1985). *Telling lies.* New York: Norton.

Ekman, P. (1989). The argument and evidence about universals in facial expressions of emotion. In H. Wagner & A. Manstead (Eds.), *Handbook of social psychophysiology.* Chichester: Wiley.

Ekman, P., Davidson, R. J., & Friesen, W. V. (1990). Emotional expression and brain physiology II: The Duchenne smile. *Journal of Personality and Social Psychology, 58*, 342–353.

Ekman, P., Friesen, W. V., & Ellsworth, P. (1972). *Emotion in the human face.* Elmsford, NY: Pergamon.

Ekman, P., Friesen, W. V., O'Sullivan, M., Chan, A., Diacoyanni-Tarlatzis, I., Heider, K., Krause, R., LeCompte, W. A., Pitcairn, T., Ricci-Bitti, P. E., Scherer, K., Tomita, M., & Tzavaras, A. (1987). Universals and cultural differences in the judgments of facial expressions of emotion. *Journal of Personality and Social Psychology, 53*, 712–717.

Ekman, P., Levenson, R. W., & Friesen, W. V. (1983, September 16). Autonomic nervous system activity distinguishes among emotions. *Science, 223*, 1208–1210.

Ekman, P., & O'Sullivan, M. (1991). Facial expression: Methods, means, and moues. In R. S. Feldman & B. Rime (Eds.), *Fundamentals of nonverbal behavior.* Cambridge, England: Cambridge University Press.

Elkin, I. (1986, May). *NIMH treatment of depression: Collaborative research program.* Paper presented at the annual meeting of the American Psychiatric Association, Washington, DC.

Elkin, I., Shea, M. T., Watkins, J. T., Imber, S. D., Sotsky, S. M., et al. (1989). NIMH treatment of depression collaborative research program: General effectiveness of treatments. *Archives of General Psychiatry, 46*, 971–982.

Elkind, D. (1981). *The hurried child.* Reading, MA: Addison-Wesley.

Ellis, A. (1962). *Reason and emotion in psychotherapy.* New York: Lyle Stuart.

Ellis, A. (1974). *Growth through reason.* Hollywood: Wilshire Books.

Ellis, A., & Dryden, W. (1987). *The practice of rational-emotive therapy (RET).* New York: Springer.

Engel, J. F., & Blackwell, R. D. (1982). *Consumer behavior* (4th ed.). Hinsdale, IL: Dryden.

Engen, T. (1982). *Perception of odors.* New York: Academic.

Engen, T. (1987, September–October). Remembering odors and their names. *American Scientist, 75*, 497–503.

Engle-Friedman, M., Baker, A., & Bootzin, R. R. (1985). Reports of wakefulness during EEG identified stages of sleep. *Sleep Research, 14*, 152.

Epperson, S. E. (1988, September 16). Studies link subtle sex bias in schools with women's behavior in the workplace. *The Wall Street Journal*, p. 19.

Epstein, L. (1986). Childhood obesity. *Science, 232*, 20–21.

Epstein, L. H., Grunberg, N. E., Lichtenstein, E., & Evans, R. I. (1989). Smoking research: Basic research, intervention, prevention, and new trends. *Health Psychology, 8*, 705–721.

Epstein, R. (1987). The spontaneous interconnection of four repertories of behavior in a pigeon. *Journal of Comparative Psychology, 101*, 197–201.

Epstein, S., & Meier, P. (1989). Constructive thinking: A broad coping variable with specific components. *Journal of Personality and Social Psychology, 57*, 332–350.

Epstein, S., & O'Brien, E. J. (1985). The person-situation debate in historical and current perspective. *Psychological Bulletin, 98*, 513–537.

Erber, R. (1991). Affective and semantic priming: Effects of mood on category accessibility and inference. *Journal of Experimental Social Psychology.*

Erickson, M. H., Hershman, S., & Secter, I. I. (1990). *The practical application of medical and dental hypnosis.* New York: Brunner/Mazel.

Erikson, E. H. (1963). *Childhood and society* (2nd ed.). New York: Norton.

Eron, L. D. (1982). Parent-child interaction, television violence, and aggression of children. *American Psychologist, 37*, 197–211.

Eron, L. D., & Huesmann, L. R. (1985). The control of aggressive behavior by changes in attitude, values, and the conditions of learning. In R. J. Blanchard & C. Blanchard (Eds.), *Advances in the study of aggression.* New York: Academic Press.

Eron, L. D., Huesmann, L. R., Lefkowitz,

M. M., & Walden, L. O. (1972). Does television cause aggression? *American Psychologist, 27,* 253–263.

Esasky, N. (1991, March). His career threatened by dizzying attacks of vertigo: A ballplayer struggles to regain his field of dreams. *People,* 61–64.

Estes, W. K. (1991). Cognitive architectures from the standpoint of an experimental psychologist. *Annual Review of Psychology, 42,* 1–28.

Evans, P. D. (1990). Type A behavior and coronary heart disease: When will the jury return? *British Journal of Psychology, 81,* 147–157.

Eveleth, P., & Tanner, J. (1976). *Worldwide variation in human growth.* New York: Cambridge University Press.

Everly, G. S., Jr. (1989). *A clinical guide to the treatment of the human stress response.* New York: Plenum.

Eysenck, H. J. (1973). *Eysenck on extraversion.* New York: Wiley.

Eysenck, H. J. (1976). Structure of social attitudes. *Psychological Reports, 39,* 463–466.

Fajardo, D. M. (1985). Author race, essay quality, and reverse discrimination. *Journal of Applied Social Psychology, 15,* 255–268.

Fanelli, R. J., Burright, R. G., & Donovick, P. J. (1983). A multivariate approach to the analysis of genetic and septal lesion effects on maze performance in mice. *Behavioral Neuroscience, 97,* 354–369.

Farley, F. (1986, May). The big T in personality. *Psychology Today,* pp. 44–52.

Fay, R. E., Turner, C. F., Klassen, A. D., & Gagnon, J. H. (1989, January 20). Prevalence and patterns of same-gender sexual contact among men. *Science, 243,* 338–348.

Fay, R. R. (1988). Comparative psychoacoustics. *Hearing Research, 34,* 295–306.

FDA (Food and Drug Administration). (1991). Denial of petition to ban Prozac. Washington, DC: Food & Drug Administration.

Fehr, B., & Russell, J. (1991). The concept of love viewed from a prototype perspective. *Journal of Personality and Social Psychology, 60,* 425–438.

Feifel, H. (1963). In N. L. Farberow (Ed.), *Taboo topics* (pp. 8–12). New York: Atherton.

Feingold, A. (1988). Cognitive gender differences are disappearing. *American Psychologist, 43,* 95–103.

Feldman, R. S. (1982). *Development of nonverbal behavior in children.* New York: Springer-Verlag.

Feldman, R. S., Philippot, P., & Custrini, R. J. (1991). In R. S. Feldman & B. Rime (Eds.), *Fundamentals of nonverbal behavior.* Cambridge, England: Cambridge University Press.

Festinger, L. (1957). *A theory of cognitive dissonance.* Stanford, CA: Stanford University Press.

Festinger, L., & Carlsmith, J. M. (1959). Cognitive consequences of forced compliance. *Journal of Abnormal and Social Psychology, 58,* 203–210.

Festinger, L., Schachter, S., & Back, K. W. (1950). *Social pressure in informal groups.* New York: Harper.

Feynman, R. P. (1988, February). An outsider's view of the *Challenger* inquiry. *Physics Today,* pp. 26–37.

Fichter, M. M. (Ed.). (1990). *Bulimia nervosa: Basic research, diagnosis and therapy.* New York: Wiley.

Fiedler, F. E., Mitchell, R., & Triandis, H. C. (1971). The culture assimilator: An approach to cross-cultural training. *Journal of Applied Psychology, 55,* 95–102.

Field, T. (1987). Interaction and attachment in normal and atypical infants. *Journal of Consulting and Clinical Psychology, 55,* 853–859.

Field, T. M. (1978). Interaction of primary versus secondary caretaker fathers. *Developmental Psychology, 14,* 183–184.

Field, T. M. (1982). Individual differences in the expressivity of neonates and young infants. In R. S. Feldman (Ed.), *Development of nonverbal behavior in children.* New York: Springer-Verlag.

Fieve, R. R. (1975). *Moodswing.* New York: Morrow.

Fink, M. (1990, April). Continuation of ECT. *Harvard Medical School Mental Health Letter, 6,* 8.

Finkelhor, D. (1979). *Sexually victimized children.* New York: Free Press.

Finkelhor, D. (1984). *Child sexual abuse: New theory and research.* New York: Free Press.

Finkelstein, N. W. (1982). Aggression: Is it stimulated by day care? *Young Children, 37,* 3–9.

Fischman, J. (1987). Type A on trial. *Psychology Today, 21,* 42–50.

Fischman, M. (1985, August). *Cocaine use: Laboratory perspective on a growing health problem.* Paper presented at the annual meeting of the American Psychological Association, Los Angeles.

Fischoff, B. (1977). Perceived informativeness of facts. *Journal of Experimental Psychology: Human Perception and Performance, 3,* 349–358.

Fisher, K. (1985, March). ECT: New studies on how, why, who. *APA Monitor,* pp. 18–19.

Fisher, P. J., & Breakey, W. R. (1991). The epidemiology of alcohol, drug, and mental disorders among homeless persons. *American Psychologist, 46,* 1115–1128.

Fisher, S., Raskin, A., & Uhlenhuth, E. H. (Eds.). (1987). *Cocaine: Classical and biobehavioral aspects.* New York: Oxford University Press.

Fiske, E. B. (1984, November 11). Learn-

ing disabled: a new awareness. *The New York Times,* Sec. 12, pp. 1, 44, 58.

Fiske, S., & Taylor, S. (1991). *Social cognition* (2nd ed.). New York: McGraw-Hill.

Fiske, S. T. (1988). People's reactions to nuclear war: Implications for psychologists. *American Psychologist, 42,* 207–217.

Fitzsimons, J. T. (1961). Drinking by rats depleted of body fluid without increase in osmotic pressure. *Journal of Physiology, 159,* 297–309.

Flam, F. (1991, June 14). Queasy riders. *Science, 252,* 1488.

Flavell, J. H., Green, F. L., & Flavell, E. R. (1990). Developmental changes in young children's knowledge about the mind. *Cognitive Development, 5,* 1–27.

Fleming, R., Baum, A., & Singer, J. E. (1984). Toward an integrative approach to the study of stress. *Journal of Personality and Social Psychology, 46,* 939–949.

Fletcher, S. W., O'Malley, M. S., & Bunce, L. A. (1985). Physicians' abilities to detect lumps in silicone breast models. *Journal of the American Medical Association, 253,* 2224–2228.

Flor, H., & Turk, D. C. (1989). Psychophysiology of chronic pain: Do chronic pain patients exhibit symptom-specific psychophysiological responses? *Psychological Bulletin, 105,* 215–259.

Flowers, J. V., & Booraem, C. D. (1990). The effects of different types of interventions on outcome n group therapy. *Group, 14,* 81–88.

Flynn, J. R. (1987). Massive IQ gains in 14 nations: What IQ tests really measure. *Psychological Bulletin, 101,* 171–191.

Foa, E. B., & Kozak, M. S. (1986). Emotional processing of fear: Exposure to corrective information. *Psychological Bulletin, 99,* 20–35.

Folkman, S. (1984). Personal control and stress and coping processes: A theoretical analysis. *Journal of Personality and Social Psychology, 46,* 839–852.

Folkman, S., & Lazarus, R. S. (1980). An analysis of coping in a middle-aged community sample. *Journal of Health and Social Behavior, 21,* 219–239.

Folkman, S., & Lazarus, R. S. (1988a). Coping as a mediator of emotion. *Journal of Personality and Social Psychology, 54,* 466–475.

Folkman, S., & Lazarus, R. S. (1988b). *Manual for the ways of coping questionnaire.* Palo Alto, CA: Consulting Psychologist Press.

Folkman, S., Lazarus, R. S., Dunkel-Schetter, C., DeLongis, A., & Green, R. J. (1986). Dynamics of a stressful encounter: Cognitive appraisal, coping, and encounter outcome. *Journal of Personality and Social Psychology, 50,* 992–1003.

Fonagy, P., & Moran, G. S. (1990). Studies of the efficacy of child psychoanalysis.

Journal of Consulting and Clinical Psychology, 58, 684–695.

Food and Drug Administration (*see* FDA)

Ford, J. G. (1991). Rogers's theory of personality: Review and perspectives. In A. Jones & R. Crandall (Eds.), Handbook of self-actualization [Special issue]. *Journal of Social Behavior and Personality, 6,* 19–44.

Fordyce, W. E. (1988). Pain and suffering: A reappraisal. *American Psychologist, 43,* 276–283.

Forer, B. (1949). The fallacy of personal validation: A classroom demonstration of gullibility. *Journal of Abnormal and Social Psychology, 44,* 118–123.

Forgas, J. P., & Bower, G. H. (1987). Mood effects on person-perception judgments. *Journal of Personality and Social Psychology, 53,* 53–60.

Foulke, E., & Sticht, T. (1969). Review of research on the intelligibility and comprehension of accelerated speech. *Psychological Bulletin, 72,* 50–62.

Fowles, D. C. (1992). Schizophrenia: Diathesis-stress revisited. *Annual Review of Psychology, 43,* 303–336.

Fox, S. (1984). *The mirror makers.* New York: Morrow.

Frable D. E. S., & Bem, S. L. (1985). If you are gender schematic, all members of the opposite sex look alike. *Journal of Personality and Social Psychology, 49,* 459–468.

Frank, S. J., Jacobson, S., & Tuer, M. (1990). Psychological predictors of young adults' drinking behaviors. *Journal of Personality and Social Psychology, 59,* 770–780.

Frankenburg, W. K., & Dodds, J. B. (1967). The Denver developmental screening test. *Journal of Pediatrics, 71,* 181–191.

Freedman, J. L. (1984). Effects of television violence on aggressiveness. *Psychological Bulletin, 96,* 227–246.

Freedman, J. L., & Fraser, S. C. (1966). Compliance without pressure: The foot-in-the-door technique. *Journal of Personality and Social Psychology, 4,* 195–202.

Freeman, P. (1990, December 17). Silent no more. *People Weekly,* pp. 94–104.

Freeman, W. (1959). Psychosurgery. In *American handbook of psychiatry* (Vol. 2, pp. 1521–1540). New York: Basic Books.

Freud, S. (1900). *The interpretation of dreams.* New York: Basic Books.

Frezz, M., di Padova, C., Pozzato, G., Terpin, M., Baraona, E., & Lieber, C. S. (1990). High blood alcohol levels in women: The role of decreased gastric alcohol dehydrogenase activity and first-pass metabolism. *New England Journal of Medicine, 322,* 95–99.

Friedman, L. (1989). Mathematics and the gender gap: A meta-analysis of recent studies on sex differences in mathematical tasks. *Review of Educational Research, 59,* 185–213.

Friedman, M., Thoresen, C. E., Gill, J. J., Powell, L. H., Ulmer, D., Thompson, L., Price, V. A., Rabin, D. D., Breall, W. S., Dixon, T., Levy, R., & Bourg, E. (1984). Alteration of type A behavior and reduction in cardiac recurrences in postmyocardial infarction patients. *American Heart Journal, 108*(2), 237–248.

Frijda, N. H. (1987). *The emotions: Studies in emotion and social interaction.* Cambridge, MA: Cambridge University Press.

Frijda, N. H. (1988). The laws of emotion. *American Psychologist, 43,* 349–358.

Frijda, N. H., Kuipers, P., & terSchure, E. (1989). Relations among emotion, appraisal, and emotional action readiness. *Journal of Personality and Social Psychology, 57,* 212–228.

Funder, D. C. (1991). Global traits: A neo-Allportian approach to personality. *Psychological Science, 2*(1), 31–39.

Funder, D. C. F. (1987). Errors and mistakes: Evaluating the accuracy of social judgment. *Psychological Bulletin, 101,* 75–90.

Funder, D. C. F., & Colvin, C. R. (1991). Explorations in behavioral consistency: Properties of persons, situations, and behaviors. *Journal of Personality and Social Psychology, 60,* 773–794.

Gabriel, M., & Moore, J. (Eds.). (1991). *Learning and computational neuroscience: Foundations of adaptive networks.* Cambridge, MA: MIT Press.

Gaertner, S. L., Mann, J. A., Dovidio, J. F., Murrell, A. J., & Pomare, M. (1990). How does cooperation reduce intergroup bias? *Journal of Personality and Social Psychology, 59,* 692–704.

Gage, N. L. (1991, January–February). The obviousness of social and educational research results. *Educational Researcher,* pp. 10–16.

Gagnon, G. H. (1977). *Human sexualities.* Glenview, IL: Scott, Foresman.

Galanter, E. (1962). Contemporary psychophysics. In R. Brown, E. Galanter, E. Hess, & G. Maroler (Eds.), *New directions in psychology* (pp. 87–157). New York: Holt.

Gale, N., Golledge, R. G., Pellegrino, J. W., & Doherty, S. (1990). The acquisition and integration of route knowledge in an unfamiliar neighborhood. *Journal of Environmental Psychology, 10,* 3–25.

Gallant, D. M. (1987). *Alcoholism: A guide to diagnosis, intervention, and treatment.* New York: Norton.

Garb, H. N. (1989). Clinical judgment, clinical training, and professional experience. *Psychological Bulletin, 105,* 387–396.

Garber, H. L. (1988). *The Milwaukee Project: Preventing mental retardation in children at risk.* Washington, DC: American Association on Mental Retardation.

Garcia, J., Brett, L., & Rusiniak, K. (1989). Limits of Darwinian conditioning. In S. B. Klein & R. R. Mowrer (Eds.), *Contemporary learning theories* (Vol. 2). Hillsdale, NJ: Erlbaum.

Garcia, J., Hankins, W. G., & Rusiniak, K. W. (1974). Behavioral regulation of the milieu intern in man and rat. *Science, 185,* 824–831.

Gardner, H. (1975). *The shattered mind: The person after brain damage.* New York: Knopf.

Gardner, H. (1983). *Frames of mind: The theory of multiple intelligences.* New York: Basic Books.

Garfield, S. L. (1983). Psychotherapy: Efficacy, generality, and specificity. In J. B. N. Williams & R. L. Spitzer (Eds.), *Psychotherapy research: Where are we and where should we go?* (pp. 295–305). New York: Guilford Press.

Garfield, S. L. (1989). *The practice of brief psychotherapy.* New York: Pergamon.

Garfield, S. L. (1990). Issues and methods in psychotherapy process research. *Journal of Consulting and Clinical Psychology, 58,* 273–280.

Garling, T. (1989). The role of cognitive maps in spatial decisions. *Journal of Environmental Psychology, 9,* 269–278.

Gartell, N. N. (1982). Hormones and homosexuality. In W. Paul et al. (Eds.), *Homosexuality: Social, psychological, and biological issues.* Beverly Hills, CA: Sage.

Gatchel, R. J., & Baum, A. (1983). *An introduction to health psychology.* Reading, MA: Addison-Wesley.

Gawin, F. H. (1991, March 29). Cocaine addiction: Psychology and neurophysiology. *Science, 251,* 1580–1586.

Gawin, F. H., & Ellinwood, E. H. (1988). Cocaine and other stimulants: Actions, abuse, and treatment. *New England Journal of Medicine, 18,* 1173.

Gazzaniga, M. S. (1970). *The bisected brain.* New York: Plenum.

Gazzaniga, M. S. (1983). Right-hemisphere language following brain bisection: A twenty-year perspective. *American Psychologist, 38,* 525–537.

Gazzaniga, M. S. (1985, November). The social brain. *Psychology Today,* pp. 29–38.

Gazzaniga, M. S. (1989, September 1). Organization of the human brain. *Science, 245,* 947–952.

Geen, R. G. (1984). Human motivation: New perspectives on old problems. In A. M. Rogers & C. J. Scheirer (Eds.), *The G. Stanley Hall lecture series* (Vol. 4). Washington, DC: American Psychological Association.

Geen, R. G., & Donnerstein, E. (1983). *Aggression: Theoretical and empirical reviews.* New York: Academic.

Geissler, H., Link, S. W., & Townsend, J. T. (1992). *Cognition, information* *processing, and psychophysics.* Hillsdale, NJ: Erlbaum.

Gelman, D. (1989a, February 20). Roots of addiction. *Newsweek, 113,* 52–57.

Gelman, D. (1989b, December 18). Alzheimer's. *Newsweek,* pp. 55–56.

Gelman, D. (1990, July 23). The mind of the rapist. *Newsweek,* pp. 46–52.

Gelman, R., & Baillargeon, R. (1983). A review of some Piagetian concepts. In J. H. Flavell & E. M. Markman (Eds.), *Handbook of child psychology: Vol. 3. Cognitive development* (4th ed.). New York: Wiley.

Gentry, W. D., & Kobasa, S. C. O. (1984). Social and psychological resources mediating stress-illness relationships in humans. In W. D. Gentry (Ed.), *Handbook of behavioral medicine.* New York: Guilford Press.

Gerbner, G., Gross, L., Jackson-Beeck, M., Jeffries-Fox, S., & Signorielli, N. (1978). Cultural indicators: Violence profile No. 9. *Journal of Communication, 28,* 176–207.

Gerrard, M. (1988). Sex, sex guilt, and contraceptive use revisited: The 1980s. *Journal of Personality and Social Psychology, 57,* 973–980.

Gerschwind, N. (1985). Cerebral lateralization: Biological mechanisms, associations, and pathology: III. A hypothesis and a program for research. *Archives of Neurology, 42,* 634–654.

Geschwind, N., & Galaburda, A. M. (1987). *Cerebral lateralization: Biological mechanism, associations, and pathology.* Cambridge, MA: MIT Press.

Getty, D. J., Pickett, R. M., D'Orsi, C. J., & Swets, J. A. (1988). Enhanced interpretation of diagnostic images. *Investigative Radiology, 23,* 240–252.

Gfeller, J. D., Lynn, S. J., & Pribble, W. E. (1987). Enhancing hypnotic susceptibility: Interpersonal and rapport factors. *Journal of Personality and Social Psychology, 52,* 586–595.

Gholson, J. B., & Rosenthal, T. L. (Eds.). (1984). *Application of cognitive development theory.* New York: Academic.

Gibbons, A. (1990, July 13). New maps of the human brain. *Science, 249,* 122–123.

Gibbons, A. (1991, March 29). Deja vu all over again: Chimp-language wars. *Science, 251,* 1561–1562.

Gibbs, M. E., & Ng, K. T. (1977). Psychobiology of memory: Towards a model of memory formation. *Behavioral Reviews, 1,* 113–136.

Gibbs, N. (1989, January 9). For goodness' sake. *Time,* 20–24.

Gibson, E. J. (1988). Explanatory behavior in the development of perceiving, acting, and the acquiring of knowledge. *Annual Review of Psychology, 39,* 1–41.

Gibson, J. J. (1979). *The ecological approach to visual perception.* Boston: Houghton Mifflin.

Gilbert, A. N., & Wysocki, C. J. (1987, October). The smell survey results. *National Geographic, 172,* 514–525.

Gilbert, D. T., & Hixon, J. G. (1991). The trouble of thinking: Activation and application of stereotypic beliefs. *Journal of Personality and Social Psychology, 60,* 509–517.

Gilbert, D. T., Jones, E. E., & Pelham, B. W. (1987). Influence and inference: What the active perceiver overlooks. *Journal of Personality and Social Psychology, 52,* 861–870.

Gill, T. J., Jr., Smith, G. J., Wissler, R. W., & Kunz, H. W. (1989, July 29). The rat as an experimental animal. *Science, 245,* 269–276.

Gilligan, C. (1982). *In a different voice: Psychological theory and women's development.* Cambridge, MA: Harvard University Press.

Gilligan, C. (1987). In a different voice: Women's conception of self and of morality. In M. R. Walsh (Ed.), *The psychology of women.* New Haven, CT: Yale University Press.

Gilligan, C., Lyons, N. P., & Hanmer, T. J. (Eds.). (1990). *Making connections.* Cambridge, MA: Harvard University Press.

Gilligan, C., Ward, J. V., & Taylor, J. M. (Eds.). (1988). *Mapping the moral domain: A contribution of women's thinking to psychological theory and education.* Cambridge, MA: Harvard University Press.

Ginsburg, H. P., & Opper, S. (1988). *Piaget's theory of intellectual development* (3rd ed.). Englewood Cliffs, NJ: Prentice-Hall.

Gladue, B. A., et. al. (1984, September 28). Neuroendocrine response to estrogen and sexual orientation. *Science, 225,* 1496–1498.

Gladue, B. A., Boechler, M., & McCaul, K. D. (1989). Hormonal response to competition in human males. *Aggressive Behavior, 15,* 409–422.

Gladwin, T. (1964). Culture and logical process. In N. Goodenough (Ed.), *Explorations in cultural anthropology: Essays in honor of George Peter Murdoch.* New York: McGraw-Hill.

Glaser, R. (1990). The reemergence of learning theory within instructional research. *American Psychologist, 45,* 29–39.

Glaser, R., Rice, J., Speicher, C. E., Stout, J. C., & Kiecolt-Glaser, J. K. (1986). Stress depresses interferon production by leukocytes concomitant with a decrease in natural killer cell activity. *Behavioral Neuroscience, 100,* 675–678.

Glass, D. C., & Singer, J. E. (1972). *Urban stress.* New York: Academic.

Glenn, N. D. (1987, October). Marriage on the rocks. *Psychology Today,* pp. 20–21.

Glick, P., Zion, C., & Nelson, C. (1988). What mediates sex discrimination in hiring decisions? *Journal of Personality and Social Psychology, 55,* 178–186.

Globe Magazine (1989, April 9).

Glover, J. A., Ronning, R. R., & Reynolds, C. R. (Eds.). (1989). *Handbook of creativity.* New York: Plenum.

Gluck, M. A., & Rumelhart, D. E. (Eds.). (1990). *Neuroscience and connectionist theory.* Hillsdale, NJ: Erlbaum.

Goate, A., Chariter-Harlin, M., Mullan, M., Brown, J., Crawford, F., Fidani, L., Giuffra, L., Haynes, A., Irving, N., James, L., Mant, R., Newton, P., Rooke, K., Roques, P., Talbor, C., Pericak-Vance, M., Roses, A., Williamson, R., Rossor, M., Owne, M., & Hardy, J. (1991, February 21). Segregation of a missense mutation in the amyloid precursor protein gene with familial Alzheimer's disease. *Nature, 349,* 703.

Gogel, W. C., & DaSilva, J. A. (1987a). A two-process theory of the response to size and distance. *Perception and Psychophysics, 41,* 220–238.

Gogel, W. C., & DaSilva, J. A. (1987b). Familiar size and the theory of off-sized perceptions. *Perception and Psychophysics, 41,* 318–328.

Gold, P. W., Gwirtsman, H., Avgerinos, P. C., Nieman, L. K., Gallucci, W. T., Kaye, W., Jimerson, D., Ebert, M., Rittmaster, R., Loriaux, L., & Chrousos, G. P. (1986). Abnormal hypothalmic-pituitary-adrenal function in anorexia nervosa. *New England Journal of Medicine, 314,* 1335–1342.

Goldberg, L. (Ed.). (1991). *Questionnaires used in the prediction of trustworthiness in pre-employ selection decisions: An APA task force report.* Washington, DC: American Psychological Association.

Goldberg, L. R. (1990). An alternative "description of personality": The big-five factor structure. *Journal of Personality and Social Psychology, 59,* 1216–1229.

Golberg, S. (1983). Parent-infant bonding: Another look. *Child Development, 54,* 1355–1382.

Goldfried, M. R., & Davison, G. (1976). *Clinical behavior therapy.* New York: Holt.

Goldfried, M. R., Greenberg, L. S., & Marmar, C. (1990). Individual psychotherapy: Process and outcome. *Annual Review of Psychology, 41,* 659–688.

Goldman, S., Salovey, P., Mayer, J. D., & Kraemer, D. (1991). Emotional intelligence and the reporting of physical symptoms in stressful situation.

Goldman-Rakic, P. S. (1988). *Neurobiology of neocortex.* New York: Wiley.

Goldstein, I. L. (1986). *Training in organizations: Needs assessment, development, and evaluation* (2nd ed.). Pacific Grove, CA: Brooks/Cole.

Goleman, D. (1985, February 5). Mourning: New studies affirm its benefits. *The New York Times,* pp. C-1 to C-2.

Goleman, D. (1988a, January 21). Physicians may bungle key part of treatment:

The medical interview. *The New York Times*, p. B-16.

Goleman, D. (1988b, February 2). The experience of touch: Research points to a critical role. *The New York Times*, pp. C-1, C-4.

Goleman, D. (1988c, March 29). Study of normal mourning process illuminates grief gone awry. *The New York Times*, pp. C-1, C-6.

Goleman, D. (1988d, October 9). When to challenge the therapist—and why. *The New York Times Good Health Magazine*, pp. 37–40.

Goleman, D. (1989, August 29). When the rapist is not a stranger: Studies seek new understanding. *The New York Times*, pp. C1, C6.

Goleman, D. (1991, October 22). Sexual harassment: It's about power, not sex. *The New York Times*, pp. C1, C12.

Goodman, N. G. (Ed.). (1945). *A Benjamin Franklin reader*. New York: Crowell.

Goodwin, F. K., & Jamison, K. R. (1990). *Manic-depressive illness*. New York: Oxford University Press.

Googans, B., & Burden, D. (1987). Vulnerability of working parents: Balancing work and home roles. *Social Work, 32*, 295–300.

Gorman, J. M., Liebowitz, M. R., Fyer, A. J., & Stein, J. (1989). A neuroanatomical hypothesis for panic disorder. *American Journal of Psychiatry, 146*, 148–161.

Gottesman, I. I., & Shields, J. (1972). *Schizophrenia and genetics*. New York: Academic.

Gottfried, A. E., & Gottfried, A. W. (Eds.). (1988). *Maternal employment and children's development*. New York: Plenum.

Gould, P., & White, R. (1974). *Mental maps*. New York: Penguin.

Gould, R. L. (1978). *Transformations*. New York: Simon & Schuster.

Gove, W. R. (1982). Labeling theory's explanation of mental illness: An update of recent evidence. *Deviant Behavior, 3*, 307–327.

Graf, P. (1990, Spring). Paper on episodic memory in *Psychonomic Science*.

Graham, J. W. (1990). *MMPI-2: Assessing personality and psychopathology*. New York: Oxford University Press.

Graham, J. W., Marks, G., & Hansen, W. B. (1991). Social influence processes affecting adolescent substance use. *Journal of Applied Psychology, 76*, 291–298.

Graham, S. (1990). Communicating low ability in the classroom: Bad things good teachers sometimes do. In S. Graham & V. S. Folkes (Eds.), *Attribution theory: Applications to achievement, mental health, and interpersonal conflict*. Hillsdale, NJ: Erlbaum.

Greeberg, M. T., Cicchetti, D., & Cummings, E. M. (Eds.). (1990). *Attachment in the preschool years: Theory, research,*

and intervention. Chicago: University of Chicago Press.

Green, D. M., & Swets, J. A. (1966). *Signal detection theory and psychophysics*. Los Altos, CA: Peninsula.

Green, D. M., & Swets, J. A. (1989). *A signal detection theory and psychophysics*. Los Altos, CA: Peninsula.

Green, R. (1978). Sexual identity of 37 children raised by homosexual or transsexual parents. *American Journal of Psychiatry, 135*, 687–692.

Green, R. (1987). *The "sissy boy syndrome" and the development of homosexuality*. New Haven, CT: Yale University Press.

Greenblatt, M. (1978). The grieving spouse. *American Journal of Psychiatry, 135*, 43–47.

Greene, B. A. (1985). Considerations in the treatment of black patients by white therapists. *Psychotherapy, 22*, 389–393.

Greeno, J. G. (1978). Natures of problem-solving abilities. In W. K. Estes (Ed.), *Handbook of learning and cognitive processes*. Hillsdale, NJ: Erlbaum.

Greenwald, A. G., Spangenberg, E. R., Pratkanis, A. R., & Eskenzai, J. (1991). Double-blind tests of subliminal self-help audiotapes. *Psychological Science, 2*, 119–122.

Gregory, R. L. (1978). *The psychology of seeing* (3rd ed.). New York: McGraw-Hill.

Greig, G. L. (1990). On the shape of energy-detection ROC curves. *Perception and Psychophysics, 48*, 77–81.

Greist-Bousquet, S., & Schiffman, H. R. (1986). The basis of the Poggendorff effect: An additional clue for Day and Kasperczyk. *Perception and Psychophysics, 39*, 447–448.

Griffith, R. M., Miyago, O., & Tago, A. (1958). The universality of typical dreams: Japanese vs. Americans. *American Anthropologist, 60*, 1173–1179.

Gross, C. G., Deimone, R., Albright, T. D., & Schwartz, E. L. (1985). Inferior temporal cortex and pattern recognition. In C. Chagas, R. Gattass, & C. Gross (Eds.), *Pattern and recognition mechanisms*. New York: Springer-Verlag.

Gross, J. (1991, June 16). More young single men hang onto apron strings. *The New York Times*, pp. 1, 18.

Grossman, H. J. (Ed.). (1983). *Classification in mental retardation*. Washington, DC: American Associations on Mental Deficiency.

Groth-Marnat, G. (1990). *Handbook of psychological assessment* (2nd ed.). New York: Wiley.

Grube, J. W., Rokeach, M., & Getzlaf, S. B. (1990). Adolescents' value images of smokers, ex-smokers, and nonsmokers. *Addictive Behaviors, 15*, 81–88.

Gruenberg, B. (1980). The happy workers: An analysis of educational and occupational differences in determi-

nants of job satisfaction. *American Journal of Sociology, 86*, 247–271.

Gubrium, J. G. (1973). *The myth of the golden years: A socio-environmental theory of aging*. Springfield, IL: Charles C Thomas.

Gur, R. C., Gur, R. E., Obrist, W. D., Hungerbuhler, J. P., Younkin, D., Rosen, A. D., Skilnick, B. E., & Reivich, M. (1982, August 13). Sex and handedness differences in cerebral blood flow during rest and cognitive activity. *Science, 217*, 659–661.

Gurin, J. (1989, July). Leaner, not lighter. *Psychology Today*, pp. 32–36.

Gurling, H. M., Sherrington, R. P., Brynjolfsson, J., Read, T., et al. (1989). Recent and future molecular genetic research into schizophrenia. *Schizophrenia Bulletin, 15*, 373–382.

Gustavson, C. R., Garcia, J., Hankins, W. G., & Rusiniak, K. W. (1974, May 3). Coyote predation control by aversive conditioning. *Science, 184*, 581–583.

Gutek, B. (1985). *Sex and the workplace*. San Francisco: Jossey-Bass.

Haber, R. N. (1983). Stimulus information processing mechanisms in visual space perception. In J. Beck, B. Hope, & A. Rosenfeld (Eds.), *Human and machine vision*. New York: Academic.

Hackman, J. R., & Oldham, G. R. (1976). Motivation through the design of work: Test of a theory. *Organizational Behavior and Human Performance, 16*, 250–279.

Hagen, E., Sattler, J. M., & Thorndike, R. L. (1985). *Stanford-Binet test*. Chicago: Riverside.

Hahn, W. K. (1987). Cerebral lateralization of function: From infancy through childhood. *Psychological Bulletin, 10*, 376–392.

Hakuta, K., & Garcia, E. E. (1989). Bilingualism and education. *American Psychologist, 44*, 374–379.

Hall, J. A. (1978). Gender effects in decoding nonverbal cues. *Psychological Bulletin, 85*, 845–857.

Hall, J. A., Roter, D. L., & Katz, N. R. (1988a). Meta-analysis of correlates of provider behavior in medical encounters. *Medical Care, 26*, 657–675.

Hall, J. A., Roter, D. L., & Katz, N. R. (1988b). Task versus socioemotional behaviors in physicians. *Medical Care, 25*, 399–412.

Halle, M. (1990). Phonology. In D. N. Osherson & H. Lasnik (Eds.), *Language*. Cambridge, MA: MIT Press.

Hamilton, D. L., Sherman, S. J., & Ruvolo, C. M. (1990). Stereotype-based expectancies: Effects on information processing and social behavior. *Journal of Social Issues, 46*, 35–60.

Hamilton, M., & Yee, J. (1990). Rape knowledge and propensity to rape.

Journal of Research in Personality, 24, 111–122.

Hammer, R. P. (1984). The sexually dimorphic region of the preoptic area in rats contains denser opiate receptor binding sites in females. *Brain Researcher, 308,* 172–176.

Hammond, L., & Fong, M. L. (1988, August). *Mediators of stress and satisfaction in multiple-role persons.* Paper presented at the annual meeting of the American Psychological Association, Atlanta.

Handler, A., Franz, C. E., & Guerra, M. (1992, April). Sex differences in moral orientation in midlife adults: A longitudinal study. Paper presented at the meetings of the Eastern Psychological Association, Boston, MA.

Hanson, S. J., & Olson, C. R. (Eds.). (1990). *Connectionist modeling and brain function.* Cambridge, MA: MIT Press.

Hardy, J., et al. (1991, February 21). *Nature.*

Harlow, H. F., & Zimmerman, R. R. (1959, August 21). Affectional responses in the infant monkey. *Science, 130,* 421–432.

Harlow, J. M. (1869). Recovery from the passage of an iron bar through the head. *Massachusetts Medical Society Publication, 2,* 329–347.

Harper, T. (1978, November 15). It's not true about people 65 or over. *Green Bay (Wis.) Press-Gazette,* D-1.

Harris, J. E., & Morris, P. E. (1986). *Everyday memory and action and absent mindedness.* New York: Academic Press.

Harris, S. L., & Handleman, J. S. (1990). *Aversive and nonaversive interventions.* New York: Springer.

Harris Poll: National Council on the Aging (1975). *The myth and reality of aging in America.* Washington, DC: National Council on the Aging.

Harsch, N., & Neisser, U. (1989). Substantial and irreversible errors in flashbulb memories of the *Challenger* explosion. Poster presented at the meeting of the Psychonomic Society, Atlanta.

Hart, N. A., & Keidel, G. C. (1979). The suicidal adolescent. *American Journal of Nursing,* pp. 80–84.

Harte, R. A., Travers, J. A., & Savich, P. (1948). Voluntary caloric intake of the growing rat. *Journal of Nutrition, 36,* 667–679.

Hartmann, E. (1967). *The biology of dreaming.* Springfield, IL: Charles C Thomas.

Hartmen, W., & Fithian, M. (1984). *Any man can.* New York: St. Martin's.

Hartup, W. W. (1989). Social relationships and their developmental significance. *American Psychologist, 44,* 120–126.

Harvard Medical School (1987, December). *Mental Health Letter,* p. 4.

***Harvard Mental Health Letter** (see HMHL)*

Haskins, R. (1985). Public school aggression among children with varying daycare experience. *Child Development, 56,* 689–703.

Hatfield, E., & Sprecher, S. (1986). *Mirror, mirror: The importance of looks in everyday life.* Albany, NY: State University of New York Press.

Hathaway, S. R., & McKinley, J. C. (1989). *MMPI-2: Minnesota Multiphasic Personality Inventory-2.* Minneapolis: University of Minnesota Press.

Hathaway, B. (1984, July). Running to ruin. *Psychology Today,* pp. 14–15.

Hatvany, N., & Pucik, V. (1981). An integrated management system: Lessons from the Japanese experience. *Academy of Management Review, 6,* 469–480.

Hauri, P. J. (Ed.). (1991). *Case studies in insomnia.* New York: Plenum.

Havighurst, R. J. (1973). Social roles, work, leisure, and education. In C. Eisdorfer & M. P. Lawton (Eds.), *The psychology of adult development and aging.* Washington, DC: American Psychological Association.

Hay, J. (1989). *Psychworld* (2nd ed. software). New York: McGraw-Hill.

Hayes, J. R. (1966). Memory, goals, and problem solving. In B. Kleinmuntz (Ed.), *Problem solving: Research, method, and theory.* New York: Wiley.

Hayes, J. R. (1989). *The complete problem solver* (2nd ed.). Hillsdale, NJ: Erlbaum.

Hayflick, L. (1974). The strategy of senescence. *Journal of Gerontology, 14,* 37–45.

Haymes, M., Green, L., & Quinto, R. (1984). Maslow's hierarchy, moral development, and prosocial behavior skills within a child psychiatric population. *Motivation and Emotion, 8,* 23–31.

Hays, R. B. (1985). A longitudinal study of friendship development. *Journal of Personality and Social Psychology, 48,* 909–924.

Hebb, D. O. (1955). Drive and the CNS. *Psychological Review, 62,* 243–254.

Heckhausen, H., Schmalt, H. D., & Schneider, K. (1985). *Achievement motivation in perspective.* (M. Woodruff & R. Wicklund, Trans.). Orlando, FL: Academic.

Heffner, R. S., & Heffner, H. E. (1983). Hearing in large and small dogs: Absolute thresholds and size of the tympanic membrane. *Behavioral Neuroscience, 97,* 310–318.

Heider, F. (1958). *The psychology of interpersonal relations.* New York: Wiley.

Heilman, M. E., & Stopeck, M. H. (1985). Attractiveness and corporate success: Different causal attributions for men and women. *Journal of Applied Psychology, 70,* 379–388.

Hellige, J. B. (1990). Hemispheric asymmetry. *Annual Review of Psychology, 41,* 55–80.

Hendrick, C. (Ed.). (1989). *Close relationships.* Beverly Hills, CA: Sage.

Hendrick, C., & Hendrick, S. S. (1986). A theory and method of love. *Journal of Personality and Social Psychology, 50,* 392–402.

Hendrick, C., & Hendrick, S. S. (1989). Research on love: Does it measure up? *Journal of Personality and Social Psychology, 56,* 784–794.

Hendrick, S. S., Hendrick, C., & Adler, N. L. (1988). Romantic relationships: Love, satisfaction, and staying together. *Journal of Personality and Social Psychology, 54,* 980–988.

Herek, G. M. (1990). Gay people and government security clearances: A social science perspective. *American Psychologist, 45,* 1035–1042.

Herman, C. P. (1987). Social and psychological factors in obesity: What we don't know. In H. Weiner & A. Baum (Eds.), *Perspectives in behavioral medicine: Eating regulation and discontrol.* Hillsdale, NJ: Erlbaum.

Herman, C. P., & Polivy, J. (1975). Anxiety, restraint, and eating behavior. *Journal of Abnormal Psychology, 84,* 666–672.

Herrnstein, R. J. (1979). Acquisition, generalization and discrimination reversal of a natural concept. *Journal of Experimental Psychology: Animal Behavior Processes, 5,* 116–129.

Herrnstein, R. J., Loveland, D. H., & Cable, C. (1976). Natural concepts in pigeons. *Journal of Experimental Psychology: Animal Behavior Processes, 2,* 285–302.

Hershenson, M. (Ed.). (1989). *The moon illusion.* Hillsdale, NJ: Erlbaum.

Hess, R., Chang, C., & McDevitt, T. (1987). Cultural variations in family beliefs about children's performance in mathematics: Comparisons among People's Republic of China, Chinese-American, and Caucasian-American families. *Journal of Educational Psychology, 79,* 179–188.

Hetherington, E. M., & Parke, R. D. (1986). *Child psychology: A contemporary viewpoint* (3rd ed.). New York: McGraw-Hill.

Hewstone, M., & Jaspars, J. (1987). Covariation and causal attribution: A logical model of the intuitive analysis of variance. *Journal of Personality and Social Psychology, 53,* 663–672.

Heyneman, N. E., Fremouw, W. J., Gano, D., Kirkland, F., & Heiden, L. (1990). Individual differences and the effectiveness of different coping strategies for pain. *Cognitive Therapy and Research, 14,* 63–77.

Heyward, W. L., & Curran, J. W. (1988, October). The epidemiology of AIDS in the U.S. *Scientific American,* pp. 72–81.

Higbee, K. L., & Kunihira, S. (1985). Cross-cultural applications of Yodni mnemonics in education. *Educational Psychologist, 20,* 57–64.

Hilgard, E. R. (1974). Imaginative involvement: Some characteristics of the highly hypnotizable and the nonhypnotizable. *International Journal of Clinical and Experimental Hypnosis, 22,* 138–156.

Hilgard, E. R. (1975). Hypnosis. *Annual Review of Psychology, 26,* 19–44.

Hilgard, E. R. (1980). Consciousness in contemporary psychology. *Annual Review of Psychology, 31*, 1–26.

Hilgard, E. R., Leary, D. E., & McGuire, G. R. (1991). The history of psychology: A survey and critical assessment. *Annual Review of Psychology, 42*, 79–107.

Hill, C. T., & Stull, D. E. (1981). Sex differences in effects of social and value similarity in same-sex friendship. *Journal of Personality and Social Psychology, 41*, 488–502.

Hinz, L. D., & Williamson, D. A. (1987). Bulimia and depression: A review of the affective-variant hypothesis. *Psychological Bulletin, 102*, 150–158.

Hiroto, D. S., & Seligman, M. E. P. (1975). Generality of learned helplessness in man. *Journal of Personality and Social Psychology, 31*, 311–327.

Hirschman, R. S., Leventhal, H., & Glynn, K. (1984). The development of smoking behavior: Conceptualization and supportive cross-sectional survey data. *Journal of Applied Social Psychology, 14*, 184–206.

HMHL (Harvard Mental Health Letter). (1992, June) Mental illness and homelessness (Pt. 1, pp. 1–4). Cambridge, MA: Harvard University.

HMHL (Harvard Mental Health Letter). (1991, February). Post-traumatic stress (Pt. 1). Cambridge, MA: Harvard University.

Hobfoll, S. E. (1989). Conservation of resources: A new attempt at conceptualizing stress. *American Psychologist, 44*, 513–524.

Hobfoll, S. E., Spielberger, C. D., Breznitz, S., Figley, C., Folkman, S., Lepper-Green, B., Meichenbaum, D., Milgram, N. A., Sandler, I., Sarason, I., & van der Kolk, B. (1991). War-related stress: Addressing the stress of war and other traumatic events. *American Psychologist, 46*, 848–855.

Hobson, J. A. (1988). *The dreaming brain*. New York: Basic Books.

Hobson, J. A., & McCarley, R. W. (1977). The brain as a dream state generator: An activation-synthesis hypothesis of the dream process. *American Journal of Psychiatry, 134*, 1335–1348.

Hoch, S. J. (1987). Perceived consensus and predictive accuracy: The pros and cons of projection. *Journal of Personality and Social Psychology, 53*, 221–234.

Hochberg, J. E. (1978). *Perception*. Englewood Cliffs, NJ: Prentice-Hall.

Hofferth, S. L., Kahn, J. R., & Baldwin, W. (1987). Premarital sexual activity among U.S. teenage women over the past three decades. *Family Planning Perspectives, 19*, 46–53.

Hoffman, C., Lau, I., & Johnson, D. R. (1986). The linguistic relativity of person cognition: An English-Chinese comparison. *Journal of Personality and Social Psychology, 51*, 1097–1105.

Hoffman, L. W. (1989). Effects of maternal employment in the two-parent family. *American Psychologist, 44*, 283–292.

Hoffman, M. (1991, June 28). A new role for gases: Neurotransmission. *Science, 252*, 1788.

Holahan, C. J., & Moos, R. H. (1987). Personal and contextual determinants of coping strategies. *Journal of Personality and Social Psychology, 52*, 946–955.

Holahan, C. J., & Moos, R. H. (1990). Life stressors, resistance factors, and improved psychological functioning: An extension of the stress resistance paradigm. *Journal of Personality and Social Psychology, 58*, 909–917.

Holden, C. (1986a, July 18). New Toyota-GM plant in U.S. model for Japanese management. *Science, 233*, 273–277.

Holden, C. (1986b, August 22). Youth suicide: New research focuses on a growing social problem. *Science, 233*, 839–840.

Holden, C. (1986c, September 19). Researchers grapple with problems of updating classic psychological test. *Science, 233*, 1249–1251.

Holden, C. (1987a, August 7). The genetics of personality. *Science, 237*, 598–601.

Holden, C. (1987b, October 9). Why do women live longer than men? *Science, 238*, 158–160.

Holden, C. (1991, January 11). Probing the complex genetics of alcoholism. *Science, 251*, 163–164.

Holing, D. (1988, October). *Discover,* 78–83.

Hollander, E. P. (1980). In K. J. Gargon, M. Greenberg, & R. Willis (Eds.), *Social exchange: Advances in theory and research*. New York: Plenum Press.

Hollingshead, A. B., & Redich, F. C. (1958). *Social class and mental illness*. New York: Wiley.

Hollingworth, H. L. (1990). *Leta Stetter Hollingworth: A biography*. Boston, MA: Anker. (Original work published 1943)

Hollingworth, L. S. (1928). *The psychology of the adolescent*. New York: Appleton.

Hollis, K. L. (1984). The biological function of Pavlovian conditioning: The best defense is a good offense. *Journal of Experimental Psychology: Animal Behavior Processes, 10*, 413–425.

Holmes, D. S. (1985). To meditate or rest? The answer is rest. *American Psychologist, 40*, 728–731.

Holyoak, K. J. (1990). Problem solving. In D. N. Osherson & E. E. Smith (Eds.), *Thinking*. Cambridge, MA: MIT Press.

Holzman, P. S., & Matthysse, S. (1990). The genetics of schizophrenia: A review. *Psychological Science, 1*, 279–286.

Honts, C. R., Hodes, R. L., & Raskin, D. C. (1985). Effects of physical countermeasures on the physiological detection of deception. *Journal of Applied Psychology, 70*, 177–187.

Honts, C. R., Raskin, D. C., & Kircher, J. C. (1987). Effects of physical countermeasures and their electromyographic detection during polygraphic tests for deception. *Journal of Psychophysiology, 1*, 241–247.

Hoon, P. W., Bruce, K., & Kinchloe, B. (1982). Does the menstrual cycle play a role in sexual arousal? *Psychophysiology, 19*, 21–26.

Horn, J. L. (1985). Remodeling old models of intelligence. In B. B. Wolman (Ed.), *Handbook of intelligence*. New York: Wiley.

Horn, J. L., & Donaldson, G. (1980). Cognitive development II: Adulthood development of human abilities. In O. G. Brim & J. Kagan (Eds.), *Constancy and change in human development*. Cambridge, MA: Harvard University Press.

Horn, M. C., & Bachrach, C. A. (1985). *1982 National Survey of Family Growth*. Washington, DC: National Center for Health Statistics.

Horowitz, F. D., & Colombo, J. (Eds.). (1990). *Infancy research: A summative evaluation and a look to the future*. Detroit, MI: Wayne State University.

Horowitz, F. D., & O'Brien, M. (Eds.). (1987). *The gifted and talented: Developmental perspectives*. Washington, DC: American Psychological Association.

Horowitz, M. J. (1990). A model of mourning: Change in schema of self and other. *Journal of the American Psychoanalytic Association, 38*, 297–324.

House, J. S., Landis, K. R., & Umberson, D. (1989, July 29). Social relationships and health. *Science, 241*, 540–545.

Houston, L. N. (1981). Romanticism and eroticism among black and white college students. *Adolescence, 16*, 263–272.

Hovland, C., Janis, I., & Kelly, H. H. (1953). *Communication and persuasion*. New Haven, CT: Yale University Press.

Howard, K. I., & Zola, M. A. (1988). Paper presented at the annual meeting of the Society for Psychotherapy Research.

Howells, J. G., & Osborn, M. L. (1984). *A reference companion to the history of abnormal psychology*. Westport, CT: Greenwood Press.

Howes, C. (1990). Can the age of entry into child care and the quality of child care predict adjustment in kindergarten? *Developmental Psychology, 26*, 292–303.

Hsu, L. K. G. (1990). *Eating disorders*. New York: Guilford Press.

Hubel, D. H., & Wiesel, T. N. (1979). Brain mechanisms of vision. *Scientific American, 241*, 150–162.

Hudson, W. (1960). Pictorial depth perception in subcultural groups in Africa. *Journal of Social Psychology, 52*, 183–208.

Huesmann, L. R., & Eron, L. D. (Eds.).

(1986). *Television and the aggressive child: A cross-national comparison.* Hillsdale, NJ: Erlbaum.

Huesmann, L. R., Eron, L. D., Klein, R., Brice, P., & Fischer, P. (1983). Mitigating the imitation of aggressive behaviors by changing children's attitudes about media violence. *Journal of Personality and Social Psychology, 5,* 899–910.

Hughes, J. (1987). *Cancer and emotion: Psychological preludes and reactions to cancer.* Chichester, England: Wiley.

Hughes, J. O., & Sandler, B. R. (1987). *"Friends" raping friends: Could it happen to you?* Washington, DC: Association of American Colleges.

Hull, J. G., VanTreuren, R. R., & Virnelli, S. (1987). Hardiness and health: A critique and alternative approach. *Journal of Personality and Social Psychology, 53,* 518–530.

Hulse, S. H., Jr., Fowler, H., & Honig, W. K. (Eds.). (1978). *Cognitive processes in animal behavior.* Hillsdale, NJ: Erlbaum.

Hunt, L., Harrison, K., & Armstrong, M. (1974). Integrating group dynamics training and the education and development of social work students. *British Journal of Social Work, 4,* 405–423.

Hunt, M. (1974). *Sexual behaviors in the 1970s.* New York: Dell.

Hurlburt, A. C., & Poggio, T. A. (1988, January 29). Synthesizing a color algorithm from examples. *Science, 239,* 482–485.

Hurst, R. (1984). *Pilot error.* London: Granada.

Hutchison, J. B. (Ed.). (1978). *Biological determinants of sexual behavior.* New York: Wiley.

Hyde, J. A., & Linn, M. C. (1988). Gender differences in verbal ability: A meta-analysis. *Psychological Bulletin, 104,* 53–69.

Hyde, J. S. (1984). How large are gender differences in aggression? A developmental meta-analysis. *Developmental Psychology, 20,* 722–736.

Hyde, J. S. (1990). *Understanding human sexuality* (4th ed.). New York: McGraw-Hill.

Hyde, J. S. (1991). *Half the human experience: The psychology of women.* Lexington, MA: Heath.

Hyde, J. S., Fennema, E., & Lamon, S. J. (1990). Gender differences in mathematics performance: A meta-analysis. *Psychological Bulletin, 107,* 139–155.

Hyman, H. H. (1991). *Taking society's measure.* New York: Russell Sage Foundation.

Iacono, W. G. (1991). Can we determine the accuracy of polygraph tests? In P. K. Ackles, J. R. Jennings, & M. G. H. Coles (Eds.), *Advances in Psychophysiology* (Vol. 4). Greenwich, CT: JAI Press.

Iaffaldano, M. T., & Muchinsky, P. M.

(1985). Job satisfaction and job performance: A meta-analysis. *Psychological Bulletin, 97,* 151–173.

Imai, M. (1986). *Kaizen: The key to Japan's competitive success.* New York: Random House.

Ingelfinger, F. J. (1944). The late effects of total and subtotal gastrectomy. *New England Journal of Medicine, 231,* 321–377.

Ingram, R. E. (Ed.). (1990). *Contemporary psychological approaches to depression: Theory, research, and treatment.* New York: Plenum.

Institute of Medicine. (1982). *Marijuana and health.* Washington, DC: National Academy Press.

Isay, R. A. (1990). *Being homosexual: Gay men and their development.* New York: Avon.

Isen, A. M., Daubman, K. A., & Nowicki, G. P. (1987). Positive affect facilitates creative problem solving. *Journal of Personality and Social Psychology, 52,* 1122–1131.

Izard, C. E. (1990a). Facial expressions and the regulation of emotions. *Journal of Personality and Social Psychology, 58,* 487–498.

Izard, C. E. (1990b). The substrates and functions of emotion feelings: William James and current emotion theory. *Personality and Social Psychology Bulletin, 16,* 626–635.

Izard, C. E., Kagan, J., & Zajonc, R. B. (Eds.). (1989). *Emotions, cognition, and behavior.* Cambridge, England: Cambridge University Press.

Jacklin, C. N. (1989). Female and male: Issues of gender. *American Psychologist, 44,* 127–133.

Jackson, J. M., Buglione, S. A., & Glenwick, D. S. (1988). Major league baseball performance as a function of being traded: A drive theory analysis. *Personality and Social Psychology Bulletin, 14,* 46–56.

Jacobs, B. L. (1987, July–August). How hallucinogenic drugs work. *American Scientist, 75,* 386–392.

Jacobs, J. (1971). *Adolescent suicide.* New York: Wiley.

Jacobs, M. K., & Goodman, G. (1989). Psychology and self-helping groups: Predictions on a partnership. *American Psychologist, 44,* 536–545.

Jacobson, N. S., & Truax, P. (1991). Clinical significance: A statistical approach to defining meaningful change in psychotherapy research. *Journal of Consulting and Clinical Psychology, 59,* 12–19.

Jacobson, P. B., Perry, S. W., & Hirsch, D. (1990). Behavioral and psychological responses to HIV antibody testing. *Journal of Consulting and Clinical Psychology, 58,* 31–37.

Jahoda, M. (1958). In G. N. Grob (Ed.), *Current concepts in positive mental health.* Ayer Co. Publishers.

James, W. (1890). *The principles of psychology.* New York: Holt.

Janis, I. (1972). *Victims of groupthink: A psychological study of foreign policy decisions and fiascoes.* Boston: Houghton Mifflin.

Janis, I. (1984). Improving adherence to medical recommendations: Descriptive hypothesis derived from recent research in social psychology. In A. Baum, J. E. Singer, & S. E. Taylor (Eds.), *Handbook of medical psychology* (Vol. 4). Hillsdale, NJ: Erlbaum.

Janis, I. L., & Mann, L. (1976). *Decision making.* New York: Holt.

Janis, I. L., & Mann, L. (1977). *Decision making: A psychological analysis of conflict, choice, and commitment.* New York: Free Press.

Jarvik, M. E. (1973). Further observations on nicotine as a reinforcing agent in smoking. In W. L. Dunn, Jr. (Ed.), *Smoking behavior: Motives and incentives.* Washington, DC: Winston.

Jarvik, M. E. (1990, October 19). The drug dilemma: Manipulating the demand. *Science, 250,* 387–392.

Jemmott, J. B., III, & Locke, S. E. (1984). Psychosocial factors, immunologic mediation, and human susceptibility to infectious disease: How much do we know? *Psychological Bulletin, 95,* 78–108.

Jencks, C., et al. (1972). *Inequality.* New York: Basic Books.

Jensen, A. (1969). How much can we boost IQ and scholastic achievement? *Harvard Educational Review, 39,* 785–795.

John, E. R., Prichep, L. S., Fridman, J., & Easton, P. (1988, January 8). Neurometrics: Computer-assisted differential diagnosis of brain dysfunction. *Science, 239,* 162–169.

Johnson, B. T. (1991). Insights about attitudes: Meta-analytic perspectives. *Personality and Social Psychology Bulletin, 17,* 289–299.

Johnson, D. M., Parrott, G. R., & Stratton, R. P. (1968). Production and judgment of solutions to five problems. *Journal of Educational Psychology Monograph Supplement, 59* (6, pt. 2).

Johnson, D. W., & Johnson, R. T. (1979). Conflict in the classroom: Controversy and learning. *Review of Educational Research, 49,* 51–70.

Johnson, J. T., Cain, L. M., Falke, T. L., Hayman, J., & Perillo, E. (1985). The "Barnum effect" revisited: Cognitive and motivational factors in the acceptance of personality descriptions. *Journal of Personality and Social Psychology, 49,* 1378–1391.

Johnson, M. G., & Henley, T. (1990). *Reflections on the principles of psychology.* Hillsdale, NJ: Erlbaum.

Johnston, L. D., Bachman, J. G., &

O'Malley, P. M. (1991). *Monitoring the future: A continuing study of the lifestyles and values of youth.* University of Michigan, Institute of Social Research.

Jones, A., & Crandall, R. (Eds.) (1991). *Handbook of self-actualization.* Corte Madera, CA: Select Press.

Jones, A., & Crandall, R. (Eds.). (1991). Handbook of self-actualization. *Journal of Social Behavior and Personality, 6,* 1–362.

Jones, E. E. (1990). *Interpersonal perception.* New York: Freeman.

Jones, G. N., Brantley, P. J., & Gilchrist, J. C. (1988, August). *The relation between daily stress and health.* Paper presented at the annual meeting of the American Psychological Association, Atlanta.

Jones, J. C., & Barlow, D. H. (1990). Self-reported frequency of sexual urges, fantasies, and masturbatory fantasies in heterosexual males and females. *Archives of Sexual Behavior, 19,* 269–279.

Jones, L. V. (1984). White-black achievement differences: The narrowing gap. *American Psychologist, 39,* 1207–1213.

Josephson, W. L. (1987). Television violence and children's aggression: Testing the priming, social script, and disinhibition predictions. *Journal of Personality and Social Psychology, 53,* 882–890.

Joyce, J. (1934). *Ulysses.* New York: Random House.

Julien, R. M. (1991). *A primer of drug action* (6th ed.). New York: Freeman.

Jusczyk, P. W. (1986). Toward a model of the development of speech perception. In J. S. Perkell & D. H. Klatt (Eds.), *Invariance and variability in speech processes.* Hillsdale, NJ: Erlbaum.

Jusczyk, P. W., & Derrah, C. (1987). Representation of speech sounds by young infants. *Developmental Psychology, 23,* 648–654.

Jussim, L., Coleman, L. M., & Lerch, L. (1987). The nature of stereotypes: A comparison and integration of three theories. *Journal of Personality and Social Psychology, 52,* 536–546.

Justice, T. C., & Looney, T. A. (1990). Another look at "superstitions" in pigeons. *Bulletin of the Psychonomic Society, 28,* 64–66.

Kagan, J. (1989a). Temperamental contributions to social behavior. *American Psychologist, 44,* 668–674.

Kagan, J. (1989b). *Unstable ideas: Temperament, cognition, and self.* Cambridge, MA: Harvard University Press.

Kagan, J. (1990). Temperament and social behavior. *Harvard Medical School Mental Health Letter, 6,* 4–5.

Kagan, J., Kearsley, R. B., & Zelazo, P. R. (1978). *Infancy: Its place in human development.* Cambridge, MA: Harvard University Press.

Kagan, J., & Moss, H. (1962). *Birth to maturity.* New York: Wiley.

Kagan, J., Reznick, J. S., & Snidman, N. (1988, April 8). Biological bases of childhood shyness. *Science, 240,* 167–171.

Kagan, J., & Snidman, N. (1991). Infant predictors of inhibited and uninhibited profiles. *Psychological Science, 2,* 40–44.

Kagehiro, D. K. (1990). Defining the standard of proof in jury instructions. *Psychological Science, 1,* 194–200.

Kahn, R. L., Wolfe, D. M., Quinn, R. P., Snoek, J. D., & Rosenthal, R. A. (1964). *Organizational stress: Studies in role conflict and ambiguity.* New York: Wiley.

Kahn, S., Zimmerman, G., Csikszentmihalyi, M., & Getzels, J. W. (1985). Relations between identity in young adulthood and intimacy at midlife. *Journal of Personality and Social Psychology, 49,* 1316–1322.

Kahneman, D., & Tversky, A. (1973). On the psychology of prediction. *Psychology Review, 80,* 237–251.

Kail, R. (1991). Processing time declines exponentially during childhood and adolescence. *Developmental Psychology, 27,* 259–266.

Kamin, L. J. (1969). Predictability, surprise, attention, and conditioning. In B. A. Campbell & R. M. Church (Eds.), *Punishment and aversive behavior.* New York: Appleton-Century-Crofts.

Kamin, L. J. (1974). *The science and politics of IQ.* New York: Wiley.

Kamin, L. J., & Eysenck, H. J. (1981). *The intelligence controversy.* New York: Wiley.

Kandel, E. R., & Schwartz, J. H. (1982, October 29). Molecular biology of learning: Modulation or transmitter release. *Science, 218,* 433–442.

Kane, J. M. (1983). Hypotheses regarding the mechanism of action of antidepressant drugs: Neurotransmitters in affective disorders. In A. Rifkin (Ed.), *Schizophrenia and affective disorders: Biology and drug treatment* (pp. 19–34). Boston: John Wright.

Kanfer, F. H., & Goldstein, A. P. (Eds.). (1985). *Helping people change: A textbook of methods* (3rd ed.). New York: Pergamon.

Kanner, A. D., Coyne, J. C., Schaefer, C., & Lazarus, R. (1981). Comparison of two modes of stress measurement: Daily hassles and uplifts versus major life events. *Journal of Behavioral Medicine, 4,* 14.

Kantrowitz, B. (1991, October 21). Striking a nerve. *Newsweek,* pp. 34–40.

Kaplan, H. S. (1974). *The new sex therapy.* New York: Brunner-Mazel.

Kaplan, H. S. (1979). *Disorders of sexual desire.* New York: Simon & Schuster.

Kaplan, J. R., & Manuck, S. B. (1989). The effect of propranolol on behavioral interactions among adult male cyunomolgus monkeys (*Macaca fascicularis*) housed in disrupted social groupings. *Psychosomatic Medicine, 51,* 449–462.

Kaplan, M. F. (1975). Information integration in social judgment: Interaction of judge and informational components. In M. Kaplan & S. Schwartz (Eds.), *Human development and decision processes.* New York: Academic.

Kaplan, M. F. (1983, May). *Effect of training on reasoning in moral choice.* Paper presented at the meeting of the Midwestern Psychological Association.

Kaplan, M. F., & Miller, C. E. (1987). Group decision making and normative versus informational influence: Effects of type and issue and assigned decision rule. *Journal of Personality and Social Psychology, 53,* 306–313.

Karasu, T. B. (1982). Psychotherapy and psychopharmacology: Toward an integrative model. *American Journal of Psychiatry, 139,* 1102–1113.

Karlins, M., & Abelson, H. I. (1979). *How opinions and attitudes are changed.* New York: Springer-Verlag.

Karoly, P., & Kanfer, F. H. (1982). *Self-management and behavior change.* New York: Pergamon.

Karp, D. A. (1988). A decade of remembrances: Changing age consciousness between fifty and sixty years old. *The Gerontologist, 28,* 727–738.

Kasa, P. (1986). The cholinergic systems in brain and spinal cord. *Progress in Neurobiology, 26,* 211–272.

Kaslow, F. W. (1991). The art and science of family psychology: Retrospective and perspective. *American Psychologist, 46,* 621–626.

Kassin, S. M. (1985). Eyewitness identification: Retrospective self-awareness and the accuracy-confidence correlation. *Journal of Personality and Social Psychology, 41,* 878–893.

Kastenbaum, R. (1975). Is death a life crisis? On the confrontation with death in theory and practice. In N. Datan & L. H. Ginsberg (Eds.), *Life-span developmental psychology: Normative life crisis.* New York: Academic.

Katz, A. N. (1989). Autobiographical memory as a reconstructive process: An extension of Ross's hypothesis. *Canadian Journal of Psychology, 43,* 512–517.

Katz, D., & Braly, K. W. (1933). Racial stereotypes of 100 college students. *Journal of Abnormal and Social Psychology, 4,* 280–290.

Katz, D., & Kahn, R. (1978). *The social psychology of organizations* (2nd ed.). New York: Wiley.

Katzell, R. A., & Guzzo, R. A. (1983). Psychological approaches to productivity improvement. *American Psychologist,* 468–472.

Katzell, R. A., & Thompson, D. E. (1990).

Work motivation: Theory and practice. *American Psychologist, 45,* 144–153.

Kazdin, A. E. (1989). *Behavior modification in applied settings.* 4th ed. Pacific Grove, CA: Brooks/Cole.

Kazdin, A. E., & Wilson, G. T. (1978). *Evaluation of behavior therapy: Issues, evidence, and research strategies.* Cambridge, MA: Ballinger.

Keating, D. P., & Clark, L. V. (1980). Development of physical and social reasoning in adolescence. *Developmental Psychology, 16,* 23–30.

Keesey, R. E., & Powley, T. L. (1986). The regulation of body weight. *Annual Review of Psychology,* p. 37.

Keith, S. J., Regier, D. A., & Rae, D. S. (1991). Schizophrenic disorders. In L. N. Robins & D. A. Regier (Eds.), *Psychiatric disorders in America.* New York: Free Press.

Keith-Spiegel, P., & Koocher, G. P. (1985). *Ethics in psychology.* San Francisco: Random House-Knopf.

Kelley, H. H. (1950). The warm-cold variable in first impressions of persons. *Journal of Personality and Social Psychology, 18,* 431–439.

Kelley, H. H. (1967). Attribution theory in social psychology. In D. Levine (Ed.), *Nebraska Symposium on Motivation.* Lincoln, NE: University of Nebraska Press.

Kemeny, M. (1985, August). *Stress and psychosocial factors predicting immunity and genital herpes recurrence.* Paper presented at the annual convention of the American Psychological Association, Los Angeles.

Kemper, T. D. (Ed.). (1990). *Research agendas in the sociology of emotions.* Albany, NY: State University of New York Press.

Kendall, P. C. (Ed.). (1991). *Child and adolescent therapy: Cognitive-behavioral procedures.* New York: Guilford Press.

Kendrick, D. T., & Funder, D. C. (1988). Profiting from controversy: Lessons from the person-situation debate. *American Psychologist, 43,* 23–34.

Kenny, D. A. (1991). A general model of consensus and accuracy in interpersonal perception. *Psychological Review, 98,* 155–163.

Kent, D. (1991, March). Speech analysis: Determining intoxication after the fact. *APS Observer, 8.*

Kerouac, J. (1959). *Mexico City blues.* New York: Grove Press.

Kertesz, A. E. (1983). Cyclofusion and stereopsis. *Perception and Psychophysics, 33,* 99–101.

Kiecolt-Glaser, J. K., & Glaser, R. (1986). Behavioral influences on immune function: Evidence for the interplay between stress and health. In T. Field, P. McCabe, & N. Schneiderman (Eds.), *Stress and coping* (Vol. 2). Hillsdale, NJ: Erlbaum.

Kienker, P. K., Sejnowski, T. J., Hinton, G. E., & Schumacher, L. E. (1986).

Separating figure from ground with a parallel network. *Perception, 15,* 197–216.

Kiesler, C. A., & Simpkins, C. (1991, June). The de facto national system of psychiatric inpatient care. *American Psychologist, 46,* 579–584.

Kihlstrom, J. F. (1987, September 18). The cognitive unconscious. *Science, 237,* 1445–1452.

Kihlstrom, J. F., Schacter, D. L., Cork, R. C., Hurt, C. A., & Behr, S. E. (1990). Implicit and explicit memory following surgical anesthesia. *Psychological Science, 1,* 303–306.

Kilborn, P. T. (1990, December 23). Workers using computers find a supervisor inside. *The New York Times,* p. A-1.

Kilborn, P. T. (1991, May 15). "Race norming" tests becomes a fiery issue. *The New York Times.*

Kimble, G. A. (1989). Psychology from the standpoint of a generalist. *American Psychologist, 44,* 491–499.

King, G. R., & Logue, A. W. (1990). Humans' sensitivity to variation in reinforcer amount: Effects of the method of reinforcer delivery. *Journal of the Experimental Analysis of Behavior, 53,* 33–46.

Kinsey, A. C., Pomeroy, W. B., & Martin, C. E. (1948). *Sexual behavior in the human male.* Philadelphia: Saunders.

Kinsey, A. C., Pomeroy, W. B., Martin, C. E., & Gebhard, P. H. (1953). *Sexual behavior in the human female.* Philadelphia: Saunders.

Kirby, D. (1977). The methods and methodological problems of sex research. In J. S. DeLora & C. A. B. Warren (Eds.), *Understanding sexual interaction.* Boston: Houghton Mifflin.

Kirsch, C. A., Blanchard, E. B., & Parnes, S. M. (1989). Psychological characteristics of individuals high and low in their ability to cope with tinnitus. *Psychosomatic Medicine, 51,* 209–217.

Klaus, H. M., & Kennell, J. H. (1976). *Maternal-infant bonding.* St. Louis, MO: Mosby.

Klein, S. B., & Mowrer, R. R. (1989). *Contemporary learning theories, instrumental conditioning theory and the impact of biological constraints on learning.* Hillsdale, NJ: Lawrence Erlbaum Associates.

Kleinman, A. (1991, July). The psychiatry of culture and culture of psychiatry. *Harvard Mental Health Letter.* Cambridge, MA: Harvard University Medical School.

Kleinmuntz, B. (1967). *Personality measurement: An introduction.* Homewood, IL: Dorsey.

Kleinmuntz, B. (1990). Why we still use our heads instead of formulas: Toward an integrative approach. *Psychological Bulletin, 107,* 296–310.

Klerman, G. L. (1984). The advantages of DSM-III. *American Journal of Psychiatry, 141,* 539–542.

Kline, P. (1987). The experimental study of the psychoanalytic unconscious. *Personality and Social Psychology Bulletin, 13,* 363–378.

Kobasa, S. C. (1979). Stressful life events, personality, and health: An inquiry into hardiness. *Journal of Personality and Social Psychology, 37,* 1–11.

Kohlberg, L. (1969). Stage and sequence: The cognitive-developmental approach to socialization. In D. Goslin (Ed.), *Handbook of socialization theory and research.* Chicago: Rand McNally.

Kohlberg, L. (1976). Stages and moralization: The cognitive-developmental approach. In T. Liskona (Ed.), *Moral development and behavior: Theory, research and social issues.* New York: Holt.

Kohlberg, L. (1984). *The psychology of moral development: Essays on moral development* (Vol. 2). San Francisco: Harper & Row.

Köhler, W. (1927). *The mentality of apes.* London: Routledge & Kegan Paul.

Kohn, A. (1988, April). What they say. *Psychology Today,* pp. 36–41.

Kohn, A. (1990). *You know what they say.* New York: HarperCollins.

Kohn, V. (1987, February). The body prison: A bulimic's compulsion to eat more, eat less, add muscle, get thinner. *Life,* p. 44.

Kolata, G. (1987a, May 15). Early signs of school-age IQ. *Science, 236,* 774–775.

Kolata, G. (1987b, August 14). What babies know, and noises parents make. *Science, 237,* 726.

Kolata, G. (1987c, November 10). Alcoholism: Genetic links grow clearer. *The New York Times,* p. C-1.

Kolata, G. (1988, February 25). New obesity studies indicate metabolism is often to blame. *The New York Times,* pp. A-1, B-5.

Kolata, G. (1991, May 15). Drop in casual sex tied to AIDS peril. *The New York Times.*

Kolb, B., & Whishaw, I. Q. (1990). *Fundamentals of human neuropsychology* (3rd ed.). New York: Freeman.

Konner, M. (1988, January 17). Caffeine high. *The New York Times Magazine,* pp. 47–48.

Koop, C. E. (1988). *The health consequences of smoking.* Washington, DC: Government Printing Office.

Korb, M. P., Gorrell, J., & VanDeRiet, V. (1989). *Gestalt therapy: Practice and theory* (2nd ed.). New York: Pergamon.

Korsch, B. M., & Negrete, V. F. (1972). Doctor-patient communication. *Scientific American,* pp. 66–74.

Kosambi, D. D. (1967). Living prehistory in India. *Scientific American, 216,* 105.

Koss, M. P. (in press). Hidden rape: Incidence, prevalence, and descriptive characteristics of sexual aggression in a national sample of college students.

In A. W. Burgess (Ed.), *Sexual assault* (Vol. 2). New York: Garland.

Koss, M. P., & Burkhart, B. R. (1989). A conceptual analysis of rape victimization. *Psychology of Women Quarterly, 13,* 27–40.

Koss, M. P., Dinero, T. E., Siebel, C. A., & Cox, S. L. (1988). Stranger and acquaintance rape: Are there differences in the victim's experience? *Psychology of Women Quarterly, 12,* 1–24.

Koss, M. P., Gidycz, C. A., & Wisniewski, N. (1987). The scope of rape: Incidence and prevalence in a nation sample of higher education students. *Journal of Consulting and Clinical Psychology, 55,* 162–170.

Kotler, P. (1986). *Principles of marketing* (3rd ed.). Englewood Cliffs, NJ: Prentice-Hall.

Kotre, J., & Hall, E. (1990). *Seasons of life.* Boston: Little, Brown.

Kotses, H., et al. (1991). Long-term effects of biofeedback-induced facial relaxation on measures of asthma severity in children. *Biofeedback and Self-Regulation, 16,* 1–22.

Koveces, Z. (1987). *The container metaphor of emotion.* Paper presented at the University of Massachusetts, Amherst.

Kraepelin, E. (1904–1968). *Lectures on clinical psychiatry.* New York: Hafner.

Kraines, S. H. (1948). *The therapy of the neuroses and psychoses* (3rd ed.). Philadelphia: Lea & Febiger.

Krantz, D. S., Glass, D. C., Schaeffer, M. A., & Davia, J. E. (1982). Behavior patterns and coronary disease: A critical evaluation. In J. T. Cacioppo & R. E. Petty (Eds.), *Focus on cardiovascular psychophysiology* (pp. 315–346). New York: Guilford Press.

Kravitz, E. A. (1988, September 30). Hormonal control of behavior: Amines and the biasing of behavioral output in lobsters. *Science, 241,* 1775–1782.

Krechevsky, M., & Gardner, H. (1990). Approaching school intelligently: An infusion approach. *Contributions to Human Development, 21,* 79–94.

Kreuger, L. E. (1989). *The world of touch.* Hillsdale, NJ: Erlbaum.

Kringlen, E. (1978). Adult offspring of two psychotic parents, with special reference to schizophrenia. In L. C. Wynne, R. L. Cromwell, & S. Matthysee (Eds.), *The nature of schizophrenia: New epidemiological-clinical twin study.* Oslo: Univesitsforlaget.

Kriphe, D. F., et al. (1979). Short and long sleep and sleeping pills: Is increased mortality associated? *Archives of General Psychiatry, 36,* 103–116.

Kronhaber, M., Krechevsky, M., & Gardner, H. (1990). Engaging intelligence. *Educational Psychologist, 25,* 177–199.

Kübler-Ross, E. (1969). *On death and dying.* New York: Macmillan.

Kucharski, D., & Hall, W. G. (1987, November 6). New routes to early memories. *Science, 238,* 786–788.

Kuhl, P. K., Williams, K. A., Lacerda, F., Stevens, K. N., & Lindblom, B. (1992, January 31). Linguistic experience alters phonetic perception in infants by 6 months of age. *Science, 255,* 606–608.

Kulik, J. A., Bangert-Drowns, R. L., & Kulik, C. C. (1984). Effectiveness of coaching for aptitude tests. *Psychological Bulletin, 95,* 179–188.

Ladd, G. W. (1990). Having friends, keeping friends, making friends, and being liked by peers in the classroom: Predictors of children's early school adjustment? *Child Development, 61,* 1081–1100.

Laird, J. D., & Bresler, C. (1990). William James and the mechanisms of emotional experience. *Personality and Social Psychology Bulletin, 16,* 636–651.

Lakey, B., & Heller, K. (1985). Response biases and the relation between negative life events and psychological symptoms. *Journal of Personality and Social Psychology, 49,* 1662–1668.

Lamal, P. A. (1979). College students' common beliefs about psychology. *Teaching of Psychology, 6,* 155–158.

Lamb, M. E. (1982a). Paternal influences on early socio-emotional development. *Journal of Child Psychology and Psychiatry and Allied Disciplines, 23,* 185–190.

Lamb, M. E. (1982b). The bonding phenomenon: Misinterpretations and their implications. *Journal of Pediatrics, 101,* 555–557.

Lambert, M. J., Shapiro, D. A., & Bergin, A. E. (1986). The effectiveness of psychotherapy. In S. L. Garfield & A. E. Bergin (Eds.), *Handbook of psychotherapy and behavior change* (3rd ed.). New York: Wiley.

Lambert, W. E., & Peal, E. (1972). The relation of bilingualism to intelligence. In A. S. Dil (Ed.), *Language, psychology, and culture.* Stanford, CA: Stanford University Press.

Landesman, S., & Ramey, C. (1989). Developmental psychology and mental retardation: Integrating scientific principles with treatment practices. *American Psychologist, 44,* 409–415.

Landis, D., Day, H. R., McGrew, P. L., Thomas, J. A., & Miller, A. B. (1976). Can a black "culture assimilator" increase racial understanding? *Journal of Social Issues, 32,* 169–183.

Landman, J., & Dawes, R. M. (1984). Reply to Orwin and Cordray. *American Psychologist, 39,* 72–73.

Landwehr, K. (1990). *Ecological perception research, visual communication aesthetics.* New York: Springer-Verlag.

Lang, J. S. (1987, April 13). Happiness is a reunited set of twins. *U.S. News and World Report,* pp. 63–66.

Langer, E. J. (1983). *The psychology of control.* Beverly Hills, CA: Sage.

Langer, E. J., Bashner, R. S., & Chanowitz, B. (1985). Decreasing prejudice by increasing discrimination. *Journal of Personality and Social Psychology, 49,* 113–120.

Langer, E.J., & Janis, I. L. (1979). *The psychology of control.* Beverly Hills, CA: Sage.

Langer, E. J., Janis, I. L., & Wolfer, J. A. (1975). Reduction or psychological stress in surgical patients. *Journal of Experimental Social Psychology, 11,* 155–165.

Langlois, J. H., Roggman, L. A., Casey, R. J., Ritter, J. M., Rieser-Danner, L. A., & Jenkins, V. Y. (1987). Infant preferences for attractive faces: Rudiments of a stereotype? *Developmental Psychology, 23,* 363–369.

Langlois, J. H., Roggman, L. A., & Rieser-Danner, L. A. (1990). Infants' differential social responses to attractive and unattractive faces. *Developmental Psychology, 26,* 153–159.

Larkin, J. H. & Chabay, R. W. (Eds.). (1991). *Computer assisted instruction and intelligent tutoring systems: Shared issues and complementary approaches.* Hillsdale, NJ: Erlbaum.

Larrick, R. P., Morgan, J. N., & Nisbett, R. E. (1990). Teaching the use of cost-benefit reasoning in everyday life. *Psychological Science, 1,* 362–370.

Larson, R. K. (1990). Semantics. In D. N. Osherson & H. Lasnik (Eds.), *Language.* Cambridge, MA: MIT Press.

Lashley, K. S. (1950). In search of the engram. *Symposia of the Society for Experimental Biology, 4,* 454–482.

Lasnik, H. (1990). Syntax. In D. N. Osherson & H. Lasnik (Eds.), *Language.* Cambridge, MA: MIT Press.

Latané, B., & Darley, J. M. (1970). *The unresponsive bystander: Why doesn't he help?* New York: Appleton-Century-Crofts.

Latané, B., & Nida, S. (1981). Ten years of research on group size and helping. *Psychological Bulletin, 89,* 308–324.

Latham, G. P. (1988). Human resource training and development. *Annual Review of Psychology, 39,* 545–582.

Lauer, J., & Lauer, R. (1985, June). Marriages made to last. *Psychology Today,* pp. 22–26.

Lazarus, R. S. (1991a). Cognition and motivation in emotion. *American Psychologist, 46,* 352–367.

Lazarus, R. S. (1991b). *Emotion and adaptation.* New York: Oxford University Press.

Lazarus, R. S., & Cohen, J. B. (1977). Environmental stress. In I. Altman &

J. F. Wohlwill (Eds.), *Human behavior and the environment: Current theory and research* (Vol. 2). New York: Plenum.

Lazarus, R. S., DeLongis, A., Folkman, S., & Gruen, R. (1985). Stress and adaptational outcomes: The problem of confounded measures. *American Psychologist, 40,* 770–779.

Lechtenberg, R. (1982). *The psychiatrist's guide to diseases of the nervous system.* New York: Wiley.

Lee, V. E., Brooks-Gunn, J., & Schnur, E. (1988). Does Head Start work? A one-year follow up comparison of disadvantaged children attending Head Start, no preschool, and other preschool programs. *Developmental Psychology, 24,* 210–222.

Lee, V. E., Brooks-Gunn, J., Schnur, E., & Liaw, F. (1990). Are Head Start effects sustained? A longitudinal follow-up comparison of disadvantaged children attending Head Start, no preschool, and other preschool programs. *Child Development, 61,* 495–507.

Leenaars, A. A. (Ed.). (1991). *Life span perspectives of suicide: Time-lines in the suicide process.* New York: Plenum.

Lefkowitz, M. M., & Tesiny, E. P. (1985). Depression in children: Prevalence and correlates. *Journal of Consulting and Clinical Psychology, 53,* 647–656.

Lehman, D. R., Lempert, R. O., & Nisbett, R. E. (1988). The effects of graduate training on reasoning: Formal discipline and thinking about everyday-life events. *American Psychologist, 43,* 431–442.

Lehman, D. R., & Taylor, S. E. (1988). Date with an earthquake: Coping with a probable, unpredictable disaster. *Personality and Social Psychology Bulletin, 13,* 546–555.

Leiber, C. S. (1990, January 11). High blood alcohol level in women. *New England Journal of Medicine, 322,* 95–99.

Leibovic, K. N. (Ed.). (1990). *Science of vision.* New York: Springer-Verlag.

Leigh, H., & Reiser, M. F. (1980). *The patient.* New York: Plenum.

Lenhardt, M. L., Skellett, R., Wang, P., & Clarke, A. M. (1991, July 5). Human ultrasonic speech perception. *Science, 253,* 82–85.

Lepore, S. J., Evans, G. W., & Schneider, M. L. (1991). Dynamic role of social support in the link between chronic stress and psychological distress. *Journal of Personality and Social Psychology, 61*(6), 889–909.

Lepper, M. R. (1983). Extrinsic reward and intrinsic motivation: Implications for the classroom (pp. 281–317). In J. M. Levine & M. C. Wung (Eds.), *Teacher and student perceptions: Implications for learning.* Hillsdale, NJ: Lawrence Erlbaum Associates.

Lepper, M. R. (1985). Microcomputers in education: Motivational and social issues. *American Psychologist, 40,* 1–18.

Lepper, M. R., & Greene, D. (1978). *The hidden costs of reward.* Hillsdale, NJ: Lawrence Erlbaum Associates.

Lerner, P. M. (1990). Rorschach assessment of primitive defenses: A review. *Journal of Personality Assessment, 54,* 30–46.

Leslie, C. (1991, February 11). Classrooms of Babel. *Newsweek,* pp. 56–57.

Lester, D. (1990). *Understanding and preventing suicide: New perspectives.* Springfield, IL: Charles C Thomas.

LeVay, S. (1991, August 30). A difference in hypothalamic structure between heterosexual and homosexual men. *Science, 253,* 1034–1037.

Levenson, R. W., Ekman, P., & Friesen, W. V. (1990). Voluntary facial expression generates emotion-specific nervous system activity. *Psychophysiology, 27,* 363–384.

Leventhal, H. (1970). Findings and theory in the study of fear communications. In L. Berkowitz (Ed.), *Advances in experimental social psychology* (Vol. 5). New York: Academic.

Leventhal, H., & Cleary, P. D. (1980). The smoking problem: A review of the research and theory in behavioral risk modification. *Psychological Bulletin, 88,* 370–405.

Leventhal, H., Nerenz, D., & Leventhal, E. (1985). Feelings of threat and private views of illness: Factors in dehumanization in the medical care system. In A. Baum & J. E. Singer (Eds.), *Advances in environmental psychology* (Vol. 4). Hillsdale, NJ: Erlbaum.

Leventhal, H., & Tomarken, A. J. (1986). Emotion: Today's problems. *Annual Review of Psychology, 37,* 565–610.

Levine, J. M. (1989). Reaction to opinion deviance in small groups. In P. B. Paulus (Ed.), *Psychology of group influence* (2nd ed.). Hillsdale, NJ: Erlbaum.

Levine, M. W., & Shefner, J. M. (1991). *Fundamentals of sensation and perception* (2nd ed.). Pacific Grove, CA: Brooks/Cole.

Levinger, G. (1983). Development and change. In H. H. Kelley et al., *Close relationships.* San Francisco: Freeman.

Levinson, D. J. (1986). A conception of adult development. *American Psychologist, 41,* 3–13.

Levinson, D. J. (1992). A theory of life structure development in adulthood. In C. N. Alexander & E. J. Langer (Eds.), *Higher stages of human development.* Oxford, England: Oxford University Press.

Levitan, I. B., & Kaczmarek, L. K. (1991). *The neuron: Cell and molecular biology.* New York: Oxford University Press.

Levy, J. (1985). Language, cognition, and the right hemisphere: A response to Gazzaniga. *American Psychologist, 38,* 538–541.

Levy, S. M., Lee, J., Bagley, C., & Lippman, M. (1988). Survival hazards analysis in first recurrent breast cancer patients: Seven-year follow-up. *Psychosomatic Medicine, 50,* 520–528.

Lewandowsky, S., Dunn, J. C., & Kirsner, K. (Eds.). (1989). *Implicit memory: Theoretical issues.* Hillsdale, NJ: Erlbaum.

Lewis, M., & Feinman, S. (Eds.). (1991). *Social influences and socialization in infancy.* New York: Plenum.

Lewis, M., Feiring, C., McGuffog, C., & Jaskir, J. (1984). Predicting psychopathology in six-year-olds from early social relations. *Child Development, 55,* 123–136.

Lewis, P. (1987). Therapeutic change in groups: An interactional perspective. *Small Group Behavior, 18,* 548–556.

Lex, B. W. (1991). Some gender differences in alcohol and polysubstance users. *Health Psychology, 10,* 121–132.

Ley, P., & Spelman, M. S. (1967). *Communicating with the patient.* London: Staples.

Lichtenstein, E. (1982). The smoking problem: A behavioral perspective. *Journal of Consulting and Clinical Psychology, 50,* 804–819.

Lidz, T., & Fleck, S. (1985). *Schizophrenia and the family* (2nd ed.). New York: International Universities Press.

Liebert, R. M., & Sprafkin, J. (1988). *The early window: effects of television on children and youth* (3rd ed.). New York: Pergamon.

Lietaer, G. (1984). Unconditional positive regard: A controversial basic attitude in client-centered therapy. In R. F. Levant & L. M. Shlien (Eds.), *Client-centered therapy and the person-centered approach.* New York: Praeger.

Lindholm, K. J. (1991). Two-way bilingual/immersion education: Theory, conceptual issues, and pedagogical implications. In R. V. Padilla & A. Benavides (Eds.), *Critical perspectives on bilingual education research.* Tempe, AZ: Bilingual Review Press.

Lindsay, P. H., & Norman, D. A. (1977). *Human information processing* (2nd ed.). New York: Academic.

Linscheid, T. R., Iwata, B. A., Ricketts, R. W., Williams, D. E., & Griffin, J. C. (1990). Clinical evaluation of the self-injurious behavior inhibiting system (SIBIS). *Journal of Applied Behavior Analysis, 23,* 53–78.

Linz, D. G., Donnerstein, E., & Adams, S. M. (1989). Physiological desensitization and judgments about female victims of violence. *Human Communication Research,* p. 15.

Linz, D. G., Donnerstein, E., & Penrod, S. (1988). Effects of long-term exposure to violent and sexually degrading depictions of women. *Journal of Personality and Social Psychology, 55,* 758–768.

Lisak, D., & Roth, S. (1988). Motivational factors in nonincarcerated sexually aggressive men. *Journal of Personality and Social Psychology, 55,* 795–802.

Liskin, L. (1985, November–December). Youth in the 1980s: Social and health concerns 4. *Population Reports, 8*(5).

Lister, R. G., & Weingartner, H. J. (Eds.). (1991). *Perspectives on cognitive neuroscience.* Oxford, England: Oxford University Press.

Livingston, M., & Hubel, D. (1988, May 6). Segregation of form, color, movement, and depth: Anatomy, physiology, and perception. *Science, 240,* 740–749.

Livingstone, M. S. (1988, January–February). Art, illusion, and the visual system. *Scientific American,* pp. 78–85.

Livson, N., & Peskin, H. (1980). Perspectives on adolescence from longitudinal research. In J. Adelson (Eds.), *Handbook of adolescent psychology.* New York: Wiley.

Lobsenz, M. M. (1975). *Sex after sixty-five.* Public Affairs Pamphlet No. 519, New York Public Affairs Committee.

Locke, E. A., & Latham, G. P. (1990). *A theory of goal setting and task performance.* Englewood Cliffs, NJ: Prentice-Hall.

Locke, E. A., & Latham, G. P. (1991). The fallacies of common sense "truths": A reply to Lamal. *Psychological Science, 2,* 131–132.

Locke, E. A., & Schweiger, D. M. (1979). Participation in decision making: One more look. In B. Staw (Ed.), *Research in organizational behavior* (Vol. 1). Greenwich, CT: JAI Press.

Loehlin, J. C. (1989). Partitioning environmental and genetic contributions to behavioral development. *American Psychologist, 44,* 1285–1292.

Loehlin, J. C., Willerman, L., & Horn, J. M. (1987). Personality resemblance in adoptive families: A 10-year follow-up. *Journal of Personality and Social Psychology, 53,* 961–969.

Loftus, E. F. (1991). The glitter of everyday memory . . . and the gold. *American Psychologist, 46,* 16–18.

Loftus, E. F., Loftus, G. R., & Messo, J. (1987). Some facts about "weapon focus." *Law and Human Behavior, 11,* 55–62.

Logothetis, N. K., & Schall, J. D. (1989, August 18). Neuronal correlates of subjective visual perception. *Science, 245,* 761–763.

Logue, A. W. (1991). *The psychology of eating and drinking: An introduction.* New York: Freeman.

Lohman, D. F. (1989). Human intelligence: An introduction to advances in theory and research. *Review of Educational Research, 59,* 333–373.

Long, A. (1987, December). What is this

thing called sleep? *National Geographic, 172,* 786–821.

Long, G. M., & Beaton, R. J. (1982). The case for peripheral persistence: Effects of target and background luminance on a partial-report task. *Journal of Experimental Psychology: Human Perception and Performance, 8,* 383–391.

Lopez, S. R. (1989). Patient variable biases in clinical judgment: Conceptual overview and methodological considerations. *Psychological Bulletin, 106,* 184–203.

Lopez, S. R., & Nunez, J. A. (1987). The consideration of cultural factors in selected diagnostic criteria and interview schedules. *Journal of Abnormal Psychology, 96,* 270–272.

LoPiccolo, L. (1980). Low sexual desire. In S. R. Leiblum & L. A. Pervin (Eds.), *Principles and practice of sex therapy.* New York: Guilford Press.

Lorenz, K. (1966). *On aggression.* New York: Harcourt, Brace, Jovanovich.

Lorenz, K. (1974). *Civilized man's eight deadly sins.* New York: Harcourt, Brace, Jovanovich.

Lorsch, J. W. (Ed.). (1987). *Handbook of organization behavior.* Englewood Cliffs, NJ: Prentice-Hall.

Lortie-Lussier, M. (1987). Minority influence and idiosyncrasy credit: A new comparison of the Moscovici and Hollander theories of innovation. *European Journal of Social Psychology, 17,* 431–446.

Lovaas, O. I., & Koegel, R. (1973). Behavior therapy with autistic children. In C. Thoreson (Ed.), *Behavior modification and education.* Chicago: University of Chicago Press.

Lublin, J. S. (1991, October 11). Companies try a variety of approaches to halt sexual harassment on the job. *The Wall Street Journal,* pp. B1, B6.

Luborsky, L. (1988). *Who will benefit from psychotherapy?* New York: Basic Books.

Luborsky, L., Barber, J. P., Crits-Christoph, P. (1990). Theory-based research for understanding the process of dynamic psychotherapy. *Journal of Consulting and Clinical Psychology, 58,* 281–287.

Luborsky, L., & Spence, D. P. (1978). Quantitative research on psychoanalytic therapy. In S. L. Garfield & A. E. Bergin (Eds.), *Handbook of psychotherapy and behavior change: An empirical analysis* (2nd ed.). New York: Wiley.

Luchins, A. S. (1946). Classroom experiments on mental set. *American Journal of Psychology, 59,* 295–298.

Ludwick-Rosenthal, R., & Neufeld, R. W. J. (1988). Stress management during noxious medical procedures: An evaluative review of outcome studies. *Psychological Bulletin, 104,* 326–342.

Ludwig, A. M. (1969). Altered states of consciousness. In C. T. Tart (Ed.),

Altered states of consciousness. New York: Wiley.

Luria, A. R. (1968). *The mind of a mnemonist.* New York & Cambridge, MA: Basic Books.

Lynch, J. G., Jr., & Cohen, J. L. (1978). The use of subjective expected utility theory as an aid to understanding variables that influence helping behavior. *Journal of Personality and Social Psychology, 36,* 1138–1151.

Lynn, S. J., & Rhue, J. (1985, September). Daydream believers. *Psychology Today,* pp. 14–15.

Lynn, S. J., & Rhue, J. W. (1988). Fantasy-proneness: Hypnosis, developmental antecedents, and psychopathology. *American Psychologist, 43,* 35–44.

Lynn, S. J., Rhue, J. W., & Weekes, J. R. (1990). Hypnotic involuntariness: A social cognitive analysis. *Psychological Review, 97,* 169–184.

Lynn, S. J., & Snodgrass, M. (1987). Goal-directed fantasy, hypnotic susceptibility, and expectancies. *Journal of Personality and Social Psychology, 53,* 933–938.

Lynn, S. J., Weekes, J. R., Neufeld, V., Zivney, O., Brentar, J., & Weiss, F. (1991). Interpersonal climate and hypnotizability level: Effects on hypnotic performance, rapport, and archaic involvement. *Journal of Personality and Social Psychology, 60,* 739–743.

Lytton, H., & Romney, D. M. (1991). Parents' differential socialization of boys and girls: A meta-analysis. *Psychological Bulletin, 109,* 267–296.

Maass, A., & Clark, R. D., III (1984). Hidden impact of minorities: Fifteen years of minority influence research. *Psychological Bulletin, 95,* 428–450.

Maccoby, E. E., & Jacklin, C. N. (1974). *The psychology of sex differences.* Stanford, CA: Stanford University Press.

MacDonald, M. L., & Tobias, L. L. (1976). Withdrawal causes relapse? Our response. *Psychological Bulletin, 83,* 448–451.

MacEvoy, B., Lambert, W. W., Karlberg, P., Karlberg, J., Klackenberg-Larsson, I., & Klackenberg, G. (1988). Early affective antecedents of adult type A behavior. *Journal of Personality and Social Psychology, 54,* 108–116.

MacKenzie, B. (1984). Explaining race differences in IQ: The logic, the methodology, and the evidence. *American Psychologist, 39,* 1214–1233.

Mackie, D. M. (1987). Systematic and nonsystematic processing of majority and minority persuasive communications. *Journal of Personality and Social Psychology, 53,* 41–52.

MacLeod, C. M. (1991). Half a century of research on the Stroop effect: An integrative review. *Psychological Bulletin, 109,* 163–203.

Maddi, S. R., Barone, P. T., & Puccetti, M. C. (1987). Stressful events are indeed a factor in physical illness: Reply to Schroeder and Costa (1984). *Journal of Personality and Social Psychology, 52,* 833–843.

Maeroff, G. I. (1977, August 21). The unfavored gifted few. *The New York Times Magazine.*

Maier, N. R. F. (1967). Assets and liabilities in group problem solving: The need for an integrative function. *Psychological Review, 47,* 239–249.

Major, B., & Konar, E. (1984). An investigation of sex differences in pay expectations and their possible causes. *Academy of Management Journal, 27,* 777–792.

Malin, J. T. (1979). Information-processing load in problem solving by network search. *Journal of Experimental Psychology: Human Perception and Performance, 5,* 379–390.

Malinak, D. P., Hoyt, M. F., & Patterson, V. (1979). Adults' reactions to the death of a parent: A preliminary study. *American Journal of Psychiatry, 136,* 1152–1156.

Malinowski, C. I., & Smith, C. P. (1985). Moral reasoning and moral conduct: An investigation prompted by Kohlberg's theory. *Journal of Personality and Social Issues, 49,* 1016–1027.

Manning, C. A., Hall, J. L., & Gold, P. E. (1990). Glucose effects on memory and other neuropsychological tests in elderly humans. *Psychological Science, 1,* 307–311.

Mapes, G. (1990, April 10). Beating the clock: Was it an accident Chernobyl exploded at 1:23 in the morning? *The Wall Street Journal, 70,* A1, A16.

Marcus, A. D. (1991, February 7). Murder trials introduce Prozac defense. *The Wall Street Journal,* p. B1.

Marks, G., & Miller, N. (1987). Ten years of research on the false-consensus effect: An empirical and theoretical review. *Psychological Bulletin, 102,* 72–90.

Marks, I. M. (1982). Toward an empirical clinical science: Behavioral psychotherapy in the 1980s. *Behavioral Therapies, 13,* 63–81.

Marlatt, G. A., Baer, J. S., Donovan, D. M., & Kivlahan, D. R. (1988). Addictive behaviors: Etiology and treatment. *Annual Review of Psychology, 39,* 223–252.

Marmar, C. R. (1990). Psychotherapy process research: Progress, dilemmas, and future directions. *Journal of Consulting and Clinical Psychology, 58,* 265–272.

Marshall, G., & Zimbardo, P. (1979). The affective consequences of "inadequately explained" physiological arousal. *Journal of Personality and Social Psychology, 37,* 970–988.

Martin, B. A. (1989). Gender differences in salary expectations. Current salary information is provided. *Psychology of Women Quarterly, 13,* 87–96.

Martin, C. L. (1987). A ratio measure of sex stereotyping. *Journal of Personality and Social Psychology, 52,* 489–499.

Martin, J. B. (1987, November 6). Molecular genetics: Applications to the clinical neurosciences. *Science, 238,* 765–772.

Martin, L., & Pullum, G. K. (1991). *The great Eskimo vocabulary hoax.* Chicago: University of Chicago Press.

Martindale, C. (1981). *Cognition and consciousness.* Homewood, IL: Dorsey.

Marvel Comics Group (1981). *See no evil.* New York: Marvel.

Marx, M. B., Garrity, T. F., & Bowers, F. R. (1975). The influence of recent life experience on the health of college freshmen. *Journal of Psychosomatic Research, 19,* 87–98.

Maslow, A. H. (Ed.). (1970). *Motivation and personality* (2nd ed.). New York: Harper & Row.

Maslow, A. H. (1987). *Motivation and personality* (3rd ed.). New York: Harper & Row.

Mason, J. W. (1974). Specificity in the organization of neuroendocrine response profiles. In P. Seeman & G. M. Brown (Eds.), *Frontiers in neurology and neuroscience research.* First International Symposium of the Neuroscience Institute. Toronto: University of Toronto Press.

Mason, J. W. (1975). A historical view of the stress field. *Journal of Human Stress, 1,* 6–12, 22–37.

Massaro, D. (1991). Psychology as a cognitive science. *Psychological Science, 2*(5), 302–306.

Massaro, D. W., & Cohen, M. M. (1990). Perception of synthesized audible and visible speech. *Psychological Science, 1,* 55–63.

Masters, W. H., & Johnson, V. E. (1966). *Human sexual response.* Boston: Little Brown.

Masters, W. H., & Johnson, V. E. (1970). *Human sexual inadequacy.* Boston: Little, Brown.

Masters, W. H., & Johnson, V. E. (1979). *Homosexuality in perspective.* Boston: Little, Brown.

Masters, W. H., Johnson, V. E., & Kolodny, R. C. (1985). *Human sexuality.* Boston: Little, Brown.

Masters, W. H., Johnson, V. E., & Kolodny, R. C. (1988). *CRISIS: Heterosexual behavior in the age of AIDS.* New York: Grove Press.

Mastropierei, M. A., & Scruggs, T. (1987). *Effective instruction for special education.* Boston: College-Hill Press/Little, Brown.

Mathews, T. (1991, January 28). The road to war. *Newsweek, 107,* 54–65.

Matlin, M. M. (1987). *The psychology of women.* New York: Holt.

Matson, J. L., & Mulick, J. A. (Eds.). (1991). *Handbook of mental retardation* (2nd ed.). New York: Pergamon.

Matsumoto, D. (1987). The role of facial response in the experience of emotion: More methodological problems and a meta-analysis. *Journal of Personality and Social Psychology, 52,* 769–774.

Matthews, K. A. (1988). Coronary heart disease and type A behaviors: Update on and alternative to the Booth-Kewley and Friedman (1987) quantitative review. *Psychological Bulletin, 104,* 373–380.

Matthews, K. A., & Siegel, J. (1987). Type A behavior pattern in children and adolescents. In A. Baum & J. Singer (Eds.), *Handbook of psychology and health.* Hillsdale, NJ: Erlbaum.

Matthies, H. (1989). Neurobiological aspects of learning and memory. *Annual Review of Psychology, 40,* 381–404.

Mawhinney, V. T., Boston, D. E., Loaws, O. R., Blumenfeld, G. T., & Hopkins, B. L. (1971). A comparison of students' studying behavior produced by daily, weekly, and three-week testing schedules. *Journal of Applied Behavior Analysis, 4,* 257–264.

May, R. (1969). *Love and will.* New York: Norton.

Mayer, R. E. (1982). Different problem-solving strategies for algebra word and equation problems. *Journal of Experimental Psychology: Learning, Memory, and Cognition, 8,* 448–462.

McAuley, E., & Duncan, T. E. (1990). The causal attribution process in sport and physical activity. In S. Graham & V. S. Folkes (Eds.), *Attribution theory: Applications to achievement, mental health, and interpersonal conflict.* Hillsdale, NJ: Erlbaum.

McCarthy, M. J. (1991a, March 18). Marketers zero in on their customers. *The Wall Street Journal,* p. B1.

McCarthy, M. J. (1991b, March 22). Mind probe. *The Wall Street Journal,* p. B3.

McCauley, C. (1989). The nature of social influence in groupthink: Compliance and internalization. *Journal of Personality and Social Psychology, 57,* 250–260.

McCauley, C., & Swann, C. P. (1980). Sex differences in the frequency and functions of fantasies during sexual activity. *Journal of Research in Personality, 14,* 400–411.

McClelland, D. C. (1978). Managing motivation to expand human freedom. *American Psychologist, 33,* 201–210.

McClelland, D. C. (1985a). How motives, skills, and values determine what people do. *American Psychologist, 40,* 812–825.

McClelland, D. C. (1985b). *Human motivation.* Glenview, IL: Scott, Foresman.

McClelland, D. C., Atkinson, J. W., Clark, R. A., & Lowell, E. L. (1953). *The achievement motive*. New York: Appleton-Century-Crofts.

McClelland, D. C., & Winter, D. G. (1971). *Motivating economic achievement*. New York: Free Press.

McCloskey, M., Wible, C. G., & Cohen, N. J. (1988). Is there a special flash-bulb-memory mechanism? *Journal of Experimental Psychology: General, 117*, 171–181.

McClusky, H. Y., et al. (1991). Efficacy of behavioral versus triazolam treatment in persistent sleep-onset insomnia. *American Journal of Psychiatry, 148*, 121–126.

McConnell, J. V. (1985). On Gazzaniga and right hemisphere language. *American Psychologist, 40*, 1273.

McDaniel, M. A., Riegler, G. L., & Waddill, P. J. (1990). Generation effects in free recall: Further support for a three-factor theory. *Journal of Experimental Psychology: Learning, Memory, and Cognition*, p. 16.

McDonald, K. (1988, March). Sex under glass. *Psychology Today*, pp. 58–59.

McDonald, S. M. (1989). Sex bias in the representation of male and female characters in children's picture books. *Journal of Genetic Psychology, 150*, 389–402.

McDougall, W. (1908). *Introduction to social psychology*. London: Methuen.

McGaugh, J. L. (1989). Involvement of hormonal and neuromodulatory systems in the regulation of memory storage. *Annual Review of Neuroscience, 12*, 255–287.

McGaugh, J. L., Weinberger, N. M., & Lynch, G. (Eds.). (1990). *Brain organization and memory: Cells, systems, and circuits*. Oxford, England: Oxford University Press.

McGrath, E., Keita, G. P., Strickland, B. R., & Russo, N. F. (Eds.). (1990). *Women and depression: Risk factors and treatment issues*. Washington, DC: American Psychological Association.

McGraw, K. M., & Bloomfield, J. (1987). Social influence on group moral decisions: The interactive effects of moral reasoning and sex-role orientation. *Journal of Personality and Social Psychology, 53*, 1080–1087.

McGuire, W. J. (1964). Inducing resistance to persuasion. In L. Berkowitz (Ed.), *Advances in experimental social psychology* (Vol. 1). New York: Academic.

McGuire, W. J. (1968). Personality and susceptibility to social influence. In E. F. Borgatta & W. W. Lambert (Eds.), *Handbook of personality theory and research*. Chicago: Rand McNally.

McGuire, W. J. (1985). Attitudes and attitude change. In G. Lindzey & E. Aronson (Eds.), *Handbook of social psychology* (Vol. 2, 3rd ed.). New York: Random House.

McKinley, J. B. (1975). Who is really ignorant—physician or patient? *Journal of Health and Social Behavior, 16*, 3–11.

McKusick, L., Horstman, W., & Coates, T. J. (1985). AIDS and sexual behavior reported by gay men in San Francisco. *American Journal of Public Health, 75*, 493–496.

McLaughlin, L. (1991, June 2). A still-young epidemic. *Boston Globe*, p. 69.

McMillan, J. R., et al. (1977). Women's language: Uncertainty or interpersonal sensitivity and emotionality? *Sex Roles, 3*, 545–560.

McNeal, E. T., & Cimbolic, P. (1986). Antidepressants and biochemical theories of depression. *Psychological Bulletin, 99*, 361–374.

McWhirter, D. P., Sanders, S., & Reinisch, J. M. (1990). *Homosexuality, heterosexuality: Concepts of sexual orientation*. New York: Oxford University Press.

Melges, F. T., & Bowlby, J. (1969). Types of hopelessness in psychopathological process. *Archives of General Psychiatry, 70*, 690–699.

Melton, G. B., & Garrison, E. G. (1987). Fear, prejudice, and neglect: Discrimination against mentally disabled persons. *American Psychologist, 42*, 1007–1026.

Melville, J. (1977). *Phobias and obsessions*. New York: Coward, McCann.

Melzack, R., & Wall, P. D. (1965, November 19). Pain mechanisms: A new theory. *Science, 150*, 971–979.

Mentzer, S. J., & Snyder, M. L. (1982). The doctor and the patient: A psychological perspective. In G. S. Sanders & J. Suls (Eds.), *Social psychology of health and illness* (pp. 161–181). Hillsdale, NJ: Erlbaum.

Messick, S., & Jungeblut, A. (1981). Time and method in coaching for the SAT. *Psychological Bulletin, 89*, 191–216.

Metcalfe, J. (1986). Premonitions of insight predict impending error. *Journal of Experimental Psychology: Learning, Memory, and Cognition, 12*, 623–634.

Metee, D. R., & Aronson, E. (1974). Affective reactions to appraisal from others. In T. L. Huston (Ed.), *Foundations of interpersonal attraction* (pp. 235–283). New York: Academic.

Meyer, J. P., & Pepper, S. (1977). Need compatibility and marital adjustment in young married couples. *Journal of Personality and Social Psychology, 35*, 331–342.

Meyer, R. G., & Macciocchi, S. N. (1989). The context of self-disclosure, the polygraph, and deception. *Forensic Reports, 2*, 295–303.

Meyer, R. G., & Osborne, Y. V. H. (1982). *Case studies in abnormal behavior* (2nd ed.). Boston: Allyn & Bacon.

Meyerhoff, M. K., & White, B. L. (1986, September). Making the grade as parents. *Psychology Today*, pp. 38–45.

Michaels, C. F., & Carello, C. (1981). *Direct perception*. Englewood Cliffs, NJ: Prentice-Hall.

Middlebrooks, J. C., & Green, D. M. (1991). Sound localization by human listeners. *Annual Review of Psychology, 42*, 135–159.

Mignard, M., & Malpeli, J. G. (1991, March 8). Paths of information flow through visual cortex. *Science, 251*, 1249–1253.

Mikhail, A. (1981). Stress: A psychophysiological conception. *Journal of Human Stress, 7*, 9–15.

Milewski, A. E. (1976). Infants' discrimination of internal and external pattern elements. *Journal of Experimental Child Psychology, 22*, 229–246.

Milgram, S. (1974). *Obedience to authority*. New York: Harper & Row.

Miller, A. G. (1986). *The obedience experiments: A case study of controversy in social science*. New York: Praeger.

Miller, D. C. (1991). *Handbook of research design and social measurement* (5th ed.). Newbury Park, CA: Sage.

Miller, E. K., Li, L., & Desimone, R. (1991). A neural mechanism for working and recognition memory in inferior temporal cortex. *Science, 254*, 1377–1379.

Miller, G. A. (1956). The magical number seven, plus or minus two: Some limits in our capacity for processing information. *Psychology Review, 63*, 81–97.

Miller, G. A. (1990). Speech perception. In D. N. Osherson & H. Lasnik (Eds.), *Language*. Cambridge, MA: MIT Press.

Miller, L. L. (Ed.). (1975). *Marijuana: Current research*. New York: Academic.

Miller, M. W. (1986, September 19). Effects of alcohol on the generation and migration of cerebral cortical neurons. *Science, 233*, 1308–1310.

Miller, N. E. (1985a, February). Rx: Biofeedback. *Psychology Today, 19*, pp. 54–59.

Miller, N. E. (1985b). The value of behavioral research on animals. *American Psychologist, 40*, 423–440.

Miller, N. E., & Brewer, M. B. (1984). *Groups in contact: The psychology of desegregation*. New York: Academic.

Miller, S. M., Brody, D. S., & Summerton, J. (1988). Styles of coping with threat: Implications for health. *Journal of Personality and Social Psychology, 54*, 142–148.

Miller, S. M., & Mangan, C. E. (1983). Interacting effects of information and coping style in adapting to gynecologic stress: Should the doctor tell all? *Journal of Personality and Social Psychology, 45*, 223–236.

Miller-Jones, D. (1989). Culture and testing. *American Psychologist, 44*, 360–366.

Milloy, C. (1986, June 22). Crack user's highs, lows. *The Washington Post*, p. A-1.

Milner, B. (1966). Amnesia following operation on temporal lobes. In C. W. M. Whitty & P. Zangwill (Eds.), *Amnesia.* London: Butterworth.

Mineka, S., & Hendersen, R. W. (1985). Controllability and predictability in acquired motivation. *Annual Review of Psychology, 36,* 495–529.

Minuchin, S. (1974). *Families and family therapy.* Cambridge, MA: Harvard University Press.

Mischel, W. (1968). *Personality and assessment.* New York: Wiley.

Mischel, W. (1990). Personality dispositions revisited and revised: A view after three decades. In L. A. Pervin (Ed.), New York: Guilford Press.

Mischel, W., & Peake, P. K. (1982a). Analyzing the construction of consistency in personality. *Nebraska Symposium on Motivation,* pp. 233–262.

Mischel, W., & Peake, P. K. (1982b). Beyond deja vu in the search for cross-situational consistency. *Psychological Review, 89,* 730–755.

Mitchell, A. (1983). *The nine American lifestyles.* New York: Macmillan.

Miyake, K., Chen, S., & Campos, J. J. (1985). Infant temperament, mother's mode of interaction, and attachment in Japan: An interim report. *Monographs of the Society for Research in Child Development, 50,* 276–297.

Molotsky, I. (1984, November 30). Implant to aid the totally deaf is approved. *The New York Times,* pp. 1, B-10.

Money, J. (1987). Sin, sickness, or status? Homosexuality, gender identity, and psychoneuroendocrinology. *American Psychologist, 42,* 384–399.

Montemayor, P. (1983). Parents and adolescents in conflict: All families some of the time and some families most of the time. *Journal of Early Adolescence, 3,* 83–103.

Moore-Ede, M. C., et al. (1982). *The clocks that time us: Physiology of the circadian timing system.* Cambridge, MA: Harvard University Press.

More, B. E., & Fine, B. D. (1990). *Psychoanalytic terms and concepts.* New Haven, CT: Yale University Press.

Morgan, M. (1982). Television and adolescents' sex-role stereotypes: A longitudinal study. *Journal of Personality and Social Psychology, 43,* 947–955.

Moscovici, S. (1985). Social influence and conformity. In G. Lindzey & E. Aronson (Eds.), *Handbook of social psychology* (3rd ed.). New York: Random House.

Moscovici, S., & Mugny, G. (1983). Minority influence. In P. B. Paulus (Ed.), *Basic group processes.* New York: Springer-Verlag.

Mosher, D. L., & Anderson, R. D. (1986). Macho personality, sexual aggression, and reactions to guided imagery of

realistic rape. *Journal of Research in Personality, 20,* 77–94.

Motley, M. T. (1987, February). What I meant to say. *Psychology Today,* pp. 25–28.

Mucha, T. F., & Reinhardt, R. F. (1970). Conversion reactions in student aviators. *American Journal of Psychiatry, 127,* 493–497.

Muehlenhard, C. L., & Hollabaugh, L. C. (1988). Do women sometimes say no when they mean yes? The prevalence and correlates of women's token resistance to sex. *Journal of Personality and Social Psychology, 54,* 872–879.

Mueller, E., & Lucas, T. (1975). A developmental analysis of peer interaction among toddlers. In M. Lewis & L. A. Rosenblum (Eds.), *Friendship and peer relations.* New York: Wiley-Interscience.

Mullins, J. (1990, June 28 approx). Nightmare life of woman who can't remember anything. *National Enquirer,* p. 53.

Munnichs, U., Mussen, P., Olbrich, E., & Coleman, P. (Eds.). (1985). *Lifespan and change in a gerontological perspective.* New York: Academic Press.

Murphy, E. (1989, July 13). Townshend, tinnitus and rock and roll. *Rolling Stone.*

Murray, D. M., Matthews, K. A., Blake, S. M., Prineas, R., et al. (1986). Type A behavior in children: Demographic, behavioral, and physiological correlates. *Health Psychology, 5,* 159–169.

Murray, J. B. (1990). Nicotine as a psychoactive drug. *Journal of Psychology, 125,* 5–25.

Mussen, P. H., & Jones, M. C. (1957). Self-conceptions, motivations, and interpersonal attitudes of late- and early-maturing boys. *Child Development, 28,* 243–256.

Nahome, L., & Lawton, M. P. (1975). Similarity and propinquity in friendship formation. *Journal of Personality and Social Psychology, 32,* 205–213.

Nash, M. (1987). What, if anything, is regressed about hypnotic age regression? A review of the empirical literature. *Psychological Bulletin, 102,* 42–52.

Nathans, J., Davenport, C. M., Maumenee, I. H., Lewis, R. A., Hejtmancik, J. F., Litt, M., Lovrien, E., Weleber, R., Bachynski, B., Zwas, F., Klingaman, R., & Fishman, G. (1989, August 25). Molecular genetics of human blue cone monochromacy. *Science, 245,* 831–838.

Nathans, J., Piantanidu, T. P., Eddy, R. L., Shows, T. B., & Hogness, D. S. (1986, April 11). Molecular genetics of inherited variation in human color vision. *Science, 232,* 203–210.

National Institute of Alcohol Abuse and Alcoholism (*see* NIAAA)

National Institute of Drug Abuse (NIDA).

(1991). Drug survey done by U. of Michigan.

Natsoulas, T. (1983). Addendum to "Consciousness." *American Psychologist, 38,* 121–122.

Navon, R., & Proia, R. L. (1989, March 17). The mutations in Ashkenazi Jews with adult G(M2) gangliosidosis, the adult form of Tay-Sachs disease. *Science, 243,* 1471–1474.

Neely, K. (1990, October 4). Judas Priest gets off the hook. *Rolling Stone,* p. 39.

Neher, A. (1991). Maslow's theory of motivation: A critique. *Journal of Humanistic Psychology, 31,* 89–112.

Neisser, U. (1982). *Memory observed.* San Francisco: Freeman.

Neisser, U. (1991). A case of misplaced nostalgia. *American Psychologist, 46,* 34–36.

Neisser, U., & Harsch, N. (in press). Phantom flashbulbs: False recollections of hearing the news about Challenger. In E. Wonograd & U. Neisser (Eds.), *Flashbulb memories: Recalling the "Challenger" explosion and other disasters.* New York: Cambridge University Press.

New York Times, The. (1984, May 20). The new addicts. p. 50.

Newell, A. (1990). *Unified theories of cognition.* Cambridge, MA: Harvard University Press.

Newman, J. P., & Kosson, D. S. (1986). Passive avoidance learning in psychopathic and nonpsychopathic offenders. *Journal of Abnormal Psychology, 95,* 252–256.

NIAAA (National Institute on Alcohol Abuse and Alcoholism). (1990). *Alcohol and Health.* Washington, DC: Government Printing Office.

Nicolson, R. I., & Fawcett, A. J. (1990). Automaticity: A new framework for dyslexia research? *Cognition, 35,* 159–182.

NIDA (*see* National Institute of Drug Abuse)

Nisbett, R. E. (1968). Taste, deprivation, and weight determinants of eating behavior. *Journal of Personality and Social Psychology, 10,* 107–116.

Nisbett, R. E. (1972). Hunger, obesity and the ventromedial hypothalamus. *Psychological Review, 79,* 433–453.

Nogrady, H., McConkey, K. M., & Perry, C. (1985). Enhancing visual memory: Trying hypnosis, trying imagination, and trying again. *Journal of Abnormal Psychology, 94,* 105–204.

Nolen-Hoeksema, S., & Morrow, J. (1991). A prospective study of depression and posttraumatic stress symptoms after a natural disaster: The 1989 Loma Prieta earthquake. *Journal of Personality and Social Psychology, 61,* 115–121.

Novak, M. A., & Petto, A. J. (Eds.). (1991). Through the looking glass: Issues of psychological well-being in captive nonhuman primates. Washington, D.C.: American Psychological Association.

Novak, M. A., & Suomi, S. J. (1988). Psychological well-being of primates in captivity. *American Psychologist, 43,* 765–773.

Nowicki, S., & Duke, M. (1978). An examination of counseling variables within a social learning framework. *Journal of Counseling Psychology, 25,* 1–7.

Oberle, I., Rousseau, F., Heitz, D., Kretz, C., Devys, D., Hanauer, A., Boue, J., Bertheas, M. F., & Mandel, J. L. (1991, May 24). Instability of a 550-base pair DNA segment and abnormal methylzation in fragile X syndrome. *Science, 252,* 1097–1102.

O'Brien, C. P., et al. (1988). Pharmacological and behavioral treatments of cocaine dependence: Controlled studies. *Journal of Clinical Psychiatry, 49,* 17.

Office of Demographic, Employment, and Educational Research. (1991). *Race/Ethnicity of Faculty in U.S. Graduate Department of Psychology: 1989–90.* Washington, DC: American Psychological Association.

Office of Demographic, Employment, and Educational Research. (1991). *Demographic characteristics of members by type of APA membership.* Washington, DC: American Psychological Association.

Office of Technology Assessment. (1990). *Unconventional cancer treatments.* Washington, DC: Government Printing Office.

O'Hare, D., & Roscoe, S. (1990). *Flight-deck performance: The human factor.* Ames, IA: Iowa State University Press.

O'Keeffe, M. K., Nesselhof-Kendall, S., & Baum, A. (1990). Behavior and prevention of AIDS: Bases of research and intervention. *Personality and Social Psychology Bulletin, 16,* 166–180.

Olds, J., & Milner, P. (1954). Positive reinforcement produced by electrical stimulation of septal area and other regions of rat brain. *Journal of Comparative and Physiological Psychology, 47,* 411–427.

O'Leary, V., & Smith, D. (1988, August). *Sex makes a difference: Attributions for emotional cause.* Paper presented at the annual meeting of the American Psychological Association, Atlanta.

Olshansky, S. J., Carnes, B. A., & Cassel, C. (1990, November 2). In search of Methuselah: Estimating the upper limits to human longevity. *Science, 250,* 634–639.

O'Neill, M. (1990, April 1). Dieters, craving balance, are battling fears of food. *The New York Times, 139,* 1, 22.

Opler, L. A., Kay, S. R., Rosado, V., & Lindenmayer, J. P. (1984). Positive and negative syndromes in chronic schizophrenic inpatients. *Journal of Nervous and Mental Disease, 172,* 317–325.

Orlafsky, J., Marcia, J., & Lasser, I. (1973). Ego identity status and intimacy vs. isolation crisis of young adulthood. *Journal of Personality and Social Psychology, 27,* 211–219.

Orne, M. T., & Holland, C. C. (1968). On the ecological validity of laboratory deceptions. *International Journal of Psychiatry, 6,* 282–293.

Ornstein, P. A., & Naus, M. J. (1988). Effects of the knowledge base on children's memory strategies. In H. W. Reese (Ed.), *Advances in child development and behavior* (Vol. 19). New York: Academic.

Ornstein, R. E. (1977). *The psychology of consciousness* (2nd ed.). New York: Harcourt, Brace, Jovanovich.

Ortony, A., & Turner, T. J. (1990). What's basic about basic emotions? *Psychological Review, 97,* 315–331.

Orwin, R. G., & Condray, D. S. (1984). Smith and Glass' psychotherapy conclusions need further probing: On Landman and Dawes' re-analysis. *American Psychologist, 39,* 71–72.

Osborne, A. F. (1957). *Applied imagination.* New York: Scribner.

Osherson, D. (Ed.). (1990). *Thinking.* Cambridge, MA.: MIT Press.

Oskamp. S. (1984). *Applied social psychology.* Englewood Cliffs, NJ: Prentice-Hall.

Oskamp, S. (1988). Nontraditional employment opportunities for applied psychologists. *American Psychologist, 43,* 484–485.

Ottoson, D. (Ed.). (1987). *Duality and unity of the brain.* London: Macmillan.

Owens, J., Bower, G. H., & Black, J. (1979). The "soap opera" effect in story recall. *Memory and Cognition, 7,* 185–191.

Paalman, M. (Ed.). (1990). *Promoting safer sex: Prevention of sexual transmission of AIDS and other STD.* Amsterdam: Swets & Zeitlinger.

Paivio, A. (1971). *Imagery and verbal processes.* New York: Holt.

Palca, J. (1989, July 28). Sleep researchers awake to possibilities. *Science, 245,* 351–352.

Palca, J. (1991, April 19). The sobering geography of AIDS. *Science, 252,* 372–373.

Palladino, J. J., & Carducci, B. J. (1984). Students' knowledge of sleep and dreams. *Teaching of Psychology, 11,* 189–191.

Palmer, S. F. (1975). The effects of contextual scenes on the identification of objects. *Memory and Cognition, 3,* 519–526.

Papalia, D., & Olds, S. (1986). *Human development* (3rd ed.). New York: McGraw-Hill.

Papini, M. R., & Bitterman, M. E. (1990). The role of contingency in classical conditioning. *Psychological Review, 97,* 396–403.

Parke, R. D. (1981). *Fathers.* Cambridge, MA: Harvard University Press.

Parlee, M. B. (1979, October). The friendship bond. *Psychology Today, 13,* 43–45.

Parmentier, M., Libert, F., Schurmans, S., Schiffman, S., Lefort, A., Eggerlek, D., Ledent, C., Mollerean, C., Gerard, C., Perret, J., Grootegoed, A., & Vassart, G. (1992, January 30). Expression of members of the putative olfactory receptor gene family in mammalian germ cells. *Nature, 355,* 453–456.

Parsons, T. (1975). The sick role and the role of the physician reconsidered. *Milbank Memorial Fund Quarterly/Health and Society, 53,* 257–278.

Paterson, R. J., & Neufeld, R. W. J. (1987). Clear danger: Situational determinants of the appraisal of threat. *Psychological Bulletin, 101,* 404–416.

Patrick, C. J., & Iacono, W. G. (1991). Validity of the control question polygraph test: The problem of sampling bias. *Journal of Applied Psychology, 76,* 229–238.

Pavlides, C., & Winson, J. (1989). Influences of hippocampal place cell firing in the awake state on the activity of these cells during subsequent sleep episodes. *Journal of Neuroscience, 9,* 2907–2918.

Pavlidis, G. T., & Fisher, D. F. (1986). *Dyslexia: Its neuropsychology and treatment.* New York: Wiley.

Pavlov, I. P. (1927). *Conditioned reflexes.* London: Oxford University Press.

Payne, D. G. (1986). Hyperamnesia for pictures and words: Testing the recall level hypothesis. *Journal of Experimental Psychology: Learning, Memory, and Cognition, 12,* 16–29.

Pedersen, P. B. (1992). Going beyond the "politically correct" debate about culture. Review of J. G. Ponterotto & J. M. Casas, *Handbook of racial/ethnic minority counseling research. Contemporary Psychology, 37,* 74.

Penfield, W., & Rasmussen, T. (1950). *The cerebral cortex of man.* New York: Macmillan.

Pennebaker, N. N., Burnam, M. A., Schaeffer, N. A., & Harper, D. C. (1977). Lack of control as a determinant of perceived physical symptoms. *Journal of Personality and Social Psychology, 35,* 167–174.

Peper, R. J., & Mayer, R. E. (1978). Note taking as a generative activity. *Journal of Educational Psychology, 70,* 514–522.

Peplau, L. A., Rubin, Z., & Hill, C. T.

(1977). Sexual intimacy in dating relationships. *Journal of Social Issues, 2,* 86–109.

Perdue, C. W., Dovidio, J. F., Gurtman, M. B., & Tyler, R. B. (1990). Us and them: Social categorization and the process of intergroup bias. *Journal of Personality and Social Psychology, 59,* 475–486.

Pereira-Smith, O., Smith, J., et al. (1988, August). Paper presented at the annual meeting of the International Genetics Congress, Toronto.

Perkins, D. N. (1983). Why the human perceiver is a bad machine. In J. Beck, B. Hope, & A. Rosenfeld (Eds.), *Human and machine vision.* New York: Academic Press.

Perkins, D. N., Lochhead, J., & Bishop, J. (Eds. (1987). *Thinking: The Second International Conference.* Hillsdale, NJ: Erlbaum.

Perlmutter, M., & Mitchell, D. B. (1986). The appearance and disappearance of age differences in adult memory. In I. M. Craik & S. Trehub (Eds.), *Aging and cognitive processes.* New York: Plenum.

Perls, F. S. (1967). Group vs. individual therapy. *ETC: A Review of General Semantics, 34,* 306–312.

Perls, F. S. (1970). *Gestalt therapy now: Therapy, techniques, applications.* Palo Alto, CA: Science and Behavior Books.

Persons, J. B. (1991). Psychotherapy outcome studies do not accurately represent current models of psychotherapy: A proposed remedy. *American Psychologist, 46,* 99–106.

Pervin, L. A. (1985). Personality: Current controversies, issues and directions. *Annual Review of Psychology,* p. 36.

Peter, J. P., & Olson, J. C. (1987). *Consumer behavior.* Homewood, IL: Irwin.

Peterson, A. C. (1988, September). Those gangly years. *Psychology Today,* pp. 28–34.

Peterson, C., & Raps, C. S. (1984). Helplessness and hospitalization: More remarks. *Journal of Personality and Social Psychology, 46,* 82–83.

Peterson, C., Seligman, M. E. P., & Vaillant, G. E. (1988). Pessimistic explanatory style is a risk factor for physical illness: A thirty-five-year longitudinal study. *Journal of Personality and Social Psychology, 55,* 23–27.

Peterson, D. R. (1991). Connection and disconnection of research and practice in the education of professional psychologists. *American Psychologist, 46,* 422–429.

Peterson, K. C., Prout, M. F., & Schwarz, R. A. (1991). *Post-traumatic stress disorder: A clinician's guide.* New York: Plenum.

Peterson, L. R., & Peterson, M. J. (1959). Short-term retention of individual items. *Journal of Experimental Psychology, 58,* 193–198.

Petitto, L. A., & Marentette, P. F. (1991, March 22). Babbling in the manual mode: Evidence for the ontogeny of language. *Science, 251,* 1493–1496.

Petri, H. L. (1991). *Motivation: Theory, research, and applications* (3rd ed.). Belmont, CA: Wadsworth.

Pettingale, K. W., Morris, T., Greer, S., & Haybittle, J. L. (1985). Mental attitudes to cancer: An additional prognostic factor. *Lancet,* p. 750.

Petty, M. M., McGee, G. W., & Cavender, J. W. (1984). A meta-analysis of the relationships between individual job satisfaction and individual performance. *Academy of Management, 9,* 712–721.

Petty, R. E., & Cacioppo, J. T. (1977). Cognitive responding and resistance to persuasion. *Journal of Personality and Social Psychology, 35,* 645–655.

Petty, R. E., & Cacioppo, J. T. (1984). The effects of involvement on responses to argument quantity and quality: Central and peripheral routes to persuasion. *Journal of Personality and Social Psychology, 46,* 69–81.

Petty, R. E., & Cacioppo, J. T. (1986). The elaboration likelihood model of persuasion. In L. Berkowitz (Ed.), *Advances in Experimental Social Psychology* (Vol. 19). New York: Academic.

Phillips, D., McCartney, K., & Scarr, S. (1987). Child-care quality and children's social development. *Developmental Psychology, 23,* 537–543.

Phillips, R. D., Wagner, S. H., Fells, C. A., & Lynch, M. (1990). Do infants recognize emotion in facial expressions?: Categorical and "metaphorical" evidence. *Infant Behavior and Development, 13,* 71–84.

Pi-Sunyer, F. X. (1987). Exercise effects on caloric intake. In R. Wurtman (Ed.), *Obesity.* New York: New York Academy of Science.

Piaget, J. (1970). Piaget's theory. In P. H. Mussen (Ed.), *Carmichael's manual of child psychology* (Vol. 1, 3rd ed.). New York: Wiley.

Piaget, J., & Inhelder, B. (1958). *The growth of logical thinking from childhood to adolescence.* (A. Parsons & S. Seagrin Trans.). New York: Basic Books.

Piccione, C., Hilgard, E. R., & Zimbardo, P. G. (1989). On the degree of stability of measured hypnotizability over a 25-year period. *Journal of Personality and Social Psychology, 56,* 289–295.

Piliavin, J. A., & Piliavin, I. M. (1972). Effect of blood on reactions to a victim. *Journal of Personality and Social Psychology, 23,* 353–362.

Pillemer, D. B. (1990). Clarifying the flashbulb memory concept: Comment on McCloskey, Wible, and Cohen (1988). *Journal of Experimental Psychology: General, 119,* 92–96.

Pinker, S. (1990). Language acquisition. In D. N. Osherson & H. Lasnik (Eds.), *Language.* Cambridge, MA: MIT Press.

Pisoni, D., & Martin, C. (1989, August). Effects of alcohol on the acoustic-phonetic properties of speech: Perceptual and acoustic analyses. *Alcoholism: Clinical and Experimental Research, 13,* 577–587.

Plomin, R. (1989). Environment and genes: Determinants of behavior. *American Psychologist, 44,* 105–111.

Plomin, R. (1990, April 13). The role of inheritance in behavior. *Science, 248,* 183–188.

Plous, S. (1991). An attitude survey of animal rights activists. *Psychological Science, 2,* 194–196.

Plutchik, R. (1980). *Emotion, a psychoevolutionary synthesis.* New York: Harper & Row.

Plutchik, R. (1984). Emotion. In K. Scherer & P. Ekman (Eds.), *Approaches to emotion.* Hillsdale, NJ: Erlbaum.

Polivy, J., & Herman, L. P. (1985). Dieting and binging: A causal analysis. *American Psychologist, 40,* 193–201.

Pollack, A. (1987, September 15). More human than ever, computer is learning to learn. *The New York Times,* pp. C-1, C-6.

Pollock, D. A., Rhodes, P., Boyle, C. A., Decoufle, P., & McGee, D. L. (1990). Estimating the number of suicides among Vietnam veterans. *American Journal of Psychiatry, 147,* 772–776.

Pomerleau, O. F., Adkins, D., & Pertschuk, M. (1978). Predictors of outcome and recidivism in smoking cessation treatment. *Addictive Behaviors, 3,* 65–70.

Pomerleau, O. F., & Pomerleau, C. S. (1989). A biobehavioral perspective on smoking. In T. Ney & A. Gale (Eds.), *Smoking and human behavior.* New York: Wiley.

Popham, S. M., & Holden, R. R. (1991). Psychometric properties of MMPI factor scales. *Personality and Individual Differences, 12,* 513–518.

Porter, R. H., Cernich, J. M., & McLaughlin, F. J. (1983). Maternal recognition of neonates through olfactory cues. *Physiology and Behavior, 30,* 151–154.

Posner, M. I., & Presti, D. E. (1987). Selective attention and cognitive control. *Trends in Neurosciences, 10,* 13–17.

Potter, M. C. (1990). Remembering. In D. N. Osherson & E. E. Smith (Eds.), *Thinking.* Cambridge, MA: MIT Press.

Potterfield, P. (1991). Trapped on Chimney Rock. *Reader's Digest, 138,* 169–197.

Power, T. G., & Parke, R. D. (1982). Play as a context for early learning: Lab and home analyses. In L. M. Laosa

& I. E. Sigal (Eds.), *The family as a learning environment.* New York: Plenum.

Pressley, M. (1987). Are keyword method effects limited to slow presentation rates? An empirically based reply to Hall and Fuson (1986). *Journal of Educational Psychology, 79,* 333–335.

Pressley, M., & Levin, J. R. (1983). *Cognitive strategy research: Psychological foundations.* New York: Springer-Verlag.

Pribram, K. H. (1984). Emotion: A neurobehavioral analysis. In K. R. Scherer & P. Ekman (Eds.), *Approaches to emotion,* Hillsdale, NJ: Erlbaum.

Price, L., Rust, R., & Kumar, V. (1986). In J. Olson & K. Sentis (Eds.), *Advertising and consumer psychology* (Vol. 3). New York: Praeger.

Pride, W. M., & Ferrell, O. C. (1987). *Marketing.* Boston: Houghton-Mifflin.

Prien, R. F. (1983). Lithium and the long-term maintenance treatment of tricyclic antidepressant drugs and therapeutic response. In P. J. Clayton & J. E. Barret (Eds.), *Treatment of depression: Old controversies and new approaches* (pp. 105–114). New York: Raven Press.

Prince, R. J., & Guastello, S. J. (1990). The Barnum effect in a computerized Rorschach interpretation system. *Journal of Personality, 124,* 217–222.

Pryor, J. B., Reeder, G. D., & McManus, J. A. (1991). Fear and loathing in the workplace: Reactions to AIDS-infected coworkers. *Personality and Social Psychology Bulletin, 17,* 133–139.

PsychINFO. (1991, January). The Psych-INFO Basic Workshop. Washington, DC: American Psychological Association. *Psychological Bulletin, 107,* 210–214.

Quinn, M. (1990, January 29). Don't aim that pack at us. *Time,* p. 60.

Rachlin, H. (1990). *Context in classical and instrumental conditioning.* G. Stanley Hall Lecture presented at the annual meeting of the American Psychological Association, Boston.

Rachman, S., & Hodgson, R. (1980). *Obsessions and compulsions.* Englewood Cliffs, NJ: Prentice-Hall.

Ragland, D. R. (1988, January 14). Type A behavior and mortality from coronary heart disease. *New England Journal of Medicine, 318,* 65.

Ragland, D. R., & Brand, R. J. (1988). Type A behavior and morality from coronary heart disease. *New England Journal of Medicine, 318,* 65–69.

Ragozin, A. S. (1980). Attachment behavior of day care children: Naturalistic and laboratory observations. *Child Development, 51,* 409–415.

Rahe, R. H., & Arthur, R. J. (1978). Life change and illness studies: Past history and future directions. *Human Stress, 4,* 3–15.

Rajecki, D. W. (1989). *Attitudes* (2nd ed.). Sunderland, MA: Sinauer.

Rasmussen, J. (1981). Models of mental strategies in process control. In J. Rasmussen & W. Rouse (Eds.), *Human detection and diagnosis of system failures.* New York: Plenum.

Ravussin, E., Lillioja, S., Knowler, W. C., Christin, L., Freymond, D., Abbott, W. G. H., Boyce, V., Howard, B. V., & Bogardus, C. (1988, February 25). Reduced rate of energy expenditure as a risk factor for body-weight gain. *New England Journal of Medicine, 318,* 467–472.

Redfield, C. A., & Steuck, K. (1991). The future of intelligent tutoring systems. In Burns, H., Parlett, J. W., & Redfield, C. L. (Eds.), *Intelligent tutoring systems: Evolutions in design.* Hillsdale, NJ: Erlbaum.

Reed, S. K. (1988). *Cognition: Theories and applications* (2nd ed.). Monterey, CA: Brooks/Cole.

Regier, D. A., Boyd, J. H., Burke, J. D., Jr., Rae, D. S., Myers, J. K., Kramer, M., Robins, L. N., George, L. K., Karno, M., & Locke, B. Z. (1988). One-month prevalence of mental disorders in the United States. *Archives of General Psychiatry, 45,* 977–986.

Register, A. C., Beckham, J. C., May, J. G., & Gustafson, D. F. (1991). Stress inoculation biliotherapy in the treatment of test anxiety. *Journal of Counseling Psychology, 38,* 115–119.

Reich, P. A. (1986). *Language development.* Englewood Cliffs, NJ: Prentice-Hall.

Reigier, D. A., Myers, J. K., Kramer, M., Robins, L. N., Blazer, D. G., Hough, R. L., Eaton, W. W., & Lock, B. Z. (1984). The NIMH epidemiological catchment area program. *Archives of General Psychiatry, 41,* 934–941.

Reis, H. T., Wheeler, L., Spiegel, N., Kerris, M. H., Nezlek, J., & Perri, M. (1982). Physical attractiveness in social interaction: II. Why does appearance affect social experience? *Journal of Personality and Social Psychology, 43,* 979–996.

Reis, S. M. (1989). Reflections on policy affecting the education of gifted and talented students. *American Psychologist, 44,* 399–408.

Reisenzein, R. (1983). The Schachter theory of emotion: Two decades later. *Psychological Bulletin, 94,* 239–264.

Reiss, B. F. (1980). Psychological tests in homosexuality. In J. Marmor (Ed.), *Homosexual behavior* (pp. 296–311). New York: Basic Books.

Reiss, I. L. (1960). *Premarital sexual standards in America.* New York: Free Press.

Reitman, J. S. (1965). *Cognition and thought.* New York: Wiley.

Rescorla, R. A. (1988). Pavlovian conditioning: It's not what you think it is. *American Psychologist, 43,* 151–160.

Reuman, D. A., Alwin, D. F., & Veroff, J. (1984). Assessing the validity of the achievement motive in the presence of random measurement error. *Journal of Personality and Social Psychology, 47,* 1347–1362.

Rexroat, C., & Shehan, C. (1987). The family life cycle and spouses' time in housework. *Journal of Marriage and the Family, 49,* 737–750.

Reynolds, R. I., & Takooshian, H. (1988, January). Where were you August 8, 1985? *Bulletin of the Psychonomic Society, 26,* 23–25.

Rhodes, N., & Wood, W. (1992). Self-esteem and intelligence affect influenceability: The mediating role of message reception. *Psychological Bulletin, 111,* 156–171.

Rhue, J. W., & Lynn, S. J. (1987). Fantasy-proneness and psychopathology. *Journal of Personality and Social Psychology, 53,* 327–336.

Rice, B. (1988, March) The selling of life-styles. *Psychology Today, 22,* 46–50.

Rice, M. L. (1989). Children's language acquisition. *American Psychologist, 44,* 149–156.

Riegel, K. F., & Riegel, R. M. (1972). Development, drop, and death. *Developmental Psychology, 6,* 306–319.

Rinn, W. E. (1984). The neuropsychology of facial expression: A review of neurological and psychological mechanisms for producing facial expressions. *Psychological Bulletin, 95,* 52–77.

Rinn, W. E. (1991). Neuropsychology of facial expression. In R. S. Feldman & B. Rime (Eds.), *Fundamentals of nonverbal behavior.* Cambridge, England: Cambridge University Press.

Rips, L. J. (1990). Reasoning. *Annual Review of Psychology, 41,* 321–353.

Ritzler, B., & Rosenbaum, G. (1974). Proprioception in schizophrenics and normals: Effects of stimulus intensity and interstimulus interval. *Journal of Abnormal Psychology, 83,* 106–111.

Rivers, P. C. (Ed.). (1986). Alcohol and addictive behavior. *Nebraska Symposium on Motivation, 34,* 1–346.

Rizley, R. C., & Rescorla, R. A. (1972). Associations in higher order conditioning and sensory pre-conditioning. *Journal of Comparative and Physiological Psychology, 81,* 1–11.

Robbins, M., & Jensen, G. D. (1978). Multiple orgasm in males. *Journal of Sex Research, 14,* 21–26.

Robbins, T. W. (1988). Arresting memory decline. *Nature, 336,* 207–208.

Robbins, W. J. (1929). *Growth.* New Haven, CT: Yale University Press.

Roberts, L. (1988a, January 1). Zeroing in on the sex switch. *Science, 239,* 21–23.

Roberts, L. (1988b, July 8). Vietnam's psychological toll. *Science, 241,* 159–161.

Roberts, R. (1989). Are neural nets like the human brain? *Science, 243,* 481–482.

Roberts, T. (1991). Gender and the influence of evaluations on self-assessments in achievement settings. *Psychological Bulletin, 109,* 297–308.

Robins, L. N., Locke, B. Z., & Regier, D. A. (1991). An overview of psychiatric disorders in America. In L. N. Robins & D. A. Regier (Eds.), *Psychiatric disorders in America.* New York: Free Press.

Robins, L. N., & Regier, D. A. (Eds.). (1991). *Psychiatric disorders in America.* New York: Free Press.

Rock, I. (1983). *The logic of perception.* Cambridge, MA: MIT Press.

Rodin, J. (1981). Current status of the internal-external hypothesis of obesity: What went wrong? *American Psychologist, 34,* 361–372.

Rodin, J. (1985). Insulin levels, hunger, and food intake: An example of feedback loops in body-weight regulation. *Health Psychology, 4,* 1–18.

Rodin, J. (1986, September 19). Aging and health: Effects of the sense of control. *Science, 233,* 1271–1276.

Rodin, J., & Janis, I. L. (1979). The social power of health care practitioners as agents of change. *The Journal of Social Issues, 35,* 60–81.

Rodin, J., & Langer, E. (1977). Long-term effects of a control-relevant intervention with the institutionalized aged. *Journal of Personality and Social Psychology, 35,* 897–902.

Rodin, J., & Salovey, P. (1989). Health psychology. *Annual Review of Psychology, 40,* 533–579.

Roediger, H. L., III. (1990). Implicit memory: Retention without remembering. *American Psychologist, 45,* 1043–1056.

Roediger, H. L., Weldon, M. S., & Challis, B. H. (1989). Explaining dissociations between implicit and explicit measures of retention: A processing account. In H. L. Roediger & F. I. M. Craik (Eds.), *Varieties of memory and consciousness: Essays in honour of Endel Tulving.* Hillsdale, NJ: Erlbaum.

Rogers, C. R. (1951). *Client-centered therapy.* Boston: Houghton Mifflin.

Rogers, C. R. (1971). A theory of personality. In S. Maddi (Ed.), *Perspectives on personality.* Boston: Little, Brown.

Rogers, C. R. (1980). *A way of being.* Boston: Houghton Mifflin.

Rogers, M. (1988a, February 15). The return of 3-D movies—on TV. *Newsweek,* pp. 60–62.

Rogers, M. (1988b, October 3). Here comes hypermedia. *Newsweek,* pp. 44–45.

Rogers, M. (1991, November 4). No more home sweet home. *Newsweek, 118,* 34–35.

Rogers, R. (1987). APA's position on the insanity defense. *American Psychologist, 42,* 840–848.

Rohter, L. (1987, July 21). Inside the operating room: A day of bold brain surgery. *The New York Times,* pp. C-17, C-20.

Roitblat, H. L. (1987). *Introduction to comparative cognition.* New York: Freeman.

Rokeach, M. (1971). Long-range experimental modification of values, attitudes, and behavior. *American Psychologist, 26,* 453–459.

Rolls, B. J., Wood, R. J., & Rolls, E. T. (1980). Thirst: The initiation, maintenance, and termination of drinking. In J. M. Sprague & Alan N. Epstein (Eds.), *Progress in psychobiology and physiological psychology* (Vol. 9). New York: Academic.

Rorschach, H. (1924). *Psychodiagnosis: A diagnostic test based on perception.* New York: Grune & Stratton.

Rosch, E. (1974). Linguistic relativity. In A. Silverstein (Ed.), *Human communication: Theoretical explorations* (pp. 95–121). New York: Halstead.

Rosch, E. (1975). Cognitive representations of semantic categories. *Journal of Experimental Psychology—General, 104,* 192–233.

Rose, R. J., Koskenvuo, M., Kaprio, J., Sarna, S., & Langinvainio, H. (1988). Shared genes, shared experiences, and similarity of personality: Data from 14,288 adult Finnish co-twins. *Journal of Personality and Social Psychology, 54,* 161–171.

Rosen, G. M. (1987). Self-help treatment books and the commercialization of psychotherapy. *American Psychologist, 42,* 46–51.

Rosenhan, D. L. (1973). On being sane in insane places. *Science, 179,* 250–258.

Rosenhan, D. L. (1975). The contextual nature of psychiatric diagnosis. *Journal of Abnormal Psychology, 84,* 462–474.

Rosenman, R. H. (1990). Type A behavior pattern: A personal overview. *Journal of Social Behavior and Personality, 5,* 1–24.

Rosenmon, R. H., Brond, R. J., Sholtz, R. I., & Friedman, M. (1976). Multivariate prediction of coronary heart disease during 8.5 year follow-up in the western collaborative group study. *American Journal of Cardiology, 37,* 903–910.

Rosenthal, E. (1991, April 23). Pulses of light give astronauts new rhythms. *New York Times,* C1, C8.

Rosenzweig, M. R., & Leiman, A. L. (1989). *Physiological psychology.* (2nd ed.). New York: Random House.

Roskies, E. (1990). Type A intervention: Where do we go from here? *Journal of Social Behavior and Personality, 5,* 419–438.

Ross, C. A. (1989). *Multiple personality disorder: Diagnosis, clinical features and treatment.* New York: Wiley.

Ross, L., Greene, D., & House, P. (1977). The false consensus effect: An egocentric bias in social perception and attribution processes. *Journal of Experimental Social Psychology, 13,* 279–301.

Rossi, P. H. (1990). The old homeless and the new homelessness in historical perspective. *American Psychologist, 45,* 954–959.

Rothblum, E. D. (1990). Women and weight: Fad and fiction. *Journal of Psychology, 124,* 5–24.

Rothenberg, R. (1990, October 5). Surveys proliferate, but answers dwindle. *The New York Times.* pp. A-1, D-4.

Rouse, W. B., & Morris, N. M. (1986). On looking into the black box: Prospects and limits in the search for mental models. *Psychological Bulletin, 100,* 349–363.

Routtenberg, A., & Lindy, J. (1965). Effects of the availability of rewarding septal and hypothalmic stimulation on bar pressing for food under conditions of deprivation. *Journal of Comparative and Physiological Psychology, 60,* 158–161.

Rowe, J. W., & Kahn, R. L. (1987, July 10). Human aging: Usual and successful. *Science, 237,* 143–149.

Rowlison, R. T., & Felner, R. D. (1988). Major life events, hassles, and adaptation in adolescence: Confounding in the conceptualization and measurement of life stress and adjustment revisited. *Journal of Personality and Social Psychology, 55,* 432–444.

Royer, J. M., & Feldman, R. S. (1984). *Educational psychology: Applications and theory.* New York: Knopf.

Rozin, P. (1977). The significance of learning mechanisms in food selection: Some biology, psychology and sociology of science. In L. M. Barker, M. R. Best, & M. Donijan (Eds.), *Learning mechanism in food selection.* Waco: TX: Baylor University Press.

Ruan, F. F. (1991). *Sex in China: Studies in sexology in Chinese culture.* New York: Plenum.

Rubeck, R. B., Dabbs, J. M., Jr., & Hopper, C. H. (1984). The process of brainstorming: An analysis with individual and group vocal parameters. *Journal of Personality and Social Psychology, 47,* 558–567.

Rubenstein, C. (1982, July). Psychology's fruit flies. *Psychology Today,* pp. 83–84.

Rubin, D. C. (1985, September). The subtle deceiver: Recalling our past. *Psychology Today, 19,* 39–46.

Rubin, D. C. (1986). *Autobiographical memory.* Cambridge, England: Cambridge University Press.

Rubin, Z. (1970). Measurement of romantic love. *Journal of Personality and Social Psychology, 16,* 265–273.

Rubin, Z. (1973). *Liking and loving.* New York: Holt.

Ruble, D. N., Fleming, A. S., Hackel, L. S., & Stangor, C. (1988). Changes in the marital relationship during the transition to first-time motherhood: Effects of violated expectations concerning division of household labor. *Journal of Personality and Social Psychology, 55,* 78–87.

Runco, M. A. (1991). *Divergent thinking.* Norwood, NJ: Ablex.

Rushton, J. P., Fulker, D. W., Neale, M. C., Nias, D. K. B., & Eysenck, H. J. (1986). Altruism and aggression: The heritability of individual differences. *Journal of Personality and Social Psychology, 50,* 1192–1198.

Russell, D. E. H., & Howell, N. (1983). The prevalence of rape in the United States revisited. *Signs, 8,* 688–695.

Russell, J. A. (1991). In defense of a prototype approach to emotion concepts. *Journal of Personality and Social Psychology, 60,* 37–47.

Russell, M. A. H. (1979). Tobacco dependence: Is nicotine rewarding or aversive? In N. A. Krasnegor (Ed.), *Cigarette smoking as a dependence process* (NIDA Research Monograph No. 23, U.S. Department of Health, Education, and Welfare, Publication No. [ADM] 79-800). Rockville, MD: National Institute on Drug Abuse.

Russo, D. C., Carr, E. G., & Lovaas, O. I. (1980). Self-injury in pediatric populations. *Comprehensive handbook of behavioral medicine: Vol. 3. Extended applications and issues.* Holliswood, NY: Spectrum.

Russo, N. (1981). In L. T. Benjamin, Jr., & K. D. Lowman (Eds.), *Activities handbook for the teaching of psychology.* Washington, DC: American Psychological Association.

Russo, N. F., & Denmark, F. L. (1987). Contribution of women to psychology. *Annual Review of Psychology, 38,* 279–298.

Rutter, M. (1982). Social-emotional consequences of day-care for preschool children. In E. F. Zigler & E. W. Gordon (Eds.), *Day-care: Scientific and social policy issues.* Boston: Auburn House.

Ryan, M. (1991, January 27). I am not alone. *Parade,* p. 14.

Sabourin, M. E., Cutcomb, S. D., Crawford, H. J., & Pribram, K. (1990). EEG correlates of hypnotic susceptibility and hypnotic trance: Spectral analysis and coherence. *International Journal of Psychophysiology, 10,* 125–142.

Sackheim, H. A. (1985, June). The case for E.C.T. *Psychology Today,* pp. 36–40.

Salber, E. J., Freeman, H. E., & Abelin, T. (1968). Needed research on smoking: Lessons from the Newton study. In E. F. Borgatta & R. R. Evans (Eds.), *Smoking, health, and behavior.* Chicago: Aldine.

Salovey, P., & Mayer, J. D. (1990). Emotional intelligence. *Imag. Cognition and Personality, 9,* 185–211.

Salovey, P., Mayer, J. D., & Rosenhan, D. L. (1991). Mood and helping: Mood as a motivator of helping and helping as a regulator of mood. In M. S. Clark (Ed.), *Prosocial behavior.* Newbury Park, CA: Sage.

Samaritans. (1989). Annual report, 1989. Boston, MA: Samaritans.

Sanders, C. M. (1988). Risk factors in bereavement outcome. *Journal of Social Issues, 44,* 97–111.

Sanders, C. M. (1989). *Grief: The mourning after.* New York: Wiley.

Sanders, M. S., & McCormick, E. J. (1987). *Human factors in engineering and design* (6th ed.). New York: McGraw-Hill.

Sarafino, E. P. (1990). *Health psychology: Biopsychosocial interactions.* New York: Wiley.

Sarasan, S., Johnson, J. H., & Siegel, J. M. (1978). Assessing the impact of life changes: Development of the Life Experiences Survey. *Journal of Consulting and Clinical Psychology, 46,* 932–946.

Sarason, I. G. (1976). A modeling and informational approach to delinquency. In E. Ribes-Inesta & A. Bandura (Eds.), *Analysis of delinquency and aggression.* Hillsdale, NJ: Erlbaum.

Sarason, I. G., Sarason, B. R., & Pierce, G. R. (1990). Anxiety, cognitive interference, and performance. *Journal of Social Behavior and Personality, 5,* 1–18.

Saul, E. V., & Kass, T. S. (1969). Study of anticipated anxiety in a medical school setting. *Journal of Medical Education, 44,* 526.

Savage-Rumbaugh, S. (1987). Communication, symbolic communication, and language: Reply to Seidenberg and Petitto. *Journal of Experimental Psychology: General, 116,* 288–292.

Savage-Rumbaugh, S., McDonald, K., Sevcik, R., Hopkins, W., & Rupert, E. (1986). Spontaneous symbol acquisition and communicative use by pygmy chimpanzees (*Pan paniscus*). *Journal of Experimental Psychology: General, 115,* 211–235.

Sawaguchi, T., & Goldman-Rakic, P. S. (1991, February 22). D1 dopamine receptors in prefrontal cortex: Involvement in working memory. *Science, 251,* 947–950.

Saxe, L., Dougherty, D., & Cross, T. (1985). The validity of polygraph testing. *American Psychologist, 40,* 355–366.

Saywitz, K., & Goodman, G. (1990). Unpublished study reported in Goleman, D. (1990, November 6). Doubts rise on children as witnesses. *The New York Times,* pp. C-1, C-6.

Scarr, S. (1986, August). *Child-care decisions and working mothers' dilemmas.* Address given at the annual meeting of the American Psychological Association, Washington, DC.

Scarr, S., & Carter-Saltzman, L. (1982). Genetics and intelligence. In R. J. Sternberg (Ed.), *Handbook of human intelligence* (pp. 792–896). Cambridge, England: Cambridge University Press.

Scarr, S., Phillips, D., & McCartney, K. (1989). Working mothers and their families. *American Psychologist, 44,* 1402–1409.

Scarr, S., Phillips, D., & McCartney, K. (1990). Facts, fantasies and the future of child care in the United States. *Psychological Science, 1,* 26–35.

Scarr, S., & Weinberg, R. A. (1976). I.Q. test performance of black children adopted by white families. *American Psychologist, 3,* 726–739.

Schab, F. R. (1990). Odors and the remembrance of things past. *Journal of Experimental Psychology: Learning, Memory, and Cognition, 16,* 648–655.

Schab, F. R. (1991). Odor memory: Taking stock. *Psychological Bulletin, 109,* 242–251.

Schachter, S. (1971). Some extraordinary facts about obese humans and rats. *American Psychologist, 26,* 129–144.

Schachter, S., Goldman, R., & Gordon, A. (1968). Effects of fear, food deprivation, and obesity on eating. *Journal of Personality and Social Psychology, 10,* 91–97.

Schachter, S., & Singer, J. E. (1962). Cognitive, social, and physiological determinants of emotional state. *Psychological Review, 69,* 379–399.

Schacter, D. L. (1983). Amnesia observed: Remembering and forgetting in a natural environment. *Journal of Abnormal Psychology, 92,* 236–242.

Schacter, D. L. (1990). Perceptual representation systems and implicit memory: Toward a resolution of the multiple memory systems debate. In A. Diamond (Ed.), *Development and neural bases of high cognition.* New York: Annals of the New York Academy of Sciences.

Schaie, K. W. (1985). *Longitudinal studies of psychological development.* New York: Guilford Press.

Schaie, K. W. (1991). Developmental designs revisited. In S. H. Cohen & H. W. Reese (Eds.), *Life-span developmental psychology: Methodological innovations.* Hillsdale, NJ: Erlbaum.

Schaie, K. W., & Willis, S. L. (1985, August). *Differential ability decline and its remediation in late adulthood.* Paper presented at annual meeting of the American Psychological Association, Los Angeles.

Scheff, T. J. (1985). The primacy of

affect. *American Psychologist, 40,* 849–850.

Scheier, M. F. (1986). Coping with stress: Divergent strategies of optimists and pessimists. *Journal of Personality and Social Psychology, 51,* 1257–1264.

Schellhardt, T. D. (1990, September 19). It still isn't dad at home with sick kids. *The Wall Street Journal,* p. B-1.

Schellhardt, T. D. (1991, October 18). Attractiveness aids men more than women. *Wall Street Journal,* B1.

Schelling, T. C. (1992, January 4). Addictive drugs: The cigarette experience. *Science, 255,* 430–433.

Scher, S. J., & Cooper, J. (1989). Motivational basis of dissonance: The singular role of behavioral consequences. *Journal of Personality and Social Psychology, 56,* 899–906.

Scherer, K. R. (1984). Les motions: Fonctions et composantes. [Emotions: Functions and components.] *Cahiers de psychologie cognitive, 4,* 9–39.

Schickedanz, J. A., Schickedanz, D. I., & Forsyth, P. D. (1982). *Toward understanding children.* Boston: Little, Brown.

Schindenhette, S. (1990, February 5). After the verdict, solace for none. *People Weekly, 33,* 76–80.

Schmeck, H. M., Jr. (1987, December 29). New light on the chemistry of dreams. *The New York Times,* pp. C-1, C-2.

Schneider, J. A., O'Leary, A., & Agras, W. S. (1987). The role of perceived self-efficacy in recovery from bulimia: A preliminary examination. *Behaviour Research and Therapy, 25,* 429–432.

Schneider, S. F. (1990). Psychology at a crossroads. *American Psychologist, 45,* 521–529.

Schneiderman, N. (1983). Animal behavior models of coronary heart disease. In D. S. Krantz, A. Baum, & J. E. Singer (Eds.), *Handbook of psychology and health* (Vol. 3). Hillsdale, NJ: Erlbaum.

Schneidman, E. S. (1987). A psychological approach to suicide. In G. R. VandenBos & B. K. Bryant (Eds.), *Cataclysms, crises, and catastrophes: Psychology in action.* Washington, DC: American Psychological Association.

Schoeneman, T. J., & Rubanowitz, D. E. (1985). Attributions in the advice columns: Actors and observers, causes and reasons. *Journal of Personality and Social Psychology, 11,* 315–325.

Schofield, W. (1964). *Psychotherapy: The purchase of friendship.* Englewood Cliffs, NJ: Prentice-Hall.

Schofield, W., & Vaughan-Jackson, P. (1913). *What a boy should know.* New York: Cassell.

Schulman, M. (1991). *The passionate mind: Bringing up an intelligent and creative child.* New York: Free Press.

Schwartz, E. L. (Ed.). (1990). *Computational neuroscience.* Cambridge, MA: MIT Press.

Schwartz, S. H., & Inbar-Saban, N. (1988). Value self-confrontation as a method to aid in weight loss. *Journal of Personality and Social Psychology, 54,* 396–404.

Schwebel, M., Maher, C. A., & Fagley, N. S. (Eds.). (1990). *Promoting cognitive growth over the life span.* Hillsdale, NJ: Erlbaum.

Schwitzgabel, R. L., & Schwitzgabel, R. K. (1980). *Law and psychological practice.* New York: Wiley.

Scott, C. R. (1990, November 7). As baby boomers age, fewer couples untie the knot. *The Wall Street Journal,* pp. B1, B8.

Sears, D. D. (1968). The paradox of de facto selective exposure without preferences for supportive information. In R. P. Abelson (Ed.), *Theories of cognitive consistency.* Chicago: Rand McNally.

Sears, D. O. (1982). The person-positivity bias. *Journal of Personality and Social Psychology, 44,* 233–250.

Sears, D. O. (1986). College sophomores in the laboratory: Influences of a narrow data base on social psychology's view of human nature. *Journal of Personality and Social Psychology, 51,* 515–530.

Sears, R. R. (1977). Sources of life satisfaction of the Terman gifted men. *American Psychologist, 32,* 119–128.

Segall, M. H., Campbell, D. T., & Herskovits, M. J. (1966). *The influence of culture on visual perception.* New York: Bobbs-Merrill.

Segraves, R. T., & Schoenberg, H. W. (Eds.). (1985). *Diagnosis and treatment of erectile disturbances: A guide for clinicians.* New York: Plenum Press.

Seidenberg, M. S., & Petitto, L. A. (1987). Communication, symbolic communication, and langauge: Comment on Savage-Rumbaugh, McDonald, Sevicik, Hopkins, & Rupert (1986). *Journal of Experimental Psychology: General, 116,* 279–287.

Sekuler, R., & Blake, R. (1990). *Perception* (2nd ed.). New York: McGraw-Hill.

Seligman, M. E. P. (1975). *Helplessness: On depression, development, and death.* San Francisco: Freeman.

Seligman, M. E. P. (1988, October). Baby boomer blues. *Psychology Today,* p. 54.

Seligmann, J. (1991, June 17). A light for poor eyes. *Newsweek,* p. 61.

Selman, R. L., Schorin, M. Z., Stone, C. R., & Phelps, E. (1983). A naturalistic study of children's social understanding. *Developmental Psychology, 19,* 82–102.

Seltzer, L. (1986). *Paradoxical strategies in psychotherapy.* New York: Wiley.

Selye, H. (1976). *The stress of life.* New York: McGraw-Hill.

Shafer, R. G. (1990, March 12). An anguished father recounts the battle he lost—trying to rescue a teenage son from drugs. *People Weekly,* pp. 81–83.

Shapley, R. (1990). Visual sensitivity and parallel retinocortical channels. *Annual Review of Psychology, 41,* 635–658.

Sharpe, L. T., Fach, C., Nordby, K., & Stockman, A. (1989, April 21). *Science, 244,* 354–356.

Shaw, C. B. (1991). Nonverbal behavior and gender in a business setting. Unpublished doctoral dissertation, University of Massachusetts, Amhert.

Shaw, M. E. (1981). *Group dynamics: The psychology of small group behavior* (3rd ed.). New York: McGraw-Hill.

Shaywitz, S. E., Escobar, M. D., Shaywitz, B. A., Fletcher, J. M., & Makuch, R. (1992, January 16). Evidence that dyslexia may represent the lower tail of a normal distribution of reading ability. *The New England Journal of Medicine, 326,* 145–151.

Shedler, J., & Block, J. (1990). Adolescent drug use and psychological health: A longitudinal inquiry. *American Psychologist, 45,* 612–630.

Shepherd, G. M. (Ed.). (1990). *The synaptic organization of the brain* (3rd ed.). New York: Oxford University Press.

Shock, N. W. (1962, January). The physiology of aging. *Scientific American,* pp. 100–110.

Shotland, R. L. (1984, March). Paper presented at the Catherine Genovese Memorial Conference on Bad Samaritanism, Fordham University.

Shotland, R. L. (1985, June). When bystanders just stand by. *Psychology Today, 19,* 50–55.

Siegel, J. M. (1990). Stressful life events and use of physician services among the elderly: The moderating role of pet ownership. *Journal of Personality and Social Psychology, 58,* 1081–1086.

Siegel, J. M., Nienhuis, R., Fahringer, H. M., Paul, R., Shiromani, P., Dement, W. C., Mignot, E., & Chiu, C. (1991, May 31). Neuronal activity in narcolepsy: Identification of cataplexy-related cells in the medial medulla. *Science, 252,* 1315–1318.

Siegler, R. S. (1989). Mechanisms of cognitive development. *Annual Review of Psychology, 40,* 353–379.

Sigerist, H. E. (1943). *Civilization and disease.* Ithaca, NY: Cornell University Press.

Signorella, M. L., & Frieze, I. H. (1989). Gender schemas in college students. *Psychology, a Journal of Human Behavior, 26,* 16–23.

Silver, R. L., & Wortman, C. B. (1980). Coping with undesirable life events. In J. Barber & M. E. P. Seligman (Eds.), *Human helplessness: Theory and application.* New York: Academic Press.

Simmons, J., & Mares, W. J. (1985). *Working together: Employee participation in action.* New York: New York University Press.

Simmons, R., & Blyth, D. (1987). *Moving into adolescence.* New York: Aldine.

Simonton, D. K. (1992). Leaders of American psychology, 1879–1967:

Career development, creative output, and professional achievement. *Journal of Personality and Social Psychology, 62,* 5–17.

Simpson, J. A. (1987). The dissolution of romantic relationships: Factors involved in relationship stability and emotional distress. *Journal of Personality and Social Psychology, 53,* 683–692.

Singer, J. L. (1975). *The inner world of daydreaming.* New York: Harper & Row.

Sinnott, J. D. (Ed.). (1989). *Everyday problem solving: Theory and applications.* New York: Praeger.

Sizemore, C. C. (1989). *A mind of my own: The woman who was known as Eve tells the story of her triumph over multiple personality disorder.* New York: Morrow.

Skinner, B. F. (1948). *Walden Two.* New York: Macmillan.

Skinner, B. F. (1957). *Verbal behavior.* New York: Appleton-Century-Crofts.

Skinner, B. F. (1975). The steep and thorny road to a science of behavior. *American Psychologist, 30,* 42–49.

Skrypnek, B. J., & Snyder, M. (1982). On the self-perpetuating nature of stereotypes about women and men. *Journal of Experimental Social Psychology, 18,* 277–291.

Slater, A., Mattock, A., & Brown, E. (1990). Size constancy at birth: Newborn infants' responses to retinal and real size. *Journal of Experimental Child Psychology, 49,* 314–322.

Slusher, M. P., & Anderson, C. A. (1987). When reality monitoring fails: The role of imagination in stereotype maintenance. *Journal of Personality and Social Psychology, 52,* 653–662.

Smith, C. A., & Ellsworth, P. C. (1987). Patterns of appraisal and emotion related to taking an exam. *Journal of Personality and Social Psychology, 52,* 475–488.

Smith, E. (1988, May). Fighting cancerous feelings. *Psychology Today,* pp. 22–23.

Smith, E. R. (1984). Attributions and other inferences: Processing information about the self versus others. *Journal of Experimental Social Psychology, 20,* 97–115.

Smith, J. (1990). *Cognitive-behavioral relaxation training.* New York: Springer.

Smith, M. B. (1990). Psychology in the public interest: What have we done? What can we do? *American Psychologist, 45,* 530–536.

Smith, M. L., Glass, G. V., & Miller, T. J. (1980). *The benefits of psychotherapy.* Baltimore, MD: Johns Hopkins.

Smith, T. W. (1990, December). *Ethnic images.* (GSS Topical Report No. 19). Chicago: National Opinion Research Center.

Smith, T. W. (1991). Adult sexual behavior in 1989: Number of partners, frequency of intercourse, and risk of

AIDS. *Family Planning Perspectives, 23,* 102–107.

Smither, R. D. (1988). *The psychology of work and human performance.* New York: Harper & Row.

Snarey, J. R. (1985). Cross-cultural universality of social-moral development: A critical review of Kohlbergian research. *Psychological Bulletin, 97,* 202–232.

Snyder, C. R., & Higgins, R. L. (1988). Excuses: Their effective role in the negotiation of reality. Psychological Bulletin, 104, 23–35.

Snyder, M. (1987). *Public appearance/private realities: The psychology of self-monitoring.* New York: Freeman.

Snyder, M., Berscheid, E., & Glick, P. (1985). Focusing on the exterior and the interior: The investigations of the initiation of personal relations. *Journal of Personality and Social Psychology, 48,* 1427–1439.

Snyder, M., & Cantor, N. (1979). Testing hypotheses about other people: The use of historical knowledge. *Journal of Experimental Social Psychology, 15,* 330–343.

Snyder, M., & DeBono, K. G. (1985). Appeals to images and claims about quality: Understanding the psychology of advertising. *Journal of Personality and Social Psychology, 49,* 586–597.

Snyder, M., & DeBono, K. G. (1989). Identifying attitude functions: Lessons from personality and social behavior. In A. R. Pratkanis, S. J. Breckler, & A. G. Greenwald (Eds.), *Attitude structure and function.* Hillsdale, NJ: Erlbaum.

Snyder, S. H. (1978). Dopamine and schizophrenia. In L. C. Wynne, R. L. Cromwell, & S. Matthysse (Eds.), *The nature of schizophrenia: New approaches to research and treatment* (pp. 87–94). New York: Wiley.

Snyder, S. H. (1987, April 30). Parkinson's disease: A cure using brain transplants? *Nature, 326,* 824–825.

Solomon, R. L., & Corbit, J. D. (1974). An opponent-process theory of motivation: I. Temporal dynamics of affect. *Psychological Review, 81,* 119–145.

Solso, R. L. (1991). *Cognitive psychology* (3rd ed.). Boston: Allyn & Bacon.

Sorkin, R. D., Wightman, F. L., Kistler, D. S., & Elvers, G. C. (1989). An exploratory study of the use of movement-correlated cues in an auditory head-up display. *Human Factors, 31,* 161–166.

Soukhanov, A. A. (1989, January). Word watch. *Atlantic,* p. 124.

Spangler, W. D., & House, R. J. (1991). Presidential effectiveness and the leadership motive profile. *Journal of Personality and Social Psychology, 60,* 439–455.

Spanos, N. P. (1986). Hypnotic behavior: A social psychological interpretation of amnesia, analgesia, and ''trance

logic.'' *Behavioral and Brain Science, 9,* 449–467.

Spanos, N. P., & Chaves, J. F. (Eds.). (1989). *Hypnosis: The cognitive-behavioral perspective.* Buffalo, NY: Prometheus Books.

Spanos, N. P., Cross, W. P., Menary, E. P., Brett, P. J., & deGroic, M. (1987). Attitudinal and imaginal ability predictors of social cognitive skill-training enhancements in hypnotic susceptibility. *Personality and Social Psychology Bulletin, 13,* 379–398.

Spear, N. E., Miller, J. S., & Jagielo, J. A. (1990). Animal memory and learning. *Annual Review of Psychology, 41,* 169–211.

Spearman, C. (1927). *The abilities of man.* London: Macmillan.

Spence, J. T. (1985, August). *Achievement American style: The rewards and costs of individualism.* Presidential address. 93rd Annual Convention of the American Psychological Association, Los Angeles.

Spence, M. J., & DeCasper, A. J. (1982, March). *Human fetuses perceive maternal speech.* Paper presented at the meeting of the International Conference on Infant Studies, Austin, TX.

Sperling, G. (1960). The information available in brief visual presentation. *Psych Monographs, 74* (whole no. 498).

Sperry, R. (1982). Some effects of disconnecting the cerebral hemispheres. *Science, 217,* 1223–1226.

Spiegel, D., Bloom, J. R., Kraemer, H. C., & Gottheil, E. (1989, October 14). Effect of psychosocial treatment on survival of patients with metastatic breast cancer. *Lancet, 2,* 888–891.

Spiegel, H. (1987). The answer is: Psychotherapy plus [Special Issue]. Is hypnotherapy a placebo? *British Journal of Experimental and Clinical Hypnosis, 4,* 163–164.

Spiegel, R. (1989). *Psychopharmacology: An Introduction.* New York: Wiley.

Spillman, L., & Werner, J. (Eds.). (1990). *Visual perception: The neurophysiological foundations.* San Diego, CA: Academic Press.

Spiro, R. J., & Jehng, J. C. (1990). Cognitive flexibility and hypertext: Theory and technology for the nonlinear and multidimensional traversal of complex subject matter. In D. Nix & R. Spiro (Eds.), *Cognition, education, and multimedia: Exploring ideas in high technology.* Hillsdale, NJ: Erlbaum.

Spitzer, R. L., Skodol, A. E., Gibbon, M., & Williams, J. B. W. (1983). *Psychopathology: A case book.* New York: McGraw-Hill.

Springer, I. (1991, April 28). Afraid to feel. *Boston Globe Health,* pp. 14, 30.

Springer, S. P., & Deutsch, G. (1985). *Left brain, right brain.* San Francisco: Freeman.

Springer, S. P., & Deutsch, G. (1989). *Left Brain, right brain.* (3rd ed.). New York: Freeman.

Squire, L. (1987). *Memory and brain.* New York: Oxford University Press.

Sroufe, L. A., Fox, N. E., & Pancake, V. R. (1983). Attachment and dependency in a developmental perspective. *Child Development, 54,* 1615–1627.

Staats, A. W. (1975). *Social behaviorism.* Homewood, IL: Dorsey Press.

Stacy, A., Newcomb, M. D., & Bentler, P. M. (1991). Social psychological influences on sensation seeking from adolescence to adulthood. *Personality and Social Psychology Bulletin, 17*(6), 701–708.

Stanley, J. C. (1980). On educating the gifted. *Educational Researcher, 9,* 8–12.

Stanley, J. C., & Benbow, C. P. (1987). SMPY's first decade: Ten years of posing problems and solving them. *Journal of Special Education, 17,* 11–25.

Steele, C. M. (1988). The psychology of self-affirmation: Sustaining the integrity of the self. In L. Berkowitz (Ed.), *Advances in experimental social psychology* (Vol. 21). New York: Academic.

Steele, C. M., & Josephs, R. A. (1990). Alcohol myopia: Its prized and dangerous effects. *American Psychologist, 45,* 921–933.

Steele, C. M., & Southwick, L. (1985). Alcohol and social behavior I: The psychology of drunken excess. *Journal of Personality and Social Psychology, 48,* 18–34.

Stein, J. A., Newcomb, M. D., & Bentler, P. M. (1987). An 8-year study of multiple influences on drug use and drug-use consequences. *Journal of Personality and Social Psychology, 53,* 1094–1105.

Steinberg, E. R. (1990). *Computer-assisted instruction: A synthesis of theory, practice, and technology.* Hillsdale, NJ: Erlbaum.

Steinberg, E. R. (1991). *Teaching computers to teach* (2nd ed.). Hillsdale, NJ: Erlbaum.

Steinberg, L., Belsky, J., & Meyer, R. B. (1991). *Infancy, childhood, and adolescence.* New York: McGraw-Hill.

Steiner, J. E. (1979). Human facial expressions in response to taste and smell stimulation. In H. Reese & L. P. Lipsitt (Eds.), *Advances in child development and behavior* (Vol. 13). New York: Academic Press.

Sternbach, R. A. (Ed.). (1987). *The psychology of pain.* New York: Raven Press.

Sternberg, R. J. (1982). Reasoning, problem solving, and intelligence. In R. J. Sternberg (Ed.), *Handbook of human intelligence* (pp. 225–307). Cambridge, MA: Cambridge University Press.

Sternberg, R. J. (1985a). *Beyond IQ: A triarchic theory of human intelligence.* New York: Cambridge University Press.

Sternberg, R. J. (1985b). Implicit theories of intelligence, creativity, and wisdom. *Journal of Personality and Social Psychology, 49,* 607–627.

Sternberg, R. J. (1986). Triangular theory of love. *Psychological Review, 93,* 119–135.

Sternberg, R. J. (1987). Liking versus loving: A comparative evaluation of theories. *Psychological Bulletin, 102,* 331–345.

Sternberg, R. J. (1988). *The nature of creativity.* Cambridge, England: Cambridge University Press.

Sternberg, R. J. (1990). *Metaphors of mind: Conceptions of the nature of intelligence.* Cambridge, England: Cambridge University Press.

Sternberg, R. J. (1991). Theory-based testing of intellectual abilities: Rationale for the STERNBERG triarchic abilities test. In H. A. H. Rowe (Ed.), *Intelligence: Reconceptualization and measurement.* Hillsdale, NJ: Erlbaum.

Sternberg, R. J., Conway, B. E., Ketron, J. L., & Bernstein, M. (1981). Peoples' conceptions of intelligence. *Journal of Personality and Social Psychology, 41,* 37–55.

Sternberg, R. J., & Davidson, J. E. (Eds.). (1986). *Conceptions of giftedness.* New York: Cambridge University Press.

Sternberg, R. J., & Detterman, D. (1986). *What is intelligence?* Norwood, NJ: Ablex.

Sternberg, R. J., & Frensch, P. A. (1991). *Complex problem solving: Principles and mechanisms.* Hillsdale, NJ: Lawrence Erlbaum Associates.

Sternberg, R. J., & Grajek, S. (1984). The nature of love. *Journal of Personality and Social Psychology, 47,* 312–329.

Sternberg, R. J., & Wagner, R. K. (Eds.) (1986). *Practical intelligence: Nature and origins of competence in the everyday world.* New York: Cambridge University Press.

Stevens, C. F. (1979, September). The neuron. *Scientific American,* p. 56.

Stevens, G., & Gardner, S. (1982). *The women of psychology: Pioneers and innovators* (Vol. 1). Cambridge, MA: Schenkman.

Stogdill, R. (1974). *Handbook of leadership.* New York: Free Press.

Storandt, M., et al. (1984). Psychometric differentiation of mild senile dementia of the Alzheimer type. *Archives of Neurology, 41,* 497–499.

Streufert, S. (1984, October). The stress of excellence. *Across the Board,* pp. 9–16.

Stricker, E. M., & Zigmond, M. J. (1976). Recovery of function after damage to catecholamine-containing neurons: A neurochemical model for hypothalmic syndrome. In J. M. Sprague and A. N. Epstein (Eds.), *Progress in psychobiology and physiological psychology* (Vol. 6). New York: Academic Press.

Stricker, G., Davis-Russell, E., Bourg, E., Duran, E., Hammond, W. R.,

McHolland, J., Polite, K., & Vaughn, B. E. (1990). *Toward ethnic diversification in psychology education and training.* Washington, DC: American Psychological Association.

Strickland, B. (1988, August). *Winning the battle against depression: Strategies for women.* Paper presented at the annual meeting of the American Psychological Association, Atlanta.

Strober, M., Lampert, C., Morrell, W., Burroughs, J., & Jacobs, C. (1990). A controlled family study of anorexia nervosa: Evidence of familial aggregation and lack of shared transmission with affective disorders. *International Journal of Eating Disorders, 9,* 239–253.

Strong, L. D. (1978). Alternative marital and family forms: Their relative attractiveness to college students and correlates of willingness to participate in nontraditional forms. *Journal of Marriage and the Family, 40,* 493–503.

Stroop, J. R. (1935). Studies of interference in serial verbal reactions. *Journal of Experimental Psychology, 18,* 643–662.

Strube, M. (Ed.). (1990). Type A behavior [Special issue]. *Journal of Social Behavior and Personality, 5.*

Suddath, R. L., Christison, G. W., Torrey, E. F., Casanova, M. F., & Weinberger, D. R. (1990, March 22). Anatomical abnormalities in the brains of monozygotic twins discordant for schizophrenia. *New England Journal of Medicine, 322,* 789–794.

Sue, D. W. (1979). Erotic fantasies of college students during coitus. *Journal of Sex Research, 15,* 299–305.

Sue, D. W. (1981). *Counseling the culturally different: Theory and practice.* New York: Wiley.

Sue, D. W., & Sue, D. (1990). *Counseling the culturally different: Theory and practice* (2nd ed.). New York: Wiley.

Sue, D. W., Sue, D., & Sue, S. (1990). *Understanding abnormal behavior* (3rd ed.). Boston: Houghton-Mifflin.

Sullivan, B. (1985). *Double standard.* Paper presented at the annual meeting of the Society for the Scientific Study of Sex, San Diego.

Sullivan, S. A., & Birch, L. L. (1990). Pass the sugar, pass the salt: Experience dictates preference. *Developmental Psychology, 26,* 546–551.

Sulzer-Azaroff, B., & Mayer, G. R. (1991). *Behavior analysis for lasting change.* New York: Holt.

Super, C. M. (1980). Cognitive development: Looking across at growing up. In C. M. Super & S. Harakness (Eds.), *New directions for child development: Anthropological perspectives on child development* (pp. 59–69). San Francisco: Jossey-Bass.

Susani, H. (1988). Concepts of ability and effort in Japan and the United

States. *Review of Educational Research, 58,* 327–345.

Sussman, N. (1976). Sex and sexuality in history. In B. J. Saddock, H. I. Kaplaw, & A. M. Freedman (Eds.), *The sexual experience.* Baltimore: Williams & Wilkins.

Suzuki, K. (1991). Moon illusion simulated in complete darkness: Planetarium experiment reexamined. *Perception and Psychophysics, 49,* 349–354.

Svarstad, B. (1976). Physician-patient communication and patient conformity with medical advice. In D. Mechanic (Ed.), *The growth of bureaucratic medicine.* New York: Wiley.

Sweeney, P. D., & Gruber, L. L. (1984). Selective exposure: Voter information preferences and the Watergate affair. *Journal of Personality and Social Psychology, 46,* 1208–1221.

Sweet, E. (1985, October). Date rape: The story of an epidemic and those who deny it. *Ms/Campus Times,* pp. 56–59.

Szasz, T. S. (1961). *The myth of mental illness.* New York: Harper & Row.

Szasz, T. S. (1982). The psychiatric will: A new mechanism for protecting persons against "psychosis" and psychiatry. *American Psychologist, 37,* 762–770.

Szasz, T. S. (1990). Law and psychiatry: The problems that will not go away. *Journal of Mind and Behavior, 11,* 557–564.

Tagiuri, R. (1958). Social preference and its perception. In R. Tagiuri & L. Petrullo (Eds.), *Person, perception, and interpersonal behavior* (pp. 316–336). Stanford, CA: Stanford University Press.

Talbot, J. D., Marrett, S., Evans, A. C., Meyer, E., Bushnell, M. C., & Duncan, G. H. (1991, March 15). Multiple representations of pain in human cerebral cortex. *Science, 251,* 1355–1358.

Tamura, T., Nakatani, K., & Yau, K. W. (1989, August 18). Light adaptation in cat retinal rods. *Science, 245,* 755–758.

Tanford, S., & Penrod, S. (1984). Social influence model: A formal integration of research on majority and minority influence processes. *Psychological Bulletin, 95,* 189–225.

Tannen, D. (1991). *You just don't understand.* New York: Ballantine.

Tanner, J. M. (1978). *Education and physical growth* (2nd ed.). New York: International Universities Press.

Tavris, C., & Sadd, S. (1977). *The Redbook report on female sexuality.* New York: Delacorte.

Taylor, A. (1991, April 8). Can Iacocco fix Chrysler—again? *Fortune, 123,* 50–54.

Taylor, S. E. (1982). Hospital patient behavior: Reactance, helplessness, or control. In H. S. Friedman & M. R. DiMatteo (Eds.), *Interpersonal issues in health care.* New York: Academic.

Taylor, S. E., & Brown, J. D. (1988). Illusion and well-being: A social psychological perspective on mental health. *Psychological Bulletin, 103,* 193–210.

Taylor, S. E., Buunk, B. P., & Aspinwall, L. G. (1990). Social comparison, stress, and coping. *Personality and Social Psychology Bulletin, 16,* 74–89.

Tellegen, A., Lykken, D. T., Bouchard, T. J., Jr., Wilcox, K. J., Segal, N. L., & Rich, S. (1988). Personality similarity in twins reared apart and together. *Journal of Personality and Social Psychology, 54,* 1031–1039.

Terman, L. M., & Oden, M. H. (1947). *Genetic studies of genius, IV: The gifted child grows up.* Stanford, CA: Stanford University Press.

Tesser, A. (1988). Toward a self-evaluation maintenance model of social behavior. In L. Berkowitz (Ed.), *Advances in experimental social psychology* (Vol. 21). New York: Academic.

Tesser, A., & Shaffer, D. R. (1990). Attitudes and attitude change. *Annual Review of Psychology, 41,* 479–523.

Thatcher, R. W., Walker, R. A., & Giudice, S. (1987, May 29). Human cerebral hemispheres develop at different rates and ages. *Science, 236,* 1110–1114.

Thienhaus, O. J., Margletta, S., & Bennett, J. A. (1990). A study of the clinical efficacy of maintenance ECT. *Journal of Clinical Psychiatry, 51,* 141–144.

Thomas, A., & Chess, S. (1980). *The dynamics of psychological development.* New York: Brunner/Mazel.

Thomas, A., Chess, S., Birch, H. G., Hartzig, M. E., & Korn, J. (1963). *Behavioral individuality in early childhood.* New York: New York University Press.

Thomas, C. B., Duszynski, K. R., & Schaffer, J. W. (1979). Family attitudes reported in youth as potential predictors of cancer. *Psychosomatic Medicine, 4,* 287–302.

Thompson, S. C. (1988, August). *An intervention to increase physician-patient communication.* Paper presented at the annual meeting of the American Psychological Association, Atlanta.

Thompson, S. C., Nanni, C., & Schwankovsky, L. (1990). Patient-oriented interventions to improve communication in a medical office visit. *Health Psychology, 9,* 390–404.

Thoresen, C. E., & Low, K. G. (1990). Women and the type A behavior pattern: Review and commentary. *Journal of Social Behavior and Personality, 5,* 117–133.

Thorndike, E. L. (1932). *The fundamentals of learning.* New York: Teachers College.

Thorndike, R. L., Hagan, E., & Sattler, J. (1986). *Stanford-Binet* (4th ed.). Chicago: Riverside.

Tierney, J. (1988, May 15). Wired for stress. *The New York Times Magazine,* pp. 49–85.

Time. (1976, September). Svengali squad: L.A. Police. p. 76.

Time. (1982, October 4). "We're sorry: A case of mistaken identity." p. 45.

Timnick, L. (1985, August 25). The *Times* poll: 22% in survey were child abuse victims. *Los Angeles Times,* pp. 1, 34.

Tjosvold, D. (1982). Effects of approach to controversy on superiors' incorporation of subordinates' information in decision making. *Journal of Applied Psychology, 67,* 189–193.

Tjosvold, D., & Deemer, D. K. (1980). Effects of controversy within a cooperative or competitive context on organizational decision making. *Journal of Applied Psychology, 65,* 590–595.

Tolman, E. C. (1959). Principles of purposive behavior. In S. Koch (Ed.), *Psychology: A study of science.* Vol. 2. New York: McGraw-Hill.

Tolman, E. C., & Honzik, C. H. (1930). Introduction and removal of reward and maze performance in rats. *University of California Publications in Psychology, 4,* 257–275.

Tomlinson-Keasey, C. (1985). *Child development: Psychological, sociological, and biological factors.* Homewood, IL: Dorsey.

Tomlinson-Keasey, C., Eisert, D. C., Kahle, L. R., Hardy-Brown, K., & Keasey, B. (1979). The structure of concrete operations. *Child Development,* 1153–1163.

Torgersen, S. (1983). Genetic factors in anxiety disorders. *Archives of General Psychiatry, 40,* 1085–1089.

Toynbee, P. (1977). *Patients.* New York: Harcourt, Brace, Jovanovich.

Trehub, S. E., Schneider, B. A., Thorpe, L. A., & Judge, P. (1991). Observational measures of auditory sensitivity in early infancy. *Developmental Psychology, 27,* 40–49.

Treisman, A., & Gormican, S. (1988). Feature analysis in early vision: Evidence from search asymmetries. *Psychological Review, 95,* 15–48.

Treisman, M. (1960). Motion sickness: An evolutionary hypothesis. *Science,* pp. 493–495.

Trinder, J. (1988). Subjective insomnia without objective findings: A pseudo-diagnostic classification. *Psychological Bulletin, 107,* 87–94.

Trost, C. (1988). Men, too, wrestle with career-family stress. *The Wall Street Journal,* p. B-1.

Tsunoda, T. (1985). *The Japanese brain: Uniqueness and universality.* Tokyo, Japan: Taishukan Publishing.

Tulving, E. (1983). *Elements of episodic memory.* New York: Oxford University Press.

Tulving, E., & Psotka, J. (1971). Retroactive inhibition in free recall: Inaccessibility of information available in the memory store. *Journal of Experimental Psychology, 87,* 1–8.

Tulving, E., & Schacter, D. L. (1990, January 19). Priming and human memory systems. *Science, 247,* 301–306.

Tulving, E., & Thompson, D. M. (1973). Encoding specificity and retrieval processes in episodic memory. *Psychological Review, 80,* 352–373.

Turkington, C. (1986, August). Pot and the immune system. *APA Monitor,* p. 22.

Turkington, C. (1987, September). Special talents. *Psychology Today,* pp. 42–46.

Turkkan, J. S. (1989). Classical conditioning: The new hegemony. *Behavioral and Brain Sciences, 12,* 121–179.

Turnbull, C. (1961). Some observations regarding the experiences and behavior of the Bambuti pygmies. *American Journal of Psychology, 74,* 304–308.

Turner, C. R., Miller, H. B., & Moses, L. E. (Eds.). (1989). *AIDS: Sexual behavior and intravenous drug use.* Washington, DC: National Academy Press.

Tversky, A., & Kahneman, D. (1974, September 27). Judgment under uncertainty: Heuristics and biases. *Science, 185,* 1124–1131.

Tversky, B. (1981). Distortions in memory for maps. *Cognitive Psychology, 13,* 407–433.

Udolf, R. (1981). *Handbook of hypnosis for professionals.* New York: Van Nostrand.

Ullman, L. P., & Krasner, L. (1975). *A psychological approach to abnormal behavior* (2nd ed.). Englewood Cliffs, NJ: Prentice-Hall.

Ulrich, R. E. (1991). Animal rights, animal wrongs and the question of balance. *Psychological Science, 2,* 197–201.

Umstot, D. D., Bell, C. H., & Mitchell, T. R. (1976). Effects of job enrichment and task goals on satisfaction and productivity: Implications for job design. *Journal of Applied Psychology, 61,* 379–394.

U.S. Bureau of Labor Statistics. (1988). *Special labor force reports.* Washington, DC: Government Printing Office.

U.S. Census Bureau. (1991). *Household and family characteristics, March 1990 and 1989.* (Current Population Reports). Washington, DC: U.S. Census Bureau.

U.S. Commission on Civil Rights. (1990). *Intimidation and violence: Racial and religious bigotry in America.* Washington, DC: U.S. Commission on Civil Rights Clearinghouse.

U.S. Department of Health and Human Services. (1981). *The health consequences of smoking for women: A report of the surgeon general.* Washington, DC: Public Health Service.

U.S. Surgeon General. (1988, May). *Report on smoking.* Washington, DC: Government Printing Office.

Ursano, R. J., Sonnenberg, S. M., & Lazar, S. (1991). *Concise guide to psychodynamic psychotherapy.* Washington, DC: American Psychiatric Press.

Valenstein, E. S. (1986). *Great and desperate cures: The rise and decline of psychosurgery and other radical treatments for mental illness.* New York: Basic Books.

Vance, E. B., & Wagner, N. W. (1976). Written descriptions of orgasm: A study of sex differences. *Archives of Sexual Behavior, 5,* 87–98.

VanSell, M., Brief, A. P., & Schuler, R. S. (1981). Role conflict and role ambiguity: Integration of the literature and directions for future research. *Human Relations, 34,* 43–71.

Viney, W., Kinn, D. B., & Berndt, J. (1990). Animal research in psychology: Declining or thriving? *Journal of Comparative Psychology, 104,* 322–325.

Vlaeyen, J. W. S., Geurts, S. M., Kole-Snijders, A. M. J., Schuerman, J. A., Groenman, N. H., & van Eek, H. (1990). What do chronic pain patients think of their pain? Towards a pain cognition questionnaire. *British Journal of Clinical Psychology, 29,* 383–394.

Voeller, B., Reinisch, J. M., & Gottlieb, M. (1991). *AIDS and sex: An integrated biomedical and biobehavioral approach.* New York: Oxford University Press.

Vonnegut, M. (1975). *The Eden express.* New York: Bantam.

von Restorff, H. (1933). Uber die wirking von bereichsbildumgen im Spurenfeld. In W. Kohler & H. von Restorff, *Analyse von vorgangen in Spurenfeld. I. Psychologische forschung, 18,* 299–342.

Vroom, V. H. (1976). Leadership. In M. D. Dunnette (Ed.), *Handbook of industrial and organizational psychology.* Chicago: Rand McNally.

Vroom, V. H., & Yetton, P. W. (1973). *Leadership and decision making.* Pittsburgh: University of Pittsburgh Press.

Wachter, K. W. (1988, September 16). Disturbed by meta-analysis? *Science, 241,* 1407–1408.

Wagner, R., & Sternberg, R. (1985). Alternate conceptions of intelligence and their implications for education. *Review of Educational Research, 54,* 179–223.

Wagner, R. K., & Sternberg, R. J. (1991). *Tacit Knowledge Inventory.* San Antonio, TX: The Psychological Corporation.

Waid, W. M., & Orne, M. T. (1982). The physiological detection of deception. *American Scientist, 70,* 402–409.

Waldrop, M. W. (1989, September 29). NIDA aims to fight drugs with drugs. *Science, 245,* 1443–1444.

Walker, E., & Emory, E. (1985). Commentary: Interpretive bias and behavioral genetic research. *Child Development, 56,* 775–778.

Wall, P. D., & Melzack, R. (Eds.). (1984). *Textbook of pain.* Edinburgh, Scotland: Churchill Livingstone.

Wall, P. D., & Melzack, R. (1989). *Textbook of pain* (2nd ed.). New York: Churchill Livingstone.

Wallace, P. (1977). Individual discrimination of humans by odor. *Physiology and Behavior, 19,* 577–579.

Wallace, R. K., & Benson, H. (1972, February). The physiology of meditation. *Scientific American,* pp. 84–90.

Waller, N. G., Kojetin, B. A., Bouchard, T. J., Jr., Lykken, D. T., & Tellegen, A. (1990). Genetic and environmental influences on religious interests, attitudes, and values: A study of twins reared apart and together. *Psychological Science, 1,* 138–142.

Wallerstein, R. S. (1986). *Forty-two lives in treatment: A study of psychoanalysis and psychotherapy.* New York: Guilford Press.

Wallis, C. (1984, June 11). Unlocking pain's secrets. *Time,* pp. 58–60.

Walster, E., & Walster, G. W. (1978). *Love.* Reading, MA: Addison-Wesley.

Walters, J. M., & Gardner, H. (1986). The theory of multiple intelligences: Some issues and answers. In R. J. Sternberg & R. K. Wagner (Eds.), *Practical intelligence.* Cambridge, England: Cambridge University Press.

Ward, W. C., Kogan, N., & Pankove, E. (1972). Incentive effects in children's creativity. *Child Development, 43,* 669–677.

Warga, C. (1987, August). Pain's gatekeeper. *Psychology Today,* pp. 51–56.

Warshaw, R. (1988). *I never called it rape: The "Ms." report on recognizing, fighting, and surviving date and acquaintance rape.* New York: Harper & Row.

Waterson, E. J., & Murray-Lyon, I. M. (1990). Preventing alcohol-related birth damage: A review. *Social Science and Medicine, 30,* 349–364.

Watkins, L. R., & Mayer, D. J. (1982). Organization of endogenous opiate and nonopiate pain control systems. *Science, 216,* 1185–1192.

Watson, D. (1982). The actor and the observer: How are their perceptions of causality divergent? *Psychological Bulletin, 92,* 682–700.

Watson, J. B. (1924). *Behaviorism.* New York: Norton.

Watson, J. B., & Rayner, R. (1920). Conditioned emotional reactions. *Journal of Experimental Psychology, 3,* 1–14.

Waynbaum, I. (1907). *La physionomie humaine: Son mecanisme et son rôle social.* Paris: Alcan.

Webb, D. (1990, November 7). Eating well. *The New York Times,* p. C-3.

Webb, W. B. (1979). Sleep and dreams.

In B. B. Wolman (Ed.), *Handbook of general psychology* (pp. 734–748). Englewood Cliffs, NJ: Prentice-Hall.

Weber, M. (1952). The essentials of bureaucratic organization: An ideal-type construction. In R. K. Merton et al. (Eds.), *A reader in bureaucracy*. Glencoe, IL: Free Press.

Weber, R., & Crocker, J. (1983). Cognitive processes in the revision of stereotypic beliefs. *Journal of Personality and Social Psychology, 45*, 961–977.

Wechsler, D. (1975). Intelligence defined and undefined. *American Psychologist, 30*, 135–139.

Wechsler, H., Rohman, M., & Solomon, R. (1981). Emotional problems and concerns of New England college students. *American Journal of Orthopsychiatry, 51*, 719.

Weinberg, M. S. (1991, February 27). Personal communication. Indiana University,

Weinberg, R. A. (1989). Intelligence and IQ: Landmark issues and great debates. *American Psychologist, 44*, 98–104.

Weiner, B. (1985a). *Human motivation*. New York: Springer-Verlag.

Weiner, B. (1985b). "Spontaneous" causal thinking. *Psychological Bulletin, 97*, 74–84.

Weiner, R. (1982). Another look at an old controversy. *Contemporary Psychiatry, 1*, 61–62.

Weinstein, C. E. (1986). Assessment and training of student learning strategies. In R. R. Schmeck (Ed.), *Learning styles and learning strategies*. New York: Plenum.

Weinstein, S., Drozdenko, R., & Weinstein, C. (1984). Advertising evaluation using brain-wave measures: A response to the question of validity. *Journal of Advertising Research, 24*, 67–71.

Weinstein, S., Weinstein, C., & Drozdenko, R. (1984). Brain wave analysis. *Psychology and Marketing, 1*, 17–42.

Weiskrantz, L. (1989). Remembering dissociations. In H. L. Roediger & F. I. M. Craik (Eds.), *Varieties of memory and consciousness: Essays in honour of Endel Tulving*. Hillsdale, NJ: Erlbaum.

Weiss, A. S. (1991). The measurement of self-actualization: The quest for the test may be as challenging as the search for the self. *Journal of Social Behavior and Personality, 6*, 265–290.

Weiss, R. S. (1988). Loss and recovery. *Journal of Social Issues, 44*, 37–52.

Weiss, R. S. (1990, February 3). Fetal-cell recipient showing improvements. *Science News, 70*.

Weitzenhoffer, A. M. (1989). *The practice of hypnotism*. New York: Wiley.

Weitzman, B. C., Knickman, J. R., & Schinn, M. (1990). Pathways to homelessness among New York City families. *Journal of Social Issues, 46*, 125–140.

Wells, G. L., & Luus, C. A. E. (1990).

Police lineups as experiments: Social methodology as a framework for properly conducted lineups. *Personality and Social Psychology Bulletin, 16*, 106–117.

Wells, R. A., & Giannetti, V. J. (1990). *Handbook of the brief psychotherapies*. New York: Plenum.

Wender, P. H., & Klein, D. F. (1981, February). The promise of biological psychiatry. *Psychology Today*, pp. 25–41.

Wertheimer, M. (1923). Untersuchungen zur lehre von der Gestalt. II. *Psychol. Forsch., 5*, 301–350. In Beardsley and M. Wertheimer (Eds.). (1958). *Readings in perception*. New York: Van Nostrand.

Westen, D. (1990). Psychoanalytic approaches to personality. In L. A. Pervin (Ed.), New York: Guilford Press.

Westoff, C. F. (1974). Coital frequency and contraception. *Family Planning Perspectives, 8*, 54–57.

Westover, S. A., & Lanyon, R. I. (1990). The maintenance of weight loss after behavioral treatment: A review. *Behavior Modification, 14*, 123–127.

Whalen, D. H., & Liberman, A. M. (1987, July 10). Speech perception takes precedence over nonspeech perception. *Science, 237*, 169–171.

Whitam, F. L. (1977). The homosexual role: A reconsideration. *Journal of Sex Research, 13*, 1–11.

Whitbourne, S. K. (1986). *Adult development* (2nd ed.). New York: Praeger.

Whorf, B. L. (1956). *Language, thought, and reality*. New York: Wiley.

Wickens, C. D. (1984). *Engineering psychology and human performance*. Columbus, OH: Merrill.

Wickens, C. D. (1991). *Engineering psychology and human performance* (2nd ed.). New York: Harper Collins.

Widiger, T. A., Frances, A. J., Pincus, H. A., & Davis, W. W. (1990). DSM-IV literature reviews: Rationale, process, and limitations. *Journal of Psychopathology and Behavioral Assessment, 12*, 189–202.

Widmeyer, W. N., & Loy, J. W. (1988). When you're hot, you're hot! Warm-cold effects in first impressions of persons and teaching effectiveness. *Journal of Educational Psychology, 80*, 118–121.

Wiebe, D. J. (1991). Hardiness and stress moderation: A test of proposed mechanisms. *Journal of Personality and Social Psychology, 60*, 89–99.

Wiederhold, W. C. (Ed.). (1982). *Neurology for non-neurologists*. New York: Academic.

Wiener, E. L., & Nagel, D. C. (Eds.). (1988). *Human factors in aviation*. New York: Academic.

Wilder, D. A. (1986). Social categorization: Implications for creation and reduction of intergroup bias. In L. Berkowitz (Ed.), *Advances in experimental social psychology* (Vol. 19). San Diego, CA: Academic.

Wilder, D. A. (1990). Some determinants of the persuasive power of in-groups and out-groups: Organization of information and attribution of independence. *Journal of Personality and Social Psychology, 59*, 1202–1213.

Wildman, R. W., Wildman, R. W., II, Brown, A., & Trice, C. (1976). Note on males' and females' preference for opposite-sex body parts, bust sizes, and bust-revealing clothing. *Psychological Reports, 38*, 485–486.

Williams, R. B., Jr., Barefoot, J. C., Haney, T. L., Harrell, F. E., Jr., Blumenthal, J. A., Pryor, D. B., & Peterson, B. (1988). Type A behavior and angiographically documented coronary atherosclerosis in a sample of 2,289 patients. *Psychosomatic Medicine, 50*, 139–152.

Williams, S. W., & McCullers, J. C. (1983). Personal factors related to typicalness of career and success in active professional women. *Psychology of Women Quarterly, 7*, 343–357.

Willis, S. L., & Nesselroade, C. S. (1990). Long-term effects of fluid ability training in old-old age. *Developmental Psychology, 26*, 905–910.

Willis, W. D., Jr. (1988). Dorsal horn neurophysiology of pain. *Annals of the New York Academy of Science, 531*, 76–89.

Wilson, G. T., Franks, C. M., Kendall, P. C., & Foreyt, J. P. (1987). *Review of behavior therapy: Theory and practice* (Vol. 11). New York: Guilford Press.

Wilson, T. D., & Schooler, J. W. (1991). Thinking too much: Introspection can reduce the quality of preferences and decisions. *Journal of Personality and Social Psychology, 60*, 181–192.

Wimbey, A., & Lochhead, J. (1991). *Problem solving and comprehension* (5th ed.). Hillsdale, NJ: Lawrence Erlbaum Associates.

Winch, R. F. (1958). *Mate selection: A study of complementary needs*. New York: Harper & Row.

Winokur, G. (1983). Alcoholism and depression. *Substance and Alcohol Actions/Misuse, 4*, 111–119.

Winson, J. (1990, November). The meaning of dreams. *Scientific American*, pp. 86–96.

Winter, D. G. (1973). *The power motive*. New York: Free Press.

Winter, D. G. (1987). Leader appeal, leader performance, and the motive profile of leaders and followers: A study of American presidents and elections. *Journal of Personality and Social Psychology, 52*, 196–202.

Winter, D. G. (1988). The power motive in women—and men. *Journal of Personality and Social Psychology, 54*, 510–519.

Witelson, S. F. (1989a). Hand and sex differences in the isthmus and genu of the human corpus callosum. *Brain, 112*, 799–835.

Witelson, S. F. (1989b, March). *Sex differ-ences*. Paper presented at the annual meeting of the New York Academy of Sciences, New York.

Wixted, J. T., & Ebbesen, E. B. (1991). On the form of forgetting. *Psychological Science, 2*(6), 409–415.

Wolman, B. B., & Stricker, G. (Eds.). (1990). *Depressive disorders: Facts, theo-ries, and treatment methods.* New York: Wiley.

Wolozin, B. L., Pruchnicki, A., Dickson, D. W., & Davies, P. (1986). A neuronal antigen in the brains of Alzheimer patients. *Science, 232,* 648–650.

Wolpe, J. (1969). *The practice of behavior therapy.* New York: Pergamon.

Wong, D. F., Gjedde, A., Wagner, H. M., Jr., Dannals, R. F., Links, J. M., Tune, L. E., & Pearlson, G. D. (1988, February 12). Response to Zeeberg, Gibson, and Reba. *Science 239,* 790–791.

Wong, D. F., Wagner, H. N., Jr., Tune, L. E., Dannals, R. F., Pearlson, G. D., Links, J. M., Tamminga, C. A., Brous-solle, E. P., Ravert, H. T., Wilson, A. A., Toung, T., Malat, J., Williams, J. A., O'Tuama, L. A., Snyder, S. H., Kuhar, M. J., & Gjedde, A. (1986, December 19). Positron emission tomography reveals elevated D2 dopamine receptors in drug-naive schizophrenics. *Science, 234,* 1558–1563.

Wong, M. M., & Csikszentmihalyi, M. (1991). Affiliation motivation and daily experience: Some issues on gender differences. *Journal of Personality and Social Psychology, 60,* 154–164.

Wood, F. B., Flowers, D. L., & Naylor, C. E. (1991). Cerebral laterality in functional neuroimaging. In F. L. Kitterle (Ed.), *Cerebral laterality: Theory and research.* Hillsdale, NJ: Erlbaum.

Wood, J. M., & Bootzin, R. (1990). The prevalence of nightmares and their independence from anxiety. *Journal of Abnormal Psychology, 99,* 64–68.

Woolfolk, R. L., & McNulty, T. F. (1983). Relaxation treatment for insomnia: A component analysis. *Journal of Consult-ing and Clinical Psychology, 4,* 495–503.

World Health Organization. (1991, March 13–17). Paper presented at meeting on HIV Disease: Pathogenesis and therapy. Grenelefe, Florida.

Wright, L. (1988). The type A behavior pattern and coronary artery disease. *American Psychologist, 43,* 2–14.

Wu, C., & Shaffer, D. R. (1987). Sus-ceptibility to persuasive appeals as a function of source credibility and prior experience with the attitude object.

Journal of Personality and Social Psychology, 52, 677–688.

Wundt, W. (1874). *Grundzuge der physio-logischen Psychologie.*

Wyden, B. (1971, December). Growth: 45 crucial months. *Life,* pp. 93–95.

Wynne, L. C., Singer, M. T., Bartko, J. J., & Toohey, M. L. (1975). Schizo-phrenics and their families: Recent research on parental communication. *Psychiatric research: The widening perspec-tive.* New York: International Universi-ties Press.

Yamamato, T., Yuyama, N., & Kawamura, Y. (1981). Cortical neurons respond-ing to tactile, thermal and taste stimu-lations of the rat's tongue. *Brain Re-search, 22,* 202–206.

Yang, N., & Linz, D. (1990). Movie ratings and the content of adult videos: The sex-violence ratio. *Journal of Communi-cation, 40,* 28–42.

Yankura, J., & Dryden, W. (1990). *Doing RET: Albert Ellis in action.* New York: Springer.

Yates, A. J. (1980). *Biofeedback and the modification of behavior.* New York: Plenum.

Youkilis, H., & Bootzin, R. R. (1981). A psychophysiological perspective on the etiology and treatment of insomnia. In S. M. Haynes & L. A. Gannon (Eds.), *Psychosomatic disorders: A psychophysiologi-cal approach to etiology and treatment.* New York: Praeger.

Yu, S., Pritchard, M., Kremer, E., Lynch, M., Nancarrow, J., Baker, E., Holman, K., Mulley, J. C., Warren, S. T., Schles-singer, D., Sutherland, G. R., & Rich-ards, R. I. (1991, May 24). Fragile X genotype characterized by an un-stable region of DNA. *Science, 252,* 1179–1181.

Yuille, J. C., & Tollestrup, P. A. (1990). Some effects of alcohol on eyewitness memory. *Journal of Applied Psychology, 75,* 268–273.

Yurek, D. M., & Sladek, J. R., Jr. (1990). Dopamine cell replacement: Parkin-son's disease. *Annual Review of Neuro-science, 13.*

Zajonc, R. B. (1968). The attitudinal effects of mere exposure. *Journal of Personality and Social Psychology, 9,* 1–27.

Zajonc, R. B. (1985, April 5). Emotion and facial efference: A theory reclaimed. *Science, 228,* 15–21.

Zajonc, R. B. (1990, August). Invited

address at the American Psychological Association annual meeting, Boston.

Zajonc, R. B., Murphy, S., & Inglehart, M. (1989). Feeling and facial efference: Implications of the vascular theory of emotion. *Psychological Review, 96,* 395–416.

Zanna, M. P., & Pack, S. J. (1974). On the self-fulfilling nature of apparent sex differences in behavior. *Journal of Experimental Social Psychology, 11,* 583–591.

Zaslow, M. J. (1991). Variation in child care quality and its implications for children. *Journal of Social Issues, 47,* 125–138.

Zautra, A. J., Reich, J. W., & Guarnaccia, C. A. (1990). *Journal of Personality and Social Psychology, 59,* 550–561.

Zevon, M., & Corn, B. (1990). Paper presented at the annual meeting of the American Psychological Association, Boston.

Zigler, E., & Glick, M. (1988). Is paranoid schizophrenia really camouflaged depression? *American Psychologist, 43,* 284–290.

Zigler, E. F., & Lang, M. E. (1991). *Child care choices: Balancing the needs of children, families, and society.* New York: Free Press.

Zika, S., & Chamberlain, K. (1987). Rela-tion of hassles and personality to sub-jective well-being. *Journal of Personality and Social Psychology, 53,* 155–162.

Zilbergeld, B., & Ellison, C. R. (1980). Desire discrepancies and arousal prob-lems in sex therapy. In S. R. Leiblum & L. A. Pervin (Eds.), *Principles and prac-tices of sex therapy.* New York: Guilford Press.

Zill, N., & Schoenborn, C. (1990). *1988 National Health Interview Survey of Child Health.* Washington, DC: National Cen-ter for Health Statistics.

Zillman, D. (1978). *Hostility and aggression.* Hillsdale, NJ: Erlbaum.

Zimmer, J. (1984). Courting the gods of sport: Athletes use superstition to ward off the devils of injury and bad luck. *Psychology Today, 18,* 36–39.

Zola-Morgan, S. M., & Squire, L. R. (1990, October 12). The primate hippocam-pal formation: Evidence for a time-limited role in memory storage. *Science, 250,* 288–290.

Zubin, J., & Spring, B. (1977). Vulner-ability: New view of schizophrenia. *Journal of Abnormal Psychology, 86,* 103–126.

Zuckerman, M. (1978). The search for high sensation. *Psychology Today,* pp. 30–46.

Figure 2-4 from Darley, B. J., & Latané, B. Bystander intervention in emergencies: Diffusion of responsibilities. *Journal of Personality and Social Psychology, 8,* 184. Copyright © 1968 by the American Psychological Association. Reprinted by permission of the authors.

Figure 3-2 by Carol Donner from The Neuron by Charles E. Stevens. *Scientific American.* Copyright 1979 by Scientific American. All rights reserved.

Figure 3-13a adapted from Nauta, W. J. H. and Feirtag, M. The Organization of the Brain. *Scientific American.* Copyright Scientific American, Inc. All rights reserved.

Figure 3-14b adapted from Geschevird, N. Specializations of the Human Brain. *Scientific American.* Copyright 1979 by Scientific American, Inc. All rights reserved.

Figure 3-15 reprinted with permission of Macmillan Publishing Company from *The Cerebral Cortex of Man,* Wilden Penfield & Theodore Rasmussen. Copyright 1950 by Macmillan Publishing Company, renamed by Theodore Rasmussen.

Figure 3-18 adapted from Rosenzweig, M. R., and Leiman, A. L. *Physiological Psychology,* 1982.

Figure 3-19 adapted from Miller, N. E., Rx: Biofeedback, *Psychology Today,* February, 1985, *54.* Reprinted with permission from *Psychology Today* magazine. Copyright © 1985.

Figure 4-3 from Coren, S., Porac, C., & Ward, L. M., *Sensation and Perception* (2nd ed.), 1984. Orlando, FL: Harcourt Brace Jovanovich.

Figure 4-5 from Lindsey, P. H., & Norman, D. A. *Human Information Processing* (2nd ed.), 1977. Orlando, FL: Harcourt Brace Jovanovich.

Figure 4-6 from Hubel, D. H., & Weisel, T. N. Brain mechanisms of vision, *Scientific American, 241,* 1979. Copyright © 1979 Scientific American.

Figure 4-8 adapted from *Visual Perception* by Tom N. Cornsweet, copyright © 1970 by Harcourt Brace Jovanovich, Inc. Reprinted by permission of publisher.

Figure 4-14 adapted from Fullard, J. H., & Barclay, R. M. R. Audition in spring species of arctiid moths . . . , *Canadian Journal of Zoology,* vol. 58, 1980, and Heffner, R. S., and Heffner, H. E.,

Hearing in mammals: The least weasel, *Journal of Mammalogy,* vol. 66, 1985. Used by permission of authors.

Figure 4-16 from *Newsweek,* June 17, 1991, after Sotoodeh. Used by permission of Newsweek.

Figure 4-17 adapted from Cain, W. S., Odor identification by males and females: Predictions versus performance. *Chemical Senses,* vol. 7, 1982. Used by permission of I. R. L. Press, Ltd.

Figure 4-19 from Meilgaard, M. C., Dalgliesch, C. E., & Clapperton, J. F. Beer Flavor Terminology. *Journal of American Society of Brewing Chemists, 37,* 47–52.

Figure 4-20 from Weinstein, S., Intensive and extensive aspects of tactile sensitivity as a function of body part, sex, and laterality. In D. R. Kenshalo (Ed.), *The Skin Senses,* 1968. Courtesy of Charles C. Thomas, Publisher, Springfield, Illinois.

Figure 5-5 from Bierderman, I. *Computer Vision, Graphics and Image Processing, 32,* 1985. Used by permission of Academic Press.

Figure 5-7 from Coren, S., Porac, C., and Ward, L. M., *Sensation and Perception,* 3rd ed. Copyright © 1989 by Harcourt Brace Jovanovich, Inc., reprinted by permission of the publisher.

Figure 5-8 from Norman, D. A., Rumelhart, D. E., and the LNR Research Group, *Explorations in Cognition,* 1975. Used by permission of W. H. Freeman and Co.

Figure 5-11 from Coren, S., Porac, C., & Ward, L. M., *Sensation and Perception* (2nd ed.), 1984. Orlando, FL: Harcourt Brace Jovanovich.

Figure 5-13a from Coren, S., Porac, C., & Ward, L. M., *Sensation and Perception* (2nd ed.), 1984. Orlando, FL: Harcourt Brace Jovanovich.

Figure 5-17 reprinted with the permission of Gerald Duckworth & Co. from *Illusion in Nature and Art* by R. L. Gregory and E. H. Gombrich, 1973.

Figure 6-3 from Hartmann, E., *The Biology of Dreaming,* 1967. Springfield, IL: Charles C. Thomas.

Figure 6-4 from *Secrets of Sleep* by Alexander Borbely. Copyright 1984 by Deutsch Verlag-Anstalt GmBH. English translation copyright 1986 by Basic Books, Inc. Reprinted by permission of Basic Books, a division of HarperCollins Publishers.

Figure 6-5 from Dement, W. C. *Sleep and Awareness,* 1989. Used with permission of Raven Press.

Figure 6-6 reproduced by permission of the American Anthropological Association from *American Anthropologist,* 60:6, pt. 1, December 1958. Not for further reproduction.

Figure 6-9 Copyright 1991 by The New York Times Company. Reprinted by permission.

Figure 6-10 from Gawin, F. H., and Kleber, H. D., *Science,* vol. 251, March 29, 1991. Used by permission of American Association for the Advancement of Science.

Figure 8-2 adapted from Atkinson, R. C., & Shiffrin, R. M., Human memory: A proposed system and its control processes. In K. W. Spence & J. T. Spencer (Eds.), *The Psychology of Learning and Motivation: Advances in Research and Theory,* (Vol. 2), 1968. Orlando, FL: Harcourt Brace Jovanovich.

Figure 8-4 from B. Kleinmuntz, *Problem Solving: Research, Method and Theory,* 1966. New York: John Wiley and Sons, Inc.

Figure 8-5 from Rubin, D. C. (1985, September). Recalling our past. *Psychology Today,* pp. 39–46. Reprinted with permission from *Psychology Today Magazine,* © 1985. (Sussex Publishers, Inc.)

Figure 8-6 from Collins, A. M., and Quillan, M. R., Retrieval times from semantic memory, *Journal of Verbal Learning and Verbal Behavior, 8,* 1969. Used by permission of Academic Press, Inc.

Figure 8-9 from Rubin, D. C., *Autobiographical Memory,* 1986. Copyright © 1986 Cambridge University Press. Used by permission of publisher.

Figure 9-2 from Solso, R. L., *Cognitive Psychology,* 3rd ed., 1991. Used by permission from Allyn & Bacon Publishers.

Figure 9-3 from *The Complete Thinker,* Barry F. Anderson. Copyright 1980. Used by permission of Prentice Hall, a Division of Simon & Schuster, Englewood Cliffs, New Jersey.

Figure 11-2 from *Motivation and Personality* by Abraham H. Maslow. Copyright 1954 by Harper & Row, Publishers, Inc. Copyright 1970 by Abraham H. Maslow. Reprinted by permission of HarperCollins Publishers.

Figure 11-6 from Plutchick, R., Emotion, in *Approaches to Emotion,* K. Scherer and

Chapter 1: *Chapter 1 opener:* Mark MacLaren. *Page 2:* J. Calson/The Sacramento Bee/Sygma. *7:* Howard Dratch/Image Works. *8:* David Ball/Picture Cube. *12:* Bettmann Archive. *14:* Archives of the History of American Psychology. *16 (top):* Bettmann Archive. *16 (bottom):* Culver. *17:* Hank Morgan/Science Source/Photo Researchers. *23:* Dion Ogust/Image Works.
Chapter 2: *Chapter 2 opener:* Innervisions. *Page 30:* Paramount Pictures/Photofest. *33:* Robert Brenner/PhotoEdit. *36:* Lee Balterman/Picture Cube. *38:* John Coletti/Picture Cube. *40:* James Wilson/Woodfin Camp & Associates. *47:* Hank Morgan/Photo Researchers.
Chapter 3: *Chapter 3 opener:* Comstock. *Page 56:* Ken Murray/The New York Times. *59 (both):* Manfred Kage/Peter Arnold. *64:* John Allison/Peter Arnold. *67 (top left):* Lynn Johnson/Black Star. *67 (bottom right):* Jim Anderson/Woodfin Camp & Associates. *68:* Willie Hill, Jr./Image Works. *69:* Blair Seitz/Photo Researchers. *74:* A. Glauberman/Photo Researchers. *75 (top left):* Dr. Richard Coppola/NIMH. *75 (top right):* Science Photo Library/Science Source/Photo Researchers. *75 (bottom left):* Dan McCoy/Rainbow. *75 (bottom right):* Courtesy of J. C. Mazziotta and M. E. Phelps, UCLA School of Medicine. *80:* A Glauberman/Photo Researchers. *83:* Courtesy of the Trustees of the British Museum of Natural History. *84:* Warren Museum, Harvard Medical School. *86:* Courtesy of J. C. Mazziotta and M. E. Phelps, UCLA School of Medicine.
Chapter 4: *Chapter 4 opener:* Fotopic/Stock South. *Page 98:* Ian Dickson/Alpha/Globe Photos. *99:* Mike Yamashita/Woodfin Camp & Associates. *101:* Michael L. Abramson/Woodfin Camp & Associates. *102:* Tom Myers. *103:* Lennart Nilsson/Behold Man/Little, Brown & Company. *113:* Joe Epstein/Design Conceptions. *116:* David Van Essen, *Science,* July 13, 1990, p. 122. *119:* Courtesy J. E. Hawkins. *122 (top):* Jim Estrin/The New York Times. *122 (bottom):* Thomas S. England/*People Weekly;* © 1991 The Time Inc. Magazine Company. *129:* Katz/Anthro-Photo. *131:* John Tlumacki/Boston Globe.
Chapter 5 *Chapter 5 opener:* George Dillon/Stock, Boston. *Page 136:* Bettmann Newsphotos. *138:* Courtesy Kaiser Porcelain. *139 (top):* Bev Doolittle. *The

Forest Has Eyes. 1985. Courtesy Greenwich Workshop, Trumbull, Connecticut. *139 (bottom):* Georges Seurat. *Sunday Afternoon on La Grande Jatte.* 1884. Oil on canvas, 207.6 × 308 cm. Helen Birch Bartlett Memorial Collection. Photograph © 1991, The Art Institute of Chicago. All rights reserved. *140:* Ronald C. James, from Carraber, R. G., and Thurston, J. B., (1966). *Optical Illusions in the Visual Arts.* New York, Von Nostrand Reinhold. *142:* Courtesy Dr. Dominic Massaro. *146:* William H. Mullins/Photo Researchers. *147:* Culver. *148 (top):* Joe Sohm/Image Works. *148 (bottom left):* Scala/Art Resource. *148 (bottom right):* © 1960 M. C. Escher/Cordon Art, Baarn Holland. Collection Haags Gemeentemuseum, The Hague. *150:* By permission of Marty Erlichman Productions. *154:* Jack Fields/Photo Researchers. *156:* Innervisions. *157:* Indian (Mughal) ms. 07.271. Rama and Lakshman Battle the Demon Bakshasas. Late 16th century. Courtesy of the Freer Gallery of Art, Smithsonian Institution. *158:* Baron Wolman/Woodfin Camp & Associates. *159:* Courtesy Chris King.
Chapter 6: *Chapter 6 opener:* Bob Daemmrich/Image Works. *Page 164:* Robert Sherbow/*People* Weekly. © 1990 The Time Inc. Magazine Company. *165 (top):* Drawing by Frascino, © 1983, The New Yorker Magazine. *165 (bottom):* Courtesy Fort Still Museum, Fort Still, Oklahoma. *166:* Courtesy Donald J. Dorff. *169:* Allan J. Hobson/Photo Researchers. *171:* The Everett Collection. *177:* National Gallery of Art, Washington; Samuel H. Kress Collection. *178:* Dan McCoy/Rainbow. *181:* John Ficara/Woodfin Camp & Associates. *194:* John Coletti/Stock, Boston.
Chapter 7 *Chapter 7 opener:* Superstock. *202:* Bruce Crummy. *204:* Culver. *207:* Courtesy of Dr. Benjamin Harris, University of Wisconsin-Kenosha. *214:* Seep Seitz/Woodfin Camp & Associates. *215:* Joe McNally/Sygma. *216:* Alan Oddie/PhotoEdit. *220:* Miro Vintoniv/Picture Cube. *223:* Gene Boyars/Focus on Sports. *224:* Drawing by M. Stevens, © 1991, The New Yorker Magazine. *226:* Graphics Express. *233:* Elsa Peterson/DDB Stock Photo. *236:* Lester Sloan/Woodfin Camp & Associates.
Chapter 8 *Chapter 8 opener:* Innervisions. *Page 243:* Drawing by Richter; © 1982 The

New Yorker Magazine, Inc. *248:* Jeffrey Muir Hamilton/Stock Boston. *249:* Charles Gupton/Stock, Boston. *252:* Joel Gordon. *256:* Wide World Photos. *259:* Wide World Photos. *263:* Bettmann Archive. *269:* Bill Bachmann/Stock South.
Chapter 9: *Chapter 9 opener:* Franz Edson/Tony Stone Worldwide. *Page 276 (top):* NASA. *276 (bottom):* Ken Regan/*People Weekly.* © 1991 The Time Inc. Magazine Company. *280:* Reuters/Bettmann Newsphotos. *290:* The Photo Source. *296:* Bob Daemmrich/Image Works. *298:* Joel Gordon. *297:* Courtesy of Dr. Laura Ann Petitto © 1991. Photo by Robert Lamarche. *300:* Georgia State University's Language Research Center, operated with the Yerkes Regional Center of Emory University.
Chapter 10: *Chapter 10 opener:* Superstock. *Page 308:* Joe McNally. *309 (left):* Joe Cavanaugh/DDB Stock Photo. *309 (right):* Joel Gordon. *311:* Bettmann Archive. *314:* Alan Carey/Image Works. *319:* Stephen Collins/Photo Researchers. *322:* Stephen Frisch/Stock, Boston. *323:* Joel Gordon. *329:* Joe Sohm/Image Works.
Chapter 11: *Chapter 11 opener:* Myrleen Ferguson/PhotoEdit. *Page 334:* Doug Gantenbein, by permission of Peter Potterfield. *337:* Erika Stone. *341:* Craig Aurness/Woodfin Camp & Associates. *348:* Courtesy of Neal E. Miller. *349:* Larry Kolvoord/Image Works. *351:* Sarah Leen *354:* © 1943 by the President and Fellows of Harvard College; © 1971 by Henry A. Murray. *356:* Bob Daemmrich/Stock, Boston. *365:* Courtesy of Donald E. Dutton. *369:* Paul Ekman. *370:* Ekman, Levenson, & Friesen, 1983.
Chapter 12: *Chapter 12 opener:* G. Veggi/Photo Researchers. *Page 376:* Courtesy of Cassandra Levin. *379 (left):* F. Lee Corkran/Sygma. *379 (right):* Jeffrey Markowitz/Sygma. *380:* Drawing by Koren; © 1988 The New Yorker Magazine, Inc. *382:* Lori Adamski-Peek/Newsweek. *388:* Courtesy of Wynmor Products Ltd. *395:* David Woo/Stock, Boston. *397:* Kindra Clineff/Picture Cube. *399:* Ellen B. Neipris/Impact Visuals. *403 (top):* Joseph Nettis/Photo Researchers. *403 (bottom):* Mary Ellen Mark Library. *404:* Bernice McWilliams/Sygma. *406:* Robert McElroy/Woodfin Camp & Associates.
Chapter 13: *Chapter 13 opener:* Elizabeth Crews/Image Works. *Page 414 (top):* Peter

NAME INDEX

SUBJECT INDEX